MW01097559

Leviticus

CONCORDIA COMMENTARY VOLUMES
Leviticus, John W. Kleinig
Joshua, Adolph L. Harstad
Ruth, John R. Wilch
Ezra and Nehemiah, Andrew E. Steinmann
Proverbs, Andrew E. Steinmann
**Ecclesiastes*, James Bollhagen
The Song of Songs, Christopher W. Mitchell
**Isaiah 40–55*, R. Reed Lessing
Ezekiel 1–20, Horace D. Hummel
Ezekiel 21–48, Horace D. Hummel
Daniel, Andrew E. Steinmann
Amos, R. Reed Lessing
Jonah, R. Reed Lessing
Matthew 1:1–11:1, Jeffrey A. Gibbs
Matthew 11:2–20:34, Jeffrey A. Gibbs
Luke 1:1–9:50, Arthur A. Just Jr.
Luke 9:51–24:53, Arthur A. Just Jr.
1 Corinthians, Gregory J. Lockwood
Colossians, Paul E. Deterding
Philemon, John G. Nordling
Revelation, Louis A. Brighton

For a current list of available Concordia Commentary volumes, visit our Web site at http://www.cph.org/commentaries.

*In preparation

CONCORDIA
COMMENTARY

A Theological Exposition of Sacred Scripture

LEVITICUS

John W. Kleinig

THE SCRIPTURES
TESTIFY TO ME

Concordia Publishing House
Saint Louis

3558 S. Jefferson Avenue
St. Louis, MO 63118-3968
1-800-325-3040 • www.cph.org

Unless otherwise indicated, Scripture quotations are the author's translation.

The SymbolGREEK II, HEBRAICA II, and TranslitLS fonts used to print this work are available from Linguist's Software, Inc., PO Box 580, Edmonds, WA 98020-0580, USA; telephone (425) 775-1130; www.linguistsoftware.com.

Manufactured in the United States of America

Library of Congress Cataloging-in-Publication Data

Kleinig, John W
Leviticus / John W. Kleinig.
p. cm. — (Concordia commentary)
Includes bibliographical references and index.
ISBN 0-570-06317-5
1. Bible. O.T. Leviticus—Commentaries. I. Title. II. Series.

BS1255.53.K53 2003
222'.13077—dc22

2003017601

---

3 4 5 6 7 8 9 10 11 12 20 19 18 17 16 15 14 13 12 11

For Claire

"He who finds a wife finds what is good
and obtains favor from the Lord."

Proverbs 18:22

Contents

Editors' Preface

What may a reader expect from the Concordia Commentary: A Theological Exposition of Sacred Scripture?

The purpose of this series, simply put, is to assist pastors, missionaries, and teachers of the Scriptures to convey God's Word with greater clarity, understanding, and faithfulness to the divine intent of the text.

Since every interpreter approaches the exegetical task from a certain perspective, honesty calls for an outline of the presuppositions held by those who have shaped this commentary series. This also serves, then, as a description of the characteristics of the commentaries.

First in importance is the conviction that the content of the scriptural testimony is Jesus Christ. The Lord himself enunciated this when he said, "The Scriptures … testify to me" (Jn 5:39), words that have been incorporated into the logo of this series. The message of the Scriptures is the Good News of God's work to reconcile the world to himself through the life, death, resurrection, ascension, and everlasting session of Jesus Christ at the right hand of God the Father. Under the guidance of the same Spirit who inspired the writing of the Scriptures, these commentaries seek to find in every passage of every canonical book "that which promotes Christ" (as Luther's hermeneutic is often described). They are Christ-centered, *Christological* commentaries.

As they unfold the scriptural testimony to Jesus Christ, these commentaries expound Law and Gospel. This approach arises from a second conviction—that Law and Gospel are the overarching doctrines of the Bible itself and that to understand them in their proper distinction and relationship to one another is a key for understanding the self-revelation of God and his plan of salvation in Jesus Christ.

Now, Law and Gospel do not always appear in Scripture labeled as such. The palette of language in Scripture is multicolored, with many and rich hues. The dialectic of a pericope may be fallen creation and new creation, darkness and light, death and life, wandering and promised land, exile and return, ignorance and wisdom, demon possession and the kingdom of God, sickness and healing, being lost and found, guilt and righteousness, flesh and Spirit, fear and joy, hunger and feast, or Babylon and the new Jerusalem. But the common element is God's gracious work of restoring fallen humanity through the Gospel of his Son. Since the predominant characteristic of these commentaries is the proclamation of that Gospel, they are, in the proper sense of the term, *evangelical.*

A third, related conviction is that the Scriptures are God's vehicle for communicating the Gospel. The editors and authors accept without reservation that the canonical books of the Old and New Testaments are, in their entirety, the inspired, infallible, and inerrant Word of God. The triune God is the ultimate author of the Bible, and every word in the original Hebrew, Aramaic, and Greek is inspired by the Holy Spirit. Yet rather than mechanical dictation, in the mysterious process by which the Scriptures were divinely inspired (e.g., 2 Tim 3:16; 2 Pet 1:21), God made use of the human faculties, knowledge, interests, and styles of the biblical writers, whose individual books surely are marked by distinctive features. At the same time, the canon of Scripture has its own inner unity, and each passage must be understood in harmony with the larger context of the whole. This commentary series pays heed to the smallest of textual details because of its acceptance of *plenary and verbal inspiration* and interprets the text in light of the whole of Scripture, in accord with the analogy of faith, following the principle that *Scripture interprets Scripture.* The entirety of the Bible is God's Word, *sacred* Scripture, calling for *theological* exposition.

A fourth conviction is that, even as the God of the Gospel came into this world in Jesus Christ (the Word incarnate), the scriptural Gospel has been given to and through the people of God, for the benefit of all humanity. God did not intend his Scriptures to have a life separated from the church. He gave them through servants of his choosing: prophets, sages, evangelists, and apostles. He gave them to the church and through the church, to be cherished in the church for admonition and comfort and to be used by the church for proclamation and catechesis. The living context of Scripture is ever the church, where the Lord's ministry of preaching, baptizing, forgiving sins, teaching, and celebrating the Lord's Supper continues. Aware of the way in which the incarnation of the Son of God has as a consequence the close union of Scripture and church, of Word and Sacraments, this commentary series features expositions that are *incarnational* and *sacramental.*

This Gospel Word of God, moreover, creates a unity among all those in whom it works the obedience of faith and who confess the truth of God revealed in it. This is the unity of the one holy Christian and apostolic church, which extends through world history. The church is to be found wherever the marks of the church are present: the Gospel in the Word and the Sacraments. These have been proclaimed, confessed, and celebrated in many different cultures and are in no way limited nor especially attached to any single culture or people. As this commentary series seeks to articulate the universal truth of the Gospel, it acknowledges and affirms the confession of the scriptural truth in all the many times and places where the one true church has been found. Aiming to promote *concord* in the confession of the one scriptural Gospel, these commentaries seek to be, in the best sense of the terms, *confessional, ecumenical,* and *catholic.*

All of those convictions and characteristics describe the theological heritage of Martin Luther and of the confessors who subscribe to the *Book of Concord* (1580)—those who have come to be known as Lutherans. The editors and authors forthrightly confess their subscription to the doctrinal exposition of Scripture in the *Book of Concord.* As the publishing arm of The Lutheran

Church—Missouri Synod, Concordia Publishing House is bound to doctrinal agreement with the Scriptures and the Lutheran Confessions and seeks to herald the true Christian doctrine to the ends of the earth. To that end, the series has enlisted confessional Lutheran authors from other church bodies around the world who share the evangelical mission of promoting theological concord.

The authors and editors stand in the exegetical tradition of Martin Luther and the other Lutheran reformers, who in turn (as their writings took pains to demonstrate) stood in continuity with faithful exegesis by theologians of the early and medieval church, rooted in the hermeneutics of the Scriptures themselves (evident, for example, by how the New Testament interprets the Old). This hermeneutical method, practiced also by many non-Lutherans, includes (1) interpreting Scripture with Scripture according to the analogy of faith, that is, in harmony with the whole of Christian doctrine revealed in the Word; (2) giving utmost attention to the grammar (lexicography, phonetics, morphology, syntax, pragmatics) of the original language of the text; (3) seeking to discern the intended meaning of the text, the "plain" or "literal" sense, aware that the language of Scripture ranges from narrative to discourse, from formal prose to evocative poetry, from archaic to acrostic to apocalyptic, and it uses metaphor, type, parable, and other figures; (4) drawing on philology, linguistics, archaeology, literature, philosophy, history, and other fields in the quest for a better understanding of the text; (5) considering the history of the church's interpretation; (6) applying the text as authoritative also in the present milieu of the interpreter; and (7) above all, seeing the present application and fulfillment of the text in terms of Jesus Christ and his corporate church; upholding the Word, Baptism, and the Supper as the means through which Christ imparts salvation today; and affirming the inauguration, already now, of the eternal benefits of that salvation that is yet to come.

To be sure, the authors and editors do not feel bound to agree with every detail of the exegesis of our Lutheran forefathers. Nor do we imagine that the interpretations presented here are the final word about every crux and enigmatic passage. But the work has been done in harmony with the exegetical tradition that reaches back through the Lutheran confessors all the way to the biblical writers themselves, and in harmony with the confession of the church: grace alone, faith alone, Scripture alone, Christ alone.

The editors wish to acknowledge their debt of gratitude for all who have helped make possible this series. It was conceived at CPH in 1990, and a couple of years of planning and prayer to the Lord of the church preceded its formal launch on July 2, 1992. During that time, Dr. J. A. O. Preus II volunteered his enthusiasm for the project because, in his view, it would nurture and advance the faithful proclamation of the Christian faith as understood by the Lutheran church. The financial support that has underwritten the series was provided by a gracious donor who wished to remain anonymous. Those two faithful servants of God were called to heavenly rest a few short years later.

During the early years, former CPH presidents Dr. John W. Gerber and Dr. Stephen J. Carter had the foresight to recognize the potential benefit of such a landmark work for the church at large. CPH allowed Dr. Christopher W. Mitchell to devote his time and energy to the conception and initial development of the project. Dr. Mitchell has remained the CPH editor and is also the Old Testament editor. Dr. Dean O. Wenthe has served on the project since its official start in 1992 and is the general editor, as well as a commentary author. Mrs. Julene Gernant Dumit (M.A.R.) has been the CPH production editor for the entire series. In 1999 Dr. Jeffrey A. Gibbs, already a commentary author, joined the editorial board as the New Testament editor.

CPH thanks Concordia Theological Seminary, Fort Wayne, Indiana, for kindly allowing its president, Dr. Dean O. Wenthe, to serve as the general editor of the series and to dedicate a substantial portion of his time to it for many years. CPH also thanks Concordia Seminary, St. Louis, Missouri, for permitting Dr. Jeffrey A. Gibbs to devote a significant share of his time to his capacity as the New Testament editor. Those two seminaries have thereby extended their ministries in selfless service for the benefit of the church.

The editors pray that the beneficence of their institutions may be reflected in this series by an evangelical orientation, a steadfast Christological perspective, an eschatological view toward the ultimate good of Christ's bride, and a concern that the wedding feast of the King's Son may be filled with all manner of guests (Mt 22:1–14).

> Now to him who is able to establish you by my Gospel and the preaching of Jesus Christ, by the revelation of the mystery kept secret for ages past but now revealed also through the prophetic Scriptures, made known to all the nations by order of the eternal God unto the obedience of faith—to the only wise God, through Jesus Christ, be the glory forever. Amen! (Rom 16:25–27)

Author's Preface

This commentary is the product of a long journey for me. That journey began at Pilgrim's Lutheran Church at Neukirch in South Australia, the church where I was baptized and confirmed. The distinctive feature of this small church is its large ornate wooden altar with three rear panels. The words "Holy! Holy! Holy!" are carved in German on these panels, which, to my childish imagination, resembled a trio of angels. In that church, during my childhood, I was often struck with awe and wonder as I knelt together with my parents and siblings during the singing of the Sanctus in the Divine Service. There too, one Christmas Eve, as we children were singing the hymn "All My Heart This Night Rejoices," the heavens seemed to open up for me, and I heard the angels singing together with us. My joy was so great that I could barely contain it.

But that vision of glory, that sense of awe at the beauty of Christ's holiness, soon faded from my consciousness. As I grew up and learned to rationalize, I became more and more insensitive to holiness. To be sure, my conscience still reminded me that some things were sacred, but that was all. God's holiness, that other, heavenly dimension, was no longer there all around me, ready at any moment to break in and stun my soul with its glorious radiance and sheer intensity.

The study of theology, as I prepared for ordination as a pastor, did little to reawaken my soul to the reality of God's holiness. But I do remember trying, rather unsuccessfully, to make sense of what the sacred Scriptures had to say on that topic. That was the era when existentialism reigned supreme, with its reduction of the Christian faith to an individual's encounter with God in a personal relationship with him. One scholar after another confidently asserted that Christ had abolished the distinction between the sacred and the secular. For those scholars, holiness was a rather naive way of referring to the transcendence of God, his otherness as absolute subject, as well as to whatever belonged to him. Since everything belonged to God, then every person and every thing must be holy. All of that was plausible, but of no use to me as a pastor!

Two significant voices, however, held me back from the peril of desecration. They too gave me some intellectual stimulus and direction in my quest for holiness. My teacher Dr. Hermann Sasse taught us that the means of grace were our means of sanctification. He used the words of the Greek Orthodox liturgy to remind us that the holy things of God were for the holy people of God. In his *Old Testament Theology,* Gerhard von Rad taught me that God's holiness was a life-giving, life-sustaining power that was opposed to the deadly power of impurity. Holiness was communicated by physical contact with the holy things at the sanctuary. Thus, when I was ordained, I accepted that I was to be a steward of the holy things of God.

Gradually, over my years of working as a pastor, God's holiness captivated me more and more. And I began to make some sense of it from experience. There were many little events, like the students who came to me when I was a chaplain at a Lutheran high school in Brisbane and rebuked me for leading services unvested and allowing the altar to be used, rather carelessly, as a prop in a chancel drama. But the main thing that jolted me to search the Scriptures to discover what they had to say about God's holiness was my ministry to people under attack by Satan and the powers of darkness. That taught me much about the demonic use of impurity, the healing power of Christ's holiness, and my own holiness in Christ as an armor of light against the powers of darkness.

When I went to Cambridge in 1979 to undertake postgraduate study in the Old Testament, I took the opportunity to write a research paper on the theological function of the rite of atonement as ordained by God in the Pentateuch. In my research for that essay, I discovered the book *Purity and Danger* by Mary Douglas. It provided me, like many other recent exegetes, with the keys to unlock the teaching of holiness in Exodus, Leviticus, and Numbers. That led, in due course, to the presentation of a paper entitled "Sharing in God's Holiness" for the general pastors conference of the Lutheran Church of Australia in 1984 in which I summarized the teaching of the Bible on that topic. The chief insight, developed in that paper, was that holiness was, of necessity, a liturgical term, for our holiness was derived from God's gracious presence and our access to him in the Divine Service. In fact, God had instituted the Divine Service to share his holiness with Israel and the church. That was followed by a paper that explored Luther's remarkably helpful teaching on our alien holiness in Christ and our ongoing reception of God's holiness.

The biblical, theological, and historical work on this topic was accompanied by my increasing involvement with Lutheran pastors from churches in animist cultures. They, in fact, have taught me more than I ever learned from all the academic books that I have read. This development began with a pastor from New Guinea who learned Hebrew from me at Luther Seminary in Adelaide, before completing an S.T.M. at an American Lutheran seminary. After his return I met with him in New Guinea. When I asked him how things had gone for him in the United States, he remained silent for a long time before he said, "John, for them nothing is sacred any longer!" His remark stunned me, and it has haunted me ever since, for I felt that he could have said the same about my seminary and my church.

That was followed by interaction with people from three different communities, all of which have given me further insights into the realities of sanctification and its importance for the mission of the church. Our own Australian Lutheran aboriginal pastors and evangelists have helped me to appreciate the function of ritual enactments in sanctification. Solomon Rajah and the pastors of the Evangelical Lutheran Church in Malaysia have helped me to see how the Old Testament speaks to the connection between the occult, blood sacrifice, and purification in Hinduism. From his own experience and study of

Simbu culture in New Guinea, Buge Ilai has helped me to understand the ritual use of blood in paganism, in the Old Testament, and in the Lord's Supper. He investigated the role of blood in his culture as the only physical substance that existed both in the material realm and the realm of the spirits as well as the implications of this for his people's understanding of Holy Communion.

All this has had a profound impact on me and my understanding of the Pentateuch. It has influenced my study of the divine service in the Old Testament and my understanding of its theology. It has also affected my understanding of spirituality and liturgics. So, when I was asked which biblical book I would like to prepare for the Concordia Commentary series, I had no hesitation in opting for Leviticus, despite its unpopularity and the neglect of it in the church. It has provided me with a golden opportunity to analyze and summarize what God has taught me about his holiness from his Word and my experience as pastor.

As I prepared this commentary, I found myself speaking mainly to three audiences. First, the commentary has been written to help missionaries and evangelists, pastors and teachers working with people in animist cultures to use the Old Testament to evangelize their compatriots and to initiate converts from that spiritual world into the riches of the Divine Service. Second, it is meant to open up the Old Testament for postmodern young people as they battle with the threat of pollution and with the menace of those dark powers that attack their stability. Third, it is dedicated to all the many orthodox Christians in the Lutheran church, and across all denominations, who love the Lord's house and revere the enactment of the holy liturgy as the theophany of the Holy Trinity (Ps 26:8).

Special thanks must go to the many people who have accompanied and supported me on the journey that has produced this commentary. I thank Dr. Christopher Mitchell, Mrs. Julene Dumit, and all the people at Concordia Publishing House for their unstinting help and encouragement. I too am most grateful for the support of many fellow pastors in the holy brotherhood of the apostolic ministry of the Gospel, but must single out my colleagues Andrew Pfeiffer, Michael Hassold, Erich Renner, and Vic Pfitzner, as well as Vernon Kleinig, my brother thrice over, for encouraging me by their brotherly love and their respect for God's holiness. I also thank God for my ancestors, who treasured the heritage of the Gospel, brought it with them to Australia, and handed it on to their descendants; my dear deceased father, Ben Kleinig, who first taught me to love God's holy Word and to kneel in awe of the triune God in the Divine Service; and my dear deceased mother, Elfriede Kleinig, whose soul was permeated with the gentleness and radiance and joy of Christ's holiness, even after her lively mind had been confused by Alzheimer's disease.

But most of all, I would like to thank the members of my own family for traveling with me and supporting me: my beloved children, Louise and her husband, Stephen; Tim and his wife, Pakan; Hilary; and Paul, who have taught me to rely on the holiness of God the Father for our protection and blessing; my grandsons, Cody and Oliver, who, I pray, will, through us, receive and treasure the heritage of our most holy faith for all God's saints; and my dear wife, Claire, whose respect for God's holiness, faith in Christ for her sanctification, and love for me have sharpened my conscience and moved me to seek closer intimacy with God, my holy Father. My prayer for all of these and for all of you who use this commentary is this prayer of Jesus: Holy Father, "sanctify them by the truth; your Word is truth" (Jn 17:17).

September 29, 2003
St. Michael and All Angels

Principal Abbreviations

Books of the Bible

Gen	2 Ki	Is	Nah	Rom	Titus
Ex	1 Chr	Jer	Hab	1 Cor	Philemon
Lev	2 Chr	Lam	Zeph	2 Cor	Heb
Num	Ezra	Ezek	Hag	Gal	James
Deut	Neh	Dan	Zech	Eph	1 Pet
Josh	Esth	Hos	Mal	Phil	2 Pet
Judg	Job	Joel	Mt	Col	1 Jn
Ruth	Ps (pl. Pss)	Amos	Mk	1 Thess	2 Jn
1 Sam	Prov	Obad	Lk	2 Thess	3 Jn
2 Sam	Eccl	Jonah	Jn	1 Tim	Jude
1 Ki	Song	Micah	Acts	2 Tim	Rev

Books of the Apocrypha

1 Esdras	Judith	Sirach	Azar/Three	Manasseh
2 Esdras	Add Esth	Baruch	Susanna	1 Macc
Tobit	Wis Sol	Ep Jer	Bel	2 Macc

Reference Works and Scripture Versions

AE	*Luther's Works*. St. Louis: Concordia, and Philadelphia: Fortress, 1955– [American Edition]
Ap	Apology of the Augsburg Confession
BDB	Brown, F., S. R. Driver, and C. A. Briggs. *A Hebrew and English Lexicon of the Old Testament.* 1906. Repr., Oxford: Clarendon, 1979
ESV	English Standard Version of the Bible
ET	English translation
FC	Formula of Concord
GKC	*Gesenius' Hebrew Grammar.* Edited by E. Kautzsch. Translated by A. E. Cowley. 2d ed. Oxford: Clarendon, 1910
HALOT	Koehler, L., W. Baumgartner, and J. J. Stamm. *The Hebrew and Aramaic Lexicon of the Old Testament.* Translated and edited under the supervision of M. E. J. Richardson. 5 vols. Leiden: Brill, 1994–2000
HS98	*Hymnal Supplement 98.* St. Louis: Concordia, 1998
KJV	King James Version of the Bible
LW	*Lutheran Worship.* St. Louis: Concordia, 1982

LXX	Septuagint
MT	Masoretic Text of the Hebrew Bible
NIV	New International Version of the Bible
NRSV	New Revised Standard Version of the Bible
NT	New Testament
OT	Old Testament
RSV	Revised Standard Version of the Bible
SC	Small Catechism of Martin Luther
SD	Solid Declaration of the Formula of Concord
TDOT	*Theological Dictionary of the Old Testament.* Edited by G. J. Botterweck, H. Ringgren, and H.-J. Fabry. Translated by J. T. Willis et al. 15 vols. Grand Rapids: Eerdmans, 1974–2006
WA	*D. Martin Luthers Werke: Kritische Gesamtausgabe.* 73 vols. in 85. Weimar: Böhlau, 1883– [Weimarer Ausgabe]

Icons

These icons are used in the margins of this commentary to highlight the following themes:

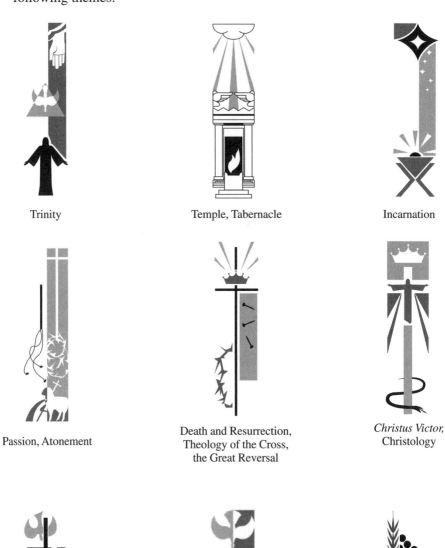

Trinity

Temple, Tabernacle

Incarnation

Passion, Atonement

Death and Resurrection, Theology of the Cross, the Great Reversal

Christus Victor, Christology

Baptism

Catechesis, Instruction, Revelation

Lord's Supper

Ministry of Word and Sacrament,
Office of the Keys

The Church,
Marriage

Worship

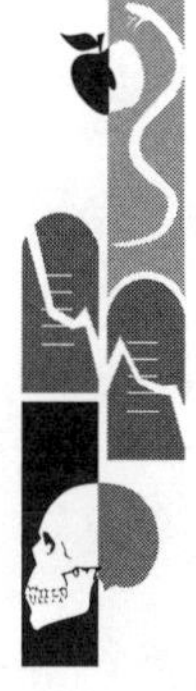

Sin, Law Breaking,
Death

Hope of Heaven,
Eschatology

Justification

Bibliography

Amit, Yairah. "The Jubilee Law: An Attempt at Instituting Social Justice." Pages 47–59 in *Justice and Righteousness: Biblical Themes and Their Influence.* Edited by Henning Graf Reventlow and Yair Hoffmann. Journal for the Study of the Old Testament: Supplement Series 137. Sheffield, England: JSOT Press, 1992.

Arens, Anton. *Die Psalmen im Gottesdienst des Alten Bundes: Eine Untersuchung zur Vorgeschichte des christlichen Psalmengesanges.* Trierer theologische Studien 11. Trier: Paulinus, 1961.

Auld, A. Graeme. "Leviticus at the Heart of the Pentateuch." Pages 40–51 in *Reading Leviticus: A Conversation with Mary Douglas.* Edited by John F. A. Sawyer. Journal for the Study of the Old Testament: Supplement Series 227. Sheffield, England: Sheffield Academic Press, 1996.

Baentsch, B. *Exodus, Leviticus, Numeri.* Handkommentar zum Alten Testament 2. Göttingen: Vandenhoeck & Ruprecht, 1903.

Bailey, Derrick Sherwin. *Homosexuality and the Western Christian Tradition.* London: Longmans, 1955.

Bailey, Lloyd R. *Leviticus.* Knox Preaching Guides. Atlanta: John Knox, 1987.

Baker, David W. "Division Markers and the Structure of Leviticus 1–7." Pages 9–15 in *Studia Biblica 1978: Sixth International Congress on Biblical Studies,* vol. 1: *Papers on Old Testament and Related Themes.* Edited by E. A. Livingstone. Journal for the Study of the Old Testament: Supplement Series 11. Sheffield, England: JSOT Press, 1979.

———. "Leviticus 1–7 and the Punic Tariffs: A Form Critical Comparison." *Zeitschrift für die alttestamentliche Wissenschaft* 99 (1987): 188–97.

Balentine, Samuel E. *The Torah's Vision of Worship.* Minneapolis: Fortress, 1999.

Bamberger, Bernard Jacob. *Leviticus.* The Torah: A Modern Commentary 3. New York: Union of American Hebrew Congregations, 1979.

Benko, Stephen. *The Meaning of Sanctorum Communio.* Studies in Historical Theology 3. London: SCM, 1964.

Bertholet, Alfred. *Leviticus.* Kurzer Hand-Commentar zum Alten Testament 3. Tübingen: Mohr, 1901.

Bibb, Bryan D. "Nadab and Abihu Attempt to Fill the Gap: Law and Narrative in Leviticus 10:1–7." *Journal for the Study of the Old Testament* 96 (2001): 83–99.

Bigger, Stephen F. "The Family Laws of Leviticus 18 in Their Setting." *Journal of Biblical Literature* 98 (1979): 187–203.

Blum, Erhard. *Studien zur Komposition des Pentateuch.* Beihefte zur Zeitschrift für die alttestamentliche Wissenschaft 189. Berlin: Walter de Gruyter, 1990.

Boer, Pieter A. H. de. "An Aspect of Sacrifice." Pages 27–47 in *Studies in the Religion of Ancient Israel.* Supplements to Vetus Testamentum 23. Leiden: Brill, 1972.

Booth, Roger P. *Jesus and the Laws of Purity: Tradition History and Legal History in Mark 7.* Journal for the Study of the New Testament: Supplement Series 13. Sheffield, England: JSOT Press, 1986.

Bretscher, Paul G. "The Covenant of Blood." *Concordia Theological Monthly* 25 (1954): 1–27, 109–25, 199–209.

Brichto, Herbert C. "On Slaughter and Sacrifice, Blood and Atonement." *Hebrew Union College Annual* 47 (1976): 19–55.

Brin, Gershon. *Studies in Biblical Law: From the Hebrew Bible to the Dead Sea Scrolls.* Translated by Jonathan Chipman. Journal for the Study of the Old Testament: Supplement Series 176. Sheffield, England: JSOT Press, 1994.

Britt, Brian, and Patrick Creehan. "Chiasmus in Leviticus 16,29–17,11." *Zeitschrift für die alttestamentliche Wissenschaft* 112 (2000): 398–400.

Brown, F., S. R. Driver, and C. A. Briggs. *A Hebrew and English Lexicon of the Old Testament.* 1906. Repr., Oxford: Clarendon, 1979.

Bruce, Frederick F. *1 and 2 Corinthians.* New Century Bible. London: Oliphants, 1971.

Brueggemann, Walter. *The Land: Place as Gift, Promise, and Challenge in Biblical Faith.* Overtures to Biblical Theology. Philadelphia: Fortress, 1977.

Budd, Philip J. *Leviticus.* New Century Bible Commentary. Grand Rapids: Eerdmans, 1996.

Cahill, Michael J. "Drinking Blood at a Kosher Eucharist? The Sound of Scholarly Silence." *Biblical Theology Bulletin* 32 (2002): 168–82.

Carmichael, Calum M. *Law, Legend, and Incest in the Bible: Leviticus 18–20.* Ithaca, N.Y.: Cornell University Press, 1997.

Carroll, Michael P. "One More Time: Leviticus Revisited." Pages 117–26 in *Anthropological Approaches to the Old Testament.* Edited with an introduction by Bernhard Lang. Philadelphia: Fortress, 1985.

Cartledge, Tony W. *Vows in the Hebrew Bible and the Ancient Near East.* Journal for the Study of the Old Testament: Supplement Series 147. Sheffield, England: JSOT Press, 1992.

Childs, Brevard S. *Introduction to the Old Testament as Scripture.* Philadelphia: Fortress, 1979.

———. *Old Testament Theology in a Canonical Context.* Philadelphia: Fortress, 1985.

Chirichigno, Gregory C. *Debt Slavery in Israel and the Ancient Near East.* Journal for the Study of the Old Testament: Supplement Series 141. Sheffield, England: JSOT Press, 1993.

Cholewinski, Alfred. *Heiligkeitsgesetz und Deuteronomium: Eine vergleichende Studie.* Analecta Biblica 66. Rome: Biblical Institute Press, 1976.

Chytraeus, David. *On Sacrifice: A Reformation Treatise in Biblical Theology.* Translated and edited by John Warwick Montgomery. St. Louis: Concordia, 1962.

Repr., Malone, Tex.: Repristination Press, 2000. Translation of *De sacrificiis,* 1569.

Clements, R. E. *God and Temple.* Oxford: Blackwell, 1965.

Coloe, Mary L. *God Dwells with Us: Temple Symbolism in the Fourth Gospel.* Collegeville, Minn.: Liturgical Press, 2001.

Cooper, Alan. M., and Goldstein, Bernard. R. "At the Entrance to the Tent: More Cultic Resonances in Biblical Narrative." *Journal of Biblical Literature* 116 (1997): 201–15.

Cotton Roger. "A Biblical Theology of Leviticus Focusing on Chapter 19." Pages 111–19 in *"Hear the Word of Yahweh": Essays on Scripture and Archaeology in Honor of Horace D. Hummel.* Edited by Dean O. Wenthe, Paul L. Schrieber, and Lee A. Maxwell. Saint Louis: Concordia, 2002.

Crüsemann, Frank. "Der Exodus als Heiligung." Pages 117–29 in *Die Hebräische Bibel und ihre zweifache Nachgeschichte: Festschrift für Rolf Rendtorff zum 65. Geburtstag.* Edited by Erhard Blum, Christian Macholz, and Ekkehard W. Stegemann. Neukirchen-Vluyn, Germany: Neukirchener, 1990.

———. *The Torah: Theology and Social History of Old Testament Law.* Translated by Allan W. Mahnke. Minneapolis: Fortress, 1996.

Cryer, Frederick H. *Divination in Ancient Israel and Its Near Eastern Environment: A Socio-Historical Investigation.* Journal for the Study of the Old Testament: Supplement Series 142. Sheffield, England: JSOT Press, 1994.

Danby, Herbert, trans. *The Mishnah: Translated from the Hebrew with Introduction and Brief Explanatory Notes.* Oxford: Oxford University Press, 1933.

Danielou, Jean. *The Bible and the Liturgy.* Notre Dame: University of Notre Dame Press, 1956.

Daube, David. *Studies in Biblical Law.* Cambridge: Cambridge University Press, 1947.

———. *The Exodus Pattern in the Bible.* Westport, Conn.: Greenwood, 1963.

Davidson, Richard M. *Typology in Scripture: A Study of Hermeneutical τύπος Structures.* Berrien Springs, Mich.: Andrews University Press, 1981.

Davies, Douglas. "An Interpretation of Sacrifice in Leviticus." *Zeitschrift für die alttestamentliche Wissenschaft* 89 (1977): 387–99.

Davies, Philip R., and David M. Gunn. "Pentateuchal Patterns: An Examination of C. J. Labuschange's Theory." *Vetus Testamentum* 34 (1984): 399–406.

Day, John. *Molech: A God of Human Sacrifice in the Old Testament.* Cambridge: Cambridge University Press, 1989.

DeGuglielmo, Antoine. "Sacrifice in the Ugaritic Texts." *Catholic Biblical Quarterly* 17 (1955): 196–216.

Dewar, Lindsay. "The Biblical Use of the Term 'Blood.' " *Journal of Theological Studies* 4 (1953): 204–8.

Dillmann, August. *Die Bücher Exodus und Leviticus.* Leipzig: Hirzel, 1880.

Douglas, Mary. *Purity and Danger: An Analysis of the Concepts of Pollution and Taboo.* London: Routledge & Kegan Paul, 1966.

———. *Natural Symbols: Explorations in Cosmology.* 2d ed. London: Barrie and Jenkins, 1973.

———. *Implicit Meanings: Essays in Anthropology.* London: Routledge & Kegan Paul, 1975.

———. "The Forbidden Animals in Leviticus." *Journal for the Study of the Old Testament* 59 (1993): 3–23.

———. "Poetic Structure in Leviticus." Pages 239–56 in *Pomegranates and Golden Bells: Studies in Biblical, Jewish, and Near Eastern Ritual, Law, and Literature in Honor of Jacob Milgrom.* Edited by David P. Wright, David Noel Freedman, and Avi Hurvitz. Winona Lake, Ind.: Eisenbrauns, 1995.

———. "Sacred Contagion." Pages 86–106 in *Reading Leviticus: A Conversation with Mary Douglas.* Edited by J. F. A. Sawyer. Journal for the Study of the Old Testament: Supplement Series 227. Sheffield, England: Sheffield Academic Press, 1996.

———. "Justice as the Cornerstone: An Interpretation of Leviticus 18–20." *Interpretation* 53 (1999): 341–50.

Driver, Godfrey R. "Birds in the Old Testament: I. Birds in the Law." *Palestine Exploration Quarterly* 87 (1955): 5–20.

———. "Three Technical Terms in the Pentateuch." *Journal of Semitic Studies* 1 (1956): 92–105.

Dunn, James D. G. *Romans 1–8.* Word Biblical Commentary 38A. Dallas: Word, 1988.

Eberhart, Christian. "Beobachtungen zum Verbrennungsritus bei Schlachtopfer und Gemeinschafts-Schlachtopfer." *Biblica* 83 (2002): 88–96.

Edelman, Diana. "The Meaning of *Qitter.*" *Vetus Testamentum* 35 (1985): 395–404.

Eerdmans, Bernardus Dirk. *Das Buch Leviticus.* Alttestamentiche Studien 4. Giessen: Töpelmann, 1912.

Eichrodt, Walter. *Theology of the Old Testament.* Vol. 1. Translated by J. A. Baker. Philadelphia: Westminster, 1961.

Elert, Werner. *Eucharist and Church Fellowship in the First Four Centuries.* Translated by Norman E. Nagel. Saint Louis: Concordia, 1966.

Elliger, Karl. "Das Gesetz Leviticus 18." *Zeitschrift für die alttestamentliche Wissenschaft* 67 (1955): 1–25.

———. *Leviticus.* Handbuch zum Alten Testament 4. Tübingen: Mohr, 1966.

Elliott-Binns, Leonard E. "Some Problems of the Holiness Code." *Zeitschrift für die alttestamentliche Wissenschaft* 67 (1955): 26–40.

Evans, Craig A. "Jesus and the Ritually Impure." Pages 353–76 in *Jesus in Context: Temple, Purity, and Restoration,* by Bruce Chilton and Craig A. Evans. Leiden: Brill, 1997.

———. " 'Do This and You Will Live': Targumic Coherence in Luke 10:25–28." Pages 377–93 in *Jesus in Context: Temple, Purity, and Restoration,* by Bruce Chilton and Craig A. Evans. Leiden: Brill, 1997.

Fager, Jeffrey A. *Land Tenure and the Biblical Jubilee: Uncovering Hebrew Ethics through the Sociology of Knowledge.* Journal for the Study of the Old Testament: Supplement Series 155. Sheffield, England: JSOT Press, 1993.

Feliks, Yehuda. "The Incense of the Tabernacle." Pages 125–49 in *Pomegranates and Golden Bells: Studies in Biblical, Jewish, and Near Eastern Ritual, Law, and Literature in Honor of Jacob Milgrom.* Edited by David P. Wright, David Noel Freedman, and Avi Hurvitz. Winona Lake, Ind.: Eisenbrauns, 1995.

Feucht, Christian. *Untersuchungen zum Heiligkeitsgesetz.* Berlin: Evangelische Verlagsanstalt, 1964.

Field, John Edward. *The Apostolic Liturgy and the Epistle to the Hebrews.* London: Rivingtons, 1882.

Firmage, Edwin. "The Biblical Dietary Laws and the Concept of Holiness." Pages 177–208 in *Studies in the Pentateuch.* Edited John A. Emerton . Supplements to Vetus Testamentum 41. Leiden: Brill, 1990.

Fishbane, Michael A. "Biblical Colophons, Textual Criticism and Legal Analogies." *Catholic Biblical Quarterly* 42 (1980): 438–49.

———. *Biblical Interpretation in Ancient Israel.* Oxford: Clarendon, 1985.

Fretheim, Terence E. "The Book of Leviticus." Pages 121–36 in *The Pentateuch.* Interpreting Biblical Texts. Nashville: Abingdon, 1996.

Frymer-Kensky, Tikva Simone. "Tit for Tat: The Principle of Equal Retribution in Near Eastern and Biblical Law." *Biblical Archaeologist* 43 (1980): 230–34.

———. "Pollution, Purification and Purgation in Ancient Israel." Pages 399–414 in *The Word of the Lord Shall Go Forth: Essays in Honor of David Noel Freedman in Celebration of His Sixtieth Birthday.* Edited by Carol L. Meyers and M. O'Connor. Winona Lake, Ind.: Eisenbrauns, 1983.

———. "Law and Philosophy: The Case of Sex in the Bible." *Semeia* 45 (1989): 90–101.

Füglister, Notker. "Sühne durch Blut: Zur Bedeutung von Leviticus 17:11." Pages 143–64 in *Studien zum Pentateuch: Walter Kornfeld zum 60. Geburtstag.* Edited by Georg Braulik. Basel: Herder, 1977.

Gabel, J. B., and C. B. Wheeler. "The Redactor's Hand in the Blasphemy Pericope in Leviticus XXIV." *Vetus Testamentum* 30 (1980): 227–29.

Gammie, John G. *Holiness in Israel.* Overtures to Biblical Theology. Minneapolis: Fortress, 1989.

Gane, Roy. " 'Bread of Presence' and Creator-in-Residence." *Vetus Testamentum* 42 (1992): 179–203.

Gennep, Arnold van. *The Rites of Passage.* Translated by Monika B. Vizedom and Gabrielle L. Caffe. London: Routledge & Kegan Paul, 1960.

Gerstenberger, Erhard S. "Er soll dir heilig sein: Priester und Gemeinde nach Lev 21:1–22:9." Pages 194–210 in *Was ist der Mensch ... ?Beiträge zur Anthropologie des Alten Testaments; Hans Walter Wolff zum 80. Geburtstag.* Edited by Frank Crüsemann, Christoff Hardmeier, and Rainer Kessler. Munich: Kaiser, 1992.

———. *Leviticus: A Commentary.* Old Testament Library. Translated by Douglas W. Stott. Louisville, Ky.: Westminster/John Knox, 1996.

Gnuse, Robert. "Jubilee Legislation in Leviticus: Israel's Vision of Social Reform." *Biblical Theology Bulletin* 15 (1985): 43–48.

Goppelt, Leonhard. *Typos: The Typological Interpretation of the Old Testament in the New.* Translated by Donald H. Madvig. Grand Rapids: Eerdmans, 1982.

Görg, Manfred. "Zum sogenannten priesterlichen Obergewand." *Biblische Zeitschrift* 20 (1976): 242–46.

———. "Die Kopfbedeckung des Hohenpriesters." *Biblische Notizen* 3 (1977): 24–26.

———. "Eine neue Bedeutung für *kăppōret." Zeitschrift für die alttestamentliche Wissenschaft* 89 (1977): 115–18.

———. "Eine rätzelhafte Textilbezeichnung im Alten Testament." *Biblische Notizen* 12 (1980): 13–17.

———. "Der Brustschmuck des Hohenpriesters." *Biblische Notizen* 15 (1981): 32–34.

Gorman, Frank H., Jr. *The Ideology of Ritual: Space, Time and Status in the Priestly Theology.* Journal for the Study of the Old Testament: Supplement Series 91. Sheffield, England: JSOT Press, 1990.

———. "Priestly Rituals of Founding: Time, Space, and Status." Pages 47–64 in *History and Interpretation: Essays in Honour of John H. Hayes.* Edited by M. Patrick Graham, William P. Brown, and Jeffrey K. Kuan. Journal for the Study of the Old Testament: Supplement Series 173. Sheffield, England: JSOT Press, 1993.

———. *Divine Presence and Community: A Commentary on the Book of Leviticus.* International Theological Commentary. Grand Rapids: Eerdmans, 1997.

Goudoever, J. van. *Biblical Calendars.* 2d rev. ed. Leiden: Brill, 1961.

Grabbe, Lester L. "The Book of Leviticus." *Currents in Research: Biblical Studies* 5 (1997): 91–110.

Gradwohl, Roland. "Das 'fremde Feuer' von Nadab und Abihu." *Zeitschrift für die alttestamentliche Wissenschaft* 75 (1963): 288–96.

Gray, George Buchanan. *Sacrifice in the Old Testament: Its Theory and Practice.* Oxford: Clarendon, 1925. Reprint edited with an introduction by Baruch A. Levine. New York: Ktav, 1971.

Grintz, Yehoshua M. "Do Not Eat over the Blood." *Annual of the Swedish Theological Institute* 8 (1972): 78–105.

Gross, Walter. "Die Herausführungsformel: Zum Verhältnis von Formel und Syntax." *Zeitschrift für die alttestamentliche Wissenschaft* 86 (1974): 425–53.

Gruber, Mayer I. *Aspects of Nonverbal Communication in the Ancient Near East.* Vol. 1. Studia Pohl: Dissertationes Scientificae De Rebus Orientis Antiqui 12. Rome: Biblical Institute Press, 1980.

———. "Women in the Cult according to the Priestly Code." Pages 35–48 in *Judaic Perspectives on Ancient Israel.* Edited by Jacob Neusner, Baruch A. Levine, and Ernest S. Frerichs. Philadelphia: Fortress, 1987.

Habel, Norman C. *The Land Is Mine: Six Biblical Land Ideologies.* Overtures to Biblical Theology. Minneapolis: Fortress, 1995.

Halbe, Jörn. "Die Reihe der Inzestverbote Lev 18:7–18: Entstehung und Gestaltungsstufen." *Zeitschrift für die alttestamentliche Wissenschaft* 92 (1980): 60–88.

Hals, Ronald M. *Grace and Faith in the Old Testament.* Minneapolis: Augsburg, 1980.

Haran, Menahem. "Uses of Incense in the Ancient Israelite Ritual." *Vetus Testamentum* 10 (1960): 113–29.

———. *Temples and Temple-Service in Ancient Israel: An Inquiry into the Character of Cult Phenomena and the Historical Setting of the Priestly School.* Oxford: Clarendon, 1977.

———. "Behind the Scenes of History: Determining the Date of the Priestly Source." *Journal of Biblical Literature* 100 (1981): 321–33.

Harms, Theodor. *Das dritte Buch Mose.* Hermannsburg: Missionshausbuchdrückerei, 1871.

Harris, Robert L. "Leviticus." Pages 499–654 in vol. 2 of *The Expositor's Bible Commentary.* Grand Rapids: Zondervan, 1990.

Harrison, Roland Kenneth. *Introduction to the Old Testament: With a Comprehensive Review of Old Testament Studies and a Special Supplement on the Apocrypha.* Grand Rapids: Eerdmans, 1969.

———. *Leviticus: An Introduction and Commentary.* Tyndale Old Testament Commentaries. Downers Grove, Ill.: InterVarsity, 1980.

Hartley, John E. *Leviticus.* Word Biblical Commentary 4. Dallas: Word, 1992.

Hartley, John E., and Dwyer, Timothy. "An Investigation into the Location of the Laws on Offerings to Molek in the Book of Leviticus." Pages 81–93 in *"Go to the Land I Will Show You": Studies in Honor of Dwight W. Young.* Edited by Joseph E. Coleson and Victor H. Matthews. Winona Lake, Ind.: Eisenbrauns, 1996.

Heider, George C. *The Cult of Molek: A Reassessment.* Journal for the Study of the Old Testament: Supplement Series 43. Sheffield, England: JSOT Press, 1985.

Heinisch, Paul. *Das Buch Leviticus.* Die Heilige Schrift des Alten Testaments. Bonn: Hanstein, 1935.

Heller, Jan. "Die Symbolik des Fettes im AT." *Vetus Testamentum* 20 (1970): 106–8.

Herman, Menahem. *Tithe as Gift: The Institution in the Pentateuch and in Light of Mauss's Prestation Theory.* San Francisco: Mellen Research University Press, 1991.

Hoenig, Sidney B. "Sabbatical Years and the Year of Jubilee." *Jewish Quarterly Review* 59 (1969): 222–36.

Hoffmann, David. *Das Buch Levitikus.* Berlin: Poppelauer, 1905/1906.

Hoffner, H. A. "Incest, Sodomy and Bestiality in the Ancient Near East." Pages 81–90 in *Orient and Occident: Essays Presented to Cyrus H. Gordon on the Occasion of His Sixty-fifth Birthday.* Edited by Harry A. Hoffner. Kevelaer, Germany: Butzon & Bercker, 1973.

Hoftijzer, Jacob. "Das sogenannte Feueropfer." Pages 114–34 in *Hebräische Wortforschung: Festschrift zum 80. Geburtstag von Walter Baumgartner.* Supplements to Vetus Testamentum 16. Leiden: Brill, 1967.

Holladay, William L., ed. *A Concise Hebrew and Aramaic Lexicon of the Old Testament: Based upon the Lexical Work of Ludwig Koehler and Walter Baumgartner.* Grand Rapids: Eerdmans, 1971.

Horton, Fred L., Jr. "Form and Structure in Laws Relating to Women: Leviticus 18:6–18." Pages 20–33 in *Society of Biblical Literature Seminar Papers.* Edited by G. MacRae. Cambridge, Mass.: Society of Biblical Literature, 1973.

Houston, Walter. *Purity and Monotheism: Clean and Unclean Animals in Biblical Law.* Journal for the Study of the Old Testament: Supplement Series 140. Sheffield, England: JSOT Press, 1993.

———. "Contrast in Tense and Exegesis: The Case of the Field Vowed and Sold, Leviticus 27:20." *Vetus Testamentum* 49 (1999): 416–20.

Houten, Christiana van. *The Alien in Israelite Law.* Journal for the Study of the Old Testament: Supplement Series 107. Sheffield, England: JSOT Press, 1991.

Houtman, C. "Another Look at Forbidden Mixtures." *Vetus Testamentum* 34 (1984): 226–28.

———. "On the Function of the Holy Incense (Exodus XXX 34–38) and the Sacred Anointing Oil (Exodus XXX 22–23)." *Vetus Testamentum* 42 (1992): 458–65.

Hudson, Michael. " 'Proclaim Liberty throughout the Land': The Economic Roots of the Jubilee." *Bible Review* 15 (1999): 26–33, 44.

Hulse, E. V. "The Nature of Biblical 'Leprosy' and the Use of Alternative Medical Terms in Modern Translations of the Bible." *Palestine Exploration Quarterly* 107 (1975): 87–105.

Hummel, Horace D. *The Word Becoming Flesh: An Introduction to the Origin, Purpose, and Meaning of the Old Testament.* St. Louis: Concordia, 1979.

Hurowitz, Victor Avigdor. "אבן משכית—A New Interpretation." *Journal of Biblical Literature* 118 (1999): 201–8.

Hurvitz, Ari. *A Linguistic Study of the Relationship between the Priestly Source and the Book of Ezekiel: A New Approach to an Old Problem.* Cahiers de la Revue biblique 20. Paris: Gabalda, 1982.

———. "Dating the Priestly Source in the Light of the Historical Study of Biblical Hebrew a Century after Wellhausen." *Zeitschrift für die alttestamentliche Wissenschaft* 100 (1988): 88–100.

Hutton, Rodney R. "The Case of the Blasphemer Revisited (Leviticus 24:10–23)." *Vetus Testamentum* 49 (1999): 532–41.

Jackson, Bernard S. "Talion and Purity: Some Glosses on Mary Douglas." Pages 107–23 in *Reading Leviticus: A Conversation with Mary Douglas.* Edited by John F. A. Sawyer. Journal for the Study of the Old Testament: Supplement Series 227. Sheffield, England: Sheffield Academic Press, 1996.

Janowski, Bernd. *Sühne als Heilsgeschehen: Studien zur Sühnetheologie der Priesterschrift und zur Wurzel KPR in alten Orient und im Alten Testament.* Wissenschaftliche Monographien zum Alten und Neuen Testament 55. Neukirchen-Vluyn, Germany: Neukirchener, 1982.

Jenson, Philip Peter. *Graded Holiness: A Key to the Priestly Conception of the World.* Journal for the Study of the Old Testament: Supplement Series 106. Sheffield, England: JSOT Press, 1992.

———. "The Levitical System." Pages 25–40 in *Sacrifice in the Bible.* Edited by Roger T. Beckwith and Martin J. Selman. Grand Rapids: Baker, 1995.

Jeremias, Joachim. *The Eucharistic Words of Jesus.* Translated by Norman Perrin. London: SCM, 1966.

Johnson, Luke T. "The Use of Leviticus 19 in the Letter of James." *Journal of Biblical Literature* 101 (1982): 391–401.

Johnston, Philip S. *Shades of Sheol: Death and Afterlife in the Old Testament.* Downers Grove, Ill.: InterVarsity Press, 2002.

Joosten, Jan. *People and Land in the Holiness Code: An Exegetical Study of the Ideational Framework of the Law in Leviticus 17–26.* Supplements to Vetus Testamentum 67, Leiden: Brill, 1996.

Jukes, Andrew John. *The Law of the Offerings.* Grand Rapids: Kregel, 1976.

Jüngling, Hans-Winfried. "Das Buch Levitikus in der Forschung seit Karl Elligers Kommentar aus dem Jahre 1966." Pages 1–46 in *Levitikus als Buch.* Edited by Heinz-Josef Fabry and Hans-Winfried Jüngling. Bonner biblische Beiträge 119. Berlin: Philo, 1999.

Just, Arthur J., Jr. *Luke 1:1–9:50.* Concordia Commentary. Saint Louis: Concordia, 1996.

———. *Luke 9:51–24:53.* Concordia Commentary. St. Louis: Concordia, 1997.

Kaiser, Walter C., Jr. "The Book of Leviticus." Pages 983–1191 in vol. 1 of *The New Interpreter's Bible.* Nashville: Abingdon, 1994.

Käsemann, Ernst. *Commentary on Romans*. Translated and edited by Geoffrey W. Bromiley. Grand Rapids, Mich.: Eerdmans, 1980.

Kaufman, Stephen A. "A Reconstruction of the Social Welfare Systems of Ancient Israel." Pages 277–86 in *In the Shelter of Elyon: Essays on Ancient Palestinian Life and Literature in Honour of G. W. Ahlström*. Edited by W. Boyd Barrick and John R. Spencer. Journal for the Study of the Old Testament: Supplement Series 31. Sheffield, England: JSOT Press, 1984.

Kaufmann, Yehezkel. *The Religion of Israel: From Its Beginnings to the Babylonian Exile*. Translated and abridged by Moshe Greenberg. Chicago: University of Chicago Press, 1960.

Kautzsch, E., ed. *Gesenius' Hebrew Grammar*. Translated by A. E. Cowley. 2d ed. Oxford: Clarendon, 1910.

Kawashima, Robert S. "The Jubilee, Every 49 or 50 Years?" *Vetus Testamentum* 53 (2003): 117–20.

———. "The Jubilee Year and the Return of Cosmic Purity." *Catholic Biblical Quarterly* 65 (2003): 370–89.

Keel, Othmar. *The Symbolism of the Biblical World: Ancient Near Eastern Iconography and the Book of Psalms*. Translated by Timothy J. Hallett. New York: Seabury, 1978.

Keil, C. F. *The Pentateuch,* vol. 2. Biblical Commentary on the Old Testament by C. F. Keil and F. Delitzsch. Translated by James Martin. Edinburgh: T&T Clark, 1869.

Kilian, Rudolf. *Literarkritische und formgeschichtliche Untersuchung des Heiligkeitsgestzes*. Bonner biblische Beiträge 19. Bonn: Hanstein, 1963.

Kiuchi, N. *The Purification Offering in the Priestly Literature: Its Meaning and Function*. Journal for the Study of the Old Testament: Supplement Series 56. Sheffield, England: JSOT Press, 1987.

Kleinig, John W. "Witting or Unwitting Ritualists." *Lutheran Theological Journal* 22 (1988): 13–22.

———. "What's the Use of Naming God?" *Lutheran Theological Journal* 26 (1992): 27–34.

———. *The Lord's Song: The Basis, Function and Significance of Choral Music in Chronicles*. Journal for the Study of the Old Testament: Supplement Series 156. Sheffield, England: JSOT Press, 1993.

———. "Sharing in God's Holiness." *Lutheran Theological Review* 8 (1995/1996): 105–18.

———. "The Blood for Sprinkling: Atoning Blood in Leviticus and Hebrews." *Lutheran Theological Journal* 33 (1999): 124–35.

———. "Where Is Your God? Luther on God's Self-Localization." Pages 117–31 in *All Theology Is Christology: Essays in Honor of David P. Scaer*. Edited by Dean O. Wenthe et al. Fort Wayne, Ind.: Concordia Theological Seminary Press, 2000.

———. "The Lord's Supper as a Sacrificial Banquet." *Logia* 12 (2003): 11–16.

Klingbeil, Gerald A. "Ritual Space in the Ordination Ritual of Leviticus 8." *Journal of Northwest Semitic Languages* 21 (1995): 59–82.

———. "The Syntactic Structure of the Ritual of Ordination (Lev 8)." *Biblica* 77 (1996): 509–19.

———. "Ritual Time in Leviticus 8 with Special Reference to the Seven Day Period in the Old Testament." *Zeitschrift für die alttestamentliche Wissenschaft* 109 (1997): 500–13.

———. *A Comparative Study of the Ritual of Ordination As Found in Leviticus 8 and Emar 369.* Lewiston, N.Y.: Mellen, 1998.

Klostermann, August. *Der Pentateuch: Beiträge zu seinem Verständnis und seiner Entstehungsgeschichte.* Leipzig: Deichert, 1893.

Knierim, Rolf P. *Text and Concept in Leviticus 1:1–9: A Case in Exegetical Method.* Forschungen zum Alten Testament 2. Tübingen: Mohr, 1992.

Knohl, Israel. "The Priestly Torah versus the Holiness School: Sabbath and Festivals." *Hebrew Union College Annual* 58 (1987): 65–117.

———. *The Sanctuary of Silence: The Priestly Torah and the Holiness School.* Minneapolis: Fortress, 1995.

Koch, Klaus. *Die Priesterschrift von Exodus 25 bis Leviticus 16: Eine überlieferungsgeschichtliche und literaturkritische Untersuchung.* Göttingen: Vandenhoeck & Ruprecht, 1959.

———. "Der Spruch 'Sein Blut bleibe über seinem Haupt und die israelitische Auffassung vom vergossenen Blut." *Vetus Testamentum* 12 (1962): 396–416.

Koehler, Ludwig, Walter Baumgartner, and Johann Jakob Stamm. *The Hebrew and Aramaic Lexicon of the Old Testament.* Translated and edited under the supervision of M. E. J. Richardson. 5 vols. Leiden: Brill, 1994–2000.

Kornfeld, Walter. "Reine und unreine Tiere im Alten Testament." *Kairos* 7 (1965): 134–47.

———. *Das Buch Leviticus.* Düsseldorf: Patmos, 1972.

Kraus, Hans Joachim. *Worship in Israel: A Cultic History of the Old Testament.* Translated by Geoffrey Buswell. Richmond, Va.: John Knox, 1966.

Kugel, James L. "On Hidden Hatred and Open Reproach: Early Exegesis of Leviticus 19:17." *Harvard Theological Review* 80 (1987): 43–61.

Kugler, Robert A. "Holiness, Purity, the Body, and Society: The Evidence for Theological Conflict in Leviticus." *Journal for the Study of the Old Testament* 76 (1997): 3–27.

Kurtz, J. H. *Sacrificial Worship of the Old Testament.* Translated by James Martin. Edinburgh : T&T Clark, 1863.

Kutsch, Ernst. "מִקְרָא." *Zeitschrift für die alttestamentliche Wissenschaft* 65 (1953): 247–53.

Labuschagne, Casper J. "The Pattern of the Divine Speech Formulas in the Pentateuch: The Key to Its Literary Structure." *Vetus Testamentum* 32 (1982): 268–96.

Laughlin, John C. H. "The 'Strange Fire' of Nadab and Abihu." *Journal of Biblical Literature* 95 (1976): 559–65.

Leeuwen, J. H. van. "The Meaning of תֻּפִינֵי in Lev 6, 14." *Zeitschrift für die alttestamentliche Wissenschaft* 100 (1988): 268–69.

Leithart, Peter J. "Attendants of Yahweh's House: Priesthood in the Old Testament." *Journal for the Study of the Old Testament* 85 (1999): 3–24.

Lemche, Niels Peter "The Manumission of Slaves—the Fallow Year—the Sabbatical Year—the Jubilee Year." *Vetus Testamentum* 26 (1976): 38–59.

Leupold, H. C. *Exposition of Zechariah.* Columbus: Wartburg, 1956.

Levine, Baruch A. "The Descriptive Tabernacle Texts of the Pentateuch." *Journal of the American Oriental Society* 85 (1965): 307–18.

———. *In the Presence of the Lord: A Study of Cult and Some Cultic Terms in Ancient Israel.* Studies in Judaism in Late Antiquity 5. Leiden: Brill, 1974.

———. "The Epilogue to the Holiness Code: A Priestly Statement on the Destiny of Israel." Pages 9–34 in *Judaic Perspectives on Ancient Israel.* Edited by Jacob Neusner, Baruch A. Levine, and Ernest S. Frerichs. Philadelphia: Fortress, 1987.

———. *Leviticus* ויקרא*. The Traditional Hebrew Text with the New JPS Translation.* Philadelphia: Jewish Publication Society, 1989.

Lewis, Theodore J. *Cults of the Dead in Ancient Israel and Ugarit.* Harvard Semitic Monographs 39. Atlanta: Scholars Press, 1989.

Lockwood, Gregory J. *1 Corinthians.* Concordia Commentary. St. Louis: Concordia, 2000.

Loewenstamm, Samuel E. "נשך *and* מ/תרבית." *Journal of Biblical Literature* 88 (1969): 78–80.

Lohfink, N. F. "Abänderung der Theologie des priesterlichen Geschichtswerk im Segen des Heiligkeitsgetzes: Zu Lev. 26, 9. 11–13." Pages 129–36 in *Wort und Geschichte: Festschrift für Karl Elliger zum 70. Geburtstag.* Edited by Hartmut Gese and Hans Peter Rüger. Alter Orient und Altes Testament 18. Kevelaer, Germany: Butzon & Bercker, 1973.

Lund, Nils Wilhelm. *Chiasmus in the New Testament: A Study in Formgeschichte.* Chapel Hill: University of North Carolina Press, 1942.

Lust, Johan. "On Wizards and Prophets." Pages 133–42 in *Studies on Prophecy: A Collection of Twelve Papers.* Supplements to Vetus Testamentum 26. Leiden: Brill, 1974.

Lyonnet, Stanislas, and Leopold Sabourin. *Sin, Redemption, and Sacrifice: A Biblical and Patristic Study.* Analecta Biblica 48. Rome: Biblical Institute, 1970.

Maccoby, Hyam. "Holiness and Purity: The Holy Place in Leviticus and Ezra-Nehemiah." Pages 153–70 in *Reading Leviticus: A Conversation with Mary Douglas.* Edited by John F. A. Sawyer. Journal for the Study of the Old Testament: Supplement Series 227. Sheffield, England: Sheffield Academic Press, 1996.

———. *Ritual and Morality: The Ritual Purity System and Its Place in Judaism.* Cambridge: Cambridge University Press, 1999.

Magonet, Jonathan. "The Structure and Meaning of Leviticus 19." *Hebrew Annual Review* 7 (1983): 151–67.

Maloney, Robert P. "Usury and Restrictions on Interest-Taking in the Ancient Near East." *Catholic Biblical Quarterly* 36 (1974): 1–20.

Marcus, David. "The Term 'Chin' in the Semitic Languages." *Bulletin of the American Schools of Oriental Research* 226 (1977): 53–60.

Martin, Ralph P. *2 Corinthians*. Word. Waco, Tex.: Word, 1986.

Mathews, K. A. "The Leviticus Scroll (11QpaleoLev) and the Text of the Hebrew Bible." *Catholic Biblical Quarterly* 48 (1986): 171–207.

Mathys, Hans-Peter. *Liebe deinen Nächsten wie dich Selbst: Untersuchungen zum alttestamentlichen Gebot der Nächstenliebe (Lev 19, 18).* Orbis biblicus et orientalis 71. Göttingen: Vandenhoeck & Ruprecht, 1986.

McCarthy, Dennis J. "Symbolism of Blood and Sacrifice." *Journal of Biblical Literature* 88 (1969): 166–76.

———. "Further Notes on the Symbolism of Blood and Sacrifice." *Journal of Biblical Literature* 92 (1973): 205–10.

McEvenue, Sean E. *The Narrative Style of the Priestly Writer.* Analecta Biblica 50. Rome: Biblical Institute, 1971.

Meacham, Tirzah. "The Missing Daughter: Leviticus 18-20." *Zeitschrift für die alttestamentliche Wissenschaft* 109 (1997): 254–59.

Meier, Samuel A. "House Fungus: Mesopotamia and Israel (Lev 14:33–53)." *Revue biblique* 96 (1989): 184–92.

———. "The Sabbath and Purification Cycles." Pages 3–11 in *The Sabbath in Jewish and Christian Traditions.* Edited by Tamara C. Eskenazi, Daniel J. Harrington, and William H. Shea. New York: Crossroad, 1991.

Meinhold, Arndt. "Zur Beziehung Gott, Volk, Land im Jobel-Zusammenhang." *Biblische Zeitschrift* 29 (1985): 245–61.

Merras, Merja. *The Origins of the Celebration of the Christian Feast of Epiphany: An Ideological, Cultural and Historical Study.* Joensuu, Finland: University of Joensuu Press, 1995.

Metzinger, Adalbert. "Die Substitutionstheorie und die alttestamentliche Opfer mit besonderer Berücksichtigung von Lev 17:11." *Biblica* 21 (1940): 159–68, 247–72.

Meyers, Carol L. *The Tabernacle Menorah: A Synthetic Study of a Symbol from the Biblical Cult.* American Schools of Oriental Research Dissertation Series 2. Missoula, Mont.: Scholars Press, 1976.

Milgrom, Jacob. *Studies in Levitical Terminology.* Vol. 1: *The Encroacher and the Levite: The Term ʿAboda.* Berkley: University of California Press, 1970.

———. "A Prolegomenon to Leviticus 17:11." *Journal of Biblical Literature* 90 (1971): 149–56.

———. "Sin Offering or Purification Offering." *Vetus Testamentum* 21 (1971): 237–39. Reprinted in *Studies in Cultic Theology and Terminology.* Leiden: Brill, 1983, 67–69.

———. "The Alleged Wave-Offering in Israel and the Ancient Near East." *Israel Exploration Journal* 22 (1972): 33–38. Reprinted in *Studies in Cultic Theology and Terminology.* Leiden: Brill, 1983, 133–38.

———. *"Hattĕnûpâ."* Pages 93–110 in *Zer Li'gevurot: President Z. Shazar Volume.* Edited by B. Z. Luria (Hebrew). Jerusalem: Kiryat Sepher, 1972. Translated in *Studies in Cultic Theology and Terminology.* Leiden: Brill, 1983, 139–58.

———. "The *Šôq hattĕrûmâ*: A Chapter in Cultic History." *Tarbiz* 42 (1972): 1–14 (Hebrew). Translated in *Studies in Cultic Theology and Terminology.* Leiden: Brill, 1983, 159–70.

———. "Akkadian Confirmation for the Meaning of the Term *tĕrûmâ*." *Tarbiz* 44 (1974/1975): 189 (Hebrew). Translated in *Studies in Cultic Theology and Terminology.* Leiden: Brill, 1983, 171–72.

———. "The Concept of *Maʿal* in the Bible and the Ancient Near East." *Journal of the American Oriental Society* 96 (1976): 236–47.

———. *Cult and Conscience: The ASHAM and the Priestly Doctrine of Repentance.* Studies in Judaism in Late Antiquity 18. Leiden: Brill, 1976.

———. "Israel's Sanctuary: The Priestly 'Picture of Dorian Gray.' " *Revue biblique* 83 (1976): 390–99. Reprinted in *Studies in Cultic Theology and Terminology.* Leiden: Brill, 1983, 75–84.

———. "Two Kinds of *ḥaṭṭāʾt*." *Vetus Testamentum* 26 (1976): 333–37. Reprinted in *Studies in Cultic Theology and Terminology.* Leiden: Brill, 1983, 70–74.

———. "The Betrothed Slave-Girl: Lev. 19:20–22." *Zeitschrift für die alttestamentliche Wissenschaft* 89 (1977): 43–50.

———. *Studies in Cultic Theology and Terminology.* Studies in Judaism in Late Antiquity 36. Leiden: Brill, 1983.

———. "The Two Pericopes on the Purification Offering." Pages 211–15 in *The Word of the Lord Shall Go Forth: Essays in Honor of David Noel Freedman in Celebration of His Sixtieth Birthday.* Edited by Carol L. Meyers and M. O'Connor. Winona Lake, Ind.: Eisenbrauns, 1983.

———. "Rationale for Cultic Law: The Case of Impurity." *Semeia* 45 (1989): 103–9.

———. "Ablutions." Pages 87–95 in *Die Hebräische Bibel und ihre zweifache Nachgeschichte: Festschrift für Rolf Rendtorff zum 65. Geburtstag.* Edited by Erhard Blum, Christian Macholz, and Ekkehard W. Stegemann. Neukirchen-Vluyn, Germany: Neukirchener, 1990.

———. "The *Modus Operandi* of the *Ḥaṭṭāʾt:* A Rejoinder." *Journal of Biblical Literature* 109 (1990): 111–13.

———. "The Composition of Leviticus, Chapter 11." Pages 183–91 in *Priesthood and Cult in Ancient Israel.* Edited by Gary A. Anderson and Saul M. Olyan. Journal for the Study of the Old Testament: Supplement Series 125. Sheffield, England: JSOT Press, 1991.

———. "The Consecration of the Priests: A Literary Comparison of Leviticus 8 and Exodus 29." Pages 273–86 in *Ernten, was man sät: Festschrift für Klaus Koch zu seinem 65. Geburtstag.* Edited by Dwight R. Daniels, Uwe Gleßmer, and Martin Rösel. Neukirchen-Vluyn, Germany: Neukirchener, 1991.

———. *Leviticus 1–16: A New Translation with Introduction and Commentary.* Anchor Bible 3. New York: Doubleday, 1991.

———. "Two Biblical Hebrew Priestly Terms: *šeqeṣ* and *ṭameʾ*." *Maarav* 8 (1992): 107–16.

———. "Does the Bible Prohibit Homosexuality?" *Biblical Review* 9 (1993): 11.

———, "Response to Rolf Rendtorff." *Journal for the Study of the Old Testament* 60 (1993): 83–85.

———. "Confusing the Sacred and Impure: A Rejoinder." *Vetus Testamentum* 44 (1994): 554–59.

———. "How Not to Read the Bible." *Biblical Review* 10 (1994): 14, 48.

———. "The Land Redeemer and the Jubilee." Pages 66–69 in *Fortunate the Eyes That See: Essays in Honor of David Noel Freedman in Celebration of His Seventieth Birthday.* Edited by Astrid B. Beck et al. Grand Rapids: Eerdmans, 1995.

———. "The Changing Concept of Holiness in the Pentateuchal Codes with Emphasis on Leviticus 19." Pages 65–75 in *Reading Leviticus: A Conversation with Mary Douglas.* Edited by John F. A. Sawyer. Journal for the Study of the Old Testament: Supplement Series 227. Sheffield, England: Sheffield Academic Press, 1996.

———. "Further on the Expiatory Sacrifices." *Journal of Biblical Literature* 115 (1996): 511–14.

———. "Law and Narrative and the Exegesis of Leviticus XIX." *Vetus Testamentum* 46 (1996): 544–48.

———. "The Antiquity of the Priestly Source: A Reply to Joseph Blenkinsopp." *Zeitschrift für die alttestamentliche Wissenschaft* 111 (1999): 10–22.

———. *Leviticus 17–22: A New Translation with Introduction and Commentary.* Anchor Bible 3A. New York: Doubleday, 2000.

———. *Leviticus 23–27: A New Translation with Introduction and Commentary.* Anchor Bible 3B. New York: Doubleday, 2001.

Miller, James E. "Notes on Leviticus 18." *Zeitschrift für die alttestamentliche Wissenschaft* 112 (2000): 401–3.

Mitchell, Bill. "Leviticus 24:6: The Bread of the Presence: Rows or Piles?" *The Bible Translator* 33 (1982): 447–48.

Mitchell, Christopher W. *The Song of Songs.* Concordia Commentary. Saint Louis: Concordia, 2003.

Möller, Hans. "Lösungsvorschlag für eine Crux Interpretum (Lev 25, 33)." *Zeitschrift für die alttestamentliche Wissenschaft* 90 (1978): 411–12.

Moloney, Francis J. *Signs and Shadows: Reading John 5–12.* Minneapolis: Fortress, 1996.

Morgenstern, Julian. "The Decalogue of the Holiness Code." *Hebrew Union College Annual* 26 (1995): 1–27.

Morris, Leon. "The Biblical Use of the Term 'Blood.' " *Journal of Theological Studies* 3 (1952): 216–27.

———. "The Biblical Use of the Term 'Blood.' " *Journal of Theological Studies* 6 (1955): 77–82.

Muraoka, Takumitsu. "A Syntactic Problem in Lev. XIX 18b." *Journal of Semitic Studies* 23 Autumn (1978): 291–97.

Nelson, Richard D. *Raising Up a Faithful Priest: Community and Priesthood in Biblical Theology.* Louisville, Ky.: Westminster/John Knox, 1993.

———. " 'He Offered Himself': Sacrifice in Hebrews." *Interpretation* 57 (2003): 251–65.

Neudecker, R. " 'And You Shall Love Your Neighbour as Yourself—I Am the Lord' (Lev 19, 18) in Jewish Interpretation." *Biblica* 73 (1992): 496–517.

Nielsen, Kjeld. *Incense in Ancient Israel.* Supplements to Vetus Testamentum 38. Leiden: Brill, 1986.

Noordtzij, A. *Leviticus.* Translated by Raymond Togtman. Grand Rapids: Zondervan, 1982.

North, Robert Grady. *Sociology of the Biblical Jubilee.* Analecta Biblica 4. Rome: Pontifical Biblical Institute, 1954.

Noth, Martin. *A History of Pentateuchal Traditions.* Translated with an introduction by Bernhard W. Anderson. Englewood Cliffs, N.J.: Prentice-Hall, 1972.

———. *Leviticus: A Commentary.* Revised edition. Translated by J. E. Anderson. Old Testament Library. Philadelphia: Westminster, 1977.

Oesterley, W. O. E. *Sacrifices in Ancient Israel: Their Origin, Purposes and Development.* London: Hodder & Stoughton, 1937.

Olyan, Saul, M. " 'And with a Male You Shall Not Lie the Lying Down of a Woman': On the Meaning and Significance of Leviticus 18:22 and 20:13." *Journal of the History of Sexuality* 5 (1994): 179–206.

———. *Rites and Rank: Hierarchy in Biblical Representations of Cult.* Princeton: Princeton University Press, 2000.

Orlinsky, Harry M. "The Hebrew Root *ŠKB.*" *Journal of Biblical Literature* 63 (1944): 19–44.

Otto, Rudolf. *The Idea of the Holy: An Inquiry into the Non-Rational Factor in the Idea of the Divine and Its Relation to the Rational.* Translated by John W. Harvey. 2d ed. London: Oxford University Press, 1958.

Paschen, Wilfried. *Rein und Unrein: Untersuchung zur biblischen Wortgeschichte.* Studien zum Alten und Neuen Testament 24. Munich: Kösel, 1970.

Pfitzner, Victor C. *Hebrews.* Abingdon New Testament Commentaries. Nashville: Abingdon, 1997.

Phillips, Anthony J. "Uncovering the Father's Skirt." *Vetus Testamentum* 30 (1980): 38–43.

Pilch, John J. "Biblical Leprosy and Body Symbolism." *Biblical Theology Bulletin* 11 (1981): 108–13.

Porter, J. R. *Leviticus.* Cambridge Bible Commentary. Cambridge: Cambridge University Press, 1976.

———. "Lev. 27:20: Some Further Considerations." *Vetus Testamentum* 50 (2000): 569–71.

Pursiful, Darrell J. *The Cultic Motif in the Spirituality of the Book of Hebrews.* Lewiston, N.Y.: Mellen, 1993.

Rabinowitz, Jacob J. "A Biblical Parallel to a Legal Formula from Ugarit." *Vetus Testamentum* 8 (1958): 95.

Rad, Gerhard von. *Old Testament Theology.* Vol. 1. Translated D. M. G. Stalker. New York: Harper, 1962.

———. "The Problem of the Hexateuch." Pages 1–78 in *The Problem of the Hexateuch and Other Essays.* Translated by E. W. Trueman Dicken. New York: McGraw-Hill, 1966.

Rainey, Anson F. "The Order of Sacrifices in Old Testament Ritual Texts." *Biblica* 51 (1970): 485–98.

Rattray, Susan. "Marriage Rules, Kinship Terms and Family Structure in the Bible." Pages 537–44 in *Society of Biblical Literature 1987 Seminar Papers.* Edited by Kent Harold Richards. Atlanta: Scholars Press, 1987.

Regev, Eyal. "Priestly Dynamic Holiness and Deuteronomic Static Holiness." *Vetus Testamentum* 51 (2001): 243–61.

Rendsburg, Gary A. "The *Inclusio* in Leviticus xi." *Vetus Testamentum* 43 (1993): 418–21.

Rendtorff, Rolf. *Die Gesetze in der Priesterschrift.* 2d ed. Forschungen zur Religion und Literatur des Alten und Neuen Testaments 62. Göttingen: Vandenhoeck & Ruprecht, 1963.

———. *Studien zur Geschichte des Opfers im alten Israel.* Wissenschaftliche Monographien zum Alten und Neuen Testament 24. Neukirchen-Vluyn, Germany: Neukirchener, 1967.

———. *Leviticus.* Biblischer Kommentar Altes Testament 3/1–3. Neukirchen-Vluyn, Germany: Neukirchener, 1985, 1990, 1992.

———. "Die Sündige noefoes." Pages 211–20 in *Was ist der Mensch … ?Beiträge zur Anthropologie des Alten Testaments; Hans Walter Wolff zum 80. Geburtstag*. Edited by Frank Crüsemann, Christoff Hardmeier, and Rainer Kessler. Munich: Kaiser, 1992.

———. "Two Kinds of P? Some Reflections on the Occasion of the Publishing of Jacob Milgrom's Commentary on Leviticus 1–16." *Journal for the Study of the Old Testament* 60 (1993): 75–81.

———. "Another Prolegomenon to Leviticus 17:11." Pages 23–28 in *Pomegranates and Golden Bells: Studies in Biblical, Jewish, and Near Eastern Ritual, Law, and Literature in Honor of Jacob Milgrom.* Edited by David P. Wright, David Noel Freedman, and Avi Hurvitz. Winona Lake, Ind.: Eisenbrauns, 1995.

———. "Is It Possible to Read Leviticus as a Separate Book?" Pages 22–35 in *Reading Leviticus: A Conversation with Mary Douglas.* Edited by John F. A. Sawyer. Journal for the Study of the Old Testament: Supplement Series 227. Sheffield, England: Sheffield Academic Press, 1996.

———. *The Covenant Formula: An Exegetical and Theological Investigation.* Translated by Margaret Kohl. Edinburgh: T&T Clark, 1998.

Renwick, David, A. *Paul, the Temple, and the Presence of God.* Brown Judaic Studies 224. Atlanta: Scholars Press, 1991.

Reventlow, Henning Graf. "Sein Blut komme über sein Haupt." *Vetus Testamentum* 10 (1960): 311–27.

———. *Das Heiligkeitsgesetz: Formgeshichtlich Untersucht.* Wissenschaftliche Monographien zum Alten und Neuen Testament 6. Neukirchen-Vluyn, Germany: Neukirchener, 1961.

Ringgren, Helmer. *Sacrifice in the Bible.* London: Lutterworth, 1962.

Rodriguez, Angel Manuel. *Substitution in the Hebrew Cultus.* Andrews University Seminary Doctoral Dissertation Series 3. Berrien Springs, Mich.: Andrews University Press, 1979.

———. "Leviticus 16: Its Literary Structure." *Andrews University Seminary Studies* 34 (1996): 269–86.

Roo, Jacqueline C. R. de. "Was the Goat Azazel Destined for the Wrath of God?" *Biblica* 81 (2000): 233–42.

Rost, Leonhard. *Studien zum Opfer im Alten Israel.* Beiträge zur Wissenschaft vom Alten und Neuen Testament 113. Stuttgart: Kohlhammer, 1981.

Rouillard, Hedwige, and Josef Tropper. "Vom kanaanäischen Ahnenkult zur Zauberei: Eine Auslegungsgeschichte zu den hebräischen Begriffen *ʾwb* und *ydʿny*." *Ugarit-Forschungen* 19 (1987): 235–54.

Rowley, Harold Henry. *Worship in Ancient Israel: Its Forms and Meaning.* London: SPCK, 1967.

Ruager, Søren. " 'Wir haben einen Altar' (Hebr 13, 10)." *Kerygma und Dogma* 36 (1990): 72–77.

Rüger, H. P. " 'Dann entfernt er seinen Kopf samt dessen Federn:' Zur Auslegungsgeschichte von Lev 1, 16." Pages 163–72 in *Wort und Geschichte: Festschrift für*

Karl Elliger zum 70. Geburtstag. Edited by Hartmut Gese and Hans Peter Rüger. Alter Orient und Altes Testament 18. Kevelaer, Germany: Butzon & Bercker, 1973.

Ruwe, Andreas. *"Heiligkeitsgesetz" und "Priesterschrift."* Forschungen zum Alten Testament 26. Tübingen: Mohr, 1999.

Sailhamer, John H. "Leviticus." Pages 323–67 in *The Pentateuch as Narrative: A Biblical-Theological Commentary.* Grand Rapids: Zondervan, 1992.

Sanders, James A. "Sins, Debts, and Jubilee Release." Pages 84–92 in *Luke and Scripture: The Function of Sacred Tradition in Luke-Acts,* by Craig A. Evans and James A. Sanders. Minneapolis: Fortress, 1993.

Sansom, M. C. "Laying On of Hands in the Old Testament." *Expository Times* 94 (1983): 323–26.

Sawyer, John F. A. "The Language of Leviticus." Pages 15–20 in *Reading Leviticus: A Conversation with Mary Douglas.* Edited by John F. A. Sawyer. Journal for the Study of the Old Testament: Supplement Series 227. Sheffield, England: Sheffield Academic Press, 1996.

Schenker, Adrian. "Der Unterscheid zwischen Sündopfer *chattat* und Schuldopfer *asham* im Licht von Lv 5, 17–19 und 5, 1–6." Pages 115–23 in *Pentateuchal and Deuteronomistic Studies: Papers Read at the XIIIth IOSOT Congress, Leuven 1989.* Edited by C. Brekelmans and J. Lust. Louvain (Leuven), Belgium: Leuven University Press, 1990.

———. "Critical Notes: Once Again, the Expiatory Sacrifices." *Journal of Biblical Literature* 116 (1997): 697–99.

———. "The Biblical Legislation on the Release of Slaves: The Road from Exodus to Leviticus." *Journal for the Study of the Old Testament* 78 (1998): 23–41.

———. "Welche Verfehlungen und welche Opfer in Lev 5, 1–6?" Pages 249–62 in *Levitikus als Buch.* Edited by Heinz-Josef Fabry and Hans-Winfried Jüngling. Bonner biblische Beiträge 119. Berlin: Philo, 1999.

Schmidt, Brian B. *Israel's Beneficent Dead: Ancestor Cult and Necromancy in Ancient Israelite Religion and Tradition.* Winona Lake, Ind.: Eisenbrauns, 1994.

Scholer, John M. *Proleptic Priests: Priesthood in the Epistle to the Hebrews*. Journal for the Study of the New Testament: Supplement Series 49. Sheffield, England: JSOT Press, 1991.

Schottroff, Willy. *Gedenken im Alten Orient und im Alten Testament: Die Wurzel zakar im semitischen Sprachkreis.* 2d ed. Wissenschaftliche Monographien zum Alten und Neuen Testament 15. Neukirchen-Vluyn, Germany: Neukirchener, 1967.

Schreiner, Thomas R. *Romans.* Baker Exegetical Commentary on the New Testament 6. Grand Rapids: Baker, 1998.

Schwartz, Baruch J. "The Prohibitions concerning the 'Eating' of Blood in Leviticus 17." Pages 34–66 in *Priesthood and Cult in Ancient Israel.* Edited by Gary A. Anderson and Saul M. Olyan. Journal for the Study of the Old Testament: Supplement Series 125. Sheffield, England: JSOT Press, 1991.

———. "The Bearing of Sin in the Priestly Literature." Pages 3–21 in *Pomegranates and Golden Bells: Studies in Biblical, Jewish, and Near Eastern Ritual, Law, and Literature in Honor of Jacob Milgrom.* Edited by David P. Wright, David Noel Freedman, and Avi Hurvitz. Winona Lake, Ind.: Eisenbrauns, 1995.

———. " 'Profane' Slaughter and the Integrity of the Priestly Code." *Hebrew Union College Annual* 67 (1996): 15–42.

Segal, Peretz. "The Divine Verdict of Leviticus 10:3." *Vetus Testamentum* 39 (1989): 91–95.

Seidl, Theodor. "Levitikus 16—'Schlußstein des priesterlichen Systems der Sündenvergebung.' " Pages 219–48 in *Levitikus als Buch.* Edited by Heinz-Josef Fabry and Hans-Winfried Jüngling. Bonner biblische Beiträge 119. Berlin: Philo, 1999.

Seow, Choon-Leong. "The Designation of the Ark in Priestly Theology." *Hebrew Annual Review* 8 (1984): 185–98.

Smend, Rudolf. *Die Mitte des Alten Testaments.* Vol. 1 of *Gesammelte Studien.* Beiträge zur evangelischen Theologie 99. Munich: Kaiser, 1986.

Smith, Christopher R. "The Literary Structure of Leviticus." *Journal for the Study of the Old Testament* 70 (1996): 17–32.

Snaith, Norman H. "Sacrifices in the Old Testament." *Vetus Testamentum* 7 (1957): 308–17.

———. "The Sin Offering and the Guilt Offering." *Vetus Testamentum* 15 (1965): 73–80.

———. *Leviticus and Numbers.* New Century Bible. London: Nelson, 1967.

———. "The Sprinkling of Blood." *Expository Times* 82 (1970): 23–24.

Speiser, E. A. "Leviticus and the Critics." Pages 123–42 in *Oriental and Biblical Studies: Collected Writings of E. A. Speiser.* Edited by J. J. Finkelstein and Moshe Greenberg. Philadelphia: University of Pennsylvania Press, 1967.

Sperber, Daniel. "A Note on Leviticus XXVII 28." *Vetus Testamentum* 16 (1966): 515–18.

Spronk, Klaas. *Beatific Afterlife in Ancient Israel and in the Ancient Near East.* Alter Orient und Altes Testament 219. Kevelaer, Germany: Butzon & Bercker, 1986.

Staubli, Thomas. "Die Symbolik des Vogelrituals bei der Reinigung von Aussätzigen (Lev 14, 4–7)." *Biblica* 83 (2002): 230–37.

Steinmann, Andrew. "Looking behind the Veil." *Concordia Theological Quarterly* 66 (2002): 368–69.

Steinmueller, John E. "Sacrificial Blood in the Bible." *Biblica* 40 (1959): 556–67.

Stevenson, William Barron. "Hebrew 'Olah and Zebach Sacrifices." Pages 488–97 in *Festschrift für Alfred Bertholet zum 80. Geburtstag: Gewidmet von Kollegen und Freunden.* Edited by Walter Baumgartner et al. Tübingen: Mohr, 1950.

Steymans, Hans-Ulrich. "Verheißung und Drohung: Lev 26." Pages 263–308 in *Levitikus als Buch.* Edited by Heinz-Josef Fabry and Hans-Winfried Jüngling. Bonner biblische Beiträge 119. Berlin: Philo, 1999.

Ströbel, August. "Die Ausrufung des Jobeljahres in der Nazarethpredigt Jesu: zur apokalyptischen Tradition Lc 4, 16–30." Pages 38–50 in *Jesus in Nazareth.* Edited by Erich Grässer et al. Berlin: Walter de Gruyter, 1972.

Stuhlmacher, Peter. *Paul's Letter to the Romans: A Commentary.* Translated by Scott J. Hafemann. Louisville, Ky.: Westminster/John Knox, 1994.

Sullivan, Kathryn. "The Book of Leviticus." *Worship* 31 (1957): 465–75.

Talley Thomas J. *The Origins of the Liturgical Year*. New York: Pueblo, 1986.

Tannehill, Robert C. "The Mission of Jesus according to Luke IV." Pages 51–75 in *Jesus in Nazareth.* Edited by Erich Grässer et al. Berlin: Walter de Gruyter, 1972.

Tawil, Hayim. "ʿAzazel, the Prince of the Steppe: A Comparative Study." *Zeitschrift für die alttestamentliche Wissenschaft* 92 (1980): 43–59.

Tosato, Angelo. "The Law of Leviticus 18:18: A Re-examination." *Catholic Biblical Quarterly* 46 (1984): 199–214.

Utzschneider, Helmut. *Das Heiligtum und das Gesetz: Studien zur Bedeutung der sinaitischen Heiligtumstexte (Ex 25–40; Lev 8–9).* Orbis biblicus et orientalis 77. Freiburg, Switzerland: Universitätsverlag, 1988.

Vanhoye, Albert. *Old Testament Priests and the New Priest: According to the New Testament.* Translated by Bernard Orchard. Petersham, Mass.: St. Bede's Publications, 1986.

Vaux, Roland de. *Studies in Old Testament Sacrifice.* Cardiff: University of Wales Press, 1964.

Vriezen, Theodore C. "The Term *Hizza*: Lustration and Consecration." Pages 201–35 in *Oudtestamentische Studiën* 7. Edited by Pieter A. H. de Boer. Leiden: Brill, 1950.

Wagner, Volker. "Zur Existenz des sogenannten 'Heiligkeitsgesetzes.' " *Zeitschrift für die alttestamentliche Wissenschaft* 86 (1974): 307–16.

Warning, Wilfried. *Literary Artistry in Leviticus.* Leiden: Brill, 1999.

Weinfeld, Moshe. *The Promise of the Land: The Inheritance of the Land of Canaan by the Israelites.* Berkeley: University of California Press, 1993.

———. *Social Justice in Ancient Israel and in the Ancient Near East.* Minneapolis: Fortress, 1995.

Wellhausen, Julius. *Prolegomena to the History of Israel.* Edinburgh: A. & C. Black, 1885.

Wenham, Gordon J. "Lev 27:2–8 and the Price of Slaves." *Zeitschrift für die alttestamentliche Wissenschaft* 90 (1978): 264–65.

———. *The Book of Leviticus.* New International Commentary on the Old Testament 3. London: Hodder & Stoughton, 1979.

———. *Numbers: An Introduction and Commentary.* Tyndale Old Testament Commentaries. Downers Grove, Ill.: Inter-Varsity, 1981.

———. "Why Does Sexual Intercourse Defile (Lev 15:18)?" *Zeitschrift für die alttestamentliche Wissenschaft* 95 (1983): 432–34.

———. "The Theology of Old Testament Sacrifice." Pages 75–87 in *Sacrifice in the Bible.* Edited by Roger T. Beckwith and Martin J. Selman. Grand Rapids: Baker, 1995.

———. "The Priority of P." *Vetus Testamentum* 49 (1999): 240–58.

Westbrook, Raymond. "The Price Factor in the Redemption of Land." Pages 90–117 in *Property and the Family in Biblical Law.* Journal for the Study of the Old Testament: Supplement Series 113. Sheffield, England: JSOT Press, 1991.

Whitekettle, Richard. "Leviticus 15:18 Reconsidered: Chiasm, Spatial Structure and the Body." *Journal for the Study of the Old Testament* 49 (1991): 31–45.

———. "Leviticus 12 and the Israelite Woman: Ritual Process, Liminality and the Womb." *Zeitschrift für die alttestamentliche Wissenschaft* 107 (1995): 395–408.

———. "Levitical Thought and the Female Reproductive Cycle: Wombs, Wellsprings, and the Primeval World." *Vetus Testamentum* 46 (1996): 376–91.

Whybray, Roger Norman. *The Making of the Pentateuch: A Methodological Study.* Journal for the Study of the Old Testament: Supplement Series 53. Sheffield, England: JSOT Press, 1987.

Wilhelm, Gernot. "Reinheit und Heiligkeit: Zur Vorstellung altanatolischer Ritualistik." Pages 197–218 in *Levitikus als Buch.* Edited by Heinz-Josef Fabry and Hans-Winfried Jüngling. Bonner biblische Beiträge 119. Berlin: Philo, 1999.

Wilkinson, John. "Leprosy and Leviticus: The Problem of Description and Identification." *Scottish Journal of Theology* 30 (1977): 153–69.

———. "Leprosy and Leviticus: A Problem of Semantics and Translation." *Scottish Journal of Theology* 31 (1978): 153–66.

Wilms. Franz-Elmar. *Freude vor Gott: Kult und Fest in Israel.* Regensburg, Germany: Pustet, 1981.

Wold, Donald J. "The *KARETH* Penalty in P: Rationale and Cases." Pages 1–45 in vol. 1 of *Society of Biblical Literature 1979 Seminar Papers.* 2 vols. Missoula, Mont.: Scholars Press, 1979.

———. *Out of Order: Homosexuality in the Bible and the Ancient Near East.* Grand Rapids: Baker, 1998.

Wright, Christopher J. H. *God's People in God's Land: Family, Land, and Property in the Old Testament.* Grand Rapids: Eerdmans, 1990.

Wright, David P. *The Disposal of Impurity: Elimination Rites in the Bible and in Hittite and Mesopotamian Literature.* Society of Biblical Literature Dissertation Series 101. Atlanta: Scholars Press, 1987.

———. "The Spectrum of Priestly Impurity." Pages 150–81 in *Priesthood and Cult in Ancient Israel.* Edited by Gary A. Anderson and Saul M. Olyan. Journal for the Study of the Old Testament: Supplement Series 125. Sheffield, England: JSOT Press, 1991.

———. "Holiness in Leviticus and Beyond: Differing Perspectives." *Interpretation* 53 (1999): 351–64.

Wyatt, Nicholas. “Atonement Theology in Ugarit and Israel.” *Ugarit-Forschungen* 8 (1977): 415–30.

Young, Edward J. *The Prophecy of Daniel: A Commentary.* Grand Rapids: Eerdmans, 1949.

Zevit, Z. “Converging Lines of Evidence Bearing on the Date of P.” *Zeitschrift für die alttestamentliche Wissenschaft* 94 (1982): 481–511.

Zimmerli, Walther. “ ‘Heiligkeit’ nach dem sogentannten Heiligkeitsgesetz.” *Vetus Testamentum* 30 (1980): 493–512.

———. *I Am Yahweh.* Translated by Douglas W. Stott. Atlanta: John Knox, 1982.

Zipor, Moshe. “Restrictions on Marriage for Priests (Lev. 21:7, 13–14).” *Biblica* 68 (1987): 259–67.

Ziskind, Jonathan R. “The Missing Daughter in Leviticus XVIII.” *Vetus Testamentum* 46 (1996): 125–30.

Zohar, Noam. “Repentance and Purification: The Significance and Semantics of חטאת in the Pentateuch.” *Journal of Biblical Literature* 107 (1988): 609–18.

Introduction

The Theological Framework of Leviticus

The voice of the Lord fills the pages of Leviticus. This book, as fully as every other in the canon, is the Word of God. It is divine speech more obviously than any other book in the Bible, for almost every section begins with "The Lord spoke to Moses." Leviticus reports what the Lord said to Moses and to the Israelites through Moses. In these speeches to Moses, God says remarkably little about himself. Instead, by his Word he institutes the sacrificial ritual for the Israelites at the tabernacle and authorizes their proper involvement with him in worship. He tells them what he does for them in the worship service and what he requires of them in their service to him.

As God speaks he gives his Gospel to Moses and the Israelites. By his word he establishes the tabernacle as the place where he dwells with his people and blesses them, just as his Son, the Word, would later become flesh and tabernacle among us, full of grace and truth (Jn 1:14). By God's provision of substitutionary atonement through the blood of the lamb for burnt offering in Leviticus, he grants forgiveness of sins, cleansing from impurity, and access to himself and his grace. By his provision of holy food from the altar, he gives his people holy communion with himself and each other. Thus the book of Leviticus foreshadows the Gospel of Jesus and proclaims it provisionally.

Jesus himself affirms this. When he appeared to his disciples on the first Easter Sunday, he used "the Law of Moses" to proclaim his death and resurrection as well as repentance and the forgiveness of sins (Lk 24:44-47). God's revelation to Moses therefore finds its fulfillment in the person and work of Jesus. Likewise, when Moses appeared in glory together with Jesus at his transfiguration, Moses spoke to Jesus about the fulfillment of God's word to him at Sinai in the greater exodus of Jesus by his sacrificial death for the sins of the world and his resurrection for the justification of sinners (Lk 9:30–31). Leviticus proclaims the same Gospel that is enacted in the Divine Service of Word and Sacrament, the same Gospel that the church is to proclaim to the world until the close of human history. This book, then, is most relevant to the life of the church because it proclaims the Gospel of Christ, the Lamb of God who takes away the sins of the world.

In keeping with the testimony of the Scriptures, we commonly speak of Leviticus as "law" or "the Law of Moses."[1] This is reinforced by the other terms

---

1 The Pentateuch was called "the Law/Torah [תּוֹרָה] of Moses" already in the first generation after Moses lived (Josh 8:31–32; 23:6). That same name for it appears in various passages throughout the OT (1 Ki 2:3; 2 Ki 14:6; 23:25; 2 Chr 23:18; 30:16; Ezra 3:2; 7:6; Neh 8:1; Dan 9:11, 13; Mal 4:4). "The Law [νόμος] of Moses" is also a common designation for the Pentateuch in the NT (Lk 2:22; 24:44; Jn 7:23; Acts 13:38 [ET 13:39]; 15:5; 28:23; 1 Cor

that are also used in Leviticus (and in some other biblical books) to describe its contents, such as "commandments," "statutes," and "ordinances." Yet all these English terms fail to do justice to the book, for they all have to do with what we need to do for God—what we are to offer to him—rather than what he does for us and gives to us. These terms seem to promote human works and works-righteousness rather than God's works, his grace. The trouble comes from a far too narrow understanding of the Hebrew word תּוֹרָה, torah.[2] While it may, at times, be translated as "law," it is rendered more accurately as "instruction," "practical direction," "guidance," or even "doctrine."[3] The torah of Moses is God's word of instruction to his people, his teaching of Law and Gospel for the divine service and the teaching that he does in it. It includes what he requires of his people as well as what he gives to them in their worship of him.

Some of the speeches in Leviticus give "commandments" (singular, מִצְוָה), authoritative mandates that authorize the ritual duties of the Israelites and so establish the liturgical tradition of Israel.[a] Others contain "ritual statutes" (singular, חֻקָּה), often called "perpetual ritual statutes" (singular, חֻקַּת עוֹלָם), that ordain an important ritual enactment or taboo and distinguish it from forbidden pagan practices.[b] These are closely related to "ritual ordinances" (singular, מִשְׁפָּט) that establish, case by case, how the sacrificial ritual is to be enacted (5:10; 9:16) as well as the conditions for right involvement in it.[c] We also have passages that give "ritual instruction" (תּוֹרָה).[d] They teach the priests and the people of Israel how to engage in the divine service without desecrating God's holiness (10:10–11; 21:23; 22:2, 9, 32). While all these terms can be used more narrowly and technically for some aspect of ritual legislation, they are also used interchangeably and generally for God's institution of the whole divine service (26:14–16, 43, 46).

(a) Lev 4:2, 13, 22, 27; 5:17; 22:31; 26:3; 27:34

(b) Lev 3:17; 7:36; 10:9; 16:29, 31, 34; 17:7; 18:4, 26, 30; 19:19, 37; 20:8, 22, 23; 23:14, 21, 31, 41; 24:3; 25:18; 26:3, 15, 43

(c) Lev 18:4, 5, 26; 19:37; 20:22; 25:18

(d) Lev 6:2, 7, 18 (ET 6:9, 14, 25); 7:1, 7, 11, 37; 11:46; 12:7; 13:59; 14:2, 32, 54, 57; 15:32

Thus Leviticus presents its readers with various kinds of ritual legislation. Yet these English terms are somewhat misleading to Lutherans and other evangelical Christians with their ingrained suspicion of legalism and ritualism. They do not give the right connotation at all to our modern religious sensibility because we do not appreciate what God actually gives to his people by his performative decrees in Exodus 24–31 and Leviticus.

First, like the words of God in Genesis 1, they are *creative decrees.* They create the tabernacle as God's residence in the midst of Israel and its services

---

9:9). In Lk 24:44 Jesus himself emphasizes that it contains abundant testimony to him: Jesus' life, suffering, death, and resurrection were in fulfillment of those things written about him in "the Law of Moses" and the rest of the OT Scriptures. Cf. "The OT Witness to Christ" in Just, *Luke 9:51–24:53,* 1021–36.

2 תּוֹרָה appears just once in Genesis (26:5) but becomes common in Exodus (seven times), Leviticus (sixteen times), Numbers (ten times), and Deuteronomy (twenty-two times).

3 See Hummel, *The Word Becoming Flesh,* 62–63. See also Hals, *Grace and Faith in the Old Testament,* 57–69, who, however, overstates his case because he seems to know nothing of the first and third uses of the Law in classic Lutheran theology.

as its means of access to him. Second, they are *sanctifying decrees.* By his Word God sanctifies the most holy things and all that is holy through them (Lev 21:23; 22:9, 16, 32). God's Word makes and keeps them holy; it empowers them with his own holiness. Third, they are *life-giving decrees.* By his Word God shares his life-giving blessing with his people and protects them from everything that diminishes their vitality (18:5). Thus, by instituting the divine service, God empowers it with his creative Word, so that it becomes a sacramental, divine-human enactment. The divine service enacts his Word; in it he works with his Word. His Word turns this human enactment in his presence into a divine enactment by which he meets and interacts with his people.

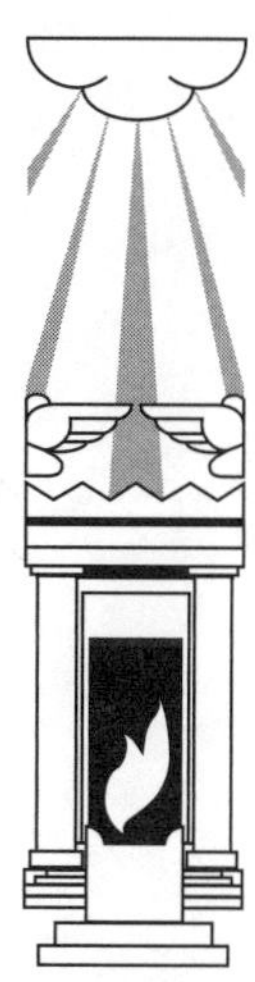

The legislation of Leviticus revolves around the mystery of the Lord's presence with his people. His Word speaks of his presence with his people in a very specific earthly location. The book begins with the shift in God's speaking from the top of Mount Sinai to the tent of meeting (1:1). There God speaks to Moses for the duration of the book. The words that are spoken there fill the whole of the book. God speaks them there because they establish his mode of presence with the Israelites. By these words God institutes the sacrificial ritual as his way of meeting and interacting with them at the altar for burnt offering. His words also reveal what he does with them there. Apart from his words, God's people have no access to his presence in the divine service and no knowledge of its theological significance.

After the portable tent had been consecrated it became God's mobile "place of residence" (מִשְׁכָּן, 8:10; 15:31; 17:4), the place where he "resided" with his people (שָׁכַן, Ex 25:8; 29:45, 46). There he made his "residence" in their midst (Lev 26:11). His presence was identified with his glory that was veiled in a cloud and concealed in the Holy of Holies (Ex 29:43; 40:34–35; Lev 9:23; 16:2). By residing with his people there, he "walked about" among them and accompanied them in their history as their God (Lev 26:11–12). Thus, when the Israelites entered the precincts of the tabernacle, they "stood before the Lord" (9:5). There they "came near" to him (9:5, 7) to "bring" their offerings "near" to him (1:2). This meant that whatever was done in that place was done "before the Lord" (e.g. 1:3, 5, 11); it was done "before his face" and in "his presence."

Yet the Lord did more than establish the tabernacle as the place for his presence with his people. Since he was holy and his people were sinful, his mere presence presented a danger to them. By itself it was never neutral, for he was present with them either in life-giving grace (Ex 33:15) or in deadly wrath (Ex 33:5). His holy presence was a cause of terror for those who served him disobediently (Lev 10:1–7), as well as joy for those who served him faithfully according to his commandments (9:24). This was why Moses had implored God to accompany his disobedient people with his forgiveness (Ex 34:9). In response to the intercession of Moses, God established the divine service to provide his people with safe access to him and his blessings through his gracious appearance to them daily in the fire on the altar for burnt offering (Lev 9:4, 6,

23–24). Through the introductory rite of atonement in the divine service, he released them from their sin, cleansed them from their impurity, and assured them of a favorable reception from him (1:4; 17:11). Through the daily burnt offering he approved of them (Ex 29:41), shared his holiness with them (Ex 29:43–44), and blessed them (Ex 20:24). During its performance he "met," first with the priests in the tent of meeting (Ex 25:22; 30:6, 36; Num 17:19 [ET 17:4]), and then with the whole congregation at the altar for burnt offering (Ex 29:42–43). Thus God established the ritual for the daily sacrifice to give the people safe access to him and his blessings. The laws that he gave to Moses in Leviticus spelled out the practical conditions and consequences of God's gracious presence with his people and their ongoing access to him and his blessings.

The book of Leviticus presupposes the presence of God with his people at the tabernacle and his gracious interaction with them in the daily service. The speeches in it did not just establish how the people were to interact with God, but they also showed them how God dealt with them in the daily service and its associated rites. The theological significance of the various ritual requirements and enactments is seldom explained in detail. Instead it is implied. The legislation develops Israel's theology of worship practically, rather than theoretically. This means that we need to be sensitive to the various theological markers that are part and parcel of the legislation.

Moreover, we need to appreciate the foundational significance of the command that God gave to Aaron in 10:8–11. This passage stands out from all the other speeches in the book because it is the only revelation that God gave exclusively to Aaron. The core of this speech is the commission of Aaron and his sons to distinguish what was holy from what was common and what was unclean from what was clean. That commission provides the key for the proper performance of the divine service with all its associated rituals, as well as for all instruction in its significance. It is the divine mandate for the priesthood and the divine warrant for the book of Leviticus.

In keeping with that commission, the book of Leviticus develops its theology of holiness. All the laws in it have to do with God's holiness and its impact on his people. Leviticus therefore teaches us the ritual grammar of holiness by showing when, where, how, and why God shared his holiness with the people of Israel.

The pagan nations that surrounded Israel had many sources of holiness, because they held that there were many different gods and spirits, each of which was holy in its own way, and none of which was holy to the exclusion of all other deities. Each gave access to some part of the supernatural realm and contact with some of its power. Like many animists, the Canaanites revered the spirits of the dead as holy entities. They therefore sought to gain supernatural knowledge and life-power through them (cf. Ps 16:3–4).

All that was repudiated by the one true God, who commanded his people to abhor idolatry and avoid any compromise with pagan practices. Since the

Lord alone is holy (1 Sam 2:2), he forbade all forms of interaction with the spirits of the dead (Lev 19:26, 31; 20:6, 27). He himself had demonstrated his exclusive holiness in his triumph over the gods of Egypt (Ex 15:11) and had repeatedly told Israel that he was holy.[e] Since his name is holy (Is 57:15), his people are to avoid desecrating it.[f] He is the Holy One (Ps 99:3, 5; Is 10:17; Hos 11:9), their holy God (Ps 99:9; Josh 24:19; 1 Sam 6:20), the Holy One of Israel.[g] He is acclaimed and adored by his angelic courtiers in his heavenly temple as the superlatively holy King of the universe (Is 6:3). He is to be treated as holy by those who approached him (Lev 10:3).

(e) Lev 11:44, 45; 19:2; 20:7, 26; 21:8

(f) Lev 18:21; 19:12; 20:3; 21:6; 22:2, 32

The Lord alone is inherently and permanently holy. His holiness is his godliness, his nature, and his power as God. It is inseparable from him and his presence. Holiness is derived only from him; it is available only by way of contact with him. People and things borrowed their holiness from their association with him at Mount Sinai and at the sanctuary. He sanctified the tabernacle and its precincts so that they became God's "sanctuary" (מִקְדָּשׁ).[h] He had called the Israelites to be holy (Ex 19:6) and had sanctified them with the blood of the covenant at Mount Sinai (Ex 24:8). He had, in fact, redeemed them from Egypt so that he could be their God and sanctify them (Lev 11:45; 22:32–33). His presence with them, his glory, made and kept them holy (Ex 29:43, 44). Yet their holiness was something that they never possessed for themselves, but kept on receiving from God. It was an acquired state of being, a contingent condition, an extrinsic power, something that was lost as soon as contact with him was lost.

(g) E.g., Pss 71:22; 78:41; 89:19 (ET 89:18); Is 1:4; 5:19, 24; 10:20; 41:14, 16, 20; 43:3, 14; 55:5

(h) Lev 12:4; 16:33; 19:30; 20:3; 21:12, 23; 26:2

Many attempts have been made to explain the concept of holiness. The most influential explanation was advanced by Otto in *The Idea of the Holy.* He defined it phenomenologically as "the totally other" which engages us as "a fearful and yet wonderful mystery."[4] Jenson defines it more helpfully as "that which belongs to the sphere of God's being or activity."[5] Like life, it is both a self-communicating power and an assimilating state of being. Yet all attempts to define holiness conceptually founder because it has to do with God's being, that which makes him God and distinguishes him from all other beings. It cannot be defined by analogy with anything in the order of creation, whether by similarity or dissimilarity, by excellence or transcendence.[6] The OT Scriptures therefore do not attempt to define God's holiness in the abstract, but treat it as something that is experienced by personal contact and ritual interaction with him at the sanctuary. Likewise, the NT reveals God's holiness through his incarnation in Jesus Christ and personal interaction with Christ.[i]

(i) E.g., Lk 1:35, 49, 75; 2:23; 4:34; Eph 4:24; 1 Thess 3:13; 4:7

God himself instructed his people quite practically in the nature of his holiness by instituting the tabernacle and its services. Since access to God's ho-

4 Otto, *The Idea of the Holy,* 25.

5 Jenson, *Graded Holiness,* 48.

6 Von Rad, *Old Testament Theology,* 1:205.

liness depended on proximity to him, his presence in the sanctuary created three concentric zones of decreasing sanctity: the Holy of Holies, the Holy Place and the altar for burnt offering, and the rest of the courtyard. All that was holy belonged in some way to these three spheres. Access to these zones created three classes of holy people: the high priest, the officiating priests, and the congregation of Israel. Thus holiness is a ritual-liturgical term in the Pentateuch. It is used to describe those persons and things that are associated in some way with God's presence in the sanctuary. The language of holiness in Leviticus is liturgical, for it has to do with God's presence and access to his favor in the divine service. Where God is available and accessible, there the Israelites share in his holiness, for his presence sanctifies the assembly of Israel and everything used in the people's service to him.

In Lev 10:10 God himself described the state of holiness in connection with what was "clean" and in contrast with what was "common" and "unclean." His holy presence in the tabernacle created three interlocking spheres and composite states of being which may be represented diagrammatically in figure 1.

Figure 1

Holy versus Common and Clean versus Unclean

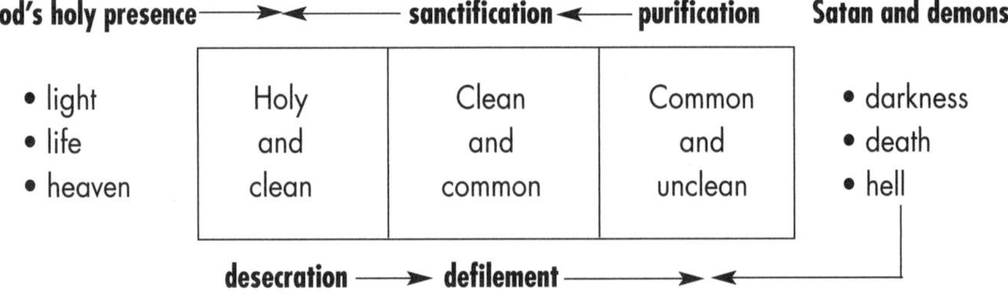

We have here a rather startling juxtaposition of two completely different systems of classification: *a theological system that distinguishes what is holy from what is common, and an anthropological system that distinguishes what is unclean from what is clean.*

Theologically, persons and things may be either holy or common. Anthropologically, persons and things may be either clean or unclean. Since the fall into sin, all people are, by nature, sinful and unholy. Most people (via their conscience and natural knowledge of God) are aware of their inherent uncleanness. Purification of unclean persons and things moves them from the state of being unclean to that of being clean. Sanctification of clean persons and things moves them from the category of being common to that of being holy. Conversely, desecration of clean things that are holy makes them common (no longer holy). And defilement of persons and things that are clean makes them unclean.

The classification of people and things as clean or unclean is presupposed and used in most cultures. It is based on the elemental human experience of the clean, healthy body that is threatened in its physical autonomy, integrity, and ecology by the invasion of unclean, alien substances and powers. Purity is therefore commonly used as an anthropological term for the self-classification of people in their physical, social, and cosmic environment. Its use for the location of the human body in its physical environment is extended by analogy to the family or clan, to caste or class, to race or nation, and, in the case of the modern ecology movement, even to the earth as a living organism. In each case human beings stand as judges at the center of the system. They assume that if they are healthy, they are clean. Their own purity determines what is included and what is excluded from their physical domain.

By the subordination of this anthropological system to the theological system of classification based on his holiness, God redefines all natural systems of purity completely. He judges purity from his own point of view as the Creator and relates all human experiences of purity to his holy presence in the sanctuary. *Therefore the classifications in Leviticus are theocentric (God himself is the point of reference) rather than anthropocentric (based on the healthy human body) or geocentric (based on the earth, environmentalism).* God's system of classification means that no person, family, race, caste, class, or nation is inherently clean. All human beings—and that includes the congregation of Israel with its priests and high priest—are, more or less, unclean and in need of constant purification. They all need to be purified before they can enter the sanctuary and share in God's holiness. Thus God alone is the source of purity, just as he alone is holy. Through his Word he determines what is holy and what is clean. He cleanses and sanctifies his people by meeting with them in the daily service at the tabernacle.

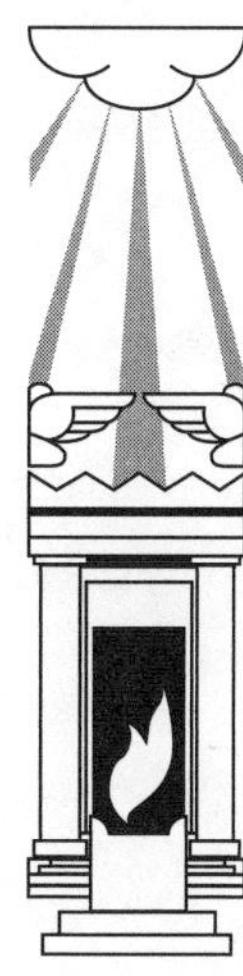

The state of holiness was the environment created by God's presence in the sanctuary. It was, so to speak, a divine bridgehead in the common world, a place where the divine domain overlapped with the human domain. God purified and sanctified every common person and thing that was properly admitted into his presence. He decided who was fit for access to him and involvement in the divine service. His holiness was the criterion for the definition of what was common as well as what was clean or unclean.

The effect of God's holiness depended on the state of the person. It was life-giving and beneficial for those who were ritually clean, but death-dealing and detrimental for those who were ritually unclean. On the one hand, contact with God's holiness had a constructive effect on those who were in a state of ritual purity. They had access to him and shared in his holiness. They enjoyed the blessings that are listed in Lev 26:3–13, such as prosperity and peace, security and fertility, victory in battle and affluence, fellowship with God, and freedom as his royal children. On the other hand, contact with God's holiness had a detrimental effect on those who defiled his tabernacle with their impurity (15:31) and desecrated his sanctuary with disobedience (20:3; 21:23). They came under God's wrath (10:6). Those who defiled any holy thing were cut off from their kinsfolk (7:20–21). Those who desecrated God's holiness died (10:1–7). The tabernacle and its services were designed to forestall both those eventualities (separation and death). They provided safe access to God's presence.

Moreover, the priests were responsible and liable for the protection of God's holiness as well as for the purification of the people. They came under God's wrath and condemnation if his holiness was desecrated. The ordinary Israelites therefore had little to fear from their appearance in God's presence, because the priests bore their iniquity before the Lord (Ex 28:38; Lev 10:17; Num 18:7, 23).

The pole opposite to holiness was the state of impurity. It was completely incompatible with God's holiness, just as darkness and death are incompatible with light and life. Like holiness, impurity was both a power and a state of being. It too was never defined in abstract terms, but was associated with those unnamed, destructive forces that were opposed to God: powers that were unleashed by the transgression of his prohibitions, such as disorder, sin, sickness, death, and the spirits of the underworld. The book of Leviticus does not attempt to list and categorize the various kinds of impurity. Instead, it instructs the Israelites to avoid common sources of impurity, such as the eating of meat from unclean animals (11:2–23) or sexual intercourse with forbidden partners (18:6–20). It also gives instructions about the treatment of common kinds of impurity, such as from contact with the carcasses of animals (11:24–28) or from an emission of semen (15:16–18).

Like holiness, impurity is a ritual-liturgical category in Leviticus. It describes those things that disqualify people and things from admission to God's presence at the sanctuary (7:20–21; 22:3). Most common kinds of impurity are relatively harmless in themselves. They become harmful only when they impinge on God's holiness, for anything that is unclean defiles and desecrates what is holy.[7] If anything unclean touches something holy, it arouses God's wrath. God's holiness destroys what is unclean, like fire that burns up gasoline, or like light that banishes darkness. If any unclean person were to eat holy meat, he would be cut off by God from his kinsfolk (7:20–21). People and things therefore had to be purified before they could come before God and share in his holiness.

The common domain lay, like a buffer zone, between the two incompatible poles of holiness and impurity. It was the normal realm, the sphere of the human body and its activity. Anything that was common could be either clean or unclean. Thus common meat was clean if it came from a fish with fins and scales (11:9), but unclean if it came from a pig (11:7). If something common

---

[7] Olyan, *Rites and Rank,* 16–17.

became holy, like the meat from a lamb that had been sacrificed as a peace offering, it ceased to be common, since it belonged to the divine domain. But if something common became unclean, like the body of a menstruating woman, it still belonged to the common domain. It spread impurity to any clean persons and objects that it touched (15:19–24). Holiness and impurity were therefore invasive and pervasive powers that exercised their influence on the people of Israel. They exercised their power most directly through the people's consumption of food and their sexual activity.

Ever since the fall into sin nothing in creation has been inherently and naturally holy. Yet God condescended to enter his creation and live among his people, and his sanctifying presence created various degrees of holiness and impurity in relation to him.[8] The closer something came to God, the holier it became. Hence in the theology of Leviticus, the high priest was holier than the ordinary Israelite, and the Holy of Holies was more sacred than the Holy Place. The meat from the sin offering that was eaten only by the priests in the sanctuary was more holy than the meat from the peace offering that could be eaten by the Israelites in any clean place.

God's presence created the following ritual topography, with circles of decreasing holiness and increasing impurity as one moves farther away from God's presence. The degree of holiness of each place corresponds to the persons and things that could and did enter or reside there. See figure 2.

Figure 2

Degrees of Holiness

Places	*Persons*
Holy of Holies	God and the high priest (16:2–17)
Holy Place and altar	Unblemished priests (21:17–23)
Courtyard	Congregation of Israel (1:4; 4:14; 8:3; 9:5; 12:4)
Israelite home	Clean Israelites (14:8)
Israelite camp/town	Israelites and resident aliens (17:8, 10, 13)
Clean dump outside the camp	Ashes and carcasses from sin offering (4:12, 21; 6:4 [ET 6:11])
Unclean area outside the camp	Unclean people and things (10:4; 13:46; 14:40, 41, 45; 16:27)
Wilderness	Azazel (16:22)

Some kinds of defilement from impurity, such as from practicing as a medium (20:27) or from sacrificing a child to Molech (20:2), were so severe and permanent that the death penalty was mandatory for them. Other kinds of impurity were temporary and readily rectified by washing, such as impurity from sex-

[8] Jenson, *Graded Holiness,* 48.

ual intercourse with a menstruating woman (which lasted seven days; 15:24) and from contact with the carcass of a dead animal (which lasted for a day; 11:28).

Like impurity, purity is a ritual-liturgical category in Leviticus. It is, at times, identical with physical purity, such as with clean water (11:36) or pure gold (24:4, 6). But even then it is a ritual term for the state that qualifies people for admission and things for use in the divine service. Those animals that were ritually clean could be offered to God and eaten by God's holy people. Only clean people were allowed to enter the sanctuary (12:4) and touch anything sacred (7:19b). Those who had become unclean had to be ritually purified before they could enter the sanctuary and touch any sacred thing. This happened corporately each day in the rite of atonement with the blood of the lamb for the daily burnt offering. In cases of minor temporary impurity, a person was purified by taking a ritual bath. If people had contracted impurity from inadvertent sins, they were cleansed by the rite of atonement with the blood from a sin offering. If they were guilty of minor acts of desecration, they were cleansed by the rite of atonement with the blood of a reparation offering. The nation, the priesthood, and the sanctuary were cleansed from impurity by the special rite of atonement on the Day of Atonement. Ritual purity is therefore not identical with holiness. It is, rather, the precondition for participation in God's holiness.[9]

God did not keep his holiness to himself, nor did he use it to distance himself from his sinful people. Instead, he joined them on their earthly journey so that he could share his holiness with them. They did not sanctify themselves; he sanctified them. He made and kept them holy. They drew their holiness from him, and him only. God emphasized this by his repeated use of the formula for divine sanctification in the book of Leviticus:

> I am the Lord, who sanctifies you. (מְקַדִּשְׁכֶם, 20:8; 21:8; 22:32)
> I am the Lord, who sanctifies them. (מְקַדְּשָׁם, 21:23; 22:9, 16; cf. 21:15)

The use of the participle ("sanctifies," not "sanctified" or "will sanctify") indicates ongoing action. God did not just sanctify them at a single point in time—at the exodus or his appearance to them at Mount Sinai. Rather, their sanctification by God was an ongoing process of receiving holiness from him, something that happened repeatedly and continually. Since he continued to share his holiness with them, they kept on receiving it from him.

---

[9] Olyan, *Rites and Rank,* 17, summarizes the system of classification in 10:11 rather helpfully in the following way:

> The contrast between holy and common establishes the limits of the sanctification of space, items, and foods; it determines the extent to which Yhwh's essential quality is distributed spatially and otherwise. The contrast between clean and unclean establishes who or what will qualify for admission to sanctified space or who might, given other necessary qualifications (for example, priestly lineage), gain access to holy items or foods. Thus, the opposition of clean to unclean pertains to persons, animals, and other items, distinguishing the admissible from the excluded. In contrast, the opposition of holy to common divides the divine and associated space, persons, animals, and other items from what is not divine or not associated with the divine through sanctification. The holy/common distinction establishes a boundary around the sanctuary; the unclean/clean distinction determines who or what may cross it.

The formula for sanctification shows that this happens in three ways, which point toward the pastoral office in the NT church, worship with Word and Sacrament, and the priesthood of all believers in Christ (cf. "I believe in … the communion of saints" [Apostles' Creed]). First, God made the altar and the sanctuary holy (8:10–16; 21:23). Through the altar he made the food from the offerings most holy or holy (Ex 29:37; Lev 22:14–16). Second, he consecrated the high priest and all the priests by their consumption of the most holy food at the sanctuary (e.g., 6:7–11, 17–22 [ET 6:14–18, 24–29]; 7:1–10; 8:31–36; 21:15; 22:9). Third, he consecrated all the Israelites through their involvement in the divine service and their consumption of the holy food from their offerings (e.g., 1:4; 4:14–15; 7:11–36; 20:8; 21:8; 22:31–33). *Thus God communicated his holiness physically with his people through the holy things.* By their access to the holy things the people shared in God's holiness.

The legislation in Leviticus distinguishes the most holy things from the holy things (21:22). The most holy food from the offerings was reserved for the priests on duty at the sanctuary. It had to be eaten in the holy place. This most holy food consisted of the showbread (24:5–9) and the bread from the grain offering (6:10–11 [ET 6:17–18]), as well as the meat from the sin offering and the reparation offering (6:18–22 [ET 6:25–29]; 7:6). God used this most holy food to communicate his holiness with the priests through its physical consumption (6:11, 20 [ET 6:18, 27]). All the other food from the offerings was merely holy. Like the most holy food, it was sanctified by its contact with the altar for burnt offering (Ex 29:37). But unlike the most holy food, it did not communicate God's holiness directly by contact with it. The main kind of holy food was the meat from the peace offering (Lev 19:8). It was the most important item of holy food that was available to the lay Israelites, a way for them to share in God's holiness. Their sacred banquets therefore revolved around the eating of that holy meat. Through it they enjoyed holy communion with God.

The purpose of God's revelation to Moses in Leviticus is summed up well by his call to the congregation of Israel: "You are/will be/shall be holy [קְדֹשִׁ֣ים תִּהְי֑וּ], as I the Lord your God am holy" (19:2; cf. 11:44, 45; 20:7, 26). This call matches the call addressed to the priest in 21:6. Its use of the Hebrew imperfect tense, considered within the context of Leviticus as a whole, can be construed as a statement of fact, a promise, and a demand.

First, it is a statement of fact by God, a Gospel declaration: "You *are* holy." At Mount Sinai God had sanctified the Israelites (Ex 19:5–6; 22:30 [ET 22:31]; 24:8; Deut 7:6; 14:2, 21). He appointed them to be his holy priestly nation (Ex 19:6). Together with the Levitical priests who performed the daily sacrifice on behalf of them, they had access to God's presence at the tabernacle. As God's royal priests, they stood between him and the peoples of the world. By meeting with them in the daily service he made and kept them holy (Ex 29:43). Unlike the priests, the lay Israelites did not share in God's holiness by eating the most holy food. They were sanctified by his name. Since that name was holy, the Lord spoke about it as "the name of [his] holiness" and warned against its desecration (Lev 20:3; 22:2, 32). The Lord's name was the only most holy thing that the people had at their disposal. It was so holy that its sanctity was protected by the Second Commandment (Ex 20:7). That holy name was placed on them by the performance of the Aaronic Benediction in which the Lord himself blessed them (Num 6:22–27; Deut 10:8; 21:5; 1 Chr 23:13). Their holiness therefore depended on him and their association with him at the sanctuary.

Second, this call is a promise of God: "You *will be* holy." He promised to make and keep his people holy. God's repeated use of the divine formula for sanctification showed that he shared his holiness with both the priests and the whole congregation of Israel through their contact with him and his holy things at the sanctuary. His promise to sanctify them was connected with his promise to be their God (22:32–33). He had rescued them from Egypt so that he could be their God and share his holiness with them. This promise of sanctification continued throughout Israel's history. His holiness never was their own possession apart from him. It was always received anew from him, like nourishment for the body from food, through their involvement in the divine service.

Third, the call to holiness is a demand from God: "You *shall be* holy." The Israelites were actively involved in their sanctification by God, for their ongoing reception of his holiness depended on their observance of his commandments (20:7–8; 22:31–33).

But this connection of Israel's sanctification with keeping God's statutes must not be misconstrued, as Milgrom does,[10] by concluding that the potentially holy Israelites generated their own holiness by observing God's performative and prohibitive commandments. That contradicts God's repeated assertions (quoted above) that *he* is the one who sanctifies his people. The people did not generate their holiness by their observance of God's commandments, such as those found in 19:3–37; they were called to observe God's commandments because they were holy and so needed to maintain their holiness (cf. Deut 28:9).

On the one hand, the prohibitions that predominate in Leviticus 19 identified those acts that defiled God's holy people and so diminished their holiness (11:44–45; 20:22–26). On the other hand, the performative commandments had to do with their membership in the holy congregation and its participation in the divine service, for only as members of the congregation and by participation in the sacrificial ritual could they continue to be recipients of God's holiness.

While it is true that some of the material in Leviticus concerns the ministry of the priests and their participation in God's holiness, the book as a whole and many of its speeches are addressed to the people of Israel, for they are the main beneficiaries of all the services that were performed by the priests. *The whole of their life in the camp and later in the land was regarded as priestly service to God.*[11] Joosten[12] rightly maintains that they were envisaged as temple servants who were called to offer holy service to God. They were therefore bound to observe a basic level of ritual purity even in their common life apart

[10] Milgrom, *Leviticus 17–22,* 1602–6.

[11] Knohl, *The Sanctuary of Silence,* 190.

[12] Joosten, *People and Land in the Holiness Code,* 135.

from the sanctuary. In fact, the meals in their homes were related to their meals at the sanctuary. Their involvement with God at the sanctuary affected their sexual behavior at home and their commercial dealings in the marketplace. Since they were part of a single priestly fraternity, they were to treat each other as sacred kinsfolk. They were obliged to observe an ethic of holiness, because their whole life was lived in God's presence. This did not mean that their holiness was reduced to morality. Instead, their moral behavior was governed by their liturgical status as people who shared in God's holiness.

Through their interaction with God at the sanctuary, the common life of the Israelites was related to the performance of the divine service there. Through it God's holiness came to pervade more and more of their common life, for God's ultimate goal is to sanctify the whole of his creation.[13] "We await new heavens and a new earth, in which righteousness dwells" (2 Pet 3:13; cf. Is 11:9; 65:17–25; Rev 21:1–5). Thus Knohl says:

> Just as profane needs enter into the Temple realm, so too holiness is apportioned to daily life. ... Holiness is no longer limited to the narrow confines of the Temple and the priesthood but emerges from the Priestly center, radiating out to all sectors of society and to all walks of life and encompassing the entire land. Israelites are called to realize the challenge of the holy life in their eating and drinking, in their relations to their families and to the stranger dwelling in the land, in their work in the fields and commerce, on the seat of judgment and in the company of friends.[14]

Origin

The book of Leviticus reports the origin of its contents. It states that God is its author, for God himself spoke all the laws and exhortations that make up its thirty-six speeches. They are *his* speeches. He spoke them to Moses at Mount Sinai (7:38; 26:46; 27:34). He addressed most of them directly to Moses, the lawgiver and founder of the divine service. But Moses was not their only recipient. God spoke some of them to Aaron as well, in his capacity as the foundational high priest, the father of the priesthood (13:1; 14:33; 15:1). In one important instance that established the role of the high priest, God spoke exclusively to Aaron (10:8–11).

The affirmation by Leviticus that it is the true record of God's words and is God's Word does more than disclose the divine origin of its contents. It indicates the book's authority and power as the divine speech that institutes the divine service, empowers that service as a divine-human enactment, and presents the terms for Israel's involvement in it. Thus the origin of Leviticus establishes its ongoing character as divine speech. The communication of that

---

13 Von Rad, *Old Testament Theology,* 1:207.

14 Knohl, *The Sanctuary of Silence,* 198. Knohl may use "Priestly" to refer to the hypothetical "P" source in the Torah. (For our view of the documentary hypothesis, see the next section on the origin of Leviticus.) However, the quote of Knohl makes a helpful point if "Priestly" is understood as a reference to the tabernacle, priesthood, and divine service with the sacrifices and rituals at the sanctuary.

speech to Israel took place through mediators who were all too human, but God's Word remains efficacious and inerrant because God himself speaks it. That comes out most clearly in God's use of Moses, Aaron, and the priests to introduce himself personally to his people with the formula of divine self-introduction (twenty-two times in the book), "I am the Lord, your God" (e.g., 11:44; 18:2; 19:2).

Yet the book goes even further than that, for it clearly establishes a chain of tradition, a divinely sanctioned process by which the divine speeches were to be handed on faithfully from God to his people from generation to generation (e.g., 3:17). Some speeches seem to be addressed exclusively to Moses and/or Aaron without any mention of their transmission,[j] but in each of those exceptional cases, the implication is that Moses and/or Aaron was meant to transmit God's instructions to the priests, who were responsible for their implementation. In most cases, God quite explicitly authorized Moses—and Aaron—to pass on his words to others.

(j) Lev 5:14, 20 (ET 6:1); 6:1 (ET 6:8); 8:1; 10:8; 13:1; 14:1; 22:26; 23:26

At the time when God spoke Leviticus he indicated that it was intended for five distinct audiences: (1) the Israelites[k] and their whole assembly (19:2); (2) Aaron as the high priest (16:2; 21:17); (3) Aaron and his sons as representatives of the priesthood (6:2, 13, 18 [ET 6:9, 20, 25]; 22:2); (4) the sons of Aaron as rank and file priesthood (21:1); and (5) Aaron together with his sons and all the Israelites (17:2; 22:18). Moses functioned as the divinely chosen lawgiver. God appointed Aaron, and the high priests that succeeded him, as the teacher of his law to the Israelites (10:8–11). He commissioned Aaron, apart from Moses and his mediation, to teach the ritual statutes that he had given to them through Moses. Aaron was therefore authorized to hand on the Word of God by interpreting it, teaching it, and supervising its enactment. After his death, that commission passed on to his successors in office.

(k) Lev 1:2; 4:2; 7:23, 29; 11:2; 12:2; 15:2; 18:2; 20:2; 23:2, 10, 24, 34; 24:2, 15; 25:2; 27:2

While the book of Leviticus discloses its divine origin and the human mediators of its data, it does not specifically state who wrote it, and when. Some passages in Exodus (Ex 17:14; 24:4; 34:27) affirm that Moses was their author, but Leviticus makes no such affirmation for any part of it. Instead, it uses the forms and language of oral tradition in a number of key places. God "commanded" Moses to pass on his words to the Israelites (צִוָּה, Lev 7:37–38; 27:34). Moses carried out this commission to hand on God's words to them (8:1–5; 9:5–7; 16:34b; 21:24; 23:44; 24:23). Leviticus is most likely the product of that commission; probably it was compiled to assist the priests in their task of handing on the law of Moses to the Israelites from generation to generation. Thus God "commanded," "spoke," and "gave" his laws to the Israelites "by the hand of Moses" (8:36; 10:11; 26:46). That may mean that Moses recorded all or some of them in writing, but we are not told. Instead, the emphasis lies on the divinely authorized process of tradition from God through Moses, the lawgiver, and Aaron, the teacher, to the Israelites.

We are not told who arranged the material into the present thirty-six speeches and incorporated them into the stream of narrative that links the canonical book of Leviticus with Exodus and Numbers. Three bits of evidence hint that it may have been composed and edited by someone besides Moses, even though he is presented as the divinely appointed lawgiver and law-speaker in it. First, there are a number of colophons (editorial summaries) at the end of some sections in the book that seem to have been composed and added by a later editor. They summarize the contents of the preceding section and, in some cases, also its origins and purpose.[1] Second, the book has a narrative framework that reports what Moses did (1:1; 8:1–10:20; 24:10–23). Like the introductions to each of the thirty-six speeches and the reports of compliance, those reports in the narrative framework speak about Moses. Third, even though the book is set in the desert at Mount Sinai, it does not just envisage the future settlement in the land (14:34; 18:3, 24–25; 19:23; 20:22–24; 23:10; 25:2), but it also speaks in 18:27–28 as if the Israelites were already residing in it. Yet none of that data contradicts its divine authorship and its place in the canon as part of the Torah ("law" or "instruction, revelation") of Moses.

(1) Lev 7:37–38; 13:59; 14:32, 54–57; 15:32–33; 23:37–38; 26:46; 27:34; cf. 7:35–36; 11:46; 12:7b

The NT confirms what the book of Leviticus says about itself and its origin. Jesus himself refers to Moses as the lawgiver in Leviticus. He recalls Lev 12:3 when he claims in Jn 7:22 that Moses "gave" the rite of circumcision to the Israelites. In Mk 7:10 he claims that Moses "spoke" the threat of the death penalty for belittling parents in Lev 20:9. Likewise, he affirms that in Lev 14:2–32 Moses "commanded" that a healed leper should show himself to the priest and present an offering for his purification (Mt 8:4; Mk 1:44; Lk 5:14). Jesus also states, more generally, that Moses "gave" the law to Israel (Jn 7:19; cf. 1:17). Christ therefore taught that the Pentateuch was "the Law of Moses" (Lk 24:44; Jn 7:23). Such references to Moses as the lawgiver through whom God spoke Leviticus are all that Jesus and the NT have to say about the authorship and composition of the book.

The simple affirmation in the NT of the role of Moses stands in sharp contrast to the obsession with the question of authorship that has characterized much of scholarship since the Enlightenment. And this is no accident. Since many historical-critical scholars denied the divine origin and revelation of the OT, they had to determine who created each part, when, and for what ideological and practical purpose.

The history of this debate is far too complicated to retrace here except in broad outline. The first stage of the debate culminated in the widely influential work of Wellhausen.[15] He held that Leviticus belonged to the last of four written sources (J, E, D, and P) that were combined to form the Pentateuch as we now have it. This was called P, since it was held to have been written by a priestly writer. It was written after the return from the Babylonian exile, in the Persian period (sixth–fifth centuries B.C.; Moses lived in the fifteenth century B.C.). While some parts of this P document are said to have been included ear-

[15] Wellhausen, *Prolegomena to the History of Israel* (1885).

lier in Genesis and Exodus, its main body stretches, uninterrupted except for Exodus 32–34, from Exodus 25 to Leviticus 10.

The documentary hypothesis proposed a different theology for the Scriptures as well as a different historical order for its parts. A basic theological presupposition of the classic documentary hypothesis was that the earliest (preexilic) forms of Israelite religion (especially J) held that individual people could interact with God personally and directly. There was little need for the mediating roles of priests or a sanctuary and sacrifices because the Israelites were not regarded as sinful before God. However, the exile, viewed as punishment by an angry God, caused the Israelites to become fixated on the problem of sin and the need for forgiveness. Hence P, with its heavy emphasis on priests, sacrifices, and atonement for sin, arose after the exile as Israel searched for relief from its collective guilty conscience.

The implication of the bias of the classic documentary hypothesis against the historic faith, then, was that pietism and liberal Protestantism are akin to the earliest (and best) forms of Israelite religion. Conversely, the Lutheran church and other churches that have a high view of the pastoral office, liturgy, and sacramental worship are following the theology of P, which is a later development (not the original biblical theology) and is driven by guilt rather than the power of the Gospel.

The documentary hypothesis advanced by Wellhausen was later modified in two significant ways. First, some scholars, beginning with Klostermann,[16] argued that Leviticus contained an earlier document, named the Holiness Code, that ran from Leviticus 18 to 26. Second, other scholars, such as Noth, von Rad, and Koch,[17] used the methods of form criticism and tradition history analysis to demonstrate that a tradition of oral transmission and combination lay behind this so-called P source. While they still agreed with Wellhausen on the composition of P in the Persian period, they and the scholars who came after them envisaged its author as an editor rather than the writer of it. This study of oral traditions, gradual inscription, and editorial activity has gone so far that some scholars, such as Whybray,[18] have reached the conclusion that the documentary hypothesis of Wellhausen and his followers is no longer useful and valid for the study of Pentateuch.

While many historical-critical scholars, such as Gerstenberger,[19] still agree with Wellhausen that Leviticus was conceived and composed by a priest or a school of priests in the Persian period, this view has been seriously challenged by other historical-critical scholars using similar modes of argumentation. The challenge began with Kaufmann.[20] He marshaled a large body of evidence to

---

[16] Klostermann, *Der Pentateuch* (1893), 385.

[17] Noth, *A History of Pentateuchal Traditions* (1972); von Rad, "The Problem of the Hexateuch" (1966); and Koch, *Die Priesterschrift von Exodus 25 bis Leviticus 16* (1959).

[18] Whybray, *The Making of the Pentateuch* (1987).

[19] Gerstenberger, *Leviticus* (1996).

[20] Kaufmann, *The Religion of Israel* (1960).

show that P was older than the book of Deuteronomy, the so-called D source. The identification of D as "the Book of the Law/Torah" (2 Ki 22:8), "the Book of the Covenant" (2 Ki 23:2) that was found in the temple during the reign of Josiah, was the main foundation of Wellhausen's hypothesis. The position of Kaufmann was supported by the work of Hurvitz,[21] who used linguistic data to show that P must have predated Ezekiel. Kaufmann's main arguments have been refined and supplemented by Haran, Knohl, and Milgrom.[22] They all argue, quite cogently, that the priestly material in the Pentateuch was edited and written down, at the very latest, during the era of Ahaz and Hezekiah, that is, between 735 and 700 B.C.

The academic debate on the historical origin of the Pentateuch from a human point of view still rages as strongly as ever. It has not produced, and is unlikely to produce, any general consensus because it rests on the varied presuppositions and suppositions of scholars and schools of scholars, their differing worldviews and ideological stances. The force of their arguments depends on value judgments about the reliability of the canonical text and data apart from the text. Moreover, the method of argumentation is, of necessity, circular, and its conclusions are, at best, tentative. Most tenuous are the works of scholars who deny any form of divine revelation and suppose that the book of Leviticus was produced by priests, without any divine intervention, to justify their own ideological stance and social position, in response to the challenge of their contemporaneous social-historical conditions.

My own position on the origin of Leviticus is similar to that of Hartley,[23] who holds that "the tradition originated in Yahweh's revelation to Moses."[24] The OT and NT affirm that Moses is the human author of the Torah. Yet no human being, not even Moses, is the ultimate author of Leviticus because it is the Lord's Word. It is not the product of human reflection on established or ideal religious practices. Rather, it is the law of God, divine ritual legislation that was meant to shape the worship and life of Israel as a holy nation. Thus even when this legislation sanctions prior religious practices, such as circumcision and animal sacrifice, God uses it to bring their "operation into alignment with his holy character."[25] What's more, the ritual statutes and instructions found in Leviticus do not truly reflect the actual practice of any particular period in Israelite history—whether the tradition in the desert before the settle-

---

21 Hurvitz, *A Linguistic Study of the Relationship between the Priestly Source and the Book of Ezekiel* (1982); "Dating the Priestly Source in the Light of the Historical Study of Biblical Hebrew a Century after Wellhausen" (1988).

22 Haran, *Temples and Temple-Service in Ancient Israel: An Inquiry into the Character of Cult Phenomena and the Historical Setting of the Priestly School* (1977), 146–47; "Behind the Scenes of History: Determining the Date of the Priestly Source" (1981); Knohl, *The Sanctuary of Silence* (1995), 199–222; Milgrom, *Leviticus 1–16* (1991), 13–35.

23 Hartley, *Leviticus* (1992), xxxv–xliii.

24 Hartley, *Leviticus,* xlii.

25 Hartley, *Leviticus,* xli.

ment, the tradition of Shiloh before its destruction, or the sacrificial ritual at Jerusalem during the monarchy or in the Persian period. Instead, they institute and regulate the performance of the divine service, more or less completely, at all stages in the history of God's people, for it is most unlikely that the law of Moses was ever fully implemented at any period in Israel's history.

This commentary examines the canonical text of Leviticus. That, after all, is the only certain datum that we possess. While all positions on its historical origin and the process of its composition are tentative and hypothetical, we stand on firm ground if we deal with the actual text of the book and accept the teaching of Israel, Jesus Christ, and the church that it is, mysteriously and yet truly, the Word of God. This focus on the canonical text results in the grammatical, literary, ritual, and theological analysis of Leviticus, first by itself and then as part of the entire Bible, culminating in its fulfillment in Christ.

Structural Analysis

The book of Leviticus is part of an extended narrative of the events that occurred at Mount Sinai. The narrative begins with the arrival of the Israelites there in Ex 19:1–2 and ends with their departure in Num 10:11–13. This narrative context is established by the recurrent summary reports of God's speeches to Moses (Lev 1:1; 7:38; 25:1; 26:46; 27:34) and sections of narrative in the book (Lev 8:6–10:20; 16:1; 24:10–12). This narrative gives the context for the sections of divine legislation in this part of the Pentateuch. They belong to a body of ritual legislation that begins in Ex 25:1 and ends in Num 10:10.

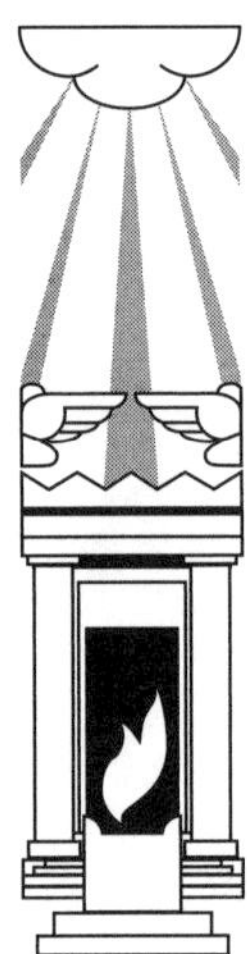

The beginning of Leviticus clearly marks off a new stage in the narrative and the law-giving with the shift of the location for God's speaking from the mountain to the tabernacle ("the tent of meeting," Lev 1:1). Yet the book is still closely connected with narrative in Exodus in four significant ways. First, God's summons to Moses from the tabernacle recalls his summons to Moses from the mountain in Ex 19:3 and 24:16 and so continues the process of revelation that began there. Second, God's speaking to Moses from the tent of meeting in Lev 1:1 presupposes the erection and consecration of the tabernacle as recorded in Ex 40:16–33, as well as the entry of God's glory into the Holy of Holies, described in Ex 40:34–38. Third, the theophany of the Lord at the altar in Leviticus 9 presupposes his preliminary appearances in glory on Mount Sinai in Ex 24:15–18 and in the tent of meeting in Ex 40:34–38. Fourth, the consecration of the priests together with the sanctuary and the inauguration of the divine service in Leviticus 8 and 9 carry out what God had commanded in Ex 29:1–46.

The introductory verse of Leviticus (1:1) sets the pattern for the rest of the book. Since the book records what God said to Moses in the tent of meeting, its contents are arranged in a series of speeches. There are, in all, thirty-six such divine speeches. Each of these begins with God's address to Moses, or, in a few cases, to Moses and Aaron (11:1; 13:1; 14:33; 15:1) or just to Aaron (10:8).

In most cases we find "Then the Lord spoke" (וַיְדַבֵּר), and the direct quotation is introduced with "saying" (לֵאמֹר).[26] In 16:2 and 21:1 we have "Then the Lord said" (וַיֹּאמֶר). God's address to Moses is followed by a formulaic commission—usually "speak to ..." (דַּבֵּר אֶל־)—which tells Moses to report God's words to the designated audience, whether that audience is Aaron (16:2; 21:17), the priests (6:2, 18 [ET 6:8, 25]; 21:1; 22:2), or the Israelites.[m] The formula of commission is absent when God speaks to Moses and the words are intended for him[n] or when God speaks words to and for Aaron (10:8–9).

The established pattern in this sequence of speeches is broken by 16:1. Chapter 16 begins with an address to Moses, but gives no subsequent speech. Instead, we have a report that this address was given after the death of Nadab and Abihu. Then in 16:2 we have the words of a new speech that is introduced by the phrase: "Then the Lord said to Moses" rather than "Then the Lord spoke to Moses, saying." Warning considers that to indicate that 16:1 and 16:2–34 are two separate speeches.[27] If 16:1 were a separate speech, then, as Warning argues, the speech about the Day of Atonement in 16:2–34 would be the center of the book, with sixteen speeches before it and sixteen after it.

It is appropriate to regard chapter 16 as a speech that is central to the message of the entire book, and hence it is a kind of centerpiece. However, Warning is wrong to regard 16:1 as a separate speech. The double introduction in 16:1–2 distinguishes chapter 16 from the rest of the book. It makes the reader understand the speech about the Day of Atonement as the culmination of the first half of the book (which revolves around the death of Nadab and Abihu from a priestly act of desecration) as well as the introduction of the second half of the book (which revolves around the danger of priestly defilement by contact with corpses in 21:1–15). Hence both 16:2 and 21:1 begin alike with the unusual phrase "Then the Lord said" (וַיֹּאמֶר) instead of the usual "Then the Lord spoke" (וַיְדַבֵּר).

Besides the use of divine speeches, the book of Leviticus employs four other prominent literary devices to structure its contents. First, we have the headings that introduce the content of a piece of legislation[o] and summaries that tell how that legislation is to be used.[p] Second, reports about the compliance of Moses and other Israelites in carrying out God's commands are inserted at the end of units in the book (8:36; 16:34; 21:24; 23:44; 24:23). Third, we have divine admonitions that introduce a new piece of legislation (18:3–5, 24–30; 19:2, 37; 22:2) or a new part of it (19:19; 20:7–8), as well as divine admonitions that conclude a speech.[q] At times, admonitions are also inserted into the body of the speech to give the reason for an injunction (21:6, 8; 22:9; 25:18–23). Fourth, the book uses stock formulae to introduce a speech and to

(m) Lev 1:2; 4:2; 7:23, 29; 11:2; 12:2; 15:2; 18:2; 19:2; 20:2; 23:2, 10, 24, 34; 24:2, 15; 25:2; 27:2

(n) Lev 5:14–15, 20–21 (ET 6:1–2); 6:12–13 (ET 6:19–20); 8:1–2; 13:1–2; 14:1–2, 33–34; 22:26–27; 24:13–14

(o) Lev 6:1, 12, 18 (ET 6:9, 19, 25); 7:1, 11; 11:2, 9, 13, 24, 29; 14:2; 17:2; cf. 8:5; 9:6

(p) Lev 7:37–38; 11:46–47; 12:7; 13:59; 14:32, 54–57; 15:32–33; 16:34

(q) Lev 3:17; 11:41–45; 15:31; 20:22–26; 22:31–33; 26:3–45

---

26 However, this commentary's translation simply renders לֵאמֹר by a colon preceding the quotation.

27 Warning, *Literary Artistry in Leviticus,* 44–46.

close a speech or a part of it, such as a declaratory formula about an offering (e.g. 1:17; 2:3, 10, 16; 3:5; 4:21; 5:19) or the formula for divine self-introduction (e.g. 11:44, 45; 18:2, 4, 5, 6, 21, 30).

If the placement of material in divine speeches is the basic device that is used to arrange the material in Leviticus, then the most perplexing part of the book is chapter 26. On the face of it, this chapter seems to function as a discrete unit. This extended admonition is introduced by three prohibitions and two commandments that have little or nothing to do with the previous chapter. Yet despite that, it is not presented as a separate speech. Instead, it seems to provide the conclusion of the speech that begins in 25:1. Chapter 26 is best taken as the conclusive summary admonition for the second half of the book. Like the previous concluding admonitions that summarize their broader and narrower context, chapter 26 provides the conclusion for chapters 17–25 as well as for chapter 25.

The function of chapter 26 is the basis for Ruwe's intriguing claim that the commandments to observe God's Sabbaths and to revere his sanctuary summarize all the requirements in chapters 17–25. Ruwe concludes that the theme of chapters 17–22 is reverence for the sanctuary, while the theme of chapters 23–25 is the observance of the Sabbaths.[28] Even though Ruwe occasionally overstates his case, his proposal does help us understand why the speeches are arranged as they are in the second half of Leviticus.

The use of divine speeches and all the other structural, literary devices combine to create a skillfully constructed work of ritual legislation. This is evident in the arrangement of Leviticus as a whole, and even more so in the arrangement of material within the speeches. As Whybray declares, judged by ancient standards, *Leviticus is a literary masterpiece.*[29] It demands that we consider and appreciate each speech as a literary construct by itself and in its context. In our exegesis we will therefore pay close attention to the literary structure of each speech, as well as the clusters of speeches in the book.

For an overview of the structure of the entire book, see the outline that forms the table of contents for this commentary.

Ritual Analysis

The book of Leviticus consists, by and large, of ritual legislation. By his Word God institutes the essential parts of the divine service for his interaction with his people at the sanctuary. In it he also indicates how their personal behavior and communal life were to harmonize with their involvement in the sacrificial ritual.

This concentration on ritual alienates most modern readers in the Western world. We have little appreciation for the function and significance of ritual, even though our daily life is, to a large extent, governed by unconscious ritu-

---

[28] Ruwe, *"Heiligkeitsgesetz" und "Priesterschrift,"* 90–120.

[29] Whybray, *The Making of the Pentateuch,* 242.

als and ritualized forms of behavior. We, rather curiously, think that ritual robs us of freedom and spontaneity. Since it imposes conventional patterns of behavior on us, we scorn it as impersonal and mechanical, empty and cold, lifeless and meaningless. At best, ritual may show what we have in common with each other and so be used to express how we feel in a conventional way. At worst, we fancy that it alienates, dehumanizes, and enslaves us; it robs us of our subjectivity and individuality.

In contrast to this modern contempt for ritual, the ancient Israelites, like most people in traditional societies, valued ritual. God himself gave them rituals that pleased him, and they rightly regarded those rituals as essential to their life as God's people. Ritual provided a secure foundation for their existence in community and an ordered basis for their interaction with each other and God in their midst. They depended on it for their sense of purpose in life and used it to find their place in the world. It affirmed their identity as the people of God and helped them to adjust to their total environment. Ritual was obviously important for them in all the aspects of their lives. Their religious life was founded on ritual. Since they were God's holy people who oriented their society around his presence with them, their existence as a holy community depended on their enactment of the sacrificial ritual that he had ordained for them. So we will not understand what they believed unless we understand how their faith was ritually enacted.

There are three presuppositions for the proper appreciation and right understanding of the ritual system that God instituted for the Israelites in Leviticus.[30]

First, we need to recognize that, whether we are aware of it or not, *we are all creatures of ritual.* Ritual is as much a part of our humanity as the use of language, for without ritual we could not coexist with each other and cooperate in any community, whether it be in a marriage, in a family, or in the church. Thus Douglas rightly maintains that "as a social animal, man is a ritual animal."[31] Rituals create and consolidate communities. Without the use of ritual, communities cannot survive the passage of time and resist the centrifugal forces of self-interest that would tear them apart. Without ritual, there is no Christian community. Ritual undergirded the life of Israel as a liturgical community, just as it governs the life of the church.

The Christian church is bonded together by regular worship on the Lord's day (usually at the same time every week), the liturgy of the Divine Service, the divinely instituted Sacraments, the Scripture readings (usually following the lectionary), the common confession of the Creeds, the sermon, the recitation of the Lord's Prayer, the singing of hymns, and many other repeated activities that might be considered rituals in a broad sense. Some of the glimpses of heaven in Revelation also hint at liturgical, ritual practices (e.g., Rev 4:8–11;

[30] See Kleinig, "Witting or Unwitting Ritualists."

[31] Douglas, *Purity and Danger,* 62.

7:9–12) and portray heavenly worship with the same imagery found in Leviticus (e.g., Rev 11:19; 15:3–8). The hosts in heaven sing "the song of Moses the servant of God and the song of the Lamb" (Rev 15:3), which links the ministry of Moses to that of Christ.

From a human point of view, the enactment of the rituals of our common faith unites us as Christians congregationally and synodically. When Christ commanded us to do the Lord's Supper in remembrance of him, he instituted our central ritual. The Augsburg Confession acknowledges the importance of ritual in Article V by teaching that the church is created and built up by the preaching of the Word and the administration of the Sacraments. It therefore, quite rightly, defines the church in ritual terms. In fact, everything that is done in the Divine Service involves some kind of ritual enactment. Without ritual there is no communal worship. We do, however, need to distinguish between those rituals that Christ has instituted and those that have been humanly devised without scriptural warrant. Furthermore, we need to distinguish the proper use of ritual from its abuse in ritualism.

Second, since we are embodied beings, *we need a ritual system to interact physically with each other.* Ritual has to do with our bodies and their involvement in our social life. But it also goes beyond the level of physical coexistence and physical interaction. We communicate our thoughts and feelings through our senses and our bodily interactions with each other and our environment. For example, in marriage and the ritual of sexual intercourse, people do not just interact physically with each other, but through their physical interaction they communicate emotionally, mentally, and personally as well.

Each community has established its own ritual system to facilitate the process of physical exchange between its members. Just as each society has its own language for verbal communication, so each society also has its own ritual code for physical communication. People use this code to reach out to others and enact their personal business with them; they use it to give and receive in their social intercourse. Religious ritual engages people bodily. Its set forms symbolize and enact some kind of personal exchange between God and people. Thus, by means of the religious rituals God gave Israel, the Israelites interacted physically with each other and their God.

Third, just as God created human beings as embodied creatures and made provision for their bodily existence on earth, *God chose to interact physically with the Israelites by instituting the rituals that made up the divine service.* Those rituals were meant to function sacramentally.[32] Just as God used human

---

[32] Hummel, *The Word Becoming Flesh,* 81. By "sacramentally" (and similar terms) we do not mean that God gave the Israelites the same two Sacraments that Jesus instituted in the NT, namely, Christian Baptism and the Lord's Supper. Rather, we mean that within the context of OT history and theology, the rites and rituals given by God to Israel served roles that were in some ways analogous to the role of the NT Sacraments in the life of the church. Many of the OT rituals were accompanied by divine promises (e.g., that a priest would be consecrated as holy for divine service, that a person would be declared clean, or that the sins of Israel or of a person were forgiven) and involved physical elements and physical actions.

speech to address his people and bless them, so he used human rituals to meet with them at the tabernacle and sanctify them for life together with him. Eichrodt therefore claims:

> The cultus is, however, not only the inwardly necessary expression of spiritual realities by means of the physical, but also *the medium by which divine power is presented* to men for their participation. Such a conception rests on the deep conviction of the ancient world, that the deity gives himself to men not merely through the subjective channels of the conscious mind, but also uses the body as a means of access by which he may effectuate weal or woe. … In the outward actions of the cult the power of the divine blessing is communicated to the actual mode of man's existence. The sacred action becomes a sacrament.[33]

In most cases, God chose the same kinds of rituals that were practiced by other peoples in the ancient Near East. Thus all the main types of offerings sanctioned in Leviticus were also offered by pagan people to their gods. However, God reshaped those rituals to suit his purposes by the ritual legislation that is found in Leviticus. God reconfigured them with his Word and promises and used them to do his work with his people. Through the reformation of these rituals, God separated the Israelites physically from their pagan neighbors and involved their whole bodily life in their service to him.

Since the book of Leviticus deals with Israel's divinely instituted ritual, it needs to be interpreted ritually. The method of interpretation must be appropriate for its contents. Yet all too often commentators of Leviticus fail to do justice to its ritual concerns. They treat it as if it were a book of theological reflections couched in ritual terms, or the program for liturgical reform at a particular period in Israel's history. Thus, on the one hand, they assume that its priestly authors used this ritual material to expound their theology or their religious ideology. On the other hand, they assume that the book describes how the Israelites were to worship God at a particular time in their religious history, such as during the reign of Hezekiah or the postexilic period. Yet even though the book was obviously used for theological reflection and for liturgical reform, it prescribes how God's people were to enact certain rituals at all times in the land of Israel. The significance of these rituals cannot be abstracted from their enactment, for their significance is determined by what they do. So any method of ritual interpretation must concentrate on the actual theological function of a ritual in the divine service.

This commentary attempts to employ such a method of ritual analysis and interpretation. Its basic assumption is that *God, through his Word, instituted and empowered the rituals in Leviticus so that they accomplished something by their enactment.* We therefore need to discover their actual function. In the secular realm, the function of a ritual enactment, like the singing of the American national anthem, is determined by custom, tradition, and convention. Peo-

---

[33] Eichrodt, *Theology of the Old Testament,* 1:99–100.

ple will only enact a ritual if it serves some recognizable function, and if it no longer has a function to perform, it is discarded. The function of the rituals in Leviticus, however, was established by God's Word, and its explanation was passed on by Moses and the priestly successors.

Even though any proper ritual enactment has a clearly recognized function in its social context, it can accomplish much more than just one thing. This element of complexity—this surplus of significance—is, in fact, its greatest asset. A single ritual enactment can serve many different purposes and mean many different things. Its full significance varies according to its context and use. A simple social-ritual enactment, like a kiss on the lips, can enact something so complex and nuanced that we cannot exhaust its full significance, no matter how much we analyze and explain it. Ritual acts can therefore initiate people into the deepest mysteries of life and give them access to the profoundest spiritual realities. Thus in the Divine Service, the Benediction conveys God's blessing by means of a performative utterance of God's Word. Yet each act of benediction may have a special force and effect, depending on who blesses whom, how, where, with what, and in what circumstances. For example, something different is enacted by saying "Bless You!" when someone sneezes, writing "God bless" at the end of a letter, and performing the Aaronic Benediction at the end of the Holy Communion service.

The basic function of a ritual enactment in Leviticus is determined by God's institution of it with his ritual legislation. However, often the actual function is not explicitly stated, but is only implied in his arrangement of it. We may infer its function from the order of the ritual, for the function of a ritual is evident in the ordered sequence of acts that are performed in the course of its enactment. We therefore need to determine who does what, to whom, where, when, and with what. All these factors work together to accomplish its intended effect.

This understanding of ritual governs the format of each section in the commentary that examines a unit of ritual legislation. The linguistic and literary analysis of the text will be followed by its ritual analysis. This will, normally, proceed with a consideration of the persons involved in the transaction of the ritual, the objects or material that they use in it, its location in the sanctuary or the Israelite camp, the time or occasion for its enactment, and the order of its enactment either in the divine service or apart from it. The process of ritual analysis will culminate in an attempt to identify the ritual function and theological significance of the enactment from two points of view. It will show what the Israelites accomplished ritually by their involvement in the divine service. It will also show how God was involved in the ritual transaction, and what he did for his people in it.

Fulfillment by Christ

The book of Leviticus consists of God's ritual legislation for the performance of the divine service at the tabernacle and, by extension, later at the temple in Jerusalem. The advent of Jesus Christ radically and irrevocably altered the way in which the OT revelation continues to speak to God's people. The Jerusalem temple was finally destroyed in A.D. 70. Therefore we who are Christians cannot appropriate Leviticus directly and must not attempt to enact it as the divine service in the NT church. We are not Israelites longing for the first advent of Christ, nor do we worship God with animal sacrifices at the temple in Jerusalem. Rather, through the Word and Meal of Christ, we are involved in the liturgy performed together with the angels in the heavenly sanctuary.

Nevertheless, both Christ and his apostles show that the ritual legislation in Leviticus is relevant for us. While the law of Moses does not prescribe what we do in the Divine Service, it helps us to understand how God interacts with us in Christ and in the Divine Service. So each section in this commentary ends with a discussion of the fulfillment of each piece of ritual legislation by Christ. In each case we will examine the function and significance of the divine service, for what God intended to achieve ritually through his law in Leviticus is accomplished fully by Christ and conveyed to the church in the Divine Service.

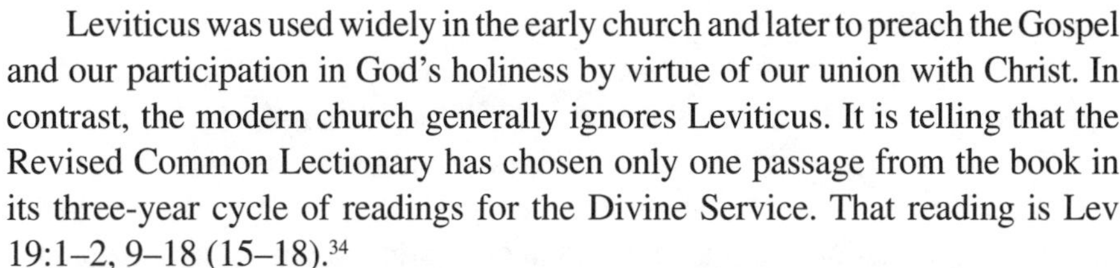

Leviticus was used widely in the early church and later to preach the Gospel and our participation in God's holiness by virtue of our union with Christ. In contrast, the modern church generally ignores Leviticus. It is telling that the Revised Common Lectionary has chosen only one passage from the book in its three-year cycle of readings for the Divine Service. That reading is Lev 19:1–2, 9–18 (15–18).[34]

The present neglect of Leviticus, however, should not surprise us. It is an accurate reflection of the status of the book in the contemporary church, an index of the embarrassment of Western Christians with its contents. It seems that this book is thought to have little or no relevance for modern people. At best, it contains outdated ancient Israelite ritual legislation that has been abolished by Christ. At worst, it is considered quite un-Christian in its promotion of ritual legalism, justification by works, the very antithesis of the Gospel. So churches that prize the Good News of free forgiveness through faith in Christ may mistakenly assume that they should no longer use Leviticus to nurture the saints, even though the entire book is concerned with forgiveness and atonement—more overtly than any other book of the Bible.[35]

Leviticus cannot be sidelined as easily as that, for much of the NT is rightly interpreted only in its light. We depend on Leviticus for the proper under-

---

[34] Lev 19:1–2, 9–18 is assigned for the Seventh Sunday after the Epiphany in Year A. Lev 19:1–2, 15–18 is an alternate reading for Proper 25 in Year A (*The Revised Common Lectionary: The Consultation on Common Texts* [Nashville: Abingdon, 1992], 28, 38).

[35] To be sure, every book of Scripture ultimately centers on the forgiveness of sins in Jesus Christ. However, Leviticus contains a disproportionately large percentage of the references in Scripture to atonement and forgiveness (e.g., the verbs כִּפֶּר, "atone, make atonement," and נִסְלַח, "be forgiven"), and the bulk of the book is about God's ritual remedies for sins and maladies.

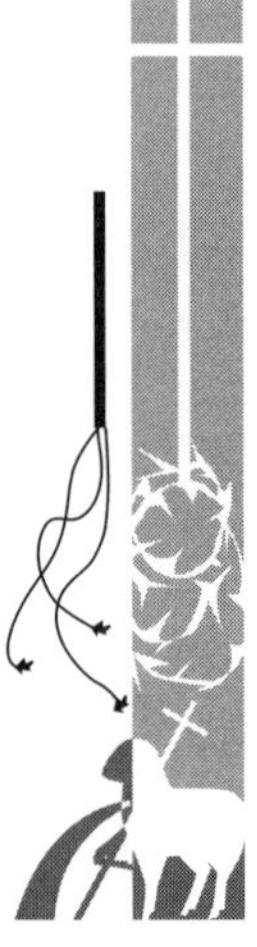

standing of Christ's death for sinners and the doctrine of his vicarious atonement, which is the heart of the NT Gospels and epistles. Christ is "the Lamb of God, who takes away the sin of the world" (Jn 1:29), "the Lamb who was slain" (Rev 5:12). The letter to the Hebrews, with its profound liturgical theology of Christ as both the great High Priest and the once-for-all sacrifice, would be inscrutable without Leviticus. From a literary point of view, it is the heart of the Pentateuch—the central book of the five that comprise the Torah, which is the foundation of the OT and indeed the entire canon.

This commentary attempts to commend this neglected part of the Holy Scriptures to the church as she reorients herself in a post-modern world. Increasingly the church is returning to her ancient roots and profound appreciation for God's gracious work in the Divine Service through the liturgy of Word and Sacrament. The contemporary church is also being called upon to confront the attacks on the exclusivity of Christ as "the Holy One of God" (Mk 1:24; Jn 6:69) from other religions and semi-animist New Age religious ideologies—the same battle fought by ancient Israel against the indigenous Canaanite religions, and by the early church against the plethora of gods and lords accepted in the Roman era.

It is our conviction that Leviticus is far from being outdated or irrelevant. It is, indeed, *most relevant for the mission of the church,* for people who sense that they live in a polluted world and so look for physical and cosmic deliverance from the powers that contaminate them. That sense of helplessness in the face of contamination is often accompanied by a longing for sanctity, a recognition of the hidden beauty and wholesome power of holiness. The solution is the cleansing that comes through Christ and the health that is obtained by participation in his holiness now, with the promise of the resurrection and complete restoration of the body on the Last Day.

Since the book of Leviticus is part of the whole Bible we will go beyond the ritual and theological analysis of its text. Each section of this commentary will conclude with a discussion on its fulfillment by Christ in the NT. Space does not permit us to explore the full canonical trajectory of interpretation that leads from Leviticus through the rest of the OT and the intertestamental period into the NT church. We will have to jump straight from Leviticus to the NT.

Our method of interpretation will be *Christological, ecclesiological,* and *typological.*

The first presupposition for our interpretation of Leviticus is that our method must be *Christological because of Christ's fulfillment of the whole law of God.* In Mt 5:17–18 Christ himself taught that he had not come to abolish the law, but to fulfill it. This claim does not just extend to the moral law as found in the second table of the Decalogue, but it also includes the whole ceremonial law of the Pentateuch. None of it will pass away until all that God has commanded in it will be accomplished by and through Christ (cf. Lk 16:17). He fulfills the whole of it by his active and passive obedience. He enacts it; he completes it all by his incarnation and glorification.

Some argue that the apostle Paul contradicts the Gospels about that. Paul declares that Christ is the end of the law (Rom 10:4); in his flesh he has "abolished the law of the commandments with its ritual decrees" (Eph 2:15). Some assert that such declarations by Paul imply that the law of Moses is no longer relevant for the church. Yet Paul himself maintains that he did not abolish the law by preaching faith in Christ; instead, he upheld the law (Rom 3:31). This was so because Christ, by his self-sacrifice as a sin offering and by the gift of the Holy Spirit, had actually accomplished everything that the law, with its ritual legislation, had required (Rom 8:3–4). Christians, therefore, are freed from the law's condemnation, and at the same time are led by the Spirit to live in harmony with the law, not in sinful violation of it (Rom 6:1–14; 8:1–11; Gal 3:13–14; 5:16–24; cf. Acts 13:39).

Christ has fulfilled the law of Moses, and we are united with him in his death and resurrection through Baptism—"the circumcision of Christ" (Col 2:11). We have been discharged from the law's implacable former demands and serve God by the power of the Holy Spirit (Rom 7:4, 6). Our service of God depends on Christ, for it is accomplished in him. The ritual legislation for purification is superseded by Christ's work as our great High Priest. He cleanses Jews and Gentiles, so that both together have access to God the Father in the church, without fear of condemnation and rejection because of ritual impurity. Christ then is the "end" of the law, because it reaches its "goal" in him. All the ritual statutes in the Pentateuch foreshadow Christ and his gifts to his baptized believers in the Divine Service (Col 2:16–17; Heb 10:1). Thus the divine service that God established through the law of Moses reaches its perfection, its consummation and fulfillment in and through Christ.

This commentary relates all the ritual legislation to Christ because he alone implemented perfectly what was commanded in Leviticus. As the Messiah, he did not just fulfill the law of Moses more completely than David and Solomon and all the other kings of Israel. Christ was like Moses but the mediator of a much greater prophetic Word from God (Deut 18:15–22). Moses built the tabernacle, and Solomon built the temple (whose glory surpassed that of the tabernacle), but Christ instituted a new and better liturgy by offering his body on the cross as the perfect sacrifice for the sins of all people. Christ raised up the new temple that grants those in him access to the heavenly sanctuary (Jn 2:19–21; Heb 8:2; cf. Mk 14:58). In the heavenly sanctuary, Christ inaugurated a new form of Divine Service in the Father's presence. There he serves as the High Priest of humanity and officiates together with the angels and on behalf of the whole church (Heb 8:2; 10:19–22; 12:22–24). By this performance of the liturgy in the heavenly sanctuary, he fulfills the law of Moses and so supersedes the OT temple and its services.

The second presupposition for our interpretation is that our exposition must be *ecclesiological because Leviticus is addressed to the NT church as well as to the OT people of Israel.* Through Christ all the members of the church—Jew and Gentile alike—are, by grace, spiritual sons and heirs of Abraham (Gal 3:29;

6:16). Gentile believers are honorary Israelites grafted into the congregation of the true Israel, which consists of all who believe in Christ (Rom 11:17–32). In Christ Gentiles therefore have equal access to the Father by the Holy Spirit together with believing Jews (Eph 2:11–19; 3:4–6). The book of Leviticus, with its legislation for the divine service and access to God's holiness and glory, is part of the legacy bequeathed to Gentile Christians from the Israelites through Christ (Rom 9:4–5). It is God's Word to the entire church. Thus all that God promised to give to his people by instituting the divine service is available to all through the ministry of Christ in the church.

This means that we will not interpret the book of Leviticus politically as a document for the establishment of the church as a theocratic community on earth, nor will we use it allegorically as a textbook on spirituality for ascent of the soul into the heavenly realm or for other kinds of spiritual experiences. We will interpret its contents canonically and liturgically. It is part of the sacred Scriptures. As such it functions properly—and canonically—when it is read in the Divine Service and applied there. It teaches those who belong to Christ how to serve God the Father as his holy priests here on earth.

The third basic presupposition for our Christian interpretation is that *the whole sacrificial system was meant typologically to foreshadow the ministry of Christ as High Priest.* Thus our method of interpretation is typological, a method of expounding the OT that is employed in the NT,[36] including Hebrews 8–9, which interprets the tabernacle, priesthood, and sacrificial cultus Christologically.[37] It does not assume that God—or even the Israelites under God's direction—established the tabernacle with its offices and services as the model for all subsequent OT and NT worship, a prototype that would have to be copied exactly thereafter by all sanctuaries, which had to conform with it in every way. Rather, it assumes that the sanctuary at Mount Sinai and the subsequent temple in Jerusalem were types: imperfect copies of the perfect antitype, which is the heavenly temple built by God himself through Christ for his eternal residence with his people (Ex 25:40; Heb 8:5).

Luther describes this use of typology for God's words and deeds most succinctly when he says:

> God always works so that the figure or type appears first, and then the true reality and fulfilment of the type follows. So the Old Testament first comes forth as a type, and the New Testament follows as the true reality.[38]

This means that even though each type resembles the antitype in some way(s), each type is also inferior to and surpassed by the greater and perfect antitype in Christ. Thus the liturgical ministry of Christ far surpasses the min-

---

[36] Davidson, *Typology in Scripture,* 336–88.

[37] Goppelt, *Typos: The Typological Interpretation of the Old Testament in the New;* Hummel, *The Word Becoming Flesh,* 16–18.

[38] Luther, *Confession concerning Christ's Supper* (AE 37:254).

istry of Aaron and his successors. Goppelt well describes a cautious and exegetically sound use of OT typology:

> Only historical facts—persons, actions, events, and institutions—are material for typological interpretation; words and narratives can be utilized only insofar as they deal with such matters. These things are to be interpreted typologically only if they are considered to be divinely ordained representations or types of future realities that will be even greater and more complete.[39]

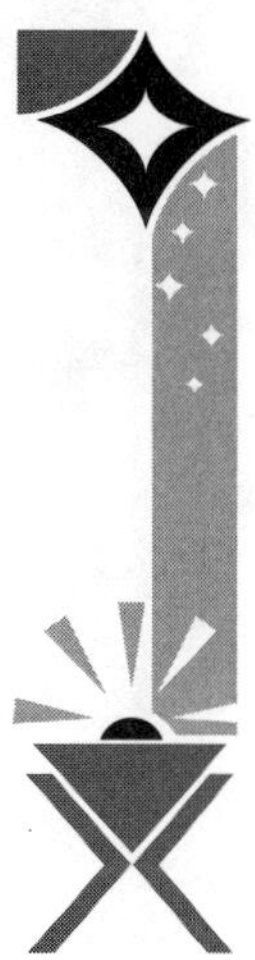

Hummel rightly maintains that this use of typology is closely related to the Christian understanding of OT prophecy.[40] Both the divinely inspired words of the prophets and divinely instituted ritual of Israel are fulfilled by Christ in history. Like prophecy, typology is both historical and eschatological, for while the type has to do with real persons and institutions in the old age, its antitype is not revealed in the eternal realm of ideas, but in the person and work of Jesus in the new age, the age of the church and its consummation in the creation of new heavens and a new earth.

A typological reading of the texts that deal with the institution of the tabernacle and its services prevents the transposition of concrete ritual realities into general theological concepts and their evaporation into mystical Gnostic states of consciousness. It does justice to the physical nature of ritual enactments as well as to the incarnation of Christ. It interprets ritual liturgically and sacramentally.

Our approach is in harmony with that of the early church, for, as Danielou[41] has shown, the early church used typology in the liturgy and in its liturgical theology. This typological approach helped the church to proclaim and confess the presence and work of Christ as High Priest in the actual ritual enactment of the liturgy. It also helps us to connect Christ's historical work of salvation with his ongoing service of us through the means of grace. Thus, "in his own person Christ takes the place of temple and sacrifice and every other OT means of salvation,"[42] and the liturgical use of typology also correlates the temple and its services with Christ's continuing work as High Priest and Mediator in the church and through the Divine Service.

In the Apology of the Augsburg Confession, Melanchthon builds on this tradition of interpretation in his discussion on the Mass. Melanchthon declares that the legislation on the divine service in Num 28:3–8 foreshadows "Christ and the whole worship [*totus cultus*] of the New Testament" (Ap XXIV 36).

The typological approach employed in this commentary ensures that the divinely instituted ritual in Leviticus is not rendered irrelevant or transformed into a system of theological ideas unrelated to bodily life as the corporate peo-

---

[39] Goppelt, *Typos,* 17–18.

[40] Hummel, *The Word Becoming Flesh,* 17.

[41] Danielou, *The Bible and the Liturgy.*

[42] Goppelt, *Typos,* 116.

ple of God. We will show how the legislation in Leviticus finds its proper fulfillment in the ministry of Christ in Word and Sacrament.

As Moses and Aaron are types of Christ and ancient Israel is a type of the NT church, so also the various sacrifices and offerings are ordained by God as types for the sacramental and sacrificial aspects of the Divine Service. Everything that God offered to his people through the daily service at the tabernacle resembles, however imperfectly, what he offers through his Son in the ministry of Word and Sacrament. So too everything that God required—and still requires—of his people is accomplished perfectly by his Son together with the faithful in the Divine Service. The offices and ritual enactments in Leviticus therefore prefigure the celebration of the Lord's Supper in the church.[43] There the triune God interacts with the saints through physical means and involves them bodily in the life and fellowship of the Son with the Father. There the triune God engages them physically and produces the bodily sacrifices that are holy and acceptable to him by animating them with his Holy Spirit (Rom 12:1; 1 Pet 2:4–5).

---

[43] See Goppelt, *Typos,* 116.

Leviticus 1:1–15:33

The Involvement of the Israelites in the Divine Service

1:1–7:38	**The Manual of Offerings**
1:1–3:17	**The Voluntary God-Pleasing Offerings**
1:1–2	Divine Legislation for the Private Offerings
1:3–17	Regulations for the Burnt Offering
2:1–16	Regulations for the Grain Offering
3:1–17	Regulations for the Peace Offering
4:1–5:26	**The Mandatory Offerings for Atonement (ET 4:1–6:7)**
4:1–5:13	Regulations for the Sin Offering
5:14–26	Regulations for the Reparation Offering (ET 5:14–6:7)
6:1–7:38	**The Consumption of the Holy Food (ET 6:8–7:38)**
6:1–11	The Daily Public Offering (ET 6:8–18)
6:12–16	The Daily Grain Offering of the High Priest (ET 6:19–23)
6:17–7:21	The Occasional Offerings of the Israelites (ET 6:24–7:21)
7:22–27	Prohibited Food: Fat and Blood
7:28–36	The Priest's Portion of the Peace Offering
7:37–38	The Conclusion of the Manual of Offerings
8:1–10:20	**The Inauguration of the Divine Service**
8:1–36	The Consecration of the Priests
9:1–24	The Inauguration of the Divine Service
10:1–20	The Penalty for Disobedience
11:1–15:33	**The Manual for Purity**
11:1–47	Instruction on Clean and Unclean Meat
12:1–8	Impurity from Childbirth
13:1–59	The Diagnosis of Impurity from Skin Diseases
14:1–32	Purification of the Skin-Diseased
14:33–57	Purification of Infected Houses
15:1–33	Purification from Genital Discharges

Leviticus 1–7

The Manual of Offerings

The first seven chapters of Leviticus form a single literary unit. They contain the various classes of offerings that the Israelites were either permitted or commanded to bring to the Lord at the tabernacle. In this first part of the book, the focus of attention shifts from the regular public sacrificial ritual that the Lord had instituted in Ex 29:38–46 to the personal offerings brought by Israelites as individuals or in their families. Some of these were voluntary, while others, such as the sin and reparation offerings in Lev 4:1–5:26 (ET 4:1–6:7), were required of the Israelites only in certain circumstances. These regulations therefore deal with those rites that involved the ordinary Israelites personally in the sacrificial ritual at the tabernacle.

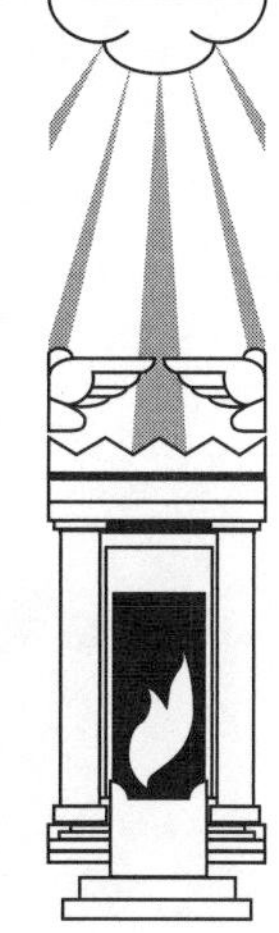

From a literary point of view, this section might seem to be out of place in the narrative. Since the book of Leviticus continues the narrative from Exodus, one might think that it would be most appropriate for it to begin with the account of the consecration of the priests and the inauguration of the sacrificial ritual, which come after this section in Leviticus 8 and 9. That would have been apt because of the pattern of instructions and fulfillments established in Exodus. The last six chapters of Exodus (Exodus 35–40) record the fulfillment of the Lord's instructions about the construction of the tabernacle in Exodus 25–27 and 30–31. Leviticus 8–9 reports how Moses fulfilled the Lord's instructions in Exodus 28 and 29. But Leviticus does not begin with that fulfillment. Instead, in Leviticus 1–7 we have a new set of divine speeches about a new topic, and God utters these speeches from a new location. Their topic is the offerings of the Israelites, and the location of these speeches is the tent of meeting.

The placement of this material here in Leviticus seems to serve two main functions: practical and theological. Practically, it prepares for the great inauguration of the full sacrificial ritual in Leviticus 9 by giving the regulations for the various classes of sacrifices that had not yet been instituted in Exodus. Those sacrifices are the sin offering for the high priest (Lev 4:3–12) and for the Israelites (4:13–21); the burnt offering for the priests and the people (1:3–13); the grain offering (2:1–16); and the peace offering for the Israelites (3:1–17).

Theologically, the location of these regulations here in Leviticus 1–7 and their character as the first revelation of the Lord from the tent of meeting emphasize the importance of the people in the sacrificial ritual. The Lord had instituted the tent of meeting to serve their needs rather than the needs of the priests. At the tent God speaks to the people through Moses and interacts with them by means of the ritual performed under the supervision of the priests. Unlike the Babylonians, the Israelites were not the temple slaves of their God. *The sacrificial ritual and all the rites associated with it were established for the benefit of God's people, rather than for the benefit of their God and his priests.*

The regulations in these seven chapters are therefore addressed to the Israelites (1:2; 4:2; 7:23, 29), even though they were all spoken to Moses,[a] and some were meant for the priests (6:2, 18 [ET 6:9, 25]). The various units in this opening section of Leviticus are arranged as a series of divine speeches to Moses. After the initial introduction in 1:1, each new section is introduced by the sentence "The Lord said to Moses." This device divides the first seven chapters into the following nine speeches:

(a) Lev 1:1; 4:1; 5:14; 5:20 (ET 6:1); 6:1, 12, 17 (ET 6:8, 19, 24); 7:22, 28

1. The God-pleasing burnt offering, grain offering, and peace offering (1:1–3:17)
2. The sin offering for atonement and forgiveness (4:1–5:13)
3. The reparation offering for the desecration of holy things (5:14–19)
4. The reparation offering for desecration from the violation of an oath (5:20–26 [ET 6:1–7])
5. Instructions for the public burnt offering and for the private grain offering (6:1–11 [ET 6:8–18])
6. The grain offering of the priests (6:12–16 [ET 6:19–23])
7. Instructions for the sin offering, the reparation offering, and the peace offering (6:17–7:21 [ET 6:24–7:21])
8. The prohibition of eating fat and blood (7:22–27)
9. The due of the priests from the peace offering (7:28–36)

The Lord is the speaker throughout Leviticus 1–7 even though, surprisingly, he refers to himself directly in the first person only in 6:10 (ET 6:17). All the regulations given here are his Word. All the rites found here are authorized, sanctified, and empowered by him through his Word; his Word determines their function and significance for his people.

The collection of nine divine speeches is marked by a general introduction (1:1–2) and rounded off by a summary conclusion (7:37–38). The reference in 7:38 to the command given by Moses to the Israelites to "offer their offerings to the Lord" echoes the introductory command in 1:2 and so serves to bracket off this section of seven chapters as a discrete unit. The editorial summary in 7:37–38 also distinguishes between two bodies of material in this section. First, 7:37 speaks about the "instruction" (תּוֹרָה) for various classes of offerings and their proper ritual performance, so that what was holy would be distinguished from what is common and clean. This verse refers to the five items of priestly instruction mentioned in 6:1–7:21 (ET 6:8–7:21): (1) the instruction for the burnt offering in 6:2 (ET 6:9); (2) the instruction for the grain offering in 6:7 (ET 6:14); (3) the instruction for the sin offering in 6:18 (ET 6:25); (4) the instruction for the reparation offering in 7:1; and (5) the instruction for the fellowship offering in 7:11. Second, mention is made in 7:38 of the offerings that the Israelites were to bring to the Lord. This refers to the body of ritual legislation in 1:3–5:26 (ET 1:3–6:7).

The division of the first seven chapters into two main parts is supported by an analysis of their content, for the same offerings are mentioned in both parts. The order of the offerings is the same except for the peace offering, which has a different location in the two parts.

Part 1	**Part 2**
1. Burnt offering (1:3–17)	1. Burnt offering (6:1–6 [ET 6:8–13])
2. Grain offering (2:1–16)	2. Grain offering (6:7–16 [ET 6:14–23])
3. Peace offering (3:1–17)	3. Sin offering (6:17–23 [ET 6:24–30])
4. Sin offering (4:1–5:13)	4. Reparation offering (7:1–10)
5. Reparation offering (5:14–5:26 [ET 5:14–6:7])	5. Peace offering (7:11–36)

It is clear that God's instructions in the second part (6:1–7:36 [ET 6:8–7:36]) presuppose and supplement what is given in the first part (1:3–5:26 [ET 1:3–6:7]). If that is so, the question arises why the data in the second part was not included in the first part and assimilated with the contents given there. What is the ritual function and theological purpose of this arrangement?

One proposal is that the two parts presuppose a different audience. While the first part is addressed to the laity (1:2; 4:2), the second part is addressed to the priests (6:2, 13, 18 [ET 6:9, 20, 25]). There is, indeed, some warrant for this proposal because the role of the laity is emphasized in the first part and the role of the priests is highlighted in the second part. But this explanation founders on the address of the two units in 7:23 and 7:29 to the Israelites as well as the address of all the regulations to them in 1:2 and 7:38.

The division into two parts seems, by and large, to correspond with the compilation of two different genres of ritual legislation. The genre in the first part is *ritual case law.* Each new law specifies either the procedure for each kind of offering or the offering for a particular person in a particular set of circumstances and the procedure for that offering. Formally speaking, each new case is introduced by a conditional clause beginning with "when" (כִּי) or "if" (אִם). The conditional clause is then followed by a series of consecutive clauses that prescribe the most significant ritual acts in the performance of that rite. In contrast, the genre in 6:1–7:36 (ET 6:8–7:34) is *statutory ritual law* that prescribes the mandatory procedure for a particular ritual performance.

That difference in genre is connected with a difference in ritual focus and purpose in each part. The first part deals with the responsibility of the layperson for the selection and presentation of each offering. Its focus is on the proper preparation and correct presentation of the offering to the Lord so that he could do his work through it. The burnt, grain, and peace offerings were to be presented so that the Lord would give his approval and demonstrate his benevolence to the people who had brought them. The sin and reparation offerings were to be presented so that the Lord would cleanse the offerers from impurity and forgive them. In keeping with the accent on lay responsibility, the offerings were ranked according to the scale of obligation, beginning with those that were voluntary and ending with those that were mandatory. The first part, then, is basically *didactic: it instructs the Israelites on which offerings could be presented to God, as well as how and why they were presented to him.* See figure 3.

The second part deals with the responsibility of the priests for the holiness of these offerings once they have been presented to the Lord. The focus is on the disposal of what has not been burnt on the altar: the ashes of the burnt offering and the unburned remains of the burnt offering and peace offering; the parts of the grain offering that must or must not be eaten by the priests; the portion of meat from the sin, reparation, and peace offerings that must be eaten by the priests; the portion of the peace offerings that must or must not be eaten by the Israelites. These regulations ensured that the most holy things (6:10, 18, 22 [ET 6:17, 25, 29]; 7:1, 6) were treated appropriately and that the Lord did not cut off his people from the congregation of Israel because they had desecrated his holy things (7:18, 20, 21, 25, 27). In keeping with these concerns, the offerings are ranked according to their holiness. What is most holy is mentioned first; what is least holy comes last. The function of the second part, then, is *administrative: it prescribes how the holy things were to be disposed of, where, when, and by whom.* See figure 4.

The first seven chapters of Leviticus codify the regulations for the offerings of the Israelites. Canonically speaking, Leviticus 1–7 parallels the covenant code in Ex 20:1–23:20 and the ritual legislation in Exodus 25–31. It therefore reports the third divine act of law-giving to the Israelites through Moses in the vicinity of Mount Sinai. Leviticus 1–7 presents God's activity in the divine service, which takes place at the tabernacle constructed according to Exodus 25–31 and which continues to provide the Israelites with the benefits of the covenant God established at Sinai (Ex 20:1–23:20). See figure 5.

Figure 3

The Didactic Order: Lay Offerings

Type of Offering	Offering	Focus of Enactment	Purpose
Burnt offering	• Young bull (1:3–9) • Male sheep or goat (1:10–13) • Turtledove or pigeon (1:14–17)	• Production of a pleasing aroma with the smoke from the whole animal	• Access to God's favor • Acceptance by God
Grain offering	• Fine flour with olive oil and frankincense (2:1–3) • Unleavened bread with olive oil (2:4–10) • Roasted fresh grain with olive oil and frankincense (2:14–16)	• Production of a pleasing aroma with the smoke from the token portion	• Provision of most holy bread for the sanctification of the priests • Acceptance by God
Peace offering	• Bull or cow (3:1–5) • Sheep (3:6–11) • Goat (3:12–16)	• Production of a pleasing aroma with the smoke from the fat, the kidneys, and the lobe of the liver	• Acceptance by God • Provision of holy meat for the priest's family and the Israelite family for holy communion with God as his guests
Sin offering for unintentional sins	• Young bull for congregation (4:1–21)	• Atonement with blood in the Holy Place	• Cleansing of the unclean congregation and forgiveness by God for admission into his presence
	• Male goat for chieftain (4:22–26) • Female goat or sheep for other lay person (4:27–35)	• Atonement with blood on the altar for burnt offering	• Cleansing of the unclean sinner and forgiveness by God for admission into his presence
Graded sin offering for some intentional sins	• Female sheep or goat (5:1–6) • Two turtledoves or pigeons for a poor person (5:7–10)	• Atonement by confession of sins and application of blood to the altar for burnt offering	• Cleansing of the unclean sinner and forgiveness by God for admission into his presence
	• Tenth of an ephah of flour for an impoverished person (5:11–13)	• Atonement by confession of sins and production of smoke from the token portion	
Reparation offering	• Ram for unintentional or suspected acts of desecration (5:14–19)	• Restitution to God by the rite of atonement	• Forgiveness by God for an act of desecration
	• Ram for the desecration of God's name by a perjured thief (5:20–26 [ET 6:1–7])	• Restitution to God by the rite of atonement	• Forgiveness by God for the desecration of his holy name

Figure 4

Administration of the Offerings

Type of Offering	Part of Offering	Manner of Disposal
Public burnt offering (6:1–6 [ET 6:8–13])	Whole animal	Burnt on the altar by the officiating priest
Public grain offering (6:7–11 [ET 6:14–18])	Token portion	Burnt on the altar by the officiating priest
	Most holy bread	Eaten in the courtyard by the priests on duty
High priest's grain offering (6:12–16 [ET 6:19–23])	Bread	Burnt on the altar by the officiating priest
Private sin offering (6:17–22 [ET 6:24–29])	Meat	Eaten in the courtyard by the officiating priest
High priest's sin offering (6:23 [ET 6:30])	Most holy meat	Incinerated at the ash dump by the officiating priest
Private reparation offering (7:1–7)	Most holy meat	Eaten in the courtyard by the officiating priest
Private burnt offering (7:8)	Skin	Property of the officiating priest
Private grain offering (7:9–10)	Bread	Eaten (at home) by the officiating priest
	Flour	Eaten (at home) by the priests on duty
Private peace offerings (7:11–36)	Unleavened loaves from thank offering	Eaten (at home) by the officiating priest
	Leavened loaf from thank offering	Eaten (at home) by the officiating priest
	Meat from thank offering	Eaten by ritually clean lay people on the day of presentation
	Meat from votive or freewill offering	Eaten by ritually clean lay people on the day of presentation and the following day
	Right thigh	Eaten (at home) by the officiating priest
	Breast	Eaten (at home) by the priests on duty

Figure 5

God's Activity in the Divine Service

A. The Rite of Atonement		B. The Rite of Burnt Offering			C. The Sacrificial Meal	
	God's cleansing and pardon	God's acceptance of intercession		God's approval: access to his favor	God's blessing	God's provision of holy food
Preparation	Disposal of Blood for Atonement	Entrance into the Holy Place	Placement of Offerings on Altar	Smoking up of Offerings	Aaronic Benediction	Sacred Meal as God's Guests
• Presentation of male lamb and other animals for sacrifice	• From public and private sin offerings as well as reparation offerings	• Attendance to lamps on lampstand	• Meat from lamb for burnt offerings and other burnt offerings	• Libation of wine on the altar	• Blessing of congregation by the priest	• Eating by priests of most holy bread from grain offerings and showbread
• Slaughter of animals for sacrifice	• From lamb for burnt offerings and other burnt offerings	• Burning of incense on incense altar	• Scattering of token portion of grain offerings	• Blowing of trumpets by the priests (Num 10:10)		• Eating by priests of most holy meat from sin and reparation offerings
• Presentation of flour, bread, and olive oil	• From private peace offerings	• Weekly presentation of showbread	• Fat, kidneys, and lobe of liver from reparation, sin, and peace offerings	• Prostration by congregation		• Eating by priests and laity of holy meat from peace offerings

Leviticus 1–3

The Voluntary God-Pleasing Offerings

Leviticus 1–3 brings together the regulations for the three most common classes of offerings in ancient Israel. All are linked together by their classification of each as קָרְבָּן, "an offering," "that which is brought near."[a] They are listed in the order that they were placed on the altar in the daily sacrificial ritual. Thus the meat from a burnt offering was always set out on the altar before the flour from the grain offering. And the fat from the peace offering was set out on the altar after the flour from the grain offering had been scattered on the burnt offering. The order of the listing, however, does not just indicate the temporal sequence of the rites, but it also shows that the burnt offering is the fundamental sacrifice. All the other sacrifices are placed on it and so are virtually incorporated into it.

(a) E.g., Lev 1:2, 3, 10, 14; 2:1, 4; 3:1, 6, 12

The material for these offerings is taken from the basic foodstuff produced by the ancient Israelites. It constituted their livelihood: the meat from their domesticated animals, the grain from their crops, the olive oil from their groves, and the syrup from their fruit trees. Generally speaking, the meat came from their firstborn male animals (cf. Deut 12:6, 17; 14:23; 15:19), while the grain, olive oil, and syrup came from the tithe of their agricultural produce (Lev 27:30; cf. Deut 12:6, 11, 17–18; 14:23). These had to be handed over entirely to the priests or eaten as part of the sacrificial banquets at the sanctuary. While the Israelites were obligated to bring these to the Lord, they could also bring other animals voluntarily as burnt and peace offerings and additional agricultural products as grain offerings.

The regulations for these offerings are formulated as a series of ritual case laws. For each of these offerings the general case is introduced first by כִּי, "When …" (1:2; 2:1, 4). This is followed by more specific instances within this general category introduced by אִם, "If …"[b] On the one hand, the three kinds of burnt offering in 1:3–17 and the three kinds of peace offering in 3:1–16 are all summarized in 1:2. On the other hand, the two cooked grain offerings in 2:5–10 and the roasted grain offering in 2:14–16 are considered as subclasses of the baked grain offering in 2:4.

(b) Lev 1:3, 10, 14; 2:5, 7, 14; 3:1, 6, 7, 12

Throughout these regulations, the conditional conjunctions ("when" and "if") and the subsequent verbs as well as the apodoses ("… then …") are linked together by the coordinating conjunction *waw*. Syntactically, we have a single sentence over these three chapters. This is interrupted only by the parenthetical appositional clauses in 2:11–13 and 3:16b–17. The three kinds of offering are therefore joined together in such a way that the animal offerings bracket and enclose the grain offerings. The grain offerings gain their ritual function from their combination with the animal offerings.

The combination of these offerings points to a deeper ritual and theological connection between them. From a ritual point of view, the rite for their presentation culminates in their transformation into smoke on the altar. The verb used to describe this last stage in the ritual enactment is הִקְטִיר, which means to "send up in smoke."[c] It is an important technical ritual term in the priestly instructions. It is used for the burning up of the meat from the victim or its fat, or a grain offering with its frankincense on the coals of the altar. It also describes the process by which the fire on the altar for burnt offering turned the sacrificial portion into a column of smoke.

(c) Lev 1:9, 13, 15, 17; 2:2, 9, 16; 3:5, 11, 16; 4:10, 19, 26, 31, 35; 5:12; 6:5, 8, 15 (ET 6:12, 15, 22); 7:5, 31; 8:16, 20, 21, 28; 9:10, 13, 14, 17, 20; 16:25; 17:6

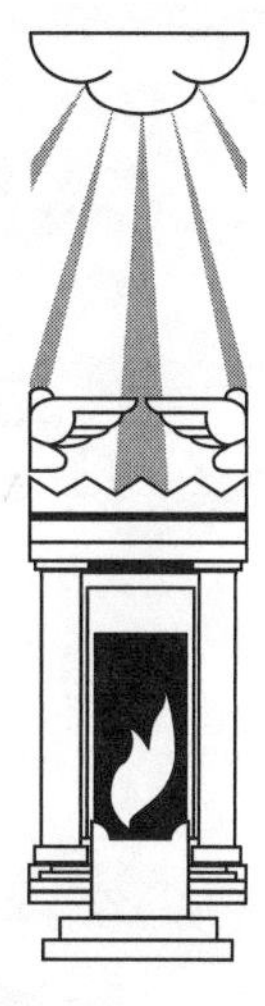

The offering thereby left the earthly human domain and made its transition into the heavenly realm. It ascended to God in heaven as a fragrant aroma, pleasing to him. It was therefore a mark of theophany, for God's glory was manifest in the fire on the altar (9:4, 6, 24), even as God had appeared in the form of a pillar of cloud by day and of fire by night to lead the Israelites during the exodus (e.g., Ex 13:21–22). When those who had brought the offering saw its ascent into the sky and smelled its sweet aroma, they were assured that it had been received by the Lord and accepted by him. Thus from a human point of view the offering was presented on the altar in order to transform it into a cloud of fragrant smoke.

The first three chapters of Leviticus go on to explain the theological purpose of the transformation of the offerings into a cloud of smoke. In each case (except for 2:16 and 3:11), the offering is turned into smoke as "a gift of a pleasing aroma to the Lord" (1:9, 13, 17; 2:2, 9; 3:5, 16). The repetition of this phrase for the divine approval of a gift highlights its importance. It shows us why the Lord instituted these offerings, and what they are meant to accomplish by their enactment. This phrase then gives us the key to understand and interpret them theologically.

That repeated affirmation of God's pleasure at the transformation of these offerings into smoke for him on the altar ("a gift of a pleasing aroma to the Lord") combines two distinct formulae, "a gift to the Lord" and "a pleasing aroma to the Lord."

The first formula is אִשֶּׁה לַיהוה, that is, "a gift for the Lord." See the textual note on אִשֶּׁה in 1:9. This formula for the assignment of a gift to the Lord is used in one of two ways. First, it occurs in the form אִשֶּׁה הוּא לַיהוה, "It is a gift for the Lord" (Ex 29:25; Lev 8:21, 28; cf. Ex 29:18). This functions as a ritual declaratory formula for designating, classifying, and so confirming an offering as a gift to the Lord. The divine designation of an offering as a gift to the Lord, as in Ex 29:18, 25, creates the precedent for the declaration by the priests that a particular offering is received as a gift to the Lord, as in the case of Lev 8:21, 28. Second, in ritual legislation the phrase אִשֶּׁה לַיהוה, "a gift for the Lord," is used together with a verb for the presentation of an offering on the altar. It stands in apposition with whatever is presented as an offering: the token portion of grain (2:16) as well as the fat from the peace offerings (3:3, 9, 11, 14; cf. 7:25). In these contexts it is an interpretive formula that defines the purpose of the performance theologically as the presentation of a gift to the Lord.

(d) E.g., Lev 6:8, 14 (ET 6:15, 21); 17:6; Num 15:3, 7, 24; 28:27; 29:2, 8

The second formula that expresses God's pleasure for a gift consists of the phrase רֵיחַ־נִיחֹחַ לַיהוה, "a pleasing aroma to the Lord."[d] It announces God's acceptance of the offering and his approval of the person who presented it to him. The combination of the formula for the ritual designation of the offering as "a gift to the Lord" with the formula for the divine approval of the "pleasing aroma" of an offering shifts the accent away from the aroma itself to the nature of the offering as a gift to the Lord. It indicates that the term "aroma" is to be understood metaphorically and symbolically, even though it still refers quite literally to the fragrance produced by the burning of the offerings. The emphasis is on the Lord's pleasure at the gift of the offering to him.

What then is the function of the combination of the two formulae? While the formula for the designation of the offering as "a gift to the Lord" describes the human side of the divine-human ritual transaction, the function of the formula for the divine approval of the "pleasing aroma" of it is not so obvious. Most commentators assume that the second formula describes what people seek to accomplish by the presentation of these offerings. If that were so, then the people would present certain offerings to the Lord in the hope that he would be pleased with them or in the certainty that they thereby would secure a favorable reception from the Lord and a positive reaction from him. The second formula is therefore taken to describe what humans seek from the Lord rather than what the Lord promises to give them in the ritual transaction. Commentators usually assume that it refers either to the intended purpose or to the assured effect of the offering—from a human point of view.

Both of those common interpretations overlook one important fact: the Lord himself is the speaker in the passages where this formula is found. (The only exception is in Lev 8:21, 28, but those verses, as 8:21 reminds us, merely repeat what the Lord has commanded in Ex 29:18, 25.) This formula gains its great significance from its use by the Lord himself to explain how he will respond and react in a particular set of ritual transactions. Human beings do not determine which gifts are acceptable to the Lord, nor can they decide by themselves if he is indeed pleased with them. The Lord himself does that for them. By his Word he establishes the rite that is to be enacted and the purpose of its enactment. *His Word not only prescribes which offering is to be presented, and how, but it also announces what he himself promises to accomplish through it.*

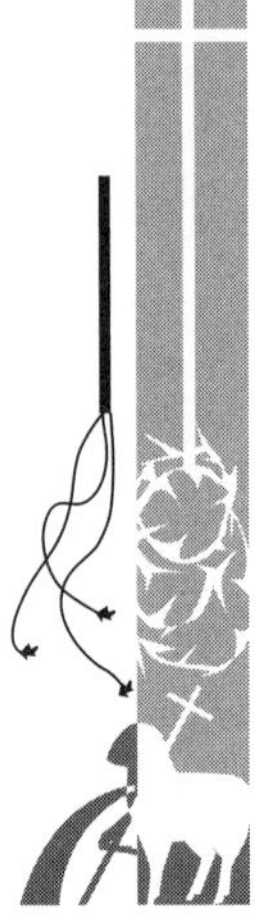

Because the Lord himself ordained that these offerings are the "gift" that produces an "aroma" that is pleasing to him, the people who presented them were assured that whenever these offerings were presented as he had ordained, *the Lord did accept them and was in fact pleased with those who brought them.* Consequently, each statement that the offering was a gift and an aroma pleasing to the Lord explains the sacrificial enactment theologically—*from God's point of view.* It explains what the Lord promised to do for those who brought these offerings to him, and it does so in general terms which are meant to cover all cases.

The Lord assured the Israelites that he would take pleasure both in them and in their offerings. He would deal favorably with them according to their particular needs, as expressed in their petitions to him. He therefore established these offerings as ritual means for seeking help from him, just as Solomon envisaged in his later prayer for the dedication of the temple (1 Ki 8:27–53). God sanctioned the presentation of the people's prayers together with these offerings and assured them that they would receive favorable hearing from him whenever they brought these offerings to him as he had prescribed.

Thus in Lev 1:9, 13, 17; 2:2, 9; 3:5, 16, we have the phrase "a gift of a pleasing aroma to the Lord," which combines the formula for the designation of an offering as "a gift to the Lord" with the formula for the divine pleasure at the "pleasing aroma" of its presentation. The phrase was used to classify an offering as an acceptable, pleasing gift to the Lord[e] and to assure his people that he would give them a favorable reception whenever they presented their offerings to him as he had prescribed.[f]

(e) Ex 29:18; Lev 1:13, 17; 8:21, 28; Num 28:6, 13; 29:6

(f) Ex 29:25, 41; Lev 1:9; 2:2, 9; 3:5, 16; 4:31; 23:13, 18; Num 15:3, 10, 14; 18:17; 28:8, 24; 29:13, 36

In sum, the first three chapters of Leviticus give us the ritual legislation for the three classes of God-pleasing offerings that the Israelites were authorized to present to the Lord. They prescribe how the Israelites as individuals or as representatives of their families were to approach the Lord. They also assured them that if they brought these offerings and presented them as he had commanded, he would be pleased with them and deal graciously with them.

Leviticus 1:1–2

Divine Legislation for the Private Offerings

Translation

1 [1]Then the Lord summoned Moses and spoke to him from the tent of meeting: [2]"Speak to the Israelites and say to them: When any of you presents an offering to the Lord, when it is of livestock, you shall present your offering from the herd or from the flock."

Textual Notes

1:1 In the Qal, קָרָא can mean "to call, summon" (*HALOT,* 5). God summons Moses to the tent of meeting, where God will regularly speak to him throughout Leviticus. See further the commentary below.

1:2 אָדָם כִּי־יַקְרִיב—This general case is introduced by a rarely used inclusive formula אָדָם כִּי, "Whenever any human being." The use of אָדָם indicates that the offering could be brought by any Israelite, male or female.[1] It includes the resident aliens and all foreigners, for they could also bring both burnt offerings and sacrifices of peace offerings to the Lord (Lev 22:18, 25; Num 15:13–16).

יַקְרִיב ... תַּקְרִיבוּ—The verb הִקְרִיב is a technical ritual term. It means to "bring near/bring forward" and so to "present" an "offering" (קָרְבָּן) to the Lord. It is a technical ritual term that indicates the location of people and objects before the altar for burnt offering as the first act in the performance of a ritual transaction.[2] The basic idea is that since the Lord is in the "midst" (קֶרֶב) of his people (Num 11:20; 14:14), they may "draw near" (קָרַב) before him (Ex 16:9; Lev 9:5; Num 17:5 [ET 16:40]) and be "near" (קָרוֹב, Lev 10:3) to him. He, in fact, authorizes certain people to "approach" (קָרַב) him (Lev 9:7, 8; 21:17, 18; 22:3) and determines their degree of access to himself (Num 16:5, 9, 10). Since the Lord dwells with his people at the sanctuary (Ex 25:8; 29:45–46), they may "bring near" or "present" (הִקְרִיב) their offerings to him there by presenting them at the entrance of the sanctuary (Lev 1:3) or to the priest officiating there (Lev 2:8). By "presenting" these offerings "before" the tent of meeting (Ex 29:10; cf. Lev 17:4), they bring them forward "before the Lord" (Lev 3:1, 7, 12; 12:7; Num 6:16; 16:17). The priests were the ones who would "present" the offerings to the Lord at the altar (Lev 1:15; 2:8; 6:7 [ET 6:14]; Num 5:25).

---

1 See also Lev 5:3, 4, 22 (ET 6:3); 7:21; 13:2, 9; 16:17; 18:5; 22:5; 24:17, 20, 21; Milgrom, *Leviticus 1–16,* 144–45.

2 Klingbeil, *A Comparative Study of the Ritual of Ordination As Found in Leviticus 8 and Emar 369,* 220–22.

The common thread that runs through this ritual terminology is God's assurance through these words that he is in fact dwelling among his people at the sanctuary. While God indeed is present everywhere, he promises favorable access to him and his benefits only at the sanctuary. There he makes himself accessible to his people by authorizing certain offerings as the proper means of access to his grace.

תַּקְרִיבוּ—Here the main case for the general rule about the choice of the animal for the offering is not couched impersonally (as is normal in ritual legislation), but is addressed personally to the Israelites in the second person plural (see also 2:11–15; 3:15). The reason may be that although the offerings are voluntary, it is mandatory that animals for sacrifice must be taken from the flock or herd of those who present them. God conveys that mandatory force by addressing the Israelites directly, "you."

Commentary

Context

These two verses serve as a heading for three bodies of material: the burnt offerings in 1:3–17, the God-pleasing offerings in 1:3–3:17, and the manual for offerings in chapters 1–7. Lev 1:1–2 also introduces an act of divine lawgiving that interrupts the flow of narrative from Exodus in two ways. First, it intrudes on the narrative sequence of Exodus 35–40 and Leviticus 8–9 that reports how Moses and the Israelites fulfilled the divine commandments about the establishment of the tabernacle and its service in Exodus 25–31. Second, it breaks into the flow of the narrative from Ex 40:16–38 to Leviticus 8–9. This reports how Moses carried out the commandment of the Lord first to set up the tabernacle with its furnishings (Ex 40:17–33) and then to anoint both its furnishings and its priests (Ex 40:9–15; Lev 8:6–13).

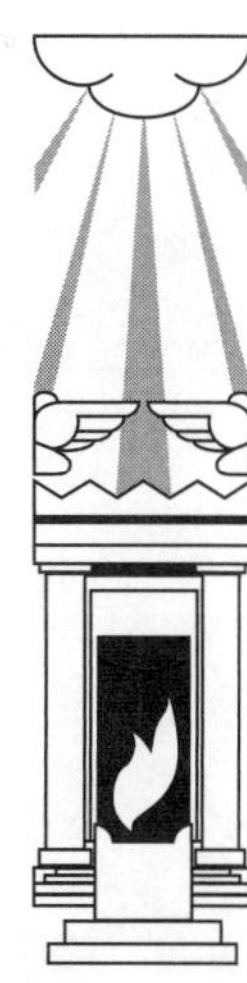

The narrative context for this piece of divine legislation determines its significance. Moses had just set up the tent of meeting with its furnishings as the Lord had commanded (Ex 40:17–33). After its erection, the glory cloud had left the top of Mount Sinai and had settled over the tabernacle. This indicated that the Lord had taken up residence there. His appearance in the tabernacle, after its construction, showed that the sacrificial ritual did not summon and evoke God's presence in a particular place. Rather, it presupposed that God was present there and gave favorable access to himself there. But, as yet, neither the tabernacle furnishings nor the priests had been anointed, and the sacrificial ritual had not yet been inaugurated. The context of this legislation then shows that the Lord had established the tent of meeting and resided there so that the Israelites could bring their offerings to him there in the divine service. They performed the divine service so that the Lord would appear to them and bless them there according to his promise (Lev 9:4, 6, 22–24).

Structure

The structure of this pericope can be outlined as follows:

I. The Lord's call to Moses from the tent of meeting (1:1)

II. The Lord's speech to Moses (1:2)
   A. The commission of Moses as ritual legislator
   B. The general regulation for the annual offerings

Content

The book of Leviticus begins with a *waw* consecutive imperfect verb followed by a preposition, וַיִּקְרָא אֶל־, "And he [the Lord] summoned" Moses. This links it closely with the end of Exodus. The choice of this particular verb, however, makes it clear that we do not have the report of just another speech in a series of divine speeches all introduced by the formula "Then the Lord said to Moses."[a] Instead, this formula serves notice that the Lord is about to commission Moses to institute a new aspect of the divine service.

(a) As in Ex 25:1; 30:11, 17, 22, 34; 31:1, 12; 32:7; 33:1; 40:1

This formula for the divine institution of Israel's ritual, "And he [the Lord] summoned Moses/him," is found only in three other places, all of which are liturgically significant. First, it appears in Ex 3:4, where the Lord summons Moses in order to reveal his holy name through Moses to his people. Second, it appears in Ex 19:3, where the Lord summons Moses to announce his intention to make the Israelites his holy, priestly people, and commissions Moses to act as the mediator of his covenant with them. Third, it appears in Ex 24:16, where the Lord institutes the tabernacle along with its priesthood and sacrificial ritual, and commissions Moses to construct it. In each of these three cases, the Lord appears to Moses on Mount Sinai, "the mountain of God" (Ex 3:1), and commissions him to serve as Israel's ceremonial lawgiver and founder of the divine service.

This pattern continues in Lev 1:1–2. According to Ex 40:35 Moses was unable to enter the tent of meeting because it had been filled with the Lord's glory. But the Lord summoned Moses into the tent. There the Lord promulgated the laws for the presentation of offerings by the Israelites and commissioned Moses to hand on these laws to them. What is new is the *location* for this law-giving. The glory of the Lord was no longer located on the mountain, but now filled the tabernacle. Since the Lord had summoned Moses and had given him access to his presence in the tabernacle, Moses no longer needed to ascend Mount Sinai. Instead, he could enter the tent of meeting and have audience with the Lord there. Moses still remains the divinely commissioned lawgiver and founder of the liturgy, but from now on the tabernacle replaces Mount Sinai as the place for divine revelation. The Lord appears to Moses in the tabernacle from this time onwards (Num 1:1; 7:89) as he had promised to do (Ex 25:22). Moses receives each new piece of ritual legislation from God in this new location.

The first verse of Leviticus combines the formula for the divine commission of Moses as the founder of the divine rituals ("And he [the Lord] summoned Moses") with the usual formula for the transmission of the Lord's Word to his people ("and the Lord spoke to him") in keeping with the people's request in Ex 20:19. The combination of these highlights the role of Moses as

lawgiver and the authority of these regulations. They are the Word of the Lord. The Lord authorized these offerings. He determined which offerings are to be presented, how, and by whom. His Word established how he was at work in and through them. Their status, efficacy, and sanctity depended on him and his Word.

The reference to "the tent of meeting" (Lev 1:1) is not just significant because it is the place where the Lord speaks to Moses and gives him the laws for the offerings of the Israelites. It is also the sacred place where these offerings must be presented if they are to be acceptable to the Lord. The laws for the offerings are therefore given at the location for their enactment.

Since the tent of meeting was the location for the presentation of the offerings, it is important that we have a clear picture of its layout and setting. See figure 6.

The holy tent was a small building divided into two rooms: the inner room, which formed a perfect cube, and the outer room, which was twice as large. Even though the phrase "the tent of meeting" could at times be used to describe the whole building, it is normally the name for the outer room. The inner room was out of bounds for anybody except the high priest on the Day of Atonement. The inner room housed the ark, which, together with the mercy seat, formed the throne of the Lord. A curtain separated the inner room from the outer room.[3] The priests had access to the outer room during the performance of the sacrificial ritual each morning and evening. It housed the altar for incense, the table for the bread, and the lampstand.

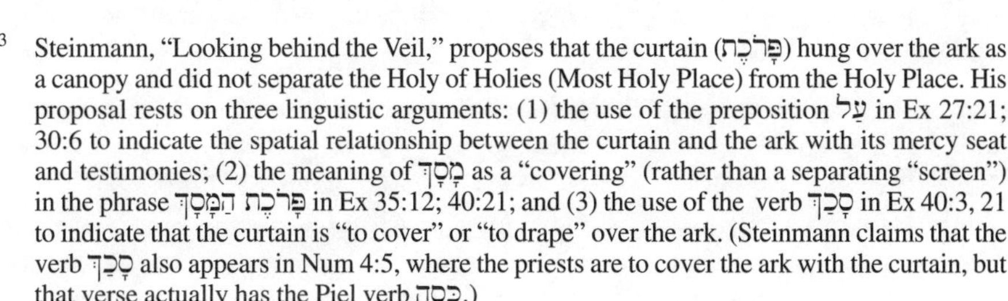

3 Steinmann, "Looking behind the Veil," proposes that the curtain (פָּרֹכֶת) hung over the ark as a canopy and did not separate the Holy of Holies (Most Holy Place) from the Holy Place. His proposal rests on three linguistic arguments: (1) the use of the preposition עַל in Ex 27:21; 30:6 to indicate the spatial relationship between the curtain and the ark with its mercy seat and testimonies; (2) the meaning of מָסָךְ as a "covering" (rather than a separating "screen") in the phrase פָּרֹכֶת הַמָּסָךְ in Ex 35:12; 40:21; and (3) the use of the verb סָכַךְ in Ex 40:3, 21 to indicate that the curtain is "to cover" or "to drape" over the ark. (Steinmann claims that the verb סָכַךְ also appears in Num 4:5, where the priests are to cover the ark with the curtain, but that verse actually has the Piel verb כִּסָּה.)

This commentary follows the traditional understanding for six reasons: (1) Ex 26:33 states that the "curtain" (פָּרֹכֶת) is to be hung so as to separate the Holy Place from the Most Holy Place. (2) In Lev 4:6, 17 the priest is to sprinkle the blood from the sin offering "against/on the surface of the curtain," which would be impossible if it were a canopy. (3) The Most Holy Place is "inside the curtain" according to Lev 16:2. (4) The altar for incense is located "in front of the curtain" according to Ex 40:26. (5) The ark and its mercy seat are "inside with respect to the curtain" (Ex 26:33; Lev 16:2, 12, 15), while the table, menorah, tent of meeting, and incense altar are situated "outside with respect to the curtain" (Ex 26:35; 27:21; 40:22; Lev 24:3). (6) While מָסָךְ can denote a covering over something, in Exodus and Numbers it is used most often for a curtain. Thus besides the phrase פָּרֹכֶת הַמָּסָךְ, the noun מָסָךְ denotes a curtain at the entrance of the tent of meeting (Ex 26:36, 37; 35:15; 36:37; 39:38; 40:28) and refers to a curtain at the entrance of the courtyard (Ex 27:16; 35:17; 38:18; 39:40; 40:8, 33; Num 3:26; 4:26).

The weight of this evidence leads to the conclusion that עַל is used in Ex 27:21; 30:6 to indicate that the curtain is "near" the ark (as a synonym of אֶל־) or else to mean that it is "opposite" (that is, "in front of") the ark and that סָכַךְ עַל in Ex 40:3, 21 means that the curtain is to "shut in, screen, shield" the ark (cf. Ps 5:12 [ET 5:11]).

Figure 6

Ground Plan of the Tabernacle

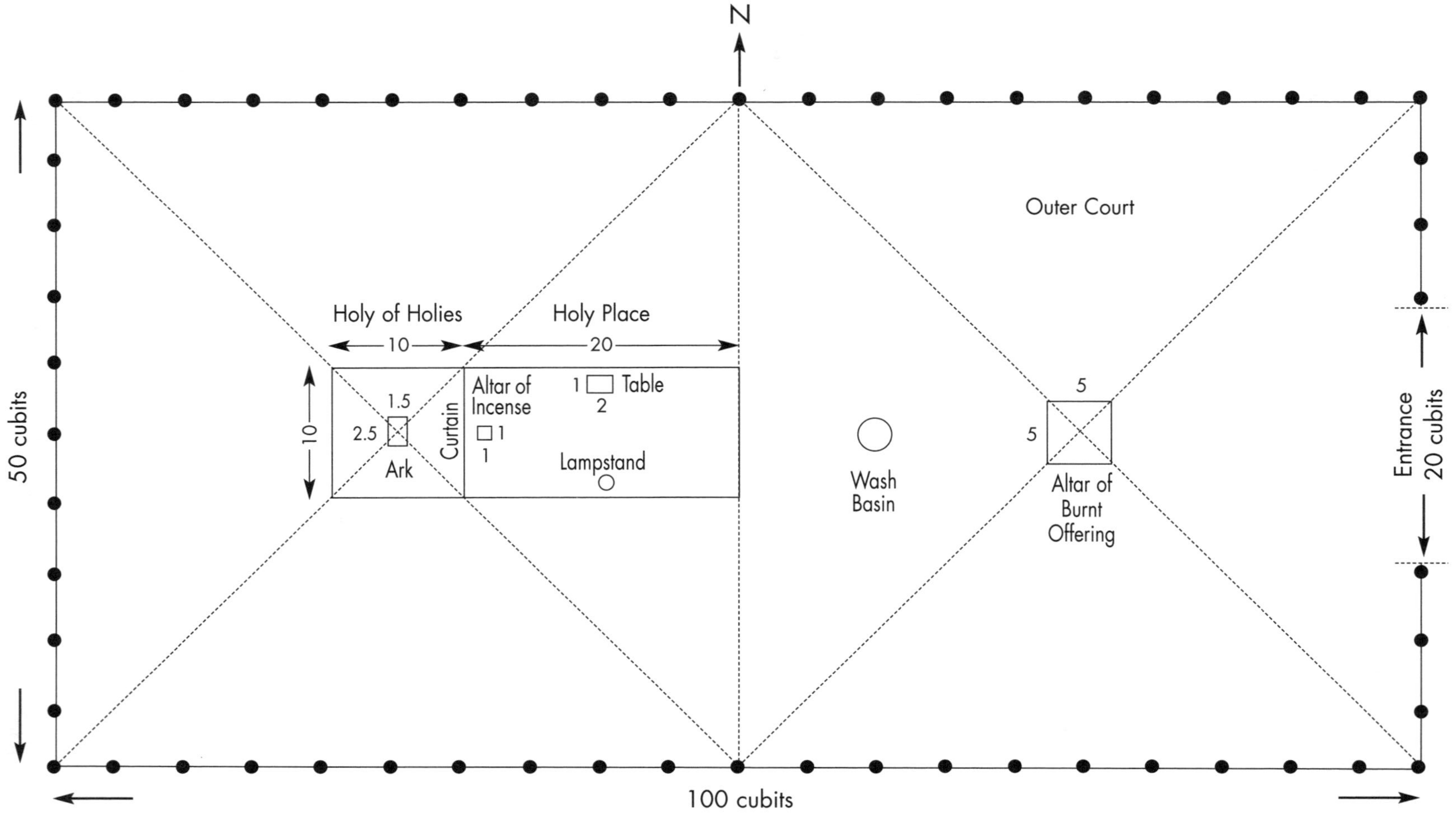

N

Holy of Holies

10

Holy Place

20

1.5

2.5

10

Ark

Curtain

Altar of
Incense

1

1

1

Table

2

Lampstand

Outer Court

Wash
Basin

5

5

Altar of
Burnt
Offering

Entrance
20 cubits

50 cubits

100 cubits

The building was set in a courtyard that was enclosed by curtains, set on metal stands, with an entrance at its eastern end. The courtyard itself formed two squares. The altar for the burnt offering, which was out of bounds to anyone except the priest on duty, most likely stood at the center of the eastern square, while the ark was most likely situated in the center of the western square. The water basin for ablutions was located somewhere between the altar for the burnt offering and the holy tent.

The spatial arrangement of the sanctuary is ritually significant. Its architecture created two focal points: (1) the incense altar in front of the curtain that hid the ark and (2) the altar for burnt offering in front of the tent. These were the two main sites for the performance of the daily sacrificial ritual, with the burning of incense on the inner altar and the burning of a lamb on the outer altar. The Lord met with Moses privately within the tent (Ex 25:22; 30:6, 36; Num 17:19 [ET 17:4]) and spoke with him from above the ark (Ex 25:22; Num 7:89). But he did not meet with his people inside the tent of meeting. He met with them at the altar for burnt offering during the performance of the burnt offering twice each day (Ex 29:38–42). The architecture of the precincts represents this symbolically by the arrangement of its east-west axis. The people entered the courtyard to approach the Lord at the altar for burnt offering, where he came from his "private residence" to meet with them.

Both the tent and its outer court are called "the tent of meeting" in Leviticus. This name is apt if it is taken to refer to the meeting of the Lord with Moses. But it would be misleading if taken to refer just to the tent proper, in which only Moses or the priest on duty met secretly with the Lord. Even though the priest met with the Lord in the rite for the burning of incense, which was hidden from public sight, the purpose of the daily sacrificial ritual was for the Lord to meet with his assembled people. That occurred publicly as part of a public enactment open to participation by all the assembly in the outer court. It took place in the daily performance of the public burnt offering each morning and evening.

The Lord commanded Moses to hand on the divine regulations to the Israelites, for they are meant primarily for them and are given for their benefit. The instruction "speak to the Israelites" (1:2; literally, "... to the sons of Israel") is repeated frequently in the book of Leviticus.[b] The entire sacrificial apparatus therefore belonged to all the Israelites, and not just the priests who were merely in charge of its administration. This differs radically from the tradition of their pagan neighbors, where the knowledge of sacred ritual and ritual texts was restricted to the priests. For Israel, the law of Moses was "the heritage of the congregation" (Deut 33:4). The book of Leviticus is therefore not a manual of "esoteric doctrine, the zealously guarded secret of the priestly guild, but an open book or, more accurately, a school textbook for all Israel."[4] Its con-

(b) Lev 4:2; 7:23, 29; 11:2; 12:2; 15:2; 17:2; 18:2; 19:2; 20:2; 22:18; 23:2, 24, 34; 24:2; 25:2; 27:2; cf. 7:38; 21:24; 23:44; 24:23; 26:46; 27:34

4 Milgrom, *Leviticus 1–16,* 144.

tents were in public domain; they had to do with the public worship of the whole nation and its citizens.

Whenever the Israelites brought an animal either as a burnt offering or as a peace offering, they were to select an animal either from their herd of cattle or from their flock of sheep and goats (1:2). No reason is given for this restriction, but these were animals that lived together with them on their land and belonged to them. They were part of the Israelite household and so were, in some way, representative of it. Unlike mules and donkeys, they were edible. Normally, the animals the people would bring (1:2) were taken from their firstborn (27:26) and tithed livestock (27:32), since those animals were reserved for ritual use. The families that did not possess any livestock were exempt from these requirements (since they would have no firstborn animals or tenth part, nor could they fulfill 1:2).

Fulfillment by Christ

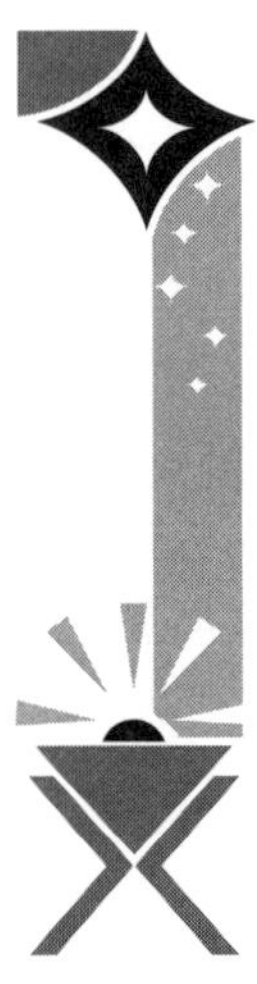

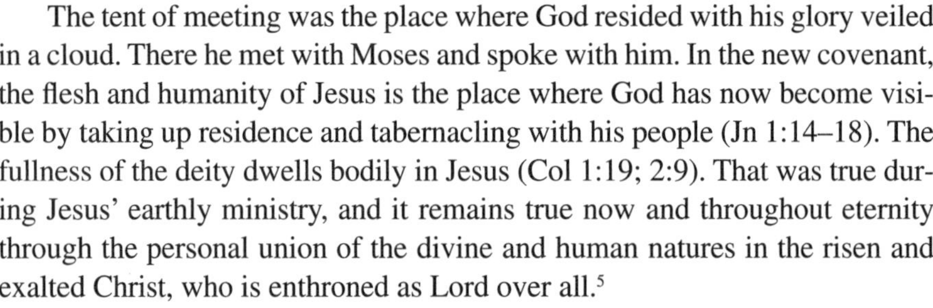

The tent of meeting was the place where God resided with his glory veiled in a cloud. There he met with Moses and spoke with him. In the new covenant, the flesh and humanity of Jesus is the place where God has now become visible by taking up residence and tabernacling with his people (Jn 1:14–18). The fullness of the deity dwells bodily in Jesus (Col 1:19; 2:9). That was true during Jesus' earthly ministry, and it remains true now and throughout eternity through the personal union of the divine and human natures in the risen and exalted Christ, who is enthroned as Lord over all.[5]

Just as the glory of God was veiled in a cloud at the Holy of Holies, so the glory of the triune God is veiled in the humanity of Jesus. The Israelites were to listen to Moses (Lev 1:1–2). When God the Father disclosed the glory of Jesus to Peter, James, and John at Jesus' transfiguration, he declared that they should listen to Jesus, for he was the incarnate Word, the place where God the Father spoke to his people—through his Son (Mk 9:2–7).

Wherever two or three are gathered in Christ's name, there the risen Lord Jesus is present with his glorified humanity (Mt 18:20; cf. Lk 24:36; Jn 20:19, 26). His humanity is our tent of meeting (Jn 1:14), the temple of the living God (Jn 2:21). The man Christ Jesus is the place where the triune God meets with us so that we too can meet with him. Through him God speaks to us. The mystery of his hidden presence with us, his saints, is made known to us through his Word (Col 1:25–27).

The preaching of the Gospel reveals Christ's divine glory so that we come to discover "the glory of God in the face of Christ" (2 Cor 4:3–6). He is our place of worship. The Divine Service is enacted in him. He is the place where we adore the Father in spirit and in truth (Jn 4:19–24). Through him we have access to God the Father (Eph 2:18; 3:12) and his grace (Rom 5:2), which is

---

[5] See, for example, Lk 24:36–43; Acts 1:9–11; Phil 2:5–11. See also FC SD VIII, "The Person of Christ."

his fullness (Jn 1:14–17). Through him we bring our offerings to God the Father (Heb 13:15; 1 Pet 2:4). His flesh is our new and living way into the Father's presence (Heb 10:20). He brings us near to the Father and presents us to him (Eph 2:13; 1 Pet 3:18).

Gracious God, I come before thee;
  Come thou also unto me;
Where we find thee and adore thee,
  There a heav'n on earth must be.
To my heart, oh, enter thou,
Let it be thy temple now!

Speak, O God, and I will hear thee,
  Let thy will be done indeed;
May I undisturbed draw near thee
  While thou dost thy people feed.
Here of life the fountain flows;
Here is balm for all our woes.[6]

---

6 From "Open Now Thy Gates of Beauty" by Benjamin Schmolck (*LW* 198:2, 5).

Leviticus 1:3–17

Regulations for the Burnt Offering

Translation

**1 3“If his offering is a burnt offering from the herd, he shall present a male
without blemish. He shall present it at the entrance to the tent of meeting for his
acceptance before the Lord. 4He shall lay his hand on the head of the burnt offering so that it may be accepted for him to perform atonement on his behalf.
5He shall slaughter the domesticated bull before the Lord. Then Aaron’s sons,
the priests, shall present the blood and dash the blood against all the sides of the
altar at the entrance to the tent of meeting. 6He shall flay the burnt offering and
cut it up into its sections. 7The sons of Aaron, the priest, shall stoke the fire on
the altar and lay out wood on the fire. 8Then Aaron’s sons, the priests, shall lay
out the sections, together with the head and the fat, on the wood that is on the
fire upon the altar, 9as he shall wash its entrails and its lower legs with water. The
priest shall turn the whole of it into smoke on the altar as a burnt offering, a gift
of a pleasing aroma to the Lord.**

**10“If his offering for a burnt offering is from the flock, from the sheep or from
the goats, he shall present a male without blemish. 11He shall slaughter it on the
north side of the altar before the Lord, and Aaron’s sons, the priests, shall dash
its blood against all the sides of the altar. 12When he has cut it up in its sections,
together with its head and its fat, the priest shall lay them out on the wood that
is on the fire upon the altar, 13as the entrails and the lower legs are washed with
water. The priest shall present the whole of it and turn it into smoke on the altar. It is a burnt offering, a gift of a pleasing aroma to the Lord.**

**14“If his offering to the Lord is a burnt offering from the birds, he shall pre-
sent a turtledove or some kind of pigeon as his offering. 15The priest shall bring
it to the altar, wring off its head, and turn it into smoke on the altar; and its blood
shall be drained out on the side of the altar. 16He shall remove its intestines by its
tail feathers and throw them at the east side of the altar into the place for the
ashes. 17He shall tear it open by its wings, without severing it. Then the priest
shall turn it into smoke on the altar, upon the wood that is on the fire. It is a burnt
offering, a gift of a pleasing aroma to the Lord.”**

Textual Notes

1:3 זָכָר תָּמִים—The sacrificed animal is to be “a male [זָכָר] without blemish [תָּמִים],” one that is “complete,” “intact,” or “perfect.” The animal is to be a perfect specimen of its species. The defects that disqualify an animal from use in the sacrificial ritual are listed in 22:22–25. This phrase (זָכָר תָּמִים) recurs in 1:10 and 4:23, and תָּמִים is frequent in Leviticus (1:10; 3:1, 6, 9; 4:3, 23, 28, 32; 5:15, 18, 25 [ET 6:6]; 9:2, 3; 14:10; 22:19, 21; 23:12, 18).

יַקְרִיבֶ֫נּוּ—The Hiphil of קָרַב is the usual technical term for bringing an offering before the Lord. In this pericope, it occurs again in 1:5, 10, 13, 14, 15. See the textual note on it in 1:2.

אֶל־פֶּ֫תַח אֹ֫הֶל מוֹעֵד—This phrase recurs in 1:5; 3:2; 4:4, 7, 18; 8:3, 4, 31, 33, 35; 10:7; 12:6; 14:11, 23; 15:14, 29; 16:7; 17:4, 5, 6, 9; 19:21. The "entrance" (פֶּתַח) to "the tent of meeting" (אֹהֶל מוֹעֵד) was a technical term for the eastern courtyard of the tabernacle in front of the altar for burnt offering. It extended from the altar to the entrance to the courtyard. This zone was the place of assembly for Israelites, the place where they came to interact with the Lord (8:3–4; 9:5). In this intermediate zone the Israelites approached God and presented their offerings to him. In Herod's temple it corresponded to the outer court that was separated from the inner court by the Nicanor Gate.

לִרְצֹנוֹ—See 19:5; 22:19, 20, 21, 29; 23:11. The noun רָצוֹן is an important term for God's grace in the OT. Often it means "favor," but "acceptance" is the most appropriate meaning here. The corresponding verb רָצָה usually means to "accept" or to "regard with favor." The noun and the verb are always used to indicate divine acceptance in liturgical contexts. The third masculine singular pronominal suffix ("his") on רְצֹנוֹ can refer either to the offering or to the person bringing the offering. The RSV and NRSV construe it as a reference to the offerer. The NIV takes it to refer to the offering, but acknowledges the other possibility in a footnote. The connection of the suffix with the offering can be supported by the parallel reference in 1:4 to the acceptance of the offering. But the use of the second masculine plural pronominal suffix on רָצוֹן in 19:5; 22:19, 29; 23:11 for the acceptance of the offerer and the lack of any suffix in 22:21 for the acceptance of the offering support the view that it refers to the person who brings the offering. So too does the formulation לִרְצוֹן ... לָכֶם in 22:20.

1:4 וְסָמַךְ יָדוֹ עַל רֹאשׁ הָעֹלָה—See also 3:2, 8, 13; 4:4, 15, 24, 29, 33; 8:14, 18, 22; 16:21; 24:14. The placement of a hand and the pressing of it on the head of the animal is the key act in the rite of presentation. Its significance is a matter of some dispute.

A first view is that by analogy with 16:21, the offerer transfers his sin and guilt to the animal. But that does not fit in this case, where the offerer places only one hand ("a hand," 1:4) on the animal. When something is transferred or conferred by the laying of hands, whether it be sins (16:21) or the pollution from hearing God cursed (24:14) or authority (Num 27:23) or the spirit of wisdom (Deut 34:9), both hands are used and some words are spoken to indicate what is imparted.

A second view is that when the offerer lays his hand on the head of the animal, he identifies himself with the animal as a vicarious substitute for him by its death. That, however, is rather unlikely, as the death of the animal by itself has no special ritual significance.

A third view is most likely correct. Based on Lev 1:3–4, which is the only passage that interprets this act, the head of the family, or his representative, laid his hand on the head of the animal to vouch that it belonged to him. It could therefore be used vicariously on his behalf to secure God's approval and acceptance.

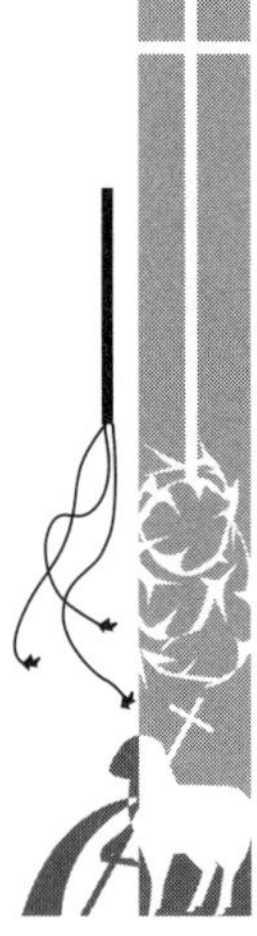

וְנִרְצָה לוֹ—The Niphal of רָצָה is related to the noun רָצוֹן (לִרְצֹנוֹ) in 1:3 (see the textual note on it above). Literally the clause means "it [the sacrifice] may be accepted for him [for the offerer]." The Niphal is best taken as a divine passive: the unnamed agent is God; the sacrifice is deemed acceptable by God. See the use of this verb also in 7:18; 19:7; 22:23, 25, 27. It usually indicates that God accepted the offering through the priests who acted on his behalf. Yet in 7:18 it also refers to God's acceptance of the person who had brought the offering.

לְכַפֵּר עָלָיו׃—The Piel of כָּפַר (usually found in the third masculine singular perfect form, כִּפֶּר) means to "atone, make atonement" and is one of the most important terms in the sacrificial theology of Leviticus. The sense of כִּפֶּר has been the matter of some dispute, because it is used in so many different ways in the OT. Consideration of its etymology does not give us much help, as it was derived from a verbal root meaning "wipe off" or "cover," as well as a denominative verb from the noun כֹּפֶר, "ransom."

כִּפֶּר is used in several different ways in Leviticus. Schwartz[1] argues that when כִּפֶּר is used with עַל־נֶפֶשׁ ("for a life/soul"), it functions as a denominative for כֹּפֶר ("ransom") and so means "to serve as a ransom for a life" (17:11; cf. Ex 30:15, 16; Num 31:50). It can also mean "to wipe away" and therefore "to purge or purify something unclean" (Lev 16:20, 33) or "to cleanse from impurity and iniquity" (5:6; 14:29; 15:15; 16:16).

The most common usage in Leviticus (including 1:4) is that כִּפֶּר is used as a technical term meaning "to perform atonement." It refers to the rite by which a priest applied the blood of a sacrificed animal to the altar for burnt offering (6:23 [ET 6:30]; 7:7; 8:15, 34; 9:7; 10:17; 14:18, 21; 16:6, 11, 24, 32, 33; 23:28). This rite was enacted to obtain acceptance (1:4), forgiveness (4:20, 26, 31, 35; 5:10, 13, 16, 18; 5:26 [ET 6:7]; 19:22), and purification from God (12:7, 8; 14:19, 20, 31, 53; 16:30).

The prepositions used with כִּפֶּר disclose its ritual function and theological purpose. The priest makes atonement "on behalf of" (עַל) those who offered the sacrificial victim (1:4; 4:20, 26, 31, 35; 5:6, 10, 13, 16, 18, 26 [ET 6:7]; 8:34; 10:17; 12:7, 8; 14:18, 19, 20, 21, 29, 31; 15:15, 30; 16:30, 33; 19:22; 23:28) or "for" (בַּעַד) himself and them (9:7; 16:6, 11, 17, 24). These two prepositions are not completely synonymous, for עַל is used only for a person other than the priest.[2] The rite was performed "by means of" (בְּ) the sacrificial victim (5:16; 7:7; 19:22) and its blood (17:11). By the application of blood, the rite of atonement was performed "upon" (עַל) the altar for burnt offering (8:15), the incense altar (16:18), the Holy of Holies (16:16), or a house free from fungus (14:53). The rite of atonement was normally performed "before" the Lord (5:26 [ET 6:7]; 10:17; 14:18, 29, 31; 15:15, 30; 16:10; 19:22; 23:28) "on account of" (עַל) the sin of the Israelites (4:35; 5:13, 18; 19:22) in order to free them "from" (מִן) sin (4:26; 5:6, 10; 16:34) and its impurity (14:19; 15:15, 30; 16:16).

---

[1] Schwartz, "The Prohibitions concerning the 'Eating' of Blood in Leviticus 17," 48–61.

[2] See Milgrom, *Leviticus 1–16,* 578.

1:5 וְשָׁחַט—The verb שָׁחַט is used for the ritual slaughter of an animal by slitting the main artery in its neck to drain off the blood from it so that the blood could be applied to the altar in the rite of atonement.[3] The verb recurs in 1:11; 3:2, 8, 13; 4:4, 15, 24 (twice), 29, 33 (twice); 6:18 (ET 6:25; twice); 7:2 (twice); 8:15, 19, 23; 9:8, 12, 15, 18; 14:5, 6, 13 (twice), 19, 25, 50, 51; 16:11, 15; 17:3 (twice); 22:28.

אֶת־בֶּן הַבָּקָר—The phrase "son of the herd" (בֶּן הַבָּקָר) is not used to describe a young bull, but a domesticated male animal that came from the herd of the person bringing the sacrifice. Therefore בֵּן (in construct, בֶּן) designates the member of a species or a class in a species. The phrase recurs in 4:3, 14; 9:2; 16:3; 23:18.

וְהִקְרִיבוּ—Literally the Hiphil of קָרַב means "to bring near." See the textual note on it in 1:2.

וְזָרְקוּ—The Qal of זָרַק is a technical term for the ritual disposal of blood. The priests "dash" the blood by splashing it sideways from a bowl against the two sides of the altar at two of its corners. The verb recurs in 1:11; 3:2, 8, 13; 7:2, 14; 8:19, 24; 9:12, 18; 17:6. It is to be distinguished from הִזָּה, the Hiphil of נָזָה, which is the term for the ritual aspersion of blood (e.g., 4:6, 17).

הַמִּזְבֵּחַ—"The altar" here is the altar for burnt offering (not the incense altar). Just in the first chapter it recurs in 1:7, 8, 9, 11 (twice), 12, 13, 15 (thrice), 16, 17.[4] In practical terms the altar for burnt offering was the most important piece of furniture at the tabernacle. It was the hearth of God's house (6:2 [ET 6:9]). The altar was the place for God's theophany (9:23–24), where God met with his people each morning and evening in the divine service (Ex 29:38–43), the place for atonement (Lev 17:11) and the presentation of offerings to God (1:9; 2:2; 3:5; 4:10) and the reception of blessing from God (9:22).

The altar was most holy; it communicated God's holiness by way of contact with it (Ex 29:37). The altar did not enable the Israelites to reach up to God in heaven;[5] it was the means by which God reached down to them and interacted with them on earth (Ex 20:24). Since the altar stood "before the Lord," the people who approached it came "before the Lord" (Lev 6:7 [ET 6:14]). Its shape and construction are described in Ex 27:1–8 and 38:1–7. It was a portable box made of acacia wood and plated with bronze. It was five cubits (about seven and a half feet) wide and deep with a height of three cubits (about four and a half feet). A horn was set on each of its four corners, and it had a grill made of bronze on its surface. Its center was filled with earth and stones whenever it was set up at the entrance to the tent of meeting.

1:7 וְנָתְנוּ ... אֵשׁ—Literally, the priests "shall put ... fire." The use of this idiom elsewhere for the placement of coals on a censer (Lev 10:1; Num 16:7; 17:11) shows that this does not refer to the lighting of fire, which would contradict God's command to keep the altar fire burning constantly (Lev 6:5–6 [ET 6:12–13]). Rather, the clause

---

3 Hartley, *Leviticus,* 271; Levine, *Leviticus,* 112–13.

4 See Milgrom, *Leviticus 1–16,* 250–51.

5 Contra Milgrom, *Leviticus 1–16,* 251.

refers to raking up the coals to receive additional wood to increase the fire.[6] Therefore we translate it "stoke the fire."

עֵצִים עַל־הָאֵשׁ׃—The singular עֵץ usually refers to a "tree," but the plural עֵצִים usually refers to pieces of wood hewn for lumber or (as here) firewood. The phrase recurs in 1:8, 12, 17; 3:5.

1:8 הַפָּדֶר—The meaning of פֶּדֶר is uncertain. In the OT it occurs only in Lev 1:8, 12; 8:20, each time together with the same other components of the burnt offering. It is usually taken as a synonym for חֵלֶב, "fat." Since חֵלֶב is used only for the suet of an animal slaughtered for a peace offering and a sin offering, פֶּדֶר could be a technical term, as Rendtorff[7] argues, for the net of fat over the intestines of an animal that was to be offered together with the head of the animal. *HALOT* defines פֶּדֶר as "suet from the kidney."

1:9 וְקִרְבּוֹ וּכְרָעָיו יִרְחַץ בַּמָּיִם—The occurrence of this disjunctive clause in a perfect consecutive sequence here (and the similar clause in 1:13) indicates that the washing was done as the priests were laying out the other parts of the animal on the altar. The singular noun קֶרֶב denotes the "entrails" of the sacrificed animal (*HALOT,* 1 a). The noun כֶּרַע or כְּרָע denotes the "lower leg" (*HALOT*) of the animal (also in 1:13; 4:11; 8:21; 9:14; 11:21). The lower leg would be the part that would be most soiled as the animal walked about on the dusty (occasionally muddy) ground, and so that is the part that would be washed.

וְהִקְטִיר—See 1:13, 15, 17. The Hiphil verb הִקְטִיר is a technical ritual term for the final act in the sacrificial ritual (1:9, 13, 15, 17; 2:2, 9, 11, 16; 3:5, 11, 16; 4:10, 19, 26, 31, 35; 5:12; 6:5, 8, 15 [ET 6:12, 15, 22]; 7:5, 31; 8:16, 20, 21, 28; 9:10, 13, 14, 17, 20; 16:25; 17:6). It means "to make smoke" or "to turn (an offering) into smoke."[8] It is to be distinguished from שָׂרַף, which is the term for incineration apart from the altar (4:12, 21; 10:16; 16:27–28). The common translation of הִקְטִיר as to "burn" (e.g., RSV; NIV) is misleading because the verb does not so much describe the incineration of an offering as the production of sweet-smelling smoke from its incineration on the altar. None of the substances that were presented as an offering burnt readily; all produced a large quantity of smoke when they were placed on a fire. All of them also produced a pungent, distinctive smell as they were burnt. Even though the verb הִקְטִיר is closely related to the common Hebrew noun for incense, קְטֹרֶת, and the verb is occasionally used to describe the burning of incense (Ex 30:7, 8; 40:27; Num 16:40), its ritual sense seems to be derived from its connection with the Hebrew word for smoke, קִיטוֹר (Gen 19:28; Pss 119:83; 148:8), and from the smoke produced from the burning of the offerings.

עֹלָה—This noun in 1:13 and 1:17 is in the phrase עֹלָה הוּא, but here the noun stands alone. Therefore this is not a declarative statement about the divine purpose of the burnt offering. Instead, it means "as a burnt offering."

---

6 Milgrom, *Leviticus 1–16,* 157–58.

7 Rendtorff, *Leviticus,* 58.

8 NRSV; Milgrom, *Leviticus 1–16,* 160–61.

:אִשֵּׁה רֵיחַ־נִיחוֹחַ לַיהוָה—The noun אִשֶּׁה (in construct, אִשֵּׁה) is frequent in Leviticus (1:9, 13, 17; 2:2, 3, 9, 10, 11, 16; 3:3, 5, 9, 11, 14, 16; 4:35; 5:12; 6:10, 11 [ET 6:17, 18]; 7:5, 25, 30, 35; 8:21, 28; 10:12, 13, 15; 21:6, 21; 22:22, 27; 23:8, 13, 18, 25, 27, 36, 37; 24:7, 9). It is usually defined as "an offering made by fire" (BDB) and explained as derived from the Hebrew noun for "fire," אֵשׁ. However, the problem with that view is that אִשֶּׁה can denote other things besides the offering burnt on the altar, such as the wine libation (Num 15:10), the showbread (Lev 24:7, 9), and some of the portions eaten by the priests (Lev 2:3, 10; 7:30, 35; Deut 18:1; Josh 13:14; 1 Sam 2:28). Conversely, the sin offerings that were burnt on the altar are never included in the category of gifts denoted by אִשֶּׁה. They are, in fact, excluded from this category in Num 15:24–25 and are distinguished from it in Lev 4:35; 5:12; and Num 28:19–22. The Targum regularly speaks about אִשֶּׁה as "a sacrifice that is favorably received by the Lord." It is best understood either as a "gift" from association with the Ugaritic word *itt,* or as a "food gift," by virtue of its use with לֶחֶם, "bread, food," and as a synonym for it in Lev 3:11, 16; 21:6, 21 and Num 28:2, 24.[9]

:רֵיחַ־נִיחוֹחַ לַיהוָה—See the discussion of this phrase in the introductory discussion of Leviticus 1–3: "The Voluntary God-Pleasing Offerings." The phrase (sometimes without לַיהוה) occurs in 1:9, 13, 17; 2:2, 9, 12; 3:5, 16; 4:31; 6:8, 14 (ET 6:15, 21); 8:21, 28; 17:6; 23:13, 18 (cf. 26:31).

The formula רֵיחַ־נִיחוֹחַ לַיהוה provides an important key to understanding the theological function of the offerings to the Lord. רֵיחַ is the normal term for "an aroma" or "an odor" that can be smelled. There is some uncertainty about the sense of נִיחוֹחַ. The LXX translates רֵיחַ־נִיחוֹחַ rather literally as ὀσμὴ εὐωδίας, "a sweet smell." נִיחוֹחַ functions in Hebrew grammar as if it is a noun, but the form really is the infinitive Polel of the verb נוּחַ.[10] The Polel would mean "to give rest" or "to put at rest." In the Hiphil the verb נוּחַ can mean "to appease" or "to soothe" an angry person (Ezek 5:13). In Prov 29:17, a son who has been disciplined will delight his father. The verbal noun נִיחוֹחַ, then, refers either to soothing and appeasing of a person in a disturbed relationship, or delighting and pleasing of a person in an undisturbed relationship.

However, our view is that the term נִיחוֹחַ is never used in contexts where it obviously refers to the appeasement of the Lord by the presentation of offerings in order to soothe his anger. To support the view that it does refer to appeasing God's anger, other interpreters adduce Gen 8:21 and Lev 26:31, but those passages do not deal with the appeasement of the Lord by the regular presentation of offerings. Instead, they have to do with his acceptance and rejection of offerings in two particular instances. Furthermore, apart from Lev 4:31, נִיחוֹחַ is not used to describe the purpose of the rite for atonement or the purpose of the sin offering, which is the sacrifice specifically employed for atonement or the restoration of a disturbed relationship. Instead, it is used in the OT for those offerings that are acceptable to the Lord and pleasurable to him.

---

[9] Hoftijzer, "Das sogenannte Feueropfer," 114–84; Milgrom, *Leviticus 1–16,* 161–62.

[10] *HALOT,* s.v. נִיחוֹחַ; De Boer, "An Aspect of Sacrifice," 45.

The term נִיחֹחַ, then, describes the positive attitude and reaction of the Lord to an offering that has been presented to him through the agency of a priest at the altar for burnt offering. This sense is confirmed by the Lord's warning in 26:31. There his decision to abhor his people is connected with his refusal to smell (cf. Amos 5:21) and so accept the pleasing aroma from the offerings bought to him in their sanctuaries. On the other hand, in Ezek 20:41 the Lord promises to accept his people, together with their offerings, "as a pleasing aroma" to him, after he has bought them back from exile and the divine service has been restored on his holy mountain, Jerusalem.

Consequently, the phrase רֵיחַ־נִיחוֹחַ לַיהוָה is the formula for the divine approval of an offering. It should be translated as "a pleasing aroma to the Lord," or "an odor that pleases the Lord."

1:10 מִן־הַכְּשָׂבִים אוֹ מִן־הָעִזִּים—This is literally "from the sheep or from the goats."

1:14 וְהִקְרִיב—The *waw* consecutive with the perfect is an alternate way of introducing an apodosis after a conditional clause.

מִן־הַתֹּרִים אוֹ מִן־בְּנֵי הַיּוֹנָה—Literally, this phrase is "from the turtledoves or from sons of (some kind of) a pigeon." However, as in 1:5, בֵּן here refers to various species ("some kind of") rather than a young animal ("son" or "child").

אֶת־קָרְבָּנוֹ׃—Since turtledoves and pigeons were domesticated to provide meat for the Israelite family, they too could be used for burnt offerings and sin offerings (5:7, 11; 12:6, 11; 14:22, 30; 15:14, 29).

1:16 וְהֵסִיר אֶת־מֻרְאָתוֹ—The term מֻרְאָה, which most authorities believe occurs only here in the OT, is usually understood to refer to the crop or "craw" (*HALOT*) of the bird. But it is not at all clear why the crop of the bird needed to be removed. Milgrom argues that מֻרְאָתוֹ represents the same noun as מֹרְאָה in Zeph 3:1, where it is used synonymously with "something filthy."[11] Therefore it may refer to the anus of the bird with its intestines. Hence the reference seems to be to the intestines of the bird together with its tail feathers. Since these are the unclean parts of the bird, they cannot be burnt on the altar.

Commentary

Structure

The regulations for the burnt offering are divided into three sections depending on whether the animal for the sacrifice is taken from the herd (1:3–9) or the flock (1:10–13) or the aviary (1:14–17). The ritual procedure for the first case is given in greater detail as it sets the basic pattern for the other two cases. Thus the regulations in 1:10–13 omit the references to the placement of hands (1:4), the presentation of blood (1:5), the skinning of the animal (1:6), the preparation of the fire (1:7), and the arrangement of wood on it (1:7). Even though the regulations for the offering of a bird modify the pattern to fit the practicalities of its sacrifice, they still conform to the basic ritual pattern of pre-

[11] Milgrom, *Leviticus 1–16,* 169–71.

sentation, slaughter, disposal of blood, presentation of the carcass, and its incineration. The most obvious formal difference between the three sections is that the appositional clause in 1:9 is reformulated as a formal declaration in 1:13 and 1:17.

The structure of this pericope can be outlined as follows:

I. Private burnt offering from the herd (1:3–9)
  A. Basic case (1:3a)
  B. Ritual procedure (1:3b–9)
    1. Presentation of unblemished male animal for acceptance (1:3b)
    2. Placement of hand on its head (1:4)
    3. Slaughter (1:5a)
    4. Presentation of blood by the priests (1:5b)
    5. Splashing of blood by the priests against the altar (1:5c)
    6. Skinning (1:6a)
    7. Cutting up (1:6b)
    8. Preparation of fire on the altar by the priests (1:7a)
    9. Arrangement of wood on the altar by the priests (1:7b)
    10. Arrangement of the pieces of the animal by the priests on the altar (1:8)
    11. Washing of intestines and lower legs (1:9a)
    12. Sending up in smoke by the priest as a pleasing gift to the Lord (1:9b)

II. Private burnt offering from the flock (1:10–13)
  A. Basic case (1:10a)
  B. Ritual procedure (1:10b–13b)
    1. Presentation of an unblemished male (1:10b)
    2. Slaughter at north side of the altar (1:11a)
    3. Splashing of blood by the priests against the altar (1:11b)
    4. Cutting up (1:12a)
    5. Arrangement of pieces of the animal by the priest on the altar (1:12b)
    6. Washing of intestines and lower legs (1:13a)
    7. Presentation of whole animal and transformation into smoke by the priest (1:13b)
  C. Declaration of its nature and purpose (1:13c)

III. Private burnt offering of a bird (1:14–17)
  A. Basic case (1:14a)
  B. Ritual procedure (1:14b–17b)
    1. Presentation of a dove or pigeon (1:14b)
    2. Bringing of the bird to the altar by the priest (1:15a)
    3. Removal of head and its transformation into smoke by the priest (1:15b)
    4. Draining of its blood by the priest against the altar (1:15c)
    5. Removal and disposal by the priest of its intestines with its tail feathers (1:16)
    6. Tearing up of its carcass by the priest (1:17a)
    7. Transformation of its carcass into smoke by the priest (1:17b)
  C. Declaration of its nature and purpose (1:17c)

Ritual Agents

The main person involved in this ritual enactment was the Israelite layperson. That person could be either a man or a woman. Normally, the head of the family brought the animal to be offered up to the Lord as a burnt offering for the benefit of his family. There was, however, no reason why anybody, whether rich enough to offer up a bull or too poor to offer anything but a pigeon or dove, should not present a burnt offering for his or her personal benefit. The ritual legislation, therefore, assumes that lay people will present these offerings.

The lay people who presented the sacrifice performed two of the four basic tasks in the performance of the rite for the burnt offering. They presented the animal by bringing it to the sanctuary and laying a hand on its head. They prepared the animal for sacrifice by slaughtering, skinning, dismembering, and washing it. Since the animal was offered up on their behalf, they did this because they were the beneficiaries from the sacrificial ritual performed with it.

The priests were involved in the ritual for the burnt offering. The role of Aaron (1:7) was distinguished from the role of his sons (1:5, 7, 8). Aaron was called "the priest." This was the designation in ritual legislation for "the high priest" or the presiding priest who deputized for him. The task of the presiding priest is distinguished from the task of his assistants. While his assistants brought the blood to the altar, splashed it against the altar (1:5b), prepared the fire on the altar, and arranged the wood on the altar (1:7–8), the presiding priest was responsible for the incineration of the burnt offering (1:9b, 13b). If the animal was a sheep or goat from the flock, the presiding priest laid its parts out by himself on the altar (1:12b), since the pieces are small enough for him to handle. But if it was taken from the herd, all the priests on duty were involved, since the pieces are too large for the presiding priest to handle by himself (1:8). For practical reasons the presiding priest performed the whole rite for the sacrifice of a pigeon or dove, since it was such a small animal.

The involvement of the priests serves to distinguish between two aspects of the ritual enactment. First, the reservation of certain acts for the priests highlights their ritual significance and theological importance. Only the priests may dispose of the blood and present the sacrificial portions on the altar, because the Lord is at work in those enactments. Second, the responsibility of the presiding priest for the incineration of the offering on the altar indicates that it was the main part of the whole ritual procedure.

The last (and most important) actor in the ritual enactment was the Lord himself. His role could be easily overlooked as the emphasis of the text is on the correct human performance of the ritual. It was the Lord, however, who had authorized this ritual and its performance in his presence (1:3, 5, 11). The offering was for him (1:2, 14) and is given as a gift to him (1:9, 13, 17). He was at work in it through the rite for atonement (1:4) and his acceptance of it (1:3, 9, 13, 17). He was, in fact, the main actor. Nothing could be accomplished by the ritual enactment apart from his Word of promise and his gracious involvement.

Ritual Substances and Materials

The animals for the burnt offering came from the domesticated or semi-domesticated livestock of the Israelites. Since they belonged to the class of animals that were clean, they were edible and were part of the normal Israelite diet. In fact, they belonged to the Israelite household. The bull was obviously regarded as the most suitable animal for the burnt offering. Yet even though lambs and goats, doves and pigeons were less valuable than a bull, these regulations give no indication that they were any less acceptable as a burnt offering. The choice of animal obviously depended on the wealth of the owner. Even though wealthy people could afford to present more expensive (and more frequent) offerings, their offerings were no more acceptable than that of a poor person. By the inclusion of pigeons and doves, the legislation made it possible for almost every Israelite to bring a burnt offering to the Lord.

The regulations give some further specifications for the choice of an acceptable offering. If the animal was taken from the herd or flock, it had to be both a male and unblemished—a male animal without any physical defects. Lev 22:17–25 explains what was meant by "unblemished" or "perfect" (the lack of any defect). The animal could not be blind or castrated, injured or maimed; it had to be a healthy specimen, without abnormal growths or open sores.

There were two possible reasons for the choice of a male. First, males were usually eaten because they were less valuable than female breeding stock, since only one male was needed for any single herd or flock. Second, the male was the head of the entire herd or flock and so was a representative of it. Symbolically, the male animal also represented the male head of the family presenting the sacrifice.

If a bird was presented as a burnt offering, it had to be either a dove or some kind of pigeon. There is no requirement that it be male. The reason is that it is almost impossible to distinguish the male of those birds from the female without killing the bird.

Neither the animals nor the birds were by themselves ritually significant. They, however, supplied the two basic substances for the burnt offering: the blood for splashing against the altar (1:5, 11, 15) and the flesh for burning on the altar (1:9, 13, 15b, 17). Even though the blood was important, the flesh was the most important part of the burnt offering since all of it was burned on the altar.

The flesh of the animal slaughtered for the burnt offering was divided into five components: its body, its head, the fat around its intestines, its lower legs, and its intestines. Of these, the lower legs and intestines had to be washed so that they were clean before they could be burnt on the altar. The division of the bird for a burnt offering corresponded, by and large, to this. Its components were the head, the body, and the intestines with the tail feathers. Yet, since the intestines could not be washed for incineration on the altar, they were thrown out on the ash heap. But even so, like the ashes, they were not treated as ritually unclean.

The regulations for the dismemberment of these animals emphasized the separation of the head and its placement on the altar (1:8, 12, 15). This was unique to the burnt offering. The head represented the whole animal. But it also represented the person who had presented the animal as a burnt offering. That's why he placed his hand on it when he presented it for sacrifice. It was offered on his behalf.

Apart from the flesh and the blood, the fire was also ritually significant. This was no ordinary fire, but holy fire that had come from the Lord's presence (9:24; cf. 10:2; Num 11:1; 16:35). Since it was holy fire, it was not allowed to go out, but had to be kept burning perpetually (Lev 6:2, 5, 6 [ET 6:9, 12, 13]). The sequence of events shows the importance of the perpetual fire. Wood was to be placed on the fire that was on the altar (1:17) so that the offerings could be placed on the wood that was on the fire that was on the altar (1:8, 12, 17). The sequence indicates that the ritual function of the fire on the altar was to turn the offerings on it into a cloud of smoke.

Ritual Location

The performance of the rite for the burnt offering gained its significance from the place of its enactment. The primary location for the presentation of the burnt offering was the altar (1:5, 7, 8, 9, 11, 12, 13, 15, 16, 17). Its basic dimensions were given in Ex 27:1–8. It originally consisted of a square bronze-covered, wooden structure about 2.3 meters (7 1/2 feet) wide and 1.3 meters (4 1/2 feet) high. It was fitted with a large grill and was probably filled with earth and stones (Ex 27:1–8; 38:1–7). The whole rite was enacted around it and on it. The blood from the burnt offerings was splashed against the sides (Lev 1:5, 11, 15). The holy fire was tended on it, and the meat from the offering was laid out for burning on it (1:8, 9, 12, 13, 17). In fact, this altar was so closely identified with the burnt offerings that it received its name from them.

The altar was the basic point of reference for the three other places mentioned in this legislation. First, there was the entrance to the tent of meeting (1:3, 5), where the altar for burnt offering was located (1:5). It consisted of the corridor from the entrance to the courtyard up to the altar for burnt offering. The bull was presented and presumably slaughtered there on the east side of the altar (1:3). Second, an ash heap was located on the same side of the altar. The intestines of any birds were thrown there together with the ashes from the altar, which were cleared out every morning (6:3–4 [ET 6:10–11]). Third, the site for the slaughter of herd animals lay on the north side of the altar. All of these places were obviously open to the Israelites, even though the altar itself was entirely out of bounds for them.

Whatever was done in these places was done before the Lord and in his presence (1:3, 5, 11). His presence was therefore connected with the altar. There he met with his people; he consecrated it by his presence (Ex 29:42–44). It was therefore most holy (Ex 29:37). It was the ritual bridge between heaven and earth, the point of contact between the Lord and his people.

Ritual Time

The legislation did not prescribe any particular time or occasion for the presentation of the private burnt offering at the sanctuary. Burnt offerings were normally presented at the great pilgrim festivals in keeping with the law given in Ex 23:14–17 and 34:18–23. Furthermore, if the reference in Lev 3:5 applies to the private burnt offerings as well as the peace offerings, they were presented in the middle of the day, after the public offerings were completed. If that were so, this temporal sequence linked the private burnt offering with the public burnt offerings as established in Ex 29:38–39. It integrated this family rite into the public sacrificial ritual.

Ritual Enactment

The legislation in this section was concerned with the correct performance of the rite for the private burnt offering. This family enactment should be distinguished from the daily public burnt offering (Ex 29:38–48; Num 28:3–6). In Lev 1:3b–9 twelve separate acts are listed as the basic components of this rite. They do not, however, describe an unbroken chronological sequence. Rather, they prescribe two sets of acts, one performed by the layperson and the other performed by the priests. While most of these acts are sequential, some are simultaneous, like the arrangement of the animal on the altar as the dirty parts were washed. Thus while the layperson presented the animal, laid his right hand on its head, slaughtered it, skinned it, cut it up, and washed some parts of it, the priests brought the blood to the altar, dashed it against the altar, prepared the fire, arranged the wood, set out the parts of the animal on the altar, and supervised its incineration.

Functionally, the rite falls into three parts: the rite of presentation, the blood rite, and the rite of incineration. Two acts are prescribed for the rite of presentation. The person who presented the burnt offering brought the animal and offered it at the entrance to the tent of meeting. If it was not a male, if it had some defect, or if it was presented anywhere else (see 17:3–4, 8–9), it was unacceptable as a burnt offering. If it was a male and had no defect, and if it was presented at the sanctuary, it was acceptable. After the person who brought the animal for sacrifice had offered it to the Lord, he laid his right hand on the head of the animal. He thereby presented it as his legal possession and part of his own household so that he and his family would gain the Lord's acceptance by its acceptance. The person who laid his hand on the animal was the ritual beneficiary of the sacrifice. In the case of a bird this was unnecessary, because he brought the beast in his own hands to the priest (1:14).

The blood rite consisted of three acts. The first act was the slaughter of the animal. Even though it was slaughtered "before the Lord" (1:5, 11), the animal was not offered to the Lord by its ritual slaughter, but was killed in such a way that all the blood was drained from it. In the case of a bird, the priest, for practical reasons, did this. He put its head on the altar with one hand and drained the blood spurting from the severed neck against the altar with his other hand (1:15). After the owner of the animal had slaughtered it, the priests brought the blood in bowls and splashed it against all sides of the altar.[12] All the blood was dispersed on the altar and so was completely excluded from human use.

The directives for the rite of incineration prescribe seven separate acts in 1:6–9. As the person presenting the offering skinned the animal and cut it up, the priests stoked up the fire and arranged the wood so as to produce the conflagration needed to burn up the entire carcass of a bull. Then either the priests (1:8) or the presiding priest (1:12b) set out the head, the fat, and the carcass of the animal on the altar as the dirty parts of the animal were washed. The presiding priest then attended to their incineration together with the rest of the animal on the altar. The whole of the animal had to be burned (1:9, 13). In the case of the bird, the priest, for practical reasons, attended to its preparation and incineration (1:16–17). The whole of the victim was turned into a cloud of smoke that rose up from the altar into the sky.

The completion of the burnt offering may have been marked by another act that was not part of the sacrifice, but announced its significance. The officiating priest, as could be implied by the occurrence of the declaratory formula in 1:13c and 1:17c, may have declared that the offering was a burnt offering, a gift that was pleasing and acceptable to the Lord. If so, this would be the only verbal part of the ritual enactment.

Ritual Theological Function

In the Pentateuch, the function of the ritual enactment was not determined by its foundational performance or by the people who performed it. Its function was determined by the Word of God—the divine legislation that authorized and regulated it. If we, then, are to establish what is accomplished by the performance of the personal burnt offering, we need to consider two pieces of legislation: the foundational legislation for the public burnt offering in Ex 29:38–46 and the foundational legislation for the personal burnt offering here in Leviticus.

The context of the directives in 1:1–17 shows that they presuppose the legislation in Ex 29:38–46. In fact, this speech to Moses from "the tent of meeting" (Lev 1:1) fulfilled God's promise in Ex 29:42, just as the mention of the presentation and slaughter of the animal "at the entrance to the tent of meeting" in Lev 1:3 recalled the reference to the performance of the daily burnt offering "at the entrance to the tent of meeting" in Ex 29:42.

The surprising theocentric accent in Ex 29:43–45 is often overlooked and reversed. That passage emphasizes *what the Lord promised to do* rather than

---

12 For Jewish traditions about how this was done, see Talmud, Mishnah, *Zebachim,* 4:1, 4; 5:1–4.

what he authorized his people to do. He established the public burnt offering as a sacramental enactment in which he was the main actor. He established the public burnt offering so that through its ritual enactment he could meet with his people there, bestow his grace and forgiveness, and serve them there as their God (Ex 29:43, 45). That was the primary function of this sacrifice. This legislation does, of course, also imply that his covenant people could therefore also approach him and meet with him through this sacrificial enactment. Yet that was secondary and dependent on his meeting with them through the public burnt offering. *The primary function of the public burnt offering was so the Lord would graciously meet with his people.* That function is presupposed here in Lev 1:1–17 and implied by the command to bring a private burnt offering "at the entrance to the tent of meeting" (1:3).

The legislation in 1:3–17 explains the particular function of the personal burnt offering in three places. First, the general function of this sacrifice is stated in 1:3. An Israelite presented the animal at the entrance to the tent of meeting "for his/its acceptance before the Lord." This compressed ritual formula is far richer than any English translation reveals. It declares that God accepted the burnt offering as well as the person who brought it (cf. Jer 14:10–12). Much more is implied than the mere acceptance of a person. When the Lord accepted people, he favored them. He did not merely regard them favorably by giving them the privilege of access to himself, but he actually treated them favorably when they approached him to present their petitions to him. That divine favor also anticipated God's acceptance of the person on the future day of judgment—the Last Day.

Since the Lord had confronted his (grumbling, idolatrous) people in judgment at various times in Exodus, the Israelites would, in certain circumstances, be uncertain whether he would meet with his people at the altar for burnt offering in an encounter that would be beneficial or detrimental to them. They were therefore authorized to bring a personal burnt offering so that they could be assured of the Lord's favorable disposition toward them and be certain of receiving favorable treatment from him. Since the Lord accepted the animal, they could also be sure that he accepted them and regarded them favorably.

Second, the function of the blood rite in the ritual is explained in Lev 1:4 by the clause "so that it may be accepted for him to perform atonement on his behalf." The use of the passive tense here indicates that it is God who accepted animals as suitable for the rite of atonement. As is evident from 17:11, the rite of atonement involved the application of blood from a ritually slaughtered animal on the altar for burnt offering. By its performance on behalf of the offerer, both he and the altar were cleansed from any ritual impurity that might otherwise result in the desecration of the Lord's holiness. The offerer was therefore qualified for entrance into the Lord's presence and the presentation of his burnt offering. The rite of atonement, however, was not the main purpose of this sacrifice; it was, in fact, a part of every animal offering. Here it ensured that the person who presented the burnt offering was acceptable to the Lord, just as the presentation of the right animal in the right place ensured that it was acceptable as a burnt offering.

Third, the repetition of the formula for divine pleasure at the voluntary burnt offering in 1:9, 13, 17 shows that this offering, like all the other voluntary offerings, was established by the Lord to demonstrate his pleasure at this offering and his delight in its giver. If we are to appreciate how this functioned theologically, we need to focus our attention, as directed by the formula for divine pleasure, on the sweet aroma that was produced by the smoke from the incineration of the offering. This aroma operated simultaneously in both a physical and a spiritual way. On a physical level, the pleasure of the Lord at the aroma from the burnt offering was shown by its physical sweetness. On a spiritual level, the physical aroma shows the delight of the Lord in the giver of this gift. Yet these two levels cannot be separated from each other and played off against each other, as if the latter could be revealed apart from the former enactment. The physical and spiritual are combined in a sacramental way. By delighting in the aroma of the gift, the Lord delighted in its giver. What's more, by smelling the aroma of the smoke and by hearing the declaration of the priest about its function, the giver experienced the Lord's pleasure at his gift and his delight in the giver of the gift. It announced God's acceptance of him.

By his acceptance of the burnt offering, the Lord showed that he was well pleased with the person who had brought it. God's pleasure in the burnt offering foreshadows his delight in the sacrifice of his Son, about whom he declared, "With him I am well pleased" (Mt 3:17; 17:5).

Fulfillment by Christ

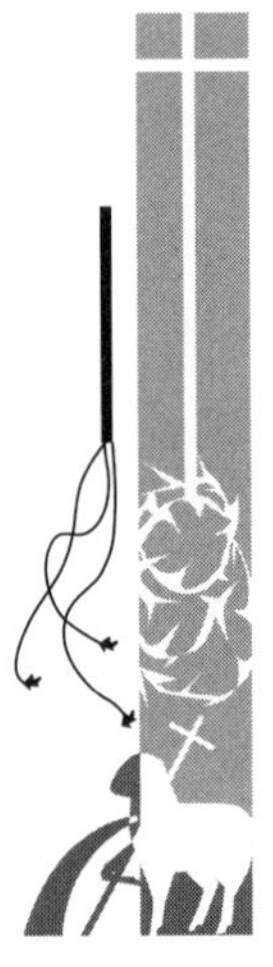

The divine service that God established for Israel at Mount Sinai was built around the daily burnt offering. When the burnt offering was offered each morning and evening at the tabernacle God met with his people. Through its daily enactment he gave them access to his favor and blessing after he had cleansed them from all impurity. By the sweet aroma that arose with the cloud of smoke from the burnt offering, he showed that he had accepted them and was pleased with them. They could therefore add their personal offerings to the public burnt offering so that they too were acceptable to him.

The Divine Service in the church is not built around the burnt offering of a lamb, but around Jesus, the Lamb of God (Jn 1:29), who is both the sacrificial victim and the priest. Like the lamb for the public burnt offering and the other animals for the private burnt offering, Christ is "a male without blemish" (Lev 1:3). His people have been redeemed "by the precious blood of Christ, as of a lamb unblemished and spotless" (1 Pet 1:18–19).[13]

[13] The requirement that the sacrificial animal be a male relates to the biblical principle of male headship. Eve was created out of Adam, and the man is the head of his wife just as Christ is the head of the man and God the Father is the head of Christ (1 Cor 11:1–16). St. Paul refers again to the headship of the man over the woman and of Christ over the church immediately before affirming that Christ gave himself up as the sacrifice that cleanses his bride, the church, so that he may present her as unblemished before God the Father (Eph 5:23–27).

No human priest offered Christ as a sacrifice to God the Father, nor does the church in its worship now offer Christ as its sacrifice. In a surprising turn of events, it was Christ who "offered himself unblemished" to God the Father for all people (Heb 9:14). All the sacrifices by which the Israelites approached God at the tabernacle and the temple foreshadowed his perfect sacrifice (Heb 10:1–4). His superseded them all (Heb 10:5–9). Jesus "offered" himself once for all to atone for the sins of the world (Heb 7:27; 9:12; 10:10; 1 Jn 2:2). He entered the heavenly sanctuary with his own blood to make atonement for sin (Heb 9:12, 24–28). That offering of his own human flesh and blood as the perfect sacrifice for all people is the "sweet aroma" that is pleasing to God (Eph 5:2).

Since Christ offered himself once and for all to God the Father, he does not now need to offer daily burnt offerings as our High Priest to gain our acceptance by God (Heb 7:27). That has been done. Perfectly, finally, completely! And so the role that he now plays in the Divine Service differs from the role played by the high priest. He offers himself and the benefits of his sacrifice for us. He comes to preach grace and peace from God the Father to both Jews and Gentiles (Eph 2:17–18). He brings the cleansing and forgiveness that has been obtained through his blood (Heb 2:17; 1 Jn 1:7). Therefore St. Paul declares that the preaching of the apostolic Gospel spreads the sweet aroma of Christ's sacrifice and the Father's acceptance of it "in every place" of worship (2 Cor 2:14–16). The apostle, however, did not just proclaim the Gospel by his words, but also by his life, which was offered in and with Christ to God the Father.[14]

Functionally speaking, in Christian worship the preaching of the Gospel in the liturgy takes the place of the burnt offering in the OT sacrificial ritual. Those who have been justified by Christ's blood and saved from death have access to the Father's life-giving grace through faith in him (Rom 5:1–2, 9; Eph 2:18). They may therefore approach God the Father with a clean conscience in the full assurance of faith (Heb 10:22), for they know that God the Father is well pleased with them and their service of him (Heb 12:28). They can come to receive mercy and grace from him (Heb 4:16).

Jesus, who once offered himself as our "burnt offering," now acts as our High Priest. He presents us holy and unblemished together with himself to God the Father in the Divine Service (Eph 5:27; Col 1:22; cf. Eph 1:4). Through Jesus and together with him, we can now approach God the Father and offer true and acceptable service to him (Heb 10:14, 19–22; 12:28). We need not (and cannot) offer a burnt offering to secure God's grace and gain acceptance for ourselves. We have that in Christ. We can therefore offer to God the Father offerings that are pleasing and acceptable to him. Paul exhorts all Christians "to offer your bodies as a living sacrifice, holy and pleasing to God" (Rom 12:1).

We offer ourselves, holy and sanctified by the Holy Spirit, rather than the body of a slaughtered animal (Rom 12:1–2; 15:16). We offer the living mem-

[14] Renwick, *Paul, the Temple, and the Presence of God,* 75–94.

bers of our bodies for sanctification and holy service rather than the dead and dismembered parts of a sacrificed animal (Rom 6:13, 19), as well as the sacrifice of our prayers and our praises (Heb 13:15), the gifts for the preachers of the Gospel (Phil 4:18) and for needy people (Heb 13:16b), and all good works (Heb 13:16a). All these offerings are only "acceptable to God through Jesus Christ" and his self-offering for us (1 Pet 2:5). Like the offerings that the Philippians gathered and sent to Paul, they are "a sweet aroma, a sacrifice acceptable and pleasing to God" (Phil 4:18).

Jesus, our High Priest and Mediator, now fulfills the role of the priest in the Divine Service. His offering of his blood and body has accomplished our "justification and sanctification, those two indispensable conditions, without which sinful man could not attain to reconciliation with God and life in God."[15] Since we sinners could not justify and sanctify ourselves before God by our own efforts, he offered himself for our justification and sanctification. In the Divine Service, he cleanses us from sin so that we can approach God the Father, unafraid, and receive his favor; he also presents us bodily together with himself to his Father, so that we may be sanctified with all our members and be made fit to participate in the life and work of the triune God.

Not all the blood of beasts
  On Jewish altars slain
Could give the guilty conscience peace
  Or wash away the stain.

But Christ, the heav'nly Lamb,
  Takes all our sins away;
A sacrifice of nobler name
  And richer blood than they.

My faith would lay its hand
  On that dear head divine
As penitently here I stand,
  Confessing guilt is mine.

Believing, we rejoice
  To see the curse remove;
We bless the Lamb with cheerful voice
  And sing his bleeding love.[16]

---

[15] Keil, *Pentateuch,* 2:281.

[16] From "Not All the Blood of Beasts" by Isaac Watts (*LW* 99:1–3, 5).

Leviticus 2:1–16

Regulations for the Grain Offering

Translation

**2 1“When a person presents an offering of grain to the Lord, his offering shall
be of fine flour; he shall pour oil upon it, lay frankincense on it, 2and bring it in
to Aaron’s sons, the priests. He shall scoop out from there a handful of its fine
flour and oil from it, as well as all its frankincense. The priest shall turn its token portion into smoke on the altar, as a gift of a pleasing aroma to the Lord.
3But what is left of the grain offering shall belong to Aaron and his sons, a most
holy part from the Lord’s gifts.**

**4“And when you present an offering of grain that has been baked in an oven,
[it shall be of] fine flour: unleavened round-loaves mixed with oil, or unleavened
wafers anointed with oil.**

**5“But if your offering is a grain offering [prepared] on a flat griddle, it shall
be of fine flour mixed with oil, unleavened. 6Crumble it into bits and pour oil on
it. It is a grain offering.**

**7“But if your offering is a grain offering of a pan, it shall be made of fine
flour with oil. 8You may bring to the Lord a grain offering made in any of these
ways. It shall be presented to the priest who shall deliver it to the altar. 9The priest
shall reserve the token portion from the grain offering and turn it into smoke on
the altar as a gift of a pleasing aroma to the Lord. 10But what is left of the grain
offering shall belong to Aaron and his sons, a most holy portion from the Lord’s
gifts.**

**11“No grain offering that you present to the Lord shall be made with leaven,
for you must not turn into smoke anything made with leaven or with fruit syrup
as a gift to the Lord. 12You may present them as a first-processed offering to the
Lord, but they shall not be offered up on the altar as a pleasing aroma. 13You
shall season all your grain offerings with salt; you shall not leave out the salt of
the covenant of your God from your grain offering. On all your offerings you
must offer salt.**

**14“But if you present a grain offering of first-ripe produce to the Lord, you
shall present milky grain parched with fire, grits of the fresh barley, as a grain
offering of your first-ripe produce. 15You shall add oil to it and place frankincense on it. It is a grain offering. 16The priest shall turn its token portion into
smoke: some of its grits and oil, with all its frankincense, as a gift to the Lord.”**

Textual Notes

2:1 וְנֶ֕פֶשׁ כִּֽי־תַקְרִ֞יב—This is literally “As for a soul, when he shall bring forward …” Like אָדָם כִּי in 1:2, נֶפֶשׁ כִּי is an inclusive phrase for any “person,” either a man or a woman (see 4:2; 5:1, 4, 15, 17, 21; 7:21; cf. 5:2; 7:20; 20:6), who presents an offering. Regarding תַּקְרִ֔יב, see 2:4, 8, 11, 12, 13, 14 (twice) and the textual note on הִקְרִיב in 1:2.

מִנְחָה֙—The term מִנְחָה is used in a number of different ways in the OT. It is used secularly for the tribute paid by vassals to their overlord (Judg 3:15, 17–18). It can denote a present given by one king to another (2 Ki 20:12) or by one person to another (Gen 32:13, 18, 20, 21; 33:10). It is also a general term for any offering to the Lord (Gen 4:3–5; 1 Sam 26:19) as well as for the daily sacrifice that consisted of a burnt offering combined with a grain offering (1 Ki 18:29; 2 Ki 3:20). As a technical term in the instructions for the divine service, it refers to the grain for the grain offering (Lev 2:1, 4, 11, 14) as well as the grain offering that was presented either as a separate sacrifice (2:4, 6, 7, 8, 9, 10, 15) or together with every burnt offering (Ex 29:41; Num 28:4–5, 8) and peace offering (Num 15:8–10).

סֹ֖לֶת—The meaning of סֹלֶת (also in Lev 2:2, 4, 5, 7) is usually given as "fine flour" (BDB) or "finely milled flour" (*HALOT*), but the definition is not completely certain. As Ex 29:2 and 2 Ki 7:16 show, סֹלֶת was produced from wheat rather than barley. In 1 Ki 5:2 (ET 4:22) it is distinguished from coarse flour and was more valuable since it is listed with luxury items such as oil and honey (cf. Ezek 16:13, 19). It was a kind of semolina, made up either of husked grits of wheat with the bran removed or of fine sifted white wheat flour which has been sieved to remove all coarse matter.[1]

לְבֹנָֽה׃—"Frankincense" is an aromatic gum resin tapped from three different species of trees in southern Arabia and Somaliland.[2] It was offered together with a grain offering (2:1, 2, 15, 16; 6:8 [ET 6:15]). It was an important ingredient of the sacred incense that was burnt twice daily on the incense altar (Ex 30:34).

2:2 וֶֽהֱבִיאָ֗הּ—The Hiphil of בּוֹא is common in Leviticus as a technical term meaning "to bring" an offering (2:2, 8; 4:4, 5, 14, 16, 23, 28, 32; 5:6, 7, 8, 11, 12, 15, 18; 5:25 [ET 6:6]; 6:14 [ET 6:21]; 7:29, 30; 10:15; 12:6; 14:23; 15:29; 17:4, 5, 9; 19:21; 23:14, 15, 17). It indicates that the person who presents the offering enters the sanctuary and personally brings the offering in there himself.

וְקָמַ֨ץ—The subject of this verb is the priest.

וְהִקְטִ֨יר—See 2:9, 11, 16 and the textual note on this verb in 1:9.

אַזְכָּרָתָהּ֙—The אַזְכָּרָה refers to the burned portion of the grain offering, but its precise meaning is uncertain. *HALOT* includes proposals that it means "remainder," "announcement (of purpose …)," "invocation," or "token-offering." The LXX and Vulgate treat it as meaning "memorial" or "remembrance." It recurs in 2:9, 16; 5:12; 6:8 (ET 6:15); 24:7; Num 5:26. Some scholars have postulated that it should be rendered as "a fragrant portion" based on the view that the noun זֵכֶר may mean "a sweet fragrance" in Hos 14:8 (ET 14:7) and the possible meaning of the Hiphil of זָכַר as "to make fragrant" in Is 66:3. But "a fragrant portion" would only hold if the אַזְכָּרָה were always offered with frankincense. But in the case of the expiatory grain offering, it was presented without any frankincense (Lev 5:12; Num 5:15).

---

1 Milgrom, *Leviticus 1–16,* 179.

2 Milgrom, *Leviticus 1–16,* 180–81.

Most likely אַזְכָּרָה is a noun (formed with prosthetic א) from the common verb זָכַר, "to remember." Three interpretations have been given for the term אַזְכָּרָה and its ritual function.

First, it has most commonly been understood as a "memorial portion" (see BDB). As such it was meant to *remind* the Lord to *remember* the givers of the offering by treating them well. However, that was the function of all offerings. Second, since the Hiphil of זָכַר was used for the invocation and proclamation of the holy name of God, some propose that this portion got its name from an act of invocation that accompanied its offering.[3] There is, however, no evidence that such an invocation was ever spoken, nor does it make sense that the holy name needed to be invoked only for the grain offering that provided bread for the priests. Why wouldn't God's name be invoked for the presentation of all offerings?

Third and most likely, the אַזְכָּרָה may be the "token portion" for the entire grain offering. This interpretation is supported by the reference to the incense in 24:7 as the אַזְכָּרָה for the show bread and the regular reference to the burnt part of the grain offering as "its" אַזְכָּרָה (2:2, 9, 16; 5:12; 6:8 [ET 6:15]; Num 5:26). This "token portion" then served as a substitute for the entire offering.[4] Only the token portion was offered to God by being burnt up on the altar. The rest of the grain offering was dedicated to God and consecrated as the most holy food that the priests (and only they) would eat.

הַמִּזְבֵּחָה—See 2:8, 9, 12 and the textual note on this word in 1:5.

אִשֵּׁה רֵיחַ נִיחֹחַ לַיהוָה׃—In this chapter, אִשֶּׁה occurs also in 2:3, 9, 10, 11, 16. Here and in 2:9 it is in construct (hence vocalized as אִשֵּׁה) as part of the construct chain "a gift of a pleasing aroma to the Lord." See the textual notes on 1:9.

2:3 קֹדֶשׁ קָדָשִׁים—This portion that is literally "a holy thing of holy things" is the "most holy part." In Hebrew such a construct phrase functions as a superlative, as in "the Song of Songs" (the best song; Song 1:1) and, negatively, "vanity of vanities" (utterly vain; Eccl 1:2). The designation of an offering, or some part of it, as "most holy" meant that it was reserved exclusively for the priests on duty and could only be eaten by them at the sanctuary. The phrase recurs in Lev 2:10; 6:10, 18, 22 [ET 6:17, 25, 29]; 7:1, 6; 10:12, 17; 14:13; 24:9; 27:28. See also the textual note on הַקֹּדֶשׁ in 4:6.

2:4 וְכִי—The use of כִּי, "when," rather than אִם, "if," indicates that 2:4 introduces a new class of offering, rather than a subcategory of the offering described in 2:1–3. In 2:4–10 the legislation is addressed directly to each individual Israelite. Almost all of the verbs and the pronouns translated "you" in 2:4–10 are second person masculine singular.

מַאֲפֵה תַנּוּר—The noun מַאֲפֶה occurs only here in the OT. It denotes "something baked" and is formed from the verb אָפָה, "to bake." It is in construct (hence מַאֲפֵה) with תַּנּוּר, "oven," which recurs in 7:9.

---

[3] H. Eising, "זָכַר *zākhar*," *TDOT* 4:80.

[4] Milgrom, *Leviticus 1–16,* 181–82.

חַלֹּת—The חַלָּה was "ring-shaped bread" (*HALOT*), a flat loaf in the shape of a ring. It recurs in 7:12, 13; 8:26; 24:5.

בַּשֶּׁמֶן ... בַּשָּׁמֶן:—The common OT term for olive oil is שֶׁמֶן, and it is used with many offerings. בַּשֶּׁמֶן (in pause, בַּשָּׁמֶן) occurs thrice in 7:12.

מְשֻׁחִים—This is the passive participle of the verb מָשַׁח, which means "to anoint." From it we get the title "Messiah." According to the teaching of the rabbis, the oil was smeared in the form of the Greek letter *chi*, χ, which resembles an "x" or cross.

2:5 עַל־הַמַּחֲבַת—This phrase recurs in 7:9. The מַחֲבַת was a flat plate or griddle made either of clay or of iron (Ezek 4:3). The bread made on it was flat and hard.

2:6 פָּתוֹת אֹתָהּ פִּתִּים—The verb פָּתַת occurs only here in the OT and means "to crumble." The cognate noun פִּתִּים follows as the second direct object and denotes the crumbled "bits" or "crumbs" (*HALOT*, s.v. פַּת, 2). The form of the verb is the Qal infinitive absolute, used as an imperative (as is זָכוֹר in Ex 20:8). Elsewhere in Leviticus, the infinitive absolute forms of various verbs occur in each instance together with a finite form of that same verb, which is not the case here, so some prefer to follow the LXX (καὶ διαθρύψεις) and read the finite (perfect) form וּפַתּוֹתָ, "and you shall crumble."

2:7 מַרְחֶשֶׁת—This term for a "baking pan" (*HALOT*) occurs also in 7:9. The bread made in it was soft and spongy. Since a pan, unlike a flat griddle (2:5), had sides to it, the bread was fried in it with the oil in the pan. (In contrast, 2:5 has the preposition עַל, indicating that the grain offering was baked "upon" the flat griddle.)

2:8 וְהִקְרִיבָהּ—The Hebrew וְהִקְרִיבָהּ is a change from second person masculine singular ("you may …") to third person masculine singular ("he shall present it"). It may be construed impersonally and rendered as a passive, which is what our translation does: "it shall be presented." Less attractive is the proposal to repoint it as a masculine singular imperative, וְהַקְרִיבָהּ.

וְהִגִּישָׁהּ—The Hiphil of נָגַשׁ (הִגִּישׁ with third feminine singular suffix) is used only here for the presentation of the baked offerings which, unlike the raw grain offerings, had to be brought forward to the altar by the priest. Thereafter the offering belonged to the priest as his personal due from the Lord (see also 6:7).

2:9 וְהֵרִים—The Hiphil of the verb רוּם (הֵרִים) can mean to "take away" (*HALOT*, 3) or to "lift up, draw away" (*HALOT*, 5), but most appropriate here is to "select" (*HALOT*, 4) or "reserve." Here it is used as a technical ritual term for the designation, reservation, and dedication of something for ritual use.[5] It recurs in 4:8, 19; 6:8 (ET 6:15); 22:15.

2:11 תַּקְרִיבוּ—Whereas the legislation in 2:4–10 is couched in second person masculine singular, the legislation in 2:11–12 is in the second person masculine plural form.

חָמֵץ—The Hebrew distinguishes between "leavened dough" (חָמֵץ) and the "leaven" (שְׂאֹר in the following phrase) that leavens it. "Leavened dough" recurs in 6:10 (ET 6:17); 7:13; 23:17.

כִּי כָל־שְׂאֹר ... לֹא־תַקְטִירוּ—Note how Amos 4:5 condemns the violation of this prohibition.

---

5 Milgrom, "The Alleged Wave-Offering in Israel and the Ancient Near East."

דְּבַשׁ—It is customary to translate דְּבַשׁ as honey. However, as Milgrom observes, this term was associated with other agricultural products (Gen 43:11; Deut 8:8; 2 Ki 18:32; 2 Chr 31:5) and is therefore best understood as the syrup produced from fruit and used to make sweet cakes from flour.[6] Throughout Leviticus we render it as "fruit syrup."

2:12 קָרְבַּן רֵאשִׁית—Often both רֵאשִׁית and בִּכּוּרִים are translated as "firstfruit(s)." However, Milgrom notes that the priestly tradition distinguishes the רֵאשִׁית (2:12; cf. Ex 23:19; Num 15:20, 21; 18:12) from the בִּכּוּרִים (Lev 2:14; 23:17, 20).[7] רֵאשִׁית is the first-processed produce from agricultural products such as grain, wine, olive oil, fruit syrup, leavened bread, and bread dough (Neh 10:37). Therefore we render רֵאשִׁית here as the "first-processed offering." בִּכּוּרִים are the first-ripe fruit and barley (Ex 23:16, 19; 34:22, 26; Neh 10:36 [ET 10:35]).

יַעֲלוּ—This form (third person masculine plural imperfect) could be either the Qal or the Hiphil of עָלָה. The context indicates that it is the Hiphil, which would mean "they [the priests] shall [not] offer up" or "they shall [not] cause to go up [in smoke]." However, since the verb has no subject, it may be understood impersonally and translated by a passive: "they [offerings with leaven or fruit syrup] shall [not] be offered up." See it also in 14:20; 17:8. The Hiphil of עָלָה is used as a technical term for offering up the meat from the burnt offering, the flour from the grain offering, and the fat from the peace offering to the Lord by burning them on the altar. It is also used, rather strikingly, for the burning of oil in the lamps overnight in the Holy Place (24:2).

2:13 וְלֹא תַשְׁבִּית—Literally, this means "you shall not cause to cease." See the Hiphil also in 26:6.

2:14 אָבִיב—The noun אָבִיב is a collective singular for the soft ears of barley that have not yet dried out, but are milky when crushed for human use. It gave its name to the first month of the year, Abib, which later was called Nisan.

גֶּרֶשׂ—The noun גֶּרֶשׂ refers to soft barley grain that was crushed after it had been roasted to harden it.

כַּרְמֶל—The noun כַּרְמֶל is used for fresh, newly ripe barley (Lev 23:14; 2 Ki 4:42).

Commentary

Structure

The legislation in this chapter is presented in two sections of ritual case laws linked together to form a single sentence, with the insertion of two appositional sentences in 2:11–13. We have two general cases introduced by "when" (כִּי) in 2:1–3 and 2:4. This divides the chapter into two parts. First, 2:1–3 deals with the raw grain offering. Then 2:4–16 deals with the cooked grain offering.

The second section has three sub-cases introduced by "if" (אִם) in 2:5, 7, 14, with a parenthesis in 2:11–13. This second section with its three subcategories differs from the first section in that it is not construed impersonally but

---

6 Milgrom, *Leviticus 1–16,* 189.

7 Milgrom, *Leviticus 1–16,* 190–91.

is addressed to the individual Israelite ("you" is singular in 2:4–10 and 2:13–16). While the procedure for the offering of the kinds of bread is set out in 2:8–10, the slightly varied procedure for offering of barley grits is covered in 2:15–16.

In 2:11–13 two general mandatory directives follow the case law for cooked grain offerings (2:4–10). The first directive about the use of yeast and syrup is addressed collectively to all Israelites: "you" is plural in 2:11–12. The second directive about the use of salt is addressed individually to each Israelite: "you" is singular in 2:13. This intrusive parenthesis of three verses (2:11–13) has been added here because it treats those substances that are not to be used in the production of the cooked grain offering mentioned in 2:4–10.

The material in chapter 2 is unified by the formal designation of each category of grain offering as "a gift to the Lord" in 2:2, 9, 16. The formula for divine pleasure ("a pleasing aroma to the Lord") is added to the first two of these instances but is omitted in the last because that offering was covered by the reference to all cooked grain offerings in 2:9. It is also used negatively in 2:12 ("they shall *not* be … a pleasing aroma") to exclude any sweetened or leavened bread from this category of grain offerings.

The structure of this pericope can be outlined as follows:

- I. Regulations for raw grain offerings (2:1–3)
  - A. The case (2:1a)
  - B. The ritual procedure (2:1b–2)
    - 1. Addition of olive oil to the flour (2:1b)
    - 2. Addition of incense to the flour (2:1c)
    - 3. Presentation to priests (2:2a)
    - 4. Removal of memorial portion with the incense (2:2b)
    - 5. Its incineration with the incense by the priest (2:2c)
  - C. The status and use of the leftover flour (2:3)
- II. Regulations for the baked grain offering (2:4–16)
  - A. The presentation of bread as a grain offering (2:4–10)
    - 1. The three cases for bread (2:4–7)
      - a. Cakes or wafers in an oven (2:4)
      - b. Flat cakes baked on a flat griddle (2:5–6)
      - c. Pancakes baked in a pan (2:7)
    - 2. The ritual procedure (2:8–9)
      - a. Transportation to the sanctuary (2:8a)
      - b. Presentation to a priest (2:8b)
      - c. Transportation by a priest to the altar (2:8c)
      - d. Removal of memorial portion by the priest (2:9a)
      - e. Incineration of memorial portion by priests (2:9b)
    - 3. The status and use of the leftover bread (2:10)
  - B. The exclusion of yeast products and the inclusion salt (2:11–13)
    - 1. The prohibition of yeast and fruit syrup in grain offerings (2:11–12)
    - 2. The use of salt in all grain offerings (2:13)

C. The case of first-ripe barley (2:14–16)
  1. The case (2:14)
  2. The ritual procedure (2:15–16)
    a. Addition of oil to the grain (2:15a)
    b. Placement of incense on the grain (2:15b)
    c. Incineration by priest of memorial portion on the altar (2:16)

Ritual Agents

These regulations were addressed to each Israelite man and woman. They anticipate the era when the Israelites will have taken possession of the land and will till it. Normally the head of the household would present the offering as a representative of the whole family unit, since the whole family had been involved in harvesting and threshing the grain, the grinding of the grain and the sifting of the flour, the baking of the bread and the roasting of the barley ears. All this, together with the production of the olive oil, was done at home before the grain offering was brought to the sanctuary. It was therefore in every way *a family offering*. These laws give us no reason to conclude that the grain offering was regarded as an inferior substitute for families that were too poor to bring a burnt offering. Farmers who lacked livestock would obviously bring this kind of offering, whether they were rich or poor. The people who brought these grain offerings belonged to agricultural communities in Israel. In this way they linked their farms with the temple and connected their families with the Lord and his priests.

The second group of people involved in this ritual enactment was the priests. The priest who officiated (2:2b, 8, 16) was distinguished from the general body of priests (2:2a, 3, 10). This comes out most clearly in the act of presentation. The raw flour was brought to the priests in general, even though only one of them officiated in its ritual incineration (2:2a). The baked bread, however, was brought to a particular priest who burned part of it on the altar (2:8). This distinction had practical implications, because the grain offerings provided the priests with their food from grain. It was their stipend. The general rule was that all leftover flour and bread belonged to all the priests, whether they officiated or not (2:3, 10). This general rule was qualified by the instruction in 7:9–10 that all baked grain belonged to the priest who officiated at its presentation, whereas the raw grain and flour was divided equally among all the priests.

The third (and most important) agent in this ritual enactment was God. He legislated how the grain offering was to be prepared and offered to him. It was therefore brought to him (2:1, 8, 14). He regarded it as one of the most holy gifts that belonged entirely to him and was given by him to his priests as their perpetual due for their service to him (2:10; 6:18). Most significantly, he showed his delight in the people presenting the grain offering by the sweet aroma that was produced as its “token portion” (2:2) was burned on the altar.

Ritual Material

The basic ritual material for this offering was the grain produced by the Israelite families on their allotted properties in the land of Israel. The grain for it was normally taken from raw first-ripened ears of barley (2:12) or their first-processed grain (2:14) or the tithe of their harvest (27:30). The grain was usually taken from the wheat harvest. The exception to this was the presentation of ears from the first barley sheaf.

The material for the grain offering was presented as fine sifted raw wheat flour (2:4–10) or as cooked flour (2:14–16). The cooked grain was made up into three different kinds of bread: loaves or wafers baked in an oven, flat cakes baked on a flat pan, and round cakes fried in a pan (2:4–7). The grain from the ears of barley had to be roasted and then crushed for presentation as coarse flour (2:14).

Three other kinds of materials were ritually significant for the production and presentation of the grain offering. First, olive oil had to be used in their preparation. In fact, the mention of it, together with the declaratory formula "it is a grain offering" in 2:6 and 2:15, shows that it was an essential ingredient. If a grain offering was presented as flour, olive oil had to be poured out on it and soaked up into it (2:2c, 15a). If the grain offering was presented as bread, olive oil had to be used in the preparation of it. The oil was mixed with the flour if the bread was baked in an oven (2:4) or on a flat plate (2:5). In the latter case, the oil also had to be poured on the pieces of crumbled flat cake before they were brought to the sanctuary (2:6). Oil was also used to fry the round cakes in a pan (2:7). Even though the use of olive oil in all these cases was part of the normal bread-making process, it also helped to make the token portion more flammable.

Second, some frankincense had to be presented together with the fine wheaten flour (2:1–2) and the coarse barley flour (2:15–16). This ordinary form of incense was distinguished from the most holy incense burnt daily by the priest on the incense altar in the Holy Place (Ex 30:1–10, 34–38). It, however, was apparently not required for the offerings of baked bread. No reason is given for this omission. While it may have been a deliberate concession for the poor, it could also have been prescribed to mask the rather acrid smell of burning flour. Whatever the reason, incense thereby came to be closely associated in the popular mind with the grain offering.[a]

(a) Is 1:13; 43:23; 66:3; Jer 17:26; 41:5; Ps 141:2; Neh 13:5, 9

Third and last, salt had to be added to every grain offering (2:13). The importance of this is highlighted by the repetition of the commandment. Salt was added for practical and symbolical reasons. Practically, it was a preservative that lessened the likelihood of mold and decay. Symbolically, it was associated with permanence, because it was a very stable substance that lent its characteristics to other substances without any change to itself.

Two substances that were commonly used in baking were excluded from ritual use in this offering. Leaven, or anything made with leaven, was prohibited for practical and symbolic reasons. Practically, the lack of leaven meant that the bread would last longer and be less subject to mold and decay. Symbolically, leaven was associated with corruption, sickness, decay, and death. Since all these were unclean, they were incompatible with God's holiness. Fruit syrup, and anything made with fruit syrup, was also banned from use in this offering because, like leavened dough, it was subject to fermentation. Both these substances could, however, be offered as first-processed agricultural produce in the form of dough and fruit syrup or in cakes made from first-processed grain (Num 15:17–21; 2 Chr 31:5; Neh 10:37). In this case, they belonged to the priests and their families. But they could not be used as a grain offering that had its memorial portion burnt on the altar.

Both the flour and the bread did not basically differ from the foodstuff for the ordinary Israelite family. But after a portion taken from them had been burnt on the altar, they became most holy. Since the flour or bread was most holy food, the priests alone were allowed to eat it, and were to eat it at the sanctuary. Through its presentation as a grain offering, common bread was transformed into most holy food for the priests. It is one of several such most holy portions to be eaten by the priests alone. See figure 7.

Figure 7

Most Holy Offerings Eaten by the Priests

Offering	*Substance*	*References*
Show bread	Flat loaves	Lev 24:9
Public grain offering	Flour	Lev 6:9–11 (ET 6:16–18); 10:12
Private grain offering	Flour	Lev 2:3; Num 18:9
Private grain offering	Bread	Lev 2:10
Sin offering	Meat	Lev 6:10, 18, 22 (ET 6:17, 25, 29); Num 18:9
Reparation offering	Meat	Lev 6:10 (ET 6:17); 7:1, 6; Num 18:9

Ritual Location

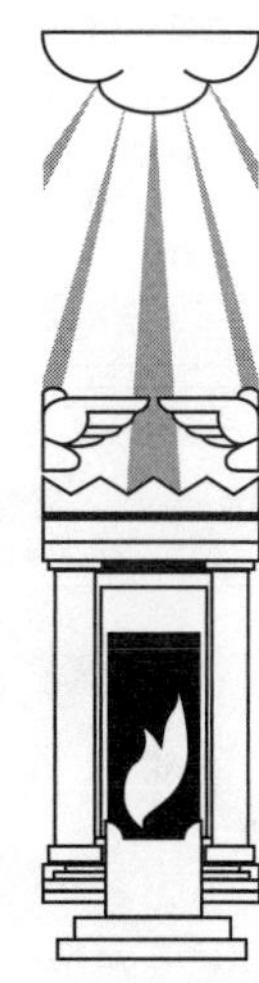

The rite for the presentation of the grain offering transferred flour and bread from the common domain to the holy, divine domain. See figure 1, "Holy versus Common and Clean versus Unclean." The offering was prepared at home by the Israelite family. The Israelites brought it from the home to the priests at the sanctuary. No location was specified for the transferal of the offering from its giver to the priests. That was unimportant. The important thing, ritually, was that the officiating priest brought a portion of it to the altar and burnt it there (2:2, 9). By means of that ritual enactment, God received the offering as a gift to him. It became his property, something most holy, part of his house, food for his table and for the members of his household. As such it could not be removed from this location; it had to be eaten there in his presence (6:9 [ET 6:16]).

Ritual Time

Like the private burnt offering, the grain offering was normally brought to the sanctuary at one of the three pilgrim festivals. This occurred most commonly either at the Feast of Weeks (Pentecost, late spring), which marked the end of the grain harvest, or at the Feast of Booths (late summer), which marked the end of the agricultural year. While the first-ripe produce (2:14–16) could have been presented on the day for the offering of the first sheaf during the Feast of Unleavened Bread following Passover (23:10–14), the first-processed grain was almost certainly offered at the Feast of Weeks (23:17). In this way the annual workaday cycle of the Israelite family was coordinated with the sacred cycle of the liturgical year that punctuated it with its holy days. Moreover, the order of legislation in chapters 1–3 implies that the grain offering was presented after the private burnt offerings. It was therefore placed together with that sacrifice on the daily public burnt offering and incorporated into the national ritual cycle at the sanctuary.

Ritual Enactment

The private grain offering must be distinguished from the grain offering that was regularly combined with the public burnt offering (Ex 29:40, 41) and the personal peace offerings (Lev 7:12–14). The ritual procedure for the public grain offering is given in 6:7–11 (ET 6:14–18). It resembled the grain offering for the priests officiating at the temple. Yet it differed from the priest's offering which was not eaten by the priests but burned up entirely on the altar.

The procedure for the offering of fine wheat flour has five acts that were performed in two stages. The first three were performed by the giver of the offering. That person poured oil into the flour, placed some incense on it, and presented it to a priest at the sanctuary. The last two acts, which were ritually the most significant, were performed by the officiating priest. He removed a handful of flour mixed together with all the incense for the offering; then he burnt it on the altar. The same ritual procedure was also followed for the coarse grain offering in 2:15–16.

This ritual procedure was modified for the bread offering in 2:4–10. Once again the rite consisted of five acts performed in two stages. The first two acts were performed by the giver, who brought the bread to the sanctuary and presented it to the officiating priest. The priest then performed three acts: he carried all the bread to the altar, removed the memorial portion, and burnt it on the altar.

The same basic procedure was followed in both cases—for the offering of fine wheat flour and the bread offering. The main difference was that no frankincense was added to the bread offering. In both cases the rite was made up of two connected transactions, two sets of acts. The Israelite presented the grain offering to the priest so that he, in turn, could hand it over to the Lord by burning up a portion of it. The formula for divine pleasure ("a pleasing aroma to the Lord") at the grain offering as a gift to him in 2:2 and in 2:9 shows that in both cases the rite was probably completed with the pronouncement of that formula by the priest to the giver of the gift.

The ritual importance of the incineration by the priest of the part that was taken from this offering is shown by its designation as the offering's "token potion." This term was used only for the parts that were burnt from the grain offering that provided food for the priests (אַזְכָּרָה).[b] Thus no "token portion" was taken from the grain offering of the priests in Lev 6:12–16 (ET 6:19–23), since all of it was burnt. The designation of the incense accompanying the showbread as its "token portion" in 24:7 is instructive, for it shows that the incense served as a substitute for the bread. In that passage the incense was burnt, while the bread was eaten by the priests.

(b) Lev 2:2, 9, 16; 5:12; 6:8 (ET 6:15); 24:7; Num 5:26

Even though the rite for the grain offering culminated in the incineration of the "token portion" on the altar, the offering's purpose was not fully accomplished by that act. As is shown by 2:3 and 2:10, the Lord established the grain offering to provide most holy food for his priests. The offering therefore ended with the consumption of the bread or grain in a sacred meal. This, as we learn from 6:9–11 (ET 6:16–18), was to be done in a holy place in the courtyard of the tent of meeting. Since it was most holy food, it had to be eaten in God's presence.

Ritual Theological Function

In this offering the Israelites brought some of their foodstuffs to the sanctuary. Some of their grain, flour, or bread—items that made up most of their diet—was handed over to the Lord. Yet unlike the pagan gods, the Lord did not eat this food, nor was he hungry for it; he did not draw nourishment from it. Rather, Israel's God gave the food to his priests to eat (6:10 [ET 6:17]). The priests were the prime beneficiaries from this ritual transaction.

The legislation, however, makes it quite clear that those who brought the offering also benefited from it. Like the personal burnt offering (1:9, 13, 17), the grain offering too was "a gift of a pleasing aroma to the Lord" (2:2, 9). The Israelites brought the firstfruits and first produce from the land as their rent to the Lord, the true owner of the land.[8] A portion of the food that God had given to the people living on his land was returned to him. And he used it to demonstrate his delight in the givers of the offering (2:2, 9). The good relationship, presupposed by the gift, was therefore consolidated and deepened by the giving and receiving of this gift. The aroma from the offering both expressed and increased their mutual delight.

The mention of "the salt of the covenant of your God" in 2:13 added another dimension to God's delight in the people who presented this offering to him. Salt was normally shared with kinsfolk at common meals in the ancient world. It was used to extend and perpetuate the ties and privileges of kinship to guests who were present but were not kinsfolk. Thus the allies of the Per-

8 Joosten, *People and Land in the Holiness Code*, 172–73.

sian king spoke about themselves in Ezra 4:14 as people who had "tasted the salt of the palace." The idiom "the salt of the covenant" seems to be related to the use of the phrase "a covenant of salt" in Num 18:19 and 2 Chr 13:5 for the perpetual privileges of hospitality that the Lord had bestowed on the priests and the royal dynasty of David by his covenant. The salt that was added to the grain offering not only expressed the permanence of the Lord's covenant with its giver, but it may also have symbolized the perpetuation of his delight in that person.

The main function of the grain offering, however, was to provide food for the priests. The offerer did not provide this food directly to the priests as guests at his own household table. Rather, God provided the food for the priests. He himself said of this offering in 6:10: (ET 6:17): "I have given it as their portion." He was their generous host, and they were his guests, who ate the food from his table, the altar. Since this food came from the Lord's altar, it was no longer ordinary bread; it had become "most holy" (2:3, 10; 6:10 [ET 6:17]). Contact with this most holy bread made a person holy (6:11 [ET 6:18]). Those priests who ate it participated in God's own holiness. By eating this bread at the sanctuary, they became holy and were kept holy. By means of the grain offerings, the Lord nourished his priests with food from his table, like a king with his courtiers, and shared his holiness with them.

Fulfillment by Christ

After his resurrection from the dead, Jesus ate and drank with his disciples (Lk 24:41–43; Acts 10:41; cf. Mk 16:14). He broke bread with them and provided food for them (Lk 24:30, 35; Jn 21:13). In fact, just as the presiding priest shared the salt of the people's offerings with God, Luke reports that Jesus "shared salt" with his disciples as a sign of his eternal covenant with them (συναλιζόμενος, Acts 1:4, related to ἅλας, "salt"). Jesus, the great High Priest, joined with his fellow priests—his disciples—in a holy meal.[9]

The early church continued to gather to share in the sacred meal that Jesus had instituted even after he had ascended into heaven and so was no longer visibly present with them. They met weekly on the day of his resurrection (Sunday) to break bread in the Lord's Supper, his holy meal (Acts 2:42, 46; 20:7; 1 Cor 11:20–32). Like the sacred meals eaten by the priests at the temple, this meal is an integral part of the Divine Service. In it Jesus' disciples meet with their risen Lord Jesus and serve with him as priests in the heavenly sanctuary

---

[9] While the context refers specifically to the "apostles" (Acts 1:2), many other disciples were among those who witnessed Jesus' resurrection appearances (e.g., 1 Cor 15:5–8), and the main concern of the text is those appearances. In the immediate context, Christ refers to the upcoming events of Pentecost (Acts 1:4–5), when all of his followers (young and old, male and female) would receive the Spirit (Acts 2). Therefore it would be in keeping with the context if Acts 1:4 implies that before his ascension Jesus shared salt with many of his disciples in addition to his apostles. This would also be consistent with their status as royal priests together with him (e.g., 1 Pet 2:5–10).

(Heb 10:19–22; 13:9–16). The food for this meal comes from a different altar than the altar at the Jerusalem temple (Heb 13:10).

From the beginning of the NT church, the presentation of gifts as a "common offering" to the Lord was part of the Divine Service.[c] As far as we can ascertain, this common contribution to the work of the church included money as well as foodstuffs such as grain, oil, bread, and wine. People brought their offerings forward and laid them at the feet of the apostles and presbyters (Acts 4:35, 37; 5:2). However, since this offering was gathered up from the congregation, it was presented as the church's communal offering to the Lord (Acts 2:44, 45; 4:32).

(c) Acts 2:42; cf. Rom 15:26; 2 Cor 8:4; 9:13; Heb 13:16

Unlike the grain for the OT grain offering, the church's offering was not consecrated by the incineration of a portion of it with some incense on the altar, but by a prayer of thanksgiving (cf. 1 Tim 4:5). That prayer performed the same function as the burning of the token portion for the grain offering. From the early church to the present day, the whole of the offering was placed on or near the communion table, the altar where the bread and wine were consecrated as the body and blood of Jesus. It was brought to God to be consecrated by him.

This holy food apparently was used in two different ways. On the one hand, some of the bread and wine from the offering was consecrated as the body and blood of Christ in Holy Communion. There Jesus was both the host and the bread. He was the true bread of life (Jn 6:35). He shared his most holy body with all the people of God because they were all priests together with him in the heavenly sanctuary. They all ate the same bread from the one loaf (1 Cor 10:10–17; Heb 13:10). They all participated equally in his holiness, for his most holy body made them all holy (Heb 10:10). Through this most holy food Jesus nourished them, so that they could serve with him as holy priests here on earth.

The second use was that the offering provided the livelihood for the pastors of the church, and the rest was distributed to the poor (Acts 2:44–45; 4:32–37).[10] Since the apostles and other ministers were engaged in holy work—the work of God—they were entitled to receive their living from his table. Thus in 1 Cor 9:13–14 Paul argues that, just as the OT priests who officiated at the temple and served at the altar received their food from what was offered on the altar, so those who preached the Gospel should receive their living from the Gospel.

Yet the ministers of the Gospel did not (and still do not today) depend on the charity of the church but on the charity of their Lord. He provided (and provides) for them through his people in this way. Paul himself gave up his right to receive his livelihood from the offerings of the congregations that he served. The only congregation that provided regularly for him was the church at Philippi. When he wrote his letter to thank them for their support of him, he

[10] See also Chytraeus, *On Sacrifice,* 130–31. Cf. Mitchell, *The Song of Songs,* 343.

referred to their gifts as "a sweet aroma, a sacrifice, acceptable and pleasing to God" (Phil 4:18), echoing the words of Lev 2:2, 9. In doing so the apostle treated it as if it were equivalent to a grain offering. It was much more than a generous human gesture. It was a holy gift from God to support him in his holy work. And that applies to all the ministers of the Gospel at all times and in all places.

> Come, risen Lord, and deign to be our guest;
> Nay, let us be Thy guests; the feast is Thine.
> Thyself at Thine own board make manifest
> In Thine own sacrament of bread and wine.
>
> We meet, as in that Upper Room they met.
> Thou at the table, blessing, yet dost stand.
> "This is My body"; so Thou givest yet;
> Faith still receives the cup as from Thy hand.
>
> One body we, one body who partake,
> One Church united in communion blest,
> One name we bear, one bread of life we break,
> With all Thy saints on earth and saints at rest.[11]

[11] From "Come, Risen Lord" (*HS98* 856:1–3). Text: George Wallace Briggs (1875–1959);

Leviticus 3:1–17

Regulations for the Peace Offering

Translation

3 1“If someone’s offering is a sacrifice of a peace offering, if he presents from the herd a male or a female, he shall present one [that is] without blemish before the Lord 2and lay his hand on the head of his offering. He shall slaughter it at the entrance to the tent of meeting. Aaron’s sons, the priests, shall dash the blood against all sides of the altar. 3From the sacrifice of the peace offering he shall then present a gift to the Lord: the fat that covers the entrails and all the fat on the entrails; 4the two kidneys and the fat around them on the sinews; and the caudate lobe on the liver, which he shall remove with the kidneys. 5Aaron’s sons shall turn it into smoke on the altar on top of the burnt offering that is upon the wood that is upon the fire, as a gift of a pleasing aroma to the Lord.

6“And if from the flock his offering for a sacrifice of a peace offering to the Lord is a male or a female, he shall present one without blemish. 7If he presents a sheep as his offering, he shall present it before the Lord 8and lay his hand upon the head of his offering. He shall slaughter it before the tent of meeting, and Aaron’s sons shall dash its blood against all sides of the altar. 9Then he shall present its fat as a gift to the Lord from the sacrifice of the peace offering: the broad tail completely removed from the base of the spine; the fat that covers the entrails and all the fat around the entrails; 10the two kidneys and the fat around them on the sinews; and the caudate lobe of the liver, which he shall remove with the kidneys. 11The priest shall turn it into smoke on the altar as food, a gift to the Lord.

12“And if his offering is a goat, he shall present it before the Lord 13and lay his hand upon its head. He shall slaughter it before the tent of meeting, and Aaron’s sons shall dash its blood against all sides of the altar. 14He shall then present a gift to the Lord as his offering from it the fat that covers the entrails and all the fat around the entrails; 15the two kidneys and the fat around them on the sinews; and the caudate lobe on the liver, which he shall remove with the kidneys. 16The priest shall turn them into smoke on the altar as food, a gift of a pleasing aroma. All fat belongs to the Lord. 17This is a perpetual ritual statute for your generations in all your settlements: you must not eat any fat or any blood.”

Textual Notes

3:1 וְאִם־זֶבַח שְׁלָמִים קָרְבָּנוֹ—This protasis is the general heading for the whole chapter.

The use of “if” (אִם) rather than “when” (כִּי) indicates that the offerings mentioned in this chapter are, like the burnt offerings in 1:3–17, another subclass of the voluntary animal offerings introduced in 1:1–2.

The phrase זֶבַח שְׁלָמִים is composed of two virtually synonymous ritual terms. The noun זֶבַח, a "sacrifice," can be used by itself for any animal that has been sacrificed to provide meat for a sacrificial banquet (7:12, 16, 17; 19:6; 23:37). The noun שְׁלָמִים (the plural of שֶׁלֶם) also can be used by itself to refer to "peace offerings" (6:5 [ET 6:12]; 7:14, 33; 9:4, 22). These two nouns may originally have designated two different classes of sacrifice (according to *HALOT,* s.v. שֶׁלֶם, 6 a δ). However, in Leviticus the only possible difference between them is given in 17:3–9, where זֶבַח could refer to any "sacrifice" at any sanctuary, in contrast to the שְׁלָמִים, which were the "peace offerings" reserved for the tent of meeting (17:5) so that their blood (7:14, 33) and fat (6:5 [ET 6:12]) could be offered on its altar (17:6).

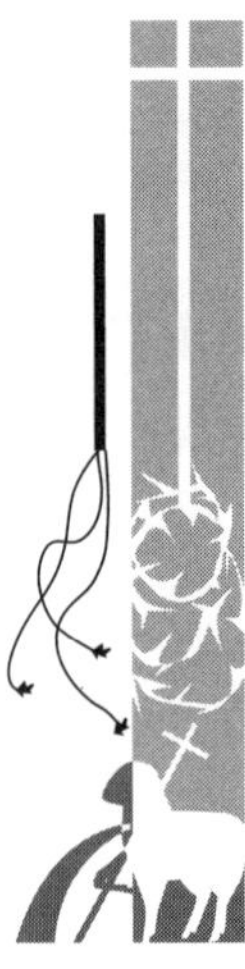

There has been much discussion of how best to render שְׁלָמִים. Three main interpretations have been proposed. We render it "peace offerings" while acknowledging the relevance of other nuances that have been advocated.

First, since this plural noun has traditionally been derived from the frequent Hebrew word for "peace," שָׁלוֹם, it has commonly been understood as the sacrifice of a "peace offering" (*HALOT,* s.v. שֶׁלֶם, 5 b; RSV) or "salvation offering" (*HALOT,* s.v. שֶׁלֶם, 5 b). This sacrifice is to establish or confirm the "peace" between the three parties involved in its enactment: God, who receives the fat; the priest who receives its forequarter; and the people who eat the meat. The saving peace that God bestowed upon his OT people foreshadowed the sacrifice of Jesus Christ and his gift of peace. The LXX normally translates זֶבַח (הַ)שְּׁלָמִים as θυσία(ς) (τοῦ) σωτηρίου, "sacrifice(s) of salvation" (e.g., Lev 3:1, 3, 6, 9). Usually the LXX renders שְׁלָמִים by itself as σωτήριον or the plural σωτήρια, "saving thing(s)" (e.g., Ex 20:24; Lev 6:5; 7:33; 9:22). Cf. *HALOT,* s.v. שֶׁלֶם, 5 a.

Second, since שְׁלָמִים may be related to the Hebrew adjective שָׁלֵם, which can mean "intact, complete, perfect, whole, healthy, harmonious," it may denote "a sacrifice for well-being" (NRSV) that promotes the well-being of its giver. Third, since it is part of a communal meal in God's presence, it has also been taken as a "fellowship offering" (NIV) or "community offering" (*HALOT,* s.v. שֶׁלֶם, 5 b β), an offering that promotes communal harmony and solidarity.

The phrase זֶבַח (הַ)שְּׁלָמִים recurs in 3:3, 6, 9; 4:10, 26, 31, 35; 7:11, 13, 15, 18, 20, 21, 29, 32, 34, 37; 9:18; 10:14; 17:5; 19:5; 22:21; 23:19.

תָּמִים—See the textual note on this adjective in 1:3. It recurs in 3:6, 9.

יַקְרִיבֶנּוּ—See the textual note on this verb in 1:2. It recurs in 3:3, 6, 7, 9, 12, 14.

3:2 וְסָמַךְ יָדוֹ עַל־רֹאשׁ קָרְבָּנוֹ—See the textual note on the similar clause in 1:4. Similar clauses recur in 3:8, 13.

וּשְׁחָטוֹ—See the textual note on this verb in 1:5. It recurs in 3:8, 13.

פֶּתַח אֹהֶל מוֹעֵד—See the textual note on this phrase in 1:3.

וְזָרְקוּ—See the textual note on this verb in 1:5. It recurs in 3:8, 13.

הַמִּזְבֵּחַ—See 3:5, 8, 11, 13, 16 and the textual notes on 1:5.

3:3 וְהִקְרִיב—The LXX translates this in the plural (προσάξουσιν), which may imply that the priests brought the fat to the altar. However, there is no reason to depart from the MT, which implies that the offerer is the one to bring forward the fat.

הַחֵלֶב—The "fat" is the technical term for the deposits of fat that cover the kidneys, liver, and intestines in the abdomen of the animal. (It does not refer to the fat on or in its meat.) The term recurs in 3:4, 9, 10, 14, 15, 16, 17. These deposits were held to be the choice food from the animal. The fat from an animal had special religious significance. Many pagan religions believed that just as the "life" of an animal was found in its blood, its spiritual power and strength lay in its fat. Those who ate these parts supposedly gained supernatural power by eating the fat from animals that had been sacrificed to a deity.[1]

Therefore the Lord proscribed that pagan practice. All the fat from all animals belonged exclusively to him (3:16). The Israelites were forbidden to eat it (3:17; 7:23–24). Anyone who ate the fat from an animal was cut off from his kinsfolk (7:25). Instead, the priests were to "offer" the fat to the Lord (3:3–4, 9–10; 6:5 [ET 6:12]; 7:3–4, 25, 33) and "turn it into smoke" on the altar (3:5, 11, 16; 4:10, 19, 26, 31, 35; 6:5 [ET 6:12]; 7:5, 31; 8:16; 9:10, 20; 17:6). The fire therefore "ate" the fat from peace offerings, the sin offerings, and the reparation offerings (9:24).

הַֽמְכַסֶּה אֶת־הַקֶּרֶב—In this phrase קֶרֶב refers to the bowel with the intestines attached to it. This phrase therefore distinguishes the network of fat covering the entrails from the deposits of fat elsewhere.

3:4 שְׁתֵּי הַכְּלָיֹת—"The two kidneys" were completely encased in fat.

אֲשֶׁר עַל־הַכְּסָלִים—The common translation of כְּסָלִים as "loins" is misleading since the kidneys are not located on the loins but in the lower ribcage. The use of cognates to this noun in other Semitic languages show that כְּסָלִים refers to the sinews or muscles close to the backbone of the animal.[2]

וְאֶת־הַיֹּתֶרֶת עַל־הַכָּבֵד—The noun יֹתֶרֶת (in form the Qal feminine singular participle of יָתַר) denotes "the **appendage of liver,** found with cow, sheep, or goat, but not with humans: *Lobus caudatus*" (*HALOT*). The caudate lobe of the liver protrudes from the liver like a finger and is located near the right kidney. In the ancient pagan world, this lobe was commonly used for augury and divination (hepatoscopy), hence it was "important when examining the liver" (*HALOT*).

עַל־הַכְּלָיוֹת יְסִירֶנָּה׃—This instruction is included because the lobe cannot easily be peeled from the liver, but must be cut off with a knife.

3:5 וְהִקְטִירוּ—See the textual note on this verb in 1:9. It recurs in 3:11, 16.

הָעֹלָה—See 6:5 (ET 6:12); 8:28. This refers to the daily burnt offering that was always placed first on the altar, before the other sacrifices were laid out upon it.

אִשֵּׁה—See the textual note on this noun (the construct of אִשֶּׁה) in 1:9. In this chapter, it occurs also in 3:3, 9, 11, 14, 16.

רֵיחַ נִיחֹחַ לַיהוָה׃—See the textual note on this phrase in 1:9. "A pleasing aroma" recurs in 3:16.

3:6 This is a general introduction for both 3:7–11 and 3:12–16.

---

1 Heller, "Die Symbolik des Fettes im AT," 107.

2 Levine, *Leviticus*, 16.

3:9 תְּמִימָה—This feminine form of the adjective תָּמִים (see 1:3; 3:1) here functions as an adverb, "completely."

3:11 לֶחֶם—The Hebrew word לֶחֶם usually means "bread," but here and in 3:16 it refers to the "meat" or "food" from the sacrificed animal.

3:16 וְהִקְטִירָם—As in 4:10, 35, the plural suffix (ָם-) refers to all the fat parts. The singular suffix in 3:5, 11 treats all of them collectively.

אִשֶּׁה לְרֵיחַ נִיחֹחַ כָּל־חֵלֶב לַיהוָה׃—This is like the regular formula for divine pleasure, "a gift of a pleasing aroma to the Lord" (אִשֶּׁה לְרֵיחַ נִיחֹחַ לַיהוָה). For the regular formula, see 1:9 and the explanation in "Leviticus 1–3." However, here the phrase "all fat" is included. The syntax indicated by Masoretic accents forms a separate phrase and clause: "… a gift of a pleasing aroma. All fat belongs to the Lord."

3:17 חֻקַּת עוֹלָם לְדֹרֹתֵיכֶם—The noun חֻקָּה comes from the root חקק, which means "carve, inscribe, incise in stone." It may reflect the ancient custom of inscribing laws in stone for their perpetual observance. In Leviticus חֻקָּה is the term for a divine decree that prescribes some ritual practice (7:36; 10:9; 16:29, 31, 34; 17:7; 23:14, 21, 31, 41; 24:3). In Leviticus it is clearly distinguished from חֹק, the term for the "due" or "stipend" of a priest which came from the offerings of the people (6:11, 15 [ET 6:18, 22]; 7:34; 10:13, 14, 15; 24:9).

See 10:9; 17:7; 23:14, 21, 31, 41; 24:3 for other perpetual ritual statutes.

בְּכֹל מוֹשְׁבֹתֵיכֶם—See 7:26. This commandment belongs to those ritual requirements that are to be observed by the common people in their homes (3:17; 23:3, 14, 21, 31).

חֵלֶב—See 7:23, 25. Like the blood, the fat belonged exclusively to the Lord (Ezek 44:7).

וְכָל־דָּם לֹא תֹאכֵלוּ׃—This prohibition against eating blood means that the blood must be properly drained from the animal after it is slaughtered so that the blood would not be eaten together with the meat. The same basic prohibition is expressed with similar wordings in 7:26, 27; 17:10, 14; Deut 12:16, 23, 24, 25.

Commentary

Structure

In Hebrew this chapter consists of a single sentence in 3:1–16a with an appositional conclusion in 3:16b–17. It gives a series of ritual case laws that are organized according to the various animals used for the peace offering. After a general heading that identifies the subject matter as "a sacrifice of a peace offering" (3:1a), the legislation distinguishes the cattle of the herd in 3:1b–5 from animals of the flock in 3:6–16a. After the subheading in 3:6, the second section distinguishes still further between the sheep in 3:6–11 and the goats in 3:12–16a. The unit is rounded off by a conclusion in 3:16b–17 dealing with the reservation of fat and blood for the Lord. Three differences are evident in the legislation for these three classes of animals: the mention of all the priests rather than only the officiating priest in 3:5; the addition of the reference to the sheep's tail in 3:9; and the insertion of "all fat" before "to the Lord" to create a new sentence in 3:16b.

The structure of this pericope can be outlined as follows:

I. The first case: sacrifice of cattle as peace offerings (3:1–5)
  A. Choice of cattle (3:1a)
  B. The ritual procedure (3:1b–5)
    1. Presentation of the animal before the Lord (3:1b)
    2. Placement of offerer's hand on its head (3:2a)
    3. Slaughter at the entrance to the tent of meeting (3:2b)
    4. Dashing of blood by the priests (3:2c)
    5. Presentation of fat portions (3:3–4)
    6. Their incineration as a pleasing gift to the Lord (3:5)
II. The second case: sacrifice of sheep and goats as peace offerings (3:6–16a)
  A. Choice of sheep and goats (3:6)
  B. The procedure for them (3:7–16a)
    1. Sheep (3:7–11)
      a. Choice of a sheep (3:7a)
      b. The ritual procedure (3:7b–11)
        i. Presentation of the sheep before the Lord (3:7b)
        ii. Placement of offerer's hand on its head (3:8a)
        iii. Its slaughter at the entrance to the tent of meeting (3:8b)
        iv. Dashing of its blood on the altar (3:8c)
        v. Presentation of its fat portions (3:9–10)
        vi. Their incineration as a pleasing gift to the Lord (3:11)
    2. Goats (3:12–16a)
      a. Choice of a goat (3:12a)
      b. The ritual procedure (3:12b–16a)
        i. Presentation of the goat before the Lord (3:12b)
        ii. Placement of offerer's hand on its head (3:13a)
        iii. Its slaughter at the entrance to the tent of meeting (3:13b)
        iv. Splashing of its blood on the altar (3:13c)
        v. Presentation of its fat portions (3:14–15)
        vi. Their incineration as a pleasing gift to the Lord (3:16a)
III. Conclusion (3:16b–17)
  A. Reservation of fat for the Lord (3:16b)
  B. Prohibition of the consumption of fat and blood (3:17)

Ritual Agents

The regulations in this chapter outline the ritual for the peace offerings from the perspective of the lay Israelite. They address the owners of livestock, who depended on them for their livelihood. Farmers who relied on agriculture for their living were therefore not in a position to present this offering. The offerers selected animals from their herd or flock and brought them to the sanctuary. They came together with the members of their families and other invited guests. Even though these guests were not mentioned in the legislation because they were not directly involved in the ritual, they joined with the givers of the offering in eating the meat from the sacrificed animal (Deut 12:7, 17–18). They played an important part in the celebration because one person could not eat all the meat provided by the sacrificed animals in the prescribed period.

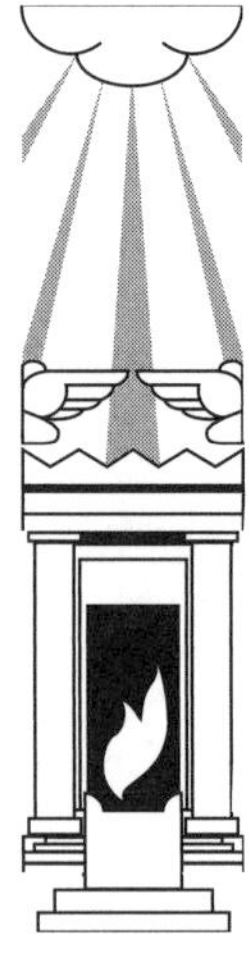

The priests played a vital part in the ritual transaction of the sacrifice. As in the case with the voluntary burnt offering and voluntary grain offering, the officiating priest is distinguished from his assistants. While his assistants dashed the blood from the animal against the altar (3:2, 8, 13), the officiating priest normally burned the fat parts of the animal on the altar (3:11, 16). In the case of a cow or a bull, additional help was required from at least one other priest (3:5). The task of the priests was to splash the blood and burn the fat on the altar (7:33; 17:6). They too were beneficiaries from this sacrifice. The breast of the animal was shared out among the priests on duty; its thigh was eaten by the officiant (7:32–34).

The third party to this ritual transaction was the Lord. He regulated the sacrifice so that it was performed correctly in his presence at the sanctuary. It could be offered nowhere else nor to any other deity (17:1–7). The animal for the sacrifice was presented "before the Lord" (3:1, 7, 12). The fat parts of the animal were "a gift to the Lord" (3:3, 5, 9, 11, 14). They belonged exclusively to him (3:16–17) and were to be used to produce a pleasing aroma for him (3:5, 11, 16).

Ritual Material

The raw material for these sacrifices was taken from the three main classes of edible animals: cattle, sheep, and goats. Their owner selected them from his own herd (3:3) or flock (3:6). They were, most commonly, the firstlings, the firstborn male animals (27:26; Deut 15:19–20). Since these domestic animals were part of a man's household they were closely associated with him and his family. Unlike the voluntary burnt offerings (1:3, 10), the animal could be either male or female (3:1, 6). But it still had to be a perfect specimen (3:1, 6), as prescribed in 22:18–25.

These animals produced three important materials for the ritual transaction. First, their blood was drained off completely for use in the rite of atonement. The Israelites were not allowed to eat blood (3:17), meaning that they could not eat the meat of an animal that still had its blood in it (7:26–27; 17:10–14). The blood was reserved exclusively for their atonement (17:11).

Second, the distinctive feature of the ritual for the peace offering was the removal of the fat from it for its incineration on the altar.[3] The importance of this can be gauged by the exact prescriptions for the fat's excision from the animal and its presentation. In fact, more than half the legislation is devoted to this part of the enactment. The fat from the cattle and the goats came from the intestines, the stomach, and the kidneys. It included the kidneys themselves and the lobe from the liver (3:3–4, 9–10). In the case of a sheep for the peace offering, the tail with its fat was also added. The inclusion of the kidneys and the liver lobe is at first sight puzzling. The kidneys were most likely included because they were regarded as the essence of the animal. The liver lobe, however, was burnt together

---

[3] Eberhart, "Beobachtungen zum Verbrennungsritus bei Schlachtopfer und Gemeinschafts-Schlachtopfer," 93–96.

with these other parts to prevent its use for divination (hepatoscopy) as elsewhere in the ancient world. Since it was removed from the liver at the slaughter of the animal and burnt by the priests on the altar, it could not be used, in violation of God's law, to attempt to foretell the future (19:26; Deut 18:10).

No reason is given for the reservation of the fat from the peace offerings for the Lord. Instead, we have a positive assertion that all the fat of an animal belongs to God followed by a prohibition of its consumption by the Israelites (3:16b–17; cf. 7:22–25). The gravity of this prohibition may be gauged from its designation as a perpetual ritual statute for all times and places (3:17). In a society where people rarely ate meat, fat was associated metaphorically with what was best and most nourishing in foodstuff, such as the produce of the land (Gen 45:18) or wheat (Deut 32:14) or grain and olive oil and wine (Num 18:12). Just as the choice parts of an animal were reserved for an honored guest, so these parts were reserved for God as the host of this sacred banquet. These fatty parts were therefore regarded as gifts of "food" for him (Lev 3:11, 16). The Israelites were also forbidden to eat the fat from any animal to distinguish them from their pagan neighbors. Just as people with animist beliefs held that the life of an animal lay in its blood (17:11, 14), so they thought that its strength and power resided in its fat. They ate the fat from animals that had been sacrificed so that they could gain spiritual power for themselves.[4] The Lord therefore proscribed this pagan practice because he gave his blessing to the Israelites by his acceptance of them and his personal interaction with them in the divine service.

The third ritual material produced by this offering was the meat that was divided between the offerer and the priests. This part of the ritual, however, is not mentioned in these regulations since that is covered later in 7:15–36. This meat was regarded as a holy thing (19:8), something sacred that could only be eaten by a ritually clean person (7:19b–21).

Ritual Location

The enactment of the rite for the presentation of the peace offerings was spread over four locations, though the first and fourth may have been the same: (1) the home of the offerer, (2) the entrance to the tent of meeting, (3) the altar for burnt offering, and (4) the place for the meal, which may have been in the home of the offerer.

Its enactment began at the home of the Israelite with the removal of the animal from the herd or the flock. Its owner presented the animal to the Lord at the sanctuary (3:1, 7, 12) and slaughtered it there somewhere in the courtyard, between its eastern entrance and the altar for burnt offering (3:2, 8, 13). Then the most important parts of the ritual were enacted at the altar for burnt offering. After the blood and the fat of the animal had been separated from its flesh, they were offered on the altar. Finally, as the prohibition in 3:17 of eating blood and fat shows, the flesh of the animal was eaten by those who had brought the offering. The legislation does not specify whether this occurred at the sanctuary or in the

---

4 Heller, "Die Symbolik des Fettes im AT," 107.

offerer's home. That would be determined by the location of the home and its distance from the sanctuary. The mention of the Israelite settlements in 3:17 indicates that the meal usually occurred in the places that they resided. Two other pieces of evidence argue for this. First, in 7:11–18 and 19:5–6 permission was given for the leftover meat from (some kinds of) the peace offering to be eaten on the day after it had been presented at the tabernacle. This meant that those who presented it would have had to take it away with them to their places of residence, where they would have eaten it on the following day. However, the meat from the thank offering was most likely eaten at the sanctuary on the day that it was presented (7:15). Second, the meat from the peace offerings that belonged to the priests could be eaten in their homes by any members of their families that were ritually clean (Num 18:11). By analogy this rule would extend to the laity also.

The location of these acts was significant for this sacrifice. A clean animal was brought from the household of the Israelite to the sanctuary for its flesh to be consecrated there. Then this consecrated flesh was brought back from the sacred domain to the household. See the following diagram. The flesh therefore bridged these two domains and connected them with each other in a tangible, physical way.

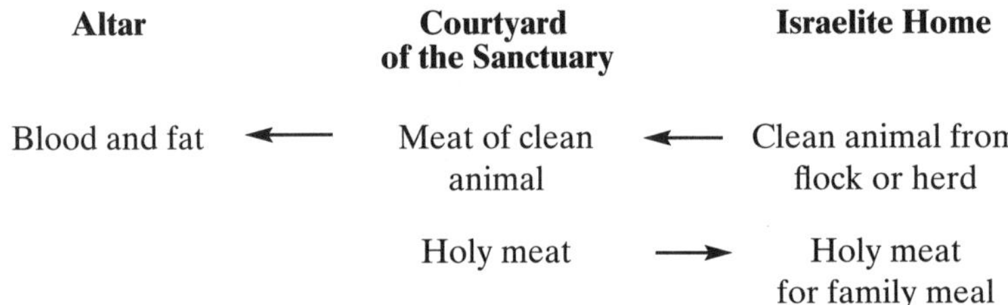

Ritual Time

Since peace offerings were voluntary sacrifices, no particular occasion was prescribed for their presentation. They were therefore most likely offered at the three annual pilgrim festivals: Passover, Pentecost, and Booths. The order of the legislation in Leviticus 1–3 shows that the peace offering was presented at the sanctuary after the voluntary burnt offering and grain offering (2 Chr 29:31c–35a). The legislation in Lev 3:5 prescribes that it had to be placed "on top of the burnt offering." If, as seems most likely, this refers to the morning sacrifice, this would have occurred around midday. This sacrifice was therefore associated with the public burnt offering and incorporated into it, since the daily burnt offering was the foundational sacrifice that provided the ritual framework for all the other sacrifices.

Since this sacrifice was meant to provide meat for consumption in a sacred banquet, the time for its consumption was regulated in 7:15–18. If it was offered as a thank offering, it had to be eaten on the day that it was presented, but if it was a votive or freewill offering, it could also be eaten on the following day.

Ritual Enactment

The peace offering was not included in the regular public sacrificial rite performed at the sanctuary each morning and evening. It was, rather, a pastoral rite ancillary to it, a rite that incorporated the Israelite families, with their own concerns and needs, into the public liturgy of the nation and so gave them a personal stake in it. A public peace offering was prescribed by the law only for the Feast of Pentecost, when two lambs were presented together with two loaves as the firstfruits of the harvest (23:19–20). Apart from that, the peace offering was a voluntary sacrifice. It was offered by Israelite families rather than by the nation as a whole, even when it was brought by a national figure such as a king who invited the whole nation as guests of the royal family on an important occasion (2 Sam 6:18, 19; 1 Ki 8:62–64). The initiative for this sacrifice therefore came from the lay people. They were its chief beneficiaries.

While the grain offering was, in all likelihood, the offering that was brought most frequently by the Israelites, the peace offering may have been the most popular sacrifice because it provided meat for a festive meal. Since animals were, by and large, too valuable to be eaten by ordinary people as part of their regular diet, they were usually eaten only on high holy days and other special occasions. In fact, firstborn male animals and all tithed animals could only be eaten after presentation at the sanctuary.[a] The meat from the peace offerings probably was a chief source of food for the sacred meals eaten at the three pilgrim festivals.

(a) Lev 27:32; Deut 12:6, 7, 17, 18; 14:23; 15:19, 20

The legislation for the peace offering institutes six separate ritual acts. These acts diverge slightly and yet quite significantly from the procedure for the burnt offering as is shown in the following table.

Ritual Acts	*Burnt Offering*	*Peace Offering*
Presentation	Yes	Yes
Laying on of hand	Yes	Yes
Slaughter	Yes	Yes
Dashing of blood	Yes	Yes
Presentation of fat	No	Yes
Incineration on altar	Whole animal	Fat, kidneys, lobe of liver

As is the case with the voluntary burnt offering, the ceremony proceeded in three stages. In the first stage, the lay Israelite presented the animal before the Lord at the sanctuary and placed his right hand on its head so that it was accepted as a peace offering on his behalf. The second stage involved the slaughter of the animal by the Israelite and the ritual disposal of the blood by the priests. They dashed the blood against the four sides of the altar in the rite of atonement. Up to this point, the procedure was the same as for the burnt offering.

But in the third stage, the peace offering diverged from the burnt offering in two ways. First, the offerer approached the altar with the fatty parts together with the kidneys and the liver lobe. The legislation from 7:29–30 fills in the details of the presentation. The offerer brought the "fat" on the brisket of the animal, in his own hands, to the priest. (The presentation of the fat was not part of the burnt offering.) Second, the ritual enactment culminated in the incineration of the fat (along with the kidneys and lobe of the liver) by the priest on the altar. He burned it up on the remains of the daily burnt offering so that they formed a single column of sweet-smelling smoke. (In the burnt offering the entire animal was incinerated.)

The ritual legislation for the peace offering does not explicitly describe the provision of meat for the sacred meal, but merely alludes to it. It prescribes what needs to be done so that the sacrifice is acceptable to God. Only then could the meal proceed. The emphasis is placed on the disposal of blood and the smoking up of the "fat" on the altar rather than the consumption of the sacred meal. The rite culminated in the transformation of the fat (with the kidneys and lobe of the liver) into smoke by incineration on the altar. The fire "ate" the fat, not the people (9:24). This part of the ritual is highlighted by the prescription in 3:15 of the procedure for the placement of the "fat" on the altar. The "fat" was to be set out on the daily burnt offering on the wood on the fire. The holy fire turned the "fat," like the memorial portion of the grain offering, into a cloud of smoke. The fire that came from God's presence (9:24) therefore brought the offering as smoke into the divine domain.

Like the burnt offering and the grain offering, the rite for the peace offering probably concluded with the declaration by the priest that the sacrifice was a gift that was acceptable to the Lord and pleasing to him (3:5, 11, 16). In the case of the peace offering, this gift was specifically designated as "food" (3:11, 16).

Ritual Theological Function

Pagan people used to bring two kinds of animal sacrifices to their gods. On the one hand, the cooked meat from choice animals was set out by their priests, together with other food, before the statues of the gods for their daily sustenance (Deut 32:38). After the gods had taken the spiritual essence from this food, the priests ate what was left over. On the other hand, ordinary people participated in the sacred banquets held at the temples of their gods. There they ate the sacred meat from the animals that had been dedicated to their gods.

St. Paul's discussion about the eating of meat offered to idols shows how temples functioned as abattoirs and restaurants for the devotees of the temple's deities into the NT era (1 Corinthians 8–10).[5] Of course, Christians are to refrain from participating in any of the pagan worship practices. In addition, it is necessary for Christians to refrain from any actions that, even if not directly idolatrous, cause offense to others. An example would be eating meat that had been sacrificed to an idol if others, viewing the meal, might conclude that the Christian was in some way affirming, acquiescing, or indifferent to idolatry since the sacrificed meat had been part of the pagan rite.

God's legislation for the peace offerings created a new kind of sacrifice that accomplished what the pagan sacrifices with their meals vainly aspired to attain. God's legislation (like that in 1 Corinthians 8–10) also protected his people and their witness to unbelievers by preventing them from engaging in customary pagan practices that incurred his wrath.

---

[5] See the commentary on those chapters by Lockwood, *1 Corinthians,* 271–355, especially pages 271–78.

The sacrifice of the peace offering created a sacred meal. The ritual for the preparation of the meat for that meal concentrated on the disposal of the blood from the animal and the incineration of its fat together with its kidneys and the liver lobe as an offering to the Lord. Both those practices (the disposal of blood and the incineration of fat, kidneys, and liver lobe) counteracted two common pagan ritual acts. Since the life of an animal was contained in its blood (17:11), in pagan rites the blood was commonly eaten together with the meat to gain the life-power of the animal, its spirit, its liveliness and vitality. But the legislation for the disposal of the blood from the peace offerings removed all the blood from human use.

The incineration of fat on the altar removed it too from human consumption. Since the fat was commonly regarded as the most nutritious part of the animal, some pagans offered it as food to their gods (Deut 32:38). To be sure, the legislation in this chapter still called the fat "bread" or "food" (Lev 3:11, 16). But in an act of ritual reversal, God did not institute it as food that was to be cooked and set out before him for his nourishment. Instead, it was to be ritually destroyed by its incineration on the altar. There it was turned into sweet-smelling smoke. The fat therefore did not provide food for the Lord to eat; it produced a sweet aroma for his enjoyment (3:5, 14; cf. 8:28; 17:6). That aroma assured the offerers that he was graciously disposed to them.

The reason for this strange ritual reversal is that the Lord, as he himself declares in Ps 50:8–13, does not need to have food provided for him. All creation belongs to him. The Creator needs no physical or spiritual sustenance from his creation or creatures. Instead, in his love he established a holy meal for his people by the institution of the peace offerings. He was their divine host at this meal; the Israelites were his honored guests. In it he provided holy meat for them (19:8; Jer 11:15). He, however, did not eat with them; they ate this meal in his presence. God himself provided this meal—a festive meal that was not necessary for his nourishment or the survival of his people, a joyful meal that celebrated the generous, royal patronage of God for his people and his lavish provision for them. The Israelites who were his guests enjoyed his divine hospitality. As his guests, they came under his care and protection. Admission to his meal meant admission to his peace and protection.

This accent on God's gracious benefaction is even more evident by the division of the peace offerings into classes according to their three main uses in 7:12–18. The peace offering could be presented as a "thank offering" together with a psalm of thanksgiving (7:12–15). In it the offerers thanked the Lord for answering their petition to him for deliverance from death. The peace offering could also be presented as a "votive offering" to the Lord in fulfillment of a vow (7:16; 27:9, 10) or as a "freewill offering" in gratitude to the Lord for the blessings received from him (7:16; Deut 16:10). In each case, the sacrifice presupposed and acknowledged God's grace and benefaction.

The rite for the presentation of the peace offerings was theologically significant in two ways. By the disposal of the blood in the rite of atonement, the

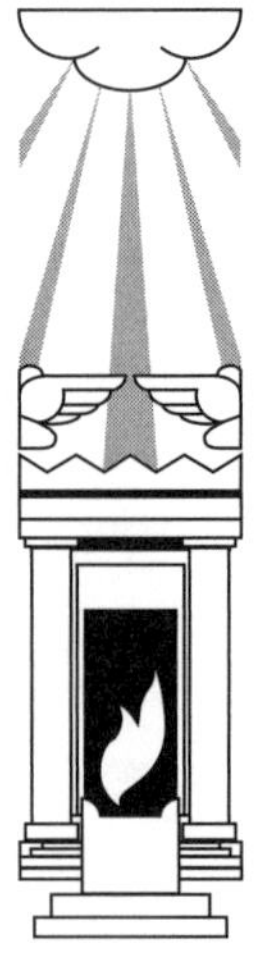

Israelites who brought this sacrifice were cleansed from ordinary ritual impurity that would otherwise have led to God's rejection of their sacrifice and of them with it. They were therefore qualified to approach the altar unafraid; they could eat the holy meat from the sacrificed animal, free from the dread of any infringement upon God's holiness. By the smoke from the fat of their offering and the declaration of its acceptance by the priest, God welcomed them as his favored guests and showed his delight in them (3:5, 16). The same God who had originally provided this animal and their whole livelihood gave them holy meat to eat in his presence so that they could "rejoice" before him (Deut 16:10, 11) and be "altogether joyful" (Deut 16:15). Best of all, as indicated by the name given to this sacrifice, he gave them the gift of "peace" through the meal—the forgiveness of sins, wellbeing, harmony, life, and salvation.

If we wish to gain a full appreciation of the theological significance of the peace offerings, we need to set them in the larger context of the ritual legislation found in Ex 23:17. This is amplified in Ex 34:23, 24 and Deut 16:16, 17. Like vassals with their overlord and royal officials with their king, the heads of each Israelite household were summoned by God to appear before him three times a year at his temple palace for audience with him. The Lord was the "owner" of their land. They, his royal servants, were dependent on him and accountable to him. The offerings brought to him were their rent for their use of his land. Their audience with him consisted of a meal held in his presence. They were his royal guests who had the honor of eating at his table together with his courtiers, the priests. By means of this meal, God acknowledged their status and reaffirmed their privileged position. He accepted their offerings, received their petitions, and blessed them.

The holy meal in which the holy meat from the peace offering was eaten united the Israelites as a holy people with their holy God; it confirmed their right to live on his land; it empowered them with his blessing to serve him as his royal priestly servants in their daily work on his land. The God of Israel, the land of Israel, and the people of Israel were all integrated harmoniously and productively by means of this pivotal sacrifice.

Fulfillment by Christ

The peace offerings that the Israelites brought to the sanctuary provided meat for their sacred meals at the three great festivals God had appointed for each year. Since the blood had been drained away and dashed against the altar and the fat had been offered to God and burned on the altar, the rest of the meat from the animal was holy. God gave this holy meat back to his guests to eat. Like the servants of a king in the ancient world, they ate the meat that came from his table, the meat from the altar. They ate and drank in his presence (cf. Ex 24:11; 1 Chr 29:22).

The scope of the banquet that the Lord had provided for them was extended in two remarkable prophecies in the OT. In Is 25:6–8 we have a promise that in the age to come the Lord would host a meal on Mount Zion that he had prepared for the benefit of all the nations of the world. This banquet would celebrate the death of death. In it God would provide the best of wine. Moreover, he would no longer reserve the fat for himself alone, but would set out a feast of שְׁמָנִים, "fat things" (KJV, RSV), for his guests.

In Ps 22:26–32 (ET 22:25–31), we have a similar scenario. In this case the messianic King whose hands and feet had been pierced (Ps 22:17 [ET 22:16]) would be the host of a great eucharistic banquet to celebrate his resurrection from death and victory over the powers of darkness. This eschatological banquet which transcends time and space would provide a feast for the poor as well as the rich. In it people from all the ends of the earth would return to the Lord and acknowledge him as their King (Ps 22:28–29 [ET 22:27–28]).

Jesus is God's peace offering to and for the world. Thus when Simeon held the baby Jesus in his hands, he thanked God because he had seen God's σωτήριον, his peace offering that provides salvation for both Jews and Gentiles (Lk 2:30).[6] Jesus, the Savior of the world, instituted his Holy Supper as the great banquet for both Jews and Gentiles based on his sacrifice.[7] In it baptized believers in Christ celebrate their deliverance from death as a foretaste of the eternal banquet that shall take place after their Lord's return and their resurrection from the dead. In it Christ is both the host and the food. As their host he furnishes the broken bread and feeds his disciples with holy food (Mt 26:26; Lk 24:30). It is his meal, his banquet (1 Cor 11:20). There they eat at his table (1 Cor 10:21).

He is also the food that all communicants receive and eat. In this meal he gives his sacrificed body to eat and his blood to drink. Unworthy communicants who do not discern that real presence still eat his body and drink his blood, but to their condemnation (1 Cor 11:27–34). Those who commune worthily believe that Christ, who gives them his broken body and shed blood, is their peace, their peace offering (Eph 2:14). He gives them his peace (Jn 14:27). Just as all the Israelites who brought their peace offerings to the altar were guests at the Lord's table, so all Christians who eat his body and drink his blood in the Lord's Supper are united in holy communion with him and with each other by eating this communal food (1 Cor 10:14–22). There he gives them his lifegiving flesh for their nourishment (Jn 6:54). It is real food (Jn 6:55), a communion in his body (1 Cor 10:16).

The blood of the peace offerings was dashed against the altar in the rite of atonement. It was reserved exclusively for that purpose. The Israelites were strictly forbidden to drink the lifeblood from the sacrificed animals.

Jesus, in a remarkable reversal, gives his blood with the wine for his disciples to drink (Mt 26:27–28). The Lord's Supper is therefore the ultimate and definitive peace offering—not a new or ongoing sacrifice, but the Meal in which the communicant receives the offering provided by God the Father through the

---

6 The textual notes on Lev 3:1 pointed out that the LXX translations of שְׁלָמִים usually include σωτήριον.

7 Kleinig, "The Lord's Supper as a Sacrificial Banquet."

(b) See Rom 1:7; 1 Cor 1:3; 2 Cor 1:2; Gal 1:3; Eph 1:2; Phil 1:2; Col 1:2; 1 Thess 1:1; 2 Thess 1:2; 1 Tim 1:2; 2 Tim 1:2; Titus 1:4; Philemon 3; 1 Pet 1:2; 2 Pet 1:2; Jude 2; Rev 1:4

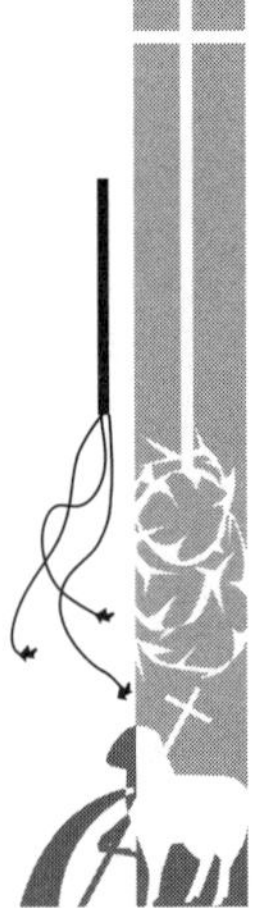

(c) Rom 15:33; Gal 6:16; Eph 6:23; 2 Thess 3:16; 1 Pet 5:14; 3 Jn 15 (some ET 14); cf. 2 Cor 13:11; Phil 4:7, 9

once-for-all sacrifice of his Son. In it Jesus comes and preaches peace to us (Eph 2:17). Through Jesus we have access to the Father's grace and peace (Rom 5:1–2). Through the body and blood of Jesus, we have peace with God the Father and with each other (Eph 2:11–18). In Holy Communion we receive the gift of peace through the body and blood of Jesus, by which God has reconciled all things to himself (Eph 2:16; Col 1:19–20).

Even though the NT does not explicitly declare that Jesus is our peace offering, it does so indirectly. The clearest evidence for this is the liturgical formulae found at the beginning and end of most epistles. These formulae show us that these letters were meant to be read in the place of the regular sermon in the Divine Service. The apostolic greeting at the beginning of these letters usually is "grace to you and peace …"[b] That greeting of peace shows that the apostles and their successors in the apostolic ministry proclaimed the gift of God's peace to the faithful in the Divine Service. Likewise, a greeting for the bestowal of peace comes at the end of many letters.[c] The closing greeting of peace may indicate that the intercessions and the Lord's Supper came after the sermon and brought God's peace to the assembled congregation.

The traditional Western liturgy for the Lord's Supper quite explicitly confesses Jesus as our peace offering in the Pax and the Agnus Dei. Before we eat this holy Meal the pastor speaks Christ's words of peace to us: "The peace of the Lord be with you always." We ask: "O Christ, the Lamb of God, who takes away the sin of the world, grant us your peace"[8] and then receive it from him through his body and blood. And we take that peace home with us as we leave his house and go about our daily service.

Here would I feed upon the bread of God,
    Here drink with you the royal wine of heav'n;
Here would I lay aside each earthly load,
    Here taste afresh the calm of sin forgiv'n.

This is the hour of banquet and of song;
    Here is the heav'nly table spread anew;
Here let me feast and, feasting, still prolong
    The brief bright hour of fellowship with you.

Feast after feast thus comes and passes by,
Yet, passing, points to that glad feast above,
Giving sweet foretaste of the festal joy,
The Lamb's great marriage feast of bliss and love.[9]

---

[8] *LW,* p. 151.

[9] From "Here, O My Lord, I See You Face to Face" by Horatius Bonar (*LW* 243:2, 3, 7).

Leviticus 4:1–5:13

Regulations for the Sin Offering

Translation

4 [1]The Lord spoke to Moses: [2]"Speak to the Israelites: When a person sins unintentionally in regard to any of the Lord's prohibitions, which should not be done, and does one of them, [3]if it is the anointed priest who sins, bringing guilt on the people, he shall present for the sin that he has committed a domesticated bull without blemish as a sin offering to the Lord. [4]He shall bring the bull to the entrance to the tent of meeting, before the Lord, and lay his hand on the head of the bull. Then he shall slaughter the bull before the Lord. [5]The anointed priest shall take some of the blood from the bull and bring it into the tent of meeting. [6]The priest shall dip his finger in the blood and sprinkle some of the blood seven times before the Lord against the curtain of the Holy Place. [7]The priest shall put some of the blood on the horns of the altar for fragrant incense that is in the tent of meeting, before the Lord; and all [the rest of] the bull's blood he shall pour out at the base of the altar of burnt offering, which is at the entrance to the tent of meeting. [8]He shall reserve all the fat from the bull of the sin offering: the fat that covers the entrails and all the fat that is around the entrails; [9]the two kidneys with the fat that is around them on the sinews; and the caudate lobe on the liver which he shall remove together with the kidneys, [10]just as it is reserved from the head of cattle for the sacrifice of the peace offering. Then the priest shall turn them into smoke on the altar of burnt offering. [11]But the skin of the bull and all its meat, together with its head and its lower legs, its entrails and its dung— [12]all [the rest of] the bull—he shall carry out to a clean place outside the camp, to the ash dump, and burn it with wood in fire; it shall be burned on the ash dump.

[13]"And if the whole congregation of Israel errs unintentionally and the matter is hidden from the eyes of [not noticed by] the assembly, so that they do one of the Lord's prohibitions, which should not be done, and they then realize their guilt, [14]when the sin that they have committed is made known to it, the assembly shall present a domesticated bull as a sin offering and bring it before the tent of meeting. [15]The elders of the congregation shall lay their hands on the head of the bull before the Lord, and the bull shall be slaughtered before the Lord. [16]The anointed priest shall bring some of the blood of the bull into the tent of meeting, [17]and the priest shall dip his finger into the blood and sprinkle it seven times before the Lord against the curtain. [18]He shall also put some of the blood on the horns of the altar that is before the Lord in the tent of meeting; and all [the rest of] the blood he shall pour out at the base of the altar of burnt offering that is at the entrance to the tent of meeting. [19]He shall reserve all its fat from it and turn it into smoke on the altar. [20]He shall perform the same ritual for the bull as he performed for the bull of the sin offering; he shall perform the same ritual for it. Thus the priest shall make atonement for them, so that they may be forgiven.

21The bull shall be carried outside the camp, and it shall be burned just as the
first bull was burned. It is a sin offering for the assembly.
22"When a chieftain sins by unintentionally doing any of the prohibitions of
the Lord his God, which should not be done, and he then realizes his guilt 23or
the sin that he has committed against it is made known to him, he shall bring a
male goat without blemish as his offering. 24He shall lay his hand on the head of
the goat; it shall be slaughtered in the place where the burnt offering is slaughtered before the Lord. It is a sin offering. 25The priest shall take some of the blood
of the sin offering with his finger and put it on the horns of the altar of burnt offering, and [the rest of] its blood he shall pour out at the base of the altar for
burnt offering. 26He shall turn all its fat into smoke on the altar, like the fat of
the sacrifice of the peace offering. Thus the priest shall make atonement for him
from his sin, so that he may be forgiven.
27"And if any ordinary person sins unintentionally by doing one of the Lord's
prohibitions, which should not be done, and he then realizes his guilt 28or the sin
that he has committed is made known to him, he shall bring as his offering a female goat without blemish for the sin that he has committed. 29He shall lay his
hand on the head of the sin offering and slaughter the sin offering at the place
for the burnt offering. 30Then the priest shall take some of the blood with his finger and put it on the horns of the altar of burnt offering; and all [the rest of] its
blood he shall pour out at the base of the altar. 31After he removes all its fat, just
as the fat was removed from the sacrifice of the peace offering, the priest shall
turn it into smoke on the altar as a pleasing aroma to the Lord. Thus the priest
shall make atonement for him, so that he may be forgiven.
32"And if he brings a sheep as his offering for a sin offering, he shall bring a
female without blemish. 33He shall lay his hand on the head of the sin offering
and slaughter it as a sin offering in the place where he would slaughter the burnt
offering. 34Then the priest shall take some of the blood of the sin offering with
his finger and put it on the horns of the altar of burnt offering; and all [the rest
of] its blood he shall pour out at the base of the altar. 35After he removes all the
fat, just as the fat of the sheep was removed from the sacrifice of the peace offering, the priest shall turn it into smoke on the altar on top of the gifts to the
Lord. Thus the priest shall make atonement for him for the sin that he has committed, so that he may be forgiven.
5 1"When a person sins in that he has heard a public adjuration and is a witness, or he saw [as an eyewitness] or is a person with knowledge, but he does not
speak up, so that he bears his iniquity; 2or when a person touches something unclean, whether it is the carcass of an unclean wild animal or the carcass of unclean livestock or the carcass of an unclean swarming creature, and it is hidden
from him that he is unclean until he realizes his guilt; 3or when he touches human impurity, any impurity by which one becomes unclean, and it is hidden from
him until he discovers it and realizes his guilt; 4or when a person blurts out an
oath for an evil or a good purpose, whatever anyone may blurt in an oath, and
it is hidden from him until he discovers it and realizes his guilt in one of these

cases; [5]when he realizes his guilt in one of these cases, he shall confess the sin of which he is guilty. [6]He shall bring as his penalty to the Lord, for the sin of which he is guilty, a female from the flock, a sheep or a goat, as a sin offering, so that the priest may make atonement for him from his sin. [7]But if he cannot afford a sheep/goat, he shall bring as his penalty for that of which he is guilty two turtledoves or two pigeons to the Lord, one for a sin offering and the other for a burnt offering. [8]He shall bring them to the priest, who shall offer first the one for the sin offering, wringing its head from its neck without severing it. [9]He shall sprinkle some of the blood as the sin offering on the side of the altar, while the rest of the blood shall be drained at the base of the altar; it is a sin offering. [10]He shall perform the ritual for the second as a burnt offering according to the regulation. Thus the priest shall make atonement for him from his sin of which he is guilty, so that he may be forgiven.

[11]"And if he cannot afford two turtledoves or two pigeons, he shall bring as his offering for that of which he is guilty a tenth of an ephah of choice flour for a sin offering; he shall not add olive oil to it or put frankincense on it, because it is a sin offering. [12]He shall bring it to the priest, and the priest shall scoop out a handful of it as its token portion and turn it into smoke on the altar upon the gifts for the Lord; it is a sin offering. [13]Thus the priest shall make atonement for him for whichever of these sins he is guilty, so that he may be forgiven. Like the grain offering, it shall belong to the priest."

Textual Notes

4:2 נֶ֫פֶשׁ—This term (literally "a soul" or "a life") indicates that the offering could be brought by any person; "a person" could be a man or a woman. The same term in the same sense occurs in, for example, 2:1; 4:27; 5:1.

תֶּחֱטָא—This verb, חָטָא, "to sin," and the corresponding noun, חַטָּאת, "a sin," are key terms that are frequent in chapters 4–5. While the verb is used elsewhere in the Scriptures for a transgression against God and humanity, it is used in the priestly legislation exclusively for sins against God. The noun חַטָּאת designates an offense against God (4:3, 14, 23, 28, 35), its impurity (4:26), the offering for it (4:3, 8, 20, 21, 24, 25, 29, 32, 33, 34, 35), and the purification from its contamination (4:33).

Since this offering cleanses from sin, it is called a "sin offering."

בִּשְׁגָגָה—The kind of sin that is forgiven by this offering is an inadvertent offense, an accidental (rather than a willful) deed. *HALOT* defines שְׁגָגָה (which recurs in 4:22, 27; 5:15, 18; 22:14) as "inadvertent sin, unintentional mistake." Its meaning is highlighted in this chapter by the use of the terms חַטָּאת (and the verb חָטָא in 4:22) and בִּשְׁגָגָה (also the verb שָׁגָה, "to sin inadvertently," in 4:13) alternately in a chiasm to introduce each new case as follows:

A Sin unintentionally (4:2)
  B Sin (4:3)
    C Err unintentionally (4:13)
  B' Sin (4:22)
A' Sin unintentionally (4:27)

In Num 15:22–31, the term בִּשְׁגָגָה is contrasted with sin "with a high hand," which is deliberate sin against God, and for which no sin offering could atone (cf. Heb 10:26). In contrast, an unintentional sin was a careless transgression from ignorance or negligence, a sin that a person did not plan to do or an act that a person did not know was an offense against God.[1]

מִכֹּל מִצְוֹת יְהוָה אֲשֶׁר לֹא תֵעָשֶׂינָה—This is literally "from any of the commandments of the Lord that should not be done." We translate it as "prohibitions, which should not be done" in 4:2, 13, 22, 27; 5:17. In the priestly legislation, the term "commandment" (מִצְוָה) did not apply to civil matters that were dealt with in human courts, but to religious laws that came entirely under God's jurisdiction (4:2, 13, 22, 27; 5:17; 22:31; 26:3, 14, 15; 27:34). These religious commandments consisted of prohibitions that averted desecration and performative decrees that established a ritual practice. If people who had violated a ritual prohibition approached God and ate the holy food without presenting a sin offering, they polluted the sanctuary and desecrated its holiness.

וְעָשָׂה מֵאַחַת מֵהֵנָּה׃—Here the conjunction *waw* is used explicatively rather than consecutively before עָשָׂה. In other words, while this phrase literally says "and he does from one from them," it does not refer to a new action. Rather, this explains the action that constitutes the inadvertent sin (שְׁגָגָה) to which the preceding part of the verse refers. Therefore we could translate it "by breaking one of them."

4:3 הַכֹּהֵן הַמָּשִׁיחַ—The anointed priest was the high priest (4:5, 16) or his successor (6:15 [ET 6:22]).

לְאַשְׁמַת—The term here, אַשְׁמָה in construct, could be the noun אַשְׁמָה, "indebtedness, guilt" (*HALOT*), which probably recurs in 5:24, 26 (ET 6:5, 7); 22:16. More likely, it may be the so-called feminine form of the infinitive construct of the verb אָשַׁם, "to be guilty" (*HALOT,* 1). *HALOT* (s.v. אשׁם, 1) considers the form in 4:3, 13, 22, 27; 5:2–5, 17, 19, 23 (ET 6:4) to be the infinite construct. It describes the subjective and objective effects of an evil deed. While it usually refers to "becoming guilty," it is used here for "suffering from guilt" and in 5:23 (ET 6:4) for "acknowledging guilt." Here the people are held to suffer from the transgression of the priest.

וְהִקְרִיב—See the textual note on this verb in 1:2. Both here and in 4:14, the ritual term הִקְרִיב is used to distinguish the ritual "presentation" of the bull as a sin offering from the act of "bringing" it to the entrance of the tent, which follows (4:4, 14b).

פַּר בֶּן־בָּקָר—See 4:14 and the textual notes on 1:5.

תָּמִים—See the textual note on this adjective in 1:3 and also "Fulfillment by Christ" in the commentary on 1:3–17. It recurs in 4:23, 28, 32.

לְחַטָּאת׃—Traditionally the חַטָּאת is called a "sin offering," which agrees with its etymology and the rendition of the LXX (περὶ τῆς ἁμαρτίας αὐτοῦ).

However, many recent commentators argue that it should be called a "purification offering" instead. They take this view for two main reasons. First, this offering

---

[1] Milgrom, *Leviticus 1–16*, 228–29.

is, in some cases, prescribed for people who have not sinned but have incurred some form of ritual impurity from physical causes, such as parturition (12:6, 8), skin disease (14:13, 19, 22, 31), sexual discharges (15:15, 30), or contact with a corpse (Num 19:9, 17). Second, the offering is not just presented for people, but also for sacred objects, such as the altar for burnt offering (Lev 8:14–15; 16:15, 18–19). In fact, the blood from this offering is said to cleanse the altar (16:19; Ezek 43:25–26).

The main exponent of the view that it is a "purification offering" is Milgrom.[2] He has proposed an elaborate interpretation of the function of the חַטָּאת as a purification offering. He argues that the חַטָּאת did not deal with the impurity of people but with the impurity of the holy things. The rite of atonement was performed with the blood from this offering to "purge" (חִטֵּא) the holy things that had been contaminated with human impurity. The Israelites generated this impurity by failing to cleanse themselves within the prescribed period after they had transgressed a divine prohibition. This failure created a miasma that gradually accumulated in the sanctuary and so polluted it. While inadvertent transgressions polluted the altar for burnt offering, the impurity from deliberate sins against God penetrated right into the Holy Place and the Holy of Holies. The purification offerings were therefore established to cleanse the sanctuary from this accumulating impurity so that it would not become irretrievably polluted, for then God would have to withdraw his protective presence from the tabernacle and so cease to dwell with his people.

Milgrom's argument is far too detailed and complex to evaluate fully here. It has been evaluated best by Maccoby.[3] He argues that people who had become ritually unclean (however that may have occurred) polluted the sanctuary by entering it and eating holy food while they were unclean. The rite of atonement was therefore performed to cleanse the sanctuary and free the people from their pollution. Since this impurity was created when people "sinned" (4:2, 3, 14, 22, 27, 28, 35; 5:1), the חַטָּאת is quite rightly called a "sin offering."

4:4 וְהֵבִיא—See the textual note on this verb in 2:2. It recurs in 4:5, 14, 16, 23, 28, 32; 5:6, 7, 8, 11, 12.

פֶּתַח אֹהֶל מוֹעֵד—See the textual note on this phrase in 1:3. It recurs in 4:7, 18.

וְסָמַךְ אֶת־יָדוֹ—See the textual note on this phrase in 1:4. It recurs in 4:15, 24, 29, 33.

וְשָׁחַט—See the textual note on this verb in 1:5. It recurs in 4:15, 24, 29, 33.

4:6 וְהִזָּה—The Hiphil of the verb נָזָה means "to sprinkle," and it is used for the ritual aspersion of a person or object or place with some liquid: the aspersion of some blood from a sin offering on the altar for burnt offering (5:9; 16:19) or the curtain in front of the Holy of Holies (4:6, 17) or the mercy seat (16:14, 15) or the floor of the Holy of Holies (16:14, 15); the aspersion of the holy anointing oil by itself on the altar for burnt offering (8:11) or with the blood from the altar on the priests and their vestments (8:30); the aspersion of blood (14:7) and olive oil (14:16, 27) on a person

---

[2] Milgrom, "Sin Offering or Purification Offering"; Milgrom, "The Concept of *Maʿal* in the Bible and the Ancient Near East"; Milgrom, *Leviticus 1–16*, 253–61.

[3] Maccoby, *Ritual and Morality,* 165–81.

who had recovered from an unclean skin disease (14:7); and the aspersion of blood on a house that had formerly been infected with unclean mold (14:51).

In Is 52:15 the verb is used of the Suffering Servant: "He shall sprinkle many peoples," meaning that the blood of Jesus Christ will atone for the sins of all people.

שֶׁ֫בַע פְּעָמִים—See also 4:17; 16:14, 19.

פָּרֹ֫כֶת—This thickly woven "curtain" separated the inner room, the Holy of Holies, from its foreroom, the Holy Place, and shut off the Holy of Holies as God's private quarters. See figure 6, "Ground Plan of the Tabernacle." The construction of this "curtain" is described in Ex 26:31–37; 36:35–38; 40:21. פָּרֹ֫כֶת recurs in Lev 4:17; 16:2, 12, 15; 21:23; 24:3.

הַקֹּ֫דֶשׁ:—This term is used specifically for the Holy of Holies here and in 16:2, 3, 16, 17, 20, 23. In reference to the tabernacle in other passages, הַקֹּ֫דֶשׁ usually is translated as "the sanctuary" and refers either to the outer room of the tabernacle (Ex 26:33; 28:29, 35; 29:30; 31:11; Lev 10:4, 18) or the inner court around the altar for burnt offering (Ex 28:43; Lev 10:18b; 14:13). The noun קֹ֫דֶשׁ is used in Leviticus for "a holy thing," something consecrated to God, something that belongs to God and can only be used ritually in the divine domain as part of the divine service (10:10). This included such things as God's name (20:3; 22:2, 32), a person (21:6), a place (4:6; 6:23 [ET 6:30]; 10:4, 18; 14:13; 16:2, 3, 16, 17, 20, 23, 27, 33), part of an offering (5:15, 16; 12:4; 22:2, 4, 6, 7, 10, 12, 14, 15, 16; 23:20; 27:9, 10, 30, 32, 33), the high priest's regalia (8:9; 16:4, 32), a time (23:2, 3, 4, 7, 8, 21, 24, 27, 35, 36, 37; 25:12), money (5:15; 27:3, 23, 25), a building (27:14), and a field (27:21).

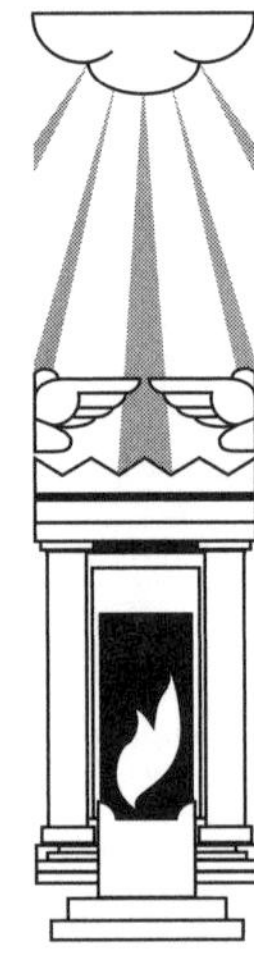

4:7 עַל־קַ֫רְנוֹת מִזְבַּח—Both the incense altar (4:7, 18) and the altar for burnt offering (4:25, 30, 34; 8:15; 9:9; 16:18) had four horns, one on each corner. Archaeologists have found ancient altars with horns. Like the head of a person, the horns represented the whole altar. Thus the sanctity of the altar depended on their sanctity. They were the place where the sacred realm of God intersected with the common realm of humanity.[4]

קְטֹ֫רֶת הַסַּמִּים—Regarding this incense, see Ex 30:1–10; 37:25–28; 40:5, 26–28.

כָּל־דַּם הַפָּר—This is literally "the whole of the blood of the bull." See 4:18, 25, 30.

יִשְׁפֹּךְ אֶל־יְסוֹד מִזְבַּח הָעֹלָה—See 4:18, 25, 30, 34; 5:9; 8:15; 9:9. Only the blood from the sin offering was disposed in this way to prevent any other use of it.

Regarding the "altar," see the textual note on מִזְבֵּחַ in 1:5. The term recurs in 4:10, 18, 19, 25, 26, 30, 31, 34, 35; 5:9, 12.

4:8 חֵלֶב—See the textual note on this word in 3:3. It recurs in 4:9, 19, 26, 31, 35. The commentary on 3:16–17 explains why the fat belonged exclusively to the Lord.

יָרִים—See the textual note on this verb in 2:9. The Hiphil recurs in 4:19.

הַחַטָּאת—See the textual notes above on 4:3.

4:9 הַכְּלָיֹת—See the textual note on the "kidneys" in 3:4.

---

[4] Klingbeil, *A Comparative Study of the Ritual of Ordination As Found in Leviticus 8 and Emar 369*, 197.

4:10 הַשְּׁלָמִים—This refers to the "peace offering" in 3:3–4.

וְהִקְטִירָם—See the textual note on this verb in 1:9. It recurs in 4:19, 26, 31, 35, 5:12.

4:11 וְאֶת־עוֹר הַפָּר וְאֶת־כָּל־בְּשָׂרוֹ עַל־רֹאשׁוֹ וְעַל־כְּרָעָיו וְקִרְבּוֹ וּפִרְשׁוֹ׃—The whole of this verse is made up of a pending phrase in Hebrew (*casus pendens*). This verse functions as the direct object of the verb וְהוֹצִיא in 4:12 and is summarized by "all the bull" in 4:12.

4:12 כָּל־הַפָּר—This is literally "all the bull." It refers to the entire bull, whose parts were described in 4:11.

אֶל־מִחוּץ לַמַּחֲנֶה—The "camp" (מַחֲנֶה) is a place of great ritual significance in Leviticus. It was a ritually clean place. Since it housed the tent of meeting where the Lord resided (cf. Num 5:1–4), care needed to be taken so that it would not be defiled by any unclean person or thing. People had to be ritually clean before they entered it (14:8; 16:26, 28). Its counterpart was the area "outside the camp" (4:12). This was a ritually ambiguous place. While some parts of it, such as the site of the dump for the ashes from the altar and remains from the sacrificed animals (4:12, 21; 6:11; 8:17; 9:11; 16:27), were ritually clean, other parts were regarded as ritually unclean: "outside the camp" included places where corpses were buried (10:4, 5), people with skin diseases were banished (13:46; 14:3), illegitimate sacrifices were offered (17:3), and blasphemers were executed (24:14, 23). The phrase here in 4:12 is repeated in 4:21.

טָהוֹר—Regarding "clean," see figure 1, "Holy versus Common and Clean versus Unclean," and the textual notes on 7:19.

שֶׁפֶךְ הַדֶּשֶׁן—We translate this phrase as "the ash dump." The noun שֶׁפֶךְ occurs only here in the OT. By etymology (from the verb שָׁפַךְ) it denotes a place where something was poured out. *HALOT* gives "outpouring," but in plain English it refers to the "dump" or "trash heap." While דֶּשֶׁן can mean "fatness" or rich food, in 1:16; 4:12; 6:3–4 it means "**fatty ashes** (of burnt wood mixed with fat on the altar)" (*HALOT,* 2).

4:13 וְאִם—The *waw* links this section to 4:3–12.

כָּל־עֲדַת יִשְׂרָאֵל—This means "the whole congregation of Israel." See 4:15; 8:3, 4, 5; 9:5; 10:6; 19:2. This speech distinguishes the עֲדַת יִשְׂרָאֵל, the actual congregation meeting with God at the sanctuary (4:13, 15), from the קְהַל יִשְׂרָאֵל, the whole liturgical community that had the right to assemble there (4:13, 14, 21; see also 16:17, 33). The "congregation" was also a legal entity that was convened by the tribal chieftains to transacted business of the whole community.[5]

יִשְׁגּוּ—"Errs unintentionally" translates the Hebrew verb שָׁגָה, "to sin inadvertently" or "to err." It is a synonym of the clause חָטָא בִשְׁגָגָה in 4:2 and 4:27.

אַחַת מִכָּל־מִצְוֹת יְהוָה—See the textual notes on 4:2.

אֲשֶׁר לֹא־תֵעָשֶׂינָה וְאָשֵׁמוּ׃—This case is best taken in tandem with 4:3–12, which is about a sin by the high priest that poses a threat to the people. Therefore the unintentional sin by the whole congregation in 4:13–21 is best understood as the consequence of an error made by the high priest.

---

5 Joosten, *People and Land in the Holiness Code*, 36–42.

4:14 וְנוֹדְעָה֙ הַֽחַטָּ֔את ... עָלֶ֑יהָ—The antecedent of the third feminine singular suffix on עָלֶ֑יהָ is הַקָּהָ֔ל, "the assembly" (4:13).

4:15 זִקְנֵ֨י הָעֵדָ֜ה—See 9:1; cf. 19:32. "The elders of the congregation" are the leaders of the tribes and clans of Israel who act on behalf of the liturgical community.

וְשָׁחַ֥ט—This impersonal verb ("he shall slaughter") is translated as a passive.

4:17 מִן־הַדָּ֑ם—This phrase, "from the blood," contrasts with "in the blood" in 4:6. The phrase here may have been brought forward from the following clause to indicate that the finger was dipped in and out "from the blood."

4:20 The Hebrew text uses the verb עָשָׂה, "perform," three times in this verse for the enactment of the ritual described in 4:8–9. As Milgrom notes,[6] this verb was often used by the priests as a technical term for "performing" a sacrifice or enacting the ritual for a sacrifice (5:10; 6:15 [ET 6:22]; 8:34; 9:7, 16, 22; 14:19, 30; 15:15, 30; 16:9, 15, 24; 17:9; 22:23; 23:12, 19). The LXX translates it by ποιέω. This may have influenced Paul's use of the same verb in 2 Cor 5:21, where he taught about Christ as a sin offering.

כַּאֲשֶׁ֤ר עָשָׂה֙ לְפַ֣ר הַֽחַטָּ֔את—This refers to what the priest did with the bull for the priest's sin offering in 4:3–12.

וְכִפֶּ֧ר עֲלֵהֶ֛ם הַכֹּהֵ֖ן—See the textual notes on 1:4.

וְנִסְלַ֥ח לָהֶֽם׃—This is literally "and it may be forgiven for them." The impersonal passive verb (the Niphal of סָלַח) in this atonement formula is a divine passive: it will be forgiven by God. This clause indicates that through this rite God did indeed grant forgiveness.[7] Since forgiveness was the purpose and result of the rite of atonement, the formula is best translated "the priest shall make atonement for them, *so that they may be forgiven.*" This formula is only used for the rite of atonement performed with the blood of the sin offering (4:20, 26, 31, 35; 5:10, 13; Num 15:25, 28) and the blood of the reparation offering (Lev 5:16, 18, 26 [ET 6:7]; 19:22).

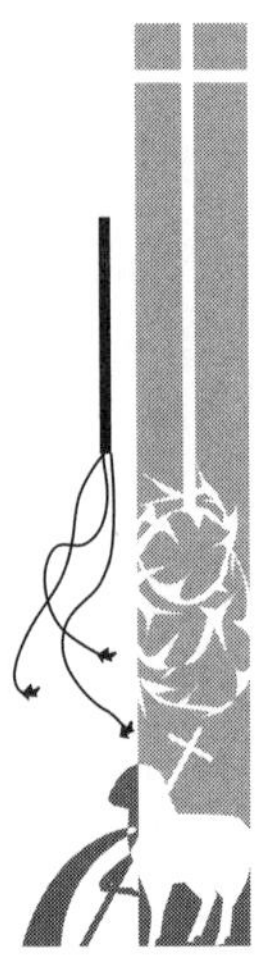

In the OT the verb סָלַח is used only with God as its subject. Even though the priests mediate God's forgiveness, it is God himself who forgives sins. The translation of סָלַח in English by words such as "pardon" or "forgive" carries some misleading connotations. Unlike these English words, סָלַח is never used for the activity of a human judge in a court of law or for the restoration of a broken human relationship. Its basic sense is to "release" a person from the burden and penalty of a sin. This is its meaning in Num 30:6, 9, 13 (ET 30:5, 8, 12), where the Lord is said to release a woman from the penalty of failing to fulfill that vow if her father or husband forbids her to fulfill it.

In Leviticus סָלַח is a ritual term which is always connected with the rite of atonement. Whenever the rite of atonement was been rightly enacted by the priest with the blood from a sin offering or a reparation offering, people were released from a sin and its destructive hold on them. When God forgave them, he removed the impurity and

---

6 Milgrom, *Leviticus 1–16*, 576.

7 Milgrom, *Leviticus 1–16*, 245.

guilt caused by the sin, freed them from its consequences and penalties, and restored communion with them. Since they were no longer tainted with sin, they could participate in the divine service at the sanctuary, without defiling its purity and desecrating its holiness.

4:21 וְהוֹצִיא אֶת־הַפָּר—Since the third person imperfect is used impersonally, it is translated by an English passive: "shall be carried outside."

4:22 After the general case which is introduced by "when" (כִּי) and followed by two related subcases headed by "if" (אִם), this section is introduced by אֲשֶׁר as a stylistic device to mark the transition to three related kinds of sin offering.

נָשִׂיא—In the premonarchical period, the "chieftain, prince" was the leader of a clan or an extended family group.

אַחַת מִכָּל־מִצְוֹת יְהוָה אֱלֹהָיו—See the textual note on the similar phrase in 4:13.

בִּשְׁגָגָה—The word בִּשְׁגָגָה been displaced for stylistic reasons, as indicated in the textual notes on 4:2 above.

4:23 הוֹדַע—The form הוֹדַע (also in 4:28) is to be parsed as the Hophal of יָדַע (rather than the Hiphil), and so it means to "be made known" to someone or for sin to be brought "to one's knowledge" (*HALOT,* Hophal, 1 and 2, respectively).

חַטָּאתוֹ אֲשֶׁר חָטָא בָּהּ—The antecedent of the third feminine singular pronominal suffix on בָּהּ is מִצְוָה in 4:22.

4:24 בִּמְקוֹם אֲשֶׁר־יִשְׁחַט אֶת־הָעֹלָה—See 1:11. Similar descriptions of this place recur in 4:29, 33.

4:26 הַשְּׁלָמִים—This refers to 3:14–15.

וְכִפֶּר עָלָיו הַכֹּהֵן מֵחַטָּאתוֹ—See the textual notes on 1:4. While the use of the preposition מִן after the verb כִּפֶּר, "to atone," may state the reason for the rite of atonement,[8] it more likely refers to the state of sin from which the offender is freed by the rite of atonement (4:26; 5:6, 10; 14:19; 15:15, 30; 16:16, 34). It should therefore be construed as an ellipsis for "making atonement for him to cleanse him from sin" (14:29; 16:30).[9] This combination of כִּפֶּר עַל with מִן is only used for the sin offering. חַטָּאת does not refer to the pollution of the altar from failure to undergo purification, as Milgrom claims,[10] but to the sin of transgressing a divine prohibition (4:2, 13, 22, 27).[11]

4:27 וְאִם־נֶפֶשׁ אַחַת ... מֵעַם הָאָרֶץ—This is literally "any single person from the people of the land." See 20:2, 4. The term עַם הָאָרֶץ refers to all the people, apart from the high priest and prince, who made up the congregation of Israel.[12]

אַחַת מִמִּצְוֹת יְהוָה—See the textual notes on 4:13.

4:28 הוֹדַע—Again, this is the Hophal of יָדַע. See the textual notes on 4:23.

4:31 הַשְּׁלָמִים—This refers to 3:14–15.

---

8 See Milgrom, *Leviticus 1–16*, 251.

9 See Hartley, *Leviticus*, 47.

10 Milgrom, *Leviticus 1–16*, 256.

11 Maccoby, *Ritual and Morality*, 178–79.

12 See Joosten, *People and Land in the Holiness Code*, 42–47.

לְרֵיחַ נִיחֹחַ לַיהוָה—See the textual note on this phrase in 1:9 and the explanation of its theology in "Leviticus 1–3." The phrase "a pleasing aroma to the Lord" occurs only here for the sin offering.[13]

4:32 כֶּבֶשׂ here refers to a sheep rather than just a lamb. The same is true of כֶּשֶׂב in 1:10; 3:7; 4:35; 7:23; 17:2; 22:19.

4:35 וְאֶת־כָּל־חֶלְבָּה יָסִיר כַּאֲשֶׁר יוּסַר חֵלֶב־הַכֶּשֶׂב מִזֶּבַח הַשְּׁלָמִים—This refers back to 3:9b–10, which refers to removal of the fat.

עַל אִשֵּׁי יְהוָה—See the textual note on אִשֶּׁה in 1:9 and the explanation in "Leviticus 1–3." אִשֶּׁה recurs in 5:12.

5:1 וְנָשָׂא עֲוֹנוֹ׃—This formula, literally "and he shall bear his iniquity," implies certain retribution and has an eschatological dimension. It is also found in 5:17; 7:18; 17:16; 19:8; 20:17, 19; 22:16. It is virtually synonymous with the related formula for "bearing sin" in 20:20; 22:9; 24:15. Sinners "bear" the inevitable destructive consequences of their iniquity and cannot rid themselves of it.[14] Only God can do that for them through his priests (Ex 28:38; Lev 10:17) and the scapegoat (16:22). When God "bears" their iniquity, he removes it and so releases them from the evil that they have brought upon themselves (Ex 34:7; Num 14:18). Unless he "bears" their iniquity, they suffer its inescapable consequences and eventually perish from it. In Lev 19:8 "he shall bear his iniquity" is closely associated with God's punishment of offenders by cutting them off from their kinsfolk, whereas in 24:15 "he will bear his sin" is contrasted with the execution of the death penalty by human hands.

This formula may have been used by a judge in a court of law to assign an evildoer or suspected evildoer to divine retribution, but it was not deployed, as Reventlow claims,[15] as a legal device by judges in cases of capital punishment to protect themselves from revenge for the illegitimate shedding of blood.

5:2 טָמֵא—Impurity, the state of being "unclean," is a key ritual-theological term in Leviticus. See figure 1, "Holy versus Common and Clean versus Unclean." The adjective טָמֵא describes the ritual "unclean" state either of persons (5:2; 13:11, 36, 44, 45, 46; 15:25, 33; 22:4) or of things (5:2 [twice]; 7:19, 21 [three times]; 10:10; 11:4, 5, 6, 7, 8, 26, 27, 28, 29, 31, 35 [twice], 38, 47; 13:15, 51, 55; 14:40, 41, 45, 57; 15:2, 26; 20:25 [twice]; 27:11, 27). Its antonym is טָהוֹר, "ritually clean." Clean persons and things could be made holy; they were fit for consecration by God and use in the divine service. People who were ritually unclean were unfit for God's presence. They were therefore unfit for contact with anything holy. If they came into contact with something holy, they both defiled and desecrated it. If they approached God in a state of ritual impurity, they forfeited their lives (15:31). Unclean people who ate the holy meat from God's table were cut off from their kinsfolk (7:20–21).

The laws in Leviticus deal with three main classes of impurity: the impurity from human beings; the impurity from livestock; and the impurity from swarming crea-

---

[13] Cf. Noordtzij, *Leviticus*, 63.

[14] Schwartz, "The Bearing of Sin in the Priestly Literature," 10–15.

[15] Reventlow, "Sein Blut komme über sein Haupt."

tures (5:2; 7:21). Like holiness, "impurity" (טֻמְאָה) is both a power and a dynamic state of being (5:3; 7:20, 21; 14:19; 15:3, 25, 26, 30, 31; 16:16, 19; 18:19; 22:3, 5). By physical contact with impurity a clean person or a thing "becomes unclean" (Qal of the verb טָמֵא, 5:3; 11:24, 25, 26, 27, 28, 31, 32 [twice], 33, 34 [twice], 35, 36, 39, 40 [twice]; 12:2 [twice], 5; 13:14, 46; 14:36, 46; 15:4 [twice], 5, 6, 7, 8, 9, 10 [twice], 11, 16, 17, 18, 19, 20 [twice], 21, 22, 23, 24 [twice], 27 [twice], 32; 17:15; 18:20, 23, 25, 27; 19:31; 22:5 [twice], 6, 8). Since the Israelites "defiled themselves" (Niphal and Hithpael of טָמֵא) by contact with unclean things (11:24, 43 [twice]; 18:24 [twice], 30; 21:1, 3, 4, 11), they were to "treat them as unclean" (20:25). Only the priests had the authority to "declare someone unclean" (Piel of טָמֵא, 13:3, 8, 11, 15, 20, 22, 25, 27, 30, 44, 59). Unclean people "defiled" (Piel of טָמֵא) themselves (11:44), the tabernacle (15:31; 20:3), and the land of Israel (18:28).

חַיָּה—See 11:27.

בְּהֵמָה—See 11:4–8.

שֶׁרֶץ—See the textual notes on 11:10. The phrase שֶׁרֶץ טָמֵא most likely refers to the eight reptiles and rodents listed in 11:29–30.

וְאָשֵׁם׃—It is more accurate to understand אָשֵׁם, "to be guilty," here and in the following verses, as a reference to the realization of guilt by the person who previously was ignorant of his guilt (which was "hidden from him"), rather than to the objective culpability for an offense or to the subjective experience of guilt. The RSV, the NIV, and the NRSV construe this clause as the apodosis of the sentence here and in the next two verses. However, it makes far better sense to take 5:5b as the summary apodosis for the four cases in 5:1–4.

5:3 בְּטֻמְאַת אָדָם—See 7:21. This applies to a person with a skin disease (14:19), a person with a venereal discharge (15:3–10, 16–17), a menstruant (15:19–24; 18:19), and anyone who has handled a corpse (Num 19:14–16). אָדָם (also in Lev 5:4) refers to any person, male or female; see the textual note on it in 1:2.

טֻמְאָתוֹ—The Hebrew noun טֻמְאָה, "uncleanness," is a key ritual-theological term in Leviticus (5:3; 7:20, 21; 14:19; 15:3, 25, 26, 30, 31; 16:16, 19; 18:19; 22:3, 5). It designates a primary source of the impurity that is spread by direct contact with people and things. They thereby become ritually unclean. They are unfit for contact with anything that is holy because God's holiness cannot coexist with impurity (15:31; 22:3).

5:4 לְהָרַע ׀ אוֹ לְהֵיטִיב—This phrase, literally "to do evil or to do good," indicates the intent of the oath: "for an evil or a good purpose." However, it could be a merism that means to swear any kind of oath.

לְאַחַת מֵאֵלֶּה׃—The phrase אַחַת מֵאֵלֶּה is repeated in 5:5 and 5:13. In 5:5 it must refer to the four cases listed in 5:1–4, but here in 5:4 it can only refer to the two kinds of oaths mentioned in this verse.

5:5 אֲשֶׁר חָטָא עָלֶיהָ׃—We understand this to mean the sin "of which he is guilty," but it could mean "which he has sinned." See also 5:6, 7, 10, 13.

5:6 אֲשָׁמוֹ—Rather than "his penalty," this could be translated "his reparation/his reparation offering." Schenker argues that this refers to a unique class of reparation offering that was to be presented for sins of omission with the performance of the blood rite in the manner of a sin offering.[16] The noun אָשָׁם can, however, be used for the penalty for a sin of commission (5:6, 7; 19:21), as well as for a reparation offering for an act of sacrilege (5:15–16).

וְכִפֶּר עָלָיו הַכֹּהֵן—See the textual notes on 1:4.

מֵחַטָּאתוֹ׃—See the textual notes on 4:26.

5:7 וְאִם־לֹא תַגִּיעַ יָדוֹ דֵּי—See 5:11. This is literally "if his hand cannot reach the sufficient amount."

שֶׂה—See 12:8; 22:28; 27:26. The term שֶׂה is a collective term for a flock of sheep and goats and a specific term for any of its members.

אֲשָׁמוֹ—As in 5:6, we take this as "his penalty," but it could mean "his reparation" or "his reparation offering."

שְׁתֵּי תֹרִים אוֹ־שְׁנֵי בְנֵי־יוֹנָה—See the textual notes on 1:14.

5:9 וְהִזָּה מִדַּם הַחַטָּאת עַל־קִיר הַמִּזְבֵּחַ—For practical reasons, the blood was not smeared on the horns of the altar (as it was in 4:25, 30, 34), but it was sprinkled directly on the side of the altar from the neck of the bird. On הִזָּה, see the textual notes on 4:6.

5:10 יַעֲשֶׂה—See the textual notes on 4:20.

כַּמִּשְׁפָּט—We render this as "according to the regulation." When מִשְׁפָּט is used in its singular, as here and in 9:16, it is the term for the ritual legislation that establishes how a ritual is to be enacted. Its plural is used more generally in Leviticus for the "ordinances" (KJV: "judgments") by which God prescribed how things were to be done. His people are therefore bound to keep these ritual and practical ordinances (18:4, 5, 26; 19:37; 20:22; 25:18).

5:11 וְאִם־לֹא תַשִּׂיג יָדוֹ—This is literally "if his hand is not able to get." See 14:22, 30, 31; cf. 25:26, 47, 49; 27:8.

עֲשִׂירִת הָאֵפָה—One tenth of an ephah amounts to 2.3 liters or 11.5 grams of flour. This would suffice as a day's ration of food for a person.

סֹלֶת—See the textual notes on 2:1.

לְבֹנָה—See the textual notes on 2:1.

כִּי חַטָּאת הִיא׃—This explains why this offering differs from the law for the grain offering in 2:1.

5:12 אַזְכָּרָתָה—This is the "token portion" or "memorial portion." Here the third feminine singular suffix lacks *mappiq* (אַזְכָּרָתָהּ). See the textual note on אַזְכָּרָה in 2:2.

וְהִקְטִיר—See the textual note on this verb in 1:9.

אִשֵּׁי יְהוָה—See the textual note on the similar phrase in 1:9 and the explanation in "Leviticus 1–3."

חַטָּאת הִוא׃—See 4:35.

5:13 This is the only case where atonement is made by a priest without the manipulation of blood.

עַל־חַטָּאתוֹ אֲשֶׁר־חָטָא מֵאַחַת מֵאֵלֶּה—This refers to the four cases in 5:1–4.

וְהָיְתָה לַכֹּהֵן—This refers to the leftover flour, which "shall belong to the priest."

---

16 Schenker, "Welche Verfehlungen und welche Opfer in Lev 5, 1–6?"

Commentary

Structure

This speech by Moses on the sin offering is a single sentence that extends from 4:1–5:13. It is only interrupted by the insertion of an appositional clause in 4:20 and the declaratory formula in 4:21b and 4:24b. Whereas 4:1–35 deals with the usual sin offering, 5:1–13 covers the graded sin offering.

The legislation for the normal sin offering begins with a general introduction in 4:2. This is followed by four sets of requirements for four different parties: the high priest in 4:3–12, the congregation in 4:13–21, the leader of a clan in 4:22–26, and the commoner in 4:27–35. The last of these is further subdivided into two parts for the two sets of animals permitted for a commoner, a female goat in 4:27–31 and female sheep in 4:32–35.

The four kinds of sin offering for unintentional sins are arranged in two classes. First, we have the two public sin offerings in 4:3–21. These are linked by the use of the conjunction וְאִם, "and if ..." in 4:3 and 13. The two are also correlated as two remedies for the same offense by a single statement of purpose in 4:20b and the concluding classification in 4:21b. In contrast with the personal sin offering in 4:22–35, both these first two sin offerings required the enactment of the major blood rite and incineration of the carcass outside the camp instead of its consumption by the priests.

Second, we have the legislation in 4:22–36 for the three different kinds of animals that could be offered as personal sin offerings by two different classes of lay people. The main parts of this single sentence are introduced by אֲשֶׁר, "which," in 4:22 and by וְאִם , "and if," in 4:27 and 4:32. Each of these three parts concludes with a similar statement of purpose. This arrangement of the material is highlighted by the use of a simple device. The same clause, "the sin that he (they) has (have) committed," that introduces each of the four kinds of sin offerings (4:3, 14, 23, 28) concludes the passage of legislation (4:35).

Three features stand out in the arrangement of Leviticus 4: the concentration on the manipulation and disposal of blood in 4:5–7, 16–19, 25, 30, and 34; the recurring statement about atonement as the purpose of this offering in 4:20, 26, 31, and 35; and the detailed legislation for the removal of fat from the bull in 4:8–10 compared to the summary character of the legislation for it elsewhere in the chapter. All this serves to call attention to the blood rite and its significance as the central enactment in this sacrifice.

Lev 5:1–13 provides an additional piece of legislation for the sin offering and is still part of the same divine speech as the previous chapter. It begins a new section that is introduced by "And if/when a person ..." (וְנֶפֶשׁ כִּי). It mentions four sins of commission that require confession and the presentation either of a sheep or a goat as a sin offering (5:6). In cases of economic hardship, this may be replaced by two other less expensive offerings (5:7–13). This unit (5:1–13) seems to have been placed here as an appendix to the personal sin offerings in 4:20–35.

The four cases in 5:1–4 form the protases before the apodosis in 5:5b–6. Three literary devices connect these four cases. First, while the first case ends with the clause "so that he bears his iniquity" (5:1), the other cases end with the clause "until he realizes his guilt" (5:2–4). A contrast is therefore made here, as in 5:17, between the experience of punishment for a known offense and the experience or consciousness of guilt for a previously hidden (unknown) offense. Second, the circumstantial clause "until he discovers it" (וְהוּא יָדַע, 5:3–4) is added in cases 3 and 4. Third, the clause "and it is hidden from him" is inserted in cases 2, 3, and 4 (5:2–4). These devices mark the transition from known sins (5:1) to unknown or unwitting sins (5:2–4).

Two other literary devices help to unify the material in this section. First, 5:1–4 and 5:5–13 are liked by resumptive repetition of the verb אָשַׁם, "to be guilty," from 5:2, 3, and 4 as a summary protasis in 5:5a. Second, the phrase אַחַת מֵאֵלֶּה, "one of these," not only introduces and concludes the legislation in 5:5 and 5:13 but also rounds off the cases for it in 5:4. This connects 5:5–13 closely to 5:1–4 and unifies these two sections.

The structure of this pericope can be outlined as follows:

- I. Introduction and commission (4:1–2a)
  - A. The Lord's address to Moses (4:1)
  - B. The commission to speak to the Israelites (4:2a)
- II. Speech with legislation for the sin offering (4:2b–5:13)
  - A. The normal sin offering (4:2b–35)
    - 1. The general case: unintentional sin against a divine prohibition (4:2b)
    - 2. The public offerings for the high priest and the congregation (4:3–21)
      - a. The case of a priest's sin with the threat to the people from his sin (4:3–12)
        - i. Bringing of a bull as sin offering (4:3)
        - ii. Ritual procedure (4:4–12)
          - Presentation of the bull (4:4a)
          - Laying on of hand (4:4b)
          - Slaughter (4:4c)
          - Disposal of blood (4:5–7)
          - Burning of fat (4:8–10)
          - Incineration of leftovers (4:11–12)
      - b. The error of the congregation due to the sin of the priest (4:13–21)
        - i. The case of the sin with the discovery of their guilt (4:13–14a)
        - ii. Bringing of a bull as sin offering (4:14b)
        - iii. Ritual procedure (4:14c–20a)
          - Presentation of the bull (4:14c)
          - Laying on of hands by the elders (4:15a)
          - Slaughter (4:15b)
          - Disposal of blood by the high priest (4:16–18)
          - Burning of fat by him as for previous offering (4:19–20a)
        - iv. Function: atonement for divine forgiveness (4:20b)
        - v. Incineration of leftovers (4:21a)
        - vi. Classification of sacrifice as congregational sin offering (4:21b)

3. The sin offering of a tribal leader (4:22–26)
    a. The case of the sin with the discovery of guilt (4:22–23a)
    b. Ritual procedure (4:23b–26a)
        i. Presentation of a male goat (4:23b)
        ii. Laying on of hand (4:24a)
        iii. Slaughter with notice of classification (4:24b)
        iv. Disposal of blood by a priest (4:25)
        v. Burning of fat by priest as for a peace offering (4:26a)
    c. Function: atonement for divine forgiveness (4:26b)
4. The sin offering for a lay Israelite (4:27–35)
    a. The case of the sin with the discovery of guilt (4:27–28a)
    b. The use of a goat as a sin offering: ritual procedure (4:28b–31a)
        i. Presentation of a female goat (4:28b)
        ii. Laying on of hand (4:29a)
        iii. Disposal of blood by a priest (4:29b–30)
        iv. Burning of fat by a priest as for a peace offering (4:30–31a)
    c. Function: atonement for divine forgiveness (4:31b)
    d. The use of a sheep as a sin offering: ritual procedure (4:32–35)
        i. Presentation of a ewe (4:32)
        ii. Laying on of hand (4:33a)
        iii. Disposal of blood by a priest (4:33b–34)
        iv. Burning of fat by a priest as for peace offering (4:35a–b)
    e. Function: atonement for divine forgiveness (4:35c)

B. The graded sin offering (5:1–13)
1. The four cases for this offering (5:1–4)
    a. Failure to obey adjuration to testify in a court case (5:1)
    b. Guilt from unwitting contact with an unclean animal (5:2)
    c. Guilt from unwitting contact with an unclean person (5:3)
    d. Guilt for forgetfulness in fulfilling a rash oath (5:4)
2. The prescribed procedure (5:5–13)
    a. Experience of guilt (5:5a)
    b. Confession of sin to the priest (5:5b)
    c. Presentation of one of the following graded sin offerings (5:6–13)
        i. Normal sin offering (5:6)
            - Presentation of female sheep or goat (5:6a)
            - Rite of atonement by priest (5:6b)
        ii. Sin offering of birds for poor person (5:7–10)
            - Presentation of two doves or pigeons for burnt offering and sin offering (5:7)
            - Presentation of birds to the priest (5:8a)
            - Offering of the first bird as the sin offering (5:8b–9)
            - Offering of the second bird as the burnt offering (5:10a)
            - Purpose: atonement for divine forgiveness (5:10b)

iii. Sin offering of flour for very poor person (5:11–13)
- Presentation of flour without oil or frankincense (5:11)
- Presentation to priest (5:12a)
- Reservation of the token portion by the priest (5:12b)
- Incineration of the token portion as the sin offering on the altar (5:12c)
- Purpose: atonement for divine forgiveness (5:13a)
- Use of leftover flour by the priest (5:13b)

The Normal Sin Offering (4:1–35)

Ritual Agents

The people involved in the performance of the public sin offering in 4:3–21 must to be distinguished from those who offer the personal sin offering in 4:22–35. Since the public sin offering was brought for some public violation of a ritual prohibition by the high priest or the congregation or both of them, they were the main actors in the ritual.

The high priest is called the "anointed priest" here in 4:3, 5, and 16, an ancient designation that is used elsewhere only in 6:15 (ET 6:22). This term was used for the high priest because, even though all priests had their vestments sprinkled with the most holy anointing oil (Ex 29:29; Lev 8:30), only the high priest and his designated successor had their heads anointed with it (Lev 8:12; cf. 16:32; Num 35:25). The use of the term here highlights the gravity of the offense. It is so severe that it requires the performance of an extraordinary rite of atonement by the ritual head of the nation in the Holy Place. When the high priest had committed a ritual transgression, he quite logically performed the entire rite, since no one else could represent him (4:3–12). When the congregation was guilty of an unintentional ritual offense, the priest attended to the manipulation of the blood (4:16–18), the burning up of the fat on the altar (4:19–20), and the disposal of the carcass (4:21). In both these cases of public ritual transgression, the high priest officiated because the rite of atonement for them had to be performed in the Holy Place.

Since the ritual transgression envisaged in 4:13–21 had been committed by Israel as a liturgical community rather than a political entity, the congregation of Israel as a ritual body was required to bring a "sin offering for the assembly" (4:21). In this it was represented by its elders (4:15), who were legally entitled to act on behalf of its tribes and clans. They brought the bull to the sanctuary, laid their right hand on it, and slaughtered it there (4:14–15). Through them as its representatives, the congregation of Israel received forgiveness (4:20):

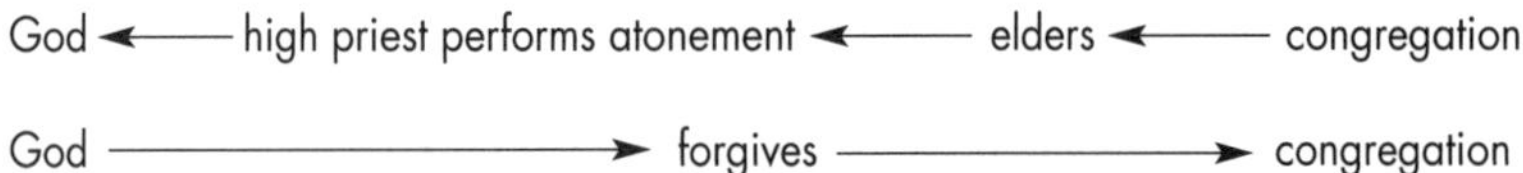

The two cases for the personal sin offering had two different sets of ritual agents. On the one hand, they envisaged two different classes of people who brought the required sacrifice. In the first case (4:22–26), the offerer of the sacrifice was a tribal chieftain, a clan leader. This term presupposed a tribal society made up of households, clans, and tribes. It refers both to the head of a clan and the head of a tribe. By virtue of his position, his sin affected him and his whole clan, as happened in the case of Korah's rebellion (Numbers 16). In the second case (Lev 4:27–35) the offerer was any Israelite, male or female. Both the tribal chieftain and the Israelite commoner were required to present the animal for the sin offering, lay their right hand on its head, and slaughter it. They therefore were the beneficiaries from the rite of atonement performed with the blood taken from the animal.

The second main actor in both these sacrifices was the officiating priest (4:25, 26, 30, 31, 34, 35). He performed the rite of atonement for them (4:26, 31, 35). He not only manipulated the blood, but also burned up the fat from the animal on the altar. He alone was permitted to eat the meat from the sacrificed animal together with the other priests from his family (6:19–22 [ET 6:26–29]). He assured the offerers that their transgressions had been forgiven.

The most significant actor in this transaction was God. By his Word he instituted these offerings to deal with the sins committed against him. All the main parts of the ritual were performed in his presence: the presentation of the animal (4:4), the laying on of hands (4:4, 15), the slaughter (4:4, 15, 24), the sprinkling of the blood (4:6, 17), and the smearing of blood on the incense altar (4:7, 17). Through the rite of atonement performed by the priest, God granted forgiveness (4:20, 26, 31, 35).

Ritual Material

As with the burnt offering and the peace offering, a ritually clean, edible, domesticated animal was required for the regular sin offering. Three kinds of animals were prescribed: a bull for a priest (4:4) and the congregation (4:14), a male goat for a tribal leader (4:23), and a female goat (4:28) or a female sheep (4:32) for a commoner. This differentiation is, at first glance, rather puzzling. The choice of animals was obviously meant to differentiate this sacrifice from the burnt offering. What's more, male lambs and rams, the most common victims for burnt offerings and peace offerings, were not authorized for use in a sin offering.

A system of ritual symbolism seems to be at work here in this legislation. Since the bull was the head of the domesticated animals, it was used for the high priest, the ritual head of the congregation. Elsewhere it was used for a sin offering at the ordination of the priests (8:14; 16:6) and the Levites (Num 8:8). If that is so, the choice of a bull for the congregational sin offering in Lev 4:14, rather than the male goat, as elsewhere, becomes explicable. It confirms the hypothesis of Milgrom that both 4:3–12 and 4:13–21 provide two complementary remedies for the one sin committed by the high priest in his official capacity.[17] Even though rams were the most aggressive and powerful animals in any flock, the dominant male goats led the flock to water and to pasture. Since the male goat represented the leaders of Israel, God's flock (Pss 74:1; 79:13; 95:7; 100:3), it was used for the sin offering of the congregation and its leaders (Lev 4:23; 16:5; Num 7:16; 28:15, 22, 30; 29:5, 11, 16). Female goats and sheep made up the bulk of any Israelite flock. They therefore symbolized the members of the congregation and so were used for the sin offerings of the ordinary people (Lev 4:28, 32; 5:6; 14:19; Num 6:14). See figure 8.

Figure 8

Animal Symbolism in the Sin Offerings

Animal	*Status of Animal*	*Symbol*
Bull	Head of livestock	Priest
Male goat	Leader of flock	Chieftain
Female goat	Member of flock	Commoner
Female sheep	Member of flock	Commoner

After their slaughter these animals produced the three most important things used in the ritual for the sin offering. First, they supplied the blood for the rite of atonement. Its significance is apparent from the unique manner of its disposal. In the public sin offering, the blood was brought by the high priest into the Holy Place, sprinkled before the curtain there, smeared on the horns of the incense altar, and then poured out at the base of the altar for burnt offering. In the ritual for the personal sin offering, however, the blood was first smeared on the horns of the altar for burnt offering and then poured out at its base. Since the sin offering was designed as a special rite of atonement, the blood from the animal was the most important ritual substance in it. Second, as with a peace offering, the fat was removed from the animal and burned on the altar. Unlike the peace offering, the fat was not classified as a "gift" to the Lord; it was regarded as his by right of possession. Third, the remains of the animal were disposed of differently, according to the kind of sacrifice. In the case of a sin offering for the priest and the congregation, all of it was incinerated in a bonfire outside the camp, while in the case of the personal sin offering, the officiating priest received the skin and the meat from it for his own use. Since the meat was most holy, it could be eaten only at the sanctuary.

The feature of this sacrifice was its use of blood in two ways unique to this offering. In the public sin offering, some of the blood was sprinkled against the curtain in the tent of meeting and smeared on the horns of the incense altar, before the rest was poured out at the base of the altar for burnt offering. In the personal sin offering, some of the blood was smeared on the horns of that al-

[17] Milgrom, *Leviticus 1–16*, 241–42.

tar before the rest of it was poured out at its base. In both cases the blood was brought, more or less closely, into God's presence and smeared on the horns of an altar. This blood was the means by which atonement was made for a transgression against God. It restored the transgressor and undid the damage done to the altar by his transgression.

Ritual Location

The location for the performance of this sacrifice is especially significant. The first place mentioned in the legislation was the location for the presentation and slaughter of the animal. The bull for the public sin offering was presented and slaughtered at the same place as the bull for the burnt offering (1:3), on the east side of the altar at the entrance to the tent of meeting (4:4, 14–15). The animals belonging to the flock were presented for the personal sin offering and slaughtered on the north side of the altar (4:24, 29, 33), where the burnt offering for the animal from the flock was to be slaughtered (1:11). Like the burnt offering, the sin offering was presented and slaughtered "before the Lord" (4:4, 15, 24).

The second ritually significant place was the location of the major blood rite for the sin offering. It was conducted in the tent of meeting itself (4:5, 16). The blood was sprinkled against the holy curtain separating the Holy Place from the Holy of Holies (4:6, 17). By being directed towards the mercy seat where the Lord was invisibly enthroned, the blood was brought as close to him as was ritually possible on any day except for the Day of Atonement. (Only on that day could the high priest enter the Holy of Holies [16:14–16].) The blood was also smeared on the horns of the incense altar situated right in front of the curtain (4:7, 18). In this way the ritual access of the congregation to the Lord's presence was publicly restored. The high priest could once again offer the incense there in the morning and evening service.

The third place for the enactment of this sacrifice was the ash dump located outside the camp. It was regarded as ritually clean place where the fat-drenched ashes and the unburned remains from the altar were deposited. The high priest got rid of the carcass of the bull for the public burnt offering by incinerating it there. He thereby ensured that it could not be used by anyone for any other ritual purpose.

The legislation prescribes the location for the performance of the sin offerings because they gain their significance from association with these holy places. The blood from them had to be sprinkled before the Lord in the Holy Place and applied to the altars because access to God's presence was either granted or refused there.

Ritual Occasion

The sin offering was the mandatory sacrifice for two clearly defined situations. Both these had to do with the unintentional transgression of a divine prohibition (4:2). Two different occasions are covered by this legislation. The first was the ritual transgression of the high priest in the performance of some ceremony involving and so implicating the congregation (4:3). No specific case is given. Whatever the error of the high priest, the congregation suffered as a result of it. Its members too became unwittingly implicated by association with his ritual transgression (4:13). When they discovered what they had done and realized that they were guilty too, both they and the high priest were required to sacrifice a bull as a sin offering.

The second occasion involved the unintentional transgression of a divine prohibition by either a chieftain (4:32) or an ordinary Israelite (4:27). Again no specific example of such a transgression is given. It may have involved something like the accidental consumption of blood or fat (3:7) or the eating of polluted food (7:19). It could also have been the failure to perform the divine service in the prescribed way, as was the case in 2 Chr 29:7, 18–24. When they realized that they were guilty or they were informed of that error, they were required to bring a sin offering, so that they could enter the sanctuary and approach God, without polluting the sanctuary with their impurity.

Ritual Enactment

The unique features of the sin offering are evident from a comparison of them with the personal burnt offering and the personal peace offering. The first stage of the ritual enactment followed the same procedure as the burnt offering and the peace offering with the presentation of the animal, the placement of the right hand on its head, and its ritual slaughter. But after that came the ritually distinctive feature of the sin offering. The simple rite of atonement common to the burnt offering and peace offering was elaborated in two different ways. Instead of "splashing" the blood against the side of the altar, as was done in the personal burnt offering (זָרַק in 1:5, 11) and in the personal peace offering (זָרַק in 3:2, 8, 13), in the sin offering the priest performed the major blood rite for animals burned outside the sanctuary or the minor blood rite for animals eaten in the sanctuary.

The major blood rite was enacted for the offering of the priest and the congregation because they had broken a ritual prohibition. Since any ritual transgression by the priest affected the daily sacrificial ritual, in which the priest entered the Holy Place and appeared before the Lord at the incense altar, the rite of atonement for it rectified the damage done to the ritual system in two ways. First, the high priest carried the blood from the sacrifice into the holy place and "sprinkled" (הִזָּה) it seven times with his right forefinger (cf. 14:16, 27) on the floor in front of the curtain (4:5–6). The blood was sprinkled seven times in this seventh act of the ritual because it is meant to achieve complete cleansing from the offense.[18] This act of sprinkling foreshadowed the sprinkling on the Day of Atonement (16:14–16). It must therefore be understood as

[18] Seven is a number of completeness, since creation was completed within seven days. Compare also Rev 1:12, 16, 20; the seven letters to the seven churches in Revelation 2–3; and the seven seals, seven trumpets, and seven censers in Revelation 4–16.

a partial fulfillment of that much more comprehensive annual enactment. Second, the priest "placed" (נָתַן, e.g., 4:7, 18) some of the blood on the four horns of the incense altar where the presiding priest burned incense as a public act of intercession, each morning and evening, during the daily performance of the public service. By daubing the horns of the altar with blood, the whole altar was purged. The priest then disposed of the leftover blood by pouring it out at the base of the altar for burnt offering.

The minor blood rite, enacted for the sin offering of a tribal leader or layperson, is much less elaborate. Since these people merely had access to the altar for burnt offering when they came to the sanctuary, the altar alone needed to be cleansed by the smearing of blood on its four horns (4:25, 30, 34). Like the public burnt offering, all leftover blood was then poured out at the base of the altar.

After the performance of the blood rite, the fat was removed from both kinds of sin offering and burned on the altar in exactly the same way as was done for the peace offering (4:8–10, 19–20, 26, 31, 35). Thereby the rest of the meat of the animal was consecrated as most holy food. But then, unlike the peace offering, the offerer ate none of the meat from the sacrifice. In the case of the public sin offering, the whole carcass was burned by the high priest at the dump for ashes outside the camp (4:11–12; cf. 6:23 [ET 6:30]). In the case of the personal sin offering, the presiding priest, together with the priests belonging to his family, ate the meat at the sanctuary (6:19, 22 [ET 6:26, 29]).

The focus of this ritual was the performance of the blood rite. It was the unique feature of this sacrifice, which distinguished it from all other sacrifices. Practically speaking, all other parts of the sin offering were related to it and functioned as part of it.

Ritual Theological Function

The legislation for the sin offering quite explicitly states its theological function. The Lord instituted this sacrifice for the performance of atonement and the reception of forgiveness from it (4:20, 26, 31, 35). By means of the sin offering, the priest as a representative of God and of the people was to "make atonement" (כִּפֶּר) for those who had unintentionally violated a divine prohibition. The sense of this verb is a matter of some dispute, because it is used in so many different ways in the OT. The consideration of its etymology does not give much help. The term could derive from a verbal root meaning "wipe off" and "cover" or else from the noun כֹּפֶר, "ransom." Both fit its use in some contexts.

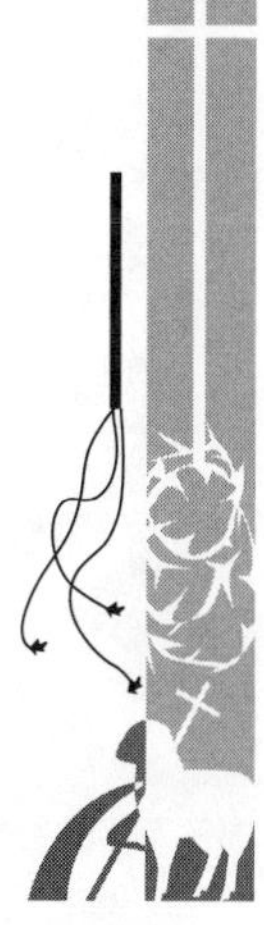

It is, however, used here, as in most liturgical contexts, as a technical ritual term for the rite of atonement performed by the manipulation of blood from a sacrificed animal. The priest "makes atonement" by means of the blood rite in the sin offering (4:20, 26, 31, 35). He performs the rite of atonement for those who have unintentionally violated some divine prohibition. As a result of this violation they had become unclean. They therefore polluted the sanctuary by their presence there. The sin offering was bought for their "sin" (4:3,

14, 23, 28, 35), its "impurity" (4:26), and their "purification" from it (4:33). It is significant that the same Hebrew word is used in all these cases. By the rite of atonement sinners are ransomed and released "from" their sin and its impurity (4:26).

The ritual act of atonement serves two related functions. On the one hand, the offender was forgiven (4:20, 26, 31, 35). God forgave the sinner through the performance of this rite by the priest. The sinner was pardoned. But that was not all. The sin had not only alienated him from God, but it had also endangered his existence. He could not approach God without polluting the holiness of the sanctuary and incurring God's wrath from the desecration of his holiness. God therefore did not just free him from the impurity of sin, but he also repaired the damaged relationship and restored the privilege of access to him. God was pleased with the sacrifice (4:20), for by it that person was once again put right with God and was made fit to share in his holiness. The opposite of receiving forgiveness for inadvertent sins, as is shown in Num 15:17–31, is to be cut off from the people of Israel and to be deprived of life with God.

The second result from the act of atonement is implied rather than stated in this legislation. The impurity from the offense had, in the case of the public ritual transgression, penetrated the Holy Place; in the case of the personal transgression, it had contaminated the altar for burnt offering. The blood from the sin offering purified the incense altar and altar for burnt offering. It counteracted the harmful effect of impurity. Since the rite of atonement removed the pollution from the sanctuary, God did not have to withdraw his presence from the tabernacle to avoid the destruction of his people for their desecration of his sanctuary. By the purification of the altar for incense and the altar for burnt offering, access to God's gracious presence was restored. The divine service could continue. The blessing of God, his goodwill and favor, was assured. God's people could approach him fearlessly and expectantly with their offerings and prayers. They could be sure that God was pleased with them and their sacrifices, because the rite of atonement had removed all the obstacles to their beneficial interaction with him.

The Graded Sin Offering (5:1–13)

Ritual Agents

The same parties are involved in this legislation as in 4:27–35. But the regulations scale down the required offerings for the ordinary Israelites in accordance with their economic status in 5:7–10 and 5:11–13. The sin offering is therefore brought within the reach of even the poorest person.

Ritual Material

The same animals are prescribed for the four cases covered in this legislation as for the personal sin offering for a normal Israelite in 4:28 and 4:32. The prescribed animal is a female sheep or goat.

In addition, two other substitutes are presented for people on the lower end of the socio-economic scale. First, as was the case with the personal burnt offering in 1:14–17, a pair of turtledoves or a pair of pigeons could be presented as a sin offering. Since a single bird would not suffice to produce some portion for incineration as well as some meat for the priest to eat, the law required one as a "sin offering" and the other as a "burnt offering." Special mention is made of the correct disposal of the blood of the bird from the sin offering. Since the blood was applied directly from the bird, it could not be smeared directly on the four horns of the altar. Instead, it is first "sprinkled" against the side of the altar and then "drained" at its base.

The second substitute for a female sheep or goat was the tenth of an ephah of fine flour. This was the amount given to a person for his ration for a single day. No oil or frankincense was to be added to the flour as was prescribed for the grain offering (2:1–2), for oil and incense were only used when people could approach God with rejoicing and petitionary prayer because God was pleased with them. A handful of the flour had to be burnt by the priest on the altar (5:12). Yet, even though the flour that was burnt on the altar was called "a token portion," it was not regarded as "a gift to the Lord," but it was placed on the "gifts to the Lord" that had been set on the altar. It therefore served a different function than in the grain offering (2:2, 9, 16), since it replaced the sprinkling of blood for the performance of atonement. Since the rest of the flour was most holy, it had to be eaten by the priest at the sanctuary (5:13; cf. 6:10 [ET 6:17]).

Ritual Occasion

The sin offering was prescribed for the unintentional violation of divine prohibitions in 4:1–35. Here it is prescribed for the alleviation of guilt from four acts of negligence affecting the divinely instituted sacred order. All of them involved a sin that infringed on God's holiness because people were unaware that they were in a state of ritual impurity.

The first case in this section has to do with the failure of a person to respond to a public oath in the name of God for an eyewitness to come forward and testify in a court of law (e.g., Judg 17:1–4; Prov 29:24). Such an oath invoked a specific curse from God on any people who failed to testify, even though they had "seen" the act or had come to "know" about it subsequently in some other way. This was an important device for the administration of justice in a close-knit society without a police force, where people often kept silent to cover up for their kinsfolk or to get back at their enemies. This sacrifice was prescribed for people who subsequently either realized that they were likely to suffer the curse invoked by the law or else were already suffering from it.

The second case deals with a people who had eaten meat from an unclean wild animal (11:5, 6) or from an unclean domesticated animal (11:4, 7) or from an unclean crawling creature (11:29–30). Even though they may have realized what they had done, they forgot what had happened and failed to do anything about it, and so remained unclean. Later they remembered what they had done and felt guilty about their failure to deal with the impurity.

The third case treats the impurity that came from contact with an unclean person, such as a person suffering from an irregular sexual discharge or a person with skin disease or a menstrual woman or a corpse. The people who had contracted uncleanness from another person were either unaware of what had happened, or they had forgotten about it. Only later did they remember what they had done. Then they felt the burden of guilt for their failure to undergo purification from it.

The fourth case involved failure to keep a carelessly uttered oath. As in the first case, such a person was guilty because he had desecrated God's holy name.

All these dealt with acts of omission that violated the sacred order and so polluted the person involved. They all needed to be rectified before that person could approach God at the sanctuary. Should any offerer fail to bring a sin offering, he would pollute the sanctuary and so incur God's wrath for desecrating its holiness. Hence the entrance liturgies mentioned both the need for purity (cf. Ps. 24:4) and for the fulfillment of oaths (cf. Ps. 15:4b) as the condition for entry into the sanctuary.

Ritual Enactment

In contrast with the sin offering for the unintentional violations of divine prohibitions in 4:1–35, the ritual for the graded sin offering for cases of omission required an act of confession (5:5; cf. 16:21; 26:40; Num 5:7). No mention is made whether this confession is made to God through a priest at the sanctuary (e.g. Ezra 10:1; Neh 9:2) or to the members of the person's family at home (e.g. Neh 1:6–7). The Hebrew verb in Lev 5:5, however, indicates that the confession had to be made out loud. Perhaps a formula such as is found in Ps 32:5 was used (cf. 1 Sam.7:6). The important thing is that the person acknowledged what he had failed to do. (In 5:5 חָטָא probably means "what he had failed to do.")

If the person brought a female sheep or goat as a sin offering, the ritual procedure was the same as in 4:27–35. The blood rite for atonement was enacted in exactly the same way. If a person brought a pair of birds, one of them was first offered as a sin offering. This was done by the high priest who wrung the neck of the bird without severing its head, "sprinkled" the blood spurting from its neck against the side of the altar, and then drained the rest of the blood at the base of the altar. Then the priest offered the second bird as a burnt offering in exactly the same way as was done for the personal burnt offering in 1:15–17. The priest, presumably, retained the first bird as his due from the sin offering and ate it in the sanctuary (cf. 6:19 [ET 6:26]). The two birds together provided what was necessary for the three essential aspects of the personal sin offering: blood for the rite of atonement, a portion of the sacrifice for burning on the altar, and meat for the priest to eat.

If some flour was offered as the substitute for the animal normally brought as the sin offering, the priest took a handful of it and burned it on the altar. The incineration of this memorial portion replaced both the normal blood rite and the incineration of the fat from the animal. Unlike the memorial portion of the grain offering, this portion, however, did not function as a "gift to the Lord," but combined the ritual function of both these acts. It sanctified the remaining flour and made atonement for the person. The leftover flour belonged to the priest as his most holy due from this offering (5:26 [ET 6:7]).

Ritual Theological Function

The graded sin offering served exactly the same theological functions as the sin offering for the unintentional violation of the divine prohibition. By its enactment the priest performed the rite of atonement which freed the "sinner" from his "sin" (5:6, 10). Through the rite of atonement, the "sinner" was also forgiven and reinstated into a favorable, harmonious relationship with God (5:10, 13). This remedy was made available to all Israelites by the authorization of cheaper substitutes for the normal prescribed animals.

The graded sin offering served two additional functions as well. On the one hand, it tackled the guilt (אָשַׁם, "to be guilty," in 5:2, 3, 4, 5) of people by authorizing a rite for the confession of their sin before God. This brought what had been hidden out into the open for God to deal with openly in the act of atonement. On the other hand, the graded sin offering was also the divinely sanctioned "compensation/reparation" for their failure, the prescribed "penalty" for it (5:6, 7). The use of the term אָשָׁם in 5:6–7 is to be understood as both "compensation" and "penalty." The act of confession and the reparatory sin offering were, therefore, instituted by God to alleviate and ease the guilty conscience of the negligent people. They were thereby freed from any penalty for actual or possible acts of sacrilege. They could approach God at the sanctuary without incurring his wrath for desecrating his holiness.

Fulfillment by Christ

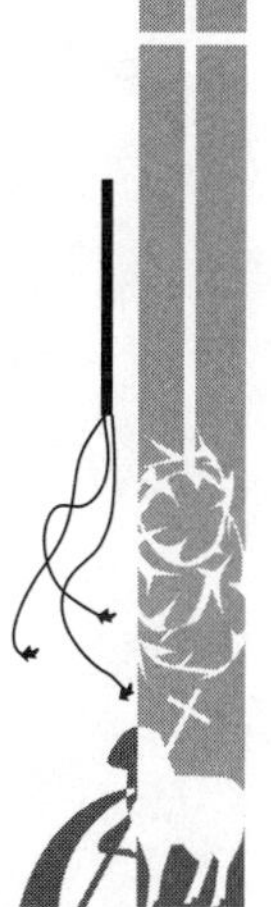

The sin offering was closely connected with the rite for atonement. God used the blood from these offerings to do two things. On the one hand, he cleansed the sanctuary (4:6, 17), the altar for incense (4:7, 18), and the altar for burnt offering (4:7, 25, 30, 34; 5:9) from impurity. On the other hand, he forgave those who had sinned inadvertently and delivered them from their sin (4:20, 26, 31, 35; 5:10). This meant that God's holiness was not desecrated by human sin, and the people who had sinned were not threatened by God's wrath. They could therefore approach God unafraid in a state of ritual purity and be certain of God's acceptance of them.

The NT teaches that Jesus sacrificed himself as the ultimate sin offering. In his parable of the Pharisee and the tax collector in Lk 18:9–14, Jesus hints at an act of atonement that goes beyond any that was established in the OT. Whereas the sin offering only provided atonement for unintentional sins and some minor sins of commission that were confessed before God, the tax collector came into the temple to seek atonement for himself *as a deliberate sinner,* an unclean person excluded from God's presence. During the performance of the daily burnt offering, he prayed, "O God, be propitiated toward me, the sinner."[19] Jesus states that this sinner was declared righteous before God. In this

[19] Just, *Luke 9:51–24:53,* 684.

way Jesus intimated that he would provide the sin offering of atonement for the justification of all overt sinners, such as the tax collector, and give them access to God's grace.

In Rom 3:22–26, the apostle Paul picks up this teaching and affirms that Christ is the means of atonement for the justification of sinners before God. Then in Rom 8:3 Paul asserts that God the Father sent Jesus to be "the sin offering" for sinful humanity.[20] Paul uses the same Greek phrase, περὶ ἁμαρτίας, to describe the purpose of Christ's mission that the LXX uses for the sin offering (Lev 4:3, 14, 28, 35; 5:6–11, 13). As a result of Christ's self-sacrifice, God accomplishes his just purposes in us through his Holy Spirit.

Paul makes the same point in a slightly different way in 2 Cor 5:21. Even though Jesus was sinless, God offered Jesus as the "sin offering" for human sin.[21] In this case Paul employs the term ἁμαρτία alone, which the LXX also uses for a sin offering in Lev 4:21, 24; 5:12; 6:10 (ET 6:17). Influenced by the use of עָשָׂה, "perform, make," as a ritual term in Leviticus, he maintains that God "made" Jesus a sin offering (see the textual note on עָשָׂה in 4:20). Those who are in Christ therefore share in his righteousness. He took on their sin so that he could give them his purity. They are righteous before God, guiltless and free from condemnation (Rom 8:1).

The letter to the Hebrews expands the same theology contained in those rather terse statements of St. Paul in a number of different directions. Hebrews notes that when the high priest offered a sin offering for himself and the people, he did not eat any of its meat, but had it burned outside the camp. So Jesus also suffered and died outside the holy city of Jerusalem (Heb 13:11–12). We therefore do not eat the flesh of his sin offering from the altar at the tabernacle as the priests did; we receive the body of Christ as a gift of grace from a heavenly altar that is outside the Israelite camp (Heb 13:9–16). In the Eucharist we go out from there, from the earthly city of Jerusalem, to him to eat his gracious body and drink his sanctifying blood in heavenly Jerusalem.[22]

In the old covenant the high priest brought the blood from the sin offering right into the Holy Place on normal occasions and into the Holy of Holies on the Day of Atonement for the sanctification of the earthly sanctuary. In contrast to that, Hebrews claims that Jesus, by his resurrection and ascension, brought the blood from his sin offering into the Father's presence (Heb 9:12). That blood was most holy and also by that action has become most holy. With it he now sprinkles the hearts of the faithful to cleanse their conscience from all impurity and to sanctify them completely as the priestly house of God (Heb 3:1–6; 9:14; 10:21–22; 12:24; 13:12).

---

[20] See the exposition of Rom 8:3 in Ap XXIV 23. See also Käsemann, *Commentary on Romans*, 216–18; Dunn, *Romans 1–8*, 422; Schreiner, *Romans*, 403.

[21] Bruce, *1 and 2 Corinthians*, 210; Lyonnet and Sabourin, *Sin, Redemption, and Sacrifice*, 250–56; Martin, *2 Corinthians*, 157.

[22] Field, *The Apostolic Liturgy and the Epistle to the Hebrews*, 415–19.

Like all the other sacrifices, the sin offering had to be offered repeatedly, because no sin offering could cleanse God's people so completely from the stain of their sin that they were fit to approach God without the need for any further sacrifices (Heb 10:1–22). But Jesus fully accomplished what those sin offerings had partly achieved. By his perfect sacrifice he has removed sin so completely that there is no longer any consciousness of sin and condemnation in God's presence. Those whom he cleanses with his blood have a good conscience before God.

The high priest used to enter the earthly sanctuary with the blood of animals to cleanse the bodies of the Israelites from physical impurity so that they could come physically into God's presence at the tabernacle. But Jesus the great High Priest entered heaven itself with his blood to cleanse our consciences so that we could perform the Divine Service together with him in the heavenly sanctuary (Heb 9:11–14). Hebrews therefore contrasts the partial physical cleansing from sin through the sin offerings presented at the tabernacle with the complete cleansing of the whole person, through the blood of Christ, for service in the heavenly sanctuary.

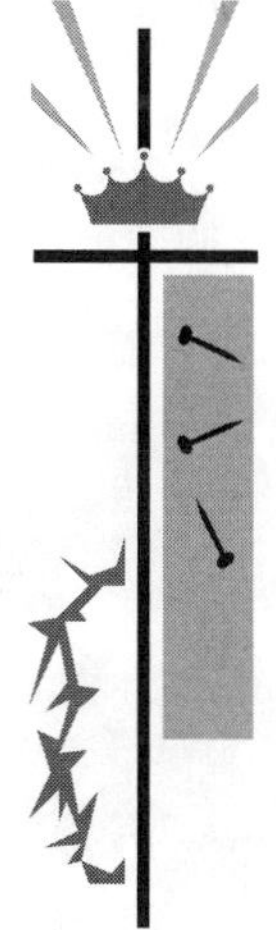

St. John affirms that Jesus is the sin offering for the sins of the whole world (1 Jn 2:2; 4:10). He uses the word ἱλασμός, "atoning offering," which the LXX uses in Ezek 44:27 for the sin offering of the high priest (cf. Num 5:8; 2 Macc 3:33). Jesus, by his blood, cleanses us from all sins. This includes the impurity that comes from the sins that we commit (1 Jn 1:7) as well as the impurity from the injustice and abuse that we have experienced from those who have sinned against us (cf. Mt 6:12). John therefore repeats the teaching of St. Paul and the letter to the Hebrews. But he also picks up another aspect of the ritual legislation in Leviticus. He emphasizes the need for the faithful to confess their sins to God the Father and so bring their impurity out into the light with him in order to receive cleansing and pardon (1 Jn 1:9).

In the old covenant, the sin offering provided blood that only atoned for the unintentional sins of God's people (Lev 4:2, 13, 22, 27). No rite of atonement was established to atone for deliberate sins, willful sins with a high hand that despised God's Word and broke his commandments (Num 15:27–31). In contrast to this, John declares that Jesus cleanses us "from all sin" and "from all injustice" (1 Jn 1:9). What's more, this sacrifice was not just made for God's people, but for the whole world (1 Jn 2:2). The apostle John also warns that "there is a sin that leads to death," the act of spiritual suicide that cuts a person off from God (1 Jn 5:16). But he does not elaborate on it as the book of Hebrews does. Hebrews contains the stern warning that in the new covenant there is but one deliberate sin that negates the efficacy of Christ's sin offering (Heb 10:26). That willful sin is the sin of apostasy from the living God (Heb 3:12; 6:6) by spurning the Son of God, desecrating his sanctifying blood, and outraging the Spirit of grace given through his blood (Heb 6:6; 10:29).[23] Those

[23] Pfitzner, *Hebrews,* 91, 98, 147.

who spurn God's Son and desecrate his blood reject the basis for repentance, restoration, and access to God's grace. That deliberate act of rejection undoes the work of Christ in them.

Since the early church, the teaching that Jesus was the sin offering that atoned for the sins of the whole world has determined the shape and content of the Divine Service. No sin offering needed to be presented before the faithful could meet with the triune God. Instead, the Divine Service often began with the confession of sins and the absolution so that the people could serve the living God with a good conscience (*Didache* 4:14). They met to celebrate the sacrificial banquet of Christ in which they ate his sacrificed body and actually drank his cleansing blood. Since they served as priests in the heavenly sanctuary together with Christ the great High Priest, they, like the priests of the old covenant, ate the most holy flesh of his sin offering.

To the present day, the orders of service based on the Latin Mass praise Christ as "the Lamb of God, who takes away the sin of the world," (Jn 1:29), for in his Holy Supper Jesus gives us the blood to drink for "the remission of sins" (Mt 26:28). The blood that atoned for our sin now frees us completely from the stain of sin and releases us from its grip. Jesus does not just sprinkle our bodies with his blood, but with it he also sprinkles our hearts, our conscience. He takes away our sin and gives us his purity. We can therefore draw near to God the Father with a true heart in the full assurance of faith (Heb 10:19). We need not fear his wrath and condemnation of us for desecrating his holiness by our impurity.

The death of Jesus Christ, our Lord,
We celebrate with one accord;
It is our comfort in distress,
Our heart's sweet joy and happiness.

He blotted out with his own blood
The judgment that against us stood;
He full atonement for us made,
And all our debt he fully paid.

That this is now and ever true
He gives an earnest ever new:
In this his holy Supper here
We taste his love so sweet, so near.

His Word proclaims and we believe
That in this Supper we receive
His very body, as he said,
His very blood for sinners shed.[24]

[24] From "The Death of Jesus Christ, Our Lord" by Haquin Spegel (*LW* 107:1–4).

Leviticus 5:14–26 (ET 5:14–6:7)

Regulations for the Reparation Offering

Translation

**5 [14]The Lord spoke to Moses: [15]"When a person commits an act of sacrilege
by unintentionally sinning against any of the Lord's holy things, he shall bring
to the Lord, as his reparation, an unblemished ram from the flock, according to
its equivalent amount in silver shekels by the sanctuary weight, as a reparation
offering. [16]He shall make restitution for the holy thing against which he sinned
by adding one-fifth of it to it and giving it to the priest. Then the priest shall make
atonement on his behalf with the ram of the reparation offering, so that he may
be forgiven.**

**[17]"If, however, a person sins, without knowing it, by doing any of the Lord's
prohibitions, which should not be done, and then realizes his guilt, he shall bear
his iniquity; [18]he shall bring an unblemished ram from the flock, or its equivalence, as a reparation offering to the priest. The priest shall make atonement on
behalf of him for his unintentional sin, which he had committed without knowing, so that he may be forgiven. [19]It is a reparation offering; he has indeed made
reparation to the Lord."**

**[20]The Lord spoke to Moses: [21]"If a person sins and commits an act of sacri-
lege against the Lord in that he dissembles to his fellow citizen about a deposit
or an investment or something stolen, or else, having extorted something from
his fellow citizen, [22]or, having found something lost, he dissembles about it; and
in that he then swears falsely about anything that a human being may do and sin
in these ways— [23]when he has sinned and then admits his guilt, he shall return
what he has stolen, or what he has extorted, or the deposit which was entrusted
to him, or the lost thing that he has found, [24]or anything else about which he has
sworn falsely, he shall repay it in its entirety and add one-fifth of it to it. He shall
pay it to its owner when he admits his guilt. [25]Then he shall bring to the priest,
as his penalty to the Lord, an unblemished ram from the flock, or its equivalence,
as a reparation offering. [26]The priest shall make atonement for him before the
Lord, so that he may be forgiven for whatever he has done to incur guilt thereby."**

Textual Notes

5:15 נֶפֶשׁ כִּי־תִמְעֹל מַעַל—See 5:21 (ET 6:2); 26:40, where the verb מָעַל and the related noun מַעַל are also used together. As Milgrom has shown, this verb and noun refer to an act of trespass on the divine domain.[1] Since this involves the misappropriation or abuse of something holy, it is an act of sacrilege. Hence we translate the use of the

[1] Milgrom, "The Concept of *Maʿal* in the Bible and the Ancient Near East"; Milgrom, *Leviticus 1–16*, 320, 345–56.

verb and noun together as "to commit an act of sacrilege." Two kinds of sacrilege are covered in 5:15–26 (ET 5:15–6:7): the desecration of something that belongs to God and the violation of an oath made with his holy name.

וְחָטְאָה—The verb חָטָא here and in 5:17 refers to failure to treat something holy in a holy way as a possession of God. It means "to sin" or "to be remiss with/to be at fault with."

בִּשְׁגָגָה—See the textual note on this in 4:2.

מִקָּדְשֵׁי יְהוָה—See the textual notes on 4:6, and see also 5:16. The plural form "the holy things of the Lord" occurs only here. See Lev 19:8 and Mal 2:11 for its singular form.

אֲשָׁמוֹ—This noun refers to the offering for "reparation" or "compensation." See the textual notes on it in 5:6. The noun אָשָׁם and verb אָשַׁם figure prominently in this section of Leviticus, with seven occurrences of the noun and four of the verb. This vocabulary recalls 5:1–13, where the noun occurs twice and the verb four times.

תָּמִים—See the textual note on this adjective in 1:3 and "Fulfillment by Christ" in the commentary on 1:3–17. It recurs in 5:18; 5:25 (ET 6:6).

בְּעֶרְכְּךָ—This is literally "to your valuation." It recurs in 5:18; 5:25 (ET 6:6); 27:2, 3, 4, 5, 6, 7, 8, 12, 13, 15, 16, 17, 18, 19, 23, 25, 27. For an explanation of this form and its meaning, see Speiser, Levine, and Milgrom.[2] The priest was required to assess the value of the ram and the value of what had been misappropriated with the addition of one-fifth of its value. He then charged the offender the amount needed for the purchase of the ram and the payment of compensation.

כֶּסֶף־שְׁקָלִים בְּשֶׁקֶל־הַקֹּדֶשׁ—The sanctuary shekel (literally "shekel of holiness") is also mentioned in, for example, Ex 30:13; Lev 27:25; Num 3:47; 18:16 (cf. Ezek 45:12). It probably differed in weight from the shekel used elsewhere. Surprisingly, the actual cost of the animal is not given. The rabbis maintained that it had to amount to at least two shekels.

לְאָשָׁם׃—The אָשָׁם has traditionally been called the "guilt offering" because of its derivation from the Hebrew verb אָשַׁם, which means "to be culpable, guilty" and often also "to feel guilty." However, "guilt offering" does not accurately describe the function of this offering.[3] It was never offered by the congregation, but was always given as a personal sacrifice. It is not prescribed for all cases where a person is guilty of offending God. The sin offering deals with such guilt. But the אָשָׁם, as Milgrom has shown, deals with the guilt from actual or suspected cases of sacrilege through the desecration of something holy or the holy name of God.[4] Such acts of trespass were regarded as a kind of theft from God, misappropriation of God's property. The offender was therefore required to present this sacrifice as an act of compensation or reparation to God for that sacred thing. If the offense remained unatoned for and no

---

2 Speiser, "Leviticus and the Critics," 124–28; Levine, *Leviticus*, 30–31; Milgrom, *Leviticus 1–16*, 336–37.

3 Hartley, *Leviticus*, 76–78.

4 Milgrom, "The Concept of *Maʿal* in the Bible and the Ancient Near East"; Milgrom, *Leviticus 1–16*, 339–73.

reparation was made, the offender would suffer divine retribution. So, since this sacrifice provides reparation for sacrilege, it is best called a "reparation offering."

5:16 וְאֵת אֲשֶׁר חָטָא מִן־הַקֹּדֶשׁ יְשַׁלֵּם—The unusual disjunctive clause indicates that the payment of compensation and the rite of atonement are not necessarily two consecutive acts.

וְהַכֹּהֵן יְכַפֵּר עָלָיו—See the textual notes on 1:4.

בְּאֵיל הָאָשָׁם—See 19:22.

וְנִסְלַח לוֹ׃—See the textual notes on 4:20, which explains that this passive implies the agency of God: "it will be forgiven (by God) to him."

5:17 וְאִם־נֶפֶשׁ כִּי—See the textual notes on 2:1. נֶפֶשׁ כִּי recurs in 5:21 (ET 6:2). The use of וְאִם with נֶפֶשׁ כִּי indicates that, even though this is a new case, it is connected ritually and theologically with the previous case. Both have to do with atonement for minor acts of sacrilege.

תֶחֱטָא—This abbreviated clause recalls the fuller expression in 5:15a.

וְעָשְׂתָה אַחַת מִכָּל־מִצְוֹת יְהוָה—The language here closely resembles the prescriptions for the sin offering in 4:13, 22, 27. The difference here is that the person is ignorant of the offense.

וְנָשָׂא עֲוֺנוֹ׃—See the textual notes on 5:1. Here the clause means that he accepts responsibility for the act.[5]

5:18 וְהוּא לֹא־יָדַע—This negated verb is repeated from 5:17 to indicate that the offense is suspected sacrilege. It stands in stark contrast to the positive clauses in 5:1, 3.

5:19 אָשָׁם אָשַׁם לַיהוָה׃—The meaning and function of this clause are uncertain. The use of the infinitive absolute (אָשֹׁם) before the finite form of the verb (אָשַׁם) makes it a very emphatic assertion. It can be construed in two ways. It could assert that the transgressor most certainly must present the reparation offering to the Lord, but that would be out of place here at the end of this section. More likely, as Hartley has shown, is that it asserts that the transgressor who presents this offering thereby most certainly makes reparation to the Lord for the offense.[6]

5:21 נֶפֶשׁ כִּי תֶחֱטָא וּמָעֲלָה מַעַל בַּיהוָה—The order of reference to sacrilege before the mention of sin in 5:15 is reversed here because this section deals with sacrilege as a secondary offense by a person who covers up his sin with an oath. In this case the use of the Lord's name in an oath is regarded as an act of sacrilege because it implicates God in defrauding an Israelite. Such an oath therefore desecrates the holy name.

Lev 5:21b–22a (ET 6:2b–3a) specifies the kinds of sins that are intended in 5:21a (ET 6:2a).

וְכִחֵשׁ בַּעֲמִיתוֹ—While the term עָמִית (5:21 [ET 6:2]; 18:20; 19:11, 15, 17; 24:19; 25:14, 15, 17) may originally have been used for a "kinsman," that is, a person who is a member of one's own clan, in Leviticus it is the designation for any fellow citizen in Israel. It is used as a synonym for אָח, "brother" (25:14), רֵעַ, "neighbor" (19:15–18), and בְּנֵי עַם, "compatriot" (19:17–18).

---

5 Milgrom, *Leviticus 1–16*, 334.

6 Hartley, *Leviticus*, 73.

בְּפִקָּדוֹן—See Gen 41:36.

בִתְשׂוּמֶת יָד—Literally this refers to "the placement of a hand." The phrase could refer either to the delivery of money for investment with another person (so we translate it as "an investment") or to a partnership in business.

עָשַׁק—The verb עָשַׁק (also in 5:23 [ET 6:4]; 19:13) is used to describe acts of extortion and exploitation against weak members of the community (Deut 24:14; 1 Sam 12:3–4; Jer 7:6; Ezek 22:29; Amos 4:1; Zech 7:10). This law covers various cases of confiscation, such as the failure to pay wages (Deut 24:14–15) and the withholding of a pledge or piece of confiscated property after the repayment of a loan (Ezek 18:7; cf. Ex 22:25–26; Deut 24:6).

5:22 וְנִשְׁבַּע עַל־שָׁקֶר—This clause does not refer the last of five transgressions but to the taking of an oath to deny these four previous crimes. That oath was the transgression that required the presentation of the reparation offering.

הָאָדָם—This refers to any person, male or female. See the textual note on it in 1:2.

5:23 כִּי־יֶחֱטָא—This resumptive clause presupposes and sums up the case laid out in 5:20–22 (ET 6:1–3).

5:24 בְּרֹאשׁוֹ—This is literally "to its head." It refers to the principal amount of money.

בְּיוֹם אַשְׁמָתוֹ׃—This is literally "on the day of his guilt." It refers to the onset of guilt rather than "the day of the reparation offering."[7] In 5:24 and 5:26 (ET 6:5 and 6:7), אַשְׁמָה is the noun meaning "guilt" (*HALOT,* s.v. אַשְׁמָה) rather than the so-called feminine form of the infinitive construct of the verb אָשַׁם, which is identical in form (אַשְׁמָה) and is frequent earlier in chapters 4–5.

5:25 אֲשָׁמוֹ—This means "as his penalty" or "as his reparation" rather than "as his guilt."

יָבִיא—See the textual note on this verb in 2:2.

5:26 וְכִפֶּר עָלָיו הַכֹּהֵן לִפְנֵי יְהוָה—See the textual notes on 1:4. The phrase "before the Lord" is also added to the atonement formula in 14:18, 31; 15:15, 30; 19:22; and in the instance of sacrilege in Num 15:28.

Commentary

Structure

This section consists of two divine speeches, both of which contain the case laws for the reparation offering (5:14–19; 5:20–26 [ET 6:1–7]) and both of which are couched in a single sentence. Both are introduced by the formula for the divine speech to Moses and both lack the formula for transmission found in 1:2 and 4:1.

The first speech gives two cases for the reparation offering, while the second speech gives only one case. The change of the sequence from sacrilege and sin to sin and sacrilege in 5:21 (ET 6:2) shows that the first deals with sacrilege as a primary transgression, while the second deals with sacrilege as a

---

[7] Contra Hartley, *Leviticus*, 73.

secondary transgression. Both speeches end with the formula for atonement and forgiveness. This formula is elaborated in three different ways: by the reference to the ram in 5:16, by the reference to ignorance and inadvertence and the classification of the ram and its presentation in 5:18b–19, and by the reference to the Lord's presence and the guilt of the offender in 5:26 (ET 6:7).

The two cases in 5:15–19 are coordinated by the unusual and rather awkward phrase וְאִם־נֶפֶשׁ כִּי, "and if a person when" (5:17). This seems to be used to indicate that, even though 5:17–19 deals with a new case, it is still an instance of sacrilege that needs to be considered together with 5:15–16. Two literary devices are used to assemble the material in 5:20–26 (ET 6:1–7). First, the complex protasis in 5:21–22 (ET 6:2–3) is arranged as a chiasm:

> If a person **sins** and commits an act of sacrilege against the Lord
> in that he *dissembles* to his fellow citizen
> about a deposit or an investment or something stolen,
> or else, having extorted something from his fellow citizen, or, having found something lost,
> he *dissembles* about it;
> and in that he then swears falsely about anything that a human being may do and **sin** in these ways …

This shows that the act of sacrilege discussed here is the false oath of denial. Second, the catchword "sin," which begins and ends 5:21–22 (ET 6:2–3), is also used in the resumptive protasis in 5:23 (ET 6:4) which ties together 5:21–22 (ET 6:2–3) and 5:23–26 (ET 6:4–7).

The structure of this pericope can be outlined as follows:

- I. The reparation offering for the desecration of holy things (5:14–19)
  - A. Introduction: the Lord's address to Moses (5:14)
  - B. The divine speech (5:15–19)
    - 1. The reparation offering for unintentional sacrilege (5:15–16)
      - a. Case (5:15a)
      - b. Procedure (5:15b–16)
        - i. Presentation of ram or its monetary equivalent (5:15b)
        - ii. Monetary restitution for the misappropriated holy thing (5:16a)
        - iii. Performance of atonement by the priest (5:16b)
    - 2. The reparation offering for suspected sacrilege (5:17–19)
      - a. Case (5:17)
        - i. Suspected sacrilege by violation of a divine prohibition
        - ii. Realization of guilt
        - iii. Assumption of responsibility
      - b. Procedure (5:18)
        - i. Presentation of a ram or its monetary equivalent
        - ii. Performance of atonement by a priest
      - c. Categorization (5:19)
        - i. Classification as a reparation offering
        - ii. Offering as reparation to God
- II. The reparation offering for the violation of an oath (5:20–26 [ET 6:1–7])
  - A. Introduction: the Lord's address to Moses (5:20 [ET 6:1])

B. The divine speech: violation of an oath (5:21–26 [ET 6:2–5])
  1. Case: sin which leads to sacrilege (5:21–23a [ET 6:2–4a])
    a. Denial of misappropriation (5:21–22a [ET 6:2–3a])
      i. Illegal possession: deposit, investment, stolen goods
      ii. Illegal acquisition: withheld goods, lost goods
    b. Denial under oath (5:22b [ET 6:3b])
    c. Realization of guilt (5:23a [ET 6:4a])
  2. Procedure (5:23b–26 [ET 6:4b–7])
    a. Restoration of misappropriated property (5:23b–24a [ET 6:4b–5a])
    b. Penalty of an additional twenty percent (5:24b [ET 6:5b])
    c. Presentation of a ram or its monetary equivalent as a reparation offering (5:25 [ET 6:6])
    d. Performance of atonement by priest for forgiveness (5:26 [ET 6:7])

Ritual Agents

Four parties interact with each other in these three cases. First, there is the person who has either committed a sacrilegious act or suspects that he may have done so. Because he has offended God directly with this act of sacrilege, he must rectify it before God. In all three cases that involves the presentation of a ram as a reparation offering. In two cases he also had to provide some repayment for the offense. If he misappropriated something holy from God, he had to repay God (5:16a). If he has misappropriated something from a fellow citizen, he had to repay that person (5:24 [ET 6:5]). The legislation centers on the offender as the guilty party.

Second, since an act of sacrilege had been committed (5:5, 17, 21 [ET 6:2]), God was involved in the ritual interaction. The ram was brought to him (5:15, 25 [ET 6:6]). He received repayment for what had been misappropriated from him (5:16a). The rite of atonement had to be performed "before the Lord," so that the offense would be forgiven by him (5:26 [ET 6:7]).

Third, even though the Lord was the main offended party in the case given in 5:21–26 (ET 6:2–7), the former owner of the misappropriated property was also involved as the primary victim of the offense. Repayment, therefore, had to be made to him in this instance (5:24b [ET 6:5b]).

Lastly, the priest was involved as the mediator between God and the offender. The offender brought the ram to the priest as to God (5:15, 25 [ET 6:6]). The priest also received the payment of reparation on God's behalf (5:16) and performed the rite on behalf of the offender in God's presence (5:16, 18, 26 [ET 6:7]). Apart from him, the offender could not make restitution to God for the sacrilege committed by him.

Holy Things

The legislation for the reparation offering protected the holy things of the Lord (5:15–16). They belonged to the Lord and were used by him in the divine service. His presence in the sanctuary made and kept them holy (Ex 29:43–44).

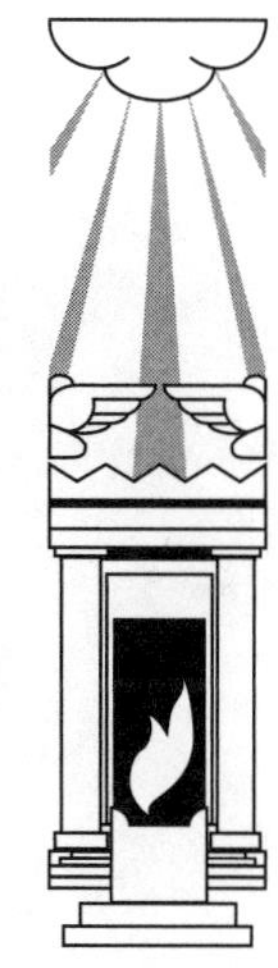

Through these holy things he made himself accessible to his people and granted them access to his gracious presence.

The priestly legislation distinguished between the most holy things and the holy things (21:22; Num 18:8–19). They differed in that only the most holy things communicated holiness by physical contact (Ex 29:37; 30:29; Lev 6:18, 27). The most holy things included the tent of meeting together with its main furnishings—the ark of the covenant, the incense altar and its incense, the lampstand, the table, the altar for burnt offering, and the laver (Ex 29:37; 30:26–29, 36)—the showbread (Lev 24:9) and the bread from the grain offering (2:3, 10; 6:10 [ET 6:17]), and the meat from the sin offering and the reparation offering (6:18, 22 [ET 6:25, 29]; 7:1, 6). Since physical contact with these things communicated holiness, they were to be kept out of bounds from everybody except a priest. The holy things consisted of all the offerings brought by the people to the sanctuary.[a] They included the meat from the peace offering (Lev 19:8) and from the firstborn male animals (Ex 13:2; Num 18:15–18), the first-ripe and first-processed agricultural produce from the land (Num 18:12–13), the tithes (Lev 27:30–33), and all votive offerings (Lev 27:9–27; Num 18:14).

(a) Num 5:9–10; 18:8, 19; cf. Lev 12:4; 19:8; 22:2, 3, 4, 6, 7, 10, 12, 14, 15, 16

The legislation in Lev 5:14–19 covers all these holy things. The penalty for their desecration was either cutting off by the Lord (cf. 19:8) or death (cf. Num 18:32). They could not therefore be abused with impunity. Any accidental or unconscious or deliberate act of desecration was potentially lethal, unless the prescribed reparation offering was presented. The legislation here does not cover the desecration of the most holy things. The penalty for that was death (cf. Num 4:19–20).

The legislation in Lev 5:20–26 (ET 6:1–7) does not just protect the holiness of some sacred object or substance, but it guards the holiness of the Lord's name. The name Yahweh was so sacrosanct that it was protected by the Decalogue itself. Abuse of it resulted in certain punishment (Ex 20:7; Deut 5:11). The abuse of the holy name in an oath to cover up the misappropriation of property was therefore an act of sacrilege (5:22 [ET 6:3]). The holy name was thereby desecrated.

The animal prescribed here for the reparation offering was a ram (5:15, 18, 25 [ET 6:6]; 19:21). It had to be without any physical blemish (5:15, 18, 25 [ET 6:6]). The reference to its monetary value in 5:15, 18 and 25 (ET 6:6) and to the temple shekel in 5:15 implies that even though the offerers could bring their own animals, they were commonly purchased at the sanctuary. This is confirmed by the mention of the money from the reparation offerings in 2 Ki 12:16. Unlike all the other sacrifices, no choice of animal was permitted for this sacrifice. It differed from the sin offering which never used any male sheep. A ram was most likely chosen because it was the head of the flock, the largest and most valuable animal in it.

Besides the animal, monetary compensation was prescribed for the first and third case of desecration. But it was not required for suspected sacrilege since the amount of compensation could not be reckoned for it as it was unknown. The compensation was fixed by the value of the misappropriated thing with the addition of twenty percent in interest (5:16, 24 [ET 6:5]; 22:27), the same amount as for the redemption of anything that had been devoted to God (27:13, 15, 19, 31). In the case of misappropriation from God, the compensation went to the priest as his representative (5:16); in the case of misappropriation from a person, it went to the owner (5:24 [ET 6:5]).

Ritual Occasion

This legislation envisages three different cases of sacrilege. The verb that describes the sacrilegious action in all three cases is מָעַל, which is used together with its noun in 5:15 and 5:21 (ET 6:1). We render the combination as "to commit an act of sacrilege." The various translations show how uncertain commentators have been about its exact sense. So, for example, the NIV translates the first occurrence by "commits a violation" and the second by "is unfaithful." Milgrom, however, points out that the use of "desecrate" (חִלֵּל) in 19:12 is synonymous with מָעַל.[8] מָעַל therefore describes an act of sacrilege against either the holy things or the holy name of God. Any act of sacrilege threatens both the community and the offender with destruction.

The sense of the verb is evident from its use in the historical narratives of the OT. See figure 9.

Figure 9

מעל as Sacrilege in OT Narrative

Text	*Offender*	*Kind of Sacrilege*
Josh 7:1 (22:20)	Achan	Misappropriation of something devoted to God
Josh 22:16, 22, 31	Eastern tribes	Construction of unauthorized altar in an unauthorized place
1 Chr 5:25	Eastern tribes	Worship of alien gods
1 Chr 9:1	People of Judah	Desecration of the temple
1 Chr 10:13	Saul	Consultation of a medium
2 Chr 12:1–2	Judah	Ritual unfaithfulness to God's law
2 Chr 26:16, 18	Uzziah	Burning of incense in Holy Place by unauthorized person
2 Chr 28:19, 22; 29:19 (29:6; 30:7)	Ahaz	Idolatry and desecration of the temple
Ezra 10:2, 10	Israel	Marriage to pagan women
Neh 1:8 (cf. Lev 26:40)	Israel	Violation of covenant by idolatry
Neh 13:27	Israel	Marriage to pagan women

[8] Milgrom, *Leviticus 1–16*, 365–67.

The gravity of these cases is evident from the consequences. Each of these offenses involved the violation of something holy. They were so severe that, unlike the acts of sacrilege described in these two speeches, they could not be expiated by any sacrifice.

The first case of sacrilege in Lev 5:15–16 deals with the unintentional desecration of something holy. In contrast with the examples in figure 9, which involve deliberate offenses that could not be undone by any sacrifice, this legislation for the reparation offering has to do with unintentional acts of desecration. An instance of this is given in 22:14–16 for a priestly family. If an unauthorized person, such as a guest or a hired worker or a daughter married to someone who is not a priest, ate some of the sacred food from the sanctuary, that person was guilty of desecration. The same applied for the inability to present a votive offering that had been dedicated to the Lord, if the animal had died or the house had been burned down (27:11–27).

The second case in 5:17–19 legislates for the presentation of a reparation offering because of a suspected sacrilege by the violation of a divine prohibition in the sacred realm. This offense differed from the violation of divine prohibitions in 4:2, 22, and 27 by virtue of the ignorance of the offender about his offense (5:17, 18). Even though he did not know whether he had committed an act of sacrilege or not, he suspected that he may have done so, because he felt guilty towards God (5:17, 19) and feared subsequent punishment. The guilt was real, even though the cause of it was unknown. And so he bore his iniquity by assuming liability for the suspected transgression and by presenting the reparation offering for it (5:17).

The third case in 5:20–26 (ET 6:1–7) prescribes the reparation offering for sacrilege from an act of perjury. This does not cover all kinds of perjury, but only the false denial, under oath, of the misappropriation of property from a fellow citizen. Two examples of illegal misappropriation are given. First, the offender has illegally retained the property of another person in one of three ways. He may have received something valuable from its owner who has entrusted it to him for safekeeping for a period of time, such as while the owner was away on a journey. He may have also received some money or property as an investment from another person in his business or in a business partnership. He may also have been in receipt of some stolen property directly or indirectly from a thief. In each case the offender had retained something that belonged to another person.

Second, the offender may have illegally acquired the property of another person in one of two ways. On the one hand, he may have improperly withheld the wages of a hired worker (Deut 24:14–15) or retained something confiscated in default of a loan after the loan had been repaid (Ezek 18:7, 12, 16). On the other hand, he may have kept lost property, such as straying livestock, which belonged to another person but which he had found and kept for himself.

The common thread in all the examples given in Lev 5:20–26 (ET 6:1–7) is that the offender denied that the misappropriated property rightly belonged to the person who had tried to repossess it. Such a case of suspected misappropriation could not, however, be tried in any normal court of law since the claimant could not prove his allegations and accusations. This situation was therefore commonly resolved in the ancient world by making the suspected party take an oath of innocence, such as is described in 1 Ki 8:31–32. If the accused person lied under oath, he would be guilty of sacrilege. By denying his offense under oath, the offender made God an accessory to his crime. God would therefore enact the curse contained in the oath and punish the person as he had threatened to do in the Second Commandment (Ex 20:7). If the offender was later struck with guilt, he could only escape this punishment by admitting his crime and making restitution to both the victim and to God, as prescribed in Lev 5:23–25 (ET 6:4–6).

Ritual Procedure

The legislation concentrates on the occasions for the reparation offering rather than the procedure for its presentation. The procedure is described in 7:1–10.

The unique feature of this sacrifice is the combination of compensation with its presentation. Before the reparation offering was presented, compensation had to be made for the offense, if it was known. If a person had misappropriated something holy from God, repayment was made in full, with twenty percent added to its value (5:16). The offender had to give the money to the priest as God's representative (5:25 [ET 6:6]). It became God's property (see also 22:14). If a person had, under oath, falsely denied any misappropriation of property from a fellow citizen, he had to repay 120 percent of its original value after he had admitted that he was guilty and decided to make amends for his offense (5:24 [ET 6:5]; see also Num 5:6–7). He gave this to the original owner.

After the reparation had been made for any act of misappropriation (Lev 5:16, 24–25 [ET 6:5–6]), or after a person felt guilty of some unspecified act of sacrilege (5:17), a ram was presented as a reparation offering. The ritual for its presentation, as described in 7:1–10, follows the procedure of the peace offering, with the exception that the priest alone ate the meat from the animal. The only part of the ritual enactment mentioned in this passage of legislation is the performance of the rite of atonement by the priest (5:16, 18, 26 [ET 6:7]). This was of special importance, for only by it could the person be freed from punishment by God from the penalties of sacrilege.

Ritual Theological Function

The reparation offering was prescribed for some cases of sacrilege (5:17, 23 [ET 6:4]). It served to eliminate "the guilt" before God for an act of desecration and to undo its fearful consequences. It has therefore commonly been called a "guilt offering." This translation has, however, been called into question since the sacrifice did not deal with common cases of guilt. That was the function of the sin offering, which freed people from the guilt of any unintentional sin (4:3, 13, 22, 27). It was prescribed to deal with the guilt from some lesser cases of sacrilege. Even though this sacrifice was offered to make restitution in cases of sacrilege, there is no mention of guilt in the case of unintentional sacrilege in 5:15–16.[9]

The connection between the "reparation offering" and sacrilege is evident from an examination of the circumstances for its presentation. In all cases those who bring this sacrifice have committed some kind of sacrilege as is evident in figure 10.

Figure 10

Occasions for the Presentation of a Reparation Offering

Text	*Offense*	*Desecrated Thing*	מעל
Lev 5:15–16	Misappropriation	Holy thing	Yes
Lev 5:17–19	Suspected violation of prohibition	Holy things	Yes?
Lev 5:20–26 (ET 6:1–7)	Perjury	Holy name	Yes
Lev 14:12, 21	Skin diseases as the cause of sacrilege	Holy status as Israelite	No
Lev 19:20–22	Sexual intercourse with a betrothed slave	Holy name	No
Num 6:7–12	Contact with a corpse	Holy status as Nazirite	No
Ezra 10:10	Marriage with pagan women	Holy seed	Yes

This sacrifice presupposes the gravity of any act of sacrilege. While all other offenses are committed against human beings, acts of sacrilege are committed directly against God. They involve acts of trespass on his domain that violate his holiness. Sins of sacrilege are an direct affront to God. They cannot therefore be overlooked, but must be dealt with by him, if he is to remain with his people as their holy God. They, in fact, threaten both the transgressor and the community with destruction. The penalty for such blatant acts of sacrilege is death.

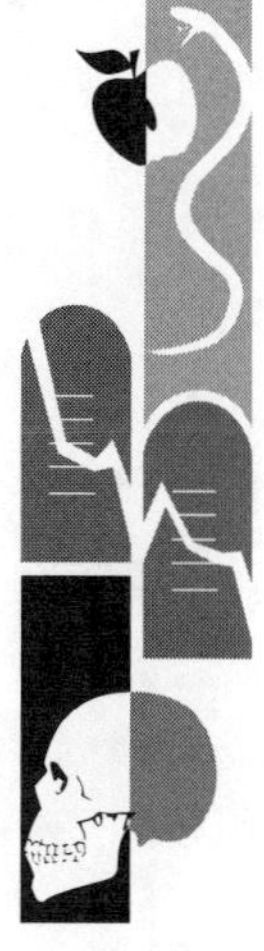

The reparation offering serves two theological functions. First, through its institution God made provision for restitution of the damage done by minor acts of sacrilege against his holy things and his holy name. Even though the ram itself was a repayment for the offense (5:15, 25 [ET 6:6]), this was reinforced by the requirement for additional compensation as restitution for sacrilegious misappropriation. The use of the verb שִׁלֵּם in 5:16 and 5:24 (ET 6:5) implies that this compensation restored something that had been disrupted. Second, and more significantly, through the rite of atonement that was performed with the blood rite from the reparation offering, the actual offender, or even

9 Milgrom, *Leviticus 1–16*, 327–28; Wenham, *Leviticus*, 104–5.

any suspected offender, was forgiven and so freed from liability before God for the act of sacrilege (5:16, 18, 26 [ET 6:7]).

The particular significance of forgiveness is emphasized by two important additions to the standard formula for divine atonement. On the one hand, the law in 5:18 says that the rite of atonement was made for the "unintentional sin, which he had committed without knowing it." Since the reparation offering was presented for the guilt of sacrilege against God, the act of atonement dealt with that guilt and released the offender from it. A scrupulous person, with the guilty conscience, could therefore be sure that he was forgiven. He was freed from the burden of attempting to discover his offense, as well as the fear of punishment for it. That seems to be the function of the two statements in 5:19. The ambiguous last clause in 5:19 declares that, even though he was truly guilty before the Lord and liable for punishment, he had made full expiation for his guilt and reparation for the unknown offense to the Lord.[10]

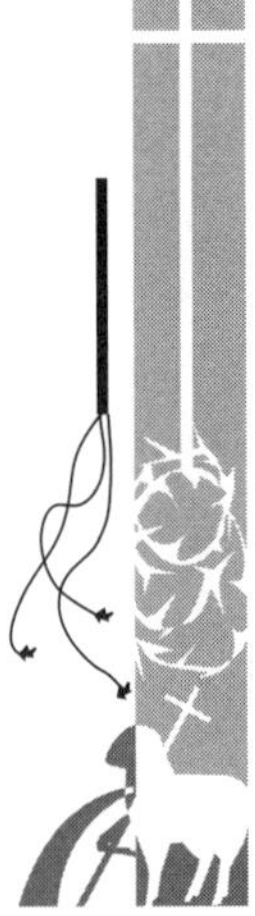

On the other hand, 5:26 (ET 6:7) prescribes that the priest make atonement "before the Lord" for the guilty person who would thereby be forgiven for whatever he had done that had made him feel guilty. Since this is the last of the three occurrences of the atonement formula in this passage, it does not just apply to the case in 5:20–26 (ET 6:1–7), but summarizes all three cases. Because any act of sacrilege was a direct offense against God, the rite of atonement, performed in his presence, freed the person both from the guilt from any such offense and from divine punishment for it.

The provision of a reparation offering for perjury in 5:21–26 (ET 6:1–7) is striking, because, unlike the two previous cases, that offense was not unintentional but deliberate. Yet despite that, atonement could still be made for it. This seems to contradict the decree in Num 15:30–31 that there was no possibility of atonement for deliberate sin. This decree, however, needs to be understood in the light of Num 5:5–10. It seems that if an offense was committed against another human being according to the second table of the Decalogue, atonement could be made, provided that the offense was confessed (Num 5:7) and full restitution was made to the wronged person (Lev 5:23; Num 5:7–8). The ritual act of confession changed the theological status of the offense, so that God no longer regarded it as a deliberate sin, but as an inadvertent offense.[11] Even though the sin remained the same, the attitude of the sinner to it had changed. And that opened the door for atonement and forgiveness.

The divine provision of the reparation offering therefore served a very clear pastoral purpose. It encouraged the Israelites to heed their consciences and repent of their sins. It also cared for troubled consciences by providing forgiveness for unintentional acts of sacrilege as well as for deliberate perjury in denying that they had misappropriated property in a court of law. By this sacrifice of restitution, God undid the destructive effect of sacrilege on the of-

[10] Wenham, *Leviticus*, 108.

[11] Milgrom, *Leviticus 1–16*, 300–3, 369–70.

fender. It ensured that God's holiness was safeguarded and that justice was done. The person who had committed this offense and had offered this sacrifice could interact with God safely at the sanctuary and expect favorable consideration by him.

Fulfillment by Christ

The reparation offering was meant to compensate God for the loss, or abuse, of something holy. Unlike the sin offering, it did not deal with the consequences of defilement, but with the desecration of something that belonged to God, whether it was an offering or his holy name. Any person who was guilty of sacrilege was in debt to God. The reparation offering both rectified what had been desecrated and paid the debt to God so that the perpetrator was released from his debt.

We find something akin to this offense in the case of Ananias and Sapphira in Acts 5:1–11. The exact circumstances of this case are difficult to establish with any certainty, but it seems that they had kept back for themselves some of the money from the sale of a piece of property that they had presented as a votive offering to the Lord. They were not obligated to offer any part of the money, but they did offer it all, and then they lied about withholding some of the money. In so doing they deliberately misappropriated for themselves the money that belonged to God. The penalty for this act shows that sacrilege is just as dangerous in the church as it was in Israel. So Paul too warns the Christians at Corinth about the peril of desecrating the body and blood of our Lord (1 Cor 11:27–30). The sin of sacrilege results in God's wrath and the withdrawal of access to his grace (cf. Heb 10:26–31).

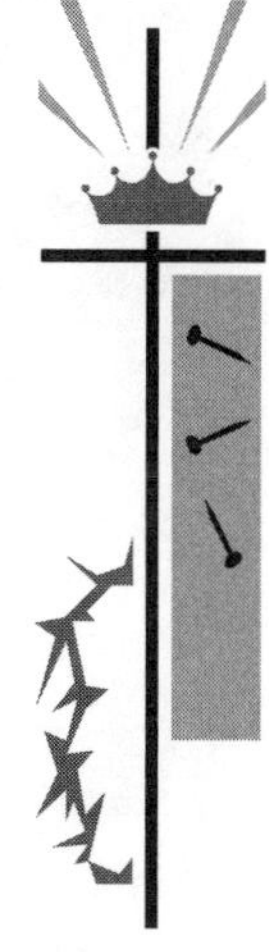

There is, however, no direct mention of the reparation offering in the NT. But we do have a possible allusion to it by way of reference to the Servant Song in Isaiah 53. In Is 53:10 we hear how God makes the life of his Servant "a reparation offering" (אָשָׁם). His Servant therefore justifies "many" by interceding for them and bringing them back to God (Is 53:11). Jesus alludes to this prophecy and applies it to himself in Mt 20:28 and 26:28. He offered his life as "a ransom for many" so that his disciples could drink his blood that had been poured out for many for the forgiveness of sins. Through his death he paid the ransom for all those who had desecrated God's holiness and gave them his blood to free them from their debt to God. Thus he was their holiness (1 Cor 1:30); they were holy in him (Phil 1:1). Since he had offered himself as the reparation offering for them, they could seek forgiveness from God the Father through him (Mt 6:12). They could approach him unafraid in the Divine Service because they were holy before him in Jesus (Eph 1:4).

Since Christ had paid their debt with God the Father, they did not have to compensate him for their abuse of his holy things. But they were still in debt to each other as the holy people of God. This was a different kind of debt than that in Leviticus, for, whereas God's people were required to pay back what they had taken from their fellow citizens in Lev 5:21–26 (ET 6:1–7), which Zacchaeus did with such extravagance in Lk 19:8, the disciples of Jesus were

to forgive their debtors just as their debt had been forgiven. Jesus did not just teach this to them in the parable of the unforgiving servant (Mt 18:21–35), but also enacted it for them in the Lord's Prayer (Mt 6:12; cf. Mk 11:25). They too were required to seek reconciliation and forgiveness from any fellow disciple that they had wronged before they approached God the Father with their gift in the Divine Service (Mt 5:23–26). They were to regard their fellow disciples as saints and respect their holiness by forgiving them repeatedly and making up to them. If they refused to do so, they forfeited their own forgiveness and holiness (Mt 6:14–15; 18:35). For next to Christ's Word and his body and blood, each disciple is the most holy thing that we have in the new covenant. We have but one debt to pay: we must continue to love one another (Rom 13:8).

Blest the children of our God,
They are bought with Christ's own blood;
They are ransomed from the grave,
Life eternal they will have:
With them numbered may we be
Here and in eternity!

They are justified by grace,
They enjoy the Savior's peace;
All their sins are washed away,
They will stand in God's great day:
With them numbered may we be
Here and in eternity.[12]

[12] From "Blest the Children of Our God" by Joseph Humphreys (*LW* 370:1–2).

Leviticus 6–7

The Consumption of the Holy Food

Even though at first sight Leviticus 6–7 seems to cover the same ground as the first five chapters, the contents and the focus differ from that in the earlier chapters. The divine legislation in 6:1–7:38 (ET 6:8–7:38) deals with the disposal of what is not burnt on the altar: the fat-drenched ashes and skin from the burnt offering for the burnt offering; the bread and grain from the grain offerings; the meat from the sin, reparation, and peace offerings. Hence, the frequent occurrence of the verb "eat" (אָכַל), which is used twenty-nine times in this section of two chapters. Since the priests are responsible for the correct disposal of what has not been burned, the instructions in Leviticus 6–7 are largely addressed to them, except in 7:22–27 and 7:28–34, where lay people are also involved.

With this shift of emphasis comes a change in genre. These directives are not couched in the form of ritual case law, but as divine ritual "instruction" to the priests (תּוֹרָה, *torah,* 7:37). As explained in the introduction to this commentary, the rendition of *torah* (including as the name of the Pentateuch, the Torah) as "law" fails to convey the rich Gospel content. God's intent is to remedy the sin of his people and convey to them his purity and holiness.

Each ritual instruction teaches a priest how to perform a ritual, so that what is sacred is distinguished from what is common, and what is unclean from what is clean (cf. 10:10, 11). This section of the book is arranged as a series of five "instructions" for sacrifice, each of which is called a תּוֹרָה (6:2, 7, 18 [ET 6:9, 14, 25]; 7:1, 11), which have their counterpart in the five "instructions" for ritual purity later in the book of Leviticus: animals (11:46), childbirth (12:7), skin disease (13:54; 14:54, 57), purification from skin disease (14:2, 32), and genital discharges (15:32).

The five "instructions" are arranged into two groups. The first group deals with regular sacrifices and the second with occasional sacrifices. The burnt offering (6:1–6 [ET 6:8–13]) is therefore linked with the grain offering (6:7–16 [ET 6:14–23]), while the sin offering (6:17–23 [ET 6:24–30]) is connected with the reparation offering (7:1–10) and the peace offering (7:11–36). We therefore have the following arrangement of material:

I. The instructions for the daily sacrifice
   A. The burnt offering (6:1–6 [ET 6:8–13])
   B. The grain offering (6:7–16 [ET 6:14–23])

II. The instructions for the occasional sacrifices
   A. The sin offering (6:17–23 [ET 6:24–30])
   B. The reparation offering (7:1–10)
   C. The peace offering (7:11–36)

The deliberate nature of this arrangement is evident from the reduction of the six instructions mentioned in 7:37 to five by the combination of the priestly grain offering of 6:12–16 (ET 6:19–23) with the daily grain offering in 6:7–11 (ET 6:14–18).

Even though the material is arranged as five instructions with the concluding summary in 7:37, another literary pattern is imposed on it so as to incorporate this material into its larger context. The subject matter is ordered as a series of five divine speeches, which, however, do not coincide with the five instructions. These divine speeches classify the divine legislation according to different categories. All these speeches are addressed to Moses (6:1, 12, 17 [ET 6:8, 19, 24]; 7:22, 28). But whereas the first and the third are to be transmitted to the priests, the last two are to be transmitted to the Israelites. The offerings are therefore also listed according to the holiness of the sacrifices. Thus the most holy sacrifices are listed before the holy sacrifices.

The result is the following literary arrangement:

I. Divine speech to priests on the daily public sacrifice (6:1–11 [ET 6:8–18])
   A. The burnt offering (6:1–6 [ET 6:8–13])
   B. The grain offering (6:7–11[ET 6:14–18])
II. Divine speech to Moses on the daily grain offering of the high priest (6:12–16 [ET 6:19–23])
III. Divine speech to the priests on the occasional offerings of the Israelites (6:17–7:21 [ET 6:24–7:21])
   A. The sin offering (6:17–23 [ET 6:24–30)
   B. The reparation offering (7:1–6)
   C. The priestly dues (7:7–10)
   D. The grain offering (7:11–21)
IV. Divine speech to the Israelites on prohibited food (7:22–27)
V. Divine speech to the Israelites on the priests' portion of the peace offering (7:28–36)
VI. Conclusion (7:37–38)

This pattern of arrangement is complicated by the intrusion of 7:7–10. It functions either as an unassimilated appendix to 7:1–6, or else, more likely, as a conclusion to the instructions for the five most holy offerings. It succinctly summarizes what belongs to the priests from each of these offerings, just as 7:28–34 prescribes the portions of the priests from the peace offering.

Leviticus 6:1–11 (ET 6:8–18)

The Daily Public Offering

Translation

6 [1]The Lord spoke to Moses: [2]"Command Aaron and his sons thus: This is the ritual instruction for the burnt offering—the burnt offering that remains on the altar hearth all the night until the morning, while the altar fire is kept burning on it. [3]After the priest has put on his linen vestments and wears linen underclothes next to his body, he shall remove the fat-drenched ashes to which the fire has reduced the burnt offering on the altar and place them beside the altar. [4]When he has taken off his vestments and put on other vestments, he shall carry the fat-drenched ashes outside the camp to a clean place. [5]But the fire on the altar shall be kept burning on it; it shall not go out. Every morning the priest shall kindle wood on it so that he may lay out the burnt offering on it and send up in smoke the fat parts of the peace offerings on the top of it. [6]A perpetual fire shall be kept burning on the altar; it shall not go out.

[7]"This is the ritual instruction for the grain offering. The sons of Aaron shall present it before the Lord, in front of the altar. [8]One of them shall remove some of the fine flour of the grain offering with a handful of it and some of its olive oil, together with all the frankincense that is on the grain offering, and turn its token portion into smoke on the altar as a pleasing aroma to the Lord. [9]Then Aaron and his sons shall eat the rest of it; it shall be eaten as unleavened cakes in a holy place; they shall eat it in the courtyard of the tent of meeting. [10]It shall not be baked with leavened dough. I have assigned it as their portion from my gifts; it is most holy, like the sin offering and the reparation offering. [11]Any male among Aaron's descendants may eat it as his perpetual due from the Lord's gifts throughout your generations; anyone who touches them will become holy."

Textual Notes

6:2 צַו—Here and in 24:2 and Num 28:2 this Piel imperative of צָוָה, "to command," begins a new section, in which provision is made for the daily sacrificial ritual.

תּוֹרַת—This is the construct state of the term תּוֹרָה. It is derived from the verb יָרָה, which normally occurs in the Hiphil (the perfect would be הוֹרָה). The Hiphil infinitive construct (לְהוֹרֹת) occurs in Lev 10:11; 14:57. While the noun תּוֹרָה, *torah,* may refer to any kind of practical instruction, it is also used as a technical term for the ritual instruction that was given by the priests at God's direction. The formula "This is the instruction" is used a heading (6:2, 7, 18 [ET 6:9, 14, 25]; 7:1, 11; 14:2) or a concluding summary (7:37; 11:46; 12:7; 13:59; 14:32, 54, 57; 15:32; cf. 26:46) in units of ritual instruction. There are in all ten collections of ritual instruction in Leviticus.[1]

---

[1] Milgrom, *Leviticus 1–16*, 382–83.

מוֹקְדָה—This may be a feminine form of the noun מוֹקֵד, "hearth" (*HALOT*). The top of the altar is called the "hearth." The noun is from the verb יָקַד, "to burn," which occurs in 6:2, 5, 6 (ET 6:9, 12, 13). Another view of מוֹקְדָה is that the ending is the third feminine singular suffix, so the form would be equivalent to מוֹקְדָהּ. In that case the antecedent of the feminine suffix would be the preceding feminine noun הָעֹלָה, and the word would mean "its hearth," that is, the hearth upon which the burnt offering was made. The Masoretes evidently were aware of some textual uncertainty about this word, for in many Hebrew manuscripts the מ is deliberately written in a small size. If the noun מוֹקֵד meant "burning," מוֹקְדָה could mean "its burning"—the burning of the burnt offering. The Samaritan Pentateuch understood the word to mean "what is burning," and the LXX has "its burning."

הַמִּזְבֵּחַ—See the textual notes on "the altar" in 1:5. In this chapter, it recurs in 6:3 (twice), 5, 6, 7, 8 (ET 6:10 [twice], 12, 13, 14, 15).

תּוּקַד בּוֹ׃—The verb תּוּקַד is the Hophal of יָקַד and means to "be kindled" (*HALOT*) or to "be burned." The verb is feminine because its subject is the feminine noun אֵשׁ, "fire." The phrase תּוּקַד בּוֹ is repeated in 6:5 (ET 6:12), and the verb alone recurs in 6:6 (ET 6:13).

6:3 מִדּוֹ בַד—The unusual Hebrew combination מִדּוֹ בַד could possibly be construed as a case of apposition: "his clothing—linen." However, the long *holem*, וֹ-, could be an archaic ending for the construct form: "clothing of linen." The Samaritan Pentateuch and Targum support that view.

וּמִכְנְסֵי־בַד—This consisted of a double apron or set of underpants fastened around the hips of the priest (Ex 28:42). It was not held to be part of his sacred vestments because it was not consecrated by having blood and oil sprinkled on it.

בְּשָׂרוֹ—"His body" is used as a euphemism or synecdoche (of the whole for a part) for the genitals, as with בָּשָׂר in 15:2, 19. The underclothes were to prevent exposure of the priest's privy members when the priest ascended the steps of the altar.

הַדֶּשֶׁן—Usually דֶּשֶׁן denotes "fat," but here the context requires that it denote the "fatty ashes" (*HALOT,* 2) or "fat-drenched ashes." This came from the suet that had been laid out for burning on the altar.

אֲשֶׁר תֹּאכַל הָאֵשׁ—In Hebrew "fire" is said "to eat." The verb אָכַל connects the burning of the offerings with the eating of the leftovers by the priests.

6:4 בְּגָדִים אֲחֵרִים—"Other vestments" are common clothing rather than the sacred vestments.

אֶל־מִחוּץ לַמַּחֲנֶה—See the textual notes on 4:12.

מָקוֹם—See 4:12; 10:14.

טָהוֹר׃—This is the ritual term for "clean." See the textual notes on 7:19.

6:5 וּבִעֵר עָלֶיהָ הַכֹּהֵן עֵצִים—The fire was rekindled from the live coals by the addition of wood.

הָעֹלָה—This refers to the regular, public morning burnt offering (Ex 29:39–40).

וְהִקְטִיר—See the textual note on this verb in 1:9. In this chapter, it recurs in 6:8, 15 (ET 6:15, 22).

עָלֶיהָ—See the textual notes on 3:5.

חֶלְבֵי—See the textual notes on 3:3.

הַשְּׁלָמִים׃—See 3:3–4.

6:6 אֵשׁ תָּמִיד—The ritual term תָּמִיד ("perpetual, always, regular") refers to the prescribed ritual acts that are regularly repeated in the divine service.[2] Like "the regular burnt offering" (Ex 29:42; Num 28:3, 6, 10), "the regular grain offering" (Lev 6:13 [ET 6:20]), "the regular incense" (Ex 30:8), "the regular light" (Lev 24:2), and "the regular bread" (Num 4:7), "the regular/perpetual fire" is part of the daily public sacrificial ritual performed at the sanctuary. The terminology may come from the royal court. Loyal courtiers had the privilege of eating "regularly" at the king's table (2 Sam 9:7, 10, 13; 2 Ki 25:29), where they received their "regular allowance" (2 Ki 25:30).

6:7 הַמִּנְחָה—There is some dispute as to whether this refers to the grain offering accompanying the daily burnt offering (Ex 29:40–41; Num 28:4–8) or the private grain offering (Lev 2:1–10). Some scholars, such as Milgrom, hold that it refers to the private grain offering because the legislation for the daily grain offering makes no mention of incense or the consumption by the priests of what was left over after its token portion had been burnt.[3] Yet five things indicate that this most likely speaks of the disposal of the daily grain offering. First, it follows immediately on the treatment of the daily burnt offering in 6:2–6 (ET 6:9–13) without a new heading. Second, a priest was required to present this offering (6:7 [ET 6:14]) rather than a lay person as in 2:1 and 2:4. Third, no mention is made of the bread that could be offered as a grain offering instead of just flour (2:4–10; 7:9). Fourth, 9:17 shows that only a handful of the daily grain offering was burnt by the priests on the altar; the rest of it was eaten by the priests (10:12–13). Fifth, frankincense is listed together with the four, oil, and wine needed for the daily burnt offering in 1 Chr 9:29. It was also linked together with the grain offering in Neh 13:5, 9.

הַקְרֵב—See the textual note on this verb in 1:2. This is the Hiphil infinitive absolute. The LXX and Samaritan Pentateuch render it as a masculine plural.

6:8 וְהֵרִים—See the textual note on this verb 2:9.

מִסָּלְתּ—See the textual note on סֹלֶת in 2:11.

הַלְּבֹנָה—See the textual notes on 2:1.

רֵיחַ נִיחֹחַ אַזְכָּרָתָהּ לַיהוָה׃—See the textual notes on 1:9 and the explanation in "Leviticus 1–3." Regarding אַזְכָּרָתָהּ, see the textual notes on 2:2.

6:9 בְּמָקוֹם קָדֹשׁ—See also "a holy place" in 6:19, 20 (ET 6:26, 27); 7:6; 10:13; 16:24; 24:9; cf. 10:17; 14:13. The priests were required to eat the most holy food in the sacred area within the courtyard around the altar for burnt offering (10:11–12). While the whole courtyard could be used for their meals, they, most likely, ate them in its western half. Thus in Ezek 42:1–14 and 46:19–20, special rooms were provided there for this purpose.

6:10 חָמֵץ—See the textual notes on 2:1.

חֶלְקָם נָתַתִּי אֹתָהּ—God speaks in the first person here, as in 17:11. That gives added weight to this statement of endowment (cf. Num 18:8, 21, 26). The noun חֵלֶק

---

2 Haran, *Temples and Temple Service in Ancient Israel*, 207.

3 Milgrom, *Leviticus 1–16*, 389–91.

was normally used for the allotment of land from God to the Israelite family. The tribe of Levi, however, received no such allotment, because the Levites received their livelihood from the offerings as their allotment from the Lord (Num 18:20).

מֵאִשֵּׁ֑י—See 6:11 (ET 6:18) and the textual notes on 1:9.

קֹ֤דֶשׁ קָֽדָשִׁים֙ הִ֔וא—See 6:18, 22 (ET 6:25, 29) and the textual notes on 2:3.

6:11 חָק־עוֹלָם֙—See 6:15 (ET 6:22); 7:34; 10:15; 24:9. The phrase חָק־עוֹלָם is used to designate a part of the offerings as the perquisite or stipend of the priests, their divinely instituted due, their ration of food for their service to the Lord at the sanctuary.[4] It is to be distinguished from חֻקַּת עוֹלָם which is a perpetual ritual statute (see the textual notes on 3:17). See figure 11 for a list of things that were the perpetual due of the priests.

Figure 11

Sacrificial Dues in the Pentateuch

Offering	*Due*	*Recipients*	*References*	*Status*
Priestly grain offering	Toasted bread	God	Lev 6:15 (ET 6:22)	Most holy?
Showbread	Baked bread	Priests	Lev 24:9	Most holy
Public grain offering	Baked bread	Priests	Lev 6:11 (ET 6:18); 10:12–13	Most holy
Private grain offering	Flour or bread	Priests	Num 18:8–9	Most holy
Private sin offering	Meat	Priests	Num 18:8–9	Most holy
Private reparation offering	Meat	Priests	Num 18:8–9	Most holy
Peace offering	Breast and thigh	Priests' families	Ex 29:28; Lev 7:34; 10:14–15; Num 18:18	Holy
Firstfruits	Grain, oil, wine	Priests' families	Num 18:11–13	Holy

כֹּ֛ל אֲשֶׁר־יִגַּ֥ע בָּהֶ֖ם יִקְדָּֽשׁ׃—The pronoun "them" (בָּהֶם) refers to meat from the sin and reparation offerings mentioned in 6:10 (ET 6:17), as well as the bread from the grain offering. This formula for contagious holiness occurs also in Ex 29:37; 30:29; and Lev 6:20 (ET 6:27).

Two parts of the formula have been the subject of debate. First, is כֹּל to be construed as "everybody" or "everything"? Both are possible linguistically. In Ex 29:37 and 30:29, as well as in Lev 6:20 (ET 6:27), it seems to refer mainly to things. Here, however, it must refer to the priests who eat these most holy offerings. Second, is

---

[4] Milgrom, *Leviticus 1–16*, 315, 618–19.

יִקְדָּשׁ to be translated as "he/it must be holy"[5] or "he/it will be holy"?[6] Milgrom shows that the Qal form of the verb קָדַשׁ, which is closely connected with the adjective קָדוֹשׁ, always means "become holy" (e.g., Ex 29:21; Num 17:2, 3 [ET 16:37, 38]).[7] This formula is used for those most holy things that communicate God's holiness by physical contact with them at the sanctuary. Its opposite is the formula for contagious pollution, for both holiness and impurity can be communicated by direct touch (Lev 11:24).

Commentary

Structure

Both 6:1–6 (ET 6:8–13) and 6:7–11 (ET 6:14–18) are introduced by a similar heading, classifying the material in each of them as a "ritual instruction" (6:2, 7 [ET 6:9, 14]). Whereas the first "instruction" maps out the procedure for ritual disposal of the fat-drenched ashes from the altar in 6:2c–6 (ET 6:9c–13), the second "instruction" outlines the procedure for the preparation and consumption of bread made from the leftover flour from the grain offering in 6:7b–11a (ET 6:14b–18a). Both units are part of a single divine speech addressed to Aaron and his sons (6:2 [ET 6:9]; cf. 6:7, 11, 13 [ET 6:14, 18, 20]).

A number of other literary devices are used to arrange the material. First, in 6:2–6 (ET 6:9–13), we have the repetition of the same sentence about the perpetual altar fire in three different forms, first as a circumstantial clause (6:2 [ET 6:9]), then as a circumstantial clause with a prohibition (6:5 [ET 6:12]), and then, finally, as a summary commandment with the same prohibition (6:6 [ET 6:13]). Second, we have the use of the term "burnt offering" as an inclusion in 6:2 (ET 6:9) and 6:5 (ET 6:12), and the "sons of Aaron" as an inclusion in 6:7 (ET 6:14) and 6:11 (ET 6:18). Third, the appositional clauses in 6:9b (ET 6:16b) form a chiasm. Lastly, two key words recur in both units: "altar" (6:2 [twice], 3 [twice], 5a, 6, 7, 8 [ET 6:9 (twice), 10 (twice), 12, 13, 14, 15) and "eat" (6:3, 9 [three times], 11 [ET 6:10, 16 [three times], 18).

The structure of this pericope can be outlined as follows:

- I. Introduction and commission (6:1–2a [ET 6:8–9a])
  - A. The Lord's address to Moses (6:1 [ET 6:8])
  - B. His commission to command the priests (6:2a [ET 6:9a])
- II. Divine speech (6:2b–11 [ET 6:9b–18])
  - A. Instruction about the disposal of the ashes from the daily burnt offering (6:2b–6 [ET 6:9b–13])
    - 1. Heading about the leftover burnt offering (6:2b [ET 6:9b])

---

5 Hartley, *Leviticus*, 97; Levine, *Leviticus*, 37–38.

6 Budd, *Leviticus*, 111–12; Wenham, *Leviticus*, 121.

7 Milgrom, *Leviticus 1–16*, 443–46.

2. Daily procedure (6:3–5 [ET 6:10–12])
    a. The vesting of the priest (6:3a [ET 6:10a])
    b. The removal of the burnt ashes and their placement next to the altar (6:3b [ET 6:10b])
    c. Removal of vestments (6:4a [ET 6:11a])
    d. Deposit of ashes outside the camp without putting out the fire (6:4b–5a [ET 6:11b–12a])
    e. The stoking of the fire on the altar with wood (6:5b [ET 6:12b])
    f. Burning of leftover offerings (6:5c [ET 6:12c])
3. Summary instruction (6:6 [ET 6:13])
    a. Commandment to keep the perpetual fire burning (6:6a [ET 6:13a])
    b. Prohibition against its extinction (6:6b [ET 6:13b])

B. Instruction on the disposal of the daily grain offering (6:7–11 [ET 6:14–18])
1. Heading (6:7a [ET 6:14a])
2. Procedure (6:7b–9 [ET 6:14b–16])
    a. Presentation of the offering by priests (6:7b [ET 6:14b])
    b. Removal and incineration of the God-pleasing token portion (6:8 [ET 6:15])
    c. Eating of leftover flour as unleavened bread by the priests in the courtyard (6:9 [ET 6:16])
3. Divine declaration of its nature and use (6:10 [ET 6:17])
    a. Prohibition of yeast in baking the cakes (6:10a [ET 6:17a])
    b. Divine bestowal of it as the priestly allotment (6:10b [ET 6:17b])
    c. Its sacrosanct status (6:10c [ET 6:17c])
4. Summary instruction (6:11 [ET 6:18])
    a. The most holy flour as the perpetual due of the priests (6:11a [ET 6:18a])
    b. Consecration from contact with it (6:11b [ET 6:18b])

The Sacred Fire and the Disposal of the Ashes (6:1–6 [ET 6:8–13])

Ritual Agents

This passage of legislation focuses exclusively on the responsibility of the priest on duty to attend to the altar. As the master of the Lord's house, he keeps the fire burning on the altar hearth by removing the ashes from it and stoking the fire each morning on it (6:3–5 [ET 6:10–12]). The importance of his task is highlighted by the requirement that he be vested with his priestly vestments for the removal of the ashes (6:3 [ET 6:10]). As the steward of the Lord's house, he served the Lord by looking after his residence. Since the hearth was regarded as the center of the house, his main task was to attend to the fire on its hearth.

Ritual Material

This legislation concentrates on the proper treatment of the sacred fire. It is described in three ways: "fire of the altar/altar fire" (6:2 [ET 6:9]), "the fire on the altar" (6:5 [ET 6:12]), and "a perpetual fire" (6:6 [ET 6:13]). This fire is significant practically and spiritually. On the practical level, it is necessary for the operation of the whole sacrificial system. The fire "ate" up the burnt offering together with all the offerings placed on the altar (6:3 [ET 6:10]). If the fire went out, the tabernacle would cease to function as the Lord's residence. No other kind of fire could be used for the altar and for the burning of incense in the Lord's presence (10:1; Num 3:4; 26:61).

Spiritually, the significance of the fire derives from its connection with the Lord's presence with his people. The perpetual fire came from the Lord's presence (Lev 9:24; cf. 1 Chr 21:26) and revealed his glory to his people through the smoke that went up from the altar (Lev 9:6, 23; cf. 2 Chr 7:1–3). The cloud of smoke, paradoxically, both concealed and revealed the presence of the fire on the altar, just as the cloud both concealed and yet revealed the Lord's glory.[a] Just as the Lord descended on Mount Sinai in smoke and fire,[b] so he appeared to his people at the altar in the smoke and the fire of the sacrifices. The fire that came from the Lord revealed his presence both in grace (Lev 9:23–24; cf. Num 16:46) and in wrath.[c] It was "a perpetual fire," a fire that could not be extinguished (Lev 6:6 [ET 6:13]). If the priests allowed it to go out, God would no longer be able to give them access to his grace (cf. 2 Chr 13:10–12; 29:6–9).

Next to the fire, the most important thing in the daily ritual preparation of the altar was the removal of the daily burnt offering that had been smoldering overnight on the altar (Lev 6:2 [ET 6:9]) until it was reduced to "fat-drenched ashes" (6:3 [ET 6:10]). Unlike the meat from the burnt offering, which was most holy, the "ashes" were not holy, but common. They therefore needed to be dumped in a clean place so that they could not be used for any ritual purpose, or abused in any way (6:4 [ET 6:11]). The removal of the ashes from the burnt offering of the previous day prepared the altar to receive the new burnt offering (6:5 [ET 6:12]).

The third thing of ritual significance was the vestments of the priest that were to be worn when the ashes were removed from the altar, but taken off when the ashes were disposed outside the sanctuary (6:3–4 [ET 6:10–11]). Besides the underskirt (Ex 28:42–43), they consisted of three items of clothing: a linen tunic, an embroidered linen sash, and a linen skullcap.[d] Because they had been sprinkled with blood and holy anointing oil (Ex 29:21; Lev 8:30), they were "holy vestments" (16:4, 32). These vestments had to be worn by the priests when they officiated at the altar in the sanctuary. In contrast to them, ordinary clothes were worn for any act performed outside the sanctuary (6:4 [ET 6:11]; cf. 16:23–24). The holy vestments were marks of the priest's sacred office and status.

(a) Ex 13:21–22; 14:19–20, 24; 16:10; 24:15–18; 40:34–38

(b) Ex 19:16–19; 24:17; 40:38; Deut 4:11–12, 33, 36; 5:22–26

(c) Lev 10:2; cf. Num 3:4; 16:35; 26:10, 61

(d) Ex 28:40; 29:8–9; 39:27–29; Lev 8:13; 16:4, 23, 32

Ritual Location

All the activity in this rite clustered around two places. First, there was the altar for burnt offering. By analogy with a normal house in the ancient world, the altar was envisaged as the sacred hearth in the Lord's residence. It was the place for the perpetual fire from the Lord. As in every household each morning in the ancient world, the ashes had to be removed from the hearth before the fire was rekindled for the day. Second, its counter-location was "the clean place" outside the camp where the ashes were to be dumped (6:4 [ET 6:11]; cf. 4:12). This rite then involves a twofold transition. On the one hand, the ashes are brought from the altar to the ash dump. On the other hand, wood was brought from outside the sanctuary to the altar.

Ritual Occasion

The time for this rite was most significant. It occurred each morning as the first ritual enactment in the daily sacrificial ritual at the sanctuary. While it was not an integral part of the morning sacrifice, it necessarily preceded it. It was therefore a preparatory rite. Until the ashes had been removed from the altar and the fire had been stoked on it, the daily morning burnt offering could not proceed.

Ritual Enactment

This preparatory rite proceeded in three stages. First, the priest, after vesting for service, removed the ashes from the altar and placed them on its east side (cf. 1:16). Second, after he had removed his vestments, he carried the ashes to the dump outside the camp. Third, he then returned and stoked the fire with firewood to burn up what remained from the sacrifices of the previous day.

Ritual Theological Function

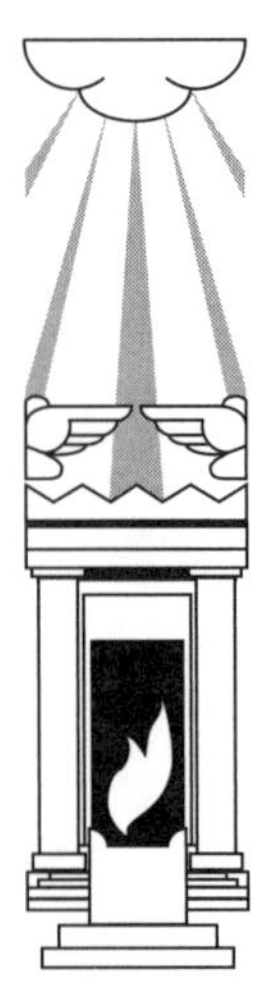

The theological function of this rite is clearly enunciated. It ensured that the fire on the altar was kept burning, without ever going out. This was not ordinary fire; it was the supernatural fire that had been kindled by the Lord rather than by any human being. It bridged heaven and earth by bringing the offerings to God, as well as by bringing God to his people. Just as Lord God, through fire, revealed his "name" to Moses (Ex 3:2–15) and his "glory" to the Israelites at Mount Sinai (Ex 24:17; 40:34), so he made himself and his glory manifest through the fire on the altar of burnt offering (Lev 9:4, 6, 23–24). Fire was an apt means for the communication of his holy presence in this daily theophany because his holiness, like fire, was life enhancing and yet life threatening, beneficial and yet destructive, enlightening and yet consuming. Since God gave his people access to himself and his grace through the fire on the altar, that fire had to be attended most diligently, for if it went out, the Lord would no longer meet with his people and make himself available to them for petition through the daily burnt offering. It was therefore the duty of the priests to make sure that the "perpetual fire" on the altar (6:6 [ET 6:13]) never went out.

Fulfillment by Christ

In Lk 12:49 Jesus declares to his disciples that he had come to bring fire from heaven to earth. But this fire could not be kindled until he had undergone the baptism of his atoning death. Only then could it be kindled to inaugurate the Divine Service in the church, the new people of God. That was accomplished on the day of Pentecost when he poured out the Holy Spirit on the mother congregation in Jerusalem (Acts 2:1–3). Just as fire had come from God's presence to kindle the altar fire at the inauguration of the divine service at the tabernacle (Leviticus 9) and then later at the temple in Jerusalem (2 Chr 7:1–3), so tongues of fire came from heaven at Pentecost and rested on the heads of each of the disciples. They were the altar in the new temple of the triune God, the place where God revealed his hidden glory and gave access to his gracious presence. The Holy Spirit therefore is the heavenly fire that must be kept alight in the church. The Holy Spirit marks and discloses the hidden presence of God the Father and the risen Lord Jesus with the faithful on earth. And they therefore serve the triune God as priests who are to make sure that this fire is kept burning in every place of worship.

That fire is not kindled by the faithful; it is kindled and kept alight by the risen Lord Jesus, the great High Priest. Just as the risen Lord Jesus appeared to his two disciples on Easter Sunday to set their hearts aflame by preaching himself from the Holy Scriptures and breaking bread with them, so he comes to the faithful in the Divine Service and kindles their hearts with his holy fire by speaking to them and filling them with his Holy Spirit (Lk 24:32). They therefore become part of Christ's offering to God the Father. Just as Jesus offered himself to the Father through the eternal Spirit (Heb 9:14), so they offer God the Father continual worship through the Holy Spirit (Jn 4:23, 24; Phil 3:3).

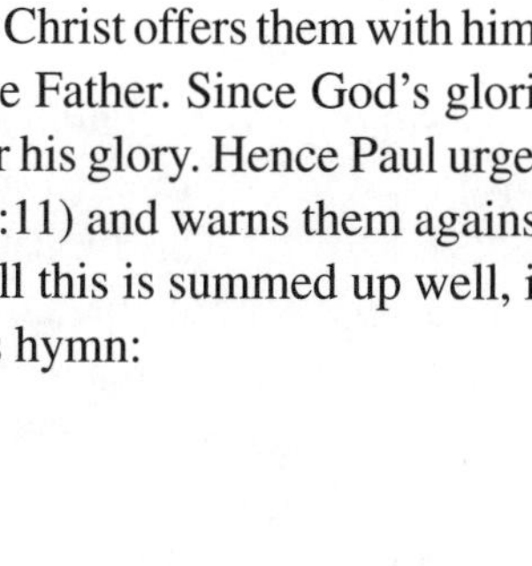

By generating faith and kindling the fire of God's love in their hearts, the Holy Spirit consecrates them as living altars where Christ offers them with himself in thanksgiving, prayer, and praise to God the Father. Since God's glorious presence is hidden in them, they are to burn for his glory. Hence Paul urges his readers to be "aglow with the Spirit" (Rom 12:11) and warns them against quenching its fire in their midst (1 Thess 5:19). All this is summed up well, if understood corporately, by Charles Wesley in this hymn:

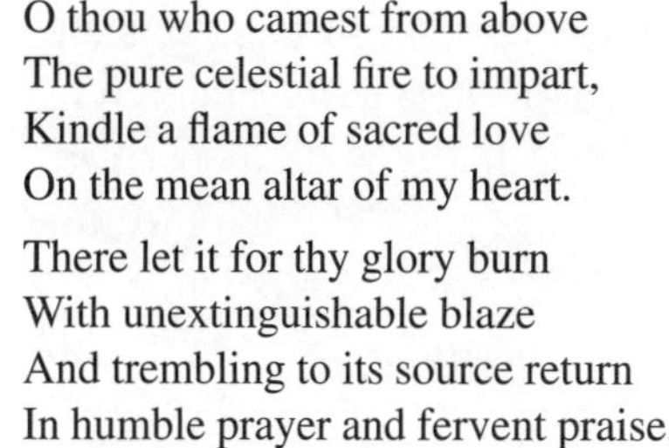

O thou who camest from above
The pure celestial fire to impart,
Kindle a flame of sacred love
On the mean altar of my heart.

There let it for thy glory burn
With unextinguishable blaze
And trembling to its source return
In humble prayer and fervent praise.

Consumption of the Daily Grain Offering (6:7–11 [ET 6:14–18])

Ritual Agents

The priests presented this offering as part of the daily burnt offering (see also 6:13 [ET 6:20] and 9:17). They brought it to the altar, on behalf of the people, and they ate what was left over from it (6:9 [ET 6:16]; cf. 9:17). But one of them, as their representative, removed the token portion and burned it on the altar for the rest of them (6:8 [ET 6:15]).

The other party to this ritual transaction was God. The grain offering was presented in his presence (6:7 [ET 6:14]), and the token portion was burnt up as a pleasing gift to him (6:8, 10, 11 [ET 6:15, 17, 18]). And he, quite explicitly and directly, assigned the leftover flour to the priests as their "portion" (6:10 [ET 6:17]), their "due" from him.

Ritual Material

The main material used in this rite was "fine flour," mixed with olive oil. It was presented as part of the daily burnt offering (Ex 29:40–41; Lev 9:17). After a portion of the grain offering had been burnt on the altar (see Lev 9:17), the rest of it was assigned to the whole priesthood as their food (6:9–11 [ET 6:16–18]; cf. 7:10). Like the meat from the sin offering and the reparation offering, this flour was most holy (6:10 [ET 6:17]). Because the flour was most holy, it had to be eaten in the Lord's presence. The bread from it had to be prepared as loaves without any yeast, even though none of them were burnt on the altar to the Lord. The prohibition of yeast for grain offerings to the Lord in 2:11 is therefore extended in 6:9–10 [ET 6:16–17] to include the bread made from them and eaten exclusively by the priests. Like the show bread (24:7) and the private grain offering of flour (2:2–3, 15–16), the public grain offering, offered each day together with the burnt offering, was presented with some frankincense (6:8 [ET 6:15]; cf. 1 Chr 9:30; Neh 13:5, 9). This masked the acrid smell of burning flour and highlighted the character of the token portion as an aroma pleasing to the Lord.

Ritual Location

Two places are significant in this legislation. It specifies that the grain offering had to be presented by the priests before the Lord, in front of the altar (6:7 [ET 6:14]). This probably refers to the east side of it. Then it tells exactly where the most holy bread was to be eaten. Since the flour from the grain offering and the bread made from it is most holy, it could only be eaten in "a holy place" (6:9 [ET 6:16]). This is further defined as "the courtyard of the tent of meeting." In 10:12–13 it is described as the area "next to the altar." While the altar stood at the center of the eastern courtyard, the western courtyard centered on the tent of meeting. The bread from the grain offering therefore had to be eaten somewhere near the altar. The exact location was not important, but it was important that it be eaten in God's presence in the courtyard of the tent of meeting. This most holy food could only be eaten in that holy place.

Ritual Occasion

The daily grain offering accompanied the public burnt offering that was presented twice a day at the sanctuary. The token portion from this offering was burnt up on the altar each morning and evening, after the burnt offering had been set out on the altar (9:16–17). The flour, however, was kept in common storage together with the flour from the private grain offerings and was used to make the daily bread for all the priests on duty at the sanctuary (7:10). It was, as it were, their daily ration from the Lord's table during their period of service with him. It was therefore eaten between the morning and the evening sacrifice as part of their midday meal in the Lord's house.

Ritual Enactment

The ritual for the presentation of the daily grain offering closely resembled the procedure for the private grain offering of flour in 2:1–3. There are, however, two significant differences. On the one hand, this offering accompanied the daily burnt offering and was connected inseparably with it. The "token portion" (6:8 [ET 6:15]) was therefore offered up as a gift to the Lord together with the meat from the lamb. The remaining flour was the priests' due from that enactment. On the other hand, the daily grain offering was brought near (6:7 [ET 6:14]; cf. 9:17) by the priests rather than an Israelite layperson (2:1, 4, 11, 14). They offered it on behalf of the congregation and for its benefit.

This passage, however, unlike the legislation in 2:1–16, highlights the ritual preparation and consumption of bread from the offering rather than its presentation to the Lord. The priests had to bake it as unleavened flat cakes without leavened dough and eat it in the courtyard of the sanctuary, for with this offering God made provision for his priests and fed them from his table. The presentation of the public grain offering therefore culminated in a holy meal eaten in God's presence as his guests.

Theological Function

The theological function of this offering has been examined in connection with the private grain offering in 2:1–16. This unit adds to that in two ways. First, it emphasizes that the flour from the public grain offering was the Lord's "portion" (6:10 [ET 6:17]) for the priests. They did not inherit a portion of land among the tribes of Israel as their livelihood from the Lord. They did not grow grain on their own land. Instead, they received their food from the Lord through the grain offerings of the Israelites. In words that resemble 17:11 and parallel 10:13b, the Lord declares: "I have assigned it as their portion from my gifts. … Any male among Aaron's descendants may eat it as his perpetual due from the Lord's gifts" (6:10–11 [ET 6:17–18]).

The Lord gave this hereditary portion personally for their livelihood (Num 18:8, 11, 12, 19, 21, 24, 26). It was their "perpetual due" (חָק־עוֹלָם, 6:11 [ET 6:18]), their stipend from the daily sacrifice.

Second, the Lord himself determined the status and function of this offering in 6:10–11 (ET 6:17–18): "I have assigned it as their portion from my gifts; it is most holy. … Anyone who touches them will become holy." Like the meat from the sin and reparation offerings, the bread from the daily flour offering was most holy. It became most holy by the incineration of its token portion on the altar. That part represented the whole of the offering. Through its contact with the altar, the whole grain offering became most holy (Ex 29:37). It was therefore reserved exclusively for priestly consumption at the sanctuary.

The use of the formula for contagious sanctification is most significant. It occurs four times in the Pentateuch. The first two describe the most holy appointments of the sanctuary: the altar for burnt offering (Ex 29:37) and the tent of meeting with its furniture (Ex 30:26–29). The second two describe the operation of the most holy offerings: the bread from the grain offerings and the meat from the sin and reparation offerings (Lev 6:11, 20 [ET 6:18, 27]; cf. Ezek 46:20). Without using this formula, Ezekiel also speaks of sanctification by contact with the vestments of the priests (Ezek 44:19; cf. 42:14). Its opposite is the formula "whoever touches it/them will become unclean" (Lev 11:24, 26, 27, 31, 36, 39; 15:10, 21, 24, 27; cf. 15:11). This formula of contagious sanctification declares that authorized contact with these most holy things makes and keeps that person or thing holy.

The Lord gave his most holy bread to the priests on duty at his residence. This most holy bread was prepared from the flour of the daily grain offering. Through this most holy bread, as well as through the holy meat from the sin and reparation offerings, the Lord conveyed his holiness to the priests officiating at the sanctuary and so sanctified them (cf. 21:15; 22:9). By eating it in that holy place, they themselves became holy and remained holy, for by the provision of that bread the Lord not only gave them nourishment but also shared his holiness with them.

Fulfillment by Christ

In the old covenant God provided daily bread for the priests during the period of service at the tabernacle. Since they served at his altar, they received their food from the altar (1 Cor 9:13). Their food came from the grain offering that was part of daily sacrifice. That bread was most holy, for it came from the Lord's table and belonged to him. They ate it in his presence at the sanctuary. Through it God shared his holiness with them.

In the new covenant all God's priests also eat the food that comes from his table. What is different is that each believer is included in this holy priesthood, and instead of a repeated sacrifice offered by the priests, Christ himself has completed the one all-availing sacrifice on the cross, whose benefits he distributes anew in each Divine Service.

All in Christ are his saints. They all serve their heavenly King; they all participate in the Divine Service together with Christ. And so they all eat the most holy food that has been consecrated on his altar (Heb 13:9, 10). Christ, the life-giving bread from heaven, gives his flesh for them to eat (Jn 6:51–58). They eat that bread together in his presence in the Divine Service.

His flesh is real food for them, holy food by which he shares his holiness with them. Through his body offered for them once and forever to God the Father, he now sanctifies all his disciples and makes them fit to serve with him in the heavenly sanctuary. He is their daily bread. By giving them his body as bread to eat, he gives them access to his Father's gracious presence; he assures them that his heavenly Father is well pleased with them. And so their hearts are strengthened by his grace (Heb 13:9). They have the privilege of eating with him as his guests.

The instruction that the most holy bread be eaten in the holy place has influenced the practice of Holy Communion in the Lutheran church. We quite commonly enter the sanctuary to receive Christ's holy body. Yet what we do far exceeds the privileges of the priests that officiated at the tabernacle and at the temple. In the Lord's Supper we enter heaven itself together with our great High Priest (Heb 10:19–22). There we eat Christ's flesh, the bread from heaven.

God's unveiled presence now we see,
As at the rail on bended knee
Our hungry mouths from Him receive
The bread of immortality.

The body of God's Lamb we eat
A priestly food and priestly meat.
On sin-parched lips the chalice pours
His quenching blood that life restores.[8]

8 From "The Infant Priest Was Holy Borne" by Chad L. Bird (*HS98* 853:5–6). © 1997 Chad L. Bird. Used with permission.

Leviticus 6:12–16 (ET 6:19–23)

The Daily Grain Offering of the High Priest

Translation

6 [12]The Lord spoke to Moses: [13]"This is the offering of Aaron and his sons that they shall present to the Lord from the day when he is anointed. A tenth of an ephah of fine flour as a regular grain offering, half of it in the morning and half in the evening, [14]shall be prepared with oil on a griddle. You shall bring it well soaked and present the pieces of the grain offering of crumbled bits as a pleasing aroma to the Lord. [15]The priest who has been anointed in his place from among his sons shall perform its ritual; it is the perpetual due of the Lord; it shall be turned entirely into smoke. [16]So too every grain offering of a priest shall be a total sacrifice; it shall not be eaten."

Textual Notes

6:13 וּבָנָ֔יו—As is clear from 6:15 (ET 6:22), this does not refer to all the priests, but to Aaron's descendants who succeeded him as high priest.

יַקְרִ֣יבוּ לַיהוָ֗ה—See the textual notes on 1:2.

בְּיוֹם֙—Literally this means "on the day" when he is anointed. However, 6:15 (ET 6:22) indicates that this offering was to be part of the regular daily service, and so we translate it "from the day" he is anointed onwards. This offering was offered daily from the time of the priest's anointing.[1]

הִמָּשַׁ֣ח אֹת֔וֹ—The direct object of the Niphal infinitive functions as its subject. On the verb מָשַׁח, "to anoint," see 8:12.

סֹ֧לֶת—See the textual notes on 2:1. This was also the amount of flour that was prescribed for the daily grain offering in Ex 29:40.

6:14 עַֽל־מַחֲבַ֗ת—See Lev 2:5–6.

תֵּעָשֶׂ֖ה—See the textual notes on 4:20.

מֻרְבֶּ֣כֶת—This Hophal participle of רָבַךְ apparently means "mixed" (*HALOT*), "well mixed," or "well soaked." Elsewhere in the OT it occurs only in 7:12 and 1 Chr 23:29. The reference in Lev 7:12 indicates that both the flour and the flat bread were soaked with oil. This aided the burning up of the bread.

תֻּפִינֵי֙—The meaning of this unique term is uncertain.

פִּתִּ֔ים—See 2:6.

רֵֽיחַ־נִיחֹ֖חַ לַיהוָֽה׃—See the textual notes on 1:9.

6:15 וְהַכֹּהֵ֨ן הַמָּשִׁ֧יחַ תַּחְתָּ֛יו מִבָּנָ֖יו—This phrase refers to the anointed priest who will (in the future) succeed the incumbent high priest. His successor is the priest who burns the offering on the altar.

---

[1] Milgrom, *Leviticus 1–16*, 397–98.

יֵעָשֶׂה אֹתָהּ—See the textual notes on 4:20.

חָק־עוֹלָם—See the textual notes on 6:11 (ET 6:18). This is the only time that חֹק is used for an offering to the Lord.

כָּלִיל—This term, which functions as an adverb here, is also used as a noun for a whole burnt offering in 6:16 (ET 6:23).

תָּקְטָר׃—See the textual notes on 1:9.

6:16 כָּלִיל—When functioning as a noun, כָּלִיל was occasionally used as a popular descriptive synonym for the burnt offering because it was burnt up entirely on the altar (Deut 33:10; cf. Deut 13:17 [ET 13:16]). כָּלִיל occurs together with עוֹלָה in 1 Sam 7:9 and Ps 51:21 (ET 51:19). Only here does כָּלִיל refer to the grain offering of the priests.

Commentary

Structure

Since this is a new divine speech, it is distinguished from the regular grain offering in 6:7–11 (ET 6:14–18). After the legislation for presentation of the offering (6:13 [ET 6:20]), we have the procedure for its presentation (6:14–15 [ET 6:21–22]), followed by a statement of its classification and a prohibition concerning all the grain offerings of the priests (6:16 [ET 6:23]).

The structure of this pericope can be outlined as follows:

I. Introduction: the Lord's address to Moses (6:12 [ET 6:19])
II. Divine speech (6:13–16 [ET 6:20–23])
  A. Description of the high priest's grain offering (6:13 [ET 6:20])
    1. Beginning of its presentation (6:13a [ET 6:20a])
    2. Material for presentation (6:13b [ET 6:20b])
    3. Times for presentation (6:13c [ET 6:20c])
  B. Procedure (6:14–15 [ET 6:21–22])
    1. Roasting of cake on a griddle (6:14a [ET 6:21a])
    2. Presentation of the oil-soaked bread in pieces as a God-pleasing aroma (6:14b [ET 6:21b])
    3. Entire incineration by high priest's successor (6:15 [ET 6:22])
  C. General summary (6:16 [ET 6:23])
    1. Definition as a total offering (6:16a [ET 6:23a])
    2. Prohibition of consumption (6:16b [ET 6:23b])

Ritual Agents

The high priest was required to present this offering. From the day of his anointing as high priest, he was responsible for its daily enactment. Since the offering was for the high priest's benefit, Aaron's designated successors burned it on the altar (6:15 [ET 6:22]).

God was the other party in this ritual enactment. The grain offering was brought to him (6:13 [ET 6:20]) as his "perpetual due" (6:15 [ET 6:22]). By receiving the offering that was burnt up for the high priest, the Lord demonstrated his pleasure in the high priest and his approval of his service (6:14 [ET 6:21]).

Ritual Material

The main substance used in this offering was fine wheat flour. The amount prescribed for each day was one-tenth of an ephah. This was the same as the daily grain offering of Israel (Ex 29:40) and the graded sin offering for a very poor person (Lev 5:11). The amount of flour for the offering therefore seems to be the daily ration for a person.

The flour was mixed with olive oil and baked as flat cakes on a griddle. These flat cakes were then soaked in olive oil and broken up in pieces for burning on the altar, just as this kind of bread was broken up and dipped in olive oil before it was eaten in ancient Israel.

Ritual Occasion

The time for this offering was most significant. The high priest began to present it regularly from the day on which he was anointed. It was therefore associated with his term of office and his vocation as high priest. Furthermore, it was to be offered each morning and each evening, at the beginning and at the end of his daily period of service. According to rabbinical tradition, the evening presentation of it was the last offering of the day.[2]

Ritual Enactment

The ritual for the grain offering of the high priest was enacted in three stages. First, the flour was mixed with oil and baked as flat cakes on a griddle (cf. 2:5–6). According to 1 Chr 9:31, this was done in the postexilic period by a family of the Levites who served as gatekeepers at the temple (cf. 1 Chr 23:29). Second, it was brought broken in pieces, soaked in oil, and presented by the high priest (Lev 6:14 [ET 6:21]). Third, all the bread made from the flour was burned on the altar by the successor of the high priest (6:15 [ET 6:22]). Unlike any other grain offering, none of it was eaten by any of the priests.

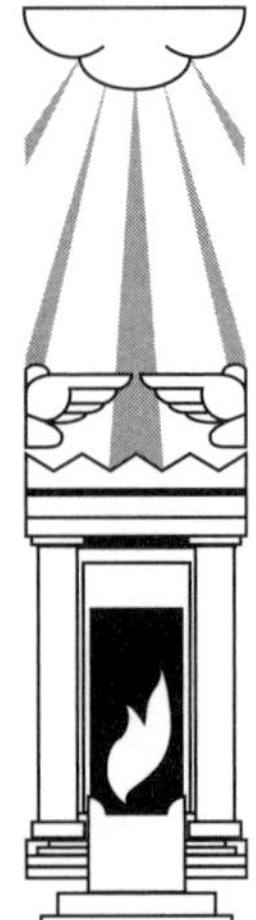

Ritual Theological Function

The unique feature of this grain offering was that none of it was eaten by any human being. It alone of all the offerings is described as "the perpetual due" of the Lord, his ration of food (6:15 [ET 6:22]). At first glance it seems to be offered as the part of the daily meal that was presented to the Lord by his priests just as the pagan priests did for their gods. But if that were the case, the bread would have been set out on the table for the show bread in the Holy Place. Instead, it was burnt entirely together with the daily burnt offerings on the altar.

We have here, then, a case of ritual reconfiguration, for the offering was brought for the benefit of the high priest rather than as sustenance for God. It had to do with the high priest's daily service as the chief courtier of the heavenly King, the King's anointed servant. It was offered "as a pleasing aroma to the Lord" (6:14 [ET 6:21]). God had instituted this offering so that the high

[2] Talmud, *Yoma,* 32b–33a.

priest could secure God's approval of him and his service each day. Through it God demonstrated his delight in the work of the high priest and so confirmed him in his status as his anointed servant. It affirmed him in his status as the high priest and in his role as the head of the priesthood. More practically, since the priest who would succeed the high priest was the one who performed the third stage of the ritual enactment (see above), this ritual also indicated who would succeed the high priest.

(a) Mt 14:23; Mk 1:35; Lk 5:16; 6:12; 9:18, 28; 11:1

Fulfillment by Christ

In his earthly ministry, Jesus did not present daily offerings for himself as our great High Priest. Instead, he "offered" prayers and supplications for himself and all people (Heb 5:7). He interacted daily with his heavenly Father.[a] He gave to his disciples his own prayer (Lk 11:1–4) and commanded them to pray "regularly" (Lk 18:1).

Now Christ serves as High Priest over "the house of God" (Heb 10:21). He appears before God the Father in heaven on our behalf (Heb 9:24). Yet he does not need to offer daily sacrifices for himself and his people (Heb 7:27). Instead he now lives to intercede constantly for his priestly people, so that they can approach God the Father through him (Heb 7:25). They are his daily offering as High Priest. Such prayers are offerings that are "pleasing" to God the Father and acceptable to him (Heb 13:15, 16). Those who served as priests together with Christ could offer prayer to God the Father each morning and evening (1 Thess 3:10; 2 Tim 1:3). They could approach him "regularly" in their daily devotions (Rom 1:9; 1 Cor 1:4; Eph 5:20; Phil 1:4; Col 1:3; 1 Thess 1:2; 2 Thess 1:3; 2:13; Philemon 4).

Pascal Lamb, by God appointed,
All our sins on you were laid;
By almighty love anointed,
You have full atonement made.
Ev'ry sin has been forgiven
Through the virtue of your blood;
Open is the gate of heaven,
Peace between mankind and God.

Jesus, hail, enthroned in glory,
There forever to abide!
All the heav'nly host adore you,
Seated at your Father's side,
Where for sinners you are pleading
While our place preparing there,
Ever for us interceding
Till we in your glory share.[3]

---

3 From "Hail, O Once Rejected Jesus" (*LW* 284:2–3; author unknown).

Leviticus 6:17–7:21 (ET 6:24–7:21)

The Occasional Offerings of the Israelites

Translation

**6 [17]The Lord spoke to Moses: [18]"Speak to Aaron: This is the ritual instruction
for the sin offering. The sin offering shall be slaughtered before the Lord in the
same place where the burnt offering is slaughtered; it is most holy. [19]The priest
who offers it as a sin offering shall eat it; it shall be eaten in a holy place, in the
courtyard of the tent of meeting. [20]Whoever touches its meat will become holy;
and if any of its blood is spattered on any vestment, you shall launder the spattered part in a holy place. [21]Any clay pot in which it has been boiled shall be
smashed; but if it is boiled in a bronze pot, it shall be scoured and rinsed with
water. [22]Any male among the priests may eat it. It is most holy. [23]But no sin offering that has had some of its blood brought into the tent of meeting to make
atonement in the Holy Place may be eaten; it must be burned with fire.**

**7 [1]"And this is the ritual instruction for the reparation offering: it is most holy.
[2]The reparation offering shall be slaughtered in the same place where the burnt
offering is slaughtered. He shall dash its blood against all sides of the altar. [3]All
the fat from it shall be presented: the broad tail; the fat that covers the entrails;
[4]the two kidneys and the fat that is around them on the sinews; and the caudate
lobe on the liver which shall be removed with the kidneys. [5]Then the priest shall
turn them into smoke on the altar as a gift to the Lord; it is a reparation offering. [6]Any male among the priests may eat it; it shall be eaten in a holy place; it
is most holy.**

**[7]"The reparation offering is like the sin offering. The same rule applies to
both: it shall belong to the priest who makes atonement with it. [8]So too the priest
who presents anyone's burnt offering shall keep the skin of the burnt offering
that he has presented. [9]Any grain offering that is baked in an oven and any that
is prepared in a pan or on a griddle shall belong to the priest who offers it. [10]Any
grain offering that has been mixed with oil or is dry shall belong to all the sons
of Aaron alike.**

**[11]"And this is the ritual instruction for the sacrifice of the peace offering that
is presented to the Lord. [12]If anyone presents it for thanksgiving, then, in addition to that offering for thanksgiving, he shall present unleavened round loaves
mixed with oil, unleavened wafers anointed with oil, and well-soaked fine flour
as flat cakes mixed with oil. [13]In addition to the sacrifice of his peace offering as
a thank offering, he shall present his offering with round loaves of leavened
bread. [14]From this he shall present one of each [kind] as a contribution to the
Lord; it shall belong to the priest who dashes the blood of the peace offering.
[15]The meat from the sacrifice of his peace offering for thanksgiving shall be eaten
on the day that it is presented; none of it shall be set aside until morning. [16]But**

if the sacrifice that he offers is a votive offering or a freewill offering, it may be eaten on the day that he offers his sacrifice; whatever is left of it may also be eaten the next day; [17]but whatever meat is left on the third day shall be burned with fire. [18]If any of the meat from the sacrifice of his peace offering is indeed eaten on the third day, the one who presented it shall not be accepted; it shall not be credited to him. Since it shall be rotten meat, the person who eats any of it shall bear his iniquity.

[19]"The meat that touches any unclean thing shall not be eaten; it shall be burned with fire. As for the other meat [from the peace offering], anyone who is clean may eat such meat. [20]But the person who eats the meat from the sacrifice of his peace offering to the Lord while in state of impurity will be cut off from his kinsfolk. [21]If a person touches any unclean thing, whether it be human impurity, or an unclean animal, or an unclean, detestable animal, and then eats some of the meat from the sacrifice of a peace offering, which belongs to the Lord, that person shall be cut off from his kinsfolk."

Textual Notes

6:18 תּוֹרַת—See the textual notes on תּוֹרָה in 6:2 (ET 6:9) and the discussion in "Leviticus 6–7."

הַחַטָּאת—See the textual notes on 4:3.

בִּמְקוֹם אֲשֶׁר תִּשָּׁחֵט הָעֹלָה—See 1:11.

תִּשָּׁחֵט הַחַטָּאת—See 7:2 and the textual notes on 1:5.

קֹדֶשׁ קָדָשִׁים הִוא׃—See also 6:10 (ET 6:17); 7:1, 6 and the textual notes on 2:3.

6:19 הַמְחַטֵּא אֹתָהּ—The Piel of the verb חָטָא functions here as a denominative verb from חַטָּאת, "sin offering." This elliptic ritual term may mean to "make a sin-offering" (BDB, 2, citing 9:15), to "perform the rite for a sin offering" (Ex 29:36; 2 Chr 29:24), or to "cleanse from impurity with a sin offering" (Lev 8:15; Ezek 43:20, 22, 23; 45:18: cf. Lev 14:49, 52; Num 19:19; Ps 51:9 [ET 51:7]).

יֹאכְלֶנָּה—"He shall eat it" means that he eats its meat.

כֹּל אֲשֶׁר—Probably this means "whoever," but it could mean "whatever."

יִקְדָּשׁ—See the textual notes on 6:11 (ET 6:18).

יִזֶּה—This use of the Qal form of נָזָה distinguishes this accidental sprinkling from the ritual sprinkling with blood which is denoted by the Hiphil of נָזָה and which was the core of the ritual for the sin offering (4:6, 17; 5:9; 16:14, 15, 19).

תְּכַבֵּס—This is the verb for the ancient practice of laundering cloth by treading, kneading, and beating it.

6:21 חֶרֶשׂ—Paul may allude to these pots in 2 Cor 4:7, where he uses the same two Greek words used by the LXX to translate כְּלִי־חֶרֶשׂ here and in Lev 14:50.

וּמֹרַק—Scouring was done with some abrasive material such as sand or ashes.

6:22 יֹאכַל אֹתָהּ—That he may eat "it" means he would eat the meat from it.

6:23 See 4:5–9, 16–18; 16:14–19.

חַטָּאת—This refers to the meat from the sin offering.

בַּקֹּדֶשׁ—See the textual notes on 4:6. "The Holy Place" here needs to be distinguished from "a holy place," a more general location in the courtyard of the sanctuary (Ex 29:31; Lev 6:9, 19, 20 [ET 6:16, 26, 27]; 7:6; 10:13; 16:24; 24:9). In this instance the reference is not to the area between the altar and the tent (Ex 28:43; Lev 10:4, 17, 18; 14:13), but to the front room of the tabernacle (Ex 26:33; 28:29, 35; 29:30; 31:11; Lev 4:6).

7:1 הָאָשָׁם—See 5:15, 18, 25.

קֹדֶשׁ קָדָשִׁים הוּא׃—See 7:6 and the textual notes on 2:3.

7:2 בִּמְקוֹם אֲשֶׁר יִשְׁחֲטוּ אֶת־הָעֹלָה—See 1:11.

יִשְׁחֲטוּ—The Qal imperfect plural is used impersonally here.

יִזְרֹק— See the textual notes on 1:5. The priest does this.

עַל־הַמִּזְבֵּחַ סָבִיב׃—See 7:5 and the textual notes on 1:5.

7:3 חֶלְבּוֹ—See 7:4 and the textual notes on 3:3.

מִמֶּנּוּ—Since a ram is prescribed as the animal for the reparation offering (5:15, 18), the fat parts correspond with the list in 3:9–10.

אֵת הָאַלְיָה וְאֶת־הַחֵלֶב הַמְכַסֶּה אֶת־הַקֶּרֶב׃—See 3:9.

7:4 This verse is virtually identical to 3:4. See the textual notes there.

7:5 וְהִקְטִיר—The syntax is significant here. After three disjunctive circumstantial clauses in 7:2–4, this is the first consecutive clause. The accent therefore falls on the incineration of the fat as the main part of the enactment. On הִקְטִיר, see the textual notes on 1:9.

אִשֶּׁה לַיהוָה—See the textual notes on 1:9.

7:6 יֹאכְלֶנּוּ—As in 6:22 (ET 6:29), this means that the priest would eat the meat from it.

7:7 הַכֹּהֵן אֲשֶׁר יְכַפֶּר־בּוֹ לוֹ יִהְיֶה׃—The meat from the reparation offering belongs to the priest who makes atonement with it. On כִּפֶּר, see the textual notes on 1:4.

7:9 בַּתַּנּוּר—See 2:4.

בַּמַּרְחֶשֶׁת—See 2:7.

מַחֲבַת—See 2:5–6.

7:10 בְלוּלָה־בַשֶּׁמֶן—See 2:1–3.

אִישׁ כְּאָחִיו׃—See 2:3.

7:11 וְזֹאת תּוֹרַת—This connects 7:11–21 with 6:18–23 (ET 6:25–30) and 7:1–6 as the third "ritual instruction" (תּוֹרָה) in this section.

7:12 עַל־תּוֹדָה—This refers not only to the reason for the offering, but also to the song of thanksgiving which was performed as the distinctive feature of "the sacrifice of thanksgiving" (Jer 33:11). The same word, תּוֹדָה, is used both for the offering of the animal that provided the meat for the banquet and for the song that was sung at its presentation. See BDB, s.v. תּוֹדָה, 2, 4 (under the root ידה).

יַקְרִיבֶנּוּ—The impersonal construction with no specified subject is translated "if anyone presents …"

עַל־זֶבַח הַתּוֹדָה—"The offering for thanksgiving" refers to the animal that was sacrificed to provide the meat for the thanksgiving banquet. The LXX makes this quite explicit by referring to it as "the sacrifice of praise." It uses this phrase for the sacrificial animal (Lev 7:12, 13, 15; cf. 2 Chr 29:31) as well as for the song of thanksgiving that accompanied its presentation (Pss 50:14, 23; 106:22; 116:17 [LXX 49:14, 23; 105:22; 115:8]). The same phrase is found in Heb 13:15, where is describes the praise that Christians offer to God the Father through Jesus Christ.

חַלּ֤וֹת מַצּוֹת֙ בְּלוּלֹ֣ת בַּשֶּׁ֔מֶן—See the textual notes on 2:4. These loaves were, most likely, made from barley rather than wheat flour.

וְסֹ֣לֶת מֻרְבֶּ֔כֶת חַלֹּ֖ת בְּלוּלֹ֥ת בַּשָּֽׁמֶן׃—This is literally "fine flour, well-soaked, flat cakes mixed with oil." On סֹלֶת, see the textual notes on 2:1. On מֻרְבֶּכֶת, see the textual notes on 6:14 (ET 6:21).

7:13 עַל־חַלֹּת֙ לֶ֣חֶם חָמֵ֔ץ—See also 23:17; Amos 4:5.

קָרְבָּנ֑וֹ—The three kinds of bread are mentioned in 7:12.

עַל־זֶ֖בַח—That is, the animal for sacrifice.

7:14 תְּרוּמָ֖ה לַֽיהוָ֑ה—See תְּרוּמָה also in 7:32, 34; 10:14, 15; 22:12. It describes both the act by which a human owner transfers some of his property as a gift to God and the gift itself. The rabbis, and most commentators since them, called it "a heave offering" because they held that it referred to a ritual act in which something was raised and then lowered vertically by the priest before the altar.[1]

However, Milgrom has shown that there are two difficulties with this view.[2] On the one hand, this term does not describe a ritual act that is performed before the Lord at the sanctuary. On the other hand, the noun תְּרוּמָה is derived from the use of הֵרִים for the reservation, removal, and dedication of something as a donation or contribution to the Lord (see the textual notes on 2:9). This happens before the offering is brought to the sanctuary and presented there. Once it has been presented to the priest, he then performs the rite of "elevation" (תְּנוּפָה) by which "the contribution/donation" (תְּרוּמָה) is transferred from the human to the divine domain (see the textual notes on 7:30). Thus every "elevation offering" is a תְּרוּמָה before it is presented as a תְּנוּפָה by the priest at the sanctuary. The offerings in figure 12 are designated as contributions to the Lord.

הַזֹּרֵ֛ק—See 7:2 and the textual note on the verb זָרַק in 1:5.

7:15 בְּי֥וֹם קָרְבָּנ֖וֹ—See 22:29–30. Since the ritual day began at sunrise, the meat could be taken home by the priest and eaten together with his family that evening (cf. Num 18:11, 19).

7:16 נֶ֣דֶר—The term נֶדֶר is used for a vow as well as the votive offering brought for its fulfillment. It recurs in 22:18, 21, 23; 23:38; 27:2.

7:17 בָּאֵ֖שׁ יִשָּׂרֵֽף׃—This clause recurs in 19:6.

7:18 וְאִ֣ם הֵאָכֹ֣ל יֵ֠אָכֵל—The use of the infinitive absolute with the verb makes this a very emphatic assertion.

לֹ֣א יֵרָצֶ֗ה—See the textual notes on 1:4.

הַמַּקְרִ֣יב אֹת֔וֹ—Even though this phrase makes best grammatical sense as a reference to God's acceptance of *the person who had brought this sacrifice,* the Masoretes indicated that it belongs to the following clause which would then be translated "*As for the one who presented it,* it will not be credited to him." They did so because the formula for divine acceptance is always used impersonally elsewhere in Leviticus for God's acceptance of an offering (1:4; 19:7; 22:23, 25, 27). Yet despite that,

---

1 Talmud, *Menahot,* Mishnah 5:6.

2 Milgrom, "The *Šôq hattĕrûmâ*"; Milgrom, *Leviticus 1–16*, 415–16, 473–81.

this may be a case of deliberate ambiguity. It affirms that when God accepts an offering he also accepts the person who brought it.

Figure 12

תְּרוּמָה Offerings in the Pentateuch

Occasion	*Offering*	*References*
Ordination of priests	Right thigh	Ex 29:27
Peace offering	Breast	Ex 29:28
	Right thigh	Ex 29:28; Lev 7:32, 34; 10:14, 15; Num 6:20
Construction of tabernacle	Materials	Ex 25:2–3; 35:5, 21, 24; 36:3, 6
Census	Money	Ex 30:13–15
Thank offering	Bread	Lev 7:14
New harvest	Dough	Num 15:19–21
Tithe	Produce	Num 18:24–29
Victory in battle	Spoils	Num 31:29, 41, 52

לֹא יֵחָשֵׁב לוֹ—The Niphal form is best taken as a divine passive, with God as the implied agent. The use of this legal term implies that God, the heavenly Judge, takes account of an act before ruling for its doer (Num 18:27, 30; Ps 106:31; cf. Gen 15:6) or against him (Lev 7:18; 17:4).

פִּגּוּל—This is the term for desecrated meat (19:7), as well as for the unclean meat from a dead animal (Ezek 4:14) and the forbidden meat of a pig (Is 65:4).

עֲוֺנָהּ תִּשָּׂא׃—See the textual notes on 5:1.

7:19 טָמֵא—See 7:21 and the textual notes on 5:2.

טָהוֹר—The adjective טָהוֹר, "clean," is an important ritual-theological term in Leviticus. While it was used to describe the physical purity of the golden lampstand and table in the Holy Place (24:4, 6), it was commonly used as the technical term for the state of ritual purity, the normal state of people and things in the order of creation (11:36, 47; 15:8). Its antonym is טָמֵא, that which is ritually "unclean" and unfit for the divine service (see the textual notes on 5:2). Related to טָהוֹר is the verb טָהֵר, which is used in the Qal to describe what is ritually clean, and in the Piel to describe the transposition from ritual impurity to ritual purity.

Ritual purity is the precondition for involvement in the divine service and participation in God's holiness, for only that which is ritually clean can become holy and used by God in the divine service. Only those who are ritually clean may eat the holy meat and bread from the offerings (7:19; Num 18:11, 13). Only those animals and birds that are ritually clean may be eaten by the Israelites and offered to God for ritual use (Lev 11:46–47; 14:4; 20:25). The holy meat from the national sin offering and the ashes from the holy altar must be disposed of in a clean place to prevent their desecration (4:12; 6:4 [ET 6:11]). God authorized the priests to distinguish what was clean and fit for divine use from what was unclean and unfit for God's presence (10:10). They therefore determined whether a person with a skin disease was clean and fit to approach God at the sanctuary without desecrating his holiness (13:13, 17, 37, 39, 40, 41).

7:20 וְהַנֶּ֫פֶשׁ—See 7:21 and the textual notes on 2:1.

וְטֻמְאָת֖וֹ עָלָ֑יו—See the textual notes on 5:2–3.This refers to those cases where a person is the source of the impurity, such as with a person who has a genital discharge (15:1–17).

וְנִכְרְתָ֛ה הַנֶּ֥פֶשׁ הַהִ֖וא מֵעַמֶּֽיהָ׃—See 7:21. The use of the passive implies that God himself is the agent, the one who will cut off the offender from his people. This was the most severe penalty for any offense. It resulted from the violation of God's holiness. Extirpation from one's kinsfolk was the penalty for failure to fast on the Day of Atonement (23:29), for involvement in prohibited worship (17:4, 9; 20:2–6) and in forbidden sexual practices (18:29), for the eating of meat with blood in it (7:27; 17:10, 14) and of meat from a peace offering in a state of ritual impurity (7:20, 21) or on the third day after its presentation (19:7–8), and for the consumption of fat from an animal that could be sacrificed (7:25).

God himself exacted this penalty (17:10; 20:3, 5, 6). He excommunicated the offenders from their kinsfolk (7:20, 21, 25, 27; 17:4, 9, 10; 18:29; 19:8; 20:3, 5, 6; 23:29). In some cases it also meant that God put an end to their families; those who were cut off died childless, or else their lineage was extirpated from Israel and from life in God's land.[3] The clause has an eschatological dimension, suggesting that even if the offender escapes obvious punishment in this life, he would be separated from God's people in the afterlife.

7:21 בְּטֻמְאַ֣ת אָדָ֗ם—See 5:2–3. This refers to minor cases of secondary contamination by a person with a genital discharge (15:4–11, 25–27), a menstruating woman (15:19–24), or a corpse (Num 19:11, 16). אָדָם (as in Lev 1:2) can refer to any person, male or female.

א֣וֹ ׀ בִּבְהֵמָ֣ה טְמֵאָ֗ה—Since mere contact with unclean animals did not contaminate a person, this must refer to the carcass of an unclean quadruped (11:4–8, 26–28; cf. 5:2).

א֣וֹ בְּכָל־שֶׁ֣קֶץ טָמֵ֔א —The noun שֶׁקֶץ is a technical term for those birds, insects, and reptiles that must not be eaten (see also 11:10, 11, 12, 13, 20, 23, 41, 42). Yet, as Milgrom has shown, unlike those quadrupeds that are "unclean" (טָמֵא), the detestable animals denoted by שֶׁקֶץ do not normally pollute by contact with their carcasses, but only by consumption of meat from them (11:9–23, 41–42).[4] If anyone ate their meat, that meat made the people detestable; it polluted them (11:43). Here, however, שֶׁקֶץ, together with the adjective "unclean," probably refers to the carcasses of the eight reptiles and rodents listed in 11:29–31 that polluted by contact with their carcasses as well as by the consumption of their meat.

Instead of שֶׁקֶץ, here the Samaritan Pentateuch and the Targum have שֶׁרֶץ, which is the term in 5:2.

---

3 Milgrom, *Leviticus 1–16*, 457–60; Wold, "The *KARETH* Penalty in P"; Wold, *Out of Order*, 144–48.

4 Milgrom, *Leviticus 1–16*, 425–26, 656–59.

Commentary

Structure

The structure of this pericope can be outlined as follows:

I. Introduction (6:17–18a [ET 6:24–25a])
  A. God's address to Moses (6:17 [ET 6:24])
  B. Commission to speak to the Israelites (6:18a [ET 6:25a])

II. Divine speech (6:18b–7:21 [ET 6:25b–7:21])
  A. Instruction about the sin offering (6:18b–23 [ET 6:25b–30])
    1. Heading (6:18b [ET 6:25b])
    2. Place of slaughter and the reason for slaughter there (6:18c [ET 6:25c])
    3. Place for the consumption of meat from the sin offering (6:19 [ET 6:26])
    4. Its holiness (6:20–21 [ET 6:27–28])
      a. Communication of holiness by contact with it (6:20a [ET 6:27a])
      b. Treatment of blood stains from it (6:20b [ET 6:27b])
      c. Treatment of cooking utensils for it (6:21 [ET 6:28])
    5. The disposal of its meat (6:22–23 [ET 6:29–30])
      a. Consumption by priests because of its holiness (6:22 [ET 6:29])
      b. Incineration of meat when its blood has been brought into the Holy Place (6:23 [ET 6:30])
  B. Instruction about the reparation offering (7:1–10)
    1. Heading (7:1a)
    2. Its status as a reparation offering (7:1b)
    3. Place of slaughter (7:2a)
    4. Place for the disposal of blood (7:2b)
    5. Presentation of its fat (7:3–4)
    6. Burning up of its fat on the altar as a food gift to the Lord (7:5)
    7. Consumption by priests in a holy place and the reason for that (7:6)
    8. Appendix on the portion for priests from the most holy sacrifices (7:7–10)
      a. Meat from the sin and reparation offerings (7:7)
      b. Skin from the burnt offering (7:8)
      c. Bread from the grain offering (7:9)
      d. Flour from the grain offering (7:10)
  C. Instruction about the peace offering (7:11–21)
    1. General heading (7:11)
    2. The material for the thank offering and the disposal of it (7:12–15)
      a. Presentation of the three kinds of unleavened bread with the animal (7:12)
      b. Presentation of leavened bread (7:13)
      c. Presentation of one loaf of each to the officiating priest (7:14)
      d. Consumption of the meat on the day of its presentation (7:15)
    3. The disposal of meat from the votive and freewill offerings (7:16–18)
      a. Consumption of the meat within two days of its presentation (7:16)
      b. The danger of eating the meat after the second day (7:17–18)

4. The consumption of the meat (7:19–21)
   a. Incineration of unclean meat (7:19a)
   b. Consumption by any clean person (7:19b–20)
   c. Disqualification from consumption by impurity or contact with impurity (7:21)

The Sin Offering (6:17–23 [ET 6:24–30])

Ritual Agents

Since this passage deals with the disposal of the blood and meat of the sin offering, the divine instruction is addressed to Aaron and his sons rather than to the people who brought it. The priests were the obvious beneficiaries from the sin offerings of the people. Since the sin offering was most holy, it belonged to the priest who performed the rite of purification with its blood (6:19 [ET 6:26]). Its meat was his property, his food. He could, however, share it with any other male priests (all priests were male) who officiated with him (Lev 6:22 [ET 6:29]; cf. 6:11 [ET 6:18]; 7:6; Num 18:10). But the priests could not be the beneficiaries of their own sin offerings by eating the flesh from them (Lev 6:23 [ET 6:30]; cf. Hos 4:8).

Ritual Material

This unit concentrates on the proper treatment of the blood and the flesh from the sin offering. Like the reparation offering, these were "most holy" (Lev 6:18, 22 [ET 6:25, 29]). Since both the blood and the meat were most holy, they sanctified anything that they touched. They should not therefore, under any circumstances, be desecrated by unauthorized use. Because the blood was most holy, the vestments of the priests had to be carefully laundered in the sanctuary if, as so easily happened when blood was "sprinkled" on the mercy seat (16:14, 15), before the curtain (4:6, 17), or on the altar (5:9; 16:19), they were spattered with blood.

Because the meat was most holy, it had to be eaten by the priests at the sanctuary (6:19 [ET 6:26]). Moreover, since the contact with it conveyed holiness, any clay pot that may have absorbed some of the meat boiled in it had to be destroyed, and any bronze pot that was used to cook the meat had to be thoroughly scoured and washed to remove any remnants of the meat from it (6:21 [ET 6:28]). The meat from the sin offerings that the priests had offered to make atonement for themselves had to be withdrawn from all human use by incineration (6:23 [ET 6:30]) on the ash dump outside the sanctuary (4:11–12, 21; 16:27; cf. 6:4 [ET 6:11]). Once it was removed from God's presence, it ceased to be holy and so was disposed of as something common. All this was done to prevent any ritual abuse of the meat.

Ritual Location

The sacrosanct status of the sin offering determined the location for the slaughter and use of it. Since it was most holy, it, like the burnt offering (1:11; cf. 4:24, 29, 33), had to be slaughtered on the north side of the altar, rather than in front of it, as was done with the peace offering (3:8, 13). Since the meat from it was most holy, it had to be eaten in "a holy place" (6:18–19 [ET 6:25–26]). As was the case with the daily grain offering (6:9 [ET 6:16]; cf. 10:13), the location for its consumption was defined rather generally as "the courtyard of the tent of meeting" (6:19 [ET 6:26]). This, most likely, was the western half of the courtyard, around the Holy of Holies, rather than the eastern half, around the altar for burnt offering. It could not therefore be removed from the Lord's presence in the sanctuary and eaten in the homes of the priests.

In contrast with this, the priests were forbidden to eat the meat from their own sin offerings whose blood had been brought into the Holy Place; it had to be burnt up at the ash dump outside the living area of the Israelites. The careful localization of these activities serves to distinguish clearly between what was holy and common, clean and unclean.

Ritual Theological Function

The careful instruction about the disposal of the blood and the meat from the sin offering both affirmed and protected their holiness. Since they were most holy, they sanctified those people and things that were authorized to come into contact with them (6:20 [ET 6:27]). As long as they remained in contact with them, they shared in their holiness and communicated it. But once that contact was lost, as happened with the laundering of vestments or the washing of a bronze pot, they could no longer communicate it, since they were no longer in contact with it.

If, however, the blood and the flesh were used by any unauthorized people, in an unauthorized place, or for an unauthorized purpose, their holiness was desecrated. God's wrath fell on those who desecrated the most holy things, as happened with Nadab and Abihu (10:1–2) and the family of Korah (Numbers 16). This instruction therefore protected the most holy things from desecration, as well as the priests from the lethal consequences of desecration.

The Reparation Offering (7:1–6)

Ritual Agents

The instruction outlines the basic ritual for the reparation offering which had not been given in 5:14–26 (ET 5:14–6:7) before it deals with the disposal of flesh from it. This, indeed, is its main concern. In keeping with that emphasis, it does not explicitly mention who was to slaughter the offering, perform the blood rite, and bring its fat to the altar. It merely specifies who should burn it up on the altar and eat the meat from it. Whereas the priest on duty burnt up the fat on the altar (7:5), the meat from the reparation offering belonged to all the priests (7:6).

Ritual Material

This instruction declares that the reparation offering is most holy by the repetition of an assertion to that effect at its beginning (7:1) and end (7:6). This assertion, however, does not apply to the animal as such, or even to its blood, which receives scant attention in 7:2. It applies to its fat parts and its meat (7:3–6).

The animal for the reparation offering is, as is mentioned in 5:15, 18 and 25 (ET 6:6), a ram. Like the peace offering (3:9–10) and the private sin offering (4:31), all the fat from the animal was burnt on the altar. The "fat" consisted of its tail, the fat around its intestines, the fat around the kidneys together with them, and the liver lobe. The significance of these parts was discussed in connection with the analysis of the peace offering. Since all these were a "gift" to God (7:5) they belonged entirely to him. But the meat from the animal belonged to the priests. Since it was most holy, the priests were required to eat it in a holy place. It was the most important part of the reparation offering.

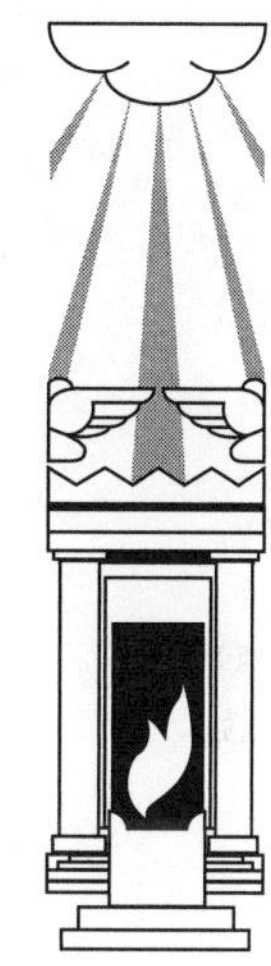

Ritual Location

The status of the reparation offering as a most holy sacrifice determined the location for its slaughter and its consumption. Like the sheep for a burnt offering, it was slaughtered on the north side of the altar. Its blood was then splashed against the sides of it and its fat was burnt on it. And more importantly, its meat, like the bread for the public grain offering and the meat from the sin offering, was eaten in a holy place. The place for its consumption was, most likely, the western courtyard around the tabernacle (cf. 6:9, 14 [ET 6:16, 21]). It could therefore not be removed from God's presence, but was eaten there in a holy place so that it was not desecrated.

Ritual Enactment

Since this passage is a ritual instruction on the treatment of holy things, it does not institute the ritual for the presentation of the reparation offering. It does, however, summarize the main parts of that ritual because they were not mentioned in 5:14–26 (ET 5:14–6:7). That ritual corresponds, in large measure, with the procedure for the presentation of a sheep as a peace offering (cf. 3:7–11). After the Israelite had slaughtered the animal and the priest had splashed its blood against the four sides of the altar, the Israelite presented the fat to the priest who burnt it all on the altar. But, in contrast with the peace offering, the priest then received all the meat as his food for the duration of his service at the sanctuary. The most significant feature in all this, from a ritual angle, is the lack of emphasis on the blood rite. Instead of that, the passage treats the burning of the fat and the eating of the meat from the offering.

Ritual Theological Function

The theological function of the reparation offering was discussed in connection with 5:14–26 (ET 5:14–6:7). This passage, however, gives divine instruction on the holiness of the meat from the sacrifice. Two things are significant in this. First, the use of the declaratory formula in 7:5 asserts that the fat is the essential part of the "reparation offering" (אָשָׁם). It is "the payment," "the compensation" (אָשָׁם), given as a "gift" (אִשֶּׁה) to the Lord for an act of sacrilege. Second, the burning up of the fat from the offering on the altar consecrated the meat from it, as a part for the whole, so that it became "most holy" (7:6). Only the priests could eat this most holy meat. Since it was most holy, it could only be eaten in God's presence at the sanctuary. Otherwise it would be desecrated.

The Lord added the meat from it to the meat from the sin offering (6:22 [ET 6:29]) and the bread from the grain offering (6:10–11 [ET 6:17–18]) as the most holy food that he provided for the priests during their service at his residence. Through this daily food, which was eaten in his presence, he nourished them physically and shared his holiness with them.

The Portions for the Priests (7:7–10)

Context and Structure

The material here is closely connected to that in 7:29–34. It has been located in this position for two reasons. First, the first sentence in 7:7, which refers to the sin offering in 6:18–23 (ET 6:25–30) and reparation offering in 7:1–6, explains that, even though all the priests could eat the meat from the reparation offering, the meat belonged to the priest who performed the ritual for it. Second, since this gives a list of the portions for the priests from the most holy offerings, it has been placed here, as a summary, at the end of the instruction for the correct disposal of them.

This summary consists of an introduction in proverbial style (7:7a) followed by four sentences, linked by a coordinating conjunction (7:7b–10). The first three of these sentences follow the same pattern: "the priest who … to him it shall belong." This is modified by the last sentence that omits any reference to the priest and maintains: "… to all the sons of Aaron it shall belong." The arrangement of these statements cleverly mirrors their content, for they clearly contrast what belongs to the officiating priest with what belongs to all the priests.

Analysis of Content

The only new piece of legislation in this summary is the assignment of the hide from the burnt offering to the officiating priest (7:8). Apart from that, it enunciates the general principle that the officiating priest receives payment for his work from a portion of the sacrifices. The only exception to this rule is the grain offering of flour. Since this did not need to be eaten immediately, it could be stored. It was therefore set aside to make bread for the priests who performed other tasks. They would otherwise have no food while on service at the temple, because they had not officiated in the presentation of grain offerings, sin offerings, and reparation offerings.

The Peace Offering (7:11–21)

Ritual Agents

Since the peace offering was the main offering of the lay Israelites, the focus in this unit shifts from the priests to them in this divine instruction. In fact, the officiating priest for the sacrifice is mentioned only as the recipient of three loaves from a sacrifice of thanksgiving. Instead, the lay Israelites receive instruction from God on what to present in addition to an animal for a thank offering (7:12–14), on when the meat from either class of peace offering must be eaten (7:15–16), on what to do with any leftover and contaminated meat (7:17–19a), and on who is qualified to eat the meat from it (7:19b–21).

The lay Israelite who eats the meat from this sacrifice must be in a state of ritual purity; "anyone who is clean" may eat it (7:19b). This enunciates a basic principle in the theology of worship in the OT, a principle that is presupposed by all the instructions on what is clean and unclean in Leviticus 11–15, as well as by the ritual for the Day of Atonement in Leviticus 16.

Ritual purity was the prerequisite for admission into God's presence and the reception of blessing from him at the sanctuary (cf. Ps 24:3–5). An unclean person who touched something holy, defiled and desecrated it so badly that it could no longer function as it should. It was therefore burned (Lev 7:19a). The penalty for those who defiled something holy was excommunication from God's presence, his people, and life with him in his land (7:20, 21). This instruction, then, sought to forestall such an eventuality by distinguishing the ritually clean people, who could safely be admitted to the holy meal, from the unclean people who, for their own good, were temporally excluded from it.

The whole of this instruction presupposes that the person who brought the offering shared the meat from the offering in a communal meal with a circle of guests from his family and community. This social dimension of the peace offering is also implied by the divine penalty for the defilement of meat from the sacrifice. Those who defiled the meat with their impurity did not enjoy greater solidarity with their kinsfolk, but they were cut off from them (7:20, 21).

Ritual Material

In this passage the Lord teaches the Israelites about the proper treatment of the holy bread and holy meat from the peace offering. When the Israelites presented a sacrifice of thanksgiving, they had to prepare four kinds of bread for presentation with it. This included three kinds of unleavened bread (7:12). It is not clear exactly how they differed from each other. All were either made with olive oil or else they had olive oil spread on them. While the third kind of bread was made of fine wheat flour, the first two kinds of bread could be made of barley flour. While the first two were probably baked as round cakes or flat wafers in an oven (cf. 2:4), the third kind of bread was probably roasted on a griddle (cf. 2:5; 6:7 [ET 6:14]). Surprisingly, the Israelites were also required to bring cakes of bread made with yeast. The only other occasion when bread made with yeast was presented at the sanctuary was for the offering of the first-processed grain at the Feast of Pentecost (23:17; cf. 2:11–12; Amos 4:5). One loaf from each of the four kinds of bread was to be presented to the officiating priest (7:14); the rest were eaten in the sacrificial banquet.

The main point of this instruction was to protect the holiness of the meat from the peace offering. In contrast with the most holy meat from the sin offering and the reparation offering, it was merely holy (cf. 19:8). Even though the meat from the peace offering did not communicate holiness directly by physical contact, it could not be treated as common meat. Restrictions were therefore placed on its consumption. It had to be eaten within a prescribed period of time (7:15–18) by ritually clean people (7:19b). It was not to be defiled through contact with anything unclean (7:19a) or from consumption by an unclean person. If the meat was held over beyond the ritually prescribed time for its consumption, it became "rotten meat" (7:18). If the flesh was defiled through contact with something unclean, it had to be burnt so that it could no longer be eaten.

The holiness of the meat from the peace offering was preserved by keeping it apart from "anything unclean" (7:19). Two common categories of impurity are identified in 7:20–21. On the one hand, there is primary self-generated ritual impurity, such as from a genital discharge. This originated in those who thereby become unclean. On the other hand, there is secondary, acquired ritual impurity. This came from direct contact with an unclean person, such as a menstruating woman, or from physical contact with the carcass of an unclean quadruped, such as a pig (11:7–8), or a detestable swarming creature, such as a lizard (11:28–31).

Ritual Time

Even though the peace offering could be presented at any time, they were most commonly brought to the sanctuary by the Israelites on the three great pilgrim festivals. They were presented in the middle of the day between the two times for the daily burnt offering. This instruction, however, is not concerned with that. Rather it establishes the time for the eating of the meat in a sacrificial banquet. While the meat for the thank offering had to be eaten on the day of its presentation, the meat from the votive offering or the freewill offering could be eaten on the following day as well. In both cases the day included the following night, for these meals most likely lasted well into the evening.

Ritual Location

No explicit ritual restrictions were placed on the location of these sacrificial banquets. It is assumed that they were eaten in the camp. This was later understood as the city of Jerusalem. But severe restrictions were placed on the time limits for their consumption to prevent the desecration of the sacred meat. The meat had to be eaten within the ritually prescribed period of time. The more holy the meat, the sooner it had to be eaten. Thus the meat from the more sacred thank offering had to be eaten at the tabernacle on the day of its presentation to make sure that the meal was connected closely with the song of thanksgiving. But the meat from the less sacred votive and freewill offerings could also be eaten on the next day.

In either case the meat could not be dissociated temporally from the ritual performed at the sanctuary. It had to be eaten in temporal proximity to the Lord's presence there. Just as the most holy meat from the sin and reparation offerings was desecrated by its removal from the sanctuary, so the sacred meat from the peace offering was desecrated by its consumption apart from the time of its presentation.

Ritual Theological Function

The peace offering served three main functions. In each case the onus for the presentation of the offering lay on the person who presented it, since it was a voluntary sacrifice. The highlight of each offering was the sacred meal with the meat from the sacrifice.

The sacrifice for thanksgiving (תּוֹדָה) receives the most attention in 7:12–14. It was offered to fulfill a promise made by people in a prayer of lament to the Lord.[a] When the Lord answered their prayer, they presented this sacrifice with music and song to celebrate their deliverance. As part of the ritual for the presentation of that offering, they, most likely, hired a Levitical singer to perform a song of thanksgiving (תּוֹדָה), such as Psalm 30 or 116, in which they formally "thanked" (הוֹדָה, the Hiphil of יָדָה) the Lord for his help and "confessed" (הוֹדָה) the Lord's goodness to his guests.[5]

Besides the song of thanksgiving, the other special feature of this sacrifice was the presentation of four kinds of bread at the sanctuary (Lev 7:12–13). One loaf from each of these kinds of bread was presented to the priest as a "contribution to the Lord," their donation to him (7:14). Unlike the grain offering, none of the four loaves was burned on the altar; all were eaten by the priest and the members of his family. The members of his family were therefore included in the sacred meal. But, more significantly, by the presentation of a portion to the Lord, the rest of the bread became holy, just as the meat was holy.

(a) E.g., Pss 7:18; 35:18; 52:11; 56:13–14 (ET 7:17; 35:18; 52:9; 56:12–13)

Peace offerings could also be presented as votive offerings or as freewill offerings (7:16). Those that were presented as votive offerings were brought to fulfill a vow made in a prayer of lament to the Lord by a person in trouble (e.g. Gen 28:20–22; 2 Sam 15:7–8), while freewill offerings were brought spontaneously in gratitude to the Lord for his blessings, even though no vow had been made to do so (cf. Deut 16:10).

All three kinds of peace offerings were offered in response to the experience of divine benefaction. Like an accountant, the Lord "credited" the offering to the offerer and accepted him together with his offering (Lev 7:18; cf. 19:7; 22:23, 25, 27). He was received as a favored guest of the Lord and ate the holy meat in the Lord's presence as part of the whole congregation of Israel. Since the meat was holy, the Israelites were forbidden to desecrate it by eating it apart from the sacred time for the meal (7:18; cf.19:7–8) and to defile it with impurity by contact with anything unclean. Its holiness was so important that anyone who desecrated the flesh from that sacrifice by eating it after the prescribed time for the meal bore his iniquity (7:18). In 19:7–8, this is

[5] Kleinig, *The Lord's Song*, 123–29.

equated with divine excommunication, the same penalty as when the peace offering was eaten by an unclean person (7:21).

In sum: this instruction was given by the Lord to protect the holiness of the meat from the peace offering from desecration and defilement. It also shielded those who ate it from the penalty for its desecration and defilement.

Fulfillment by Christ

All the sacrifices that were offered at the tabernacle were part of a single ritual enactment. There were three main stages to that enactment: the disposal of blood in the rite of atonement; the incineration of the offerings on the altar for burnt offering; and the sacred meal with the bread and meat from the offerings.[6] Only after the removal of impurity by the rite of atonement and the acceptance of the people by God in the burnt offering could the priests and the people eat the sacred food from the table. They had to be ritually clean before they could participate in that meal (7:19–21).

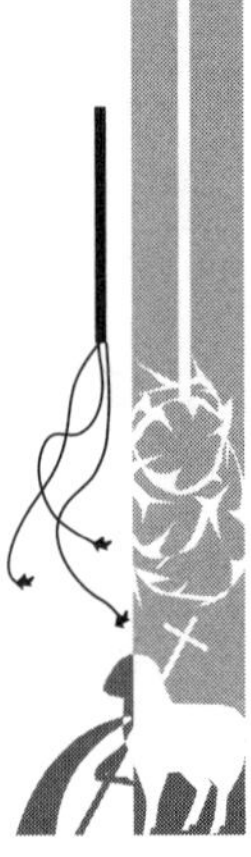

The ritual instructions in 6:17–7:21 (ET 6:24–7:21) deal with the meat for that meal that came from the sin offering, the reparation offering, and the peace offering. These varied offerings all find their fulfillment in the one sacrifice of Christ (Heb 7:27; 10:12). He fulfilled all these functions completely and perfectly. Since Christ has removed all impurity by his blood and has gained our acceptance by God the Father through the offering of his body, we now no longer need to offer up sin offerings or reparation offerings or burnt offerings for our justification before God. Instead, we are invited to participate in the sacrificial meal that Christ has established. In it he gives us his own body to eat.

That meal resembles and yet differs from the sacrificial meals eaten by the priests and the people in the old covenant. We all eat the most holy food from Christ's offering. There is therefore now no difference between the lay people and the priests, for all God's people are priests (1 Pet 2:9). In the old covenant the rule was given that neither the priests nor the people could eat the meat from the sin offerings and reparation offerings that had been sacrificed to atone for their sins. In a remarkable reversal, all God's people eat the flesh of Christ that was sacrificed for their atonement, even though those who ministered at the tabernacle had no right to eat the meat from their sin offerings (Heb 13:10).[7]

Since Christ's body has been offered up as a sin offering and a reparation offering to God the Father, it is now most holy. It is therefore eaten as part of the Divine Service in a holy place, the assembly of the saints in the heavenly sanctuary (Heb 10:19–22). This is typified for us by our reception of the Lord's Supper in the sanctuaries of our churches. Contact with that most holy flesh makes and keeps God's people holy (Heb 10:10). In this way we come to share more and more in God's life-giving holiness.

---

6 Kleinig, *The Lord's Song*, 101–8, 132.

7 See Pursiful, *The Cultic Motif in the Spirituality of the Book of Hebrews*, 140.

In the Lord's Supper Christ is also the host of a banquet that fulfills all the functions of the peace offering. It is our Eucharist, our offering of thanksgiving in which we both receive the gift of peace from God the Father and thank him for that great eschatological gift (Mt 26:26, 27, 30; Lk 22:19–20). As we participate in that meal we offer our sacrifice of praise to him through our Lord Jesus Christ (Heb 13:15), just as the people of Israel combined their sacrifice of thanksgiving with a song of thanksgiving and praise (7:12–17). The Lord's Supper is both an act of thanksgiving and a Eucharistic banquet; it is our offering of thanksgiving that is well pleasing to God the Father (Heb 13:15–16).

In Jer 33:10–11, the prophet Jeremiah had announced that when God restored his people, they would bring thank offerings to him. The rabbis understood this as a prophecy of the messianic age. Thus *Midrash Rabbah Leviticus,* § 9.7, declares that in the age to come all sacrifices would cease, except the offering of thanksgiving. So, after Christ's great sacrifice of atonement, the church has no sacrifice to bring to God the Father except the sacrifice of praise.

Melanchthon makes a similar affirmation in Ap XXIV 9–77. There in his discussion on whether the Mass is a sacrifice or not, he distinguishes the eucharistic sacrifices from the propitiatory sacrifices. He argues that since Christ has offered himself to atone for all our sins, we can only offer God a sacrifice of thanksgiving. The whole of the Divine Service is therefore an offering of thanksgiving and praise to God the Father as we receive Christ's body and blood. The heart of that service is our reception of the Lord's Supper; it is in itself an act of thanksgiving and praise, for as often as we eat that meal we rejoice in God's grace and proclaim Christ's death for our redemption (1 Cor 11:26; Ap XXIV 35–36).

Like the Israelites, the members of the church have to be in state of ritual purity to receive the most holy body of Christ (Mt 7:6).[8] And we more so than the Israelites! Not only our bodies, but our consciences must be washed clean through Holy Baptism (Heb 9:14; 10:22). Thus normally the Eucharist begins with the rite of confession and absolution. Great care also needs to be taken to make sure that those who eat Christ's body do not profane its holiness and so come under God's judgment for sacrilege (1 Cor 11:27–32). But those who receive it in faith with a clear conscience receive grace and peace, life and blessing from it. They feast on Christ and share in him (Heb 3:14). In that meal they have a foretaste of the great heavenly banquet that celebrates the union of the Messiah with his holy people (Rev 19:6–9).

More generally, those who lose faith in God's kindness and reject Christ will be cut off from the new people of God (Rom 11:22). And worse than that, those who try to justify themselves by observing the law cut themselves off from Christ and lose access to God's grace (Gal 5:4), for only in Christ are we part of God's kinsfolk.

8 See *Didache* 9:5.

Jesus Christ, our blessed Savior,
Turned away God's wrath forever;
By his bitter grief and woe
He saved us from the evil foe.

He, to pledge his love undying,
Spreads this table, grace supplying,
Gives his body with the bread,
And with the wine the blood he shed.

Firmly hold with faith unshaken
That this food is to be taken
By the sick who are distressed,
By hearts that long for peace and rest.[9]

---

[9] From "Jesus Christ, Our Blessed Savior" by John Hus; translated by Samuel Janzow (*LW* 236:1; 237:2; 236:5; translation © 1980 Concordia Publishing House; all rights reserved).

Leviticus 7:22–27

Prohibited Food: Fat and Blood

Translation

7 [22]The Lord spoke to Moses: [23]"Speak to the Israelites: You shall not eat any fat from a head of cattle, a sheep, or a goat. [24]The fat of an animal that has died naturally or has been mauled by wild animals may be put to any [other] use, but you must never eat it. [25]Indeed, if anyone who eats the fat from an animal from which someone may present a gift to the Lord, the person who eats [it] will be cut off from his kinsfolk.

[26]"You must not eat any blood from birds or animals in any of your settlements. [27]Any person who eats any blood will be cut off from his kinsfolk."

Textual Notes

7:23 חֵלֶב—See 7:24–25 and the textual notes on 3:17.

7:24 וְחֵלֶב נְבֵלָה—Literally this phrase is "the fat of a carcass." See 17:15.

טְרֵפָה—This refers to an animal that has been killed by another. It recurs in 17:15; 22:8.

יֵעָשֶׂה לְכָל־מְלָאכָה—Literally this means "it may be prepared for any task."

וְאָכֹל לֹא תֹאכְלֻהוּ׃—The use of the infinitive absolute from the same root as the verb makes this a very emphatic prohibition.

7:25 כִּי—כִּי is used here as an emphatic particle ("indeed") rather than a conjunction.

יַקְרִיב—See the textual note on this verb in 1:2.

אִשֶּׁה לַיהוָה—See the textual notes on 1:9 and the explanation in "Leviticus 1–3."

וְנִכְרְתָה הַנֶּפֶשׁ הָאֹכֶלֶת מֵעַמֶּיהָ׃—See the textual notes on 7:20. The use of the term נֶפֶשׁ here and in 7:27 also implies that the "life" of that person will come to an end.

7:26 וְכָל־דָּם לֹא תֹאכְלוּ—See the textual notes and commentary on 3:17. See 7:27.

בְּכֹל מוֹשְׁבֹתֵיכֶם—See 3:17.

7:27 כָּל־נֶפֶשׁ ... הַנֶּפֶשׁ—By repeating the noun נֶפֶשׁ with the article (הַנֶּפֶשׁ), the Hebrew text emphasizes that the person will lose his life. A literal translation of the verse would be this: "Any person who eats any blood—that person/life will be cut off from his kinsfolk."

Commentary

Context and Structure

This unit consists of a new divine speech that, like 7:7–10, is somewhat intrusive. It interrupts the divine instruction about the disposal of meat from the peace offering, beginning with 7:11–21 and ending with 7:29–34. Even though it gives general prohibitions about the eating of fat and blood from all animals, it has been placed here because it asserts that the Israelites must never eat the fat and the blood from the peace offering.

The speech is divided by its subject matter and structure into two parts. While 7:23–25 prohibits the eating of fat, 7:26–27 forbids the eating of meat with blood in it. The warning in 7:25 and 7:27 that those who eat fat and blood will be "cut off" connects these verses with 7:20 and 7:21, just as the key word "eat" links this unit with the discussion on eating meat in 7:15–21.

The structure of this pericope can be outlined as follows:

I. Introduction (7:22–23a)
   A. The Lord's address to Moses (7:22)
   B. His commission to speak to the Israelites (7:23a)
II. Divine speech (7:23b–27)
   A. The fat from animals (7:23b–25)
      1. Prohibition of eating the fat of cattle, sheep, and goats (7:23b)
      2. Permission to use the fat from a dead animal for other purposes (7:24)
      3. Divine excommunication for the consumption of fat (7:25)
   B. The blood from animals (7:26–27)
      1. Prohibition of eating blood from any animal (7:26)
      2. Divine excommunication for the consumption of blood (7:27)

Analysis of Content

The prohibition of the consumption of fat and blood has already been discussed in connection with 3:16b–17. This speech adds two things to the general prohibition in 3:17. First, it extends the prohibition of eating fat of sacrificed animals to the fat taken from all animals which have died from natural causes or which have been killed by a beast of prey. The fat from these animals could be used for other purposes, such as fuel for a lamp or as polish or as a base for an ointment, but it could not be eaten by any Israelite. Its meat, however, could be eaten, even though the animal had not been sacrificed at the altar. Second, the consumption of fat from a sacrificed animal (7:25) and the consumption of blood from any animal (7:26) was an offense against God which resulted in divine excommunication of the offender from the people of Israel and life with them in God's presence. The offender and his family would cease to exist in Israel.

Leviticus 7:28–36

The Priest's Portion of the Peace Offering

Translation

**7 [28]The Lord spoke to Moses: [29]"Speak to the Israelites: Anyone who presents
his sacrifice of peace offering to the Lord shall bring some of his sacrifice of peace
offering as an offering to the Lord. [30]His own hands must bring the gifts of the
Lord; he shall bring the fat upon the breast in order to offer the breast as an elevation offering to the Lord. [31]The priest shall turn the fat into smoke on the altar, but the breast shall belong to Aaron and his sons. [32]But you shall give the
right thigh to the priest as a donation from your sacrifices of peace offering; [33]the
right thigh shall be the portion that belongs to the son of Aaron who offers the
blood and the fat of the peace offering. [34]For I have taken the breast of the elevation offering and the donated thigh from the Israelites, from the sacrifices of
their peace offerings, and I have assigned them to Aaron, the priest, and to his
sons as a perpetual due from the Israelites."**

**[35]This is the perquisite for Aaron and the perquisite for his sons from the
gifts to the Lord after the day when he presents them to serve the Lord as priests,
[36]which the Lord commanded the Israelites to give to them from the day when
he anoints them. It is a perpetual ritual statute throughout your generations.**

Textual Notes

7:29 זֶבַח שְׁלָמָיו—See the textual notes on 3:1.

יָבִיא—See the textual note on this verb in 2:2. It recurs in 7:30.

מִזֶּבַח שְׁלָמָיו׃—This refers to the breast and the thigh of the animal.

7:30 אִשֵּׁי יְהוָה—These gifts consist of the fat, breast, and thigh of the animal. See the textual note on this phrase in 1:9 and the explanation in "Leviticus 1–3." The phrase recurs in 7:35.

הַחֵלֶב—See the textual notes on 3:3 and the commentary on 3:16–17. See 7:31, 35.

עַל־הֶחָזֶה—The preposition עַל could also be translated as "with" or "as well as." חָזֶה most likely designates the rib cage of the animal without the lower spine.

תְּנוּפָה—This is a technical term for the ritual act of offering to God as well as what was offered in it (7:34; 8:27, 29; 9:21; 10:14, 15; 14:12, 21, 24; 23:15, 17, 20). It is used with its cognate verb, the Hiphil of נוף (הֵנִיף), to describe the ritual by which it is offered (8:27, 29; 9:21; 10:15; 14:12, 24; 23:20; cf. 23:11, 12). Traditionally, it has been called a "wave offering" or "heave offering," since it was held to have been presented by extending it, in a horizontal motion, away from the body before bringing it back to the body.[1] But, as Milgrom has shown, this term describes the ritual el-

---

1 Talmud, Mishnah, *Menahot,* 5:6.

evation of an offering before the Lord in the sanctuary to transfer it from human possession to the divine domain.[2] By its enactment something that by right belonged to human beings was dedicated to God. Whatever was thus dedicated could be used only by him and his priests. It should therefore be called an "elevation offering." Figure 13 shows the elevation offerings in the Pentateuch.

Figure 13

Elevation Offerings in the Pentateuch

Occasion	*Offering*	*References*
Peace offering	Breast	Lev 7:30, 34; 9:21;10:14, 15 Num 18:18
Ordination of priests	Fat from ram	Ex 29:22–24; Lev 8:25–27
	Thigh of ram	Ex 29:22–24; Lev 8:25–27
	Three loaves of bread	Ex 29:23–24; Lev 8:26–27
	Breast of ram	Ex 29:26; Lev 8:29
Construction of tabernacle	Gold and bronze	Ex 35:22; 38:24, 29
Cleansed leper	Lamb for reparation offering	Lev 14:12, 21, 24
	Oil for anointing	Lev 14:12, 24
Day of Firstfruits	Sheaf of first grain	Lev 23:11, 15
Pentecost	Two leavened loaves	Lev 23:17
	Two lambs	Lev 23:20
Installation of Levites	Levites	Num 8:11, 13, 15
Suspected adultery	Barley flour	Num 5:25
Completion of Nazirite term	Shoulder of ram	Num 6:19–20
	Unleavened cake and wafer	Num 6:19–20

7:31 וְהִקְטִיר—See the textual note on this verb in 1:9.
הַמִּזְבֵּחָה—See the textual notes on 1:5.
7:32 שׁוֹק—This is the hindquarter. In Deut 18:3, however, the forequarter is assigned to the priest.
תְּרוּמָה—This refers to the "donation" or "contribution." See Lev 7:34 and the textual notes on 7:14.
7:34 חֲזֵה הַתְּנוּפָה—See also Ex 29:27; Lev 10:14, 15; Num 6:20; 18:8.

---

[2] Milgrom, *"Hattĕnûpâ";* Milgrom, *Leviticus 1–16,* 461–73.

שׁוֹק הַתְּרוּמָה—Literally "the thigh of the donation." See Ex 29:27; Lev 10:14, 15; Num 6:20.

וָאֶתֵּן—This is literally "I have given." The combination of "take" with "give" may be adapted from a legal formula by which a king assigned a reward to his faithful servant.

לְחָק־עוֹלָם—See the textual notes on 6:11 (ET 6:18).

7:35 זֹאת—This collective ("this" meaning "these") refers to the things mentioned in 7:30–34.

מִשְׁחַת—The term מִשְׁחָה occurs only here in the OT. It could be construed as "an anointed right" (the view of the LXX), under the influence of the reference to the "anointing" of the priest in 7:35, or else as "a due," "a perquisite," like מָשְׁחָה in Num 18:8, from a homonym meaning "measure, apportion."

מֵאִשֵּׁי יְהוָה—See the textual notes on 1:9.

בְּיוֹם—This is literally "on the day." See the textual notes on 6:13 (ET 6:20).

הִקְרִיב אֹתָם לְכַהֵן לַיהוָה׃—This refers to the rite of presentation, in which Moses brought the priests forward for their ceremonial investiture at the altar (Ex 29:4, 8; 40:12, 14; Lev 8:6, 13).

7:36 צִוָּה יְהוָה—As in all the priestly material of the Pentateuch, the verb "command" is used in Leviticus for God's institution of various aspects of the divine service. It is used in two main ways: to report what God had instituted (7:36, 38 [twice]; 8:5, 34, 35; 9:6; 10:1, 13; 17:2; 27:34) and to report its fulfillment with the so-called formula of execution (8:4, 9, 13, 17, 21, 29, 36; 9:7, 10; 10:15; 16:34; 24:23).

לָתֵת לָהֶם ... מֵאֵת בְּנֵי יִשְׂרָאֵל—This is literally "for giving to them from the Israelites."

בְּיוֹם מָשְׁחוֹ אֹתָם—בְּיוֹם is literally "on the day." See the textual notes on 6:13 (ET 6:20). The high priest was anointed on his head with anointing oil (Ex 29:7; Lev 8:12; 21:10). All the priests had their bodies and vestments anointed with anointing oil which had been mixed with blood from the altar (Lev 8:30; cf. Ex 28:41; 30:30–33; 40:13–15). The pronoun on מָשְׁחוֹ (the Qal infinitive construct) refers to Moses, since "he" is the one who will anoint the priests (8:12, 30).

חֻקַּת עוֹלָם—See the textual notes on 3:17.

Commentary

Structure

The divine speech in 7:29–34 is an appendix to the instruction about the peace offering in 7:11–21. Whereas 7:11–21 had covered the correct procedure for the disposal of the bread and meat from the peace offering, 7:29–34 outlines the parts that had to be presented to the Lord. The passage ends with an editorial summary in 7:35–36 that emphasizes the divine origin of this system of apportionment.

The structure of this pericope can be outlined as follows:

I. Introduction (7:28–29a)
   A. The Lord's address to Moses (7:28)
   B. His commission to speak to the Israelites (7:29a)
II. Divine speech about the priestly dues from the peace offering (7:29b–34)
   A. Personal presentation of the Lord's offering from the peace offering (7:29b–33)
      1. Presentation of the fat on the breast in the right of elevation before the Lord (7:29b–30)
      2. Burning of the fat by the priest (7:31a)
      3. Retention of the breast for the priesthood (7:31b)
      4. Gift of the thigh to the officiating priest (7:32–33)
   B. Divine decree (7:34)
      1. God's appropriation of the breast and thigh (7:34a)
      2. God's endowment of them on the priest (7:34b)
III. Postscript about the priestly portions from the peace offering (7:35–36)
   A. God's institution of these dues for the priests (7:35–36a)
   B. Their perpetuity (7:36b)

Ritual Agents

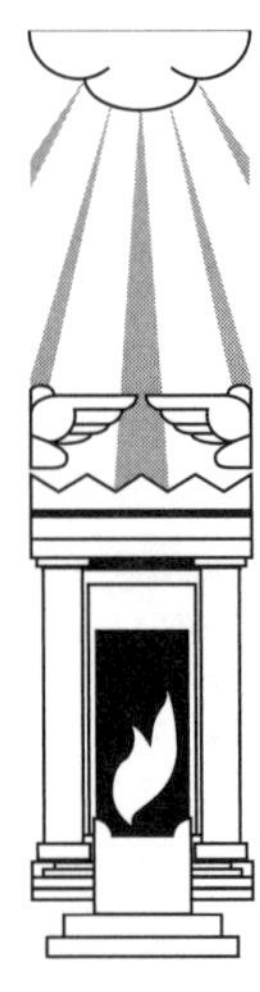

This divine instruction is addressed to the Israelites who presented their peace offerings at the sanctuary. Since the peace offering by right belonged to the offerer, he himself brought it personally to the Lord with "his own hands" as a gift to the Lord (7:30). He handed the breast with the fat on it over to God by elevating it before the altar and donated the right hind thigh directly to the priest who ate it (7:32).

Since the fat from all the sacrificed animals belonged exclusively to the Lord, he received the breast and the thigh from the owner of the animal and gave them to the priests as their due from the offerings (7:34). The breast that had been elevated before the Lord was assigned to all the priests (7:31), while the thigh was assigned to the officiating priest (7:32–33). They were God's gift to them, their endowment from him.

Ritual Materials

This passage mentions the parts of the peace offering that the Israelites brought as their offering to the Lord (7:29). This offering was made up of three kinds of "gifts" (7:30, 35): the fat that belonged to the Lord; the breast cage of the animal that served as the holder for the fat; and the right hindquarter. God reassigned the breast and the thigh as food to the priests and their families (Num 18:18–19).

Ritual Enactment and Function

The ritual statutes in 7:28–36 expand on the ritual legislation for the peace offering in 3:1–17 and the ritual instruction about the bread and meat from it in 7:11–21. While the legislation in 3:3, 9, 14 had mentioned the presentation of the fat, 7:29–34 describes the full procedure for this rite. The offerer brought the fat heaped on the breast cage with his own hands and performed the act of elevation with it in front of the altar so that the priest could remove the fat and burn it on the altar (7:30–31a). By the act of elevation and the rite for the burning of the fat, both the breast cage and the right thigh were handed over to God (cf. Ex 29:27). After they had been transferred into the divine domain, the offerer handed the breast to a representative of the priesthood and the thigh to the officiating priest (7:31b–33). The fat had to be burned before the priests received their portions. This is theologically significant, for God had to receive his three gifts before he himself could reapportion the meat as food to his servants.

These ritual statutes ordained who should receive which portion of the peace offering. Since the peace offering was the most common of all the sacrifices, it constituted a large part of the diet of the priests and their families (cf. 10:14–15; Num 18:18–19). The vexing problem of inequity was lessened by the exact prescriptions for the distribution of the breast and the thigh. While the officiating priest received the thigh of the animal (7:32–33), the ribcage was divided among the rest of the priests (7:31). Both the breast and the thigh were the Lord's personal provision for them (7:34). They were their "due," their stipend as the servants of the heavenly King. Just as a king paid his courtiers from his royal revenue, so the Lord provided for his servants from his holy offerings.

The assignment of the breast and the thigh from the peace offering was established by the divine precedent in the ritual for the ordination of the priests at Mount Sinai (7:35–36). The rite for the presentation of the ram for ordination set the precedent for all subsequent peace offerings (Ex 29:22–28; Lev 8:25–29). It was the archetypal peace offering that determined the operation and significance of all other peace offerings.

Most significantly, the ordination offering clearly distinguished the thigh that was burnt with the fat on the altar (Ex 29:22–26; Lev 8:25–28) from the breast that was eaten by Moses in his capacity as priest (Ex 29:26; Lev 8:29). This connection between the rite for ordination and the priestly dues from the peace offering is reinforced by a pun. Since the priests were "anointed" to serve the Lord (7:36), they received the breast and the thigh as their "anointed right" and their "hereditary portion" from the gifts of the Lord (7:35). He provided for them and their families from his own resources. Their livelihood came from him.

Fulfillment by Christ

Since the priests were God's courtiers, the keepers of his house, and the administrators of his affairs, they received their livelihood directly from God rather than the land. He assigned certain portions of the offerings to them and their families so that they could devote themselves fully to God's service, without working the land or seeking other supplementary employment.

When Jesus sent out his apostles, he decreed that they too were to receive food and other necessities as a free gift from those who heard the Gospel (Mt

10:8–10). Those who were ministers of the Gospel were entitled to receive their livelihood from it (1 Cor 9:13–14). Since they were involved in God's holy work, they got their living from the holy offerings that were offered to God in the Divine Service and consecrated for sacred use (Gal 6:6; cf. Phil 4:15–18). In fact, those preachers who did their work well were entitled to receive double the normal honorarium (1 Tim 5:17). The ministers of the Word therefore depend on God for their living. He supports them through the sacred gifts that he receives as an offering from the congregation.

O Lord, we praise you, bless you, and adore you,
In thanksgiving bow before you.
Here with your body and your blood you nourish
Our weak souls that they may flourish.
O Lord, have mercy!
May your body, Lord, born of Mary,
That our sins and sorrows did carry,
And your blood for us plead
In all trial, fear, and need:
O Lord, have mercy![3]

[3] This stanza of "O Lord, We Praise You" is a German folk hymn (*LW* 238:1).

Leviticus 7:37–38

The Conclusion of the Manual of Offerings

Translation

7 [37]This is the ritual instruction for the burnt offering, the grain offering, the sin offering, the reparation offering, the ordination offerings, and the sacrifice of the peace offerings, [38]which the Lord commanded Moses on Mount Sinai, when he commanded the Israelites to present their offerings to the Lord, in the Wilderness of Sinai.

Textual Notes

7:37 זֹאת הַתּוֹרָה—See the textual notes on 6:2 (ET 6:9) and the discussion in "Leviticus 6–7."

וְלַמִּלּוּאִים—See the textual notes on 8:22. The ordination offerings were instituted in Ex 29:19–28 and enacted in Lev 8:22–29. There is no other reference to them in Leviticus 6–7. Yet מִלּוּאִים occupies its proper place here in the list of offerings that are arranged according to the order of holiness. It could recall the instruction on the priest's portion of the peace offering in 7:29–36, which echoes the ritual for the ram of ordination in Ex 29:22–28 and was derived from it. This is shown by the use of the following words and phrases:

1. "Elevate it [the breast] as an elevation offering before the Lord" (Ex 29:26; Lev 7:30).
2. "It belongs/will belong to you/him as a share" (מָנָה, Ex 29:26; Lev 7:33).
3. "The breast for elevation and the thigh for contribution" (Ex 29:27; Lev 7:34).
4. "A perpetual due from the Israelites" (Ex 29:28; Lev 7:34).
5. "A donation … from the sacrifices of their/your peace offerings" (Ex 29:28; Lev 7:34).

7:38 צִוָּה יְהוָה—See the textual notes on 7:36. This verse distinguishes the commandments given by the Lord on Mount Sinai (Ex 31:18; 34:32; Lev 25:1; 26:46; 27:34) from the commandments given by Moses at the tent of meeting in the Desert of Sinai.

בְּיוֹם צַוֹּתוֹ—This could refer to Moses or to God. The former makes better sense.

Commentary

Analysis of Content

These verses summarize the content of Leviticus 1–7. On the one hand, they classify the material in chapters 6–7 as God's instruction about the various categories of offerings. On the other hand, they distinguish the commandments that the Lord gave to Moses at Mount Sinai from the commandments that God gave to the Israelites in the Desert of Sinai. While these verses could distinguish between Mount Sinai as the place for the revelation in chapters 6–7 and the tent in the Desert of Sinai as the place for the revelation in chapters 1–5 (see 1:1; cf. Num 1:1; 9:1), they, more likely, distinguish between Mount Sinai as the place where Moses received divine instruction about the offerings of Israel and the tabernacle as the place where the Israelites were to bring their offerings to the Lord. The place for the institution of the divine service was not the location for its performance.

Leviticus 8–10

The Inauguration of the Divine Service

This is the first section of extended narrative in the book of Leviticus. It tells how Moses executed the commands that God had given in Ex 29:1–37. It also expands on the brief report in Ex 40:12–16 about the ordination of the priests and the note in Ex 40:29 about the commencement of the sacrificial ritual.

The action of the narrative is initiated by the Lord's command to Moses in Lev 8:2–3. A series of seven commands is given by Moses as the founder of the divine service: in 8:5, 31–35; 9:2–4, 7; 10:4, 6–7, 12–15. Each of those commands is followed by a report of its execution, except in the case of 10:12–15, where compliance is assumed. Even though this narrative consists largely of a report on how the divine service was inaugurated by Moses, it also contains the report of God's speech to Moses in 10:3 and to Aaron in 10:8–10. In addition, we find a short dialogue between Moses and Aaron in 10:16–20.

The narrative unfolds in three stages. It begins with the consecration of the priests in 8:1–36, proceeds to the inauguration of the divine service in 9:1–24, and then concludes with the report of the tragic death of Nadab and Abihu from a careless act of sacrilege in 10:1–20. Their death provides the occasion for a discussion on the need for the priests to respect the Lord's holiness by performing the divine service exactly as the Lord had commanded, by refraining from certain acts of mourning and abstaining from alcohol during their period of service, and by properly disposing of the food from the offerings. But the narrative does not have its climax in the death of the two brothers. The climax comes with the report of the Lord's appearance to the congregation in 9:23–24. Everything else centers on and revolves around that event.

Chapters 9 and 10 are connected thematically by the contrast between the presentation of divinely instituted offerings by Aaron in 9:8–21 and the presentation of unauthorized fire by his sons in 10:1.[1] In both cases the appearance of fire from the Lord's presence is described with the same words (9:24 and 10:2). This shows that the presence of God's glory brought blessing and joy to those who approached him as he had commanded, but also dealt out death and destruction to those who did not approach him as he had commanded. These chapters prepare the reader for the rest of Leviticus, since the ensuing legislation seeks to ensure that Israel's encounter with the Lord in his glory will result in life and blessing rather than in death and destruction.

The main motif in Leviticus 8–10 is, quite appropriately, the recurring formula that affirms the execution of the Lord's commands "just as the Lord had commanded Moses/him" in 8:4, 9, 13, 17, 21, 29; 9:10 and the variations of it in 8:5, 31, 34, 35, 36; 9:5, 6, 7, 21; 10:13, 15. The narrative therefore depicts

---

[1] Ruwe, *"Heiligkeitsgesetz" und "Priesterschrift,"* 47–52.

the inauguration of the divine service as a exemplary act of obedience by Moses, Aaron, and the people of Israel. What the Lord commanded is vividly and fatally contrasted with that "which he [the Lord] had not commanded them" in 10:1, as well as what Moses had commanded in 10:18 without divine authorization.

Leviticus 8:1–36

The Consecration of the Priests

Translation

8 1The Lord spoke to Moses: 2"Take Aaron and his sons with him, the vestments, the anointing oil, the bull for the sin offering, the two rams, and the basket of unleavened bread, 3and assemble the whole congregation at the entrance to the tent of meeting."

4Moses did just as the Lord had commanded him. When the whole congregation had assembled at the entrance to the tent of meeting, 5Moses said to the congregation: "This is what the Lord has commanded to be done."

6Then Moses presented Aaron and his sons and washed them with water. 7He put the tunic on him, girded him with the sash, clothed him with the robe, put the ephod on him, girded him with the decorated band of the ephod, and tied it to him with it. 8He placed the breast piece on him and put the Urim and Thummim into the breast piece. 9Then he placed the turban on his head; and on the turban, in front, he placed the golden plate, the holy diadem, just as the Lord had commanded Moses.

10Then Moses took the anointing oil and anointed the tabernacle and everything in it, to consecrate them. 11He sprinkled some of it on the altar seven times and anointed the altar with all its utensils and the basin with its stand, to consecrate them. 12He poured out some of the anointing oil upon the head of Aaron and anointed him, to consecrate him. 13Then Moses presented the sons of Aaron, clothed them with tunics, fastened a sash around them, and put caps on them, just as the Lord had commanded Moses.

14After the bull of the sin offering had been presented, Aaron and his sons laid their hands on the head of the bull of the sin offering. 15After it had been slaughtered, Moses took the blood and smeared it with his finger all around the horns of the altar, purifying the altar. Then he poured out [the rest of] the blood at the base of the altar. Thus he consecrated it by performing the rite of atonement upon it. 16Then, taking all the fat around the entrails and the caudate lobe of the liver and the two kidneys with their fat, Moses turned [them] into smoke on the altar. 17But the bull, with its hide, its flesh, and its dung, was burnt with fire outside the camp, just as the Lord had commanded Moses.

18After the ram of burnt offering had been presented, Aaron and his sons laid their hands on the ram's head. 19After it had been slaughtered, Moses dashed the blood against all sides of the altar. 20After the ram had been cut into its sections, Moses turned the head, the sections, and the fat into smoke. 21After the entrails and the legs had been washed with water, Moses turned all the ram into smoke on the altar; it was a burnt offering for a pleasing aroma, a gift to the Lord, just as the Lord had commanded Moses.

**22Then the second ram, the ram of ordination, was presented. Aaron and his
sons laid their hands on the ram's head, 23and it was slaughtered. Moses took
some of its blood and put [it] on the lobe of Aaron's right ear, on the thumb of
his right hand, and on the big toe of his right foot. 24After he presented Aaron's
sons, Moses put some of the blood on the lobes of their right ears, on the thumbs
of their right hands, and on the big toes of their right feet. Then Moses dashed
[the rest of] the blood against all the sides of the altar. 25Next he took the fat—
the broad tail, all the fat around the entrails, the caudate lobe of the liver, and
the two kidneys with their fat—and the right thigh. 26From the basket of unleavened bread that was before the Lord, he took one round loaf of unleavened
bread, one round loaf of bread made with olive oil, and one wafer, and he placed
them on the fat and the right thigh. 27He put all these on the palms of Aaron and
on the palms of his sons, and raised them as an elevation offering before the Lord.
28Then Moses took them from their palms and turned [them] into smoke on the
altar on top of the burnt offering. They were an ordination offering for a pleasing aroma; it was a gift to the Lord. 29Moses took the breast and raised it as an
elevation offering before the Lord; it was the portion for Moses from the ram of
ordination, just as the Lord had commanded Moses.**

**30After Moses had taken some of the anointing oil and some of the blood that
was on the altar, he sprinkled [them] on Aaron, his vestments, and his sons, and
the vestments of his sons with him. Thus he consecrated Aaron, his vestments,
and his sons, and the vestments of his sons with him.**

**31Then Moses said to Aaron and his sons: "Boil the meat at the entrance to
the tent of meeting. You shall eat it there with the bread that is in the basket of
ordination, just as I commanded when I said, 'Aaron and his sons shall eat it.'
32What is left over from the meat and the bread you shall burn with fire. 33You
shall not go outside the entrance to the tent of meeting for seven days, until the
period of your ordination is completed; for it will take seven days to ordain you.
34The Lord has commanded that the ritual done on this day is to be done to make
atonement for you, 35while you reside at the entrance to the tent of meeting day
and night for seven days. You shall keep the Lord's watch, so that you do not die,
for so I have been commanded." 36Aaron and his sons did all the things that the
Lord had commanded through Moses.**

Textual Notes

8:2 אַהֲרֹן֙ וְאֶת־בָּנָ֣יו אִתּ֔וֹ—See Ex 29:4.

הַבְּגָדִ֔ים—See Exodus 28. Haran provides an excellent description of these vestments and an analysis of their significance.[1]

שֶׁ֣מֶן הַמִּשְׁחָ֑ה—See Ex 29:7; 30:22–33; 37:29.

פַּ֣ר הַֽחַטָּ֔את—See Ex 29:1.

שְׁנֵי֙ הָֽאֵילִ֔ים—See Ex 29:1.

סַ֖ל הַמַּצּֽוֹת׃—See Ex 29:2–3, 23.

---

1 Haran, *Temples and Temple-Service in Ancient Israel,* 165–74.

8:3 כָּל־הָעֵדָה הַקְהֵל—See the textual notes on 4:13. See 8:4, 5.

אֶל־פֶּתַח אֹהֶל מוֹעֵד׃—See the textual notes on 1:3. See 8:4, 31, 33, 35.

8:5 זֶה הַדָּבָר אֲשֶׁר־צִוָּה יְהוָה—The same formula is found in Ex 16:16, 32; 35:4; Lev 9:6; 17:2; Num 30:2 (ET 30:1); 36:6. Here it recalls Ex 29:1–37 and 40:9–15 and refers to the whole ritual enactment in Lev 8:6–30. This therefore completes what Moses had begun on Ex 40:16–33.

8:6 The material in Lev 8:6–13 is arranged in the form of a simple chiasm.[2]

וַיַּקְרֵב—See the textual note on this verb in 1:2. In this chapter, it recurs in 8:13, 18, 22, 24.

וַיִּרְחַץ אֹתָם בַּמָּיִם׃—See Ex 29:4 and 40:12.

8:7 הַכֻּתֹּנֶת—See Ex 28:39; 29:5a; 39:27. The tunic was made of linen.

בָּאַבְנֵט—See Ex 28:4, 39; 39:29; Lev 16:4. The sash was made of linen embroidered with blue, purple, and scarlet yarn.

הַמְּעִיל—See Ex 28:31–34; 39:22–26. The robe was made of blue wool and constructed as a single garment with an opening at the neck, like a poncho or a surplice.

הָאֵפֹד—See Ex 28:15–30; 39:2–7. The ephod was made of gold thread, interwoven with fine linen and with blue, purple, and scarlet woolen yarn. It was a kind of apron, suspended over the loins of the high priest from two shoulder straps. This ephod is most likely different from the linen ephod which, in texts other than the Pentateuch, was also worn by any priest (1 Sam 2:18; 22:18) and even King David (2 Sam 6:14). The term אֵפֹד seems also to have been used for a sacred metallic robe (Judg 8:27), an image or cult object covered with a sacred metallic robe (1 Sam 23:6, 9; Hos 3:4), and the robe that covered it (Judg 17:5; 18:14, 17, 18, 20).

בְּחֵשֶׁב—See Ex 28:8, 27–28; 39:5, 20–21. This band was made of the same material as the ephod and was part of it.

וַיֶּאְפֹּד—The verb אָפַד occurs only here and in Ex 29:5. It is denominative from אֵפֹד and so means to "gird on [an] ephod" (BDB).

8:8 הַחֹשֶׁן—See Ex 28:15–28; 29:5b; 39:8–21. The breast piece was made of the same material as the ephod and was part of it.

אֶת־הָאוּרִים וְאֶת־הַתֻּמִּים׃—See Ex 28:30; Deut 33:8; Ezra 2:63; Neh 7:65. There has been much debate about what exactly these were, how they were used, and what their names ("Urim" and "Thummim") signified. Probably they were two sacred lots, placed in the pocket of the ephod. They were used by the high priest to obtain an oracle from the Lord (Num 27:21). Each lot could give one of two possible answers (perhaps yes or no), resulting in three possible combinations for the two when they were cast on the ground. Hence the two together could give a positive, negative, or neutral answer to any question put to God (1 Sam 14:36–42; 23:6–12; 28:6). The response was neutral (God did not answer) if the two lots each gave a different answer.

8:9 הַמִּצְנֶפֶת—See Ex 28:4, 37, 39; 29:6; 39:28, 31; Lev 16:4. The turban was a royal headdress (cf. Ezek 21:31 [ET 21:26]), made of fine linen and wound around the head of the high priest.

---

[2] Klingbeil, *A Comparative Study of the Ritual of Ordination As Found in Leviticus 8 and Emar 369,* 132.

צִ֥יץ הַזָּהָ֖ב—See Ex 28:36–37; 39:30–31. This gold plate was called a צִיץ, "a flower" or "a rosette." The words קֹדֶשׁ לַיהוָה, "YHWH's holiness," were engraved on it (Ex 28:36). It was about two fingers wide. It was attached to the turban with a blue cord and extended from ear to ear across the forehead.

נֵ֣זֶר הַקֹּ֑דֶשׁ—See the textual notes on הַקֹּדֶשׁ in 4:6. The Hebrew word נֵזֶר designates some thing that distinguishes a person as sacrosanct. Here it refers to the sacred diadem of the high priest (cf. Ex 29:6 and 39:30). It can also refer to the diadem of a king (2 Sam 1:10; 2 Ki 11:12; Pss 89:40 [ET 89:39]; 132:18). In Lev 21:12 it refers to the holy anointing oil on the forehead of the priest. It refers to the uncut hair of a Nazirite in Num 6:4, 5, 7, 8, 9, 12, 13.

כַּאֲשֶׁ֛ר צִוָּ֥ה יְהוָ֖ה אֶת־מֹשֶֽׁה׃—This formula refers to all the ritual acts in 8:6–9. They fulfill the commands given by the Lord in Ex 29:4–6 and 40:12–13.

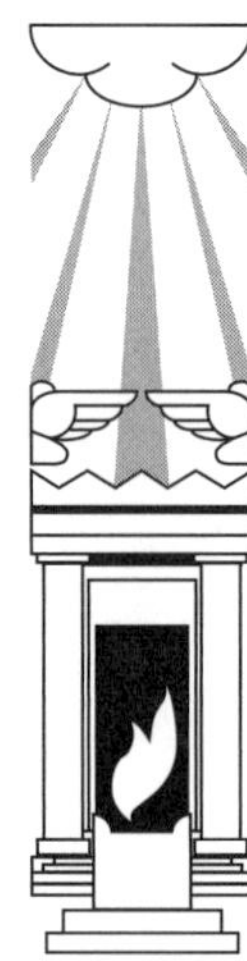

8:10 הַמִּשְׁכָּ֖ן—The term מִשְׁכָּן, "tabernacle" or "residence," is used here for the first time in Leviticus. It will recur in 15:31; 17:4; 26:11. It was the portable tent where the Lord "resided" in the midst of his people. This tent had an inner room, which was called the Holy of Holies, and an outer room, which was called the Holy Place or the tent of meeting. See figure 6, "Ground Plan of the Tabernacle."

כָּל־אֲשֶׁר־בּ֑וֹ—See Ex 40:9. Moses anointed the ark with the mercy seat, the table for the bread with its bowls (cf. Ex 25:29; 37:16), the lampstand with its utensils (cf. Ex 25:38; 37:23), and the altar for incense (cf. Ex 30:26–27).

וַיְקַדֵּ֖שׁ אֹתָֽם׃—The *waw* consecutive is epexegetical or purposive. It gives the reason for the anointing: to sanctify them.[3] The Piel verb יְקַדֵּשׁ will recur in 8:11, 12, 15, 30. The Piel of קָדַשׁ is used in Leviticus for God's activity in taking objects and persons that were common and making them holy. He transferred them from the human domain to the divine domain and "sanctified" them with the most holy anointing oil and the blood from the sin offerings (8:10, 11, 12, 15, 30; 16:19). Through the most holy things that he had "sanctified" by his presence at the sanctuary (21:23; 22:16), he "sanctified" the priests (21:15; 22:9) and the whole congregation of Israel (20:8; 21:8; 22:32). In Leviticus only in 25:10 is God not the subject of the verb: the Israelites were to "sanctify" the Jubilee by proclaiming it as a holy year for the land of Israel.

8:11 וַיַּ֥ז—See the textual note on this verb (the Hiphil of נָזָה) in 4:6. It recurs in 8:30.

הַמִּזְבֵּ֖חַ ... הַמִּזְבֵּ֗חַ—See the textual notes on 1:5. "The altar" recurs in 8:15 (three times), 16, 19, 21, 24, 28, 30. Since 8:11 mentions the altar twice and distinguishes the sprinkling of the altar from the anointing of the altar, Klingbeil concludes that the first altar that was sprinkled seven times was the altar for incense, while the second was the altar for burnt offering.[4] Thus while both were anointed, the altar for incense was anointed as comprehensively as possible, because it was even more holy than the other altar. It was associated with the sevenfold sprinkling of blood in the major rite of atonement for a sin offering (4:6–7, 17–18).

---

3 Milgrom, *Leviticus 1–16,* 516.

4 Klingbeil, *A Comparative Study of the Ritual of Ordination As Found in Leviticus 8 and Emar 369,* 191–95.

שֶׁבַע פְּעָמִים—This was a unique act of anointing. Its closest parallel was the sevenfold sprinkling of olive oil for the purification of a "leper" in 14:27.

כָּל־כֵּלָיו—See the list of utensils in Ex 27:3; 38:3.

הַכִּיֹּר—See Ex 30:18–21; 38:8; 40:7, 11, 30–32.

8:12 וַיִּמְשַׁח—See Ex 29:7.

8:13 וַיַּחְבֹשׁ לָהֶם—See Ex 28:40; 29:9; 39:27–29.

מִגְבָּעוֹת—See Ex 28:40; 29:9; 39:28. These were most likely a kind of skullcap, made of fine linen.

כַּאֲשֶׁר צִוָּה יְהוָה אֶת־מֹשֶׁה׃—This formula refers to all the ritual acts in 8:10–13, which fulfill the commands given in Ex 29:7–9; 40:9–11, 14–15.

8:14 וַיַּגֵּשׁ—Since the third person form of the verb without a subject is used impersonally here, it is translated in the passive. Likewise, some of the verbs in 8:15–23 are impersonal third person singular verbs and are translated as passives. Here in 8:14 and in some of the later verses, the LXX adds Moses as the subject of the verb, but it may have been Aaron or one of his sons who performed some of the priestly actions.

8:15 עַל־קַרְנוֹת הַמִּזְבֵּחַ סָבִיב—See the textual notes on 1:5 and 4:7. The phrase עַל־הַמִּזְבֵּחַ סָבִיב is repeated in 8:19, 24. Milgrom holds that since the adverb סָבִיב modifies the "altar," the ritual is identical with that described in 4:18, 25, 30, 34.[5] Rodriguez quite rightly argues that the adverb modifies the "horns."[6] Thus when the altar is purified at its consecration (8:15) and on the Day of Atonement (16:18), the blood from the sin offering is not just placed on the horns of the altar, but it is also smeared all around them.

וַיְחַטֵּא אֶת־הַמִּזְבֵּחַ—We translate this as "purifying the altar," but it could also mean "performing the ritual for the sin offering on the altar." See the textual notes on 6:19 (ET 6:26).

וְאֶת־הַדָּם יָצַק—The verb יָצַק is used only here and in 9:9 for the disposal of blood. The usual verb for pouring out blood is שָׁפַךְ. The disjunctive construction here indicates that the pouring out of blood is closely connected with its placement on the altar for purification.

לְכַפֵּר—See the textual notes on 1:4. This phrase could also be translated "for performing the rite of atonement."[7] Thus the altar was consecrated by the rite of atonement for the purpose of making atonement upon it.

עָלָיו׃—This could also be translated "for him" or "by means of it." See the textual notes on 1:4.

8:16 וַיִּקַּח—Literally "he took."

כָּל־הַחֵלֶב ...—See 3:3–4 and the textual notes and commentary on 3:3, 16–17.

וַיַּקְטֵר—See the textual note on this verb in 1:9. It recurs in 8:20, 21, 28.

8:17 See 4:11–14. Since the blood for this sin offering was not brought into the Holy Place (cf. 6:23 [ET 6:30]), Moses should have eaten the meat from it. But since he

---

5 Milgrom, *Leviticus 1–16*, 254–55, 521.

6 Rodriguez, *Substitution in the Hebrew Cultus*, 137–39.

7 Levine, *Leviticus*, 52; Milgrom, *Leviticus 1–16*, 524–25.

was not a priest, he was not allowed to eat any of it. He could only eat the less sacred portion from the ordination offering (cf. 8:29).

מִחוּץ לַמַּחֲנֶה—See the textual notes on 4:12.

כַּאֲשֶׁר צִוָּה יְהוָה אֶת־מֹשֶׁה׃—This refers to all the ritual acts listed in 8:14–17, which fulfilled God's commands in Ex 29:10–14.

8:19 וַיִּזְרֹק—See the textual note on this verb in 1:5. It recurs in 8:24.

8:20 וְאֶת־הָאַיִל נִתַּח לִנְתָחָיו—The disjunctive construction of this clause indicates complementary activity. The cutting up of the animal was closely connected with the burning up of its parts.

8:21 וְאֶת־הַקֶּרֶב וְאֶת־הַכְּרָעַיִם רָחַץ בַּמָּיִם—See 1:9, 13. Similar will be 9:14.

עֹלָה הוּא לְרֵיחַ־נִיחֹחַ—See the textual notes on 1:9 and the explanation in "Leviticus 1–3." "For a pleasing aroma" will be repeated in 8:28.

אִשֶּׁה הוּא לַיהוָה—See the textual notes on 1:9 and the explanation in "Leviticus 1–3." This phrase too will be repeated in 8:28.

כַּאֲשֶׁר צִוָּה יְהוָה אֶת־מֹשֶׁה׃—This refers to the ritual acts listed in 8:18–21, which fulfill God's commands given in Ex 29:15–18.

8:22 הַמִּלֻּאִים—See Ex 29:22, 26, 27, 31, 34; Lev 7:37. The Hebrew word used for the ordination offering and the rite of ordination is מִלּוּאִים, "filling." It is derived from the idiom "to fill the hand of [someone]," מִלֵּא יָד (Ex 28:41; 29:9, 29, 35; 32:29; Lev 8:33; 16:32; 21:10; Num 3:3; Judg 17:5, 12; 1 Ki 13:33; 1 Chr 29:5; 2 Chr 13:9; 29:31). Most likely, it refers to the installation of priests by the inaugural performance of their role in the sacrificial ritual in which they first offered and received their portion from the sacrifices (Lev 8:27).[8] While the LXX translates the noun מִלּוּאִים by τελείωσις, "perfection" (Lev 7:37; 8:22, 28, 31, 33; cf. Ex 29:22, 26, 27, 31, 34), it uses the verb τελειόω to describe the rite of ordination (Lev 8:33; 16:32; 21:10; cf. Ex 29:9, 29, 33, 35; Num 3:3), for by the reception and presentation of the ordination offering the process of ordination was completed; it had reached its goal. The hands of the candidate for the priesthood were fully qualified to receive and present the offerings to God.

8:23 This resembled the rite for the cleansing and reinstatement of a healed "leper" with oil and the blood from a sin offering in 14:14–17.

8:25 הַחֵלֶב ...—See 3:3–4, 9–10, 16–17.

שׁוֹק הַיָּמִין׃—This is the right hind quarter. It normally belongs to the officiating priest as his due.

8:26 הַמַּצּוֹת—The LXX reads "the ordination" rather than "the unleavened bread."

חַלַּת מַצָּה ... וְחַלַּת לֶחֶם—See the textual notes on 2:4.

וְעַל שׁוֹק הַיָּמִין׃—Instead of the breast that normally held the fat and the bread in a peace offering (7:30; 9:19–20), the thigh served as their carrier in this case. This was done because the thigh was burned together with the bread and the fat since Moses was not a priest and so could not eat it.

8:27 וַיָּנֶף אֹתָם—Older translations render this as "he waved them," but more accurate is "he elevated them" or "he raised them."

---

[8] Gorman, *The Ideology of Ritual*, 128.

תְּנוּפָה—See the textual notes and commentary on 7:30. This term is repeated in 8:29. In this case the thigh and the cakes had to be consecrated to the Lord by a special rite of elevation because in all other peace offerings they belonged to the officiating priest.

8:29 הֶחָזֶה—See 7:30.

לְמָנָה—See 7:33.

כַּאֲשֶׁר צִוָּה יְהוָה אֶת־מֹשֶׁה׃—This refers to the ritual acts listed in 8:22–29, which fulfill God's commands in Ex 29:19–20, 22–29.

8:30 וּמִן־הַדָּם אֲשֶׁר עַל־הַמִּזְבֵּחַ—The blood for the consecration of the priests needed to be taken from the altar, because the altar made it most holy and so able to communicate holiness (Ex 29:37).

וַיַּז—The rite of ordination was the only occasion when the blood from a sacrificed animal was mixed with oil so that it could be sprinkled on the priests. The rite of sprinkling associated the consecration of the priests with the consecration of the altar in 8:11.

וַיְקַדֵּשׁ אֶת־אַהֲרֹן ...—This fulfills God's command in Ex 29:21.

8:31 See Ex 29:11.

הַבָּשָׂר—The meat comes from the ram for ordination.

צִוֵּיתִי—This is the (active) Piel, "I commanded," but the LXX and the Peshitta translate it as if it should be vocalized as the (passive) Pual, צֻוֵּיתִי, "I was commanded [by God]." Moses uses the Pual צֻוֵּיתִי in 8:35 and 10:13. Ezekiel uses the phrase כַּאֲשֶׁר צֻוֵּיתִי in Ezek 12:7; 24:18; 37:7.

אַהֲרֹן וּבָנָיו יֹאכְלֻהוּ׃—The command is found in Ex 29:31–34.

8:32 וְהַנּוֹתָר בַּבָּשָׂר וּבַלָּחֶם—Ex 29:34 makes clear the sense of "what is left over ..." by adding "until morning." The ordination offering was therefore subject to the same temporal restrictions for the consumption of its meat as the thank offering (7:15).

8:33 וּמִפֶּתַח אֹהֶל מוֹעֵד לֹא תֵצְאוּ שִׁבְעַת יָמִים—The process of purification from major defilement usually lasted for seven days. See also "seven days" in 8:35; 12:2; 13:4, 5, 21, 26, 31, 33, 50, 54; 14:8, 38; 15:13, 19, 24, 28. Here the purification of the priests involved their transition from a common state to a holy state. Seven days also marked the transition from one half of the year to the other (23:6, 8, 34, 36, 39, 40, 41, 42).

כִּי שִׁבְעַת יָמִים יְמַלֵּא אֶת־יֶדְכֶם׃ —Literally this says, "for he shall fill your hand for seven days." See the textual notes on 8:22. The three kinds of offerings described in 8:26 were placed in the hands of the ordinands and offered to the Lord on each of the seven days. From this concrete usage, the idiom "to fill the hand" came to be used as a technical term for the ordination of priests (16:32; 21:10; cf. Ex 28:41; 29:9, 29, 33, 35; 32:29; Num 3:3; Judg 17:5, 12; 1 Ki 13:33; 1 Chr 29:5; 2 Chr 13:9; 29:31) and for the consecration of the altar (Ezek 43:26).

8:34 עָשָׂה—See the textual notes on 4:20. The active verb עָשָׂה is best taken impersonally and translated in the passive voice.

לְכַפֵּר עֲלֵיכֶם׃—This refers to Ex 29:35–37 with its command for the presentation of a sin offering on each of the seven days so that the rite of atonement could be performed daily for the ordinands.

8:35 וּפֶתַח אֹהֶל מוֹעֵד תֵּשְׁבוּ יוֹמָם וָלַיְלָה שִׁבְעַת יָמִים—The disjunctive clause implies that their week of residence coincided with the performance of atonement for them. They resided with the Lord at his residence for the period of ordination.

וּשְׁמַרְתֶּם אֶת־מִשְׁמֶרֶת יְהוָה—We render this "You shall keep the Lord's watch." It could also be translated "You shall do the sentry duty of the Lord." See 18:30; 22:9. This idiom was used for the performance of guard duty by guards at a royal palace (2 Ki 11:5, 6) or at the temple (2 Ki 11:7). Since the tabernacle was conceived as the Lord's royal residence, the priests were held to do sentry duty before him there (Num 1:53).[9] But whereas the royal guard protected the king from attack by his enemies, the priests protected the holiness of the Lord and his sanctuary. If they desecrated the sanctuary or even allowed it to be desecrated by the intrusion of any unclean person or thing, they would die, as did Nadab and Abihu in Lev 10:1–2. If they left their sentry post during the period of service, they forfeited their lives, just as soldiers did when they abandoned their sentry posts (cf. 10:7).

8:36 This echoes 8:5 and forms an inclusio with it.

Commentary

Structure

This narrative is deeply embedded in its context. It carries on the discussion from 7:11–36 about the proper disposal of the bread from the peace offerings in 8:31–32 and culminates in the inauguration of the divine service in 9:1–24 on the eighth day after the commencement of the process for ordination.

The narrative itself is structured by the use of three literary devices. The first device is the repetition in the formula for the execution of the Lord's commands seven times in 8:4, 9, 13, 17, 21, 29, 36. As in the narrative for the manufacture of the holy vestments in Ex 39:1–31 and the narrative for the construction of the tabernacle in Ex 40:17–33, the repetition of the formula divides the process of ordination into seven acts of obedience. Strikingly, the formula separates the investiture of Aaron in Lev 8:7–12 from the investiture of his sons in 8:13. It also associates the sprinkling of the vestments in 8:30 with the eating of the bread and meat from the sacrificial ritual.

The second device is the arrangement of the chapter in the form of a chiasm with the report of the sacrificial ritual in 8:14–29 at its center.[10]

A Preparation of material and persons for ordination: command and execution (8:1–5)
  B Anointing of the sanctuary and the high priest (8:6–13)
    C The sacrificial service (8:14–29)
  B' Anointing of the priests and their vestments (8:30)
A' Continuation of the ritual for a week: command and execution (8:31–36)

---

9 Milgrom, *Studies in Levitical Terminology,* 8–10.

10 Klingbeil, "The Syntactic Structure of the Ritual of Ordination (Lev 8)"; Klingbeil, *A Comparative Study of the Ritual of Ordination As Found in Leviticus 8 and Emar 369,* 111–14; Milgrom, *Leviticus 1–16,* 542–44.

The divine command to Moses and the report of his compliance with it in 8:1–4 correspond to the contrasting command from Moses to the priests and the report of their compliance with it in 8:31–36. Likewise, the vesting of the priests and the anointing of Aaron in 8:6–13 correspond with the contrasting anointing of priests and their vestments in 8:30. This verse therefore completes what was begun in 8:13, once the blood has been provided for this act by the sacrifices in 8:14–29. This arrangement stresses that the priests were ordained to perform the divine service, just as they were ordained by performing it. They were not in themselves holy; they derived their sanctity from the service.

The third device is the use of "take" (לָקַח) and "give" (נָתַן) as catchwords. In the enactment of this rite Moses "takes" ten significant things for the rite of ordination: the candidates for ordination and the material for their ordination (8:2); the anointing oil (8:10); the blood from the sin offering (8:15); the fat from the sin offering (8:16); the blood from the ram for ordination (8:23); the fat from the ram for ordination (8:25); the three loaves from the basket (8:26); the thigh with the fat and loaves on it (8:28); the breast of the ram for ordination (8:29); and the mixture of the oil with the blood from the altar (8:30). It is significant that three of these things are the normal priestly dues from the peace offering. Moses also "gives" seven things to the priests and the Lord: the vestments to Aaron (8:7a); the ephod to Aaron (8:7b); the breastplate to Aaron (8:8); blood from the sin offering to the altar (8:15); blood from the ram for ordination for Aaron (8:23) and for his sons (8:24); and the thigh with fat and loaves into the hands of the priests (8:27). The process of endowment, therefore, culminates, as one would expect from the technical term for ordination, in the fitting of the priests' hands. The use of these two words ("take" and "give") in this narrative indicates that the rite of ordination involved a complex series of interchanges between the Lord, the priests, and Moses.

The structure of this pericope can be outlined as follows:

I. Preparation for ordination (8:1–5)
  A. The Lord's speech to Moses (8:1–3)
    1. The Lord's address to Moses (8:1)
    2. Command for Moses to take the priests and the material for ordination (8:2)
    3. Command for Moses to assemble the congregation (8:3)
  B. Compliance of Moses and the obedience of the congregation (8:4)
  C. Announcement by Moses of God's authorization of the ceremony (8:5)

II. Description of the ceremony for the ordination (8:6–30)
  A. Preparatory rite (8:6–13)
    1. Washing of the candidates (8:6)
    2. Investiture of Aaron as high priest (8:7–9)
    3. Anointing of tabernacle, altar, basin, and Aaron (8:10–12)
    4. Investiture of Aaron's sons (8:13)

B. Sacrificial ritual (8:14–29)
   1. Sacrifice of a bull as a sin offering (8:14–17)
      a. Presentation and slaughter (8:14–15a)
      b. Purification and consecration of the altar with the blood rite (8:15b)
      c. Burning up of fat by Moses (8:16)
      d. Incineration of leftovers (8:17)
   2. Sacrifice of a ram as a burnt offering (8:18–21)
      a. Presentation and slaughter (8:18–19a)
      b. Disposal of blood by Moses (8:19b)
      c. Burning up by Moses as a pleasing aroma (8:20–21)
   3. Sacrifice of a ram as an ordination offering (8:22–29)
      a. Presentation and slaughter (8:22–23a)
      b. Placement of blood on priests and disposal by Moses (8:23b–24)
      c. Elevation of thigh with fat and loaves (8:25–27)
      d. Burning of these by Moses as a pleasing aroma (8:28)
      e. Appropriation of the breast by Moses (8:29)
C. Concluding rite (8:30)
   1. Sprinkling of the priests and their vestments with oil and blood (8:30a)
   2. Result: consecration of the priests and their vestments (8:30b)

III. Completion of the ordination (8:31–36)
   A. Speech by Moses to the priests (8:31–35)
      1. Address by Moses to the priests (8:31a)
      2. Command about the consumption of meat and bread by them (8:31b–32)
      3. Command for weeklong seclusion with the daily repetition of the sacrifices (8:33–35)
   B. Compliance of the priests (8:36)

Ritual Agents

The main character in this narrative was Moses.[11] As the divinely appointed founder of the OT divine service he conducted the inaugural rite of ordination for Aaron and his sons.[12] Even though he himself was not a priest, he officiated in this rite as the divine lawgiver and so established the priesthood as an institution in Israel. As the ritual founder of the cultus, he performed those acts that were normally performed by the priests. He handled the blood of the sacrifices and burnt the offerings on the altar. Yet, since he was not a priest, he was not able to eat the meat from the sin offering (8:16), and the thigh from the ram for ordination (8:27–28). But as a relative of the priests, he was allowed to eat the breast (8:29). His position was therefore unique and without parallel. Even

---

[11] Klingbeil, *A Comparative Study of the Ritual of Ordination As Found in Leviticus 8 and Emar 369,* 208–11.

[12] This analysis of the rite of ordination as a founding ritual and Moses as founder of the service owes much to the perceptive exegesis of Gorman, *The Ideology of Ritual*, 103–39.

though he did all this only once, his actions set a precedent for all subsequent rites of ordination.

The rite itself obviously centered on Aaron and his sons.[13] Symbolically, they represented all the candidates for the office of high priest and all the candidates for the priesthood. The ceremony distinguished the status and role of the high priest from all other priests by the bestowal of the special regalia on him (8:7b–9), the anointing of his head with oil (8:12), and the daubing of him with blood before all the other priests (8:23).

The priestly candidates for ordination in fact did very little in this ceremony. They were on the receiving end of the rite. They were merely required to lay their hands on the animals for sacrifice (8:14, 18, 22), boil the meat from the ram for ordination (8:31a), eat it together with the bread (8:31b), and remain sequestered in the sanctuary for the entire week of ordination (8:33–35).

The third party to the ceremony of ordination was the whole congregation of Israel.[14] The people assembled before the altar in the courtyard of the sanctuary on this momentous occasion (8:3–4), even as they had assembled for the briefing on their contribution to the construction of the tabernacle (Ex 35:1), and as they would later assemble for the national census (Num 1:18) and the installation of the Levites (Num 8:9). As witnesses to the ceremonial enactment, the people of Israel learned what the Lord commanded (Lev 8:5). The members of the congregation were present for the ordination because the priests were ordained to represent them before God and deputize for God with them.

God is the most important agent because he ultimately is the one who ordained the priestly candidates. He gave the instructions that are carried out in the ordination rite. He authorized the priests to minister on his behalf to Israel, and to represent them before him.

Ritual Animals and Materials

At the beginning of the narrative, the Lord himself listed the four basic things needed for the act of ordination (8:2b). Each of these was in its own way an essential part of the rite.

First, the vestments of the priests, worn by them when they officiated at the altar, made their own special contribution to the ceremony.[15] Apart from the linen underskirt, each priest received three items of clothing: a white linen tunic; a sash made of embroidered linen with blue, purple, and scarlet yarn; and a linen cap, or, in the case of the high priest, a linen turban. The high priest also received four additional items of clothing which constituted his full regalia:

---

[13] Klingbeil, *A Comparative Study of the Ritual of Ordination As Found in Leviticus 8 and Emar 369,* 213–16.

[14] Klingbeil, *A Comparative Study of the Ritual of Ordination As Found in Leviticus 8 and Emar 369,* 211–13.

[15] Haran, *Temples and Temple-Service in Ancient Israel,* 169–71; Klingbeil, *A Comparative Study of the Ritual of Ordination As Found in Leviticus 8 and Emar 369,* 177–91.

- The blue woolen robe was made with a single piece of cloth, with an opening for the neck like a surplice. It had bells and pomegranates around the fringes of its skirt.
- The ephod was shaped like a circular apron and worn over the robe. It was made with gold interwoven with blue, purple, and scarlet yarn mixed with fine linen. Straps attached it to the shoulders. It reached from the breast to the shoulders.
- The breast piece was worn over the ephod. It was attached to the shoulder of the ephod with gold cord on the top and the strap of the ephod on the bottom with blue cord. It was constructed as a pouch for the sacred lots and was made of the same material as the ephod. Four rows of three precious stones engraved with the names of the twelve tribes were set in it.
- The holy diadem was a gold plate inscribed with the words "YHWH's holiness." It stretched from ear to ear across the forehead and was attached to the turban with blue bands of cloth.

These four articles of clothing, worn by the high priest as he officiated daily in the Holy Place, resembled the material used to construct the tabernacle and so corresponded in their sanctity to its inner parts.[16] By means of his regalia, the high priest was "clothed" with God's holiness on his head (the holy diadem), just as he bore the whole nation on his heart (the breast piece) before the Lord in the Holy Place.

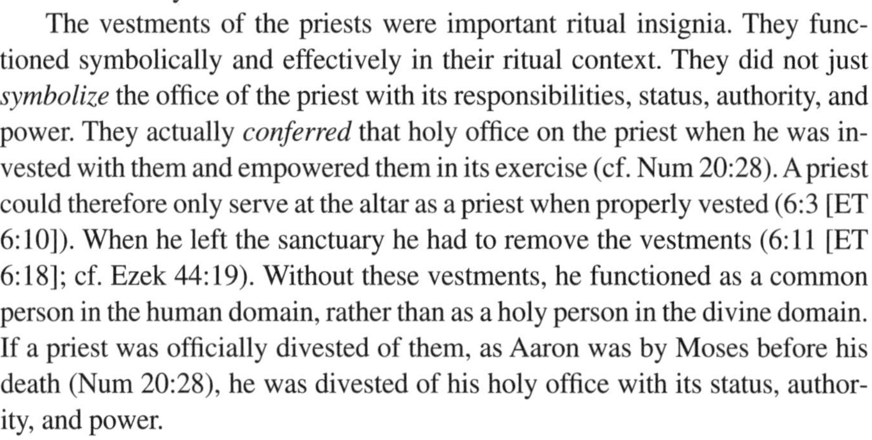

The vestments of the priests were important ritual insignia. They functioned symbolically and effectively in their ritual context. They did not just *symbolize* the office of the priest with its responsibilities, status, authority, and power. They actually *conferred* that holy office on the priest when he was invested with them and empowered them in its exercise (cf. Num 20:28). A priest could therefore only serve at the altar as a priest when properly vested (6:3 [ET 6:10]). When he left the sanctuary he had to remove the vestments (6:11 [ET 6:18]; cf. Ezek 44:19). Without these vestments, he functioned as a common person in the human domain, rather than as a holy person in the divine domain. If a priest was officially divested of them, as Aaron was by Moses before his death (Num 20:28), he was divested of his holy office with its status, authority, and power.

Second, the holy anointing oil was essential for the rite of ordination, which consecrated the sanctuary and the priests. It sanctified an object or a person by its application (cf. Ex 30:22–33; 40:9–15). It was used in two different ways in the ceremony. On the one hand, it was used by itself as a means of consecration. Since it was poured on the high priest after it had been applied to the tabernacle, altar, and basin, it consecrated the high priest, together with these most holy things, for service with these most holy things. On the other hand,

---

[16] Haran, *Temples and Temple-Service in Ancient Israel,* 166–69.

it was mixed with the holy blood from the altar and was sprinkled on the vestments of all the priests. In this way they became "holy garments," which, thereafter, consecrated those who were clothed with them (cf. Ezek 44:19–20). It vested them with God's own holiness.

Third, three animals provided the raw material for the rite of ordination. In keeping with the regulation in Lev 4:3, a bull was presented as a sin offering for the priests. Because the priests were leaders of the congregation, rams were required for the burnt offering (cf. 1:10–13; 9:2) and the ordination offering (cf. 3:7–11).

On the one hand, these three animals provided the blood for the blood rite (8:15–19, 24). The blood from these animals played a special role in this ceremony. The blood from the sin offering purified the altar in its consecration and as the place for all subsequent rites of atonement. The blood from the ram for ordination was used to daub the right ears, thumbs, and big toes of the ordinands, just as the blood from the sin offerings of the priest and the congregation was daubed on the four horns of the incense altar (4:7, 18). Most remarkably, blood from all three of the sacrifices was taken from the altar, mixed with the anointing oil, and sprinkled on the vestments of the priests (8:30), just as the blood from the sin offerings of the high priest and the people was sprinkled on the curtain of the sanctuary (4:6, 17).

On the other hand, the ram provided the holy meat for the priests to eat during the week of their ordination (8:31). Like the meat from the thank offering, it had to be eaten on the day of its presentation. Any leftover meat had to be burnt, so that it could not be used by anyone else for any other purpose.

Finally, there was the basket of bread. It consisted of three kinds of unleavened bread made from fine wheat flour: cakes baked without oil; cakes made of flour baked with oil; and wafers spread with oil (8:2, 26; cf. Ex 29:2). Only one piece of bread from each class was presented with the fat from the ram for the ordination (cf. Lev 7:12). The rest were to be eaten by the ordinands on the day of presentation.

Ritual Location

Ritual space highlighted the function and significance of the ordination rite.[17] The priests were ordained at the entrance to the tent of meeting (8:2–4). This was the area in front of the altar for burnt offering. Their ordination took place there because that is the primary location for their operation as priests. Thus, their status as priests was conferred on them ritually in the very place where they served as priests (8:13, 27–28, 30). The congregation was also gathered there around them. This, in fact, was the first full liturgical assembly of the congregation at the sanctuary. It set a precedent for all subsequent assem-

---

[17] Klingbeil, "Ritual Space in the Ordination Ritual of Leviticus 8"; Klingbeil, *A Comparative Study of the Ritual of Ordination As Found in Leviticus 8 and Emar 369,* 143–66.

blies for the participation of the congregation in the regular sacrificial ritual. The assembly of the congregation in that place therefore also established its ritual location in the divine service as well as its ritual status.

The entrance to the tent of meeting was the place for the priests' ordination and their place of residence for the whole week of their ordination (8:33–35). They were to remain there for seven days and seven nights. They cooked the meat there and ate their meals there. They could not, under any circumstance, leave that place until the ceremony was complete (cf. 10:7). Their location in that place showed that they did not derive their holiness from a series of random rites that could be conducted anywhere, but from their presence with the Lord himself, who shared his holiness with them there at the sanctuary through these rites.

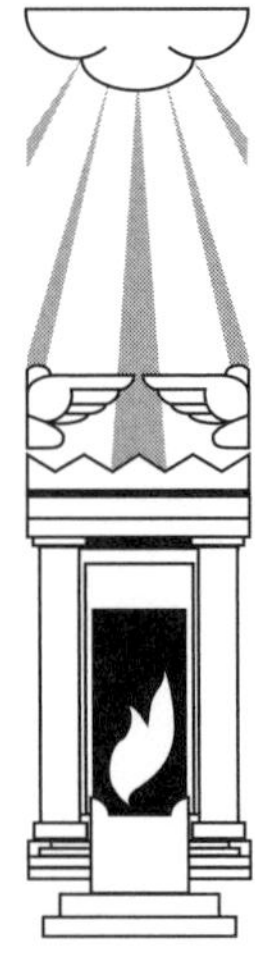

The correlation between ritual status and ritual space, sacred office and sacred space, is also evident in the rite of anointing. The high priest was anointed together with the tabernacle, the altar, and the basin (8:10–12). He was, in fact, anointed after they received their anointing. Their common anointing gave them a common status. The places where the high priest exercised his vocation were consecrated together with him. His anointing located him in their sacred ambit and gave him access to them. His sacred status that derived from that context was given for his service in it. The priests could not operate as priests apart from the sanctuary, just as the sanctuary could not function as a sanctuary without their ministry in it.

Ritual Time

This story is a foundational narrative set on the first day of Nisan in the second year of Israel's stay at Mount Sinai (cf. Ex 40:2, 17). It describes the inaugural consecration of the sanctuary and the priesthood. That ritual lasted seven days and culminated in inauguration of the sacrificial ritual on the eighth day. These seven days were a transitional period of time, a period of purification and initiation. They, in themselves, were neither sacred nor common, but they brought the priests, through a rite of passage, fully into the sacred domain.[18] This foundational occasion did not then establish a regular time for ordination in the liturgical calendar. It set the precedent for all subsequent rites of ordination that lasted for seven days and prepared the priests for service at the altar on the eighth day (9:1).

Ritual Enactment

The ceremony for the ordination of priests was a complex ritual enactment. Its complexity comes from its foundational function and significance.[19] It pre-

---

[18] Klingbeil, "Ritual Space in the Ordination Ritual of Leviticus 8"; Klingbeil, *A Comparative Study of the Ritual of Ordination As Found in Leviticus 8 and Emar 369,* 166–76.

[19] Gorman, *The Ideology of Ritual,* 103–4.

pared for the regular services, but did not itself, for that reason, follow the regular pattern for these services.

The ceremony began with a public assembly of the congregation at the tent of meeting. In this assembly Moses took the candidates for priesthood and everything that was needed for their ordination and made a public announcement to the congregation about divine authorization for the subsequent proceedings.

Then came the preliminary rite for the preparation of the priests and the sanctuary for the act of ordination. It consisted of four separate enactments:

First, Moses bought Aaron and his sons forward to the basin, removed their ordinary clothes, and washed them in an act of ritual cleansing (8:6).

Second, Moses dressed Aaron with the vestments and ritual insignia of the high priest (8:7–9).

Third, Moses then performed the rite for the anointing with the most holy oil (8:10–13). He began with what was most holy and closest to the Lord. He anointed the tabernacle with its furnishings as listed in Ex 30:26–28 (cf. Ex 40:9), the altar with its utensils (cf. Ex 40:10), and the basin (cf. Ex 40:11). The altar was singled out for special attention, for Moses did not just smear oil on it, but sprinkled oil on it seven times, in an additional act of consecration, so that it became most holy (cf. Ex 40:10). After that, he anointed Aaron by pouring out some of the oil onto his head (cf. Lev 21:10, 12; Ps 133:2).

Fourth, Moses clothed the sons of Aaron with their vestments. He did not, however, anoint them on their forehead with oil. That was reserved for Aaron.

The rite of ordination was enacted with three sacrifices presented for the priests.

The first sacrifice in the rite of ordination was the bull for the sin offering (8:14–17). The procedure for its presentation did not conform exactly to the sin offering for the high priest in 4:4–12, because its blood could not yet be brought into the Holy Place. Nor did it correspond with the offering for an Israelite leader in 4:22–26, because the meat from the offering was not eaten by Moses, but was burned instead. It functioned as a preparatory sacrifice rather than an independent offering (cf. 9:2, 8–11). It was designed to perform the inaugural rite of atonement on the altar by smearing the horns with the blood of that sin offering (cf. Ezek 43:19–21). The altar was therefore "purified" and "consecrated" for the acts of atonement that were subsequently performed on it (8:15).

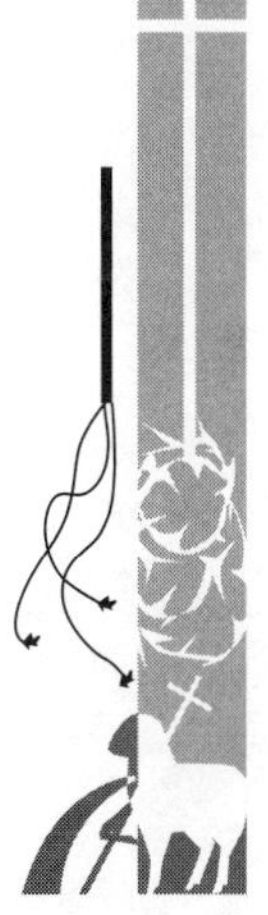

The second sacrifice in the rite of ordination was the burnt offering (8:18–21). It was the centerpiece of every complete sacrificial enactment. On this occasion, it was performed according to the normal procedure for it (cf. 1:10–13). As the founder of the divine service, Moses splashed the blood from it on the altar and burnt up all its parts on the altar.

The sacrificial ritual for the rite of ordination culminated in the third sacrifice, the presentation of the ram for ordination. This sacrifice occupied the slot that normally was for the peace offering and resembled it in many ways.

This sacrifice was, in fact, regarded as the archetypal peace offering (cf. 7:35–36). Yet despite that, it diverged from the peace offering in three ways that corresponded with its special role as the offering for ordination.

The first difference is that before Moses splashed the blood from it against the sides of the altar, he placed some of it on the right ears, right thumbs, and right big toes of the candidates for the priesthood. This was without parallel in any regular sacrifice. The only ritual enactments that resembled it was the smearing of blood of a public sin offering on the four horns of the altar (4:7, 18; 16:18) and placement of blood from the sin offering on the right ear, thumb, and toe of a cleansed "leper" (14:14–17).

The second difference is that a unique rite of elevation was performed with the fat from the ram for ordination. Instead of the breast, Moses took the ram's thigh which would have normally belonged to the officiating priest, put the fat on it, with the three loaves which, in a thank offering, would also have belonged to the officiating priest, and placed it on the hands of Aaron and his sons in the rite of elevation before the Lord (8:26–27). By thus filling their hands with the tokens of their priestly dues, he ordained them as priests. Then he took these things from them and burned them. By being burnt on the altar in this original offering, the meat from the thighs and the loaves from all subsequent peace offerings were designated as holy food for the priests.

The third difference is that in this ordination sacrifice Moses received as his due the breast, rather than the thigh, since he himself was not a priest, even though he belonged to the tribe of Levi.

After the central act, in which the elevation offering had been placed in the hands of the priests, came the fourth and final stage of the ceremony. Moses took the anointing oil, mixed it with the blood from the altar, and sprinkled it on the vestments of the priests (8:30). The blood from all three sacrifices had itself been made holy by its contact with the altar (Ex 29:37). Two potent holy substances (the anointing oil and blood) were therefore uniquely combined for this final, conclusive act of consecration. With that rite of anointment, the ordination ceremony was complete.

The anointing of those vestments was a rather strange and unexpected ritual act. Unlike Aaron, whose head was anointed with the anointing oil (8:12), the priests were not themselves anointed. No sacred oil was poured out on their bodies. Instead, both their vestments and the vestments of the high priest received this unique type of anointing with blood and oil. The anointing of the vestments shifted the accent away from the person to the office of the priest. The vestments physically represented that holy office. They "consecrated" the priest who wore them. The priests were holy only as long as they wore the vestments. The priests, therefore, did not personally acquire inherent holiness by virtue of their ordination. They derived holiness from the office that had been conferred on them at their ordination.

The ordination ceremony ended with the consecration of the vestments and the sacred banquet at the tabernacle. For the rest of the week none of the priests left the sanctuary, but ate the holy bread and the holy meat from the ordination offerings in that sacred place. As is indicated by 8:33–34, which needs to be understood in the light of Ex 29:35–37, the basic service for their ordination was repeated on each of the subsequent days of that week. While Ex 29:35 (see also 29:1–34) tells that the ram for the burnt offering and the ram for ordination was sacrificed on each day, Ex 29:36–37 prescribes the daily sacrifice of a bull as a sin offering, so that the rite of atonement could be performed daily, at the altar, on behalf of the priests (Lev 8:34). This came to the end on the eighth day when Aaron, rather than Moses, finally presented all the sin offerings and burnt offerings with the peace offerings rather than the ram for the ordination offering (9:8–21).

Ritual Theological Function

The narrative quite clearly and explicitly explains the basic theological function for this ceremony. If we take 8:30b as a summary statement at the end of the narrative for all the events from the washing of the candidates in 8:6 to the anointing of their vestments in 8:30a, the whole ceremony was an act of consecration. Through it Aaron and his sons were consecrated as priests with the holy anointing oil and the holy blood from the altar.

The process of consecration with the holy anointing oil and the blood from the sacrifices unfolded in five subsidiary acts of consecration. First and most centrally, the tabernacle was consecrated together with all its most holy furnishings (8:10). Second, Moses consecrated the altar and the basin (8:11). Third, he consecrated Aaron as the high priest, the Lord's deputy who shared in the Lord's holiness (8:12). Fourth, Moses consecrated the already-consecrated altar with blood for the rite of atonement for the performance of atonement on behalf of the priests (8:15). Lastly, the vestments of the priests were consecrated with oil and blood so that they, in turn, consecrated those who wore them (8:30).

Neither the altar nor Aaron was consecrated by a single act, but by this whole process. Thus the consecration of Aaron that began with his anointing ended with the sprinkling of his vestments with blood and oil. Likewise, the consecration of the altar that began with its anointing was completed by the application of blood on its horns. In fact, as Ex 29:37 shows, it needed to have blood applied to its horns for seven days before its consecration was complete (cf. Ezek 43:18–27).

The rite for ordination also involved a process of purification. On the one hand, the altar was purified by means of the blood that was applied to its horns for the week of ordination (8:15; cf. Ex 29:36; Lev 8:34). On the other hand, the candidates for the priesthood were purified in three different ways. First, Moses washed them with water, in a simple rite of cleansing, so that they could enter the sacred precincts (8:6). Second, they were freed from impurity by the rite of atonement that was performed on their behalf (8:15, 34). They were thereby qualified for access to the altar. Third, Moses cleansed them with the blood from the ram for ordination (8:23–24). In this unique act of purification, they were specifically cleansed for their service as priests. By the purification of these body parts, the priests were purified so completely that they were qualified to share in the Lord's holiness, without desecrating it by their impurity:

- The right ear of each candidate was purified to hear and obey the Word of the Lord.
- The right thumb of each candidate was purified to handle the holy things of God.
- The right big toe of each candidate was purified to walk on holy ground.

The rite of ordination involved the Lord's admission of the priests into his presence and his acceptance of them as his priests. Thus they were "brought near" by Moses as if they themselves were his offering to the Lord; he presented them to the Lord (8:6, 13). He offered the burnt offering and the ram for ordination as a "pleasing aroma" to the Lord, so that he would receive the priests as his privileged servants and take pleasure in their service to him (8:21, 28). Through his anointing, the high priest received the right of access to the tabernacle, the altar, and the basin. Through the anointing of their vestments, the priests received their right of access to the altar and the food from the altar. Hence, each day during the week of ordination, the daily ritual for their ordination ended with a sacred meal in the sanctuary. As the guests of the Lord, they ate the bread and meat that came from his table (8:31–32).

The rite of ordination was enacted exactly as the Lord had commanded in Ex 29:1–37, without any improvisation or deviation from God's Word. This is emphasized by the repetition of the formula for execution six times: "just as the Lord had commanded Moses/him" (Lev 8:4, 9, 13, 17, 21, 29). Since God had instituted this ceremony by his Word, his Word empowered it, so that, by its power, the Lord himself consecrated the priests and admitted them as his servants into his presence. As his servants they were under his orders and obligated to "keep watch" (8:35) at his residence as guardians of his holiness until their period of ordination was over—and not just then, but whenever they were on duty there (Num 18:5). They performed guard duty at the entrance to the tent of meeting to ensure that God's holiness was not desecrated and his wrath unleashed against those who had desecrated his sanctuary.

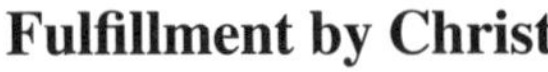

Fulfillment by Christ

Jesus is the great High Priest in the church (Heb 2:17; 3:1; 4:14, 15; 5:5; 6:20; 7:26; 8:1; 9:7, 11). He was anointed by the Holy Spirit at his Baptism (Acts 10:38) and consecrated himself as priest by his sacrificial death (Jn 17:19). By raising him from the dead, God appointed him as his chief and eternal priest in the order of Melchizedek, rather than the order of Levi (Heb 5:1–10; 7:1–28). He serves God the Father in the heavenly sanctuary (Heb 8:1–2; 9:11–12; 10:19–21) as our intercessor (Heb 7:25) and mediator (Heb 12:24; cf. 1 Tim 2:5). There he appears before God on our behalf (Heb 9:24).

God's Son did not become a man to serve as a solitary priest for the whole human family; he became a man so that he could include all human beings in his priestly work (Heb 2:11). He is therefore the founder of a new priesthood whose character and function is derived from him. He consecrated himself as priest so that he could consecrate his disciples by his Word to serve together with him in his mission to the world (Jn 17:17–19). All baptized people are therefore ordained as priests together with Christ; in this new age the church is God's holy priesthood (1 Pet 2:5, 9). The baptized serve God the Father as his royal priests together with Christ on earth and in heaven, each according to his or her station and vocation (Rev 1:6; 5:10; cf. 20:6).

The letter to the Hebrews may allude to the appointment of the saints to serve as priests together with Christ by borrowing from the terminology from the LXX to describe their ordination as "perfection." By his offering of himself to the Father, Christ has been "perfected" and so "ordained" as our great High Priest (Heb 2:10; 5:9; 7:28). All the faithful are likewise "perfected" by his self-sacrifice to "serve" as priests together with him with a "perfect" conscience, rather than just "perfect" hands, in the heavenly sanctuary (Heb 9:9; 10:14; cf. 7:11, 19).

Through Baptism Christ appoints people as his priests. In Baptism he washes their bodies with pure water and cleanses their consciences from the stain of sin (1 Cor 6:11; Eph 5:26; Heb 10:22). He anoints them with his Holy Spirit just as he was anointed (2 Cor 1:21–22; 1 Jn 2:20, 27). He consecrates them as his holy priests (1 Cor 6:11; Eph 5:26). They are therefore sanctified in Jesus (1 Cor 1:2) and through faith in him (Acts 26:18). He is the source of their holiness (1 Cor 1:30). They are holy in him (Phil 1:1). Thus their priesthood is derived from his and is inseparable from him.

Like Jesus himself (Heb 8:6), Christians have a priesthood that is far greater than that of Aaron and his descendants. They are far better equipped than Aaron ever was to fulfill even greater responsibilities. At the ordination of Aaron and his sons, Moses went to the altar of burnt offering and took some of the blood from it and mixed it with the holy anointing oil to consecrate Aaron and his sons by "sprinkling" it on their vestments (Lev 8:30). In contrast to their physical consecration for imperfect service in an earthly sanctuary, Jesus consecrates his priests with his own blood and his Holy Spirit for perfect service in the heavenly sanctuary (Heb 9:13; 10:22; 1 Pet 1:2).[20] He "sprinkles" them inwardly in their conscience, so that they are completely holy. He does not do this just once, but repeatedly, for he provides "the blood for sprinkling" to them in the Divine Service (Heb 12:24). In Holy Communion he gives them his holy blood to drink, so that they can share in his holiness and serve God the Father perfectly together with him.

[20] Compare Pursiful, *The Cultic Motif in the Spirituality of the Book of Hebrews*, 128, 146.

The disciples of Christ have unique priestly vestments. Through Baptism they are clothed in Christ himself (Gal 3:27; cf. Rom 13:14; Col 3:10–11). He provides them with a breastplate of faith and love (1 Thess 5:8). He clothes them in the armor of light (Rom 13:12). He gives them his own righteousness and holiness as their priestly dress (Eph 4:20–24). Since God has chosen them to be his holy priests in Christ, they are urged to vest themselves with his qualities, as gifts from him, for their eucharistic service of God the Father (Col 3:12–17). They wear the white robes of his holiness that qualify them for access to the divine presence in the heavenly Jerusalem (Rev 7:9, 13, 14; 22:14; cf. 3:4–5). These robes have been washed with his own blood (Rev 7:14). They can therefore stand before the throne of God and serve him in his holy temple (Rev 7:15–17). They offer prayers to him with "holy hands" (1 Tim 2:8).

Since they are holy priests they have "access" to God the Father through Jesus the Son (Rom 5:2; Eph 2:18; 3:12). They can "approach" him in the heavenly sanctuary together with Christ (Heb 4:16; 7:19, 25; 10:1, 22).[21] They are involved in the Divine Service together with the angels in the heavenly sanctuary (Heb 9:14; 12:22–24). There they stand before God the Father and offer their bodies and their gifts, their prayers and their praises, as sacrifices that are acceptable to him through Jesus Christ (Rom 12:1; Heb 13:15–16; 1 Pet 2:5, 9). As priests they use their access to God's grace in the Divine Service for themselves and for others (Heb 4:16).

Like the high priest with the twelve tribes of Israel (Ex 28:9–12), they can stand in for others before God and offer prayers on behalf of them (1 Tim 2:1–10). They can also stand in for God before others in their daily routine and make him and his deeds known to others (1 Pet 2:9). By their access to the light of God's presence, they become children of the light (Eph 5:8), theophanic people who are the light to the world (Mt 5:14–16). They therefore represent God to other people in their vocations and represent them before God in the Divine Service. As priests together with Christ they have "a holy vocation" (2 Tim 1:9), "a heavenly calling" (Heb 3:1). They serve God as his royal priesthood on earth.

Church of God, elect and glorious,
Holy nation, chosen race;
Called as God's own special people,
Royal priests and heirs of grace:
Know the purpose of your calling,
Show to all His mighty deeds;
Tell of love that knows no limits,
Grace that meets all human needs.

Church of God, elect and holy,
Be the people He intends;
Strong in faith and swift to answer

---

[21] Compare Pfitzner, *Hebrews*, 88, 111; Scholer, *Proleptic Priests*, 91–149.

Each command your master sends:
Royal priests, fulfill your calling
Through your sacrifice and prayer;
Give your lives in joyful service—
Sing His praise, His love declare.[22]

[22] From "Church of God, Elect and Glorious" by James E. Seddon (*HS98* 864:1, 4).

Leviticus 9:1–24

The Inauguration of the Divine Service

Translation

9 [1]On the eighth day Moses summoned Aaron and his sons and the elders of Israel. [2]He said to Aaron: "Take a bull calf of the herd for a sin offering and a ram for a burnt offering, both without blemish, and present [them] before the Lord. [3]Then speak to the Israelites and say: 'Take a male goat for a sin offering; a calf and a lamb, both a year old and without blemish, for a burnt offering; [4]a head of cattle and a ram for peace offerings to be sacrificed before the Lord; and a grain offering mixed with oil, for today the Lord will appear to you.' "

[5]They took what Moses had commanded to the entrance of the tent of meeting. Then the whole congregation approached and stood before the Lord.

[6]Moses said: "This is what the Lord has commanded you to do, so that the glory of the Lord may appear to you."

[7]Then Moses said to Aaron: "Approach the altar and perform the ritual for your sin offering and your burnt offering; make atonement for yourself and for the people. Then perform the ritual for the offering of the people; make atonement for them—just as the Lord has commanded."

[8]Aaron approached the altar and slaughtered the calf for his sin offering. [9]Then Aaron's sons presented the blood to him. After he had dipped his finger in the blood, he put [it] on the horns of the altar, and he poured out [the rest of] the blood at the base of the altar. [10]Then he turned the fat, the kidneys, and the caudate lobe of the liver from the sin offering into smoke upon the altar, just as the Lord had commanded Moses. [11]But the meat and the skin were burned with the fire outside the camp. [12]After he slaughtered the burnt offering, Aaron's sons brought to him the blood, and he dashed it against all sides of the altar. [13]They brought to him the burnt offering, piece by piece, and the head; and he turned [them] into smoke on the altar. [14]He washed the entrails and the legs and turned [them] into smoke on top of the burnt offering upon the altar.

[15]Then he presented the offering of the people. He took the male goat for the sin offering of the people, slaughtered it, and performed the rite of purification with it as with the previous [sin offering]. [16]He then presented the burnt offering and performed the ritual according to the regulation. [17]Next he presented the grain offering. Taking a handful of it, he turned it into smoke, in addition to the morning burnt offering. [18]When he had slaughtered the head of cattle and the ram as the people's sacrifice of peace offerings, Aaron's sons brought to him the blood, which he dashed against the sides of the altar, [19]and the fat pieces from the head of cattle and the ram—the broad tail, the layer [of fat], the kidneys, and the caudate lobe of the liver. [20]They laid the fat pieces on the breasts, and he turned the fat pieces into smoke on the altar. [21]Aaron raised the breasts and the right thigh as an elevation offering before the Lord—just as Moses had com-

manded. 22Then Aaron lifted up his hands toward the people and blessed them.
After he had performed the ritual for the sin offering, the burnt offering, and
the peace offerings, he came down.
23Then Moses and Aaron entered the tent of meeting. When they came out,
they blessed the people, and the glory of the Lord appeared to all the people.
24Fire came out from the presence of the Lord and consumed the burnt offering
and the fat pieces on the altar. When all the people saw [it], they shouted for joy
and fell on their faces.

Textual Notes

9:1 בַּיּוֹם הַשְּׁמִינִי—The eighth day is the first day of a new week. In ritual transactions the eighth day marks the inauguration of something new, a new way of life, the beginning of a clean or holy state after a period of purification or consecration. The original creation was completed within seven days, and so the eighth day in Scripture represents the start of God's new creation, his work of redemption. Circumcision took place on the eighth day to mark the start of the infant's new life as a member of God's covenant people. Jesus Christ rose from the dead on the first day of the week—the start of God's new creation. See the "eighth day" also in 12:3; 14:10, 23; 15:14, 29; 22:27; 23:36, 39.

וּלְזִקְנֵי יִשְׂרָאֵל׃—These are the leaders of the tribes and clans of Israel who act on behalf of the liturgical community. See 4:15; cf. 19:32.

9:2 קַח—This imperative of לָקַח could also be translated as to "select." The plural imperative, קְחוּ, occurs in 9:3.

עֵגֶל—On this occasion a "calf" replaced the bull as the animal for the sin offering of the priests (4:3; 8:2; 16:3).

בֶּן־בָּקָר—See the textual notes on 1:5.

תְּמִימִם—See the textual notes on this adjective (singular: תָּמִים) in 1:3 and the explanation in "Fulfillment by Christ" in the commentary on 1:3–17. The word recurs in 9:3.

וְהַקְרֵב—See the textual note on this verb, the Hiphil of קָרַב, "to present, bring near," in 1:2 and the explanation in "Leviticus 1–3." The Hiphil recurs in 9:9, 15, 16, 17.

9:3 שְׂעִיר־עִזִּים—The noun שָׂעִיר denotes a "billy-goat, buck" (*HALOT,* s.v. שָׂעִיר II). In construct with the plural of עֵז, this phrase literally is "a buck of the goats," that is, a male goat. The phrase recurs in, for example, 16:5; 23:19; Num 28:15, 30; 29:5, 11, 16, 19, 25.

וְעֵגֶל—The "calf" was sacrificed instead of the bulls that were sacrificed on the regular festive occasions listed in Num 28:11, 19, 27; 29:2, 8, 13, 17, 20, 23, 26, 29, 32, 36.

וָכֶבֶשׂ—The "lamb" or "kid" may be the same as the regular burnt offering instituted in Ex 29:38.

9:4 לִזְבֹּחַ—Literally the infinitive construct with לְ means "to sacrifice." The verb recurs in 17:5 (twice), 7; 19:5 (twice); 22:29 (twice).

וּמִנְחָה—The daily grain offering, mentioned in Ex 29:40, was part of the daily burnt offering.

הַיּוֹם יְהוָה נִרְאָה אֲלֵיכֶם׃—נִרְאָה is the Niphal participle of רָאָה, so literally the clause means "today the Lord is appearing to you." The Niphal of רָאָה refers to the Lord's theophany also in 9:6, 23; 16:2.

9:5 וַיִּקְחוּ—The subjects of the verb "they took" are the elders who were mentioned in 9:1.

אֶל־פְּנֵי אֹהֶל מוֹעֵד—See the textual notes and commentary on 1:3, 5.

וַיִּקְרְבוּ—This is the first instance in Leviticus of the Qal of קָרַב, which is intransitive and means "to approach." Here it refers to approaching God at his sanctuary (9:5), and in 9:7, 8 it will refer to Aaron approaching the altar. See the textual note and commentary on the Hiphil of קָרַב, "to present, bring near," in 1:2. See too the analysis of this important ritual term by Milgrom.[1]

וַיַּעַמְדוּ לִפְנֵי—The royal idiom "to stand before" was used for the audience of a person or persons before a king (e.g., 1 Ki 1:28) and for entry into the king's service (e.g., Gen 41:46; 1 Sam 16:21; 1 Ki 1:2). Normally it was used for the service of the Lord by priests (e.g., Deut 10:8; 2 Chr 29:11) or the prophets (e.g., 1 Ki 17:1; 18:15; 2 Ki 3:14; 5:16). Here it is used for the audience of the congregation with the Lord and its entry into his service.

9:6 זֶה הַדָּבָר אֲשֶׁר־צִוָּה יְהוָה—This formula for the introduction of a divine command (Ex 16:16, 32; Lev 17:2) or for the summary of it (Ex 35:4; Num 30:1; 36:6) is used here and in Lev 8:5 to introduce the enactment of a divinely prescribed ceremony.

תַּעֲשׂוּ—See the textual notes on the verb עָשָׂה in 4:20. It recurs in 9:7, 16, 22. The verb is used here as a ritual term for the performance of a ritual.

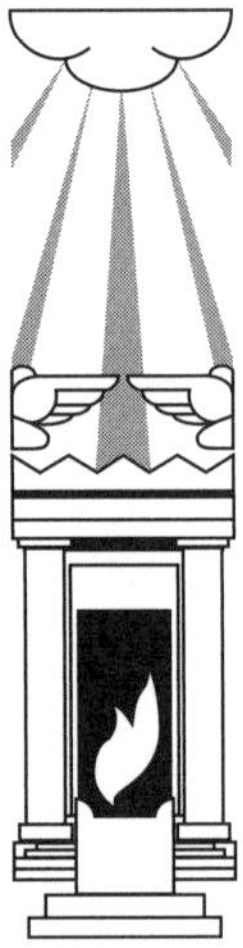

וְיֵרָא אֲלֵיכֶם כְּבוֹד יְהוָה׃—The conjunctive *waw* with the jussive indicates that this is the purpose of the enactment: "so that the glory of the Lord may appear to you."

כְּבוֹד יְהוָה׃—"The glory of the Lord" (also in 9:23) was the radiance that surrounded him, his visible and accessible presence as revealed in a theophany. It was not associated with an idol, as was normally the case with pagan gods, but enclosed in a cloud and revealed at the altar, like fire within smoke. The glory cloud of the Lord had first appeared to the Israelites in the desert when they had complained about their lack of food (Ex 16:7, 10). Then the Lord's glory settled on Mount Sinai (Ex 24:16–17), where Moses was granted a limited vision of him (Ex 33:18, 22). When the tabernacle had been consecrated, the Lord's glory filled the tabernacle and covered it with his enveloping cloud (Ex 40:34–35). After that foundational theophany the tabernacle then became the place for the Lord's regular theophany (e.g., Num 14:10; 16:19, 42; 20:6).

9:7 קְרַב אֶל־הַמִּזְבֵּחַ—Similar phrases that refer to approaching (the verb קָרַב) the altar (אֶל־הַמִּזְבֵּחַ) occur in Ex 40:32 and Lev 9:8 (cf. Num 18:3; 2 Ki 16:12; Ezek 44:15–16). This is the only occasion when such a command to approach the altar is given to Aaron. By means of that command Aaron was granted access to the altar and authorized to officiate there. Unauthorized approach to the Lord and his most holy

[1] Milgrom, *Studies in Levitical Terminology*, 16–33.

things resulted in death (Numbers 16; 18:1–7). On מִזְבֵּחַ, see the textual note on it in 1:5. In this chapter it recurs in 9:8, 9 (twice), 10, 12, 13, 14, 17, 18, 20, 24.

וְכַפֵּר בַּעַדְךָ וּבְעַד הָעָם—See the textual notes and commentary on the Piel verb כִּפֶּר in 1:4; 4:20. A similar phrase, "and he shall make atonement for himself and for his house," occurs in 16:6, 11, 17. The same clause that is here in 9:7 recurs in 16:24. Here the LXX reads "for your house" instead of "for the people." The LXX reading harmonizes 9:7 to agree with 16:6, 11, 17, but it is an inferior reading.

קָרְבַּן הָעָם—"The offering" of the people is a collective term for the four classes of offerings mentioned in 9:3–4.

כַּאֲשֶׁר צִוָּה יְהוָה׃—This refers to the Lord's commands in 9:2–5. This clause recurs in 9:10.

9:8 וַיִּשְׁחַט—See the textual note on this verb in 1:5. It recurs in 9:12, 15, 18.

9:9 קַרְנוֹת הַמִּזְבֵּחַ—See the textual notes on 4:7.

יָצַק—As in 8:15, the verb used here is יָצַק rather than the usual שָׁפַךְ.

9:10 הַחֵלֶב—See the textual notes and commentary on 3:3, 16–17. "The fat" recurs in 9:19, 20, 24.

הַחַטָּאת—See 4:8–10.

הִקְטִיר—See the textual note on this verb in 1:9. It recurs in 9:13, 14, 17, 20.

9:11 מִחוּץ לַמַּחֲנֶה׃—See the textual notes and commentary on 4:11–12.

9:12 וַיַּמְצִאוּ—The Hiphil of מָצָא is uncommon in the OT. In Leviticus it occurs only in 9:12, 13, 18, where it means to "bring something" (*HALOT,* s.v מָצָא, Hiphil, 1). In all three verses, it takes the preposition אֶל, and the combination means "to bring something to someone."

וַיִּזְרְקֵהוּ—See the textual note on this verb in 1:5. It recurs in 9:18.

9:15 קָרְבַּן הָעָם—"The offering of the people" refers to the following four offerings.

וַיְחַטְּאֵהוּ—See the textual note on the Piel of חָטָא in 6:19 (ET 6:26).

כָּרִאשׁוֹן׃—This refers to what was done in 9:8–11.

9:16 See 1:3–13.

כַּמִּשְׁפָּט׃—See the textual notes on 5:10.

9:17 וַיְמַלֵּא כַפּוֹ מִמֶּנָּה—Literally this clause means "and he filled his hands with some of it." The normal terminology for the presentation of the memorial portion is in 2:2. The different terminology used here may be intended to associate this act with the ordination of Aaron as a priest by the use of the same idiom, "to fill the hand of the ordinand"; see the textual notes and commentary on 8:22.

עֹלַת הַבֹּקֶר׃—This refers to the lamb for the regular public morning burnt offering (Ex 29:38–40; Num 28:3–4).

9:19 See Lev 3:3–4, 9–10.

9:20 הֶחָזוֹת—See 7:30.

9:21 שׁוֹק—The singular "thigh" is unexpected after the plural "breasts." It may be that on this occasion only the right thigh of the ram was waved to correlate it with the ram for ordination in 8:26–27. Normally, the fat pieces were placed on the breast of the animal and raised as an elevation offering (7:30). The fat pieces from the ram of ordination, however, were brought on its right thigh and elevated on it, because the thigh was not to be eaten by Moses but burned with the fat (8:28). On this occasion,

which Moses recalls in 10:15, both the breasts and the right thigh were raised in an elevation offering.

תְּנוּפָה—See Ex 29:22–26; Lev 7:30; and the textual notes on 7:30.

9:22 וַיִּשָּׂא אַהֲרֹן אֶת־יָדָיו אֶל־הָעָם—The Qere is "Aaron lifted up his hands," while the Kethib is "… his hand [יָדוֹ]." While the Israelites raised their hands in a gesture of receptivity to God in prayer (Ps 28:2; Lam 2:19), they also raised them in a gesture of homage when they "blessed" him (Pss 63:5 [ET 63:4]; 134:2). But since the hands of Aaron were raised toward the people, this, like the laying on of hands in Gen 48:14, was a gesture of bestowal.

וַיְבָרְכֵם—The Piel of בָּרַךְ is repeated in 9:23. This could refer to one of the three ritual acts. First, Aaron may have congratulated the people as the recipients of God's blessing (Ps 118:26). Second, he may have praised and proclaimed God as the giver of blessing to his people (1 Ki 8:14–16, 55–56; Ps 135:19–21). Third, and most likely, he may have pronounced a benediction which conferred God's blessing on them (Num 6:23–26; 1 Sam 2:20; Pss 115:14–15; 128:5–6; 134:3). The pronouncement of the Aaronic benediction was one of the priest's main duties (Num 6:22–26; Deut 10:8; 21:5; 1 Chr 23:13).

וַיֵּרֶד—This indicates that Aaron came down the ramp from the altar.

9:23 וַיָּבֹא מֹשֶׁה וְאַהֲרֹן אֶל־אֹהֶל מוֹעֵד—Even though Moses could not "enter" the tent after God's glory had filled it (Ex 40:35), he now "enters" it together with Aaron, just as he had previously entered the cloud on Mount Sinai (Ex 24:18; 34:34, 35) and would subsequently enter the tent to speak with God (Num 7:89; cf. Num 17:23 [ET 17:8]). By bringing Aaron into the tent, Moses, founder of the divine service, set the precedent for the daily entry of the high priest into the Holy Place (Ex 28:29, 30, 35; 29:30; Lev 10:9) to burn incense before the Lord (Ex 30:7–8; cf. Ex 28:43; 30:20; 40:32).

וַיֵּרָא כְבוֹד־יְהוָה אֶל־כָּל־הָעָם׃—The presence of God, normally veiled in a cloud, is now revealed in this theophany as fire that issued from the Holy of Holies.

9:24 See 6:1–6 (ET 6:8–13); 2 Chr 7:1, 3; cf. Num 11:1, 3; 16:35; Judg 6:21; 1 Ki 18:38; 1 Chr 21:26.

וַתֹּאכַל—Literally the fire "ate" the sacrifices. See also Lev 6:3 (ET 6:10); 10:2.

הָעֹלָה—Here the term "burnt offering" is used either generically for all the burnt offerings or inclusively for the daily burnt offering together with all other burnt offerings.

הַחֲלָבִים—The fat pieces came from the sin offerings (9:10, 15) and the peace offerings (9:19–20).

וַיָּרֹנּוּ—The Qal of רָנַן here means "to give out a cry of jubilation, break out in rejoicing" (*HALOT,* 2). Compare a similar worshipful vocal response (described with different vocabulary) by the Israelites when God's glory descended upon Solomon's temple in 2 Chr 7:3.

וַיִּפְּלוּ עַל־פְּנֵיהֶם׃—This will also be the reaction of Moses and Aaron to the reappearance of God's glory in Num 16:22; 20:6, as well as the reaction of the people to the consumption of sacrifices with divine fire in Judg 13:20 and 2 Chr 7:3.

Commentary

Structure

The events in this chapter are linked chronologically with the previous chapter as the culmination of the seven days of ordination as well as with the next chapter, which reports further events on the eighth day, when the divine service was inaugurated at the sanctuary. There is, in fact, no break in the sequence of narrative from 9:24 to 10:1.

Like 8:1–36, the narrative is arranged according to the pattern in which a divine command (9:2–4, 7) is followed by its execution (9:5, 8–24). But whereas Moses normally fulfills God's commands, here Aaron executes the commands that Moses gives to him. By his fulfillment of these commands, Aaron begins to officiate as the high priest with his sons as priests. This pattern of command and fulfillment is modified by the inclusion of an explanation of the divinely instituted purpose of the ritual in 9:4b and 9:6 and the results of its execution in 9:23–24.

The sequence of acts in the performance of the sacrificial ritual follows the content of the commands given in 9:2–4 and 9:7. The offerings of the priests (9:2, 7a) were brought first (9:8–14). Then the offerings of the people (9:3, 7b) were brought together with the lamb for the daily burnt offering and the daily grain offering (9:15–22). The report of inaugural service focuses on what happens at the altar. This is highlighted in the narrative by the repetition of the Hebrew word for "altar" (מִזְבֵּחַ) twelve times in 9:7–24.

The structure of this pericope can be outlined as follows:

I. Preparation for the inaugural service (9:1–5)
   A. The command of Moses to Aaron (9:1–4)
      1. The summoning of the priests and elders by Moses (9:1)
      2. His commission to Aaron (9:2–4)
         a. Instruction about Aaron's offerings and the people's offerings (9:2–4a)
         b. Announcement of the Lord's appearance as the purpose of the service (9:4b)
   B. Report of their compliance (9:5)
      1. Presentation of the offerings at the tent of meeting (9:5a)
      2. Assembly of the congregation (9:5b)

II. Inauguration of the divine service at the altar (9:6–24)
   A. Announcement by Moses of the Lord's appearance as the purpose of the ritual (9:6)
   B. Authorization by Moses of Aaron's access to the altar (9:7)
      1. Command to approach the altar (9:7a–b)
      2. Command to sacrifice the offerings for the priests (9:7c)
      3. Command to sacrifice the offerings for the people (9:7d)

- C. Aaron’s execution of the commands (9:8–22)
    - 1. His approach to the altar (9:8a)
    - 2. The sacrifice of the offerings for the priests (9:8b–14)
        - a. A calf as a sin offering (9:8b–11)
        - b. A ram as a burnt offering (9:12–14)
    - 3. The sacrifice of the offerings for the people (9:15–22a)
        - a. A goat as a sin offering (9:15)
        - b. A calf and a lamb as burnt offerings (9:16)
        - c. Flour as a grain offering (9:17)
        - d. A head of cattle and a ram as peace offerings (9:18–22a)
    - 4. His benediction of the people and descent from the altar (9:22b)
- D. The ritual conclusion of the service (9:23a–b)
    - 1. Entry of Moses and Aaron into the tent and their exit from it (9:23a)
    - 2. Their benediction of the people (9:23b)
- E. The result of the ritual enactment (9:23c–24)
    - 1. The appearance of the Lord in glory with fire on the altar (9:23c–24a)
    - 2. The jubilation and homage of the people (9:24b)

Ritual Agents

Moses continued to function as the divinely chosen founder in the ritual for the inauguration of the divine service. His role, however, was much more limited than in the rite for the ordination of the priests (Leviticus 8), because in chapter 9 Aaron begins to officiate for the first time in this service. Moses summoned the priests and the elders for the official ceremonial instruction of Aaron on his duties for the day (9:1–4). He also announced the purpose of the ceremony to the people (9:6), authorized Aaron to officiate at the altar (9:7), entered the Holy Place together with him (9:23a), and blessed the people together with him (9:23b). All these were official public enactments, in which Moses recognized Aaron as high priest, installed him in his office, and sanctioned his service at the altar and in the tent. He thereby handed over the responsibility for the altar, the tent, and the divine service to Aaron.

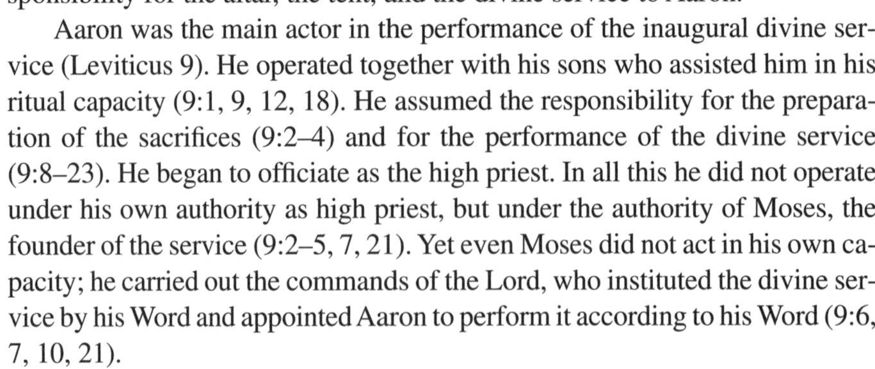

Aaron was the main actor in the performance of the inaugural divine service (Leviticus 9). He operated together with his sons who assisted him in his ritual capacity (9:1, 9, 12, 18). He assumed the responsibility for the preparation of the sacrifices (9:2–4) and for the performance of the divine service (9:8–23). He began to officiate as the high priest. In all this he did not operate under his own authority as high priest, but under the authority of Moses, the founder of the service (9:2–5, 7, 21). Yet even Moses did not act in his own capacity; he carried out the commands of the Lord, who instituted the divine service by his Word and appointed Aaron to perform it according to his Word (9:6, 7, 10, 21).

The congregation, led by its elders, was also involved in this divine service. In fact, the divine service was instituted for the benefit of the congregation. Here for the first and only time in the history of Israel, the glory of the

Lord—unveiled, without its protective cloud—appeared to "the whole congregation" (9:5). Here the congregation, for the first time, "approached" the altar, assembled there as a liturgical community, and entered the service of its heavenly King (9:5). The importance of the congregation can easily be overlooked by the little space given to it and its activity in the narrative. Yet the narrative clearly emphasizes its role in the introduction (9:1–6) and conclusion (9:22–24). Through its leaders, the congregation presented its offerings to Aaron (9:1–5a). He, in turn, presented them to the Lord (9:15–21) and performed the rite of atonement on behalf of the congregation (9:7b). The assembled congregation received the Lord's blessing in the service and saw the fiery theophany (9:22–24). The congregation responded to that divine epiphany with a shout of jubilation and an act of prostration. The elders were, most likely, also involved in the sacred meal in which they ate the meat from the peace offerings.

Ritual Material

The raw material for the divine service is listed in the introduction given by Aaron in 9:2–4a. On the one hand, Aaron was required to bring two animals for his offerings: a young bull as the calf for his sin offering and a ram for his burnt offering. A ram was required because Aaron was the leader of the Lord's flock (cf. 8:18; 16:3). But the prescription of a male calf for the sin offering, instead of a bull, was most unusual. It may be because Aaron had not begun to officiate as a priest. On the other hand, the congregation was required to bring a male goat as its sin offering, a calf in addition to the usual lamb as its daily burnt offering, flour mixed with oil as its daily grain offering, and a head of cattle and a ram as its peace offerings. The only unusual thing about this list was the choice of a calf rather than a bull for its burnt offering as was normally the case on festive occasions. This too may be because it was the inaugural service for the congregation.

As one would expect for such an inaugural service, the narrative mentions the application of the blood (9:9, 12, 18), the burning up of the flesh from the burnt offering (9:13–14) and of fat portions from the other sacrifices (9:10, 19–20), and the incineration of the flesh and hide from the sin offering of the priests (9:11). The only abnormal treatment of anything was the burning of the meat from the people's sin offering instead of its consumption by the priests. Moses calls attention to this anomaly in the following chapter (10:16–20).

Ritual Location

This narrative shows how closely ritual location is connected with ritual status and ritual activity. It identifies three main places as the significant locations for the performance of the daily sacrificial ritual. This foundational narrative assigns the place for each part of the service in sacred space and sets the precedent for the location of the performance of each.

First, the area in the courtyard in front of the tent of meeting was the place for the assembly of the congregation (9:5). They brought their offerings there and "stood" in the Lord's presence. They had access to the Lord and served him there. There they received the Lord's blessing. There they acclaimed the Lord's gracious presence with them and prostrated themselves before him. Their location in the sanctuary was consistent with their status as the Lord's people and compatible with their ritual responsibilities.

Second, the altar was the focal point for the whole inaugural service, as for every service at the sanctuary. Only Aaron and his sons had access to the altar. The high priest and his fellow priests were authorized to approach the altar and go up onto it (9:7, 8). They alone put the blood from the sacrifices on the altar and burned up the offerings on the altar. Only they were allowed to bless the people from the altar (9:22). The altar was the priests' station in the sanctuary. Their status was derived from it, for their vocation was to perform the rites associated with it.

Third, the inaugural service culminated in the entry of Aaron into the tent of meeting (9:23). He did not do this by himself, but entered together with Moses. The entry by Aaron into that holy place pioneered and inaugurated the daily entrance of the high priest for the burning of incense on the altar. That was his unique place of service in the sanctuary. It determined his status and ritual responsibility as high priest. He had access to that place only in his ritual capacity as high priest during the performance of the daily service.

Ritual Time

The newly consecrated priests inaugurated the divine service at the newly consecrated altar on the eighth day (9:1). The seven previous days for the ordination of the priest were preparation for this momentous event. Calculating from the date given in Ex 40:17, it would have fallen on the eighth day of Nisan, the first month of the liturgical year. Yet that day for the inaugural service did not establish an annual festival or the pattern of worship for any festive occasion. It established the precedent for the daily burnt offering, which followed the pattern set on that day on each day of the year.

Ritual Enactment

Rainey correctly recognized that, whereas most legal texts in Leviticus deal with aspects of ritual according to their administrative order, this narrative describes the actual procedural order for the whole sacrificial ritual.[2] The center of that ritual, as listed in 9:16–17, was the daily burnt offering with its grain offering. This provided the framework for the other occasional sacrifices that were built onto it and around it. Thus the rite for the sin offering prepared for the daily burnt offering, while the rite for the peace offering followed its enactment.

---

2 Rainey, "The Order of Sacrifices in Old Testament Ritual Texts."

The ritual for the inauguration of the divine service began with the presentation of the offerings by Aaron and by the elders of the congregation. This was done in the context of the public assembly of the whole congregation in front of the altar. After the congregation had been convened and the offerings had been brought there, Moses announced that God had instituted the service so that he could appear in his glory to the congregation through the performance of the sacrificial ritual (9:6).

The main part of the service proceeded in three stages. First, Moses formally ordered Aaron to approach the altar and to perform the sacrificial ritual for himself and the people. This charge to Aaron served an important ritual function. By it Moses, as the Lord's representative, publicly authorized Aaron's access to the altar and officially commissioned him to perform the divine service.

Second, after Aaron had been publicly entrusted with the performance of the divine service, he performed the complex sacrificial ritual for it. Assisted by his sons, he slaughtered the calf for his sin offering, performed the rite of atonement with its blood, burned its fat portions on the altar, and attended to the incineration of the leftover flesh and hide (9:8–11). Then he also slaughtered a ram for his burnt offering, splashed its blood against the altar, and burnt up its remains (9:12–14). By these enactments he was freed from all impurity and accepted by the Lord as the people's representative. Then Aaron brought up the four offerings of the people: the sin offering; the burnt offering for the occasion together with the daily burnt offering; the grain offering; and the peace offerings.

The ritual for the presentation of the peace offerings culminated in the act of blessing, performed by Aaron from the altar, after the peace offerings had been presented. On this occasion the blessing was therefore closely associated with the presentation of the peace offerings. As far as we can gather, the Aaronic benediction was not normally performed from the altar in the daily service. Sirach 50:19–23 reports that, at least in the postexilic era, the high priest delivered the Aaronic benediction at the close of the service from the front of the altar for burnt offering. That, most likely, was the regular location for its performance.

Third, the last stage of the service was the entry of Aaron, together with Moses as his mentor, into the tent of meeting. We are not told whether he entered it, as he did twice daily, to burn incense on the altar in the Holy Place (Ex 28:29, 30, 35; 29:30) or else, as Moses did, to pray on behalf of the people (Num 7:89; cf. Ex 33:8, 9). Whatever the case, his entry clearly established the precedent for that daily rite. In this case the entry occurred after the presentation of the burnt offering on the altar rather than after the rite of atonement and before the burnt offering as was normally the case. In this case the normal order was reversed to connect the final benediction with Aaron's entry into the tent of meeting. Aaron entered God's presence in order to bring his blessing to the assembled congregation.

The significance of that final benediction is highlighted by its association with the theophany. The coincidence of the blessing and the theophany is ritually and theologically significant, because, after this foundational event, the presence of God was not revealed by means of repeated theophanies, but by smoke from the altar and the performance of the Aaronic benediction in front of it. The jubilation of the congregation at the Lord's appearance and their prostration before him set a precedent for the regular response of the people to God's meeting with them for the daily burnt offering (2 Chr 7:3; 29:29; Ps 96:7–10). It may even have been taken to set a precedent for the performance of the Lord's song as the burnt offering was sent up in smoke from the altar.[3]

Ritual Theological Function

The foundational narrative for the inauguration of the divine service was obviously meant to interpret the ritual function and theological significance of the daily service at the sanctuary. It did not just report how the ritual was to be enacted, but clearly announced what God accomplished through its performance. What happened at that service happens at each subsequent service. It revealed how God was at work in each performance of the daily burnt offering.

The service was performed so that God could appear in a new and previously unprecedented fashion to his people, both in and through that service (9:4). Through the service God revealed himself in his glory to the assembled congregation (9:6). His glory was his visible, accessible presence. Previously, the people had only seen the glory of the Lord encased and veiled in a cloud (Ex 16:10). The glory cloud, which had appeared on Mount Sinai (Ex 24:15–18), had filled the tabernacle after its construction (Ex 40:34–38). But now the glory of the Lord appeared, for the first and last time, unclouded and unveiled as sacred fire, to the people of Israel, through the performance of the service. That sacred fire came from the Lord's presence in the tent of meeting and consumed all the sacrifices.

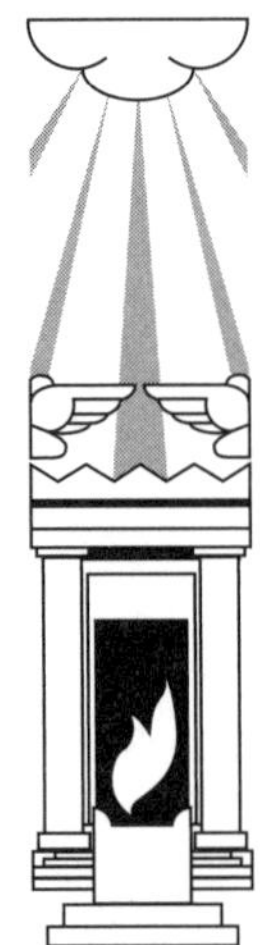

This unique, unrepeated fiery theophany, at the climax of the inaugural service, announced the Lord's acceptance of the service and so disclosed the significance of every service. Every service was a divine theophany. The place of the Lord's appearance was the altar. The time for his appearance was at the burning up of the daily burnt offering. The manner of his appearance was through the holy fire on the altar, a fire that was normally veiled and encased in a cloud of smoke.

The service, which was performed for the theophany of the Lord, was also meant to prepare the congregation for that theophany. Moses told Aaron to present the sacrifices in order to make atonement (9:7). This was necessary because the presence of the Lord in glory was ambivalent in its effect on the people. If they were ritually unclean and so unfit for his presence, he encoun-

[3] Arens, *Die Psalmen im Gottesdienst des Alten Bundes*, 34–54.

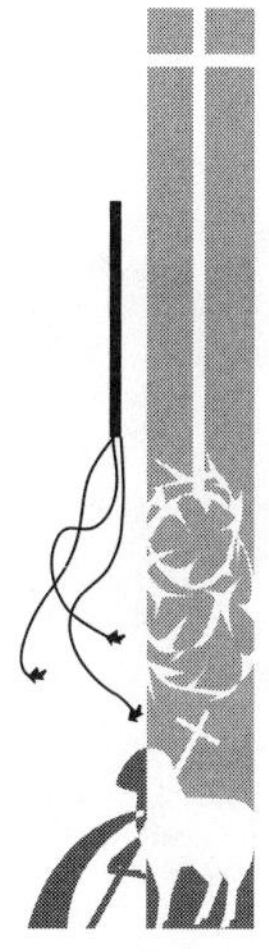

tered them in wrath and disfavor to prevent the desecration of his holiness. If they were ritually clean and so fit for his presence, he accepted them and gave them access to his grace. So then, the rite of atonement was enacted first in each part of this service, as in all subsequent services. It was the preparatory rite for the burnt offering and all the other offerings burnt with it on the altar.

Aaron made atonement in two stages. First, he made atonement for himself in his office as priest by the ritual manipulation of the blood from his own sin offering and burnt offering (9:7, 9, 12). Since he, on this occasion, formally represented the people, his sin offering was not a personal sacrifice, as was instituted in 4:3–12, but a public sacrifice for the benefit of the people. Second, Aaron then made atonement for the people directly by the ritual disposal of the blood from their sacrifices (9:7, 18).

Through the performance of atonement, Aaron and the people were cleansed from all impurity and prepared for the theophany of the Lord. Since they had been cleansed, they received blessing and joy, rather than wrath and death from their desecration of God's holiness by their impurity. It is, then, theologically significant that the theophany was associated with the entry into the tent of meeting and the burning of the burnt offering with the fat portions from the other offerings, rather than with the rite of atonement. That rite was not meant to mediate the Lord's presence, but to prepare the way for his advent. It did not give the people access to the Lord, but prepared them for his theophany.

The relation between the theophany of the Lord at this inaugural service and his regular meeting with the congregation in all subsequent services is disclosed by the emphasis in the narrative on the two concluding acts of benediction. The first abnormal benediction, performed by Aaron upon the altar at the end of the rite for the peace offerings of the people, shows that the blessing of the Lord was normally conveyed to the people in and through their peace offerings. The second benediction by Moses and Aaron occupies the normal position of the Aaronic benediction at the end of the regular service. Its function is therefore much more profound than that of the first benediction. It is deliberately associated with the theophany and identified with it.

That closing benediction served two functions in connection with the theophany. First, it announced the theophany and interpreted it as God's gracious act of benediction and approval. Both the service as a whole and the theophany of the Lord at the end of it conveyed the Lord's blessing to his people. This fulfills the promise of the Lord in Ex 20:24 that he would come to his people and bless them at the place where they offered their burnt offerings and peace offerings.

Second, the benediction with the theophany shows how the Lord would subsequently "appear" to his people in the regular service. As the Lord had revealed his glory during the performance of the benediction in the inaugural service, so he would reveal his face and manifest his gracious presence to the people through the performance of the regular Aaronic benediction at the conclusion of the regular service (Num 6:22–27; 1 Chr 23:13). In every subsequent service the Lord would disclose his presence verbally to the Israelites by blessing them (but normally not visually by showing himself to them). The narrative therefore identifies the benediction as the moment of theophany in the regular service. It was, quite rightly, to be received with jubilation by the congregation and acknowledged by the performance of prostration before the Lord.

The report of the inaugural service explained the significance of that service and depicted it as the paradigm for what would happen in every subsequent service. In every service God came to his people to bless them. In every service the people of God brought their offerings so that they might be cleansed from their impurity and receive God's favor rather than his wrath. In every service the altar was the place where the Lord met with his people through the fire on the altar. It was the daily sign of his gracious presence with them.

Fulfillment by Christ

As Moses inaugurated the OT service, Jesus inaugurated the Divine Service in the new covenant. He was its ritual pioneer, its founder who blazed the way for others into the heavenly sanctuary (Heb 6:20) and led them with him into glory (Heb 2:10; 12:2).

Yet the service that Jesus inaugurated was not completely new. In fact, St. Paul claims that the church has received "the service [ἡ λατρεία] and the promises" from the people of Israel (Rom 9:4). But the Divine Service that Christ has given to the NT church is the fulfillment of the OT service, its perfection. Christ brought the OT service to its divine goal. The law of Moses established its purpose, but it was not able to bring it to its goal (Heb 7:19): open access to God's presence in the heavenly sanctuary.[4]

Jesus, who was made the perfect Priest through his sufferings (2:10; 5:9; 7:28), inaugurated a new and living way into his Father's presence (Heb 10:20). He perfected the conscience of his fellow priests (all baptized believers in Christ) so that they could be involved with him completely and perfectly in the service of God (Heb 9:9; 10:1). He is therefore both the pioneer and perfecter of the Christian faith (Heb 12:2). Just as Moses initiated Aaron and his sons into the divine service at the tabernacle, so Jesus initiates his fellow priests into the acceptable service of God with the angels in the heavenly sanctuary (Heb 9:14; 12:28). There Jesus, the mediator of a better covenant than Moses, based on better promises, performs a more excellent liturgical ministry than Aaron and his sons did at the tabernacle (Heb 8:1–2, 6).

The Gospel of Luke shows us how Jesus established the Divine Service in the church. Five key events relate to the corresponding events in Leviticus 9:

- At the beginning of the Gospel, Zechariah, the priest on duty, was prevented from bringing God's blessing to the people assembled at the temple for the daily service (Lk 1:8–22).

---

[4] Scholer, *Proleptic Priests*, 185–200.

- In the middle of the Gospel, God's glory was revealed in Jesus to Peter, James, and John on the eighth day on the mountain (Lk 9:28–36). In this theophany God the Father established Jesus as the new place of worship, where listening to his Word is the central requirement.
- Before his crucifixion, Jesus established the Divine Service of Holy Communion, in which he is present with his disciples to serve them (22:14–30).
- On the eighth day—the first day of the new week, the start of the new creation inaugurated by his resurrection—the Lord Jesus revealed himself and his hidden glory to the disciples through the exposition of the sacred Scriptures and the breaking of the bread with them (Lk 24:13–35).
- At the close of the Gospel, Jesus, the new and greater High Priest, blessed his disciples from heaven itself at the completion of his sacrificial service of God on earth (24:50–51). And so with his ascension he began to serve as High Priest in the heavenly realm.

The Divine Service of the church straddles heaven and earth through the priestly mediation of the exalted Lord Jesus. God had instituted the divine service in ancient Israel so that he could manifest his glory to his people on earth and bless them. That glory was revealed each day in the fire that blazed on the altar and in the smoke that ascended from it. There he made himself graciously available and accessible to his people in the sacrificial ritual that removed their impurity and brought them into his presence.

In the new covenant, God's glory is hidden in the humanity of Jesus (Jn 1:14, 18; 2 Cor 4:6; Heb 1:3) and revealed to the saints through God's Word (Col 1:25–27). In the risen Lord Jesus, the fullness of the Deity dwells in bodily form with his people so that they can come into the fullness of God's life through him (Col 2:9–10). He is present wherever two or three are gathered in his name (Mt 18:20). He is their new place of worship. He involves them in a new way of worship that is Trinitarian. In it they worship God the Father through Jesus by the power of the Holy Spirit (Jn 4:19–24; Eph 2:18). They approach God the Father through Jesus, for he intercedes for them as their High Priest (Heb 7:25).

By his presence and activity as High Priest, the exalted Lord Jesus changes the orientation and shape of the Divine Service. Since he has made purification for the sins of the world by his sacrifice of atonement (Heb 1:13), there is now no need for any further acts of atonement for those involved in the Divine Service. Instead, Jesus now brings his fellow priests the benefits of that sacrifice by removing their sin and cleansing them from its stain (Heb 2:17).[5] They do not need to atone for their sin before they can approach God. Rather they can "approach" him, like a generous king, to receive mercy and grace from him (Heb 4:16). Since Jesus has cleansed them completely, they can "approach"

---

5 Pfitzner, *Hebrews*, 69.

God the Father with a clear conscience in the heavenly sanctuary with the full assurance of faith (Heb 10:19–22). Since Jesus their mediator sprinkles them with his blood that speaks pardon and acceptance, they can, already here on earth, participate by faith in the heavenly liturgy together with the angels, all the church on earth, and all the saints in heaven (Heb 12:22–24).

The sacred meal was only a small part of the sacrificial ritual at the tabernacle, but by Christ's institution, the new Meal is the heart of the Divine Service in the NT church. In the Lord's Supper, the triune God reveals his glory to the assembled congregation and blesses his people with every spiritual blessing in the heavenly realms (Eph 1:3–14). The congregation shouts for joy and rejoices at that mysterious theophany. The people of God kneel before the altar to receive the body and blood that manifest God's glory and convey his blessings to them. And the Meal ends with a benediction. The pronouncement of the Aaronic benediction at the end of each Eucharist recalls this foundational story and acknowledges our liturgical connection with the ancient people of Israel—the OT church.

How blessed is this place, O Lord,
Where you are worshiped and adored!
In faith we here an altar raise
To your great glory, God of praise.

Here let your sacred fire of old
Descend to kindle spirits cold;
And may our prayers, when here we bend,
Like incense sweet to you ascend.

Here let the weary one find rest,
The troubled heart, your comfort blest,
The guilty one, a sure retreat,
The sinner, pardon at your feet.[6]

---

6 From "How Blessed Is This Place, O Lord" by Ernest E. Ryden (*LW* 327:1–3). Copyright © Board of Publications, Lutheran Church in America. Used with permission of Augsburg Fortress.

Leviticus 10:1–20

The Penalty for Disobedience

Translation

**10 [1]Now Aaron's sons Nadab and Abihu each took a pan, put coals on it, and
laid incense on it; and they presented unauthorized fire in the Lord's presence,
which he had not commanded them. [2]Then fire came out from the Lord's presence and consumed them; thus they died in the Lord's presence.**

[3]Moses said to Aaron: "This is what the Lord said:

'When I am treated as holy by those who are near me,
I appear in glory in the sight of all the people.' "

And Aaron remained silent.

**[4]Then Moses summoned Mishael and Elzaphan, sons of Uzziel, Aaron's un-
cle, and said to them: "Come forward and carry your kinsmen outside the camp
away from the sanctuary." [5]They came forward and carried them outside the
camp by their tunics, just as Moses had ordered. [6]Then Moses said to Aaron and
to Eleazar and Ithamar, his sons: "Do not dishevel your hair and do not tear your
vestments, so that you will not die and he will not have wrath against the whole
congregation. But your kinsmen, all the household of Israel, may weep for the
burning that the Lord has kindled. [7]You must not go outside the entrance to the
tent of meeting, or you will die; for the anointing oil of the Lord is upon you."
And they did as Moses had ordered.**

**[8]The Lord spoke to Aaron: [9]"When you enter the tent of meeting, you and
your sons shall not drink any wine or beer, so that you will not die. This is a perpetual ritual statute throughout your generations: [10]you must distinguish between what is holy and what is common, what is unclean and what is clean, [11]and
you must teach the Israelites all the statutes that the Lord has spoken to them
through Moses."**

**[12]Moses spoke to Aaron and to Eleazar and Ithamar, his remaining sons:
"Take the grain offering that is left over from the gifts for the Lord and eat it as
unleavened bread beside the altar, for it is most holy. [13]You shall eat it in a holy
place, because it is your due and the due of your sons from the gifts for the Lord;
for that is as I have been commanded. [14]But you, and your sons and your daughters with you, may eat the breast that is elevated and the thigh that is contributed
in any clean place, for they have been assigned as a due to you and your children
from the sacrifices of the peace offerings of the Israelites. [15]In addition to the gifts
of the fat pieces, they must bring the thigh that is contributed and the breast that
is elevated, to raise them as an elevation offering before the Lord; they shall be
a perpetual due for you and your children with you—just as the Lord has commanded."**

**[16]When Moses made inquiry about the goat of the sin offering, he discovered
that it had already been burned. He was angry with Eleazar and Ithamar, Aaron's**

remaining sons, and said, 17"Why did you not eat the sin offering in the holy place? It is certainly most holy, and he has assigned it to you for bearing the guilt of the congregation by making atonement for them in the Lord's presence. 18Since its blood was not brought into the inner precinct of the Holy Place, you should most certainly have eaten it in the sanctuary, just as I commanded."

19Aaron replied to Moses: "Even though they presented their sin offering and burnt offering in the Lord's presence today, such things have happened to me! Would the Lord have approved if I had eaten the sin offering today?"

20When Moses heard this, he approved.

Textual Notes

10:1–2 This incident is referred to in Lev 16:1; Num 3:2–4; 26:60–61; 1 Chr 24:1–2.

10:1 נָדָב וַאֲבִיהוּא—These two sons are also mentioned in Ex 6:23; 24:1, 9; 28:1.

קְטֹרֶת—See 16:12, 13. We are not told whether this was the most holy incense that was offered on the altar for incense (Ex 30:7–8, 34–38) or the frankincense that was offered with the grain offerings (Lev 2:1, 2, 15, 16; 5:11; 6:8 [ET 6:15]; 24:7).

לִפְנֵי יְהוָה—It is not clear where they went to burn their incense "before the Lord." Did they enter the Holy Place as Uzziah later did (2 Chr 26:16–20), or did they do so before the altar for burnt offering as Korah and his company did (Num 16:5–11, 16–19, 35–40)?

אֵשׁ זָרָה—The adjective זָר means "strange, different, heterogeneous, illicit" (*HALOT*). It is feminine (זָרָה) because אֵשׁ is a feminine noun. The meaning of this phrase is explained by the following clause: the "fire" did not belong in the divine service because the Lord had not authorized it.

10:2 וַתֵּצֵא אֵשׁ מִלִּפְנֵי יְהוָה וַתֹּאכַל—These words are identical to those in 9:24. See also Num 16:35.

10:3 הוּא אֲשֶׁר־דִּבֶּר יְהוָה—This introduction to a word from God is found only here.

בִּקְרֹבַי—The adjective קָרוֹב means "close, near." Often it refers to kinship. Here it serves as a substantive, "those who are near" to God. It refers to the priests who have access to God and therefore can approach him (see Ezek 42:13; 43:19; *HALOT,* s.v. קָרוֹב I, 3 a). It can also be a royal term for an official who had direct access to his king (Ezek 23:12; Esth 1:14 ; cf. 1 Ki 2:7; 5:7).

אֶקָּדֵשׁ—This could mean either "When I am treated as holy" or "When I show myself as holy." This may be a case of deliberate ambiguity as both make good sense. The same is true for the Niphal of קָדַשׁ in Lev 22:32.

אֶכָּבֵד—When the Niphal of כָּבֵד has God as its subject, it means either that God will "gain glory" for himself (Ex 14:4, 17, 18; Is 26:15; Ezek 28:22; 39:13), or, more likely here in the context of Lev 9:6, 23, that he will "appear in glory" (Hag 1:8).

וַיִּדֹּם אַהֲרֹן׃—The Qal of דָּמַם can mean to "keep quiet" (*HALOT,* 2). We are not told why Aaron was silent. Did he remain silent from dread (Job 31:34)[1] or from rightly

---

1 Elliger, *Leviticus*, 137.

refusing to mourn (Ezek 24:17)[2] or from acceptance of God's Word and deed (Job 29:21)?[3] The last seems most likely.

10:4 אֶל־מִישָׁאֵל וְאֶל אֶלְצָפָן בְּנֵי עֻזִּיאֵל—See Ex 6:18.

קִרְבוּ—This literally means "approach." This is parallel to the command in 9:7.

פְּנֵי־הַקֹּדֶשׁ—See the textual notes on 4:6. This refers to the court of the tabernacle or the area between the altar and the tent (7:6; 10:17, 18; 14:13).

אֶל־מִחוּץ לַמַּחֲנֶה׃—See the textual notes on 4:12. The phrase recurs in 10:5.

10:6 וּלְאֶלְעָזָר וּלְאִיתָמָר—With the death of Nadab and Abihu, these two sons are now Aaron's assistants.

רָאשֵׁיכֶם אַל־תִּפְרָעוּ—The verb פָּרַע, "to loose, let free," with the direct object רֹאשׁ, "head," means "to let the hair on the head hang loosely" (*HALOT,* s.v. פרע, Qal, 2 a) or "be disheveled." That was a custom for those in mourning. In 13:45, a "leper" is to leave his hair disheveled as a sign of his uncleanness. Lev 21:10 uses the same idiom to prohibit the high priest from disheveling his hair.

וּבִגְדֵיכֶם לֹא־תִפְרֹמוּ—Tearing the garments was another custom for a person in mourning. Again, compare 13:45 and 21:10.

אֶת־הַשְּׂרֵפָה אֲשֶׁר שָׂרַף יְהוָה׃—This is literally "the burning that the Lord has burnt."

10:7 וּמִפֶּתַח אֹהֶל מוֹעֵד לֹא תֵצְאוּ— See the textual notes on 1:3. This is not a permanent prohibition but applies to their departure to engage in mourning and funeral rites (21:11–12).

כִּי־שֶׁמֶן מִשְׁחַת יְהוָה עֲלֵיכֶם—Normally only the high priest was anointed on his head (Ex 29:7; Lev 8:12; 21:10). However, this phrase may indicate that the sons who deputized for him may also have been anointed in the same way (Ex 29:29; 30:30; 40:15; Lev 16:32; Num 3:3).

10:8 וַיְדַבֵּר יְהוָה אֶל־אַהֲרֹן—This is the only direct revelation by God to Aaron in Leviticus (cf. Num 18:1, 8, 20).

10:9 יַיִן וְשֵׁכָר אַל־תֵּשְׁתְּ—See the extension of this prohibition in Ezek 44:21 to the inner court. Wine was offered on the altar as a libation with the burnt offering and the peace offering (Ex 29:40; Lev 23:13; Num 15:5, 7, 10; 28:14). The Israelites also offered tithes of wine to the priests and drank some of the tithed wine in their sacrificial banquets (Num 18:12; Deut 12:17; 14:23, 26; 18:4). Nevertheless, the priests were not allowed to drink any of the holy wine while they were on duty.

The term שֵׁכָר was normally used for beer and similar fermented alcoholic beverages. Even though it is used in Num 28:7 for wine, here and in Num 6:3 it is distinguished from wine.

בְּבֹאֲכֶם אֶל־אֹהֶל מוֹעֵד—See Ex 28:29, 30, 35; 29:30; 40:32; Lev 9:23. There were four things that disqualified a priest from entry into the sacred precincts: the lack of vestments (Ex 28:43); the lack of ritual washing (Ex 30:20); drunkenness (Lev 10:9); and a physical blemish (Lev 21:23). These did not defile the priest, but they dese-

---

2 Milgrom, *Leviticus 1–16,* 604.

3 Hartley, *Leviticus*, 134.

crated the holiness of the sanctuary. The penalty for transgression in each of these cases was death.

וְלֹא תָמֻתוּ—See also 10:2, 6, 7.

חֻקַּת עוֹלָם לְדֹרֹתֵיכֶם׃—See the textual notes on 3:17.

10:10 וּֽלֲהַבְדִּיל—The use of the infinitive with prefixed *waw* is best construed as a statement of obligation (GKC, § 114 l). The Hiphil of בָּדַל was an important ritual term for the Israelite priests. Just as God had distinguished day from night and light from darkness in creation (Hiphil of בָּדַל in Gen 1:14, 18), so the priests were to distinguish holy from common and clean from unclean (Lev 10:10; 11:47) and teach the Israelites to do so (10:11). Likewise, just as God had distinguished the Israelites as his holy people from the unclean nations (20:24, 26) and had distinguished certain unclean animals from clean animals (20:24), so they were to distinguish clean animals from unclean animals (20:25).

הַקֹּדֶשׁ—See the textual notes on 4:6.

הַחֹל—See 1 Sam 21:5–6 (ET 21:4–5); Ezek 22:26; 42:20; 44:23; 48:15. While holiness describes the state of people or things in God's domain, the term חֹל, "what is common," describes their state in the natural created realm, the human domain. If something common became holy it ceased to be common. Yet it could be either clean or unclean, depending on whether or not it functioned as it should in the order of creation. See figure 1, "Holy versus Common and Clean versus Unclean," and the accompanying explanation.

וּבֵין הַטָּמֵא וּבֵין הַטָּהוֹר׃—See the textual notes on 5:2 and 7:19. The same pair of antonyms, "unclean" and "clean," occurs in Lev 11:47; 14:57; 20:25; Deut 12:15, 22; 15:22; Ezek 22:26; 44:23; Job 14:4; Eccl 9:2.

10:11 וּלְהוֹרֹת—This verb, the Hiphil of יָרָה, occurs with the same meaning in the similar verse 14:57. See also the textual note and commentary in 6:2 (ET 6:9) regarding תּוֹרָה, the noun "instruction," which is related to this verb.

הַחֻקִּים—See 26:46 for the only other use in Leviticus of the plural of חֹק as a general term for God's legislation.

אֲשֶׁר דִּבֶּר יְהוָה אֲלֵיהֶם בְּיַד־מֹשֶׁה׃—This is literally "which the Lord has spoken through the hand of Moses."

10:12 הַמִּנְחָה—See 9:4, 17.

הַמִּזְבֵּחַ—See the textual notes on 1:5.

כִּי קֹדֶשׁ קָדָשִׁים הִוא׃—See the textual notes on 2:3. This phrase recurs in 10:17.

10:13 בְּמָקוֹם קָדֹשׁ—See the textual notes on 6:9 (ET 6:16).

חָקְךָ—See the textual notes on 6:11 (ET 6:18). The noun חֹק recurs in 10:14, 15.

מֵאִשֵּׁי יְהוָה—See the textual notes on 1:9 and the explanation in "Leviticus 1–3."

10:14 הַתְּנוּפָה—See the textual notes on 7:30. The term recurs in 10:15.

שׁוֹק הַתְּרוּמָה—This is literally "the thigh of the contribution." See the textual notes on 7:14.

בְּמָקוֹם טָהוֹר—This "clean place" is the house of the priest rather than the sanctuary (which is holy). Cf. 22:10–13; Num 18:11–20.

כִּי־חָקְךָ וְחָק־בָּנֶיךָ—See 7:34.

10:15 הַחֲלָבִים—See the textual notes on 3:3.

יָבִ֫יאוּ—See the textual notes on 2:2.

וּלְבָנֶ֣יךָ אִתָּ֑ךְ—This refers to the children living in the house of the priest.

כַּאֲשֶׁ֖ר צִוָּ֥ה יְהוָֽה׃—See 7:34.

10:16 שְׂעִ֣יר הַֽחַטָּ֗את—See 9:15.

דָּרֹ֥שׁ דָּרַ֖שׁ—The verb is introduced by its infinitive absolute for emphasis to indicate diligence and persistence on the part of Moses.

וַיִּקְצֹ֗ף—Moses was angry because the priests did not strictly follow either of the two contingencies for the sin offering in 6:19–23 (ET 6:26–30). Normally the priest who offered the sin offering was to eat the meat from it in a holy place (6:19, 22 [ET 6:26, 29]). But if the priests presented the sin offering to make atonement for themselves, they brought blood from the offering into the tent of meeting to atone for themselves, and then the priests were not to eat the sin offering; it had to be burnt (6:23 [ET 6:30]). In 10:16 Moses finds that the priests had burnt the sin offering (and did not eat the meat from it) even though the blood from it had not been used to make atonement for the priests.

10:17 הַֽחַטָּאת֙—This refers to the meat from the sin offering.

בִּמְק֣וֹם הַקֹּ֔דֶשׁ—This is literally "in the place of the sanctuary."

קֹ֥דֶשׁ קָדָשִׁ֖ים הִ֑וא—See 6:10, 18, 22 (ET 6:17, 25, 29); 14:13; and the textual notes on 2:3.

נָתַ֣ן—The implied subject is God. See the textual notes on 17:10.

לָשֵׂאת֙ אֶת־עֲוֺ֣ן—See the textual notes on 5:1. The idiom נָשָׂא עָוֺן is used in three different ways in liturgical texts.[4] If God is the subject, then it means "to remove/forgive iniquity" (Ex 34:7; Num 14:18; cf. Hos 14:3 [ET 14:2]; Micah 7:18). If the offender is the subject, it means "to bear the guilt" or "experience the evil consequences/suffer the penalty" from the offense as afflicted by God (Ex 28:43; Lev 5:1, 17; 7:18; 17:16; 19:8; 20:17, 19; see the related idiom נָשָׂא חֵטְא in Lev 19:17; 20:20; 22:9; 24:5; Num 9:13; 18:22, 32). If a priest (Ex 28:38; Lev 10:17; Num 18:1) or a Levite (Num 18:23) or a scapegoat (Lev 16:22) is the subject, then it refers to them "bearing/removing the iniquity" of sinners from the sanctuary.

הָֽעֵדָ֔ה—See 9:5; 10:6.

לְכַפֵּ֥ר עֲלֵיהֶ֖ם—See the textual notes on 1:4. We render this as "by making atonement for them." However, Rodriguez argues that it means "to make atonement for them" and that the priests removed the people's sin by eating the meat that had absorbed their impurity.[5] But that is most unlikely, for the meat was most holy (6:18 [ET 6:25]; 7:1) and so had to be eaten in a holy place (6:19 [ET 6:26]). Janowski quite rightly argues that the priests bore the guilt of the congregation by performing the rite of atonement with the blood from the sin offering.[6]

---

4 Schwartz, "The Bearing of Sin in the Priestly Literature."

5 Rodriguez, *Substitution in the Hebrew Cultus*, 130–36; compare Rendtorff, *Studien zur Geschichte des Opfers im alten Israel,* 215–16, and Milgrom, *Leviticus 1–16,* 623–25.

6 Janowski, *Sühne als Heilsgeschehen*, 238–39, n. 272; compare Kiuchi, *The Purification Offering in the Priestly Literature*, 47; Hartley, *Leviticus*, 136; and Schwartz, "The Bearing of Sin in the Priestly Literature," 15–16.

10:18 אֶל־הַקֹּ֖דֶשׁ פְּנִ֑ימָה—This is literally "into the Holy Place inside."

אָכ֨וֹל תֹּאכְל֥וּ אֹתָ֛הּ בַּקֹּ֖דֶשׁ—This was prescribed for the sin offering for the inadvertent sin of the congregation.

כַּאֲשֶׁ֥ר צִוֵּֽיתִי׃—As in 8:31, the versions translate the verb as if it were the passive Pual, צֻוֵּיתִי, "I was commanded [by God]," instead of the active Piel, "I commanded." The Pual occurs in 8:35; 10:13.

10:19 הֵ֣ן—The particle הֵן can mean "suppose," "granted that," or "if." Here it is used to introduce the following three verbs as the basis for this conclusion: "the Lord would not have been pleased." The argument could be paraphrased as follows: "Even though my sons offered their sin offering and burnt offering before the Lord, the Lord killed them. Well, then, since that was the Lord's reaction to them, he would not have been pleased with me if I had eaten the meat from that sin offering whose atoning affect was annulled by their act of disobedience."

עֹלָתָם֙—See 9:2, 8–14.

הַיִּיטַ֖ב בְּעֵינֵ֥י יְהוָֽה׃—This is literally "Would it have been good in the eyes of the Lord?" (cf. 1 Ki 3:10). This is a negative assertion in the form of a rhetorical question.

10:20 וַיִּיטַ֖ב בְּעֵינָֽיו׃—This is literally "it was good in his [Moses'] eyes." This echoes the question in the previous verse (10:19) about the Lord's reaction. Moses' approval here implies that the Lord approved of their incineration of the offering instead of eating it.

Commentary

Structure

This chapter continues the narrative of the events on the day for the inauguration of the divine service (chapters 8–10). The unhappy events in 10:1–3 stand in stark contrast with the happy events in 9:23–24. The rest of the chapter deals with the practical and theological aftermath of the event. The pattern of instruction on the avoidance of desecration, followed by the report of compliance with that instruction, which begins in 10:3 and continues in 10:4–5 and 10:6–7, is interrupted by God's speech to Aaron in 10:8–11 and results in the break of the pattern of divine instruction followed by human compliance. That pattern is not followed in 10:12–20. The commands of Moses in 10:12–15 result in disputation rather than compliance in 10:16–20.

In this dispute Aaron acts on the divine commission received in 10:10–11 and teaches Moses about the correct application of the Lord's decrees, in the case of the sin offering, so that what was holy was properly distinguished from what was common in that case. Three other features are significant in this narrative. The report about the coming out of fire from the Lord's presence in 9:24 is repeated in 10:2. But in this case the fire "ate up" the two priests, rather than eating the offerings on the altar. The word "eat" (אָכַל) then becomes an important word in this chapter.[a] The other key word is "die" (מוּת). It appears four times in the first nine verses (10:2, 6, 7, 9). The same fire that brought blessing to the people in the previous episode (9:24) now brought death to two priests (10:2).

(a) Lev 10:2, 12, 13, 14, 17, 18, 19

The structure of this pericope can be outlined as follows:

I. The report of the death of Nadab and Abihu (10:1–5)
   A. The Lord's reaction to their unauthorized offering (10:1–3)
      1. The offering of incense with unauthorized fire (10:1)
      2. Their death by the holy fire from the Lord (10:2)
      3. Instruction by Moses to Aaron on respect for the Lord's holiness (10:3a)
      4. Compliance of Aaron with silence (10:3b)
   B. The arrangement of the burial of Nadab and Abihu by Moses (10:4–5)
      1. The summoning by Moses of Mishael and Elzaphan (10:4a)
      2. His directive to them about the removal of the corpses (10:4b)
      3. Their compliance (10:5)
II. The aftermath of the event (10:6–20)
   A. The instruction of the priests by Moses (10:6–7)
      1. His address to Aaron and his sons (10:6a)
      2. His speech (10:6b–7a)
         a. Prohibition of ritual mourning by the priests with the threat of death
         b. Permission for mourning by the Israelites
         c. Prohibition of the departure of the priests from the sanctuary for the funeral
      3. Their compliance (10:7b)
   B. The Lord's instruction to Aaron (10:8–11)
      1. His address to Aaron (10:8)
      2. His speech on the duties of the priests (10:9–11)
         a. Prohibition of alcoholic beverages during service (10:9)
         b. Commission of the priests as teachers of God's law (10:10–11)
   C. The instruction of the priests by Moses on their consumption of the holy food (10:12–20)
      1. His address to Aaron and his sons (10:12a)
      2. His speech (10:12b–15)
         a. The consumption of bread from the grain offering (10:12b–13)
         b. The consumption of meat from the peace offerings (10:14–15)
      3. His dispute with Aaron over meat from the priests' sin offering (10:16–20)
         a. Moses' anger at the incineration of the meat from their sin offering (10:16)
         b. His challenge to Aaron (10:17–18)
         c. The reply of Aaron (10:19)
         d. Moses' satisfaction (10:20)

Ritual Agents

In this chapter the priests are the focus of the narrative. It distinguishes the ordinary priests from Aaron and from two other pairs of priests, each of which were, in some way, representative of the Levitical priesthood.

The narrative begins with Nadab and Abihu, the two oldest of Aaron's sons, who were anointed together with him. They were killed by the Lord's fire for disobeying the Lord by offering up incense with "unauthorized fire" (10:1).

They therefore symbolize the priests who, to use the later rabbinical term, performed "unauthorized service" to the Lord. Even though they were legitimate priests, they exceeded their ritual authority by introducing an illegitimate ritual innovation. They failed to distinguish the common fire from holy fire.

In contrast with them, Aaron is portrayed as the faithful high priest. Because he, as high priest, entered the tent of meeting, he was subject to extraordinary taboos on mourning (10:6–7) and the consumption of alcohol (10:9). He faithfully obeyed the Lord who spoke to him through Moses (10:3, 7). In a remarkable affirmation of his status after the death of his two oldest sons, the Lord spoke to him directly, for the first and last time in Leviticus, to authorize him to interpret and apply the divine ritual statutes in accordance with the ritual-theological principles enunciated in 10:10. In this sphere he was directly accountable to God rather than to Moses. He therefore exercised that authority in the subsequent dispute with Moses on the priestly sin offering (10:16–19).

The role of Aaron as high priest is defined in comparison to the role of Moses, the other main actor in this episode. As the lawgiver, Moses instructed Aaron in divine law (10:3, 6–7, 12–15) and challenged him on its implementation (10:16–18). Yet at the same time, he deferred to Aaron in the interpretation and application of these ritual ordinances. He came to accept the authority of Aaron in this domain and to respect his judgment (10:20). Like all the Israelites, he was taught by Aaron on how to distinguish between the holy and the common, the clean and the unclean.

Eleazar and Ithamar, the two surviving sons of Aaron, had the same ritual status and responsibilities as Aaron. Like Aaron, and unlike all the other priests, they had their heads anointed (10:7). They could therefore enter the tent of meeting together with their father. They, remarkably, performed the same tasks as their father (10:9–11). They received the same food from the altar (10:12–15). They were therefore subject to the same ritual restrictions on mourning (10:6–7) and on the consumption of alcohol (10:8–9). Since they officiated with their father, he spoke for them and defended them (10:16–19). Moses therefore addressed them together with their father, for they represented the Aaronic priesthood (10:6, 12).

Mishael and Elzaphan are distinguished by Moses from Eleazar and Ithamar (10:4–5). They were cousins of Moses and Aaron (Ex 6:18, 22; 1 Chr 23:20). Since they were Levites, they had access to the courtyard of the sanctuary. But as Levites they were not subject to the same ritual restrictions as Aaron and his sons. They did not have access to the altar and could not enter the tent of meeting; their task was to care for the purity of the sanctuary (cf. Num 18:2–4, 6). Moses therefore commanded them to remove the corpses of Nadab and Abihu from the sanctuary.

The death of Nadab and Abihu provided the occasion for clarifying the basic responsibilities of the priests. Aaron and his sons put their lives on the line by doing guard duty at the sanctuary (8:35). Not only were they to respect the Lord's holiness (10:3), but they were also to teach the people to do so as well

(10:10–11). They were the custodians of the holy fire. That fire brought blessing to those who faithfully performed the divine service, but it also consumed the priests who did not distinguish it, and everything associated with it, from whatever was common and unclean.

Ritual Material and Objects

The action in this narrative had to do with fire as a powerful ritual element. It was related to three ritually significant materials: incense, flour, and meat. Unclean human corpses were not allowed to remain in the vicinity of the sacred fire, nor could alcohol be consumed by those who tended it.

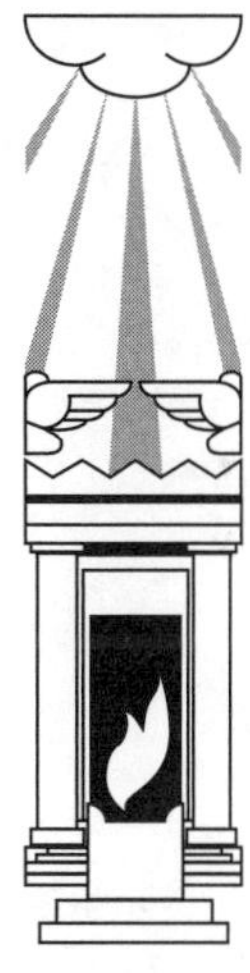

Nadab and Abihu failed to distinguish between the Lord's fire and "unauthorized fire" (10:1). The Lord's fire came from his presence and burnt up offerings on the altar (9:24). It was to be kept burning as a perpetual fire that never went out (6:2–6 [ET 6:9–13]). That fire turned the offerings into smoke (cf. 1:8, 12, 17; 3:5). Coals, set alight with it, were used for burning incense twice each day on the altar in the Holy Place (cf. 16:12–13). But, instead of using coals with holy fire from the altar, Nadab and Abihu offered "alien fire" (10:1; cf. Num 3:4; 26:61). Just as "alien incense" was unauthorized incense (Ex 30:9), so "alien fire" was unauthorized fire.

They therefore brought incense and censers with common fire taken from some other source than the altar for burnt offering. Exactly how they did so we are not told. But we do know that the fire was not taken from the altar of burnt offering. So, in a startling reversal, the same fire that had come from the Lord's presence to "consume" the sacrifices on the altar (9:24), came out of his presence to "consume" that unauthorized fire and those who had brought it (10:2). That holy fire was the effectual symbol, the powerful medium, of the Lord's holy presence in grace and in wrath. As it had formerly brought blessing and joy, it now dealt out death and grief. God appeared to his people as "a consuming fire" (see Ex 24:17; cf. Deut 5:22).

The fire came to "consume" the offerings. On the one hand, it consumed the incense. In all, three kinds of incense were customarily presented at the sanctuary: the most holy incense burnt by the high priest each day on the incense altar (Ex 30:1–10, 34–38; cf. 2 Chr 2:4; 13:11; 29:7); the frankincense offered up with the grain offerings (Lev 2:1–12, 15–16) and the showbread (24:7); and the unspecified incense burnt by the priests on censers, as in this case, in an act of supplication before the altar for the burnt offering (see Num 16:6, 17–18; Deut 33:10; Is 1:13). On the other hand, the most holy flour from the grain offering, the holy meat from the peace offerings, and the most holy meat from the people's sin offerings that the fire did not "consume," were to be consumed by the priests (Lev 10:12–18). All these derived their holiness from the holy fire. None was holy apart from that fire.

This narrative also defines the ritual status of alcoholic beverages. Even though wine and beer were poured out as libations to the Lord on the altar as part of the regular divine service (Num 15:5, 7, 10), the officiating priests were forbidden to drink them while on duty at the sanctuary (Lev 10:8–9). The power that came from these beverages was not divine but natural. Since it was not a holy substance, alcohol could not be used to induce holy intoxication and spiritual ecstasy, as may have happened in some Canaanite cults. It is mentioned here in this context because mourners customarily drank from "the cup of consolation" at funeral meals (see Jer 16:7). Service by a priest under the influence of alcohol was an act of sacrilege. It resulted in the penalty of death for those who flouted the divine prohibition of its consumption.

On this occasion Moses also defined the ritual status of corpses. The concern for their status is rather difficult for us to grasp, because we are largely unaware of the way they were regarded by animists and those who were influenced by animism. Since the spirits of the people were held to enter the divine realm after death, the bodies became spiritually powerful and sacrosanct for their kinsfolk after their death. Their physical remains were the point of contact between them and the living. Hence regular banquets and other rites were conducted at their graves, by which they were thought to be fed, and through which they were thought to share their supernatural powers with the living. From an animist point of view, it could be argued that the corpses of Nadab and Abihu were clearly holy. They were not just holy because they had died, but they were most holy because their corpses had been consecrated by their death from holy fire in that holy place as they were engaged in the service of God.

The ritual status of corpses was reversed by the Lord in his legislation for the divine service. They were not holy, but unclean. Contact with corpses was incompatible with service to the living God. Their impurity was primary and contagious. It was not derived from some other source, but it was, in itself, a source of impurity (Num 19:11–16). The corpses of Nadab and Abihu were therefore unclean, even though they had been touched with sacred fire. They had to be removed from the sanctuary and buried outside the camp, so that they did not pollute the camp or the sanctuary.

This story then affirms the ritual status of the altar fire that consecrated the incense of the priests, the bread from the grain offerings, and the meat from the reparation and peace offerings. They thereby ceased to be common and became holy. In contrast to these substances, neither corpses nor alcoholic beverages could be consecrated by contact with holy fire. Contact with corpses and the consumption of wine and beer were therefore forbidden to the priests.

Location

This narrative shows how dangerous it was to bring something alien into the sanctuary in the divine service. The events that it describes take place in the sanctuary at the altar for the burnt offering. There Nadab and Abihu presented "alien fire" before the Lord (10:1). There they were burnt to death (10:2). Their corpses were removed from that place in the sanctuary and buried outside the camp (10:4–5).

Two things were ritually misplaced in this incident. The fire that Nadab and Abihu used to burn their incense was common fire. It could not be used in the sanctuary. It had to be extinguished otherwise it would continue to desecrate the sanctuary. The corpses of Nadab and Abihu were also misplaced. Since they were unclean and transmitted impurity by contact with them, they threatened to defile the priests and desecrate the sanctuary. They were therefore removed by their tunics, without being touched, and buried in the cemetery outside the camp.

This gave rise to the legislation for the protection of the sanctity of the sanctuary and the holy things in it. Aaron and his sons could not observe any rites of mourning there. Such rites were out of place there (10:6). They could not leave "the entrance to the tent of meeting" to become involved with the funeral of Nadab and Abihu, because their place as anointed priests was within the sanctuary (10:7). Should they leave it for the funeral, they would desecrate their holiness and incur God's wrath. Since they entered the tent of meeting daily to conduct the divine service, they were not allowed to drink any alcoholic beverages while they were on duty. Those beverages were out of bounds as long as they were officiating at the sanctuary (10:9).

They also had to be careful where they ate which class of holy food. While the most holy bread from the grain offering and the most holy meat from the sin offering had to be eaten in the sanctuary (10:12–13, 17–18), the holy meat from the peace offering could be eaten by them together with their families in any clean place, such as in their homes (10:14). In all this, they had to distinguish what was most holy, such as the meat from a sin offering, from what is holy; what was holy, such as the meat from the peace offering, from what was common; and what was common, such as wine, from what was unclean, such as a corpse.

This meticulous care for the placement of things in their right location arose from the lethal peril of sacrilege, which involved the mislocation of something holy into the human domain and the mislocation of something common into the divine domain.

Ritual Enactment

The ritual context of this chapter was the inaugural performance of the divine service. Whereas the previous chapter had presented the model for the benefits of its right performance, 10:1–3 provides a stark example of the peril from its wrong performance.

The ritual catalyst for the events and the discussions in this chapter was the presentation by Nadab and Abihu of incense with unauthorized fire. The burning of incense was, in itself, a rather insignificant, marginal enactment. It was not, as far as we can gather, a regular part of the divinely instituted sacrificial ritual. In this case, the right persons performed a permissible rite at the right time and in the right place, but it was done in the wrong way. The incense was not burned with fire from the altar, but with ordinary fire. And Nadab and Abihu paid for that infringement with their lives. That act of disobedience is the archetype for all unauthorized ritual enactments.

The ritual blunder of Nadab and Abihu served as the basis for the instruction of the priests by God and Moses on the necessity to avoid two kinds of desecration. First, the observance of mourning rites by the priests, their departure from the sanctuary for the funeral of their kinsfolk, and the consumption of alcohol during their time of service were strictly forbidden at the pain of death. These three sets of prohibitions had to do with their involvement in mourning at the death of Nadab and Abihu. Like a shaved head (Deut 14:1), a disheveled head was the mark of mourning (cf. Lev 21:10). So too were torn clothes. Both seem to have been associated with pagan rites of mourning for the dead. The priests therefore could not leave the sanctuary to attend the funeral. They were not only forbidden to drink the "cup of consolation" (Jer 16:7) at the funeral, but were forbidden to drink any wine or beer at any time during their period of service. In this way, the regular service at the sanctuary was totally dissociated from funerary rites and all the other rites for the veneration of ancestral spirits.

Second, Moses instructed Aaron and his sons on how to avoid desecrating the holy food from the Lord's altar (10:12–18). The first two cases presented no difficulties. While the priests ate the bread from the grain offering in the sanctuary, the priestly portion of the meat from the peace offering could be eaten by the whole family of the officiating priest in a ritually clean place. The third case of the people's sin offering, however, was a borderline case. If the strict letter of the law was to be observed, Aaron and his sons should have eaten its meat in the sanctuary. But they burned it instead as if it were the meat from an animal whose blood had been brought into the Holy Place (6:23 [ET 6:30]). The reason for this ritual anomaly lay in the death of Nadab and Abihu and its ritual implications for them.

The argument of Aaron in 10:19 ran as follows. Even though he had offered a burnt offering and sin offering to cleanse and safeguard himself and his sons in their work of service, Nadab and Abihu had desecrated the Lord's holiness and had been put to death by God. The ritual status of Aaron and his sons was therefore uncertain. Were they implicated with the two dead sons in this act of sacrilege? Were Aaron and his other two sons also defiled by this act of sacrilege, or even by their corpses? Was God perhaps displeased with them too? Was it right for them to feast on meat from the sin offering on that day if they themselves were guilty of sacrilege?

In these circumstances, it was better to err on the side of caution rather than that of presumption, even if it meant the letter of the law was not observed. God would be more pleased with those who were too scrupulous to claim a divine due than with those who were disrespectful of his holiness, as Nadab and Abihu had been.[7]

This chapter then uses the death of Nadab and Abihu to warn the priests of desecration in their performance of the sacrificial ritual. The performance of

[7] Wenham, *Leviticus*, 160.

any forbidden or even unauthorized ritual was an act of sacrilege that endangered the lives of the priests who desecrated God's holiness.

Ritual Theological Function

The appearance of the Lord to his people at the climax of the regular service was ambiguous and equivocal. His glory was revealed as a fire that "consumed" the offerings of the congregation (9:24) as well as Nadab and Abihu (10:1). While it brought blessing to the people, it too dealt out death to these two priests. It could result in communal weeping (10:6) as well as communal jubilation (9:24).

Since the holy God was a consuming fire (Ex 24:17), his presence was potentially lethal. All the material in this chapter develops the ritual, theological ramifications of that threat as is shown by the recurring reference to the danger of death from the desecration of God's holiness by the priests (Lev 10:2, 6, 7, 9).

The effect of God's holy presence was not indiscriminate. On the one hand, he appeared in grace to the congregation and blessed the people as they stood in his presence. They were completely protected from the threat of death by the rites of atonement. They therefore received nothing but blessing from God in the divine service. On the other hand, God appeared in wrath to those priests who desecrated his holiness. Thus, just as he extended his grace to the priests, his wrath also fell on the priests. They stood as a buffer between God and his people. They protected the people from the threat of God's holiness. They bore the iniquity of the congregation (10:17). They removed that iniquity by performing the rite of atonement for them (cf. 9:7). By their obedience to the Lord and their observance of his prohibitions (10:6–9), they protected the congregation from God's wrath at their iniquity. If they desecrated the holy things of God, they alone lost their lives. But the people would be spared.

The priests bore the iniquity of the people. The significance of this is explored in connection with another act of sacrilege, the rebellion of Korah and his associates in Numbers 16–18. That event led the congregation to complain to Moses (Num 17:27–28 [ET 17:12–13]): "We are perishing; we are lost; all of us are lost! Everyone who approaches the tabernacle of the Lord will die. Are we all to perish?" The sin of sacrilege was so dangerous that the Israelites decided to avoid contact with God. He therefore acted to allay their fears and to shield them from the dire consequences of desecration whenever they approached the tabernacle. The priests insulated the people from God's wrath. They were made accountable for the holiness of God and the purity of the people. They were to prevent the people from desecrating the holy things by performing the rites of atonement; they too bore the brunt of God's wrath for any act of desecration. If the people desecrated the most holy things of God, the priests would have to die instead of the people, just as Nadab and Abihu had died.

Thus God set up a chain of accountability. The Levites "bore the iniquity" of the people (Num 18:23). The Aaronic priests "bore the iniquity" of the whole priesthood (Num 18:1). The high priest "bore the iniquity" from any act of sacrilege that was committed in the divine service (Ex 28:38). Then, on the Day of Atonement, a day that God had instituted as a result of the death of Nadab and Abihu (Lev 16:1), the scapegoat "bore all the iniquities" of the priests and the people, so that they would not have to die if they desecrated God's holiness with their impurity (16:21–22).[8]

Moses explained the theological significance of both divine manifestations by quoting the Lord's Word:

> When I am treated as holy by those who are near to me,
> I appear in glory in the sight of all the people.

This little couplet explains the connection between God's holiness and his glory. It also links the people's experience of God's glory with the faithfulness of the priests.

Since the Lord was holy and the source of all holiness, he had to be regarded and treated as holy by his priests. They respected his holiness by performing the divine service as he had commanded, by observing the divine prohibitions for them in their service, and by treating the holy offerings appropriately. If the priests failed to respect God's holiness, he would show his holiness by his judgment of them for the desecration of his holiness (cf. Num. 20:12–13). If they treated him as holy, he would appear in his glory to the whole congregation and bless the people as he had at the culmination of the inaugural service. So, the manner in which the priests performed the sacred ritual determined whether the Lord's glory would be manifest in grace or in wrath to the congregation.

The awesome responsibility of the priests is clarified by the remarkable Word of the Lord to Aaron in 10:8–11. This unique divine speech is the charter of the priesthood in Israel. After the Lord had forbidden the consumption of alcoholic beverages, he gave a two-part commission to Aaron and his descendants.

First, he charged them to distinguish what was holy from all that was unholy in their performance of the sacrificial ritual. This decree was not given to them as a foundational principle for the construction of a theological system, but as practical ritual-theological criteria for the right operation and development of the divine service. Everything holy was in some way connected with God's presence in the divine service. It had to be distinguished ritually from what was common and available for human use, as well as from what was unclean and incompatible with God's holiness. This was not done in an abstract, theoretical way. It was done quite practically by diagnosing impurity and performing the proper rites for purification, by performing the proper rites for the sanctification of those people and things that God had chosen, and by keeping what was holy apart from whatever desecrated and defiled it. The priests were required to perform the sacred ritual in such a way that they safeguarded God's

---

[8] Compare Kiuchi, *The Purification Offering in the Priestly Literature*, 77–85.

holiness and protected the people from the dire consequences of desecration. The divine service was to be conducted in accordance with the ritual-theological criteria given in 10:10.

Second, the Lord authorized Aaron and his sons to teach his ritual decrees to the people. Unlike pagan religions whose priests kept the knowledge of their esoteric rituals hidden from the common people, the Lord's priests were to share their ritual knowledge with the people of God. It was common knowledge. They were to catechize them by teaching them all the Lord's decrees to Moses, by showing them how they were to be ritually observed, and by explaining their significance. If we want to get some idea of how this was done, we need go no further than to study the book of Leviticus. It was addressed primarily to the Israelites (1:2; 26:46; 27:34). Lev 1:1–8:36 and 19:1–27:34 teaches them to distinguish what was holy from what was common. Leviticus 11–18 instructs them on how to distinguish what was clean from what was unclean. This was most important, for the Lord had instituted the divine service for their benefit. They therefore had a vested interest in its proper operation.

This great charter that the Lord gave to Aaron in 10:8–11 is therefore the key to origin and purpose of Leviticus. It not only teaches the priests how to conduct the sacred ritual in a sacred way, but it also catechizes the people liturgically, so that they would benefit from God's interaction with them in the divine service.

Fulfillment by Christ

The presence of the living God may have one of two effects upon people, for God is either present in grace to the righteous or present in wrath to the unrighteous. That is so in the church just as it was in ancient Israel. Those who believe in Christ have eternal life from him; those who reject him remain under God's wrath (Jn 3:36). The messengers of the Gospel bring justification and life as well as condemnation and death to their hearers (2 Cor 2:14–16). Those who desecrate the body and blood of Christ in Holy Communion come under God's judgment (1 Cor 11:27–32). They do not receive strength, health and life; instead they suffer the same kinds of penalties for desecration as did the Israelites—infirmity, sickness, and death (1 Cor 11:30). The letter to the Hebrews therefore warns its readers about the dreadful consequences of desecration (Heb 6:4–6; 10:26–31).

When the people of God assemble for the Divine Service, they come into the heavenly realm, heavenly Jerusalem, the holy city of God. There they approach God, who is the Judge of all (Heb 12:23)—the God who justifies sinners but condemns unbelievers for their unbelief. Since the living God is a consuming fire that devours all that is unclean and ungodly, his people, as beneficiaries of his grace, should serve him acceptably with reverence and awe (Heb 12:28–29). Thus involvement in the Divine Service is a matter of life or death, life for the righteous who seek cleansing, and death for the unrighteous who refuse to repent.

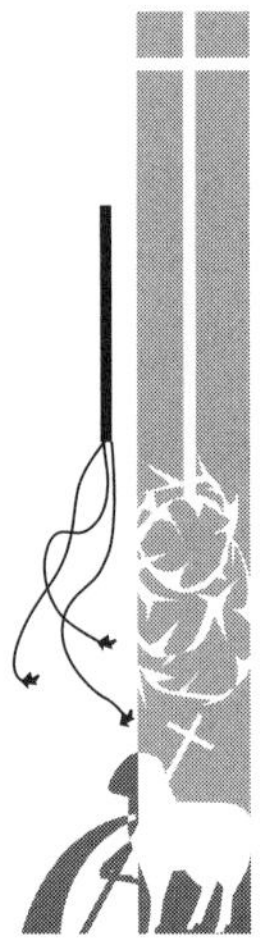

The possibility of desecration is even greater in the new covenant than in ancient Israel, since God became a man and lived among sinful men. Yet God has undone the devastation of desecration in an even more remarkable way. He himself bore the brunt of sacrilege and provided the divine remedy for it. He did not require any group of human beings or even a scapegoat to bear the iniquity of the people who came into his presence with their impurity; he appointed his Son as their great High Priest.

As Isaiah had prophesied (Is 52:13–53:12), Jesus bore the sins of the people with his own body so that they could be free from sin and live by his justification of them (Jn 1:29; Heb 9:28; 1 Pet 2:24; 1 Jn 3:5). As their priest he bore their sins; as their sacrifice he provided the blood for their atonement. Like the blood of the Passover lamb (Heb 11:28), his blood protects them from God's wrath against their impurity and the desecration of his holiness by their impurity. They, therefore, can approach God the Father without any fear of condemnation and death (Rom 5:1–2; 8:1), for Christ has "removed" their sin by his death on their behalf (Heb 9:26; cf. 10:4).

Unlike Aaron and his sons, the ministers of the Word, who preside at the Lord's Table, do not bear the iniquity of the people whom they serve. They are nevertheless required to be faithful stewards of God's holy mysteries (1 Cor 4:1–5). They should not be drunkards (1 Tim 3:3; 2 Tim 4:5). They must take care that they do not desecrate the holy things of God by offering them carelessly to unbelievers (Mt 7:6). Like the priests in the OT, they are called to teach the saints to distinguish what is holy from what is common and unclean (Mk 7:17–23; Acts 10:1–29; 11:1–18). They are authorized to admit forgiven sinners to the Lord's Table and to exclude those who are impenitent and unclean (Jn 20:23; 1 Cor 6:9–11; Rev 22:14–15).

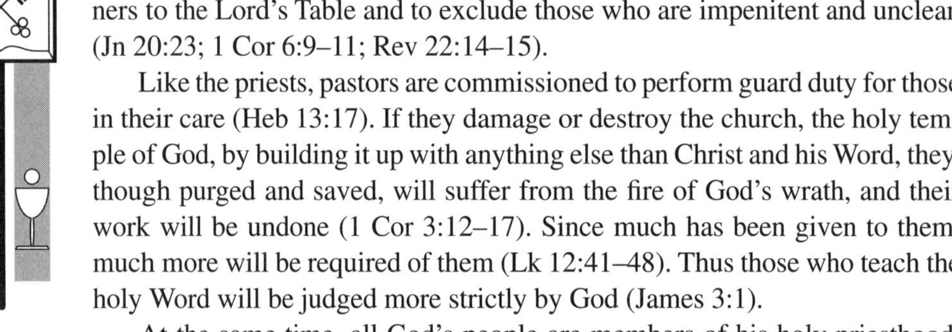

Like the priests, pastors are commissioned to perform guard duty for those in their care (Heb 13:17). If they damage or destroy the church, the holy temple of God, by building it up with anything else than Christ and his Word, they, though purged and saved, will suffer from the fire of God's wrath, and their work will be undone (1 Cor 3:12–17). Since much has been given to them, much more will be required of them (Lk 12:41–48). Thus those who teach the holy Word will be judged more strictly by God (James 3:1).

At the same time, all God's people are members of his holy priesthood. They must all treat him as holy and hallow his name (Mt 6:9; 1 Pet 3:15). They are all called to pursue God's holiness (Heb 12:14) and avoid pollution by the sinful world (James 1:21). They are all expected to be sober people who avoid drunkenness (Eph 5:18; 1 Thess 5:6, 8; 1 Pet 1:13; 4:7; 5:8). They are all called to serve God acceptably as he himself has commanded (Heb 12:28). As holy people they are all corporately accountable to God the Father (1 Pet 1:16–17; 4:17–18).

The Law of God is good and wise
And sets his will before our eyes,
Shows us the way of righteousness,
And dooms to death when we transgress.

Its light of holiness imparts
The knowledge of our sinful hearts
That we may see our lost estate
And seek escape before too late.

To Jesus we for refuge flee,
Who from the curse has set us free,
And humbly worship at his throne,
Saved by his grace through faith alone.[9]

[9] From "The Law of God Is Good and Wise" by Matthias Loy (*LW* 329:1, 2, 6).

Leviticus 11–15

The Manual for Purity

The flow of narrative from Leviticus 8–10 to Leviticus 16 is interrupted by the manual for purity. It consists of six speeches, four addressed to Moses and Aaron (11:1; 13:1; 14:33; 15:1) and two to Moses (12:1; 14:1). The content of three speeches was to be passed on to the Israelites because they dealt with matters of concern for them and their purity as God's holy people (11:2; 12:2; 15:2). Each speech gives ritual instruction to the priests and the Israelites on how to distinguish what was unclean from what was clean (10:10–11). Each speech ends with a summary formula about the content of the ritual instruction that was given in it.[a] The purpose of this manual is stated as the conclusion of the last speech in 15:31. The priests and the people were to make sure that they did not defile the tabernacle with their impurity, or else they, like Nadab and Abihu, would die in their impurity. These chapters prepare for the institution of the comprehensive ritual of cleansing on the Day of Atonement in Leviticus 16, in which the sanctuary was cleansed from the accumulated impurity of the Israelites. This annual rite of atonement was meant to prevent the recurrence of what had happened to Nadab and Abihu.

(a) Lev 11:46–47; 12:7b; 13:59; 14:32, 54–57; 15:32–33

Leviticus 11:1–47

Instruction on Clean and Unclean Meat

Translation

11 [1]The Lord spoke to Moses and Aaron and said to them: [2]"Speak to the Israelites: These are the creatures that you may eat. Of all the quadrupeds on the land, [3]you may eat any quadruped that has hoofs, with splits between the hoofs, and that brings up the cud. [4]But you shall not eat the following of those that only bring up the cud or have hoofs: the camel, for although it brings up the cud, it has no hoofs: it is unclean for you; [5]and the rock badger, for although it brings up the cud, it has no hoofs: it is unclean for you; [6]and the hare, for although it brings up the cud, it has no hoofs: it is unclean for you; [7]and the pig, for although it has hoofs, with splits between the split hoofs, it does not regurgitate the cud: it is unclean to you. [8]You shall not eat any of their meat or touch their carcasses: they are unclean for you.

[9]"These are [the creatures] that you may eat from all that live in water: you may eat anything in water, whether in the seas or in the streams, that has fins and scales. [10]But as for everything, in the seas or in the streams, that does not have fins and scales, every swarming creature in the water and every [other] living creature in the water: they are detestable to you [11]and shall remain detestable to you. You shall not eat any of their meat, and you shall detest their carcasses. [12]Every [creature] in the water that does not have fins or scales is detestable to you.

[13]"You shall detest the following among the birds; they shall not be eaten; they are detestable: the eagle, the black vulture, the bearded vulture, [14]the kite, and all species of falcons; [15]all species of ravens; [16]the eagle owl, the short-eared owl, the long-eared owl; all species of hawks; [17]the tawny owl, the fisher owl, the screech owl, [18]the white owl, and the scops owl; the osprey, [19]the stork, and all species of herons; the hoopoe and the bat.

[20]"As for all winged swarming insects that walk on all fours: they are detestable for you. [21]But among all the winged swarming insects that walk on all fours you may eat those that have their jointed legs above their feet, with which to leap on the ground. [22]You may eat the following of them: all species of locusts; all species of bald locusts; all species of crickets; and all species of grasshoppers. [23]But as for all other winged swarming insects that have four feet: they are detestable for you.

[24]"By these you will make yourselves unclean; whoever touches their carcass will remain unclean until sunset, [25]and whoever carries any part of their carcass shall launder his clothes and remain unclean until sunset: [26]all quadrupeds that have hoofs without splits between the hoofs or that do not chew the cud are unclean for you; whoever touches them will become unclean; [27]all animals that go on all fours and walk on their paws are unclean for you; whoever touches their

carcass will remain unclean until sunset, 28and whoever carries their carcass shall launder his clothes and remain unclean until sunset. They are unclean for you.

29"These are the most unclean for you of the creatures that swarm on the land: the rat, the mouse, and all species of large lizards; 30the gecko, the spotted lizard, the lizard, the skink, and the chameleon. 31These are the most unclean for you of the creatures that swarm. Whoever touches them when they are dead will remain unclean until sunset. 32Any article, made of wood or fabric or leather or sackcloth, on which one of them falls when they are dead will become unclean; any article that is used for any task shall be put in water and remain unclean until sunset; then it will be clean. 33You shall smash any clay pot into which any of them falls; everything in it will become unclean; 34if any water from it comes upon any food that could be eaten, it will become unclean, and if any drink that could be drunk is in any such clay pot, it will become unclean. 35Anything else on which the carcass of any of them falls will become unclean; an oven or stove shall be broken up; they are unclean and shall remain unclean for you. 36But a spring or a cistern with a reservoir of water will remain clean, even though anyone who touches their carcass will become unclean; 37if any part of their carcass falls upon any seed grain that is about to be sown, it is clean, 38but if water has been added to the seed and part of their carcass falls on it, it shall become unclean for you.

39"If a quadruped that you may eat has died, anyone who touches its carcass will remain unclean until sunset; 40anyone who eats any part of its carcass shall launder his clothes and remain unclean until sunset; anyone who carries its carcass shall launder his clothes and remain unclean until sunset.

41"As for any swarming creature that swarms on the land: it is detestable; it shall not be eaten. 42You shall not eat any swarming creature that swarms on the land, from anything that goes on its belly and anything that goes on all fours, to anything that has many legs, for they are detestable. 43You shall not disgust your throats with any creature that swarms, nor shall you pollute yourselves with them, so that you become polluted by them, 44for I am the Lord your God. Sanctify yourselves, therefore, so that you may be holy, for I am holy; you shall not make your throats unclean with any swarming creature that crawls on the land, 45for I am the Lord who brought you up from the land of Egypt to be your God. You therefore shall be holy, for I am holy."

46This is the ritual instruction concerning quadrupeds, flying creatures, all living creatures that move in the water, and all creatures that swarm on the land, 47for distinguishing between what is unclean and what is clean, as well as between creatures that may be eaten and creatures that may not be eaten.

Textual Notes

11:1 וַיְדַבֵּר יְהוָה אֶל־מֹשֶׁה וְאֶל־אַהֲרֹן לֵאמֹר—This clause is repeated in 13:1; 14:33; 15:1, where the Lord again speaks to both Moses and Aaron.

11:2 זֹאת הַחַיָּה אֲשֶׁר תֹּאכְלוּ—This heading serves a double function. It introduces

11:2c–3 and is a heading for the whole of 11:2c–23.[1] Here חַיָּה is used as a generic term for all living creatures. It is used more narrowly in 11:27 for all wild quadrupeds (cf. 5:2; 17:13). A similar list of clean and unclean animals is found in Deut 14:3–20. See Hartley for a concise analysis of the differences between these two lists.[2]

הַבְּהֵמָה—While some other passages use בְּהֵמָה more narrowly for a domesticated quadruped (e.g., 1:2; 7:24–26), this chapter uses this term more broadly for any quadruped.

11:3 מַפְרֶסֶת פַּרְסָה—Literally this phrase refers to an animal "that hoofs a hoof." See Deut 14:6.

וְשֹׁסַעַת שֶׁסַע פְּרָסֹת—This is literally "that splits a split of hoofs."

תֹּאכֵלוּ׃—This verb, which is repeated from 11:2, comes last in 11:3 as an inclusion for emphasis. A list of edible game animals, as found in Deut 14:4–5, is not included here, even though they may be eaten (Lev 17:13).

11:4 אַךְ אֶת־זֶה לֹא תֹאכְלוּ—As in 11:21, אַךְ אֶת־זֶה gives the exceptions to a rule.

וּמִמַּפְרִיסֵי הַפַּרְסָה—The LXX adds "with split hoofs," as in 11:3 and Deut 14:7.

הַגָּמָל—A camel has a sole of hardened skin with two toes, but does not have a hoof.

טָמֵא הוּא לָכֶם׃—The declarative formula "it is unclean/ they are unclean" was used by the priests to identify what was permanently unclean and unable to be cleansed by human actions. Examples include the meat of certain animals (11:4, 5, 6, 7, 8), the carcasses of all animals (11:8, 26, 27, 28), carcass-infected objects (11:35) and seed grain (11:38), scaly skin disease (13:11, 15, 36, 44, 46), fungus-infected fabrics (13:51, 55), mold-infected houses (14:44), and the irregular genital discharge from a man (15:2). But this declarative formula was never used to classify a person as unclean; the formula for that was given in 5:2. The formula here recurs in 11:5, 6, 7, 8, 26, 27, 28, 29, 31, 35, 38, 47.

11:7 יִגָּר—The verb גָּרַר refers to the dragging up of the cud from the stomach to the mouth.

11:8 לֹא תֹאכֵלוּ—This forms an inclusion with 11:4a.

וּבְנִבְלָתָם—The term נְבֵלָה, "carcass," is used in this chapter to refer to the remains of an animal that has died a natural death—the only case in which God forbids contact with their carcasses. If they died, the Israelites were therefore forbidden to dispose of their carcasses.

11:9 בַּיַּמִּים—In addition to "seas," this includes any lake or marsh.

11:10 מִכֹּל שֶׁרֶץ הַמַּיִם וּמִכֹּל נֶפֶשׁ הַחַיָּה אֲשֶׁר בַּמָּיִם—The repetition of מִכֹּל in these two phrases operates inclusively and so specifies what is included by the first word of the verse, וְכֹל, "and everything."

שֶׁרֶץ—The term שֶׁרֶץ comes from verbal root (שָׁרַץ) that means to "teem, crawl, swarm." It is collective noun for small animals such as fish that swim in shoals, insects that move in swarms, and small creatures that crawl about in the sea or on the ground. In Leviticus it was used in 5:2 and recurs in 11:20, 21, 23, 29, 31, 41, 42, 43, 44; 22:5.

---

1 Houston, *Purity and Monotheism*, 33.

2 Hartley, *Leviticus*, 155–56.

נֶפֶשׁ הַחַיָּה—See this phrase in Gen 1:30.

שֶׁקֶץ הֵם לָכֶם׃—The declarative formula "it is/they are a detestable thing to you" was used by the priests to identify those animals that the Israelites had to shun for ritual reasons. This formula recurs in 11:12, 20, 23. See the textual note on שֶׁקֶץ in 7:21.

11:11 תְּשַׁקֵּצוּ׃—The Piel of שָׁקַץ means both "to detest" (11:11, 13) and "to make detestable" (11:43; 20:25).

11:13–19 Lev 11:13–19 names twenty unclean birds (counting the bat, which comes last). See figure 14 below. The identification of many of these birds is uncertain. The list in Deut 14:12–18 includes twenty-one unclean birds, most of which are the same as in Lev 1:13–19. The one that is included in Deut 14:12–18 but is absent from Leviticus is דַּיָּה in Deut 14:13. (Some English translations, such as RSV and ESV, omit a rendition of דַּיָּה in Deut 14:13 and so reduce the number in the list in Deut 14:12–18 to twenty.) One of the birds probably is the same but is spelled differently (perhaps due to a scribal error in Deut 14:13): where Lev 11:14 has דָּאָה, Deut 14:13 has רָאָה. One of the birds is in a different location in the two lists: Deut 14:12–18 places שָׁלָךְ (Deut 14:17) in the seventeenth position, whereas שָׁלָךְ (Lev 11:17) is twelfth in Lev 11:13–19.

The following classes of birds could be eaten: doves and pigeons (columbiformes), geese and ducks (anserines), hens and quails (galliformes), and sparrows (fringillides or passerines). But the list here specifies which could not be eaten.

וְאֶת־אֵלֶּה תְּשַׁקְּצוּ מִן־הָעוֹף—This first part of the verse could also be taken as a heading for the whole of 11:13–23. It would then be translated "These you shall detest: of the birds …"

הַנֶּשֶׁר—This "eagle" is the bald-headed (Micah 1:16) griffon vulture that lives in the desert (Deut 32:10–11) and feeds on carrion (Prov 30:17; Job 9:26). See also Deut 28:49; Jer 48:40; 49:22.

הַפֶּרֶס—This term, rendered as the "black vulture," might instead be the "bearded vulture" or "lamb vulture."

הָעָזְנִיָּה׃—This, rendered "bearded vulture," might instead be the "black vulture."

11:14 הָאַיָּה—This is a generic term for all members of the falcon family.

11:15 עֹרֵב—This is a generic term for ravens and crows (Gen 8:7; 1 Ki 17:4; Ps 147:9; Prov 30:17).

11:16 בַּת הַיַּעֲנָה—Literally "the daughter of the desert," we translate this as "the eagle owl." It occurs also in Is 13:21; 34:13; 43:20; Jer 50:39; Micah 1:8; Job 30:29. The traditional rendering of it by "ostrich" (LXX) does not fit the context here and elsewhere, since ostriches do not haunt ruins.

הַתַּחְמָס—This ("short-eared owl") might instead be the "barn owl," "screech owl," or "night owl."

הַשָּׁחַף—For the "long-eared owl," the LXX has "sea gull," which would place it among the water birds in 11:18–19.

הַנֵּץ—This ("hawks") is a generic term for all the smaller members of accipiters. Here it precedes the list of smaller owls in 11:17–18. The larger accipiters were listed as the first four birds in Lev 11:13–14.

11:17 הַכּוֹס—See Ps 102:7 (ET 102:6).

הַשָּׁלָךְ—This ("fisher owl") might instead be the "cormorant" or "pelican." But since the שָׁלָךְ is placed with the stork and heron in Deut 14:17, it most likely is a water bird of the owl family.

הַיַּנְשׁוּף׃—See Is 34:11.

11:18 הַתִּנְשֶׁמֶת—This ("white owl") might instead be the "barn owl." A homograph, תִּנְשֶׁמֶת, denotes the "chameleon" in 11:30.

הַקָּאָת—This ("scops owl") might be the "horned owl." See Is 34:11; Zeph 2:14; Ps 102:7 (ET 102:6).

הָרָחָם׃—This water bird ("osprey") might instead be the "Egyptian vulture."

11:19 הַחֲסִידָה—This ("stork") is a migratory, fresh-water bird. See Job 39:13; Jer 8:7; Zech 5:9; Ps 104:17.

הָאֲנָפָה—This is a generic term for any kind of "heron."

הַדּוּכִיפַת—The "hoopoe" is a large crested bird that feeds on insects and worms found in manure heaps and secretes a foul odor to protect its messy nest. It was revered as sacred by the Egyptians.

הָעֲטַלֵּף׃—See Is 2:20. Even though bats are flying rodents, they are listed here because they fly.

11:20 If 11:13a is taken as the heading for 11:13–23, the translation of this verse would be "As for every winged swarming insect … it is something detestable for you."

כֹּל שֶׁרֶץ הָעוֹף—This is literally "every swarmer of the flying kind."

הַהֹלֵךְ עַל־אַרְבַּע שֶׁקֶץ הוּא לָכֶם׃—Deut 14:19 omits "walk on all fours," which then more closely associates the unclean insects with the unclean birds.

11:21 אַךְ אֶת־זֶה תֹּאכְלוּ—As in 11:4, אַךְ אֶת־זֶה gives an exception to the rule. In contrast to the preceding unclean animals, the following insects can be eaten. Cf. Deut 14:20.

לֹא [לוֹ]—The Qere is לוֹ, "belonging to it," which is the reading required by the context. The Kethib is לֹא, "not."

11:22 הָאַרְבֶּה—Aedipoda migratoria.

הַסָּלְעָם—Acrydum peregrinum.

הַחַרְגֹּל—Aedipoda cristata.

הֶחָגָב—See Num 13:33; Is 40:22; 2 Chr 7:13; Eccl 12:5.

11:24–25 These verses are a summary for 11:26–28.

11:24 וּלְאֵלֶּה תִּטַּמָּאוּ—The term "these" does not refer to the animals in the previous verses but obviously anticipates the two cases in 11:26–28.[3] This sentence is also the heading for the whole of 11:24–43. תִּטַּמָּאוּ is the Hithpael of טָמֵא, meaning to "defile oneself" (*HALOT*). The Hithpael recurs in 11:43; 18:24, 30; 21:1, 3, 4, 11. People pollute themselves by eating unclean meat or by touching something unclean. In the form תִּטַּמָּאוּ, the ת that normally would be part of the Hithpael conjugation (תִּתְטַמְּאוּ) has been assimilated, hence the *daghesh* in the *tet* (-טּ-).

כָּל־הַנֹּגֵעַ … יִטְמָא—This formula for defilement by direct contact with something unclean is the opposite of the formula for contagious sanctification (see 6:11 [ET 6:18]

3 Wenham, *Leviticus*, 177.

and the textual notes on that verse). A similar formula first occurred in 5:2, and in this chapter variations recur in 11:25, 26, 27, 28, 31, 32, 33, 34, 35, 36, 39, 40.

עַד־הָעָֽרֶב׃—"Until the evening" recurs in 11:25, 27, 28, 31, 32, 39, 40; 14:46; 15:5, 6, 7, 8, 10, 11, 16, 17, 18, 19, 21, 22, 23, 27; 17:15; 22:6. This formula implies that the unclean people must take a bath before they become clean again,[4] as shown by the comparison of 11:39 with 17:15 and 22:6.

11:25 וְכָל־הַנֹּשֵׂא מִנִּבְלָתָם יְכַבֵּס בְּגָדָיו—The people need to wash their clothes because they have been touched by the carcass. Washing (11:28, 40; 13:6, 34, 35, 54, 55, 58; 14:8, 9, 47; 15:5, 6, 7, 8, 10, 11, 13, 21, 22, 27; 16:26, 28; 17:15, 16) was done by treading, kneading, and beating the clothes.

11:26 לְכָל־הַבְּהֵמָה אֲשֶׁר הִוא מַפְרֶסֶת פַּרְסָה וְשֶׁסַע ׀ אֵינֶנָּה שֹׁסַעַת— This refers to quadrupeds such as a horse or donkey or mule. The preposition *lamed* at the beginning of this verse can be construed a *lamed* of specification, specifying what the preceding two verses are about. We render the *lamed* by a colon (:). See לְכָל־ also in 5:3, 4; 11:42, 46; 16:16; 22:5.

וְגֵרָה אֵינֶנָּה מַעֲלָה—An example would be the pig.

כָּל־הַנֹּגֵעַ בָּהֶם—Touching "them" means touching their carcasses.

11:28 טְמֵאִים הֵמָּה לָכֶם׃—This serves as a summary for all of 11:24–28.

11:29 וְזֶה לָכֶם הַטָּמֵא בַּשֶּׁרֶץ—We translate this as "These are the *most* unclean for you of the creatures that swarm on the land" because the use of the definite article with an adjective (הַטָּמֵא), followed by בְּ with a noun (בַּשֶּׁרֶץ), can indicate the superlative degree.

הַשֹּׁרֵץ עַל־הָאָרֶץ—This is added to distinguish these land-swarmers from the water-swarmers (11:10) and air-swarmers (11:20, 23). See figure 15 below.

הַחֹלֶד—Probably this means "rat," but it could be the "weasel" (LXX) or "mole."

וְהַצָּב—Probably this denotes any "large lizard," but the LXX renders it "crocodile."

11:30 וְהָאֲנָקָה—This probably means "gecko," but the LXX has "ferret."

וְהַכֹּחַ—Probably this is the "spotted lizard," but LXX has "chameleon."

וְהַלְּטָאָה—We simply render this as "lizard," while the LXX has "newt."

וְהַחֹמֶט—This may be the "skink" or perhaps "salamander."

וְהַתִּנְשָֽׁמֶת׃—*HALOT* has a long discussion of תִּנְשֶׁמֶת (in pause, תִּנְשָׁמֶת), which concludes that it probably denotes the "chameleon" but might perhaps denote a kind of "owl," which would agree with the LXX.

11:31 אֵלֶּה הַטְּמֵאִים לָכֶם בְּכָל־הַשָּׁרֶץ—This forms an inclusion with 11:29a.

11:32 כְּלִי—This general term for an "article"—a vessel, clothing, and so on—provides the name for the tractate in the Mishnah that is called *Kelim,* which codifies the elaborate system of purity in Judaism that was based on 11:32–38.

מְלָאכָה—This has most likely been added to distinguish these objects that are used for the storage of food and drink from the following objects that are used for cooking.

---

[4] Milgrom, *Leviticus 1–16*, 667.

וְטָהֵר׃—This is the stative verb טָהֵר, "to be clean." See figure 1, "Holy versus Common and Clean versus Unclean," in the introduction and also the textual note and commentary on the adjective טָהוֹר, "clean," in 7:19. In Leviticus the Qal of טָהֵר is used to indicate that an unclean thing (11:32; 13:58; 14:53) or an unclean person (12:7, 8; 13:6, 34; 14:8, 9, 20; 15:13, 28; 16:30; 17:15; 22:4, 7) had become "ritually clean." These became clean by undergoing the prescribed process for purification, whether it be by washing for a minor impurity (11:32; 13:6; 14:8) or by the rite of atonement for a major impurity (12:7, 8; 14:20, 53; 16:30). While the Piel of the verb טָהֵר describes the process of purification (14:11; 16:19, 30), as well the declaration of its completion by the priests (13:6, 13, 17, 23, 28, 34, 37, 59; 14:7, 48), the Hithpael is used for those who undergo ritual purification (14:4, 7, 8, 11, 14, 17, 18, 19, 25, 28, 29, 31). Those who had become ritually clean (14:9) could eat common food with their families and enter the sanctuary (12:4) to eat the sacred food there (7:19; 22:4, 7).

11:36 אַךְ—See the textual notes on 11:4.

מִקְוֵה־מַיִם—The Hebrew refers to two sources of water: (1) a spring and (2) a cistern that is or has a reservoir of water. The LXX adds "and" to "reservoir" and so treats "a reservoir of water" as a third and separate source of water.

טָהוֹר—This adjective, "clean," recurs in 11:37, 47. See the textual note on it in 7:19 and the textual note above on the verb טָהֵר in 11:32.

וְנֹגֵעַ—This can mean "anyone" or "anything that touches."

11:37 טָהוֹר הוּא׃—The formula "it/he is clean" was used by the priests to pronounce something clean that had been threatened with impurity (11:37) or to declare someone clean who had previously been unclean (13:13, 17, 37, 39, 40, 41).

11:39–45 Although these verses fit more naturally after 11:28, the mention of eating in 11:40 builds a bridge to the discussion on eating meat from swarming land animals in 11:41–45.

וְכִי יָמוּת מִן־הַבְּהֵמָה אֲשֶׁר־הִיא לָכֶם לְאָכְלָה—This functions as the heading for the three following cases.

11:40 עַד־הָעָרֶב׃—See 17:15–16.

11:41 וְכָל־הַשֶּׁרֶץ הַשֹּׁרֵץ עַל־הָאָרֶץ שֶׁקֶץ הוּא—We take this as a heading and so render it as "As for any swarming creature ..." If it were not meant to function as a heading, it could be rendered as this: "Any swarming creature that swarms on the land is detestable." It is a résumé of 11:29.

11:42 This verse lists the three main classes of swarming land animals as defined by their method of locomotion. The verse literally reads like this: "From everything that goes on its belly and everything that goes on all fours to everything that has many legs, every swarming creature that swarms on the land, you shall not eat them for they are detestable."

כֹּל הוֹלֵךְ עַל־גָּחוֹן—An example of a creature that goes on its belly would be a snake. The ו in גָּחוֹן is written as a larger letter because it is the center letter in the Pentateuch (GKC, § 5 n). The marginal Masoretic note, חצי אותיות בתורה, means "the halfway point of the letters in the Torah." The Masoretes would count the letters in a manuscript they had copied to make sure that they had copied it exactly. If the copy contained a different number of letters than the original, then they would know that they had made an error and the copy was unreliable and unfit for use.

וְכֹל ׀ הוֹלֵךְ עַל־אַרְבַּע—Animals that go on all fours would include crocodiles and tortoises.

עַד כָּל־מַרְבֵּה רַגְלַיִם—Those animals with a multiplicity of legs would include centipedes and millipedes.

לְכָל־הַשֶּׁרֶץ—Regarding the use of לְ in לְכָל־, see the textual notes on 11:26.

11:43 תְּשַׁקְּצוּ—The causative sense of the Piel verb here, "to make [one's throat] be disgusting," recalls the different use of the same verb in 11:11, 13, where it means "to detest, to regard as detestable."

נַפְשֹׁתֵיכֶם—See 20:25. Even though נֶפֶשׁ can be used reflexively for oneself, it is used in its much more concrete sense of "throat" with שִׁקֵּץ, as with טִמֵּא in 11:44, for it is the throat that is polluted by eating the meat from these animals.[5]

תִטַּמְּאוּ—This repeats the Hithpael of טָמֵא from 11:24 and forms an inclusion with it.

וְנִטְמֵתֶם—This is the Niphal of טָמֵא, with the א elided. The Niphal could have the middle meaning "to defile oneself" (*HALOT*). However, more likely it has the passive meaning "to become polluted, to be made unclean." The Niphal recurs in 18:24.

11:44 כִּי אֲנִי יְהוָה אֱלֹהֵיכֶם—This means "for I am the Lord your God" or "for I, the Lord, am your God." This important theological declaration combines the formula of divine self-introduction, "I am Yahweh" (18:5, 6, 21), with the promise of divine self-commitment, "I will be your God" (Ex 6:7; Lev 26:12; see also Gen 17:8).[6] God used this declaration to introduce himself by name to his people and to commit himself to them as their God at Mount Sinai (Ex 20:2). Thereafter he used it to introduce himself to his people through Moses, the lawgiver, and Aaron, the law-teacher, before or after, he gave his decrees to them (Lev 18:2, 4, 21, 30; 19:3, 4, 10, 25, 31, 34, 36; 20:7, 24; 23:22, 43; 24:22; 25:17, 38, 55; 26:1, 13, 44).

Since Moses and Aaron spoke for God, the Lord addressed his people through them and Aaron's successors in the office of the priesthood.[7] The formula for self-introduction and self-commitment is expanded by other relative clauses that make other important theological declarations. God used it to declare that he was holy (19:2; 20:26; 21:8) and that he had freed his people from slavery in Egypt (11:45; 19:36; 26:13). God also used it to declare that he had distinguished Israel from the nations (20:24) so that he could sanctify them (20:8; 21:8, 15, 23; 22:9, 16, 32) and be their God (11:45).

וְהִתְקַדִּשְׁתֶּם—This is the Hithpael perfect of קָדַשׁ with *waw,* used as an imperative. The Hithpael can have a middle voice, meaning "to keep oneself sanctified" (*HALOT,* 1) or "sanctify oneself." It recurs in 20:7. The Israelites sanctified themselves by performing the divinely instituted rites through which God shared his holiness with them.

---

5 Milgrom, *Leviticus 1–16*, 684.

6 See Hartley, *Leviticus*, 291–93; Zimmerli, *I Am Yahweh*, 1–28.

7 Kleinig, "What's the Use of Naming God?" 29.

וִהְיִיתֶם קְדֹשִׁים—"You shall be holy" recurs in 11:45; 19:2; 20:7, 26; Num 15:40; cf. Lev 21:6, 7, 8.

כִּי קָדוֹשׁ אָנִי—This formula, "for I am holy," recurs in 11:45; 19:2; 20:26; 21:8. By means of this formula, God declares that he is the source of holiness for his people. In 21:8 this clause is combined with the formula for sanctification ("for I the Lord, who sanctifies you, am holy"). That combination shows that the Lord presented himself to Israel as their sanctifier in the divine service.

תְטַמְּאוּ—In Leviticus the Piel of the verb טָמֵא can mean (1) "to make unclean" something that previously was clean, to defile it (11:44; 15:31; 18:28; 20:3); (2) verbally "to declare as unclean" something that formerly was clean (13:3, 8, 11, 15, 20, 22, 25, 27, 30, 44, 59); or (3) to treat something unclean as unclean (20:25).

נַפְשֹׁתֵיכֶם—See the textual notes on נֶפֶשׁ in 11:43.

11:45 כִּי ׀ אֲנִי יְהוָה הַמַּעֲלֶה אֶתְכֶם מֵאֶרֶץ מִצְרַיִם לִהְיֹת לָכֶם לֵאלֹהִים—This summarizes an important theological theme that extends throughout the Pentateuch. God promised Abraham, the first patriarch of Israel, that his descendants would be afflicted in another land for four hundred years, but after that God would bring them out (from Egypt), and they would inherit the promised land (Gen 15:13–16). When the Lord reiterated and reconfirmed his covenant with Abraham, he promised that he would "be the God" of Abraham and his descendants (Gen 17:7–8). He repeated this promise to Moses (Ex 6:7) and fulfilled it by residing with the Israelites in the tent of meeting and meeting with them there (Ex 29:42–45). There he met with them twice a day and acted as their God. There he came to them and said: "I am the Lord your God" (Lev 11:44). His daily self-presentation was the purpose of his people's deliverance from Egypt (Ex 29:46; Lev 22:33; 25:38; 26:45).

11:46 זֹאת תּוֹרַת—See the textual note on תּוֹרָה in 6:2 (ET 6:9).

הַבְּהֵמָה—See 11:2b–8, 24–28, 39–40.

וְהָעוֹף—Instead of "flying creatures" in general, this might specifically refer to "birds." See 11:13–23.

וְכֹל נֶפֶשׁ הַחַיָּה הָרֹמֶשֶׂת בַּמָּיִם—See 11:9–12.

וּלְכָל־נֶפֶשׁ הַשֹּׁרֶצֶת עַל־הָאָרֶץ׃—See 11:29–38, 41–45 and the textual notes on 11:26. The use of a *lamed* at the end of a list emphasizes the final item.

11:47 לְהַבְדִּיל—See the textual notes on 10:10.

בֵּין הַטָּמֵא וּבֵין הַטָּהֹר—See 11:24–40.

וּבֵין הַחַיָּה הַנֶּאֱכֶלֶת וּבֵין הַחַיָּה אֲשֶׁר לֹא תֵאָכֵל׃—See 11:2b–23, 41–45.

Commentary

Structure

Like the other five speeches of ritual instruction in chapters 11–15, the speech in chapter 11 has a subscript that summarizes its content and purpose (11:46–47). The body of the speech falls into three parts. The instruction on the consumption of meat from clean and unclean animals in 11:2b–23 and 11:41–45 frames the instruction on the treatment of impurity from contact with the carcasses of animals (11:24–40).

The arrangement of material in this speech is governed by the scribal conventions for the construction of lists for administrative purposes in the ancient world. Thus, most obviously, we have a series of lists: unclean quadrupeds in 11:4b–7; detestable birds in 11:13b–19; edible grasshoppers in 11:22b; quadrupeds whose carcasses are unclean in clean in 11:26–27; unclean land-swarmers in 11:29b–30. Each new unit has a phrase or sentence that functions as its heading.[a] Most of these units are also rounded off by words, phrases, or clauses at the end that function as a frame or inclusion around the body of the unit, such as "you may eat" in 11:2 and 11:3; "you shall not eat" in 11:4 and 11:8; "everything in the waters" in 11:9 and 11:12; "every winged swarmer … is detestable to you" in 11:20 and 11:23; "unclean" in 11:24 and 11:28; "unclean for you" in 11:29 and 11:31a as well as 11:38. As is usually the case in Hebrew lists, the objects of verbs are almost always placed before their verbs, often in the form of pending clauses.

(a) Lev 11:2b, 4a, 9a, 13a, 20a, 24a, 29a, 39a, 41a

The material is arranged according to a number of different systems of classification. Thus the animals are listed according to their habitat: the land creatures in 11:2b–8; the sea creatures in 11:9–12; and the sky creatures in 11:13–23. If Driver is right in his identification of the twenty birds in 11:13b–19,[8] they are listed according to their habitat, with the land birds (numbers 1–15) followed by the sea birds (numbers 16–18). Another factor in the classification is their size, with the larger owls (numbers 7–9) before the smaller owls (numbers 11–15), with the smaller hawks (number 10) listed between them. The clean insects in 11:22b are, most likely, also listed by size. Most significantly, the meat from certain animals and contact with their carcasses are classified as unclean. This results in the repetition of the formula for impurity in consecutive clauses in 11:4b–8 and the repetition of the formula for secondary pollution in 11:24–28, 31–38, 39–40.

Two other significant literary devices are employed in this speech. The material in 11:24–28 is arranged as a chiasm—with its pivot in 11:26a—by the repetition of the verbal root for "unclean" and of the verb "touch." The concluding admonition in 11:43–45 is shaped by four motive clauses introduced by "for" (כִּי), in which God speaks about himself. The admonition is also shaped by the parallelism created by the contrast between the two prohibitions followed by the single commandment in 11:43 and two commandments followed by a single prohibition in 11:44.

The structure of this pericope can be outlined as follows:

I. Introduction (11:1–2a)
   A. God's address to Moses and Aaron (11:1)
   B. God's commission of them (11:2a)
II. Speech about clean and unclean meat (11:2b–45)

[8] Driver, "Birds in the Old Testament."

A. Instruction about edible and inedible meat (11:2b–23)
 1. Four-legged land animals (11:2b–8)
  a. Criteria for the identification of edible animals (11:2b–3)
  b. Classification of four inedible animals as unclean (11:4–8)
 2. Sea creatures (11:9–12)
  a. Criteria for the identification of edible fish (11:9)
  b. Classification of inedible sea life as detestable (11:10–12)
 3. Detestable birds (11:13–19)
  a. Commandment about the detestation of certain birds (11:13a)
  b. List of twenty detestable birds (11:13b –19)
 4. Detestable flying insects (11:20–23)
  a. Classification of all flying insects as detestable (11:20)
  b. Exceptions to the rule (11:21–22)
   i. Criteria for the identification of edible insects (11:21)
   ii. List of four edible insects (11:22)
  c. Restatement of the rule (11:23)
B. Instruction about the impurity from the carcasses of dead animals (11:24–40)
 1. Impurity from the carcass of an inedible four-legged animal (11:24–28)
  a. Introduction on the contraction and treatment of impurity from carcasses (11:24–25)
  b. Treatment for the impurity from the carcass of a four-legged animal (11:26–28)
   i. Animals with unsplit hooves (11:26)
   ii. Animals with paws (11:27–28)
 2. Impurity from the carcass of a swarming land animal (11:29–38)
  a. List of eight rodents and reptiles (11:29–31a)
  b. Pollution by their contact with people (11:31b)
  c. Pollution by their contact with objects (11:32–38)
   i. An article onto which a carcass falls (11:32)
   ii. A container into which a carcass falls (11:33)
   iii. Food or drink by water from a polluted container (11:34)
   iv. Oven or stove onto which part of a carcass falls (11:35)
   v. Water in a spring or cistern into which a carcass falls (11:36)
   vi. Seed onto which part of a carcass falls (11:37–38)
 3. Impurity from the carcass of an edible four-legged animal (11:39–40)
C. Instruction about the consumption of meat from swarming land animals (11:41–45)
 1. Classification of all swarming land animals as detestable and inedible (11:41–42)
 2. Final prohibitions and commands about purity and sanctification (11:43–45)
  a. Prohibition of throat-contamination and self-pollution with divine self-introduction (11:43–44a)
  b. Command for self-consecration and call to holiness with declaration of God's holiness (11:44b)

c. Prohibition of throat-pollution with formula of divine deliverance (11:44c–45a)
d. Call to holiness with declaration of God's holiness (11:45b)

III. Summary subscript (11:46–47)
  A. Topics covered in this ritual instruction (11:46)
  B. Purpose of this instruction (11:47)

Literary Ritual Analysis

The Lord gave these ritual instructions to Moses and Aaron (11:1). This is the first time that Aaron was also included as the custodian of this teaching. He had just been ordained as the high priest and had begun to act in that capacity (Leviticus 8–9). He had also been commissioned to distinguish what was clean from what was unclean so that God's holiness would not be desecrated (10:10–11). As he had been commissioned, Aaron was to pass on to the Israelites this instruction about the consumption of meat (11:2–23, 41–45) and the treatment for impurity from the carcasses of animals (11:24–40).

The speech begins with the first topic for legislation: edible, four-footed land animals (11:1). Then follow the two criteria for their identification: they had to be cud-chewing animals (like sheep, goats, and cattle), and they also had to have split hooves (11:2–3). Those two complementary criteria are then used negatively to exclude four borderline cases that fitted only one of them: the camel; the rock badger; the hare; and the pig (11:4–8). Since they failed to fulfill the two criteria, they were unclean; their meat could not be eaten, and their carcasses could not be touched. No remedy is given for the contraction of impurity from them.

The second unit begins with a heading before it gives the criteria for distinguishing edible fish from all water creatures (11:9). These criteria apply to all creatures that live in streams and lakes and the sea. The Israelites were only allowed to eat meat from fish with fins and scales. All other fish life was classified as "detestable" for ritual reasons (11:10). Whether they were caught alive or taken dead, they could not be eaten. They always remained "detestable" (11:11–12). There is, however, no prohibition against touching their carcasses, nor is there any mention of any impurity from eating them. Their consumption was forbidden, even though their meat did not convey ritual impurity.

After a heading, the third unit lists twenty birds whose meat was "detestable" and not allowed to be eaten (11:13–19). It is taken for granted that all other birds may be eaten. No criteria are given to distinguish the inedible birds from other, edible birds, even though most likely all the inedible ones are carnivorous scavengers. Although the identification of some of these birds is rather uncertain, they seem to be classified according to their zoological classes and their size. The large accipitrides, such as eagles and vultures, come first (numbers 1–3). Then follow the larger falcons (numbers 4–5); the ravens (number 6); the larger owls (numbers 7–9); the smaller falcons (number 10); the smaller owls (numbers 11–15); the water birds (numbers 16–18); the hoopoe (number 19); and last of all, the bats (number 20).

Figure 14 shows the various identifications of the Hebrew terms as particular species according to our modern names of those species.

Figure 14

Proposed Identifications of Unclean Birds

	MT	*LXX*	*Driver*	*Milgrom*	*Hartley*
1.	נֶשֶׁר	Eagle	Griffon vulture	Eagle	Griffon vulture
2.	פֶּרֶס	Lammergeier	Black vulture	Black vulture	Bearded vulture
3.	עָזְנִיָּה	Osprey	Bearded vulture	Bearded vulture	Black vulture
4.	דָּאָה	Vulture	Kite	Kite	Kite
5.	אַיָּה	Kite	Saker falcon	Falcon	Buzzard
6.	עֹרֵב	Raven	Raven/rook	Raven	Crow
7.	יַעֲנָה	Ostrich	Eagle owl	Eagle owl	Eagle owl
8.	תַּחְמָס	Little owl	Short-eared owl	Short-eared owl	Short-eared owl
9.	שַׁחַף	Gull	Long-eared owl	Long-eared owl	Long-eared owl
10.	נֵץ	Hawk	Kestrel/sparrow hawk	Hawk	Hawk
11.	כּוֹס	Long eared owl	Tawny owl	Tawny owl	Little owl
12.	שָׁלָךְ	Sea bird	Fisher-owl	Fisher-owl	Cormorant
13.	יַנְשׁוּף	Ibis	Screech owl	Screech owl	Long-eared screech owl
14.	תִּנְשֶׁמֶת	Water hen	Little owl	White owl	Barn owl
15.	קָאַת	Pelican	Scops owl	Scops owl	Scops owl
16.	רָחָם	Swan	Osprey	Osprey	Egyptian vulture
17.	חֲסִידָה	Heron	Stork/heron	Stork	Stork
18.	אֲנָפָה	Plover	Cormorant	Heron	Heron
19.	דּוּכִיפַת	Hoopoe	Hoopoe	Hoopoe	Hoopoe
20.	עֲטַלֵּף	Bat	Bat	Bat	Bat

These unclean birds are closely associated with four-legged insects that fly in swarms above the ground (11:20–23). These unclean insects are something of an anomaly because of their mode of locomotion. Like the birds, they have wings and are therefore able to fly in the sky, but like quadrupeds, they also have four legs to walk on the ground. Like the forbidden fish and inedible birds, they are classified as "detestable" for ritual reasons and therefore unfit for human consumption, even though Leviticus 11 does not state that they convey ritual impurity (11:20). The only exceptions to this rule about unclean insects are the four classes of grasshoppers that could be used for human consumption (11:21–22). The criterion for their identification was their possession of jointed legs for leaping on the ground.

The second part of the speech shifts from the consumption of meat to the treatment of impurity from the carcasses of animals (11:24–40). Even though living animals (including the four unclean animals in 11:4–7) did not convey impurity by touch, the carcasses of all animals did do so. Just as the corpse of a person was a source of impurity (22:4; Num 19:11–13), the carcasses of all land animals communicated impurity by contact with them. While most carcasses spread it by direct contact or by transportation, a special group of swarming creatures also conveyed their virulent impurity by the contact of their carcasses with objects (Lev 11:29–38). However, 11:24–40 is not as concerned about the spread of impurity from these animals as in its treatment.

The instruction on the treatment of impurity from contact with the carcasses of animals begins with a general statement in 11:24–25 that provides the framework for what follows in 11:26–40. The general statement distinguishes the treatment of impurity from contact with a carcass (11:24) from the treatment of impurity contracted from transporting any part of a carcass (11:25). Both cases assume that the Israelites could not leave the carcass of any animal unburied in their environment, but they had to dispose of it in some way. Contact with a carcass communicated daylong impurity that was removed by taking a ritual bath before sunset (11:24). Transportation of any part of a carcass required the laundering of clothes as well, since they too had come into contact with it (11:25). The general principle is then illustrated by two cases in 11:26–27: (1) the carcasses of the hoofed land animals that are not regarded as edible by the criteria given in 11:3, such as horses, donkeys, and mules and (2) the carcasses of land animals with paws such as lions, bears, and wolves. The impurity from contact with them needed to be treated as outlined in 11:24–25. This is emphasized by the repetition of 11:24b–25 in 11:27b–28a.

Next follows a unit on the treatment of impurity from the carcasses of eight swarming land animals (11:29–38). A heading that classifies them as "most unclean" introduces their list in 11:29–31. As with the list of unclean birds, the identification of many of them is uncertain. See figure 15.

Figure 15

Proposed Identifications of Unclean Swarming Land Animals

	MT	*LXX*	*NRSV*	*Hartley*	*Milgrom*
1.	חֹלֶד	Weasel	Weasel	Mole rat	Rat
2.	עַכְבָּר	Mouse	Mouse	Mouse	Mouse
3.	צָב	Lizard	Great lizard	Dabb lizard	Large lizard
4.	אֲנָקָה	Shrew	Gecko	Gecko	Gecko
5.	כֹּחַ	Chameleon	Land crocodile	Monitor lizard	Spotted lizard
6.	לְטָאָה	Newt	Lizard	Lizard	Lizard
7.	חֹמֶט	Salamander	Sand lizard	Skink	Skink
8.	תִּנְשֶׁמֶת	Mole rat	Chameleon	Chameleon	Chameleon

This list seems to consist of those rodents and reptiles that invaded human houses and storage areas.[9] Since they were also often found dead in these places, they had to be removed by the Israelites.

The list begins with the assertion that these were the "most unclean" of all the creatures that swarmed on the land (11:29). Their carcasses not only polluted those who touched them (11:31b), but they also polluted whatever they fell onto and into (11:32–38). The treatment for human pollution from them (11:31b) was the same as for any other carcass of a clean (11:24) or an unclean animal (11:39). But the treatment for the things that they polluted varied.

There were three general rules. First, any polluted article of wood, cloth, leather, or sacking had to be dipped in water before it could be used again for any purpose in the house (11:32). Second, any polluted earthenware container had to be smashed, while anything in it was unclean and unfit for human consumption (11:33). Since water from such a polluted container polluted the food and drink that it touched, that food and drink was unclean and unfit for human consumption (11:34). Third, cooking utensils, such as an oven or a stove, were so polluted by any carcass that fell on them that they had to be smashed (11:35).

There were, however, two exceptions to these rules. On the one hand, if a carcass fell into a spring or a cistern, it did not pollute it, but only the person or object that removed it from the water (11:36). On the other hand, if a carcass fell onto some seed grain, it did not pollute the grain unless it had been watered to start the process of germination (11:37–38). In that case the carcass of the dead animal contaminated the seed that was sprouting. It could not therefore be used to provide human food.

The third unit in 11:24–40 gives instructions on the treatment of impurity from the carcass of a clean, edible domesticated animal, such as a cow, sheep, or goat (11:39–40). The meat from these animals could be eaten, even if they had not been slaughtered but had been killed by a wild animal or had died of natural causes. Their meat was too valuable to be wasted. Nevertheless the carcass was still unclean. Those who touched it and ate the meat from it became unclean and so stood in need of the same procedure for purification as those who touched the carcass of any unclean animal. If they carried it, they had to launder their clothes as well (cf. 11:15–16).

The third part (11:41–45) of the speech in Leviticus 11 continues the instruction from 11:2–23 on the eating of meat from animals. Like the list of birds in 11:13–19 and most of the swarming insects in 11:20–23, all the swarming land animals are classified as "detestable" and therefore inedible (11:41). They are divided into three groups according to their mode of locomotion: the no-footed slitherers, the four-footed walkers, and the many-footed walkers (11:42).

The repeated prohibition of their consumption introduces a final theological exhortation. On one hand, it forbids self-pollution: "You shall not disgust

9 See Carroll, "One More Time," 121.

your throats with any creature that swarms, nor shall you pollute yourselves with them, so that you become polluted by them" (11:43). The reason for the prohibition is that the Lord is the God of Israel, who brought them up out of Egypt to be their God (11:44–45). On the other hand, the concluding exhortation calls on the Israelites to consecrate themselves and be holy (11:44–45). The reason for this call to holiness is the holiness of God (11:45).

The Israelites are *not* called to imitate God by generating their own holiness and achieving it for themselves, for that is beyond human ability, since God alone is holy. Rather they are to *receive* holiness from God himself and share in his holiness. So, whereas the prohibition recalls the need to avoid the consumption of unclean meat from swarming land animals, *the call to holiness caps off the whole speech.* It gives the reason for all the rulings in this piece of ritual instruction. It defines what is unclean and clean in relation to God rather than any class of people.

The subscript in 11:46–47 is not part of the speech. It summarizes the content and purpose of the instruction. The declaration of its purpose to distinguish unclean meat from clean meat recalls and carries out the charge given to Aaron in 10:10–11. That is the duty of the priests. That too is the duty of the people under their supervision.

Theological Significance

The ritual instructions in this chapter obviously teach that the avoidance of eating unclean meat and the treatment of impurity from the carcasses of animals are matters for religious observance. They do, of course, deal with physical matters, such as nutrition, health, and animal husbandry. But that is not the concern of this legislation. The consumption of meat by the Israelites has to do with their standing before God, their status as his people, and their access to him. This is implied by the classification of meat from some animals as unclean (11:4, 5, 6, 7, 8) and from other creatures as detestable (11:10, 11, 12, 13, 20, 23, 41, 42), as well as by the classification of the carcasses of all creatures as unclean (11:8, 26, 27, 28, 29, 31). Both the terms "unclean" and "detestable" are ritual-theological terms. While impurity disqualified a person from involvement in the sacrificial ritual at the sanctuary, the designation of something as detestable indicated that it should be avoided for ritual reasons.

It may have been obvious to the ancient Israelites that their relationship with God demanded that they needed to avoid the meat from some animals and to purify themselves after touching the carcass of an animal. The reason(s) why may have been plain to them. But the rationale is not obvious to us. Why was the meat from some animals unclean or even detestable? Were they inherently unclean, or unclean for ritual reasons? Why did eating unclean meat or touching the carcasses of animals disqualify the Israelites from contact with the holy things of God?

The answer is that these things disrupted the work of God in two domains: the common domain of human life in the natural order and the holy domain of God's life-giving presence in the supernatural order. Both the sanctuary of the

Lord and the Israelite home—the Lord's table and the family table—were threatened by the life-diminishing, life-destroying power of impurity that emanated from the underworld, the demonic realm of chaos and death. Because the holiness of the temple was connected with the purity of the home, both were damaged by all that was unclean and unacceptable in God's eyes. Conversely, God desired to extend his holiness through his people further into the common realm by purifying and sanctifying it.[10]

The meat from creatures was not unclean because they were misfits, anomalies that were out of place in the theological system of classification in ancient Israel, contrary to what Douglas maintains.[11] Rather, it became unclean when it was served as food on the Israelite table, or misused by the Israelites. It was unclean if its natural function was abused and misplaced domestically or ritually. Misplaced, abused meat did not generate ritual impurity; it conveyed impurity from the unclean realm into the human realm. Once it gained a foothold there, it was able to enter the sacred realm. Thus, no living creature was in itself unclean. In itself a pig was not unclean. Its meat became a medium for transmission of impurity when it was misplaced and abused. Since pigs were banned as animals for sacrifice, their meat was out of place on the table of the Israelites since they too ate holy meat as guests at God's table.

In the order of creation, God had given the land as the common habitat for human beings and for three classes of land animals: the wild animals, the domestic animals, and the swarming animals (Gen 1:26). Each had its own God-given niche and function. The domestic animals were the only creatures that were created to share the human domain; they had their place as members of a human household. So from a human point of view they were both common and clean.

In general, all other creatures were out of place in the domestic realm. They were therefore potentially bearers of impurity.

Some of the domesticated animals, such as sheep and goats and cattle, were to be used for food, while others, such as horses and donkeys, were to be used for haulage and transportation. The animals that were used for food provided the criteria for determining which of the other creatures could be eaten. Thus any game that had split hooves and chewed its cud could be eaten. Birds that lived off grain and grass could also be eaten, while, as was recognized by the Jewish sages,[12] carnivorous birds of prey were to be shunned. Members of the locust family that had four legs with knees, like sheep, were also edible. It is, however, difficult to ascertain how the possession of fins and scales qualified fish for human consumption. It may merely be that they had always been used as food, or that they could be farmed in ponds.

---

[10] See figure 1, "Holy versus Common and Clean versus Unclean" in the introduction.

[11] Douglas, *Purity and Danger,* 49–57.

[12] Talmud, Mishnah, *Hullin* 3:6.

Whatever the specific reasons for this system of classification may have been, it is clear that the meat that was regarded as either "unclean" or "detestable" was unfit for consumption by the Israelites; it could not serve as food in the common domain. This applied too for meat from the carcass of a dead animal. It was out of place on an Israelite table. Moreover, the meat from the carcasses of eight swarming land animals was so unclean that it polluted human food and drink by polluting those things that were used to store them and prepare them for human consumption. These carcasses were out of place in the domestic domain, the habitat of the Israelite family. Those who touched any carcass had to undergo purification before they could eat clean, common food together with their family in the evening meal. God instituted these rites of purification with water so that he could thereby preserve the common purity of the Israelite household and the holiness of its members. This was necessary because impurity disqualified a person from sharing common food, and some sources of impurity were unavoidable in Israelite society, such as that contracted from contact with animal carcasses, which could defile the family.

The domestic aspect of impurity, however, is not the main concern in this ritual instruction. The focus throughout is on the ritual aspect of impurity and on its implications for those who ate holy meat at the sanctuary (cf. 7:21). To understand this concern, we need to realize that the Israelites usually ate meat only at sacred meals in God's presence during the three pilgrim festivals. In fact, very little meat was eaten as part of their normal diet. When it was eaten, the animals had to be slaughtered in the same way as at the sanctuary by draining off the blood (17:13; cf. Deut 12:15). But the Israelites were not encouraged to use the meat from domesticated animals as common food.

Their meat was meant for the Lord's table, for the Israelites were a priestly people who lived with him as his holy servants. Since the sanctuary was the proper place for eating meat, its standards and taboos governed the consumption of meat in the Israelite home. The household meals of the Israelites were thereby associated with their meals at the sanctuary. The family table became an extension of the Lord's altar, for the sanctity of the home was dependent on the sanctity of the sanctuary.

This instruction does not, then, provide general regulations about the best diet for all human beings, so that they can live harmoniously, healthily, and productively in the order of creation. Instead, *it provides specific regulations for the Israelites* (11:1) *so that they could live as holy people in God's presence and be his guests in the meals that he hosted for them at the sanctuary* (11:44–45). God had brought them up out of Egypt so that he could be their God by residing and interacting with them at the tabernacle (11:45; cf. Ex 29:43–46). They were not just common people, clean people who lived harmoniously with each other and their environment. Rather, they were holy people, ritually clean people who lived with God and shared in his holiness. They, therefore, had to be ritually clean, fit for God's table and for participation in his holiness. If they ate the sacred meat from their peace offerings in a state of ritual impurity from eating unclean meat or touching the unclean carcass of an animal, they polluted it and forfeited their place in Israel (7:20–21).

This means that these rules for impurity applied only to the Israelites as God's holy, priestly people. They did not apply to people from other nations. Thus the meat from certain animals was unclean "for" the people of Israel (11:4, 5, 6, 7, 8) or detestable "for" them (11:11, 12, 20, 23). The carcasses of all animals were unclean "for" them (11:26, 27, 28, 29, 31). Any polluted stove or oven or seed was unclean "for" them (11:35, 37). This impurity mattered only because it disqualified the Israelites from eating the sacred meat and sharing in God's holiness. It had to be dealt with before they could enter the sanctuary.

Houston has shown that the Israelites did not differ very much at all from their pagan neighbors in their diet of meat.[13] That is as we would expect. Yet they did differ from them in a few instances for theological reasons. Two cases are most noteworthy. First, the consumption of meat from carcasses was forbidden because they still had their blood in them (17:14–16). The Israelites therefore did not gain supernatural life-power from their meat; instead, they contracted life-diminishing impurity.

Second, the Israelites also shunned everything that belonged in any way to the realm of the death and the cult of the dead. The carcasses of dead animals belonged to the realm of death. So too did all animals and birds that lived off dead animals. Since the sea, the lakes, and the rivers were associated with the underworld, the creatures that lived in them were regarded with suspicion. The animals that burrowed in the ground, like pigs and badgers, may also have been shunned for the same reason. Many of the detestable birds may have been shunned because they were used in augury and regarded as birds of ill omen.[14] Owls may also have been regarded with suspicion because they were birds of the night. Reptiles were most likely regarded as detestable because, as is shown by the ritual use of the bronze serpent in 2 Ki 18:4 as well as of the painted swarming creatures in Ezek 8:7–13, they were used as idols or were symbols in the service of underworld deities and demonic powers. Likewise, the meat from pigs was regarded as unclean because it was used in the cult of the dead or the goddesses of fertility (Is 65:2–5; 66:3, 17).[15]

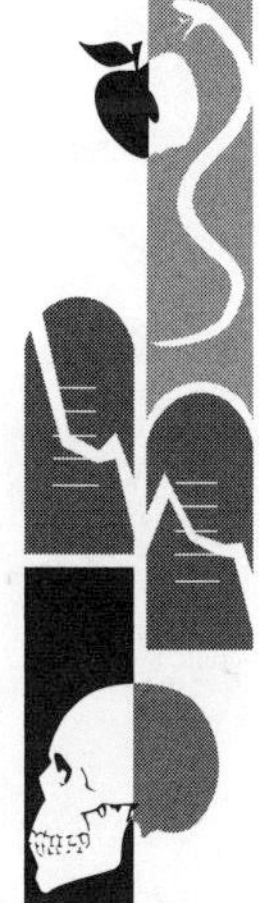

The theological rationale for the avoidance of impurity from eating unclean or detestable meat is summarized by the conclusion of the speech in 11:43–45. Here God enters the discussion directly. He warns against self-defilement and calls on the Israelites to share in his holiness. He shares his holiness with them by giving them holy meat to eat at his table. The same throats that ate that sacred meat should not, under any circumstances, be contaminated by unclean meat, for they would then defile and desecrate the holy food.

---

[13] Houston, *Purity and Monotheism*, 124–77.

[14] Houston, *Purity and Monotheism*, 193–99.

[15] Houston, *Purity and Monotheism*, 168, 177.

God also commands the Israelites to consecrate themselves by eating holy food, so that they could continue to receive his holiness. Since he was holy, he made them holy. He therefore called on them to share in his holiness by eating the meat from his table and by avoiding impurity from the consumption of unclean meat.

(b) Is 4:4; Jer 33:8; Ezek 36:29, 33; 37:23

Fulfillment by Christ

In the OT, the prophets announced that in the age to come God himself would cleanse his people from impurity by washing it away and purifying them with his Spirit.[b] This would involve the total transformation of them so that they would have a new heart and serve him by the power of his Spirit (Ezek 36:25–27). This purification from sin was accomplished by Jesus (Heb 1:3). He offered himself as the sacrifice that purifies the new people of God (Titus 2:14). He purifies his disciples by his Word (Jn 15:3) and through the waters of Baptism (1 Cor 6:11; Eph 5:26). His blood cleanses them from the taint of sin and the stain of abuse (1 Jn 1:7, 9). His body and blood, given and shed for them for the forgiveness of sins, are received by them in his holy Supper.

Christ does not merely cleanse the bodies of his baptized believers so that they could approach him in an earthly sanctuary, but he has cleansed their conscience, their heart, the whole of their being, so they could serve as priests with him in the heavenly sanctuary (Heb 9:13–14; 10:19–22). God has purified their hearts through faith in Jesus (Acts 15:9). Thus in the church, purity of the heart qualifies a person ritually for participation in God's holiness.[c]

(c) Mt 5:8; 1 Tim 1:5; 2 Tim 2:22; cf. 2 Cor 7:1; 1 Tim 3:9; 2 Tim 1:3; Heb 13:18

This cleansing of the heart for participation in God's holiness is presupposed by the teaching on purity in the NT. Jesus criticized the Pharisees and the scribes because they were not concerned with the purification of the whole person (Mt 23:25–26; Lk 11:37–41). They took such care to strain out tiny unclean gnats from their water that they unwittingly swallowed larger, more unclean camels (Mt 23:24). Jesus did not, as some suppose, replace ritual purity with moral purity or with subjective piety. Rather, he demanded a far higher and much more comprehensive level of ritual purity than was required for the people and the priests in Leviticus.

When the scribes and Pharisees criticized him for allowing his disciples to eat food with unwashed hands, he taught a far more radical form of purification than they had ever envisaged (Mt 15:1–20; Mk 7:1–23). He did not ridicule their concern for purity and abolish the rules for purity in Leviticus. Instead, he reaffirmed them and deepened them. His teaching on purity presupposes that his disciples shared in his holiness with their hearts rather than just with their bodies. They were therefore not "desecrated" and so "defiled" by the unclean food that they ate and absorbed into their bodies; they were "desecrated" by what came from their hearts (Mt 15:11, 18, 20; Mk 7:15, 19, 20, 23). Since they, by faith, shared in God's holiness, their hearts were the site of the battle between purity and impurity; unclean thoughts and desires, which produced unclean acts, desecrated their holiness (Mt 15:19; Mk 7:21–23).

Since Jesus has cleansed the hearts of his disciples, he has fulfilled the purpose of the laws in Leviticus 11 about the need to avoid eating unclean meat. By his cleansing of their hearts, he made all food clean for them (Mk 7:19). The eating of "unclean meat" did not desecrate their holiness and so disqualify them from eating at his table. Thus he intensified the demand for purity and extended it from the body to the "heart," the conscience of his disciples that he himself had purified and sanctified. They no longer shared in God's holiness by eating the consecrated meat of clean animals, but by eating the holy body of Christ. His body strengthened their hearts with God's grace (Heb 13:9–12).

Christ's cleansing of his disciples through the waters of Baptism and the gift of the Holy Spirit is presupposed by two further discussions on the eating of unclean meat in the NT. First, the vision of Peter before his visit to the household of Cornelius in Acts 10:9–15 applied the teaching of Jesus on purity to the Baptism of Gentiles and their inclusion in the church. By commanding Peter in that vision to eat the meat of animals that were common and ritually unclean, God showed Peter that through the Gospel of Jesus, he cleansed the hearts of Gentiles, just as he had cleansed the hearts of the Jews (Acts 10:15, 28; 11:9). They could therefore eat together from the same table as members of the same holy community. Peter later used the same vision at the council of Jerusalem to argue for the inclusion of the Gentiles in the church (Acts 15:7–11).

Second, Paul builds on the teaching of Jesus about the ritual status of the meat that had been declared unclean in Leviticus. He argues that by itself "unclean meat" does not desecrate those who are in Christ (Rom 14:14). All food is therefore to be treated as ritually clean (Rom 14:20). In fact, all the regulations about clean and unclean food foreshadowed the work of Christ; he fulfilled them by his priestly ministry and so superseded them (Col 2:16–17, 20–22). The righteousness, peace, and joy that Christ gives to us through the Holy Spirit make us acceptable to God (Rom 14:17–18). We are holy in him. Our purity therefore has to do with our faith in him and our love for each other (1 Tim 1:5).

At the same time, the apostle Paul does relate one of the theological concerns in Leviticus 11 to participation in the Lord's Supper. Just as the Israelites were not to eat meat from those unclean animals that were associated with idolatry and the demonic, so St. Paul states: "You cannot drink the cup of the Lord and the cup of demons. You cannot share in the Lord's Table and the table of demons" (1 Cor 10:21). It is not simply the eating of a kind of meat, but involvement in demonic and idolatrous worship that is incompatible with participation at the holy Table of the Lord.[16]

---

[16] The issue of eating meat sacrificed to idols extends throughout 1 Corinthians 8–10 and involves implications for church fellowship and attendance at Holy Communion, which the apostle addresses in greater detail in 1 Cor 11:17–34. This is discussed more fully by Lockwood, *1 Corinthians,* 271–410.

We are called to "be separate" from every unclean thing that threatens to desecrate our holiness as the temple of the living God (2 Cor 6:14–7:1). The holy people of God must not touch any unclean thing. Only those whose names are written in the Lamb's book of life (Rev 21:27), those who washed their robes and shared in Christ's purity (Rev 22:14), will be permitted to enter the holy city, the heavenly Jerusalem, the eternal bride of Christ. Using the language of Leviticus 11 ("unclean," "detestable"), God warns: "No unclean thing may enter her, nor anyone who does a detestable thing or a lie" (Rev 21:27; cf. 21:8; 22:15).

Come to Calv'ry's holy mountain,
Sinners, ruined by the fall;
Here a pure and healing fountain
Flows for you, for me, for all,
In a full perpetual tide,
Opened when our Savior died.

Come in sorrow and contrition,
Wounded, impotent, and blind;
Here the guilty, free remission,
Here the troubled, peace may find.
Your true health it will restore,
So that you need thirst no more.

Come with hurts and guilts and meanness,
Come, however soiled within;
From the most ingrained uncleanness,
From pollution by your sin,
Wash your robes and make them white;
You shall walk with God in light.[17]

---

[17] From "Come to Calvary's Holy Mountain" by James Montgomery (*LW* 96:1–3).

Leviticus 12:1–8

Impurity from Childbirth

Translation

**12 [1]The Lord spoke to Moses: [2]"Speak to the Israelites: When a woman pro-
duces seed and gives birth to a male, she will become unclean for seven days just
as she is unclean during the period of her menstrual infirmity. [3]On the eighth
day, the flesh of his foreskin shall be circumcised. [4]She shall remain in [a state
of] blood purification for thirty-three days; she shall not touch any holy thing
nor enter the sanctuary until her period of purification is complete.**

**[5]"If she gives birth to a female, she will become unclean for two weeks as in
her menstrual period. She shall remain in [a state of] blood purification for sixty-
six days.**

**[6]"At the completion of her period of purification for either a son or a daugh-
ter, she shall bring a lamb in its first year as a burnt offering and a pigeon or turtledove as a sin offering to the priest at the entrance to the tent of meeting. [7]He
shall present it before the Lord and make atonement for her, so that she may be
clean from her flow of blood. This is the ritual instruction for the woman who
gives birth to a male or female.**

**[8]"If, however, she cannot afford a sheep/goat, she may bring two turtledoves
or two pigeons, one as a burnt offering and the other as a sin offering. The priest
shall make atonement for her, so that she will be clean."**

Textual Notes

12:2 תַזְרִ֔יעַ—Literally the Hiphil of זָרַע means "to produce seed, produce offspring."

וְטָֽמְאָה֙—See the textual notes on 5:2. The verb recurs in 12:5.

שִׁבְעַ֣ת יָמִ֔ים—See the textual notes on 8:33.

נִדַּ֥ת—In Leviticus the term נִדָּה (here in construct) is used for the menstrual period with its discharge (12:2, 5; 15:20, 25, 26, 33; 18:19) and the impurity from it (15:19, 24) or from a man marrying his brother's wife (20:21).

דְּוֺתָ֖הּ—This is the Qal infinitive construct of the verb דָּוָה, "to be weak, sick." The adjective from this verb , דָּוֶה, is found in 15:33; 20:18.

See 15:19–24 for the legislation on menstrual impurity. After seven days, the mother is therefore able to resume normal life and sexual relations because she no longer defiles common things by her contact with them.

12:3 וּבַיּ֖וֹם הַשְּׁמִינִ֑י—See the textual notes on 9:1.

יִמּ֖וֹל—See Gen 17:10–14; Jn 7:22–23.

בְּשַׂ֥ר עָרְלָתֽוֹ׃—As in 15:2, 3, 19, here ("the flesh of his foreskin") the term בָּשָׂר is used as a euphemism for the genitals. Milgrom rightly construes this as an explicative genitive.[1]

---

[1] Milgrom, *Leviticus 1–16*, 748.

12:4 וּשְׁלֹשִׁים יוֹם וּשְׁלֹשֶׁת יָמִים—These thirty-three days added to the earlier seven make a total of forty days. Whitekettle argues plausibly that the forty days mirror the forty days from the opening of the cosmic springs in Gen 7:12 to their closure in Gen 8:2.[2] Thus, just as the earth was washed clean and thereby once again rendered habitable, so the womb becomes habitable after this transition of time.

תֵּשֵׁב—The exact sense of יָשַׁב here is uncertain. Some argue that it means "to remain home" in social seclusion (cf. Deut 21:13),[3] while others hold that it means "to remain sexually inactive" (cf. Hos 3:3).[4] But most likely it means "to remain" in a state of transition where she may have contact with common things, but does not yet have access to the sacred domain.

בִּדְמֵי טָהֳרָה—This is literally "in the bloods of purification." The term טָהֳרָה is used for the purification of a mother after childbirth (12:4, 5), the purification of the healed "leper" (13:7, 35; 14:2, 23, 32), and the purification of a man with a venereal discharge (15:13). It refers to the prescribed ritual process for purification (12:4, 5; 14:2, 32; 15:13) and for the declaration of purity by the priest (13:7, 35; 14:23). Blood purification seems to be a technical term here and in 12:5 for the intermediate state of a mother after childbirth. While she is physically clean with respect to the common domain, she is not yet ritually clean with respect to the sacred domain. The LXX translates it incorrectly with "her unclean blood." The use of this Hebrew phrase indicates that by its discharge the womb is reconstituted and cleansed for further reproductivity. The plural form for blood seems to be used to describe the various kinds of discharge, the lochia, from the womb. These vary in color from bright red to lighter degrees of brown over the forty or so days after childbirth.

בְּכָל־קֹדֶשׁ—See the textual notes on 4:6.

הַמִּקְדָּשׁ—The term מִקְדָּשׁ is used in two different ways in Leviticus. It most commonly refers to the "sanctuary," the sacred area around the altar and the tent of meeting (12:4; 16:33; 19:30; 20:3; 21:12; 26:2) and that is its meaning here. It can also be used for the sacred furnishings and objects that belong there (21:23; 26:31; cf. Num 3:38; 10:21; 18:1).

טָהֳרָהּ׃—This is best construed as an infinitive construct of the verb טָהֵר.

12:5 וְאִם—As elsewhere (e.g., 1:10, 14), the subsidiary case is introduced by וְאִם. See also 12:8.

12:6 תָּבִיא—See the textual note on this verb in 2:2.

כֶּבֶשׂ בֶּן־שְׁנָתוֹ— Literally "a lamb, the son of its year," this refers to a lamb that is less than a year old. This idiom recurs in 14:10; 23:12.

לְעֹלָה—For the sacrificial procedure, see 1:10–13.

וּבֶן־יוֹנָה אוֹ־תֹר—See the textual notes on 1:14.

פֶּתַח אֹהֶל־מוֹעֵד—See the textual notes on 1:3 and the explanation in "Leviticus 1–3."

---

2 Whitekettle, "Levitical Thought and the Female Reproductive Cycle," 387–88.

3 Hartley, *Leviticus*, 168.

4 See the references in Milgrom, *Leviticus 1–16*, 748.

12:7 וְהִקְרִיבוֹ—See the textual note on this verb in 1:2.

וְכִפֶּר—See the textual note on this verb in 1:4.

וְטָהֲרָה—See the textual note on this verb in 11:32. It recurs in 12:8. By the act of atonement, a people were cleansed from major impurities (14:19). Once they had been cleansed from impurity (12:7; 16:30), they were ritually clean (12:8; 14:20).

מִמְּקֹר—In the OT מָקוֹר usually refers to a "source" or "spring" of water (*HALOT*). It is used in Leviticus for the womb as a spring (20:18) as well as the flow of blood from the womb (12:7). Whitekettle investigates the significance of this analogy.[5]

זֹאת תּוֹרַת—See the textual note on תּוֹרָה in 6:2 (ET 6:9).

12:8 וְאִם־לֹא תִמְצָא יָדָהּ דֵּי—Literally this clause says "if her hand does not find sufficiency of resources for" (cf. 5:7; 25:26, 28).

שֶׂה—See the textual note on שֶׂה in 5:7.

וְלָקְחָה—We translated this as "she may bring," but literally it is "and she will take."

אֶחָד לְעֹלָה וְאֶחָד לְחַטָּאת—See 5:7–10; 15:14–15, 29–30 for the combination of the same two sacrifices.

Commentary

Structure

This short speech is divided into two clear parts. It begins with the legislation of the time schedule for the purification of a woman after the birth of a son (12:2b–4) or a daughter (12:5). The connection between these is highlighted by the repetition of יָלַד (12:2, 5), נִדָּה (12:2, 5), and דְּמֵי טָהֳרָה (12:4, 5). The second part, which is closely joined to 12:4 by the repetition of clause מְלֹאת יְמֵי טָהֳרָהּ (12:6), gives the normal prescribed sacrifices for presentation by the mother at the completion of this period of purification (12:7a), followed by the concession of a less burdensome sacrifice for a poor woman (12:8). The exceptional status of this concession is confirmed by the placement of the concluding summary before it in 12:7b.

The structure of this pericope can be outlined as follows:

I. Introduction (12:1–2a)
  A. God's address to Moses (12:1)
  B. God's commission of Moses (12:2a)
II. Speech about the purification of a woman after childbirth (12:2b–8)
  A. The schedule for purification (12:2b–5)
    1. The schedule for a male child (12:2b–4)
      a. Primary period of menstrual impurity for a week (12:2b)
      b. Circumcision on the eighth day (12:3)
      c. Secondary period of purification (12:4)
        i. Length: thirty-three days
        ii. Prohibition of access to the sacred domain

5 Whitekettle, "Levitical Thought and the Female Reproductive Cycle," 382–89.

      2. The schedule for a female child (12:5)
         a. Primary period of menstrual impurity for two weeks (12:5a)
         b. Secondary period of purification for sixty-six days (12:5b)
   B. The prescribed sacrifices for ritual restoration (12:6–8)
      1. The normal sacrifices (12:6–7a)
         a. Offering of a lamb as a burnt offering and a bird as a sin offering to the priest (12:6)
         b. Presentation by priest for atonement for her purification (12:7a)
      2. Summary statement (12:7b)
      3. The sacrifice for a poor woman (12:8)
         a. Offering of a bird for a burnt offering and a bird for a sin offering (12:8a)
         b. Performance of atonement for her purification (12:8b)

Ritual Theological Analysis

Even though the legislation in this chapter was addressed to all the Israelites, the main actor in it was the mother who had just given birth to a child. She was required to note and observe the time schedule for her purification and ritual reintegration into the congregation of Israel. Two main events in this process concerned her. She gave birth to the child; she offered the sacrifices that completed the passage from parturition to renewed participation in the divine service. She obviously did not act alone. All this involved her husband and her family too. But they merely went along with her. She brought the offerings to the tent of meeting and interacted with the priest there (12:6).

This speech of Moses outlines the ritual transition of a mother from parturition to normal life after the birth of a child. It describes a typical rite of passage with its three stages: an initial act of separation; a liminal stage of transition; and a final rite of reincorporation into society.[6] It concentrates on two things: the time schedule for this period of transition (12:1–5) and the rite of reintegration at the end of it (12:6–8). Even though this period of transition includes the physiological and social changes in the status of the mother during that period, that is not the main concern of this legislation. It has to do with her religious status, her access to the sanctuary and her contact with holy things. That overrides all the other aspects of childbearing.

The ritual passage began with the birth of the child. Immediately after that had occurred, the mother remained in social seclusion for a week if she had given birth to a son (12:2) or a fortnight if she had given birth to a daughter (12:5). During this period she remained in a state of ritual impurity. The postnatal discharge of blood from her womb was considered the same as her normal menstrual discharge. That discharge made her "unclean" (12:2, 5). Unlike some animistic pagans, she was not to regard it as a substance full of supernatural life-power that could be used in ritual, magical spells, and sorcery. On

---

[6] Van Gennep, *The Rites of Passage*, 10–11.

the contrary, it defiled her husband and children and made them unfit for contact with anything holy. Like menstrual blood (15:19–24), it conveyed impurity to people and things by contact with them. She could not therefore engage in sexual intercourse, the preparation of food, or any other domestic activities during this initial stage of separation. Her impurity disqualified her from normal involvement with others in the common domestic domain. As with menstruation, this period presumably ended with a ritual act of washing. Thereafter, she was free to resume her normal domestic role in the family.

This period of social separation for one week was followed by a longer period of ritual quarantine. If she had a male child, that lasted an additional thirty-three days; if she had a female child, it was sixty-six days. During this time she was not allowed to have any contact with the sacred domain (12:4b). Her ritual status was somewhat indeterminate. She was no longer ritually unclean because she did not transmit impurity through her postnatal discharge. The term that is used for her condition shows that she was not held to be unclean. Any further discharges after the initial week (or two) are called "the blood of purity" or "the blood for purification" (12:4–5).

Nevertheless, during this period she was also not yet ritually clean because she was not yet allowed to have access to anything that is holy. She was not allowed to touch any holy thing in her household, such as the meat from a peace offering or anything that had been dedicated as an offering to the Lord or, if she is the wife of a priest, any of the holy food from the sanctuary. She was also forbidden to enter the sacred precincts of the tabernacle and participate there in the sacrificial ritual.

If she had given birth to a male, her period of quarantine lasted for a total of forty days. If she had given birth to a female, it lasted for a total of eighty days. No rationale is given for the length of this transitional state and the difference between the sexes. A number of reasons have been proposed.[7]

The simplest solution is that the periods of forty and eighty days were customary lengths of time for ritual transition, as was the case with Moses, who spent forty days on Mount Sinai (Ex 24:18). This practice merely reflected what was common custom in the ancient world. Physiologically, it marked the maximum length for the postnatal discharge that could last longer for a female baby than a male. Ancient biology held that while a male embryo was fully formed in forty or forty-one days, the female embryo took up to eighty days to develop.

Many modern scholars ascribe the difference to a priestly obsession with impurity and evidence of "the cultic inferiority of the female sex."[8] This last judgment is inaccurate, for greater defilement did not indicate inferior status or worth. For example, the rabbis held that the holy OT Scriptures written in their original languages rendered the hands unclean, whereas common writ-

---

7 See Milgrom, *Leviticus 1–16*, 750–51.

8 Noth, *Leviticus*, 97.

ings or the Scriptures not written in their original languages did not render the hands unclean.[9] It could, in fact, be argued that the longer period of separation resulted from the importance of the daughter as a potential mother.[10] Whatever the case, the sacrifice is the same for both males and females (12:6–8).

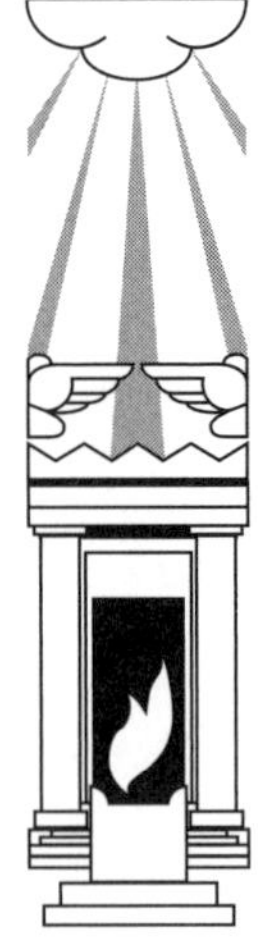

The period of religious quarantine was concluded by an act of sacrifice. The woman who had given birth to a child offered a lamb as a burnt offering and a turtledove or pigeon as a sin offering (12:6). If she was too poor to afford a lamb, she brought a bird instead (12:8). She entered the sacred precincts and brought the offerings to the priest on duty at the entrance. These two sacrifices performed two specific functions. Through the rite of atonement with the blood from both sacrifices, the woman was cleansed from any impurity that she had incurred from her flow of blood (12:7). Through the burning up of the lamb on the altar she was accepted by God and reinstated as a member of the congregation. She was once again ritually clean. She therefore had access to God's holiness and his blessing. That meant too that she was once again open to the gift of another child from him.

The observance of this rite of passage had a profound impact on the life of every mother. It connected her life as a mother with her participation in the divine service and her reception of blessing from God. Negatively, it ensured that she did not become involved as a woman in pagan practices that affirmed her status as a child-producer and sought to empower her by giving her access to cosmic life-power. Positively, it affirmed her status as a full member of the holy congregation and recognized her role as a bearer of blessing from God.

The reference in 12:2 to the mother as the seed-bearer, the offspring-producer, hints at this (see "Fulfillment by Christ" below). Her vocation as a mother then was connected with her call to holiness. What's more, the continuity and survival of her family—and, more broadly, of Israel—depended on her and her access to the blessing gained from the presence of God in the sacred domain. See figure 16.

By this legislation the menstrual and reproductive cycle of a mother was coordinated and incorporated into the liturgical calendar with its ordered enactment of the sacrificial ritual. Her time was synchronized with God's time.

While this chapter deals mainly with the state of a mother after childbirth, it also mentions, in passing in 12:3, the requirement for her to attend to the circumcision of any son that she produced. His circumcision occurred after her initial week of social seclusion. It marked her social reengagement on the eighth day after his birth. In the rite of circumcision, the foreskin was removed.

Whereas in many tribal societies circumcision had traditionally been, and still often is, a rite of passage that was performed at the onset of puberty to turn a boy into a man fit for marriage and adult life (cf. Gen 17:25), God had made it the mark or sign of his covenant with Abraham (Gen 17:9–14). By his Word

---

9 Talmud, Mishnah, *Yadayim* 4:5–6.

10 Gruber, "Women in the Cult according to the Priestly Code," 43, n. 13.

he established it as a rite in which an infant male became a member of his clan, a beneficiary of his covenant with Abraham (Gen 17:10–11) and a member of the liturgical community (Ex 12:48). This involved two powerful ritual reversals to the traditional pattern. The rite was not performed by the future father-in-law of the boy, but by his own father, the head of his family (Gen 17:23). It was not done to an adolescent boy in early puberty to make a man of him, but to an eight-day old infant (Gen 17:12; Lev 12:3) to make him part of God's kinsfolk, a male called on to pass on the seed and the blessing of Abraham to his descendants.

Figure 16

The Rite of Passage for the Purification of a Mother

	Gestation	Postnatal Period	Fecund State
Physiological condition	Pregnancy	Menstrual irregularity	Regular menstruation
Symptom	No menstruation	Vaginal discharge	Menstruation
Reproductivity	Reproduction	Reproductive incapacity	Reproductive capacity
Uterine condition	Inhabited womb	Uninhabitable womb	Habitable womb
Common time	Nine months	Week or fortnight	Monthly periods
Social-sexual status	Common purity	Menstrual impurity	Common purity
Ritual status	Ritual purity	Ritual ambiguity	Ritual purity
Ritual involvement	Access to sanctuary	Quarantine from holiness	Access to sanctuary

Fulfillment by Christ

The description of the mother as one who "produces seed" (תַזְרִיעַ, Lev 12:2) may recall the promise to Eve, the "mother of every living person" (Gen 3:20), that her "Seed" (זֶרַע) would crush the serpent's head (Gen 3:15). God repeated to the patriarchs his promise that through the Seed of Abraham all nations of the earth would be blessed (Gen 22:18; 26:4; 28:14). The apostle Paul expounds the fulfillment of this promise about the "Seed" by Christ and in all those who are baptized into Christ and thereby become the "seed" of Abraham (Gal 3:15–29).

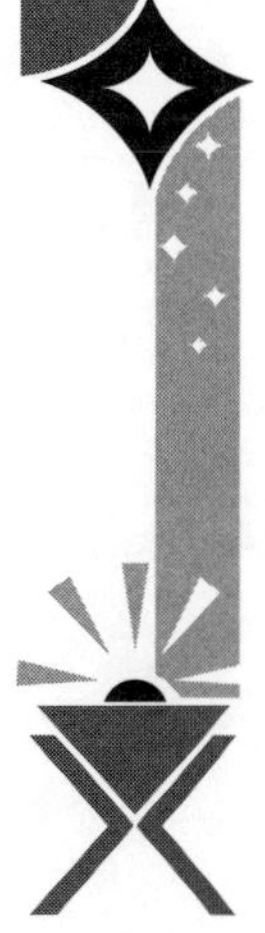

In keeping with the law in Lev 12:3, Jesus was circumcised on the eighth day after his birth (Lk 2:21). He fulfilled this aspect of the law just as he fulfilled the whole of it, for, as Just notes, "in the circumcision of the one who represents all humanity, all people are circumcised once and for all."[11] He entered into the covenant that God had made with Abraham and received the blessing that had been promised to him.

11 Just, *Luke 1:1–9:50*, 119.

Christ, in turn, replaced the rite of circumcision with his own circumcision, the circumcision performed by God the Father rather than by human hands (Col 2:11–13). That supernatural act of circumcision is enacted in Baptism. In Baptism the whole "body of flesh" is "put off" by burial with Christ and resurrection with him (Col 2:11–12). All baptized believers, whether male or female, Jew or Greek, are members of the one body of Christ (Col 3:11–15). Those who undergo this circumcision are qualified to participate in the service of God the Father by the Holy Spirit (Phil 3:3).

Mary, the mother of Jesus, involved him in her purification after his birth (Lk 2:22–24). She and Joseph brought him to the temple for the first time to include him in her purification on the fortieth day after his birth, even though the law did not require the son (Jesus) to be present for this. Since he was her firstborn son, he was offered to God at the same time as she was purified by the sacrifice of two birds (cf. Ex 13:2, 12; Neh 10:36). Yet no mention is made of his redemption then or later. Luke thereby indicated that the whole of his life was consecrated to the service of God (cf. Lk 1:35). Luke quite deliberately connected Mary's purification to Christ's consecration, for she was purified by her son—as are all the saints—for access to the heavenly sanctuary.

The circumcision of Jesus is commemorated in the church on New Year's Day, which is the eighth day after the Feast of the Nativity. On that day the church traditionally prays for the true circumcision of the Spirit, so that the hearts of the faithful may be pure from all sinful desires and lusts.

The purification of Mary is celebrated on the day for the presentation of our Lord on February 2. On that day the church prays for cleansing by Christ so that, like Mary, the people of God may be brought and presented to him with clean hearts.

The law for the purification of a mother after childbirth has led to the creation of a pastoral rite for the churching of mothers. In recent times the emphasis in that rite has shifted from purification and readmission to the Sacrament to thanksgiving for the safe delivery of the child and the blessing of the mother and the child together with the family.

Jesus, by your presentation,
When they blessed you, weak and poor,
Make us see your great salvation,
Seal us with your promise sure;
And present us in your glory
To your Father, cleansed and pure.[12]

---

[12] From "In His Temple Now Behold Him" by Henry J. Pye (*LW* 186:3).

Leviticus 13:1–59

The Diagnosis of Impurity from Skin Diseases

Translation

13 1The Lord spoke to Moses and Aaron: 2"When a person has a discoloration or a scab or a shiny patch on the skin of his body that may become an infection of a scaly skin disease on the skin of his body, he shall be brought to Aaron the priest or to one of his sons, the priests. 3The priest shall examine the infection on the skin of the body: if the hair on the infection has turned white and if the infection appears to be deeper than the skin of his body, it is an infection of a scaly skin disease; after the priest has examined it, he shall declare it unclean. 4But if there is a white shiny patch on the skin of his body that does not appear to be any deeper than the skin and if its hair has not turned white, the priest shall quarantine [the person with] the infection for seven days. 5On the seventh day the priest shall examine it, and if, in his observation, the infection has stayed the same and the infection has not spread in the skin, the priest shall quarantine him for seven days a second time. 6On the seventh day the priest shall examine it a second time: if the infection has faded and the infection has not spread in the skin, the priest shall declare it clean. It is only a scab. After he launders his clothes, he will be clean. 7But if the scab on his skin should spread out after he has shown himself to the priest for his purification, he shall show himself to the priest once again. 8The priest shall make an examination: if the scab has spread in the skin, the priest shall declare him unclean; it is a scaly skin disease.

9"When a person has an infection of a scaly skin disease, he shall be brought to the priest. 10The priest shall make an examination: if there is white discoloration in the skin that has turned the hair white, with a sore of raw flesh in the discoloration, 11it is a chronic scaly skin disease on the skin of his body. The priest shall declare him unclean; he shall not quarantine him, because he is unclean. 12But if the scaly condition breaks out all over the skin, so that scaly condition covers all the skin with the infection from his head to his foot, as far as the priest can see, 13then the priest shall make an examination. If the scaly condition covers the whole of his body, he shall declare the infection clean, since the whole of it has turned white; he is clean. 14But as soon as raw flesh reappears on him, he shall become unclean; 15the priest shall examine the raw flesh and declare it unclean. The raw flesh is unclean; it is a scaly skin disease. 16If, however, the raw flesh once again turns white, he shall come to the priest; 17the priest shall examine it: if the infection has turned white, the priest shall declare the infection clean; he is clean.

18"When the body of someone has a boil on its skin that has healed, 19and a white discoloration or shiny, reddish-white patch develops on the site of the boil,

**he shall show himself to the priest. 20The priest shall make an examination: if it
appears lower than the skin and if its hair has turned white, the priest shall declare him unclean; it is an infection of a scaly skin disease; it has broken out in
the boil. 21But if the priest examines it and finds that the hair in it is not white,
nor is it lower than the skin, but it has faded, the priest shall quarantine him for
seven days. 22If it should spread out in the skin, the priest shall declare him unclean; it is an infection. 23But if the shiny patch stays stationary and it does not
spread, it is the scar of a boil; the priest shall declare him clean.**

**24"Or, when the body of someone has a burn by fire on its skin, and the sore
from the burn becomes a shiny, reddish-white or white patch, 25the priest shall
examine it. If the hair in the shiny patch has turned white and it appears deeper
than the skin, it is a scaly skin disease; it has broken out in the burn. The priest
shall declare him unclean; it is an infection of a scaly skin disease. 26But if the
priest examines it and finds that the hair in the shiny patch is not white or it is
not lower than the skin, but it has faded, the priest shall quarantine him for seven
days. 27On the seventh day the priest shall examine it: if it should spread out on
the skin, the priest shall declare him unclean; it is an infection of a scaly skin disease. 28But if the patch stays stationary, without spreading, and if it has faded, it
is the discoloration from a burn. The priest shall declare him clean, because it is
the scar of a burn.**

**29"When a man or a woman has an infection on the head or on the chin, 30the
priest shall examine the infection. If it appears deeper than the skin and if the hair
in it is yellow and thin, the priest shall declare him unclean; it is a rash; it is the
scaly skin disease of the head or the chin. 31If the priest examines the infection of
the rash, and it appears no deeper than the skin and there is no black hair in it,
the priest shall quarantine [the person with] the infection of the rash for seven
days. 32On the seventh day the priest shall examine the infection. If the rash has
not spread, and there is no yellow hair on it, and the rash appears no deeper than
the skin, 33he shall get himself shaved, without shaving the rash. The priest shall
quarantine the rash for seven days a second time. 34On the seventh day the priest
shall examine the rash. If the rash has not spread on the skin, and it appears no
deeper than the skin, the priest shall declare him clean. After he launders his
clothes, he will be clean. 35If, however, the rash should spread out on the skin after his purification, 36the priest shall examine it: if the rash has spread on the skin,
the priest does not need to look for the yellow hair; he is unclean; 37but, if, in his
observation, the rash stays the same, and the black hair has grown in it, the rash
is healed; that person is clean. The priest shall declare him clean.**

**38"And when a man or a woman has many shiny white patches on the skin
of their bodies, 39the priest shall make an examination: if the patches on the skin
of their bodies are fading white, it is vitiligo that has broken out on the skin; that
person is clean.**

**40"When a man's head loses hair, he is bald, but he is clean. 41If his head loses
hair from his forehead, he has a receding hairline, but he is clean. 42But if he has
a reddish-white infection on his bald crown or on his bald forehead, it is a scaly**

skin disease that has broken out on his bald head or on his bald forehead. [43]The priest shall examine it: if the discoloration of the infection is reddish-white on his bald head or on his bald forehead, like the scaly skin disease on the skin of the body in appearance, [44]he is a skin-diseased man; he is unclean. The priest shall declare him utterly unclean; his infection is on his head. [45]The skin-diseased person who has the infection on him shall wear torn clothes and let his head be disheveled; he shall cover his upper lip and cry out, "Unclean! Unclean!" [46]For as long as the infection is on him he shall remain unclean. He is unclean. He shall reside apart; his place of residence shall be outside the camp.

[47]"When an infection of mold occurs on any piece of clothing, on woolen or linen cloth, [48]on the warp or the woof of linen or wool, on leather or anything made of leather, [49]and if the infection on the cloth or the leather or the warp or the woof or any article made of leather is bright yellow-green or bright red, it is an infection of mold. It shall be shown to the priest. [50]The priest shall examine the infection and shall quarantine the infection for seven days. [51]On the seventh day he shall examine the infection: if the infection has spread on the cloth or the warp or the woof or the leather or any article that is made of leather, the infection is a persistent mold; it is unclean. [52]He shall burn the clothing or the warp or the woof, whether it is made of wool or of linen, or whether it is any article made of leather that has the infection on it; because it has a persistent mold, it shall be burned in fire. [53]But if the priest makes an examination and discovers that the infection has not spread in the clothing, or on the warp or the woof, or on any leather article, [54]the priest shall command them to launder the material with the infection on it, and he shall quarantine it for seven days a second time. [55]Then after the infected material has been laundered, the priest makes an examination and even if he discovers that the infection has not changed its appearance and the infection has not spread, it is unclean. You shall burn it in fire; it is a rot on its front or its back. [56]But if the priest makes an examination and discovers that the infection has faded after it has been laundered, he shall tear it out of the clothing or the leather or the warp or the woof. [57]If it reappears in the clothing or the warp or the woof or any leather article, it is a new outbreak; you shall burn the material with the infection on it in fire. [58]If, however, the infection vanishes from the clothing or the warp or the woof or any leather article that you launder, it shall be washed a second time; then it will be clean."

[59]This is the ritual instruction for the infection of mold in woolen or linen clothing, in the warp or woof, or in any leather article, in order to determine whether it is clean or unclean.

Textual Notes

13:1 וַיְדַבֵּר יְהוָה אֶל־מֹשֶׁה וְאֶל־אַהֲרֹן—See this clause also in 11:1; 14:33; 15:1.

13:2 אָדָם—This term refers to any "person," male or female. See the textual note on it in 1:2. It recurs in 13:9.

שְׂאֵת—The noun שְׂאֵת is one of three key diagnostic terms in this section. It recurs in 13:10, 19, 28, 43; 14:56. It could be derived from the verb נָשָׂא, "to raise," and mean "a swelling." But most likely it comes from a different root and is best understood as "a mark, a discoloration."[1] *HALOT* gives "spot, blemish on the skin."

סַפַּחַת—The noun סַפַּחַת is the second key diagnostic term. It occurs in 13:2; 14:56. *HALOT* defines it as "scabs, flaking skin" and notes that in modern Hebrew it refers to psoriasis. It is synonymous with מִסְפַּחַת (13:6, 7, 8) and comes from the same root (ספח). It is regarded as benign if it does not spread (13:6).[2]

בַהֶרֶת—The noun בַּהֶרֶת is the third key diagnostic term. It occurs in 13:2, 4, 19, 23, 24, 25, 26, 28, 38, 39; 14:56. It is most likely a shiny, bright mark that is regarded as benign if it fades in color (13:6, 21, 26, 39). *HALOT* defines it as a "white spot on the skin."

לְנֶגַע—Often in the OT נֶגַע is used as a generic term for an "affliction, plague" (*HALOT,* 1 a). In the pagan world (ancient and modern), the common conviction is that gods and demons afflicted people with sickness by their touch. However, the Israelites knew that the one true God is in control of all things. They held that some infectious diseases were to be understood as a blow of punishment from the hand of God (Gen 12:17; Ex 11:1; Pss 39:11 [ET 39:10]; 89:33 [ET 89:32]; Is 53:8). Yet only once in Leviticus, with the case of mold on the walls of the house in 14:34, does God say that he has sent an infection.

In Leviticus 13–14 the term נֶגַע is used for three different kinds of infection: (1) the visible infection of a person with a skin disease (13:2, 3b, 9, 20, 22, 25, 27, 31, 32, 44, 45, 46; 14:3, 32, 54), the infected area (13:3a, 5, 6, 17a, 29, 30, 42, 43), and the infected person (13:4, 12, 13, 17b, 31); (2) the visible infection of cloth with a fungus (13:47, 49b, 51c, 52, 53, 54, 59), the infected area (13:49a, 50a, 51a, 55, 56, 58), and the infected material (13:50b, 51b, 57); and (3) the visible infection of a house with mold (14:34, 35, 40, 43, 44, 48) and the moldy area (14:36, 37, 39). A tractate of the Mishnah, *Nega'im,* gets its name from this term.

צָרַעַת—The noun צָרַעַת (in pause, צָרָעַת) is a general term for those kinds of infection (14:54, 57) that grow on the human skin (13:2, 3, 8, 9, 11, 12, 13, 15, 20, 25, 27, 30, 42, 43; 14:3, 7, 32) or cloth (13:47, 49, 51, 52, 59; 14:55) or house walls (14:34, 44, 55). *HALOT* gives for it the broad definition "skin disease." It means something like "scaliness, scabiness, moldiness." While KJV translated it as "leprosy," it is not the designation for what we now call leprosy. The LXX translates it by λέπρα, which means "a scaly condition," rather than by ἐλεφαντίασις, "leprosy." Since it was also used for fungus in clothes and mold in houses, it did not refer to any particular skin disease, such as psoriasis,[3] but covered a number of different diseases and conditions.[4] It is impossible to find a single English word that covers all these cases. It is derived from a verb that occurs in the OT only in the form of the Qal passive participle, צָרוּעַ

[1] Milgrom, *Leviticus 1–16*, 773.

[2] Milgrom, *Leviticus 1–16*, 774.

[3] Hulse, "The Nature of Biblical 'Leprosy' and the Use of Alternative Medical Terms in Modern Translations of the Bible," 98.

[4] Milgrom, *Leviticus 1–16*, 774–76, 816–26.

(Lev 13:44, 45; 14:3; 22:4), and the Pual participle, מְצֹרָע (14:2). Both forms of the verb mean "afflicted with a rash" (*HALOT*).

וְהוּבָא—Probably this (Hophal of בּוֹא) means that the infected person "shall be brought" to the priest, but it could mean that "it [the fact that the man is sick] shall be reported."[5] Lev 13:7 and 13:19 state that the man shall show himself to the priest, so probably this verse states that he shall be brought to the priest.

13:3 עָמֹק—This important diagnostic term describes soft, hollowed-out flesh under the infection or a thickened patch of skin that reached below the surface. *HALOT,* 2, defines it as "**deep-seated** (a patch of skin infection)." It occurs in 13:3, 4, 25, 30, 31, 32, 34. Its synonym שָׁפָל occurs in 13:20, 21, 26; 14:37.

נֶגַע צָרַעַת הוּא—The declaratory formula "it is an infection of a scaly skin disease" and its shortened form "it is a scaly skin disease" occur seven times in this section and eight times in this chapter (13:3, 8, 15, 20, 25 [twice], 27, 49). It was used officially by the priests to certify that a person had an unclean skin disease. Variations on it and other similar formulae of certification are found in 13:11, 22, 30, 39, 42, 57.

וְרָאֵהוּ—This could mean that the priest has examined "it" (the disease) or has examined "him" (the diseased person). Throughout this chapter the third masculine singular pronouns can refer to the disease or the diseased person.

וְטִמֵּא—See the textual note on this Piel verb in 11:44. It recurs in 13:8, 11, 15, 20, 22, 25, 27, 30, 44, 59.

13:4 וּשְׂעָרָה לֹא־הָפַךְ לָבָן—The LXX adds "but it is dull."

וְהִסְגִּיר—The Hiphil of סָגַר means "to quarantine" infected materials and houses as well as infected people (13:4, 5, 11, 21, 26, 31, 33, 50, 54; 14:38, 46). The purpose of the quarantine was not to prevent the spread of infection but to keep a suspected infection under surveillance before declaring it either clean or unclean.

שִׁבְעַת יָמִים׃—See the textual notes on 8:33. This phrase recurs in 13:5, 21, 26, 31, 33, 50, 54.

13:5 בְּעֵינָיו—Literally this means "in his eyes." See 13:37, 55. Milgrom argues that in this chapter עַיִן means "color."[6]

פָּשָׂה—This Qal verb means to "spread" (*HALOT*). It is a key diagnostic term. In the OT it occurs only in Leviticus 13–14, where it is frequent (13:5, 6, 7, 8, 22, 23, 27, 28, 32, 34, 35, 36, 51, 53, 55; 14:39, 44, 48).

13:6 כֵּהָה—This is the feminine form of the adjective כֵּהֶה, which means "**colourless,** dull" (*HALOT,* 1 a) or "faded." It is an important criterion for the diagnosis of the purity of a person with a skin infection. It recurs in 13:21, 26, 28, 39, 56.

וְטִהֲרוֹ—See the textual note on this verb in 11:32. As well as here, the Piel occurs in 13:13, 17, 23, 28, 34, 37, 59. The Qal form טָהֵר occurs later in 13:6 and then again in 13:34, 58.

וְכִבֶּס בְּגָדָיו—See the textual notes on 11:25. The verb recurs in 13:34, 54, 55, 56, 58.

---

5 Milgrom, *Leviticus 1–16*, 776.

6 Milgrom, *Leviticus 1–16*, 780–81.

13:7 פָּשֹׂה תִפְשֶׂה—An emphatic infinitive absolute is used before the verb פָּשָׂה in 13:7, 22, 27, 35.

הֵרָאֹתוֹ ... וְנִרְאָה—These two Niphal forms of רָאָה have a reflexive or middle meaning: "to present oneself" (*HALOT,* Niphal, 2) or "show oneself" to the priest. The Niphal of רָאָה has the same meaning in 13:19. See Lk 17:14.

לְטָהֳרָתוֹ—See the textual notes on 12:4.

13:9 נֶגַע צָרַעַת כִּי תִהְיֶה בְּאָדָם—Literally this means "As for an infection of scaly skin disease, when it is on a person …"

13:10 וּמִחְיַת בָּשָׂר—The exact sense of מִחְיָה here and in 13:24 is hard to pin down. It refers to a raw sore with raw flesh.

חַי בַּשְׂאֵת׃—Literally this phrase means "live flesh." "Live" recurs in 13:14, 15, 16. Cf. 1 Sam 2:15.

13:11 נוֹשֶׁנֶת—Literally this Niphal participle of יָשֵׁן means "aging, becoming old." This participle is not used to indicate that the condition was old, but that it was likely to persist for a long time: a "chronic skin disease" (*HALOT,* s.v. ישׁן II, Niphal, 2).

כִּי טָמֵא הוּא׃—See the textual notes on 5:2 and 11:44. This formula is used seven times in this chapter for unclean people and unclean things (13:11, 15, 36, 44, 46, 51, 55).

13:12 וְאִם־פָּרוֹחַ תִּפְרַח—See also 13:20, 25, 39, 42, 57; 14:43. An emphatic infinitive absolute is used here before the verb.

הַצָּרַעַת—The term צָרַעַת here and in the next verse does not refer to the infection, but to the condition of the skin.

לְכָל־מַרְאֵה עֵינֵי הַכֹּהֵן׃—Literally "with respect to all the appearance of the eyes of the priest," this means "as far as the priest can see."

13:13 הַנֶּגַע—This can mean that the priest declares "the infection" or "the infected person" to be clean.

כֻּלּוֹ הָפַךְ לָבָן—This could also be translated "since it has turned completely white."

טָהוֹר—See the textual notes on this adjective in 4:12 and 7:19. It recurs in 13:17, 37, 39, 40, 41; 14:4, 57.

13:16 אוֹ כִי יָשׁוּב הַבָּשָׂר הַחַי וְנֶהְפַּךְ לְלָבָן—This could also be translated "if the raw flesh recedes and becomes white." See 2 Ki 20:9 for the use of שׁוּב to mean "recede."

13:18 וּבָשָׂר כִּי־יִהְיֶה בוֹ־בְעֹרוֹ שְׁחִין—Literally this means "As for the body, when there is a boil on it, on its skin …"

13:20 שָׁפָל—This term occurs in 13:20, 21, 26; 14:37. It means "deeply imbedded" (*HALOT,* 1). It is a synonym of עָמֹק (see the textual note above on it in 13:3).

13:23 וְאִם־תַּחְתֶּיהָ תַּעֲמֹד הַבַּהֶרֶת—This clause literally means "if the shiny patch stands under it." It recurs in 13:28.

צָרֶבֶת—This term recurs in 13:28.

13:29 וְאִישׁ אוֹ אִשָּׁה—See the use of the same inclusive formula in 13:38.

בְּזָקָן׃—Literally this means "on the beard." However, since women are also addressed here, it is best translated as "on the chin" (see 1 Sam 17:35; Ezek 5:1).[7]

---

7 See Marcus, "The Term 'Chin' in the Semitic Languages," 54–55.

13:30 נֶתֶק—This refers to an itchy rash that makes hair fall out. The condition corresponds to what is now called favus.[8] This is an important diagnostic term in this unit (13:30, 31 [twice], 32 [twice], 33 [twice], 34 [twice], 35, 36, 37 [twice]). It comes from a verb that means "to tear off."

13:33 וְהִתְגַּלָּח—This Hithpael verb means "to have oneself shaved." The Piel occurs later in this verse as well as in 14:8, 9; 21:5. Milgrom notes that the use of elongated *gimel* in this word in many manuscripts indicates that some scribes regarded this as the middle verse of the Pentateuch.[9] However, the marginal Masorah on the first word of 8:8 indicates that it is the middle verse of the Torah in terms of verses. The marginal Masorah notes that the ו in גָּחוֹן in 11:42 is the middle letter of the Torah.

13:34 וְכִבֶּס בְּגָדָיו—See the textual note on this verb in 11:25.

13:35 טָהֳרָתוֹ׃—See the textual note on this term in 12:4.

13:36 יְבַקֵּר—See 27:33.

13:38 בֶּהָרֹת בֶּהָרֹת—Milgrom suggests that the Masoretic cantillation should be disregarded and these two words should go together.[10] This repetition indicates that there are many such patches (see GKC, § 123 e).

13:39 בֹּהַק—This term, which is found only here in the OT, is most likely the term for what is now called vitiligo or leukoderma, an unsightly, noncontagious rash common in warm and hot climates.[11]

13:40 וְאִישׁ כִּי יִמָּרֵט רֹאשׁוֹ—Literally this means "as for a man, when his head becomes bare …"

קֵרֵחַ—This is the term for baldness that begins at the crown rather than the forehead.

13:41 וְאִם מִפְּאַת פָּנָיו יִמָּרֵט רֹאשׁוֹ—Literally this means "if his head becomes bare from the fringe of his face …"

גִּבֵּחַ—This is the term for the baldness that begins at the forehead rather than the crown.

13:42 בַקָּרַחַת—Literally this means "on his crown-baldness."

בַגַּבַּחַת—Literally this means "on his forehead-baldness."

13:43 כְּמַרְאֵה צָרַעַת עוֹר בָּשָׂר׃—This is literally "like the appearance of the scaly skin disease of the skin of the body."

13:44 צָרוּעַ—This is the Qal passive participle of the verb צָרַע. See the textual note on צָרַעַת above in 13:2.

טַמֵּא יְטַמְּאֶנּוּ— An emphatic infinitive absolute precedes the verb.

בְּרֹאשׁוֹ נִגְעוֹ׃—This phrase, "his infection is on his head," seems to function as a declaratory formula akin to the formula of responsibility for one's own death: "his blood on his head" in Josh 2:19; 1 Ki 2:32; Ezek 33:4. It declares that the whole per-

8 Hulse, "The Nature of Biblical 'Leprosy' and the Use of Alternative Medical Terms in Modern Translations of the Bible," 103.

9 Milgrom, *Leviticus 1–16*, 796.

10 Milgrom, *Leviticus 1–16*, 799.

11 Hulse, "The Nature of Biblical 'Leprosy' and the Use of Alternative Medical Terms in Modern Translations of the Bible," 95.

son is totally affected by the disease. We have a case of this with the trespass of Uzziah into the Holy Place to burn incense in 2 Chr 26:19–20.

13:45 בְגָדָ֞יו יִהְי֣וּ פְרֻמִ֗ים—See Lev 10:5; 21:10.

וְרֹאשׁוֹ֙ יִהְיֶ֣ה פָר֔וּעַ—See 10:5; 21:10.

שָׂפָ֖ם—This could also be translated "moustache" (2 Sam 19:25 [ET 19:24]; Ezek 24:17, 22; Micah 3:7).

13:46 כָּל־יְמֵ֞י אֲשֶׁ֨ר הַנֶּ֥גַע בּ֛וֹ—This is literally "all the days that the infection is on him."

מִח֥וּץ לַֽמַּחֲנֶ֖ה—See the textual notes on 4:12.

13:47 נֶ֣גַע צָ֑רַעַת—This is the same phrase that was used for an infection of skin disease in 13:2–46. It is used in 13:47–59 for an infection of mold on clothes.

13:48 א֥וֹ בִשְׁתִי֙ א֣וֹ בְעֵ֔רֶב—The mold is either found on the vertical, down threads on the loom or the horizontal, cross thread in the shuttle or the loom.[12]

13:51 מַמְאֶ֧רֶת—See 13:52; 14:44. The sense of this term is uncertain. The LXX translates it by "persistent/incurable."

13:54 אֵ֥ת אֲשֶׁר־בּ֖וֹ הַנָּ֑גַע—This is literally "that on which the infection is." See 13:57.

13:55 הַנֶּ֗גַע—This is literally "the infection."

פְּחֶ֣תֶת—This unique term is most likely used for a fungus that eats away the cloth so that it rots.

בְּקָרַחְתּ֖וֹ—This is literally "on his forehead-baldness." The mold on the outside of the cloth is equivalent to the skin disease on the forehead of the person in 13:42–43.

בְגַבַּחְתּֽוֹ׃— This is literally "on his head-baldness." The mold on the inside of the cloth is equivalent to the skin disease on the crown of the person in 13:42–43.

13:56 וְקָרַ֣ע—This could be "cut," as in Jer 36:23.

אֹת֗וֹ—What is to be torn out is the infected area.

13:57 פֹּרַ֖חַת הִ֑וא—This is literally "it is breaking out." See 13:42.

13:59 This is the subscript for 13:47–58.

זֹ֞את תּוֹרַ֣ת—See the textual notes on 6:2 (ET 6:9).

לְטַהֲר֖וֹ א֥וֹ לְטַמְּאֽוֹ׃—This could also be translated "to declare it clean or unclean."

Commentary

Structure

(a) Lev 13:2–8, 9–17, 18–23, 24–28, 29–37, 38–39, 40–46

This speech is divided into two main parts. The first part covers the diagnosis of unclean skin diseases (13:2–46). The second part covers the diagnosis and treatment of mold in clothing (13:47–59).

The first section is made up of seven subunits, each of which begins with כִּי, "when."[a] In each case the subject matter of the subunit is introduced by the placement of a pending noun or a phrase before כִּי. This creates the following pattern:

[12] Milgrom, *Leviticus 1–16*, 809–10.

1. "When a *person* ..." (13:2)
2. "When an infection of scaly skin disease ... on a *person* ..." (13:9)
3. "When a *body* ..." (13:18)
4. "Or, when a *body* ..." (13:24)
5. "When *a man or a woman* ..." (13:29)
6. "When *a man or a woman* ..." (13:38)
7. "When *a man* ..." (13:40)

This device pairs off the first six statements and links them together as complementary units. The coupling of 13:18–23 and 13:24–28 is reinforced by a chiastic reversal in the use of three key diagnostic terms: שְׂאֵת, "discoloration," פָּשָׂה, "to spread," and בַּהֶרֶת, "a shiny patch." The three occur in that order in 13:19, 22, 23, and then in reverse order in 13:24, 27, 28.[13]

The seventh instruction culminates in the prescriptions for the person with a certified scaly skin disease on his head in 13:45–46. Most interpreters regard these two verses as a separate unit that provides the conclusion for the seven units of instruction that precede it. But it, more evidently, belongs to the seventh instruction for four reasons.

First, these verses are linked by the use in 13:45 of the catchword צָרוּעַ, "skin-diseased," from 13:44. In fact, the use of this term in 13:44 is unexpected because, from what has gone before, we have come to expect the certification of the infection rather than the infected person.

Second, the unique occurrence of the infinitive absolute with the verb טָמֵא in 13:44 signals that this is the worst case of pollution from skin disease. It is matched by the double cry of warning in 13:45.

Third, the pronouncement in 13:44 "his infection is on his head" is echoed in the following verses by the repeated affirmation that "the infection is on him."

Fourth and last, the fact that the infection is said to be on the head of the person requires him to go about with a disheveled head in 13:45. Thus 13:45–46 does not provide a general prescription for all people with a certified skin disease, but only for those who have skin disease on their heads.

The second section of the speech, which deals with moldy clothing, is introduced by וְהַבֶּגֶד כִּי, "As for clothing, when ..." (13:47). It forms a separate unit and is connected with the material around it by the classification of fabric mold as an infection of skin disease. Since this unit is complete in itself, it has its own subscript in 13:59.

Most of the material in this chapter is presented casuistically. All the main cases follow the same pattern, which identifies the main steps in the diagnosis of each case. This consists of five elements that occur as follows:

---

[13] Fishbane, "Biblical Colophons, Textual Criticism and Legal Analogies," 443.

1. Statement of symptoms:13:2, 9, 18–19, 24, 29, 38, 42, 47–49
2. Examination by priest:13:3, 10, 20, 25, 30, 39, 43, 50–51
3. Identification of symptoms:13:3, 10, 20, 25, 30, 39, 43, 51
4. Certification of disease:13:3, 11, 20, 25, 30, 39, 44, 51
5. Declaration of ritual status:13:3, 11, 20, 25, 30, 39, 44, 51

The order for the certification of the disease and the declaration of ritual status is reversed in 13:20 and 13:30. This basic pattern is modified to fit the requirements of all the subsequent cases for diagnosis. Each diagnosis culminates in two kinds of pronouncements: the certification of the disease and the declaration of ritual status. In each case the disease is officially certified with a stock formula.[b] The declaration of ritual status is indicated by reference to the pronouncement of a person as unclean[c] or clean[d] and by the use of the declaratory formula "he/it is unclean" (13:36, 44, 51, 55) or "he/it is clean" (13:17, 37, 39).

(b) Lev 13:3, 8, 11, 20, 22, 25, 27, 30, 39, 42, 51, 57

(c) Lev 13:3, 8, 11, 15, 20, 22, 25, 27, 30, 44

(d) Lev 13:6, 13, 17, 23, 28, 34, 37

The structure of this pericope can be outlined as follows:

I. Introduction: God's address to Moses and Aaron (13:1)
II. Speech about their diagnosis of infected skin and clothing (13:2–59)
  A. Seven cases of clean skin disease (13:2–46)
    1. Diagnosis of a person with suspected skin disease (13:2–8)
      a. Presentation of person with symptoms to a priest (13:2)
      b. Initial diagnosis (13:3–4)
        i. Certification of impurity after a positive diagnosis (13:3)
        ii. Quarantine after an uncertain diagnosis (13:4)
      c. Subsequent examination and further quarantine with a negative diagnosis (13:5)
      d. Final examination and certification of quarantined person (13:6)
        i. Certification of purity with negative diagnosis (13:6a)
        ii. Purification by laundering of clothing (13:6b)
      e. Diagnosis of person with subsequent infection (13:7–8)
        i. Appearance before priest for examination (13:7)
        ii. Certification of impurity after a positive diagnosis (13:8)
    2. Diagnosis of a person with skin disease (13:9–17)
      a. Presentation of infected person to a priest (13:9)
      b. Initial diagnosis (13:10–13)
        i. Certification of impurity after a positive diagnosis (13:10–11)
        ii. Certification of purity after a negative diagnosis (13:12–13)
      c. Diagnosis of person with subsequent infection (13:14–15)
        i. Appearance of infection (13:14)
        ii. Certification of impurity after a positive diagnosis (13:15)
      d. Diagnosis of unclean person with subsequent change of symptoms (13:16–17)
        i. Visit to a priest (13:16)
        ii. Certification of purity after a negative diagnosis (13:17)

3. Diagnosis of infected boils for possible skin disease (13:18–23)
    a. Presentation of person with an infected boil to a priest (13:18–19)
    b. Initial diagnosis (13:20–21)
        i. Certification of impurity after a positive diagnosis (13:20)
        ii. Quarantine after an uncertain diagnosis (13:21)
    c. Subsequent diagnosis of quarantined person (13:22–23)
        i. Certification of impurity after a positive diagnosis (13:22)
        ii. Certification of purity after a negative diagnosis (13:23)
4. Diagnosis of infected burns for possible skin disease (13:24–28)
    a. Initial diagnosis by a priest (13:24–26)
        i. Certification of impurity after a positive diagnosis (13:24–25)
        ii. Quarantine after an uncertain diagnosis (13:26)
    b. Subsequent diagnosis of quarantined person (13:27–28)
        i. Certification of impurity after a positive diagnosis (13:27)
        ii. Certification of purity after a negative diagnosis (13:28)
5. Diagnosis of head rash for possible skin disease (13:29–37)
    a. Initial diagnosis by a priest (13:29–31)
        i. Certification of impurity after a positive diagnosis (13:29–30)
        ii. Quarantine after an uncertain diagnosis (13:31)
    b. Subsequent examination of quarantined person (13:32–33)
        i. Examination of symptoms by a priest (13:32)
        ii. Shaving of the hair around the infection (13:33a)
        iii. Further quarantine (13:33b)
    c. Final diagnosis of quarantined person (13:34)
        i. Certification of purity after a negative diagnosis (13:34a)
        ii. Purification by laundering of clothing (13:34b)
    d. Diagnosis of person with subsequent infection (13:35–37)
        i. Certification of impurity after a positive diagnosis (13:35–36)
        ii. Certification of purity after a negative diagnosis (13:37)
6. Diagnosis of skin patches for possible skin infection (13:38–39)
    a. Description of symptoms (13:38)
    b. Certification of purity by priest after a negative diagnosis (13:39)
7. Diagnosis of hair loss for possible skin disease (13:40–46)
    a. Two cases of clean baldness (13:40–41)
    b. Diagnosis of unclean baldness (13:42–44)
        i. Symptoms of skin disease on the head (13:42)
        ii. Certification by priest of impurity with positive diagnosis (13:43–44)
    c. Restrictions for an unclean skin-diseased person (13:45–46)

B. Diagnosis and treatment of moldy clothing (13:47–59)
    1. The presentation of moldy clothing to a priest (13:47–49)
    2. Their initial examination and quarantine by the priest (13:50)

3. The diagnosis and treatment of quarantined clothing (13:51–58)
   a. Positive diagnosis (13:51–52)
      i. Confirmation of impurity by a priest (13:51)
      ii. Burning of the infected clothing (13:52)
   b. Negative diagnosis (13:53–58)
      i. Further quarantine after a negative diagnosis (13:53–54)
      ii. Treatment of quarantined clothing (13:55–58)
         - Laundering of quarantined clothing (13:55a)
         - Burning of clothing after a positive diagnosis (13:55b)
         - Removal of infected area after a negative diagnosis (13:56)
         - Burning of clothing with subsequent infection (13:57)
         - Purification of clothing by laundering (13:58)
4. Concluding subscript (13:59)

Ritual Analysis

These instructions are addressed to Moses and Aaron (13:1). Aaron was included because the priests were to diagnose and certify the cases of skin disease and fabric mold. But they were not commissioned to hand on these instructions to others who were not priests.

The first instruction deals with the case of suspected skin disease (13:2–8). Three primary symptoms are listed as possible precursors to infectious skin disease: discoloration, a scab, and a bright patch. If a person had one of these, that person was brought to a priest who then examined the infection. If the hair in the infected area had turned white and the area appeared deeper than the surrounding skin, the priest certified that it was "an infection of a scaly skin disease" (13:3).

Those two key symptoms for its identification indicated that the infection was eating away the flesh of the person. The priest then declared that person ritually unclean. But if those two verifying symptoms were absent, the person was kept under observation in quarantine for fourteen days. At the end of the first and second weeks, the priest made an examination to discover whether the infection had spread. If it had faded and not spread at all over those two weeks, the priest certified that it was a scab, and he declared the person ritually clean after he had laundered his clothes (13:6). If, however, the scab began to spread once again, the person reappeared before the priest for diagnosis of his symptoms, certification of his disease, and declaration of his ritual status (13:7–8). The diagnostic scheme of 13:2–8 is set out in figure 17.

The second instruction outlines the procedure for the certification of a person with skin disease (13:9–17). As in the previous case, the priest performed the diagnosis of the person (13:9). Two symptoms verified the presence of skin disease: the appearance of white hair in the discolored area and the appearance of an ulcer with raw flesh. If both these symptoms were present, there was no need for any period of quarantine, for the flesh was obviously decaying. The priest therefore certified that it was "a chronic scaly skin disease" and declared that the person was ritually unclean (13:10–11).

If, on the other hand, an infection covered the whole body with a white skin disease, the priest pronounced both the infection and the person ritually clean (13:12–13). But if ulcerating flesh appeared on the person who had been pronounced clean, the priest reexamined it, recertified the infection, and reclassified the person as ritually unclean (13:14–15). Likewise, if the ulcerating flesh subsequently turned white, the priest reexamined the infection and recertified the infection and the person as ritually clean (13:16–17).

Figure 17

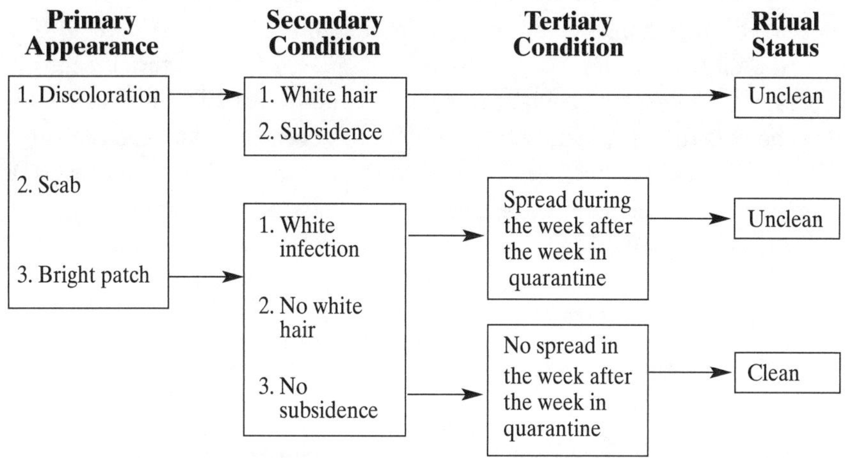

The third subunit outlines the procedure for the diagnosis of the scars from boils for evidence of possible skin disease (13:18–23). The initial primary symptoms for this condition were the appearance of white discoloration or a reddish-white inflamed patch on the scar from the boil. If these primary symptoms were evident, the person came before the priest for diagnosis (13:18–19). If the same two verifying symptoms were evident as for suspected skin disease (13:4), the priest certified that it was "an infection of a scaly skin disease" and declared the person unclean (13:20). But if these symptoms were absent and the color of the patch had faded, the priest quarantined the person for a week before he reexamined the infected area and passed his judgment on the infection and the person by considering whether it had spread or remained just as it was (13:21–23).

The fourth subunit is a variation on the previous case and closely related to it. It deals with diagnosis of scars from burns for evidence of possible skin disease (13:24–28). The symptoms for this condition were the appearance of a reddish-white or white inflamed patch on the burnt area (13:24). Apart from that, the procedure for diagnosis and certification was exactly the same as for scars from boils.

The fifth section of the instruction addresses the procedure for the diagnosis of an infection on the head or jaw for evidence of possible skin disease in men and women (13:29–37). The symptoms for the confirmation of the infection as a skin disease were the subsidence of the infected flesh below the level of the surrounding skin together with the change in the color of the hair on the infected area so that it became yellow and straggly. If these two symptoms were evident, the priest certified that it was a "scaly skin disease of the head or the chin" (13:29–30).

If, however, there was no subsidence in the level of the affected area and no black hair in it, the person with the infection of rash was quarantined for a fortnight. At the end of the first week, the priest reexamined the infected area to discover whether the infection had spread, produced yellow hair, and subsided. If none of these things had happened, the hair around the infected area was shaved off and the person was put in quarantine for another week. If the infected area had not spread or subsided, the priest declared him clean. Like the person with suspected skin disease, that person then laundered his clothes before he was ritually clean (13:31–34). If, however, the rash began to spread again, the priest reexamined the condition. If the rash had spread, the priest declared the person unclean, even if no yellow hairs had appeared on the rash. But if the rash remained as it was and it had dark hair on it, the priest declared the rash and the person clean (13:35–37). The diagnostic procedure is set out in figure 18.

Figure 18

Diagnostic Procedure for Infection on the Head or Chin

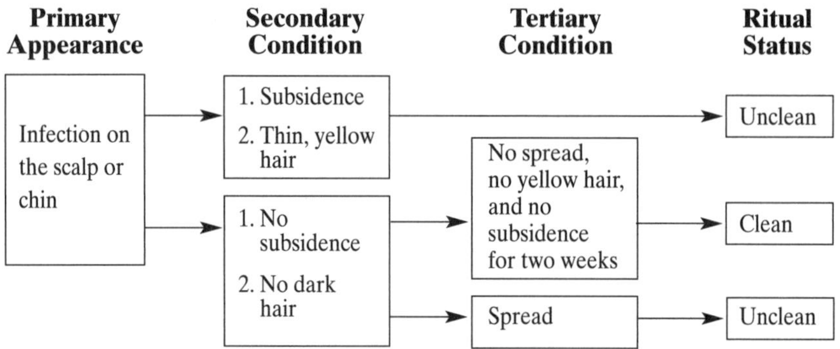

The sixth instruction deals rather briefly with the outbreak of white inflamed patches all over the body of a man or woman (13:38–39). If the patches were a dull white color that faded around the edges, the priest pronounced the person clean.

The last instruction on skin infection outlines the procedure for the diagnosis of hair loss from possible skin disease (13:40–46). First, the primary symptoms were identified. Ordinary hair loss with a patch of baldness that began either at the crown or the forehead was excluded from further consideration. In this case hair loss was associated with reddish-white infection on the crown or the forehead. If the priest discovered that the infection had produced a reddish-white discoloration, like that for a boil or a burn (13:19, 24), he declared the person doubly unclean because he had an infection on his head. He was both "a skin diseased man" and "unclean" (13:42–44).

Such a skin-diseased person with an infection on his head was subject to severe restrictions. First, he had to conduct himself like a person in mourning by wearing torn clothes and having his head disheveled. Second, he had to protect other people from his severe impurity by covering his lower face and crying out, "Unclean! Unclean!" when anyone approached him. Third, since he remained unclean for as long as the infection was on his head, he had to reside by himself, apart from his kinsfolk, outside the camp of Israel.

These seven instructions are therefore concerned with the certification of a skin infection as either unclean or clean. The criteria for this judgment by the priests are carefully defined. The primary symptoms for consideration vary from case to case. There are, however, five secondary symptoms that confirm the presence of a defiling skin disease:

1. Change of skin color from the normal pink-white
2. Change of hair color from dark to white or yellow
3. Subsidence to the flesh under the infected area
4. Spread of the infected area
5. Ulceration of the skin in a discolored area

The second part of the speech outlines the procedure for the diagnosis and treatment of fungus in clothing (13:47–59). The infection of clothing is treated in this speech rather than, as we might expect, in the speech on fungus in houses in 14:33–57 because clothing was closely associated with human skin. It was a kind of second skin for the human body. This instruction begins by identifying the primary symptoms of "skin disease" in clothing and fabrics. They are a greenish or reddish infection (13:47–49). If these symptoms appeared in any fabric or any piece of clothing, the item with the infection was brought to the priests for examination. After the priest had examined it, he kept it in quarantine for a week. If the infection had spread, then he certified that it was a "skin disease" or a "persistent mold" and declared that it was unclean. The piece of clothing was therefore burned (13:52). But if the infection had not spread during the first week of quarantine, the piece of clothing was thoroughly laundered and kept in quarantine for another week before reexamination by the priest.

If, on the one hand, the infection had not changed, even though it had not spread, the priest declared the clothing unclean and had it burned (13:55). If, on the other hand, the infection had faded, the priest removed the formerly infected area from the clothing. But if it reappeared and spread, the whole item of clothing was burned (13:56–57). If the infection had disappeared from any piece of cloth after it had been laundered, it was laundered a second time before it was regarded as clean and available for human use (13:58). The purpose of this instruction was to help the priests distinguish between ritually clean and ritually unclean clothing (13:59).

Ritual Theological Analysis

The ritual instruction in this chapter does not provide a medical diagnosis of skin diseases, nor does it deal with the ritual status of people who have certain kinds of skin disease. While most kinds of skin infection are not held to be ritually significant, there is one kind that makes the Israelites and their clothes unclean. That class of infection is called צָרַעַת, "a scaly skin disease." This technical term covers a number of different kinds of infection, all of which are identified in this speech. While the initial symptoms for them varied, all kinds of צָרַעַת had one thing in common: they ate away at the flesh of the body or the fabric of a piece of clothing. The key symptoms for identification of it were the loss of flesh beneath the infection, its spread across the body, and raw ulceration on flesh of the infected area. This applied to fabrics as well, for the infection ate away at the fabric and rotted it.

Thus the "skin disease" (צָרַעַת) was an infection that killed off the flesh in the body and made it decay. It was the mark of death on a person. It turned some part of the body into a corpse before the actual death of the person; it brought with it a kind of impurity like the impurity of carcasses and corpses. The deadly character of this kind of skin disease for human beings was evident from the secondary symptom of its presence. It destroyed the hair that lived on it so that it lost its color and died. The healthy dark hair on the body became white (13:3, 10, 20, 25; cf. 13:4, 21, 26) or yellow and wispy (13:30; cf. 13:31, 32, 37).

Yet all kinds of skin disease were not equally deadly. While ordinary skin disease rotted away the flesh under the skin, chronic skin disease broke through the skin and opened up raw ulcers on the body (13:11). The worst form of skin disease broke out on the head of a person. Since it was located on the head, it defiled the whole body and made the whole person unclean. He did not just have "a skin disease," he was "skin-diseased." The infection was the mark of death on his head (13:42–44). This kind of skin disease had its equivalent in the infection of clothing that could not be stopped by thorough laundering. Like the skin disease that had "broken out" on the "forehead" or "crown" of a man (13:42), it was a rot that had symbolically appeared on the forehead or crown of the cloth (13:55). The cloth was therefore burned, since it could not be purified (13:57; cf. 13:42).

Those who had a skin disease were declared unclean by the priest as God's representative, because it was a kind of death that disqualified them from God's presence. This pronouncement affected people in two ways. On the one hand, they were excluded from the sanctuary and were not allowed to eat any holy food (22:4; 2 Chr 26:21). On the other hand, they were also excluded from participation in common meals and the common life of the holy community, because their skin disease transmitted impurity by direct and indirect contact with it. They were, in some cases, required to live outside the camp (Num 5:1–4) or outside the city (2 Ki 7:3). But those who had skin disease on their heads were also required to act as if they were in mourning by tearing their clothes and having their hair disheveled; they were required to avoid contact with other people by covering their mouth and warning others that they were doubly unclean (13:45–46).

The singling out of that group for those sanctions is hard for us to comprehend. Two keys are needed for making sense of the sanctions. First, the head had special ritual significance in Leviticus. It represented the whole person; it was the place of distinction on the human body. Thus Aaron and every high priest after him had their heads anointed with holy oil (8:12; 21:10). He wore the turban with the holy plate on his head (8:9). Neither the high priest nor any priest was allowed to dishevel his hair in mourning (10:6; 21:10). When a person who had recovered from skin disease was reinstated as a member of the congregation, the priest put the leftover oil on his head (14:18, 29). But, when a person was sentenced to death for blasphemy, those who heard him blaspheme laid their hands on his head (24:14). Second, 2 Chr 26:16–21 shows how King Uzziah's act of sacrilege by his entry into the Holy Place to burn incense resulted in an outbreak of skin disease on his forehead. This kind of skin disease was therefore regarded as an act of God, the punishment for the desecration of his holiness and for refusal to submit to his headship.

The focus on the purity of the body in 13:1–46 is matched by an equal emphasis in 13:47–59 on the purity of the clothing that was worn by the Israelites. This concern for clothing is a surprising feature in this chapter. Yet it pervades the whole of Leviticus, for clothing is, as it were, a second skin for the human body.

The priestly legislation therefore holds that clothing can be holy, common, or unclean. Common clothing needs to be clean if those who wear it engage in common activities within their communities and enter the sanctuary. Clean and common clothing can be consecrated by the application of holy anointing oil and the blood from the ram for ordination (8:30). These items of clothing thereby become the sacred vestments of the priests (16:4, 32). But common clothing can also be polluted by contact with something unclean, such as a carcass (11:28, 40), skin disease (13:6), a genital discharge (15:6), semen (15:17), menstrual blood (15:21), or an irregular menstrual discharge (15:27). It therefore had to be laundered before the person who wears it could use it for common or sacred purposes (13:6, 34).

In fact, the laundering of clothes was often connected with the washing of the body as the basic rite for purification from a secondary source of impurity (15:8, 11, 13, 27). Just as the consecrated vestments of the priest were holy by virtue of the holy oil and blood on them, so common clothes were unclean if they had an irremovable infection of mold on them (13:51, 55). They could not be worn any more, for they polluted their wearers. They had to be destroyed. But if the mold was removed, they were washed so that they became clean once again (13:58).

Fulfillment by Christ

Since the fulfillment of the laws on skin disease is covered at the end of Leviticus 14, here we only deal with the Christological significance of infected clothing.

In Leviticus, clothing was associated with the bodily purity that qualified a person for access to the sanctuary and contact with the food that came from the Lord's table. That level of purity, however, did not suffice for human access to God the Father in the heavenly sanctuary that was granted in the new covenant. All human beings are "far from God's glory" (Rom 3:23) because they all are sinners; they are, as it were, clothed in unclean and dying flesh, the old Adam.

That deadly deficiency has, however, been rectified by God's Son in his incarnation, for he took on our sin-infected humanity in order to clothe us with his own sinless and pure humanity. In Baptism we have put off our old self, like a piece of dirty clothing (Col 2:11), and we have been clothed with Christ (Gal 3:27; Col 3:9–10). We have received our new self in him. We are clothed in "his righteousness and holiness" (Eph 4:23–24). In him we have access to God the Father (Rom 5:1–2; Eph 2:18). He gives us the wedding garment that we need to eat at his table (Mt 22:11–12). As saints—people who are holy in Christ—we are required to let him strip us of all the evil that is in us (Eph 4:22) and to clothe ourselves with him (Rom 13:14) and his virtues (Col 3:12–14), so that we can live in his presence and fulfill our vocation as his holy people, now and for eternity.[e]

(e) Rev 3:4–5, 18; 4:4; 6:11; 7:9, 13–14; 16:15; 22:14

All mankind fell in Adam's fall,
One common sin infects us all;
From sire to son the bane descends,
And over all the curse impends.

Through humankind corruption creeps
And them in dreadful bondage keeps;
In guilt they draw the infant breath
And reap its fruits of woe and death.

But Christ, the second Adam, came
To bear our sin and woe and shame,
To be our life, our light, our way,
Our only hope, our only stay.

As by one man all mankind fell
And, born in sin, was doomed to hell,
So by one Man, who took our place,
We all received the gift of grace.[14]

[14] From "All Mankind Fell in Adam's Fall" by Lazarus Spengler (*LW* 363:1, 2, 4, 5).

Leviticus 14:1–32

Purification of the Skin-Diseased

Translation

**14 1The Lord spoke to Moses: 2“This is the ritual instruction for a skin-diseased
person at the time of his purification. When it is reported to the priest, 3the priest
shall go outside the camp. The priest shall make an examination: if the infection
of the skin disease has become healthy on the skin-diseased person, 4the priest
shall command that two wild clean birds, some cedar wood, some crimson yarn,
and hyssop be taken for the person who is being purified. 5The priest shall command one bird to be slaughtered into an earthen pot over living water. 6After
taking the live bird, along with the cedar wood, the crimson yarn, and the hyssop, he shall dip them, along with the live bird, in the blood of the bird that was
slaughtered over the living water. 7He shall sprinkle [the blood] seven times on
the person who is being purified of the skin disease. When he has declared him
clean, he shall release the live bird into the open country. 8The person who is being purified shall launder his clothes, shave off all his hair, and bathe in water;
then he will be clean. After that he may enter the camp, but he must reside outside his tent for seven days.**

**9“On the seventh day he shall shave off all his hair; he shall shave his head,
his chin, his eyebrows, and all [the rest of] his hair. He shall launder his clothes
and bathe in water; then he will be clean. 10On the eighth day he shall take two
male lambs without blemish, one yearling ewe without blemish, three-tenths [of
an ephah] of fine flour for a grain offering mixed with olive oil, and one measure
of olive oil. 11The priest who performs the rite of purification shall station the
person who is being purified, together with them, before the Lord at the entrance
to the tent of meeting. 12The priest shall take one of the male lambs, bring it forward as a reparation offering, together with the measure of olive oil, and raise it
as an elevation offering before the Lord. 13The lamb shall be slaughtered in the
holy place, the place where the sin offering and the burnt offering are slaughtered, for the reparation offering is like the sin offering; it belongs to the priest;
it is most holy. 14The priest shall take some of the blood of the reparation offering and put [it] on the right lobe of the ear of the person who is being purified,
on the thumb of his right hand, and on the big toe of his right foot. 15The priest
shall take some of the olive oil from the measure and pour [it] out on the palm
of the priest’s left hand. 16Then the priest shall dip his right finger into some of
the olive oil that is on his left palm and sprinkle some of the olive oil with his finger seven times before the Lord; 17and some of the rest of the olive oil on his palm
the priest shall put on the lobe of the right ear of the person who is being purified, on the thumb of his right hand, and on the big toe of his right foot—over
the blood of the reparation offering; 18the priest shall put the rest of the olive oil
that is on his palm upon the head of the person who is being purified. Then the**

priest will make atonement for him before the Lord. 19The priest shall perform
the ritual for the sin offering and make atonement for the person being purified
from his impurity. After that, the burnt offering shall be slaughtered, 20and the
priest shall offer up the burnt offering and the grain offering on the altar. Thus
the priest shall make atonement for him so that he will be clean.

21"If, however, he is poor and his means are insufficient, he shall take one
male lamb as a reparation offering for elevation to make atonement for him, one-
tenth [of an ephah] of fine flour mixed with olive oil for a grain offering, and one
measure of olive oil, 22as well as two turtledoves or two pigeons, whichever are
within his means, the one as a sin offering and the other as a burnt offering. 23On
the eighth day he shall bring them for his rite of purification to the priest at the
entrance to the tent of meeting before the Lord. 24The priest shall take the lamb
for the reparation offering and the measure of olive oil, and the priest shall raise
them as an elevation offering before the Lord. 25After the lamb for the repara-
tion offering has been slaughtered, the priest shall take some of the blood of the
reparation offering and place it on the lobe of the right ear of the person who is
being purified, on the thumb of his right hand, and on the big toe of his right
foot. 26After the priest has poured out some of the olive oil on the palm of the
priest's left hand, 27the priest shall sprinkle with his right finger some of the olive
oil from his left palm seven times before the Lord; 28the priest shall also put some
of the olive oil which is on his palm on the lobe of the right ear of the person
being purified, on the thumb of his right hand, and on the big toe of his right
foot—on the place of the blood of the reparation offering; 29then the priest shall
put the rest of the olive oil that is on his palm upon the head of the person who
is being purified by making atonement for him before the Lord. 30The priest shall
then perform the ritual with one of the turtledoves or pigeons that are within his
means— 31whichever he can afford—the one as a sin offering and the other as a
burnt offering, together with the grain offering. Thus the priest shall make atone-
ment before the Lord for the person being purified."

32This is the ritual instruction for anyone who has the infection of skin dis-
ease on him [and] whose means are insufficient at [the time of] his purification.

Textual Notes

14:2 זֹ֣את תִּהְיֶה֙ תּוֹרַ֣ת—See the textual note on תּוֹרָה in 6:2 (ET 6:9).

הַמְּצֹרָ֔ע—This Pual participle of צָרַע is used for someone who has been certified as afflicted with an unclean skin disease. See the textual note on צָרַ֫עַת in 13:2.

טָהֳרָת֑וֹ—See the textual note on this noun (טָהֳרָה) in 12:4. It recurs in 14:23, 32.

וְהוּבָ֖א—This Hophal of בּוֹא could mean "when it [the fact that the man is healed] is reported" or "when he is brought." See the textual note on the same verb in 13:2. However, since a diseased person who had been declared unclean was to reside outside the camp (13:46), probably he would not be brought to the priest within the camp. Therefore we translate this "when it is reported."

14:3 מִח֖וּץ לַֽמַּחֲנֶ֑ה—See the textual note on this phrase in 4:12. See 14:8.

נִרְפָּ֥א—Instead of the middle voice, "has become healthy," the Niphal of the verb רָפָא could mean "has been healed" with God as the implied agent of healing.

הַצָּרוּעַ:—This is the Qal passive participle of צָרַע. The Pual participle occurred in 14:2. See the textual note on צָרַעַת in 13:2.

14:4 וְלָקַח—See the textual note on this verb in 9:2.

לַמִּטַּהֵר— This Hithpael participle of טָהֵר (the assimilated ת is marked by the *daghesh* in the *tet* [-טּ-]) is used to describe the person undergoing the rites for purification. It recurs in 14:7, 8, 11, 14, 17, 18, 19, 25, 28, 29, 31. See the textual note on this verb in 11:32.

צִפֳּרִים—Most likely this denotes some kind of sparrow.[1]

חַיּוֹת—The adjective חַי usually means "live, alive," and that is its meaning in 14:6–7, where it (חַיָּה) refers to the "live bird." However, often with animals it means "wild, undomesticated," and that is its sense in 14:4.

טְהֹרוֹת—These "clean" birds are birds that could be eaten. See 11:13–19. See also the textual note on this adjective, טָהוֹר, in 7:19.

וְעֵץ אֶרֶז—This could also be "a stick of cedar/a twig of cedar." See Num 19:6. Cedar may have been used because it is fragrant, red, and not subject to decay.

וּשְׁנִי תוֹלַעַת—This is literally "the crimson of the worm." See Num 19:6. This refers to woolen yarn colored with a crimson-scarlet dye made from the female chochmial worm (cf. 2 Chr 2:6, 12 [ET 2:7, 13]; 3:14). This dye was used to make the furnishings of the tabernacle and the vestments of the high priest (Ex 25:4; 26:1; 28:5).

וְאֵזֹב:—Most likely this is the herb marjoram (see Ex 12:22; Num 19:6, 18; Ps 51:9 [ET 51:7]).

14:5 וְשָׁחַט—See the textual note on this verb in 1:5. It recurs in 14:6, 13, 19, 25. The third person singular is used impersonally and so is translated with a passive verb, "is slaughtered." Even though the term for ritual slaughter is used, this is not a sacrifice, since the bird is not slaughtered at the sanctuary.

מַיִם חַיִּים:—This is literally "living waters." This refers to running water taken from a spring or a flowing stream (14:6, 50, 51, 52; 15:13). The water that is mentioned most likely refers to water in the pot. The pot, however, may also be held over running water.

14:6 וְטָבַל אוֹתָם—He is to dip the cedar stick, the crimson thread, and the bunch of hyssop.

14:7 וְהִזָּה—See the textual note on this verb in 4:6.

שֶׁבַע פְּעָמִים—See the textual note on this phrase in 4:6. It recurs in 14:16, 27, 51.

וְטִהֲרוֹ—See the textual note on this verb in 11:32. See also 14:8, 9, 11, 23, 28, 34, 37, 58, 59.

וְשִׁלַּח אֶת־הַצִּפֹּר הַחַיָּה—Levine and Milgrom regard the release of the "live bird," like the release of the scapegoat in 16:21, as a rite of elimination in which the disease is carried away from the person.[2] However, in ancient Israel birds symbolized human vitality. Therefore it is more likely that this rite announces and symbolizes the return of the healed person from social death to life.[3]

---

1 See Talmud, Mishnah, *Nega'im,* 14:5.

2 Levine, *Leviticus*, 85; Milgrom, *Leviticus 1–16*, 838.

3 Keil, *Pentateuch*, 2:385–86; Staubli, "Die Symbolik des Vogelrituals bei der Reinigung von

עַל־פְּנֵי הַשָּׂדֶה׃—This phrase recurs in 14:53; 17:5.

14:8 וְכִבֶּס הַמִּטַּהֵר אֶת־בְּגָדָיו—See the textual notes on 11:25.

וְגִלַּח אֶת־כָּל־שְׂעָרוֹ—See 13:33; 14:9.

וְרָחַץ בַּמַּיִם—A ritual bath is often prescribed for priests (8:6; 16:4, 24, 26, 28; 22:6) or lay people (14:8, 9; 15:5, 6, 7, 8, 10, 11, 13, 16, 18, 21, 22, 27; 17:15, 16) whose bodies had been ritually polluted by contact with impurity.

וְטָהֵר—See the textual note on this verb in 11:32. See also its use in 14:9, 20, 53.

שִׁבְעַת יָמִים׃—See the textual notes on 8:33.

14:9 וְאֶת־כָּל־שְׂעָרוֹ—This would include the pubic hair.

14:10 וּבַיּוֹם הַשְּׁמִינִי—See the textual notes on 9:1. The phrase recurs in 14:23.

תְּמִימִים—See the textual note on this adjective in 1:3.

וְכַבְשָׂה—The female lamb was for the sin offering (4:32; 5:6).

בַּת־שְׁנָתָהּ—See the textual notes on 12:6.

וּשְׁלֹשָׁה עֶשְׂרֹנִים—This was the same amount of flour as for the public offerings at the festivals (Num 28:12, 20, 28; 29:3, 9, 14). Three-tenths of an ephah amounts to about thirty-five grams.

סֹלֶת—See the textual note on this term in 2:1. It recurs in 14:21.

וְלֹג—The Hebrew לֹג is the term for a small liquid measure of about three-tenths of a liter or about two cups.

14:11 וְהֶעֱמִיד—This verb is used to indicate the location of this person and his offerings in a sacred place before the Lord. It is used in rites that involve a change of status, in connection with the goats on the Day of Atonement (16:7, 10), a person or animal vowed to the Lord (27:8, 11), Levites at their installation (Num 3:6; 8:13), a woman suspected of adultery (Num 5:16, 18, 30), and Joshua as the successor of Moses (Num 27:19, 22).

הַכֹּהֵן הַמְטַהֵר—This phrase means "the purificatory priest" or "the priest who performs the rite of purification."

וְאֹתָם—This refers to the animals, the flour, and the oil.

פֶּתַח אֹהֶל מוֹעֵד׃—See the textual note on this phrase in 1:3. It recurs in 14:23, 38. During the later era of the temple, the rabbis held that this did not refer to the area before the altar, but to the Nicanor Gate.[4]

14:12 הַכֶּבֶשׂ—As for the purification of a Nazirite defiled by a corpse (Num 6:12), the male lamb replaced the normal ram for the reparation offering (5:15, 16, 18; 5:25 [ET 6:6]; 19:21, 22).

וְהִקְרִיב—See the textual note on this verb in 1:2. See also 14:21, 24.

לְאָשָׁם—The reparation offering was required for the actual or suspected desecration of a holy thing (5:14–19). But it is not clear how this applies to a person with a certified skin disease. Four reasons have been proposed. First, the reparation offering compensated God for the offerings that he had not received for the duration of the disease.[5] This is most unlikely because desecration is a sin of commission. Second,

---

Aussätzigen (Lev 14, 4–7)."

4 See Talmud, Mishnah, *Nega'im,* 14:8.

5 Wenham, *Leviticus*, 210.

the person defiled with the skin disease had desecrated the priest who ministered to him.[6] This is also unlikely because it would mean that anybody who brought a sin offering to a priest for purification would also need to present a reparation offering. Third, the disease had desecrated the holiness of the person.[7] This too is unlikely because it would apply to any Israelite with any impurity. Last, and most likely, the infection with the skin disease was associated with the sin of sacrilege. Thus King Uzziah was punished with it for presuming to enter the Holy Place in the temple to offer incense there (2 Chr 26:16–19). The reparation offering was therefore required in this case for the suspected desecration of holy things.[8]

תְּנוּפָה— This is the only case where a whole animal is dedicated to the Lord in a rite of elevation. See the textual note and commentary on this noun in 7:30. It recurs in 14:21, 24.

14:13 בִּמְקוֹם אֲשֶׁר יִשְׁחַט אֶת־הַחַטָּאת וְאֶת־הָעֹלָה—See 1:11; 4:24, 29, 33; 7:2.

בִּמְקוֹם הַקֹּדֶשׁ—This is literally "the place of the sanctuary." See 10:17 and the textual notes on 4:6.

הוּא—"It," what belonged to the priest, was the meat from the offering.

קֹדֶשׁ קָדָשִׁים—See the textual notes on 2:3.

14:14 See the parallel ritual application of blood for the ordination of priests in 8:23–24.

14:15 עַל־כַּף הַכֹּהֵן—See 14:26. The priest is mentioned again to ensure that the oil was not poured out on the hand of the person being purified.

14:16 It is not clear whether the oil was to be sprinkled on the altar or on the floor of the courtyard before it. The Mishnah claims that the priest sprinkled it while facing the Holy of Holies, and that would imply that he sprinkled it on the floor.[9]

14:18 יִתֵּן—Whereas the holy oil was "poured out" on the head of the high priest (8:12; 21:10), this oil is "put" on the head of the person being purified.

עַל־רֹאשׁ—This placement of oil on the head stands in contrast with pollution of the head in 13:43–44. The head of a person governs his body and so represents the whole person. It is the place for distinction or dishonor; it is the index of a person's status.

וְכִפֶּר עָלָיו הַכֹּהֵן—See the textual note on the Piel verb כִּפֶּר in 1:4. See the formula of atonement also in 14:19, 20, 29, 31. It is not certain whether the formula of atonement refers to the splashing of the leftover blood from the reparation offering against the altar, the placement of blood and oil on the person in 14:14–18, or the application of blood on the altar from the following sin and burnt offerings. We take it to refer to the disposal of the remaining blood from the reparation offering because there is otherwise no mention of it.

14:19 וְעָשָׂה—See the textual note on this verb in 4:20.

הַחַטָּאת—See 4:32–35.

---

6 Budd, *Leviticus*, 206.

7 Hartley, *Leviticus*, 197.

8 Milgrom, *Leviticus 1–16*, 263–64, 856–57.

9 See Talmud, Mishnah, *Nega'im,* 14:10.

וְכִפֶּ֥ר עַל־הַמִּטַּהֵ֖ר—See the textual notes on 11:32 and 12:7.

מִטֻּמְאָתֽוֹ—See the textual notes on 5:3.

14:20 וְהֶעֱלָ֧ה—See the textual notes on 2:12. This means that the whole grain offering was burnt up on the altar with the burnt offering.

הַמִּנְחָ֖ה—This is not a separate offering, but was burned together with the burnt offering (23:13, 18). This term recurs in 14:21, 31.

הַמִּזְבֵּ֑חָה—See the textual note on הַמִּזְבֵּחַ in 1:5. Here it has the locative or directional ending ־ָה, but instead of "toward the altar" it means "on the altar."

14:21 וְאֵ֣ין יָדוֹ֮ מַשֶּׂ֒גֶת֒—This is literally "his hand is not reaching." It means that the poor man is not able to acquire the goods for the full sacrifice. See the textual note on this idiom in 5:1. It recurs in 14:22, 30, 31, 32.

וְלָ֠קַח—See the textual note on this verb in 9:2.

וְעִשָּׂר֨וֹן—This amounts to about twelve grams.

14:22 וּשְׁתֵּ֣י תֹרִ֗ים א֛וֹ שְׁנֵ֥י בְּנֵ֖י יוֹנָ֑ה—See 5:7; 15:29.

14:23 וְהֵבִ֨יא—See the textual note on this verb in 2:2.

14:29 לְכַפֵּ֥ר—See also 8:15 and 10:17 for this use of the gerundial infinitive (see GKC, § 114 o). The rite of atonement was not enacted by the application of oil in 14:26–29, nor were its benefits conveyed by the application of oil, since that rite had not yet been performed. Rather, as is shown in 14:31b, the person was purified by rite of atonement with the blood from the reparation offering, the sin offering, and the burnt offering.

עָלָ֖יו לִפְנֵ֥י יְהוָֽה׃—The LXX reads "and the priest shall make atonement for him." This agrees with 14:31 and the formula that is frequently used elsewhere at the end of legislation for a sin offering (4:20, 26, 31) or a reparation offering (5:16, 18, 26 [ET 6:7]).

14:30 וְעָשָׂ֣ה—See the textual note on this verb in 4:20.

14:31 אֵ֣ת אֲשֶׁר־תַּשִּׂ֗יג—This is absent from the LXX. It may be in the MT because of dittography, or it may have been skipped by the LXX because of haplography.

עַל־הַמִּנְחָ֑ה—This can mean either "together with the grain offering" or "in addition to the grain offering." See the textual notes on 14:20.

14:32 זֹ֣את תּוֹרַ֔ת—See the textual note on תּוֹרָה in 6:2 (ET 6:9). This verse forms an inclusion with 14:2.

אֲשֶׁר־בּ֖וֹ נֶ֣גַע צָרָ֑עַת—See 13:44–46.

Commentary

Structure

This speech is framed by a heading in 14:2a and a subscript in 14:32. The instruction on the cleansing of a person healed from an unclean skin disease falls into two parts: the preliminary rite for his readmission to the community in 14:2b–8 and the main rite for his readmission to the congregation in 14:9–31. This latter section is in turn divided into two parallel parts: the normal rite in 14:9–20 and its modified form for a poor person in 14:21–31.

Both of these two parts are arranged to form a carefully crafted inverted chiasm.[10] The instruction in 14:11–20 is constructed as follows with the repetition of the listed words and phrases:

A 14:11–12 and 14:20b: "priest," "purification/purify/clean"

B 14:12b–13 and 14:18–20a: "oil," "before the Lord," "sin offering," "burnt offering"

C 14:14a and 14:17c: "the blood of the reparation offering"

D 14:14b and 14:17b: identical material

E 14:15 and 14:17a: "oil," "palm"

The pivot in this section is 14:16, which includes "palm" and "oil" from E and "before the Lord" from B. This arrangement highlights the consecration of the oil in 14:16 and the rite of anointing with oil. It also emphasizes the application of blood from the reparation offering as well as the parallel between its application and the application of the oil. It indicates that all this is done in the Lord's presence for the purification of this person.

The instruction about the modified ritual for a poor person is also arranged as a chiasm with a slightly different emphasis.

A 14:21a and 14:32: "means are insufficient"

B 14:21b–23 and 14:30–31: "make atonement," "grain offering," "turtledoves," "pigeons," "within his means," "sin offering," "burnt offering," "priest," "before the Lord"

C 14:24 and 14:29: "priest," "oil," "before the Lord"

D 14:25a and 14:28c: "the blood of the reparation offering"

E 14:25b and 14:28b: almost all the same material

F 14:26 and 14:28a: "priest," "some of the oil," "on the palm/from his palm"

The pivot in this instruction is 14:27, which includes "some of the oil from his palm" from F, "before the Lord" from B and C, and the "priest" from B, C, and F. Once again, the pivotal verse highlights the consecration of the oil. The rest is much the same as the first instruction apart from the emphasis in A and B that the offering must be within the means of the poor person and on atonement in B.

The structure of this pericope can be outlined as follows:

I. God's address to Moses (14:1)
II. Speech about purification of a person from skin disease (14:2–32)
  A. Heading (14:2a)
  B. Preliminary rite for admission to the community (14:2b–8)
    1. Examination by the priest and preparation of animals and material for the rite (14:2b–4)

[10] Lund, *Chiasmus in the New Testament*, 53–56; Milgrom, *Leviticus 1–16*, 846–48, 859–60.

2. Preliminary rite of purification (14:5–8)
    a. Slaughter of one bird over a pot with fresh water (14:5)
    b. Sprinkling of the person by the priest with the blood from that bird (14:6–7a)
    c. Release of the other blood-stained bird (14:7b)
    d. Laundering of clothing, shaving, and bathing for purification (14:8a)
    e. Readmission into the camp but not into the tent for a period of seven days (14:8b)

C. Main rite for the readmission to the sanctuary (14:9–31)
1. The normal rite (14:9–20)
    a. Preparation by shaving, laundering, and bathing on the seventh day (14:9)
    b. Presentation of animals and material for the rite on the eighth day (14:10)
    c. Location of the person and his offerings in the prescribed place (14:11)
    d. Enactment of the reparation offering (14:12–18)
        i. Dedication of the lamb and the oil by the priest (14:12)
        ii. Slaughter of the lamb at the right place (14:13)
        iii. Application of the blood by the priest on the person (14:14)
        iv. Application of oil on the person (14:15–18a)
        v. Performance by priest of the rite for atonement (14:18b)
    e. Enactment of the sin offering (14:19a)
    f. Enactment of the burnt offering with the grain offering (14:19b–20a)
    g. Declaration of ritual purity from the combined rites of atonement (14:20b)
2. The alternative rite for a poor person (14:21–31)
    a. Preparation and presentation of alternative animals and materials (14:21–23)
    b. Enactment of the reparation offering (14:24–29)
        i. Dedication of the lamb and the oil by the priest (14:24)
        ii. Application of the blood by the priest (14:25)
        iii. Application of oil by the priest (14:26–29)
    c. Enactment of the sin offering and burnt offering (14:30–31a)
    d. Declaration of ritual purity from the combined rites of atonement (14:31b)

D. Summary subscript (14:32)

Ritual Analysis

The instruction about the purification of a skin-diseased person was addressed only to Moses, the founder of the OT divine service, because it, like 12:1–8, dealt with the sacrificial ritual for purification rather than the distinction of impurity from purity. The main human actor was the priest who enacted the two stages of the ritual for purification. He was called "the purificatory priest" (14:11). This indicates that he was, most likely, a specialist in this area of ritual.

He dominated the whole procedure. The other human actor was "the person who is being purified."[a] He provided the materials and animals for the rite (14:4, 10, 21), laundered his clothes, shaved his hair, and took a ritual bath (14:8, 9).

(a) Lev 14:4, 7, 8, 11, 14, 17, 18, 19, 25, 28, 29, 31

Since the rite of purification reinstated a person into his community and his place before God, the location and timing of the various enactments were significant. The process of reinstatement began with the movement of the priest to the healed person outside the camp where the first part of the ritual was enacted (14:3). After the completion of this stage, the person entered the camp. But he was not yet allowed to reside in his tent with the rest of his family for the space of a week (14:8). After that week was over, he could enter the sanctuary on the eighth day, a day that marked the end of that period of transition and the beginning of his state of ritual purity. On that day the priest stationed him and his offerings "before the Lord" at the entrance to the tent of meeting (14:11, 23). After he had slaughtered the lamb for the reparation offering in the holy area on the north side of the altar (14:13), he returned there and stood in that place before the Lord while the rest of the rites were performed for him "before the Lord" (14:12, 16, 18, 24, 27, 29, 31). His relocation in sacred space therefore confirmed his change of status before God and the holy congregation.

A large number of things were used in this rite of purification. Two wild birds played a key role in the preliminary rite. One of them provided the blood for the purification, and the other was dipped in that blood. The blood from the first bird was mixed with fresh water taken from a spring or a running stream. The brush for sprinkling the watered-down blood was made of three symbolically significant things: a stick or twig of cedar with some branches of hyssop tied to it with crimson thread. Two things were required for the main act of purification: the male lamb for the provision of blood for application on the person undergoing purification and the olive oil for its application on him. As well as that, he was required to supply a male lamb for a burnt offering, a female yearling lamb for a sin offering, and three measures of fine flour for a grain offering, if he was affluent enough. But if he could not afford that, he provided a pair of turtledoves or pigeons and one measure of fine flour instead.

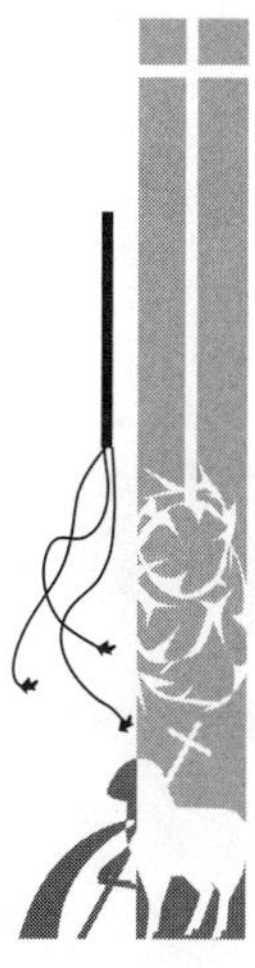

The ritual procedure for the reinstatement was enacted in two stages. These corresponded with the transition of the person back into his home and the sanctuary. The first stage began with the examination of the healed person by the priest outside the camp (14:2b–3). If the healing was confirmed, the preliminary rite was enacted in three steps. First, after the person who was to be purified had presented the two birds and the material for the rite, one of the wild birds was slaughtered by wringing its neck over an earthen pot filled with fresh water. Then the priest dipped the live bird and the hyssop brush into the pot. With that brush he sprinkled the watered down blood on the healed person seven times to cleanse him from his skin disease, and he formally declared him clean (14:4–7b), just as the person had formerly been pronounced unclean. Second, the live bird that had been dipped in the blood was then set free to return to its habitat in the open country to symbolize and announce the return of the healed person from social death to life in the community (14:7c). Third, the person who had been declared clean then laundered his clothes, shaved his hair, and bathed in water. After that, he was clean enough to enter the camp, but was not yet ready to enter his home (14:8–9). He remained in this ambiguous transitional state for a week, like a man or a woman with an irregular venereal discharge (15:13, 28).

The first stage of purification did not culminate in the readmission to the home, as might be expected, but in readmission to the sanctuary. The main rite of purification was enacted in three steps. First, the healed person prepared himself for that event on the seventh day after the initial rite of purification. Once again he shaved himself, this time of all his hair; then he laundered his clothes again and took another bath to complete this stage in the process of ritual purification, so that he was ritually clean and fit to enter the sanctuary (14:9).

Second, on the eighth day, he brought the required offering of animals, oil, and flour to the sanctuary. After the priest stationed him and his offerings before the altar, the priest brought the lamb for the reparation offering and the olive oil forward to the altar and dedicated them to the Lord with the rite of elevation. By this act both the lamb and the oil were transferred from the human domain to the divine domain (14:10–12, 21–24).

Third, the priest performed the ritual for the three classes of sacrifices (14:13–20, 25–31). This began with the slaughter of the male lamb for the reparation offering at its place on the north side of the altar. The normal procedure for this sacrifice, as outlined in 7:1–8, was modified at one point. All the blood from the animal was not dashed against the altar, but some of it was first applied to the person together with the olive oil, before its residue was dashed against the altar in the rite of atonement (14:14–18). Like the blood from the ordination offering for the priest (8:23–24), the priest applied the blood to the right ear, right hand, and right foot of the person. Before the priest applied the oil to the same places as the blood, he sprinkled the oil seven times on the floor of the courtyard or on the altar to consecrate it. The priest then smeared the holy oil on the right ear, right hand, and right foot, before he put the rest of it on the head of the person. Then the rest of the blood was used to perform the first rite of atonement.

The leftover meat from the lamb belonged to the priest (14:13b). The priest then performed the normal ritual for the sin offering with a female yearling, as outlined in 4:32–35, in the rite of atonement for the purification from the impurity of skin disease. After that, the ritual for the burnt offering and its adjunct grain offering completed the process of atonement and established the person as clean and acceptable to God. He could therefore eat the sacred meat from the peace offerings as a guest at God's table. He, presumably, was also free to reside in his home and engage in the common life of his family. The ritual brought about a change of status for him from a ritually unclean person to a ritually clean person.

This extraordinary rite of purification combined elements from four other ritual enactments. First, the use of a bird resembled the use of the scapegoat on the Day of Atonement (16:21–22). Yet, unlike the scapegoat, it did not remove the impurity of the person that had been healed.

Second, the rite resembled the rite for the purification of pollution from contact with a corpse. Cedar, crimson thread, and hyssop were used to prepare the ashes that were mixed with fresh water and sprinkled with a hyssop brush on the body of the person (Num 19:6, 17–18). This resemblance suggests that the impurity from skin disease was similar to impurity from contact with a corpse. The theological status of a skin-diseased person was therefore the same as that of a corpse (Num 12:12).

Third, just as the blood from the ram for ordination was put on the right ear, right thumb, and right big toe of the priests for their ordination (8:22–24), so the blood from the reparation offering was put on the same places of the person being purified from skin disease. But whereas the holy anointing oil was poured out on the head of the high priest and sprinkled on vestments of the priests (8:12, 20), it was put on the head and the same places as the blood for the person who had been healed of skin disease.

Fourth, this rite of purification included the shaving of the head on the seventh day and the presentation of the same three sacrifices as the rite for the purification of a Nazirite whose holiness had been defiled by contact with a corpse (Num 6:9–12).

The combination of these sacrifices, which are unique to these two rites, shows how similar the rites are in their function and theological significance. They do not merely remedy the pollution from contact with a corpse, but they also remedy the guilt from the pollution of something holy. Yet the rite for the purification of the skin-diseased person also differs from the rite for the defiled Nazirite by requiring five additional things: the laundering of clothes and bathing in water on the first day and seventh day (14:8, 9); the additional shaving of all hair from the body on the seventh day (14:9) after the initial shaving on the first day (14:8); the presentation of male lambs for the sin offering and burnt offering rather than two birds (14:10); and the presentation of a large grain offering with a measure of olive oil (14:10).

In all this, one sacrifice is conspicuous by its absence, the peace offering. It has no place here because this ritual of purification merely prepares the person for its presentation and the consumption of the holy meat from it.

Theological Significance

In this instruction God instituted the rite by which he purified and reinstated a skin-diseased person. His Word established this ritual enactment and authorized the priests to enact it on his behalf. The priests that were authorized in the previous chapter to declare a person unclean are here authorized to declare the same person as clean after he had recovered. In doing so, they acted as God's representatives. But much more was required than just that, for purification involved both the removal of impurity and the full restoration of purity for the person as a member of the holy congregation of Israel.

The removal of impurity proceeded in three main stages that corresponded to three aspects and levels of purity (14:8, 9, 20).[11] The first level was the purity that qualified the person to reenter the camp (14:8). This was accomplished by sprinkling him with blood from a slaughtered wild bird and releasing the other blood-stained bird. He was also required to wash his clothes, shave his hair, and bathe his body in water.

The second level was the degree of purity that qualified him for entry into the sanctuary. This was accomplished by shaving off all his hair, washing his clothes, and bathing in water.

The third level was the degree of purity that qualified him to stand before God once again in the divine service and share in God's holiness by eating the holy meat from the peace offerings. This was accomplished for him by the offering of three sets of sacrifices, the chief of which was the reparation offering. Each of these culminated in the application of its blood in the rite of atonement for the person. Thus the first two acts of purification with their ablutions executed the rites of passage for him to the camp and then to the sanctuary. The third rite of purification, which was not preceded by ablutions, completed the process of restoration to life with God and reincorporation into the holy congregation.[12]

The theological significance of this sacrificial enactment is evident in its unusual use of the reparation offering and its combination with the application of consecrated olive oil. Both the lamb for the reparation offering and the oil for application were handed over to God in a special rite of elevation (14:12). Moreover, the oil was specially consecrated by sprinkling it seven times before the Lord (14:16, 27).[13] By that extraordinary act of consecration, it became the means for divine endowment and empowerment.

Before most of the blood was splashed against the altar to free the person from the guilt of actual or suspected sacrilege, some of it was placed on his extremities to purify him. It was put on his right ear so that he would be fit to hear the holy voice of God; it was put on his right hand so that he could touch the holy meat from the peace offerings; it was put on his right foot so that he could stand unscathed on holy ground. Then, rather strangely, the holy oil that had been consecrated was put on these places, together with the blood, to protect him from further defilement, to sustain his health, and to empower him with divine strength (14:17, 25).[14] After that, the priest put the rest of the oil on the person's forehead to restore his status in the holy congregation of Israel and to honor him as a guest at God's table (Ps 23:5; cf. Eccl 9:8; Lk 7:38, 46).

---

[11] Milgrom, *Leviticus 1–16*, 859.

[12] Milgrom, *Leviticus 1–16*, 859.

[13] Vriezen, "The Term *Hizza*: Lustration and Consecration."

[14] Milgrom, *Leviticus 1–16*, 854–55.

The act of atonement with the blood from the reparation offering "before the Lord" came last (Lev 14:18, 29), because, by it and the other acts of atonement, the person that had been unclean was freed "from his impurity" (14:19a) and made entirely acceptable before God (14:20, 31b; cf. 1:4–5). Thus, when the process of purification was over, the theological status of the healed person was restored; he was a full-fledged member of the congregation and a well-qualified participant in the divine service. He was once again clean and so fit to enjoy the Lord's food at his table. The once doomed outcast became a privileged guest. He no longer belonged to the realm of death as he had formerly; he now belonged to the realm of life.

Fulfillment by Christ

Unlike the priests in ancient Israel, Jesus did not diagnose whether people had an unclean skin disease or whether they had been healed from it. Neither did he perform rites to heal them. Instead, by means of his word and touch he simply and powerfully healed all manner of diseases; that included cleansing lepers by healing them. He did this frequently in his ministry. His cleansing of lepers was one of the six signs by which he announced that he was the Messiah (Mt 11:5; Lk 7:22).

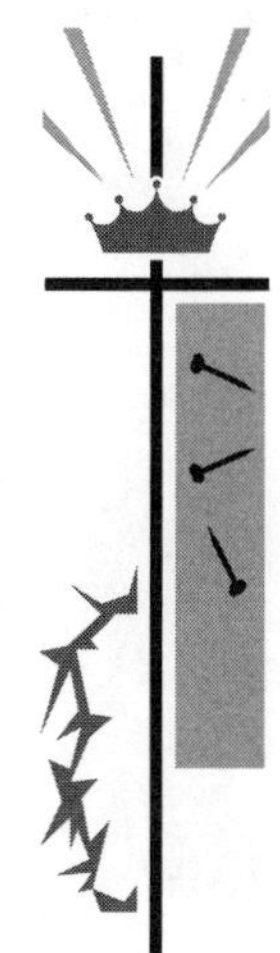

Many of the messianic prophecies found in the OT refer to his ministry of healing. However, none of them mention the healing specifically of lepers. Yet the wording of Isaiah 53 points in that direction. This prophecy declared that the Servant of the Lord would be deemed to have been "stricken[נָגוּעַ] by God" like a leper (Is 53:4). "Because of the rebellion of my people a strickenness[נֶגַע] would be to him" (Is 53:8). That is the same Hebrew term that is frequent in Leviticus 13–14, where it refers to the "infection" of skin diseases.[15] Therefore the Suffering Servant would heal people with unclean diseases by being afflicted for them and with them. He would take on their sickness and impurity and give them his purity and health. The Servant would be stricken even unto death (Is 53:8–9) and give his life as a reparation offering (Is 53:10). By doing so he would justify the many sinners and make intercession for them (Is 53:11–12).

The significance of Christ's treatment of people with skin diseases is evident from the location of the story about the healing of a leper in the Synoptic Gospels. In Mt 8:1–4 it comes at the head of the two chapters that list Jesus' mighty works as the Messiah. After these two chapters, he commissions the apostles to perform the same mighty deeds, including the cleansing of lepers, by preaching the Gospel (Mt 10:8). In Mk 1:40–45 and Lk 5:12–16, this story introduces a section that culminates in a meal with Levi, the tax collector. The most remarkable feature of this story is that Jesus does not just speak the word that cleanses the unclean man, but he actually reaches out and touches him (Mt 8:3; Mk 1:41; Lk 5:13). He, the holy Messiah, takes on the impurity of the man whom he chose to cleanse. Then he commands him to fulfill the law by presenting himself to a priest at the

[15] See the textual note on נֶגַע in 13:2.

temple and offering the sacrifices for his reinstatement as a ritually clean person with access to God's presence at the sanctuary. This story therefore shows how Jesus cleanses unclean people so that they can approach God without desecrating his holiness with their impurity.

The story of the cleansing of the ten lepers in Lk 17:11–19 reinforces this teaching and adds a further dimension to it. In it Luke distinguishes the Samaritan from the other nine lepers, who apparently were Jewish. Since the nine Jewish men were cured of leprosy, they were readmitted to the congregation of Israel after the certification of their ritual purity by the priest. The Samaritan, however, gained something more than that. Since he was a Samaritan, he could not gain admission to the congregation of Israel. So he turned back to Jesus instead and thanked him by prostrating before Jesus. He received the gift of salvation in addition to his healing from leprosy. Even though he was a Samaritan, he had access to God the Father through faith in Jesus. He became a member of the church, the congregation of those who have faith in Jesus as their Lord. He entered into communion with God in a way that unbelieving Jewish people could not.

Since lepers were regarded as the preeminent exemplars of unclean people in Judaism and the early church, these accounts imply that Jesus deals with all unclean people in the same way as he dealt with those lepers. The Gospel records are, as it were, paradigms of cleansing. What applied to the people cleansed in those accounts applies to all unclean people. Jesus cleanses them and makes them fit for God's holy presence. In Baptism he removes their impurity, like unclean clothing, and takes it on himself; then he gives them his purity and holiness as their new dress, so that they can clothe themselves in him (Gal 3:27; Eph 4:24; Col 3:9–10). Through faith in Christ they therefore have access to God the Father in the Divine Service. They join in the Eucharist, the great thanksgiving for healing that comes through physical reception of the body and blood of the risen Lord Jesus.

This great High Priest in human flesh
Was icon of God's righteousness.
His hallowed touch brought sanctity;
His hand removed impurity.

The holy Lamb undaunted came
To God's own altar lit with flame;
While weeping angels hid their eyes,
This Priest became a sacrifice.

But death would not the victor be
Of Him who hung upon the tree.
He leads us to the Holy Place
Within the veil before God's face.[16]

---

[16] From "The Infant Priest Was Holy Borne" by Chad L. Bird (*HS98* 853:2–4). © 1997 Chad L. Bird. Used with permission.

Leviticus 14:33–57

Purification of Infected Houses

Translation

14 [33]The Lord spoke to Moses and Aaron: [34]“When you enter the land of Canaan, which I am giving you as a possession, and I put an infection of fungus on a house in the land that you possess, [35]the owner of the house shall come and tell the priest: ‘There seems to me to be some sort of an infection in my house.’ [36]The priest shall order the house to be cleared, before the priest comes to examine the infection, so that nothing in the house may become unclean; after that the priest shall enter to examine the house. [37]If, when he examines the infection, the infection on the walls of the house consists of depressions that are bright green or bright red and that appear deeper than the wall, [38]the priest shall come out of the house to the entrance of the house and quarantine the house for seven days. [39]On the seventh day the priest shall return and make an examination; if the infection has spread on the walls of the house, [40]the priest shall order that they rip out the stones with the infection on them and throw them into an unclean place outside the city. [41]The house shall be scraped off all around inside, and they shall dump the mud that is scraped off in an unclean place outside the town. [42]They shall take other stones and bring them to replace those stones; and other mud shall be taken to plaster the house.

[43]“If the infection returns and breaks out in the house, after the stones have been ripped out and after the house has been scraped and replastered, [44]the priest shall enter [it] and make an examination; if the infection has spread in the house, it is a persistent mold in the house; it is unclean. [45]The house shall be demolished with its stones and timber and all its mud, and brought out to an unclean place outside the city. [46]Whoever enters the house at any time during its quarantine shall be unclean until sunset. [47]Whoever sleeps in the house shall launder his clothes; and whoever eats in the house shall launder his clothes.

[48]“If, however, the priest does enter and sees that the infection has not spread in the house after the house was plastered, the priest shall declare the house clean, because the infection has been healed. [49]To purify the house, he shall take two birds, some cedar wood, some crimson yarn, and hyssop. [50]He shall slaughter one of the birds over living water in an earthen pot. [51]He shall take the cedar wood, the hyssop, the crimson yarn, and the live bird, and dip them in the blood of the slaughtered bird and in the living water and sprinkle [it] on the house seven times. [52]Having purified the house with the blood of the bird, the living water, the live bird, the cedar wood, the hyssop, and the crimson yarn, [53]he shall release the live bird into the open country outside the town. Thus he shall make atonement on the house, so that it is clean.”

[54]This is the ritual instruction for every infection of skin disease, for rash, [55]for mold on clothing or a house, [56]for discoloration and a scab and a shiny patch— [57]to give instruction about when it is unclean and when it is clean.

This is the ritual instruction for skin disease.

Textual Notes

14:33 וַיְדַבֵּר יְהוָה אֶל־מֹשֶׁה וְאֶל־אַהֲרֹן—See 11:1; 13:1; 15:1.

14:34 אֶרֶץ כְּנַעַן—Later references to entry into the land of Canaan are in 19:23; 23:10; 25:2.

לַאֲחֻזָּה—This "possession" is the technical term for inalienable land that is received and possessed as a perpetual grant from a king, rather than נַחֲלָה, "inheritance," the patrimony that was transmitted by inheritance. See the use of אֲחֻזָּה also in 25:10, 13, 24, 25, 32, 33, 41; 27:16, 21, 22, 28, where often it refers to a person's "landholding."

נֶגַע—See the textual notes on 13:2. The term נֶגַע occurs ten more times in this speech (14:35, 36, 37 [twice], 39, 40, 43, 44, 48 [twice]).

צָרַעַת—See the textual note on this term in 13:2.

בְּבֵית אֶרֶץ אֲחֻזַּתְכֶם׃—This is literally "in the house of the land of your possession."

14:35 לַכֹּהֵן—The priest is mentioned nine times in this speech (14:35, 36 [twice], 38, 39, 40, 44, 48 [twice]).

14:36 וּפִנּוּ—Here and in the following verses the impersonal third person forms (here: "they shall clear") are translated with the passive (here "shall be cleared").

יִטְמָא—See the textual notes on 5:2. The verb recurs in 14:46.

14:37 שְׁקַעֲרוּרֹת—See Milgrom for a discussion on the derivation and sense of this unique word.[1] The etymology and translations of it by the ancient versions indicate that it means "**depressions,** hollows, cavities (damage to a wall)" (*HALOT*).

יְרַקְרַקֹּת—See 13:49.

אֲדַמְדַּמֹּת—See 13:19, 24, 42, 43, 49.

שָׁפָל—See the textual notes on 13:3.

14:38 וְהִסְגִּיר—See the textual note on this verb in 13:4.

שִׁבְעַת יָמִים׃—See the textual notes on 8:33.

14:39 פָּשָׂה—See the textual notes on 13:5.

14:40 אֶל־מָקוֹם טָמֵא׃—This phrase recurs in 14:41, 45.

14:41 יַקְצִעַ—This singular, impersonal verb and the ones in 14:42–46 are translated as passives. The dried off mud plaster was scraped from the walls to ascertain whether the fungus had penetrated below the surface of the wall.

הֶעָפָר—The term עָפָר is used here for the clay that was mixed with water and used in building the house. It was used as mortar to build the wall with timber and stones (14:45) and as plaster to cover the inside of the walls (14:41, 42).

14:44 מַמְאֶרֶת—See the textual notes on 13:51.

---

1 Milgrom, *Leviticus 1–16*, 870–71.

טָמֵא הוּא׃—"It is unclean" means that the house is unclean.
14:46 עַד־הָעָרֶב׃—See the textual notes on 11:24.
14:47 יְכַבֵּס אֶת־בְּגָדָיו—See the textual notes on 11:25.
14:48 וְטִהַר—See the textual notes on 13:6.
14:49 לְחַטֵּא—See the textual note on this verb in 6:19 (ET 6:26). It recurs in 14:52.
וְאֵזֹב׃—See the textual note on this noun in 14:4.
14:50 וְשָׁחַט—See the textual note on this verb in 1:5. It recurs in 14:51.
עַל־מַיִם חַיִּים׃—See the textual notes on 14:5.
14:51 וּבַמַּיִם הַחַיִּים—See 14:6.
וְהִזָּה—See the textual notes on 4:6.
שֶׁבַע פְּעָמִים׃—See the textual notes on 4:6.
14:52 וּבַצִּפֹּר הַחַיָּה—The bird is mentioned here rather than later, as in 14:51, to fit in with the chiastic arrangement of 14:51–52.
14:53 הַצִּפֹּר הַחַיָּה—See 14:7.
אֶל־פְּנֵי הַשָּׂדֶה—See 14:7; 17:5.
וְכִפֶּר עַל־הַבַּיִת—See the textual notes on 1:4.
14:54 See 13:29–37, 42–44.
זֹאת הַתּוֹרָה—See the textual notes on 6:2 (ET 6:9).
לְכָל־נֶגַע הַצָּרַעַת—While some commentators consider that this phrase is used as an inclusive term for all that follows, it is most likely used here as a technical term for the diseases on the skin of the body in 13:2–28.[2]
14:55 וּלְצָרַעַת—צָרַעַת is the same Hebrew word as is used for skin disease in the previous verse.
הַבֶּגֶד—See 13:47–59.
וְלַבָּיִת׃—See 14:34–53.
14:56 This verse forms an inclusion with 13:2 and so rounds off chapters 13–14.
14:57 לְהוֹרֹת—See the use of the same verb (Hiphil of יָרָה) in 10:11 and Deut 24:8. This phrase recalls Lev 11:47.
בְּיוֹם ... וּבְיוֹם—This is literally "on the day of." See the textual notes on 7:19.
וּבְיוֹם הַטָּהֹר—This forms an inclusion with 14:2.
זֹאת תּוֹרַת הַצָּרָעַת׃—This sentence recalls 13:59 and forms an inclusion with 14:54.

Commentary

Structure

The speech on the treatment of fungus in houses is divided into three clear sections: 14:34–42; 14:43–45; 14:48–53. The basic case of diagnosis and treatment is introduced by כִּי, "when," in 14:34; the two subsequent cases are introduced by וְאִם, "and if," in 14:43 and 14:48. The unit on the cleansing of people in 14:46–47 that is attached as an appendix to 14:43–45, seems out of place there. According to its subject matter, it would fit better after 14:38, since

2 Milgrom, *Leviticus 1–16*, 883.

it deals with entry into a quarantined house. It was most likely placed before the instruction on the purification of the house in 14:48–53 for thematic reasons because it deals with the purification of people who had been polluted by the house. By its placement it connects 14:43–45 with 14:34–42.

The arrangement of the cases in this instruction follows the pattern established in the two previous speeches. Thus the instruction on the treatment of an infected house in 14:34–47 follows the pattern of the instruction on infected fabrics in 13:47–58, while the ritual for the cleansing of the house in 14:48–53 is similar to the preliminary ritual for the cleansing of a skin-diseased person in 14:2–7. The core of the ritual for the cleansing of the house in 14:51–52 is arranged as a carefully constructed chiasm to emphasize the sprinkling of the house with the blood of the bird.[3] It is arranged as follows with these key words:

A 14:51a and 14:52d: "the cedar wood," "the hyssop," "the crimson yarn"

B 14:51b and 14:52c: "the live bird"

C 14:51c and 14:52b: "in/with the blood of the bird," "in/with the living water"

D 14:51d and 14:52a: "the house"

X 14:51e: "seven times"

As in the instruction for the purification of a skin-diseased person (14:16b–27), the pivot of the chiasm focuses our attention on the sevenfold sprinkling of the house. It defines the act of sprinkling as a rite of purification.

The speech is followed by an elaborate subscript to chapters 13–14 in 14:54–57. It lists the various cases of unclean infection and states the common purpose of these three units of instruction. By its use of inclusion it draws these units together as a subsection in Leviticus.

The structure of this pericope can be outlined as follows:

- I. God's address to Moses and Aaron (14:33)
- II. Speech about the treatment of fungus in houses (14:34–53)
  - A. The case of a house with suspected unclean fungus (14:34–47)
    - 1. Notification of the priest (14:34–35)
      - a. Appearance of a fungus in the house (14:34)
      - b. Report by the owner to the priest (14:35)
    - 2. Initial examination by the priest (14:36–38)
      - a. Removal of contents from the house (14:36)
      - b. Quarantine of house with red or green fungus (14:37–38)
    - 3. Second examination by the priest (14:39–42)
      - a. Inspection for the spread of the fungus (14:39)
      - b. Removal of the infected area (14:40–41)
      - c. Repair of the wall (14:42)

---

[3] Lund, *Chiasmus in the New Testament*, 52; Milgrom, *Leviticus 1–16*, 880–81.

4. Treatment for the recurrence of fungus (14:43–45)
   a. Examination for its outbreak and spread (14:43–44a)
   b. Identification of the infection and declaration of the house as unclean (14:44b)
   c. Demolition of the house (14:45)
5. Purification of people polluted by entry into the house (14:46–47)

B. The purification of a formerly infected house (14:48–53)
1. Examination by priest and declaration as clean (14:48)
2. Preparation of material for the rite (14:49)
3. Rite of purification (14:50–53a)
   a. Slaughter of one bird (14:50)
   b. Dipping of live bird and hyssop in the blood (14:51a)
   c. Sprinkling of the house with the blood (14:51a–52)
   d. Release of the live bird (14:53a)
4. Result: purification of the house (14:53b)

III. Summary subscript for chapters 13–14 (14:54–57)
A. List of unclean infections (14:54–56)
B. Purpose of their identification (14:57a)
C. General summary (14:57b)

Ritual Analysis

This instruction on the treatment of houses infected with fungus was addressed to Moses as the founder of the divine service and the lawgiver and to Aaron as the priest and judge who was commissioned to distinguish between what was clean and what was unclean. The instruction deals with two people: the owner of the house who reports the infection and follows the directions of the priest (14:35) and the priest who diagnoses the infection, attends to the removal of impurities, and performs the rite of purification. The priest, presumably, is an expert in dealing with unclean infections. He alone has the authority to declare a house unclean (14:44) or clean (14:48).

The location for the enactment of these directives is significant. They anticipate the settlement of the Israelites with God in the land of Canaan. That land belonged to God (14:34). Even though he gave it as a permanent possession to the Israelites, it was still his land; they were tenants on his royal estate. Since they lived together with God on the land, their houses and their towns were kept ritually clean. Anything that was unclean belonged in an unclean place outside the town (14:40, 41, 45).

The legislation in this speech describes two things. First, it tells how the priest identified and treated an unclean infection in an Israelite home (14:36–45). After the owner had reported a suspected infection, the priest visited him. He ordered the owner to empty all the contents of the house so that they did not become ritually unclean. If the infected area was bright red or bright green, and if it reached below the surface of the mud-plastered wall, the house was quarantined for a week. On the seventh day the priest made a further inspection of the house to ascertain whether the infection had spread on the wall. If it had not, the house presumably was clean. But if it had spread, the infected area with its stones and all the plaster on the walls inside the house was removed and dumped in an unclean place outside the town. After that, the walls were repaired and replastered. Then it was considered clean. If, however, the fungus broke out again, the priest, after making an inspection of it, identified it as "a persistent mold in the house" and declared it "unclean" (14:44). The house was totally demolished, and its rubble was dumped in an unclean place outside the town. The diagnostic procedure is set out in figure 19.

Figure 19

Diagnostic Procedure for Fungus in Houses

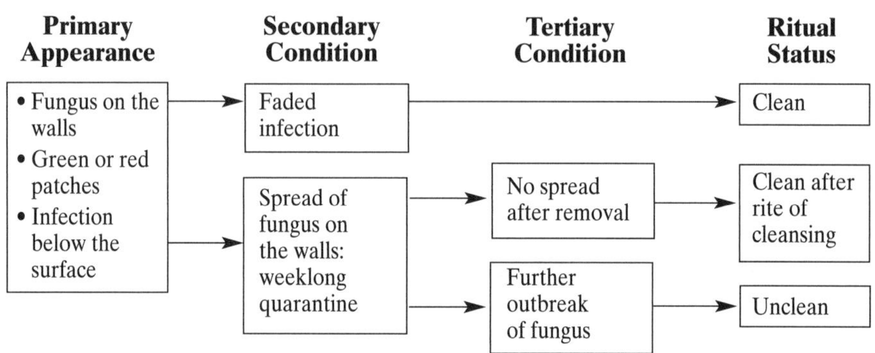

This legislation also describes the prescribed procedures for purification from pollution by contact with the mold (14:46–53). Those who had entered the house during its period of quarantine were unclean until sunset; they became clean by taking a bath. Those who slept or ate in the polluted house had to launder their clothes as well (14:46–47). The rite for the purification of the house was identical with the preliminary rite for the purification of a person who had recovered from an unclean skin disease (14:48–53; cf. 14:4–7). This was not an act of sacrifice but an extraordinary rite of atonement. Since the house could not be brought to the sanctuary, the blood could not be applied to the altar as was normally the case with all other rites of atonement.

The elaborate subscript ties together the material from the three sets of instruction in two ways. On the one hand, it classifies the various kinds of unclean infection from chapters 13–14 in a number of different ways: specifically, as cases of skin disease or of head rash or of disease in fabric and in a house; symptomatically, as discolorations or scabs or shiny patches; and generally, as cases of צָרַעַת, unclean disease. On the other hand, it states that the common purpose of these sets of instruction is to teach when these kinds of infection are either clean or unclean.

Theological Significance

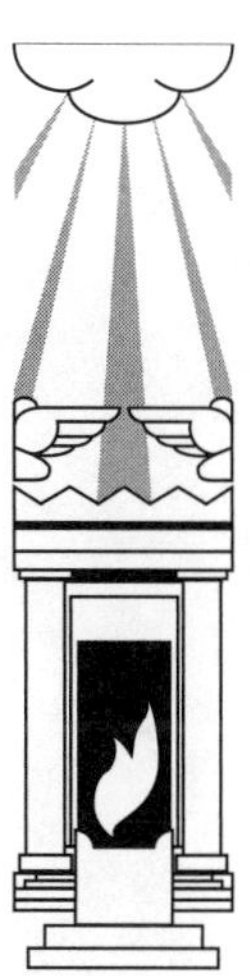

The purpose of this instruction on the treatment of impurity is largely pastoral. It presupposes that the home of each Israelite was connected with the temple in the land of Israel. The land belongs to God, who expelled the Canaanites from it because of their sins and pollution (see Leviticus 18). God's indwelling presence was centered in the tabernacle and, later, the temple. God's presence sanctified the land (the Holy Land) and its inhabitants and dwellings.

The house was also closely connected with each Israelite household. Just as a person's clothing was an extension of his body, so the house was an extension of the family. Thus what happened to the house had an impact on the people in it. Since most people in Israel and the surrounding countries lived in houses made from mud, they were liable to infection with mold.

The infection of houses with fungus had religious significance for the pagan people that surrounded Israel. The Hurrians and Hittites held that the impurity of the infection was a manifestation of evil and a sign that the gods were displeased with the members of the household. In Hurrian rites the impurity was removed by invoking the deities of the underworld by the sacrifice of a bird.[4] The Babylonians held that all impurity came from demons and was thus associated with demonic activity. For them the appearance of red or white or green fungus inside a house was an omen of disaster and death for the people who lived in it. Its residents were therefore required to wash themselves, and the house was anointed with substances that absorbed the impurity.[5] It was therefore natural for the Israelites to regard the infection of their houses as signs of divine displeasure and omens of disaster.

The treatment prescribed in this speech deals pastorally with that problem without sanctioning the superstitions that were often associated with it. In this speech God acknowledged that he, at times, sent an infection on the house (14:34). But he did not do so either to warn or to punish the household. It was an unclean infestation that polluted the house and the people in it. Even though the mold did not bring bad luck, it was still ritually significant. Since it was potentially dangerous, it had to be dealt with appropriately. But it was not the sign of the demonic infestation of the house or of a crime committed in the house. It was therefore treated simply as a source of impurity, something that needed to be removed from the house.

Besides that, the house itself needed to be cleansed after the infection had been healed and the priest had declared it clean (14:48). The cleansing of the house involved the sprinkling of it with the blood from a bird and the release of another bird that had been dipped in the blood of the first bird. By means of a modified rite of atonement, in which the blood was sprinkled on the house rather than the altar, God purified the house (14:49, 52). It thereby became rit-

---

4 Milgrom, *Leviticus 1–16*, 864–65; Wilhelm, "Reinheit und Heiligkeit."

5 Meier, "House Fungus"; Milgrom, *Leviticus 1–16*, 864.

ually "clean" (14:53). It could no longer pollute those who resided in it and make them unfit for entry into the sanctuary. They had no cause to fear misfortune and disaster if they remained in that house.

Fulfillment by Christ

At first glance this legislation might seem to have little or no relevance for the church or for Christian households. We consider the occurrence of mold in our houses to have no spiritual significance; instead, it is a hygienic or esthetic concern. Nevertheless, this legislation connects the homes of God's people with the temple. That connection is matched by the way in which Jesus visits homes in the NT. He does not just visit the homes of the righteous. Christ quite deliberately enters the unclean homes of sinners, such as Levi the tax collector (Mk 2:14–15), and unclean people, like Simon the leper (Mt 26:6; Mk 14:3). He brings salvation to these houses as he did to the home of Zacchaeus (Lk 19:9). He purifies and blesses these homes by his presence in them.

Since Christian homes are places where families call on the triune God, hear God's Word, and pray, they are theologically significant. In fact, many Lutherans at every meal ask Christ to be their guest. Since ancient times, Christians have had their homes blessed. Pastors may follow Jesus' example by visiting church members in their homes. Many churches continue to have rites in which a pastor blesses a home for the family's sacred service of Christ. Likewise, some churches have rites of exorcism in case a home has been the site of demonic activity. In such ways the homes of Christians are sanctified by the Word of God and prayer (cf. 1 Tim 4:5). Christ's holy presence protects them from the evil one and all the powers of darkness.

> Our Father, by whose name
> All fatherhood is known,
> Who dost in love proclaim
> Each family thine own,
> Bless thou all parents, guarding well,
> With constant love as sentinel,
> The homes in which thy people dwell.[6]

[6] From "Our Father, by Whose Name" by F. Bland Tucker (*LW* 465:1).

Leviticus 15:1–33

Purification from Genital Discharges

Translation

15 [1]The Lord spoke to Moses and Aaron: [2]"Speak to the Israelites and say to them: If any man at all has a discharge from his flesh, his discharge is unclean. [3]This is his impurity by means of his discharge: whether his flesh runs with his discharge or his flesh is obstructed from his discharge, it is his impurity. [4]Any bedding that the man with a discharge lies on is unclean, and every object on which he sits becomes unclean; [5]anyone who touches his bedding shall launder his clothes, bathe in water, and remain unclean until sunset; [6]whoever sits on any object that the man with a discharge has sat on shall launder his clothes, bathe in water, and remain unclean until sunset. [7]Whoever touches the body of the man with a discharge shall launder his clothes, bathe in water, and become unclean until sunset.

[8]"If the man with a discharge spits on someone who is clean, that person shall launder his clothes, bathe in water, and remain unclean until sunset.

[9]"Any saddle on which the man with a discharge rides becomes unclean; [10]everyone who touches anything that was under him will become unclean until sunset, and whoever carries these things shall launder his clothes, bathe in water, and become unclean until sunset. [11]Anyone whom the man with a discharge touches when he has not washed his hands with water shall launder his clothes, bathe in water, and remain unclean until sunset; [12]any piece of pottery that the man with a discharge touches shall be broken, and any wooden implement shall be rinsed with water.

[13]"When the man with a discharge is cleansed from his discharge, he shall count off seven days for his purification, launder his clothes, and bathe his body in living water; then he will be clean. [14]On the eighth day he shall take two turtledoves or two pigeons and come before the Lord at the entrance to the tent of meeting and give them to the priest. [15]The priest shall perform the ritual for them—one [bird] as a sin offering and the other one as a burnt offering. Thus the priest shall make atonement on his behalf, from his discharge, before the Lord.

[16]"When a man has an emission of semen, he shall bathe his whole body in water and remain unclean until sunset; [17]any garment or leather with an emission of semen on it shall be laundered in water and remain unclean until sunset.

[18]"[This also applies] to a woman with whom a man lies and has an emission of semen; they shall bathe in water and remain unclean until sunset.

[19]"When a woman has a discharge and her discharge is blood from her flesh, she will be in her menstrual impurity for seven days. Anyone who touches her will become unclean until sunset. [20]Everything on which she lies in her menstrual period is unclean, and everything on which she sits becomes unclean; [21]anyone

who touches her bedding shall launder his clothes, bathe in water, and remain unclean until sunset, 22and anyone who touches any object on which she sat shall launder his clothes, bathe in water, and remain unclean until sunset; 23if it is on the bed or anything else on which she is sitting when he touches it, he shall become unclean until sunset. 24And if a man definitely lies with her, her menstrual impurity will be on him, and he will become unclean for seven days; any bedding on which he lies will be unclean.

25"When a woman has a discharge of blood for many days not at the time of her menstrual period, or when she has a discharge beyond her menstrual period, she will be unclean for the duration of the discharge of her impurity, as during her menstrual period. 26Any bedding on which she lies during her discharge shall be regarded by her like the bedding during her menstrual period; and every piece of furniture on which she sits will be unclean, as [during] the impurity of her menstrual period; 27everyone who touches them will become unclean; he shall launder his clothes, bathe in water, and remain unclean until sunset. 28If she is cleansed from her discharge, she shall count off seven days, and after that she will be clean. 29On the eighth day she shall take for herself two turtledoves or two pigeons and bring them to the priest at the entrance to the tent of meeting. 30The priest shall perform the ritual for the one as a sin offering and the other as a burnt offering. Thus the priest shall make atonement on her behalf, from the impurity of her discharge, before the Lord.

31"Thus you shall separate the Israelites from their impurity, so that they do not die in their impurity when they defile my tabernacle that is in their midst."

32This is the ritual instruction for those who have a discharge: for him who has an emission of semen by which he becomes unclean, 33for her who is unwell in her menstrual period, for anyone, male or female, who has a discharge, and for the man who lies with an unclean woman.

Textual Notes

15:1 וַיְדַבֵּר יְהוָה אֶל־מֹשֶׁה וְאֶל־אַהֲרֹן—Both Moses and Aaron are also addressed in 11:1; 13:1; 14:33.

15:2 אִישׁ אִישׁ—The repetition means "any man" and is used as an all-inclusive formula here and elsewhere in Leviticus (17:3, 8, 10, 13; 18:6; 20:2, 9; 22:4, 18; 24:15).

יִהְיֶה זָב—This is literally "becomes discharging."

מִבְּשָׂרוֹ—Here, as in 12:3, בָּשָׂר is a euphemism for the penis. Milgrom[1] argues that one should disregard the Masoretic accents and read מִבְּשָׂרוֹ זוֹבוֹ as belonging together, just as זָבָה בִּבְשָׂרָהּ go together in 15:19 (as indicated by the Masoretic accents there). The translation would then be "with his discharge from his member." The verb טָמֵא would refer to the person rather than the discharge. But that view does not fit the context, since 15:2b–3 deals with the discharge as the source of impurity. Therefore our translation follows the MT.

---

1 Milgrom, *Leviticus 1–16*, 906.

טָמֵא הוּא:—See the textual note on the adjective טָמֵא in 5:2. It is used also in 15:25, 26, 33.

15:3 וְזֹאת תִּהְיֶה טֻמְאָתוֹ—The LXX has καὶ οὗτος ὁ νόμος τῆς ἀκαθαρσίας αὐτοῦ ("And this is the law for his impurity"). Apparently the LXX misread תִּהְיֶה as if it were תּוֹרָה.

טֻמְאָתוֹ בְּזוֹבוֹ— This phrase means "his impurity by means of his discharge" or "his impurity from his discharge." The term טֻמְאָה is used here for the discharge as the cause of "impurity," rather than the unclean state the comes from it. See the textual note on it in 5:3. The term recurs in 15:25, 26, 30, 31.

רָר בְּשָׂרוֹ אֶת־זוֹבוֹ אוֹ־הֶחְתִּים בְּשָׂרוֹ מִזּוֹבוֹ—This appositional clause with its perfect verbs gives the two characteristic symptoms for the diagnosis of the malady. The LXX takes them as connected symptoms and holds that the discharge results in blockage to the flow of urine.

טֻמְאָתוֹ הִוא:—הִוא refers to the discharge. The LXX adds "he has impurity all the days of the discharge from his flesh by which his flesh is blocked because of the discharge." This reading is supported by the Samaritan Pentateuch and 11QpaleoLev. It also corresponds to the pattern in 15:16, 19, 25, which all give the duration of unclean state.

15:4 הַזָּב—This is literally "the discharging one."

יִטְמָא—See the textual notes on 5:2. The verb recurs in 15:5, 6, 7, 8, 9, 10, 11, 16, 17, 18, 19, 20, 21, 22, 23, 24, 27, 31, 32. See the similar declarations about polluted objects in 15:9, 20.

15:5 וְאִישׁ אֲשֶׁר יִגַּע—See the similar clauses in 15:7, 10, 11, 21, 23, 27.

יְכַבֵּס בְּגָדָיו—See the textual notes on 11:25.

וְרָחַץ בַּמַּיִם—See the textual notes on 14:8. The clause recurs in 15:6, 7, 8, 10, 11, 13, 16, 18, 21, 22, 27.

עַד־הָעָרֶב:—See the textual note on this phrase in 11:24. It recurs in 15:6, 7, 8, 10 (twice), 11, 16, 17, 18, 19, 21, 22, 23, 27.

15:6 This is the only case in this chapter of contamination by sitting on a polluted object.

15:7 בִּבְשַׂר הַזָּב—Literally this refers to "the flesh of the discharging man." See the parallel case in 15:19b. In both these cases this refers to direct contact with some uncovered part of the body of the person with a discharge, rather than indirect contact through the clothing.

15:8 וְכִי—The shift to וְכִי (rather than וְאִם, as is normally the case for a subunit) indicates a change of subject in 15:8–9 back to the man with the discharge.

בַּטָּהוֹר—See the textual notes on 7:19.

15:10 וְכָל־הַנֹּגֵעַ בְּכֹל אֲשֶׁר יִהְיֶה תַחְתָּיו—This obviously refers to the saddle and its trappings. Milgrom claims that it may also refer to anything else on which the man has sat.[2] While that interpretation is possible, it overlooks the fact that while 15:9 de-

2 Milgrom, *Leviticus 1–16*, 916–18.

fines the source of contamination, 15:10 defines the mode of contamination from that source.

יִטְמָא עַד־הָעָרֶב—An instruction about the need to launder clothing and to take a bath is omitted here. These acts are, most likely, to be assumed by analogy with the parallel case in 15:6 and their mention in the latter part of the verse. Milgrom, however, argues that even though the reference to the duration of impurity until evening always implies the need for a ritual bath, it does not imply the need to launder clothing.[3]

וְהַנּוֹשֵׂא אוֹתָם—The direct object, אוֹתָם, refers to any saddle or seat upon which the discharging man had sat.

15:11 It is assumed that when the man urinates, his hands are polluted by contact with the uncleanness.

15:13 יִטְהַר—Here, as well as in 13:35, cleansing is almost synonymous with healing.

שִׁבְעַת יָמִים—See the textual note on this phrase in 8:33. It recurs in 15:19, 24, 28.

לְטָהֳרָתוֹ—See the textual note on this noun in 12:4.

בְּמַיִם חַיִּים—This could also be "running water." See the textual notes on 14:5.

וְטָהֵר׃—See the textual note on this verb in 11:32. It recurs in 15:28. The person who now is clean no longer communicates any impurity by contact with clean people and objects.

15:14 וּבַיּוֹם הַשְּׁמִינִי—See the textual notes on 9:1 and the use of this phrase in 9:1; 12:3; 14:10, 23; 15:29; 22:27; 23:36, 39.

שְׁתֵּי תֹרִים אוֹ שְׁנֵי בְּנֵי יוֹנָה—See 5:7; 14:22; 15:29.

אֶל־פֶּתַח אֹהֶל מוֹעֵד—See the textual notes on 1:3 and the explanation in "Leviticus 1–3." This phrase recurs in 15:29.

15:15 וְעָשָׂה—See the textual notes on 4:20.

וְכִפֶּר עָלָיו—See the textual notes on 1:4 and 4:26.

15:16 וְאִישׁ כִּי—The shift to וְאִישׁ כִּי indicates the beginning of a new unit in the speech.

שִׁכְבַת־זֶרַע—This is literally "outpouring of seed." This phrase is used for both nocturnal ejaculation in a so-called "wet dream" (15:16, 17, 32; 22:4), as well as ejaculation in sexual intercourse (15:18, 32; 19:20; Num 5:13). As Orlinsky has shown, שִׁכְבָה is most likely to be derived from the root "pour/pour out" rather than the common root "lie."[4]

כָּל־בְּשָׂרוֹ—The mention of the whole body ensures that the term "flesh" is not understood as a euphemism for the penis.

וְטָמֵא—He is merely ritually unclean. A nocturnal emission is therefore not to be regarded (as it was in pagan religions) as an act of intercourse with a succuba, a female spirit or the ghost of a female ancestor.

15:17 וְכָל־בֶּגֶד וְכָל־עוֹר—This refers to his bedding.

---

3 Milgrom, *Leviticus 1–16*, 917–18, 935–36.

4 Orlinsky, "The Hebrew Root *ŠKB*."

15:18 וְאִשָּׁה אֲשֶׁר—As Milgrom has shown, the phrase וְאִשָּׁה אֲשֶׁר is used here to mark this verse as a pivot in the chiastic arrangement of the speech.[5] It links back to the two cases of male discharges, introduced by אִישׁ כִּי in 15:2 and 15:16, and anticipates the two cases of female discharges, introduced by וְאִשָּׁה כִּי in 15:19 and 15:25.

יִשְׁכַּב אִישׁ אֹתָהּ—This clause with the verb שָׁכַב is a euphemistic idiom for sexual intercourse. This idiom recurs in 15:24, 33; 18:22; 19:20; 20:11, 12, 13, 18, 20.

וְטָמְאוּ עַד־הָעָרֶב׃—They are therefore forbidden to enter the sanctuary and eat holy food. Why should semen that is spilled during sexual intercourse be regarded as a ritual pollutant? A number of answers have been proposed. Wenham proposes that it, like the flow of blood during menstruation, involves the loss of a life fluid and is therefore to be associated with the realm of death.[6] Whitekettle argues, quite correctly, that during sexual intercourse life-giving semen is not wasted but transferred from husband to wife as one flesh.[7] Whitekettle goes on to say that it pollutes because it is transmitted by the penis that functions both to produce life-giving semen and to dispose of unclean urine. But, as Hartley notes, those two functions of the penis are not confused during sexual intercourse.[8]

Hartley holds, most plausibly, that it was declared unclean for religious reasons. Animists commonly regarded semen as a substance that had supernatural life-power. Israel's pagan neighbors practiced ritual sex and had sacral prostitutes at places of worship. But the divine legislation in Leviticus 15 that pronounced spilled semen as unclean meant that sexual intercourse therefore could never occur in the sanctuary and so become sacralized. Israel could never adopt these pagan sexual practices at the place of the worship of the one true God.

Leviticus 15 does not, however, imply that marital sexual intercourse is to be regarded as sinful. It is an act that for spouses is in the ritual category of the common realm and that can be either clean or unclean.

15:19 יִהְיֶה זֹבָהּ בִּבְשָׂרָהּ—This appositional clause identifies the characteristic feature for the definition of menstruation. Here בָּשָׂר, literally "flesh," is a euphemism for the female genitals.

בְנִדָּתָהּ—See the textual notes on 12:2.

וְכָל־הַנֹּגֵעַ בָּהּ—This is parallel to the case in 15:7. See the textual note on 15:7. However, it may be that, unlike a man with a discharge in 15:11, she does not communicate impurity by touching people or things with her hands.

15:23 הוּא—This refers to any object that is located on the bed or a seat together with the menstruant.

15:24 שָׁכֹב יִשְׁכַּב—This is an emphatic infinitive absolute with the finite verb.

וְטָמֵא שִׁבְעַת יָמִים—The leniency of this penalty stands in such stark contrast to the penalty of extirpation in 20:18 (cf. 18:19; Ezek 18:6; 22:10) that, as Wenham argues, this law may refer to accidental intercourse at the hidden onset of menstruation rather than the deliberate violation of the prohibition against sexual intercourse dur-

---

5 Milgrom, *Leviticus 1–16*, 905, 930–31.

6 Wenham, "Why Does Sexual Intercourse Defile (Lev 15:18)?"

7 Whitekettle, "Leviticus 15:18 Reconsidered."

8 Hartley, *Leviticus*, 210–11.

ing menstruation.[9] That interpretation is reinforced by the additional reference in 20:18 to uncovering the nakedness of the menstruant and laying bare her flow of blood.

וְכָל־הַמִּשְׁכָּב אֲשֶׁר־יִשְׁכַּב עָלָיו יִטְמָא׃—This is similar to the clause in 15:20 that opened 15:20–23. The similarity indicates that what is decreed there applies to the man here. This shows that he is in exactly the same state as the menstruant and subject to the same restrictions.

15:25 וְאִשָּׁה כִּי־יָזוּב זוֹב דָּמָהּ יָמִים רַבִּים—This is literally "if the discharge of a woman's blood discharges for many days."

אוֹ כִי־תָזוּב עַל־נִדָּתָהּ—This is literally "if she discharges beyond her menstrual period."

זוֹב טֻמְאָתָהּ—This abnormal discharge is called "her impurity" to distinguish it from the normal flow of blood during menstruation.

15:27 See 15:21–23. The LXX reads "her" instead of "these things." This, however, breaks the pattern in which the mention of polluted objects always introduces the contraction of impurity through them (15:5–6, 10, 21–23).

15:28 The requirement to take a bath is presupposed by its mention in 15:13.

15:29 וְהֵבִיאָה—See the textual note on this verb in 2:2.

15:30 מִזּוֹב טֻמְאָתָהּ׃—This is literally "from the discharge of her impurity." This unclean discharge is therefore to be distinguished from the normal menstrual discharge.

15:31 וְהִזַּרְתֶּם—This final verse is addressed to Moses and Aaron as the custodians of this tradition. In this context this Hiphil of נָזַר means to *"keep the sons of Isr[ael] sacredly separate from their uncleanness"* (BDB). See Lev 22:2; Ezek 14:7; Hos 9:10 for the use of the Niphal of נָזַר in similar senses.[10]

מִטֻּמְאָתָם—See Lev 16:16, 19. It is uncertain whether this refers to the genital impurities from chapter 15 or all the impurities from chapters 11–15. The mention of death from defilement supports the second interpretation.[11]

וְלֹא יָמֻתוּ—See the textual notes on 8:35.

בְּטַמְּאָם—This could also be translated "by defiling." This warning links the laws for purity with the death of Nadab and Abihu for sacrilege (10:2; cf. 8:35; 10:6, 7, 9; 22:9) and its remedy by the ritual for the Day of Atonement (16:1, 2, 13). Ritual impurity defiles the sanctuary when an unclean person enters its precincts and comes into contact with the holy things. Compare 20:3.

15:32 זֹאת תּוֹרַת—See the textual notes on תּוֹרָה in 6:2 (ET 6:9). Lev 15:32–33 serves a similar function to the summary subscript in 7:37.

הַזָּב—This is literally "a discharging person." It is therefore the general term for all the cases summarized next in 15:32–33.

לְטָמְאָה־בָהּ׃—This is literally "for becoming unclean by it."

15:33 וְהַדָּוָה בְּנִדָּתָהּ—This is a résumé of 15:19–23.

וְהַזָּב אֶת־זוֹבוֹ לַזָּכָר וְלַנְּקֵבָה—This is a résumé of 15:2–15 and 15:25–30.

וּלְאִישׁ אֲשֶׁר יִשְׁכַּב עִם־טְמֵאָה׃—This is a résumé of 15:24.

---

[9] Wenham, *Leviticus*, 220; cf. Keil, *Pentateuch*, 2:394.

[10] Milgrom, *Leviticus 1–16*, 945.

[11] Elliger, *Leviticus*, 196.

Commentary

Structure

In this chapter the speech to Moses and Aaron is framed by an introductory commission in 15:1–2a and a concluding statement in 15:31–33. The main body of the speech is arranged as a chiasm. The laws about abnormal male and female genital discharges in 15:2b–15 and 15:25–30 frame the laws about the normal male and female discharges in 15:16–17 and 15:19–24 and center attention on sexual intercourse between males and females in 15:18, the pivot of the chiasm.[12] The chiasm emphasizes the formal equivalence in the ritual status of men and women with respect to impurity from genital discharges and the treatment for it.

Repetition marks the presentation of the various cases in the speech. These cases follow two main patterns. On the one hand, there is the pattern for the treatment of a person with a venereal discharge. The basic pattern gives a definition of the impurity and its duration (15:2b–3, 19a, 25). This is modified by additional mention of the mode of purification in 15:16, 18, and it is altered in 15:13–15 and 15:28–30 by the prescription of the time for the process of purification and its culmination in the ritual for purification.

On the other hand, there is the pattern for the contraction and treatment of secondary impurity. The basic pattern deals with contamination by direct contact of a person (15:7, 8, 11, 19b, 24) or an object (15:12) with an unclean person. In it the definition of the mode of contact, whether it be by touching, being touched, being spat on, or sexual intercourse, is followed by the prescription for purification. This is modified for the contamination of a person with a contaminated object. In this case the definition of the mode for the contamination of the object (15:4, 9, 20, 26) is followed by reference to the mode of contamination from the object, its duration, and the prescribed form of purification (15:5–6, 10, 21–23, 27).

We also find the repetition of many key words and phrases. The most important of these is the root טמא, "unclean," as a verb,[a] an adjective (15:2, 25, 26, 33), and a noun (15:3 [twice], 25, 26, 30, 31). The result is a masterpiece of ritual composition.

(a) Lev 15:4, 5, 6, 7, 8, 9, 10 (twice), 11, 16, 17, 18, 19, 20 (twice), 21, 22, 23, 24 (twice), 27 (twice), 31, 32

The structure of this pericope can be outlined as follows:

- I. Introduction (15:1–2a)
  - A. God's address to Moses and Aaron (15:1)
  - B. God's commission of them (15:2a)
- II. Speech on the treatment of impurity from genital discharges (15:2b–30)
  - A. Impurity of a male from discharges (15:2b–17)
    - 1. Treatment for an abnormal venereal discharge (15:2b–15)
      - a. The nature of the impurity (15:2b–3)
        - i. The discharge as the cause of impurity (15:2b)

[12] Whitekettle, "Leviticus 15:18 Reconsidered," 34–37.

ii. The symptoms for the identification of this impurity (15:3)

b. Its transmission, duration, and treatment (15:4–12)

i. Contact with polluted bedding and a polluted seat (15:4–6)

ii. Contact with a polluted body (15:7)

iii. Contact with polluted spittle (15:8)

iv. Contact with a polluted saddle and its trappings (15:9–10)

v. Touch of people and vessels by a polluted hand (15:11–12)

c. Restoration to a clean state at the end of the infection (15:13–15)

i. Laundering of clothes and bath after a week (15:13)

ii. Presentation of sacrifices for ritual purification on the eighth day (15:14–15)

2. Treatment for a normal seminal discharge (15:16–17)

a. Cleansing of body with a bath (15:16)

b. Laundering of cloth or leather stained with semen (15:17)

B. Impurity of male and female from sexual intercourse (15:18)

C. Impurity of a female from discharges (15:19–30)

1. Treatment for normal menstrual discharge (15:19–24)

a. The duration of impurity from menstruation (15:19a)

b. Its transmission, duration, and treatment (15:19b–24)

i. Direct contact with the menstruant (15:19a)

ii. Contact with polluted bedding and anything on which she has sat (15:19b–23)

iii. Sexual intercourse (15:24)

2. Treatment for abnormal menstrual discharge (15:25–30)

a. Its characteristics and the duration of impurity from it (15:25)

b. Its transmission by bedding and seating, duration, and treatment (15:26–27)

c. Restoration to a clean state at the end of the discharge (15:28–30)

i. Transitional period of seven days (15:28)

ii. Presentation of sacrifices for ritual purification on the eighth day (15:29–30)

III. Summary instruction to Moses and Aaron (15:31)

IV. Summary subscript (15:32–33)

Ritual Analysis

Moses and Aaron are introduced as the custodians of the legislation in this chapter (15:1). The Lord commissions them to hand it on to the Israelites (15:2) and to enforce it (15:31). Their task is connected with the duty of the priest to perform the ritual for the reinstatement of a person after recovery from an abnormal genital discharge (15:14, 15, 30). But the main actors in this legislation are the Israelites. They are required to attend to their own diagnosis and treatment.

As often happens in ritual legislation, the first case in 15:2b–15 is presented in detail, because it provides the pattern for the cases that follow. These are abbreviated to avoid unnecessary repetition. The first case legislates for the treatment of a male with genital infection. This infection produced an irregular flow of fluid from the penis that obstructed the process of urination. That pathological discharge was itself unclean; it was the source of impurity (15:2). It generated the ritual impurity that disqualified the man from contact with holy things. The impurity from this discharge could be communicated directly or indirectly by contact with other people and objects.

Three kinds of secondary contamination are mentioned. First, another person could be contaminated by contact with the bedding on which he had lain, the seat on which he had sat, or the saddle on which he had ridden. Those who touched the polluted bedding became unclean (15:5). Those who sat on the polluted seat became unclean (15:6). Those who touched or carried a polluted saddle became unclean (15:10). Second, another person could become unclean by touching the body of the person with the discharge (15:7). Third, the person with the discharge could communicate its impurity by spitting on a clean person (15:8) and by touching another person (15:11) or object (15:12) with unrinsed hands. This secondary form of impurity from a genital discharge was rather trivial and short-lived. It lasted until sunset provided that it was treated by the appropriate method of purification. Those who became unclean laundered the clothes that they wore when they contracted the impurity and took a bath so that they became ritually clean again (15:5–8, 10). Any piece of pottery that they touched was smashed, while anything made of wood was rinsed with water (15:12; cf. 11:32–33).

The process of purification for the man with the discharge was much more complex (15:13–15). He waited for a week after the cessation of the discharge. This seven-day period marked his ritual passage from a state of impurity to a state of ritual purity. This week culminated in two important enactments. On the seventh day, he laundered his clothes and bathed in fresh water taken from a flowing spring or a running stream. Then on the eighth day, which marked the beginning of his new condition, he brought two turtledoves or two pigeons to the sanctuary and presented them there to the priest. The priest offered the first bird as a sin offering for his ritual cleansing and the second as a burnt offering for ritual readmission and reintegration into the holy congregation. While the rite of atonement removed his impurity, the sending up of the second bird as smoke restored the privilege of access to God and his blessings. The priest ate the meat from the first bird as his due from the offering.

The second case in 15:16–17 legislates for the treatment of impurity that was contracted by a male from the emission of semen apart from normal sexual intercourse. The semen that was ejaculated was the source of the ritual impurity that contaminated the man and his bedding. Both required purification. While the man had to take a bath before he became ritually clean again at sunset, the bedding had to be laundered before it too became clean at sunset.

The third pivotal case in 15:18 legislates for the treatment of impurity from sexual intercourse between a woman and a man. The emission of semen from it made both of them ritually unclean. Since, presumably, both of them were naked for intercourse, they did not launder their clothing; they took a bath so that they became clean again at sunset.

The fourth case in 15:19–24 legislates for the treatment of a woman with impurity from her regular flow of blood during menstruation. Like the semen from the man in 15:16–18, the menstrual blood was the cause of her ritual impurity. Like her period, the impurity lasted for a week. During her period she could communicate its impurity to others by her bedding or by any seat that had some of her menstrual blood on it (15:20–23). While anyone who touched her body became unclean (15:19b), she was able to touch people and things without communicating any impurity because she would not normally have any trace of menstrual blood on her hands.[13] She could therefore still attend to cooking and other housework.

If, however, a man had sexual intercourse with her at the onset of menstruation and so got some of her menstrual blood on his body, he shared her condition (15:24). Like her (15:20–23), he communicated impurity through his bedding and anything that he had sat on (15:24). The method of purification differed for each of these instances. Apart from the duration of impurity for the week of her menstrual period, no rite was prescribed for the menstruant at the end of her period. But its parallel with the situation of the man with the emission of semen in 15:16 implies that she, and any man who had engaged in sexual intercourse with her, had to take a bath.[14] This seems also to apply for anyone who had touched her (15:19b). Those who had touched any bedding or a seat with some of her menstrual blood on it laundered their clothes and took a bath, so that they would be ritually clean again (15:21–23).

The final case in 15:25–30 legislates for the treatment of impurity from prolonged or irregular menstruation. Any woman with such an abnormal discharge of blood from her vagina was unclean for the duration of the discharge, just as for the week of her period (15:25). Any of her bedding or any seat of hers that had some of her discharge on it communicated impurity to others, as during her period (15:26). Those who touched these things were required to purify themselves by laundering their clothes and taking a bath (15:27). The final process of ritual purification and restoration after she had recovered from her irregular discharge in 15:28–30 was exactly the same as for the man with an abnormal genital discharge.

Theological Significance

This speech, which comes at the end of the manual of impurities, provides us with a theological grammar of bodily impurity. As such, it is typical for the theological understanding of impurity in Leviticus, for the sense of impurity

---

[13] Milgrom, *Leviticus 1–16*, 936–37.

[14] Milgrom, *Leviticus 1–16*, 934–35.

has to do with threats to the integrity and health of the human body. It is exemplified, most characteristically and universally, by the attitude of women and men to their genitals and their use in sexual activity. Human beings oscillate between a sense of spiritual awe at their sexuality and a sense of physical disgust with their sexual organs, between a belief in the possible supernatural power of sexuality and the fear of actual contamination from it.

The rulings in this chapter work on the rather indiscriminate, raw sense of sexual impurity that is often associated with sexual intercourse, menstruation, seminal ejaculations, and genital infection. They use five different cases to reinterpret impurity theologically and so reshape the attitude of the Israelites to their genitals and their sexual use. They do not try to explain away the common human sense of bodily impurity and sexual defilement as primitive and irrational, but they treat it positively by discriminating between various degrees of impurity and prescribing appropriate pastoral rites of purification.

The most significant feature of this legislation is that it does not locate the source of genital impurity in either of the sexes or in their sexual organs. People do not generate impurity; it is something extrinsic to them and their sexual organs, an invasive and infective power. It is identified quite practically with the genital discharges found outside the human body. It belongs to the unclean domain that is associated with the underworld and its powers, the realm of death and of anti-god. So, even though impurity is experienced most tangibly as something physical, it is in itself as much a spiritual as a physical state of being, a power that impinges on the sexuality of men and women.

The Israelites lived together as a community in the common domain that was caught between two realms, the holy realm of God and the counter-realm of impurity—the fallen, sinful world. Consequently, they were all more or less unclean from their involvement in various kinds of impurity, just as they were all more or less clean from their involvement with God and his holiness. None of them were inherently clean and so capable of making others clean. Only God could do that. The laws in this chapter distinguish major long-term impurity from minor short-term impurity, just as they distinguish minor rites of purification from major rites of purification.

This theological grammar of bodily purity explores three different dimensions of impurity. The first had to do with the physical vitality and integrity of the body with its reproductive organs in the order of creation. God created the genitals for the purpose of reproduction. They could fail to fulfill their potential for procreation by pathological malfunction (15:2b–12, 25–27) or operational dysfunction (15:16–24). If the sexual organs had an abnormal discharge, they had lost their power to achieve reproduction; if they had an external discharge of semen or blood apart from sexual intercourse, they thereby failed to achieve reproduction. Thus God's creative purpose for them was frustrated. The flow of life from God did not pass through them to another person.

The second dimension had to do with the use of male and female organs in sexual intercourse. The classification of abnormal and normal genital discharges as unclean and the cause of impurity served to regulate sexual activity in Israelite marriages and families. It stopped those who had abnormal discharges from having sexual intercourse with their partners, so spreading their infection. While it prevented a man from having sex with a woman during her period, relieving her of his sexual demands, it also encouraged sex during the other three weeks of the month.

Most importantly, the classification of clean and unclean gave a structure for handling the vague sense of sexual impurity and limited the scope for the spread of impurity by people with normal sexual discharges, in sexual intercourse or apart from it. This is most evident in the careful formulation of the rules for a menstruating woman. She did not by herself pollute anybody; only her discharge did that. As she went about her household work, she could safely touch anyone and anything in her home, without contaminating them. The members of her household did not need to fear her and shun her with disgust as a danger to them. These rules therefore freed people with some form of sexual impurity to engage in their normal business with each other in their families.

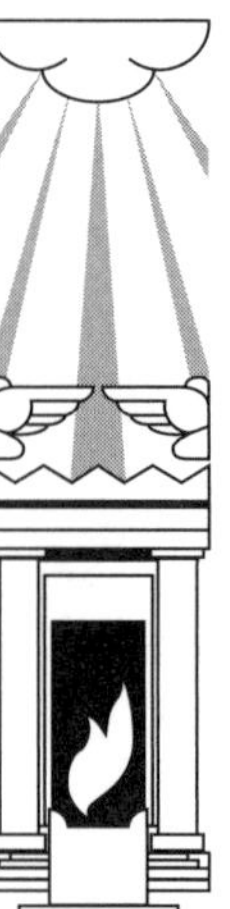

The third and most significant dimension of these rulings had to do with the ritual status of men and women before God. It involved the Israelites as members of the liturgical community. These rulings defined impurity ritually and theologically. Thus, if people were unclean from any genital discharge, they were not allowed to come before God at the sanctuary and touch anything that is holy (cf. 12:4). If they brought their impurity with them into the sacred realm, they defiled the sanctuary (15:31). This form of defilement was the worst kind of sacrilege; it resulted in death from God. Those who defiled God's holiness died in their impurity.

This theological understanding of impurity helps to explain some of the most puzzling features of this chapter. If we operate only with hygienic and social notions of impurity, we will not be able to figure out why semen and menstrual blood are held to be pollutants. They are, after all, normal and natural substances emitted by healthy people. But impurity is a ritual, theological category.

The classification of semen and menstrual blood as pollutants makes good sense in a pagan, animist environment such as ancient Israel faced. They were commonly regarded as supernatural substances with life-giving power if rightly used, but dangerous if used in the wrong way or by the wrong person. They were therefore often used in ritual, magic, and sorcery. Many people in the ancient world also believed that certain families and nations were bearers of "holy seed" and "divine blood" because they traced their origin mythologically to an ancestor who had sexual intercourse with a god or goddess.

God's classification of semen and menstrual blood as impurities desacralized them and prevented the Israelites from engaging in pagan and occult practices. Since the emission of semen made people unclean, no couple could ever have sexual intercourse at the sanctuary as part of any ritual enactment, nor could any man present his "seed" as an offering to the Lord. Thus these laws located sexual intercourse securely in the common realm. Sex was not, under any circumstance, sacred; it was not at all divine. Yet this teaching still associated reproduction with the will of God and the flow of life that came from him into Israelite homes and families.

This ritual-religious definition of sexual impurity resulted in a corresponding ritual-religious definition of sexual purity. If people were clean, they were fit for God and contact with the holy things of God. They could enter the sanctuary without defiling it. They received life and blessing from God; he empowered them to procreate. He too instituted the rites of purification for them, whether it was by laundering their clothes and taking a bath or by presenting sacrifices for their release from impurity and restoration. His Word empowered these rites. Through them he purified his people, so that they could once again stand in his presence and share in his holiness.

Fulfillment by Christ

In harmony with the OT, Christ and his apostles taught that sex and sexual intercourse belonged to the common realm. God had created and blessed the marital union and procreation (Gen 1:27–28; 9:1, 7). In itself sex is neither unclean nor holy in a ritual or liturgical sense. But it can be defiled. Thus, since all God's people are holy, they are required to avoid sexual impurity (Eph 5:3; Col 3:5; 1 Thess 4:7). The marriage bed is to be kept undefiled (Heb 13:4). But the focus of concern for sexual purity is shifted from the physical purity of the body to the purity of the heart, since a clean conscience qualifies a person for access to the heavenly sanctuary (Heb 9:14). The washing of the whole person, body and soul, by the waters of Baptism, includes the complete cleansing from all kinds of sexual impurity (1 Cor 6:11; Eph 5:26–27).

Since Christ was concerned with the purification of the conscience for service in the heavenly sanctuary, there is no discussion on pollution from sexual discharges in the NT. There is one account of a woman with a continuous menstrual discharge. That story is repeated in all three Synoptic Gospels (Mt 9:20–22; Mk 5:25–34; Lk 8:43–48). She had suffered from this condition for twelve years. This meant that she was in a state of perpetual ritual impurity. This impurity excluded her from access to God's holy presence in the temple and from participation in services of the synagogue. Yet she came from behind Jesus in the press of the crowd and touched his clothing. According to Lev 15:25–27 and the teaching of the rabbis, her touch would have rendered Jesus ritually unclean.[15] But by her touch the purity of Jesus was also conveyed to her.[16] He took on her impurity in exchange for his purity. She was not just healed and so delivered from her disease, but she was also saved and restored to the community of God's people. By her faith in Jesus she was cleansed from all

---

[15] Talmud, Mishnah, *Zabim,* 5:1–6.

[16] Evans, "Jesus and the Ritually Impure," 368.

her impurity. She was no longer disqualified from participation in the divine service. She began to live in community with God once again.

In all three Synoptic Gospels this incident is framed by the account of Jesus' resurrection of a dead girl—the twelve-year-old daughter of Jairus. Just as the unclean woman had touched Jesus, so Jesus touched the unclean corpse of that dead girl to restore her to life. His life-giving power was not diminished by contact with impurity. In fact, his power to cleanse from impurity was connected with his power to give life to those who were dead. Both stories therefore deal with the treatment of human impurity by Jesus. In them Jesus treats two typical cases of impurity. The healing of the woman with the continuous menstrual bleeding shows how he deals with all kinds of sexual impurity. Through word and touch he takes away the cause of impurity and conveys his own purity to those who are unclean and unfit for God's presence. Those who were once disqualified from contact with the holy things of God gained access to them through faith in Jesus.

It is remarkable that there is no debate in the NT about whether menstruating women were disqualified from attending the Divine Service and receiving the Sacraments. It seems that this was not an issue in the NT era, even though it was raised later in the history of the church. The NT therefore implies that women and men with venereal discharges did not desecrate the body and blood of Christ; as baptized believers, they had been cleansed and remained clean. The blood of Jesus, which they drank at the Lord's Table, conferred the forgiveness of sins upon the worthy communicants and further cleansed them from all impurity (cf. 1 Cor 10:16; 11:23–32; 1 Jn 1:7, 9).

In 1 Tim 2:15 St. Paul asserts that a Christian woman "shall be saved through childbearing"—which involves menstruation and childbirth—if she remains "in faith and love and holiness." Therefore the natural cycle and discharges do not in any way disqualify Christian women from participation in salvation. Instead, they continue to participate in God's holiness (even during menstruation and childbirth) and will be saved. The whole process of the bearing of children is sanctified through faith in Christ, just as he, by his incarnation, purified and sanctified the whole human life cycle from conception to the grave.

> Sin, disturb my soul no longer:
> I am baptized into Christ!
> I have comfort even stronger:
> Jesus' cleansing sacrifice.
> Should a guilty conscience seize me
> Since my Baptism did release me
> In a dear forgiving flood,
> Sprinkling me with Jesus' blood?[17]

---

[17] Stanza 2 of "God's Own Child, I Gladly Say It" by Erdmann Neumeister; translated by Robert E. Voelker (*HS98* 844:2). © 1991 Robert E. Voelker. Used with permission.

Leviticus 16:1–34

The Ritual for the Day of Atonement

Leviticus 16:1–34

The Ritual for the Day of Atonement

Translation

16 [1]The Lord spoke to Moses after the death of the two sons of Aaron; when they approached the presence of the Lord they died. [2]The Lord said to Moses: "Tell your brother Aaron that he should not enter just at any time into the Holy Place, inside the curtain, in front of the mercy seat that is upon the ark, so he will not die; for I appear in the cloud over the mercy seat.

[3]"This is how Aaron shall enter into the Holy Place: with a bull from the herd for a sin offering and a ram for a burnt offering; [4]he shall put on a sacred linen tunic, have linen underclothes over his body, gird with the linen sash, and wrap [his head] with the linen turban. These are the sacred vestments. He shall wash his body with water and then put them on. [5]From the congregation of the Israelites, he shall also receive two male goats for a sin offering and one ram for a burnt offering.

[6]"Aaron shall present the bull for the sin offering that is for him to make atonement for himself and for his household. [7]He shall take the two he-goats and station them before the Lord at the entrance to the tent of meeting. [8]Aaron shall place tags upon the two goats, one tag [marked] 'for the Lord' and the other tag [marked] 'for Azazel.' [9]Aaron shall bring forward the goat that the tag 'for the Lord' had come upon, to prepare it as a sin offering, [10]while the goat that the tag 'for Azazel' had come upon shall be stationed alive before the Lord, to make atonement upon it in order to send it off into the wilderness to Azazel.

[11]"After Aaron has presented the bull for his sin offering to make atonement for himself and his household, he shall slaughter the bull for his sin offering. [12]Then he shall take a full pan of glowing coals from the top of the altar before the Lord, and two handfuls of finely ground aromatic incense, and bring them inside the curtain. [13]He shall put the incense on the fire before the Lord so that the cloud from the incense covers the mercy seat that is over the written stipulations, so he will not die. [14]He shall take some of the blood of the bull and sprinkle it with his finger upon the surface of the mercy seat on its east side; he shall also sprinkle some of the blood seven times with his finger in front of the mercy seat.

[15]"He shall then slaughter the goat for the sin offering of the people, bring its blood inside the curtain, and perform the ritual with its blood as he had done with blood of the bull; he shall sprinkle it upon the mercy seat and in front of the mercy seat. [16]Thus he shall perform the rite of atonement in the Holy Place [to cleanse it] from the impurities of the Israelites and from their rebellions and all their sins.

"He shall perform the same ritual for the tent of meeting which resides with them in the midst of their impurities. [17]When he enters to make atonement in the Holy Place, no other human being may be in the tent of meeting until he has come out. Thus he shall make atonement for himself and his household as well as for the entire assembly of Israel.

**18“He shall then come out to the altar that is before the Lord and make atone-
ment on it. He shall take some of the blood of the bull and some of the blood of
the goat and smear it all around the horns of the altar. 19With his finger he shall
sprinkle some of the blood upon it seven times. Thus he shall purify it and consecrate it from the impurities of the Israelites.**

**20“When he has finished making atonement [to cleanse] the Holy Place, the
tent of meeting, and the altar, he shall present the live goat. 21Then Aaron shall
lay his two hands on the head of the live goat and confess over it all the iniquities of the Israelites and all their rebellions and all their sins. Thus he shall put
them on the head of the goat and send it away into the desert by means of an appointed man. 22In this way the goat will carry upon itself all their iniquities to an
inaccessible region.**

**“After he has released the goat in the wilderness, 23Aaron shall enter the tent
of meeting, take off the linen vestments that he had put on for entry into the Holy
Place, and leave them there. 24He shall bathe his body in water in a holy place and
put on his vestments; then he shall go out and perform the ritual for his burnt offering and the burnt offering of the people, making atonement for himself and for
the people. 25He shall turn the fat from the sin offering into smoke on the altar.**

**26“The person who releases the goat for Azazel shall launder his clothes and
bathe his body in water; after that he may reenter the camp. 27The bull for the
sin offering and the goat for the sin offering, whose blood has been brought in to
make atonement in the Holy Place, shall be brought outside the camp; their hide
and flesh and dung shall be burned in fire. 28He who burns them shall launder
his clothes and bathe his body in water; after that he may reenter the camp.**

**29“This shall be a perpetual ritual statute for you: In the seventh month, on
the tenth day of the month, you shall humble yourselves, and you shall not do
any kind of work, neither the native-born nor the alien who resides among you.
30For on this day atonement will be made on your behalf to purify you; you will
become clean from all your sins before the Lord. 31It shall be a Sabbath of complete rest, and you shall humble yourselves; it is a perpetual ritual statute. 32The
priest who is anointed and ordained to serve as priest in his father’s place shall
make atonement, wearing the linen vestments—sacred vestments. 33He shall
make atonement [to purge] the holiest part of the Holy Place, and he shall make
atonement [to cleanse] the tent of meeting and the altar; he shall make atonement on behalf of the priests and all the people of the assembly. 34This shall be a
perpetual ritual statute for you to perform atonement for the Israelites from all
their sins once a year.”**

Then he did as the Lord commanded Moses.

Textual Notes

16:1 See 10:1–3 for the incident referred to in this verse.

בְּקָרְבָתָם—This is the so-called feminine form (קָרְבָה) of the Qal infinitive construct of קָרַב. Instead of “when they approached” it could mean “when they encroached upon” the Lord’s presence.

16:2 הַקֹּ֫דֶשׁ—This term is used elsewhere in this chapter for the Most Holy Place (16:16, 17, 20, 23, 27, 33; see also 4:6; Ezek 41:21, 23; and the textual notes on Lev 4:6). But in 16:3 it also refers to the area in the courtyard around the altar for burnt offering (as in 10:4, 17, 18b; 14:13).

לַפָּרֹ֫כֶת—See the textual note on this term in 4:6. It recurs in 16:12, 15.

הַכַּפֹּ֫רֶת—This object has traditionally been called "the mercy seat" (KJV) by virtue of the derivation of כַּפֹּרֶת from כִּפֶּר, "to atone, make atonement," and the rite of atonement that was performed on it. "Seat" in this phrase refers to the location that was the source, the place where mercy was procured. The mercy seat was the place of atonement. Atonement for sins was necessary before God would display his mercy toward his people.

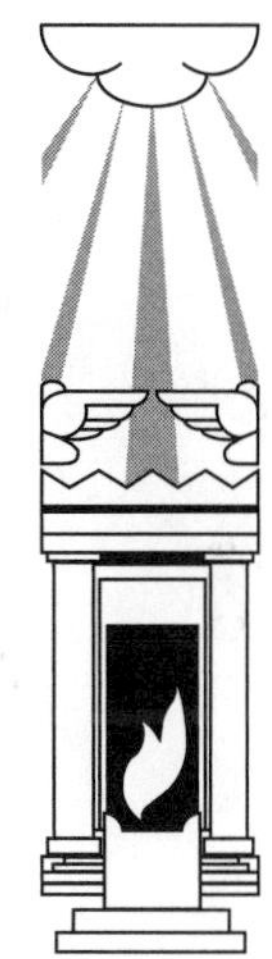

The mercy seat consisted of a solid gold slab that covered the ark of the covenant. This cover for the ark had one cherub attached to each side, so that the cherubim were facing each other with heads bowed down and with outstretched wings. Since this apparatus was commonly regarded as the seat for God's throne, it was identified with his presence. It was the place where God appeared (16:2), the place where he met and spoke with Moses (Ex 30:6; Num 7:89).

וְלֹ֣א יָמ֔וּת—This is literally "lest he die." See 16:13.

בֶּֽעָנָ֔ן—While this "cloud" resembles the glory cloud which both revealed and concealed the divine presence, it is most evidently the cloud of smoke from the incense burnt by the high priest as he entered the inner shrine (16:13).[1]

אֵרָאֶ֖ה—See the textual note on the Niphal of רָאָה in 9:4. It refers to theophany also in 9:6, 23.

16:3 בְּזֹ֛את יָבֹ֥א אַהֲרֹ֖ן אֶל־הַקֹּ֑דֶשׁ—This heading does not refer to the entry of the high priest into the Most Holy Place in 16:12–17 with the blood from these animals, but to the presentation of these animals as his offerings on this day.

בְּפַ֨ר בֶּן־בָּקָ֛ר—See the textual notes on 1:5.

לְחַטָּ֖את—See the use of a bull as a sin offering also in 4:3.

לְעֹלָֽה׃—See the use of a ram as a burnt offering also in 8:18; 9:2.

16:4 See also the descriptions of the vestments in Ex 28:40; 29:8–9; 39:27–29.

קֹ֫דֶשׁ—See the textual note on this noun in 4:6. It is also used in 16:32 in the same sense as here in 16:4.

עַל־בְּשָׂרוֹ֒—"Next to his body" is literally "over his flesh." בָּשָׂר may be a euphemism for the genitals, as in 6:3 (ET 6:10), which prescribes that the priest on duty must wear the undergarments, and also 15:2–3, 19.

16:5 לְחַטָּ֑את—See the use of a goat as a sin offering also in 9:3.

16:6 וְהִקְרִ֧יב—See the textual note on this verb in 1:2. It means "to present" or literally "to bring near." It recurs in 16:11, 20.

וְכִפֶּ֥ר בַּעֲד֖וֹ וּבְעַ֥ד בֵּיתֽוֹ׃—See the textual note on כִּפֶּר in 1:4. See the identical or similar clauses in 16:11, 17, 24.

16:7 פֶּ֖תַח אֹ֥הֶל מוֹעֵֽד׃—See the textual notes on 1:3.

[1] Milgrom, *Leviticus 1–16*, 1014–15.

16:8 וְנָתַן אַהֲרֹן ... גּוֹרָלוֹת—The RSV, NIV, and NRSV mistakenly refer to the casting of lots rather than to the placing of lots on each goat to distinguish them. These lots were attached as tags to the animals. The verb here is the Qal of נָתַן, which means "to place." In contrast, the common verb for the casting of lots is the Hiphil of נָפַל (e.g., Jonah 1:7; Ps 22:19 [ET 22:18]; Prov 1:14). The "lots" (גּוֹרָלוֹת) were two tags. One had the inscription "Belonging to the Lord" and the other had "Belonging to Azazel." Each tag was attached to one of the goats.

לַעֲזָאזֵל׃—The term "Azazel" (the transliteration of עֲזָאזֵל) has long puzzled exegetes. Four main interpretations have been advanced.[2]

First, the LXX, followed by the Vulgate and most exegetes, takes it as the combination of the noun עֵז, "goat," and the verb אָזַל, "to go away" (*HALOT*). Therefore "Azazel" means "a departing goat." From this we get the traditional English term "(e)scape goat."

Second, some rabbis explained it as referring to "a precipice" as the goat's destination.[3]

Third, by virtue of its parallel with the other goat "for YHWH," most modern scholars hold that it is a proper name for the demon that inhabits the desert.[4] In fact, later Jewish interpreters identify Azazel with Azael, the leader of the fallen angels (*1 Enoch* 8:1; 10:4–8; 13:1; cf. 4Q180, 1, 7–8).

Fourth, the name is held to be a metathesized form of the combination of a form of עזז and אֵל, "God/a god." The adjective עַז from the root עזז can mean "strong, fierce," and can describe anger as "fierce" (Gen 49:7; Prov 21:14). "Azazel" would then mean either "a fierce god"[5] or, more likely, "divine anger."[6] However, that fourth possibility is improbable because it would be unlikely for a Hebrew theophoric name that ends with אֵל to undergo metathesis that obliterates "God."

16:9 אֲשֶׁר עָלָה עָלָיו הַגּוֹרָל לַיהוָה—Literally this means the goat "upon which the lot 'for the Lord' had come up."

וְעָשָׂהוּ חַטָּאת׃—This could also be translated "to perform the ritual for it as a sin offering." Even though עָשָׂה could be used here as a technical term for the performance of the ritual for the sin offering, as in 4:20; 9:7; 14:19, 30; 15:15, 30; 16:15; 23:19, it makes better sense to understand it in this case as a reference to the preparation of the animal for slaughter.

16:10 אֲשֶׁר עָלָה עָלָיו הַגּוֹרָל לַעֲזָאזֵל—Literally this means the goat "upon which the lot 'for Azazel' had come up."

יָעֳמַד—This is the rare Hophal of עָמַד. Its meaning ("be stationed") is the passive of the Hiphil in 16:7.

לְכַפֵּר עָלָיו—See the textual note on this verb in 1:4. עָלָיו could also be translated "by means of it." See the use of the same idiom in 8:15; 14:53; 16:10, 18. In this case

---

2 De Roo, "Was the Goat Azazel Destined for the Wrath of God?"

3 Talmud, *Yoma,* 67b. Compare Driver, "Three Technical Terms in the Pentateuch," 97–98.

4 Milgrom, *Leviticus 1–16*, 1020–21.

5 Tawil, " ʿAzazel, the Prince of the Steppe," 58–59.

6 De Roo, "Was the Goat Azazel Destined for the Wrath of God?" 234–37.

the rite of atonement involves the confession of sins with the laying on of hands and the driving of the goat out into the desert rather than the application of blood.

16:11 וְהִקְרִ֨יב אַהֲרֹ֜ן אֶת־פַּ֤ר הַֽחַטָּאת֙ אֲשֶׁר־ל֔וֹ וְכִפֶּ֥ר בַּעֲד֖וֹ וּבְעַ֣ד בֵּית֑וֹ—This resumptive repetition of 16:6 indicates that 16:6–10 does not deal with the rite for atonement, but with the preparation of the animals for it.

וְשָׁחַט—See the textual note on this verb in 1:5. It recurs in 16:15.

16:12 הַמַּחְתָּה—See 10:1. The pan was, most likely, a small golden shovel with a handle.[7]

הַמִּזְבֵּחַ֙—See the textual note on this ("the altar") in 1:5. It recurs in 16:18 (twice), 20, 25, 33.

הַמִּזְבֵּחַ֙ מִלִּפְנֵ֣י יְהוָ֔ה—"The altar from before the Lord" refers to the altar for burnt offering with its perpetual fire (6:5–6 [ET 6:12–13]) rather than the incense altar.

קְטֹ֥רֶת סַמִּ֖ים דַּקָּ֑ה—See Ex 30:34–38 for the ingredients of the incense. In contrast to the "ground" (הָדֵק) incense burnt each day on the incense altar (Ex 30:36), the incense for this day was "finely ground" (דַּקָּה).[8]

וְהֵבִ֖יא מִבֵּ֥ית לַפָּרֹֽכֶת׃—According to the rabbis, the incense was brought with a ladle into the Holy of Holies.[9]

16:13 עַל־הָאֵ֖שׁ—This ("on the fire") means upon the live coals from the altar. In opposition to the Sadducees, who taught that the incense was kindled before the entry into the Holy of Holies, the Pharisees held that the incense was kindled in it.[10]

עַל־הָעֵד֖וּת—This means "over the written stipulations" or "over [the tablets of] the covenant." עֵדוּת is the term for the two tablets of stone which had the Decalogue inscribed on them (see, e.g., Ex 16:34; 25:21; 26:34; 27:21; 30:6, 36; 40:20; Lev 24:3; Num 17:19, 25 [ET 17:4, 10]). It has traditionally been translated by "testimony" by virtue of its supposed derivation from עֵד, "witness." עֵדוּת, however, was an ancient Semitic term for a formal, written agreement made by a suzerain with a vassal.[11] It is the term used by the priests for the stipulations of the Decalogue that were inscribed on "the tablets of the agreement" (Ex 31:18; 32:15; 34:29) and stored in the "ark of the agreement" (Ex 25:16, 22; 26:33; Num 7:89).

16:14 וְהִזָּ֥ה—See the textual note on this verb in 4:6. It recurs in Lev 16:15, 19.

קֵ֑דְמָה—This could mean either the "east side" or the "front side."

וְלִפְנֵ֣י הַכַּפֹּ֗רֶת—"Before the mercy seat" means on the floor of the Most Holy Place.

16:15 This verse prescribes that Aaron should bring all the blood of the goat, rather than some of it as in 16:14, into the Most Holy Place to consecrate the blood for its subsequent use.

וְעָשָׂ֤ה—See the textual note on this verb in 4:20.

---

7 Milgrom, *Leviticus 1–16*, 1024–25.

8 See Talmud, Mishnah, *Yoma,* 4:4, and Milgrom, *Leviticus 1–16*, 1025–26.

9 Talmud, Mishnah, *Yoma,* 5:1.

10 Milgrom, *Leviticus 1–16*, 1028–30.

11 Seow, "The Designation of the Ark in Priestly Theology," 192–95.

עַל־הַכַּפֹּ֖רֶת וְלִפְנֵ֥י הַכַּפֹּֽרֶת׃—Two acts of sprinkling were therefore performed: the one on the mercy seat and the other on the floor in front of it.

16:16 עַל־הַקֹּ֗דֶשׁ—This is literally "upon the Holy Place." See 16:10, 18.

מִטֻּמְאֹת֙—The blood was sprinkled in the Most Holy Place to cleanse it "from the impurities" of the people. See the use of the idiom כִּפֶּר מִן in 4:26; 5:6, 10; 14:19; 15:15, 30; 16:34. On טֻמְאָה, see the textual notes on it in 5:3. It recurs in 16:19.

וּמִפִּשְׁעֵיהֶ֖ם לְכָל־חַטֹּאתָ֑ם—Literally this means "all their acts of rebellion with respect to all their sins." See also 16:21. Schwartz argues that since atonement is made for impurity and for deliberate rather than inadvertent sins, these phrases should be translated as "and of their transgressions, among all their sins."[12]

וְכֵ֤ן יַעֲשֶׂה֙ לְאֹ֣הֶל מוֹעֵ֔ד—The blood was to be sprinkled seven times on the floor and daubed on the four horns of the altar as prescribed in Ex 30:10.

לְאֹ֣הֶל מוֹעֵ֔ד הַשֹּׁכֵ֣ן אִתָּ֔ם—The tent of meeting "resides" or "dwells" with the Israelites. This is a play on the designation of the tabernacle as "the dwelling place" of the Lord (8:10; 15:31; 17:4; 26:11). Since God, rather than the tabernacle, is usually said to "reside" among his people, some propose that הַשֹּׁכֵן could refer to God as "the one who dwells" with his people. If the Masoretic accents were disregarded to form a long construct chain, the phrase could mean "for the tent of meeting of the one who resides with them."

16:17 וְכָל־אָדָ֞ם לֹא־יִהְיֶ֣ה ׀ בְּאֹ֣הֶל מוֹעֵ֗ד—That is, no other priest may be in the tent of meeting.

בְּאֹ֣הֶל מוֹעֵ֗ד—See 6:23 (ET 6:30); 16:27.

כָּל־קְהַ֥ל יִשְׂרָאֵֽל׃—This could also be translated "the entire congregation of Israel." See the textual note on קָהָל in 4:13. See also 16:21.

16:18 וְיָצָ֗א אֶל־הַמִּזְבֵּ֛חַ אֲשֶׁ֥ר לִפְנֵי־יְהוָ֖ה—The altar referred to in this verse is the altar for burnt offering. See the textual notes on 1:5.

וְכִפֶּ֣ר עָלָ֑יו—See 8:15.

מִדַּ֤ם הַפָּר֙ וּמִדַּ֣ם הַשָּׂעִ֔יר—The blood of the bull was therefore mixed with the blood of the goat for this part of the rite.

וְנָתַ֛ן—This is literally "give." See also 4:7, 18; 8:15.

עַל־קַרְנ֥וֹת הַמִּזְבֵּ֖חַ—See the textual notes on 4:7.

סָבִֽיב׃—See the textual notes on 8:15.

16:19 וְטִהֲר֣וֹ—This is the Piel of טָהֵר, which first occurred in Leviticus in 13:6. Compare the textual note on the Qal in 11:32. The Piel recurs in 16:30.

וְקִדְּשׁ֔וֹ—See 8:15 and the textual notes on 8:10.

16:20 מִכַּפֵּ֤ר—The verb כִּפֶּר, "atone," is used transitively only here and in 16:33, with the parts of the sanctuary as its object (cf. Ezek 43:20, 26; 45:20). Apart from these ritual texts, it is also used transitively with "guilt" as its object in Pss 65:4 (ET 65:3); 78:38; Dan 9:24. In this context כִּפֶּר is used with the sense "to perform the rite of atonement so as to cleanse" something sacred.

16:21 וְסָמַ֨ךְ אַהֲרֹ֜ן אֶת־שְׁתֵּ֣י יָדָ֗ו—See the textual notes on 1:4.

---

12 Schwartz, "The Bearing of Sin in the Priestly Literature," 6–7.

אִישׁ עִתִּי—The adjective עִתִּי is derived from the noun עֵת, "time," and means "timely" (*HALOT*), that is, a man who has been appointed for this particular role, which is performed only once each year. Therefore we translate the phrase as "an appointed man." It could also be translated "a man in waiting."[13]

16:22 וְנָשָׂא ... עֲוֹנֹתָם—See the textual notes on 10:17.

16:24 בְּשָׂרוֹ—This is literally "his flesh."

בַמַּיִם בְּמָקוֹם קָדוֹשׁ—The location for this is uncertain. It could most likely be anywhere within the courtyard of the sanctuary.

בְּגָדָיו—These were his normal vestments.

וְעָשָׂה—See the textual notes on 4:20.

16:25 חֵלֶב—See the textual notes on 3:3, 16–17.

הַחַטָּאת—This refers to both the sin offerings.

יַקְטִיר—See 4:26, 31, 35 and the textual notes on 1:9.

16:26 Since 16:26–28 consists of disjunctive clauses outside the consecutive sequence, they are meant to be taken as parenthetical instructions rather than as part of the main ritual enactment.

הַמַּחֲנֶה׃—See the textual notes on 4:12. This term recurs in 16:27, 28.

16:27 פַּר—This refers to the carcass of the bull.

שְׂעִיר—This refers to the carcass of the goat.

דָּמָם—Whereas the direct object normally becomes the subject in a passive construction, "their blood" remains in the accusative case, even though it functions as a subject (GKC, § 121 b).

יוֹצִיא—This is literally "he shall bring out." However, we translate this impersonal verb as a passive, "shall be brought out."

וְשָׂרְפוּ—This is literally "and they shall burn." This impersonal verb too is translated as a passive.

16:29 לְחֻקַּת עוֹלָם—See the textual notes on 3:17.

תְּעַנּוּ אֶת־נַפְשֹׁתֵיכֶם—This could also be translated "deny yourselves." See 16:31; 23:27, 29, 32; Num 29:7. This lasted for a full twenty-four hours (Lev 23:29, 32). It included the total abstention from food, drink, bathing, anointing, and sexual intercourse.[14]

הָאֶזְרָח—Even though אֶזְרָח could be used more broadly for any native-born inhabitant of the land, Leviticus contrasts the native with the resident alien and so uses this term for an Israelite citizen.[15] The term recurs in 17:15; 18:26; 19:34; 23:42; 24:16, 22.

וְהַגֵּר—The גֵּר was an alien resident in the land of Israel.[16] Since aliens could not own land, they were economically vulnerable (19:10) and likely to be cheated in com-

---

[13] Milgrom, *Leviticus 1–16*, 1045.

[14] Milgrom, *Leviticus 1–16*, 1054.

[15] Joosten, *People and Land in the Holiness Code*, 35–36.

[16] Joosten, *People and Land in the Holiness Code*, 54–73; Milgrom, *Leviticus 17–22*, 1493–1501.

merce (19:33–34). The Israelites were therefore commanded to love and care for them as for themselves (19:33–34). Even though resident aliens did not belong to the people of Israel, they could join with them by presenting offerings at the altar (17:8; 22:18). They could therefore become members of the liturgical assembly (cf. Ex 12:19). They were also governed by the same prohibitions as the Israelites, such as work on the Day of Atonement (Lev 16:29), the consumption of blood (17:10, 12, 13), sexual immorality (18:26), sacrifice to Molech (20:2), blasphemy (24:16), and the injury of animals and people (24:22). These prohibitions ensured that they did not defile the land and the sanctuary. But since they were not Israelites, they were not obliged to observe the performative commandments.[17] The term גֵּר recurs in 17:8, 10, 12, 13, 15; 18:26; 19:10, 33, 34; 20:2; 22:18; 23:22; 24:16, 22; 25:23, 35, 47.

16:30 יְכַפֵּר עֲלֵיכֶם—Since there is no preceding subject, the verb can be construed impersonally as a passive: "atonement will be made." See the textual notes on 1:4.

לְטַהֵר ... תִּטְהָרוּ׃—See the textual notes on the Qal of טָהֵר in 11:32.

16:31 שַׁבַּת שַׁבָּתוֹן—The construct phrase שַׁבַּת שַׁבָּתוֹן can be best understood as a superlative expression for "a sabbatical Sabbath," "a restful day of rest," "a Sabbath day of complete rest."[18] It is used for the complete cessation of work each seventh day of the week (Ex 31:15; 35:2; Lev 23:3), the complete cessation of work each seventh month on the Day of Atonement (16:31; 23:32), and the complete cessation of cultivation for the land each seventh year (25:4). It therefore connects the Sabbath month and Sabbath year with the weekly Sabbath day.

16:32 אֲשֶׁר־יִמְשַׁח אֹתוֹ וַאֲשֶׁר יְמַלֵּא אֶת־יָדוֹ—This refers to the priest who is anointed to succeed his father as high priest. It is literally "whom he anoints and whose hand he fills." These verbs are used impersonally and so are best translated by the passive. See the textual notes on 8:22 and 8:33.

בִּגְדֵי הַבָּד בִּגְדֵי הַקֹּדֶשׁ׃—This is literally "the linen vestments, the sacred vestments."

16:33 וְכִפֶּר ... יְכַפֵּר—This is literally "he shall atone." See the textual notes on 16:20.

מִקְדַּשׁ הַקֹּדֶשׁ—This could also be translated "the sacred precinct of the Holy Place." This is the only occurrence of the phrase מִקְדַּשׁ הַקֹּדֶשׁ. The noun מִקְדַּשׁ (the construct of מִקְדָּשׁ) is best taken to mean the "holiest part," as in Num 18:29, rather than its usual meaning, the "sacred precinct."

כָּל־עַם הַקָּהָל—This is the only occurrence of the phrase עַם הַקָּהָל, "the people of the assembly." It combines the previous references to "the people" in 16:15 and 16:24 with the reference to "the assembly" in 16:17.

16:34 לְכַפֵּר עַל־בְּנֵי יִשְׂרָאֵל מִכָּל־חַטֹּאתָם—See the use of the same idiom in 4:26; 5:6, 10; 14:19; 15:15, 30; 16:16.

וַיַּעַשׂ כַּאֲשֶׁר צִוָּה יְהוָה אֶת־מֹשֶׁה׃—This follows from 16:28 and refers to what Aaron had been commanded to do in 16:2–28. On צִוָּה, see the textual notes on 7:36.

---

17 Milgrom, *Leviticus 1–16*, 1055.

18 Levine, *Leviticus*, 155.

Commentary

Context and Structure

This chapter stands out from the rest of Leviticus. The importance of this chapter is emphasized by a curious literary device. The chapter begins like any other speech with the report of God's address to Moses. But no speech follows "The Lord spoke to Moses" in 16:1. Instead we have the report that this occurred after the death of Nadab and Abihu. Then in 16:2 we have a new introduction to the speech that follows.

Warning claims that 16:1 is to count as the eighteenth speech, which would then make 16:2–34 the central and nineteenth speech in thirty-seven speeches.[19] We believe that Leviticus has thirty-six speeches, but we agree that the literary device indicates the pivotal role of this chapter. It is indeed the central chapter of the book. As the eighteenth speech, it is the last speech of the first half of the book. It also is the essential preparation for the second half of the book.

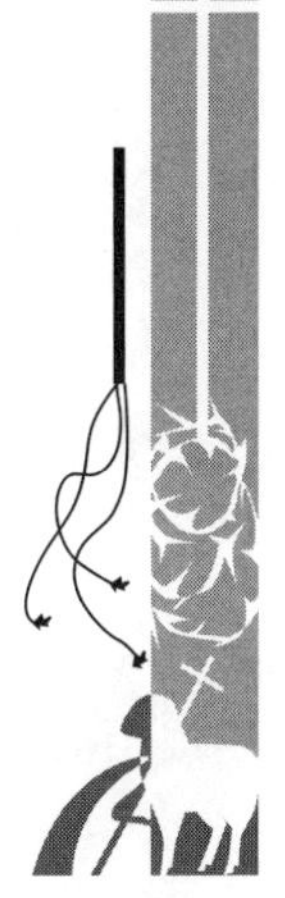

This chapter stands at the heart of Leviticus, which, in turn, is the center book of the Pentateuch. The ritual for the Day of Atonement cleansed the people from all the sins for which the normal sacrifices prescribed in chapters 1–7 did not atone. It also purged the sanctuary from the classes of impurity mentioned in chapters 11–15. Once this had been done the Israelites could continue to bring their offerings to the Lord under the leadership of the priests in the divine service, as established in chapters 8–10, and so have access to the Lord's gracious presence at the sanctuary. The service of that day also qualified them for their ongoing participation in the Lord's holiness at the sanctuary and in their daily life, as elaborated in the second half of the book, chapters 17–27.

The narrative in 16:1 gives the occasion for the speech of the Lord to Moses in 16:2–34a. The death of Nadab and Abihu for approaching the Lord in the wrong way with unauthorized fire in 10:1–3 results in the legislation on how Aaron is to enter the Holy Place with fire from the altar to perform a rite of atonement for the defiled sanctuary. The five instructions on impurity intervened in chapters 11–15 because the rite that was instituted in chapter 16 was meant to cleanse both the sanctuary and the people from impurity (16:16, 19, 30, 34). Most of the speech, which was given to Moses to report to Aaron (16:2–28), deals with cleansing the sanctuary after the death of Aaron's sons. The last part of the speech appears to be an appendix to this legislation. It is not addressed to Aaron, but is spoken to the Israelites in the second person plural form (16:29–34a; cf. similar forms in 1:2; 2:11–12; 7:23–27, 32; 11:2–45). It legislates the annual performance of this rite and the participation of the Israelites in it.

A number of devices serve to structure the ritual legislation in 16:3–28. The resumptive repetition of 16:6 in 16:11a marks off the intervening section

---

[19] Warning, *Literary Artistry in Leviticus*, 40–46.

as a preparatory enactment before the performance of the main rite in 16:11–20. This rite is framed by the references to the sin offering and burnt offering in 16:3 and 16:24b–25, to the ritual act of clothing and bathing in 16:4 and 16:23–24a, and to the scapegoat in 16:7–10 and 16:20–22. The performance of the blood rite in each of the three key locations in the sanctuary is concluded by a summary statement of purpose in 16:16a, 17b, and 19b.

The addendum in 16:29–34 is both framed and divided into two parts by the reference to its contents as a perpetual ritual statute in 16:29, 31, 34. Furthermore, the material in 16:29–31 is arranged chiastically so that it focuses and hinges on the cleansing of the Israelites of their sins in 16:30. The material in 16:32–34a is tied together by the repetition of the verb "atone" five times in four different senses. The mention in 16:34 of the annual rite of atonement, performed by the high priest once a year, recalls the Lord's warning in 16:2 about unauthorized entry by the high priest at any time. Thus, whereas 16:3–28 explains how Aaron should enter the sanctuary and the Most Holy Place on that first Day of Atonement, 16:29–34a explains when and why it is to be done annually.

Number symbolism is evident in the composition of this chapter.[20] It focuses on seven, the divine number of completeness and perfection.[21] Blood is sprinkled seven times in the comprehensive act of atonement (16:14, 19). Two significant things are mentioned seven times in 16:2–28: "the Holy Place" (16:2, 3, 16, 17, 20, 23, 27) and "the mercy seat" (16:2 [twice], 13, 14 [twice], 15 [twice]).The word חַטָּאת, the term for sin offering and for sin, occurs fourteen times in this chapter,[a] while the key verb "enter" (בּוֹא) is used ten times.[b]

(a) Lev 16:3, 5, 6, 9, 11 (twice), 15, 16, 21, 25, 27 (twice), 30, 34

(b) Lev 16:2, 3, 12, 15, 17, 23 (twice), 26, 27, 28

The combination of the historical report in 16:1 and 16:34b with the divine speech in 16:2b–34a (as well as the combination of the particular charge to Aaron for the cleansing of the sanctuary after the death of his sons in 16:2b–28 with the general charge to the congregation about an annual day of atonement in 16:29–34a) means that this chapter does more than establish the ritual for the Day of Atonement. It also reports its first observance as a precedent for its subsequent observance. It therefore gives us the foundational legislation for the ritual as it tells us the foundational reason for its observance.

The structure of this pericope can be outlined as follows:

I. Introduction (16:1–2a)
    A. The occasion: the death of Aaron's sons (16:1)
    B. The Lord's address to Moses (16:2a)
II. Speech with the legislation for Aaron's entry into the Holy of Holies (16:2b–28)

---

[20] Warning, *Literary Artistry in Leviticus*, 124–26.

[21] For example, God completed his work of creation in seven days. In Revelation, the exalted Christ is depicted with the number seven (Rev 1:12, 16, 20; 2:1; 3:1). The entire church is represented by the seven churches in Revelation 2–3 (cf. 1:4, 11). Cf. Dan 9:25, 27; Zech 3:9; 4:2, 10.

- A. Warning about unauthorized entry (16:2b–c)
  - 1. Danger of intrusion: death (16:2b)
  - 2. Reason for the danger: theophany (16:2c)
- B. The preparation for entry by the high priest (16:3–10)
  - 1. Sacrifice of animals by the high priest: bull and ram (16:3)
  - 2. Ritual bathing and clothing (16:4)
  - 3. Reception of the people's sacrificial animals: two goats (16:5)
  - 4. The presentation of the high priest's sin offering (16:6)
  - 5. The preparation of the two goats as the people's sin offering (16:7–10)
- C. The rite for the cleansing of the sanctuary (16:11–19)
  - 1. The blood rite for the Most Holy Place (16:11–16a)
    - a. The sin offering of the high priest (16:11–14)
      - i. The slaughter of the bull (16:11)
      - ii. Burning of incense in the Most Holy Place (16:12–13)
      - iii. Sprinkling of its floor and the atonement cover (16:14)
    - b. The sin offering of the people (16:15)
      - i. Slaughter of the goat (16:15a)
      - ii. Sprinkling of the floor and the atonement cover (16:15b)
    - c. Purpose: atonement for the purging of the Most Holy Place (16:16a)
  - 2. The blood rite in the tent of meeting (16:16b–17)
    - a. Repetition of the two blood rites (16:16b)
    - b. Exclusion of the other priests (16:17a)
    - c. Purpose: atonement for the priesthood and the congregation (16:17b)
  - 3. The blood rite at the altar for burnt offering (16:18–19)
    - a. Smearing of the blood from the sin offerings on its horns (16:18)
    - b. Sprinkling of blood on the altar (16:19a)
    - c. Purpose: cleansing and consecration of the altar (16:19b)
- D. The rite for the removal of sin (16:20–22)
  - 1. Presentation of the scapegoat by high priest (16:20)
  - 2. Confession of sins over it (16:21a)
  - 3. Its dispatch to the desert by an assistant (16:21b)
  - 4. Its release by him there (16:22)
- E. Presentation of the offerings on the altar (16:23–25)
  - 1. Removal of vestments in the tent of meeting (16:23)
  - 2. Bathing and clothing with normal vestments (16:24a)
  - 3. Bathing of the two burnt offerings (16:24b)
  - 4. Burning of fat from the sin offering (16:25)
- F. Readmittance of assistants (16:26–28)
  - 1. Bathing of person who dispatched the scapegoat (16:26)
  - 2. Bathing of person who burnt up the sin offerings (16:27–28)

III. The Lord's legislation for the Israelites about the Day of Atonement (16:29–34a)
- A. Date for the annual day of fasting and rest (16:29–31)
- B. Performance of atonement by Aaron's successor (16:32–34a)

IV. Report of Aaron's compliance (16:34b)

Ritual Agents

Everything in this chapter focuses on Aaron in his capacity as the high priest. In fact, he functioned as the high priest of Israel most evidently and distinctively in the performance of the rites for atonement on the Day of Atonement, for only he was authorized to enter the Most Holy Place, and on no other day except that day. He alone entered that dangerous place to perform the annual rite of atonement there.

The legislation, recorded here in this chapter, prescribes how and when the high priest was to "enter" the Most Holy Place on that day (16:2, 3, 17, 23). It also states quite explicitly that no one else was to accompany him as he performed the blood rite in the Most Holy Place and the tent of meeting (16:17). By himself Aaron fulfilled the commandments that the Lord gave to his brother, Moses (16:2, 34). As the sole celebrant he acted on behalf of the people and represented them before the Lord. He approached the Lord on behalf of them. He performed the rite of atonement for all the Israelites (16:34), for himself and the priesthood, and for the congregation (16:5, 11, 17, 24, 33). As the representative of the people, he atoned for all their sins and cleansed the sanctuary from all their impurity (16:16); as their representative he also confessed their sins and laid them on the scapegoat (16:21). He therefore embodied the whole sinful nation and acted vicariously on its behalf before the Lord.

The role that Aaron took on that first Day of Atonement was passed on to his successors who were anointed and ordained to officiate as high priests after him (16:32–33). They too were to wear the sacred vestments that were only to be worn on that day. They too were to perform the comprehensive rite of atonement for all the Israelites on the Day of Atonement.

Both Aaron and his successors were to receive help from only two people for two peripheral aspects of the ritual for that day. One person was appointed to take the scapegoat into the desert and release it there (16:21, 22, 26). Another person was to get rid of the leftovers by burning them up outside the camp (16:27–28; cf. 4:11–12, 21; 6:23 [ET 6:30]). So sacred was the day and everything associated with it that they, like the high priest (16:23–24), had to bathe and wash their clothes before they could return to the camp and resume their normal status (16:26–28).

While Aaron played the main role in the ritual for that day, the next most important part was played by the congregation. From its representatives he received the goats for their sin offerings and the ram for their burnt offering (16:5). Whether they were present or not, they, along with all the foreigners who lived with them, participated in the ritual by fasting and abstaining from all kinds of work (16:29–31). The ritual for this day was therefore so inclusive that it was the only ritual occasion, apart from the Feast of Unleavened Bread (Ex 12:19), which automatically included all resident aliens in its observance.

Ritual Materials and Objects

There were four kinds of materials and objects that were used in the ritual for the Day of Atonement. First, there were the animals presented as the sin offerings and burnt offerings. The animals for the sin offerings were especially significant since they provided the blood for the rite of atonement. Because the high priest represented the nation, a bull was prescribed on this occasion as his sin offering, just as at his ordination (16:3; cf. 4:3; 8:2). As was usually the case for festive occasions (9:3; Num 28:15, 22, 30, etc.), male goats were offered as sin offerings (Lev 16:5). The unusual thing about this day was that of the two male goats that were offered as sin offerings, the second was used as a scapegoat. A ram was presented for the burnt offering for the high priest (16:3), just as at his ordination (8:18) and at the inaugural service (9:2), as well as for the burnt offering of the congregation (16:5). The unusual choice of the ram for both parties probably affirmed the solidarity of the priest with the congregation.

Second, special vestments were prescribed for the high priest only on the Day of Atonement. They are described as "the sacred vestments" (16:4), "the sacred linen vestments" (16:32). These plain linen garments are to be distinguished from his normal ornate vestments (16:24; cf. Ex 28:1–19). They consisted of a holy linen tunic, linen underpants, a plain linen sash, and a linen turban. They resembled the garments worn by the ordinary priests (8:13; cf. Ex 28:40; 29:8–9; 39:27–29) and yet differed from them in two ways. The sash was made of linen rather than an embroidered fabric; the cap was replaced by a linen turban.

These plain vestments, which were normally kept in the tent of meeting (16:23), were worn by the high priest only for the rite of atonement. After that was finished, he put on his normal garments. There was then a dramatic contrast between the vestments worn by the high priest while he presented the sin offering in 16:6–22 and the royal vestments worn by him as he burnt the offering on the altar for the burnt offering. In the former case he functioned as the representative of the sinful people before God, "stripped of all honor ... the servant of the King of kings."[22] He was dressed like God's courtiers, the angels,[c] for, like them, he was admitted to the heavenly council on that day (Zech 3:3–7) and was "given access to the divine presence."[23] In the latter case he functioned as a representative of the holy Lord before the people, clothed in glory and honor, the ambassador of the heavenly King, dressed in royal robes. The vestments of the high priest starkly portrayed his equivocal status as the great mediator between the holy God of Israel and his sinful people.

(c) Ezek 9:2–3, 11; 10:2, 6–7; Dan 10:5; 12:6–7

Third, two pieces of sacred furniture, found in two separate locations, were the focus of the extraordinary rite of atonement on that day. The first of these was the כַּפֹּרֶת, the "mercy seat" that was fixed on top of the ark (16:2, 13, 14, 15). This object, which was made of pure gold, consisted of a flat cover with a cherub at either end (Ex 25:17–20; 37:6–9). It formed the seat of God's throne. It was the place where the Lord was "enthroned upon the cherubim,"[d] the place

(d) 1 Sam 4:4; 2 Sam 6:2; Pss 80:2 (ET 80:1); 99:1; Is 37:16

[22] Wenham, *Leviticus*, 230.

[23] Milgrom, *Leviticus 1–16*, 1016.

(e) Ex 25:22; 30:6, 36; Num 7:89; 17:4

where he met with Moses and spoke to him.[e] The rite of atonement, in which the high priest appeared twice before the mercy seat in the Most Holy Place to sprinkle blood seven times on it and on the floor in front of it, was the central act in the ritual for the Day of Atonement when the Lord appeared there in a cloud over it. This was, in fact, the only rite that involved the mercy seat in its enactment.

The second main piece of sacred furniture, used for the rite of atonement on that day, was the altar for burnt offering (16:18–19). This was the place where the regular rites of atonement were enacted in the daily services. On this day, however, it was not the place for the performance of the rite; instead, it benefited from the rite performed in the Most Holy Place. Its purity and holiness were restored so that it could function as the place where atonement was made and where God met with his people to bless them (Ex 29:42–43). As is indicated in Lev 16:16, which echoes the legislation in Ex 30:10, the blood rite was also performed on the altar for incense. It, however, was not explicitly mentioned here because it was peripheral to the main ritual that connected the appearance of God over the mercy seat with the presence of his sinful people at the altar for burnt offering.

Fourth, incense and blood were needed for the performance of the ritual. The priest had to burn incense to produce a cloud of smoke as he entered the Most Holy Place (16:2, 16). He used the same incense that was burnt twice each day on the altar for incense, except that it was more finely ground for this occasion. Two handfuls of it, made as prescribed in Ex 30:34–35, had to be brought into the Most Holy Place in a ladle, together with live coals from the altar for burnt offering on a pan. According to the Pharisees, a smoke raiser was added to the coals by the high priest as he entered the Most Holy Place, and the incense was added to the coals as he stood "before the Lord" in the Most Holy Place.[24] Both the high priest and the Lord were therefore hidden in a cloud of smoke and incense as they met there on that day.

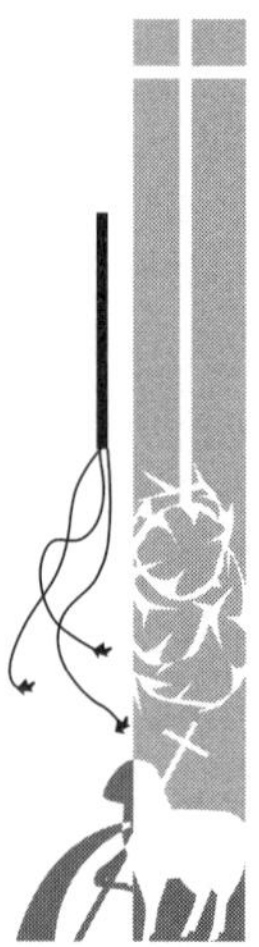

The actual rite of atonement was performed with the blood from the two sin offerings. While "some of the blood" from the sin offering of the high priest was brought into the Most Holy Place (16:14), all the blood from the sin offering of the people was taken there (16:15).[25] The two lots of blood, which were kept apart for the performance of the blood rite in the Most Holy Place and the tent of meeting (16:14–16), were combined for the final blood rite at the altar for burnt offering (16:18–19). The blood, which had become most holy by virtue of its contact with the atonement cover, was used to reconsecrate the altar for burnt offering. It was the most holy thing in the enactment of the ritual.

---

[24] Milgrom, *Leviticus 1–16*, 1029–31.

[25] Milgrom, *Leviticus 1–16*, 1033.

Ritual Location

The location of the ritual for the Day of Atonement was the most important element in its performance, for it was the only ritual performed in the Most Holy Place. It involved the annual entry of the high priest there (16:2, 3). He entered the Most Holy Place to perform the special rite of atonement there and in the tent of meeting. Thus he did not just perform this rite on the mercy seat and the incense altar, but he also sprinkled the Most Holy Place and the tent of meeting (16:14–16) and thereby "atoned" for them (16:20, 33); he cleansed these places from all impurity (16:16).[26] The ritual performed in these most holy places was therefore performed for them and the preservation of their sanctity.

The most significant location for the atonement ritual was the Most Holy Place, for the Day of Atonement was the only time that the high priest entered this special place and performed a rite there. In this chapter it is called "the Holy Place" (16:2, 3, 16, 17, 20, 23, 27), rather than "the Most Holy Place." This cube-shaped inner room of the tabernacle was separated from the outer room by a curtain (16:2, 12, 15). It contained nothing but the ark with its mercy seat (16:13). It was the place where the Lord appeared to the high priest in a cloud on that day (16:2). In all, the priest was required to enter it three times: to burn incense there before the Lord (16:12–13), to sprinkle the blood from his sin offering (16:14), and to sprinkle the blood from the sin offering of the people (16:15).

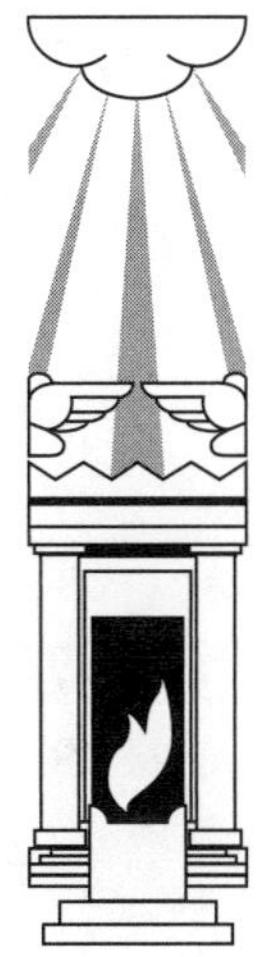

Two other places were involved in the entry and exit of the high priest from the Most Holy Place. The first of these was the tent of meeting, the outer room of the tabernacle (16:16, 17, 20, 23, 33). He also returned there to remove his vestments and deposit them there after he had completed the special ritual for the day (16:23). The second of the places associated with the exit and entry of the high priest from the Most Holy Place was the altar for burnt offering that stood at the center of the eastern courtyard of the tabernacle. The final blood rite was performed on it (16:18–19). As well as that, the high priest took live coals from it for his first entry into the Most Holy Place (16:12). He also burned the burnt offering and the fat from the sin offerings on it at the conclusion of the ritual for the Day of Atonement (16:24–25).

Three other places played an important role in the atonement ritual. The two special goats for the sin offering of the people were "stationed" before the Lord at the entrance to the tent of meeting (16:7). This area in front of the altar was the site for most of the transactions involving the congregation. The Lord's goat was presented before the altar to be sacrificed there (16:9); the scapegoat which had been stationed there for the blood rite (16:10) was also presented there (16:20) and sent out into the desert from there (16:21–22). While the blood for the Lord's goat was brought into the Most Holy Place, the

[26] Milgrom, *Leviticus 1–16*, 1032, 1034.

other goat for Azazel was sent out to an "inaccessible region" in the desert (16:21–22). That place was the counter location to the Most Holy Place. It was part of the unclean, demonic realm that belonged to Azazel rather than to the Lord. The third location was the ash heap outside the camp where the leftovers from the sin offerings were burned (16:27; cf. 4:12).

Whereas the altar for burnt offering was the usual point of orientation for the performance of the daily services, the Most Holy Place was the point of orientation for the ritual performed on the Day of Atonement. This point of orientation meant that the ritual for the day consisted of movements in two opposite directions. On the one hand, there was the inward movement of sacrificial animals into the courtyard, the transition of animal blood from the courtyard into the Most Holy Place, and the transportation of animal meat and fat from the courtyard to the altar. On the other hand, there was the counter-movement of blood from the Most Holy Place to the tent of meeting and the altar for burnt offering, of the scapegoat from the courtyard to the desert, and of the leftovers from the sin offerings from the courtyard to the ash dump outside the camp. Thus the main ritual movement into the Most Holy Place prepared the way for the counter-movement from it outwards with the extension of holiness to the altar and the expulsion of impurity from the sanctuary.

Ritual Time

The occasion for the institution of this special ritual and its first enactment was the death of Aaron's two sons for approaching the Lord with unauthorized fire (10:1–4). In response to this disaster, the Lord warned Aaron about unauthorized entry "at any time" into the Most Holy Place (16:2). The subsequent legislation prescribed the ritual for the most comprehensive rite of atonement on that day (16:3–28), as well as on the annual Day of Atonement on the tenth day of the seventh month (16:29–31). The seventh month was the first month in the secular Babylonian calendar. The festivals of the seventh month began with the Day of Acclamation (23:23–25) and culminated in the Feast of Booths in the middle of the month (23:33–35). Thus the ritual for the cleansing of the sanctuary after the death of Aaron's sons established the precedent for the annual day of cleansing that prepared the sanctuary and the people for that great festival.

Ritual Enactment

The central ritual for the Day of Atonement was an extraordinary rite of atonement. It was performed by the high priest on behalf of the congregation. The legislation for that day covers five aspects of its enactment: the preparation for the rite in 16:3–10, the main rite in 16:11–25, the concluding acts in 16:26–28, the involvement of the people in 16:29–31, and the responsibility of the high priest for its annual performance in 16:32–33.

The high priest first prepared himself and the animals for the ceremony. He prepared for his role by bathing in water and putting on the vestments for the occasion (16:4). Both these acts were exceptional measures. Whereas the priests on duty normally washed their hands and feet before they entered the tent of meeting or officiated at the altar (Ex 30:19–20; 40:30–32), the high priest had to wash his whole body, like the candidates for ordination to the priesthood (Ex 29:4; Lev 8:6). After that ritual bath, he put on the special vestments that corresponded with his marginal status as a representative of sinful Israel with access to the heavenly realm together with the angels. Then he received the two goats and the ram from the congregation, presented the bull for his sin offering, and stationed the two goats before the altar, allotting one goat to the Lord and the other to Azazel (16:5–10).

The main rite for the day consisted of three enactments: the cleansing of the sanctuary with the blood from the sin offerings (16:11–19), the removal of sin (16:20–22), and the performance of the burnt offering (16:23–25). The cleansing of the sanctuary proceeded in three stages.

First, the blood rite was performed in the Most Holy Place. After the high priest had slaughtered the bull for his sin offering, he did not bring the blood from it immediately into the Most Holy Place, but first entered it with incense and coals from the altar to create a cloud of smoke and to burn incense before the Lord. This cloud of incense screened the mercy seat and protected the priest from the lethal danger of visual intrusion on God's presence. After the first entry, he brought in the blood from his own sin offering and sprinkled it with his forefinger, once on the surface of the mercy seat, and then seven times on the floor of the Most Holy Place. He repeated the same rite with the blood from the sin offering of the people.

Second, he also performed the blood rite in the tent of meeting (16:16). The details are omitted because they had been given in 4:6–7 and 4:17–18. As was the case with his own sin offering and the sin offering of the congregation, he sprinkled the blood from his sin offering seven times on the floor in front of the curtain. Then he smeared some of it on the four horns of the incense altar (Ex 30:10). He did the same with the blood from the sin offering of the people.

Third, he brought the remaining blood from both sin offerings to the altar for burnt offering, mixed it together, placed some of it on the four horns, and sprinkled it on the altar seven times with his forefinger (Lev 16:18–19). In this way the high priest performed the rite of atonement in these three places for these three places.

The blood rite for the Day of Atonement was an expanded version of the rite for the sin offering of the high priest and the congregation in 4:5–7 and 4:16–17. Like that rite, it concentrated on the manipulation and use of blood. In all, the blood was manipulated forty-nine times, that is, seven times seven. This symbolizes the perfection of this comprehensive act of cleansing.[27] Yet for all that, its orientation was quite different. It did not involve Aaron's move-

---

[27] Milgrom, *Leviticus 1–16*, 1039.

ment inward to God's presence as much as his movement outward from it, from the Most Holy Place to the altar for burnt offering. The blood brought in to God was brought out, sanctified, to the people.

After the sanctuary had been cleansed, the high priest conducted the rite for the removal of sin (16:20–22). He brought the second goat before the altar, laid both his hands on its head in a gesture of transference (cf. Num 27:18, 23; Deut 34:9), and performed an act of confession over it. The goat was then taken into an inaccessible place in the desert and released there. The significant thing about this extraordinary enactment was the vicarious act of confession by the high priest. Normally, individual sinners (Lev 5:5; cf. Num 5:7) confessed their unintentional sins to God. They did not confess their deliberate acts of rebellion, because the normal sin offerings did not provide atonement for them (Num 15:22–31). In this case, however, the high priest performed a comprehensive rite of confession for the acts of rebellion and all the other sins committed by the Israelites. He did this on their behalf and acted as if their sins were his sins. He "placed" their sins on the head of the goat so that it would remove the sin from God's presence in the sanctuary.

Once the rite for the removal of sin was over, the high priest performed two other unusual acts before he offered the burnt offerings for the day and the fat from the sin offerings. He entered the tent of meeting for the fourth time, removed the special holy vestments for the day, and left them there, for they were to be used on that day only to perform the special rite for that day. Then rather unusually, he took a second ritual bath somewhere in the sanctuary, where we are not told, and put on his normal priestly regalia. This is the only occasion when a priest took a bath after the completion of a sacrifice. It was taken to "remove the superholiness that he contracted" by his entry into the Most Holy Place.[28] By removing these vestments and bathing, the high priest protected himself, his fellow priests, and the congregation from sacrilegious contact with the Lord's holiness.

The regulations for the readmission of the high priest and the two attendants to normal life in the camp highlights the sanctity of the day and everything associated with it (16:26–28). Both the person who released the scapegoat in the desert and the person who burnt up the remains of the sin offerings had to wash their clothes and bathe their whole bodies to remove whatever holiness they had received through contact with the offerings.[29]

The conclusion of the chapter shows how the people were involved in the observance of the day. They were not required to be present at the sanctuary, but were to refrain from all forms of work and deny themselves (16:29, 31; cf.

---

[28] Milgrom, *Leviticus 1–16*, 1048.

[29] Milgrom, *Leviticus 1–16*, 1051–52, argues that these two assistants had to bathe because they were contaminated by the animals that had become contaminated with Israel's sins. However, the animals were used to make atonement, and so the assistants were part of the holy rite for Israel's sanctification.

23:28, 32; Num 29:7). The nature of their self-denial remains unspecified. It probably involved them fasting from food and drink, avoidance of sexual intercourse, and abstention from bathing and anointing the body.[30] They often wore sackcloth and covered themselves in ashes as if they had been bereaved. Thus they mourned for themselves as people who were doomed to die and appealed to God for cleansing and forgiveness. On this day, the only mandatory fast for Israel, they were to refrain completely from all work, so that the Lord could perform his work on them by freeing them from their iniquity.

Ritual Theological Function

The legislation for the Day of Atonement is quite explicit about the function and significance of the ritual for that day. It was enacted to perform a comprehensive act of atonement for the sanctuary and for the congregation. The performance of atonement was in fact so central to the ritual that the verb כִּפֶּר, "atone," is used sixteen times in this chapter.[f] The day is therefore called "the Day of Atonement," יוֹם (הַ)כִּפֻּרִים, later in 23:27, 28, and 25:9.

(f) Lev 16:6, 10, 11, 16, 17 (twice), 18, 20, 24, 27, 30, 32, 33 (three times), 34

Scholars have tried to pin down the exact meaning of the verb כִּפֶּר from its etymology and use that as the key to understanding this and all other rites of atonement.[31] Most argue that it can mean either "to ransom," or "to purge away." Even though much of this work is useful, it tends to reduce a complex set of ritual enactments to an abstract theological principle that is all too easily removed from its concrete referents. So, instead of asking what is meant by this term in its context, we seek to determine what was accomplished by the performance of atonement. This chapter is most suited for this exercise, since it uses the term "atone" most discriminately and in the most varied manner of any part of the Pentateuch.

The purpose of this rite was to perform an act of atonement. This is indicated by the use of the verb כִּפֶּר without direct or indirect object (16:17, 27, 32). It involved the manipulation and disposal of the blood from the sin offerings (16:27) and the burnt offerings (16:24), as well as the expulsion of the scapegoat from the sanctuary (16:10). The act of atonement was performed "on behalf of" (בְּעַד) Aaron (16:6, 11, 17, 24), his household (16:6, 11, 17), and the people (16:24) and "for" (עַל) them (16:30, 33). They were therefore the beneficiaries of it. But it did not just involve the people of Israel. The act of atonement was performed "upon" (עַל) the scapegoat (16:10) by the rite of confession, as well as with the blood rite "upon" the Most Holy Place (16:16), the incense altar in the tent of meeting (16:16; see also Ex 30:10), and altar for burnt offering (Lev 16:18; see also Ex 29:36, 37; Lev 8:15). By the ritual application of the blood from the sin offerings, the high priest, in 16:20 and 16:33 is said to have "atoned" the Most Holy Place, the tent of meeting, and the al-

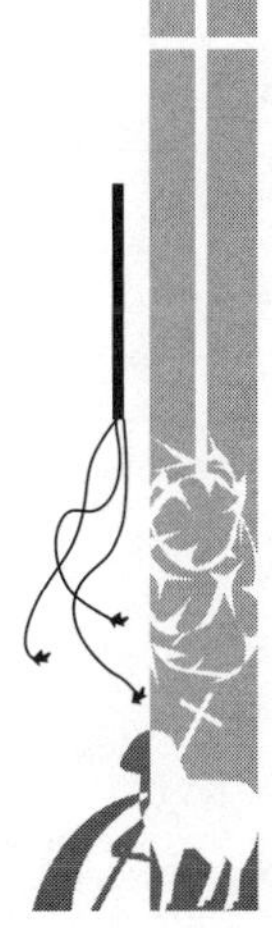

[30] See Num 30:14; Ps 35:13; Dan 10:12; Talmud, Mishnah, *Yoma,* 8:1.

[31] For example, see Hartley, *Leviticus,* 63–66; Milgrom, *Leviticus 1–16,* 1079–84; Schwartz, "The Prohibitions concerning the 'Eating' of Blood in Leviticus 17," 51–58.

tar for burnt offering. In both these cases the verb כִּפֶּר is used as a transitive verb, which is unusual.

Two things were accomplished by this act of atonement. First, it dealt with the "impurities" of the Israelites (16:16 [twice], 19). That uncleanness resulted from their deliberate acts of rebellion against God, as well as from all their other sins. Their misdeeds not only polluted the people who had sinned and had been sinned against, but they also defiled and desecrated the sanctuary (15:31). Since God had chosen to establish the tabernacle as a holy bridgehead in a polluted world, so that he could reside there with his people "in the midst of their impurities" (16:16), he instituted this rite to rid the sanctuary of the impurity that had penetrated with them into his presence.

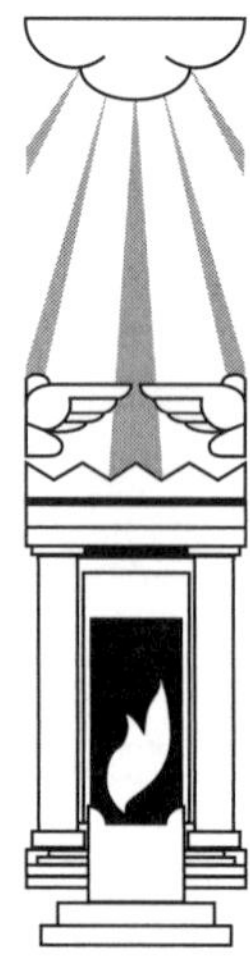

Through the blood rite performed by the high priest in the sanctuary, God himself purged and cleansed the Most Holy Place and the tent of meeting (16:16). All impurity was eradicated from his presence, so that it could not defile and desecrate his holy dwelling place. But that was not all. The main point of the rite was to perform the rite of atonement on the altar for burnt offering, the regular place of atonement. By means of the blood that had been sanctified by contact with the mercy seat, the high priest first cleansed the altar from impurity by smearing its horns and then reconsecrated it by sprinkling it seven times (16:19; cf. 8:15).

Since the altar for burnt offering was the place where the holy God of Israel met with his sinful people, it was most subject to defilement by them. Its cleansing and reconsecration ensured that God would not withdraw their right of access to him and his grace there. It meant that they could continue to meet with him there and share in his holiness, without the fear of his wrath and punishment for the desecration of his holiness. The altar was made safe for the people, for by the performance of the blood rite God's holiness overcame the malignant power of human impurity and so restored the sanctity of the altar.

Since the annual rite of atonement cleansed the sanctuary of impurity, God remained present with his people. He did not have to withdraw his gracious presence from the desecrated sanctuary and deliver his people over to instability and insecurity. They continued to have access to his blessings. Their ongoing existence as his redeemed people was assured. On the Day of Atonement, the Sabbath day of the Sabbath month, the Israelites rested from all work, so that, like the Sabbath, the sanctuary could serve as a link between heaven and earth.[32] God cleansed and reconsecrated the sanctuary, so that he could work together with the Israelites in extending the range of his holiness and his blessings further into the order of creation as he had planned when he had created the world (Gen 2:2–3; Ex 20:8–11).

Second, the rite for the Day of Atonement dealt with the sins of the Israelites (16:34). The normal rite of atonement with the blood from their sin offerings treated their unintentional sins, while the blood rite for the burnt

[32] Balentine, *The Torah's Vision of Worship*, 165.

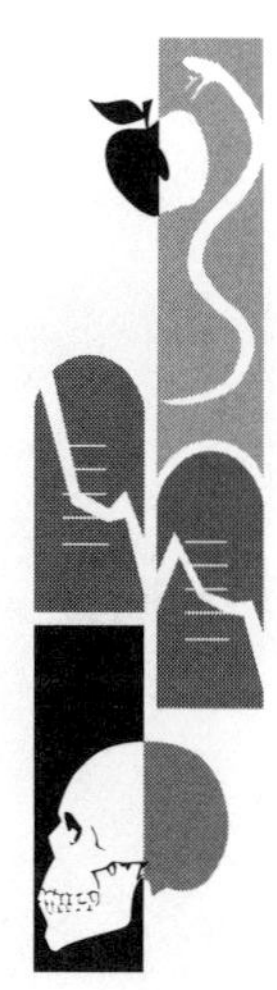

offerings and peace offerings treated their general impurity. This rite, however, dealt comprehensively with all their iniquities and acts of rebellion against God. This is made clear by the comprehensive listings in 16:16 and 16:21. The rite for the expulsion of the scapegoat was therefore attached to the blood rite for the sin offerings (16:14–19) and the blood rite for the burnt offerings (16:24), to remove the burden of corporate guilt from the congregation.

Normally, the Levites "bore the guilt" from any act of defilement of the people (Num 18:23). While the priests "bore the guilt" for any act of sacrilege committed by the priests (Num 18:1) as well as for the sins of the people (Lev 10:17), the high priest "bore the guilt" of the Israelites as he led the daily service (Ex 28:38).[33] On this day, however, the high priest placed all the sins of Israel on the head of the scapegoat (16:21). The scapegoat took over from the high priest and "bore all their iniquities" away from God's presence in the sanctuary (16:22) to the desert, the place of the demonic Azazel.[34] The scapegoat therefore removed the iniquity of the people. The high priest atoned for the Israelites from their sins (16:34); that is, they were ransomed and released from them by the rite of atonement (cf. 4:26; 5:6, 10). By this combination of the rite for the expulsion of the scapegoat with the blood rite, the whole congregation of Israel was cleansed (16:30), just as the altar had been cleansed (16:19). They were therefore "clean from all [their] sins" "before the Lord" (16:30; cf. 12:7; 15:13, 28). Since they were in a state of ritual purity, they could approach the altar and meet with him there; they had ongoing access to his grace and blessing.

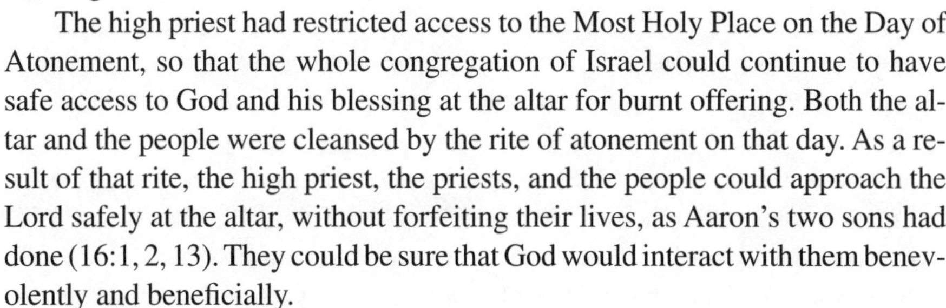

The high priest had restricted access to the Most Holy Place on the Day of Atonement, so that the whole congregation of Israel could continue to have safe access to God and his blessing at the altar for burnt offering. Both the altar and the people were cleansed by the rite of atonement on that day. As a result of that rite, the high priest, the priests, and the people could approach the Lord safely at the altar, without forfeiting their lives, as Aaron's two sons had done (16:1, 2, 13). They could be sure that God would interact with them benevolently and beneficially.

Thus on this most holy day, the most holy person in Israel performed the most holy rite in the Most Holy Place with the most holy blood from the most holy animals, so that the sinful Israelites could have safe access to their most holy God.

Fulfillment by Christ

The NT teaches that the death of Jesus is to be understood in the light of the Day of Atonement.[35] Thus the Synoptic Gospels relate that when Jesus died,

---

[33] See Kiuchi, *The Purification Offering in the Priestly Literature*, 49–52, 98–99.

[34] Milgrom, *Leviticus 1–16*, 1020–21; Wenham, *Leviticus*, 234–35.

[35] In addition to Jesus' atoning death, his temptation by the devil in the wilderness may be explained in part by the Day of Atonement. The goat that bore the sins of Israel was sent into the wilderness "to Azazel," to the devil, who had plunged humanity into sin. The wilderness,

the veil of the temple was split from top to bottom (Mt 27:51; Mk 15:38; Lk 23:45). This showed what Jesus had accomplished by his death. As a result of his self-sacrifice, the way into the Father's presence lay open to all his disciples. In the OT era only the high priest, on one day per year, could enter the Holy of Holies. But because of the death of Jesus, all peoples at all times have open access to God the Father through faith in him.

In Rom 3:25 Paul alludes to the Day of Atonement to describe the purpose of Christ's death. God appointed Jesus as the new ἱλαστήριον, the "mercy seat," the place of atonement and God's gracious presence.[36] Through his blood Jesus gained redemption for sinners. Those who trust in his blood are justified by grace. So Jesus is both the place of atonement and the priest who makes atonement before God with his blood. God justifies those who have faith in Jesus and grants them access to his gracious presence (Rom 5:1–2).

The book of Hebrews elaborates on this. The high priest entered the Holy of Holies once a year on the Day of Atonement. There he performed the rite of atonement in God's presence. But that access was limited and temporary. His work prefigured the ministry of Jesus who fulfilled what the high priest had begun on that day (Heb 9:7–14). By his death Jesus offered himself as the perfect sin offering for the whole world so that, exalted by God, he could enter the heavenly sanctuary with his blood (Heb 9:12) and open the way for his brothers into the divine presence (Heb 6:20).

The work of Jesus resembles and yet differs from the ministry of the high priest on the Day of Atonement in four ways. First, the high priest entered the Holy of Holies in an earthly sanctuary to perform the rite of atonement in God's presence once a year (Heb 9:7). However, Jesus entered heaven itself, the heavenly sanctuary, only once at his ascension, to appear before God on behalf of his brothers (Heb 9:12, 24).

Second, the high priest entered the Holy of Holies with the alien blood of animals to make atonement before God (Heb 9:7, 25). But Jesus brought his own blood into his Father's presence to make atonement for sinners (Heb 9:12). Since Jesus' blood had been brought into heaven, it was most holy. It had the power to cleanse and sanctify perfectly.

Third, the high priest brought the blood from the Holy of Holies and sprinkled the earthly altar for incense and the earthly altar for burnt offering (Heb 9:21). In this way he cleansed and consecrated these most holy things. Jesus, the great High Priest, sprinkles the heavenly things with his blood (Heb 9:23); with his own blood he sprinkles the hearts and consciences of those who serve the living God in the heavenly sanctuary (Heb 9:13–14; 10:2, 22; cf. 9:9).[37] In

---

as his abode, was a barren wasteland, devoid of life. But after Jesus' Baptism and the descent of the Spirit upon him, he went forth into the wilderness to do battle with the devil, and Jesus prevailed against him (Mt 4:1–11). Mark notes that there in the wilderness Jesus "was with the wild beasts" (Mk 1:13).

[36] Stuhlmacher, *Paul's Letter to the Romans,* 60–61.

[37] Scholer, *Proleptic Priests*, 171.

his Holy Supper he brings his blood from his Father's presence and gives it to his guests to drink for their cleansing and sanctification. Thus, as Pfitzner has shown, Jesus performs an "ongoing ministry of atonement" by the application of his blood on his people.[38]

Fourth and most remarkably, the high priest was the only person who ever passed through the curtain into the Holy of Holies. No one else was ever allowed to approach the throne of grace. But Jesus entered the heavenly sanctuary to open up a new and living way into the heavenly sanctuary for all his fellow priests (Heb 10:20). He is therefore our ritual forerunner (Heb 6:20). As his fellow priests we can tread where no Israelite priest had ever trod. Through the flesh and blood of Christ, we can approach "the throne of grace" with a clear conscience. We who have the privilege of open access to God the Father can receive mercy and help from him for ourselves and for others (Heb 4:16; 10:19–22). By faith we have access to heavenly Jerusalem while we are residing here on earth (Heb 12:22–24).

Since Christ has made atonement for us, once and for all, on Good Friday, Christians have no need for any annual Day of Atonement. Through Jesus we are justified before God the Father and are reconciled with him (Rom 5:9–11). Unlike the people of Israel, we have no need to fast in order to lament God's sentence of death on us for our sins and to seek atonement from those sins by our self-abasement before him. We do, however, fast in Lent and on Good Friday in order to celebrate his death for us and to rejoice in our redemption (Mt 6:16–18; Mk 2:18–22).

This theology of atonement has influenced the shape of our worship and the architecture of our churches. We have no barrier between the nave and the sanctuary. We all enter the sanctuary to receive the body and blood of our heavenly High Priest in Holy Communion. The altar symbolizes the throne of grace. It reminds us of the mercy seat, with the cherubim, that was set over the ark of the covenant in the Holy of Holies, as well as the altar for burnt offering in the courtyard of the tabernacle. But they are no longer kept apart, for Christ has opened up the way into the heavenly sanctuary for us through his body and blood. The altar is the mercy seat where we come to receive mercy and grace from God for ourselves and others (Heb 4:16). And so by faith we enter the heavenly realm whenever we celebrate the Sacrament of the Altar.

No temple now, no gift of price,
No priestly round of sacrifice,
Retain their ancient pow'rs.
As shadows fade before the sun
The day of sacrifice is done,
The day of grace is ours.

---

[38] Pfitzner, *Hebrews*, 69.

The dying Lord our ransom paid,
One final full self-off'ring made,
Complete in ev'ry part.
His finished sacrifice for sins
The covenant of grace begins,
The law within the heart.

In faith and confidence draw near,
Within the holiest appear,
With all who praise and pray;
Who share one family, one feast,
One great imperishable Priest,
One new and living way.[39]

[39] From "No Temple Now, No Gift of Price" by Timothy Dudley-Smith (*HS98* 861:1–3).

Leviticus 17:1–27:34

The Participation of the Israelites in God's Holiness

17:1–22:33 Reverence for the Sanctuary

The Structure of Leviticus 17–22

17:1–16 Ritual Use and Abuse of Blood

The Structure of Leviticus 18–20

18:1–30 Ritual Defilement of the Land by Sexual Immorality

19:1–37 The Holiness of the Congregation

20:1–27 Penalties for the Ritual Defilement of the Sanctuary and the Land

21:1–22:16 Holy Priests and Holy Offerings

- 21:1–15 Protecting the Holiness of the Priests
- 21:16–24 Causes of Disqualification from Priestly Service
- 22:1–16 Consumption of Holy Food by the Priests and Their Families

22:17–33 Acceptable Offerings for the Israelites

23:1–25:55 Observance of the Sabbaths

The Structure of Leviticus 23–26

23:1–44 Calendar of Holy Times

24:1–9 Holy Oil and the Holy Bread

24:10–23 The Penalty for the Abuse of God's Holy Name

The Structure of Leviticus 25–26

25:1–55 Sabbatical Years and the Jubilee

26:1–46 Promises and Warnings: God's Policy for Israel

27:1–34 Votive Offerings and Consecrated Things

The Structure of Leviticus 17–22

After Leviticus 16, which is the pivotal chapter in the book, the following chapter introduces the speeches that follow. These speeches culminate in an extended admonition in 22:31–33 that is obviously much more than a conclusion to the speech in 22:26–30. The use of the elaborated formula for divine sanctification in 22:32, its seventh and last occurrence (previously used in 20:8; 21:8, 15, 23; 22:9, 16), shows that the speeches in chapters 20–22 must be taken together. Likewise, the repetition of the call to holiness from 19:2 in 20:7 and 21:6 connects chapter 19 with chapters 20–22. Chapter 20 obviously presupposes and mirrors chapter 18 with its prohibitions of those acts that pollute the Israelites and the land.

What then is the function of chapter 17? Does its prohibition of the abuse of blood stand in contrast with the right use of blood on the Day of Atonement? Or is it connected thematically with chapters 18–22, as is shown by the recurrent threat of being "cut off" from kinsfolk in it (17:4, 9, 10, 14) and in the chapters after it (18:29; 20:3, 5, 6, 17, 18)?

Ruwe offers a helpful solution to this question.[1] He takes God's command to revere his sanctuary in 26:2 as a summary of all the laws in Leviticus 17–22. The speeches in 18:1–22:16 tell how the Israelites were to orient their lives around the sanctuary by avoiding defilement and relating all that they did to God's sanctifying presence with them in it. These speeches are framed by laws that deal with eating meat from their animals. While chapter 17 deals with the ritual use and abuse of the blood from their animals, 22:17–30 considers which animals are acceptable for sacrifice and for the provision of holy meat at the sanctuary. Ruwe's analysis is reinforced by the mention of the tabernacle (17:4), the tent of meeting (17:4, 5, 6, 9; 19:21), and the sanctuary (19:30; 20:3; 21:12 [twice], 23) in these chapters.

The material in this section of Leviticus is arranged in a loose chiasm as follows:

A Use of blood from animals for atonement (17:1–16)
  B Defilement of the land (18:1–30)
    C Holiness of the congregation (19:1–37)
  B' Penalties for defilement of the land (20:1–27)
    C' Holiness of the priesthood (21:1–22:16)
A' Animals acceptable for sacrifice (22:17–33)

1 Ruwe, *"Heiligkeitsgesetz" und "Priesterschrift,"* 100–20.

Leviticus 17:1–16

Ritual Use and Abuse of Blood

Translation

17 1The Lord spoke to Moses: 2"Speak to Aaron, his sons, and all the Israelites and say to them: This is what the Lord has commanded: 3If anyone from the household of Israel slaughters a head of cattle or a sheep or a goat in the camp or slaughters it outside the camp 4without bringing it into the entrance to the tent of meeting, to present it as an offering to the Lord before the Lord's tabernacle, bloodguilt shall be imputed to that man; he has shed blood; that man will be cut off from the midst of his people. 5This is so the Israelites will bring the sacrifices which they have been offering on the surface of the fields. They should bring them to the Lord at the entrance to the tent of meeting, to the priest, and offer them as sacrifices of peace offerings to the Lord 6so that the priest may dash the blood against the altar of the Lord at the entrance to the tent of meeting and turn the fat into smoke as a pleasing aroma to the Lord; 7and that they may no longer offer their sacrifices to the goat-demons, after which they have been prostituting themselves. This shall be a perpetual ritual statute for them throughout their generations.

8"Say to them: If anyone from the household of Israel or from the aliens who reside among them offers up a burnt offering or a sacrifice 9and does not bring it into the entrance to the tent of meeting to perform its ritual for the Lord, that man will be cut off from his kinsfolk.

10"If anyone from the household of Israel and from the aliens who reside among them eats any blood, I will set my face against the person who eats the blood, and I will cut him off from among his people. 11For the life of the flesh is in the blood, and I myself have assigned it to you to make atonement for your lives upon the altar, because it is the blood that makes atonement by means of the life. 12Therefore I have said to the Israelites: None of you shall eat blood, nor shall any alien who resides among you eat blood.

13"If any of the Israelites or any alien who resides among them hunts down as game an animal or a bird that may be eaten, he shall pour out its blood and cover it with earth. 14For the life of every animal is its blood: it is its life. Therefore I have said to the Israelites: You shall not eat the blood of any flesh, for the life of all flesh is its blood; whoever eats it will be cut off.

15"If any person, whether native or alien, eats what has died or has been mauled by wild animals, he shall wash his clothes, bathe in water, and remain unclean until evening; then he shall be clean. 16But if he does not wash [his clothes] and bathe his body, he shall bear his iniquity."

Textual Notes

17:2 דַּבֵּר אֶל־אַהֲרֹן וְאֶל־בָּנָיו וְאֶל כָּל־בְּנֵי יִשְׂרָאֵל—The same audience is addressed here as in 22:18. In both cases the speech has to do with the offering of private sacrifices. The statement about the compliance of Moses with this command is found in 21:24. This statement serves to gather together all the intervening data in 17:2–21:23 as a single block of material.

אֲשֶׁר־צִוָּה יְהוָה—See the textual notes on 7:36. The same formula is found in 8:5 and in 9:6. It is used in both these places to introduce a foundational ritual enactment. Here it introduces an instruction about the tabernacle as the only place for sacrifice as well as the only place for the disposal of blood from the sacrificed animals.

17:3 אִישׁ אִישׁ—See the textual note on this phrase in 15:2. It recurs in 17:8.

מִבֵּית יִשְׂרָאֵל—This formula is used in Leviticus only in this chapter. Under the influence of 17:13, the LXX reads "the sons of Israel" here, as well as in 17:8 and 17:10. The LXX adds "or resident aliens living among you" here to bring this verse into line with 17:8, 10, 13.

יִשְׁחַט ... יִשְׁחָט—See the textual note on this verb in 1:5.

מִחוּץ לַמַּחֲנֶה׃—See the textual notes on 4:12. The LXX adds "he does not bring it to the entrance of the tent of meeting to perform the ritual for it as a burnt offering or a peace offering to the Lord for acceptance as a pleasing aroma, and he slaughters it outside."

17:4 וְאֶל־פֶּתַח אֹהֶל מוֹעֵד—See the textual note on this phrase in 1:3. It recurs in 17:5, 6, 9.

לֹא הֱבִיאוֹ—See the textual note on this verb in 2:2. It recurs in 17:5, 9.

לְהַקְרִיב—See the textual note on this verb in 1:2.

לִפְנֵי מִשְׁכַּן יְהוָה—See also 8:10; 15:31; 26:11.

יֵחָשֵׁב—See the textual notes on 7:18. This Niphal is best construed as a divine passive: "to be imputed [by God]." For a positive use of this same verb, see Gen 15:6: Abraham believed God, and "it was imputed to him as righteousness."

דָּם שָׁפָךְ—Normally, the pouring out of blood refers to murder as a capital crime. But the idiom "to pour out blood" is also used for the disposal of leftover blood from the peace offerings and sin offerings at the base of the altar (Ex 29:12; Lev 4:7, 18, 25, 30; Deut 12:27). It is used here to assert that the ritual slaughter of animals and the disposal of their blood at any other place except the tabernacle is regarded by God as a capital crime.

וְנִכְרַת הָאִישׁ הַהוּא מִקֶּרֶב עַמּוֹ׃—This verb is most likely a divine passive, "cut off [by God]," and should therefore be regarded as threat of extirpation by God. See the textual note on the Niphal of כָּרַת in 7:20. See also 17:8, 9, 10, 14. The singular noun עַם denotes the "people" from whom the offender is extirpated (17:4, 10; 18:29; 20:3, 5, 6, 18; 23:30). The plural noun עַמִּים in other verses indicates that the offender will be extirpated from his "relatives" or "kinsfolk" (7:20, 21, 25, 27; 17:9; 19:8; 23:29).

17:5 זִבְחֵיהֶם—The end of the verse shows that these sacrifices are peace offerings.

זֹבְחִים—Literally this participle means "sacrificing." See 17:5b, 7.

עַל־פְּנֵי הַשָּׂדֶה—This phrase occurred in 14:7, 53. In light of 17:7, 17:5 points to the idolatrous practice of the ritual disposal of the blood from the slaughtered animals upon the earth for the appeasement of its "spirits" and its consequent fertility. God prohibits that practice.

וֶהֱבִיאֻם—The *waw* introduces the apodosis of this sentence.

17:6 וְזָרַק—See the textual note on this verb in 1:5.

מִזְבַּח יְהוָה—See 17:11 and the textual notes on 1:5. Only here in book of Leviticus is the altar called "the altar of the Lord" to distinguish it from every other altar.

וְהִקְטִיר—See the textual note on this verb in 1:9.

הַחֵלֶב—See the textual notes on 3:3, 16–17.

לְרֵיחַ נִיחֹחַ לַיהוָה׃—See the textual notes on 1:9 and the explanation in "Leviticus 1–3."

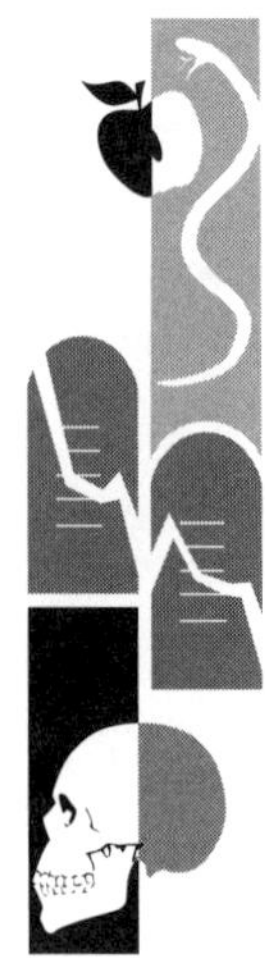

17:7 לַשְּׂעִירִם—In Lev 17:7 and some other OT passages (Is 13:21; 34:14; 2 Chr 11:15), שְׂעִירִם denotes demons, earth spirits that were envisaged as he-goats, like the satyrs of classical mythology. Hence the NIV refers to them in this verse as "the goat idols." *HALOT* defines שָׂעִיר III as "the hairy one, a goat (buck) demon." The noun שָׂעִיר II means "billy-goat, buck" (*HALOT;* see, e.g., Gen 37:31). The feminine form שְׂעִירָה denotes a female goat (Lev 4:28; 5:6). The related noun שֵׂעָר means "hair."

אֲשֶׁר הֵם זֹנִים אַחֲרֵיהֶם—See also 20:5, 6. The idiom of "prostituting themselves" (the Qal participle of זָנָה) suggests that the sacrifices offered in the fields had to do with fertility rites of some kind, even if it may not have involved ritual prostitution. The OT and NT depict unfaithfulness to God as adultery, fornication, and harlotry (e.g., Jeremiah 2–3; Ezekiel 16 and 23; 2 Cor 11:2–3; Rev 2:14, 20–22; 17:1–19:3).

חֻקַּת עוֹלָם—See the textual notes on 3:17.

17:8 הַגֵּר—We translate this as a plural ("aliens") because it refers to anyone from a class of people. See the textual note on this term in 16:29. It recurs in 17:10, 12, 13, 15.

יַעֲלֶה עֹלָה אוֹ־זָבַח׃—Here זָבַח apparently refers to a peace offering. זָבַח is not a verb, but the pausal form of the noun זֶבַח. Hartley rightly maintains that the phrase "a burnt offering or sacrifice" could also be used inclusively for all public and private sacrifices.[1]

17:9 לַעֲשׂוֹת—See the textual note on the verb עָשָׂה in 4:20.

17:10 וְאִישׁ אִישׁ—See the textual notes on 17:3.

יֹאכַל כָּל־דָּם—See the textual notes on 3:17. Similar clauses recur in 17:12 (twice), 14 (twice).

וְנָתַתִּי פָנַי בַּנֶּפֶשׁ—A change occurs in 17:10–14 as the Lord speaks of himself directly in the first person. By setting his face ("my face") against the people, the Lord did not merely oppose them, but he set out to bring about their destruction (20:3, 6; 26:17; Ezek 14:8; 15:7).

In some contexts נֶפֶשׁ concretely refers to the "gullet" of an animal or human being. It can also refer to the "life breath" of any animate creature. More abstractly, it is used as a term for the "life force," "soul," or "spirit," of any animate creature, as

---

[1] Hartley, *Leviticus*, 273.

is the case in 17:11 and 17:14. It is also used to refer to any "living person" both here and in 17:12, 15. Since it is a feminine noun, the pronominal suffixes on אֹתָהּ and עַמֶּהָ later in the verse are feminine even though we translate them as masculine.

17:11 הַבָּשָׂר֒—The term "flesh," here and in 17:14, refers both to an animal and to the meat from it.

וַאֲנִ֞י נְתַתִּ֤יו לָכֶם֙—This is a formula of divine assignment. God uses similar formulas elsewhere to grant a portion of the offerings to the priests (7:34; Num 18:8, 11, 12, 19; cf. Lev 10:17) or to the Levites (Num 18:21, 24, 26) as their due for their service to him. Here God uses it to grant the blood from the sacrificed animals to all the Israelites for their use in the rite of atonement.

לְכַפֵּר—This means "to make atonement" or "to perform the rite of atonement." The verb כִּפֶּר can mean "to purify" (16:20, 33) or "to cleanse from ritual impurity" (4:26, 35; 5:6, 10, 13). When it is used together with עַל נֶפֶשׁ, it functions as a denominative of כֹּפֶר ("ransom") and means "to provide a ransom for a life" (Ex 30:15, 16; Num 31:50). It is, however, most commonly used in Leviticus as a technical ritual term for the performance of the rite of atonement (4:20, 26, 31; 5:16; 6:23 [ET 6:30]). See the textual notes on it in 1:4.

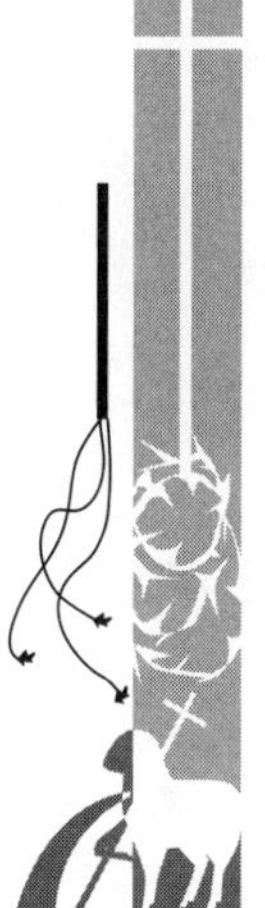

עַל־הַמִּזְבֵּ֔חַ לְכַפֵּ֖ר עַל־נַפְשֹׁתֵיכֶ֑ם—This compact formula indicates that the blood which was reserved for application on the altar was also given for the reception of atonement from the altar. Through this formula God grants the people both the blood for atonement and atonement through that blood.

הַדָּם—Milgrom claims that this applied only to the blood from peace offerings.[2] The blood needed to be offered back to God to ransom the life of the person who had killed the animal. This, however, is unlikely, because mention is made in 17:10 of "all of the blood" and the burnt offering is mentioned together with the peace offering in 17:8.

בַּנֶּפֶשׁ—The phrase בַּנֶּפֶשׁ has been construed in three main ways.[3]

First, some believe the phrase identifies the life of an animal with its blood. The phrase therefore is translated similarly to "the blood as life makes atonement" (see the similar translation in the NRSV). However, since the noun has the definite article (-בַּנ) the preposition probably is not the so-called *bet essentiae* (so it does not mean that the blood *is* the life).

Second, since the LXX translated בְּ with ἀντί, some understand it as the *bet pretii,* and the phrase is taken to indicate the cost of atonement: "the blood at the cost of the life" or "the blood in exchange for the life." This interpretation is based on the phrase נֶפֶשׁ בְּנֶפֶשׁ in Deut 19:21. But the sentence in Leviticus is not at all analogous to that verse, since Lev 17:11 speaks of blood atoning for life rather than life atoning for life. The NIV follows that general line of interpretation and mistranslates the phrase by "for one's life." It therefore is taken as a reference to the beneficiary of atonement rather than the means or basis for its performance. It presupposes that the life of the animal substitutes for the life of those who present the animal for sacrifice.

---

2 Milgrom, "A Prolegomenon to Leviticus 17:11," 150.

3 Hartley, *Leviticus*, 273.

Third, since כִּפֶּר is commonly used with the preposition בְּ to indicate the means of atonement (Ex 29:33; Num 5:8; 35:33; 1 Sam 3:14; Is 27:9; Prov 16:6), the phrase is best understood as the assertion that the blood atones by means of, or on the basis of, the life power in it. This is analogous to the instrumental use of בְּ with כִּפֶּר in Lev 5:16; 7:7; 19:22. Hence RSV has "for it is the blood that makes atonement, by reason of the life." Our rendition is "… by means of the life."

17:12 אָמַ֙רְתִּי֙—Since God here paraphrases what he has previously said in 17:10 as well as in 3:17 and 7:26–27, this verb is best translated in the perfect tense. The same is true in 17:14.

17:13 Deut 12:15–16, 20–25 and 15:21–23 use this law to sanction the secular slaughter of domestic animals for the provision of meat for human consumption.

17:14 כִּֽי־נֶ֣פֶשׁ כָּל־בָּשָׂ֗ר דָּמ֣וֹ בְנַפְשׁוֹ֮ הוּא֒—Following the syntax indicated by the Masoretic accents, this literally says "for the life of all flesh—its blood is its life." This use of the preposition בְּ without the definite article (whereas בַּנֶּ֫פֶשׁ in 17:11 had the article) is best taken as the *bet essentiae,* "its blood *is* its life." This verse then corresponds to Deut 12:23.

The LXX translates, "For the life of all flesh is its blood," which omits or ignores בְנַפְשׁוֹ֮ הוּא֒. The Peshitta and Vulgate are similar to the LXX. The NIV likewise fails to translate בְנַפְשׁוֹ֮ הוּא֒.

וָאֹמַר֙ לִבְנֵ֣י יִשְׂרָאֵ֔ל …—This self-quotation refers back to 17:10–12. The assertion about blood as the seat of life in 17:11 is reworded as a declaration about blood as the life power of the animal.

17:15 תֹּאכַ֤ל נְבֵלָה֙ וּטְרֵפָ֔ה—See 7:24 and 11:40 for additional references to the eating of carrion. Lay people could eat carrion, but priests are forbidden to do so (22:8). Both Ex 22:31 and Deut 14:21 are more restrictive. They decree that, since all Israelites are holy, they were not allowed to eat meat from an animal torn by wild beasts or from any dead animal.

בָּאֶזְרָח—See the textual note on this term in 16:29.

וְכִבֶּ֨ס בְּגָדָ֜יו—See 11:39–40.

וְטָמֵ֥א—See the textual notes on 5:2.

וְטָהֵֽר׃—See the textual notes on 11:32.

17:16 In 17:15 the direct object of "he shall wash" was stated as "his clothes," which is implied as the direct object here too.

וְנָשָׂ֖א עֲוֺנֽוֹ׃—See the textual note on this clause in 5:1.

Commentary

Context and Structure

The legislation in Leviticus 17 about the use of blood for atonement is connected thematically with the legislation for the Day of Atonement in Leviticus 16. This thematic connection is underlined by the chiastic arrangement of the material in 16:29–17:11.[4] It links the self-denial of those who fast with their atonement in the following way:

---

4 Britt and Creehan, "Chiasmus in Leviticus 16,29–17,11."

A **Atonement** and denial of **selves** (16:29–31)
  B **Perpetual ritual statute** (16:31)
    C The role of the **priest** in performing the rite of atonement (16:32)
      D Atonement for the **tent of meeting** (16:33)
        E Atonement for the **children of Israel** (16:34a)
          F The fulfillment of the **Lord's** command to **Moses** (16:34b)
          F' The **Lord's** speech to **Moses** (17:1)
        E' Speaking to the **children of Israel** (17:2)
      D' Offerings at the **tent of meeting** (17:4)
    C' Offerings to the **priest** (17:5)
  B' **Perpetual ritual statute** (17:7)
A' **Atonement** for your **selves/lives** (17:11)

In this way the regular use of blood for atonement was associated with the fasting of the Israelites on the Day of Atonement.

In Leviticus 17, God orders Moses to make five proclamations about the correct use of blood in connection with the consumption of meat from edible animals. The first of these proclamations is separated from the rest by introductory and concluding summaries in 17:2b and 17:7b, as well as by the repetition of God's commission to Moses in 17:8a. Each of the five proclamations consists of a single, compound sentence with two main clauses. In each case the first clause mentions the subject of the proclamation in an introductory phrase. This is followed by a relative clause that describes the case for consideration. The second consecutive clause enunciates the divine decree for the case. This is followed in all cases except for 17:8–9 with the reasons for the decree.

The five proclamations are unified by means of two literary devices. On the one hand, the first four sections begin with the same inclusive formula (17:3a, 8b, 10a, 13a). The last section, however, breaks the pattern by beginning with "any person." This introduction echoes the introduction to the reported speech in 17:12b. In this way 17:15–16 is attached as an expansion and development of 17:13–14. In fact, 17:15–16 could be construed as part of the reported speech in 17:14b and regarded as a quotation from 11:39–40. Apart from the first paragraph, each of these sections also addresses both the Israelites and the resident aliens as the subjects of these decrees.

On the other hand, each of these sections contains the threat of divine punishment. In the first three paragraphs the proclamation culminates in the threat of divine extirpation (17:4d, 9c, 10c). Strikingly, the impersonal form of the threat in the first two cases gives way to the direct speech from God himself in 17:10. In the fourth proclamation, which culminates in the declaration about the proper disposal of blood from edible game, the threat of extermination is mentioned as an explanatory warning in the quotation from 17:10 in 17:14. Most remarkably, this pattern is broken by the warning in the last paragraph that anyone who fails to undergo purification after the consumption of carrion "shall bear his iniquity."

Apart from these structural elements, certain key words are used to powerful effect in the text. The most prominent of these is נֶפֶשׁ, "life." It refers to three related things: the life of animate creatures, human life, and the life of slaughtered animals.[5] It is the key term in this discussion. It is used to create a chiasm in 17:10–12. The repetition from 17:10 of references to "eating blood" and to any "alien living among them/you" in 17:12 serves to frame 17:11 with its emphasis on the proper, God-ordained use of blood. A chiasm is formed by the interplay between נֶפֶשׁ and "blood" with its pivot on this key statement: "I myself have assigned it to you to make atonement for your lives/persons upon the altar."

A The "Israelite" or "alien" **person** who eats blood (17:10)
  B The **life** of flesh in its blood (17:11a)
    C Your **persons/lives** (17:11b)
  B' Blood by means of the **life** (17:11c)
A' No "Israelite" or "alien" **person** shall eat blood (17:12)

As Schwartz observes, the last three paragraphs with their discussion on the eating of blood are linked together by means of wordplay on נֶפֶשׁ with its sense both of "life" and of "gullet."[6]

The other key word is the term "blood." It occurs thirteen times in the chapter.[a] Its sense is defined in connection with the term "life" by the construction of three similar assertions.

(a) Lev 17:4 (twice), 6, 10 (twice), 11 (twice), 12 (twice), 13, 14 (three times)

- The life of the flesh is in the blood (17:11a).
- The life of all flesh is its blood (17:14a).
- The life of all flesh is its blood (17:14d).

The illegitimate pouring out of blood in the slaughter of a domesticated animal (17:4) is contrasted with the legitimate pouring out of blood from a wild animal (17:13). The illegitimate consumption of blood (17:10, 12, 14) is distinguished from the legitimate use of it in the rite of atonement (17:6, 11).

This chapter is, as Schwartz has shown, a very skillful, balanced composition.[7] The first three paragraphs announce the penalties for the incorrect sacrifice of animals in ascending order of severity, while the last two paragraphs give instructions on the correct use of blood with warnings of penalties for noncompliance in descending order of severity. This formal pattern is reinforced by the arrangement of content. All five paragraphs deal with the proper use of blood from edible animals. The first two speak of animals that must be sacrificed before their meat is eaten, while the last two speak of the animals that may be eaten even though they are not sacrificed. The central paragraph deals with the prohibition of blood consumption because of God's reservation of it for sacrificial atonement. This is "the axis upon which the chapter revolves."[8] Its core is the divine mandate for the use of blood in the rite of atonement in

[5] Hartley, *Leviticus*, 276.

[6] Schwartz, "The Prohibitions concerning the 'Eating' of Blood in Leviticus 17," 41.

[7] Schwartz, "The Prohibitions concerning the 'Eating' of Blood in Leviticus 17," 36–43.

[8] Schwartz, "The Prohibitions concerning the 'Eating' of Blood in Leviticus 17," 43.

17:11. All four paragraphs depend on this mandate. The first two provide the rationale for it; the last two draw the consequences from it for the consumption of meat from animals that have not been sacrificed. Thus the five paragraphs form an inverted "V" with 17:11 at its zenith:

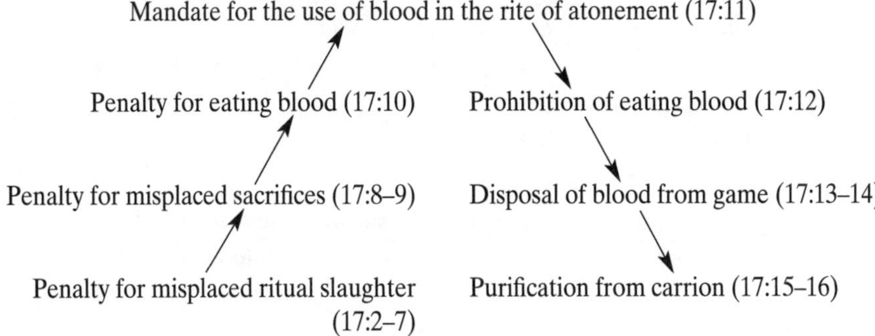

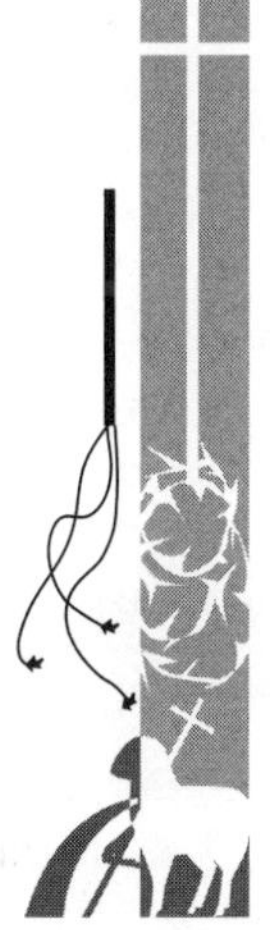

Leviticus 17 is a transitional chapter. On the one hand, it is linked with the previous chapter structurally by the chiasm in 16:29–17:11 and thematically by the repeated references to "blood" and "atonement." On the other hand, it also introduces the following chapters. The address of the legislation in 17:2 to all the priests and the Israelites is recalled in 21:24, which reports the compliance of Moses in transmitting the material in the intervening chapters to them. This indicates that Leviticus 17 introduces this section and forms a parallel with Leviticus 21. While chapter 17 deals with the desecration of sacred blood from the sacrifices, chapter 21 deals with the desecration of the sacred food from the offerings. Leviticus 17 also resembles the following chapters by giving motivation for the laws against consuming blood (17:5–7, 11) and penalties for infringing this prohibition (17:4, 9, 10, 14, 16). Some scholars, such as Milgrom, therefore regard it as the beginning of the Holiness Code.[9] Yet, as Milgrom admits, it does not mention holiness at all, nor does it use the recurrent refrain that is common in chapters 18–26: "I am the Lord."

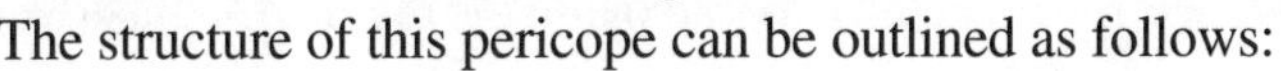

The structure of this pericope can be outlined as follows:

- I. God's address and commission to Moses (17:1–2a)
- II. Speech on the place for ritual slaughter (17:2b–7)
  - A. Superscription: divine command (17:2b)
  - B. Proclamation of the penalty for ritual slaughter apart from the tabernacle (17:3–7a)
    - 1. Case of ritual slaughter for peace offerings (17:3–4a)
    - 2. Extirpation as the penalty for illegitimate slaughter (17:4b)
    - 3. Reasons for the penalty (17:5–7a)
      - a. Offering of blood and fat at the tabernacle rather than in the field (17:5–6)
      - b. Prevention of sacrifice to the demons (17:7a)

---

[9] Milgrom, *Leviticus 17–22*, 1450.

C. Subscription: perpetual ritual statute (17:7b)

III. God's second commission to Moses (17:8a)

IV. Speech about the legitimate sacrifice and consumption of meat (17:8b–16)

A. Proclamation of the penalty for sacrifice apart from the tabernacle (17:8b–9)

1. Case of sacrifice apart from the tabernacle (17:8b–9a)
2. Extirpation as the penalty for infringement (17:9b)

B. God's personal threat of punishment for the consumption of blood (17:10–12)

1. Case of blood consumption (17:10a)
2. Personal threat of extirpation by God (17:10b)
3. Reasons (17:11–12)
   a. God's provision of blood for the rite of atonement (17:11)
   b. God's repetition of his prohibition of eating blood (17:12)

C. Instruction about the disposal of blood from edible game (17:13–14)

1. Case of slaughter of game for food (17:13a)
2. Instruction on the burial of blood (17:13b)
3. Reasons for burial (17:14)

D. Instruction about purification after the consumption of carrion (17:15–16)

1. Case of eating meat from carrion (17:15a)
2. Purification by washing and bathing (17:15b)
3. Reason: threat of guilt from failure to undergo purification (17:16)

Ritual Agents

Apart from 22:18, this is the only place in Leviticus where Moses is commanded to address Aaron, his sons, and the Israelites. This inclusive form of address emphasizes that the teaching applies to all Israelites without exception, for it has to do with the most important ritual observance of Israel as a congregation. The focus is therefore on the ritual responsibility of the whole community. All the people were to serve God by offering animal sacrifices to him—and to him only. Their personal sacrifices were to be offered together with the communal sacrifices and incorporated into the regular ritual performed by the priests. No private sacrificial cult was to exist apart from the national cult. The national cult was established to include all the sacrifices of all the people. Those who offered private sacrifices apart from it were cut off from the community of Israel (17:4, 9, 10). The inclusive, communal orientation of this teaching is underscored by the repeated use in 17:3, 8, 10, and 13 of the inclusive formula אִישׁ אִישׁ ... אֲשֶׁר, "each and every person who" (a formula that is rare outside of Leviticus and Numbers). Thus all Israelites are addressed personally and communally as the primary ritual agents in this central chapter.

The range of this teaching is extended beyond the Israelite community to include all the resident aliens in its midst (17:10, 12, 13, 15). Since they lived together with the Israelites, they too were to observe the prohibition of sacrifice apart from the tabernacle, the taboo on the consumption of blood, and the need for purification after the consumption of carrion. They stood in ritual solidarity with the Israelites and suffered the same communal penalties for any transgression. God granted them equal status with his people in the sacrificial ritual (cf. Num 15:14–16). They too could be guests of the Lord and his people at the sacrificial banquets for the peace offerings.

Both the Israelites and the resident aliens were to bring all their animals for sacrifice to the priest who officiated at the tabernacle. He was the Lord's ritual representative. By bringing their sacrifices to him, they brought them to the Lord (17:5). The priest performed the rite of atonement by splashing the blood against the Lord's altar; he sent up the smoke from the fat of their peace offerings as a pleasing aroma to the Lord (17:6).

The other main actor was the Lord. Everything revolved around his presence and interaction with the people. The tent of meeting was his residence; its altar belonged to him (17:4). All the peace offerings were to be brought to him by the priest (17:5, 6) and performed for him (17:9). He instituted the rite of atonement by the application of blood to the altar (17:11). The fat was burnt as a pleasing aroma to him (17:6). He warned that he himself would reject and extirpate those who misused the blood from animals (17:4, 9, 10, 14).

The teaching also refers to "goat-demons" (17:7), who were worshipped as rivals to the Lord. Apparently they were earth spirits who were venerated as part of pagan fertility worship. Like the satyrs of classical mythology, they were envisaged as hairy he-goats. Since they were associated with the earth and the underworld, they were believed to reside in the open fields and the uninhabited grazing lands (Is 13:21; 34:14). As earth spirits, they were held to control the fertility of the animals that grazed on their terrain. They therefore had some claim on those animals. The blood from the firstborn cattle, sheep, and goats may have been drained out into the earth to feed and appease them. In fact, the apostate Jeroboam appointed priests to perform the sacrifices for them (2 Chr 11:15). By offering the blood from the peace offerings to them, the Israelites rejected the Lord as the giver of life and prostituted themselves after the demons in an act of spiritual harlotry (Lev 17:7).

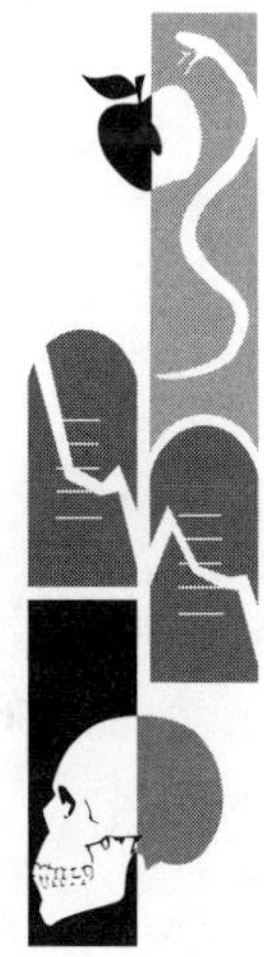

The Lord did not deny the existence or power of these demonic recipients of idolatrous worship. Instead, he forbade all ritual involvement with them (see also 1 Cor 10:20–21).

Ritual Location

These laws assert that it was not enough to offer the right sacrifices to the Lord; they had to be offered to him in the right place. They explicate the altar law in Ex 20:24 and are related to the decrees about the centralization of worship in Deuteronomy (e.g., Deut 12:5–7, 10–14). Here, however, the focus is on the location for the disposal of blood from slaughtered animals.

First, mention is made of the wrong places for ritual slaughter and sacrifice. The Israelites were not allowed to slaughter their domestic animals as peace offerings either in the camp or outside the camp (Lev 17:3). The camp was the common domain, the sphere for human habitation and activity, as distinct from the divine sphere. Practically speaking, it was the obvious place for slaughter since it was the natural location for the consumption of the meat from the sacrifice. Nevertheless, no peace offering could be slaughtered there. Even though it was a ritually clean place where the holy meat could be eaten, it was not the right place for the sacrifice of domestic animals. The area outside the camp is described as "the surface of the fields" (17:5). It was an ambiguous place. On the one hand, the fields were the home of the wild animals whose meat could be eaten if their blood was drained from them and buried in the earth (17:13). On the other hand, it was also the domain of the "goat-demons" (17:7), an unclean area. The blood from any animal ritually slaughtered there was not given to the Lord but to demons.

The place that God authorized for the ritual slaughter of the peace offerings was the entrance to the tent of meeting (17:3–7). It was a ritually clean, transitional area that stood between the common domain and the sacred domain. It led from the camp to the holy altar and back again. The Israelites were required to bring all the peace offerings to "the entrance to the tent of meeting" for presentation there as an offering to God in front of his residence, "the Lord's tabernacle" (17:4). They brought them for slaughter as sacrifices at "the entrance to the tent of meeting" (17:5). The animals were slaughtered there so that the priest could dash the blood taken from them "against the altar of the Lord at the entrance to the tent of meeting" (17:6).

The repetition of references to this location and its exact specification is unique in Leviticus. It connects private ritual slaughter most emphatically with communal access to the Lord's presence and public disposal of the blood and fat from the slaughtered animal by the priest on the altar. By decreeing that the animals be slaughtered at the entrance to the tent of meeting, the Lord claimed the blood from animals for himself; the blood, by being splashed against the altar, was transferred from the human to the divine domain. Thus, even though the animals for the peace offering were domestic, and even though the meat from the peace offerings was eaten at home (3:17; 7:26), the animals could not be ritually slaughtered there.

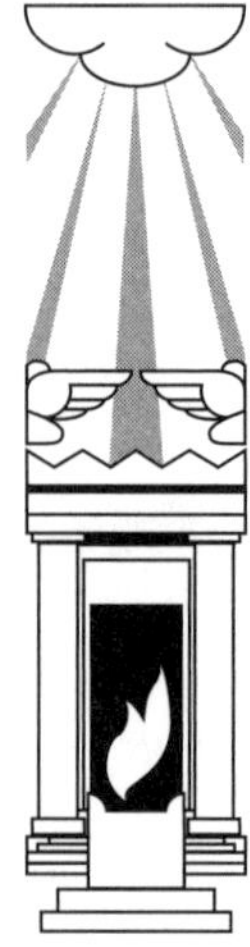

This applies too for the presentation of all animals for sacrifice (17:8–9). All private sacrifices were brought to "the entrance to the tent of meeting." They had to be offered up there on the altar. The ritual for them was to be performed there to the Lord. All other places of sacrifice were forbidden. Those who sacrificed any animals elsewhere misplaced them and so were misplaced by them; God dislocated those people by cutting them off from himself and his people.

The reason for the localization of private sacrificial slaughter and of all private sacrifices at the entrance to the tent of meeting is given in 17:11. This was the site of the Lord's altar (17:6). This altar was the place where God met with his people. By his Word God established its unique, ritual function for his people and all the aliens resident with them. It was the place for the disposal of the blood from the private burnt and peace offerings. There God gave the blood that belonged to him back to them to perform the rite of atonement for their lives. That was why it could not be eaten.

However, blood by itself did not atone. Nor did blood atone through the ritual slaughter of the animal and through its removal from a living animal. It atoned by being applied to the altar. By the ritual application of the blood to his altar, God released the people assembled there in the sacred precincts from their sin. Blood offered at any other place resulted in extirpation by God. The altar then was the place for sacrificial atonement as well as the place for the reception of its benefits from God.

Ritual location is most significant for the teaching in this chapter. Since God has given access to himself and his grace through the rite of atonement performed at the altar situated in front of the tabernacle, his people must sacrifice their animals there, and only there.

Ritual Material

The whole of this chapter has to do with blood and its legitimate use in ancient Israel. It is true that mention is also made of the fat from the peace offerings (17:6). Like the blood, it was reserved exclusively for God (cf. 3:16–17; 7:23–25). It therefore had to be burnt up on the altar together with the meat from the burnt offerings. But the reason for this is not given here. Instead, the focus is on blood.

The concern for blood in this chapter is alien and repulsive to modern readers who lack the cultural background to appreciate its significance for people from animist and semi-animist societies, such as still exist in many parts of the world. The basic premise of all animist societies is that all living things have a spirit. More significantly, all animals and humans are animated by a soul, their life spirit. It is their life-power, their life-breath, the supernatural life-force that enlivens and empowers them. The Hebrew word for this is נֶפֶשׁ. It gives "life" to the flesh of humans and animals and resides in their blood. It is therefore axiomatic for people with an animist worldview that "the life of the flesh is in the blood" (17:11). Loss of "blood" therefore results in loss of "life."

The blood, however, is not merely the seat of "life"; it *is* "life." Hence "the life of all flesh is its blood" (17:14). Thus, while "live blood" may be distinguished from "dead blood," the "life" of animals or people cannot exist and be had apart from their blood. Blood is therefore the most precious, powerful, and spiritual substance in the world. It is living and life-giving. It belongs to both the natural and supernatural realm.

This explains the ritual use of blood in animist societies and by Israel's pagan neighbors. In fact, many animists regard blood as the most potent of all ritual substances. The blood of an animal was either drunk or, more commonly, eaten with its meat to gain its life-power, its vitality and health, its virility and fertility, its energy and strength. The priestly writers refer to this as "eating blood." Deut 12:23 claims that those who eat blood eat "the life with the flesh." As indicated in Lev 17:5, 7, in idolatrous practice the blood was also poured out on the ground and given to plants to enhance agricultural production.

More significantly, blood was the only substance that was both material and spiritual. The blood from sacrificed animals was therefore used to "feed" the spirits of the dead (see a possible allusion to this practice in Ps 16:4), as well as the "deities" residing in the earth or in the underworld (Deut 32:17). It was also given to appease evil spirits, such as the goat-demons mentioned in Lev 17:7, in order to ward off infertility and other forms of bad luck. Lev 19:26 seems to imply that the blood from a sacrificed animal was at times drained into a trench to invoke the gods of the earth or the earth spirits for the purpose of divination. Most extremely, children were sacrificed to feed parasitic gods, such as Molech, with human blood (Ps 106:36–39; cf. Lev 20:1–5).

All those ritual practices presuppose the connection of blood with life, as well as the power of blood to give life.

The teaching in this chapter forbids all those ritual uses of blood. God reserved all blood for himself as the life-giver. It had to be given back to him. People could not use blood to gain supernatural life-power for themselves, nor could they manipulate it to grant life-power to those who lacked it. It could not be handed over to other gods and demons, since they had no right to use it, nor were they allowed to acquire life-power from it. Above all, no Israelite was allowed to consume the blood from any animal. Instead, God ordained that it was to be used ritually only in the rite of atonement and the practices associated with it. Yet the power of blood in that rite did not come from the life in it, but from God's Word which had instituted its use. That Word determined its function in the rite of atonement.

Blood in itself was not holy; it became holy only by virtue of its contact with the altar (Ex 29:37). God did not establish the sanctity of animal life in Lev 17:4, as some maintain.[10] Rather God declared that he protected the life of domestic animals, even as he protected human life. He did not allow anyone to take the life of any animal unless he himself had sanctioned it (Gen 9:3–4). Since he had not sanctioned the ritual slaughter of animals apart from the tabernacle, those who did so were guilty of bloodshed. He considered them to be murderers, for they had stolen life for themselves from the animal and so from God.

The total ban on the consumption of blood created two problems. These are dealt with in the last two parts of the chapter. The first was the consumption of meat from edible game birds and animals (17:13–14). These did not need be sacrificed; indeed, they could not be brought to the tabernacle and slaughtered there. Instead, the hunter drained out the blood from them onto the earth and buried it in the earth, before the meat was eaten.

The second problem was the consumption of meat from an edible animal that had died from natural causes or from attack by a wild animal. Since the animal was already dead, its blood lacked "life." Its flesh had no "life" in it. The meat from it was therefore not banned, but merely regarded as unclean. It communicated low level ritual impurity, like the discharge of semen (15:16).

---

[10] For example, Gorman, *The Ideology of Ritual*, 188–89.

Consumption of its meat was treated as a minor act of defilement rather than as a serious act of desecration (11:39–40). Those who ate carrion had to purify themselves by taking a ritual bath and by washing their clothes. If they failed to do so, they remained unclean and would have to bear their iniquity (17:16). This meant that if they came to the tabernacle without undergoing purification they defiled it. God would sentence them to death for the desecration of his sanctuary (15:31).

Ritual Theological Function

This chapter lays the foundation for one of the most important acts of God in the sacrificial ritual. In 17:11 God himself founds the rite of atonement as a sacrificial enactment. By his divine decree he establishes the practice of ritual atonement. Its importance is highlighted by God's speech to his people in the first person. By employing the formula of assignment and bestowal, God gives them permission to use the blood from all sacrificed animals in the rite of atonement and decrees that the blood applied to the altar in that rite makes atonement for their lives. His Word, his decree, empowered the rite, so that, thereafter, he worked atonement for them through their faithful performance of it. It gave the mandate for that important transaction.

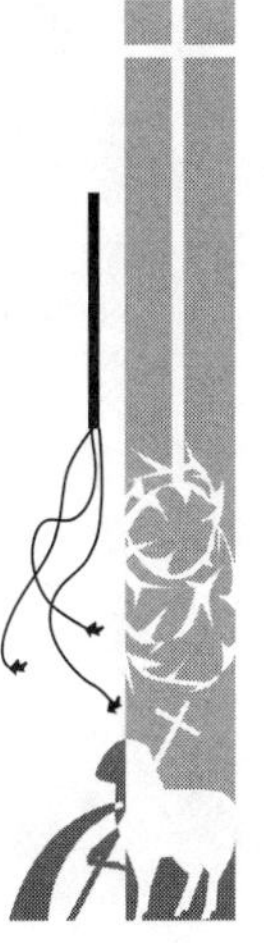

The laws earlier in Leviticus had established how the blood from the different sacrifices was to be used. They had also announced that cleansing and forgiveness would result from the performance of the rite for atonement. This chapter gives the rationale for it. In this body of teaching, God announced what was transacted in the rite of atonement. In this rite his people did not give the lives of their animals to God in exchange for their own lives. The blood and the life in the blood was not theirs to give. Rather, God gave them the life of these animals to make atonement for their own lives. He could do this because he was the life-giver. The life of the sacrificed animal belonged to him. But he did not, as might well be expected, give them that life to eat and drink by their consumption of its blood. They did not, in fact, receive life-power from God. Rather, they received the gift of atonement from God through the blood from the altar. That blood ransomed and so freed them.

But from what were they ransomed? We are not given the answer to that question here. From the discussion on atonement earlier in the book, we may infer that they were ransomed and released from impurity or pollution (e.g., 4:26; 5:6; 15:31; 16:16, 19). They were also thereby freed from the threat of death for the desecration of God's holiness by their impurity. They therefore had access to God's gracious presence. They could approach him with their petitions and receive his life-enhancing blessing. Their vitality then did not come from the consumption of animal blood, but from their access to God's blessing as result of atonement.

The teaching in this chapter could be seen as the culmination of all the legislation on the presentation of offerings in chapters 1–10 and on purification in chapters 11–15. Like the previous chapter, it deals with ritual atonement. But whereas in that chapter God established the ritual for the Day of Atonement, here he explained what was accomplished by the use of blood in the rite of atonement. Both these chapters show that the book of Leviticus understands atonement as a divine-human ritual transaction. The ritual context is of paramount importance. By instituting the rite of atonement, God himself provided the solution to the problem created by his desire to have his people meet and interact with him at the tabernacle. The problem was this: how could his sinful, unclean people come before their holy God to receive blessing from him without desecrating his holiness by their impurity and so suffering the penalty of death as threatened in 15:31?

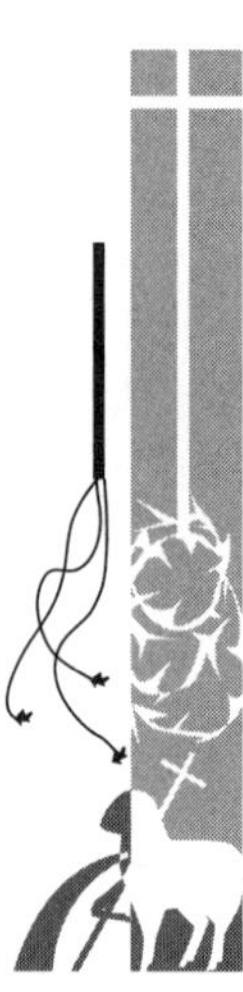

God solved that problem by establishing the rite of atonement. It removed the obstacles to their harmonious, productive interaction at the tabernacle. It qualified them for access to God's grace at the tabernacle. Just as the priests on duty each day could enter the Holy Place only after they had dashed the blood from the lamb for burnt offering on the altar, so God's people could eat the holy meat at his sanctuary only after the rite of atonement had been performed with the blood from the slaughtered animal. By means of the blood from the sacrificed animals, God's people were ransomed from impurity and sin. Their bodies were cleansed from its stain. They could therefore approach God boldly in prayer and be confident that they would receive nothing but blessing from him. By their contact with God they shared in his life-giving, life-protecting, life-enhancing holiness. Thus ritual purification through the rite of atonement qualified God's people for their participation in his holiness.

The ban on any sacrifice apart from the Lord's altar, the prohibition of blood consumption, and the threat of extirpation—these all follow from God's gift of blood for atonement. According to God's decree, the blood of a sacrificed animal ransomed the lives of his people through its application to the altar (17:11). It did so by virtue of the life contained in it. Both the blood from a slaughtered animal and the life in the blood could be used only in the rite of atonement. Blood could not be used for any other sacral or secular purpose. The Israelites were not allowed to appropriate that life for themselves by their consumption of blood. They were not allowed to gain life-power from God for themselves and use that supernatural life-power for their own ends. That ban applied to both sacrificial and non-sacrificial animals (17:12, 14).

In ironic contrast to the rite of atonement, the misapplication and misappropriation of blood did not lead, as was supposed, to enhanced vitality and fertility, but to the extirpation of the offender by God himself from his people and from life with him (17:9, 10, 14). Life-giving blessing could not be obtained from the blood of animals, but only from God and from contact with him in worship. All other methods of acquiring life-power were suicidal.

Fulfillment by Christ

The prohibition of consuming blood and eating meat that had not been ritually slaughtered was and remains a key observance for every pious Jew. It therefore became a burning issue in the early church with the inclusion of Gentiles as members of the liturgical community. There was a vigorous debate about which ritual regulations the Gentile converts were bound to observe. This matter was debated and resolved in the council of Jerusalem (Acts 15:1–21). It was decided that the Gentiles did not have to be circumcised. But they had to abstain from four things: pollution from idols, sexual immorality, the meat from strangled animals, and the consumption of blood (Acts 15:20, 29; 21:25).

All four of these requirements reflect the concerns in Leviticus 17. The first two also draw on the decrees in Lev 18:6–23 and 19:4–8. The prohibition of pollution from idols, which echoes the sanctions against the offerings to goat-demons in Lev 17:7, is connected by St. Paul to the eating of meat offered to idols. The apostle describes non-Christian worship as demonic and forbids Christians from participating in it or in syncretistic combinations of Christianity with other religions: "What they sacrifice—to demons and not to God they sacrifice. I do not wish you to be participants in fellowship with demons. You are not able to drink the cup of the Lord and the cup of demons" (1 Cor 10:20–21). Just as the offering of worship to false deities is considered to be religious self-prostitution in Lev 17:7, so the Revelation of St. John regards false doctrine and the eating of food offered to idols as spiritual fornication and adultery (Rev 2:14, 20–23). Thus false worship is closely associated with sexual immorality.

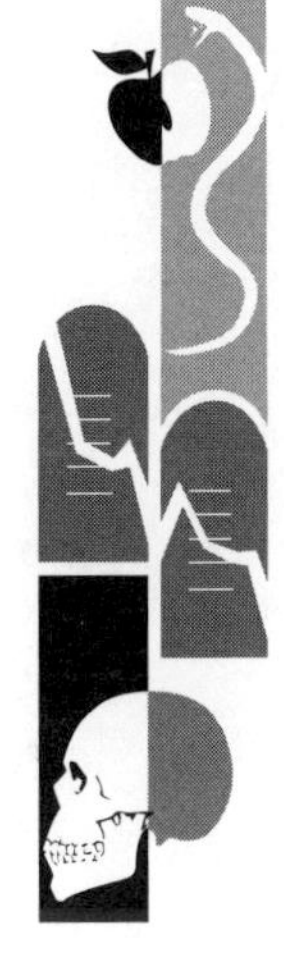

The last two apostolic prohibitions for Gentile Christians (the meat from strangled animals and the consumption of blood) draw on the prohibitions in Leviticus 17 that applied to resident aliens as well as Israelites. Since Jewish Christians could not enjoy table fellowship with anyone who consumed blood, Gentile Christians were required to observe these restrictions in any congregation that had Jewish converts. Yet both Jews and Gentiles were saved by God's grace, rather than the observance of the law (Acts 15:7–11).

This chapter in Leviticus has influenced the church in other ways as well. On the one hand, the centralization of all sacrificial ritual and the rite of atonement at the altar at the entrance to the tent of meeting culminated in the incarnation of God's Son and the establishment of his body as the temple of God. On the other hand, the restriction of the use of the blood from animals prepared God's people for Christ's gift of his own blood for their redemption.

The tent of meeting, later replaced by the temple in Jerusalem, was the only place where the Israelites could present animals as offerings to God. That was the only place where God had promised to make himself available and accessible to them. He had located himself there for them. They were to perform the rite of atonement there, because they had access to his grace and blessing there.

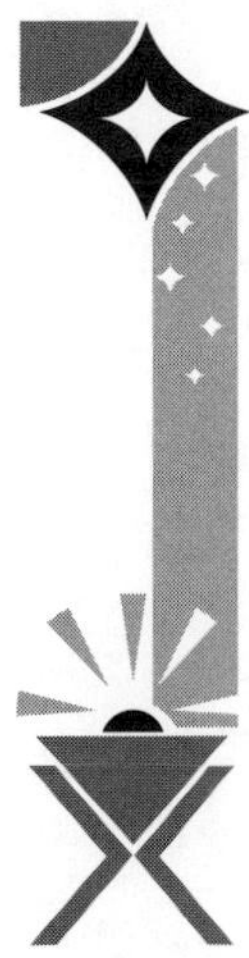

By the incarnation of his Son, God localized himself in time and space for the Israelites and all the nations of the world.[11] The body of Jesus is therefore the temple of the living God (Jn 2:21), the place where he dwells with all his fullness (Col 1:19; 2:9). Since the fullness of God dwells bodily in the glori-

[11] Kleinig, "Where Is Your God?"

fied body of Jesus, those who are united bodily with him in Baptism receive more and more of that fullness in him (Col 2:9–15). The man Jesus, whose glorified body is no longer bound by the limits of time and space, is the place where we can come near to God the Father (Eph 2:13). He is the gate, the entrance to the Father's saving presence (Jn 10:7–9; cf. Heb 7:25). This means that no one can come to God the Father anywhere else except through him (Jn 14:9–10). Through Jesus we have access to God the Father and his grace (Rom 5:2; Eph 2:18); through him we offer sacrifices that are pleasing to God the Father (Heb 13:15; 1 Pet 2:5). Apart from the incarnate Son of God, all human worship is idolatry; our prayers and everything else that we offer in the Divine Service are acceptable to God the Father only if they are brought in and through Jesus.

When the Samaritan woman asked Jesus about the proper place for the worship of God, he told her that in the new age God's people would no longer pay homage to him either on Mount Gerizim or in Jerusalem (Jn 4:19–24). Instead they would pay homage to the Father in him, the truth, and by the power of the Holy Spirit. He, the Messiah, would not just build the new temple of God; he would be that temple. Luther explains this most aptly when he says:

> In the NT we have been freed from attachment to external places. … Our spiritual place is Christ, because God has determined that he will not hear [anyone] except through this place, Christ. … Christ is our one and only place, our time, and everything else required for prayer. Just as the Jews had no other sanctuary than the one in Jerusalem, so we have no other sanctuary than this one, Jesus, the Son of Mary.[12]

The incarnate Son of God, the one and only place for the worship of God the Father, is also our great High Priest who makes atonement for us with his own blood (Rom 3:25). God the Father has sent him to make atonement for the sins of the whole (1 Jn 2:2; 4:10). By the blood that he shed on the cross, he has ransomed people from a futile existence (1 Pet 1:18–19; cf. Heb 9:12) and has freed them from their sins (Rev 1:5). By his blood he has "purchased" people from all over the world for God (Rev 5:9) and "obtained" them as the members of his flock (Acts 20:28).

Yet his astonishing achievement for humanity includes more. He does something that, scandalously, might appear to violate the divine prohibition against drinking blood.[13] Yet Christ's institution does not really violate that taboo, because it is the ultimate reason for it. He gives his own blood to drink in Holy Communion (Mt 26:28; Mk 14:24; Lk 22:20; 1 Cor 10:16; 11:25), the blood by which he made peace on a cosmic scale with his death on the cross (Col 1:20), the most holy blood that he brought with him at his ascension into the heavenly sanctuary (Heb 9:11–12). In Jn 6:53–56 Jesus speaks to the Jews four times about the need for them to "drink" his blood; that blood gives life,

---

[12] WA 40^{III}.53.19–35, quoted by Kleinig, "Where Is Your God?" 128.

[13] Cahill, "Drinking Blood at a Kosher Eucharist?"; Jeremias, *The Eucharistic Words of Jesus*, 170–71.

his own divine life, eternal life through the Holy Spirit (Jn 6:61–63). His blood is a Spirit-filled drink (1 Cor 10:4); by receiving it we drink in Christ's life-giving Spirit (1 Cor 12:13; cf. Heb 6:4; 10:29).[14]

Christ's gift of his blood to drink, in the sacrificial banquet established by him, marks what is different and new about the Divine Service in the church. By means of his blood he conveys to worthy communicants (1 Cor 11:27–32) all the eternal blessings that he gained for the faithful through his self-sacrifice. By giving his blood to drink, he sprinkles their hearts, their consciences (Heb 9:13–14; 10:22; 12:24; 1 Pet 1:2). Through his blood they have redemption, the forgiveness of sins (Mt 26:28; 1 Cor 11:25; Eph 1:7). His blood justifies them before God the Father (Rom 5:9) and cleanses them from all impurity (Heb 9:14; 1 Jn 1:7). They can therefore approach God the Father through his blood in Holy Communion (Eph 2:13; Heb 10:19). By means of that blood they are consecrated as priests together with Christ (Heb 10:29; 13:12) and equipped well for their priestly service of him (Heb 13:20–21). As priests whose robes have been washed with his holy blood (Rev 7:14), they can use his blood to overcome Satan and triumph over the powers of darkness (Rev 12:11).

In the light of all this, it comes as no surprise that the description of the Divine Service in Heb 12:22–24 culminates in "the blood for sprinkling." Our involvement in the heavenly liturgy is only possible through the blood of Jesus. Through his blood the risen Lord Jesus gives God's holy people access to the heavenly city here on earth; through it he unites them with the angels and the whole communion of saints and presents them as purified sinners before God the Judge. There is therefore great power in the life-giving blood of the Lamb. His cleansing, sanctifying blood is our most precious possession, for by it we have access to the heavenly sanctuary here on earth.

Here we have come to a place that is holy,
    the mountain of God,
    the city of light.
Here we cross over from earth into heaven,
    receiving by faith
    things hidden from sight.

Here we can join with ten thousands of angels
    who lead us in praise
    for what Christ has done.
Here we are part of a worldwide assembly,
    in which we are all
    joint heirs with God's Son.

Here is our Father, the judge of all people,
    who pardons our sin
    and shows us his face.

[14] Cf. Luther, WA 15.607–8.

Here we are close to the saints gone before us,
who rest in the light
of God's holy place.

Here we have Jesus, our one mediator,
who brings God to us
and us back to him.
Here is the blood that makes us sinners holy,
by giving us life
and washing us clean.[15]

[15] By John W. Kleinig (2000).

The Structure of Leviticus 18–20

These three chapters with their three speeches are linked together in a number of ways. Most obviously, the prohibitions of defilement in chapter 18 correspond with the penalties for desecration through defilement in chapter 20, just as the admonition to avoid defilement in 18:24–30 matches the call to holiness in 20:22–26. The formula of divine self-introduction and self-commitment runs as a recurring motif through this whole part of Leviticus.[a] The repetition of the call to holiness in 19:2 and 20:26 frames all the intervening legislation and highlights God's demand for holiness and promise of sanctification in 20:7–8.

(a) Lev 18:2, 5, 6, 21, 30; 19:3, 4, 10, 11, 14, 16, 18, 25, 30, 32, 34, 36, 37; 20:7, 24; cf. 19:2; 20:8, 26

The most significant structural device is the repetition of the admonition by God to keep his statutes and ordinances in 18:5, 26; 19:37, and 20:22 (cf. 19:19; 20:8). God's appeal for the Israelites to observe them in order to receive life from him introduces the legislation in 18:3–5. This culminates in the appeal in 20:8 to observe God's ritual statutes in order to share in his holiness. The gift of life is thereby connected with participation in his holiness. Each of the three speeches concludes with the plea for the observance of God's ritual statutes and social ordinances (18:26; 19:37; 20:22). In fact, in 19:36–37 God asserts that he has brought the Israelites out from Egypt so that they would observe his statutes and ordinances. The focus on their observance in 18:3–5 and 20:22–26 frames the body of legislation in these chapters and suggests that all the laws need to be interpreted ritually and theologically. This means that the call to holiness in 20:22–26 is not just the conclusion of that chapter, but the climax of this whole section.

These three chapters also introduce the second half of Leviticus. They deal with reverence for the sanctuary and participation in God's holiness. The legislation in Leviticus 18–27 therefore carries out the command of God to Aaron in 10:10–11 that he and his fellow priests must distinguish what is holy from what is common and what is clean from what is unclean and teach the Israelites to do so as well.

Leviticus 18:1–30

Ritual Defilement of the Land by Sexual Immorality

Translation

18 [1]The Lord spoke to Moses: [2]"Speak to the Israelites and say to them: I am the Lord your God.

[3]"You shall not copy the customs of the land of Egypt, in which you resided; nor shall you copy the customs of the land of Canaan, to which I am bringing you; you shall not walk according to their ritual statutes. [4]You shall enact my ordinances and keep my ritual statutes by walking according to them. I am the Lord your God.

[5]"You shall keep my ritual statutes and my ordinances; any person who does them will have life by them. I am the Lord.

[6]"None of you shall approach the flesh of his relative to uncover nakedness. I am the Lord.

[7]"You shall not uncover your father's nakedness, which is the nakedness of your mother; she is your mother; you shall not uncover her nakedness.

[8]"You shall not uncover the nakedness of your father's wife; it is the nakedness of your father.

[9]"You shall not uncover the nakedness of your sister, whether she is your father's daughter or your mother's daughter, whether born into the household or outside it.

[10]"You shall not uncover the nakedness of your son's daughter or your daughter's daughter; indeed they are your nakedness.

[11]"You shall not uncover the nakedness of the daughter of your father's wife, the offspring of your father; she is your sister; [it is] her nakedness.

[12]"You shall not uncover the nakedness of your father's sister; she is your father's flesh.

[13]"You shall not uncover the nakedness of your mother's sister, for she is your mother's flesh.

[14]"You shall not uncover the nakedness of your father's brother by approaching his wife; she is your aunt.

[15]"You shall not uncover the nakedness of your daughter-in-law. She is your son's wife; you shall not uncover her nakedness.

[16]"You shall not uncover the nakedness of your brother's wife; it is the nakedness of your brother.

[17]"You shall not uncover the nakedness of a woman and her daughter. You shall not marry her son's daughter or her daughter's daughter and so uncover her nakedness. They are her flesh; it is a depraved act.

18“You shall not marry a woman and her sister, thereby making her a rival
wife and uncovering her nakedness, in addition to her during her lifetime.
19“Nor shall you approach a woman during the period of her impurity to un-
cover her nakedness.
20“Nor shall you give to the wife of your fellow citizen your copulation for
seed, so that you become unclean by her.
21“Nor shall you give any of your seed for dedication to Molech, thereby des-
ecrating the name of your God; I am the Lord.
22“You shall not lie with a male as lying with a woman; it is an abomination.
23“Nor shall you give your copulation to any animal, so that you become un-
clean by it, nor shall any woman stand before an animal to crouch down for it;
it is a perverted act.
24“Do not defile yourselves in any of these ways, for in all these ways the na-
tions that I am casting out before you defiled themselves. 25Thus the land became
unclean; and I visited its iniquity on it, and the land vomited out its inhabitants.
26“You yourselves must keep my ritual statutes and ordinances; you must
not practice any of these abominations, neither the native nor the alien who re-
sides among you; 27for the people of the land who were before you practiced all
these abominations, so that the land became unclean. 28So do not let the land
vomit you out for defiling it as it vomited out the nation that was before you.
29Surely as for anyone who does any of these abominations—the lives of those
who practice them will be cut off from the midst of their people. 30So keep watch
for me by not enacting any of the ritual statutes that are abominations which
were done before you, so that you do not defile yourselves by them. I am the Lord
your God.”

Textual Notes

18:2 אֲנִי יְהוָה אֱלֹהֵיכֶם׃—See the textual note on this clause in 11:4. It recurs in 18:4, 30.

18:3 כְּמַעֲשֵׂה … לֹא תַעֲשׂוּ—Literally God commands, “According to the deeds of … you shall not do.”

וּבְחֻקֹּתֵיהֶם—See the textual note on this term in 3:17. The plural חֻקֹּת recurs in 18:4, 5, 26, 30. Since God’s statutes prescribe important ritual practices, this most likely refers to the religious laws of the Egyptians and the Canaanites.

לֹא תֵלֵכוּ׃—This idiom of walking in statutes, which recurs in 18:4 and 20:23, may derive from the involvement of pagan people in religious processions with the idols of their gods and the traditions of their involvement in those processions.

18:4 מִשְׁפָּטַי—See the textual note on this term in 5:10. It recurs in 18:5, 26.

18:5 וּשְׁמַרְתֶּם אֶת־חֻקֹּתַי וְאֶת־מִשְׁפָּטַי—For further use of this idiom, see 18:26; 19:37; 20:22.

הָאָדָם—See the textual notes on 1:2. The use of הָאָדָם here indicates that this applies to all human beings, not just the Israelites.

אֲשֶׁר יַעֲשֶׂה אֹתָם הָאָדָם וָחַי בָּהֶם—This is quoted in Ezek 20:11, 13, 21, and Neh 9:29. חַי is the Qal third masculine singular perfect of the verb חָיָה, “to be alive, to

stay alive," or with the preposition בְּ (בָּהֶם), "to live by something" (*HALOT,* s.v. חיה, Qal, 1 and 2, respectively). This clause can be construed as a result clause: "the man shall do them *so that he may live/have life by them.*" The promise of life here goes beyond mere physical survival. It has to do with the possession of God-given life in its fullness: liveliness and vitality, prosperity and blessing (Deut 30:15–20). This abundant life continues into the age to come (Jn 10:10).

אֲנִי יְהוָה׃—See the textual notes on 11:4. By this formula, the Lord introduces himself by name to his people and gives them access to himself through the ritual use of his name (e.g., 18:6, 21; 19:12, 14, 16, 18, 30, 32, 37; 22:30, 31, 33; 26:2, 45).[1]

18:6 אִישׁ אִישׁ—The MT uses part of the same inclusive form here as in 15:2; 17:3, 8, 10, 13.

שְׁאֵר בְּשָׂרוֹ—Literally this construct phrase means "the intimate flesh of his body" (see also 25:49). שְׁאֵר is used as a designation for a person's sexual organs, as well as for all close blood relatives, such as a person's father, mother, brother, sister, son, daughter, and grandchild (18:12, 13; 20:19; 21:2–3; cf. 18:17). Close blood relatives are therefore conceived metaphorically as internal parts of a person's body. While בָּשָׂר is also used in Leviticus for the genitals of a man (15:2, 3, 7) and of a woman (15:19), it is most commonly used for a person's body as a whole, rather than the sexual organs.

תִקְרְבוּ—This verb is also used for approaching God at the tabernacle and having access to him there. See the textual notes on it in 1:2.

לְגַלּוֹת עֶרְוָה—The Piel of the verb גָּלָה means "to uncover, reveal, expose." "Nakedness" is a euphemism for a person's genitals. Just as people "cover" their nakedness with their clothing (Gen 9:23; Ex 28:42), their nakedness is revealed or uncovered when they are undressed. To uncover the nakedness of a woman means much more than to engage in an act of sexual intercourse with her. The improper uncovering that is prohibited is understood as an act by which she is shamefully exposed and publicly seen (Gen 9:22; Lev 20:17; Lam 1:8; Is 47:2–3; Ezek 16:36–37). She is thereby violated and shamed as a woman. Her nakedness then involves her personal honor as a woman, her sexual identity, modesty, and self-esteem.

This is tied up with her position in the family and her relationship with her husband. A man shares in the nakedness of his wife (Lev 18:8, 16; 20:11, 20, 21) and the nakedness of his granddaughter (18:10). Thus when a son has sexual intercourse with his mother, he also uncovers his father's nakedness, but when a grandfather has sexual intercourse with his granddaughter, he uncovers his own nakedness as well as hers. Improper sexual intercourse is envisaged in the first case as a shameful act of public sexual exposure by a son of his father through his mother, in the second case, as a shameful act of public sexual self-exposure of a grandfather through his granddaughter.

18:7 See Lev 20:11; Deut 27:20; Ezek 22:10.

---

[1] See Kleinig, "What's the Use of Naming God?"; Zimmerli, *I Am Yahweh*, 10.

עֶרְוַת אָבִיךָ וְעֶרְוַת אִמְּךָ לֹא תְגַלֵּה—Literally this prohibition is "The nakedness of your father and the nakedness of your mother you shall not expose." The second clause is best construed as an explicative clause: it explains that uncovering the father's nakedness takes place when the mother's nakedness is uncovered. That interpretation is confirmed by Lev 20:11.[2]

18:9 אֲחוֹתְךָ—In a polygamous society a man may have full sisters and paternal or maternal half sisters. This prohibition applies to both full and half sisters.

בַת־אָבִיךָ אוֹ בַת־אִמֶּךָ—See 20:17; Deut 27:22.

מוֹלֶדֶת חוּץ—This refers most naturally to a half sister from the prior marriage of a man's mother. She could have been brought up with him in his home or left behind in the mother's previous home.[3]

עֶרְוָתָן׃—The syntax of the verse as it stands in the MT is a *casus pendens* that literally says, "The nakedness of your sister, your father's daughter or your mother's daughter, whether born into the household or outside it—you shall not uncover their nakedness." The main part of the next verse has the same syntax (18:10, except for the last three Hebrew words). Some interpret עֶרְוָתָן in 18:9 to be a separate clause (not the direct object of the verb) that means "[it is] their nakedness" by way of apposition with the preceding clause.

18:10 כִּי עֶרְוָתְךָ הֵנָּה׃—This translation construes כִּי as an emphatic particle, "indeed," rather than a causal conjunction.

18:11 It is uncertain how this law differs from the law in 18:9. Most take it to apply to a girl born to the man's father from a woman other than the man's mother, whether she was the father's wife, his concubine, or a maid. But the phrase "the daughter of your father's wife," standing as it does in contrast to "your father's daughter" in 18:9, indicates that this speaks of the daughter born to a man's stepmother in a previous marriage. She has accompanied her mother into the new marriage and has been adopted by her stepfather.[4]

מוֹלֶדֶת אָבִיךָ—If the second interpretation given above is correct, then מוֹלֶדֶת here does not refer to the man's father as her father, but to her membership in the household of her stepfather.[5]

עֶרְוָתָהּ׃—The third feminine singular pronominal suffix refers to the mother rather than the daughter.

18:15 אֵשֶׁת בִּנְךָ—See Lev 20:12; Ezek 22:11.

18:16 עֶרְוַת אֵשֶׁת־אָחִיךָ לֹא תְגַלֵּה—See Lev 20:21. In Mt 14:4 John the Baptist used these passages to rebuke Herod for marrying his brother's wife.

---

2 Phillips, "Uncovering the Father's Skirt," 39, proposes an alternative interpretation. He claims that the uncovering of a father's nakedness, like the uncovering of his skirt in Deut 23:1 (ET 22:30), refers to homosexual intercourse with him. However, the immediate context here is concerned about marriage and incest. God will forbid homosexual activity in Lev 18:22; 20:13.

3 Wenham, *Leviticus*, 255–56.

4 Wenham, *Leviticus*, 256–57.

5 Hartley, *Leviticus*, 295–96.

18:17 וּבִתָּהּ—This refers to a man's stepdaughter.

תִּקַּח—Literally, "take," the verb לָקַח here refers to taking a woman in marriage. The verb recurs in the same sense in 18:18; 20:14, 17, 21.

שַׁאֲרָה הֵנָּה—This is literally "they are your flesh."

זִמָּה—This ("a depraved act") is a technical term in ritual legislation for a deliberate act of sexual depravity, such as incest (20:14; Ezek 22:9), rape (Judg 20:16), and prostitution (Lev 19:29; Jer 13:17; Ezek 16:27, 43, 58; 23:21, 27, 29, 35, 48, 49; 24:13).

18:18 From here through 18:23, each of the following laws is introduced in Hebrew by "and." These verses are thereby joined together to form a separate series of laws from 18:7–17.

לִצְרֹר—This is the Qal infinitive construct of denominative verb צָרַר, to "make a rival-wife" (BDB), which occurs only here in the OT.

עֶרְוָתָהּ—The third feminine singular pronominal suffix refers to the first wife.

עָלֶיהָ בְּחַיֶּיהָ׃—The preposition עַל has the same force here, "in addition to," as with עַל־נָשָׁיו in Gen 28:9. The prohibition in this verse is limited to "during her lifetime," meaning that marriage to a sister-in-law would be permitted after the death of her sister.

18:19 בְּנִדַּת טֻמְאָתָהּ—See the textual notes on 5:3; see also 15:26.

לְגַלּוֹת עֶרְוָתָהּ׃—See 20:18; Ezek 22:10.

18:20 עֲמִיתְךָ—See the textual notes on 5:21 (ET 6:2).

לֹא־תִתֵּן שְׁכָבְתְּךָ—Literally this means "you shall not give your lying down" or "you shall not give your emission." The noun שְׁכֹבֶת occurs in the OT only in Lev 18:20, 23; 20:15; Num 5:20 and means either "an emission of semen" or lying down for "copulation" (*HALOT*). It is related to שִׁכְבָה in Lev 15:16–18, 32; 19:20; 22:4.

לְזָרַע—Literally this is "for seed" or "for offspring." The mention of זֶרַע, "seed," "semen," "offspring," may indicate that this particular law does not refer to a secret act of adultery, but to a consensual act of sexual intercourse to impregnate the wife of an infertile man.

לְטָמְאָה־בָהּ׃—See the textual notes on 5:2. This is the so-called feminine form of the Qal infinitive absolute. Qal forms of the verb recur in 18:23, 25, 27. The use of the preposition לְ prefixed to the infinitive indicates the result of the previous action: "so that you become unclean by her."

18:21 וּמִזַּרְעֲךָ—This could also be translated "from your offspring." Note the mention of seed in the previous verse.

לְהַעֲבִיר—This is literally "to hand them over." This verb is used for the dedication of firstborn animals to the Lord (Ex 13:12) and for the offering of children to a heathen god (Deut 18:10; 2 Ki 16:3; 17:17; 21:6; Jer 32:35; Ezek 16:21; 20:31; 23:37), such as Molech (Jer 32:35). In pagan cults this seems to have involved the slaughter of a child (Ezek 16:21) or the child's incineration by fire (Deut 18:10). Child sacrifice seems to be envisaged here as an act of ritual masturbation by the offering of semen to Molech. Alternatively, the prohibition in this verse could be connected with the prohibitions in Lev 18:20 and 18:22. The giving of seed to Molech would then involve either adulterous sexual intercourse with a woman or homosexual intercourse with a man as part of the worship of Molech. That somewhat speculative interpretation is backed up by the description of Molech worship as ritual prostitution in 20:5. It would explain why this verse was inserted here in this list of forbidden sexual acts.

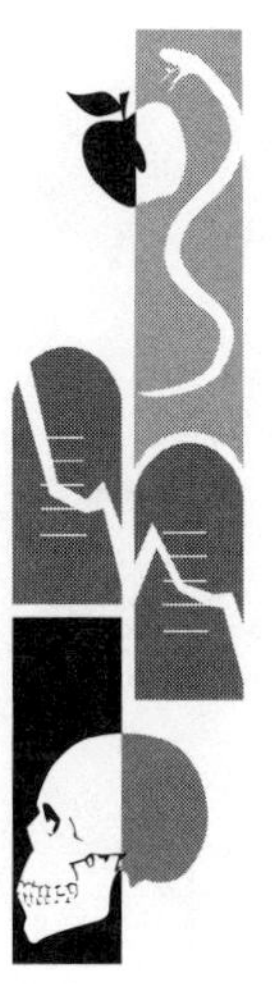

לַמֹּלֶךְ—Molech was most likely an underworld deity. In the OT he is associated with child sacrifice and the worship of the dead. See Hartley for an up-to-date summary of the recent discussion on the nature of Molech and his connection with child sacrifice.[6]

וְלֹא תְחַלֵּל אֶת־שֵׁם אֱלֹהֶיךָ—Even though this second clause could be understood grammatically as a separate prohibition of the abuse of God's name, as in 18:21, in this case it refers to the desecration of God's name by the act of child sacrifice. The verb חָלַל recurs in 19:8, 12, 29; 20:3; 21:4, 6, 9, 12, 15, 23; 22:2, 9, 15, 32.

People "desecrate" something holy by treating it as if it were common and so transferring it from the divine to the human domain. A person most obviously desecrated the holy name Yahweh by abusing it in some way, like employing it to swear a false oath (19:12). But this is not how this idiom is used here and elsewhere in Leviticus. It occurs in ritual contexts where the holy name is not apparently used at all, let alone abused, such as when a father sacrificed a child to Molech (18:21; 20:3), when a priest cut his hair and mutilated his body for a dead person (21:5–6), or when priests who were unclean ate the sacred food from God's table (22:2).

It is important to understand why the name of the Lord was desecrated in each of these cases. The striking thing about the idiom "to desecrate the name of God" is its use together with the formula for divine self-introduction and self-presentation, here as well as in 19:12; 22:2, 32. All these occurrences have one thing in common: they all connect the desecration of the Lord's name with involvement in some form of forbidden ritual activity (22:31–32). Thus God introduced himself by name in those decrees that forbade idolatry and instituted how he presented himself to his people as their holy, sanctifying God in the divine service. In fact, these decrees often begin or end with the Lord's use of his holy name in the formula of self-introduction. Thus anyone who violated them desecrated that holy name (cf. Ezek 20:9, 14, 22, 39; 36:20, 21, 22, 23).

18:22 לֹא תִשְׁכַּב מִשְׁכְּבֵי אִשָּׁה—See 20:13 and the textual notes on 15:18. The verb שָׁכַב, "to lie with" a person, is the usual term for an act of heterosexual intercourse. This command uses the related noun מִשְׁכָּב, which could refer to the "marriage bed" (*HALOT,* 2) but more likely refers to the act of lying down (BDB, 2 b). This command with the periphrastic phrase מִשְׁכְּבֵי אִשָּׁה, "acts of lying down with a woman," does not just prohibit some positions for homosexual acts, as some modern commentators have attempted to claim.[7] Rather, it forbids all forms of sexual intercourse between male persons.[8]

תּוֹעֵבָה—"Abomination" is the standard term for behavior repugnant to God and prohibited for God's people. It recurs in 18:26, 27, 29, 30. Since this behavior disgusts God, it disqualifies people from ritual association with him. Both Deuteronomy and Ezekiel use this term for activities that contaminate God's people or desecrate his

---

6 Hartley, *Leviticus*, 333–37.

7 For example, Bailey, *Homosexuality and the Western Christian Tradition*, 58–59, 156.

8 Wold, *Out of Order*, 104–7.

holiness.[9] This term is used in Leviticus for sexual practices that defile the people engaging in them, as well as defiling their environment. This eventually leads to God withdrawing his presence from people. As Wold has shown, Boswell's claim that תּוֹעֵבָה is used in Leviticus only to prohibit temple prostitution cannot be sustained because ritual impurity is not just generated by ritual transgressions, but by the effect of sexual, moral disorder on the sacred domain.[10]

18:23 וּבְכָל־בְּהֵמָה לֹא־תִתֵּן שְׁכָבְתְּךָ—This is literally "and with any animal you shall not give your lying down [or: your emission]." See the textual notes on 18:20. See also Deut 27:21.

לְרִבְעָהּ—The verb רָבַע may mean "to lie in position" or "to copulate" (*HALOT,* Qal, 1 and 2, respectively). The third feminine singular suffix on the infinitive construct refers to בְּהֵמָה.

תֶּבֶל הוּא׃—The noun תֶּבֶל comes from the verb בָּלַל which means "to mix, confuse" (see also 20:12). It therefore denotes "a perverted act" and describes the perversion of the divinely established order by the admixture and union of what should be kept apart.

18:24 See also 20:23.

תִּטַּמְּאוּ—This is the Hithpael of טָמֵא with a middle or reflexive meaning, to "defile oneself" (BDB). The second, prefixed *taw* has been assimilated and is marked by the *daghesh* in the *tet* (-טּ-). The following Niphal, נִטְמְאוּ, may have either a middle meaning, "defile oneself," or a passive meaning, "be defiled" (BDB).

18:25 וַתִּטְמָא הָאָרֶץ—This clause recurs in 18:27.

וָאֶפְקֹד עֲוֹנָהּ עָלֶיהָ—Iniquity here refers to the evil effect of people's sexual disorder on their habitat, the pollution of the land by its human inhabitants. This is the only place where God is said to "visit the iniquity [of people]" on the land. This idiom is used for an act of divine intervention in human affairs by which God calls people to account for their deeds and lets them suffer the evil consequences of their acts (Ex 20:5; 34:7; Num 14:18; Deut 5:9).

וַתָּקִא הָאָרֶץ אֶת־יֹשְׁבֶיהָ׃—See also 18:28; 20:22. The land is here depicted as a human body with its stomach. Just as a stomach vomits up what nauseates it, so the land vomits out its inhabitants who poison it with their sexual depravity. וַתָּקִא could be either the Qal or Hiphil third feminine singular imperfect of קִיא. The verb recurs in 18:28; 20:22. (In 18:28 קָאָה is the Qal third feminine singular perfect.)

18:26 וּשְׁמַרְתֶּם אַתֶּם אֶת־חֻקֹּתַי וְאֶת־מִשְׁפָּטַי—See also 18:5; 19:37; 20:22.

הָאֶזְרָח וְהַגֵּר הַגָּר בְּתוֹכְכֶם׃—See the textual notes on 16:29.

18:27 הָאֵל—This is an abbreviated form of הָאֵלֶּה, the plural demonstrative pronoun with definite article.

אַנְשֵׁי־הָאָרֶץ אֲשֶׁר לִפְנֵיכֶם—This is literally "the men of the land before you."

---

9 Hartley, *Leviticus*, 283.

10 Wold, *Out of Order*, 107–20, countering John Boswell, *Christianity, Social Tolerance, and Homosexuality* (Chicago: University of Chicago Press, 1980), 100–2.

18:28 וְלֹא—The NIV construes לֹא as an emphatic particle rather than a negative particle. The sentence could also be understood as a subordinate negative result clause (RSV; NRSV).

בְּטַמַּאֲכֶם אֹתָהּ—See the textual notes on 5:2 and 11:44. Similar statments are in Num 35:34; Deut 21:23; Jer 2:7; Ezek 36:17, 18.

18:29 כִּי—This is used here as an emphatic particle.

וְנִכְרְתוּ ... מִקֶּרֶב עַמָּם:—See the textual notes on 7:20.

הַנְּפָשׁוֹת—Instead of "lives," this could mean "persons" or "souls."

18:30 וּשְׁמַרְתֶּם אֶת־מִשְׁמַרְתִּי—This could also be translated "you shall keep my guard" or "do guard duty for me" (8:35; 22:9). See the textual notes on 8:35. This idiom was used for the performance of guard duty by guards at a royal palace (2 Ki 11:5, 6) or at the temple (2 Ki 11:7). Since the tabernacle was conceived as the Lord's royal residence, members of the priesthood were held to do sentry duty there (e.g., Lev 8:35; Num 1:53). Whereas the royal guard protected the king from attack by his enemies, the priesthood protected the people from destruction by God for the desecration of his holiness. Here all the people are commissioned by God to perform guard duty for God's land, just as the priests were employed to do guard duty for God's residence.

Commentary

Structure

The core of this speech is the two sets of laws dealing with human sexuality in 18:7–17 and 18:18–23. God addresses them to each adult male personally in the second person singular mode of address. The first set of laws, however, is introduced by a general prohibition of incest, addressed to the Israelites (in the plural) as a community (18:6), rather than to each male citizen.

In Hebrew, the eleven prohibitions in 18:7–17 all begin with the word עֶרְוָה, "nakedness." Each of them follows one of two chiastic patterns.[11] The first ABA' pattern is illustrated by 18:8:

A The nakedness of your father's wife
  B do not uncover;
A' it is your father's nakedness.

While the first part defines the prohibited relationship, the third part gives the reason for the relationship with a declaratory formula. This formulation centers on the prohibition of sexual involvement. This pattern is copied by the laws in 18:12, 13, 16 and is modified in 18:9, 10, 17.

The second ABCB'A' pattern is illustrated by 18:15:

A The nakedness of your daughter-in-law
  B do not uncover;
    C she is your son's wife;
  B' do not uncover
A' her nakedness.

---

[11] Halbe, "Die Reihe der Inzestverbote Lev 18:7–18."

The feature of this pattern is the repetition of "nakedness" and "uncover." The repeated prohibition centers on the declaratory formula that gives the reason for the prohibition. The law in 18:7 is drafted in this pattern, while the laws in 18:11 and 18:14 modify it.

The first set of prohibitions (18:7–17) is joined to the second set (18:18–23) by the catchword "take/marry" in 18:17 and 18:18. In Hebrew the seven prohibitions in 18:18–23 are linked as a series by the use of "and." Each of the first three prohibitions begins with the word "wife/woman." So too does the last one (18:23b). Apart from that, the prohibitions are connected by the use of catchwords and catchphrases: "seed/semen" in 18:20 and 18:21; "to become unclean by her/it" in 18:20 and 18:23; "do not give your seminal emission" in 18:20 and 18:23; and "animal" in 18:23a and 18:23b.

These two sets of laws are framed by two passages of admonition. They are addressed directly by God to all the Israelites and are interspersed with the formula for God's self-introduction in 18:2b, 4c, 5c and 30d. In both passages, prohibition (18:3, 24) precedes commandment (18:4, 5, 26, 30). This framework is reinforced by repetition: the sentence "I am the Lord your God" from 18:2 and 18:4 in 18:30; the verb עָשָׂה, "do, copy, enact, practice" from 18:3–5 in 18:26–30; the paired terms "ordinances" and "statutes" from 18:4–5 in 18:26; the word "land" from 18:3 in 18:25, 27, 28. The final admonition begins and ends with a warning against self-defilement (18:24, 30).

The structure of this pericope can be outlined as follows:

- I. Introduction (18:1–2a)
  - A. God's address to Moses (18:1)
  - B. God's commission of Moses (18:2a)
- II. Speech by Moses to the Israelites (18:2b–30)
  - A. Introductory admonition (18:2b–5)
    1. God's self-introduction (18:2b)
    2. Prohibitions against following the pagan customs and laws of the land (18:3)
    3. Commands to observe God's laws with God's self-introduction (18:4)
    4. Promise of life from observance with God's self-introduction (18:5)
  - B. Legislation for human sexual activity (18:6–23)
    1. Heading (18:6)
       - a. Prohibition of incest (18:6a)
       - b. God's self-introduction (18:6b)
    2. Prohibition of incest in an extended family (18:7–17)
       - a. With a mother (18:7)
       - b. With a stepmother (18:8)
       - c. With a full sister or half sister (18:9)
       - d. With a granddaughter (18:10)
       - e. With a stepsister (18:11)
       - f. With a paternal aunt (18:12)
       - g. With a maternal aunt (18:13)

h. With a paternal aunt-in-law (18:14)
i. With a daughter-in-law (18:15)
j. With a fraternal sister-in-law (18:16)
k. With a mother and her daughter (18:17a)
l. With a mother and her granddaughter (18:17b)

3. Prohibition of sexual malpractices (18:18–23)
    a. Marriage to the sister of a wife during her lifetime (18:18)
    b. Sexual intercourse with a women during menstruation (18:19)
    c. Sexual intercourse with a neighbor's wife (18:20)
    d. Sacrifice of offspring to Molech (18:21)
    e. Homosexual intercourse (18:22)
    f. Sexual intercourse of a man with an animal (18:23a)
    g. Sexual intercourse of a woman with an animal (18:23b)

C. Concluding admonition: rationale for compliance (18:24–30)
    1. Avoidance of the defilement and expulsion from the land (18:24–25)
    2. Avoidance of expulsion and extirpation by God (18:26–29)
    3. God's commission of the Israelites to protect the land (18:30a)
    4. God's concluding self-introduction (18:30b)

Ritual Agents

As we come to this chapter, we cannot but be struck by its personal tone. It is composed in such a way that God himself spoke directly to his people in an unprecedented way. He did so in two ways. First, he introduced himself by name to the Israelites and assured them that he was bound to them as their God (18:2, 4, 5, 6, 21, 30). Thereby he not only reminded them of his covenant with them as his holy people at Mount Sinai, but he also spoke to them through Moses and his priestly successors as one who was present with them. Through his name he gave them access to himself.

Second, he addressed them directly, corporately in 18:2–6, 24–30 and individually in 18:7–23. His personal interest in them and their welfare is shown by his admonition of them and his legislation for them. This legislation establishes the conditions for their enjoyment of life in the promised land. It connects their sexual relationships with his provision for them as his people in his land.

This speech is addressed first to the Israelites as God's people and then to each adult male Israelite. All adult males were required to observe God's laws about their sexuality. This may seem to belittle the responsibility of Israelite women, for they were not explicitly addressed as moral agents, but merely spoken about in the law on bestiality (18:23).

However, it would be wrong to conclude that this male orientation excluded women. They are obviously included in the promise in 18:5, the general law annunciated in 18:6, and the warning in 18:29. All Israelites were to protect the land from defilement (18:30) by avoiding defilement (18:24). Moreover, the prohibitions are not primarily concerned with individual rights (as Westerners are today) but with the integrity and survival of the extended family, for it was threatened most radically by incest and disordered sexual relationships.

This extended family, commonly called a "father's house," consisted of three to five generations of people, living and working together on a plot of land. Its members were linked physically to each other as a body with the same flesh (18:6, 12, 13, 17). All adult males were equally responsible for the integrity and productivity of this community, with its network of intergenerational relationships between men and women. They represented their family and were obliged to act in its best interests.

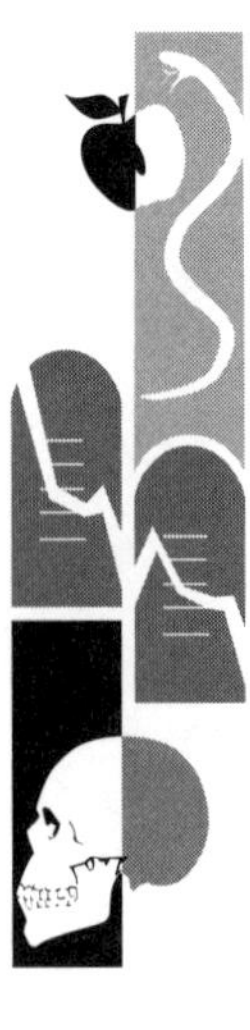

This chapter draws a sharp contrast between the sexual responsibilities of the Israelites, on the one hand, and the sexual shortcomings of their pagan neighbors, on the other hand—the Egyptians with whom they once lived (18:3a) and the people who lived in the land of Canaan before them (18:3b, 24, 27, 30). Since the Canaanites polluted themselves and their land by their sexual abominations, God removed them from the land and gave it to the Israelites.

The point of this comparison was not just to establish the moral inferiority of those nations, but to warn the Israelites of a similar fate if they too failed to respect the universal sexual taboos that are known, by the testimony of creation and the human conscience, to be wrong (e.g., Romans 1). God adds his own specific revelation so that his people will have no doubt about what behaviors are sinful and about the temporal and eternal consequences of disobeying his commands.

Ritual Location

If we are to interpret the teaching in this chapter rightly, we must pay due regard to the location for the enactment of these laws. They do not envisage the existence of the Israelites as nomadic people living in a camp around the tabernacle, but as a settled community in the land of Canaan. These laws are given for Israel as a nation and a network of families in that location.

At the beginning of the chapter, God addresses the Israelites at the point of transition from Egypt to Canaan (18:3). They have left the land of Egypt where they once resided. They must therefore also leave the customs of Egypt behind them. More significantly, God is about to bring them into the land of Canaan. When they enter that land, they must not (as often happens to immigrants) adopt and live according to the customs and norms of the people who had lived there (18:3, 24, 27). Rather, they must live according to the laws of their God, who would live with them in that land (18:4, 5, 26, 30). Life there was to revolve around him and his coexistence with them.

The land of Canaan was the ritually significant place for the observance of these prohibitions. It was regarded as a good place, a clean land that its former inhabitants had polluted by their involvement in incest and other sexual deviations. The land had therefore become ritually unclean (18:25, 27). But the land was much more than a healthy environment that had been ecologically disturbed by its inhabitants. It belonged to God. He therefore visited the iniquity of its inhabitants upon it, so that, though innocent of transgression, it suffered from the wickedness of its people (18:25). Like the stomach of a human body, the land "vomited out" its inhabitants who had polluted and poisoned it (18:25, 28; see also 20:22; 26:41). In this way God had cast them out and so purged the land of its pollutants (18:24).

All this presupposes a close bond between God and the land, as well as between the land and its inhabitants. God deals with the land and its people. The land is the arena of his activity; it is responsive to him as it is to its inhabitants. It depends on him for its purity, as do the Israelites. Because of its association with Israel's holy God, its purity must be preserved, like the purity of the tabernacle and its precincts. The land then was the context for the observance of the prohibitions in this chapter. It was the place where the Israelites were required to do guard duty for the Lord by keeping out sexual impurity from it and from their community in it (18:30), just as the priests were required to do guard duty at the tabernacle to protect it from desecration and themselves from death (cf. 8:35).

Ritual Taboos

The legislation in this chapter consists entirely of prohibitions. They cover two topics: taboos against incest in an extended family (18:6–17) and taboos against other sexual practices and child sacrifice (18:18–23).

The first group of prohibitions in 18:6–17 sets the main boundaries for sexual activity in the extended family. These prohibitions have often been taken to specify which persons may not be married to each other.[12] It does, of course, entail this. But that is not its main concern. Its main concern lies in the avoidance of incest. Although the prohibitions define incest from a man's point of view, the heading in 18:6 gives the general rule that includes both men and women. No one shall have any form of sexual intercourse with a flesh-relative in an extended family. This rule is applied in the cases listed in 18:7–17. It is obviously meant to be followed in all the other cases.

The range of these taboos is best described by figure 20.

It is noteworthy that there is no mention of a man's daughter, even though she would obviously be covered by the general definition in 18:6. The reason for this omission is not obvious and has become a matter of some speculation. The most satisfactory solution is that it was so self-evident that it did not need to be mentioned.

The prohibition of incest had nothing to do, as is sometimes claimed, with the misappropriation of another man's property, since the laws in this chapter do not regard women as the property of men. Nor does it have to do with preserving the honor of the head of the family by protecting his women. Two other reasons are given for the prohibition of incest.

The first reason is that all the members of an extended family are the same flesh (18:6, 12, 13, 17). This does not just apply to the direct descendants of a couple, but to the couple itself and those linked by their sexual union. Sexual

[12] For example, Wenham, *Leviticus*, 253.

intercourse in marriage joins a husband and wife as closely as parents and children. They become one flesh (Gen 2:24). People do not just become one flesh with their spouse, they also become flesh-and-blood relatives with everybody who has been incorporated into their extended family by other marriages. Thus, a girl who married into a family became connected to all its members. The children and grandchildren that she brought with her from her former marriage also became a physical part of that family (18:17).

Figure 20

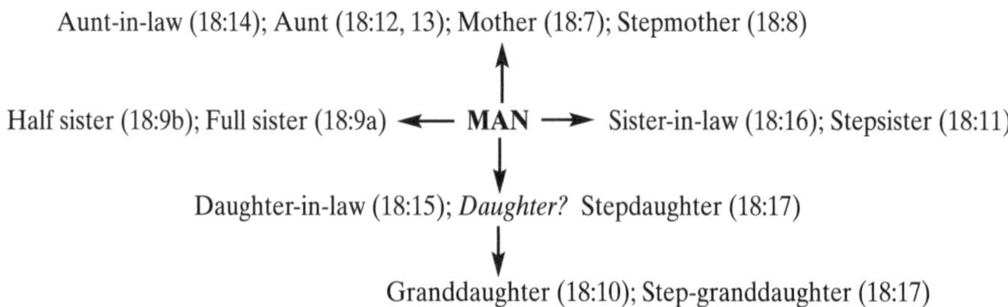

Thus her new family did not regard her as a daughter-in-law, but as a daughter of her husband's parents, a sister to her husband's brothers, and an aunt to her nephews by marriage.[13] If her husband died or if he divorced her, she still remained physically related to her in-laws and so continued to be subject to the prohibition of incest. All this presupposes the physical solidarity and integrity of an extended family. Incest is prohibited because it disrupts the foundational relationships in a family; it threatens to destroy it as a basic unit in the land of Israel and among the people of Israel. The survival of the family depends on the avoidance of incest.

The second reason for the taboo on incest has to do with the significance of nakedness. In an extended family the nakedness of its members is to be respected; it is to be neither flaunted nor violated. The sexual nakedness of another person in the family is associated with each person's own nakedness. It is, in some sense, shared by that person—the nakedness of the mother by the father (18:7); the nakedness of a granddaughter by her grandfather (18:10); the nakedness of an aunt by her husband (18:14); the nakedness of a sister-in-law by her husband (18:14); and the nakedness of a granddaughter by her grandmother (18:17).

This prohibition, most concretely, prohibits the visual exposure of the genitalia of any member of the family outside of each person's own marriage (20:17). But it goes beyond that. It has to do with the need for sexual modesty

[13] Wenham, *Leviticus*, 255.

and visual privacy in the family. It protects the personal sexual identity of each man and woman in the family as symbolized by their sexual organs and as confirmed by their engagement in sexual intercourse or avoidance of it. Incest violates the nakedness of a family, its ordered intimacy; it exposes the sexuality of its members and confuses its sexual ecology. It shames the family publicly. It takes what is most private and reserved for married couples and puts it on display in the public domain (see Ezek 16:37; 23:18). Incest therefore degrades those who engage in it, as well as the family to which they belong.

The second set of prohibitions, in Lev 18:18–23, is much more varied in content. Apart from the prohibition of child sacrifice, they all prohibit certain kinds of sexual activity—marriage to the sister of a woman as a rival wife, a replacement for her, while she is still alive (18:18); sexual intercourse with a woman during menstruation (18:19); adultery with the wife of a neighbor (18:20); homosexual intercourse (18:22); and sexual intercourse by a man or a woman with an animal (18:23).

Unexpected here is the reference to child sacrifice. As its link by catchword with 18:20 shows, it seems to have been included because it, like adultery, involves the abuse of "seed." In the OT the term "seed" refers both to semen and to offspring. It links the family with Abraham, identifies it as part of Israel, and represents its continuity. The seed of Abraham belongs to God. Through it God promises to give his blessing to that family. It is passed down through the men in that family from generation to generation. It must therefore not be given to another family by adultery or to Molech by child sacrifice. The "seed" of a family is contained and embodied in that family. It connects the members of that family to each other and to God. All the prohibitions in 18:18–23 deal with the improper use of "seed."[14]

The reasons for these prohibitions vary. Marriage to the sister of a woman uncovers the nakedness of the woman (18:18), just as intercourse with a woman during menstruation uncovers her nakedness (18:19). Men who engage in adultery and bestiality become unclean (18:20, 23). Homosexual activity is an abomination because it reverses what is normal and natural; it treats a man as if he were a woman (18:22). Bestiality is a perversion; it violates the boundaries between human beings and animals and so creates confusion in the natural realm (18:23). Sacrifice of children to Molech desecrates the holy name of God by taking one of his holy people and giving that child to a demon (18:21; cf. 17:7).

Ritual Theological Significance

This chapter most obviously seeks to regulate human sexuality by a series of sexual prohibitions. But it does more than that. It explains why these taboos are to be observed. From a modern point of view, it is remarkable that there is no discussion of the biological or economic reasons for these prohibitions.

---

[14] Miller, "Notes on Leviticus 18," 402.

There is no mention of the genetic effects of incest. There is also no suggestion that women and children are economic assets, part of a man's property. Instead, four other arguments are given.

The first is evident in the prohibitions in 18:7–17. They forbid incest for social reasons. They presuppose the existence of an extended family and its solidarity as a body of people created by kinship. Incest does not respect the sexual boundaries in this body; it disrupts the relationships that constitute and maintain it. It is therefore to be avoided for the sake of the family.

The second argument, used in the case of bestiality (18:23), is based on an understanding of the natural, created order. It presupposes that when God created the world, he established order in it. In this natural realm he separated the various species of animals from each other and from humans (Gen 1:20–28). People are therefore distinguished and separate from the animals. Sexual intercourse with an animal confuses the animal realm with the human realm and so disrupts the divinely established natural order. In a similar fashion, since homosexual intercourse violates the distinction between men and women in the human sphere, it is an abomination (18:22). The laws against incest belong to the same category. As is recognized by Hoffner,[15] God forbids those sexual acts that are against his created order, for bestiality violates the order of the species, homosexuality violates the order of the sexes, and incest violates the order of kinship.

The third level of argument is based on the human sense of ordered embodiment and its disruption by pollution. It rests on the identification of people with their bodies and the consequent distinction of bodily purity from bodily impurity. People feel uneasy and unwell if their bodies are somehow polluted. Thus, since contact with menstrual blood communicates impurity, a man is defiled by sexual intercourse with a woman during menstruation (18:19). If a man has sexual intercourse with his neighbor's wife, he thereby becomes unclean. Both he and his body are polluted (18:20). The integrity of his body has been violated. He has been tainted by physical contact with something alien to it.

The fourth level of argument is theological. This is the most important because it includes the other three categories and transcends them. This argument is developed by the incorporation of all the prohibitions into a divine speech with an introductory and concluding admonition from God. This gives the theological reasons for their observance and so interprets the prohibitions theologically. We discern three theological reasons.

The first and main theological reason for their observance is that God himself has created the Israelites as his people and identifies himself with them as their God. He gives them his name and commits himself to them by the repeated use of the formula for divine self-introduction (18:2, 4, 5, 6, 21, 30). His association with them and his commitment to them is the main reason for their observance of these taboos.

---

[15] Hoffner, "Incest, Sodomy and Bestiality in the Ancient Near East."

The second theological reason for their observance is that God has given these laws so that they may live and have life from him (18:5). Life here means much more than mere physical existence and the power to procreate. It includes a full life in family and community, peace and prosperity, health and happiness, vitality and longevity. The implication from this is that sexual disorder curtails and disrupts the flow of life from God to his people and through people to each other.

The third theological reason for the observance of these prohibitions is to prevent the pollution of God's land. The concluding admonition in 18:24–30 picks up the notion of personal defilement from 18:19–23 and interprets it theologically. The sexual defilement of individuals leads to the defilement of the nation (18:24, 30) and the land (18:25, 27, 28). This way of thinking assumes that people belong to the divinely created biological order. This biological order is dependent on the land as its habitat. Just as the land supports life in this order, that life must not pollute and so disorder the land.

What's more, since God lives with his people in the land, the land must be kept free from pollution, or else it will forfeit its life-giving connection with its divine owner. Thus God's holy name is desecrated by the sexual pollution of his land and his people, just as it was desecrated by the sacrifice of the lives of his people's children to Molech, the god of the underworld, the realm of impurity and death (18:21). All sexual aberrations were abominations to God, abhorrent to him and incompatible with his holiness (18:24, 26, 27, 29, 30). The Israelites therefore were commissioned by God to protect God's land, his physical environment, from contamination by sexual pollution (18:30). Should they fail to do so, God would make the land expel them as a nation from itself (18:28) and extirpate those who had polluted the land (18:29).

The references to the Egyptians and Canaanites (18:3, 24–30) and to God's punishment of them for their sins make it clear that the sexual ethics commanded by God in this chapter are relevant for all human societies. The main purpose of the chapter, however, is to reveal God's decrees about what he requires of Israel as his holy people—people who live with him in his land and interact with him at the tabernacle. He sketches out for them a theological ethics of sexuality, the ethics of holiness. The aim of these prohibitions is not to create a genetically or morally superior nation. Rather, they are meant to preserve the holiness of the Israelites as the holy "seed" and to enable them to share more fully in his holiness. By keeping this divine charge, they serve him as his holy, priestly people and enjoy a full life with him on his land.

Fulfillment by Christ

The laws in Leviticus 18 affirm the sexual integrity of the families of God's people, with the sexual union of husband and wife at its core. They protect the natural flow of life through the family from generation to generation. While these laws were given to OT Israel, they express God's will for all peoples in all times and places. God punished the Canaanites, for example, for indulging in the sexual sins prohibited here (Lev 18:3, 24–30; 20:23). The prohibitions against incest, adultery, homosexuality, and bestiality continue to apply to God's NT people and indeed to all people.

Christ and his apostles reaffirm those laws and also reapply them to fit the life of the church, deepening them in keeping with the new situation created by the death and resurrection of Christ (e.g., 1 Corinthians 5–6). Both Christ and his apostles presuppose that the new people of God will not live in the same way and follow the same sexual practices as their pagan neighbors. In fact, the attitude of Christians toward sexuality distinguishes them as the holy people of God (1 Cor 6:14–20). Since they have been joined to Christ through the Word and Sacraments, they are members of Christ's body. Their bodies are temples of the indwelling Holy Spirit now, and the same God who raised Jesus will raise their bodies on the Last Day. Sexual immorality does not just damage them physically, mentally, and socially, but it desecrates their holiness and defiles members that belong to Christ. "You were bought at a price; therefore glorify God with your body!" (1 Cor 6:20).

The NT broadens the scope of the promise of life in Lev 18:5: "You shall keep my ritual statutes and my ordinances; any human being who does them will have life by them." This promise originally pertained to God's people and their practice of sexuality in the old covenant as they lived in the orders of creation and redemption prior to the first advent of Christ. Jesus expounded this promise of life through God's Word in relation to all of God's commandments and to the inheritance of the righteous in the age to come.[16] When a teacher of the law asked Jesus, "What shall I do to inherit eternal life?" Jesus directed him to the Law or Torah: "What is written in the Law?" After the man quoted from Lev 19:18 and Deut 6:5, Jesus affirmed with this promise that he was to love God and his neighbor: "Do this, and you shall live" (Lk 10:25–28).

The reaction of the man, however, reveals the problem with all men. While this teaching is true, it is also impossible for any sinful person to display such perfect and continual love. The man therefore sought to justify himself for his failure to love every neighbor by asking Jesus to define and so limit what God meant by his neighbor. In the story of the Good Samaritan, Jesus extends the teaching about life in the Israelite family on its hereditary estate in the land of Israel to life of a disciple within the whole human family on earth (Lk 10:30–37). By the juxtaposition of the story about Mary and Martha in Lk 10:38–42, Luke explains how love for God is fulfilled by listening to the life-giving Word of Jesus.

In John's Gospel Jesus goes further than this and applies the promise of Lev 18:5 to himself and his Word. He has been sent to give life to all people on earth (Jn 3:16; 5:26; 10:10; 17:2). He therefore teaches and enacts the life-giving commandment of his heavenly Father (Jn 12:50). Those who seek eternal life should search the OT Scriptures with the knowledge that they testify

---

[16] Evans, "Do This and You Will Live."

to Jesus himself, who is the sole source of life (Jn 5:39–40). "If you believed Moses, you would believe me, for he wrote of me" (Jn 5:46). Jesus speaks "the words of eternal life," the life-giving words that bring the Holy Spirit to those who hear them (Jn 6:63, 68). This means that those who believe in him have eternal life already in this age (Jn 3:36; 5:24).

In his letters to the Galatians and the Romans, St. Paul corrects the misuse of Lev 18:5 by his opponents. They used it to argue that a person would be justified before God the Judge and so receive eternal life only if he kept the whole of God's law. In Gal 3:12 and Rom 10:5, Paul quotes the promise from Lev 18:5 in that context. He teaches that the observance of God's life-giving decrees is not the means by which a person is justified before God, but is the fruit of justification.

The teaching of Leviticus on sexual morality is therefore confirmed in the NT. Thus both Jesus (Mt 5:27–30; 19:18; Mk 10:19; Lk 18:20) and the apostles (Rom 13:9; James 2:11; cf. 1 Cor 6:9) repeat the prohibition of adultery in the Sixth Commandment. Jesus also widens the scope of adultery by regarding sexual lust as adultery (Mt 5:27–30). He teaches that a person is defiled by the secret acts of adultery and sexual immorality that are committed imaginatively within the human heart (Mt 15:19; Mk 7:22).

St. Paul forbids the incestuous liaison of a man with his stepmother and urges a congregation to excommunicate an incestuous man so that he would no longer defile the whole congregation (1 Cor 5:1–8). The apostle also teaches that homosexual and lesbian activity perverts the natural order of creation and incurs the wrath of God (Rom 1:26–27). The practice of sodomy is not only forbidden in God's law, but is also contrary to the healing doctrine that conforms to the Gospel (1 Tim 1:9–11). It disqualifies people from participation in the heavenly inheritance:

> Or don't you know that unrighteous people will not inherit the kingdom of God? Do not be deceived: neither the sexually immoral nor idolaters nor adulterers nor catamites nor sodomites … will inherit the kingdom of God. (1 Cor 6:9–10)[17]

Yet at the same time, the apostle makes it quite clear that those who had engaged in homosexual acts and other sexual sins could—like all other sinners—receive pardon, cleansing, and a new way of life in Christ:

> And such *were* some of you. But you were washed, but you were sanctified, but you were justified in the name of the Lord Jesus Christ and by the Spirit of our God. (1 Cor 6:11)

---

[17] "Catamites" and "sodomites" refer to subservient and dominant male homosexuals, respectively. One may see further the commentary on these verses by Lockwood, *1 Corinthians,* 196–203. Lockwood includes a survey and affirmation of OT and NT teaching in the excursus "Homosexuality" on pages 204–9.

(a) Mt 5:32; 15:19; 19:9; Acts 15:20, 29; 21:25; 1 Cor 5:1; 6:13, 18; 7:2; 2 Cor 12:21; Gal 5:19; Eph 5:3; Col 3:5; 1 Thess 4:3; Rev 2:21; 9:21

More generally, the NT classifies all the sexual sins mentioned in Lev 18:6–23 as πορνεία, "fornication" or "sexual immorality."[a] Fornication is a cause of impurity (2 Cor 12:21; Gal 5:19; Eph 5:3; Col 3:5). Just as the practice of sexual immorality polluted the land and prompted God to expel the Canaanites before the Israelites and God warned that the Israelites must not practice the same sins or they would be disqualified from the possession of the inheritance in that land, so involvement in fornication also disqualifies the saints from participation in their heavenly inheritance (1 Cor 6:9–10; Eph 5:5; cf. Rev 21:8; 22:15).

The punishments that God inflicted on unfaithful Israel were types and examples for Christians not to be seduced into fornication (1 Cor 10:5–13). God's wrath and judgment come on those Christians who persist in sexual immorality (Eph 5:5–6; Heb 13:4). The members of the church are therefore required to dissociate themselves from the impenitent sinners and their misbehavior (1 Cor 5:9–13; Eph 5:7).

All this is summed up succinctly in Heb 13:4: "Marriage is honorable in all respects and the marriage bed undefiled." Those who confess Christ are to make sure that the estate of marriage is honored in their midst. Sexual intercourse between a married husband and wife is a clean act approved by God. If they are Christians both they and their marriage are holy. Therefore they are forbidden from defiling the marriage bed in any way, either by sexual immorality or by adultery. God's will for his holy people is to keep them and their marriages clean and holy. Since he has established and sanctified marriage, he will also defend it. "The sexually immoral and adulterers God will judge" (Heb 13:4).

Oh, that the Lord would guide my ways
To keep his statutes still!
Oh, that my God would grant me grace
To know and do his will!

Assist my soul, too apt to stray,
A stricter watch to keep;
If ever I forget your way,
Restore your wand'ring sheep.

Make me to walk in your commands,
A most delightful road;
Nor let my head or heart or hands
Offend against my God.[18]

---

[18] From "Oh, That the Lord Would Guide My Ways" by Isaac Watts (*LW* 392:1, 3, 4).

Leviticus 19:1–37

The Holiness of the Congregation

Translation

19 1The Lord spoke to Moses: 2"Speak to the whole congregation of the Israelites and say to them: You will be holy, because I, the Lord your God, am holy.

3"Each of you shall fear his mother and his father, and you shall keep my Sabbaths; I am the Lord your God.

4"You shall not turn to godlings, nor shall you make gods of cast metal for yourselves; I am the Lord your God.

5"When you offer a sacrifice of peace offerings to the Lord, you shall offer it for your acceptance. 6It shall be eaten on the day that you offer it or on the next day, but whatever is left over on the third day shall be burned in fire. 7If it is eaten at all on the third day, it is rotten meat; it is not acceptable. 8Whoever eats it shall bear his iniquity, because he has desecrated what is holy to the Lord; any such person will be cut off from his kinsfolk.

9"And when you reap the harvest of your land, you shall not finish reaping to the edge of the field, nor shall you gather up the gleanings of your harvest. 10You shall not strip your vineyard, nor shall you pick up the fallen grapes from your vineyard, but you shall leave them for the poor and the alien; I am the Lord your God.

11"You shall not steal; and you shall not dissemble nor lie, each of you against his compatriot; 12and you shall not swear falsely by my name so that you do not desecrate the name of your God; I am the Lord.

13"You shall not exploit your neighbor, nor shall you commit robbery. You shall not keep the wages of a day laborer overnight with yourself until morning. 14You shall not curse a deaf person, nor shall you put an obstacle in front of a blind person, but you must fear your God; I am the Lord.

15"You shall not act unjustly in judgment; you shall not show favoritism to a poor person, nor shall you show [undue] honor to a great person; you shall judge your compatriot in righteousness. 16You shall not go about as a slanderer among your kinsfolk; you shall not stand against the blood of your neighbor; I am the Lord.

17"You shall not hate your brother in your heart; you must openly rebuke your compatriot so that you do not bear sin because of him. 18You shall not take revenge, nor shall you bear a grudge against the members of your people, but you must love your neighbor as yourself; I am the Lord.

19"You must keep my ritual statutes. You shall not cause two kinds of livestock to mate; you shall not sow your field with two kinds of seed; you shall not bring up upon yourself clothing [made] with two kinds of yarn.

20"If a man lies with a woman [and has] an emission of semen and she is a slave woman already assigned to another man, even though she has not yet been

fully ransomed or freedom has not been given to her, an inquest shall be held. They shall not be put to death, because she has not been freed. [21]But he must bring his reparation offering to the Lord to the entrance to the tent of meeting—a ram for reparation. [22]The priest shall perform atonement on his behalf before the Lord with the ram for the reparation offering for his sin that he has committed, so that he may be forgiven from his sin that he has committed.

[23]"And when you enter the land and plant any kind of fruit tree, you shall treat its foreskin [bud] with its fruit as if it were a foreskin; for three years you shall regard it as uncircumcised; it shall not be eaten. [24]In the fourth year, all its fruit shall be a holy offering of rejoicing to the Lord. [25]You may eat its fruit in the fifth year, so that its yield may be increased for you; I am the Lord your God.

[26]"You shall not eat [meat] over its blood; you shall not practice augury, nor shall you perform divination. [27]You shall not round off the side [hair] of your heads, nor shall you spoil the edge of your beard; [28]and you shall not make a gash in your flesh for the dead, nor shall you put tattoos on yourselves; I am the Lord your God.

[29]"You shall not desecrate your daughter by making her a prostitute, so that the land will not be prostituted and the land be filled with depravity. [30]You must keep my Sabbaths, and you must fear my sanctuary; I am the Lord.

[31]"You shall not turn to ghosts, nor shall you seek out spirits, becoming unclean by them; I am the Lord your God.

[32]"You shall rise in the presence of a gray-haired person and show honor before an elder, so that you fear your God; I am the Lord.

[33]"When an alien resides with you in your land, you shall not oppress him. [34]The alien that resides with you shall be regarded by you as a native from among you; you shall love him as yourself, for you were aliens in the land of Egypt; I am the Lord your God.

[35]"You shall not act unjustly in a legal transaction, whether by measure of weight or of volume. [36]Instead you must use a just scale, just weights, a just ephah, and a just hin. I am the Lord your God who brought you out of the land of Egypt, [37]so you should keep all my ritual statutes and my ordinances and enact them; I am the Lord.

Textual Notes

19:2 דַּבֵּ֞ר אֶל־כָּל־עֲדַ֧ת בְּנֵֽי־יִשְׂרָאֵ֛ל—See the textual notes on 4:13. This is the only occasion where God commissions Moses to speak directly to the congregation.

קְדֹשִׁ֣ים תִּהְי֑וּ—See 11:44, 45; 20:26. This use of the imperfect form in this clause ("You will be holy") could also be construed as a command, "You shall be holy," or even as a statement of fact, "You are holy."

כִּ֣י קָד֔וֹשׁ אֲנִ֖י יְהוָ֥ה אֱלֹהֵיכֶֽם׃—See the textual notes on 11:44.

19:3 אִמּ֤וֹ וְאָבִיו֙—As in 21:2, the placement of the mother before the father is unusual and most emphatic in a patrilineal society.

תִּירָ֔אוּ—The verb יָרֵא means "to fear" and here the parents are the direct object (*HALOT,* s.v. ירא I, Qal, 2 d). In this context it has the nuance of showing reverence and honor. The use of the same verb with God (19:14, 32) and his sanctuary (19:30) as the objects connects reverence of parents with reverence for God and his sanctuary. Likewise, יָרֵא in 25:17, 36, 43; 26:2 (its only other occurrences in Leviticus outside chapter 19) refers to fearing God or his sanctuary. Compare Ex 20:12 and Deut 5:16, which use the Piel of כָּבֵד, "to honor," with the father and mother (in that order) as the direct objects.

שַׁבְּתֹתַי—See also 19:30 and 26:2. The plural is used because this refers to the weekly Sabbaths (e.g., 23:3), the festive Sabbaths (e.g., 16:31), and the Sabbatical Years (e.g., 25:4).

19:4 אַל־תִּפְנוּ אֶל־הָאֱלִילִים—See 19:31; 20:6. "Turning" to a god involves approaching another deity for help or blessing.[1]

הָאֱלִילִים—This noun, translated as "godlings," is a diminutive, derogatory term for idols as puny, weak deities (Lev 26:1; 1 Chr 16:26; Pss 96:5; 97:7; Is 2:8, 18, 20; 10:10, 11; 19:1, 3; 31:7; Ezek 30:13; Hab 2:18).

מַסֵּכָה—See Ex 34:17; cf. Ex 20:23.

19:5 The case in Lev 19:5–8 summarizes the material given to the priests in 7:16–18 with a number of significant differences. First, the positive part of the law is addressed directly to the Israelites who present the offering and eat the holy meat from it (19:5–6). Second, this command is inserted after the protasis in 19:5b: "you shall offer it for your acceptance." This stands in contrast to the warning about the rejection of the meat eaten on the third day in 19:7b. Lastly and most significantly, a motive clause about the reason for the penalty for desecration and a new clause about the penalty's exact nature are added in 19:8b.

תִּזְבָּחֻהוּ—See 19:5b, 6. Literally this verb means "to sacrifice."

שְׁלָמִים לַיהוָה—See 3:1–17; 7:11–18, 29–36; 22:21–26.

לִרְצֹנְכֶם—See the textual notes on 1:3.

19:7 פִּגּוּל—See the textual notes on 7:18.

19:8 עֲוֹנוֹ יִשָּׂא—See the textual notes on 5:1. Because this clause refers to one eater, we render the preceding participle (אֹכְלָיו) as singular ("whoever eats") even though the participle is plural ("those who eat it").

קֹדֶשׁ יְהוָה—See 19:24 and the textual notes on 4:6.

חִלֵּל—See the textual note on this verb in 18:21. It recurs in 19:12, 29.

וְנִכְרְתָה הַנֶּפֶשׁ הַהִוא מֵעַמֶּיהָ׃—See the textual notes on 7:20.

19:9–10 See Milgrom for an analysis of the symmetrical arrangement of 19:9–10.[2] The law on gleanings is repeated in 23:22 with the omission of the reference to the vineyards. See also the parallel in legislation in Deut 24:19–22.

19:9 פְּאַת—This is the construct form of פֵּאָה, "**side, edge** of a field" (*HALOT,* 1 a). According to the rabbis, this refers to the last furrow of a field or at least one-sixteenth of the field.[3] The term will recur in 19:27 in reference to the hair on the side of the head.

---

1 Milgrom, *Leviticus 17–22*, 1613.

2 Milgrom, *Leviticus 17–22*, 1624.

3 Milgrom, *Leviticus 17–22*, 1625–26.

19:10 וְכַרְמְךָ֙ לֹ֣א תְעוֹלֵ֔ל—This could also be translated "You shall not go over your vineyard a second time." The noun עֹלֵלוֹת in Is 24:13 and Obad 5 is related to the verb here and shows that the clause here refers to leftover grapes.

וּפֶ֥רֶט—This noun, a collective meaning "grapes" (*HALOT*), occurs in the OT only here.

לֶֽעָנִ֤י וְלַגֵּר֙—See the textual notes on 16:29. See also 19:33, 34.

תַּעֲזֹ֣ב אֹתָ֔ם—The pronoun refers to the four items mentioned in 19:9–10: the edge of the field; the fallen stalks; the leftover grapes; and the fallen grapes.

19:11 תִּגְנֹ֑בוּ—This is the term for furtive theft rather than open robbery.

וְלֹא־תְכַחֲשׁ֥וּ וְלֹֽא־תְשַׁקְּר֖וּ—While כחשׁ refers to the denial of truth, שֶׁקֶר is used for the assertion of something false.[4]

בַּעֲמִיתֽוֹ׃—See the textual notes on 5:21 (ET 6:2). This term also occurs in 18:20; 19:15, 17; 24:19; 25:14, 15, 17.

19:12 שֵׁ֥ם אֱלֹהֶ֖יךָ—See the textual notes on 18:21.

19:13 לֹא־תַעֲשֹׁ֥ק—See the textual notes on 5:21 (ET 6:2).

רֵֽעֲךָ֖—The term רֵעַ, "neighbor," is normally used for a fellow Israelite. But since hired workers were often aliens (Deut 24:14), here it probably refers to any person living in Israel. The same more inclusive use of the term is also found in Gen 38:12, 20; Ex 11:2. It recurs in Lev 19:16, 18; 20:10.

תָלִ֞ין—This could be the third feminine singular Qal imperfect of לִין, in which case the subject is the feminine noun פְּעֻלָּה: "the wages … shall not remain overnight with you." But since the preceding verbs are second person, more likely this is the Hiphil second masculine singular imperfect: "you shall not cause the wages … to remain overnight with you."

שָׂכִ֛יר—See 22:10; 25:6, 40, 50, 53.

עַד־בֹּֽקֶר׃—See Deut 24:14–15.

19:14 לֹא־תְקַלֵּ֣ל חֵרֵ֔שׁ—The verb קִלֵּל means to "curse" someone verbally. The prohibition here would also proscribe ridicule, disparagement, and insults. See 20:9; 24:11, 14, 15, 23. A deaf person (חֵרֵשׁ) could neither hear what was said nor who had said it.

וְלִפְנֵ֣י עִוֵּ֔ר לֹ֥א תִתֵּ֖ן מִכְשֹׁ֑ל—A blind person could neither see the obstacle nor discover who had made him stumble. See the similar case in Deut 27:18.

וְיָרֵ֥אתָ מֵּאֱלֹהֶ֖יךָ—The commandment to fear God implies that God will avenge those who take advantage of the deaf and the blind. See the textual note on יָרֵא in 19:3.

19:15 The four clauses in this verse are in chiastic order. The first and fourth phrases have מִשְׁפָּט and תִּשְׁפֹּט, respectively. The second and third phrases have פְּנֵי.

לֹא־תַעֲשׂ֥וּ עָ֙וֶל֙ בַּמִּשְׁפָּ֔ט—See the identical sentence in 19:35. Here מִשְׁפָּט refers to the local court of law.

לֹא־תִשָּׂ֣א פְנֵי־דָ֔ל—Literally this command is "You shall not lift up the face of a poor person." See Gen 19:21; 32:20; 1 Sam 25:35; Job 32:21; 34:19; Lam 4:16. The

---

[4] Milgrom, *Leviticus 17–22*, 1631.

idiom נָשָׂא פָּנִים in this context means "to show favoritism, to favor unfairly, to be biased toward" a person (cf. *HALOT,* s.v. נשׂא, Qal, 6 c). Regarding דַּל, see Ex 23:3.

וְלֹא תֶהְדַּר—See Lev 19:32; Lam 5:12. Since Lev 19:32 uses the same verb to command showing proper honor (to an elder), here the negated verb must refer to showing undue honor or favoritism.

גָדוֹל—Normally "great" is used in contrast to "small" (Deut 1:17), but here, as Magonet observes, גָּדוֹל, "great" (instead of עָשִׁיר, "rich"), is used as the antonym to דַּל, "poor," for reasons of assonance.[5]

19:16 רָכִיל—See Prov 11:13; 20:19; Jer 6:28; 9:3 (ET 9:4).

בְּעַמֶּיךָ—This is the plural of עַם meaning "**clan,** kin" (*HALOT,* s.v. עַם, B). The plural can be rendered as "kinsfolk."

לֹא תַעֲמֹד עַל־דַּם רֵעֶךָ—Four interpretations have been proposed for this commandment, which literally is "You shall not stand beside/over/against the blood of your neighbor":

- It could refer to standing by idly or silently when a person was threatened with death.
- It could refer to a person's survival or promotion to a position of power at the expense of the life of another.
- It may refer to arising to carry out a physical or verbal attack that threatened the life of the neighbor.
- Most likely it refers to indifference to the fatal consequences of slander that could lead to the neighbor's conviction in a court of law.

19:17 לֹא־תִשְׂנָא אֶת־אָחִיךָ בִּלְבָבֶךָ—The "brother" is a fellow Israelite.

הוֹכֵחַ תּוֹכִיחַ—The infinite absolute before the verb makes this a very emphatic commandment in contrast to the previous prohibition. While הוֹכִיחַ can be used for laying charges against another person in a court of law, it is used here for a personal rebuke of an offender that seeks to correct him and to get him to rectify the offense.

וְלֹא־תִשָּׂא עָלָיו חֵטְא׃—See 22:9; Num 18:32. The offender ("you" is singular) would "bear sin" in one of three ways: by failing to warn the compatriot of his offense, thereby becoming an accomplice to his offense; by not giving him a chance to make up for the offense privately; or else, most likely, by harboring hatred and ill will in the heart against the offending compatriot.

19:18 לֹא־תִקֹּם—The verb נָקַם is used for extra-judicial (unauthorized, not explicitly legal) acts of retribution.

בְּנֵי עַמֶּךָ—This is literally "the sons of your people." See 20:17.

וְאָהַבְתָּ לְרֵעֲךָ כָּמוֹךָ—The verb אָהַב refers to a person's attitude of love and also to his loving activity as well. The preposition לְ is used with the verb אָהַב again only in 19:34 and 2 Chr 19:2.

There has been some debate on the interpretation of כָּמוֹךָ.[6] Three interpretations have been proposed. First, this term has been understood reflexively to indicate the

---

5 Magonet, "The Structure and Meaning of Leviticus 19," 158.

6 Mathys, *Liebe deinen Nächsten wie dich Selbst*, 6–9; Milgrom, *Leviticus 17–22*, 1655–56.

motivation for loving the neighbor. Thus it asserts the priority of self-care as the basis for love of the neighbor. The sense would be this: "If you love yourself, you will be able to love your neighbor as yourself."[7]

Second, it has been understood adjectivally as modifying the noun "neighbor" and as an assertion of his similarity to "you" (singular in Hebrew) either as a fellow Israelite or as a fellow human being created in God's image. The sense would then be "Love your neighbor as a person like yourself."[8] This interpretation, however, does not fit the context here and in 19:34, for כָּמוֹךָ only makes good sense if it describes the equal manner in which one loves one's neighbor.

Third and most likely, the traditional interpretation understands this word adverbially as modifying the verb "love." It therefore prescribes the manner and measure of that love. The Israelite should love his neighbor in the same way—to the same degree and extent—that he loves himself. This view presupposes that each person naturally (and selfishly) loves himself. The command is for each person to display at least as much love for his neighbor as he already has for himself.

19:19 חֻקֹּתַי—See the textual note on this term in 3:17. See also its use in 18:4, 5, 26; 19:37; 20:8, 22.

בְּהֶמְתְּךָ לֹא־תַרְבִּיעַ כִּלְאַיִם—The dual noun כִּלְאַיִם means "of two kinds" (*HALOT*, 1). A slightly different version of the prohibition of mixtures is found in Deut 22:9–11. Deut 22:10 interprets this as a reference to ploughing with the ox and ass rather than to sexual copulation. While the first part of Lev 19:19 had a plural verb, this clause reverts to the singular. (Most of 19:13–18 was phrased with singular Hebrew forms translated as "you," but most of 19:2–5, 9, 11, 12 was plural.)

שָׂדְךָ לֹא־תִזְרַע כִּלְאָיִם—The LXX, in harmony with Deut 22:9, interprets this as growing another crop in a vineyard.

וּבֶגֶד כִּלְאַיִם שַׁעַטְנֵז לֹא יַעֲלֶה עָלֶיךָ׃—Deut 22:11 interprets this as weaving wool and linen together in one cloth. The meaning of שַׁעַטְנֵז is uncertain; see *HALOT*. It may mean false or adulterated fabric.

19:20 וְאִישׁ כִּי־יִשְׁכַּב אֶת־אִשָּׁה שִׁכְבַת־זֶרַע—Literally this means "If a man lies with a woman with an emission of semen." See Lev 15:16–18, 32. Cf. Lev 22:4; Num 5:13.

נֶחֱרֶפֶת—See Milgrom for a discussion on the etymology of this unusual term, which probably means that the woman has been assigned in advance to a man.[9] Even though negotiations may have taken place to secure her as a wife, she had not yet been ransomed from slavery and the dowry had not yet been paid to formalize the betrothal.

וְהָפְדֵּה לֹא נִפְדָּתָה—See Ex 21:8.

בִּקֹּרֶת—Wenham and Levine adopt Speiser's proposal that the unique term בִּקֹּרֶת is related to an Akkadian word for indemnity.[10] Milgrom, however, has shown that

---

[7] Hartley, *Leviticus*, 318.

[8] Muraoka, "A Syntactic Problem in Lev. XIX 18b."

[9] Milgrom, *Leviticus 17–22*, 1666–67.

[10] Wenham, *Leviticus*, 270–71; Levine, *Leviticus*, 130; Speiser, "Leviticus and the Critics," 128–31.

there is no secure basis for that derivation.[11] It is related to the Piel verb בִּקֵּר (13:36; 27:33) and is, most likely, the term for a formal inquest or inquiry.

לֹא יוּמְתוּ—See the textual notes on 20:2.

19:21 וְהֵבִיא—See the textual notes on 2:2.

אֲשָׁמוֹ—This could also be translated "his compensation" or "his penalty." See the textual notes on 5:6.

אֶל־פֶּתַח אֹהֶל מוֹעֵד—See the textual notes on 1:3.

אָשָׁם׃—See 5:14–19 and the textual notes on 5:15.

19:22 וְכִפֶּר עָלָיו—See the textual notes on 1:4.

וְנִסְלַח לוֹ מֵחַטָּאתוֹ—See the textual notes on 4:20. This is the only place where the preposition מִן is used with נִסְלַח.

19:23 וְכִי־תָבֹאוּ אֶל־הָאָרֶץ—The LXX adds "which the Lord your God will give to you."

עֵץ מַאֲכָל—This is literally "a tree of food" (Deut 20:20; Neh 9:25; Ezek 47:12).

עָרְלָתוֹ—The bud for the fruit of the tree was regarded as the "foreskin" of the tree. It was therefore removed to prevent the production of fruit by the tree.

עֲרֵלִים—The adjective עָרֵל, "uncircumcised," is also used metaphorically for uninitiated, inept, and unbelieving hearts (26:41; Ezek 44:7, 9), lips (Ex 6:12, 30), and ears (Jer 6:10).

19:24 קֹדֶשׁ הִלּוּלִים—Regarding קֹדֶשׁ, see the textual notes on 4:6. The only other OT occurrence of הִלּוּלִים is in Judg 9:27, where it means "festival exultation" (*HALOT*). Here the combination of these two terms probably means an "offering of praise" (*HALOT,* s.v. הִלּוּלִים) or "a holy offering of rejoicing."

19:26 לֹא תֹאכְלוּ עַל־הַדָּם—This idiom is also found in 1 Sam 14:33, 34, and in Ezek 33:25. (The LXX reads "on the mountains" instead of "upon the blood.") Three interpretations have been advanced for this obscure expression.

First, it could refer to the eating of meat "with" blood in it. Therefore it would be a synonym for "eating blood" (Gen 9:4; Lev 17:10, 12, 14; Deut 12:16, 23, 24). This is most unlikely because in those passages where אָכַל עַל means "to eat with" (Ex 12:8; Num 9:11), the other thing that is eaten is a direct object (and is not introduced by the preposition עַל, which precedes "blood" here).[12]

Second, it could refer to eating meat "near" the blood, that is, before the blood had been offered to God on the altar. This may fit the incident in 1 Samuel 14, but makes no sense in this context in Leviticus, nor does it explain why the consumption of blood is connected with idolatry in Ezek 33:25.

Third and most likely, the prohibition is a command not to engage in the pagan practice of eating the meat of a sacrificed animal "over the blood" from the sacrifice. The practice was to slaughter an animal over a pit, drain its blood into that pit to attract the ancestral spirits from the underworld, and eat the meat as a meal around the pit and hence "over" the blood that was down in the pit. This practice was supposed

[11] Milgrom, *Leviticus 17–22*, 1668.

[12] Hartley, *Leviticus*, 320–21.

to summon the spirits for the purpose of divination.[13] The rest of 19:26 clearly refers to occult practices.

לֹא תְנַחֲשׁוּ—The verb נָחַשׁ occurs only in the Piel and means "to **seek** and **give omens, foretell**" (*HALOT*). Augury involves the reading of omens, such as the liver of a sacrificial animal or the position of the stars and constellations to foretell the future.[14] See נָחַשׁ in Gen 30:27; 44:5; Deut 18:10; 1 Ki 20:33; 2 Ki 17:17; 21:6.

וְלֹא תְעוֹנֵנוּ׃—The verb עָנַן (עוֹנֵן is the Po'el) is closely related to נָחַשׁ and is probably a technical term for some form of divination (see BDB, s.v. עָנַן II). *HALOT* defines the Po'el as "to interpret signs." Alternatively, it could refer to necromancy, the conjuring up of spirits of the dead.[15] The Po'el occurs in Deut 18:10, 14; 2 Ki 21:6; 2 Chr 33:6; Is 2:6; 57:3; Jer 27:9; Micah 5:11 (ET 5:12).

19:27 לֹא תַקִּפוּ פְּאַת רֹאשְׁכֶם—Here פֵּאָה in construct with רֹאשׁ refers to the "side of the head … meaning the hairline" (*HALOT,* 1 b i). While lay Israelites were forbidden to remove their side growth and shave their foreheads, the priests were not allowed to shave any part of their heads (Lev 21:5; Ezek 44:20). Heads were often shaved in the rites for mourning in the ancient world (Deut 14:1; Jer 16:6).

וְלֹא תַשְׁחִית אֵת פְּאַת זְקָנֶךָ׃—While the lay Israelites were forbidden to spoil their beards by tearing hair out from them in grief, the priests were not even allowed to shave the edges of their beards (Lev 21:5).

19:28 וְשֶׂרֶט לָנֶפֶשׁ לֹא תִתְּנוּ בִּבְשַׂרְכֶם—See 21:5; Deut 14:1. The practice of self-mutilation was common in mourning rites (Jer 16:6; 41:5; 47:5; 48:37). While נֶפֶשׁ usually denotes "a living being," "a live person," here it is used for a person who has died, as in various other verses (Lev 21:1; 22:4; Num 5:2; 6:11; 9:6, 7, 10; 19:11; Hag 2:13). It functions as an abbreviation for נֶפֶשׁ מֵת, "a dead person" (Lev 21:11; Num 6:6; cf. Num 19:13).

וּכְתֹבֶת קַעֲקַע לֹא תִתְּנוּ בָּכֶם—The noun כְּתֹבֶת refers to a mark or inscription as a tattoo. קַעֲקַע denotes a "tattoo" (*HALOT*), though the derivation and precise sense of the word is unknown. Both words occur in the OT only here. It is not certain whether the prohibition of tattoos refers to mourning rites, to the use of tattoos to mark slaves, or to inscribing oneself with the name of a god.[16]

19:29 אַל־תְּחַלֵּל אֶת־בִּתְּךָ לְהַזְנוֹתָהּ—Milgrom maintains that חִלֵּל is used for degradation figuratively here and in 21:9.[17] But Milgrom assumes that the Israelites were not actually holy but rather were merely called to attempt to achieve holiness. It is best to affirm the holiness of the Israelites according to God's pronouncement (as in, e.g., 19:2) and to take the term "profane" literally here and elsewhere in Leviticus. The Israelites were holy but would profane themselves by the practices described here.

---

13 Füglister, "Sühne durch Blut," 151–52; Grintz, "Do Not Eat over the Blood"; Hartley, *Leviticus*, 320; Milgrom, *Leviticus 17–22*, 1490–93, 1685–86.

14 Milgrom, *Leviticus 17–22*, 1686–88.

15 Holladay, *A Concise Hebrew and Aramaic Lexicon of the Old Testament*, 278.

16 Milgrom, *Leviticus 17–22*, 1694–95.

17 Milgrom, *Leviticus 17–22*, 1696–97.

Traditionally the verb זָנָה has been interpreted as referring specifically to prostitution: "Do not prostitute thy daughter, to cause her to be a whore" (KJV). However, *HALOT* (1) defines the Qal of זָנָה more generally as "to commit fornication." The Hiphil here (לְהַזְנוֹתָהּ is the Hiphil infinitive construct) may mean "to encourage to commit fornication" (*HALOT,* Hiphil, 1). However, the commandment may be aimed more specifically at the prevention of making one's daughter into a prostitute for the sake of financial gain.

וְלֹא־תִזְנֶה הָאָרֶץ—See Hos 1:2.

וּמָלְאָה הָאָרֶץ זִמָּה׃—See Lev 18:17; 20:14.

19:30 אֶת־שַׁבְּתֹתַי תִּשְׁמֹרוּ—This positive injunction stands in contrast to the preceding prohibitions. See 19:3; 26:2.

וּמִקְדָּשִׁי תִּירָאוּ—Fearing God's sanctuary is tantamount to fearing God himself, since God dwells there in the midst of his people. Similar to 19:30 is 26:2. See the textual note on יָרֵא in 19:3. It will recur in 19:32. (The LXX translates מִקְדָּשִׁי as "holy things.")

19:31 אַל־תִּפְנוּ אֶל־הָאֹבֹת וְאֶל־הַיִּדְּעֹנִים אַל־תְּבַקְשׁוּ—The first part of this verse (אַל־תִּפְנוּ אֶל־) is the same as the prohibition in 19:4, "You shall not turn to" pagan gods. See also 20:6, 27.

While the exact sense of the two terms אוֹב and יִדְּעֹנִי is uncertain, most authorities agree that they refer to the spirits of the dead.[18] The term אוֹב probably means "spirit of the dead" (*HALOT,* s.v. אוֹב II) and is used for the spirit of an ancestor (Lev 19:31; 20:6; Is 29:4), the person who conjures up such spirits (Lev 20:27; Is 8:19; 19:3), and any object used in conjuring them (1 Sam 28:3, 7; 2 Ki 21:6; 23:24). Throughout the OT, the term אוֹב is almost always used together with יִדְּעֹנִי (Lev 20:6, 27; Deut 18:11; 1 Sam 28:3, 9; 2 Ki 21:6; 23:24; 2 Chr 33:6; Is 8:19; 19:3).

יִדְּעֹנִי is derived from the verb יָדַע, "to know," and so KJV rendered it as "familiar spirit." יִדְּעֹנִי is used for a person skilled in spiritism (Lev 20:6; 1 Sam 28:3, 9), as well as any spirit conjured by him (Lev 20:27). This may refer to some other spirit than that of an ancestor. *HALOT* believes that in Lev 20:27 יִדְּעֹנִי means "spirit of divination" (*HALOT,* 1), that is, a spirit that enters or dwells in a person and enables him to engage in occult practices, and that in Lev 19:31 and other OT passages יִדְּעֹנִי refers to a person "in whom that spirit dwells" (*HALOT,* 2).

לְטָמְאָה בָהֶם—See the textual notes on 5:2.

19:32 מִפְּנֵי שֵׂיבָה תָּקוּם—Rising was a gesture of respect for old people, which treated them as kings or royal officials (Job 29:7–10). שֵׂיבָה is literally "gray-headedness."

וְהָדַרְתָּ—See Lev 19:15.

פְּנֵי זָקֵן—See 4:15; 9:1. The term זָקֵן is used both for an "elderly person" and a "leader" in a tribal society.

---

18 Hoffner, "Incest, Sodomy and Bestiality in the Ancient Near East"; Lust, "On Wizards and Prophets"; Milgrom, *Leviticus 17–22*, 1768–72; Rouillard and Tropper, "Vom kanaanäischen Ahnenkult zur Zauberei"; Spronk, *Beatific Afterlife in Ancient Israel and in the Ancient Near East.*

וְיָרֵאתָ מֵּאֱלֹהֶיךָ—As with 19:14, this clause gives the reason for reverent fear and respect for the elderly.

19:33 גֵּר—See the textual notes on 16:29.

לֹא תוֹנוּ אֹתוֹ׃—See 25:14, 17, where the Hiphil of יָנָה (הוֹנָה) is used for cheating an alien in business transactions. The same prohibition is found in Ex 22:20 (ET 22:21). See Deut 23:17 (ET 23:16) for the application of this law to an escaped slave.

19:34 כְּאֶזְרָח—See the textual notes on Lev 16:29.

וְאָהַבְתָּ לוֹ כָּמוֹךָ—See 19:18.

כִּי־גֵרִים הֱיִיתֶם בְּאֶרֶץ מִצְרָיִם—See Ex 22:20 (ET 22:21); 23:9; Deut 10:19; 23:8 (ET 23:7).

19:35 The same law reappears in reworded form in Deut 25:13–16 and Ezek 45:10–11.

בַּמִּשְׁפָּט—Whereas מִשְׁפָּט meant a court of law in Lev 19:15, it is used here for legal transactions and business dealings.

בַּמִּדָּה בַּמִּשְׁקָל וּבַמְּשׂוּרָה׃—מִדָּה is the general term for all measures, while מִשְׁקָל and מְשׂוּרָה are specific terms for two different kinds of measures.[19]

19:36 מֹאזְנֵי צֶדֶק—The dual noun מֹאזְנַיִם is the name for a crossbar with two cups, forming a scale or balance. It was either held in the hand or placed on a stand. A stone weight was placed in one cup and the goods to be weighed in the other.

אַבְנֵי־צֶדֶק—Weights were normally made of stone. "Stones of righteousness" are stones with accurate, fair weights so that the purchaser would not be cheated. If a lighter stone were placed in the balance, the purchaser would receive fewer (less, lighter) goods.

אֵיפַת צֶדֶק—See 5:11; 6:13 (ET 6:20). The ephah was the measure used for grain. It amounted to about twenty-three liters.

וְהִין צֶדֶק—A hin was the measure of liquids such as olive oil (Ex 29:40) and wine (Lev 23:13). It amounted to about four liters.

אֲשֶׁר־הוֹצֵאתִי אֶתְכֶם מֵאֶרֶץ מִצְרָיִם׃—See 11:45; 22:44; 25:38; 26:13; and the textual notes on 11:45. As Daube has shown, הוֹצִיא מִן is a technical legal term for the release of slaves or property.[20] In the introduction to the Decalogue in Ex 20:2, God used this formula for the emancipation of the Israelites to lay claim on his people and their allegiance to him.

19:37 וּשְׁמַרְתֶּם אֶת־כָּל־חֻקֹּתַי וְאֶת־כָּל־מִשְׁפָּטַי—See 18:5, 26. This clause introduced with *waw* is a result clause. God redeemed his people from Egypt, and as a result of his salvation they are to keep his statutes and ordinances. The keeping of his commands is not what saved them, nor were their works what elicited his salvation. Rather, God takes the initiative and saves his people. Their new and renewed lives are the result of his action.

וַעֲשִׂיתֶם אֹתָם—See 20:22.

---

19 Milgrom, *Leviticus 17–22*, 1708–9.

20 Daube, *The Exodus Pattern in the Bible*, 31–34.

אֲנִי יְהוָה׃—The formula of divine self-introduction concludes the chapter, as also in 18:30; 22:33; 25:55. Regarding the formula, see the textual notes on 11:44–45 and the commentary below.

Commentary

Context and Structure

At first sight the modern reader might think that the material in this chapter has been assembled in a rather haphazard fashion. Ritual laws are interspersed with moral laws, without any apparent rhyme or reason. But closer examination discloses evidence of much more careful composition. The main structural device is the repetition of the formula for divine self-introduction. The shorter form of it, "I am the Lord," is used in 19:12, 14, 16, 18, 28, 30, 32, 37, and in some of those cases it marks off subunits. The longer form, "I am the Lord your God," is found in 19:3, 4, 10, 25, 31, 34, 36 (cf. 19:2), sometimes closing off major units.

The content of the speech in Leviticus 19 is framed by the use of an admonition at its beginning in 19:2b, its middle in 19:19, and its end in 19:36b–37. This divides the speech into two clear parts. In these two parts the main sections correspond. Thus both sets of case law in 19:5–10 and 19:20–25 deal with animal sacrifices and agriculture. The moral commandments in 19:11–18 correspond with the religious commandments in 19:26–32. The foundational laws in 19:3–4 match the concluding laws about the treatment of resident aliens in 19:33–36a.

In addition, the repeated key words, phrases, and sentences serve to connect the two parts of the speech in a complex pattern of association. Thus the command is repeated to "keep" (שָׁמַר in 19:3, 19, 37) God's statutes. That repetition divides the speech into two halves. The first of those commands (19:3) emphasizes the observance of the Sabbath as the most important of all God's statutes. The recurrence of the verb "to fear," יָרֵא, associates reverence for the Lord (19:14, 32) with reverence for parents (19:3) and the sanctuary (19:30). The repetition of the command to keep the Sabbaths in 19:3 and 19:30 in two different contexts shows that Sabbath observance connects the family with the sanctuary.

Likewise, the command "you shall not turn to" idols in 19:4 is associated with the command "you shall not turn to" the spirits of the dead in 19:31. The varied use of the root "holy," קדשׁ, connects God's holiness (19:2) with the meat from the peace offerings (19:8), the fruit from a young tree (19:24), and the sanctuary (19:30). By repetition, the *desecration* of God's name in 19:12 is connected with a father's *desecration* of his daughter in 19:29. The repetition of the command to do nothing unjust links judicial injustice in 19:15 with commercial injustice in 19:35. The recurrence of command to love another as oneself extends the love of the neighbor in 19:18 to the love of resident aliens in 19:34.

Wenham has also shown that in the four subunits in 19:11–18 four different synonyms are employed to build a sense of climax so that this whole section culminates in the command to love your neighbor as yourself:[21]

19:11–12:	X	Compatriot	X	X
19:13–14:	X	X	X	Neighbor
19:15–16:	X	Compatriot	Kinsfolk	Neighbor
19:17–18:	Brother	Compatriot	Kinsfolk	Neighbor

This construction serves to highlight God's desire to extend the values of the kin group to the whole liturgical community as God's family.

The speech as whole is quite deliberately connected with chapters 18 and 20. This is done in three ways: (1) by the recollection of the admonition to "keep" God's "statutes" from 18:5, 26 in 19:19a and 19:37a; (2) by the repetition of the admonition to "enact" them from 19:37b in 20:22; and (3) by the recurrence of the call to share in God's holiness from 19:2 in 20:26b.

The structure of this pericope can be outlined as follows:

- I. Introduction (19:1–2a)
  - A. God's address to Moses (19:1)
  - B. God's commission to Moses (19:2a)
- II. Speech by Moses to the congregation of Israel (19:2b–37)
  - A. Introductory call to share in God's holiness (19:2b)
  - B. Basic requirements for sharing in God's holiness (19:3–4)
    - 1. Respect for parents and observance of the Sabbaths with divine self-introduction (19:3)
    - 2. Prohibition of idolatry with divine self-introduction (19:4)
  - C. Two cases of offerings (19:5–10)
    - 1. Right use of the meat from the peace offerings (19:5–8)
    - 2. Right provision of food for the disadvantaged (19:9–10a)
      - a. Leftover grain for gleaning in the fields (19:9)
      - b. Leftover grapes for picking in the vineyards (19:10a)
    - 3. Divine self-introduction (19:10b)
  - D. Justice and love as the basis for communal solidarity (19:11–18)
    - 1. Prohibition of deceptive misappropriation of property with divine self-introduction (19:11–12)
    - 2. Prohibition of the oppression and abuse of the disadvantaged with divine self-introduction (19:13–14)
    - 3. Maintenance of justice in local courts with divine self-introduction (19:15–16)
    - 4. Positive rather than negative retaliation with divine self-introduction (19:17–18)
  - E. Central admonition (19:19)
    - 1. Admonition on the observance of God's statutes (19:19a)

---

[21] Wenham, *Leviticus*, 267.

2. Proverbial instruction on the avoidance of mixtures (19:19b)

F. Two cases on mixtures (19:20–25)

1. Sexual intercourse between an Israelite and a betrothed slave girl (19:20–22)
2. The use of fruit from a young fruit tree or vine (19:23–25a)
3. Divine self-introduction (19:25b)

G. Areas of conflict between God's holiness and family solidarity (19:26–32)

1. Involvement in spiritism and the cult of the ancestors with divine self-introduction (19:26–28)
2. Respect for God's Sabbaths and sanctuary rather than desecrating daughters by making them prostitutes with divine self-introduction (19:29–30)
3. Respect for live elders rather than dead ancestors with repeated divine self-introduction (19:31–32)

H. The generous treatment of resident aliens (19:33–36a)

1. Loving treatment rather than oppression of aliens (19:33–34)
2. Use of correct weights and measures in trade and commerce (19:35–36a)

I. Final admonition on the observance of God's laws (19:36b–37)

Ritual Agents

Through Moses as his mouthpiece, God addresses the Israelites directly as a liturgical community, the congregation of Israel. Apart from the ritual case law in 19:20–22, all the laws in this chapter are couched either in the second person plural or the second person singular form. Thus, while God speaks to the congregation as a whole, he also addresses each person individually in 19:9–10, 12b, 13–14, 15b–18, 19b, 29, 32, 34b.

The liturgical community of Israel is envisaged in two ways. First, it is understood as an ethnic community made up of families governed by parents (19:3a) and elders (19:32). The members of these landed families are the "great" (19:15), the native-born residents in the land (19:34). This society is engaged in agriculture (19:9, 19c), viticulture (19:10), fruit growing (19:23–25), animal husbandry (19:5, 19b, 22, 26), and trade (19:35–36a). In it certain people are marginalized and economically vulnerable, such as the day laborers (19:13) and poor Israelites (19:10, 15), landless aliens (19:10, 33, 34), and slave girls (19:20). Second, since all classes of people are included in the liturgical community, the whole community is understood as an extended family, the family of God.[22] Each member is not just regarded as a neighbor (19:13, 16, 18), but as a brother (19:17), a compatriot (19:11, 15, 17), or a relative (19:16, 18). Thus the language of kinship is extended to all members of the liturgical community as part of a large extended family.

Even though Israel was an ethnic community that would, once it entered the land, consist of landowning families, the Lord regarded it primarily as a liturgical community. Its communal solidarity did not derive from its social or

---

[22] Gerstenberger, "Er soll dir heilig sein," 285.

political structure, but from its common worship of one God (19:3, 30), its common rejection of idolatry (19:4), and its common ritual connection with the sanctuary (19:22). While the priests played an important role at the sanctuary, the community was the main actor there. As a corporate religious body it was responsible for the promotion of right worship and the administration of justice. God envisaged it as a holy community, a community of people called to share in his holiness (19:2). He therefore applied the commandments of the Decalogue to their life in the land.[23] We find allusions to them in the following places:

Ten Commandments	*Leviticus 19*
First (Ex 20:3)	19:4; cf.17:26–28, 31
Second (Ex 20:7)	19:12
Third (Ex 20:8)	19:3, 30
Fourth (Ex 20:12)	19:3, 32
Fifth (Ex 20:13)	19:16–17
Sixth (Ex 20:14)	19:29
Seventh (Ex 20:15)	19:11, 35–36
Eighth (Ex 20:16)	19:14–16
Ninth and tenth (Ex 20:17)	19:17–18, 33–36 (?)

Ritual Location

Even though God gave these laws to his people at Mount Sinai, they anticipated Israel's life in the promised land (19:9, 23, 29, 33). There they would no longer be landless aliens, as they had once been in Egypt (19:34). Since that land belonged to God, he apportioned part of its produce to the poor and the alien (19:9–10), just as he reserved the fruit from a four-year-old fruit tree for himself (19:23–24). There he would establish his sanctuary (19:30) and interact with them at the tent of meeting (19:21). He was giving them that land so that they could interact with him there as his holy people in all aspects of their life on it (19:2).

Holy and Unholy Things

Since this chapter deals with the participation of all Israelites in God's holiness (19:2), it mentions the holy things that were available to the lay people. The most important of these was the meat from the peace offering. Since it was holy to the Lord (19:8), it had to be eaten either on the day that it was offered or the day after it had been offered (19:5–6). The fruit from a four year-old fruit tree was also holy. It could not be eaten, but had to be given to the priests as an offering to the Lord (19:24). Thereafter its fruit was available for common use (19:25). The Israelites were instructed to respect God's holy Sabbaths (19:3, 30), his sanctuary (19:30), and his holy name (19:12). The Lord used the

---

[23] Kaiser, "The Book of Leviticus," 1131; Morgenstern, "The Decalogue of the Holiness Code."

meat from the peace offering, the sanctuary, the Sabbaths, and his name to make and keep his people holy.

These holy things are contrasted with the idols made of cast metal (19:4), the desecrated meat from the peace offering (19:8), and the meat from the sacrifices offered to the spirits of the dead (19:26). God's holy people were called to shun these unholy things, because such things desecrated their holiness.

Theological Analysis

Call to Holiness (19:1–2)

All the statutes and ordinances in this chapter need be understood in the light of the repeated formula for divine self-introduction. The Lord used this formula to address the Israelites directly. It occurs in four different forms, each of which is significant. First, the Lord used the short formula eight times to introduce himself by name so that his people had access to him (19:12, 14, 16, 18, 28, 30, 32, 37). Second, he used the longer formula six times to commit himself to them as their God (19:3, 4, 10, 25, 31, 34). Third, he used this longer formula in combination with the formula of deliverance from Egypt in 19:36 to claim their allegiance to him as his subjects. Fourth and most importantly, he used the longer formula with the declaration of his own holiness to claim them as his holy people (19:2). Since they were holy, they were to keep his statutes and enact his ordinances (19:19a, 37).

This passionate speech of the Lord begins with the assertion that Israel's holiness derives from his holiness (19:2; cf. 11:44). God's call to holiness (19:2) can be understood in three ways: as a promise: "you will be holy"; as a statement of fact: "you are holy" (11:45); and/or as a demand: "you shall be holy" (11:44). Since God shares his holiness with his people, all the Lord's demands in this chapter are based on the people's participation in his holiness. These demands presuppose that God makes and keeps them holy. They, therefore, were to keep on receiving holiness from him and do nothing to block its spread throughout their community. God wanted to extend his holiness out into the world through his presence with his people. His holiness protected the congregation of Israel from all evil, ungodly powers, built it up as his sacred kinsfolk, and promoted its communal life. Thus the Israelites could only enjoy his holiness as long as they were members of the sacred congregation of Israel.

Only God was intrinsically holy. He was the generator and source of all holiness. He communicated his holiness to his people by his presence with them. By giving the Israelites his holy name, he gave them access to his holiness in the divine service. They never possessed his holiness; they received it from him, just as we receive light from the sun. He did not give them the list of prohibitive and performative commandments in 19:3–36 for them to generate and so achieve holiness, as Milgrom[24] and many others claim. That view is based on a theology of self-sanctification that contravenes the teach-

[24] Milgrom, *Leviticus 17–22*, 1603–5.

ing of St. Paul that righteousness is through faith alone and not through works (Rom 3:20–5:21). Instead, the theology in this chapter (and in Leviticus as a whole) teaches that purification and sanctification (which are often equated with justification in the NT) are by grace alone. These laws deal with the people's reception of God's holiness and their ongoing participation in it.

Most of the laws in this chapter are prohibitions. They identify the activities that either desecrated God's holiness or defiled the Israelites as his holy people. Together with positive commandments, they map out an ethic of holiness. Since the Israelites were holy just as God was holy, they were to act in a godly way and avoid whatever was ungodly. He did not call them to imitate his holiness so that they could become more and more holy like him. Rather, he called them to obey him because they were holy. That is the presupposition for all that follows this speech.

Participation in God's Holiness (19:3–4)

Since the Lord was the source of holiness for the whole congregation of Israel, this chapter begins with four commandments that were meant to protect the flow of holiness from the Lord and out to and through his congregation. They restate the content of the Fourth (Ex 20:12), Third (Ex 20:8), and First (Ex 20:3) Commandments.

Positively, the Israelites kept on receiving holiness from the Lord as long as they respected their parents and observed the Sabbath. In a practical reversal of the order from the Decalogue, the Israelites were commanded to fear and revere their parents as God's representatives, for they shared in God's holiness by belonging to an Israelite family. The mother may be mentioned first in Lev 19:3 because, even though she was the heart of the family, she was most prone to be neglected if her husband died before her. Parents also played a vital role in promoting the holiness of each family that made up the congregation of Israel. They led the family in its observance of the Sabbaths, whether they were the regular weekly days of rest in their homes or the annual festive holy days at the sanctuary. The Sabbath is mentioned because it was the basic regular ritual enactment of the laity. By refraining from work, each Israelite family acknowledged that they did not make themselves holy but that the Lord made them holy by what he did for them (Ex 31:13). They did not generate holiness, but received their holiness from him.

The Israelites were also forbidden to turn to other gods and make idols of the Lord. The prohibition of apostasy in Lev 19:4 uses a derisive term for deities other than the Lord. Such deities were "godlings," feeble entities that did not deserve to be called gods. Because the Israelites had access to the Lord and enjoyed his provision for them, they did not need to "turn" to these ineffectual entities for help and blessing. They were not even allowed to make idols of cast metal as a means of access to the Lord, because they already had the use of the Lord's name as their means of access to him and his blessings. In an echo of Ex 34:17, the second prohibition in Lev 19:4 uses the derisive term "gods of cast metal" for any idol of the Lord. This, most likely, refers to household statues, such as that of Micah in Judg 17:4. They were made by pouring gold, silver, or bronze in a mold or by plating wooden statues with silver or gold. By turning to other gods and by making idols of the Lord for their homes, the Israelite families cut themselves off from the Lord and his holiness.

Two Kinds of Offerings (19:5–10)

This unit comes first in the main body of the speech because the meat from the peace offering was the only holy object that the lay people were allowed to handle.[25] They ate this meat as part of a sacred meal together with their family and their guests. They usually took it home from the sanctuary and ate it there. That would explain why the meat from the ordinary peace offering, unlike the thank offering, could also be eaten on the day after its presentation. That would allow for two meals, one at the sanctuary on the first day and the other at home on the second day. The holy meat from the peace offering conveyed the Lord's life-giving blessing to the families that ate it. The sanctity of this meat accounts for the severe warning about the consequences of its desecration. Those who disobeyed God's Word by treating it as common meat forfeited the Lord's gracious acceptance of them. They cut themselves off from the flow of life and blessing from God through their families and out into the whole community. This act of sacrilege was a kind of spiritual suicide, an act of self-destruction.

The second subunit, 19:9–10, part of which recurs in the legislation for Pentecost in 23:22, deals with the provision of gleanings for those who owned no land and had no harvest of their own, the poor and the aliens. When the Israelites reaped their grain, they were forbidden to harvest the whole field and to gather up the stalks that had fallen to the ground in the process of harvesting. Likewise, when they picked their grapes, they were forbidden to gather all their grapes, whether it be the small bunches or the second crop of late-ripe fruit, and to pick up the grapes that had fallen to the ground during the harvest. All these were God's provision for the poor. Through these four kinds of surplus produce, God established his welfare system for the Israelite community.

The laws about the meat from the peace offerings are closely connected with the laws about the gleanings. This is shown in the lack of the formula of divine self-introduction between these two units. But it is not clear why they were joined together. As Milgrom notes, 19:9–10 serves as a bridge between the holy ritual realm in 19:5–8 and the moral social realm in 19:11–18.[26] The requirement to leave some of the grain and grape harvest behind for the poor is both a religious and a moral duty. These gleanings were an offering given by God from his land to those who had no land. They were a kind of tithe that

[25] Milgrom, *Leviticus 17–22*, 1615.

[26] Milgrom, *Leviticus 17–22*, 1623–24.

was not given, as one would expect, to the priests, but to the poor and the aliens. God thereby treated them as if they were his priests.

God's Protection of His Holy People from Abuse (19:11–18)

The four units in this section consist mainly of prohibitions. By these prohibitions the Lord covered the members of his holy community with the canopy of his holiness and protected them from abuse by their associates. The prohibitions deal with those kinds of abuse and injustice that could not be treated in a normal court of law, but could only be judged by God. By prohibiting them, God made these acts of injustice sins against himself and his holiness. He therefore upheld the integrity of the community and protected the sanctity of its members with his holy Word. His holiness supported and sustained those who were socially vulnerable and economically disadvantaged in the congregation of Israel.

The list of prohibitions culminates in four performative commandments: to fear God in 19:14, to judge justly in 19:15, to rebuke an offender in 19:17, and to love the neighbor in 19:18. These commandments tell how the Israelites were to treat each other as God's holy people.

The prohibitions in 19:11–12 protected the property of each Israelite. They recall the Seventh Commandment (Ex 20:15) and deal with secret acts of theft and their subsequent denial. The first prohibition ("you shall not steal") forbids the secret theft and furtive misappropriation of property. The next three forbid the subsequent covering up of the theft by denial, deception, and perjury. The second prohibition ("you shall not dissemble") forbids the denial of the theft by dissembling or telling lies, while the third prohibition ("nor lie") forbids the affirmation of the lie as the truth by the thief, for often, when challenged, the thief would not only deny the theft, but claim ownership to what he had stolen. The fourth prohibition ("you shall not swear falsely …") prohibits the use of God's name in an oath on a witness stand, at the sanctuary (1 Ki 8:31–32), or in personal self-defense in an attempt to cover up the theft. By doing so, the thief broke the Second Commandment (Ex 20:7) and so desecrated the holy name of God. Thus the act of theft could result in the terrible sin of sacrilege.

The second set of commandments, in 19:13–14, protected each member of the holy congregation from exploitation by powerful people. Three common forms of exploitation are singled out for consideration. First, the Lord warns his people against legal exploitation by withholding property or payment from another person, as well as the illegal use of position and influence to gain property by robbery from a vulnerable person. While these first two prohibitions may refer to two separate cases, they may also be joined to indicate that the retention of another's property was, in fact, robbery.

Second, the Lord warns against any delay in paying day laborers. Day laborers could be either Israelites or foreigners (Deut 24:14–15). They were among the poorest members of Israelite society. Since they had no property and since they lacked permanent employment, they needed their daily wages to support themselves and their families. God protected their livelihood by requiring their employers to pay them at the end of each day.

Third and last, the Lord warns against hidden abuse of disadvantaged people. God's people were forbidden to insult a deaf person or put an obstacle before a blind person. These acts took secret advantage of these people's handicaps in order to harm them publicly, either out of spite or for personal gain. It was safe to do so because they did not know what was said or done. They were therefore unable to defend themselves by retaliation. By analogy with this, the Israelites were forbidden to insult each other in secret behind each other's back or to bring about someone's downfall by setting a hidden obstacle before him.[27] This kind of malicious behavior was common in any close community that was riddled with jealousy and rivalry. In it powerful people often worked secretly to shame others who were weak or who did not support them. They had no reason to fear retaliation from those who were "deaf" and "blind" to them and their scheming. But they had good reason to fear God, for he protected the weak from exploitation with his own holiness and avenged them (Ex 22:21–23 [ET 22:22–24]; Deut 24:15).

In Lev 19:15–16 the Lord prohibits the perpetration of injustice in Israel. This unit presupposes that all Israelites were involved in the local administration of God's justice. This operated on two levels. On the one hand, all adult males served as judges in the courts convened to hear legal cases in the gates of their villages. In 19:15 the Lord warns them against acting unjustly in passing judgment in their courts by either favoring the poor, just because they were weak, or deferring to the "great men" in the community, just because they were powerful (cf. Ex 23:2–3). Like God, the Israelites were to show partiality to neither (cf. Deut 1:17; 10:17). They were to judge according to what is right before God (Lev 19:15).

On the other hand, all Israelites served as witnesses for others both in their communal life and in the local courts of law. In 19:16 the Lord warns them against peddling slander about others. A slander-monger secretly attacked the reputation of others and so destroyed their life in that community. Slander bred injustice, because it passed an unjust sentence on another, without the observance of due process; it was a kind of murder. The Lord's warning against slander-mongering is coupled with a warning against indifference to slanderous attacks on a person's reputation among his peers, as well as against the toleration of the destruction of a slandered person's life by a wrong conviction in a court of law (cf. Ex 23:7). The two were closely related. Both those who slandered and those who tolerated slander were equally culpable for the loss of that person's life. They had blood on their hands.

The three subunits in 19:11–16 culminate in 19:17–18 with the Lord's remedy for injury and abuse, whether it be from theft of property, exploitation, or

---

[27] Milgrom, *Leviticus 17–22*, 1639–41.

injustice. The material in 19:17–18 presupposes a tribal society made up of close blood clans, a society governed by payback. In such a society each offense had to be avenged to preserve the society's social and moral ecology. Payback operated positively as benefaction within the blood clan; it also operated negatively as revenge and hatred against those who stood outside it. The Lord therefore undermined the cycle of revenge by forbidding hatred and commanding love for all members of the Israelite congregation.

God forbade any person who had been injured to hate the offender secretly in his heart. Instead, he was required to confront the offender openly and directly with his offense. He was to rebuke his fellow Israelite to give him a chance to admit his wrongful deed and put it right. If, however, anybody failed to reprimand the wrongdoer, but hated him instead and plotted his downfall, that person became a party to that evil deed. Hatred of the wrongdoer turned the victim into a wrongdoer. It devoured the hateful person. The offended person was therefore required to rebuke the wrongdoer or else he himself would be guilty of hatred and suffer the penalty of hatred. We are not told what the penalty was. It is, however, clear that such a person came under God's judgment.

The prohibition of vengeance in 19:18 follows directly from the prohibition of hatred in 19:17, for the desire for revenge and the nursing of grudges were the products of hatred. Even if the reproof of the evildoer did not produce a positive response, the Lord did not permit his people to take revenge, or even to bear a grudge against the evildoer.[28] God alone "paid back" evildoers (Nah 1:2; cf. Ps 94:1) and "bore a grudge" against them (Nah 1:2; cf. Ps 103:9; Jer 3:5, 12). These two prohibitions contradicted the most basic tenet of a tribal society, the principle of personal retaliation. Those who had been injured could neither pay back the offender by an extra-judicial act of retribution, nor could they even indulge in secret mental scenarios of hatred and revenge. All thoughts of revenge and acts of vengeance were equally forbidden. Instead, they were required to practice positive retaliation by showing love to those who had wronged them. The Israelites were required to treat those who wronged them as well as they treated themselves.

The love that the Lord commands is not basically an emotional attitude, a matter of sentiment, but an act of benevolence, a matter of the will, for feelings cannot be commanded. The Lord commands his people to act in a loving way toward their neighbors and care for them as they cared for themselves. This commandment does not, then, promote self-love, as if people had to love themselves before they could love others. Instead, it assumes that all people seek their own advantage, their own good, and that without limitation or discrimination. The "neighbor" who was to be loved in this way was most obviously an Israelite wrongdoer. But, as is shown in 19:34, it also extended to the

[28] Cf. Milgrom, *Leviticus 17–22*, 1646–47.

aliens resident with the Israelites in the land. Benevolent love was therefore to replace malevolent hatred as the response to slights and acts of injustice.

All the prohibitions in this section culminate in the commandment to love the neighbor as oneself. This is the basic social duty of the Israelites as God's holy people, for God's holiness encouraged and fostered brotherly love in his holy congregation. The kind of loving benevolence that applied to close blood relatives in a tribal society was extended to the whole congregation of Israel. All its members were to be regarded as close spiritual kinsfolk, holy brothers and sisters in the Lord's holy family, people who all equally shared in God's holiness and who all equally came under its protection.

The Prohibition of Mixtures (19:19)

The admonition to observe the Lord's statutes introduces the second half of the speech. It is followed by three puzzling prohibitions. All of them have to do with the mixture of species: mating two different species of livestock, such as a horse and a donkey; sowing a field with two different species of grain, such as wheat and barley; and wearing clothes made of two different kinds of yarn, such as wool and linen. These three prohibitions have to do with three different natural-cultural orders: the order of domestic animals; the order of cultivated grains; and the order of processed produce. Interbreeding produces confusion with a hybrid species; sowing two kinds of seed produces disorder in agriculture; wearing two kinds of clothes produces ambiguity in religious status. All three are violations of order, all fail to distinguish and separate things that are different and meant to be kept apart.

While the general sense of these prohibitions is clear, it is difficult to determine how they are to be applied. Two applications are possible. On the one hand, they could be taken as literal prohibitions. If that were so, then it is difficult to discern how they were to be applied and why. None of the livestock on an Israelite property could be crossbred; no farmer would ever want to mix different kinds of grain; the Israelites had no reason to produce fabrics of mixed yarn like those worn by the high priest (Ex 28:6, 15; 39:29) and the other priests (Ex 39:29). On the other hand, these prohibitions could be understood metaphorically as a kind of riddle to forbid intermarriage,[29] to avoid the use of mixtures that belong to the sacred sphere,[30] to distinguish between the various spheres in the divinely instituted cosmic order,[31] or, most likely, proverbially to distinguish what was holy from what was common and unclean.

It is not obvious whether the three prohibitions were meant to function as a separate unit or as an introduction to the rest of the chapter. The latter is more likely, as 19:19 seems to be parallel to the call to holiness in 19:2. It introduces

[29] Wenham, *Leviticus*, 269.

[30] Milgrom, *Leviticus 17–22*, 1660–65.

[31] Ruwe, *"Heiligkeitsgesetz" und "Priesterschrift,"* 116, 219.

a section that deals with various borderline cases for the maintenance of Israel's holiness. In each case, care was to be taken to avoid the confusion of the sacred with the common and the clean with the unclean.

Two Cases of Sacral Disorder (19:20–25)

These two cases are the counterpart to the two instances in 19:5–10 in the first part of the speech.

The first case, in 19:20–22, deals with an ambiguous social situation. A free male Israelite had, allegedly, engaged in sexual intercourse with a slave girl who was betrothed to a man other than her owner. If she were a free woman, both she and her lover should be put to death (Deut 22:23–24); if she were unbetrothed, her lover would have to pay compensation to her owner and marry her (cf. Deut 22:28–29). But since she has not yet been ransomed and set free by her husband-to-be, her master, who was only her partial owner, was not entitled to receive compensation. She and her lover were also not liable to the penalty for adultery. An inquest therefore needed to be held to determine the truth of the allegations.

If they were substantiated, her lover was required to present a reparation offering to the Lord. No compensation was paid either to the Lord, since she was not God's property (5:16), or to her owner, since she no longer belonged to him (5:24 [ET 6:5]). Reparation offerings were normally required when something holy had been desecrated. But in this case it is not clear what holy thing had been violated, whether it was the Lord's name in an oath of betrothal or, more likely, the Lord's name in Israel's promise to keep the Decalogue.[32] An unintentional act of adultery, such as this, would therefore be regarded as a case of sacrilege that required expiation by a reparation offering, as commanded in 5:15. The procedure was the same as outlined in 5:14–5:26 (ET 5:14–6:7). The priest made atonement with the blood from the reparation offering so that the offender was released from the sin that he had committed. His holy status was therefore restored by that offering.

The second case prescribes that all the produce from a newly planted fruit tree was to be offered to God in the fourth year of its life (19:23–25). Thereafter the Israelites offered the firstfruits of their produce, such as dates, figs, pomegranates, almonds, and grapes, annually to the Lord as their "rent" for the land (Neh 10:35, 37). The Israelites were forbidden to eat any fruit from a young tree during the first three years of its life. In fact, this law seems to imply that all the green fruit was plucked from the trees so that the young tree did not waste its energies producing premature fruit.[33] The yield of the fourth year belonged to the Lord; since it was a holy thing, like each firstborn animal, the fruit had to be taken to the sanctuary and eaten by the priests. It was "an offering of rejoicing" (Lev 9:24) to the Lord, for the Israelites used it to rejoice

---

[32] Milgrom, *Leviticus 17–22*, 1673–74.

[33] Milgrom, *Leviticus 17–22*, 1679.

in the Lord's presence. The offering of the firstfruits of the tree freed the subsequent fruit for common use by the Israelites. It belonged to them, provided that they offered the firstfruits from each year as tithes to the Lord (27:30). In this way the Israelites acknowledged that the land and its produce belonged to the Lord, even if he reserved only a small part of the land and its produce for his own exclusive use.

This theological understanding is underscored by use of circumcision as an analogy for a young tree. Each new fruit tree is compared to a young Israelite male whose foreskin is removed so that the penis was "opened" for sexual intercourse. The law in 19:23 regards the fruit as the penis of the tree with the bud and its petals as its foreskin and the stone as its seed. For the first three years the Israelites were to treat the buds as the foreskin by plucking them off, before the fruit emerged and produced seed.[34] The dedication of the fruit as a sacred thing to the Lord from the fourth year resembled the circumcision of the male infant on the eighth day. Its consecration made it available for common use, so that it could bring God's blessing to his people. Once the first produce had been offered as a holy thing to the Lord, the tree was blessed. It increased its yield for God's people (cf. Prov 3:9–10; Ezek 44:30). The productivity of the land came from the Lord as Israel's God. It was enhanced by Israel's respect for his holiness.

The Sacral-Social Disorder of the Congregation (19:26–32)

This section of the speech is the structural counterpart to 19:11–18. Thematically, the prohibitions in it forbade those acts that violated the sacral and social order of the congregation, while the performative commandments highlighted the means by which its sacral (19:30) and social (19:32) order was upheld. In a world where people held that each human family was made up of living people and the spirits of their dead ancestors, these prohibitions served to cut the links between these two realms. They helped to reform Israel as a community that drew its life from the Lord, rather than from its dead ancestors.

This concern for separating the realm of the living from the realm of the dead is evident in all the prohibitions in 19:26–28. First, the Israelites were forbidden to eat meals around the graves of their ancestors (19:26). In such meals people in the ancient world offered up the blood of an animal to conjure up the spirits of their ancestors for the purpose of divination. Second, the Israelites were forbidden to observe those mourning customs that involved mutilation either of their hair (19:27) or of their bodies (19:28). No reason is given for these prohibitions, except that gashes were not to be made on their bodies for the dead (19:28; cf. Deut 14:1). These acts of self-mutilation were meant to link the living mourners ritually with the dead. They thereby demonstrated their

---

[34] Milgrom, *Leviticus 17–22*, 1679.

solidarity with them and proved their loyalty to them.[35] These common pagan practices were forbidden because they encouraged ancestor worship and the cult of the dead. The realm of the living was not to be mixed with the realm of the dead. They were to be kept quite separate from each other.

The focus in 19:29–30 shifts to the sacral order of the family and its disruption by fornication and the commercialization of sex. No matter how poor and desperate they were, Israelite fathers were not allowed to prostitute their daughters. Their daughters could not be treated as the property of the family or as a commercial asset. Daughters were not family property, like livestock, or commercial assets, like slaves. Two reasons were given. First, like the fathers, daughters were holy. Prostitution (like other sexual sins) desecrated their holiness. Hence it was forbidden. Second, by the people's involvement in prostitution, the land was prostituted and defiled (cf. 18:25, 27, 28), for sexual disorder polluted the natural environment, the order of creation, just as it disturbed the sacral order. The whole land became full of depravity. The delicate balance between the sacral, social-familial, and natural realms was upset. Disorder and confusion set in.

This prohibition of prostitution is followed by the performative commandments in 19:30. Both of these deal with the means by which God shared his holiness with the Israelites. They participated in God's holiness by observing his Sabbaths (cf. 19:3; 26:2) and by revering his sanctuary (cf. 26:2). They revered the sanctuary by entering it in a state of ritual purity and by presenting the divinely instituted offerings there. By observing the Sabbath, they distinguished sacred time from common time; by respecting the sanctuary they distinguished sacred space from common space. In this way both spheres were rightly distinguished from each other, without any ambiguity or confusion.

In 19:31–32 the legislation shifts back to the need for the separation of the living from the dead. The Israelites were forbidden to turn to the spirits of the dead for knowledge and help, power and blessing (cf. 20:6). The spirits of the dead were not holy, nor did they confer supernatural help. Instead, they were contagiously unclean. They polluted those who turned to them and sought their help. They could not consolidate and enrich their descendents who respected them. In fact, God himself threatened to cut off from their kinsfolk those who employed the help of the dead, because they disrupted the solidarity of Israelite families. The Israelites were therefore not allowed to consult their dead ancestors. Rather, they were required to respect the living elders (19:32). These elders had knowledge and wisdom. They conveyed blessing. They were therefore to be honored. Deference should be paid to them, for they represented the living God.[36] The Israelites were therefore to fear God by revering them (cf. 19:3). The solidarity of each family and the whole congregation depended

---

[35] Ruwe, *"Heiligkeitsgesetz" und "Priesterschrift,"* 213–14.

[36] Ruwe, *"Heiligkeitsgesetz" und "Priesterschrift,"* 216.

largely on its elders. The sanctity of the congregation was threatened when they were disregarded and treated with contempt.

Generosity to Aliens as Fellow Servants of God (19:33–36a)

This final section of legislation deals with the marginal case of the foreigners who were resident in the land of Israel. They could join the Israelites in presenting offerings to the Lord and so were in some sense regarded as members of the liturgical assembly, the holy congregation of Israel. They therefore also had some access to God's holiness. Legally speaking, they did not belong to the people of Israel. Since they could not own any land, they had to work for their living as laborers, artisans, and traders. They were then, to some extent, dependent on the goodwill of their hosts. They were also open to commercial exploitation by the Israelites. In 19:33–34 the commandment to love one's neighbor from 19:18 is therefore extended and applied specifically to them. The holy people of God were forbidden to cheat them in their commercial dealings with them. Instead, the Israelites were to regard the aliens as their fellow Israelites and show the same love to them as they did to themselves.

The reason given for this extraordinary treatment of aliens is striking. No appeal is made to their legal status as guests, nor, as might be expected in a society governed by payback, to the principle of reciprocal benefaction. Rather, the plea is made to the common plight of the aliens and the Israelites when they were in Egypt and, implicitly, to the Lord's generosity to Israel. Since the Israelites too were aliens in the land of Egypt before the Lord rescued them, he urged them to be sympathetic and compassionate to the landless aliens in their community as if these aliens were members of their holy community (cf. Ex 23:9). What is implied here is clearly articulated in Deut 10:18–19. The Israelites were to love the aliens resident with them because the Lord loved them and provided for them. What had been received from the Lord was to be shared with those who resided as aliens among them.

The last unit in 19:35–36a illustrates what was meant by the prohibition of exploitation in 19:33. It picks up the prohibition in 19:15 of injustice in a court of law and applies is to unjust dealing in business transactions. The prohibition of false measures that applies to all Israelites is here connected specifically with the legislation for the generous treatment of aliens because aliens were most likely to suffer from this kind of commercial exploitation. They too were to use correct weights and measures in commerce and trade.

Summary Admonition (19:36b–37)

The speech ends with the divine formula for deliverance from Egypt coupled with the call to observance of God's law. In the formula for deliverance, the Lord not only gave the Israelites access to himself through his holy name, but also claimed their allegiance as a people liberated by him. He did not lay claim to their allegiance to him on the basis of his legal rights, but on his benefaction of them as his clients. He was their divine patron. They therefore were to do as he had commanded because he had dealt so generously with them.

Since they were his holy people, he gave them these commandments so that they could participate more fully in his holiness.

Fulfillment by Christ

Like the Israelites, all the members of the church are called to be holy (1 Cor 1:2; 1 Thess 4:7) and share in God's holiness (Heb 12:10). Each congregation is a community of saints or "holy ones" (1 Cor 14:33), people with angelic status and a priestly vocation (e.g., Acts 9:13, 32, 41; 26:10; Rom 1:7; 8:27; 12:13). These saints are true Israelites (Romans 9–11; Gal 3:26–29; 6:16). They are united with Christ in a fuller covenant and communion. He is their holiness (1 Cor 1:30). They are sanctified by him (1 Cor 1:2), holy in him (Phil 1:1; 4:21; Col 1:2). Since they are holy and blameless before God the Father in Christ, they have access to every spiritual blessing in the heavenly realm (Eph 1:3–4). The goal of their sanctification in Christ is participation in eternal life, the divine life of the Holy Trinity (Rom 6:19–23). All this is a corporate, communal reality, something that all Christians have in common because they all belong to Christ.

Since they are holy in Christ, the promise and admonition of Lev 19:2 applies to them. They are to live and act as holy, priestly people here on earth (1 Pet 1:15). Their lifestyle is governed by the ethic of holiness. Their liturgical participation in God's holiness shapes the life of the community and their dealings with each other in it. Apart from the laws that dealt with the temple services rather than the Divine Service in the church, the prohibitions and the commandments are even more relevant to Christians than the Israelites. Hence this chapter is used more often in the NT and the early church than any other part of Leviticus.

The NT does not repeat God's commandment to observe his Sabbaths (Lev 19:3b, 30a) because Christ had fulfilled the Sabbath (Col 2:16–17). The Sabbaths foreshadowed him and the sanctifying rest that he provides (Mt 11:28–30). His most holy Word sanctifies all things (Jn 17:17–19; 1 Tim 4:5). His disciples therefore enter his sanctifying rest by trusting in him and listening to his Word (Heb 4:1–13). That is why Luther gives this explanation of the Third Commandment: "We should fear and love God so that we do not despise preaching and his Word, but hold it sacred and gladly hear and learn it."[37] Thus those who participate faithfully in the Divine Service receive what God ordained for them in the Third Commandment. By hearing his holy Word, they participate in his holiness.

All the commandments in Leviticus about the sanctuary are fulfilled by Christ. He is greater than the temple (Mt 12:6); his body is the new heavenly temple constructed by God the Father (Jn 2:21). All those who are joined to him in Baptism comprise the temple of the living God here on earth—his sanc-

[37] *Luther's Small Catechism with Explanation* (St. Louis: Concordia, 1986), 10.

tuary, the place where he dwells and gives access to himself (1 Cor 3:16–17; 2 Cor 7:1; Eph 2:19–22; 1 Pet 2:4–8). The commandment to revere God's sanctuary (Lev 19:30b) therefore applies to the church. Those who form his holy temple must take care to build it up on Christ and do nothing to destroy it (1 Cor 3:9–17). They must respect its sanctity by withholding his holy things from those who are unclean (Mt 7:6) and keeping themselves free from every defilement of body and spirit (2 Cor 7:1).

God the Father shares his holiness with the congregation through the body and blood of Jesus (1 Cor 11:20–28). Just as the Israelites were guests at God's table when they ate the meat from the peace offerings (Lev 19:5–8), so communicants are the guests of the Lord (1 Cor 10:14–22). If they desecrate that holy food and drink, they, like the Israelites (Lev 19:8), come under God's judgment (1 Cor 11:27–32).

The members of the church have turned from the service of idols and become involved in the service of the living God (1 Thess 1:9). They therefore must avoid all forms of idolatry (1 Cor 10:7; 1 Jn 5:21), for even though idols are dedicated to nonentities (1 Cor 8:4), they are not neutral or benign pagan artifacts, but instruments for demonic influence (1 Cor 10:20–21; 12:2; Rev 9:20). The saints cannot participate in the Table of the Lord and eat meat at temple with an idol (1 Cor 10:14–22). All those who are idolaters are excluded from the church, the holy city of God (1 Cor 6:9; Rev 22:15). The members of the church are the temple of the living God, his living sanctuary here on earth (1 Cor 3:17). They therefore dissociate themselves from idols (2 Cor 6:14–16). Idolatry is forbidden because it desecrates their holiness.

Like idolatry, all kinds of involvement in the occult are forbidden for the holy people of God.[38] Occult practices are works of the devil which Christ has undone.[39] All the practices mentioned in Lev 19:26–29, 31 were dead works that defiled the conscience and led to spiritual death (Heb 9:14). Since Christ has cleansed the hearts of the faithful from these life-destroying works, magic, sorcery, astrology, and soothsaying no longer have any hold over them (Acts 16:16–18; 19:19).

Their participation in God's holiness also governs their treatment of each other in the church, the priestly fraternity of Christ, their Brother and High Priest (Heb 2:11–12; 3:1; 1 Pet 2:17). It determines their interaction with each other (Eph 4:22–5:6; Col 3:12–14). By their treatment of each other, they either promote or undermine the holiness of their community (1 Pet 1:14–2:10). While desecration leads to spiritual sickness and death (1 Cor 11:30), their common holiness results in their communal participation in the eternal life of the Holy Trinity (Rom 6:22). Thus acts of desecration and defilement are to be shunned by all for the benefit of the whole community (2 Cor 7:1).

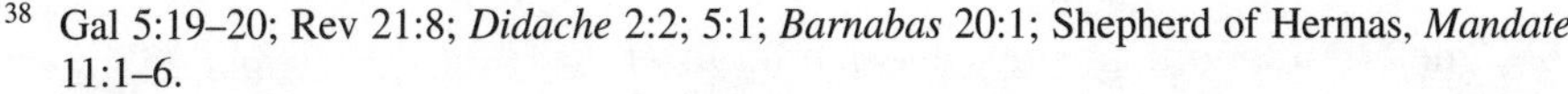

38 Gal 5:19–20; Rev 21:8; *Didache* 2:2; 5:1; *Barnabas* 20:1; Shepherd of Hermas, *Mandate* 11:1–6.

39 1 Jn 3:8; Ignatius, *Epistle to the Ephesians* 19:3.

Christ and his apostles used Leviticus 19 to catechize the saints on what kinds of behavior either undermined or promoted their mutual participation in God's holiness. Thus we have the following prohibitions that echo those given in this chapter.

- The prohibition of theft coupled with the admonition to work hard to provide for those who were needy with the offering that they presented in the Divine Service (Lev 19:11a reflected in Eph 4:28)
- The prohibition of deceptive and fraudulent dealing with fellow Christians coupled with the admonition to speak honestly (Lev 19:11b reflected in Eph 4:25; Col 3:9)
- The prohibition of oaths among the holy people of God coupled with the admonition to speak the plain truth (Lev 19:12 reflected in Mt 5:33–37; James 5:12; cf. Mt 23:16–22)
- The prohibition of exploiting workers and other disadvantaged people coupled with the admonition to put up with personal injustice from fellow Christians (Lev 19:13 reflected in 1 Cor 6:7–8; James 5:1–6)
- The prohibition of cursing others coupled with the admonition to bless those who abused them (Lev 19:14a reflected in Lk 6:28; 1 Cor 4:12; James 4:11–12; 1 Pet 3:9)
- The prohibition of putting a stumbling block before young saints coupled with the admonition to welcome them (Lev 19:14b reflected in Mt 18:1–6; Mk 9:42; Lk 17:2; Rom 14:13; 16:17; 1 Cor 8:13)
- The prohibition of partiality in the church coupled with the admonition to judge mercifully (Lev 19:15 reflected in James 2:12–13; 3:7–12)
- The prohibition of gossip and slander coupled with the admonition to use gracious and constructive speech (Lev 19:16 reflected in 1 Cor 5:11; 6:10; 2 Cor 12:20; Eph 4:29; James 4:11–12; 1 Pet 2:1; cf. Rom 1:29, 30)
- The prohibition of hatred against the fraternity of Christ coupled with the admonition to love each other (Lev 19:17a reflected in 1 Jn 2:9–11; 3:15; 4:20)
- The prohibition of revenge coupled with the admonition to repay evil with good (Lev 19:18a reflected in Rom 12:19–21 and 1 Thess 5:15)
- The prohibition of sexual sins, particularly prostitution, since they desecrate God's holy people (Lev 19:29 reflected in 1 Cor 6:13–20)

The remarkable thing in each of these cases is that Christ and his apostles also added corresponding positive commands. The prohibitions of the misbehavior that contradicts the holiness of the body of Christ correspond to positive exhortations to the good behavior that promotes it. Thus it comes as no surprise that almost all the positive commandments in this chapter are repeated in the NT.

- The commandment for Christian children to respect their parents (Lev 19:3a reflected in Eph 6:1–3; Col 3:20)

- The commandment to provide food and other necessities for the needy members of the church from the offerings presented to the Lord (Lev 19:9–10 reflected in Rom 12:13; Eph 4:28; James 2:14–16; 1 Jn 3:14–17; cf. Acts 2:45; 4:34–35; Rom 15:26–27; 1 Cor 16:1–2; 2 Cor 8:4; 9:1, 12; Gal 2:10)
- The commandment to fear God (Lev 19:14b, 32b reflected in Mt 10:28; 1 Pet 2:17; cf. 2 Cor 7:1; 1 Pet 1:17), which is qualified by the assurance of salvation (1 Jn 4:14–18)
- The commandment for pastors and all disciples to rebuke those who had sinned (Lev 19:17 reflected in Lk 17:3; Eph 5:11–14; Gal 6:1–5; 1 Tim 5:20; 2 Tim 4:2; Titus 1:9, 13; 2:15)
- The commandment to love their neighbors as themselves (Lev 19:18b reflected in Mt 19:19; 22:39; Mk 12:31; Lk 10:27; Rom 13:9; Gal 5:14; James 2:8)
- The commandment to submit to the elders of the church and to honor them (Lev 19:37 reflected in 1 Pet 5:5a; 1 Tim 5:1–2)[40]

Christ and his apostles emphasize the crucial importance of the commandment to love your neighbor. It is second only in rank to the commandment to love God (Mt 22:39; Mk 12:31). It is the kingly law that informs the life of God's royal family (James 2:8). Its enactment results in the fulfillment of the whole law of God (Rom 13:8–10; Gal 5:13–14). Jesus taught that it was one of the two hinges on which the whole of the OT hung, like a door on a doorpost (Mt 22:40). Yet by making that claim he did not abolish the liturgical foundation for human participation in God's holiness, nor did he redefine holiness in ethical terms. Rather, he taught that since he had fulfilled the whole law by his self-sacrificial love so that he could share God's holiness with his disciples (Jn 17:17–19), they, in turn, were to love their fellow saints as people who were all alike loved by God (1 Jn 4:9–11).

The commandment to love your neighbor applies first and foremost to the congregation, the community of faith. The people of God are called to love their fellow saints (Eph 1:15; Col 1:4; Philemon 5, 7; cf. Heb 6:10), their brothers in Christ (1 Pet 2:17; 1 Jn 2:10; 3:10, 14; 4:20–21), each other (Jn 13:34; 15:12, 17; Rom 13:8; 1 Thess 4:9; 1 Pet 1:22; 1 Jn 3:11, 23; 4:7, 11–12; 2 Jn 5). By increasing their love for each other, the Lord Jesus strengthens and establishes them in his holiness so that they remain blameless before God the Father (1 Thess 3:12–13). Their common participation in Christ and his holiness provides the basis and stimulus for their mutual love.

Yet the range of their love is to reach even further than the church. Just as in Leviticus the love for the neighbor was meant to extend to the needy aliens who resided with God's people and so were potential beneficiaries of his grace (Lev 19:18, 33–34), so the love of Christ's disciples is to reach beyond the

[40] See also *1 Clement* 1:3; 21:6.

boundaries of the church. Hence in the story of the Good Samaritan, Jesus turned the question of the young lawyer around to challenge him to be a neighbor to those in need, no matter who they were (Lk 10:25–37).

The saints are therefore called to copy Christ and reflect his merciful holiness by interceding for others and showing mercy to those who lack God's grace, which comes only through faith in Christ. All unbelievers are potential recipients and beneficiaries of God's grace and holiness (Gal 6:10; 1 Thess 3:12; 1 Tim 2:1–6; Heb 13:16; Rev 5:8–10). The love of Christians is to reach out even to their enemies (Mt 5:43–48; Lk 6:27–36). Since Christians belong to the holy priesthood of Christ, they are to use their access to God the Father to intercede for those who abuse them (Mt 5:44; Lk 6:28). Thus, when God calls on the church to share in his life-giving holiness, he also commissions it to serve as his holy, compassionate priesthood, seeking to reconcile lost humanity to God.

Where charity and love prevail
There God is ever found;
Brought here together by Christ's love
By love we are thus bound.

Forgive we now each other's faults
As we our faults confess,
And let us love each other well
In Christian holiness.

Let us recall that in our midst
Dwells Christ, His only Son;
As members of His body joined
We are in him made one.

For love excludes no race or clan
That names the Savior's Name:
His family embraces all
Whose Father is the same.[41]

---

[41] From "Where Charity and Love Prevail," a Latin hymn translated by Omer Westendorf (*HS98* 878:1, 3, 5, 6). Text copyright © 1960 World Library Publications. All rights reserved. Used with permission. For permission to reprint, contact WLP at 800-566-6150.

Leviticus 20:1–27

Penalties for the Ritual Defilement of the Sanctuary and the Land

Translation

20 [1]Then the Lord spoke to Moses: [2]"Say further to the Israelites: Any of the Israelites or any of the aliens who reside in Israel who gives any of his seed to Molech shall be put to death; the people of the land shall stone him with stones. [3]I myself will set my face against that man and will cut him off from among his people, because he gave some of his seed to Molech, so polluting my sanctuary and desecrating my holy name. [4]Moreover, if the people of the land deliberately shut their eyes to that man when he gives any of his seed to Molech and do not put him to death, [5]I myself will set my face against that man and against his clan; I will cut off from among their people both him and all those who whore after him in prostituting themselves to Molech.

[6]"If any person turns to ghosts and familiar spirits, prostituting himself to them, I will set my face against that person and cut him off from among his people.

[7]"You shall sanctify yourselves, and you shall be holy, for I am the Lord your God.

[8]"You shall keep my ritual statutes, and you shall enact them; I am the Lord who sanctifies you.

[9]"Indeed, if anybody curses his father and his mother, he shall be put to death; since he has cursed his father and his mother, his blood is upon him.

[10]"If a man commits adultery with the wife of another man, if he commits adultery with the wife of his neighbor, both the adulterer and the adulteress shall be put to death.

[11]"If a man lies with his father's wife, it is the nakedness of his father that he has uncovered; both of them shall be put to death; their blood is upon them.

[12]"If a man lies with his daughter-in-law, both of them shall be put to death; they have committed a perverse act; their blood is upon them.

[13]"If a man lies with a male as lying with a woman, both of them have committed an abomination; they shall be put to death; their blood is upon them.

[14]"If a man marries a woman and her mother, it is an act of depravity; both he and they shall be burned in fire, so that there may be no depravity among you.

[15]"If a man gives his emission with an animal, he shall be put to death; and you shall kill the animal.

[16]"If a woman approaches any animal to mate with it, you shall kill the woman and the animal; they shall be put to death; their blood is on them.

[17]"If a man marries his sister, the daughter of his father or the daughter of his mother, he will see her nakedness and she will see his nakedness; it is a shame-

ful act; they will be cut off in the sight of the members of their people. He has uncovered his sister's nakedness; he will bear his iniquity.

18"If a man lies with a menstruating woman and uncovers her nakedness, he exposes her flow, and she uncovers her flow of blood; both of them will be cut off from the midst of their people.

19"You shall not uncover the nakedness of your mother's sister or your father's sister, for that would expose his own flesh; they will bear their iniquity.

20"If a man lies with the wife of his father's brother, he uncovers the nakedness of his father's brother. They shall bear their sin; they will die childless.

21"If a man marries his brother's wife, it is an act of pollution. It is the nakedness of his brother that he has uncovered; they will remain childless.

22"You shall keep all my ritual statutes and all my ordinances and enact them, so that the land to which I am bringing you to settle in may not vomit you out. 23You shall not walk according to the ritual statutes of the nation which I am driving out before you, for it is because they did all these things that I was disgusted with them 24and said to you: 'You will possess their land. I myself will give it to you to possess, a land flowing with milk and syrup. I, the Lord, am your God, who has distinguished you from the peoples. 25You shall therefore distinguish the clean animal from the unclean, and the unclean bird from the clean. You shall not make your throats detestable with an animal or a bird or anything that crawls on the ground that I have distinguished by declaring it unclean for you. 26You will be holy to me, for I, the Lord, am holy, and I have distinguished you from the peoples to belong to me.

27"A man or a woman who has a ghost or a familiar spirit in them—they shall be put to death; they shall stone them with stones; their blood is on them."

Textual Notes

20:2 וְאֶל־בְּנֵי יִשְׂרָאֵל תֹּאמַר—This clause indicates that chapter 20 continues the speech to the Israelites in chapter 18, which had an introduction similar to this one. Therefore we translate it as "Say further …" The intervening speech, chapter 19, was introduced with a somewhat different clause: "Speak to the whole congregation of the Israelites" (19:2).

אִישׁ אִישׁ—See the textual note on this phrase in 15:2.

הַגֵּר—See the textual note on this term in 16:29.

לַמֹּלֶךְ—See the textual notes on 18:21.

מוֹת יוּמָת—The same formula is repeated in 20:9, 10, 11, 13, 15, 16. It refers to execution by human hands.

עַם הָאָרֶץ—See 4:27; 20:4. This referred to all adult men who had a voice in the public affairs of the community and who together acted as its representative assembly with official status.[1]

---

1 Joosten, *People and Land in the Holiness Code*, 42–47.

יִרְגְּמֻהוּ בָאָבֶן:—See 20:27; 24:14, 16; Num 15:35, 36. Stoning to death was a communal form of execution for acts of sacrilege that threatened the existence of the community as God's people.

20:3 וַאֲנִי אֶתֵּן אֶת־פָּנַי בָּאִישׁ הַהוּא—See the textual notes on 17:10.

וְהִכְרַתִּי אֹתוֹ מִקֶּרֶב עַמּוֹ—See the textual notes on 7:20. This clause recurs in 20:5, 6.

טַמֵּא—See the textual notes on 5:2. See also Num 19:20; Ezek 5:11; 23:38; 28:18. The sacrifice of a child to Molech desecrated the sanctuary by defiling it.

מִקְדָּשִׁי—See the textual notes on 12:4.

וּלְחַלֵּל אֶת־שֵׁם קָדְשִׁי:—See the textual notes on 18:21. See also 21:6; 22:2, 32. The use of the infinitive construct with a *waw* and the preposition לְ is best construed as an explicative instrumental phrase: "that is, by desecrating my holy name." The Samaritan Pentateuch reads וְחִלֵּל, "he profanes."

20:4 הַעְלֵם יַעְלִימוּ—The use of the infinitive absolute before the verb indicates that this is a deliberate act.

20:5 וְשַׂמְתִּי אֲנִי אֶת־פָּנַי בָּאִישׁ הַהוּא—See the textual notes on 17:10.

וּבְמִשְׁפַּחְתּוֹ—The "clan" was the basic sociological unit in ancient Israel. It consisted of a group of extended families linked together by kinship.

וְהִכְרַתִּי אֹתוֹ ... מִקֶּרֶב עַמָּם:—See 17:10; 20:3.

הַזֹּנִים ... לִזְנוֹת—See the textual notes on 17:7.

20:6 וְהַנֶּפֶשׁ—See the textual notes on 2:1.

אֶל־הָאֹבֹת וְאֶל־הַיִּדְּעֹנִים—See the textual notes on 19:31.

20:7 וְהִתְקַדִּשְׁתֶּם—See the textual note on this Hithpael verb in 11:44. People sanctified themselves by performing the rituals that God had instituted. Through those means God made and kept his people holy.

כִּי אֲנִי יְהוָה אֱלֹהֵיכֶם:—See the textual notes on 11:44. This clause recurs in 20:24.

20:8 חֻקֹּתַי—See the textual note on this term in 3:17. It recurs in 20:22, 23. These statutes are the ritual decrees by which God established the rites of consecration.

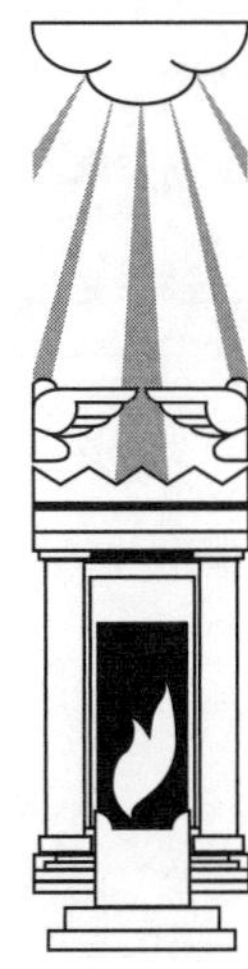

אֲנִי יְהוָה מְקַדִּשְׁכֶם:—See the textual notes on 8:10. This formula that affirms that the Lord is the one who sanctifies his people occurs seven times in Leviticus (20:8; 21:8, 15, 23; 22:9, 16, 32; see also Ex 31:13; Ezek 20:12; 37:28). The number seven is significant, for it shows that these instances, when taken together, are the sum of God's sanctifying activity. The formula for sanctification was always combined with the formula for divine self-introduction by which the Lord presented himself to his people (see the textual notes on 11:44 and 18:5). It was also combined with God's declaration of himself as holy in 21:8, as well as the formula for the deliverance of Israel from slavery in Egypt in 22:32–33. The use of the participle in 22:32 is not meant to identify the Lord's sanctification of Israel with the deliverance from Egypt, as Crüsemann maintains,[2] but with the continuous reception of his holiness. The participle indicates that this is an ongoing process,[3] for the Lord shared his own holiness

---

2 Crüsemann, "Der Exodus als Heiligung."

3 Knohl, *The Sanctuary of Silence,* 182–83; Joosten, *People and Land in the Holiness Code*, 94–96; Olyan, *Rites and Rank*, 174.

with his people by their contact with the holy things in the divine service. Thus the Lord declares that he sanctifies the tabernacle with its furnishings (21:23) and the offerings of food (22:16), as well as the high priest (21:15), the priests (22:9), and the Israelites (20:8; 21:8; 22:32) through these holy things. The goal of God's dealings with Israel is his sanctification of his people. Thus in 22:32–33 his desire to be their God is connected with his ongoing sanctification of them.

20:9 כִּי—The initial כִּי here in the MT is an emphatic particle. The previous two verses (20:7–8) therefore do not introduce the following section, but are the conclusion of 20:2–6.

יְקַלֵּל—See the textual note on the Piel verb קִלֵּל in 19:14. Cursing one's parents is the opposite of honoring them, which is what the Fourth Commandment prescribes (Ex 20:12; Deut 5:16).

מ֥וֹת יוּמָ֖ת—Capital punishment for cursing one's parents is also the penalty in Ex 21:17 (cf. Deut 27:16).

דָּמָ֥יו בּֽוֹ׃—This declaration is repeated in Lev 20:11, 12, 13, 16, 27; cf. Ezek 18:13. It means that like any murderer, the sinner has brought the penalty of death upon himself. Anyone who killed him would therefore not be guilty of murder; the executioner would have no cause to fear revenge from the kinsfolk of the executed person.[4]

20:10 אִ֗ישׁ אֲשֶׁ֤ר יִנְאַף֙ אֶת־אֵ֣שֶׁת רֵעֵ֔הוּ—See Ezek 18:6, 11, 15; 22:11. This clause is repetitious because it basically says the same thing as the first clause of the verse. The repetition may emphasize that adultery involves the betrayal of friendship in a close community. Alternatively, it may limit the jurisdiction of the law to an Israelite by defining the "man" in the preceding phrase as "his neighbor" (רֵעֵ֔הוּ).[5]

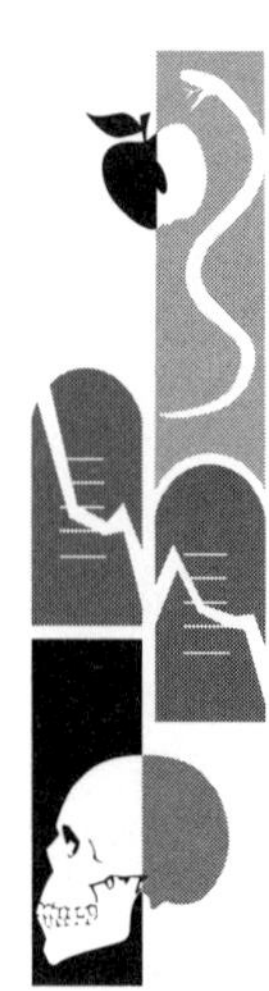

מֽוֹת־יוּמַ֥ת הַנֹּאֵ֖ף וְהַנֹּאָֽפֶת׃—See Deut 22:22 and Jn 8:3–5.

20:11 וְאִ֗ישׁ אֲשֶׁ֤ר יִשְׁכַּב֙ אֶת־אֵ֣שֶׁת אָבִ֔יו—See the textual notes on 15:18. See Deut 27:20.

גִּלָּ֑ה—See 18:7 and Ezek 22:10.

20:12 כַּלָּת֔וֹ—See Ezek 22:11.

תֶּ֥בֶל—See the textual notes on 18:23.

20:13 See the textual notes on 18:22.

וְאִ֗ישׁ—The term אִישׁ is used here in the sense of any male person, not just a husband. This verse forbids all homosexual intercourse. It does not just forbid the intercourse of a married man with another male person.

20:14 וְאִ֗ישׁ אֲשֶׁ֨ר יִקַּ֧ח אֶת־אִשָּׁ֛ה וְאֶת־אִמָּ֖הּ זִמָּ֣ה הִ֑וא—See the textual notes on 18:17. The verb לָקַח literally means that a man "takes" a woman, but in this context it denotes marriage. This refers to the public, legal side of marriage that coincides with sexual cohabitation (rather than just betrothal).

בָּאֵ֞שׁ יִשְׂרְפ֤וּ אֹתוֹ֙ וְאֶתְהֶ֔ן—See also 21:9. Literally the command is that "in fire they shall burn him and them." אֶתְהֶ֔ן, "them," is feminine, referring to the women. In the

---

4 See also Milgrom, *Leviticus 17–22*, 1746–47.

5 Milgrom, *Leviticus 17–22*, 1747.

ancient world, the worst kind of incest was when a man had sexual intercourse with two women related in the first degree of kinship, such as with a woman and her daughter.[6] The cremation of the man together with the two women was the most extreme sanction in ancient Israel because it deprived them of burial in the family tomb and removed all traces of those defiled people from the face of the earth.

20:15 See Deut 27:21.

יִתֵּן שְׁכָבְתּוֹ—Literally, the man "gives his emission," meaning that he copulates. See the textual notes on 18:20.

וְאֶת־הַבְּהֵמָה תַּהֲרֹגוּ׃—See 20:16. The animal was executed summarily without the need for due judicial process.

20:16 לְרִבְעָה—See the textual note on this verb in 18:23.

20:17 See Deut 27:22. As with Lev 18:9, this law is probably meant to apply to a full sister as well as to both a paternal and a maternal half sister.

וְרָאָה אֶת־עֶרְוָתָהּ וְהִיא־תִרְאֶה אֶת־עֶרְוָתוֹ—The double expression of mutual sexual intimacy is used to show that sexual intercourse was sought and enacted by both parties.[7]

חֶסֶד—In the OT only here and in Prov 14:34 does חֶסֶד mean "shame" (BDB; *HALOT*), a shameful act that brings disgrace. This term in these two OT verses is a homograph that is a different word than the common term חֶסֶד, "faithfulness, mercy."

וְנִכְרְתוּ—See the textual note on this Niphal verb in 7:20.

לְעֵינֵי—Since they cohabited in secret, God would punish them in public.[8]

בְּנֵי עַמָּם—This is literally "the sons of your kinsfolk." See 19:18.

עֲוֹנוֹ יִשָּׂא׃—See the textual notes on 5:1.

20:18 וְאִישׁ אֲשֶׁר־יִשְׁכַּב אֶת־אִשָּׁה דָּוָה—See Ezek 18:6; 22:10; and the textual notes on Lev 15:24. This law refers to deliberate sexual intercourse during the menstrual period.

מְקֹרָהּ—This is literally "her fountain."

וְהִוא גִּלְּתָה אֶת־מְקוֹר דָּמֶיהָ—This indicates that the woman consented to the act. מְקוֹר דָּמֶיהָ is literally "the fountain of her blood."

20:19 הֶעֱרָה—This Hiphil of עָרָה is literally "he exposed." The third person form is used impersonally.

20:20 חֶטְאָם יִשָּׂאוּ—See Lev 22:9; 24:15; Num 9:13; 18:22; Ezek 23:49; and the textual notes on Lev 5:1.This means that the sinners will eventually die as a result of their misdeeds.

עֲרִירִים יָמֻתוּ׃—The adjective עֲרִירִי means "childless" in Gen 15:2 and Sirach 16:3. Yet, as Hartley argues, its occurrence in Jer 22:30 shows that it could also refer to older people who were abandoned by their (adult) children so that they no longer had anybody to care for them and bury them.[9]

---

6 Douglas, "Justice as the Cornerstone," 350.

7 Milgrom, *Leviticus 17–22*, 1753.

8 Milgrom, *Leviticus 17–22*, 1754.

9 Hartley, *Leviticus*, 328–29.

20:21 נִדָּה—The term נִדָּה, which refers elsewhere to the menstrual flow of a woman (12:2, 5; 15:19, 20, 24, 25, 26, 33; 18:19), is used here metaphorically for an act of pollution.

20:22 תָקִיא—See this verb also in 18:25, 28.

20:23 הַגּוֹי—Here "the nation" is a collective singular for all of the nations that inhabited Canaan before God drove them out and gave the land to Israel. הַגּוֹי has the same meaning in 18:28.

אֲשֶׁר־אֲנִי מְשַׁלֵּחַ מִפְּנֵיכֶם—See 18:24.

20:24 See 25:46. The promise to inherit "a land flowing with milk and syrup" occurs only here in Leviticus, but is frequent in Numbers and Deuteronomy.

לָרֶשֶׁת—This is the infinitive construct of יָרַשׁ.

חָלָב—This refers to the milk from goats, which was used to make a kind of yogurt.

וּדְבָשׁ—This refers to the syrup from dates and other fruit, rather than the honey from bees.

הִבְדַּלְתִּי—See the textual note on this verb in 10:10. It recurs in 20:25, 26.

20:25 הַטְּהֹרָה—See the textual notes on 7:19.

לַטְּמֵאָה—See the textual notes on 5:2.

תְשַׁקְּצוּ—See the textual notes on 7:21 and 11:11.

נַפְשֹׁתֵיכֶם—Rather than "your throats," this could be translated "yourselves." See the textual note on it in 11:43.

אֲשֶׁר־הִבְדַּלְתִּי לָכֶם לְטַמֵּא׃—This could also be translated "which I have set apart for you to treat as unclean."

20:26 וִהְיִיתֶם לִי קְדֹשִׁים—See 11:45; 19:2; 20:7. We render this as a future indicative: "You will be holy to me." It could also be translated as a present indicative: "You are holy to me."

כִּי קָדוֹשׁ אֲנִי יְהוָה—See the textual notes on 11:44.

20:27 אוֹב אוֹ יִדְּעֹנִי—See the textual notes on 19:31.

Commentary

Structure

This chapter could be regarded as an appendix to Leviticus 18. Its connection with that chapter is emphasized editorially by its address to the same audience, "to the Israelites" (18:2; 20:2). It covers some of the same topics as the two chapters before it but treats them in the following order.

- Child sacrifice to Molech in 20:2–5 from 18:21
- Spiritism in 20:6 from 19:31
- Being holy in 20:7 from 19:2
- Cursing parents in 20:9 from 19:3
- Adultery in 20:10 from 18:20
- Sexual intercourse with mother in 20:11 from 18:8
- Sexual intercourse with daughter-in-law in 20:12 from 18:15

- Homosexual intercourse in 20:13 from 18:22
- Marriage with a woman and her mother in 20:14 from 18:14
- Bestiality in 20:15–16 from 18:23
- Marriage to one's sister in 20:17 from 18:9
- Sexual intercourse during menstruation in 20:18 from 18:19
- Sexual intercourse with aunt in 20:19 from 18:12–13
- Sexual intercourse with aunt-in-law in 20:20 from 18:14
- Sexual intercourse with sister-in-law in 20:21 from 18:16

Leviticus 18 and 19 forbid these offenses. Leviticus 20 announces God's penalties for them in a series of case laws. The one exception to this is the apodictic decree in 20:19, which fits the kinds of laws in chapter 18.

These laws follow the same basic pattern with some variations.[10] This pattern consists of four basic elements: the case; the penalty; the reason; and the status of the offense. See figure 21.

As is evident from figure 21, these case laws are arranged according to their subject matter and the severity of the penalty. The first three cases in 20:2–6 deal with religious offenses. Each results in divine extirpation. The first one also carries the penalty of communal stoning. The second series of thirteen cases in 20:9–21 deals with moral offenses arranged in decreasing order of severity in the penalty for them. They are all linked together as a series of *waw* clauses.

A number of other literary devices are used in the arrangement of these laws. The five noncapital offenses involving the disclosure of nakedness in 20:17–21 are arranged as a chiasm by the mention of "take" (marry) in 20:17 and 20:21, as well as the mention of "lies with" in 20:18 and 20:20. The laws are also interconnected by the repetition of two key declarations: "his/their blood is upon him/them" (20:9, 11, 12, 13, 15, 16), as well as "he/they shall be put to death."[a] We also have the repetition of the phrases "a man lies with" (20:11, 12, 13, 15, 20), "uncovers the nakedness of" (20:11, 17, 18, 19, 20, 21), "gives his seed to Molech" (20:2, 3, 4), and "set my face against" (20:3, 5, 6), as well as the words "cut off" (20:3, 5, 6, 17, 18) and "take as wife/marry" (20:14, 17, 21).

(a) Lev 20:2, 9, 10, 11, 12, 13, 15, 16, 27

The two sets of laws culminate in two similar admonitions in 20:7–8 and 20:22–26. These admonitions are linked together structurally by the repetition of the formula for divine self-introduction in 20:7 and 20:24, the command to keep God's decrees in 20:7 and 20:22, and the call to be holy in 20:7 and 20:26. Thus the two sets of laws and the two admonitions divide the chapter into two parallel sections. As a result of this arrangement the final verse (20:27) is highlighted and emphasized. It forms an inclusion with the first set of laws by its reference to spiritism (20:6) and death by stoning (20:2).

[10] Hartley, *Leviticus*, 330–31.

Figure 21

Penalties for Offenses in Leviticus 20

Offense	*Penalty*	*Reason*	*Status of Offense*
Child sacrifice (20:2–3)	Divine extirpation Death by stoning	Defilement of sanctuary	Profanation of God's name
Tolerance of child sacrifice (20:4–5)	Divine extirpation	Ritual prostitution	
Consultation of spiritists (20:6)	Divine extirpation	Ritual prostitution	
Cursing of parents (20:9)	Execution	Bloodguilt	Bloodguilt
Adultery (20:10)	Execution of couple		
Sex with stepmother (20:11)	Execution of couple	Uncovering of father's nakedness	Bloodguilt
Sex with daughter-in-law (20:12)	Execution of couple	Bloodguilt	Perversion; bloodguilt
Homosexual intercourse (20:13)	Execution of couple	Bloodguilt	Abomination; bloodguilt
Marriage to a woman and her mother (20:14)	Burning	Prevention of obscenity	Act of obscenity
Male bestiality (20:15)	Execution of man and animal		
Female bestiality(20:16)	Execution of woman and animal	Bloodguilt	Bloodguilt
Marriage to sister (20:17)	Divine extirpation	Mutual viewing of nakedness Uncovering of sister's nakedness	Disgraceful act Bearing of iniquity
Menstrual intercourse (20:18)	Divine extirpation	Uncovering of woman's nakedness Uncovering of blood flow by man Exposure of blood flow by woman	
Sex with aunt (20:19)		Uncovering of nakedness Exposure of uncle's flesh	Bearing of iniquity
Sex with paternal aunt-in-law (20:20)	Childlessness	Uncovering of uncle's nakedness	Bearing of sin
Marriage with sister-in-law (20:21)	Childlessness	Menstrual impurity Uncovering of brother's nakedness	
Practice of spiritism (20:27)	Death by stoning	Bloodguilt	Bloodguilt

The structure of this pericope can be outlined as follows:

I. Introduction (20:1–2a)
  A. God's address of Moses (20:1)
  B. Commission to speak to the Israelites (20:2a)
II. Speech (20:2b–27)
  A. Religious offenses and participation in God's holiness (20:2b–8)
    1. Cases of the death penalty for religious offenses (20:2b–6)
      a. Sacrifice of children to Molech (20:2b–3)
      b. Communal tolerance of child sacrifice (20:4–5)
      c. Consultation of spiritists (20:6)
    2. Participation in God's holiness (20:7–8)
      a. Call to self-consecration with formula of divine self-introduction (20:7)
      b. Call for ritual observance with formula of divine consecration (20:8)
  B. Moral offenses and the preservation of holiness (20:9–26)
    1. Penalties for moral offenses (20:9–21)
      a. Cases for execution by humans (20:9–16)
        i. Cursing of parents (20:9)
        ii. Adultery (20:10)
        iii. Incest with stepmother (20:11) and daughter-in-law (20:12)
        iv. Homosexual intercourse (20:13)
        v. Marriage to a woman and her mother (20:14)
        vi. Bestiality: male (20:15) and female (20:16)
      b. Cases for divine extirpation (20:17–18)
        i. Marriage to sister or half sister (20:17)
        ii. Sexual intercourse during menstruation (20:18)
      c. Case for bearing iniquity: intercourse with paternal or maternal aunt (20:19)
      d. Cases for childlessness (20:20–21)
        i. Sexual intercourse with aunt-in-law (20:20)
        ii. Sexual intercourse with sister-in-law (20:21)
    2. Avoidance of defilement and participation in God's holiness (20:22–26)
      a. Admonition for observance of God's decrees in the land (20:22–23)
      b. Promise of possession of the land as a gift from God (20:24a)
      c. Call for separation from impurity (20:24b–26)
        i. Formula for God's self-presentation as Israel's creator (20:24b)
        ii. Command to avoid defilement with unclean animals and birds (20:25)
        iii. Promise of participation in God's holiness (20:26)
  C. Death penalty for the practice of spiritism (20:27)

Ritual Agents

The legislation in this chapter focuses on the extended family as the basic social and religious unit in Israel. The casuistic laws in it protect the family

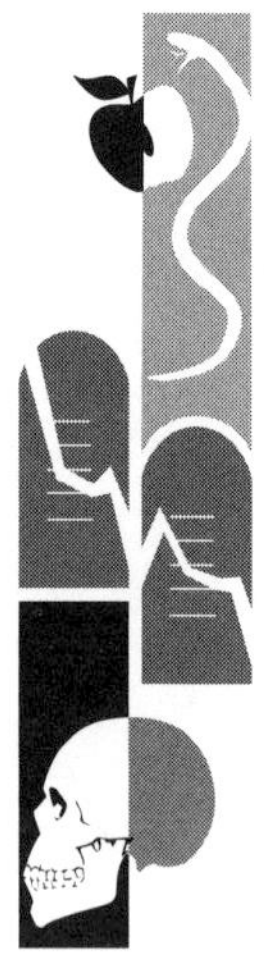

from disintegration from four potential threats to its survival. The first threat comes from the spiritual apostasy of the family by the sacrifice of children to Molech and the practice of necromancy (20:1–6, 27). The second threat comes from the displacement of parents as the heads of the family (20:9). The third threat comes from improper sexual activity in the family (20:10–21). The fourth threat comes from the possible embroilment of the family in destructive acts of vengeance for the execution of its members by people belonging to other families.

Since the penalty of death had to be carried out by people from outside the family, they and the family itself were protected from vengeance by the divine decree that the offenders brought this penalty on themselves by their offense (20:9, 11, 12, 13, 16). God himself prohibited revenge in these cases by asserting that their blood was on them; they brought the death penalty on themselves. All the laws in this chapter were meant to preserve the family as a part of Israel.

One might have expected these laws, which lay down the penalties for these offenses, to be addressed to the heads of the extended families. Instead, they were given to "the sons of Israel" (20:2). The sons of Israel formed the assembly of the landed families that constituted the people of Israel.[11] As such they had political and judicial power in their communities. These men were called "the people of the land."[12] Together they acted representatively as "the assembly of Israel" (19:2; 24:16). As 20:4 shows, they were responsible for the local administration of justice. In each of the cases mentioned in this chapter, they were required to intervene where the normal leaders of the family would either be unable or unwilling to act because they were hampered by the ties of kinship, obligation, and solidarity in the family.

The male heads of the local community were therefore commissioned by God to act as a corporate body on his behalf. They were empowered to carry out the sentence of death, if necessary, by stoning (20:2, 27), burning (20:14), or public execution (20:9–13, 15–16). They, presumably, were to warn offenders and possible offenders in those cases where God himself exacted the penalty. So God addressed them directly and required them to protect the families in their communities from possible self-destruction (20:7, 8, 19, 22–26).

God resided in his sanctuary at the center of this community (20:3). He made his people holy (20:8) and set them apart from the nations around them (20:24, 26). He promised to bring them into the land of Canaan and give it to them (20:22–24). He was Israel's divine head who gave the Israelites these laws to enact for him (20:8, 22). But he did not just execute justice through them. When they, in their families, secretly committed a capital offense that could not be dealt with in a human court, he himself carried out the penalty for

---

[11] Joosten, *People and Land in the Holiness Code*, 30–33.

[12] Joosten, *People and Land in the Holiness Code*, 42–47.

it by either cutting off the offenders (20:3, 5, 17, 18) or by making them bear their iniquities (20:17, 19, 20).

God is clearly distinguished from the pagan god Molech and the spirits of the dead. Molech was a deity who resided in the underworld. He required child sacrifice as the price for the fertility of a family and the prosperity of its land. Molech may have been associated by the Canaanites with the spirits of their ancestors, the ghosts of the people who formerly lived on that tract of land and were buried there. That land could therefore be held to belong to them spiritually. They had the power to bless or harm those who occupied their territory. They were related to the other earth-spirits residing there. They were, perhaps, even identified with them. They could be conjured up by necromancers or mediums, who were therefore said to have "a ghost or a familiar spirit in them" (20:27).

Ghosts seem to have been regarded as ancestral spirits with supernatural power to do good or evil. The familiar spirits, "the knowers" as they are termed in Hebrew, were people who were possessed by spirits and who therefore could foretell the future. Families were tempted to turn to these mediums and consult them to secure their family's survival (20:6). Both 20:2–5 and Deut 18:9–12 imply that necromancy was connected in some way with Molech and the sacrifice of children to Molech. Whatever the connection, this chapter regards both Molech and these spirits as the rivals to the Lord in the land. Child sacrifice and the practice of spiritism were completely incompatible with the worship of the Lord and life with him in his land.

Ritual Location

As in chapter 18, these laws are framed for enactment in a very specific ritual situation. They envisage the residence of the Israelites in the land of Canaan. They were therefore addressed proleptically to "the people of the land" (20:2, 4) even though the Israelites would not inherit the land until later under Joshua.

God regarded this land as his own land. It did not belong to "the nation" which had formerly occupied it (20:23), even though God spoke of its territory as "their land" (20:24). As the rightful owner of the land, he treated the former inhabitants as bad tenants who had forfeited their right to occupy the land by their abuse of it. He therefore announced that he would evict them from the land and promised that he would bring the Israelites into it, so that they could settle there. As he had promised Abraham and his descendants, he would "give" them his land to "possess" (20:23–24). They would inherit the land from him and occupy it as his tenants. By giving them this land, he "set them apart" and so "distinguished" them from all other nations (20:26). Their occupation of his land therefore reflected their unique identity. It was the presupposition for all the sanctions in this chapter.

The land was significant in two ways. First, it was "a land flowing with milk and syrup" (20:24). It was therefore a fertile, productive land that did not just supply the mere necessities for human life, but, in fact, supplied its people with luxuries, and that in abundance. Its characteristic luxuries were milk from goats for yogurt and butter and syrup from grapes and dates for sweets and sweet-cakes. So, through this land God promised to provide an abundant life for his people.

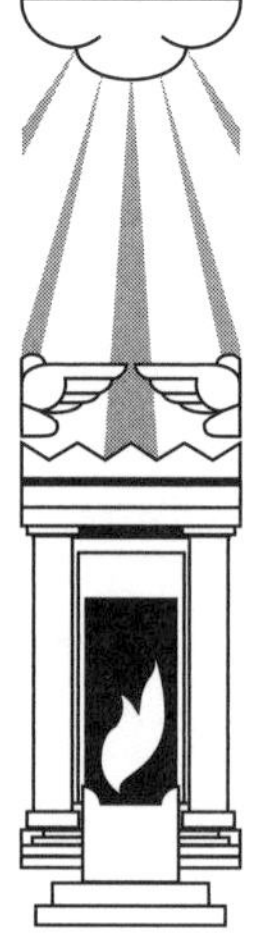

Second, it was God's land, the land where he resided with them in his sanctuary (20:3). He set the terms for its occupation and use by them (20:22–23). It was sacrosanct land, temple property, divine rather than human territory. The land was an extension of the sanctuary, part of it and inseparable from it. And the Israelites were his temple servants, holy people who worked with him and shared in his bounty.[13] They lived with him on his estate and feasted with him at his table. They therefore had to rid the land of everything that desecrated his sanctuary and so disrupted the flow of life from him to his people through the land. Indeed, since the Lord lived in this land, the land itself would "spew out" those who polluted it by following the sacrilegious, life-threatening customs of its former residents (20:22; see also 18:25, 28). As the stomach showed its disgust at anything that polluted it, so the land also sympathetically shared God's disgust at the pollution of the land by its inhabitants (20:23).

The location of the Israelites on this land had a further, even more profound implication. Their bodies were to be regarded ritually as a microcosm of the land. Their treatment of their bodies was to match their life in the land (20:25–26). Both the land and their bodies were to be kept ritually clean; both were to avoid all that would defile them. Just as God had "distinguished" his people by separating them from all the unclean nations and giving them his land (20:24, 26), so in their diet they were to "distinguish" clean, edible animals and birds from unclean, inedible animals and birds (20:25). Their diet was therefore to mirror their sexual behavior in the land. As God was "disgusted" with the people who polluted his land (20:23), so the Israelites were forbidden to contaminate themselves disgustfully by eating unclean meat (20:25).

Penalties for Ritual Defilement

Whereas the apodictic statutes in Leviticus 18 had prohibited certain dangerous acts of defilement to the land of Israel, these casuistic laws laid down the penalties for them. These penalties are listed on a descending scale, according to the severity of the sanction and the responsibility for its exaction. They weave together the demand for human punishment with the threat of divine retribution. From a human point of view, they list capital crimes that required ritual communal execution by stoning (20:2, 27), public juridical execution (20:9–13, 15–16), or public juridical execution with the ritual burning of the culprits (20:14). From the divine point of view, they list crimes that incurred a range of supernatural sanctions: God's opposition to the law-break-

---

[13] Joosten, *People and Land in the Holiness Code*, 176–92.

ers by his setting his face against them (20:3, 5, 6); his extirpation of them from their kinsfolk (20:3, 5, 6, 17, 18); his visitation of their iniquity (20:17, 19) and their sin (20:20) as a burden on them until it was expiated; and the curse of childlessness (20:20, 21).

This chapter deals generally with penalties for two classes of evildoing. The first class consists of capital offenses against the holy Lord and his holy people. They are child sacrifice to Molech and the consultation with spiritists (20:2–6, 27). The sacrifice of a child to Molech and the practice of spiritism incurred the mandatory sentence of death and the public execution of the criminal by the ritual act of stoning. God also declared that he himself would set his face implacably against three groups of evildoers in order to extirpate them: the father who sacrificed his child to Molech (20:3); the family and supporters of that man if they did not bring him to justice (20:4–5); and the person who consulted a spiritist (20:6).

The second class consists of offenses against the Israelite family (20:9–21). The first eight of these are capital offenses: the rejection of parents (20:9); adultery (20:10); sexual intercourse with one's stepmother (20:11) or daughter-in-law (20:12); homosexual intercourse (20:13); polygamous sexual cohabitation with a woman and her daughter (20:14); and male (20:15) and female bestiality (20:16). These all alike incurred the death penalty. In the case of polygamous cohabitation all three parties were to be burned as well (20:14). The next five offenses incurred a divine penalty only, because they, by and large, occurred in secret and in private within the confines of the family: extirpation by God for marriage to a sister (20:17) or for deliberate sexual intercourse with a menstruating woman (20:18); retribution by God for sexual intercourse between a man and his aunt (20:19); childlessness for sexual intercourse between a man and his paternal aunt-in-law (20:20) or between a man and his fraternal sister-in-law (20:21).

These laws combine three kinds of penalties: the penalty of capital punishment by human beings for public crimes against the family; the penalty of retribution by God for secret crimes in the family; and the penalty of extirpation from the family or through childlessness for secret crimes. All were, in a sense, crimes against life. They disrupted the flow of life from God through the family. Since they violated life, they were lethal and suicidal. And so they, appropriately, incurred either the penalty of death from the people of Israel (20:2, 10–16, 27) or the threat of diminishment of life from God (20:3–6, 17–21).

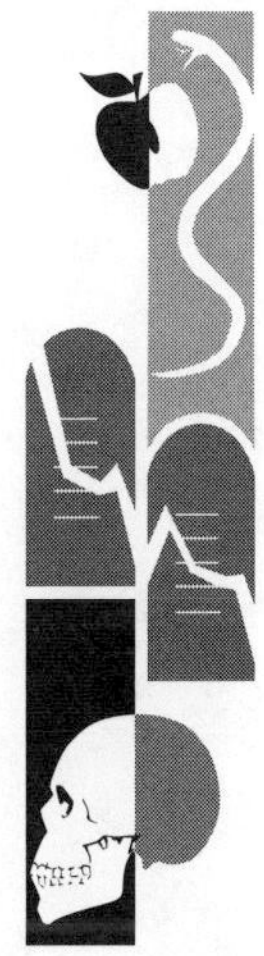

Child sacrifice and the consultation of spiritists incurred such severe penalties because they involved the worst kinds of ritual offenses against God. They were acts of faithlessness by which the Israelites prostituted themselves with Molech (20:5) and the spirits of the dead (20:6). The Israelites did not just defile themselves by this form of contact with occult powers, but they also defiled God's sanctuary (20:3). Worse than that, since they were God's holy people who had access to his holiness, they desecrated his holy name. Ritually, they therefore cut themselves off from the divine source of life in the land and aligned themselves with the powers of the underworld and death. By this suicidal behavior, they brought the penalty of death upon themselves.

The penalties for the sexual offenses in 20:11–21 are given for the same reasons as in 18:6–23. Incestuous sexual activity was to be punished because it would "expose" and so endanger the "flesh" of relatives beyond those of just the participants in the sin. The vulnerable flesh of the family, its physical unity and intimacy, was invaded; it lost its protective covering. Thus sexual intercourse by a man with his mother uncovered his father's nakedness (20:11). Sexual intercourse by a man with an unmarried aunt uncovered her nakedness and exposed his own flesh (20:19). Sexual intercourse by a man with a married aunt uncovered the nakedness of his uncle (20:20). In the same way the cohabitation of a man with his widowed sister-in-law uncovered the nakedness of his brother, even if he was no longer alive (20:21). The cohabitation of a man with his sister or half sister was a special case (20:17). The man not only uncovered her nakedness; both of them exposed themselves sexually to each other so that they "saw" each other's nakedness. And this was regarded as something disgraceful. It violated the taboo on visual sexual intimacy in the nuclear family apart from marriage.

If a man deliberately had sexual intercourse with a menstruating woman, he too uncovered her nakedness (18:19). But something else was also involved. He "bared" and "exposed" her "fountain." The term fountain refers to the womb that produced the menstrual blood (cf. Prov 5:18) and to the blood that it produced (Lev 12:7). The womb of a woman was thus envisaged as a well for water, a life-giving spring, the source of life.[b] Like a well that needed to be protected by covering its mouth so that it did not become polluted or blocked with debris, the womb of a woman needed to be covered and protected if it was to remain fertile and productive.

(b) Cf. Ps 36:10 (ET 36:9); Prov 10:11; 13:14; 14:27; 16:22; Jer 2:13; 17:13

Sexual intercourse during menstruation did not, as is believed in some animist societies, open up the fountain of life, nor did it increase fertility by mixing the living seed of a man with the life-giving blood of a woman. Intercourse during menstruation did not increase the virility of a man or the fertility of a woman, but actually endangered the flow of life in a family. By engaging in sexual intercourse at this time, the man "exposed" and so dissipated its flow. The woman who sought to have sexual intercourse during her menstrual period also "uncovered the fountain of her blood" and threatened the regular, secret flow that kept her womb fertile and healthy. Sexual intercourse during menstruation was not a sacred act by which a couple participated in the cosmic current of life, its divine flow, as some pagan religions held. On the contrary, it contaminated both parties and cut them off from God's life. Menstrual blood did not have supernatural life-power. It was a unique source of pollution, resembling the pollution arising from the cohabitation of a man with his widowed sister-in-law (20:21). God forbade the use of it by men through the taboo against contact with it. He did not allow them to attempt to gain life-power from women by any kind of sexual contact with menstrual blood.

The category of perversity, used for the evaluation of bestiality in 18:23, is also used in 20:12 to pass judgment on sexual intercourse by a man with his daughter-in-law. This act created inevitable confusion within the family, since it violated the divinely created order of succession of life from father to son through the son's mother. As in 18:17, the polygamous cohabitation of a man with a woman and her mother was regarded as "something obscene." In fact, it was so contagiously obscene that it required all parties to be burnt with fire to remove its evil influence from Israel (20:14; cf. 19:29).

As in 18:22, homosexual intercourse is an abominable act (20:13). God does not give a humanistic or moral reason for his judgment; the reason is theological. God abhors it. It cannot enhance male virility, the life-power of men, by the reception or even exchange of semen, as some animists may have believed. Instead, it cuts off the offenders from God and God's life. They are to be put to death.

This chapter makes the best sense as a unified composition if we assume that all the offenses mentioned in it are remnants of the pagan religious customs and ritual practices of those who occupied the land of Canaan before the Israelites (20:23; cf. 18:3). From a religious point of view, all these prohibited practices were attempts by people in an animist environment to gain or increase supernatural life-power, a prescientific form of Viagra. The pagan belief was that this life-power could be acquired by the head of a family for his family through child sacrifice to Molech or through contact with the life-giving spirits of the dead. It could also be gained from the clan by cursing one's parents (20:9), from another man by sleeping with his wife (20:10–12), and from another man (20:13) or the mother of a woman (20:14) or an animal (20:15–16) by sexual intercourse with them. The mistaken view was that the life-power of a family could be conserved and increased by cohabitation with one's sister (20:17) or widowed sister-in-law (20:21), by sexual intercourse with a menstruating woman (20:18), and by sexual intercourse with an unmarried aunt (20:19) or even married aunt (20:20).

However, the Lord declares that all those acts incur his wrath and lead to sterility, death, the destruction of the family, and ultimately to punishment in hell. They are incompatible with God's gifts of fertility, life, and the prosperity of the family.

Theological Significance

The legislation in this chapter is interpreted theologically by a simple literary device. The penalties for the various offenses are framed by two sets of passages that relate all the offenses to God.

The first of these is the bracket formed by the laws on spiritism in 20:6 and 20:27. This device indicates that all the intervening material is to be connected implicitly with the practice of spiritism. But how does that material relate to it? The solution to this problem lies in the insight that ghosts and familiar spirits belonged to the realm of impurity rather than the divine sacral realm, as an-

imists believed. Like Molech, they resided in the underworld, the place of death. These spirits were not regarded as the allies of God and the agents of his blessing; they were unclean spirits, malign powers that destroyed life and disordered the world. They exercised their power through those who conjured them (20:27) or who had them conjured for their benefit (20:6). Through the practice of child sacrifice these evil powers most obviously made inroads into a land and its people (20:2–5). But they also invaded the families in a land more secretly through their rejection of parental authority (20:9) and their involvement in sexual malpractices (20:10–21).

These sins were penalized so severely because they opened up the people of Israel to evil spirits. God aimed to keep these powers at bay by the threat of expulsion (Deut 18:9–14; 1 Sam 28:3) and capital punishment (Ex 22:18; Lev 20:27) of those who trafficked in them. They were best kept from the land by the removal of the impurity that provided a hospitable cover for them.

The second set of passages is the summary admonitions in 20:7 and 20:22–26. Both these texts explicate the theological presuppositions for the preceding legislation. All the sanctions were required because the Lord was holy (20:26). Since he had introduced and committed himself to his people with his holy name, he was their God who dwelt with them in his sanctuary (20:3, 7, 24). He declared, most emphatically, that he made them holy (20:8), just as he also made the priests holy; since the Israelites could not make themselves holy enough to enter the divine realm, he came to them to share his own unique holiness with them. That gave them their unique status and extraordinary vocation on earth.

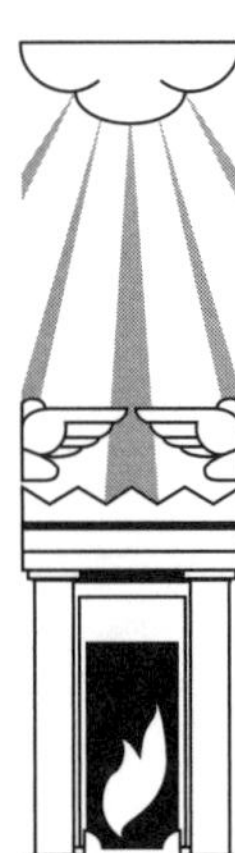

His sanctification of them was not just a past historical event, something that he did to them by rescuing them from slavery in Egypt (Deut 7:6–8) or by meeting with them at Mount Sinai (Ex 19:6). Rather, it involved the ongoing process of the reception of holiness from him in the divine service (Ex 29:43–44), like light and warmth and energy from the sun. As such it had three sides to it.

First, God set his people apart by giving them his land as their place of residence with him (20:24, 26).

Second, he made them holy and kept them holy by his presence with them in the land. He consecrated them by residing in the sanctuary and giving them access to his holiness there (20:3, 7).

Third, they themselves were to "be holy" (20:26) by consecrating themselves to him (20:7). They consecrated themselves to God and received holiness from him by observing his ritual statutes. Positively, these sanctifying statutes established the rituals by which the Lord made the people holy and prescribed how they were to be involved in these rituals. Negatively, they prohibited those activities that desecrated and profaned God's holiness. If the Israelites were to remain holy, they had to avoid the offenses listed in 20:2–6 and 20:9–21.

God imposed these penalties on the Israelites because they shared in his holiness. Since they were his holy people, they had access to him and his life-giving blessing. They were a priestly people who lived and worked with him in his holy land. This great privilege, however, came with great responsibilities. The imposition of capital punishment for the sexual offenses in 20:10–16 and the prohibition of menstrual intercourse in 20:18 all presuppose that the Israelites were a holy, priestly people. If they observed God's rules for their ritual purity, they would receive life from him and be blessed by him (26:1–13). But if they desecrated his holiness by their impurities, they would face temporal and eternal death and come under his curse (26:14–39). Ongoing participation in God's holiness was a matter of life or death for his people.

Fulfillment by Christ

Jesus did not explicitly abolish any of the laws and penalties for their infringement in Leviticus 20. In Mt 15:4 and Mk 7:10 he confirmed the decree from Lev 20:9 that those who cursed their parents should be put to death. When the scribes and the Pharisees brought a woman to him who had been caught in adultery, he did not disagree with their judgment from Lev 20:10 that such a person should be put to death (Jn 8:2–11). He did not repeal these laws or even lighten the weight of the penalties given in this chapter. If anything, he extended the scope of offenses that merit the death penalty from the offenses described in Leviticus 20 to include all sins. His message is that since everyone has sinned, everyone is under the divine sentence of death. They (we) all will perish unless they (we) all repent (Lk 13:5).

Paul too follows Jesus in this. He includes homosexuality and lesbianism in the list of offenses against God in Rom 1:18–32 and concludes with this statement: "those who practice such things deserve to die."

In fact, God's law reveals that every human being has sinned against God and is therefore under the sentence of death (Rom 3:9–20). Every sin is a capital offense before God, and "the wages of sin is death" (Rom 6:23).

All this serves to highlight the Gospel side of the ministry of Jesus and his apostles. Jesus did not come to abolish the law, but to fulfill it. And that in a strange way! He did not establish a theocratic state that enforced the letter and the spirit of God's law. Instead, the sentence of death that should have been carried out on all the descendants of Adam—not just those who do the kinds of evil described in Leviticus 20—fell on Jesus. In fact, God the Father sentenced him to death through the high priest. The divine curse for human sin was inflicted on him (Gal 3:10–14). God the Father made him the sin offering for all people so that all those who were joined with Jesus could receive pardon and justification (2 Cor 5:21).

Jesus made it quite clear that he had not come to condemn sinners to death, but to save them from the sentence of death (Jn 3:17–18; 12:47). He therefore did not condemn the woman caught in adultery, but pardoned her (Jn 8:2–11), just as he forgave the sinful woman who anointed his feet (Lk 7:36–50). He did not shun the people with unclean spirits, but delivered them from the spirits that had possessed them. In this he set the pattern for the early church. Thus in Acts 16:16–18 Paul exorcised the woman who had a spirit of divination. The apostle also taught that through Baptism into Christ people who formerly were guilty of sexual immorality and had engaged actively and passively in homosexual intercourse have now been cleansed, justified, and consecrated as God's holy people. Since they have died to sin with Christ, they no longer engage in those evil behaviors. Instead, they lead a new life in the Spirit in conformity to God's Word (Rom 6:1–11; 1 Cor 6:9–11).

Jesus also fulfilled the just requirements of God's law by making and keeping his disciples holy. He consecrated himself on their behalf so that he could consecrate them (Jn 17:19). He is the Holy One of God (Mk 1:24; Jn 6:69). Like God who had declared to the Israelites in Lev 20:8, "I am the Lord who makes you holy," he sanctifies all the members of the church by his embodied presence with them in the Divine Service and his ministry as their exalted High Priest (Heb 2:11). He sanctifies them through his holy body and blood (Heb 10:10, 14, 29; 13:12). He therefore is their sanctification (1 Cor 1:30). In him and through their faith in him, they are sanctified (Acts 26:18; 1 Cor 1:2). They are holy in him (Phil 1:1).

Just as God sanctified the Israelites by his ritual statutes by which he instituted and empowered the divine service at the tabernacle (Lev 20:8), so Jesus makes and keeps his disciples holy with his Word (Jn 17:17). They sanctify themselves by their participation in the Divine Service. There he shares his holiness with them through his Word and the Sacrament. Since they are saints, holy people with a priestly vocation, they are called to be holy in all their behavior (1 Pet 1:14–15). Their lifestyle reflects their ritual status.

Like the book of Leviticus, the NT does not inculcate a system of natural ethics based on universal human values that promote harmony within the order of creation. Instead, the NT proclaims a system of liturgical ethics—the ethics of holiness—a heavenly lifestyle for God's people on earth. The NT presupposes that all Christians are involved in the Divine Service that is enacted by the church together with Christ in the heavenly sanctuary. They are all priests who serve together with Christ their High Priest (1 Pet 2:5; Rev 1:6; 5:10). They are also God's earthly sanctuary, the temple of the living God (1 Cor 3:16–17; 2 Cor 6:16).

Since they all share bodily in Christ's holiness, their bodies too are temples of the Holy Spirit (1 Cor 6:19). As holy sons of God they seek to hallow God's name (Mt 6:9; Lk 11:2). They must not desecrate his temple by defiling themselves in body or spirit (2 Cor 6:14–7:1). If they desecrate his holiness they come under God's wrath and judgment (Eph 5:3–6; 1 Thess 4:7–8; Heb 10:26–31). If they defile themselves, they lose their inheritance in God's kingdom (1 Cor 6:9–10), just as those Israelites who followed the evil customs of the Canaanites lost their place in the land and their status as God's people (Lev 20:22–23; 1 Cor 10:1–13).

The avoidance of sexual immorality and occult practices does not, in itself, make people holy. Rather, God's people are to avoid those sins so that they do not lose their holiness by their involvement with impurity. Since they are holy, they are called to shun all that is unholy, everything that is incompatible with their ritual status (2 Tim 2:20–22). They are to separate themselves from unclean people and avoid "every defilement of body and spirit," for defilement opens up their bodies and spirits to the influence of unclean spirits and the powers of darkness (2 Cor 6:14–7:1).

This applies, most obviously, to their sexuality, for sexual impurity mirrors and matches all other kinds of impurity. The holiness of God's people determines their sexual behavior, their talk about sex, and their attitude toward sexually immoral people (Eph 5:3–14). In fact, God intends his holiness to pervade and transform their sexuality (1 Thess 4:3–5). The call of God to share in his holiness affects them in three ways. They avoid immorality; they do not exploit their spouse for their own sexual gratification, but use their sexuality honorably and considerately; and they respect the God-pleasing sexuality of others.

God's judgment on two cases of sexual impurity in Leviticus 20 are hard for some modern people to accept. The first of these is homosexuality, which is now promoted as a natural and legitimate mode of sexuality in many parts of the Western world and even in some parts of the visible church. The prohibition of homosexual intercourse was imposed on the Israelites as a condition for their residence with God in the land of Israel. Homosexual intercourse was practiced and condoned in some parts of the ancient world. The Pentateuch states that homosexuality was one of the reasons for the eviction of the Canaanites from the land of Israel (Lev 18:3, 24–25, 27–28; 20:23). Therefore these laws did not pertain only to Israel; all peoples are held accountable to them, as affirmed in the NT (e.g., Rom 1:18–32).

God prohibits his people from engaging in homosexual activity for religious, theological reasons. Such behavior is inconsistent with their holy status as God's people. It defiles their holiness and disqualifies them from involvement in the Divine Service. Even if there is a general consensus in our secular society that it should be tolerated or approved, the church cannot sanction it for its members, for that would contravene the clear teaching of God through St. Paul in 1 Cor 6:9–11 and 1 Tim 1:8–11. The church must condemn it on the basis of the Scriptures. As for those individuals and church bodies that condone the practice, the apostle's warning stands: those who do such things will not inherit the kingdom of God (1 Cor 6:9–10).[14]

The second case in Leviticus 20 that is hard for some to accept is the prohibition of sexual intercourse during menstruation and the harsh penalty for any contravention (20:18). There may indeed be good hygienic, aesthetic, and

---

[14] See also Rev 21:8; 22:15; and the discussion of homosexuality in Lockwood, *1 Corinthians*, 204–9.

psychological reasons for this prohibition, but those are not the reasons why God forbade it. Behind the command lies the teaching that menstrual blood is unclean because it was used for magic and for ritual purposes in pagan cults. Intercourse during the flow of that blood was therefore forbidden for religious reasons. The question is whether these reasons still apply to Christian couples in our modern secular culture. The NT says nothing about this (unlike homosexuality, which the NT does condemn). Because of the silence of the NT, the church has not made a decision on this, but has left the matter to the conscience of its members. It could be argued that we need to revisit this issue and affirm the prohibition in Leviticus in the light of the modern, pagan sacralization of sex and menstrual blood by some proponents of the New Age Movement.

The need for all Christ's disciples to avoid doing anything that desecrates their holiness applies to all the other matters mentioned in this chapter. The members of the church do not sacrifice their children for their own gain by exposing them at the shrine of a god. Neither do they abort their children. The abomination of wanton sacrifice of (untold millions of) children by their parents through abortion is the closest modern equivalent to the Canaanite practice of parents sacrificing their children to the god Molech.

Christian parents treasure their children as a gift from God and raise them as children of God (Eph 6:4). Under no circumstances do they have anything to do with spiritism, nor do they traffic in the occult. They do not belittle their own parents, but honor them in every possible way (Eph 6:1–3; Col 3:20). They live as in God's presence and resolve to lead holy lives since Christ himself has made them holy. They wear Christ's holiness as their armor of light that protects them and their families from the powers of darkness (Rom 13:12).

Renew me, O eternal Light,
And let my heart and soul be bright,
Illumined with the light of grace
That issues from your holy face.

Remove the pow'r of sin from me
And cleanse all my impurity
That I may have the strength and will
Temptations of the flesh to still.

Create in me a new heart, Lord,
That gladly I obey your Word.
Let what you will be my desire,
And with new life my soul inspire.[15]

[15] From "Renew Me, O Eternal Light" by Johann F. Ruopp (*LW* 373:1–3).

Leviticus 21–22

Holy Priests and Holy Offerings

Whereas chapters 18–20 had shown how the Israelites were to avoid defilement and participate in God's holiness, chapters 21–22 show how the priests were to do so. The focus in these chapters is on the holiness of the priests and their food.

These two chapters make up a discrete unit in Leviticus. They bring together six sections that conclude with the same formula: "I am the Lord who sanctifies you/them" (21:8, 15, 23; 22:9, 16, 32). A general summary admonition in 22:31–33 rounds off this unit. Like 20:22–26 in chapters 18–20, this admonition provides the conclusion for 22:26–30, as well as all the material in chapters 21–22.

This basic pattern of arrangement is complicated by the insertion of these six sections in five speeches that do not coincide entirely with them (beginning in 21:1, 16; 22:1, 17, 26). The first speech logically joins the code for the priests in 21:1–9 with the code for the high priest in 21:10–15, while the third speech combines the list of defects that disqualify a priest from eating sacred food in 22:1–9 with the list of those residents of a priest's household who are forbidden to eat sacred food in 22:10–16. The sixth section with its list of the animals that are acceptable as private sacrifices by lay people is divided into two separate speeches: 22:17–25 and 22:26–33. This distinguishes the disqualification of some animals for sacrifice because of their physical defects from the temporal restrictions placed on the presentation of an animal for sacrifice and the consumption of meat from an animal sacrificed as a thank offering.

The arrangement of these six units is complicated still further by the separation of the first three sections from the next three by the formula for compliance in 21:24. This formula echoes the introduction in 17:2. It associates the material in 21:1–23 with the body of legislation collected in chapters 17–21 or with the legislation on the disposal of blood in 17:1–16.

Leviticus 21:1–15

Protecting the Holiness of the Priests

Translation

**21 1The Lord said to Moses: "Say to the priests, the sons of Aaron, and you will
say to them: No one shall make himself unclean for a dead person among his kinsfolk, 2except for his closest relative—his mother, his father, his son, his daughter,
and his brother; 3and for his virgin sister, who is close to him because she does not
belong to a man—for her he may make himself unclean. 4But he shall not make
himself unclean as a husband among his kinsfolk and so desecrate himself.**

**5"They [priests] shall not shave off a bald patch on their heads or cut off the
edges of their beards or gash gashes in their bodies. 6They shall be holy to their
God, and they shall not desecrate the name of their God; because they present
the gifts of the Lord, the food of their God, they possess holiness.**

**7"They shall not marry a prostitute or a woman who has been desecrated;
neither shall they marry a woman divorced from her husband, for he [each priest]
is holy to his God; 8and you shall treat him as holy, since he presents the food of
your God; he shall be holy to you, for I, the Lord, who sanctifies you, am holy.**

**9"When the daughter of a man who is a priest desecrates herself through
prostitution, she is desecrating her father; she shall be burned in fire.**

**10"The priest who is greater than his brothers, on whose head the anointing
oil is poured and who has been ordained to wear the vestments, shall not dishevel
his hair nor tear his vestments; 11nor shall he enter any place on account of a dead
person; he may not [even] make himself unclean for his father or his mother. 12He
shall not leave the sanctuary so that he will not desecrate the sanctuary of his
God, for the mark of consecration with the anointing oil of his God is upon him;
I am the Lord.**

**13"He [the high priest] shall marry a woman who is in her state of virginity.
A widow or a divorcée or a desecrated woman or a prostitute—these he shall not
marry. Instead, he shall marry a virgin from his own kinsfolk as a wife, 15so that
he does not desecrate his offspring among his kinsfolk; for I am the Lord who
consecrates him."**

Textual Notes

21:1 וַיֹּ֤אמֶר יְהוָה֙ אֶל־מֹשֶׁ֔ה—This is the same unusual introductory formula as in 16:2. Both introduce passages that have to do with the office of the high priest.[1] See also Ezek 44:25. The following imperative אֱמֹ֤ר, "say," is also unusual because the usual imperative that follows the usual introductory formula is דַּבֵּר (e.g., 18:2; 19:2; 22:2).

---

1 Warning, *Literary Artistry in Leviticus*, 42–43.

לְנֶפֶשׁ—The term נֶפֶשׁ is used here for both the corpse and soul of a dead person (cf. 19:28; 21:11; Num 5:2; 6:11; 9:6, 7, 10; 19:11, 13; Hag 2:13). While it obviously refers to the dead body, it can also be used for the soul or spirit of a person that leaves the body at death (Gen 35:18; 1 Ki 17:21, 22).

יִטַּמָּא—The Hithpael of טָמֵא is used here and in 21:3, 11 for ritual defilement of oneself through physical contact with a corpse. The assimilated ת is marked by the *daghesh* in the *tet* (-טּ-).

בְּעַמָּיו׃—In this chapter (21:1, 4, 14, 15) the plural of עַם is used in its narrower sense for the "kinsfolk" or people who make up a person's clan rather than "peoples."

21:2 כִּי אִם־לִשְׁאֵרוֹ הַקָּרֹב אֵלָיו—In Hebrew שְׁאֵר, "flesh," refers to a close consanguinal relative in an extended family. It excludes the spouse of the person. The adjective קָרוֹב, "near," also implies dependency and indicates that the relative lives close by as part of the extended family.

לְאִמּוֹ וּלְאָבִיו—As in 19:3, the mother comes before the father. Here it could be because physically the priest is closest to her.

21:3 הַבְּתוּלָה—The noun בְּתוּלָה here and in 21:14 refers to a young woman who is mature enough for marriage. In some contexts, as in 21:3, 14, it can indicate that she is still a virgin, so we translate it as "virgin." (עַלְמָה, the term used in Is 7:14, in the OT always means "virgin.")

לֹא־הָיְתָה לְאִישׁ—This refers to her legal status as a single woman. Because she is not married, she legally is still part of the priest's family.

21:4 לֹא יִטַּמָּא בַּעַל—The sense of בַּעַל here is debated. Most likely it refers to the priest as a "husband," which is the meaning of בַּעַל in various other passages (e.g., Ex 21:3, 22). This prohibition means that the priest could not prepare his wife for burial, because she is not his "flesh" relative. (שְׁאֵר, the term for "flesh" in Lev 21:2, is a different term than בָּשָׂר in Gen 2:24, which affirms that husband and wife become "one flesh.") An Israelite husband was normally responsible for the burial of his wife (cf. Genesis 23; 48:7; 49:31–32). But in the case of a priest that was not allowed.

Some commentators have interpreted this prohibition more broadly to refer to involvement in the burial of any relative by marriage apart from the priest's wife.[2] Elliger and Hartley argue that the text should read בְּעֻלַת־בַּעַל (cf. Deut 22:22), under the assumption that בְּעֻלַת was omitted by haplography, and so the phrase refers to a woman married to any of the priest's kinsfolk.[3]

לְהֵחַלּוֹ׃—The verb חִלֵּל, "desecrate," is a key technical ritual term in this section. See the textual note on it in 18:21. The form here is the Niphal infinitive construct. The priests (21:4) and their daughters (21:9) are forbidden to "desecrate" something holy by treating it as if it were something "common," such as God's name (21:6), his sanctuary (21:12), themselves (21:4), and their seed (21:15). An adjective derived from this verb, functioning as a noun, is also used disparagingly for a cult prostitute in 22:7, 14.

---

2 For example, Hartley, *Leviticus*, 343.

3 Elliger, *Leviticus*, 279; Hartley, *Leviticus*, 343.

21:5 [יִקְרְחוּ] לֹא־יִקְרְחָה—Our translation follows the Qere, יִקְרְחוּ, "they shall not shave off."

קָרְחָה בְּרֹאשָׁם—Under the influence of Deut 14:1, the LXX adds "for the dead."

וּבִבְשָׂרָם לֹא יִשְׂרְטוּ שָׂרָטֶת׃—See Lev 19:27–28 and Deut 14:1.

21:6 קְדֹשִׁים יִהְיוּ לֵאלֹהֵיהֶם—See Lev 11:44, 45; 20:7, 26.

וְלֹא יְחַלְּלוּ שֵׁם אֱלֹהֵיהֶם—See the textual notes on 18:21.

אִשֵּׁי יְהוָה—See the textual notes on 1:9 and the explanation in "Leviticus 1–3."

לֶחֶם אֱלֹהֵיהֶם—See 21:8, 17, 22; 22:25; Num 28:2, 24; cf. Lev 3:11, 16. According to Ezek 44:7, the bread of God was the fat and the blood from the sacrificed animals. But that definition is too narrow for the usage in the Pentateuch. In the Torah it includes everything that was offered as an אִשֶּׁה, a gift of food to the Lord (3:11, 16; 21:6, 21; Num 28:2, 24), as well as the meat that the priests received from God as their due from the sacrificed animals (Lev 21:22).

מַקְרִיבִם—See the textual note on this verb in 1:2. (This is the Hiphil participle.) It recurs in 21:8.

וְהָיוּ קֹדֶשׁ׃—The perfect consecutive here introduces the apodosis of the preceding causal clause. Literally it reads "and they are holiness." See the textual notes on 4:6. In Leviticus the noun קֹדֶשׁ refers to God's holiness, as well as to something that is permanently holy because it is reserved exclusively for use by God or the priests or the people in the divine service. Only here is it used for priests, rather than God and the (non-human) things of God.

21:7 אִשָּׁה זֹנָה וַחֲלָלָה—The participle זֹנָה is a term for a prostitute (e.g., Josh 2:1; 6:17). It recurs in Lev 21:14. The term חֲלָלָה occurs in the OT only here and in 21:14. As Zipor has shown, it could be construed in three different ways.[4]

First, it could be derived from חָלַל, to "pierce" or "wound" (see BDB, s.v. חָלַל I; *HALOT,* s.v. חלל II). It would then refer to a woman who had lost her virginity. However, this interpretation would make redundant the mention of marriage to a prostitute or a divorcée. It might also refer to a woman who had been raped.[5]

Second, it could be derived from חָלַל, to "profane, defile" (*HALOT,* s.v. חלל I). The term could refer to a woman who has been profaned by becoming a prostitute. If so, the combination of זֹנָה with חֲלָלָה should then be regarded as a hendiadys. It could also refer to a woman from a priestly family who has been profaned by the marriage of her father to a forbidden woman.

The third possibility too assumes that it is derived from חָלַל, to "profane, defile." This view is the one that is most likely. If we take this reference together with 19:29, it is probably a polemical and pejorative term for a cult prostitute as a "defiled woman," "a woman who has been desecrated." This term condemns and counteracts the pagan designation of a cultic prostitute as "a sacred woman" (קְדֵשָׁה, Gen 38:21–22; Deut 23:18; Hos 4:14). Such a woman does not become holy, but actually loses her holiness by her involvement in sacral prostitution.

---

4 Zipor, "Restrictions on Marriage for Priests (Lev. 21:7, 13–14)."

5 Milgrom, *Leviticus 17–22*, 1807.

גְּרוּשָׁה—The verb גָּרַשׁ means "to drive out" or "expel" in the Qal and Piel. Hence the feminine singular Qal passive participle גְּרוּשָׁה denotes a woman who has been cast out—a divorcée. The verb recurs in 21:14 and 22:13. Ezek 44:22 will forbid all priests from marrying divorcées or widows except for the widows of priests. However, that more stringent regulation, given during the exile, envisions an eschatological state (Ezekiel 40–48), and so it probably was never implemented in the OT era.

21:8 וְקִדַּשְׁתּוֹ—The speech shifts to the direct second person singular form of address. קִדַּשְׁתּוֹ is the Piel second masculine singular perfect with third masculine singular suffix. The suffix refers to the priest. But it is not clear who the implied subject of the verb is—the person addressed ("you"). It cannot be the priest. It seems that the Israelites are addressed collectively in the second person singular as "you." This is confirmed by 21:24. The Piel of קָדַשׁ has this sense, "to treat as holy," only here in Leviticus. *HALOT* (Piel, 6 b) defines it as "to treat someone (something) as sanctified, consecrated."

קָדֹשׁ יִהְיֶה־לָּךְ—Normally this and similar clauses state that the priests (21:6, 7), the Nazirites (Num 6:8), and the Israelites (Lev 20:26; Num 15:40) are to be "holy" to *God.* Only here in the OT is this idiom used to describe the status of priests in relation to the people of Israel: the priests are "holy to you [Israel]."

קָדוֹשׁ—See the textual notes on 11:44. This is the only place where the formula for God's declaration of himself as holy (11:44, 45; 19:2; 20:7, 26) is combined with the formula for him as the sanctifier (20:8; 21:15, 23; 22:9, 16, 32).

מְקַדִּשְׁכֶם׃—See the textual notes on 20:8. The pronominal suffix on it addresses the Israelites in the second person masculine plural (not singular). This participle is repeated in 21:15. 11QpaleoLev, the Samaritan Pentateuch, and the LXX take this to refer to the priests and so read "who sanctifies them" instead of "who sanctifies you."

21:9 The LXX holds that the involvement in prostitution by the daughter of a priest desecrates her father's name by sullying his reputation. More obviously, she thereby disqualifies him from serving as a priest at the sanctuary. He therefore forfeits his status as a priest and becomes a common person.

בָּאֵשׁ תִּשָּׂרֵף׃—See 20:14; cf. Gen 38:24. Cremation was not normal practice in Israel because it was deemed to show disrespect for the human body and was associated with animism. Normally burial was the practice so that the body would await the resurrection from the dead (e.g., Is 26:19; Dan 12:2–3). Burning the body was the most severe sanction against any evildoer, for it removed all traces of the person from the face of the earth.

21:10 יוּצַק—The use of the imperfect implies that even though the high priest was anointed at a particular point of time in the past, that anointing continues in force and in its effect as a ongoing condition and a lasting state of being. The priest continues to be an anointed person.

שֶׁמֶן הַמִּשְׁחָה—See Ex 29:7; Lev 8:12; 10:7; 21:12; Num 35:25. Since this oil was most holy, the anointing of the high priest on his head made him continue to be holy.

וּמִלֵּא אֶת־יָדוֹ—See the textual notes on 8:22 and 8:33. Literally this is "and he filled his hand." We translate the impersonal construction as a passive: "has been ordained."

לִלְבֹּשׁ אֶת־הַבְּגָדִים—See 8:6–9 and Ex 28:1–29:9.

וּבְגָדָיו לֹא יִפְרֹם׃—See 10:6.

21:11 וְעַל כָּל־נַפְשֹׁת מֵת לֹא יָבֹא—The use of עַל in this clause instead of אֶל, as in Num 19:14 and Ezek 44:25, is unusual, but the prepositions are sometimes used interchangeably. Levine proposes that this preposition be understood as "on account of."[6]

נַפְשֹׁת מֵת is literally "souls of a dead." The term מֵת here serves as a collective singular or generic noun. Perhaps the singular was used to avoid the possibility that its plural, מֵתִים, might be confused with מְתִים, "persons."

21:12 וּמִן־הַמִּקְדָּשׁ לֹא יֵצֵא—See the textual notes on 12:4.

וְלֹא יְחַלֵּל אֵת מִקְדַּשׁ אֱלֹהָיו—See 21:23.

נֵזֶר—The term נֵזֶר ("mark of consecration") is derived from the verb נָזַר, which means to "distinguish" and so mark for sacred use (15:31; 22:2). It refers to the consecration of a person to God and to the mark of that consecration. The distinctive mark of consecration to God—such as the holy anointing oil for the high priest, as in this verse, or his sacred diadem (Ex 29:6; 39:30; Lev 8:9) or the uncut hair of a Nazirite (Num 6:18, 19)—was called the נֵזֶר of the consecrated person. It marked the heads of people to show their total dedication to God.

אֲנִי יְהוָה׃—Levine interprets this use of the short formula for divine self-introduction and self-presentation as God's mark of ownership on the high priest and so interprets it as saying that the high priest is "mine, the Lord's" (cf. Ex 28:36; 39:30).[7]

21:13 בִבְתוּלֶיהָ—The abstract plural noun בְּתוּלִים means "state of virginity" (*HALOT,* 1). Hence the high priest must only marry a woman who is a virgin.

21:14 Apart from the prohibition of marriage to a widow, this repeats the list from 21:7 in reverse order of desirability.

אַלְמָנָה—In Ezek 44:22 all the priests will be forbidden to marry any widow except the widow of a priest. That passage, spoken by God during the exile, looks forward to an eschatological temple and priesthood, an ideal that was never realized in earthly Israel.

וַחֲלָלָה זֹנָה—See the textual notes on 21:7. Our translation reflects the view that these are two distinct terms, as they clearly are in 21:7. The first refers specifically to a cultic prostitute (חֲלָלָה) and the second refers to any kind of prostitute (זֹנָה). The alternative view is that the two terms form a hendiadys and denote a woman who has become profane by being a prostitute.

מֵעַמָּיו יִקַּח אִשָּׁה׃—This command means that the wife of the high priest must come from the family of Aaron. This is an extra stipulation that is not included in the command for priests in general in 21:7. See Ezek 44:22.

21:15 וְלֹא־יְחַלֵּל זַרְעוֹ—A son born from the marriage of the high priest to a forbidden woman is therefore regarded as a common person and so disqualified from be-

---

6 Levine, *Leviticus*, 144–45.

7 Levine, *Leviticus*, 145.

coming a high priest, and perhaps even from being a priest. The "seed" of the priests was holy. This affirmation was later extended to all the "seed" of Israel (Ezra 9:2).

Commentary

Structure

The content of this speech divides it into two clear parts. The speech deals first with the holiness of the priests (21:1c–9) and then with the holiness of the high priest (21:10–15). Both parts follow the same basic pattern of arrangement. First, they prohibit the involvement of the priests in certain funerary practices and then list the classes of women who are unsuitable for marriage to a priest. In each case, reasons are given for the prohibitions. Both parts end with the formula for the self-presentation of the Lord as the sanctifier of his people (21:8, 15). By means of this pattern, the speech isolates and highlights the command in 21:9 to burn the daughter of a priest who had been involved in prostitution. That command was, most likely, placed there to indicate the gravity of this offense and to show that it applies to both the priests and the high priest.

A number of key words and roots help to connect the material in this speech. The most significant of these is the verb חָלַל, "desecrate." It links the self-desecration of a priest (21:4) and of his daughter (21:9) with his desecration of God's name (21:6), God's sanctuary (21:12), and his (the priest's) children (21:15), as well as with the desecration of a priest by his daughter (21:9). An adjective from that verb, functioning as a noun, is also used in the prohibition of marriage to a "desecrated woman" (21:7, 14).

Its antonym, קָדַשׁ, "to be holy," and words derived from it, also feature prominently in this chapter. Since the Lord is "holy" (21:8), he resides in his "sanctuary" (21:12) and "sanctifies" his people (21:8, 15). Since the priests have the same status as "something holy" (21:6), they too are "holy" both to God (21:6, 7) and to the Israelites (21:8). They, therefore, should be "regarded as holy" by them (21:8).

The recurrence of forms of the verb טָמֵא, meaning "to defile" or "to be defiled," in 21:1, 3, 4, 11 also links the two parts of the speech together. So too does the repetition of the list of prohibited classes of women for marriage from 21:7 in reverse order in 21:14.

The structure of this pericope can be outlined as follows:

- I. Introduction (21:1a–b)
  - A. God's address to Moses (21:1a)
  - B. God's commission of Moses (21:1b)
- II. Speech by Moses to the priests (21:1c–15)
  - A. The holiness of the priests (21:1c–8)
    - 1. Their involvement in funerary practices (21:1c–6)
      - a. Prohibition of desecration by contact with the dead except for "flesh" relatives (21:1c–4)

- b. Prohibition of involvement in certain mourning rites (21:5–6)
  - i. Prohibition of three kinds of self-abasement for the dead (21:5)
  - ii. Their sanctity as the reason for these prohibitions (21:6)
- 2. Their choice of a wife (21:7)
  - a. Prohibition of marriage to prostitutes, cult prostitutes, and divorcées (21:7a)
  - b. Their sanctity as the reason for this prohibition (21:7b)
- 3. Call for the Israelites to respect the holy status of the priests (21:8a)
- 4. God's self-presentation as Israel's sanctifier (21:8b)

B. Penalty for a priest's daughter who desecrates her father by prostitution (21:9)

C. The holiness of the high priest (21:10–15)
- 1. His involvement in funerary practices (21:10–12)
  - a. Prohibition of disheveled hair and torn clothes because of his sacred anointing and investiture (21:10)
  - b. Prohibition of involvement in the funeral of a consanguinal relative (21:11–12a)
    - i. Prohibition of entry to the place of the deceased (21:11a)
    - ii. Prohibition of defilement from contact with deceased parents (21:11b)
    - iii. Prohibition of departure from the sanctuary for a funeral (21:12a)
  - c. His consecrated status as the reason for these prohibitions (21:12b)
  - d. God's self-introduction (21:12c)
- 2. His choice of a wife (21:13–15)
  - a. Virgin rather than widow, divorcée, cult prostitute, or prostitute (21:13–14)
  - b. Desecration of children as the reason for not choosing from prohibited women (21:15a)
  - c. God's self-introduction as Israel's sanctifier (21:15b)

Ritual Location

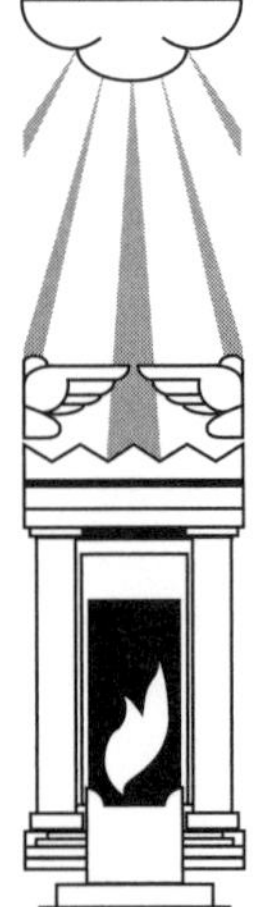

The legislation for the participation of the priests in God's holiness is determined by their location in sacred space. Thus the funeral and marital restrictions for the priests result from their calling to "present" the gifts of the people to God (21:6, 8). Since they bring these gifts to God at the altar, they are holy. Their access to the altar confers their sacred status. It is the reason for the prohibition of their involvement in certain funerary practices and the ban on their marriage to certain classes of women. The same applies for the high priest. He, however, not only has access to the altar, but the whole sanctuary (21:12). This consists of the Holy of Holies, the Holy Place, and the altar for burnt offering. The sanctuary is the place where he serves as high priest. He, therefore, is not allowed to "leave" it for the funeral of any relative (21:12). In fact, if he does leave it, he desecrates it.

The implied counter location to the sanctuary, in this speech, is the home of the priests. There the priests engage in sexual intercourse with their wives. Since the corpse of a deceased person remains there until it is buried, they "enter" it when they mourn for that person and prepare the corpse for burial (21:11; cf. Num 19:14).

Holy Things

The laws in this speech legislate for the protection of the holy things of God. The most significant of these holy things is the holy name of God, by which the Lord gives access to himself in the sacrificial ritual (21:6). In fact, he instituted the ritual so that he could present himself to his people by name in it. Through the sacrificial ritual he sanctifies them by means of that holy name (21:8, 15).

Second, there is the most holy anointing oil that was poured out on the head of the high priest (21:10; cf. Ex 30:22–33; Lev 8:10–12). It consecrated him and gave him his unique sanctity. The sweet smell of the incense identified him with God and associated him with God's gracious loving kindness.

Third, the sacred vestments, which the high priest donned when he served in his office as high priest, invested him with God's own holiness (21:10; cf. 10:6). He was not allowed to tear these vestments in mourning for a close relative.

Last, the holy "gifts" that filled his hands at his ordination[8] and whenever he officiated at the altar were the holy "food" of God (21:6, 8). Only priests were allowed to eat this most holy food (21:22). Since they were God's guests, they ate at his table and shared in his holiness, because the most holy bread and meat communicated his holiness.

In addition to these sanctifying holy things, this section mentions the things that were sanctified by virtue of their contact with the most holy things.

The body of the priest was holy. The priest himself had the same status as "something holy" (21:6). Since his body was holy, he was not allowed to defile it by contact with the corpse of any person, except a close relative (21:1–4); he was not allowed to mutilate it as a mark of his devotion to a deceased person (21:5); nor was he allowed to marry a forbidden woman (21:7–8).

The body of the high priest was even holier than the body of any ordinary priest. Since his head had been anointed with the most holy anointing oil, he could not touch the corpse of his father or mother (21:11) or even marry a widow (21:14). Ritually speaking, the most significant part of the body was the head with its crop of hair. It represented the whole body, as a part for the whole of it. Because a priest was dedicated to God, his head belonged to God. The hair on it was, therefore, not shaved at the forehead or cut at its side-locks (21:5; cf. Deut 14:1) as an act of devotion to a deceased person. In fact, since the head of the high priest had been anointed with the most holy oil, he was not even allowed to dishevel it in mourning for the dead (Lev 21:10; cf. 10:6).

---

[8] The idiom "to fill the hand," a technical term for the ordination of priests, is used in 21:10. See the textual note on that idiom in 8:33.

The "seed" of the high priest was also holy. He was, therefore, not allowed to desecrate it by marrying a forbidden woman (21:15).

The holiness of these sacred things was desecrated by two unclean things. The first of these was the corpse of a deceased person. The animist neighbors of the Israelites seem to have believed that on death the spirit of a person entered the supernatural world, the spiritual realm. The spirits of the dead were much more "alive," more influential than ever after death. Their corpses were regarded as sacred, for they provided a physical bridge into that realm. This led to common involvement of people in the cult of the dead. The Lord, however, totally banned the cult of the dead, together with all other forms of spiritism in Israel. Death was not to be regarded as something sacred, part of the supernatural cosmic process, but as something unclean, a prime source of defilement. Direct contact with a corpse therefore contaminated a person (21:1, 3, 11). This meant that people who had touched a corpse had to be purified before they could approach God (Num 19:11–13).

The second source of contamination mentioned in this speech is the body of a forbidden woman (21:7, 14). Marriage and sexual cohabitation with such a woman desecrated the holiness of a priest (21:7–8) as well as the holiness of his offspring (21:15).

Ritual Agents

Moses addresses this speech to the Aaronic priests (21:1). The laws in it do not deal with their ritual activity as priests, but with implications of their priesthood for their family life in two key areas, marriage and bereavement. Both these occasions were most significant for the continuity and integrity of any family. In fact, the most important duties for the head of any family were to provide a proper burial for his next of kin, especially his parents, and to arrange the marriage of his sons. The duty of the priest to his family, however, clashed with his duty as a priest. As a priest he was responsible for the divine service at the sanctuary. As a family man he needed to be married and attend to the burial of his "flesh relatives," his mother and father, his son and daughter, his brother and unmarried sister (21:2). Yet even in these aspects of his life, his attachment to God overrode his loyalty to his family.

While the high priest was totally debarred from involvement in the burial even of his closest kinsfolk (21:11), ordinary priests were permitted to defile themselves by contact with the corpses of their closest "flesh relatives" (21:1–3). But they could not do so for their wives, for that would disqualify them from the priesthood (21:4). A priest could mourn for his wife and attend her funeral, but he could not prepare her for burial and actually bury her, because she was not a "flesh relative."

A priest was also forbidden to marry three classes of women, a prostitute, a cult prostitute, and a divorcée (21:7). These women had been desecrated and defiled by what had happened to them (cf. 19:29; Deut 24:4). In addition to these, the high priest was not allowed to marry a widow because she had been previously attached to another man (21:14). The purpose of all these restrictions was to protect the sanctity of the priesthood by protecting the holiness of the priests (21:7–8) and their children (21:15).

Ritual Theological Significance

The restrictions placed on a priest in funerary practices had to do with the preservation of his holiness. He was forbidden to engage in the funerary rites and customs that were popularly associated with the cult of the dead and spiritism. The prohibition of physical contact with a corpse; the prohibition against shaving the forehead and cutting the side-locks and marking the body with tattoos; the prohibition of entry into the place where a person had died; and the prohibition against the disheveling of hair and the tearing of vestments: all these served to exclude a priest from any kind of formal leadership or ritual participation in the cult of the dead.

This counter-cultural religious stance was theologically most significant and far-reaching in its implications, for in ancient religions priests played a leading role in funerals, mourning rites, and commemorations of the dead. These prohibitions completely dissociated the divine service of the Lord from the cult of the dead. The living God did not share his domain with the dead. The spirits, named and evoked in the cult of the dead, were not regarded as denizens of the divine realm, like the angels, but, as 19:26–31 shows, they were identified with the unclean spirits and evil powers. Contact with the dead defiled the priest. It disqualified him from involvement in the performance of the sacrificial ritual at the tabernacle. These prohibitions therefore helped to break the hold of spiritism on Israel. They ensured that animism, with its belief in the power of the living dead over their human descendants, would not take hold in Israel.

The extraordinary marital and sexual restrictions for the priests were also connected with the maintenance of their holiness. They were forbidden to marry women who had engaged in sexual activity with other men, such as prostitutes, cult prostitutes, divorcées, and, in the case of the high priest, widows (21:7, 14). Marriage with such women desecrated the sanctity of the priestly family (21:14–15). It meant that any male children from such a union were disqualified from the priesthood, for the holy seed of Aaron had thereby been desecrated (21:15). Similarly, if the daughter of a priest became a cult prostitute or a common prostitute, she profaned the sanctity of her father, as well as her own sanctity as a member of a priestly family. She was therefore to be burnt to death for this act of sacrilege (21:9). Thus the holiness of the priest was closely linked with the holiness of his family.

While participation in forbidden funerary practices and marriage to forbidden women desecrated the holiness of a priest and his family, contact with the holy things of God made and kept a priest and his family holy. God had instituted the divine service so that he could share his holiness with them through these holy things. He presented himself to them as their holy God and gave them access to his holiness by means of his holy name. He linked the holy food with his sanctification of them (21:8). This bestowal of holiness on them did not just happen once, as a single historical event in the remote past, but it was

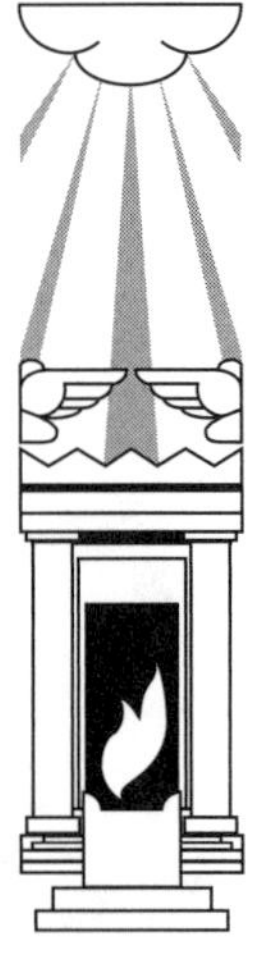

an ongoing ritual occurrence. Every time the sacrificial ritual was enacted, God presented himself with his holiness to the priests. As the priests ate the holy offerings, God animated them with his holiness. Contact with these holy things conveyed his holiness to them, like an electric current through copper wire.

The priests received their holiness from God through their presentation of the sacred offerings and their consumption of food from them (21:6, 8). The priests were, in a sense, nourished by God's holiness. The high priest was even more privileged than the ordinary priests. They depended for their holiness on his holiness. He participated even more fully in God's holiness than they did, for he was anointed with the high holy oil, and he wore the sacred vestments. God covered him with the sweet fragrance of his holiness that showed how sweet and beautiful and ennobling it was; God dressed him with the beauty of his own holiness (cf. Ps 96:9). So the high priest borrowed his holiness from God and shared it with all his fellow priests. They too were regarded as "something holy" (21:6).

The sanctity of the priests was not just limited to the time of service at the sanctuary, for they were not only "holy to [their] God" (21:7), but also holy to the Israelites (21:8). The Israelites were therefore required to treat them at all times as holy people, for they ate the holy food of God at home as well as at the sanctuary. In their life apart from the sanctuary, the priests had to avoid doing anything that desecrated their holiness, so that they would not also desecrate God's holy name (21:6) and his holy sanctuary (21:12). Since they were always holy, they were required to be holy in their lifestyle and behavior.

Fulfillment by Christ

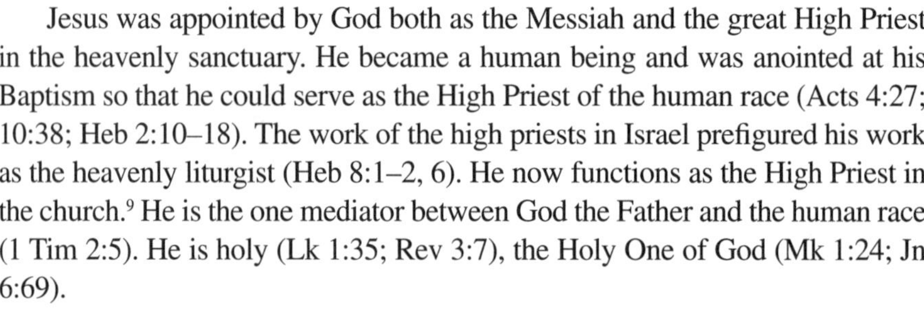

Jesus was appointed by God both as the Messiah and the great High Priest in the heavenly sanctuary. He became a human being and was anointed at his Baptism so that he could serve as the High Priest of the human race (Acts 4:27; 10:38; Heb 2:10–18). The work of the high priests in Israel prefigured his work as the heavenly liturgist (Heb 8:1–2, 6). He now functions as the High Priest in the church.[9] He is the one mediator between God the Father and the human race (1 Tim 2:5). He is holy (Lk 1:35; Rev 3:7), the Holy One of God (Mk 1:24; Jn 6:69).

Just as the high priest served together with his fellow priests in Israel, so Jesus shares his holiness with his disciples and sanctifies them so that they serve God the Father together with him (Heb 2:11–13). In Baptism he anoints them with the Holy Spirit (2 Cor 1:21–22; 1 Jn 2:26–27), just as he was anointed, and consecrates them as priests (Acts 26:18; 1 Cor 1:2; 6:11; Eph 5:26). They derive their holiness from him (1 Cor 1:30); they are holy in him (Phil 1:1; 4:21). They therefore serve as priests together with him in the heavenly sanctuary (1 Pet 2:9; Rev 1:6; 5:10; 20:6). They are involved with him and the angels in the heavenly liturgy (Heb 12:22–24). Like the high priest in Israel, they never leave the heavenly sanctuary, but always remain on service there (Rev 7:15).

---

[9] Heb 2:17; 3:1; 4:14, 15; 5:5, 10; 6:20; 7:26; 8:1; 9:11; see also *1 Clement* 36:1; 61:3; 64.

Unlike the priests in the OT, the disciples of Jesus have the same degree of access to God the Father as their High Priest does, for they come to God the Father in him and together with him.[a] Since they have access to the presence of the Father, they can bring people and their needs to him and bring him and his blessings to them. They are therefore much more privileged than any of the priests at the tabernacle, for they share the status of Jesus and participate in his work as High Priest.

(a) Jn 14:6; 16:23–24; 17:24; Eph 2:18; Heb 7:25

As members of God's heavenly priesthood, Christians receive the holy food that comes from their Lord's Table (1 Cor 10:16–22). They eat the bread of God that comes down from heaven, the life-giving flesh of Christ (Jn 6:33, 51). Since they serve the living God they must not once again become involved in "dead works," deeds that defile and deaden their conscience (Heb 9:14). They are therefore required to separate themselves from every defilement of body and spirit (2 Cor 7:1). They are to avoid spiritism and all forms of contact with unclean spirits (1 Cor 10:14–22). Since so much has been given to them, much is expected of them (Lk 8:18; 12:48). Their obedience to Christ's call takes precedence over their responsibility to bury their parents (Lk 9:60).

Because Christians are NT priests robed with Christ's holiness, they are given higher standards for holiness in their marital relations than the OT priests, who were forbidden to marry a divorced woman but were allowed to divorce their wives. Christians are forbidden to divorce their spouses, except for sexual immorality or malicious desertion. Yet even in such cases God does not encourage divorce but desires the spouses to reconcile in Christ and the marriage to last, if at all possible. Anyone who wrongly divorces his or her spouse and then remarries commits adultery. Anyone who wrongfully divorces his or her spouse also defiles the spouse's holiness, treating the divorced party as if he or she had committed adultery (Mt 5:31–32; 19:3–12; Lk 16:18; 1 Cor 7:10–16).

God has called all Christians to share in his holiness. He shares his life-giving holiness with them through the holy things. They are therefore required to avoid all kinds of sexual impurity (1Thess 4:2–8), as well as all other forms of impurity (Eph 5:3–6). They are to be holy and to treat each other as holy.

Come, gracious Spirit, heav'nly dove,
With light and comfort from above.
Come, be our guardian and our guide;
At ev'ry thought and step preside.

The light of truth to us display,
And make us know and choose your way;
Plant holy fear in ev'ry heart
That we from God may not depart.

Lead us to Christ, the living way,
Nor let us from his pastures stray;
Lead us to holiness, the road
That we must take to dwell with God.[10]

---

[10] From "Come, Gracious Spirit, Heavenly Dove" by Simon Browne (*LW* 161:1–3).

Causes of Disqualification from Priestly Service

Translation

21 [16]The Lord spoke to Moses: [17]"Speak to Aaron: Any man from your offspring throughout their generations who has a defect may not approach to present the food of his God. [18]Indeed, any man who has a defect shall not approach—a man who is blind or lame, or who has a limb too short or too long, [19]or a man who has a crippled foot or a crippled hand, [20]or who is a hunchback or a dwarf, or who has a growth in his eye, or a festering boil, or eczema, or a damaged testicle. [21]Any man among the offspring of Aaron the priest who has a defect shall not draw near to present the gifts of the Lord. He has a defect, so he shall not draw near to present the food of his God. [22]But he may eat the food of his God from the most holy things and from the holy things. [23]Nevertheless, he shall not enter before the curtain and shall not draw near the altar because he has a defect, so that he does not desecrate my holy things; for I am the Lord, who sanctifies them."

[24]So Moses spoke to Aaron and his sons and to all the Israelites.

Textual Notes

21:17 מִזַּרְעֲךָ—See 21:15 and 21:21.

מ֔וּם—This could also be translated "blemish/ injury." See 21:18, 21 (twice), 23; 22:20, 21, 25; 24:19, 20. This is the term for a physical defect or injury that disqualified a priest from ritual service and an animal for use as an offering to God. A person or animal that had no defect was תָּמִים, "complete, perfect, without blemish" (see the textual notes on 1:3).

יִקְרַ֔ב—See 9:7, 8; 21:18; 22:3.

לְהַקְרִ֖יב—See 21:21 (twice) and the textual notes on 1:2.

לֶ֥חֶם אֱלֹהָֽיו׃—See 21:21, 22 and the textual notes on 21:6.

21:18 This list corresponds, in large measure, to the list of defects for the sacrificial animals in 22:22–24.

עִוֵּר֙—See 22:22.

פִסֵּ֔חַ—This does not mean that he is a cripple, but rather that he cannot walk properly.

א֥וֹ חָרֻ֖ם א֥וֹ שָׂרֽוּעַ׃—Even though these two categories seem to be related, their sense is uncertain. As in 22:23, שָׂר֫וּעַ probably refers to a leg that is too long. Most scholars derive חָרֻם from a verbal root meaning "split." It is therefore commonly taken to refer to a split nose or a cleft palate or a scarred face. Levine argues that it refers to a truncated or shortened leg. It is the human equivalent of קָלוּט in 22:23.[1]

[1] Levine, *Leviticus*, 146.

21:19 This could also refer to a hand or a foot that has not set properly after being broken.

21:20 דַּק—This is literally "thin" or "small."

תְּבַלֻּל בְּעֵינוֹ—This seems to be the human equivalent of יַבֶּלֶת in 22:22. It refers either to a growth or some kind of discoloration on the pupil of the eye.

גָרָב—See 22:22 and Deut 28:27. It could also refer to an open wound or a festering sore.

יַלֶּפֶת—See 22:22. This refers to some kind of flaky skin from dermatitis or some kind of eczema.

מְרוֹחַ אָשֶׁךְ׃—This is literally "one whose testicle is crushed." See 22:24; cf. Deut 23:2 (ET 23:1).

21:21 יִגַּשׁ ... יִגַּשׁ—Twice here and once in 21:23 נָגַשׁ is used, in this ritual sense, as a synonym for קָרַב.

לְהַקְרִיב—See the textual notes on 1:9.

21:22 לֶחֶם אֱלֹהָיו—See the textual notes on 21:6.

מִקָּדְשֵׁי הַקֳּדָשִׁים—See the list in Num 18:9–10 and the textual notes on Lev 2:3.

וּמִן־הַקֳּדָשִׁים—See Num 18:11–19, 26–32.

21:23 הַפָּרֹכֶת—See the textual notes on 4:6.

יָבֹא—See the textual notes on 10:9. This refers to the entry of the priest into the Holy Place each morning and evening to attend to the lamps and to burn the incense (Ex 28:29, 30, 35, 43; 29:30; 30:20; Lev 9:23; 10:9).

הַמִּזְבֵּחַ—See 9:7–8 and the textual notes on 1:5.

מִקְדָּשַׁי—This could also be translated "my sanctuaries." See the textual notes on 12:4; cf. Ps 68:36 (ET 68:35); Jer 51:51. The plural may refer to the various parts of the sacred precincts or, more likely, to the furnishings and objects in the sacred precinct around the altar for burnt offering and in the outer room of the tabernacle. These holy things are out of bounds for everyone, except the priests on duty.

כִּי אֲנִי יְהוָה מְקַדְּשָׁם׃—See the textual notes on 20:8. The pronominal suffix refers to the tabernacle and the altar for burnt offering.[2] It also includes the holy and most holy offerings mentioned in 21:22.

21:24 This report of compliance matches the previous reports in 8:36; 10:7b; and 16:34b.

אֶל־אַהֲרֹן וְאֶל־בָּנָיו וְאֶל־כָּל־בְּנֵי יִשְׂרָאֵל׃—This list echoes 17:2. Thus the laws for the conduct of the priests are also a matter of concern for the Israelites as is emphasized in 21:8.

Commentary

Structure

This speech to Moses is built up rather skillfully by the repetition of the same basic prohibition four times: "No one ... may approach/draw near." Twice it has the verb קָרַב, "to approach" (21:17–18a), and twice it has the synonym

---

2 Hartley, *Leviticus*, 345; Milgrom, *Leviticus 17–22*, 1832.

הַגִּישׁ, "to draw near" (21:21). Those repetitions frame the list of disqualifying blemishes in 21:18b–20. They culminate in the significant concession about the consumption of sacred food in 21:22. The two final prohibitions in 21:23 restate the initial prohibition of ritual activity in spatial-ritual terms.

The repetition of the same prohibition in six different ways is reinforced by the repetition of certain key words and phrases: בּוֹ מוּם, "blemish in him" (21:17, 18, 21a, 21b, 23); אִישׁ, "man" (21:17, 18, 19, 21); לֹא יִגַּשׁ, "he shall not draw near" (21:21a, 21b, 23); לְהַקְרִיב, "to present" (21:17, 21a, 21b); לֶחֶם אֱלֹהָיו, "the food of his God" (21:17, 21, 22); לֹא יִקְרָב, "he shall not approach" (21:17, 18); and זֶרַע, "seed" (21:17, 21).

This speech is rounded off by the formula for divine self-introduction in 21:23b. This corresponds to its summary use in 21:8 and 21:16. There is, in fact, a progression in these, from the sanctification of the Israelites in 21:8 and the sanctification of the high priest in 21:16 to the sanctification of the holy places in 21:23.

The structure of this pericope can be outlined as follows:

- I. Introduction (21:16–17a)
  - A. God's address to Moses (21:16)
  - B. God's commission of Aaron (21:17a)
- II. Speech about the disqualification of blemished priests from sacred service (21:17b–23)
  - A. Prohibition of service by a blemished priest (21:17b–21)
    - 1. Repeated prohibition of presentation of offerings (21:17b–18a)
    - 2. List of disqualifying blemishes (21:18b–20)
    - 3. Repeated prohibition of approach with God's food (21:21)
  - B. Privilege of consumption of sacred food by a blemished priest (21:22)
  - C. Prohibition of access to the sacred places to avoid their desecration (21:23a)
  - D. God's self-introduction as the sanctifier of the holy things (21:23b)
- III. The compliance of Moses (21:24)

Ritual Location

This speech defines the disqualification of a priest from involvement in the enactment of the sacrificial ritual in spatial terms. A blemished priest was debarred from approaching the altar with the offerings, to "present" them to the Lord. He was not allowed to "draw near" to the altar with them (21:17, 21, 23). He was also disqualified from entering the Holy Place to burn incense and to sprinkle the blood before the curtain. His blemishes debarred him from God's "sanctuaries," his "holy places," the altar for burnt offering in the courtyard and the altar for incense in the Holy Place (21:23). God sanctified these sacred sites by his residence there in them. They were desecrated by the intrusion of any blemished priest on them. Yet even a blemished priest could eat the most holy food in the sacred precincts, just as he could perform any other task at the tabernacle except that which involved service at the altar for incense and the altar for burnt offering.

Holy Things

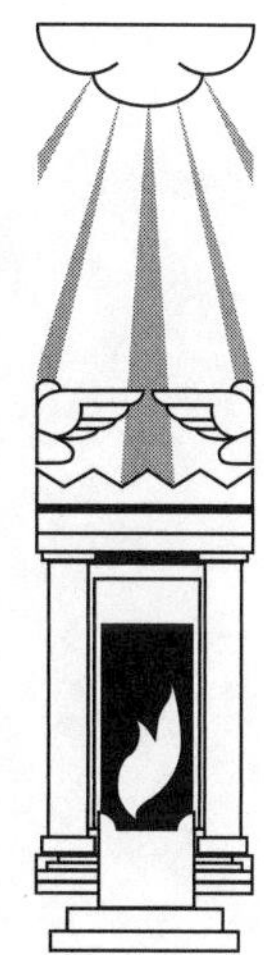

This speech distinguishes between two kinds of ritual contact by the priests with the holy things of God. The first was the regular presentation of offerings to God at the altar for burnt offering and at the incense altar. These consisted of "the gifts of the Lord," which were presented to him for his exclusive use (21:21a), and the "food of God," which was also presented to him for him to distribute as he pleased (21:17, 21, 22). Blemished priests were not allowed to bring these offerings to the sacred place, to present them to the Lord. The second kind of ritual contact with the holy things was the consumption of the holy food that was taken from these offerings. Even though a blemished priest did not present any offering to the Lord in the divine service, he, like any unblemished priest, ate God's food at the sanctuary. Both shared the same privilege as guests at the Lord's table; both ate the same holy food from God; both received their livelihood from God (21:22).

Like any unblemished priest, a blemished priest had access to food from the two classes of holy things (21:22). He ate "the most holy things." This consisted of the meat from the sin offering and the reparation offering (6:2 [ET 6:9]; 7:6), as well as the bread or flour from the grain offering (2:3, 10). Contact with these most holy offerings communicated holiness (6:11 [ET 6:18], 27). Since these offerings could not be removed from God's presence, they were eaten by the priests in the sacred precincts (6:9, 19 [ET 6:16, 26]; 7:6). This meat and bread were their rations from God while they were on duty at the sanctuary.

The blemished priest also ate the food that came from the "holy things" (21:22). They consisted of the forequarter of meat from the peace offerings; the first-ripe fruits of grain; the first-processed offerings of olive oil, grain, and wine; all votive offerings of food; and the tithes of agricultural produce. The blemished priest could take them home and share them with the members of his household. Despite any blemish, the Lord made and kept him holy by his consumption of holy food. Thus eligibility of a priest for the presentation of offerings was clearly distinguished from his eligibility for the consumption of sacred food from them.

Holy People

The prohibition of service by a blemished priest was addressed to Aaron as the original high priest (21:17; cf. 21:21). As the high priest he determined whether his "offspring" were eligible for service as priests. He too supervised the distribution of the offerings to the priesthood. These regulations, however, did not just apply to him and his family, but to all priests after him, "throughout their generations" (21:17).

Ritual Theological Significance

This speech draws out some of the practical, ritual implications of God's residence at the tabernacle. He sanctified his "sanctuaries" by his presence there (21:23). His sanctuaries were to be treated with respect and not desecrated by the priests, for they alone had access to them. He sanctified his priests so that they could serve him by approaching him and presenting his gifts to him at the altar (21:17, 21). He admitted them into his presence at the altar for burnt offering and at the incense altar (21:23). Since they were his courtiers, they ate his food (21:22). There were two kinds of food, the most holy food that was eaten at the sanctuary and the holy food that was eaten by the priests at home together with their families. By means of this food, God sanctified his priests, just as he sanctified the Holy Place and the altar for burnt offering (21:23).

Since God was the owner of the tabernacle, his residence, he determined what disqualified a priest from serving him there. If a priest was to officiate in God's presence, he had to be without any bodily defect (21:17, 18, 21, 23), just as no defective animal could be offered in sacrifice to God (22:18–25). Like animal, like priest! The body of the priest was therefore regarded as an offering to God. It was claimed by God and used by him.

The defects that disqualified a priest from service were all rather obvious: blindness and obscured sight, lameness and broken limbs, an elongated leg and an amputated leg, dwarfishness and a hunchback, boils and eczema and damaged testicles. The priest who officiated had to be a physically complete man.

But astonishingly, both the blemished priest and unblemished priest were on the same footing as guests at God's table (21:22), even though the blemished priest could not serve at the altar and burn incense in the tent of meeting. Both ate the same food. Both shared equally in God's holiness. The blemished priest and his family therefore benefited from the physical integrity and service of the unblemished priests.

Fulfillment by Christ

Jesus has been anointed as the Christ, the new Aaron, the unblemished High Priest in the heavenly sanctuary (Heb 7:26). He offered himself as an unblemished sacrifice to purify and sanctify his fellow priests—all believers in Christ (Heb 9:14; 1 Pet 1:19). Like Aaron and his successors with their kinsmen, Christ takes responsibility for all his fellow priests. He rids them of every blemish that would otherwise disqualify them from involvement in the Divine Service by washing them in the waters of Baptism (Eph 5:25). By virtue of their union with him, all his disciples stand before God the Father unblemished and have access to the heavenly realm with all its blessings (Eph 1:4). Christ presents them together with himself unblemished in his sight (Col 1:22).

Since all baptized believers are in Christ and share in his perfect humanity, there is nothing about their physical body that disqualifies them from the Father's presence. Christ himself sanctifies them with his most holy things, his body and his blood (Heb 10:29; 13:12). As God's holy children who serve the Father together with Christ himself in the heavenly sanctuary, they are called to be unblemished in their behavior on earth (Phil 2:15). In Christ's holy meal they eat "the bread of God," the life-giving flesh of Christ (Jn 6:33, 51). By their priestly service on earth Christ himself prepares them to be unblemished members of the eternal, heavenly choir (Rev 14:5).

Those kinds of people who had previously been disqualified from the priestly banquets at the temple—such as the blind, the maimed, and the lame laity—are qualified in Christ for participation in the future heavenly banquet (Lk 14:21). All those who heed the Gospel invitation to the banquet are, through faith, fit for it and will be accepted into it. Conversely, those who had previously been qualified by virtue of their outward standing (family lineage and physical body) are excluded from it if they reject the invitation that comes only through Christ (Lk 14:18–20).

Thus faith in Christ and his Gospel qualifies all believers for priestly service together with him in the heavenly sanctuary. They are without blemish in him.

O living Bread from heaven,
How well you feed your guest!
The gifts that you have given
Have filled my heart with rest.
Oh, wondrous food of blessing,
Oh, cup that heals our woes!
My heart, this gift possessing,
With praises overflows.

My Lord, you here have led me
Within your holiest place
And here yourself have fed me
With treasures of your grace;
For you have freely given
What earth could never buy,
The bread of life from heaven,
That now I shall not die.[3]

3 From "O Living Bread from Heaven" by Johann Rist (*LW* 244:1–2).

Leviticus 22:1–16

Consumption of Holy Food by the Priests and Their Families

Translation

22 [1]The Lord spoke to Moses: [2]"Tell Aaron and his sons to be scrupulous with the holy things of the Israelites, which they consecrate to me, so that they may not desecrate my holy name; I am the Lord.

[3]"Say to them: If anyone among your offspring throughout your generations approaches the holy things, which the Israelites consecrate to the Lord, while he is in a state of uncleanness, that person will be cut off from my presence; I am the Lord.

[4]"Any man of Aaron's offspring who has a skin disease or a bodily discharge shall not eat any of the holy things until he is clean.

"Any man who touches anything unclean from a dead person, or any man from whom an emission of semen goes out, [5]or any man who touches any swarming creature by which he becomes unclean or any human being by whom he becomes unclean, whatever his uncleanness may be— [6]that person who touches it shall be unclean until evening and shall not eat any of the holy things unless he has washed his body with water. [7]When the sun has gone down, he will be clean; after that he may eat from the holy things, for it is his food. [8]But he shall not eat anything that has died or been torn by wild animals, becoming unclean by it. I am the Lord.

[9]"They shall therefore keep watch for me, so that they do not bear sin on account of it and die for it, because they have desecrated it. I am the Lord, who sanctifies them.

[10]"Any unauthorized person may not eat anything holy. No guest or employee of a priest may eat anything holy. [11]But if a priest purchases anyone [by] a purchase with his money, that person may eat of it; and one who is born into his household—they may eat of his food. [12]If a priest's daughter belongs to a husband who is an unauthorized person, she may not eat any of the holy things that have been donated. [13]But if a priest's daughter is widowed or divorced and she has no children and returns to her father's house as in her youth, she may eat of her father's food. No unauthorized person, however, may eat of it.

[14]"If anyone eats a holy thing unintentionally, he shall add one-fifth of it to it and give the holy thing to the priest.

[15]"They shall not desecrate the holy things of the Israelites that they donate to the Lord [16]and so make them bear the penalty of the reparation offering by eating their holy things; for I am the Lord who sanctifies them."

Textual Notes

22:2 וְיִנָּזְרוּ—The Niphal of נָזַר here means "to **deal respectfully** מִן with" (*HALOT,* 3) or "*hold sacredly aloof* from" (BDB). Those priests who are unclean are to refrain from handling or eating the sacred things. See the textual notes on 15:31, where the Hiphil means to "*keep ... sacredly separate from*" (BDB).

מִקָּדְשֵׁי—See the textual notes on 4:6. This term recurs in 22:3, 4, 6, 7, 10, 12, 14, 15, 16.

יְחַלְּלוּ—See the textual note on this verb in 18:21. It recurs in 22:9, 15.

שֵׁם קָדְשִׁי—See 18:21; 19:12; 20:3; 22:2, 32.

מַקְדִּשִׁים—The Hiphil of קָדַשׁ is used here and in 22:3 for the consecration of those things that, unlike the firstlings (27:26), do not by right belong to God, such as a person's field (27:16, 17, 18, 19, 22) or his house (27:14, 15).

22:3 יִקְרַב—See the textual notes on 1:2.

וְטֻמְאָתוֹ עָלָיו—This is literally "and his uncleanness is upon him." See the textual notes on 5:3. The clause recurs in 22:5.

וְנִכְרְתָה הַנֶּפֶשׁ הַהִוא מִלְּפָנַי—This varies the usual formula for extirpation from one's kinsfolk or people. In this case the priest would no longer have access to the altar, but would be excluded from God's presence.

22:4 אִישׁ אִישׁ—See the textual notes on 15:2.

צָרוּעַ—See the legislation for this condition in chapters 13 and 14.

זָב—See the legislation for discharges in chapter 15.

עַד אֲשֶׁר יִטְהָר—See the textual notes on 11:32. The verb recurs in 22:7. As is explained in 14:1–20 and 15:13–15, 28–30, this refers to the eighth day in the ritual process of purification.

וְהַנֹּגֵעַ בְּכָל־טְמֵא—This introduces four kinds of minor impurity which make a person unclean for the length of a day. The verb נָגַע, "to touch," often takes the preposition בְּ attached to what is touched.

טְמֵא־נֶפֶשׁ—Regarding טָמֵא, see the textual notes on 5:2, and Num 19:10–12. As in Lev 19:28 and 21:1, 11, the term נֶפֶשׁ is used here to refer to the soul of a deceased person.

שִׁכְבַת־זָרַע׃—See the case in 15:16–17 and the textual notes on 15:16.

22:5 שֶׁרֶץ—See the textual notes on 11:10 and the use of this word in 11:29–31.

יִטְמָא־לוֹ—See the textual notes on 5:2. This clause, which occurs twice in this verse, literally is "it will become unclean to him." However, we translate the impersonal construction as intransitive: "he becomes unclean" by it.

בְאָדָם—See the textual notes on 1:2.

אֲשֶׁר יִטְמָא־לוֹ—See 15:4–12, 20–24, 26–27.

22:6 נֶפֶשׁ —Here this term refers to the person (the priest) who touches and becomes unclean. Since it is grammatically feminine, the following two verbs are feminine (תִּגַּע and וְטָמְאָה).

22:8 וּטְרֵפָה—See Ezek 44:31. The legislation in Lev 11:39–40 and 17:15–16 allowed lay people to eat the meat from these animals provided that they purified themselves afterwards.

אֲנִי יְהוָה׃—The formula of divine self-introduction gives the reason for the preceding and also for the following admonition in 22:9. It is linked to the following verse by the *waw* that begins 22:9.

22:9 This verse applies to the laws in 22:3–8 and understands care for ritual purity by the priests as keeping watch for the Lord at the sanctuary.

וְשָׁמְרוּ אֶת־מִשְׁמַרְתִּי—See 8:35 and 18:30.

וְלֹא־יִשְׂאוּ עָלָיו חֵטְא—See 19:17; 20:20; 24:15 for this synonym of נָשָׂא עָוֹן. See also the textual notes on 5:1.

וּמֵתוּ בוֹ—The desecration of something holy by a priest results in the penalty of death (8:35; 10:2, 6, 7, 9; 16:1, 2; Num 18:32; cf. Lev 15:31). This clause literally reads "and they die in it," that is, in their sin (see Num 27:3; 2 Ki 14:6). The NRSV interprets this clause as a reference to death in the sanctuary as happened to Nadab and Abihu in Lev 10:2. However, that does not fit the context here because the priests ate the holy things at home with their families rather than at the sanctuary (where Nadab and Abihu died).

כִּי יְחַלְּלֻהוּ—It is not clear what "it" (the third masculine singular suffix הוּ-) is that "they [unclean priests] have desecrated." Most likely "it" refers to the food taken from the holy things, mentioned in 22:7, but it could also refer to God's holy name in 22:2.

מְקַדְּשָׁם׃—See 21:15 and the textual notes on 20:8.

22:10 וְכָל־זָר—See 10:1; 22:12, 13. The term זָר, "unauthorized person," is literally a "stranger" or "outsider" or "intruder," and refers to a layperson. Unlike the priests and their families, the laity were not allowed to eat the sacred food.

קֹדֶשׁ—The collective singular קֹדֶשׁ here and in 22:14 is synonymous with its plural in 22:2, 3, 7, 12, 15.

תּוֹשַׁב כֹּהֵן—A תּוֹשָׁב is a resident alien (25:6, 23, 35, 40, 45, 47). Such a person would be residing with a priest as a member of his household if he defaulted in repaying a loan and so had to live with his creditor as an indentured servant until he had discharged his debt.

וְשָׂכִיר—As is evident from 19:13, a שָׂכִיר is an employee, a hired laborer who works for a daily wage (25:6, 40, 50, 53).

22:11 קִנְיַן כַּסְפּוֹ—This is literally "the purchase of his money." As is explained in 25:39–46, this refers to a non-Israelite slave who had been bought by the priest and had therefore become part of his family.

וִילִיד בֵּיתוֹ—As in Gen 17:12–13, 23, 27 and Jer 2:14, this refers to children born to the slaves of a priest while they resided in his household.

22:12 זָר—This is the same term as in 22:10 and is literally "a stranger" or "an outsider." The priest's daughter has married a layman.

בִּתְרוּמַת הַקֳּדָשִׁים—The phrase תְּרוּמַת הַקֳּדָשִׁים is an unusual combination of terms (see also Num 18:19). The term תְּרוּמָה is used for the donation of a gift to God (see the textual notes on 7:14). In this case it refers to the sacred offerings that could be eaten at home by the priest together with his family (see 7:14, 32 and the comprehensive list in Num 18:11–19).

22:13 Since a widow did not inherit the estate of her husband, she had no livelihood unless she had a son who looked after her.
22:14 See the law on this in 5:14–16. In this case the second "holy thing" is the money for the misappropriated food, together with the addition of twenty percent interest for it. It belonged to the priest on duty.
22:15 This refers to the priests who were to make sure that all the offerings were properly stored and accounted for. They were to police themselves so that none of them became involved in selling or trading or abusing these offerings.

יְחַלְּלוּ—See 19:8; Num 18:32; Ezek 22:8, 26.

יָרִימוּ—See the textual notes on 2:9.[1] The verb הֵרִים is used as a technical ritual term to refer to those parts that were *removed from* the sacrifices by the priest for burning on the altar (2:9; 4:8, 19; 6:8 [ET 6:15]) or, as in this verse, that were *donated* as an offering to the Lord (see also Num 15:19, 20; 18:19).

22:16 וְהִשִּׂיאוּ אוֹתָם עֲוֺן—Usually the expression is that an offender bears the iniquity for his offense. Yet here, most unusually, the priests are said to "make" the people "bear iniquity" by failing to prevent them from eating the holy food. This refers either to the Israelites who had brought the offerings or, more likely, to any unauthorized people who had eaten any of the sacred food.

עֲוֺן אַשְׁמָה—Regarding עָוֺן, see the textual notes on 5:1. The combination of the two terms here, עֲוֺן אַשְׁמָה, is unique in the OT. The noun אַשְׁמָה may refer to an act of sacrilege (5:26 [ET 6:7]), the guilt from it (4:3), and the compensation for it (5:24 [ET 6:5]). This idiom probably refers both to the sin of sacrilege and the penalty for that sin. Both the NIV and the NRSV rightly interpret this as guilt from an act of sacrilege that requires compensation by means of a guilt offering.

קָדְשֵׁיהֶם—"Their holy things" refers to the sacred food which belongs to the priests.

כִּי אֲנִי יְהוָה מְקַדְּשָׁם׃—As in 21:23, the Lord here affirms that he sanctifies the holy food from the offerings of the Israelites. Milgrom claims that the pronominal suffix here (ָם-), as in 22:9, refers to the priests rather than the holy food, and that God did not consecrate the offerings but those who offered them.[2] His view is improbable because the nearest antecedent is "the holy things." Moreover, in 21:23 and 22:15, God quite clearly asserts that he sanctifies the holy things. How else could they become holy?

Commentary

Structure

This speech is part of the legislation in chapters 21–22 on the responsibility of the priests for the holy things of God. While chapter 21 dealt with who could officiate in the divine service, this speech indicates who was allowed to

---

1 See also Milgrom, *Leviticus 1–16*, 474–75.

2 Milgrom, *Leviticus 17–22*, 1870.

eat the sacred food. After the concluding formula of compliance in 21:24, chapter 22 gives an explanation of what was meant in 21:22 by the eating of the holy things. This chapter deals with the handling and consumption of the sacred food that constituted the livelihood of the priests, God's payment for their service.

The speech, rather unusually, repeats the commission of Moses to speak to Aaron and his sons, first as an introduction to the general command about the proper treatment of the holy things in 22:2, and then as an introduction to its elaboration in 22:3–16. This elaboration makes up the body of the speech. The body of the speech itself is divided into two parts by the formula for the divine self-introduction of the Lord as the sanctifier of the priests and the offerings in 22:9 and 22:16, as well as by the general admonitions to the priests about their responsibility for the holy things in 22:9 and 22:15–16.

The first of these parts indicates what kinds of impurity disqualify a priest from eating the sacred food (22:3b–9). This is divided into three sections by the recurrence of the formula for divine self-introduction in 22:3, 8, 9. The second part tells which members of the priest's household are disqualified from eating sacred food (22:10–16). The repetition in 22:10a and 22:13b of the prohibition of consumption of sacred food by any unauthorized person marks off these verses and highlights the provision in 22:14 for restitution in cases of accidental consumption of this food by such a person.

The main units in this speech are linked by the repetition of the reference to desecration in 22:2, 9, 15. The repetition of other key terms also serves to unify the speech rhetorically and thematically: "a holy thing" (22:10, 14 [twice]), "holy things" (22:2, 3, 4, 6, 7, 12, 15, 16), "sanctify"(22:2, 3, 9, 16), "eat,"[a] and a word from the root טמא, "to be unclean" (22:3, 4, 5 [three times], 6, 8).

(a) Lev 22:4, 6, 7, 8, 10 (twice), 11 (twice), 12, 13 (twice), 14, 16

The structure of this pericope can be outlined as follows:

- I. Introduction (22:1–3a)
  - A. The Lord's address to Moses (22:1)
  - B. First commission to speak (22:2)
    - 1. General directive to Aaron and his sons about the holy things (22:2a)
    - 2. God's self-introduction (22:2b)
  - C. Second commission to speak (22:3a)
- II. Speech about the protection of the holy things (22:3b–16)
  - A. General prohibition (22:3b–d)
    - 1. Prohibition of access to the holy things by an unclean priest (22:3b)
    - 2. Threat of divine excommunication (22:3c)
    - 3. God's self-introduction (22:3d)
  - B. Laws about the consumption of food (22:4–16)
    - 1. Laws for the priests (22:4–9)
      - a. Prohibition of consumption of holy food by an unclean priest (22:4–7)
      - b. Prohibition of defilement from eating animals found dead (22:8a)

        c. Responsibility of the priests for the holy things (22:8b–9)
            i. God's self-introduction (22:8b)
            ii. Command for vigilance to prevent desecration (22:9a)
            iii. God's self-introduction as the sanctifier of the priests (22:9b)
    2. Laws for the members of a priest's household (22:10–16)
        a. Persons forbidden or permitted to consume holy food (22:10–13)
            i. Layperson (22:10a)
            ii. Employee (22:10b)
            iii. Slave (22:11)
            iv. Daughter (22:12–13a)
            v. Layperson (22:13b)
        b. Law of restitution for accidental consumption by a disqualified person (22:14)
        c. Responsibility of the priests for the holy things (22:15–16)
            i. Desecration by the carelessness of the priests (22:15)
            ii. Guilt offering for lay people who eat forbidden holy food (22:16a)
            iii. God's self-introduction as the sanctifier of the holy things (22:16b)

Ritual Location

This speech restricts contact with the holy things in two different locations. On the one hand, it prohibits any priest who is unclean from approaching any holy thing at the sanctuary (22:3). If he did so, he was cut off from God's presence at the sanctuary and excluded from subsequent access to him there. On the other hand, it also prohibits an unclean member of the priest's family (22:4–8) and any unauthorized person in his household (22:10–13) from eating any of the sacred food in a meal at the home of the priest. The presence of the sacred food in the home of the priest therefore made its table an extension of the Lord's table. His house became a holy place. The same rules for purity applied to the eating of the sacred food in both locations.

Holy People

This unit treats the personal offerings that the Israelites "donated to the Lord" (22:15) and "dedicated" to him (22:2, 3). Although they belonged to the Lord, only a portion of them was set out on the altar for him. The rest was given to the priests as their recompense for performing the divine service, their livelihood from the Lord. In this speech, the Lord addresses Aaron and his sons and directs them on the proper treatment of these "holy things" (22:3). On the one hand, all the priests were corporately responsible for guarding the holy things and ensuring that they were not desecrated (22:9, 15–16). However, those who were in a state of uncleanness were disqualified from handling and presenting these offerings at the sanctuary as long as they remained unclean. On the other hand, all the priests' offspring (22:4), the male and female members of their families, received these holy things as their food from the Lord's table.

Two classes of members, however, were excluded from eating this holy food. The members of a priest's family who were unclean could not eat it as long as they remained unclean (22:4–8). Nor could any unauthorized member of his household (22:10a, 13b). All indentured servants and employees (22:10b) and any daughters who were married to laymen (22:12) were not allowed to eat this food because they were not members of the family, even if they happened to be residing temporally in it. But all slaves of the priests and any children born of their slaves (22:11b), as well as any widowed or divorced daughter who did not have any sons to support her (22:13), could eat this food because they were regarded as members of the priest's family.

This speech treats the priesthood as the extended family of Aaron. Each person in each family was therefore envisaged as part of that holy family. All of the family members could eat the sacred food from the Lord's table provided that they were clean. The Lord sanctified them through the holy bread and the holy meat that he provided for them (22:9).

Holy Things

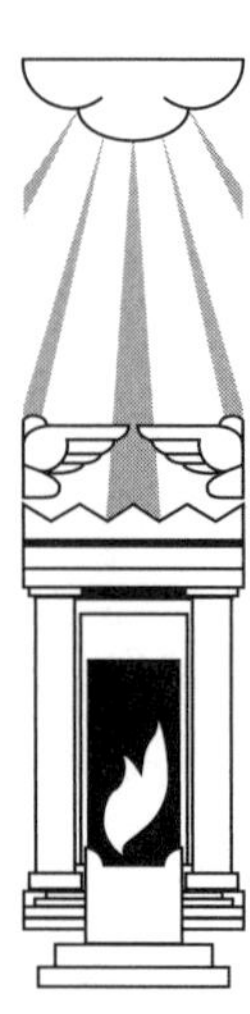

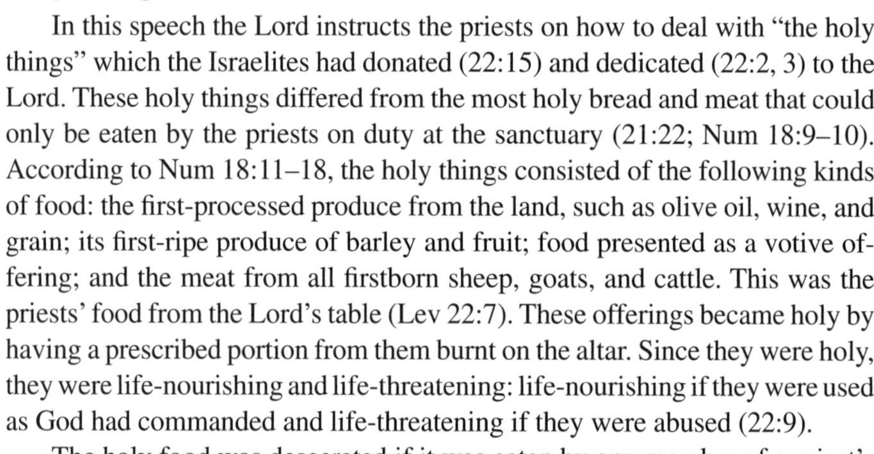

In this speech the Lord instructs the priests on how to deal with "the holy things" which the Israelites had donated (22:15) and dedicated (22:2, 3) to the Lord. These holy things differed from the most holy bread and meat that could only be eaten by the priests on duty at the sanctuary (21:22; Num 18:9–10). According to Num 18:11–18, the holy things consisted of the following kinds of food: the first-processed produce from the land, such as olive oil, wine, and grain; its first-ripe produce of barley and fruit; food presented as a votive offering; and the meat from all firstborn sheep, goats, and cattle. This was the priests' food from the Lord's table (Lev 22:7). These offerings became holy by having a prescribed portion from them burnt on the altar. Since they were holy, they were life-nourishing and life-threatening: life-nourishing if they were used as God had commanded and life-threatening if they were abused (22:9).

The holy food was desecrated if it was eaten by any member of a priest's family who had been defiled by contact with something unclean. Three kinds of impurity are mentioned. The first came from skin diseases and abnormal sexual discharges (22:4a). The impurity from them was so severe that the people who had been healed from these maladies had to wait a week before they could present the offering for their purification. The second came from contact with corpses, spilt semen, swarming creatures, and the body of a person with a contagiously unclean sexual discharge (22:4b–7). The impurity from these lasted only for the day of contact. It was removed by bathing in water on the evening of that day. The third was the meat from an animal that had died a natural death or had been killed by wild animals (22:8). The priests were not allowed to eat the meat from such animals or else they would become irreparably unclean.

Ritual Theological Significance

The legislation in this chapter shows how the families of the priests participated in God's holiness. God provided them with holy food so that he could share his holiness with them. He sanctified the holy things (22:16) so that he could present himself to the priests and sanctify them through these holy things (22:9). This meant that the priests desecrated his holy name by their abuse of these holy things, for the offerings belonged to him; they could not be enjoyed apart from him (22:2). In fact, through the holy things the home of a priest became a holy place, a secondary sanctuary, whose sanctity was threatened by ritual impurity.

Since the food that the priests received from God was holy, they had to treat it as he had instructed. The holy things were only available to the members of a priest's family who were in a state of ritual purity. The priests therefore had to keep watch to ensure that these holy things were not desecrated (22:9). Any act of desecration had severe consequences. If a priest handled the holy things at the sanctuary while he was unclean, he was cut off from God's "presence" and disqualified from the priesthood (22:3). If the members of a priest's family ate the holy food while they were unclean, they were likely to die because they desecrated it (22:9).

If any unauthorized people accidentally misappropriated some of the holy food and ate it, they too desecrated the holy things of God (22:14–15). Since they had taken something that belonged to God, they had to repay him for what they had misappropriated. They paid the priest as God's representative the monetary value of what they had taken from God and a surcharge of a fifth of its value. As instructed in 5:14–16, they also presented a ram as a reparation offering to the Lord to compensate him for their misappropriation of his holy property.

All these restrictions presuppose that God himself shared his holiness with the priests and their families by giving them holy food. The responsibility of the priests for the proper use of this holy food came from the wonderful privilege of their access to his table and from their status as his courtiers. Because they ate at his table, they served as his holy bodyguards who prevented the desecration of his holiness (22:9). They were the stewards of the life-giving, holy things of God.

Fulfillment by Christ

All Christians belong to the royal priesthood of God. As priests they receive the spiritual food and drink that the Lord provides for the sustenance of their faith. Many biblical passages speak of such food and drink in a spiritual sense[b] or eschatologically (e.g., Mt 22:1–14; Lk 14:16–24). This spiritual food and drink are most holy things that they have from God. Just as he sanctified the food for the Israelite priests and their families, so he consecrates this food and drink for those who are sanctified by his blood (Heb 10:29; 13:12).

(b) E.g., Is 55:1–2; Jn 4:10–15; 6:32–40; 1 Pet 2:2–3

Whereas the members of the priestly families had to be physically clean, the saints in the new covenant must be pure in heart (Mt 5:8; Heb 9:14; 10:22). This all-embracing purity comes through faith in Christ and results in love for all the saints (1 Tim 1:5). The distinctive feature of this purity, its index, is a good, clear conscience before God as revealed in the light of his Word.[c]

(c) 1 Tim 1:5, 19; 3:9; 2 Tim 1:3; 1 Pet 3:16, 21

The early church affirmed that the saints, the holy people of God, have fellowship with God through their participation in the holy things.[3] Thus the Apostles' Creed confesses faith in the *sanctorum communionem,* the "communion of saints" or "communion in the holy things," that arose from their common faithful reception of the Word and Sacraments. Lutherans still think in these terms when they speak about *communio in sacris*, "communion in sacred things."

The Lord's Supper is a real meal in which the communicant receives the very body and blood of Jesus Christ, given and shed for the forgiveness of sins. This feast at the Lord's Table may be the most specific NT fulfillment in Christ of Lev 22:1–16. Since the body and blood of Jesus are most holy, they must be treated with respect. Like the holy offerings of the Israelites, they may be eaten only by authorized people.

Christ's body and blood in the Sacrament are to be eaten only by those who belong to the priesthood of all believers and are in a state of purity in Christ. The NT adds further stipulations regarding participation in the Lord's Supper: self-examination, belief in the real presence of Christ's body and blood, and agreement with the doctrine and practice the Lord has mandated for the church (1 Cor 11:17–34).[4]

As early as the *Didache,* the Lord's Supper was closed to all except those who had been baptized (*Didache* 9:5), for in Baptism they were purified from sin by God's Word and consecrated as priests together with Christ (Jn 15:3; Eph 5:25–27; 1 Pet 3:21). Since unrepented sin before God and enmity against a fellow saint polluted the conscience, they confessed their sins and were reconciled with those whom they had offended before approaching the Lord's Table. By doing this, they made sure that they did not pollute and desecrate Christ's holy body and blood (*Didache* 14:1–3; cf. Mt 5:23–26).

Throughout its history, the Christian church has practiced closed Communion to prevent the desecration of Christ's body and blood and God's judgment upon unworthy communicants (1 Cor 11:27–34).[5] Both the ministers of the Sacrament and the members of the congregation bear responsibility for this. The pastors who administer the Sacrament are to take care that they do not give what is holy to those who are unclean because they are unbaptized, impenitent,

---

3 Benko, *The Meaning of Sanctorum Communio;* Elert, *Eucharist and Church Fellowship in the First Four Centuries*, 1–22.

4 One may see the commentary on these verses in Lockwood, *1 Corinthians,* 380–410.

5 Lockwood, *1 Corinthians,* 396–410, discusses unworthy reception of the Sacrament and the church's historic practice of closed Communion.

or heretics (Mt 7:6; Rom 16:17–20; 1 Cor 11:27–34; *Didache* 9:5). Since their master has set them over his household to give its residents their food at the proper time, they are required to be wise, faithful stewards of his holy things (Lk 12:41–43). Like the Israelite priests (Lev 22:9), they therefore are appointed to keep watch so that God's holiness is not desecrated (Heb 13:17; cf. Eph 6:17–18).

All the members of the congregation are also required to make sure that they do not desecrate the body and blood of Christ by failing to discern them or by the discord between their confession of faith in Christ's body and blood and their mistreatment of other members of his body (1 Cor 11:17–34). Those who desecrate his body and blood do not receive God's blessing, but come under his judgment (1 Cor 11:29). They do not receive life, strength, and health from Christ, but are threatened by infirmity, sickness, and death (1 Cor 11:30). Their unbelief and sin is compounded by their sacrilegious misappropriation of the Sacrament.

Thus both pastors and all the members of the church must be most scrupulous in their treatment of Christ's body and blood so that they do not desecrate God's holy name.

Like the Israelite priests, the ministers of the Word too receive their livelihood from the offerings of the congregation (1 Cor 9:3–14; Gal 6:6; 1 Tim 5:17–18), for they are involved in the priestly ministry of the Gospel by which all the saints are made holy (Rom 15:15–16). These offerings are holy. They must therefore not be misappropriated or abused or squandered by those who receive them. If pastors do misuse and desecrate them, they should rectify their misdeeds by confession and appropriate compensation, just as the Israelite priests did with the presentation of a reparation offering (Lev 22:16; cf. 22:14).

Draw near and take the body of the Lord,
And drink the holy blood for you outpoured;
Offered was he for greatest and for least,
Himself the victim and himself the priest.

He who his saints in this world rules and shields,
To all believers life eternal yields;
With heav'nly bread he makes the hungry whole,
Gives living waters to the thirsting soul.[6]

---

6 From "Draw Near and Take the Body of the Lord," a Latin hymn translated by John M. Neale (*LW* 240:1–2).

Leviticus 22:17–33

Acceptable Offerings for the Israelites

Translation

22 [17]The Lord spoke to Moses: [18]"Speak to Aaron and his sons and all the Israelites and say to them: When anyone of the house of Israel or of the alien in Israel presents his offering, whether it be as any of their votive offerings or as any of their freewill offerings, which they may present to the Lord as a burnt offering, [19]for your acceptance [it must be] a male without blemish, from the cattle or the sheep or the goats. [20]You shall not present any animal with a defect in it, for it will not be acceptable on your behalf.

[21]"If anyone presents a sacrifice of a peace offering to the Lord from the herd or the flock, to discharge a vow or as a freewill offering, it must be without blemish for your acceptance; there must not be any defect in it.

[22]"Any animal that is blind, injured, or maimed; with a growth in the eye, a festering boil, or scabs—these you shall not present to the Lord; you shall not put any of these on the altar as a gift to the Lord. [23]You may, however, make a freewill offering with a head of cattle or a sheep/goat that has a long or short leg; but it will not be accepted as a votive offering. [24]You shall not present to the Lord any animal that has its testicles bruised or crushed or torn out or cut off; you shall not do this in your land. [25]You shall not present any from these animals from a foreigner as the food of your God. Because they are corrupted, with a defect in them, they will not be accepted on your behalf."

[26]Then the Lord spoke to Moses: [27]"When a head of cattle or a sheep or a goat is born, it shall remain under its mother for seven days. From the eighth day on, it shall be accepted as an offering of a gift to the Lord. [28]But you shall not slaughter a head of cattle or a ewe with its young one on the same day.

[29]"When you sacrifice a sacrifice of thanksgiving to the Lord, you shall sacrifice it for your acceptance. [30]It shall be eaten on the same day; you shall not leave any of it over until the morning. I am the Lord.

[31]"You shall therefore keep my commandments by doing them. I am the Lord.

[32]"You shall therefore not desecrate my holy name, so that I may be sanctified among the Israelites.

"I am the Lord, who sanctifies you, [33]who brought you out of the land of Egypt to be your God.

"I am the Lord."

Textual Notes

22:18 דַּבֵּר אֶל־אַהֲרֹן וְאֶל־בָּנָיו וְאֶל כָּל־בְּנֵי יִשְׂרָאֵל—See the textual notes on 17:2.

אִישׁ אִישׁ—See 22:4 and the textual notes on 15:2.

מִבֵּית יִשְׂרָאֵל—See 17:3, 8, 10. This includes women as well as men.

הַגֵּר—See the textual notes on 16:29.

יַקְרִיב—See the textual note on this verb in 1:2. It recurs in 22:20, 21, 22, 24, 25.

קָרְבָּנוֹ—See the textual note on this noun in 1:2. See 22:19, 20, 21, 22, 23, 24, 25.

נִדְרֵיהֶם—See the textual notes on 7:16. This noun recurs in 22:21, 23.

נִדְבוֹתָם—Even though the burnt offering was the basic public sacrifice, it could also be offered by the lay Israelites as a individual votive offering or an individual freewill offering (Num 15:3).

22:19 לִרְצֹנְכֶם—See the textual note on this noun in 1:3. It recurs in 22:20, 21, 29.

תָּמִים—See the textual note on this adjective in 1:3. It recurs in 22:21.

22:20 מוּם—See the textual note on this noun in 21:17. It recurs in 22:21, 23.

לֹא תַקְרִיבוּ—The plural form of the verb is used inclusively for all Israelites.

22:21 לְפַלֵּא—See also Num 15:3, 8 for this use of פָּלָא in the Piel.

לִנְדָבָה—See Lev 7:16–18; Num 15:1–12.

22:22 Some commentators hold that Lev 22:22–25 lists blemishes that make an animal unsuitable for presentation as a peace offering.[1] These verses would then elaborate on the prohibition in 22:20 by specifying what was meant by a blemish in 22:21. But the arrangement of the material in 22:22–24 syntactically as a single sentence, with seven coordinated clauses, indicates that the blemishes also applied to personal burnt offerings. This is reinforced by the division of the material in 22:18b–25 into three parts by the repetition of the word מוּם, "defect, blemish," in 22:20, 21, and 25b.

עַוֶּרֶת—See 21:18.

שָׁבוּר—This probably refers to a poorly healed broken leg.

יַבֶּלֶת—See the textual notes on 21:20.

גָרָב—See Deut 28:27.

יַלֶּפֶת—See the textual notes on 21:20.

וְאִשֶּׁה—See the textual notes on 1:9.

22:23 תַּעֲשֶׂה—The subject can include both males and females. The verb is literally "do." See the textual note on it in 4:20.

וָשֶׂה—This is the common term for either a sheep or a goat. See the textual note on it in 5:7. In 22:28 it is used for specifically female animals.

שָׂרוּעַ—This is literally "extended" or "contracted."

יֵרָצֶה:—See the textual notes on 1:4. This term recurs in 22:25, 27.

22:24 וּמָעוּךְ וְכָתוּת וְנָתוּק וְכָרוּת—These are the four ways of de-sexing a male animal.

וּבְאַרְצְכֶם לֹא תַעֲשׂוּ:—The interpretation of this prohibition is disputed. Some understand this sentence as a prohibition of castrating animals in the land of Israel.[2] But, as Dillmann has shown, if that were so, there would be no need to prohibit the sacri-

---

[1] Hartley, *Leviticus*, 361; Gorman, *Divine Presence and Community*, 125.

[2] Elliger, *Leviticus*, 300; Wenham, *Leviticus*, 295.

fice of castrated animals.[3] This sentence therefore seems to prohibit the sacrifice of castrated animals in Israel. Such animals may have been accepted, and perhaps even preferred, in other religions.

22:25 לֶחֶם אֱלֹהֵיכֶם—See the textual notes on 21:6.

מִכָּל־אֵלֶּה—This is literally "any of these." While this may refer only to castrated animals bought from foreigners, it most likely refers to all the blemishes listed in 22:22–24.

כִּי מָשְׁחָתָם בָּהֶם מוּם בָּם לֹא יֵרָצוּ לָכֶם׃—This is a summary sentence for 22:22–25.

The term מָשְׁחָת occurs only here in the OT. It may be a noun meaning "fault, blemish," or it may be the Hophal masculine singular participle of the verb שָׁחַת (*HALOT,* s.v. מָשְׁחָת). It occurs here with the third masculine plural pronominal suffix. The similar noun מִשְׁחַת, "disfigurement," occurs only in Is 52:14 in reference to the Suffering Servant. If the term here is a noun, and if one disregards the Hebrew accents, then the two words מָשְׁחָתָם בָּהֶם could go together; they would literally mean "their corruption in them." However, we follow the view that the term is the Hophal participle. The clause then literally is "their corrupted one is in (or among) them." A fragment from Qumran, 11QpaleoLev, supports the reading מָשְׁחָתִם הֵם, which has the Hophal masculine plural participle (with no suffix): "they have been spoiled."

The simple clause מוּם בָּם, "a blemish is in them," helps clarify the rather obscure previous clause.

22:27 אִשֶּׁה—See the textual notes on 1:9.

לַיהוָה׃—See Ex 22:29 (ET 22:30).

22:28 See the similar law in Deut 22:6–7 for a mother bird and her chicks.

שֶׂה—See the textual notes on 5:7. This applies to a she-goat as well as a female sheep.

תִשְׁחֲטוּ—See the textual note on this verb in 1:5.

22:29 וְכִי־תִזְבְּחוּ—The lay Israelites seem to be addressed from here on.

זֶבַח־תּוֹדָה—See 7:12–15.

22:30 אֲנִי יְהוָה׃—See the textual notes on 18:5. One may see this clause as the conclusion of the section from 22:27–30 or 22:29–30. The *waw* at the beginning of 22:31 and the arrangement of 22:31–33 also suggest that it is linked to the next verse.

22:31 מִצְוֺתַי—See the textual notes on 4:2.

וַעֲשִׂיתֶם—This is literally "and do them."

22:32 וְלֹא תְחַלְּלוּ—See the textual notes on 18:21.

אֶת־שֵׁם קָדְשִׁי—See 18:21; 19:12; 20:3; 22:2; and the textual notes on 4:6.

וְנִקְדַּשְׁתִּי—See 10:3.

אֲנִי יְהוָה מְקַדִּשְׁכֶם׃—See the textual notes on 20:8.

22:33 הַמּוֹצִיא אֶתְכֶם מֵאֶרֶץ מִצְרַיִם—See 19:36; 23:43; 25:38, 42, 55.

לִהְיוֹת לָכֶם לֵאלֹהִים—See the textual notes on 11:45.

---

3 Dillmann, *Die Bücher Exodus und Leviticus*, 628; compare Hartley, *Leviticus*, 362.

Commentary

Structure

This section has two related speeches about which animals were acceptable for private sacrifices. The repetition of the terms רָצוֹן, "acceptance," and רָצָה, "accept," divides the first speech into four parts (22:19, 20, 21, 23, 25) and the second speech into two parts (22:27, 29). These seven references create the following pattern:

- "For your acceptance" (לִרְצֹנְכֶם, 22:19)
- "It will not be acceptable on your behalf" (לֹא לְרָצוֹן יִהְיֶה לָכֶם, 22:20)
- "For your acceptance" (יִהְיֶה לְרָצוֹן, 22:21)
- "It will not be accepted" (לֹא יֵרָצֶה, 22:23)
- "They will not be accepted on your behalf" (לֹא יֵרָצוּ לָכֶם, 22:25)
- "It shall be accepted" (יֵרָצֶה, 22:27)
- "For your acceptance" (לִרְצֹנְכֶם, 22:29)

Thus 22:29 forms an inclusion with 22:19. The first speech is divided into three parts by the repetition of מוּם, "defect, blemish," in 22:20, 21, and 25. It also features the recurrence of the verb הִקְרִיב, "to present" (22:18 [twice], 20, 21, 22, 24, 25), while the second speech repeats the noun יוֹם, "day(s)" (22:27 [twice], 28, 30).

The second speech ends with an admonition (22:30b–33) that provides a conclusion for the speeches in chapters 21–22. Similarly, admonitions concluded some of the earlier divine speeches (e.g., 18:24–30; 19:36b–37; 20:22–26). This admonition is constructed, rather skillfully, with the repetition of the formula for divine self-introduction four times. The first is with a positive commandment; the second is with a prohibition; the third is with a statement of self-predication; and the fourth is by itself without any addition.

The structure of this pericope can be outlined as follows:

I. First speech on acceptable animals for sacrifice (22:17–25)
   A. Introduction (22:17–18a)
      1. God's address to Moses (22:17)
      2. God's commission of Moses (22:18a)
   B. Speech of Moses to the Israelites (22:18b–25)
      1. Prohibition of defective male animals as personal votive and freewill burnt offerings (22:18b–20)
      2. Prohibition of defective animals as votive and freewill peace offerings (22:21)
      3. Classes of defective animals (22:22–25)
         a. General blemishes (22:22)
         b. Animals with a stunted leg for votive offerings but not for freewill offerings (22:23)
         c. Male animals with damaged testicles (22:24)
         d. Blemished animals obtained from foreigners (22:25)

II. Second speech on temporal restrictions for sacrifices (22:26–33)
  A. Introduction: the Lord's address to Moses (22:26)
  B. God's speech to Moses (22:27–33)
    1. Temporal restrictions on the sacrifice of young animals (22:27–28)
    2. Temporal restriction on eating meat from a thank offering (22:29–30a)
    3. Concluding admonition (22:30b–33)
      a. God's self-introduction with an instruction to keep commandments (22:30b–31a)
      b. God's self-introduction with a prohibition of desecration (22:31b–32a)
      c. God's self-introduction as Israel's sanctifying redeemer (22:32b–33a)
      d. God's self-introduction (22:33b)

Acceptable Animals for Sacrifice (22:18–25)

Ritual Agents

The legislation in this section is addressed to the priests and the Israelites (22:18). The reason for this is obvious. This speech determines which animals may be presented by the Israelites and the aliens residing with them as acceptable burnt and peace offerings to the Lord. It is significant that both groups are on an equal footing with these voluntary, personal sacrifices (cf. 1 Ki 8:41–43). Their personal offerings must be distinguished from the official, public sacrifices of the congregation and the prescribed personal offerings for each Israelite family. Like them the personal offerings were offered at the sanctuary as part of the regular sacrificial ritual.

Even though these burnt offerings and peace offerings were brought by the lay Israelites and the aliens in their community, the laity did not have the final responsibility to determine whether the animals were acceptable for sacrifice or not. This was the task of the priests. They had to ensure that the right animals were presented. They had to examine the animals to discover whether there was any defect in them or not. The approval of the priests was needed. Through them God gave his approval of the animal for sacrifice.

Nevertheless, the lay people still played an important role in the enactment of these sacrifices. They "presented" them (22:18, 20, 21, 22, 25), so that they could "give a gift" to the Lord (22:22) and so gain his acceptance (22:19, 20, 25). It was, after all, their ritual enactment, their divinely sanctioned means of access to the Lord.

Ritual Material

This speech specifies the animals that could be presented by the Israelites as their personal votive and freewill offerings to the Lord. It also establishes the criteria for determining the acceptability of an animal for sacrifice.

Normally the Israelites were not required to present any burnt offerings as personal sacrifices to the Lord because the burnt offering was the public sacrifice for the whole congregation. But if any Israelite wished to present an animal as a voluntary, personal burnt offering, it had to be a perfect male head of cattle or a perfect male sheep or goat (22:18–19). If any Israelite wished to pre-

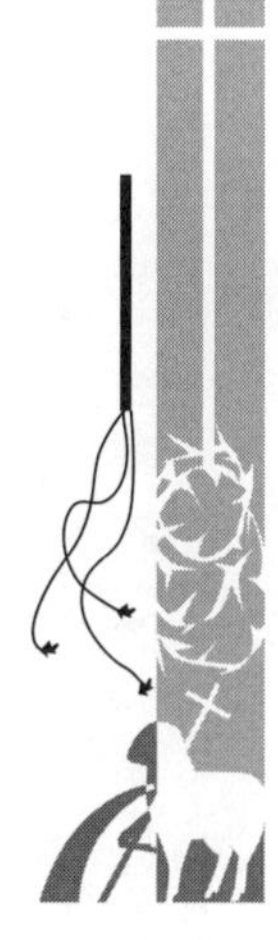

sent some other animal than the prescribed firstborn male animals from his herd or flock as a peace offering, it had to be a perfect male specimen taken from his own herd or flock (22:21a). If any Israelite wished to make a freewill burnt offering or a freewill peace offering, he could present a head of cattle or a sheep or a goat with a stunted or deformed leg (22:23). Generally speaking, the animal had to be תָּמִים, "perfect, without blemish," a normal, healthy animal without any physical defects (22:19, 21, as in 1:3). It had to be complete and whole.

Any abnormal animal was unacceptable for sacrifice. Any "defect," any blemish that made an animal less than whole, disqualified the animal (22:20, 21, 25). These defects are divided into three classes: six general defects that disqualified all animals from consideration for sacrifice (22:22); a stunted or extended limb that disqualified it from use as a votive offering (22:23); and damaged testicles that disqualified male animals from presentation as a sacrifice (22:24). These prohibitions prevented Israelite farmers from using the sacrifices to cull out inferior animals and non-breeders from their flocks and herds. No second-rate animals could be used for sacrifice (cf. Mal 1:8).

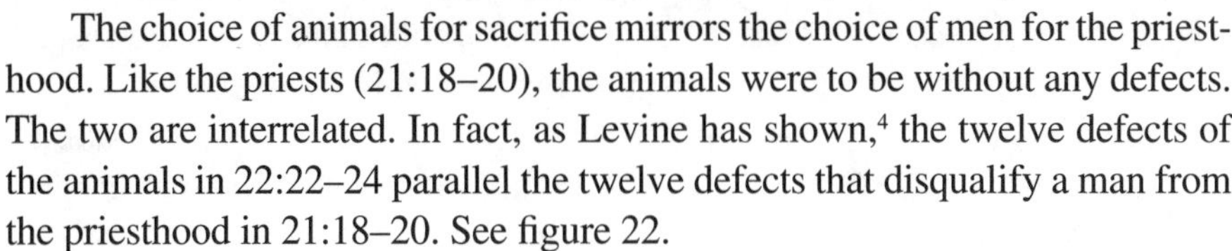

The choice of animals for sacrifice mirrors the choice of men for the priesthood. Like the priests (21:18–20), the animals were to be without any defects. The two are interrelated. In fact, as Levine has shown,[4] the twelve defects of the animals in 22:22–24 parallel the twelve defects that disqualify a man from the priesthood in 21:18–20. See figure 22.

Figure 22

Disqualifying Defects in Priests and Sacrificial Animals

Priests	*Sacrificial Animals*
Blindness (21:18a)	Blindness (22:22a)
Lameness (21:18b)	Injured limb (22:22b)
Extended or shortened leg (21:18c)	Extended or shortened limb (22:23)
Crippled foot or hand (21:19)	Maimed limb (22:22c)
Hunchback or dwarf (21:20a)	
Growth in the eye (21:20b)	Growth in the eye (22:22d)
Festering boil (21:20c)	Festering boil (22:22e)
Eczema (21:20d)	Scabies (22:22f)
Crushed testicles (21:20e)	Four kinds of damaged testicles (22:24)

Apart from the deformity of a hunchback or a dwarf, there is a close parallel between the defects of the priests and the defects of the sacrificial animals. This indicates that just as the priests represented the people of Israel, ritually the sacrificial animals represented their herd or flock.

---

4 Levine, *Leviticus*, 141.

Ritual Theological Function

In this speech, the Lord set out the criteria for determining which animals were acceptable to him as personal burnt offerings and peace offerings. The Israelites were, of course, required to bring their firstborn animals as offerings to the Lord (27:26–27). But these case laws do not deal with those offerings, since the criteria for their selection was self-evident. Instead, these laws cover those animals that were brought voluntarily as personal burnt offerings (22:18) or as peace offerings (22:21). They came in two categories: the votive offerings that were presented to discharge a vow[a] after a person had experienced the desired divine intervention (Ps 61:6 [ET 61:5]) and the freewill offerings that were presented spontaneously to the Lord.[b]

(a) Lev 7:16; 23:38; 27:9–13; cf. Pss 22:26 (ET 22:25); 50:14; 61:9 (ET 61:8); 66:13

(b) Lev 7:16; 23:38; cf. Ps 54:8 (ET 54:6); Amos 4:5

These sacrifices were presented to the Lord for a clearly identified ritual-theological purpose. The Israelites presented them wholly, in the case of the burnt offering, or partially, in the case of the peace offering, with the rest of the meat left over for a banquet, as "a gift to the Lord on the altar" (22:22), so that the Lord would accept both the offerings and those who presented them. Since the animal was presented for acceptance on behalf of them (22:20), it was presented for their acceptance (22:19). But the acceptability of the animal depended on its physical perfection (22:21). No abnormal or defective animal was acceptable as an offering (22:19); an animal with a defect was not accepted by God on behalf of those who brought them (22:25).

God therefore established the criteria for their acceptance so that his people could have access to his favor. By presenting acceptable animals to him, they could approach God with certainty; they could be sure of receiving favorable treatment from him. But the bestowal of his favor was not automatic. They had to present the right animals to the priests, and those animals had to be without any defects. Through the priests God declared whether the animals were acceptable or not. Through the priests God also declared that he had favorably accepted the offerers. If they offered the sacrifices that he ordained in his Word, they could be certain that he was pleased with them.

Fulfillment by Christ

See the end of the next section.

Temporal Restrictions for Sacrifices (22:26–30a)

Ritual Agents

These ritual case laws are addressed to Moses as the priestly founder of the cultus without any direction to transmit them to the Israelites[c] because the priests were responsible for their enforcement. Nevertheless the inclusive second person plural is still used for the reference to the slaughter of the animal (22:28, 29) and the prohibition against keeping some meat over from the day of its presentation (22:30). This shows that these cases deal with the sacrifices presented by the laity for their acceptance by God.

(c) Cf. Lev 5:14; 5:20 (ET 6:1); 6:12 (ET 6:19); 14:1

Ritual Material

The Lord's speech in 22:27–30 instructs Moses on how to deal with two practical ritual problems. The first restricts the use of young domesticated animals from the herd or the flock for sacrifice (22:27–28). This was necessary because the Israelites most commonly slaughtered young animals to provide choice meat for their sacrificial banquets. These rules protected the relationship between the young animal and its mother, as well as the integrity of the herd and the flock by ensuring that a particular breeding line was not exterminated as a family of animals. The second part of the speech restricts the consumption of meat from a thank offering to the day of its presentation.

Ritual Time

The common thread in both these cases is the three kinds of temporal restriction.

First, a young animal had to remain with its mother for at least seven days before it was presented for sacrifice. Like the seven days before the circumcision of a male child in 12:2–3, this was the normal time for ritual transition from one state into another. By the observance of this ritual week, the young animal was separated from its mother before slaughter. It had to become an animal in its own right before it was used as an offering on behalf of its owner.

Second, a young animal was not sacrificed on the same day as its mother. While this may originally have been designed to counter some pagan practice that was meant to enhance the fertility of the herd or the flock,[5] it meant that both the mother and her young were to be regarded as two separate sacrificial animals. They were not to be confused with each other by their presentation on the same occasion.

Third, the meat from the thank offering was eaten on the same day that it was presented. The sacrificial banquet was thereby connected ritually with the presentation of the animal and the performance of the song of thanksgiving at the sanctuary. The thanksgiving meal was associated with the act of thanksgiving. Even if the meal was separated spatially from the Lord's presence, it was not separated temporally from it and the sanctuary. The Israelites were not allowed to treat the holy meat from this sacrifice as common food.

Ritual Theological Function

The purpose of these case laws is the same as the previous section. The Lord set these temporal restrictions so that the people could be sure that he would accept their sacrifices as gifts to him (22:27) and them together with their gifts (22:29). God also protected the holy meat from ritual abuse. He gave these instructions so that the Israelites were certain that their offerings were acceptable to him.

---

[5] Compare Noth, *Leviticus*, 163.

Fulfillment by Christ

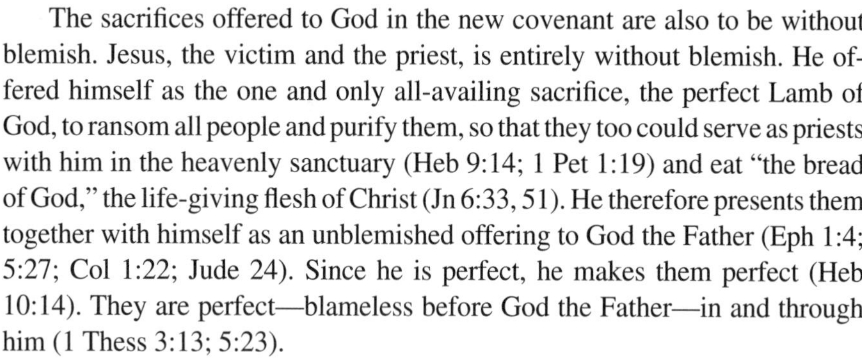

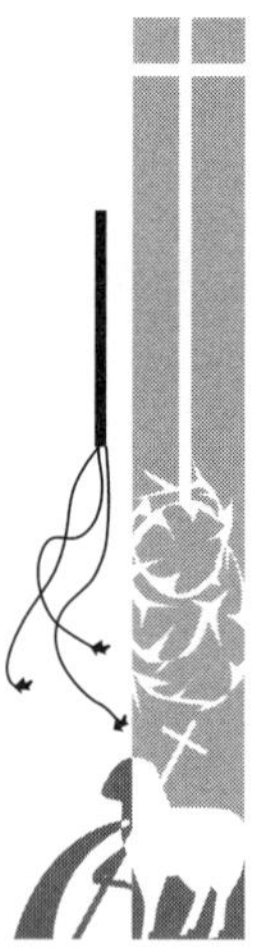

The sacrifices offered to God in the new covenant are also to be without blemish. Jesus, the victim and the priest, is entirely without blemish. He offered himself as the one and only all-availing sacrifice, the perfect Lamb of God, to ransom all people and purify them, so that they too could serve as priests with him in the heavenly sanctuary (Heb 9:14; 1 Pet 1:19) and eat "the bread of God," the life-giving flesh of Christ (Jn 6:33, 51). He therefore presents them together with himself as an unblemished offering to God the Father (Eph 1:4; 5:27; Col 1:22; Jude 24). Since he is perfect, he makes them perfect (Heb 10:14). They are perfect—blameless before God the Father—in and through him (1 Thess 3:13; 5:23).

In the church, as in Israel, God declares which sacrifices are acceptable and well-pleasing to him. He determines what blemishes make sacrifices unacceptable and establishes how they are to be offered to him. Most wonderfully, he himself provides the perfect remedy for the defects of his people and their offerings through the perfect priesthood and sacrifice of his Son, Jesus. Since Jesus pleased his heavenly Father in every possible way (Jn 8:29),[6] God the Father was pleased with him (Mt 3:17; 17:5; 2 Pet 1:17). Thus the offerings of the saints are pleasing to God because they are offered through Jesus and together with him (Heb 13:15–16; 1 Pet 2:5; *1 Clement* 64).

Through the preaching of the Gospel and the gift of the Holy Spirit, Jesus sanctifies all people who believe in him. He makes them and their Spirit-produced offerings acceptable to God the Father in and through him (Rom 15:15–16). Jesus determines how they are to serve his heavenly Father. By his commands, he institutes the right mode of worship. Their liturgical service is acceptable to God the Father if they perform it as he has ordained (1 Jn 3:22; *1 Clement* 40:1–4). They can therefore worship him in an acceptable way in the Divine Service (Rom 14:18; Heb 12:28). They can offer him a pure sacrifice each Sunday as they gather together to break bread and give thanks to the Father together with their great High Priest (*Didache* 14:1–3).

Since the saints are purified by the blood of Christ, their bodies and their souls, their offerings and their good works, their prayers and their praises, their acts of thanksgiving and their confessions of faith are well-pleasing to God the Father (Rom 12:1–2; Phil 4:18; Heb 13:16; 1 Pet 2:5, 9). He takes delight in them and enjoys them. The saints can therefore be sure that he is pleased with them and their service of him. They enjoy his approval of them and delight in his gracious acceptance of their offerings to him, for in Christ they have the righteousness and peace and joy that come from the Holy Spirit (Rom 14:17–18). Everything that they do is pleasing to him, an acceptable thank offering to him (Col 3:17). Their whole life on earth is therefore included in the service that they offer together with Jesus in the heavenly sanctuary.

---

[6] See also Ignatius, *Epistle to the Magnesians* 8:2.

Conclusion (22:30b–33)

This section functions most obviously as the conclusion of God's speech to Moses in 22:27–30. But it also reaches back much further than that. This is shown in three ways.

First, the admonition on the observance of God's commands in 22:31 parallels the similar introductory admonition in 18:2–4 as well as the summary admonitions in 18:30; 19:37; and 20:22. This suggests that 22:30b–33 is the conclusion for chapters 21–22, dealing with the holiness of the priests and the holy things of God, as well as chapters 18–20, dealing with the avoidance of ritual defilement.

Second, in 22:32b we have the seventh and final occurrence of the formula for the self-introduction of the Lord as the sanctifier of his priests and his people (20:8; 21:8, 15, 23; 22:9, 16). This implies that the ritual legislation in chapters 18–22 deal with the participation of the Israelites in God's holiness through the holy things.

Third, the prohibition against the profanation of the holy name in 22:32 not only forms an inclusion with 22:2, but it also echoes the same concern articulated in 18:21; 19:12; 20:3; and 21:6. Thus the conclusion of this chapter draws together the main theological strands from chapters 18–22.

This theological summary reminded the Israelites that God's great demands on them were based on his even greater gifts to them, their God-given privileges. In these verses, God introduced himself by name to them four times to give them access to himself and his blessings. In the third self-introduction, he also presented himself to them for the seventh and last time as the one who sanctifies them (22:32). They did not make themselves holy; he made them holy.

After that he reminded them how he shared his holiness with them by repeating his statement from 11:45. In this he combined the formula for deliverance from Egypt, "the God/the Lord who brought you/them out of the land of Egypt," with the formula for divine self-commitment to them, "I am the Lord your God." Thus he recalled his promise to Abraham in Gen 17:7–8 and its fulfillment by his residence with Israel through the performance of the divine service in Ex 29:42–46. God had freed his people from slavery in Egypt so that he could sanctify them by dwelling with them and acting as their God in the divine service. He therefore presented himself to them as the God who shared his own holiness with his people by his interaction with them in the sacrificial ritual. There he made and kept them holy.

The immense privilege of access to God and participation in his holiness brought with it two fundamental demands. Both presupposed that the Israelites were holy. Both followed logically from the gift of God and his holiness to them in the divine service.

First, God expected them to keep his ritual commandments, for apart from the divinely mandated ritual they had no access to his holiness (22:31). His Word instituted, governed, and empowered the enactment of the divine service. These sanctifying commandments established the means by which God shared his holiness with his people. They also prohibited anything that damaged the divine service and compromised its sanctity.

Second, God forbade the desecration of his holy name (22:32). The Israelites desecrated his holy name most obviously by swearing a false oath (19:12). But they also desecrated it less obviously by their participation in the cult of Molech (18:21; 20:3) and their involvement in any forbidden ritual practice (21:6). They observed this prohibition positively by respecting the sanctity of the holy things of God and by acknowledging that he dwelt in their midst in the tabernacle to sanctify them by his presence with them (22:32a). They observed it negatively by avoiding any activity that defiled and desecrated his holiness, for such behavior prevented God from demonstrating his holiness beneficially in their midst and sharing it benevolently with them (22:32b). Thus God's gift of himself to Israel as the source of its holiness brought with it his demand for the observance of his sanctifying commandments and his prohibition of desecration.

Fulfillment by Christ

The triune God has rescued his new Israel from slavery to sin and the devil (1 Cor 10:1–4; 1 Pet 1:14–21; Rev 5:9–10). He has brought his people to himself in the church, so that he could dwell with them there on earth and give them access to his heavenly presence in the Divine Service (Eph 2:17–22). He has blessed them with every spiritual blessing in the heavenly realm (Eph 1:3). He has given them his holy name and access to himself through his triune name (Jn 17:6, 26). By his Word he sanctifies them and keeps them holy (Jn 17:17; Eph 5:26).

Everything that they receive from him is sanctified by the use of his Word and name in worship and prayer (1 Tim 4:4–5). Through the name and Word of the triune God they share in his holiness. Without his Word and name they have no access to his presence and his holiness. They are therefore required to hallow his name (Mt 6:8; Lk 11:2) and enact his Word faithfully.[d] They are to observe and enact his sanctifying commandments, for through them he institutes and empowers and sanctifies their service of him.[e]

(d) Mt 7:24; 13:23; Lk 8:21; 11:28; Jn 8:31

(e) Mt 28:20; Jn 12:47–50; 14:21–24; 15:10; 1 Cor 7:19; 1 Jn 2:2–3; 3:21–24; 5:2–4; Rev 12:17; 14:12

This applies most obviously to what they do in the Divine Service. There they are to invoke the triune name and enact his Word in proclamation and confession, Baptism and Holy Communion, absolution and benediction, prayer and praise, self-offering and the presentation of offerings. Everything must be done in the name of Jesus and by the power of his Word (Col 3:16–17). Thus as Luther reminds us in his Small Catechism, God's name is hallowed when his Word is rightly taught and enacted in the holy liturgy and the whole of our lives are lived in consonance with that Word.[7] His Word makes everything else holy.

---

7 SC, Lord's Prayer, 3–5.

Dearest Jesus, at your word
We have come again to hear you;
Let our thoughts and hearts be stirred
And in glowing faith be near you
As the promises here given
Draw us wholly up to heaven.

Radiance of God's glory bright,
Light of light from God proceeding,
Jesus, send your blessed light;
Help our hearing, speaking, heeding,
That our prayers and songs may please you
As with grateful hearts we praise you.[8]

---

[8] From "Dearest Jesus, at Your Word" by Tobias Clausnitzer (*LW* 202:1, 3).

The Structure of Leviticus 23–26

Since the speeches in chapters 17–22 form a discrete whole, the question arises whether chapters 23–26 too are interconnected structurally and thematically. At first glance two things make this rather unlikely. First, each section has its own clear conclusion apart from the speech in 24:1–9 (23:44; 24:23b; 26:46). Second, there is no conclusive summary. In addition, chapter 26 seems an anomaly. It seems to serve as the conclusion of the speech that begins in the previous chapter. Yet it does not function as part of the discussion about the Sabbatical and Jubilee Years apart from a passing reference in 26:43.

Ruwe argues quite convincingly that chapter 26 is, in fact, the conclusion for the whole of Leviticus 17–25.[1] Just as God's command in 26:2 to revere his sanctuary states the theme of chapter 17–22, so his command in 26:2 to observe his Sabbaths summarizes the laws in chapters 23–26. Hence just as the Israelites were to orient their lives spatially around the sanctuary, they were also to orient their work and rest temporally around the observance of the Sabbath and the other holy times. This theory is backed by the prominence given to the Sabbath as the foundation for the liturgical calendar in 23:3 and the repeated mention of the various Sabbaths in this section of the book.[a] While this theory does not explain the placement of the account of the blasphemer in 24:10–23, it does make sense of the sequence of these speeches.

(a) Lev 23:3 (twice), 11, 15 (twice), 16, 32 (twice), 38 (twice); 24:8 (twice); 25:2, 4 (twice), 6, 8 (twice); cf. 26:2, 34 (twice), 35, 43

[1] Ruwe, *"Heiligkeitsgesetz" und "Priesterschrift,"* 90–97.

Leviticus 23:1–44

Calendar of Holy Times

Translation

23 1The Lord spoke to Moses: 2"Speak to the Israelites and say to them: The
appointed times of the Lord which you shall proclaim as proclaimed holy days—
these are my appointed times. 3On six days work may be done, but on the seventh day there shall be a Sabbath of total rest, a proclaimed holy day. You shall
not do any work; it shall be a Sabbath to the Lord throughout all your places of
residence. 4These are the appointed times of the Lord, the proclaimed holy days
which you shall proclaim at their appointed time. 5In the first month, on the fourteenth day of the month, at twilight, is the Lord's Passover, 6and on the fifteenth
day of this month is the Feast of Unleavened Bread for the Lord. You shall eat
unleavened bread for seven days. 7On the first day there shall be a proclaimed
holy day for you; you shall not do any work in your occupation. 8You shall present a gift to the Lord for seven days. On the seventh day there shall be a proclaimed holy day; you shall not do any work in your occupation."

9The Lord spoke to Moses: 10"Speak to the Israelites and say to them: When
you enter the land that I am giving to you and you reap its harvest, and when
you bring the first sheaf of your harvest to the priest 11so that he may raise the
sheaf before the Lord for your acceptance, the priest shall raise it on the day after the Sabbath. 12On the day that you elevate the sheaf, you shall perform the
ritual for the burnt offering to the Lord with a lamb without blemish in its first
year. 13The grain offering with it shall be two-tenths [of an ephah] of fine wheat
flour mixed with oil, a gift to the Lord, a pleasing aroma; the libation with it shall
be a fourth of a measure of wine. 14You shall not eat any [new] bread or roasted
grain or fresh ears until this very day, until you have brought the offering of your
God. This is a perpetual ritual statute throughout your generations in all your
places of residence. 15Then you shall count off for yourselves from the day after
the Sabbath, from the day that you bring the sheaf for elevation, seven weeks;
they must be complete. 16Until the day after the seventh Sabbath-week, you shall
count fifty days; then you shall present an offering of new grain to the Lord.
17From your places of residence you shall bring two loaves of bread as an elevation offering; they shall be made of two-tenths [of an ephah] of fine wheat flour,
baked with leaven, as first-ripe produce for the Lord. 18Then with the bread you
shall present seven lambs without blemish and a year old, one bull from the herd,
and two rams; they shall be a burnt offering for the Lord, together with their
grain offerings and their libations, a gift of a pleasing aroma to the Lord. 19You
shall also perform the ritual for the sin offering with one male goat and for the
peace offering with two year-old male lambs. 20The priest shall raise them, together with the bread from the first-ripe produce, as an elevation offering before

the Lord, in addition to [the] two lambs; they shall be a holy thing to the Lord for the priest. 21On this very same day you shall make a proclamation; it shall be a proclaimed holy day for you; you shall do no work in your occupation. This is a perpetual ritual statute in all your places of residence throughout your generations. 22When you reap the harvest of your land, you shall not completely reap the edges of your field or gather the dropped stalks from your harvest; you shall leave them for the poor and for the alien. I am the Lord your God."

23The Lord spoke to Moses: 24"Speak to the Israelites: In the seventh month, on the first of the month, you shall have a rest, a commemoration with acclamation, a proclaimed holy day. 25You shall not do any work in your occupation, and you shall present a gift to the Lord."

26The Lord spoke to Moses: 27"However, on the tenth day of this seventh month is the Day of Atonement; it shall be a proclaimed holy day for you, and you shall humble yourselves, and you shall present a gift to the Lord. 28You shall not do any work on this very day, because it is the Day of Atonement, to make atonement for you before the Lord your God. 29Indeed, anyone who is not humbled on this very day will be cut off from his kinsfolk; 30as for anyone who does any work on this very day, I will exterminate that person from the midst of his people. 31You shall do no work; this is a perpetual ritual statute throughout your generations in all your places of residence. 32It is a Sabbath of total rest for you; you shall humble yourselves; on the ninth day of the month at evening, from evening to evening, you shall rest on your day of rest."

33The Lord spoke to Moses: 34"Speak to the Israelites: On the fifteenth day of this seventh month [there shall be] the Feast of Booths for seven days for the Lord. 35On the first day there shall be a proclaimed holy day; you shall not do any work in your occupation. 36For seven days you shall bring a gift to the Lord; on the eighth day there shall be a proclaimed holy day for you, and you shall present a gift to the Lord; it is a closing ceremony; you shall not do any work in your occupation. 37These are the appointed times of the Lord, which you shall proclaim as proclaimed holy days, for the presentation of gifts to the Lord: burnt offerings and grain offerings, sacrifices and libations, the daily quota for each day, 38apart from the Sabbaths of the Lord and apart from your personal donations and apart from all your personal votive offerings and apart from all your personal freewill offerings that you give to the Lord. 39Moreover, on the fifteenth day of the seventh month, when you have gathered in the produce of the land, you shall go on pilgrimage [to celebrate] the Feast of the Lord for seven days; there shall be a time of rest on the first day and a time of rest on the eighth day. 40On the first day you shall take up for yourselves the fruit from majestic trees—branches of palm trees, boughs from leafy trees, and willows from the brook—and you shall rejoice before the Lord your God for seven days 41and go on pilgrimage with it [to celebrate] the Feast for the Lord for seven days in each year. This is a perpetual ritual statute throughout your generations. On the seventh month you shall go on pilgrimage with it. 42You shall reside in the booths for seven days—every native-born person in Israel shall reside in the booths—

[43]so that your generations may know that I housed the Israelites in booths when I brought them out of the land of Egypt. I am the Lord your God."

[44]Thus Moses declared the appointed times of the Lord to the Israelites.

Textual Notes

23:2 The sentence beginning "These are my appointed times" and 23:4 are arranged as a chiasm in Hebrew to emphasize that the Lord sets the time for these occasions.

מוֹעֲדֵי יְהוָה—The Hebrew noun מוֹעֵד, "appointed time," comes from the root יָעַד, "to appoint a time to meet" or "to arrange a place for meeting." A number of important ritual terms come from this root. The "tent of meeting" is the place where God has arranged to "meet" with his priests (Ex 25:22; 30:6, 36; Num 17:4). Since he desires to "meet" with his people at the altar during the performance of the burnt offering (Ex 29:42–43), he has also fixed "the appointed times for meeting" with them there (Lev 23:4, 37, 44). The people who meet with him there are his עֵדָה, his "meeting," his congregation (4:13, 15; 8:3, 4, 5; 9:5; 10:6, 17; 16:5; 19:2; 24:14, 16). The phrase מוֹעֲדֵי יְהוָה occurs also in 23:4, 37, 44; 2 Chr 2:3 (ET 2:4); Ezra 3:5.

מִקְרָאֵי קֹדֶשׁ—Literally this phrase is "proclamations of holiness" or "days proclaimed as holy" (Ex 12:16; Lev 23:2, 3, 4, 7, 8, 21, 24, 27, 35, 36, 37; Num 28:18, 25, 26; 29:1, 7, 12). Usually מִקְרָא is defined as an "assembly" (BDB, 1; *HALOT,* 1 b) or "convocation" (BDB, 1), that is, the congregation of people who are called or invited to meet together. However, we prefer the view that this phrase does not refer to "sacred convocations" or "sacred assemblies" of people for worship at the sanctuary,[1] but to the official proclamation of certain days of the month as extraordinary holy days.[2] God told his people to "proclaim" (קָרָא, 23:2, 4, 21, 37; cf. Is 1:13) the days for certain occasions by the sounding of trumpets (Num 10:10) because these occasions did not occur regularly, like the Sabbath, or obviously, like the full moon. The appointed time for them was determined by astronomical observance and calculation. They clustered around the spring and autumn equinoxes. By virtue of their proclamation, they became holy days when no work could be done (Ex 12:16; Lev 23:3, 7, 8, 21, 25, 31). The people were obliged to assemble at the sanctuary on some of these days. The use of this term for the Sabbath in 23:3 is rather unusual because it did not need to be officially promulgated again as a holy day. It may specifically refer to the Sabbath at the end of the Feast of Unleavened Bread (23:8).

23:3 שֵׁשֶׁת יָמִים תֵּעָשֶׂה מְלָאכָה—See Ex 31:15; 35:2.

וּבַיּוֹם הַשְּׁבִיעִי שַׁבַּת שַׁבָּתוֹן—See the textual notes on Lev 16:31. שַׁבַּת שַׁבָּתוֹן recurs in 23:32. The term שַׁבָּתוֹן is used for four different occasions in this chapter: the weekly Sabbath (23:3; cf. Ex 16:23; 31:15; 35:2), the Day of Atonement (Lev 23:32; cf. 16:31), and the first and last days in the Feast of Booths (23:39).

מִקְרָא־קֹדֶשׁ—This is the only place where the Sabbath is designated as (literally) "a day *proclaimed as holy.*"

---

1 Contra Levine, *Leviticus*, 154; Wenham, *Leviticus*, 301; NIV; NRSV.

2 Hartley, *Leviticus*, 375; Milgrom, *Leviticus 1–16*, 20–21; Milgrom, *Leviticus 23–27*, 1956–59.

כָּל־מְלָאכָה לֹא תַעֲשׂוּ—See Ex 20:10; Deut 5:14.

שַׁבָּת הִוא לַיהוָה—See Ex 20:10; 35:2; Deut 5:14; cf. Lev 25:2, 4.

בְּכֹל מוֹשְׁבֹתֵיכֶם׃—See 3:17; 7:26; 23:14, 17, 21, 31.

23:4 בְּמוֹעֲדָם׃—See Ex 13:10; 23:15; Num 9:2, 3, 7, 13; 28:2; 29:39.

23:5 בֵּין הָעַרְבָּיִם—This is literally "between the two evenings." This is the term for the period between sunset (the first of the two evenings) and nightfall (the second of the two evenings). We translate the phrase as "twilight." This phrase occurs also in Ex 12:6; 16:12; 29:39, 41; 30:8; Num 9:3, 5, 11; 28:4, 8.

פֶּסַח—This could also be translated "Passover offering."

23:6 חַג הַמַּצּוֹת—The feminine plural noun מַצּוֹת is literally "loaves of unleavened bread." The noun חַג refers to a communal pilgrim feast. There were three such feasts: the Day of Unleavened Bread, the Day of Weeks (Pentecost), and the Week of Booths (Ex 23:14–17). On these the male heads of each Israelite family were obliged to appear with their offerings before the Lord at his residence.[3]

There is some uncertainty about which day was to be observed as the time for pilgrimage in the week of Unleavened Bread. If the Passover was celebrated at home, the seventh day was the time for pilgrimage (Ex 13:6). But when the Passover was celebrated at the central sanctuary, its commemoration was combined with the festival of Unleavened Bread, and the first day became the day for pilgrimage (Ex 12:14, 17; Lev 23:6; Num 28:17; Deut 16:16). This day became identified with the Passover and was also called the Feast of the Passover (Ex 34:25). In the postexilic period, the whole week was observed as a communal festival with the result that the term חַג was no longer used exclusively for a communal pilgrimage to the temple in Jerusalem (Ezra 6:22; 2 Chr 30:13, 21; 35:17; Ezek 45:21, 23).

On the Feast of Unleavened Bread, see Ex 12:17; 23:15; 34:18. The feast derived its name from the prohibition of leavened bread during the week of its observance. For other legislation of this celebration, see Ex 12:1–28, 43–50; 13:3–10; 23:15; 34:18, 25; Num 28:16–25; Deut 16:1–8.

שִׁבְעַת יָמִים—See Lev 23:8 and the textual notes on 8:33.

מַצּוֹת תֹּאכֵלוּ׃—See Ex 12:15, 18; 13:6, 7; 23:15; 34:18; Num 28:17; Deut 16:3.

23:7 כָּל־מְלֶאכֶת עֲבֹדָה לֹא תַעֲשׂוּ׃—This clause recurs in 23:8, 21, 25, 35, 36; Num 28:18, 25, 26; 29:1, 12, 35. The phrase מְלֶאכֶת עֲבֹדָה is literally "work of labor," meaning the work that a person does for his job or occupation. In contrast with the total ban on all work for the Sabbath (Lev 23:3) and for the Day of Atonement (16:29; 23:28, 31; Num 29:7), here God only prohibits the work done in pursuit of a person's occupation.[4]

23:8 וְהִקְרַבְתֶּם—See the textual note on this verb in 1:2. It recurs in 23:16, 18, 25, 27, 36, 37.

אִשֶּׁה—See the textual note on this noun in 1:9 and the explanation in "Leviticus 1–3." It recurs in 23:13, 18, 25, 27, 36, 37.

---

3 Haran, *Temples and Temple-Service in Ancient Israel*, 289–300; Milgrom, *Leviticus 23–27*, 1974–76; Wenham, *Leviticus*, 303.

4 Milgrom, *Leviticus 1–16*, 1054–55.

שִׁבְעַת יָמִים—See Num 28:19–24.

כָּל־מְלֶאכֶת עֲבֹדָה לֹא תַעֲשׂוּ׃—See Num 28:25.

23:10 כִּי־תָבֹאוּ אֶל־הָאָרֶץ—See Lev 14:34; 19:23; 25:2.

וַהֲבֵאתֶם אֶת־עֹמֶר רֵאשִׁית קְצִירְכֶם אֶל־הַכֹּהֵן׃—This fills out the ritual mentioned in Ex 23:19 and 34:26.

עֹמֶר רֵאשִׁית—This could also be translated "sheaf of firstfruits/first-produce." See Milgrom[5] and the textual notes on 2:12.

23:11 וְהֵנִיף—See the textual note on this verb in 7:30. It recurs in 23:12, 20.

לִרְצֹנְכֶם—See the textual notes on 1:3.

מִמָּחֳרַת הַשַּׁבָּת—This phrase is repeated in 23:15, 16. The sense of מִמָּחֳרַת הַשַּׁבָּת and the date for this enactment has long been disputed in Jewish circles, since the Hebrew text does not specify which Sabbath provided the basis for its reckoning. Milgrom gives a comprehensive overview of all positions.[6] There are four possible interpretations.[7]

First, as the LXX shows, the Sabbath before the day for the presentation of the barley sheaf could be the first day of the feast, the extraordinary day of rest on the fifteenth of Nisan. This is the position of the Pharisees.[8] Josh 5:10–12, with its mention of eating parched grain on the day after the Passover, is incorrectly adduced to support this date, for it refers to the fifteenth rather than the sixteenth of Nisan. The Council of Nicaea assumed that this day was a regular Sabbath for the year of Christ's death.

Second, the Sabbath could be the extraordinary day of rest of the last day of the feast, the twenty-first of Nisan.[9]

Third, it could be the regular weekly Sabbath during the week of the feast. The designation of the day before the Feast of Weeks as a Sabbath in 23:16 may be adduced to support this view. This was the view of the Samaritans and Karaites.

Fourth, and least likely, it could be the first regular weekly Sabbath after the week of Unleavened Bread was over. This was the view of the Boethians and the Qumran community. Thus for both of them the day for the elevation of the first sheaf and the Day of Pentecost always fell on a Sunday.

23:12 וַעֲשִׂיתֶם—See the textual note on this verb in 4:20. It recurs in this sense in 23:19.

תָּמִים—See the textual note on this adjective in 1:3. It recurs in 23:18.

בֶּן־שְׁנָתוֹ—This is literally "the son of its year." See the textual notes on 12:6.

23:13 שְׁנֵי עֶשְׂרֹנִים—See 23:17; cf. 14:10, 21; 24:5.

סֹלֶת—See the textual notes on 2:1. This recurs in 23:17.

רֵיחַ נִיחֹחַ—See the textual notes on 1:9 and the explanation in "Leviticus 1–3." This phrase recurs in 23:18.

---

5 Milgrom, *Leviticus 1–16*, 190.

6 Milgrom, *Leviticus 23–27*, 2056–63.

7 Van Goudoever, *Biblical Calendars,* 18–29; Hartley, *Leviticus*, 385–86.

8 Cf. Josephus, *Antiquities,* 3.250 (3.10.5).

9 Gerstenberger, *Leviticus*, 344.

יַיִן רְבִיעִת הַהִין׃—See also Ex 29:40; Num 15:5; 28:14. The libations of wine were used in the ritual for the burnt offering (Ex 29:40; Lev 23:18; Num 15:5, 24) and in the ritual for the peace offering (Num 15:8–10).

23:14 וְכַרְמֶ֗ל—See 2:14.

עֶ֫צֶם—When עֶצֶם is used, as here, with "day," it can refer either to the exact day for a celebration (23:14, 21) or the entire duration of the day of an observance (23:29, 30).

הֲבִיאֲכֶ֔ם—See the textual note on the Hiphil of בּוֹא in 2:2. It recurs in 23:15, 17.

חֻקַּת עוֹלָם—See the textual notes on 3:17. This phrase recurs in 23:21, 31, 41.

בְּכֹל מֹשְׁבֹתֵיכֶם׃—See the textual notes on 3:17. This phrase recurs in 23:21, 31.

23:15 מִמָּחֳרַת הַשַּׁבָּת—See 23:11.

הַתְּנוּפָה—See the textual notes on 7:30. This noun refers to the ritual presentation in 23:10–11. It recurs in 23:17, 20.

שֶׁבַע שַׁבָּתוֹת—This is literally "seven Sabbaths." The seven Sabbaths may be understood either as seven weekly Sabbaths or as seven weeks. If this refers to the regular Sabbaths, then the day for the elevation of the first sheaf and the Day of Pentecost would always fall on Sunday. But as Deut 16:9 shows in its reference to this day, the term "Sabbath" can also be taken more generally as a period of seven days by analogy with its use for seven years in Lev 25:8.[10]

23:16 מִמָּחֳרַת הַשַּׁבָּת הַשְּׁבִיעִת—This is literally "the day after the seventh Sabbath."

וְהִקְרַבְתֶּם מִנְחָה חֲדָשָׁה לַיהוָה׃—See the parallel legislation in Num 28:26–31.

מִנְחָה חֲדָשָׁה—This is literally "a new grain offering." This annual grain offering needs to be distinguished from the other grain offerings brought by each Israelite household in Lev 2:14 on other occasions.

23:17 It is not clear whether the two loaves were presented by each household[11] or by the congregation as a national offering.[12] While the reference to bringing the loaves from their places of residence is taken as evidence for the former view, their presentation with the public sacrifices in 23:18–19 and their elevation with the two lambs support the latter view.

חָמֵץ—Since none of this bread was burnt on the altar, it, like the bread for the thanksgiving offering (7:13) and the first loaf from the new harvest (Num 15:18–21), was made from leavened dough.

בִּכּוּרִים—This term recurs in 23:20.

23:18 שִׁבְעַת כְּבָשִׂים—The presentation of seven lambs corresponds to the day as the culmination of the seven weeks of harvest.

וּפַר בֶּן־בָּקָר—See the textual notes on 1:5.

וּמִנְחָתָם—See Num 28:28–29.

וְנִסְכֵּיהֶם—See Num 28:7, 14.

---

[10] Keil, *Pentateuch*, 2:442; Levine, *Leviticus*, 442.

[11] Noth, *Leviticus,* 172; Gerstenberger, *Leviticus*, 345.

[12] Keil, *Pentateuch*, 2:442–43; Levine, *Leviticus*, 159.

23:19 This contrasts with the schedule in Num 28:27–31, which makes no mention of the two lambs for the peace offering and prescribes two bulls, one ram, and seven male lambs for the burnt offering. The LXX adds "with the bread of the firstfruits."

שְׁלָמִים׃—This seems to be the only occasion for which animals were presented as a public peace offering to provide meat exclusively for the priests to eat in a sacrificial banquet.

23:20 That the priest shall raise the two lambs is not stated, but understood in the Hebrew text.

עַל־שְׁנֵי כְּבָשִׂים—Since the bread and the meat from the lambs were raised as an elevation offering, they were holy and reserved for consumption by the priests.

לַכֹּהֵן׃—The LXX has "the priest who presents them to him." This was most likely the high priest.

23:22 This verse repeats what God commanded in 19:9–10. The reference to the grape vintage in 19:10 is omitted here because it is irrelevant in this context.

וְלַגֵּר—See the textual notes on 16:29.

אֲנִי יְהוָה אֱלֹהֵיכֶם׃—See the textual notes on 11:44. This clause is repeated in 23:43.

23:24 שַׁבָּתוֹן—See Ex 16:23; Lev 23:39; 25:5. The noun שַׁבָּתוֹן is used for a time of rest from work for people and the land.

זִכְרוֹן—The noun זִכָּרוֹן designates a "commemoration" that is, most commonly, instituted by God. Three such divinely ordained commemorations are accompanied by a promise of his grace and salvation for those who perform them: the blood of the Passover lamb (Ex 12:14); the breast piece of the high priest (Ex 28:12, 29); and the sounding of the trumpets (Num 10:10).[13] By their enactment God's people remembered him. At the same time he "remembered" them by giving them the help that he has promised to give to them. While there is no specific promise of grace in this instance, it is probably meant to recall God's promise of salvation to Israel in connection with the sounding of the trumpets over the sacrifices at the beginning of each month in Num 10:10.

תְּרוּעָה—See Num 28:1, where this day is called the Day of Acclamation. It received this name from the sounding of the trumpets by the priests on this occasion. Hence this celebration was also called the Day of Trumpets. The noun תְּרוּעָה, "acclamation," is derived from the verb רוּעַ, which usually occurs in the Hiphil meaning "to shout." The verb refers to the shouting of a routed enemy (Judg 7:21), shouting in battle (Judg 15:14), and the shouting of acclamation for a king (1 Sam 10:24). The noun was used for the ritual acclamation of the Lord as King in the divine service (Num 23:21) by a shout (Ps 89:16 [ET 89:15]) or by the blast of a ram's horn together with a shout (Ps 47:6–8 [ET 47:5–7]). The verb was used for acclaiming the Lord as King by the sounding of the sacred trumpets and a ram's horn (Ps 98:6; cf. Num 10:10). The priests sounded the sacred "trumpets for acclamation" (Num 31:6) in the divine

---

[13] H. Eising, "זָכַר *zākhar,*" *TDOT* 4:82.

service to announce the presence of the divine King and to call his people to acknowledge him as their King (Num 10:1–10).[14]

23:25 וְהִקְרַבְתֶּם אִשֶּׁה לַיהוָה׃—The public offerings for this day are listed in Num 29:2–6.

23:27 אַךְ—This emphatic particle draws a contrast between this day and the previously mentioned first day of the month. This connection is reinforced by the omission of God's commission to report the contents of the speech to the Israelites.

יוֹם הַכִּפֻּרִים—This designation of "the Day of Atonement" recurs in 23:28; 25:9.

וְעִנִּיתֶם אֶת־נַפְשֹׁתֵיכֶם—This could also be translated "you shall deny yourselves." See the textual notes on 16:29. It recurs in 23:29, 32.

וְהִקְרַבְתֶּם אִשֶּׁה לַיהוָה׃—The public offerings for the day are listed in Num 29:8–11.

23:28 לְכַפֵּר עֲלֵיכֶם—See the textual notes on 1:4.

23:29 כִּי—Our translation takes כִּי as an emphatic particle.

לֹא־תְעֻנֶּה—This could also be translated "does not humble himself" if the Pual is understood reflexively.

וְנִכְרְתָה מֵעַמֶּיהָ׃—See the textual notes on 7:20.

23:32 מֵעֶרֶב עַד־עֶרֶב—The mention of the precise length of time for the observance underscores the importance of the occasion. The day begins at evening (cf. Gen 1:5) and lasts until the following evening.

תִּשְׁבְּתוּ שַׁבַּתְּכֶם׃—This is literally "you shall sabbath your Sabbath." This unique use of the verb with its cognate accusative emphasizes the need for total rest from all work.

23:34 See the other legislation for this celebration in Num 29:12–40 and Deut 16:13–17.

חַג הַסֻּכּוֹת—This could also be translated "the Feast of Tabernacles." See also Deut 16:13, 16; 31:10; 2 Chr 8:13; Ezra 3:4; Zech 14:16, 18, 19.

שִׁבְעַת יָמִים—See Lev 23:36, 39, 40, 41, 42 and the textual notes on 8:33.

23:36 תַּקְרִיבוּ אִשֶּׁה לַיהוָה—See the list of offerings in Num 29:13–34.

בַּיּוֹם הַשְּׁמִינִי—See the list of offerings in Num 29:35–38.

אִשֶּׁה לַיהוָה—See Lev 23:37 and the textual notes on 1:9.

עֲצֶרֶת—Our translation ("closing ceremony") follows the LXX, which renders עֲצֶרֶת by ἐξόδιος, "finale, recessional." It is difficult to determine the precise sense of the Hebrew term. Even though it is used rather generally for a ritual occasion outside the Pentateuch (Amos 5:21; cf. the form עֲצָרָה in 2 Ki 10:20; Is 1:13; Joel 1:14; 2:15), the Pentateuch uses it exclusively for the eighth day of Booths (Lev 23:36; Num 29:35; cf. 2 Chr 7:9; Neh 8:18) and the last day of Unleavened Bread (Deut 16:8) to describe the closing ceremony or closing assembly of a time of celebration.

23:37 אֵלֶּה מוֹעֲדֵי יְהוָה אֲשֶׁר־תִּקְרְאוּ אֹתָם מִקְרָאֵי קֹדֶשׁ—This résumé of 23:2 closes off the intervening material that deals with the times appointed for the presentation of offerings at the sanctuary.

זֶבַח—This refers to peace offerings. This and several of the nearby terms are collectives in this verse and so are translated as plurals.

---

[14] Compare Kleinig, *The Lord's Song*, 36–37, 79–82.

דְּבַר־י֥וֹם בְּיוֹמֽוֹ׃—This idiom originally referred to the daily roster of work for servants (Ex 5:13, 19; Neh 11:23) or the daily quota of rations for dependants (Ex 16:4; 2 Ki 25:30; Neh 12:47; Dan 1:5). The phrase was also used in ritual contexts, as here, for the daily quota of sacrifices for God (2 Chr 8:13; Ezra 3:4) and the roster for the performance of liturgical music (1 Chr 16:37; 2 Chr 8:14).

23:38 שַׁבְּתֹ֣ת יְהוָ֑ה—This refers to the regular Sabbaths with their prescribed offerings in Num 28:9–10.

מַתְּנֽוֹתֵיכֶ֗ם—This term is used for the gifts that were not burned on the altar (Ex 28:38; Num 18:6, 7, 29; Deut 16:17).

כָּל־נִדְרֵיכֶם֙—See the textual notes on 7:16.

כָּל־נִדְבֹ֣תֵיכֶ֔ם—See 7:16; 22:18, 21, 23.

אֲשֶׁ֥ר תִּתְּנ֖וּ לַיהוָֽה׃—See Num 29:39b. This refers to all the offerings listed in Lev 23:38a.

23:39 אַ֡ךְ—Since 23:39–44 is located after the subscription in 23:37–38, most critical scholars regard this as a later addition.[15] However, there are three good reasons for regarding this section as an integral part of the whole chapter. First, the use of אַךְ in 23:39 echoes its occurrence in 23:27, where it links the Day of Atonement with the Day of Acclamation. Second, the designation of the first and eighth days as times of rest recalls 23:3, 24, 32, while the perpetual ritual statute for the observance of the feast in the Lord's presence at the sanctuary stands in contrast with the perpetual statutes for the observance at home of the Festival of Weeks in 23:21 and the Day of Atonement in 23:31. Third, unlike the legislation in 23:4–38, which prescribes the appointed times for the presentation of gifts by the priests to the Lord (23:8, 18, 25, 27, 36, 37), these verses deal with popular observances that are not an integral part of the divine service for these celebrations.

בְּאָסְפְּכֶם֙—Because of this use of the verb אָסַף, "to gather (in)," the feast was also called "the Feast of the Ingathering" in Ex 23:16 and 34:22 (cf. Deut 16:13).

תָּחֹ֥גּוּ אֶת־חַג־יְהוָ֖ה—This is literally "you shall go on a pilgrimage on the Feast of the Lord" or "you shall proceed on a procession on the Feast of the Lord." See too Lev 23:41.

חַג־יְהוָ֖ה—While this celebration is designated as "the Feast for the Lord" in 23:34 and 23:41, this is the only place where it is called "the Feast of the Lord."

23:40 וּלְקַחְתֶּ֨ם—The people are to "pick" up the branches with their hands (cf. Ex 12:3) and "carry" them in procession.

פְּרִ֨י עֵ֤ץ—Traditionally, "the fruit of the tree" is taken to be the citron.[16] Neh 8:15, however, lists the olive, wild olive, myrtle, and palm as four specific kinds of branches from leafy trees. Milgrom therefore proposes that the word "fruit" be understood as the branches of the trees in contradistinction to their stock.[17]

---

[15] Elliger, *Leviticus*, 305–6; Noth, *Leviticus*, 175.

[16] Talmud, Mishnah, *Sukkah,* 3:4.

[17] Milgrom, *Leviticus 23–27*, 2041.

עֵץ—This is the general category which is followed by three specific species.[18]

עֵץ־עָבֹת—The kinds of trees are purposely left unspecified.

וְעַרְבֵי־נָחַל—Traditionally this was identified with the poplar tree.

וּשְׂמַחְתֶּם—This is the only occasion in this chapter on which God commands his people to "rejoice." The calendar in Deuteronomy emphasizes rejoicing as the distinctive feature of this festival (Deut 16:14, 15). This was fulfilled by the daily processions with the branches around the altar, which, no doubt, were accompanied by music and song.

23:41 וְחַגֹּתֶם אֹתוֹ חַג לַיהוָה שִׁבְעַת יָמִים—This is absent from the LXX, which may have omitted it by way of haplography from 23:39.

וְחַגֹּתֶם—The verb חָגַג is used here in the ancient sense of a communal procession into the sanctuary and around the altar (see Ps 42:5 and the use of חַג in Ps 118:27).

אֹתוֹ—Our translation takes the "it" with which they were to go on pilgrimage as a bunch of branches made from the "fruit" from the trees. "It" could also refer rather generally to the day of celebration, as in Ex 12:14, without any exact antecedent. The translation would then be "you shall celebrate it as a pilgrim festival to the Lord for seven days."[19]

חַג לַיהוָה—Elsewhere the Feast of Booths is simply called "the Feast" (הֶחָג) because it is the main pilgrim festival, the archetypal feast (1 Ki 8:2, 65; 12:32; 2 Chr 5:3; 7:8, 9; Neh 8:14; Ezek 45:25).

חֻקַּת עוֹלָם לְדֹרֹתֵיכֶם—This is the only perpetual ritual statute in this chapter that did not require the Israelites to observe a day of rest in their places of residence.

בַּחֹדֶשׁ הַשְּׁבִיעִי תָּחֹגּוּ אֹתוֹ׃—This sentence is the subheading for 23:42–43.

23:42 בַּסֻּכֹּת—This is literally "in the booths." The article indicates that their purpose is well-known (GKC, § 126 n).

שִׁבְעַת יָמִים—See Neh 8:13–18, where Ezra extends the law to include the people in their homes as well as the people in Jerusalem.

הָאֶזְרָח—See the textual notes on 16:29.

23:43 דֹרֹתֵיכֶם—This could also be translated "your descendants."

בְּהוֹצִיאִי אוֹתָם מֵאֶרֶץ מִצְרָיִם—See 19:36; 25:38, 42, 55; 26:45.

23:44 For the use of a similar formula of compliance, see 8:36; 16:34; 21:24; 24:23.

Commentary

Structure

The material in this chapter is arranged as a speech with five sub-speeches. The report of God's address to Moses and commission of him introduces the speech as a whole, which is rounded off with the formula of compliance in 23:44. It also introduces the first of five speeches. Apart from the fourth of these, each begins with the same introduction. The fourth speech, however, lacks a commission to speak, but is linked to the third speech by the use of אַךְ, "however" (23:27).

---

[18] Keil, *Pentateuch*, 2:448; Milgrom, *Leviticus 23–27*, 2041–42.

[19] Milgrom, *Leviticus 23–27*, 2047.

Three other devices serve to subdivide the chapter. First, the general heading in 23:2b is followed by the subscription in 23:37–38. This distinguishes the regulations in 23:39–43 about lay involvement in the Feast of Booths from the preceding list of the appointed times for God's meetings with his people. Second, the subheading in 23:4 distinguishes the regulations for the Sabbath in 23:3 from the regulations for the other appointed times in 23:5–36. It thereby shows that, unlike them, the Sabbath did not need to be fixed by astronomical observance. It also indicates that the Sabbath was the archetypal holy day. Third, the occurrence of the formula for divine self-introduction in 23:22 and 23:43 separates the celebrations in spring from the celebrations in autumn.

The contents of the calendar are linked together by the repetition of certain key words and phrases.

- "Appointed times of the Lord" (23:2, 4, 37, 44)
- "Sabbath(s)" (23:3, 11, 15 [twice], 16, 32 [twice], 38)
- "A [time of] rest" (23:3, 24, 32, 39)
- "The seventh day" (23:3, 8); "the seventh month" (23:24, 27, 34, 39, 41)
- "Seven days" (23:6, 8, 34, 36, 39, 40, 41, 42)
- "A proclaimed holy day/proclaimed holy days" (23:2, 3, 4, 7, 8, 21, 24, 27, 35, 36, 37)
- "Present a gift/gifts to the Lord" (23:8, 13, 18, 25, 27, 36 [twice], 37)
- "You shall not do any work in your occupation" (23:7, 8, 21, 25, 35, 36)
- "You shall not do any work" (23:3, 28, 31)
- "A perpetual ritual statute throughout your generations" (23:14, 21, 31, 41)
- "To the Lord" (23:3, 5, 6, 8, 12, 13, 16, 17, 18 [twice], 20, 25, 27, 34, 36 [twice], 37, 38, 41)

The legislation for the appointed times also follows two similar patterns. The first specifies the dates for the day and its observance.[20] See figure 23.

The second pattern prescribes the duration of the observance. See figure 24.

In a few instances, the first formula also mentions the duration of the celebration (23:3, 34, 39).

---

[20] Hartley, *Leviticus*, 372.

Figure 23

Date and Observance of Appointed Feasts

Reference	*Date*	*Occasion*	*Lay Observance*	*Work Prohibition*	*Offerings/Gifts to the Lord*
23:3	Sabbath			Total	
23:5	14th day of first month	Passover			
23:6, 8	15th–21st days of first month	Feast of Unleavened Bread	Eating of unleavened bread		Yes
23:6–8	15th day of first month	First day of Feast of Unleavened Bread, a holy day	Eating of unleavened bread	Partial	Yes
23:8	21st day of first month	Last day of Feast of Unleavened Bread, a holy day	Eating of unleavened bread	Partial	Yes
23:15–21	50th day after elevation of first sheaf	Holy day (Day of Pentecost)		Partial	Yes
23:24–25	1st day of seventh month	Day of Acclamation, a holy day		Partial	Yes
23:27–32	10th day of seventh month	Day of Atonement, a holy day	Fasting	Total	Yes
23:34–43	15th–21st days of seventh month	Feast of Booths, Feast of the Lord, holy days	Going on pilgrimage, residing in booths, rejoicing		Yes
23:35	15th day of seventh month	First day of Feast of Booths, a holy day	Going on pilgrimage, residing in booths, rejoicing	Partial	Yes
23:36	22d day of seventh month	Closing ceremony of Feast of Booths, a holy day		Partial	Yes

Figure 24

Length of Commanded Observances

Reference	*Length*	*Observance*
23:3	Six days	Work
23:6	Seven days	Consumption of unleavened bread
23:8	Seven days	Presentation of offerings
23:32	Evening to evening	Sabbath rest
23:36	Seven days	Presentation of offerings
23:40	Seven days	Rejoicing
23:42	Seven days	Residing in booths

The chapter also employs inclusion and chiasm as devices for ordering the data in this calendar. The regulations for the elevation of the first sheaf and the Feast of Weeks are enclosed by references to the reaping of the harvest in 23:10 and 23:22. The mention of the place of residence for the Israelites in 23:17 and 23:21 brackets off the laws about the bringing of the first-ripe produce. The repeated command to keep "the Feast of the Lord" in 23:39 and 23:41 brackets the command to carry branches. The introduction to the chapter is arranged as a chiasm with its central pivot in 23:3b.[21]

A and A' Appointed time(s), proclaim (23:2b and 23:4c)
B and B' Sacred occasion (23:2c and 23:4b)
C and C' These, appointed times (23:2d and 23:4a)
D and D' Work, do (23:3a and 23:3c)
X Sacred occasion (23:3b)

The laws for the Day of Atonement are arranged in the form of a chiasm to emphasize the key observances for this day.

A[1] Demand for **self-deprivation** (23:27)
 B[1] Prohibition of *work* (23:28)
A[2] Lack of **self-deprivation** (23:29)
 B[2] Prohibition of *work* (23:31)
A[3] Demand for **self-deprivation** (23:32)

The structure of this pericope can be outlined as follows:

I. Speech about the Sabbath and the Feast of Unleavened Bread (23:1–8)
 A. Introduction (23:1–2a)
  1. God's address to Moses (23:1)
  2. God's commission of Moses (23:2a)
 B. Speech of Moses to the Israelites (23:2b–8)
  1. Heading with instructions for the dating of the Sabbath (23:2b–3)
   a. Heading about the proclamation of the times appointed by God (23:2b)
   b. Proclamation of the seventh day as a time for rest (23:3)

[21] Milgrom, *Leviticus 23–27*, 1952–53.

        2. The dates for the Feast of Unleavened Bread (23:4–8)
            a. Subheading about the proclamation of the times appointed by God (23:4)
            b. Dating the week of Unleavened Bread (23:5–8)
                i. Date for the Passover (23:5)
                ii. Date for the Feast of Unleavened Bread (23:6a)
                iii. Length of time for eating unleavened bread (23:6b)
                iv. Proclamation of the first day as holy day (23:7)
                v. Length of time for the presentation of offerings (23:8a)
                vi. Proclamation of the seventh day as a holy day (23:8b)

II. Speech about the Feast of Weeks (23:9–22)
    A. Introduction (23:9–10a)
        1. God's address to Moses (23:9)
        2. God's commission to Moses (23:10a)
    B. Speech by Moses to the Israelites (23:10b–22)
        1. Date the day for the elevation of the first sheaf (23:10b–14)
            a. Its occurrence after the Sabbath during week of Unleavened Bread (23:10a–11)
            b. Prescription of its offerings (23:12–13)
            c. Prohibition of consumption of new grain before that day (23:14)
        2. Date of the Feast of Weeks (23:15–21)
            a. Calculation of the date for the feast (23:15–16)
            b. List of offerings for that day (23:17–20)
            c. Proclamation of a day free from work as a perpetual statute (23:21)
        3. Commandment to leave the gleanings for the needy (23:22a)
        4. God's self-introduction (23:22b)

III. Speech about the Day of Acclamation (23:23–25)
    A. Introduction (23:23–24a)
        1. God's address to Moses (23:23)
        2. God's commission of Moses (23:24a)
    B. Speech by Moses to the Israelites (23:24b–25)
        1. Date for the proclamation of the Day of Acclamation (23:24b)
        2. Prohibition of work and requirement to present offerings on that day (23:25)

IV. Speech about the Day of Atonement (23:26–32)
    A. Introduction: God's address to Moses (23:26)
    B. Continuation of the previous speech (23:27–32)
        1. Date for the proclamation of the Day of Atonement (23:27a)
        2. Instruction on the observance of that day (23:27b–32a)
            a. Practice of self-deprivation and presentation of offerings (23:27b)
            b. Prohibition of all work (23:28)
            c. Warnings about noncompliance (23:29–30)
            d. Prohibition of work as a perpetual ritual statute (23:31)
            e. Establishment of the day as a time for rest and self-deprivation (23:32a)

3. Length of rest for that day (23:32b)

V. Speech about the Feast of Booths (23:33–43)
  A. Introduction (23:33–34a)
    1. God's address to Moses (23:33)
    2. God's commission of Moses (23:34a)
  B. Speech by Moses to the Israelites (23:34b–43)
    1. Dates for the Feast of Booths (23:34b–36)
      a. Date and duration of the feast (23:34b)
      b. Proclamation of the first day as a holy time free from work (23:35)
      c. Requirement to present offerings for seven days (23:36a)
      d. Proclamation of the eighth day as time for offerings and a day free from work (23:36b)
    2. Subscription about the times appointed by God for offerings (23:37–38)
    3. Additional dates for the lay observance of the Feast of Booths (23:39–43a)
      a. The carrying of branches in festal procession during the feast (23:39–41a)
        i. Date and duration of the feast with its first and eighth days as times of rest (23:39)
        ii. Length of time for carrying branches in rejoicing as a perpetual ritual statute (23:40–41a)
      b. Residing in booths during the feast (23:41b–43a)
        i. Date for the feast (23:41b)
        ii. Length of time for residing in booths (23:42–43a)
    4. God's self-introduction (23:43b)

VI. Statement of Compliance (23:44)

Ritual Agents

In Leviticus 23 God commissions Moses, the founder of the divine service, to establish the sacred times for the Israelites. This is the third of five liturgical calendars in the Pentateuch. (The others are in Ex 23:14–17; 34:18–26; Numbers 28–29; Deut 16:1–17.) Like the rest of them, it is addressed to the Israelites rather than the priests (Lev 23:2, 10, 24, 34, 44), because these times were given to govern the whole life of the nation, week by week and year by year. The accent falls on the times for Israel's involvement in annual cycles of celebration.

The Israelites were responsible for maintaining the divine service. They proclaimed the dates for holy times (23:2, 4, 21, 37) and calculated the time for the Feast of Weeks (23:16). They kept the Day of Atonement as a Sabbath (23:32) and went on pilgrimage for the Feast of Booths (23:39, 41). They presented the public sacrifices for each holy day,[a] as well as the first sheaf (23:10) and the family sacrifices (23:17; cf. 23:38). They refrained from work on these holy days.[b] They ate unleavened bread during the week after the Passover (23:6) and refrained from eating the new season's grain until after the presentation of

(a) Lev 23:8, 12, 14, 16, 18, 19, 25, 27, 31, 36

(b) Lev 23:3, 7, 8, 21, 25, 28, 35, 36

the first sheaf (23:14). They fasted on the Day of Atonement (23:27, 32) and observed the Feast of Booths by carrying branches with rejoicing (23:40) and by living in booths for seven days (23:42). The days were ordained for them (23:7, 21, 27, 36). Likewise, the time of rest was for their benefit (23:24, 32). The day of rest for the Day of Atonement was their Sabbath (23:32).

In all this, the priests took the second place, for they represented the congregation and performed the rituals on its behalf. In fact, the high priest was only mentioned in connection with the elevation of the first sheaf (23:10, 11) and the elevation of the loaves for the Feast of Weeks (23:20).

Ritual Location

This codification of Israel's ritual calendar links the sacred times with three specific locations. First, it obviously connected the sacred times with the sanctuary, for these times were the appointed days for the presentation of offerings to the Lord there (23:37–38). The holy days were associated with the Lord's domain.[c] The people went there on pilgrimage for the Feast of Unleavened Bread (23:6), as well as for the Feast of Booths (23:34, 39, 41). At that place the two loaves are elevated (23:20), atonement is made (23:28), and rejoicing is done (23:40) "before the Lord."

(c) Lev 23:2, 3, 4, 7, 8, 24, 27, 35, 36, 37

The second location for the observance of sacred time is the מוֹשָׁב, the "place of residence" where the Israelite family resided. There they were to observe the Sabbaths (23:3), the Day of Pentecost (23:21), and the Day of Atonement (23:31) as days of rest from work. They were forbidden to eat any of the new grain there until the sheaf had been presented at the sanctuary (23:14). They were to bring two loaves of leavened bread from their homes to the sanctuary on the Day of Pentecost (23:17). Thus the sacred calendar linked the homes of the Israelites temporally with the sanctuary.

The third location for the observance of sacred time was the land of Israel. This was the land that God gave to them (23:10). Three celebrations depended on it for their enactment: the presentation of the first sheaf during the Feast of Unleavened Bread (23:10); the presentation of the two loaves at the Feast of Weeks (23:10, 15–16); and the carrying of branches in rejoicing at the Feast of Booths (23:39–40). Since the land belonged to God, he received the first portion of its harvest (23:10, 17, 20) and reserved the gleanings from it for the poor and the aliens (23:22). Thus the sacred calendar connected the land and its produce with the sanctuary and its ritual.

Ritual Things

This ritual calendar fixed the times that God appointed for the presentation of the offerings at the sanctuary (23:37–38). A comprehensive schedule of offerings is given with the calendar in Numbers 28–29. Yet, since this calendar is concerned mainly with the times for the offerings, they are mentioned summarily as "a gift to the Lord" (23:8, 25, 27, 36) and listed according to their categories in 23:37–38. There are, however, two notable exceptions to this.

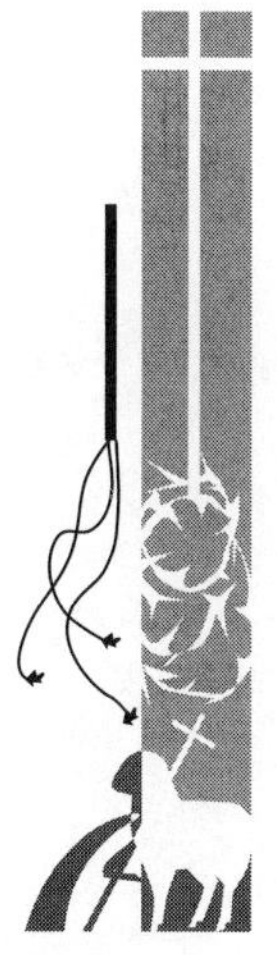

When the first sheaf was elevated, an unblemished lamb was presented as a burnt offering, together with a grain offering of flour mixed with oil and a libation of wine (23:12–13). When the two loaves from the first produce of the new harvest were elevated on the Day of Pentecost, the sacrificial ritual required three classes of animals: a burnt offering made up of seven unblemished lambs, two rams, and one bull, together with their normal grain offerings and libations; a sin offering with a male goat; and a peace offering with two yearling male lambs (23:18–19).

These offerings are connected with two ceremonies that figure prominently in the calendar: the elevation of the first sheaf and the elevation of the two loaves made from the first produce of the wheat harvest. They show that the sacred times in spring were closely connected with the production of grain in an agrarian community. During the whole week for Unleavened Bread the Israelites were required to eat unleavened bread (23:6). During that week a first sheaf of the new barley harvest was presented and elevated. It was thereby dedicated to the Lord, the owner of the land. Its dedication released the new grain for consumption by the Israelites, either as holy bread at the sanctuary or as common bread in their homes (23:14).

At the end of the wheat harvest, the Israelites were to present two loaves of leavened bread as the firstfruits of their harvest (23:17). After they and the two lambs had been dedicated to the Lord by the rite of dedication, both the loaves and the lambs belonged to the high priest. All the bread and meat was holy; it belonged to the Lord who reserved it for the priests (23:20). Unlike the meat from the other peace offerings that could be shared with the members of the priests' families, they had to be eaten at the sanctuary. The dedication of the loaves of leavened wheat bread released the rest of the produce of the land to the Israelites as God's gift to them from his land.

Ritual Times

In this sacred calendar, God instituted the "appointed times" for ritual observance by the Israelites (23:2, 4, 37, 44). In the broader sense of the word as occasions for God to meet with his people, they included the weekly celebration of the Sabbath (23:3). Seven of these "appointed times" needed to be officially proclaimed as holy days: the regular Sabbaths, because their occurrence did not fit in with the phases of the moon, and the six annual holy days, because they were calculated from the movement of the sun rather than just the phases of the moon. In the stricter sense of the word as a day determined by the movements of the heavenly bodies (Gen 1:14), the appointed times included the Passover with the week of Unleavened Bread, the day for the elevation of the first sheaf, the Day of Weeks, the Day of Acclamation, the Day of Atonement, and the eight days of Booths. Two of these sacred times were called pilgrim feasts: the first day of Unleavened Bread (23:6) and the seven days of Booths (23:34, 39, 41), because on them the heads of each Israelite household were obliged to go on pilgrimage to the sanctuary.

The calendar begins with the Sabbath because it sets the pattern of alternation between work on common days and rest on holy days that was established by the observance of sacred times (23:3). Each Sabbath was "a time of rest," for on it, as on the Day of Atonement (23:28, 31), no work was to be done. It belonged to the Lord, while the other days of the week belonged to the Israelites. The Sabbath was the archetypal holy day. All other holy days were, as it were, derived from it and extensions of it. Its position in the temporal order corresponded to the place of Holy of Holies in the spatial order and the role of the daily sacrifice in the ritual order. It was especially significant because it did not require any ritual enactment by each Israelite or attendance by them at the sanctuary. By their temporal observance of rest, they participated ritually in it and received the benefit from the divine service enacted on it at the sanctuary. Hence it is placed in its special position between the headings at the beginning of the calendar.

The next item in the calendar is the week of Unleavened Bread (23:5–8). Three times are singled out for special observance during this week: the evening of the fourteenth when the Passover lamb was offered and eaten in a banquet; the Feast of Unleavened Bread on the following day when no work was to be done on the farm or in the family business; and the seventh day when no work was to be done on the farm or in the family business. The day of the Passover vigil, with its consumption of the Passover lamb, inaugurated the seven days of Unleavened Bread and seven weeks of Pentecost. It introduced the festive half of the liturgical year that was concluded by the eighth day in the Feast of Booths. Representatives of the family had to be present at the sanctuary only on the first day of Unleavened Bread. During the whole week, all Israelites, whether they were present at the sanctuary or not, had to eat unleavened bread. They could also present their own offerings during that week, together with the additional public offerings, listed in Num 28:19–24.

The third item on the calendar is the day for the presentation of the first sheaf to mark the beginning of the barley harvest (23:9–14). The day for this ceremony and its offerings occurred during the week of Unleavened Bread. It fell either on the sixteenth after the extraordinary Sabbath on the fifteenth or on the Sunday that occurred during that week. The elevation of the first sheaf was a public ceremony enacted by the high priest on behalf of the nation. Its elevation was accompanied by the presentation of a lamb as a burnt offering with its required grain offering and libation of wine. That day was important for each family in Israel, because only after that day could the Israelites eat any of the grain from the new harvest. This requirement was a perpetual ritual statute that applied to the eating of grain at home as well as at the sanctuary. It synchronized the eating of ordinary meals at home with sacred meals at the sanctuary.

The fourth item in the calendar is the Day of Weeks (23:15–22). It was closely connected with the Feast of Unleavened Bread by its calculation from the time for the elevation of the first sheaf. It completed what began then. It occurred forty-nine days, that is, on the fiftieth day, after that ceremony. The numbers have symbolic significance. In Hebrew the name for a week is "seven." Just as there was a "week" of days, so this constituted a "week" of weeks. In symbolic terms, the fiftieth day, the Day of Weeks, was the eighth day. It therefore corresponded to the eighth day of the Feast of Booths. This ritual calendar does not give a name to the fiftieth day, because the emphasis in it falls on the full seven weeks as the season of weeks. As Jeremiah notes, these were the weeks that God had appointed for harvest (Jer 5:24). Hence the references to the harvest in 23:10 and 23:22. The only "ritual" observance for this season was the requirement to leave the corners of the fields unreaped and the fallen stalks of grain lying on the ground for the poor and the alien to gather (23:22). This was God's provision for them from his land. It also ensured that they too could observe the weeks of harvest.

Since the fiftieth day closed this season, later Jewish tradition called it the Azareth by analogy with the eighth day of Booths (עֲצֶרֶת, 23:36). On this day the Israelites brought two loaves of leavened wheat bread made with yeast as the "first-ripe produce" from their harvest (23:17). These loaves were presented together with a burnt offering made up of seven lambs, two rams, and one bull, a sin offering with a male goat, and a sacrifice of a peace offering with two male lambs. The seven lambs were obviously connected with the completion of the seven weeks. A bull and two rams were sacrificed because this was a national enactment. A male goat was sacrificed as a sin offering to make atonement for the congregation (cf. Num 28:30). The high priest elevated the two lambs together with the two loaves to dedicate them to the Lord. The two lambs provided the meat for the only public peace offering in the liturgical year. Their meat and the loaves of leavened bread were eaten by the high priest and the other priests on duty with him. The Israelites kept this day free from the work done in pursuit of their occupations. This day of rest marked the ritual end of the grain harvest.

The fifth item in the calendar is the Day of Acclamation (23:23–25). It fell on the first day of the important seventh month. This day in the seventh month corresponded to the position of the Sabbath in the seven days of the week and the Day of Pentecost in the seven weeks of harvest. It was a "time of rest" for all the people, a day free from the work done in pursuit of their occupations. The prescribed offerings are outlined in Num 29:2–6. It was a day of "commemoration" of the Lord by "acclamation" (Lev 23:24). According to Ps 81:4 (ET 81:3), this was done by blowing a ram's horn on the new moon, the first day of the month. The blast of the ram's horn ushered in this ritually significant month with the Day of Atonement on its tenth day and the beginning of the Feast of Booths on the fifteenth day. This was done throughout the land to tell the people to prepare for these two significant occasions. In later Jewish tradition this day was celebrated as New Year's Day.

The sixth item in the calendar is the Day of Atonement. It fell on the tenth day of the seventh month, the "Sabbath month." On this day the high priest performed the rite of atonement on behalf of the whole nation (23:28). This was connected with the presentation of the offerings prescribed for the day in Num 29:8–11. Whether the people were present at the sanctuary or not, they observed a day of fasting (Lev 23:27, 32) and refrained from all work (23:28, 31). The importance of this day is highlighted in four ways. First, it was called a "sabbatical Sabbath," the great day of rest on the Sabbath month (23:32). This meant that on this day, as on every Sabbath, no work whatsoever could be done for the entire day. Second, the length of the day and its observance did not stretch from dawn to dusk as with all other holy days, but from dusk to dusk (23:32). Third, it alone was accompanied by the threat of divine extirpation for anybody who failed to observe the day (23:29–30).

The seventh item in the calendar is the Feast of Booths. It was "the Feast of the Lord" (23:39, 41), which lasted for seven days. It was one of the two pilgrim feasts, but unlike the Feast of Unleavened Bread, when the heads of the Israelite households were required to be at the sanctuary only on the first day, the pilgrimage for Booths lasted all seven days of the feast. The first of these seven days and the eighth concluding day were "high holy days" (23:35, 36), "days of rest" (23:39), with the prohibition of all occupational work. The public offerings, prescribed in Num 29:13–38, were presented, according to the quota for the day, on each of the eight days (Lev 23:36, 37).

The seven days of the Feast of Booths were observed in two unique ways. The first is that on each of the seven days, the pilgrims carried a collection of branches from three kinds of trees in a festal procession into the sanctuary, and they "rejoiced before the Lord" (23:40) by walking in procession around the altar (cf. Ps 118:27). This compulsory observance for the feast was fixed by a perpetual ritual statute (Lev 23:41). This procession around the altar was the culmination of the pilgrimage to the sanctuary. The second unique feature is that all the Israelites made makeshift shelters for themselves around the sanctuary to reside in during the seven days of the feast (23:42–43). The final, eighth day stood apart from the seven days of the feast. No processions were held on it. The people did not reside in booths on it as they returned home at the end of it. It was the Azareth, the day for the closing ceremony, the day of transition from the seven days for rejoicing back to the regular rhythm of six days for work and one for rest. It also marked the close of the festive half of the liturgical year that began with the Passover.[22]

Even though the calendar lists each of these seven appointed times separately in chronological sequence, the calendar needs to be taken as a whole. It established an annual cycle of observance that coordinated the work of the Israelites on their properties in the land with the work of the Lord in the divine service at the sanctuary. It established a pattern of alternation between workdays and holy days. This ran according to two separate cycles: the weekly cy-

---

[22] Keil, *Pentateuch*, 2:447.

cle with its Sabbaths (23:3) and the annual cycle with its seven extraordinary days of rest (23:5–36, 39–43). While the weekly cycle operated apart from the natural astronomical order created by the movement of the sun, the moon, and the stars in the sky, the annual order was synchronized with it. Through the sun, the moon, and the stars, God governed the seasons for the agricultural, horticultural, and animal-rearing year and determined the appointed times for annual rest and ritual celebration (Gen 1:14; Ps 104:19).

The annual cycle was divided into two halves by the cluster of celebrations around the two critical times for an agrarian community in the temperate Mediterranean zone: the spring equinox and the autumn equinox. While the period between spring and autumn was the dry season, the rainy period between autumn and spring was the growing season for wheat and barley and grass. The appointed times in spring corresponded, in part, with the appointed times in autumn. Thus the seven days of Unleavened Bread after the spring equinox corresponded to the seven days for the Feast of Booths, and the Day of Pentecost was matched by the eighth day of Booths. The appointed times in autumn also culminated in the great autumn festival. This is evident from the establishment of the Day of Acclamation and the Day of Atonement as times of preparation for this important occasion.

Even though the holy times for the Israelites were embedded in the natural order and partly synchronized with it, the calendar transcended the natural temporal order. This is shown by the sabbatical principle that governed the calendar (23:3). This operated symbolically, with the identification of seven as the complete holy number. Just as the seventh day of the week was a holy day, so the seventh month of each year was the holy month (23:24, 27, 34, 39, 41). Just as there were seven days to the week, so there were seven days of Unleavened Bread (23:6, 8), seven days for the Feast of Booths (23:34, 39, 41, 42), and seven weeks between the elevation of the first sheaf and the Day of Weeks (23:15). Just as the seventh day of the week was the weekly day of rest, so there were seven extraordinary annual days of rest that began with the first day of Unleavened Bread. These seven extraordinary annual days are designated in 23:7, 8, 21, 24–25, 32, 34–36, 39, and they culminate in the Feast of Booths. Thus the divinely instituted calendar harmonized the work of the Israelites with the natural cosmic order and their worship with the supernatural life of God. Each Sabbath was an eternal moment in the temporal order, a foretaste of heaven on earth.

Ritual Theological Function

Just as God had, through his Word, established a holy place for his people, so he also instituted the holy times for his people through his Word. On these days the Israelites were to rest from their work and present gifts to the Lord from the result of their work. Whether they were actually present on these days at the sanctuary or not, by their rest from work they were involved in the divine service and so benefited from it.

(d) Lev 23:3, 7, 8, 21, 24, 27, 35, 36

But these days were not naturally or intrinsically holy. They had to be proclaimed as "holy" (23:2, 21, 37). How this was done we are not told, but it probably occurred by the blowing of the trumpets at the sanctuary (Num 10:10). By their proclamation these days become holy days.[d] Through their proclamation by Israel, in obedience to God's Word through Moses, those days were removed from common use and located in the divine domain. They were thereby offered to God, made over to him. They became days that belonged to the sanctuary, days for the presentation of gifts to God, days "for the Lord" (Lev 23:3, 34, 41). Through his Word God therefore made these days holy, so that on them he could share his holiness with his people.

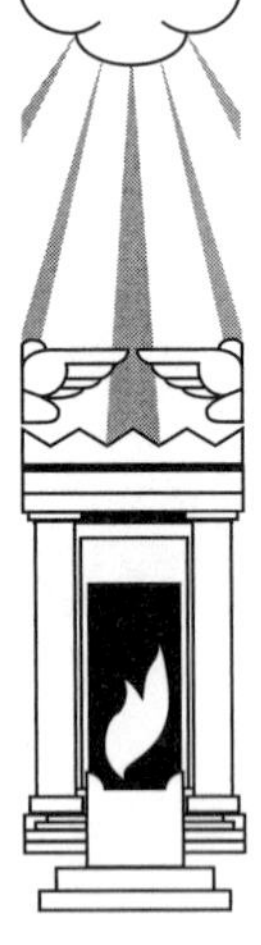

These holy days were the times that God had appointed to meet with his people (23:2, 4, 37, 44). He met with them at the sanctuary through the performance of the sacrificial ritual in the divine service. Hence the reference to the presentation of offerings on these days. Through the rite of atonement on the Day of Atonement, God removed their guilt and impurity (23:28). Through the divine service and the rituals associated with it, God took pleasure in his people and gave them access to his grace (23:13, 18). There he introduced himself to them by name and committed himself to them (23:22, 43).

The calendar highlights the presentation of the "first sheaf' of barley (23:10–11) and the presentation of two loaves as the first-ripe produce of the grain harvest (23:17, 20). The Israelites presented them to the Lord as their rent for the land. They thereby acknowledged that God had given them the land and the produce of the land (23:10). Since he was the owner of the land, its produce, by right, belonged to him. Yet, when they dedicated the first-ripe produce of the land to God, he released the rest of the harvest for their use (23:11, 14). Once its first-ripe produce had been consecrated for divine use, God used the rest of the produce to let his blessing rest on their households (Deut 16:15; Ezek 44:30–31). Just as God provided bread for the priests through the grain offering (Lev 23:20), so he provided food for the landless people in Israel by the gleanings of the harvest (23:22).

Ritually, the Israelites acknowledged the work of God for them on these occasions in and through the divine service in a number of different ways. Most significantly, they did no work on these holy days, for their work did not make the day holy. God gained nothing from their ritual work. Rather, through the divine service that the priests enacted on their behalf, God did his work on them and through them. Twice a year they also went on pilgrimage to the sanctuary and appeared before the Lord. The first pilgrim feast was on the first day of Unleavened Bread (23:6), and the second pilgrim feast was for the whole week of Booths (23:34, 39, 41).

The appendix to the calendar in 23:39–43 highlights the theological significance of the second feast in two ways. First, on each day of the Feast of Booths, the Israelites appeared before the Lord as pilgrims in procession, with a bouquet of tree branches, around the altar, and rejoiced together with the whole congregation in God's presence with music and song (23:40; cf. Ps

81:2–6 [ET 81:1–5]). They did not just rejoice in God's gifts to them, but in God himself as their source of joy and their reason for rejoicing. They were altogether joyful (Deut 16:15).

Second, during the seven days of the feast they also lived in booths to acknowledge that when God had brought them from Egypt, he had not settled them in permanent homes, but had housed them in temporary shelters. They were his people apart from the land; the land did not make them his people. Nor did they ever own the land; it belonged to God. By living in booths, they acknowledged their resident status on God's land each year during the Feast of Booths (25:23). From generation to generation, they also recalled their time in the desert and their entry into the land. In this way they shifted the theological focus on this festival away from God as the owner of the land to God as their deliverer from slavery in Egypt. They celebrated their holy status and royal freedom under God, their heavenly King (cf. Zech 14:16, 17).

Fulfillment by Christ

The life and work of Jesus was profoundly shaped by the liturgical calendar that had been instituted by God in Leviticus 23. It was Jesus' custom to attend the synagogue each Sabbath (Lk 4:16). Much of his ministry was connected with the observance of the Sabbath and attendance at the synagogue on that day. On the Sabbath he taught in the synagogues[e] and at the temple (Jn 5:14–47) and in houses where he was an honored guest for the festive banquets (Lk 14:1–24). On the Sabbath he also exorcised a man with an unclean spirit (Mk 1:21–27 || Lk 4:31–36) and healed people who were sick (Mk 1:29–31 || Lk 4:38–39; Lk 14:1–6), disabled,[f] and blind (Jn 9:1–41).

Jesus also belonged to a family that went up regularly each year on pilgrimage to Jerusalem for the Passover (Lk 2:41). When he was twelve he went with them and learned his Father's business from the teachers at the temple (Lk 2:42–50). During his ministry he went up to Jerusalem for the festivals: the Passover (Jn 2:13–23), an unnamed feast (Jn 5:1), the Feast of Booths/Tabernacles (Jn 7:2–10), and the Dedication of the Temple (Jn 10:22). But, most significantly, he went up on pilgrimage to Jerusalem for the last time to sacrifice himself in connection with the Passover and the Feast of Unleavened Bread.[g] He was crucified on the eve of the Passover, rested in the tomb on the following Sabbath, and rose on Sunday, the day of the first sheaf. In fact, the Synoptic Gospels envisage the ministry of Jesus as an extended pilgrimage of Jesus with his disciples to Jerusalem for that climactic Passover.[h]

By his observance of the times for worship that were fixed by the liturgical calendar, Jesus both fulfilled and transformed them. Everything that God had promised to grant to his people through their faithful participation in the divine service at the appointed times was given to them in full measure through his incarnate Son. Thus Paul claims that all the festivals and the Sabbaths prefigured Jesus' incarnation and exaltation (Col 2:16). He fulfilled them and embodied their fulfillment. This teaching is elaborated most fully in John's Gospel.

(e) Mk 1:21 || Lk 4:31; Mk 6:1–6; Lk 4:16–31; 13:10

(f) Mt 12:9–13 || Mk 3:1–6 || Lk 6:6–11; Lk 13:10–17; Jn 5:1–13

(g) Mt 26:2, 17; Mk 14:1, 12; Lk 22:1, 7; Jn 11:55; 12:1, 12; 13:1

(h) Mt 20:17–19 || Mk 10:32–34; Lk 9:51; 13:31–35; 17:11; 18:31–33; 19:28

It unfolds the teaching and miracles of Jesus within the framework of the festive calendar. His ministry begins and ends with his pilgrimage to Jerusalem to celebrate the Passover (Jn 2:13–25; 13:1). Between these two pilgrimages, John shows how the whole festive cycle of the liturgical calendar reaches its goal in Jesus, the incarnate Son of God. Coloe sums this up well:

> During the cycle of Israel's feasts, throughout chapters 5 to 10, Jesus has come up to his Father's House in obedience to the requirements of Torah. He has celebrated Israel's festivals and revealed himself as the one fulfilling Israel's festal traditions. He has offered life and judgment on Sabbath, bread during the Passover, light and water at Tabernacles, and his own consecrated presence, which is the presence of Israel's God, during Dedication.[23]

The NT interprets the divinely instituted sacred times Christologically and eschatologically: the Sabbath, the Passover and Unleavened Bread, Pentecost, the Day of Atonement, and Booths. Thus Jesus declared that he was the Lord of the Sabbath in his controversy with the Pharisees over the plucking of grain on the Sabbath by his disciples (Mk 2:23–28). As a man and an Israelite, Jesus was required to observe the Sabbath. But as the Messiah, the Son of God, he was the Lord of the Sabbath. It belonged to him; it was "a Sabbath to the Lord" (cf. Lev 23:3). On it he provided holy food for his disciples; on it he healed a disabled man. He worked on the Sabbath because his Father also worked on the Sabbath. Just as God the Father worked on the Sabbath in the order of creation by giving life to those who were born on that day and by judging those who died on that day,[24] so, on the Sabbath, Jesus too, in the order of redemption, gave eternal life to his disciples and passed judgment on those who did not listen to him. Since he was the Lord of the Sabbath, he provided rest for his disciples (Mt 11:28). Those who believed in him entered the heavenly rest that God had promised (Heb 4:3, 9–10).

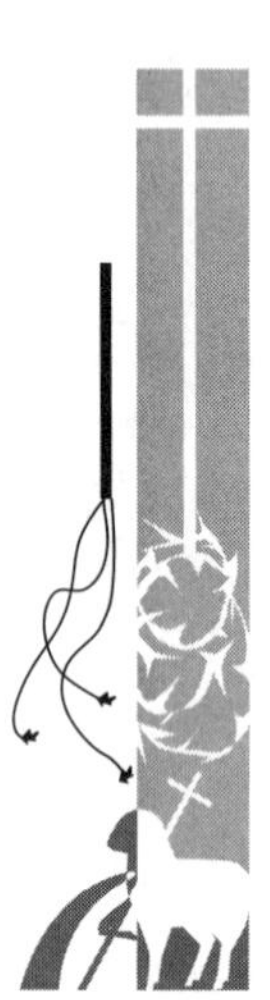

By Christ's resurrection on Sunday—the first day of the new week, the eighth day—he inaugurated the new calendar for the new creation, the eternal Sabbath that never ends. That is why the first (Jewish) Christians did not gather to conduct the Divine Service on Saturday, as the unbelieving Jews continued to do, but on Sunday, the Lord's Day, the day of resurrection (Acts 20:7; 1 Cor 16:1; Rev 1:10). As the Sabbath was foundational for the liturgical calendar of the old covenant, Sunday became the archetypal holy day for the NT church.

By his death on the eve of the Passover, Jesus sacrificed himself as "the Lamb of God," the paschal lamb of the new covenant (Jn 1:29, 36; 1 Pet 1:19; Rev 5:6–10). On the night before he died, Jesus gave his disciples his body to eat in the new paschal banquet (Lk 22:14–20). He thereby became their Passover (1 Cor 5:6–8). They celebrated this paschal meal each Sunday, rather than just once a year. They were encouraged to remove "the leaven of malice and evil" from their midst so that they could enjoy its full blessings (1 Cor 5:8).

---

[23] Coloe, *God Dwells with Us*, 155.

[24] See Just, *Luke 1:1–9:50*, 255.

Thus the celebration of the Feast of Unleavened Bread was deepened to include the removal of all corruption and extended to embrace the whole of life. The whole of the life of the church was an ongoing celebration of the new Passover, a continuous Easter festival. Just as Christ established the new Passover, so Christ, by his resurrection on the day of the elevation of the first sheaf, became the firstfruits of the new creation, God's harvest of holy people for himself (1 Cor 15:23). Jesus' resurrection marked the beginning of the harvest time that will not end until the close of the age (Mt 13:36–43).

Jesus appeared to his disciples for forty days during the seven weeks of Pentecost, the seven weeks that culminated in the gift of the Holy Spirit on the Day of Pentecost (Acts 2:1–42). At Pentecost God the Father poured out the Holy Spirit on the disciples of Christ. He did not give them the blessings of a bountiful harvest from the land, but conveyed the firstfruits of the Spirit to them as his priests through the risen Lord Jesus (Rom 8:23). Since they were members of his holy priesthood, they were to use their gifts in his service. After the Day of Pentecost Jesus began to gather in the firstfruits of holy people as converts from Israel and the nations of the world.[i] He sanctified them so that he could offer them together with himself to God the Father (Col 1:22). The martyrs were the firstfruits of these converts (Rev 14:4). Just as the Israelites presented the firstfruits of their harvest to the priests, so the church presented the firstfruits of its offerings to their pastors as their stipend (*Didache* 13:3, 6–7). They, like all its offerings, were produced and sanctified by the Holy Spirit (1 Pet 1:2).

(i) Rom 16:5; 1 Cor 16:15; 2 Thess 2:13; *1 Clement* 42:2–4

The Day of Atonement prepared the Israelites for the celebration of Booths. The NT, however, as was shown in the comments on Leviticus 16, associated this day with Christ's death on Good Friday and his entry as High Priest into the heavenly sanctuary at his ascension. It therefore prepared the faithful for their pilgrimage to the heavenly city.

The Feast of Booths is also understood Christologically in the NT. Thus John includes a major discourse of Jesus on his visit to the temple on the occasion of this feast (Jn 7:14–52; 8:12–59). The climax of that visit came on the eighth day, the last great day of the feast (Jn 7:37). On that day Jesus alluded to two of its most popular ceremonies: the lighting of a large candelabrum on the first night of the feast[25] and the daily ritual pouring out of water on the altar. He declared that he was the well of the life-giving Holy Spirit (Jn 7:37–39) and proclaimed that he was the light of the world (Jn 8:12). That occasion was the theophany of Jesus at the temple. He, as it were, filled the space that had been left at the end of the feast, the end of the festive part of the liturgical calendar. By his proclamation, he brought the feast and the whole liturgical calendar to its intended goal. His self-proclamation as the light of the world opened the door for the fulfillment of Zechariah's prophecy about the inclu-

[25] See the description of this practice in the Talmud, Mishnah, *Sukkah,* 5:1–4.

sion of the Gentiles with the Israelites in their celebration of the Feast of Booths (Zech 14:16–21). His body was the new tabernacle of God, the place of theophany and blessing. His presence therefore brought heavenly joy and everlasting rejoicing to God's people.[j]

(j) Jn 8:56; 15:11; 16:20–24; 17:13; 20:20

In a similar fashion, Luke interprets the transfiguration of Jesus in the light of the Feast of Booths.[26] He alone of the Gospel writers relates that the transfiguration occurred on the eighth day after Peter's confession of faith (Lk 9:28). The transfiguration was the epiphany of Jesus as God's Son. It showed Peter, James, and John that the age of the Messiah had come when the righteous would be overshadowed by God's presence and dwell with him in "heavenly shelters" (cf. Lk 16:9), just as the Israelites had dwelt with him in earthly shelters in the desert and at Jerusalem during Booths. And so Peter offered to build "shelters" for Jesus, Moses, and Elijah (Lk 9:33).

The NT also interprets Booths eschatologically. On the one hand, both Paul and Peter regard the shelters that were built for that occasion as an image of the earthly bodies that housed the faithful on their journey to the heavenly homeland, where God would give them glorified bodies as their permanent residences (2 Cor 5:1–5; 2 Pet 1:13–14). On the other hand, in Rev 7:9–17 St. John recalls the festivity of Booths to describe the never-ending procession of the redeemed around the heavenly altar.[27] They celebrate the heavenly Feast of Booths with palm branches in their hands (Rev 7:9) and sing a song of praise that was inspired by Ps 118:14 (Rev 7:10). Traditionally, this psalm was sung during the daily processions around the altar at the feast. The redeemed also have access to the springs of living water that flow from God's presence (Rev 7:17).

Thus the NT shows how Christ fulfilled the whole of the liturgical calendar. Sacred time was no longer determined by the meeting of God with his people at the tabernacle or the temple, but it was created by the presence of the risen Lord Jesus bodily with his people in the church. The church therefore established a new liturgical calendar to reflect this reality. This calendar was based on Sunday rather than Saturday as the archetypal holy day. It was the eighth day, the Lord's Day, the day of resurrection and the Holy Spirit, the first day of the new aeon, the day for the beginning of eternity.

Nevertheless, the church still retained the weekly cycle of work and rest from the OT. Like the people of Israel, it observed three great feasts: the Easter Passover, which was originally celebrated as a single day that was eventually extended to three days;[28] Pentecost, which ended the fifty Easter days of rejoicing;[29] and Epiphany, which replaced the Feast of Booths.[30] The focus in all

---

[26] Danielou, *The Bible and the Liturgy*, 339–40.

[27] Danielou, *The Bible and the Liturgy*, 342.

[28] Talley, *The Origins of the Liturgical Year*, 1–57.

[29] Talley, *The Origins of the Liturgical Year*, 57–66.

[30] Merras, *The Origins of the Celebration of the Christian Feast of Epiphany*.

this was on the risen Lord Jesus. Each Sunday and all the feasts centered on him and his ongoing ministry in the Divine Service. Thus the Christian liturgical calendar celebrated the eternal day of the Lord within the annual cycle of seasons and years.

Christ Jesus lay in death's strong bands
    For our offenses given;
But now at God's right hand he stands
    And brings us life from heaven.
Therefore let us joyful be
And sing to God right thankfully
Loud songs of alleluia!
Alleluia!

So let us keep the festival
    To which the Lord invites us;
Christ is himself the joy of all,
    The sun that warms and lights us.
Now his grace to us imparts
Eternal sunshine to our hearts;
The night of sin is ended.
Alleluia!

Then let us feast this Easter Day
    On Christ, the bread of heaven;
The Word of grace has purged away
    The old and evil leaven.
Christ alone our souls will feed;
He is our meat and drink indeed;
Faith lives upon no other!
Alleluia![31]

[31] From "Christ Jesus Lay in Death's Strong Bands" by Martin Luther (*LW* 123:1, 4, 5).

Leviticus 24:1–9

Holy Oil and the Holy Bread

Translation

24 [1]The Lord spoke to Moses: [2]"Command the Israelites that they bring to you clear oil from beaten olives for the luminary to offer up a regular lamp. [3]Aaron shall set it in the tent of meeting, outside the curtain of the testimony, regularly from the evening to the morning; it is a perpetual ritual statute throughout your generations. [4]He shall set the lamps regularly on the pure [gold] lampstand before the Lord.

[5]"You shall take fine flour and bake it [in the form of] twelve round-loaves; two-tenths [of an ephah] shall be [in] each round-loaf. [6]You shall put them in two piles, six to each pile, on the pure [gold] table before the Lord. [7]Upon the pile you shall place clear frankincense, and it shall be a token portion for the bread; it is a gift to the Lord. [8]On every Sabbath day, he shall set it before the Lord regularly; it is a perpetual covenant on behalf of the Israelites. [9]It shall belong to Aaron and his sons, who shall eat it in a holy place, for it belongs to him as a most holy thing from the gifts to the Lord, a perpetual due."

Textual Notes

24:2–3 These verses repeat almost verbatim Ex 27:20–21.

24:2 צַו—For this imperative (Piel of צָוָה), see 6:2 (ET 6:9); compare other commands to the Israelites in Num 5:2; 28:2; 34:2; 35:2.

וְיִקְחוּ—See Lev 24:5. The verb לָקַח is used here, as in 9:5 and 12:8, in the sense of bringing by hand and handing over something as an offering personally to Moses.

שֶׁמֶן זַיִת זָךְ כָּתִית—Literally this is "oil of olive, clear, crushed." See Ex 27:20; 29:40; Num 28:5. This was the first, choicest kind of strained olive oil that was produced by beating the olives before they were crushed in an olive press. Like the frankincense for the incense altar (Ex 30:34) and the frankincense for the showbread (Lev 24:7), the oil for the lamps had to be "clear" (זָךְ) and so "pure" (cf. Ex 27:30).

לַמָּאוֹר— "The luminary" was the lampstand with the seven lamps to which 24:4 refers. See Ex 25:6; 27:20; 35:8, 14, 28; 39:37; Num 4:9, 16; cf. Num 8:2.

לְהַעֲלֹת—This could also be translated "by setting up." The Hiphil form of עָלָה refers to the placement of each lamp on its holder in the lampstand (Ex 25:37; 27:20; 30:8; 40:4, 25; Num 8:2, 3). It may have been used to suggest that the "offering up" of the oil in the tabernacle corresponded to the "offering up" of the burnt offering in the courtyard (see the textual notes on Lev 2:12). As Ex 30:7–8 shows, the priest trimmed the lamps in the morning and set them up alight with fresh oil each evening.

נֵר—This singular form (Ex 27:20; 1 Sam 3:3) seems to be a technical, collective term for the seven "lamps" on the lampstand.[1] Each of these cup-shaped bowls, with

1 Haran, *Temples and Temple-Service in Ancient Israel*, 208, n. 4.

a spout for a wick, was placed on a saucer-like holder on one of the seven branches of the lampstand. The plural will occur in Lev 24:4 (הַנֵּרוֹת).

תָּמִיד׃—See the textual note on this term in 6:6 (ET 6:13). It recurs in 24:3, 4, 8.

24:3 לְפָרֹכֶת הָעֵדֻת—See the textual notes on 4:6 and 16:13. This is an abbreviated form of the phrase found in Ex 27:21 and 30:6.

בְּאֹהֶל מוֹעֵד—According to Ex 40:24, the lampstand was located opposite the table on the south side of this room. Like the mercy seat for the ark, it was made as a single piece of pure beaten gold (Num 8:4). According to Num 8:1–3, it was to meant to light up the table with the bread for the Lord.

יַעֲרֹךְ אֹתוֹ אַהֲרֹן—Aaron shall set "it" (אֹתוֹ), which refers to the "lamp" (נֵר) in 24:2, which, in turn, designates the lampstand with its seven lamps. The LXX expands the subject to be "Aaron and his sons."

חֻקַּת עוֹלָם—See the textual notes on 3:17.

24:4 הַמְּנֹרָה—The making of the menorah is described in Ex 25:31–40 and 37:17–24.[2]

הַטְּהֹרָה—See Ex 31:8; 39:37. The reason for the use of this adjective, "clean, pure, bright," for the lampstand and the table (Lev 24:6) is uncertain. Most likely it meant that these furnishings were made of gold that was to be kept "pure" in appearance by being bright and clean.

תָּמִיד׃—The LXX has "until morning."

24:5 וְלָקַחְתָּ—The use of לָקַח, "take," indicates that Moses is to receive the flour from the Israelites.

סֹלֶת—See the textual notes on 2:1.

חַלּוֹת—See the textual notes on 2:4.

שְׁנֵי עֶשְׂרֹנִים—The noun עִשָּׂרוֹן means "one-tenth." It is implied that the measure is the ephah, so this phrase refers to "two-tenths" of an ephah, which amounts to about four liters or one gallon. One-tenth of an ephah seems to have been the same as an עֹמֶר (see *HALOT,* s.v. עֹמֶר II), and according to Ex 16:16, an עֹמֶר was the daily ration of grain for one person.

24:6 מַעֲרָכוֹת—This could also be translated "rows." See 24:7; 1 Chr 9:32; 23:29; 28:16; 2 Chr 2:4; 13:11; 29:18; Neh 10:33.

שֵׁשׁ הַמַּעֲרָכֶת—Since the table was not large enough to accommodate two rows of six loaves, they were most likely stacked in two piles with six in each pile.[3]

הַשֻּׁלְחָן—The table, described in Ex 25:23–30; 37:10–16; 39:36; 40:22–23, was about ninety centimeters or three feet long and about forty-five centimeters or eighteen inches wide. It was made of acacia wood and was overlaid with pure gold. Whereas 1 Ki 7:48 mentions only one table in the temple, Chronicles refers to ten tables (1 Chr 28:16; 2 Chr 4:8, 19).

24:7 לְבֹנָה—See the textual notes on Lev 2:1. The LXX adds "and salt." The frankincense was most likely put in the dishes mentioned in Ex 25:29 and placed on the two piles of bread.

---

2 See Meyers, *The Tabernacle Menorah,* 17–34, for an analysis of the data on its construction and shape.

3 Milgrom, *Leviticus 23–27,* 2096; Mitchell, "Leviticus 24:6: The Bread of the Presence."

לְאַזְכָּרָה—See the textual notes on Lev 2:2. It is not stated whether the incense was burnt on the altar for incense or on the altar for burnt offering.

אִשֶּׁה לַיהוָה׃—See the textual notes on 1:9 and the explanation in "Leviticus 1–3."

24:8 יַעַרְכֶנּוּ—The subject is the priest on duty. In this case it was Aaron.

מֵאֵת בְּנֵי־יִשְׂרָאֵל—See 7:34. The bread was offered "on behalf of the Israelites" for the priests, just as the breast and thigh were offered on their behalf for the priests as their perpetual due from the peace offerings.[4]

בְּרִית עוֹלָם׃—This is the only offering that is called "a perpetual covenant" (cf. Gen 9:16; 17:7, 13, 19; Ex 31:16). Its closest parallel is the use of the term "a perpetual covenant of salt" for the offerings assigned by the Lord to the priests in Num 18:19. This term in Lev 24:8 corresponds to חֻקַּת עוֹלָם, "perpetual ritual statute," in 24:3. It therefore is used in the sense of an obligation. God's covenant with the Israelites obliges them to present this bread to him.

24:9 וְהָיְתָה—The use of the feminine singular form may refer back to the feminine noun הַמַּעֲרֶכֶת in 24:6 or הַחַלָּה in 24:5.

בְּמָקוֹם קָדֹשׁ—See the textual notes on 6:9 (ET 6:16).

קֹדֶשׁ קָדָשִׁים—See the textual notes on 2:3.

חָק־עוֹלָם׃—See the textual notes on 6:11 (ET 6:18).

Commentary

Context and Structure

The whole of chapter 24 seems to interrupt the sequence of legislation about the sacred times, beginning with the annual ritual calendar in chapter 23 and continuing with the laws for the celebration of the Sabbatical Year and the Jubilee Year in chapter 25. It deals with three most holy things: the holy oil for the lamps; the holy bread for the Lord; and the holy name of the Lord. The material in this chapter would, it seems, be better placed after chapter 22 as the end of the discussion on the use of the holy things and the need to avoid the profanation of the holy name. This chapter, however, may serve as the culmination in the arrangement of holy things in Leviticus 19–24. These holy things are arranged in ascending order for increasing holiness with closer proximity to God. There is a progression from the Israelites (chapters 19–20) to the priests (21:1–22:16), from the sacrifices offered on the outer altar (22:17–33) to the sacred times (chapter 23), from the oil and bread offered in the tent of meeting (24:1–9) to the name of the Lord residing in the Holy of Holies (24:10–23).

These two units (24:1–4 and 24:5–9), which cover the provision of oil and flour for the tent of meeting, are linked by the repetition of certain key words and phrases: תָּמִיד, "regular, regularly" (24:2, 3, 4, 8); לָקַח, "bring, take" (24:2, 5); זַךְ, "clear"(24:2, 7); עָרַךְ, "set, arrange"(24:3, 4, 8) and its related noun מַעֲרֶכֶת, "arrangement, pile" (24:6, 7); לִפְנֵי יְהוָה, "before/in the presence of the Lord" (24:3, 4, 6, 8); and טָהוֹר, "pure, clean, bright" (24:4, 6).

---

[4] Gane, " 'Bread of Presence' and Creator-in-Residence," 198.

The structure of this pericope can be outlined as follows:

I. God's address to Moses (24:1)
II. God's speech to Moses (24:2–9)
   A. God's commandment to the Israelites about the holy lamps (24:2–4)
      1. Provision of olive oil by the Israelites (24:2)
      2. Care of the lamps by Aaron (24:3–4)
         a. Setting them up to burn overnight in the tent of meeting (24:3)
         b. Setting them up regularly on the lampstand (24:4)
   B. God's commandment to Moses and Aaron about the holy bread (24:5–9)
      1. Arrangement of the bread by Moses (24:5–7)
         a. Preparation of the twelve loaves (24:5)
         b. Setting out the loaves with frankincense on the table (24:6–7)
      2. Replacement of the bread by the priests (24:8–9)
         a. Setting out new loaves each Sabbath (24:8)
         b. Assignment of the old bread to the priests (24:9)

Ritual Location

Both the ritual acts instituted by the Lord in this speech were enacted in the tent of meeting. Their location there indicated their significance. Thus both the lamps and the bread were set out by Moses, the founder of the divine service, and the priests "before the Lord" (24:3, 6, 8). This place is described more precisely as the area outside the curtain, before the ark in the tent of meeting (24:3), the place where God, the heavenly King, met with his priests on duty. The speech regards the tent as the Lord's residence. While the inner room was his private quarters, the outer room of the tent was his office, the place where he transacted his business each morning and evening with his servants, like a king with his courtiers or a general with his staff officers. The speech also identifies the more general sacred area outside the tent as the place where the priests ate the bread each Sabbath. This was located in the western part of the courtyard around the tabernacle. See figure 6, "Ground Plan of the Tabernacle."

Ritual Agents

In this speech the Lord spoke to Moses as the archetypal priest, the founder of the divine service. God addressed him as the recipient, rather than the mediator of his Word. He commissioned Moses to command the Israelites (24:2) and Aaron (24:3, 4) to perform their ritual duties. Moses received the oil for the lamps (24:2) and the flour for the bread (24:5) from the Israelites. He set up the lamps (24:2), baked the bread (24:5), and set it out with the incense on the table in the tent of meeting (24:6, 7). After this inaugural activity, Aaron took over from Moses. Aaron or his deputy attended to the lamps each morning and evening (24:3, 4) and changed the bread every Sabbath (24:8). Yet, even though Moses and Aaron were responsible for the foundation and continuation of the rites enacted in the tent of meeting, the speech did not concentrate on them, but on the Israelites. They supplied the oil and the flour. By their provision of oil, they kept the lamp burning (24:2). The twelve loaves of bread, which were set out before the Lord and eaten by his priests, came from them; the loaves were offered on their behalf (24:8). Even though they themselves did not enter the tent, all that the priests did in it was done for them.

Ritual Material and Furniture

God commanded the Israelites to bring oil and fine flour to Moses for the rites performed in the tent of meeting. The oil was the best grade of olive oil, clear in color and made by beating olives rather than crushing them. Its quality meant that it gave little smoke as it was burnt. It was accompanied by fine wheat flour that was used to bake twelve large, round loaves. These were placed in two piles with containers of frankincense on the table in the tabernacle. While all the oil was burnt in the lamps, the priests burnt the frankincense and ate the bread. The bread became most holy by the burning of the frankincense as its token portion (24:9), just like the grain from the grain offerings (2:3, 10).

The oil and the bread were connected with two most holy items of furniture in the tent of meeting, the lampstand on its south side and the table on its north side (Ex 40:22–25). (See figure 6, "Ground Plan of the Tabernacle.") The oil was burnt in the lamps (נֵרֹת) set up on the lampstand (מְנֹרָה, Lev 24:4). The lampstand was made up of a central column with six shafts, paired on opposite sides of the shaft. Cups were fixed as holders for the lamps on top of the central column and the six shafts. The seven lamps were put out on these bowls. The bread was set out on the table (24:6). It was made of acacia wood and was overlaid with gold. Like all the furniture in the tabernacle, both the lampstand and the table were made of bright, pure gold to show their holiness.[5]

Ritual Time

The lighting of the lamps and the setting out of the bread were part of the תָּמִיד, the regular ritual at the tabernacle. The "regular lamp" (24:2) had to be set up "regularly" (24:3, 4) by the priest on duty each evening (Ex 30:8), so that it would burn overnight in the tent of meeting (Lev 24:3). Its burning inside the tabernacle at night corresponded to the burning of the offerings outside on the altar of burnt offering during the day. A new batch of bread was set out on the table "regularly" each Sabbath (24:8) and eaten by the priests the following Sabbath. So, just as the lighting of the lamp marked off the daily cycle, the setting out of the bread marked off the weekly cycle of service at the tabernacle.

Ritual Theological Significance

This speech deals with the involvement of the Israelites in the rite that the high priest performed, hidden from their sight, in the Holy Place.[6] They supplied the olive oil for the lamps and the flour for the bread. The high priest

---

[5] Haran, *Temples and Temple-Service in Ancient Israel*, 159.

[6] Haran, *Temples and Temple-Service in Ancient Israel*, 205–10.

served on their behalf and for their benefit (24:8). He represented them as he entered the Holy Place each morning and evening from Sabbath to Sabbath.

Each day the high priest entered the Holy Place after he had performed the rite of atonement at the altar for burnt offering and before he offered the daily sacrifices on it. In the Holy Place he did three things. Each day he attended to the lamps on the lampstand and burnt the incense on the golden altar; on the Sabbath he also changed the bread on the table. This speech concentrates on the first and last of these because the Israelites were to provide the material for their enactment. They were regarded as a parallel enactment to the ritual for the daily burnt offering. The regular lamp was "offered up" (לְהַעֲלֹת, 24:2), just as the regular burnt offering was "offered up" (Ex 40:29). Like the token portion of the daily grain offering (2:1–10), the frankincense from the bread was burned before the bread was eaten by the priests in a holy place.

These rites presuppose that the tabernacle was the residence of God.[7] They were performed there in his presence. Yet they were kept at a distance from him by the curtain that divided his private quarters from the Holy Place. They resembled the rites that pagan priests performed to provide food and light for their deities. And yet they differed from those pagan rituals because in them God provided for his people and his priests. They are not envisaged as a daily meal for God, but as his nightly provision for his people and weekly food for his priests.

The lamps were lit each evening to provide light during the night in the Holy Place. From a human perspective, this requirement is rather puzzling. The light did not serve any practical purpose for the priests, since they did not enter the Holy Place at night. Neither did the light in the Holy Place directly benefit God, since he resided in the Holy of Holies. He does not need any light to see even in darkness, for the darkness is as light to him (Ps 139:12).

The lamp served a symbolical ritual function. The speech gives two hints of its significance. First, it was for "light" or "illumination" (24:2), like the sun and the moon (Gen 1:14–16). It was the light that came from God's presence and proclaimed that presence with his people in the menacing darkness of the night. More precisely, it was the light of his presence (Ps 90:8) that shone on his people with his grace and blessing (Num 6:25). It was a little theophany, the nightly theophany that corresponded to his daily theophany in fire at the altar (Lev 9:23, 24). Second, the lamp was also connected with the ark of the covenant and its two tablets of stone with the Decalogue inscribed on them. It was set before "the curtain of the written stipulations" (24:3). The lamp was therefore associated with God's Word that enlightened his people (cf. Ps 19:9 [ET 19:8]). Hence in Num 7:89–8:4, God's speaking to Moses coincided with Aaron's care for the lamps.

All of this is reinforced by the symbolism of the lampstand. As Meyers has shown, it was constructed to represent the tree of life, the life-giving tree that

---

[7] Haran, *Temples and Temple-Service in Ancient Israel*, 218.

proclaimed God's life-giving presence with his people.[8] It was also constructed as a flaming tree that was connected symbolically with the sun and the constellations. Its flowers were seven lamps that gave light. The vision of Zech 4:1–14 described them as the eyes of the Lord that ranged through the whole world. The lampstand with its lights was therefore meant to manifest the life-giving, enlightening presence of the Lord in the tabernacle for his people. He was the tree of life for his people. In the light of his presence they saw light (Ps 36:10 [ET 36:9]). Since the lamps proclaimed God's gracious presence with his people (2 Chr 13:10–12), their extinction proclaimed Israel's apostasy and resulted in his wrath (2 Chr 29:6–9).

The bread gained its function and significance from its location in the Lord's presence (Lev 24:8). It was therefore called the "bread of (the) Presence" (Ex 25:30; 35:13; 39:36; 1 Sam 21:7 [ET 21:6]; 1 Ki 7:48; 2 Chr 4:19). Its table was called "the table of the Presence" (Num 4:7). It was the only food offering that was set before the Lord in the tabernacle. But, unlike the food offered to pagan gods, it did not provide a meal for the Lord. None of it was offered to God by being burned on the incense altar or the altar for burnt offering. Only the incense that accompanied it was burnt. All the bread was eaten by the priests on duty in the sanctuary on the Sabbath.

We therefore have a case of ritual reversal. The divine service instituted by the Lord is the reverse of pagan rites. There was indeed a meal, but God was the host of the meal. In that meal he provided bread each Sabbath for his servants the priests.[9] But he did so through his people. As part of his covenant with them (24:8), the people provided the flour as an offering to the Lord. The twelve loaves represented the twelve tribes of Israel. The placement of those loaves in God's presence for a week and the burning of the frankincense as their token portion made them "most holy" (24:9). At the end of their week of service at the sanctuary, the priests on duty ate them as God's gift to them, their rations from him. Since the bread was most holy, the priests shared in God's holiness by eating them.

So, then, God instituted the lighting of the lamps and the setting out of the bread for the benefit of his people. He used these ritual enactments to make himself available to his people. Through the lamp and the bread he gave them access to his life-giving, enlightening, sanctifying presence. The daily service of the priests in the Holy Place culminated in a special weekly meal that God hosted for them. In that meal he gave them his most holy bread to eat.

Fulfillment by Christ

Both the lampstand and the table for the bread of the Presence are described in Heb 9:2 and interpreted in light of Christ in Hebrews 9. Like the whole outer tent and its rituals, they were parabolic for the present age and lasted until the

---

8 Meyers, *The Tabernacle Menorah,* 133–81.

9 Gane, " 'Bread of Presence' and Creator-in-Residence."

coming of the Messiah (Heb 9:8–9). They prefigured the work of Jesus with his establishment of the new way into the heavenly sanctuary by means of the holy things. He therefore fulfilled the function of the Holy Place and the ritual that was enacted there in the OT era.

In the Divine Service of the new covenant, Jesus replaces the lampstand and the bread for the Presence. Christ is the light of the world (Jn 8:12; 9:5). He is the light that shines in the darkness, the perpetual light that never goes out (Jn 1:5). Those who see him see the gracious face of God the Father (Jn 12:45; 14:9), his glory in Christ's face (2 Cor 4:6). They no longer remain in the darkness, but have the life-giving light (Jn 8:12; 12:46). Since they have been called out of the darkness into the light of God's marvelous presence, they stand before him and serve him as his holy priesthood (1 Pet 2:9). This is symbolized liturgically in our churches by the candles that are lit and placed on or near the altar. Like the perpetual sanctuary lamps that are kept burning in some churches, they proclaim the gracious presence of the triune God with his holy people in the Divine Service.

In the book of Revelation, the apostle John describes a vision of the risen Lord Jesus as the lampstand in the church (Rev 1:12–13; cf. Rev 21:23). By his presence he bridges heaven and earth. He, the lampstand in the heavenly sanctuary, stands in the midst of the seven lamps (Rev 1:20). These seven lamps (or lamp holders) are the seven churches of Asia Minor. He walks among them, just as God had promised in Lev 26:12, and illumines them with the light of his presence (Rev 2:1). Should he remove them from their place with him in the heavenly sanctuary, like lamps removed from a lampstand, they would be plunged into darkness; they would no longer have access to God's grace and would not be able to participate in the Divine Service together with their angel in the heavenly realm (Rev 2:5).

Jesus therefore fulfills the prophecy found in the vision of Zech 4:1–14. In that vision Zechariah had seen how the seven lamps on the golden lampstand were provided with a permanent supply of oil. On top of the lampstand was a bowl of oil with seven pipes to the seven lights on it. This bowl, in turn, was supplied with oil from the two olive trees that flanked the lampstand. The olive trees were the two servants of God who stood before God in his temple. They were able to supply the oil of God's Spirit because they themselves had been supplied with it (Zech 4:6, 14). These two servants of God represented the combination of the office of the anointed high priest and the anointed king in the vision of Zechariah. This was symbolized by the coronation of Joshua the high priest with a double crown (Zech 6:9–15) and embodied by Jesus.[10] The prophetic and apostolic ministers of the Gospel bear witness to Jesus as the light of God's presence in the midst of the church, the temple of the living God (Rev 11:1–12).

---

[10] Leupold, *Zechariah*, 96.

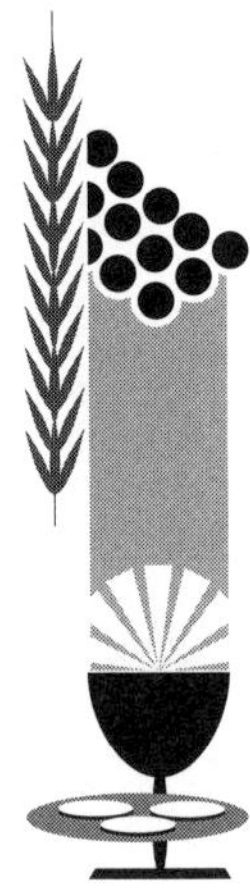

Jesus is also the bread of life (Jn 6:35, 48). He gives his flesh as bread for the life of the world (Jn 6:51). Those who eat his flesh receive divine life from him; they have eternal life in their own bodies (Jn 6:53–55). In the divine service at the tabernacle, the priests were the only guests at the Lord's table on the Sabbath; they ate the most holy bread of the Presence that communicated his holiness to them. But in the Divine Service of the church, all God's people receive Christ's sanctifying body; they are all guests at his royal table together with the twelve apostles (Lk 22:27–30); they all eat the bread of the Presence in the heavenly sanctuary. Thus, when the writer to the Hebrews declares in Heb 6:18–19 that we have strong encouragement from the hope that is "spread before us" in the inner sanctuary behind the curtain, he may allude to Lev 24:8 and the showbread as a type of the eucharistic bread that we have in our hands and in our mouths in the Lord's Supper.[11] It anchors our souls in the heavenly realm through the everlasting covenant of our Lord.

Jesus explained the priestly status of his disciples in connection with the criticism of them by the Pharisees for plucking and eating grain on the Sabbath (Mt 12:1–8 || Mk 2:23–28 || Lk 6:1–5). He defended what they had done by recalling how David had entered the sanctuary at Nob and had eaten the bread of the Presence there together with his companions during his flight from Saul in 1 Sam 21:2–7 (ET 21:1–6). Jesus took this incident as a messianic sign. David and his companions acted as if they were priests, holy men engaged in the holy work of God. So Jesus and his disciples too had priestly status, because he was the Messiah. As the Messiah he made them holy and involved them in his priestly work. He fed them with holy bread. As God's royal Son, the heir of David and Solomon, he was greater than the old temple; he built a new temple and inaugurated the Divine Service in which God did not demand sacrifices from his people but showed his mercy to them (Mt 12:6–7).

In his commentary on Luke, Just explores this important incident at some length. He notes how Luke alone emphasizes the eucharistic significance of this event by telling us that David, "taking" the bread of the Presence, "ate" it and "gave" it to his companions (Lk 6:4). Just sums up the theology of the story thus:

> What David did with the bread of the Presence in the tabernacle, Christ now does with grain that is not yet bread on the Sabbath. And as Lord of the Sabbath, he will soon institute a Meal in which he gives his body and blood together with bread and wine. This new Meal will be celebrated not on the Sabbath, but on Sunday (Acts 20:7), the eighth day, the time of the new creation. …
>
> In the new Sabbath era, the Lord of the Sabbath will give the bread of God's presence to his disciples to eat.[12]

---

[11] Field, *The Apostolic Liturgy and the Epistle to the Hebrews*, 170–73.

[12] Just, *Luke 1:1–9:50*, 257–58.

Some Christian commentators hold that the oil used in the lamps in the tabernacle prefigured the gift of the Holy Spirit, who enlightens the hearts of the faithful (Eph 1:17–18). Harms adds a Lutheran nuance to this interpretation. Just as the oil produced light by being burnt on the lampstand in the tabernacle, so the Holy Spirit illumines the people of God through his Word. God gives the Holy Spirit and his enlightenment through the ministry of Word and Sacrament in the church. The members of the church are therefore called to be light-bearers, like lamps in a lampstand, that shine with the light of God in the world by holding on to the life-giving Word of God (Phil 2:15–16).[13]

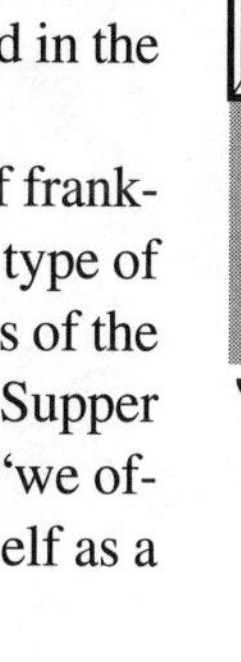

Harms also gives a sacramental interpretation to the presentation of frankincense with the showbread. Just as the bread that the priests ate was a type of Christ's body, so the incense that was offered with it typified the prayers of the faithful. Our reception of the body and blood of our Lord in his holy Supper for the forgiveness of our sins is accompanied by our prayer in which "we offer ourselves to Christ the Lord as his possession, just as he gives himself as a sacrifice to us for our possession."[14]

Abide with us, Redeemer,
O Light, eternal Light;
Your truth direct and guide us
To flee from error's night.

Abide in princely bounty
With us, large-hearted Lord,
Our lives with grace and wisdom
Enriching through your Word.[15]

---

13 Harms, *Das dritte Buch Mose*, 151–52.

14 Harms, *Das dritte Buch Mose*, 152.

15 From "Abide with Us, Our Savior" by Josua Stegmann (*LW* 287:3–4).

Leviticus 24:10–23

The Penalty for the Abuse of God's Holy Name

Translation

24 [10]A man who was the son of an Israelite woman and the son of an Egyptian man came out among the Israelites, and they fought in the camp—the Israelite woman's son and a certain Israelite. [11]The Israelite woman's son blasphemed the Name, cursing it. They brought him to Moses. Now his mother's name was Shelomith, daughter of Dibri, belonging to the tribe of Dan. [12]They put him in the place of custody for [God] to give a decision to them according to the mouth of the Lord.

[13]Then the Lord spoke to Moses: [14]"Take the cursing man outside the camp, and all those who heard [it] shall lay their hands on his head, and the whole congregation shall stone him, [15]and speak to the Israelites: If anyone curses his God, he shall bear his sin; [16]but if anyone blasphemes the name of YHWH, he shall be put to death; the whole congregation shall stone him; whether he is an alien or a citizen, when he has blasphemed the Name, he shall be put to death.

[17]"If anyone strikes [takes] the life of a human being, he shall be put to death; [18]but as for one who strikes [takes] the life of an animal, he shall make restitution for it, a life for a life. [19]If anyone gives an injury to his fellow citizen, he shall have the same thing done to him as he has done, [20]fracture for fracture, eye for eye, tooth for tooth; as he gave an injury to that human being thus it shall be given to him.

[21]"One who strikes [kills] an animal shall make restitution for it; but one who strikes [kills] a human being shall be put to death. [22]You shall have one standard of justice which shall be for the alien as for the citizen, for I am the Lord your God."

[23]Moses spoke [thus] to the Israelites. Then they took the cursing man outside the camp and stoned him with stones. The Israelites did as the Lord had commanded Moses.

Textual Notes

24:10 וַיֵּצֵא—This man either came out from his tent (e.g., Num 16:27) or appeared in public (e.g., Jer 37:4; Ezek 3:25).

וַיִּנָּצוּ—The Niphal of נָצָה means "to fight" (*HALOT*).

בַּמַּחֲנֶה—See the textual notes on Lev 4:12. This term recurs in 24:14, 23.

וְאִישׁ הַיִּשְׂרְאֵלִי׃—Literally this phrase is "a man, the Israelite." The definite article indicates that he was known to be an Israelite.

24:11 וַיִּקֹּב—This Qal verb could be from either נָקַב or קָבַב. (Those two verbs are related to each other since both are from an original biliteral root קב that has been expanded to become a triliteral root, either by the addition of נ to form נָקַב or by the doubling of the second radical to form קָבַב.) Since it is clearly the verb נָקַב that occurs twice in 24:16, most likely the verb וַיִּקֹּב here in 24:11 too is from נָקַב. In other OT passages, the Qal of נָקַב may mean "to designate a person by name" (Is 62:2). The Niphal of נָקַב can therefore refer to people who are "designated by name" to fulfill a task (Num 1:17; Ezra 8:20; 1 Chr 12:32 [ET 12:31]; 16:41; 2 Chr 28:15; 31:9).

Only in Lev 24:11, 16 does נָקַב mean "to curse a person by name" or "to use a name in a curse." But the related verb קָבַב means "to curse" and occurs often in the Pentateuch in the narrative of Balaam, who was hired to curse Israel (Num 22:11, 17; 23:8, 11, 13, 25, 27; 24:10). In Job 3:8 קָבַב refers to ritual cursing by practitioners of the occult. See also קָבַב in Prov 11:26; 24:24. In addition, the Piel of קָלַל, which is the usual OT Hebrew verb for "to curse," occurs in Lev 24:11, 14, 15, 23 as a synonym of נָקַב in Lev 24:11, 16. Hutton has argued that נָקַב in Lev 24:11, 16 is used as a euphemism ("designate" for "curse") for the abuse of the divine name.[1]

הַשֵּׁם—Literally this means "the Name." It is a reference to the personal name of God, the Tetragrammaton, יהוה. Its use here means that the man abused the holy name Yahweh (cf. Deut 28:58). הַשֵּׁם recurs in Lev 24:16. God refers to his personal name with שֵׁם in the phrase "my holy name" in 20:3; 22:2, 32. In rabbinic and modern Hebrew הַשֵּׁם, "the Name," is one of the most common ways of referring to God.

וַיְקַלֵּל—Literally this is "and he cursed." See Ex 22:27 (ET 22:28). The Piel verb קִלֵּל may be used for any form of verbal abuse that degrades a person (Lev 19:14). It can also be used more specifically for the pronouncement of a curse on a person (20:9) or for cursing God (24:11, 14, 15, 23). Even though קִלֵּל is a transitive verb, its direct object, which would be the Name or YHWH, is omitted here. Moses, the inspired writer of Leviticus, refrains from writing a specific description of the curse so as to avoid prompting any blasphemous thoughts in those who hear or read the passage.

This verse literally says that the man "blasphemed the Name and cursed." Hutton argues that this expression does not refer to two acts, but to two aspects of the same pronouncement.[2] Thus the man misused the holy name by cursing God by name.

וַיָּבִיאוּ אֹתוֹ—This impersonal plural verb could be translated as a passive: "and he was brought."

24:12 וַיַּנִּיחֻהוּ—This impersonal plural verb too could be translated as a passive: "and he was put."

בַּמִּשְׁמָר—See Gen 40:3, 7; 41:10; 42:17, 19; Num 15:34.

לִפְרֹשׁ לָהֶם עַל־פִּי יְהוָה׃—This is literally "for explaining to them according to the mouth of the Lord." See Num 15:34. The Qal of פָּרַשׁ means "to give a clear decision" (*HALOT*). "According to the mouth of the Lord" means that the people awaited a word from the Lord about what exactly to do. For the use of this idiom in the priestly tradition for a divine directive or legal pronouncement, see Ex 17:1; Num 3:16, 39, 51; 4:37, 41, 45, 49; 9:18, 20, 23; 10:13; 13:3; 33:2, 38; 36:5.

---

1 Hutton, "The Case of the Blasphemer Revisited (Leviticus 24:10–23)," 534–37.

2 Hutton, "The Case of the Blasphemer Revisited (Leviticus 24:10–23)."

24:14 אֶל־מִחוּץ֙ לַֽמַּחֲנֶ֔ה—This phrase is repeated in Lev 24:23. See the textual note and commentary on it in 4:12.

וְסָמְכ֧וּ כָֽל־הַשֹּׁמְעִ֛ים אֶת־יְדֵיהֶ֖ם עַל־רֹאשׁ֑וֹ—For the laying on of hands, see the textual notes and commentary on 1:4.

וְרָגְמ֥וּ אֹת֖וֹ—See the textual notes on 20:2.

כָּל־הָעֵדָֽה׃—See the textual notes on 4:13. This phrase is repeated in 24:16.

24:15 וְאֶל־בְּנֵ֥י יִשְׂרָאֵ֖ל תְּדַבֵּ֣ר לֵאמֹ֑ר—The use of a disjunctive clause indicates that taking the man outside the camp (24:14) and speaking to the Israelites are two aspects of the same event.

אִ֥ישׁ אִ֛ישׁ כִּֽי־יְקַלֵּ֥ל אֱלֹהָ֖יו—See Ex 22:27 (ET 22:28). Lev 24:15 describes a case where the person cursed God without using his holy name. Lev 24:16 will describe the case where the blasphemer does use God's holy name.

וְנָשָׂ֥א חֶטְאֽוֹ׃—For this idiom, see the textual notes and commentary on 20:20; 22:9. See also the similar idiom "he shall bear his iniquity" in 5:1.

24:16 וְנֹקֵ֤ב שֵׁם־יְהוָה֙—This refers to the use of the holy name to curse God.[3]

מ֣וֹת יוּמָ֔ת—See the textual notes on 20:20. This verb recurs in 24:17, 21, 29.

רָג֥וֹם יִרְגְּמוּ־ב֖וֹ—The infinitive absolute is used with its verb for emphasis.

כַּגֵּר֙—See 24:22 and the textual notes on 16:29.

כָּֽאֶזְרָ֔ח—See the textual notes on 16:29. This recurs in 24:22.

24:17 וְאִ֕ישׁ כִּ֥י—This is literally "as for a man, if."

יַכֶּ֖ה—The Hiphil of נָכָה literally is "strikes." Here it means to strike so as to kill. The Hiphil participle occurs in 24:18, 21.

כָּל־נֶ֣פֶשׁ אָדָ֑ם—See Num 35:30; Deut 19:6, 11; and the textual notes on Lev 1:2. The term אָדָם is used in 24:17, 20, 21 to bring aliens within the scope of this law.

24:18 וּמַכֵּ֥ה—Literally this Hiphil participle of נָכָה means "one who strikes."

נֶֽפֶשׁ־בְּהֵמָ֖ה—The term בְּהֵמָה here and in 24:21 refers to a domesticated animal.

יְשַׁלְּמֶ֑נָּה—See Ex 21:36, 37; 22:4.

נֶ֖פֶשׁ תַּ֥חַת נָֽפֶשׁ׃—See Ex 21:23; cf. Deut 19:21. This phrase applies to both cases of killing (Lev 24:17–18). It has been separated from the rest of the rule of retaliation to distinguish the penalty for taking life from the penalty for bodily injury (24:19).

24:19 וְאִ֕ישׁ כִּֽי—This is literally "as for a man, if."

מ֖וּם—See the textual notes on 21:17. This term recurs in 24:20.

בַּעֲמִית֑וֹ—See the textual notes on 5:21 (ET 6:2).

כַּאֲשֶׁ֣ר עָשָׂ֔ה כֵּ֖ן יֵעָ֥שֶׂה לּֽוֹ׃—See 24:20. This is literally "As he has done, so shall it be done to him." This could also be understood as a divine passive: God is the one who, indirectly or directly, will make sure that "it shall be done to him."

24:20 שֶׁ֚בֶר תַּ֣חַת שֶׁ֔בֶר—The term "fracture" includes and interprets the reference to the "hand" and the "foot" in Ex 21:24. תַּחַת could be translated "instead of."

עַ֚יִן תַּ֣חַת עַ֔יִן—See Ex 21:24; Deut 19:21.

שֵׁ֖ן תַּ֣חַת שֵׁ֑ן—See Ex 21:24; Deut 19:21.

כַּאֲשֶׁ֨ר יִתֵּ֥ן מוּם֙ בָּֽאָדָ֔ם כֵּ֖ן יִנָּ֥תֶן בּֽוֹ׃—This is literally "As he gave an injury to a human being, so shall it be given to him."

---

[3] Wenham, *Leviticus*, 311.

יִנָּתֶן—This could also be translated "will be given." As in the previous verse, this may be a divine passive: "it shall be given to him by God."

24:21 וּמַכֵּה ... וּמַכֵּה—As in 24:18, this participle is literally "one who strikes."

24:22 מִשְׁפַּט אֶחָד—This could also be translated "one justice" or "one ordinance." This term refers to divine law that applies to the civil realm of God's people (cf. Num 15:16). The terms תּוֹרָה, "instruction" (Ex 12:49; Num 15:16, 29), and חֻקָּה, "statute" (Num 9:14; 15:15), are used for religious law.

כַּגֵּר כָּאֶזְרָח—See the use of these terms together also in 16:29; 17:15; 18:26; 19:34; 24:16.

כִּי אֲנִי יְהוָה אֱלֹהֵיכֶם׃—See the textual notes on 11:44.

24:23 וַיְדַבֵּר מֹשֶׁה אֶל־בְּנֵי יִשְׂרָאֵל—This carries out the command of God in 24:15.

וַיִּרְגְּמוּ אֹתוֹ אָבֶן—This is literally "and they stoned him with stones." This carries out the command of God in 24:14.

וּבְנֵי־יִשְׂרָאֵל עָשׂוּ כַּאֲשֶׁר צִוָּה יְהוָה אֶת־מֹשֶׁה׃—See the textual notes on 7:36. For the use of a similar formula of compliance, see 8:36; 16:34; 21:24; 23:44.

Commentary

Structure

The story of the blasphemer is told in three stages: the referral of the case to God for adjudication in 24:10–12; the ruling from God on the case in 24:13–22; and the compliance of Moses and the Israelites in 24:23. As Fishbane has shown, this story proceeds according to the pattern of three similar legal cases in Numbers (9:6–14; 15:32–36; 27:1–11).[4] Each of these cases dealt with unprecedented problems that were not covered by previous legislation. In each instance, the case was brought to Moses and referred to God for a ruling.

The ruling from God is given in two parts: the command to execute the blasphemer in 24:14 and the legal argument in support of the penalty in 24:15–22. The legal argument contains seven laws, six of which are paired for contrast. The first two deal directly with the case of blasphemy. The last five laws are set apart from the first two laws by the reference to "alien and/or citizen" in 24:16 and 24:22. They are also arranged as a chiasm by the repetition of the laws about killing from 24:17–18 in reversed order in 24:21.[5] This arrangement serves to highlight the law of retaliation in 24:19–20.

The report of the Lord's ruling on the case and the implementation of it are constructed rather intricately in the shape of two interlocking, interacting chiasms that focus attention on two different points. The first chiasm deals directly with the case of the blasphemer in 24:13–16 and 24:23. It has as its pivot the command to stone the blasphemer in 24:16b. It is arranged as follows:

A and A'	"Yahweh/the Lord," "Moses" (24:13 and 24:23c)
B and B'	"Take out," "blasphemer," "outside the camp," "stone" (24:14 and 24:23b)
C and C'	"Speak to the Israelites" (24:15a and 24:23a)
D and D'	"Blaspheme the Name," "put to death" (24:16a and 24:16c)
X	"The whole congregation shall without fail stone him" (24:16b)

4 Fishbane, *Biblical Interpretation in Ancient Israel*, 98–102.

5 Milgrom, *Leviticus 23–27*, 2128–31; Wenham, *Leviticus*, 311–12.

The second chiasm is created by the insertion of 24:17–22 into the middle of the first chiasm. Its counter-pivot is the rule of retaliation in 24:20a. Its inclusion shifts the focus of the first chiasm and creates the following pattern:

E and E'	"God," "Yahweh," "alien and citizen alike" (24:15b–16 and 24:22)
F and F'	"Strikes/kills," "human being," "put to death" (24:17 and 24:21b)
G and G'	"Strikes/kills an animal," "he shall make restitution for it" (24:18 and 24:21a)
H and H'	"Gives an injury," "the same," "to/on him" (24:19 and 24:20b)
X	"Fracture for fracture, eye for eye, tooth for tooth" (24:20a)

This complex construction therefore juxtaposes the death penalty for the blasphemer with the law of retaliation.

The structure of this pericope can be outlined as follows:

- I. The case of the blasphemer (24:10–12)
  - A. The fight between the half-Israelite and the full Israelite (24:10)
  - B. The blasphemy of the half-Israelite (24:11a)
  - C. The blasphemer's confinement until the Lord's direction (24:11b–12)
- II. The Lord's decision in the case of blasphemy (24:13–22)
  - A. The Lord's address to Moses (24:13)
  - B. The Lord's speech to Moses (24:14–22)
    - 1. Instruction for Moses to arrange for the execution of the blasphemer (24:14)
    - 2. Commission of Moses to instruct the Israelites (24:15a)
    - 3. Speech to the Israelites (24:15b–22)
      - a. Penalties for the verbal abuse of God (24:15b–16)
        - i. Divine retribution for the utterance of a curse (24:15b)
        - ii. Execution for the abuse of the holy name (24:16)
      - b. Penalties for killing and personal injuries (24:17–21)
        - i. Death penalty for a person but restitution for an animal (24:17–18)
        - ii. Retaliation for personal injuries (24:19–20)
        - iii. Restitution for animals and death penalty for a person (24:21)
      - c. Use of the same standard of justice for aliens as for citizens (24:22a)
      - d. God's self-introduction (24:22b)
- III. The compliance of Moses and the Israelites (24:23)

General Analysis

This is the second time we have had an extended piece of narrative in the book of Leviticus. The first narrative is found in Leviticus 8–10. It tells about the inauguration of the divine service and God's reaction to its desecration by the two sons of Aaron. This story tells of God's reaction to the desecration of his name after he had instituted the ritual for the lighting of the lamps and the setting out of the bread before him (24:1–9). In both cases an incident is reported in order to give the setting for divine legislation and its implementation.

In this case the legal problem is a specific act of blasphemy. During the course of a fight that occurs in the camp, the half-Israelite uses the holy name YHWH to curse God himself. It is self-evident that the act cannot go unpunished, for it is an attack on God, as well as on Israel as his holy people. The problem is that God had given no law to cover such a case. The judgment of the case is complicated by three extraordinary factors.

First, the act of blasphemy involved the use of the holy name. The blasphemer had cursed God by name. This was a terrible act of sacrilege. How then should it be punished? The Second Commandment had warned the Israelites that the Lord would punish all those who abused that name (Ex 20:7). Furthermore, through Moses God had forbidden them to curse him in any way (Ex 22:28). Since the offense was a direct attack on God, should it be left to God to punish the offender or were the Israelites required to do so?

Second, the blasphemer was a half-Israelite, a man with an Egyptian father. Legally, therefore, he was an alien in Israel. Did the prohibition against cursing God also apply to aliens who were resident in Israel?

Third, the act occurred within the camp. It was therefore heard by a number of Israelites. Did the public utterance of the curse implicate its hearers? How did it affect the whole community? Was the congregation required to undo the damage that had been done to it by this act of sacrilege?

Since the leaders of the community were uncertain how to deal with the man, they brought him to Moses as the supreme judge. Since Moses too was unable to give a clear ruling on this case, he referred the matter to God for adjudication. The blasphemer was kept in custody until the matter was settled.

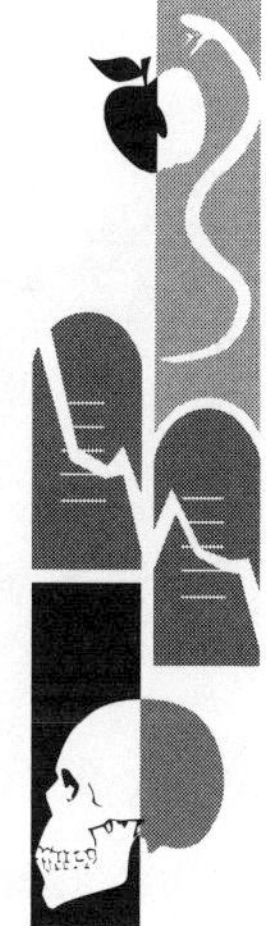

The ruling from God came in two parts. First, God instructed Moses on how to deal with the blasphemer (24:13–14, 23). Since the man had polluted the camp by his act of blasphemy, he had to be removed from the camp and executed outside the camp. The location for the execution was ritually significant. Neither the man nor his corpse was to be allowed to contaminate the camp any further. Those who had heard the curse were to lay their hands on his head before he was ritually executed by stoning. The reason for this ritual gesture is not given. They most likely transferred "the pollution generated by the blasphemy back on its producer."[6] As witnesses to the crime, they also thereby took responsibility for his death and exculpated themselves of bloodguilt for his death (Deut 13:10; 17:7). Thus the evil done by the blasphemer came back upon his own head. After that ritual transaction, the whole community was required to put him to death by stoning. That was the normal mode of execution for sacrilege. Since the life of the community was threatened by this act of blasphemy, it was involved in the execution of the blasphemer. It purged the evil from its midst.

The second part of God's ruling was that in it he also commissioned Moses to brief the Israelites on the legal basis for the execution of the blasphemer (24:15–22). Three points were made. First, God distinguished a general curse against him, without the use of his proper name, from a curse that involved the

[6] Milgrom, *Leviticus 23–27*, 2113.

use of his holy name. While anyone who cursed God without naming him would be punished by God himself, the whole congregation was required to stone anyone who had cursed God by name (24:15b–16). The gravity of the offense was emphasized by the repetition of the death penalty in three separate commandments in 24:16. Second, God decrees that in religious law, as in civil law, all resident aliens in Israel were subject to the same prohibitions as the Israelites (24:16, 22). Third, the laws in 24:17–22 justify the death penalty for the blasphemer as an application of the *lex talionis,* the rule of commensurate retribution, that had been given in Ex 21:23–25.

The ruling from God implies that cursing of him by name is similar to the murder of a person. The legal argument runs as follows. The law of equivalent retribution in Ex 21:23 is used to distinguish an attack on the "life" of a person or an animal from the bodily injury of a person. If a "life" is taken, a "life" is required. The kind of life-payment depends on the status of the creature whose life has been taken. Since human beings ranked above animals in the order of creation, the penalty for murder was more severe than the penalty for killing livestock. A murderer was to be put to death, but the killer of an animal was to compensate its owner for the "life" of the animal (Lev 24:17–18, 21).

The implied legal argument proceeds from the lesser to the greater. If the death penalty was required to compensate for the murder of a human being (the lesser crime), it was even more necessary to "compensate" for cursing God by name (the greater crime). What's more, the whole community needed to carry out this penalty, because the desecration of God's name polluted the camp just as murder polluted the land (Num 35:33). The principle of retaliation from Ex 21:24 is used to distinguish the injury that is inflicted on the body of a person from the loss of life by killing that person (Lev 24:19–20). Anyone who injured a person physically was punished in like kind—no more and no less! The punishment must not be more severe than the injury. Yet at the same time, it must not be lighter than the injury.

Even if a human court did not exact this penalty for the bodily injury of a person, God would do so in his own time, and in his own way (24:20). The same principle applied for those who repudiated or cursed God without employing his proper name (24:15). Their deed was not an attack on the "life" of God, but it was similar to an injury inflicted on the body of a person. It did indeed injure God, but it did not threaten his existence with his people. The offenders therefore were not punished by any human court. Instead, they bore their iniquity. God dealt with them in like kind; they would be repudiated and cursed by God (cf. Mt 25:41), and perhaps too by the people of God.

Theological Significance

The legal focus in this story is on the *lex talionis,* the "law of retribution" or the principle of commensurate punishment. The *lex talionis* is not a legal prescription, but a legal principle that is couched in proverbial form. As a legal principle, it was not applied literally and indiscriminately in all cases. Rather, it enshrined the notion of equivalence in the administration of justice.

Because modern people regard this principle as a legal decree, they also frequently misunderstand and misrepresent it as a primitive, barbaric form of punishment. Yet it was anything but that in ancient Israel and in the ancient Near East.

It is, in fact, the basis for all civilized legal systems. The *lex talionis* was already elaborated quite explicitly in Mesopotamia long before it was mentioned in the OT.[7] It performed two very important functions there and in ancient Israel. First, it limited the scope for revenge, which always tended to escalate indiscriminately and endlessly in any tribal society. By it, the principle of equivalence was enshrined in the administration of justice. Second, it treated the life and the body of every person as equal in value regardless of social, racial, and economic status. It therefore ensured that the loss of human life and the bodily injury of any person were not treated as commercial matters in a civil court, but as crimes against humanity in a criminal court in the ancient world.[8]

God's ruling in this story goes further than that. It makes the murder and bodily injury of a human being a sin against God. What's more, God not only sanctioned this legal principle in the Pentateuch (Ex 21:23–25; Lev 24:19–20; Deut 19:21), but he also indicated that, since he himself administered his justice according to this principle in the order of creation, the Israelites were to use this principle in their administration of his justice by their courts of law.

While the legal focus of this story is on the principle of retaliation, the theological focus is on the abuse of God's holy name. Milgrom is right in his claim that this story is the counterpart to the story about the desecration of the sanctuary by Aaron's sons in Lev 10:1–4. Both stories are exemplary. While the first story warns the priests about the desecration of the sanctuary, this story warns the laity about the desecration of God's name. That name was the most holy thing available to them. Just as the priests approached God by the presentation of incense and other offerings, so the laity had access to him and received help from him by means of his holy name. The desecration of the name YHWH was therefore the worst act of sacrilege possible for a layperson.

The legal ruling in 24:15–22 implies that the use of God's name to curse him was in fact an attack on his "life." This is not as farfetched as it sounds, because anyone who cursed God damned him and so, in a sense, condemned him to death. It is, of course, true that no one could put God to death by cursing him. Yet by using the holy name to curse God, this blasphemer attacked the means by which God gave the Israelites access to himself and his life: his name.

God had introduced himself by name to them so that they could live with him as his holy people (24:22). Any attack on that name not only threatened the life of the blasphemer, it also endangered the life of Israel as God's people.

---

7 Frymer-Kensky, "Tit for Tat."

8 Hartley, *Leviticus*, lxii.

It desecrated God's holiness and polluted the congregation. It therefore threatened God's life with his people and their life with him. If that crime was left unpunished, God would be forced to withdraw his gracious, life-giving presence from his people, or else they would be destroyed by his holiness. So, since the blasphemer had attacked the "life" of Yahweh as Israel's God, his own life was forfeit. He was to be put to death for attempted deicide.[9]

Fulfillment by Christ

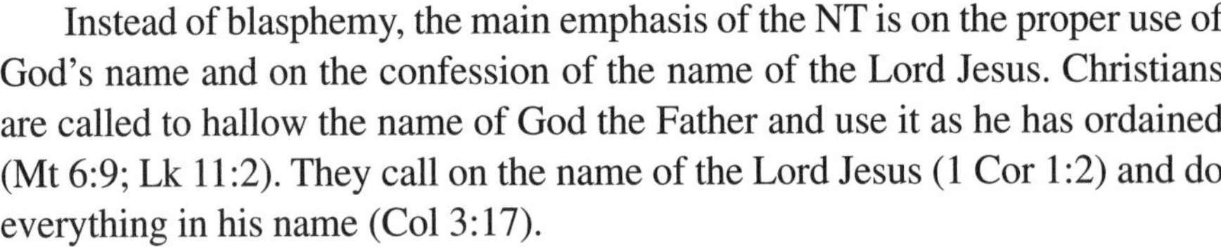

Instead of blasphemy, the main emphasis of the NT is on the proper use of God's name and on the confession of the name of the Lord Jesus. Christians are called to hallow the name of God the Father and use it as he has ordained (Mt 6:9; Lk 11:2). They call on the name of the Lord Jesus (1 Cor 1:2) and do everything in his name (Col 3:17).

The teaching of Jesus on blasphemy is most surprising. On the one hand, he declares that people can receive forgiveness from God for every kind of blasphemy except blasphemy against the Holy Spirit (Mt 12:31–32). This is so because they depend on the Holy Spirit for their justification—since the Spirit creates faith in Christ, through whom alone comes the forgiveness of sins—and their sanctification. On the other hand, Jesus extends the scope of blasphemy to include all careless words that people utter about him and against him (Mt 12:33–37). People are either saved or damned by what they say; their salvation hinges on their confession of Jesus as Lord (Rom 10:9–13).

Yet despite that, Jesus does not ever demand that blasphemers should be put to death. He is, in fact, more concerned about the blaspheming heart than blasphemous speech (Mt 15:19; Mk 7:22). He aims to transform the evil heart by his Word and the Holy Spirit so that the believer, like a fruitful tree, will confess him as Lord and praise God wholeheartedly (Mt 12:33–35; Heb 13:15; cf. Eph 4:31; Col 3:8).

Just as Jesus does not sanction the exercise of the death penalty by his disciples for those who curse God, so he does not endorse the rule of retaliation for them when they suffer an injury. In fact, he instructs them to practice nonresistance and positive retaliation against those who exploit or hurt them (Mt 5:38–42). They are to repay evil with good. This hard teaching is repeated by Paul (Rom 12:17–21). Those who follow Christ are commissioned to overcome evil with good. The administration of civil justice is the business of the civil authorities, to whom God has given the authority of the sword (Rom 13:4; 1 Pet 2:14). The church, however, is to follow Christ's example by accepting suffering and blessing those who persecute its members (1 Pet 2:21–25; 4:12–16). Christ's disciples are called to love their enemies by praying for them and for God's forgiveness of them (Mt 5:43–48).

Ironically, unbelieving Jewish people considered Christ himself (Jn 10:33,

---

[9] Milgrom, *Leviticus 23–27*, 2141.

36) and Christians (Acts 6:11; 13:45; 18:6) to be blasphemers (cf. the Gentiles in Acts 19:37; Rom 2:24). Since the rise of Islam, Muslims too have often accused Christians of blasphemy because of the biblical doctrines of Christ's incarnation and the Trinity.

The rich are said to blaspheme the name of the Lord by their oppression of their poor brothers and sisters in Christ (James 2:7).

While false prophets "blaspheme the glories" by speaking against Christ the Lord and the holy angels (2 Pet 2:10), in return the angels themselves do not carry out the *lex talionis;* they "do not pronounce a blasphemous judgment against them before the Lord" (2 Pet 2:11 ESV). Rather, they wait for God to carry out the just punishment of the destruction of the blasphemers (2 Pet 2:10–14; cf. Jude 8–10).

Paul confesses that when he was a zealous unbeliever, he fiercely persecuted the church and sought to compel Christians "to blaspheme" (Acts 26:11), which would take place if they were to deny the name and lordship of Jesus Christ (cf. Rom 10:8–13; 1 Cor 12:3). Moreover, Paul confesses that by being such a persecutor of the church of Christ, he himself was a "blasphemer" (1 Tim 1:13).

St. Paul names two men, Hymenaeus and Alexander, who may formerly have been coworkers of the apostle but who "made shipwreck of their faith" and became blasphemers (1 Tim 1:19–20). Paul says nothing about stoning them or any other physical punishment that would correspond to Lev 24:10–23. Instead, he excommunicated them from the church: "... whom I have delivered to Satan, that they may learn not to blaspheme" (1 Tim 1:20). Paul excommunicated these two men in the same way he prescribed for the incestuous man in 1 Cor 5:1–5.[10] The hope was to bring them to repentance and restore them to faith in Christ before Judgment Day. But if they refused to repent, they, like the blasphemers in Rev 16:9, 11, 21, would belong to Satan forever.

St. John describes how the beast (Rev 13:5–6) and impenitent people who experience God's wrath against their iniquity (Rev 16:9, 11, 21) blaspheme the name of God. Ironically, those people blaspheme the name of the very God who has the authority to relieve them of their suffering (Rev 16:9, 11, 21). As in 1 Tim 1:19–20, Revelation too gives no indication that the church is to attempt to punish the blasphemers or the beast physically. In accord with Lev 24:15, God himself carries out the proper judgment upon the blasphemous beast and the blasphemers who refuse to repent. The beast and those people are delivered to the lake of fire for eternity (Rev 19:20; 20:10, 14–15; 21:8).

---

[10] See Lockwood, *1 Corinthians,* 161–70. Excommunication from the church is delivery to Satan, since those outside the church are under the dominion of the devil and on their way to hell. The goal of excommunication is to move the offender to repentance and then return him to faith in Christ and communion with the church before the Last Day: "Deliver this man to Satan for the destruction of the flesh, that his spirit may be saved in the day of the Lord" (1 Cor 5:5).

Jesus! Name of wondrous love,
Name all other names above,
Unto which must ev'ry knee
Bow in deep humility.

Jesus! Name of priceless worth
To the fallen sons of earth
For the promise that it gave,
"Jesus shall his people save."

Jesus! Only name that's given
Under all the mighty heaven
Whereby man, to sin enslaved,
Bursts his fetters and is saved.

Jesus! Name of wondrous love
Human name of God above;
Pleading your redemption true,
We flee, helpless, Lord to you.[11]

---

[11] From "Jesus! Name of Wondrous Love" by William W. How (*LW* 182:1, 3, 5–6).

The Structure of Leviticus 25–26

These two chapters are addressed as a single speech by Moses to the Israelites. They are set apart from their context by an introduction and a conclusion, which assert that their contents were given by the Lord to Moses at Mount Sinai (25:1; 26:46). The chapters are connected thematically by their focus on life in the land and their concern for the observance of its Sabbatical Years. What's more, no new introduction (e.g., "The Lord spoke to Moses") is given for the commandments in 26:1–2 and the promises and threats in 26:3–45. Indeed, according to the Masoretic tradition, 25:47–26:2 comprises a single paragraph (as indicated by the ס that precedes 25:47 and the ס that follows 26:2).

Yet for all that, chapter 26 is much more than the conclusion of the previous chapter. Apart from the summary commandments in 26:1–2, which restate what had already been given in 19:3b–4, 30 and summarize the laws in chapters 17–25, it contains no new legislation.[1] It is, instead, an extended admonition by God to his people. Like 18:24–30; 19:37; 20:22–26; and 22:31–33, it functions as the conclusion to the preceding legislation. It is the subscript for the whole of chapters 17–25 as well.[2] It could therefore be taken as the climax of the whole book, for in it God outlines his policy for Israel as his holy people in the promised land.

---

[1] Ruwe, *"Heiligkeitsgesetz" und "Priesterschrift,"* 90–120.

[2] Ruwe, *"Heiligkeitsgesetz" und "Priesterschrift,"* 98–100.

Leviticus 25:1–55

Sabbatical Years and the Jubilee

Translation

25 1The Lord spoke to Moses at Mount Sinai: 2"Speak to the Israelites and say to them: When you enter the land that I am giving to you, the land shall observe a Sabbath for the Lord. 3Six years you may sow your field, and six years you may prune your vineyard and gather its produce. 4But in the seventh year there shall be a Sabbath of complete rest for the land, a Sabbath for the Lord; you shall not sow your field, and you shall not prune your vineyard; 5you shall not reap the self-sown growth from your harvest or pick the grapes from your unpruned vine; it shall be a Sabbath of complete rest for the land. 6The Sabbath of the land will be [provide] for you food—for you, for your male slave and for your female slave, for your hired worker and for your indentured servant who reside as aliens under your authority, 7for your livestock and for the wild animals which are in your land; all its produce will be to eat.

8"You shall count off seven weeks of years, seven years seven times, so that the days of the seven weeks of years amount to forty-nine years. 9Then you shall sound the ram's horn of acclamation; in the seventh month on the tenth day, on the Day of Atonement, you shall have a ram's horn sounded throughout the land, 10so that you may consecrate the fiftieth year and proclaim release throughout the land for all its inhabitants. It shall be a Jubilee for you, so that each of you may return to his landholding and each of you may return to his kin group. 11The fiftieth year shall be a Jubilee for you; you shall not sow [the field], and you shall not reap its self-sown grain, and you shall not pick its unpruned vines. 12Because it is a Jubilee, it shall be holy for you; from the field you may eat its produce. 13In this Year of Jubilee each of you shall return to his landholding.

14"When you sell some [land] that is for sale to your fellow countryman, or when you buy from your fellow countryman, each of you shall not cheat his brother. 15According to the number of years since the Jubilee you shall buy from your fellow countryman; according to the number of years of produce he shall sell to you. 16According to the multitude of the years you shall multiply its purchase price, and according to the paucity of the years you shall diminish its purchase price, for it is the amount of produce that he is selling to you. 17So each of you shall not cheat his fellow countryman, but you shall fear your God, for I am the Lord your God.

18"You shall enact my statutes, and you shall observe my ordinances, and you shall do them, so that you may reside on the land in security. 19The land will yield its fruit, and you will eat your fill and reside in security on it. 20If you should ask, 'What shall we eat on the seventh year, since we may not sow and we may not gather our produce?' 21I will ordain my blessing for you in the sixth year, so

that it will yield the produce for three years. 22When you sow in the eighth year,
you will still be eating from the produce old [food]; until the ninth year, when its
produce comes in, you will eat old [food].

23"But the land must not be sold beyond reclaim, for the land belongs to me;
you are indeed resident aliens under my authority. 24Therefore, throughout all
the land of your possession, you shall grant the right of redemption for the land.

25"When your brother becomes so impoverished that he has to sell some of
land that he holds, his closest kinsman shall come and redeem what his brother
has sold. 26When the man who has no kinsman prospers and acquires enough for
the price of his redemption, 27he may calculate the years since its sale, refund the
difference to the man to whom he sold it, and return to his landholding. 28But if
he does not acquire a sufficient amount to return [the land] to himself, what he
has sold shall remain under the control of the one who bought it until the Year
of Jubilee; it shall become free in the Jubilee, so that he may return to his landholding.

29"When a man sells a place of residence [in] a walled town, his right of redemption shall last until the end of the year of its sale; its time of redemption
shall be a year. 30But if it is not redeemed before the completion for it of a full
year, the house which is in a town which has a wall shall belong to its buyer and
his descendants beyond reclaim; it will not become free in the Jubilee. 31But as
for the houses in the villages that have no wall around them: each of them shall
be classed as a field of the land; it has the right of redemption, and it shall become free in the Jubilee. 32As for the towns of the Levites and the houses in the
towns of their possession: the Levites have a perpetual right of redemption. 33No
matter who of the Levites redeems [it], the house and his town property that has
been sold shall become free in the Jubilee, because the houses in the towns of the
Levites are their possession among the Israelites. 34But the paddocks around their
towns may not be sold, for that is their possession forever.

35"When your brother becomes so impoverished that his hand is under your
authority and you take hold of him as a resident alien, let him retain his livelihood under your authority. 36You shall not exact from him advance interest or
compound interest, but you shall fear your God and let your brother retain his
livelihood under your authority. 37You shall not lend him your money on advance
interest, or lend him your foodstuff on accrued interest. 38I am the Lord your
God, who freed you from the land of Egypt to give you the land of Canaan, to be
your God.

39"When your brother who is impoverished under your authority is sold to
you, you shall not make him work in service as a slave. 40He shall remain under
your authority as a resident hired laborer; he shall work under your authority
until the Year of Jubilee. 41Then he and his children with him shall become free
from your authority; he shall return to his kin group and return to his ancestral
landholding, 42for they are my servants, whom I freed from the land of Egypt;
they shall not be sold in a slave sale. 43You shall not rule over him harshly, but
you shall fear your God. 44As for your male slave and female slave that you may

**own: it is from the nations around you that you may buy a male slave or a fe-
male slave. [45]You may also buy some of the children of those residents who reside as aliens under your authority and some of their kin groups under your
authority that they cause to be born in your land, so that they become your property. [46]You may bequeath them to your children after you to inherit as property;
in perpetuity you may make them work as slaves. But as for your brothers, the
Israelites, each man shall not rule over his brother harshly.**

**[47]"When a resident alien under your authority prospers, and when your
brother was so impoverished under his authority that he was sold to a resident
alien under your authority or to a branch of the alien's kin group, [48]after he has
been sold, he shall have the right of redemption. One of his brothers may redeem
him, [49]or his uncle or his uncle's son may redeem him, or anyone from his flesh
and kin group may redeem him, or if he prospers, he may redeem himself. [50]To-
gether with his buyer, he shall calculate the total from the year that he was sold
to him until the Year of Jubilee, and the price of his sale shall be applied to the
number of years; he shall be under his authority as if it were the term of a hired
laborer. [51]If many years remain, in proportion to them he shall pay back some
of the money for his purchase as the price of his redemption; [52]and if a few years
remain until the Year of Jubilee, he shall calculate it in this way; according to his
years [of work] he shall pay the price of his redemption. [53]He shall be under his
authority as a worker hired year by year. You shall see to it that he does not rule
over him harshly. [54]If he has not been redeemed in any of these ways, he and his
children with him shall become free in the Year of Jubilee, [55]because the Israelites
are servants who belong to me; they are my servants whom I freed from the land
of Egypt. I am the Lord your God."**

Textual Notes

25:1 וַיְדַבֵּר יְהוָה אֶל־מֹשֶׁה בְּהַר סִינַי—See 7:38; 26:46; 27:34.

25:2 כִּי תָבֹאוּ אֶל־הָאָרֶץ אֲשֶׁר אֲנִי נֹתֵן לָכֶם—See 14:34; 23:10; cf. 19:23.

וְשָׁבְתָה הָאָרֶץ שַׁבָּת—This clause with the verb שָׁבַת and noun שַׁבָּת is literally "the land shall sabbath a Sabbath." See 23:32. Other references to the land resting from its work are in 25:4, 6; 26:34, 35; and 2 Chr 36:21.

שַׁבָּת לַיהוָה׃—See Ex 16:23, 25; 20:10; 31:15; Lev 23:3; 25:4; Deut 5:14.

25:3 See Ex 23:10–12 for an earlier version of this law.

כַּרְמֶךָ—This could also be translated "orchard."

וְאָסַפְתָּ—This verb is used for gathering in the grain, oil, and wine for storage (Deut 11:14), which was completed by the Feast of Booths (Lev 23:39).

תְּבוּאָתָהּ׃—This word occurs in 19:25; 23:39; 25:3, 7, 12, 15, 16, 20, 21, 22 (twice). The produce of the land consisted of grain, olive oil, fruit, and wine.

25:4 שַׁבַּת שַׁבָּתוֹן—See 16:31; 23:3, 32; 25:5; and the textual notes on 16:31.

25:5 סְפִיחַ—The "second growth" (*HALOT*) or "self-sown growth" refers to the grain that grows of itself during the year after the harvest from the seed of the previous year. The word recurs in 25:11 (cf. 2 Ki 19:29; Is 37:30).

נְזִירֶךָ—This noun comes from the root נזר, which means "to restrain, abstain, separate from" (15:31; 22:2). Its use suggests that the grapevines with their untrimmed branches (cf. Jer 7:29), with their forbidden fruit (cf. Lev 22:2), or with their consecrated fruit (LXX; cf. Num 6:5; Is 65:8) are held to resemble a Nazirite. This term recurs in Lev 25:11.

25:6 וְ֠הָיְתָה שַׁבַּ֨ת הָאָ֤רֶץ לָכֶם֙ לְאָכְלָ֔ה—This is literally "The Sabbath of the land will be for you for food." See also 25:7 (cf. Gen 1:29).

וּלְעַבְדְּךָ֖—The noun עֶבֶד can be used for a chattel slave (Lev 25:6, 39, 44; 26:13), an indentured servant, or a devotee to God (25:42, 55). This chapter studiously avoids the use of this term for the indebted Israelite who worked as a servant to pay off his creditor.

וְלַאֲמָתֶ֑ךָ—This term recurs in 25:44.

וְלִשְׂכִֽירְךָ֙ וּלְתוֹשָׁ֣בְךָ֔—See 22:10; 25:40. Even though Milgrom argues that these two terms form a hendiadys,[1] they are parallel to the preceding two distinct terms "your male slave" and "your female slave." Therefore it is more likely that these two terms refer to two different groups of workers: hired employees (cf. 25:53) and laborers indentured to work off a debt (cf. 25:35).

הַגָּרִ֖ים עִמָּֽךְ׃—This could refer just to the two classes of residents (the previous two Hebrew words) or to the male and female slaves as well (the previous four words). For גֵּר, the Qal participle of גּוּר (here in the plural), see 19:33–34. The term recurs in 25:45.

עִמָּֽךְ׃—The preposition עִם is used as a technical term for the control of a bankrupt debtor by his creditor. It therefore means "under the authority, under the power, in the service of."[2] It recurs often in this chapter (25:35, 36, 39, 40, 41, 45, 47, 50, 53, 54; cf. 25:23).

25:7 תִּהְיֶ֥ה כָל־תְּבוּאָתָ֖הּ לֶאֱכֹֽל׃—See 25:6. This may indicate that the produce of the land may only be gathered as food for eating.

25:8 The Jubilee cycle is based on the annual pentecostal period in 23:15–16 of fifty days, from the beginning of the barley harvest in the week of Unleavened Bread to the end of the wheat harvest at Pentecost.

שַׁבְּתֹ֣ת—This could also be translated "Sabbaths" (instead of "weeks"). See the textual notes on 23:15.

25:9 וְהַעֲבַרְתָּ֞ ... תַּעֲבִ֥ירוּ—The verb הֶעֱבִיר (the Hiphil of עָבַר) is used twice in this verse, rather that the usual verb תָּקַע, to indicate that ram's horns were blown in sequence all over the land.

שׁוֹפַ֤ר ... שׁוֹפָ֖ר—The ram's horn needs to be distinguished from the sacred trumpets of the priests (Num 10:2–6). The ram's horn was used for giving signals to an army (e.g., Joshua 6), for gathering the nation for the coronation of a king (e.g., 2 Sam 15:10; 2 Ki 9:13; Ps 47:6 [ET 47:5]), and for announcing the assembly of the congregation for a sacred occasion (e.g., Ex 19:16, 19; 2 Sam 6:15; Ps 81:4 [ET 81:3]; Joel 2:15).

תְּרוּעָה֙—This could also be translated "as an acclamation" (rather than "with a cry of acclamation"). See Lev 23:24. The use of תְּרוּעָה with the ram's horn indicates

---

[1] Milgrom, *Leviticus 23–27*, 2161.

[2] Milgrom, *Leviticus 23–27*, 2205–6; Speiser, "Leviticus and the Critics," 134–35.

that the sounding of the horn was accompanied by a loud shout of acclamation of God as King (Num 23:21; Pss 47:6 [ET 47:5]; 89:16 [ET 89:15]; cf. Ps 98:6).

בְּיוֹם הַכִּפֻּרִים—See Lev 23:27, 28.

25:10 וְקִדַּשְׁתֶּם—See Joel 2:15 and the textual notes on Lev 8:10. See GKC, § 112 m (α), for the use of a perfect verb with *waw* consecutive to introduce a purpose clause following an imperfect verb (here תַּעֲבִירוּ in 25:9).

שְׁנַת הַחֲמִשִּׁים שָׁנָה—There are two main issues in determining the date of the Jubilee. First, it is not clear whether it was reckoned by the liturgical calendar, which began the year in spring (cf. Ex 12:2), or by the agricultural calendar, whose year began in autumn. According to Lev 25:9, the trumpet was sounded on the Day of Atonement in the seventh month of the forty-ninth year. If, as seems most likely, the Jubilee was announced then, it followed the agricultural calendar. If it announced the coming of the Jubilee in the following spring, it followed the liturgical calendar.

Second, there has been some debate whether the Jubilee was the year that followed the seventh, Sabbatical Year, whether the Jubilee coincided with that seventh, Sabbatical Year, or even whether the Jubilee was the day of its proclamation at the beginning of that year. Most scholars have held that the Jubilee lasted for the year after the seventh, Sabbatical Year.[3] But if that were so, the seven-year cycles would be disrupted by the addition of a fiftieth year.

Other modern scholars argue that the Jubilee was meant to coincide with the seventh, Sabbatical Year.[4] In that case, what we would call the forty-ninth year was reckoned as the fiftieth year by counting inclusively. Other OT examples of counting inclusively are circumcision on the eighth day,[5] the fifty days of Pentecost in 23:16, the chronology of the kings in the Northern Kingdom, and the 490 years for the cycle of ten Jubilees in Dan 9:24. If that were so, then, strictly speaking, the Jubilee was the day of its proclamation, as is indicated by Lev 27:23, rather than the year that followed it. The forty-ninth year was called the Year of Jubilee because the Jubilee was proclaimed in it (25:13, 28, 40, 50, 52, 54; 27:17, 23, 24).

דְּרוֹר—See Is 61:1; Jer 34:8, 15, 17; Ezek 46:17. This word, which means "a release" (LXX), is derived from the Akkadian terms *duraru/anduraru.* In ancient Mesopotamia the release of people from debt and the release of land to its original owners was connected with the declaration of a *misarum,* a program of socioeconomic reform by a king at his ascension to his throne or at a time of national crisis.[6]

יוֹבֵל—The name for the Year of Jubilee is derived from the "horn" that was sounded to inaugurate it (cf. Ex 19:13; Josh 6:4, 5, 6, 8, 13). We agree with those who

---

3 Milgrom, *Leviticus 23–27*, 2181–83, 2248–51.

4 Hartley, *Leviticus,* 434–36; North, *Sociology of the Biblical Jubilee*, 129–34; Schenker, "The Biblical Legislation on the Release of Slaves," 25. This proposal has been examined and refuted by Kawashima, "The Jubilee, Every 49 or 50 Years?"

5 The birthday is considered the first day, and so the eighth day is the same day of the week as the birthday, one week later. We would say that the circumcision took place one week after the birth, but the OT reckons it as the eighth day.

6 Weinfeld, *Social Justice in Ancient Israel and in the Ancient Near East*, 152–78; Hudson, "Proclaim Liberty throughout the Land."

maintain that the Jubilee was not the year itself, but the proclamation at the beginning of the year.[7] Thus the Year of Jubilee was the year on which the Jubilee was proclaimed. The term יֹובֵל occurs often (Lev 25:10–13, 15, 28, 30, 31, 33, 40, 50, 52, 54; 27:17, 18, 21, 23, 24; Num 36:4).

וְשַׁבְתֶּ֗ם אִ֚ישׁ אֶל־אֲחֻזָּתֹ֔ו—This is a legal expression for the restoration of a person to his landholding. A similar expression refers to the landholding reverting to its original owner. See 25:13, 27, 28, 41; 27:24.

אֲחֻזָּתֹ֔ו—See the textual notes on 14:34, where אֲחֻזָּה is translated as "possession." This term recurs in 25:13, 24, 25, 27, 28, 32, 33, 34, 41, 45, 46.

מִשְׁפַּחְתֹּ֖ו—This could also be translated "clan." It recurs in 25:41, 45, 47, 49.

25:12 קֹ֖דֶשׁ—This is literally "holiness." See the textual notes on 4:6.

25:14 תִמְכְּר֤וּ—As Milgrom notes, the verb מָכַר can be used for leasing as well as buying property.[8] The context here implies that these things are for lease. The verb recurs in 25:15, 16, 23, 25, 27, 29, 34, 39, 42, 47, 48, 50; 27:20, 27, 28.

מִמְכָּר֙—The noun מִמְכָּר is used for property that is for lease or sale (25:14), the lease or sale of property (25:27, 29, 33, 50), and property that has been leased or sold (25:25, 28).

לַעֲמִיתֶ֔ךָ—See the textual notes on 5:21 (ET 6:2). This term recurs in 25:15, 17.

קָנֹ֖ה—The infinitive absolute is used instead of a finite verb.

מִיַּ֣ד עֲמִיתֶ֑ךָ—This is literally "from the hand of your fellow countryman."

אַל־תֹּונ֖וּ—See the textual note on the Hiphil of יָנָה in 19:33. It recurs in 25:17 (cf. Ex 22:20 [ET 22:21]).

אָחִֽיו׃—See the textual notes on 19:17. This term recurs in 25:25 (twice), 35, 36, 39, 46 (twice), 47, 48.

25:15 בְּמִסְפַּ֥ר שְׁנֵֽי־תְבוּאֹ֖ת—This is literally "according to the number of years of produce."

25:16 מִקְנָתֹ֑ו—This is literally "its purchase, acquisition." See 25:51; 27:22. It refers to the amount paid for the rental and use of a piece of land.

25:17 וְיָרֵ֖אתָ מֵאֱלֹהֶ֑יךָ—See the textual notes on 19:14. The appeal to the fear of God shows that even if the measures taken in each of these cases were technically legal, they were nevertheless immoral. This clause recurs in 25:36, 43.

כִּ֛י אֲנִ֥י יְהוָ֖ה אֱלֹהֵיכֶֽם׃—See the textual notes on 11:44.

25:18 חֻקֹּתַ֔י—See the textual notes on 3:17.

מִשְׁפָּטַ֖י—See the textual notes on 5:10.

לָבֶֽטַח׃—This recurs in 25:19; 26:5.

25:19 וְנָתְנָ֤ה הָאָ֙רֶץ֙ פִּרְיָ֔הּ—See 26:4.

לָבֶ֖טַח—See 26:5.

25:21 וְצִוִּ֤יתִי אֶת־בִּרְכָתִי֙—See Deut 28:8.

וְעָשָׂת֙—עָשָׂת is the archaic form of עָשְׂתָה, the Qal third person feminine singular perfect of עָשָׂה. See GKC, § 75 m. The implied subject may be בִּרְכָתִי֙ since בְּרָכָה is

---

7 Kaufmann, "A Reconstruction of the Social Welfare Systems of Ancient Israel," 284, n. 1.

8 Milgrom, *Leviticus 23–27*, 2177.

a feminine noun. If so, God's blessing is pictured as a gracious, life-giving entity that produces an extraordinarily abundant harvest in the sixth year. Alternatively, the subject of the verb could be implied to be הָאָרֶץ or הָאֲדָמָה, since both are feminine nouns.

לִשְׁלֹשׁ הַשָּׁנִים׃—The produce lasted for two whole years, from the harvest in the late spring of the sixth year to the harvest in the late spring of the eighth year.

25:22 מִן־הַתְּבוּאָה יָשָׁן—See Lev 26:10.

עַד־בּוֹא תְּבוּאָתָהּ—This refers to the autumn, when all the produce of the land has been brought in and stored away.

תֹּאכְלוּ יָשָׁן׃—This is promise of plenty: "you shall be eating old store" because God will have given an especially abundant harvest in the prior year. It is not a restriction of consumption of grain as is implied by the translation of the verb as a command in the NRSV and by Milgrom.[9]

25:23 לִצְמִתֻת—The term צְמִתֻת, found only here and in 25:30, is connected with the root צמת, which means "to exterminate, annihilate." Rabinowitz demonstrates that it was an ancient legal term that was used for real estate transactions to indicate that the seller had forfeited the title to the land.[10]

כִּי ...—The כִּי that introduces this sentence is best construed as an emphatic particle.

גֵרִים וְתוֹשָׁבִים—This is literally "aliens and residents." As in 25:35, 47, this is a hendiadys (cf. 25:45). See 1 Chr 29:15 for an echo of the declaration "You are indeed resident aliens under my authority."

עִמָּדִי׃—Milgrom observes that, like עִם in 25:6, 35, 36, 39, 40, the preposition עִמָּד means "under the authority, under the control of, in the service of."[11]

25:24 גְּאֻלָּה—The noun גְּאֻלָּה occurs in 25:24, 26, 29 (twice), 31, 32, 48, 51, 52; Ruth 4:6, 7; Jer 32:7, 8; Ezek 11:15. It is a technical legal term for the payment of money or goods for the restoration of land to its former owner, and for the liberation of an enslaved person. In this chapter, it is used to describe three different aspects of the process: the right of redemption (Lev 25:24, 29a, 31, 32, 48); the price of redemption (25:26, 51, 52); and the time during which redemption can take place (25:29b).

25:25 יָמוּךְ—This verb, the Qal imperfect of מוּךְ, means "become impoverished" (*HALOT*). It recurs in 25:35, 39, 47; 27:8.

אָחִיךָ—This could also be translated "fellow Israelite." It recurs in 25:35, 36, 39, 46, 47, 48.

גֹּאֲלוֹ—A גֹּאֵל (also in 25:26), "a kinsman-redeemer," was the oldest, close male blood relative, as defined in 25:48–49. Together with the other adult males, he was responsible for the solidarity, protection, and survival of the family, with its members, as a viable social and economic unit on its plot of land.

הַקָּרֹב—See 21:2, 3.

---

9 Milgrom, *Leviticus 23–27*, 2181–82.

10 Rabinowitz, "A Biblical Parallel to a Legal Formula from Ugarit."

11 Milgrom, *Leviticus 23–27*, 2188.

וְגָאַל—This verb was used for buying back land or a house that had been sold and for ransoming the freedom of a person enslaved for debt. It recurs in 25:30, 33, 48, 49 (three times), 54; 27:13, 15, 19, 20 (twice), 27, 28, 31, 33.

25:26 וְהִשִּׂיגָה יָדוֹ—This is literally "his hand has reached, has enough." See the textual notes on 5:11. The expression recurs in 25:47, 49.

25:27 הָעֹדֵף—This could also be translated "the remainder." See Ex 16:23; 26:12, 13; Num 3:46, 48, 49.

25:28 וְאִם לֹא־מָצְאָה יָדוֹ דֵּי הָשִׁיב לוֹ—This is literally "if his hand does not gain the sufficient amount to return [the land] to himself."

בְּיַד—This is literally "in the hand of."

וְיָצָא—This is literally "and it shall go out." We render it "it shall become free." It could also be translated "and it shall be released." See 25:30, 31, 33, 41, 54. The use of this term for release from debt echoes its use to describe the exodus from Egypt as a release from slavery. This is reinforced by its juxtaposition with the Hiphil forms of it in the formula for divine emancipation in 25:38, 41–42 and 25:54–55.

25:29 בֵּית־מוֹשַׁב עִיר חוֹמָה—This is literally "a house of a settlement of a city of [with a] wall."

מִמְכָּרוֹ ... גְּאֻלָּתוֹ׃—The pronominal suffixes on these nouns may refer either to the seller ("his sale [of the house]," "his time of redemption [during which he can redeem the house]") or to the house itself ("its sale," "the time of its redemption"). Our translation follows the second option.

יָמִים—The term יָמִים, "days, "functions as a collective noun for a year (as also in Ex 13:10; Judg 17:10; 1 Sam 27:7).

25:30 וְקָם—The term קָם לְ is a commercial idiom for the transferal of property from one owner to another (27:19; cf. Gen 23:17, 20).[12]

אֲשֶׁר־לֹא [לוֹ]—The Kethib is the negative particle לֹא, which would mean "a town with *no* wall." The Qere is לוֹ, yielding "a town which there is *to it* a wall" (i.e., "a town which has a wall"). The preceding verse (25:29) requires that we follow the Qere, which is supported by the Samaritan Pentateuch and the versions.

לְדֹרֹתָיו—This is literally "for his generations," but we render it "to ... his descendants."

25:31 הַחֲצֵרִים—This could also be translated "homesteads, farm buildings." See Gen 25:16; Deut 2:23; Josh 13:23, 28.

עַל־שְׂדֵה הָאָרֶץ—This is literally "as a field of the land."

יֵחָשֵׁב—The singular form of the verb is used in a distributive sense.

25:32 וְעָרֵי הַלְוִיִּם בָּתֵּי עָרֵי אֲחֻזָּתָם—This is literally "As for the towns of the Levites, the houses of the towns of their possession." For the towns of the Levites, see Num 35:1–8; Josh 21:1–42; 1 Chr 6:54–81.

25:33 מִן־הַלְוִיִּם—This could also be translated "from the Levites." In that case this would refer to a lay Israelite redeeming his house from a Levite and the translation of the clause would be this: "Whoever redeems it from any of the Levites." But this

---

[12] Milgrom, *Leviticus 23–27*, 2199.

does not fit the context with its discussion of houses in Levitical towns and the rationale in 25:33b.

מִמְכַּר־בַּיִת וְעִיר אֲחֻזָּתוֹ—This is literally "the sale of the house and town of his possession." In this case עִיר, "town, "is best taken as any other part of the town apart from his residence (see 2 Sam 5:7; 12:27; and 2 Ki 10:25 for the use of this noun as a part or quarter of a town or city). Alternatively, the *waw* on וְעִיר could be explicative: "that is, in the town of his possession."

25:34 מִגְרַשׁ—See Num 35:2, 3, 4, 5, 7. The usual translation for מִגְרָשׁ is "pastureland." But that is too broad. The term here refers to the areas around the towns that are fenced off as enclosures for livestock.

25:35 אָחִיךָ—This could also be translated "fellow Israelite."

וּמָטָה יָדוֹ—The exact sense of this unique clause, "and his hand totters/fails," is difficult to ascertain. מָטָה is the Qal third feminine singular perfect of מוט, which here means "to be in economic difficulties, 'be shaky' " (*HALOT,* 2). The verb's subject, יָד, is a feminine noun. The LXX translates the clause as "and he is powerless with the hands." It seems to be a commercial idiom that is used for a bankrupt person.[13] In this case the farmer who had sold off part of his land fell further into debt and lost all of his land to his creditor. He became a tenant who worked his own land for his creditor for a share of the harvest. He was thus totally dependent on his creditor for his livelihood.

עִמָּךְ—See the textual notes on 25:6.

וְהֶחֱזַקְתָּ בּוֹ—The combination here of the Hiphil of חָזַק (הֶחֱזִיק) and the preposition בְּ is usually construed as "supporting" or "providing help" for the person (LXX).[14] Thus *HALOT* defines it here as "to sustain a person in debt" (s.v. חזק, Hiphil, 1; see also BDB, s.v. חָזַק, Hiphil, 6 c). However, the Israelites were also not obliged to offer interest free loans to resident aliens. Therefore it is preferable to see this as a reference to the seizure of a person (an impoverished fellow Israelite) who has failed to repay a debt. *HALOT* includes this possible meaning for the use of the verb in this verse: "to 'seize' and employ as a domestic" (s.v. חזק, Hiphil, 1).

גֵּר וְתוֹשָׁב—See the textual note on this expression in 25:23. Since the former landholder has lost the use of his land, he now has the economic status of a resident alien, a person without land and the livelihood that comes from having land to farm.

וָחַי עִמָּךְ׃—We render this as "let him retain his livelihood under your authority." Literally it is "and he lives with you." This is the command that pertains to the situation described in the preceding part of the verse. An alternative view is that the whole of 25:35 could be construed as the protasis for 25:36. In that case this last clause of 25:35 would be translated "so that he retains his livelihood under your authority."

Regarding וָחַי, the Qal third masculine singular perfect of חָיָה with *waw* consecutive, see the textual note on the same form in 18:5. A similar form occurs in 25:36.

---

[13] Milgrom, *Leviticus 23–27*, 2205.

[14] Milgrom, *Leviticus 23–27*, 2206, argues that that meaning would require בְּיָדוֹ rather than בּוֹ. See the various syntactical constructions in *HALOT,* s.v. חזק, Hiphil, 1.

Here the verb means "to subsist, live, have one's livelihood." The LXX and most commentators interpret this to mean that the debtor resides in the household of the creditor, but חָיָה is never used in that sense. It indicates that the debtor may still live as a tenant on his land and draw what he needs to live from its produce before he repays his debt from his share of its produce.[15]

25:36–37 See the similar laws in Ex 22:24 (ET 22:25) and Deut 23:20–21 (ET 23:19–20). Like Ex 22:24 (ET 22:25), Lev 25:36–37 forbids the extraction of interest from loans to an impoverished Israelite, rather than from any Israelite, as in Deut 23:20 (ET 23:19).

25:36 נֶשֶׁךְ—This term here refers to interest taken in advance when the loan is made. The term recurs in 25:37; see its use also in Ex 22:24 (ET 22:25); Deut 23:20 (ET 23:19); cf. Ezek 18:8, 13, 17; 22:12; Prov 28:8.

וְתַרְבִּית—See Ezek 18:8, 13, 17; 22:12; and Prov 28:8 for the use of תַּרְבִּית and its synonym מַרְבִּית in Lev 25:37. These terms may originally have been used in a subsistence economy for the repayment of a loan with an increased amount of foodstuff, but they seem eventually to have become the terms for interest collected at the end of the loan.[16]

וְחֵי אָחִיךָ—*HALOT* (s.v. חיה, Qal) includes this form (חֵי) in this verse as a different vocalization of the same Qal third masculine singular verb form (חַי) that occurred in 25:35. GKC, § 76 i, suggests that this should be repointed as וָחַי as in 25:35, but that emendation is unnecessary.

25:38 אֲנִי יְהוָה אֱלֹהֵיכֶם אֲשֶׁר־הוֹצֵאתִי אֶתְכֶם מֵאֶרֶץ מִצְרָיִם—See the textual notes on 19:36. Similar clauses recur in 25:42, 55; 26:13, 45.

הוֹצֵאתִי—This literally means "who brought you out." We translate it as "who freed you" because it is the Hiphil of the Qal verb יָצָא, which in 25:28 and other verses refers to property that goes free in the Jubilee.

לָתֵת לָכֶם אֶת־אֶרֶץ כְּנַעַן—This is the only time that the formula for deliverance from Egypt and emancipation from slavery is combined with the formula for the bestowal of the land.

לִהְיוֹת לָכֶם לֵאלֹהִים׃—See the textual notes on 11:45 and 26:12.

25:39 וְנִמְכַּר—This Niphal of מָכַר is best understood as a passive, "is sold," rather than as a reflexive; it should not be translated as "he sells himself." The Niphal recurs in 25:42, 47, 48, 50. The Niphal of מָכַר is used for the sale of property in 25:23, 34, and it should have the same passive meaning when used for the sale of people.

לֹא־תַעֲבֹד בּוֹ עֲבֹדַת עָבֶד׃—See Ex 1:14.

25:40 This law differs from the legislation in Ex 21:2–6 and Deut 15:12–18 that provides for the release of slaves on the seventh year.

25:41 מִשְׁפַּחְתּוֹ—This could also be translated "his clan."

אֲחֻזַּת אֲבֹתָיו—This is literally "the holding/possession of his fathers."

25:42 עֲבָדַי—This could also be translated "slaves." See 25:55b.

---

15 Milgrom, *Leviticus 23–27*, 2208–9.

16 Loewenstamm, "נשך *and* מ/תרבית"; Milgrom, *Leviticus 23–27*, 2209–10.

אֲשֶׁר־הוֹצֵאתִי—This could also be translated "whom I brought out."

מִמְכֶּרֶת עָבֶד׃—This could also be translated "as slaves are sold/at the price of a slave."

25:43 תִרְדֶּה בוֹ—See רָדָה, "to rule," also in 25:46, 53; 26:17.

בְּפָרֶךְ—See 25:46, 53; cf. Ex 1:13, 14.

25:44 הַגּוֹיִם—See 18:24, 28; 26:33, 38, 45.

25:45 וְגַם מִבְּנֵי הַתּוֹשָׁבִים הַגָּרִים עִמָּכֶם מֵהֶם תִּקְנוּ—This is literally "And also from the children of the residents who live as aliens under your authority, from them you may buy."

וּמִמִּשְׁפַּחְתָּם—This could also be translated "clan."

הוֹלִידוּ—This is literally "they cause to be born" or "they beget."

25:46 וְהִתְנַחַלְתֶּם אֹתָם לִבְנֵיכֶם אַחֲרֵיכֶם—This could also be translated "And you may have them as your own inheritance for your children after you."

לָרֶשֶׁת—See 20:24.

לְעֹלָם בָּהֶם תַּעֲבֹדוּ—See the same use of עָבַד בְּ in 25:39 and Ex 1:14.

לֹא־תִרְדֶּה בוֹ בְּפָרֶךְ׃—This reprise of 25:43a marks the end of an extended parenthesis and the return to the main topic.

25:47 וְכִי תַשִּׂיג יַד גֵּר וְתוֹשָׁב—This is literally "And when the hand of a resident alien reaches out." See the textual notes on 5:11 and 25:23.

אָחִיךָ—This could also be translated "fellow Israelite."

מִשְׁפַּחַת גֵּר׃—This could also be translated "the alien's clan."

25:49 דֹדוֹ—See 10:4; 20:20. The term דּוֹד is used for a paternal uncle.

מִשְּׁאֵר בְּשָׂרוֹ—This is literally "who is from the intimate flesh of his body." See the textual notes on 18:6.

מִמִּשְׁפַּחְתּוֹ—This could also be translated "from his clan." This refers to any blood relative.

25:53 לֹא־יִרְדֶּנּוּ בְּפֶרֶךְ לְעֵינֶיךָ׃—This is literally "He shall not rule over him harshly in your eyes."

25:55 כִּי־לִי בְנֵי־יִשְׂרָאֵל—The use of לִי here for the Israelites mirrors its use for the land in 25:23.

אֲנִי יְהוָה אֱלֹהֵיכֶם׃—See 25:17, 38; 26:1, 2, 13, 44, 45.

Commentary

Structure

The divine speech of Leviticus 25 comes in two parts. The first part of the speech (25:1–22) consists of two units of legislation, 25:2b–7and 25:8–17, which culminate in the formula of divine self-introduction in 25:17b and in the admonition of 25:18–22. In fact, the promise of a good harvest on the sixth year in 25:18–22 harks back to the legislation of the Sabbatical Year in 25:2b–7 and so frames the discussion of the Jubilee in 25:8–17.

The second part of the speech (25:23–55) is introduced by a general prohibition of the sale of land and the institution of the right of redemption in 25:23–24. This is elaborated in three main sections: (1) 25:25–34; (2) 25:35–38; and (3) 25:39–54. Each of those three sections is introduced by

כִּי־יָמוּךְ אָחִיךָ, "when your brother is impoverished." Three parentheses, introduced by means of pending cases, are inserted in these sections. While the first of these deals with the houses in rural villages (25:31), the second considers the houses of the Levites in their towns (25:32–34). The third deals with the right of the Israelites to own slaves (25:44–46). The first two sections (25:25–34 and 25:35–38), which treat the redemption of the land, culminate in an elaborate formula of divine self-introduction in 25:38, while the third section (25:39–54) and the second part of the speech as a whole (25:23–55) culminate in a declaration of the status of the Israelites as God's servants and the formula of divine self-introduction in 25:55.

Many of the units in this speech are arranged as chiasms. Thus we have parallel chiasms in 25:6–7; 25:9; 25:10b–13; 25:14–17; 25:37; 25:38; and 25:50–53.[17] In addition we have introverted pivotal chiasms in 25:18b–19; 25:20–22; 25:22; 25:36–43; and 25:47–49.[18] Besides that, many key clauses are repeated, such as the declaration of Jubilee (25:10, 11, 12), the admonition to fear God (25:17, 36, 43), the formula for emancipation from Egypt (25:38a, 42a, 55b), the warning against trampling on any Israelite (25:43a, 46b, 53b), and the declaration that the Israelites are God's servants (25:42a, 55a).

The material in this speech is interwoven with recurring key words. Thus the main word אֶרֶץ, "land," appears twenty times. It is accompanied by יוֹבֵל, "Jubilee," which occurs fourteen times; מָכַר, "sell," thirteen times; אֲחֻזָּה, "holding," thirteen times; שׁוּב, "return," eleven times; גָּאַל, "redeem," ten times; גְּאֻלָּה, "redemption," nine times; the root שׁבת, "sabbath," nine times; and מִמְכָּר, "sale," seven times.

The structure of this pericope can be outlined as follows:

- I. Introduction to Leviticus 25–26 (25:1–2a)
    - A. God's address to Moses at Mount Sinai (25:1)
    - B. God's commission of Moses (25:2a)
- II. Speech about rest for the land and its redemption (25:2b–55)
    - A. Institution of the Sabbatical Year and the Jubilee (25:2b–22)
        - 1. The Sabbatical Year (25:2b–7)
            - a. Institution of rest for the land (25:2b)
            - b. Explication of the basic regulation (25:3–7)
                - i. Normal agriculture for six years (25:3)
                - ii. Rest from agriculture on the seventh year (25:4–7)
        - 2. The enactment of the Jubilee (25:8–17)
            - a. Institution of the Jubilee (25:8–10)
                - i. Its date (25:8)
                - ii. Its proclamation (25:9–10a)
                    - • Sounding of a ram's horn throughout the land (25:9)
                    - • Consecration of the year and proclamation of release (25:10a)

---

[17] See Milgrom, *Leviticus 23–27*, 2159, 2163, 2170, 2176–77; 2211; 2212; 2234.

[18] See Milgrom, *Leviticus 23–27*, 2180, 2219, 2233.

            iii. Purpose: the return of people to their land and kin group (25:10b)
        b. Explication of the basic regulation (25:11–13)
            i. Cessation of agricultural work for that holy year (25:11–12a)
            ii. Consumption of self-grown produce from the land (25:12b)
            iii. Return of people to their landholdings (25:13)
        c. Terms for leasing land before the Jubilee (25:14–17)
            i. Prohibition of cheating in leasing the land (25:14)
            ii. Payment according to the years until the next Jubilee (25:15–16)
            iii. Fear of God as motivation for not cheating (25:17a)
            iv. God's self-introduction (25:17b)
    3. Admonition for the observance of the Sabbatical Year (25:18–22)
        a. Observance of these laws as the condition for security and good harvests (25:18–19)
        b. God's promise of blessing on the harvest of the sixth year (25:20–22)
B. Institution of redemption for the land and its tenants (25:23–55)
    1. God's institution of the right of redemption (25:23–24)
        a. Prohibition of the sale of the title to God's land (25:23a)
        b. Status of Israelites as resident aliens under God (25:23b)
        c. God's provision for the redemption of the land (25:24)
    2. The redemption of land forfeited to pay for a debt (25:25–28)
        a. Duty of redemption of land by the closest kinsman (25:25)
        b. Right of redemption by the landholder (25:26–27)
        c. Release of the land on the Jubilee (25:28)
    3. The redemption of houses forfeited to pay for a debt (25:29–34)
        a. Houses in walled towns (25:29–30)
            i. Right of redemption during the year after the sale (25:29)
            ii. Ownership of the unredeemed house by the buyer after that year (25:30)
        b. Houses in rural villages (25:31)
            i. Their classification as land with the right of redemption (25:31a)
            ii. Release on the Jubilee (25:31b)
        c. Houses of Levites (25:32–34)
            i. Right of redemption with release at the Jubilee for the houses in their towns (25:32–33)
            ii. Embargo on the sale of the stock paddocks around their towns (25:34)
    4. The treatment of an indebted Israelite who had lost all his land (25:35–38)
        a. Permission to retain his livelihood as a tenant on his land (25:35)
        b. Prohibition of taking interest on the loan (25:36)
        c. Prohibition of lending money or foodstuff with interest (25:37)
        d. God's self-introduction as Israel's emancipator, land-giver, and God (25:38)

5. The redemption of indebted servants (25:39–55)
   a. An indebted Israelite held by an Israelite (25:39–43)
      i. Treatment as hired worker rather than a slave (25:39–40a)
      ii. Release with children at the Jubilee (25:40b–41)
      iii. Emancipation of the Israelites as the reason for their release (25:42a)
      iv. Prohibition of their sale and mistreatment motivated by the fear of God (25:42b–43)
   b. Excursus on the ownership of slaves by the Israelites (25:44–46)
      i. Permission for acquisition of foreign slaves (25:44–45a)
      ii. Status of slaves as part of the patrimony (25:45b–46a)
      iii. Prohibition of the mistreatment of Israelite servants (25:46b)
   c. The redemption of an indebted Israelite from slavery to foreigners (25:47–54)
      i. Right of redemption by the kinsman or the debtor (25:47–49)
      ii. Computation of the price of redemption (25:50–52)
      iii. Status of the Israelite as a hired worker (25:53a)
      iv. Warning against the toleration of mistreatment (25:53b)
      v. Release with children at the Jubilee (25:54)
   d. Reason for the redemption of Israelites (25:55)
      i. Status of Israelites as God's servants (25:55a)
      ii. God's self-introduction (25:55b)

Theological Analysis

The importance of these laws is shown by the reference to God's gift of them to Moses at Mount Sinai. This legislation anticipates the settlement of the Israelites in the land of Canaan. In this speech God establishes three interrelated institutions for their life with him on his land: the Sabbatical Year, the Jubilee, and the redemption of the land with its tenants. All of these are part of the same complex arrangement by which God links the agricultural calendar for work on the land with the liturgical calendar for the enactment of the divine service at the sanctuary.

The speech begins with the institution of a year of rest for the land (25:3). Just as the Israelites were to rest on the Sabbath from their work, so the land was given a time of rest from its work of production (25:4–7). On each seventh year, the landholders let the land lie fallow. The fields were left unsown, and the vineyards were left unpruned; their owners too did not harvest their produce for commercial use. The self-sown grain and the self-grown grapes were not gathered up for storage and sale. They were treated as common property that was available to be gleaned as food by all the people and animals that resided on the land. Thus the land was given a time of rest from human cultivation.

The institution of a Sabbath for the land was coupled with the institution of the Jubilee for those who worked it. On the seventh, Sabbatical Year (or on each fiftieth year; see the textual notes on 25:10), the Israelites were to proclaim a holy year throughout the land. This was called the Jubilee. Just as God had ordained seven weeks of harvest that culminated in the Feast of Pentecost (23:15–16), so the years of harvest culminated in this Jubilee (25:8–10). It was proclaimed on the Day of Atonement with the sounding of a ram's horn throughout the land. The blowing of the horn accomplished two things. First, it announced God's amnesty to all debtors, the release from debt for all the inhabitants of his land (25:10). This meant that the Israelites who had lost the use of their land and had been forced to work off their debt with their creditors could "return" to their land and their kin group (25:10, 13). They thereby regained their patrimony, unencumbered by the burden of debt. Second, the horn consecrated the whole year on which the Jubilee was enacted (25:10a). It was to be treated by the Israelites as a holy year, a holiday from agriculture, a year for all inhabitants to eat what the land provided for them by itself without their work (25:11, 12).

The institution of the Jubilee is followed in 25:14–17 by the consideration of the case in which a person "sold" some part of his landholding to raise money or pay a debt. That legislation emphasized three things. First, the case was introduced and concluded by the prohibition of cheating by the seller or the buyer in the transaction. This, however, was a matter of morality, something that could not be enforced by any human court, an obligation that was motivated by the fear of God. Second, it was made clear that the person who "bought" the land did not gain the title to it; he only purchased the use of it for a limited period of time. He became its usufructuary, with the right to cultivate it and obtain its produce for a certain number of harvests. In effect, he leased the land. Third, the value of the land depended on the number of harvests and years until the Jubilee. The greater the number of years until the Jubilee, the more the land was worth; the less years, the less it was worth.

The legislation that instituted and regulated the Sabbatical Year and the enactment of the Jubilee concluded with an admonition that encouraged the Israelites to observe the Sabbatical Years (25:18–22). God made two promises to those who observed these statutes. First, the land would be so productive that the Israelites would be secure and have more than enough to eat. Second, God allayed their understandable fears about making ends meet in the Sabbatical Years. He personally promised them that he would bless them so richly and provide such a bumper harvest for them on the sixth year so that they would not just have enough to last until the eighth year, but into the ninth year as well. He therefore called on them to trust in his provision for them by observing the Sabbatical Years.

In the second part of the speech, God elaborated on what he had said in 25:10b about the return of the Israelites to their patrimony by instituting the right of redemption for the land and its tenants. The particular cases of redemption were introduced by a general decree from God in 25:23–24. The right of redemption was based on God's ownership of the land. It was his royal estate. This meant that the Israelites too belonged to God as his royal servants. They, then, were not landowners. Rather, they resided on the land at his discretion, as if they were resident aliens. So, since both the land and the people belonged to God, he decreed that the people should provide for the redemption of the land. The cases that follow show that this has two sides to it. On the one hand, all leased land returned to its original holders (25:25–38). On the other hand, all landholders returned to their holdings (25:39–55).

The speech first outlines how the right of redemption applied to land and houses in 25:25–28. It begins with the case of a man who "sold" part of his land to raise money to support his family in a time of need or to pay a debt (25:25–28). In that case, his paternal next of kin was obliged to act as his redeemer. If the redeemer could afford to redeem the land, he was bound to buy it back to make sure that it remained in the family. The law, however, did not indicate how he was repaid for this intervention. He presumably had the use of it until the Jubilee (25:33). If the man had no one to redeem the land for him, he could, if he prospered, reclaim the land at any time, provided that he paid for it. The price that he paid was determined by the criteria enunciated in 25:15–16. After he had redeemed the land, he returned to his holding and reclaimed it for himself as his patrimony. But even if no one could afford to redeem the land, it was released at the Jubilee, so that its former holder could return to it. In this case God himself acted as the Redeemer of the land.

The next case considers the right of redemption for houses (25:29–34). They differed from rural property in that they were not necessary for the economic support and livelihood of the family. The general rule was that, unlike the land, a house in a walled town could only be redeemed for the period of a year after its "sale." If it was not redeemed within that year, the right of redemption lapsed; it became the property of its "buyer." It became his patrimony that was passed on to his descendants. Since the title to the house was thereby forfeited, it was not released and returned to its former owner at the Jubilee.

There were, however, two exceptions to this rule. The first was the case of houses in rural villages that had no walls to enclose them (25:31). Since those houses belonged to the land on which they stood, they were treated like the land. They were therefore redeemed like the land; if they had not been redeemed beforehand, they were released at the Jubilee. The second exception was the houses of the Levites in their towns (25:32–34). Since they had no plot of land, the houses that belonged to them were their holdings from God in the land. They therefore retained an unlimited right of redemption. In fact, if they had to "sell" their houses or any of the urban property, that property could not be purchased by strangers, but could only be redeemed by a kinsman, a fellow Levite. Like the land, these holdings reverted to their owners at the Jubilee. Yet even though the Levites could "sell" their houses, they could not "sell" the paddocks, fenced off for their livestock, around their towns. This was their perpetual holding, part of their livelihood from God.

Whereas 25:25–34 considers the plight of an impoverished landholder who had been forced to sell off some of his land or his house in a town, 25:35–37 deals with an even more extreme case of impoverishment. In this instance an Israelite had become so indebted that he lost control of all his land. He had therefore lost his livelihood. His status was the same as a resident alien, a landless person. Two extraordinary provisions were made for him. First, the creditor let him reside on his holding as its manager with the right to take what he needed for his livelihood from the produce of the land. He therefore continued to receive what he and his family needed to survive. Second, the creditor was forbidden either to demand any payment of interest up front or at the end of a loan, or to lend money or foodstuff at interest up front or demand interest at the end of the loan. Thus the creditor was not allowed to take advantage of the impoverished person in his vulnerable state to rob him of his livelihood and push him even deeper into debt. These obligations to an impoverished family were motivated by the fear of God and Israel's experience of him as their emancipator and land-giver.

After considering the redemption of the land, 25:39–55 deals with the status and treatment of Israelites who sold themselves to pay off a debt. It begins with the case of Israelites who worked off a debt to their fellow Israelites (25:39–43). The Israelites were not allowed to treat such people as their slaves. Instead, they employed them as hired laborers who lived with them on their land and used their wages to pay off their debt (cf. 25:6). Even if they had not yet paid off their full debt, they and their children were released from service at the Jubilee, so that they could return to their kin group free from debt and reclaim their holding from its buyer or its redeemer.

They were to be released then, because they were God's royal servants, his slaves. They belonged to him because he had released them from slavery in the land of Egypt. Since they belonged to God, they could not be sold as slaves. Their Israelite employers were therefore to fear God and take care not to trample on them "harshly" as the Israelites had been trampled on in Egypt (cf. Ex 1:13, 14). But even though the Israelites could not enslave their fellow Israelites, they were allowed to own slaves that had been purchased from foreigners or from aliens living with them in the land of Canaan (25:44–46). Such slaves were part of their patrimony, permanent property that they could bequeath together with their landholding as an inheritance to their descendants. While they could work these foreigners as slaves, they were not allowed to trample harshly over any Israelite bond servant.

The case of Israelites in debt to their fellow Israelites is followed by the case of Israelites in debt to foreigners (25:47–55). Their plight was to be alleviated in three ways. First, they retained the right of redemption. Their closest kinsman or any of their kinsfolk were obliged to redeem them. If the debtor prospered, he could, like the man who had lost his land, redeem himself. Two criteria were set down to determine the price of redemption: the length of time from the sale of the person to the Jubilee (cf. 25:15–16, 27) and the wages that he would have earned if he were a hired laborer. The foreigner was thereby compensated for the loss of work from the indebted Israelite. Second, the foreigner was to treat the indebted Israelite as a hired worker, rather than a slave. And the Israelites were to make sure that he was not treated harshly as if he were a chattel slave. The yearly work of the Israelite was therefore sold, just as the yearly produce of the land was sold (cf. 25:15–16). Third, even if they had not been redeemed beforehand, they and their children were released, free of debt, on the Jubilee, because they, like all the Israelites, were God's royal servants. They did not belong to any foreigners; they belonged to him, since he had released them from servitude in Egypt.

Theological Significance

The legislation in this chapter develops a theology of the land. It shows how God, the clans of Israel, and the land are interconnected. This theological understanding of the land is spelled out against the backdrop of a program of reform that was implemented occasionally by kings in ancient Mesopotamia. When a new king came onto his throne, he, quite often, proclaimed a kind of amnesty for his kingdom, called a *misarum.* It involved the cancellation of debts, the liberation of slaves, the restoration of land, and the rectification of economic injustices. At Sinai the Lord, the King of Israel, instituted something similar to that for his people. But he did not do it as a political gesture to gather support at the beginning of his reign; he instituted it as a liturgical benefaction that recurred periodically on each seventh year and fiftieth year. By means of it, the God who released Israel from slavery continued to release his people from slavery. It was part of his gracious provision for them in the land that he provided for them.

Three times in the chapter God reminded the Israelites that he had committed himself to them as their God (25:17, 38, 55). He had freed them from slavery in Egypt (25:38, 42, 55). He had brought them out of the land of Egypt so that he could give them the land of Canaan (25:2, 38) and be their God, a God who resided with them and gave them access to himself in the divine service (25:38; cf. Ex 29:45). The Israelites, who had been slaves in Egypt, had been freed from all human masters by being transferred into God's realm and taken into his service.

God's speech develops the implications of his treatment of his people for the land and for the Israelites as its inhabitants. The land that God promised to give to them was his land (25:23). He owned it. It was his royal estate. The land of Israel belonged to him, just as in the ancient world temple cities and tracts of land around them commonly belonged to the local gods and their sanctuaries. Like the kings in the ancient world, God granted his land to his royal servants, the Israelites, as their livelihood. Through the land he provided what was necessary for the livelihood of his people and the solidarity of their families

(25:18–19). He did not give the land to individual persons, but to kin groups, the clans and fathers' houses that made up Israel as a tribal society (25:10, 41, 45, 47, 49). Yet the land still belonged to him. The Israelites held it in fealty, under the condition of loyalty and service to him. They did not own the land, but received it as their "holding" from God.[a] Theologically speaking, they were not landowners, but "resident aliens," tenants who had received the land from God; they worked it as shareholders and depended on him for their livelihood in it (25:23).

(a) Lev 25:10, 13, 24, 25, 27, 28, 41

Since the land belonged to God, the Israelites were to return it to him every seven years. Thus, just as God had rested on the seventh day after creation (Gen 2:2–3) and had provided a regular day of rest for Israel on each Sabbath, so the land too was to observe a Sabbath to the Lord once every seven years (25:2, 4, 5). Like the Israelites on the Sabbath, the land was to acknowledge its God by resting from its work of agricultural production. For that to happen, the Israelites were forbidden to cultivate their fields for the duration of that Sabbatical Year. Since the land belonged to God, the Israelites were also forbidden to sell it (25:23). At the most, they could lease it out and thus sell off its produce for a limited number of years (25:14–16).

What's more, God ensured that the land would not be alienated from him and the kin groups who held it by making two further provisions for his people. First, he established the right of redemption for the land (25:24). This meant that the owner or any member of his kin group could, at any time, buy back the land that had been claimed by a creditor. Second, God himself acted as the Redeemer of the land by proclaiming its remission, the release of the land every fifty years (25:10). This meant that the landholders and their families could return to their ancestral holding once again (25:10, 13, 27, 28, 41). Since God himself provided release for his people on the Jubilee, it was consecrated by the sounding of the horn (25:9) and observed as a holy time (25:10). The sound of the horn was, as it were, the voice of God proclaiming release and calling his people to return to their homeland (cf. Is 27:13).

Like the land (Lev 25:23), the Israelites too belonged to God (25:55). Since he had freed them from slavery in Egypt, they were his "servants" (25:42, 55). Even though the same word was used in Hebrew (עֶבֶד) for a "slave" and a "servant," it could also be used to describe a person who was God's devotee, someone involved in the divine service, as well as God's deputy or his royal courtier. Thus, when God declared that the Israelites were his servants, he did not enslave them to himself. Rather, he appointed them as his royal courtiers, the administrators of his royal estates, his priestly servants.

Since they were his royal servants who lived on his royal estate, the land of Canaan, they retained their holdings, even if they fell into debt and lost the use of their land (25:35). They were also exempt from slavery to anyone else. The Israelites were therefore forbidden to charge interest on loans to any impoverished Israelites (25:36–37), enslave them (25:39), sell them as slaves (25:42), or allow aliens to mistreat them (25:53b). No Israelite was to be a slave.

At the most, an impoverished Israelite could lease out his labor to another Israelite or an alien creditor for a number of years to discharge a debt (25:39, 47). Such impoverished Israelites would then be employed as hired laborers who resided in the households of their creditors and worked for a set wage (25:40, 53). Their employers were also forbidden to treat them harshly, as if they were slaves (25:43, 46, 53).

God also made two provisions for those Israelites who had lost their freedom for a period of time, just as he had done for the land. First, he established the right of redemption for the Israelites who had been indentured for service to foreign creditors. Either their kinsfolk or they themselves could pay for their release from service at any time (25:47–52). Second, God also provided for their release from servitude on the Jubilee so that they could return to their kin groups and ancestral holdings (25:40–41, 54). At the Jubilee he freed them, just as he had freed Israel at the exodus (25:42, 55), so that they could return to their patrimony.

By instituting the Jubilee, God not only curbed the scope of injustice in the land, but also linked his provision of social and economic justice for the Israelites and their clans with the divine service and their worship of him. It is significant that the release of debtors was proclaimed on the Day of Atonement (25:9). The cancellation of the debts that the Israelites owed to their fellow Israelites issued from God's cancellation of their debts to him on that day. The restoration of sinful Israel to God resulted in the restoration of the debtor to his family. Through the gift of the Jubilee, God served the Israelites as their Redeemer and gave them freedom in the land. There he made himself available to them as their God in the divine service (25:17, 38, 55). In turn, he called on them to "fear" him as their God by treating his servants with respect (25:17, 36, 43). The exploitation of God's servants was an attack on God. He also called on the Israelites to redeem their kinsfolk, just as he had redeemed them. They were expected to treat each other as God had treated them.

Fulfillment by Christ

In Is 61:1–3 we have a remarkable prophecy. There, in words that recall Isaiah 35, the Suffering Servant of the Lord declares that he was sent by God to proclaim an extraordinary Jubilee. In the regular years of Jubilee, creditors released debtors from their debts and returned their land to them and their families. But in this year of Jubilee, God himself would free his people from their debt to him and avenge their enemies. Through his Messiah he would announce a royal amnesty, a year of divine favor that inaugurated his reign as King. He would free his people from oppression, enslavement, and imprisonment. He would comfort the bereft citizens of Zion by rebuilding their ruined city and reinstating them as a liturgical community.

Dan 9:24–27 picks up the main point of that prophecy and develops it further. Daniel had been meditating on the prophecy of Jeremiah that Jerusalem would remain desolate for seventy years. In answer to Daniel's prayer for un-

derstanding, the angel Gabriel came to him and explained that this referred to seventy Sabbatical Years. The messianic age—in which God would deal with iniquity and put an end to sin, atone for wickedness and usher in righteousness, fulfill all prophecy and anoint the most holy Messiah—would begin on the year of the tenth Jubilee after the rebuilding of Jerusalem (49 x 10 = 490 years). Thus the celebration of the Jubilee was taken as a type for the messianic age (cf. *Jubilees* 1:29; 11QMelchizedek). As Ströbel has shown, it inspired the chronological speculation that eventually led to the Jewish revolt against the Romans in A.D. 67.[19] However, that revolt was crushed by the Romans in A.D. 70. It was actually the ministry of Jesus of Nazareth, culminating in his atoning death and resurrection, that ushered in the messianic age about which the prophets had spoken.[20]

Luke's Gospel shows us that Jesus explained his ministry in the light of the prophecy in Is 61:1–3.[21] In Lk 4:16–30 the evangelist reports that after Jesus had been baptized, he returned to Nazareth and declared that he was ushering in the ultimate Jubilee. Jesus deliberately selected Is 61:1–2, with its allusion to Lev 25:10, as part of his Scripture reading in the synagogue for his inaugural sermon at the start of his public ministry (Lk 4:17–19). Luke reports this event because he regards it as "programmatic and foundational for the rest of Jesus' teaching," for Jesus released creation from its bondage to sin, sickness, and Satan and restored it to *"its proper state of harmony with the Creator."*[22]

(b) Lk 4:43; 7:22; 8:1; 16:16; 20:1; Acts 10:36; cf. Lk 9:6; Acts 5:42; 8:4, 12, 25, 35, 40; 11:20; 13:32; 14:7, 15, 21; 15:35; 16:10; 17:18

The ministry of Jesus fulfilled the prophecy of Isaiah in four ways.[23] First, Luke shows that Jesus was the Christ because he had been "anointed" by God's Spirit (Lk 4:18; Acts 4:27; 10:38). Second, as the Christ, the Anointed One, he was endowed with the Holy Spirit (Lk 4:1, 14) and operated by the power of the Spirit (Lk 4:14, 36; 5:17; Acts 10:38). Third, he was commissioned by God to "evangelize" the poor.[b] Fourth, in his preaching he proclaimed the "release" of those who had been enslaved by sin and oppressed by Satan. By his word of amnesty he freed them from blindness and death, sickness and the unclean

---

[19] Ströbel, "Die Ausrufung des Jobeljahres in der Nazarethpredigt Jesu."

[20] The chronology of the prophecy is a complicated topic. Dan 9:24–27 was not intended to give a timeline by which one could calculate the date of the first or second advent of Christ. He was born "in the fullness of time" (Gal 4:4), and no one knows the day of his return. See the discussion of this in Young, *Daniel,* 195–221, and in *The End Times: A Study on Eschatology and Millennialism* (a report of the Commission on Theology and Church Relations of The Lutheran Church—Missouri Synod, September 1989), 50–52.

[21] Is 61:1–3 may be regarded as the fifth Suffering Servant Song of Isaiah because in it the Servant himself speaks in the first person, even though the noun עֶבֶד, "servant," is absent from the passage. The previous four Suffering Servant Songs in Isaiah (42:1–9; 49:1–13; 50:4–11; and 52:13–53:12) also are prominent in the NT due to abundant quotations from and allusions to them. They too are cited by Jesus and the apostles to explain how Christ's ministry fulfills the OT Scriptures.

[22] Just, *Luke 1:1–9:50*, 191, 193.

[23] Tannehill, "The Mission of Jesus according to Luke IV," 68–72.

spirits. He accomplished all this by releasing them from their sins, their debts to God.[c] God's amnesty was his word of pardon for sinners.

(c) Lk 5:23–24; 7:47–49; 24:47; Acts 2:38; 5:31; 10:43; 13:38–39

The story of the sinful woman in Lk 7:36–50 shows how closely Jesus associated the forgiveness of sins with God's amnesty. The woman was both a sinner and a debtor to God.[24] Because Jesus was the Messiah, he cancelled her debt to God; he announced God's pardon by declaring: "Your sins are forgiven" (Lk 7:48). Jesus used the passive to indicate that God the Father had forgiven her. Like all debtors on the Jubilee, she could therefore go home in peace. What she had lost had been restored.

A second incident confirms the connection of Christ's ministry with the celebration of God's Jubilee. When John the Baptist was in prison, he sent two of his disciples to ascertain whether Jesus was indeed the Messiah (Mt 11:2–6; Lk 7:18–25). After Jesus healed many sick, blind, and demonized people, he sent the disciples back to John with the report that he was restoring the blind, the lame, the leprous, the deaf, and the dead while preaching the Good News to the poor. In this response Jesus alluded to Is 61:1–3; he claimed to usher in the new age of God's favor, the Jubilee of God. He did not release the Jewish people from economic indebtedness and restore their portion of land in Israel. Instead, he freed all people from all the evil powers that had oppressed and dehumanized them—even death itself—and so restored them to their place in the new order of creation that he established by his messianic ministry.

All those who trust in Jesus are beneficiaries of God's grace, his royal amnesty to his rebellious subjects. Just as the Jubilee issued from the Day of Atonement in ancient Israel, so their release from sin and all the powers of darkness is the result of Christ's sacrificial death (Acts 10:39–43; 13:26–39). They are released from all debts to God. They are therefore called to release others from their debts (Mt 6:12; 18:21–35). Through the death and resurrection of Jesus, they receive an eternal inheritance (1 Pet 1:3–5), their place in the "new heavens and new earth in which righteousness dwells" (2 Pet 3:13). They therefore await the time of universal restoration that had been foreshadowed by the celebration of the Jubilee in Israel (Acts 3:21).

Oh, for a thousand tongues to sing
  My great Redeemer's praise,
The glories of my God and King,
  The triumphs of his grace!

He breaks the pow'r of canceled sin;
  He sets the pris'ner free.
His blood can make the foulest clean;
  His blood avails for me.[25]

[24] Sanders, "Sins, Debts, and Jubilee Release."

[25] From "Oh, for a Thousand Tongues to Sing" by Charles Wesley (*LW* 276:1, 4).

Leviticus 26:1–46

Promises and Warnings
God's Policy for Israel

Translation

26 [1]"You shall not make godlings for yourselves, and you shall not set up a carved image or a pillar for yourselves, and you shall not place a figured pavement of stone on your land, to make prostration upon it, for I am the Lord your God. [2]You shall observe my Sabbaths and fear my sanctuary; I am the Lord.

[3]"If you walk according to my statutes and keep my commandments and enact them, [4]I will give your rains in their season, so that the land will yield its produce and the tree of the field will yield its fruit. [5]Threshing will overtake for you the vintage, and the vintage will overtake the sowing; you will eat your food to satiety and reside securely in your land. [6]I will give peace in the land so that you may lie down without anyone frightening you; I will eliminate the evil beast from the land, and a sword will not pass through your land. [7]You will pursue your enemies, and they will fall before you by the sword; [8]five of you will pursue a hundred, and a hundred of you will pursue ten thousand, and your enemies will fall before you by the sword. [9]I will turn my face to you, and I will make you fruitful and multiply you, and I will keep my covenant with you. [10]You will eat old [grain] long stored until you remove the old [grain] for the new. [11]I will place my dwelling in your midst, and my soul will not loathe you. [12]I will walk about in your midst, and I will be your God, and you will be my people. [13]I am the Lord your God, who freed you from the land of Egypt from being slaves to them. I broke the bars of your yoke so that I could make you walk along erectly.

[14]"But if you will not listen to me and do not enact all these commandments, [15]if you reject my statutes and your soul loathes my ordinances so that you do not enact all my commandments, so that you annul my covenant, [16]I, in turn, will do this to you: I will visit upon you panic, consumption, and fever, with failing eyes and pining away of life. You will sow your seed in vain, for your enemies will eat it. [17]I will set my face against you; you will be beaten by your enemies, and those who hate you will rule over you. You will flee, even though nobody pursues you.

[18]"If, despite these things, you will not listen to me, I will go on to discipline you seven times for your sins. [19]I will break your proud strength and make your sky like iron and your land like bronze, [20]so that your strength will be spent in vain; your land will not yield its produce, and the tree on the land will not yield its fruit.

[21]"If you still walk contrary to me and you are not willing to listen to me, I will add to you a smiting sevenfold according to your sins. [22]I will send against you the beast of the field so that it will bereave you and cut off your livestock; it will decimate you, so that your roads will be deserted.

[23]"If by these things you still will not be disciplined by me, but walk contrary to me, I myself will also walk contrary to you. [24]I too will strike you sevenfold for your sins; [25]I will bring on you an avenging sword with the vengeance of the covenant. If you withdraw into your cities, I will send an epidemic among you, so that you will be delivered into the hand of the enemy. [26]When I break your supply of bread, ten women will bake your bread in a single oven; they will distribute your bread by weight, and though you eat, you will not be satisfied.

[27]"But if, for all this, you will not listen to me and walk contrary to me, [28]I will walk contrary to you in anger; I myself will discipline you sevenfold for your sins. [29]You will eat the flesh of your sons, and the flesh of your daughters you will eat. [30]I will destroy your cult places, cut down your incense burners, and place your corpses on the corpses of your idols; my soul will loathe you. [31]I will turn your towns into a wasteland, make your holy places desolate, and will not smell your pleasing aroma. [32]I myself will make your land so desolate that your enemies who settle in it will be appalled at it, [33]while I scatter you among the nations and unsheath my sword after you. Then your land will be a desolation, and your cities will be a wasteland.

[34]"The land will then enjoy its Sabbaths all the days of its desolation, while you are in the land of your enemies. Then the land will rest and enjoy its Sabbaths. [35]All the days of its desolation it will rest, because it did not rest on your Sabbaths when you resided on it. [36]As for those of you who survive, I will bring despondency in their hearts in the lands of their enemies, so that the sound of a scattered leaf will pursue them. They will flee as though fleeing from a sword, and they will fall though no one pursues. [37]They will stumble, each over his brother, as if from a sword, even though no one pursues [them]. You will have no power to stand against your enemies, [38]and you will perish among the nations. The land of your enemies will devour you. [39]Those of you who survive will rot away in the lands of your enemies because of their iniquity; they will also rot away because of the iniquities of their ancestors as well. [40]They will confess their iniquity and the iniquity of their ancestors in the sacrilege that they committed against me and also that they walked contrary to me; [41]I, in turn, had to walk contrary to them, and I brought them into the land of their enemies. So their uncircumcised heart will then be humbled, and they will then accept the punishment for their iniquity.

[42]"I will remember my covenant with Jacob; I will also remember my covenant with Isaac and with Abraham. I will remember the land, [43]for the land will be deserted by them, so that it may enjoy its Sabbaths in its desolation without them, as they come to accept the punishment for their iniquity, because, and only because, they rejected my ordinances and their soul loathed my statutes. [44]Yet, for all that, when they are in the land of their enemies, I will not reject them, and I will not loathe them so as to exterminate them, annulling my covenant with them, for I am the Lord their God. [45]I will remember in their favor the covenant with their founders whom I freed from the land of Egypt, in the sight of the nations, to be their God; I am the Lord."

[46]These are the statutes, the ordinances, and the ritual instructions that the Lord instituted between himself and the Israelites at Mount Sinai through Moses.

Textual Notes

26:1 This is a continuation of God's speech in the previous chapter.

אֱלִילִם—See the textual note on this term in 19:4. This verse rewords the prohibition in Ex 20:23. The two clauses that follow the first prohibition indicate that these are not separate acts but are all part of the process of establishing an idolatrous cult.

וּפֶסֶל—See Ex 20:4; Deut 5:8. A פֶּסֶל is a statue carved out of wood or stone. It was often covered with gold or silver (Deut 7:25).

וּמַצֵּבָה—See Deut 16:22. A מַצֵּבָה was a stone stele. In ancient Israel steles were originally used as markers next to the altar in a sanctuary, as at Bethel (Gen 28:18, 22; 31:13; 35:14, 20; Hos 3:4; 10:1), or around the altar, as at Mount Sinai (Ex 24:4). Even though they were originally only forbidden if they had been used as idols in pagan cults (Ex 23:24; 34:13; Deut 7:5; 12:3), later all of them were forbidden as idolatrous in the reforms of Hezekiah and Josiah (1 Ki 14:23; 2 Ki 17:10; 23:14; Micah 5:13; see also 2 Ki 18:4).

וְאֶבֶן מַשְׂכִּית—This is literally "a stone of relief work." See Num 33:52; Ezek 8:12. This term refers to pictures of pagan gods and their symbols that were carved in relief on a flat stone surface. Whereas in Ezek 8:12 the relief was carved on the walls of a chamber in the temple, this prohibition in Leviticus envisages engravings that were carved on a pavement of stone before an idol to mark the place for prostration "upon it."[1]

לְהִשְׁתַּחֲוֹת—See Ex 20:5; Deut 5:9. This is the infinitive construct of the Hishtaphel conjugation (which adds the prefix -הִשְׁתַּ) of the verb חָוָה, which means "to bow down" in worship (*HALOT,* s.v. חוה II; *HALOT* calls the conjugation eshtafel). It is the technical ritual term for an act of submission and homage performed before the statue of a god. This ritual was enacted in three stages by bowing, kneeling, and then falling with hands and face upon the ground.[2]

כִּי אֲנִי יְהוָה אֱלֹהֵיכֶם׃—See the textual notes on 11:44. This clause is repeated in 26:13, 44 (cf. 26:2, 45).

26:2 שַׁבְּתֹתַי—See 19:3, 30. The root שׁבת appears eight times in this chapter, five times as the noun שַׁבָּת (26:2, 34 [twice], 35, 43) and three times in the Qal conjugation of the verb (26:34, 35 [twice]).

וּמִקְדָּשִׁי—See 19:30.

26:3 בְּחֻקֹּתַי—See the textual notes on 18:3. This noun is repeated in 26:15, 46. Cf. Ezek 5:6; 11:12, 20; 20:13, 16, 19, 21.

תֵּלֵכוּ—The metaphor of walking runs through this whole chapter. It is used for Israel's walk with God (26:3, 21, 23, 27, 40) and God's walk with Israel (26:12, 24, 28, 41). In fact, God declares that he wants to cause his people to "walk" (Hiphil of

---

1 Hurowitz, "אבן משכית—A New Interpretation."

2 Gruber, *Aspects of Nonverbal Communication in the Ancient Near East*, 1:90–145, 187–201; Keel, *The Symbolism of the Biblical World*, 309.

הָלַךְ) with him (26:13), like a person leading a blind man by the hand (Is 42:16), just as he "walked" the Israelites through the Red Sea (Ps 106:9) and the desert (Deut 8:2; 29:4 [ET 29:5]; Ps 136:16; Is 48:21; 63:13; Jer 2:6).

מִצְוֹתַי—See Lev 22:31 and the textual notes on 4:2.

26:4 וְנָתַתִּי גִשְׁמֵיכֶם בְּעִתָּם—See Deut 11:14; Jer 5:24; and the reworking of this promise in Ezek 34:26. The most important times for rain in the agricultural calendar were in late autumn and early winter for the opening rains before ploughing and sowing, and in early spring for the heading and filling out of the grain.

The verb נָתַן, "give, appoint," is used seven times in this chapter for God's activity in carrying out his promises and threats (26:4, 6, 11, 17, 19, 30, 31; cf. 26:46).

יְבוּלָהּ—See 26:20 and the reappearance of this promise in Ezek 34:27.

וְעֵץ הַשָּׂדֶה—This is the term for a cultivated fruit tree (Ex 9:25; Deut 20:19; Is 55:12; Jer 7:20; Ezek 17:24; 31:4, 5, 15; 34:27; Joel 1:12, 19).

פִּרְיוֹ—See Lev 25:19, 21.

26:5 The time for threshing was in June and July, after the grain had been gathered up and stored near the threshing floor.

בָּצִיר—See Judg 8:2; Is 24:13; 32:10; Jer 48:32; Joel 1:12, 19; Micah 7:1. The grape harvest was in July and August.

זָרַע—Crops were sown after the opening rains in November and December.

וַאֲכַלְתֶּם—The verb אָכַל, "eat," occurs seven times in this chapter (26:5, 10, 16, 26, 29 [twice], 38).

לָשֹׂבַע—This is literally "for satiation."

וִישַׁבְתֶּם לָבֶטַח בְּאַרְצְכֶם׃—See 25:18, 19 and Ezek 34:25, 28.

26:6 וְנָתַתִּי שָׁלוֹם—See Hag 2:9.

וְאֵין מַחֲרִיד—See Ezek 34:28; 39:26.

וְהִשְׁבַּתִּי חַיָּה רָעָה מִן־הָאָרֶץ—Note the quotation of this clause in Ezek 34:25. An "evil beast" (חַיָּה רָעָה) is a potential predator of human beings, such as a lion. See the use of the phrase חַיָּה רָעָה also in Ezek 5:17; 14:15, 21.

וְחֶרֶב לֹא־תַעֲבֹר בְּאַרְצְכֶם׃—See 26:25 and the allusion to the threat from that verse in Ezek 14:17.

וְחֶרֶב—The term "sword" is used seven times in this chapter as a synecdoche (of a part for the whole) for warfare (26:6, 7, 8, 25, 33, 36, 37).

26:8 מֵאָה—A "hundred" is equivalent to a later Roman century. It was the basic military unit in an Israelite army (Amos 5:3; cf. 1 Sam 29:2).

רְבָבָה—See Deut 32:30; Josh 23:10. "Ten thousand" made up an army, a legion that consisted of one hundred hundreds (Num 10:36; Judg 20:10).

26:9 וּפָנִיתִי אֲלֵיכֶם—See Num 16:15; 1 Ki 8:28; 2 Ki 13:23; Ezek 36:9.

וְהִפְרֵיתִי אֶתְכֶם וְהִרְבֵּיתִי אֶתְכֶם—See Gen 1:28; 9:1, 7; 17:6, 20; 26:4, 24; 28:3; 35:11; 48:4; Ex 1:7.

וַהֲקִימֹתִי אֶת־בְּרִיתִי—See Gen 17:19, 21; Ex 6:4; Deut 8:18; Ezek 16:60, 62; and the analysis of the idiom הֵקִים בְּרִית by Milgrom.[3] *HALOT* lists this idiom under the

---

[3] Milgrom, *Leviticus 23–27*, 2343–45.

meaning "keep" for the Hiphil of קוּם (Hiphil, 2 c). Also appropriate is "to **fulfil,** cause to happen what has been promised" (*HALOT,* s.v. קוּם, Hiphil, 3).

בְּרִיתִ֖י—See the textual notes on 24:8. The term "covenant" occurs eight times in this chapter (26:9, 15, 25, 42 [three times], 44, 45).

26:10 יָשָׁ֣ן—See 25:22.

נוֹשָׁ֑ן—See 13:11; Deut 4:25.

26:11 וְנָתַתִּ֥י—This is literally "I will give, grant."

מִשְׁכָּנִ֖י—See Ezek 37:27. The term מִשְׁכָּן refers to God dwelling with his people (rather than to the tabernacle as God's residence), which had already been granted in fulfillment of his promise in Ex 29:45 (cf. Ex 25:8; Num 5:3; 35:34; Zech 8:3, 8).

וְלֹֽא־תִגְעַ֥ל נַפְשִׁ֖י אֶתְכֶֽם׃—This is literally "my gullet will not expel you" or "my soul will not loathe you." The feminine noun נֶפֶשׁ is the subject of the verb גָּעַל, "to **loathe,** to feel disgust" (*HALOT,* Qal), which recurs in 26:15, 30, 43, 44. This strong idiom is used both for God's personal disgust with his people (26:11, 30, 44 [without נַפְשִׁי]) and for Israel's disgust at his ordinances (26:15, 43). Its synonym is "reject" (מָאַס, 26:15, 43).

26:12 וְהִתְהַלַּכְתִּי֙ בְּת֣וֹכְכֶ֔ם—See Gen 3:8; 2 Sam 7:6; Deut 23:15 (ET 23:14).

וְהָיִ֤יתִי לָכֶם֙ לֵֽאלֹהִ֔ים וְאַתֶּ֖ם תִּֽהְיוּ־לִ֥י לְעָֽם׃—The initial *waw* could also be translated "so that." These clauses literally say this: "And I will be God for you, and you will be a people for me." This so-called covenant formula has been closely examined by many scholars, including Smend and Rendtorff.[4] While this formula is anticipated in Ex 6:7, this is the first occurrence of the full formula in the canonical text in the Pentateuch. The full formula is repeated in various forms in Deut 26:17–18; 29:11–12 (ET 29:12–13); 2 Sam 7:24; Jer 7:23; 11:4; 24:7; 30:22; 31:1, 33; 32:38; Ezek 11:20; 14:11; 36:28; 37:23, 27; and Zech 8:8. In it God states the purpose of Israel's deliverance from Egypt (Ex 6:7; Lev 11:45; 22:32–33; 25:38; 26:45).

The first part of the formula ("I will be your God") is found by itself in Gen 17:7, 8; Ex 29:45; Lev 11:45; 22:33; 25:38; 26:45; Num 15:41; and Ezek 34:24. God's foundational promise in Gen 17:7–8 that he would be a God for Abraham and his descendants is fulfilled with the establishment of the divine service (Ex 29:44–45). The Lord acted as God for the Israelites by dwelling with them (Ex 29:45; Lev 26:45; cf. Ezek 37:26)[5] to sanctify them (Lev 11:45; 22:32–33; Num 15:40–41; cf. Deut 7:6; 14:2; 26:18–19; 28:9) and by giving them his land for them to live with him (Gen 17:8; Lev 25:38).

The second part of the formula ("you will be my people") occurs by itself in Deut 4:20; 7:6; 14:2; 27:9; 28:9; 1 Sam 12:22; 2 Ki 11:17; and Jer 13:11. It may be explicated in Lev 20:26, where God declares that he has separated the Israelites "for" himself so that they may "be holy to him." In Ezekiel the full formula appears in reversed order in all instances (Ezek 11:20; 14:11; 36:28; 37:23) apart from 37:27 which quotes Lev 26:12. Ezek 37:23 and 37:27 declare that the Israelites could only be God's

---

4 Smend, *Die Mitte des Alten Testaments,* 11–39; Rendtorff, *The Covenant Formula*; see also the summary in Joosten, *People and Land in the Holiness Code*, 101–7.

5 See Blum, *Studien zur Komposition des Pentateuch*, 318.

people and worship him as he had ordained after he had cleansed them from their impurity.

26:13 אֲשֶׁר הוֹצֵאתִי אֶתְכֶם מֵאֶרֶץ מִצְרַיִם—This could also be translated "who brought you out of the land of Egypt." See 26:45 and the textual notes on 19:36.

מִהְיֹת לָהֶם עֲבָדִים—This could also be translated "to be their slaves no more." This phrase has as its counterpart לִהְיֹת לָהֶם לֵאלֹהִים, "to be their God," in 26:45.

וָאֶשְׁבֹּר מֹטֹת עֻלְּכֶם—See the allusion to this in Ezek 34:27. Israel is envisaged as a beast of burden. It had been bowed down with a horizontal yoke placed on its neck and forced to go where it was steered by its master. This yoke was fastened to its neck by vertical bars and leather thongs. Once the yoke had been removed, Israel could stand upright once again and walk about freely wherever it pleased. (See the next textual note.)

וָאוֹלֵךְ אֶתְכֶם קוֹמְמִיּוּת׃—The verb אוֹלֵךְ (Hiphil first common singular imperfect of הָלַךְ, "to make someone walk") could also be translated "(I will/might) lead." See the textual notes on 26:3.

The term קוֹמְמִיּוּת occurs in the OT only here. Clearly it derives from the verb קוּם, "to rise, stand up." In form קוֹמְמִיּוּת is an abstract noun meaning "uprightness, erectness," but in this verse it functions as an adverb, to walk "in an upright position" (*HALOT*) or "erectly." The LXX translates קוֹמְמִיּוּת with μετὰ παρρησίας, "with outspokenness, confidence, boldness, freedom of access." That Greek phrase occurs in a similar sense in Heb 4:16, and the noun παρρησία is used with a similar meaning in 2 Cor 3:12; Eph 3:12; Heb 3:6; 10:19, 35; 1 Jn 3:21; 5:14.

The promises of Lev 26:4–13 provide the basis for the prophecy about the restoration of Israel in the messianic age in Ezek 34:24–31.[6] The following six promises are applied to God's flock, his redeemed people:

- Rains in season: Lev 26:4a referred to in Ezek 34:26
- Produce of the land and the fruit trees: Lev 26:4b referred to in Ezek 34:27
- Secure residence in the land: Lev 26:5b referred to in Ezek 34:25c, 28c
- Peace without any evil beast and anything to fear: Lev 26:6a referred to in Ezek 34:25, 28
- Presence of God with his people: Lev 26:12 referred to in Ezek 34:24, 30
- Deliverance from slavery and the breaking of its yoke: Lev 26:13 referred to in Ezek 34:27

26:14 וְאִם־לֹא תִשְׁמְעוּ לִי—This could also be translated "but if you do not obey me." See Lev 26:18, 21, 27.

וְלֹא תַעֲשׂוּ אֵת כָּל־הַמִּצְוֺת הָאֵלֶּה׃—This could refer to the commandments in 26:1–2 that summarize the legislation in the book of Leviticus.

הַמִּצְוֺת—See the textual notes on 4:2.

26:15 וְאִם־בְּחֻקֹּתַי תִּמְאָסוּ וְאִם אֶת־מִשְׁפָּטַי תִּגְעַל נַפְשְׁכֶם—Similar clauses are found in 26:43.

בְּחֻקֹּתַי—See the textual notes on 3:17, and Ezek 20:24.

---

6 Milgrom, *Leviticus 23–27*, 2348–49.

מִשְׁפָּטַי—See the textual notes on 5:10.

לְהַפְרְכֶם אֶת־בְּרִיתִי׃—לְהַפְרְכֶם (Hiphil infinitive construct of פָּרַר with לְ and second masculine plural suffix), "(by your) annulling," could also be translated "(by your) breaking." See 26:44.

This does not mean that the people can terminate God's covenant. Rather, by their disobedience they annul its proper operation and so forfeit its blessings. Thus God's covenant with Abraham could be annulled by failure to undergo circumcision (Gen 17:14), and God's covenant with Israel could be annulled by apostasy (Deut 31:16, 20; Jer 11:10; 31:32; Ezek 16:59) and sacrilege (Ezek 44:7).

26:16 אַף—This conjunction introduces the apodosis, as also in 26:41.

וְהִפְקַדְתִּי עֲלֵיכֶם בֶּהָלָה—God is here envisaged as a king who appoints "panic" as his inspector to attend to the misbehavior of his civil servants in his royal bureaucracy. בֶּהָלָה could also be translated "terror, calamity." It is used also in Ps 78:23; Is 65:23; Jer 15:8.

הַשַּׁחֶפֶת—See Deut 28:22.

הַקַּדַּחַת—See Deut 28:22.

מְכַלּוֹת עֵינַיִם וּמְדִיבֹת נָפֶשׁ—See Deut 28:65; 1 Sam 2:33. מְכַלּוֹת is the Piel feminine plural participle of כָּלָה, which here means "to cause to fail" (*HALOT,* Piel, 4 b). However, this participle lacks a subject, and so it functions as a verbal noun, "failure" of eyes or "failing" eyes. מְדִיבֹת is the Hiphil feminine plural participle of דּוּב, "making life pine away" (*HALOT*), which is found only here in the OT. It too functions as a verbal noun rather than as a verb.

וַאֲכָלֻהוּ אֹיְבֵיכֶם׃—See Deut 28:33.

26:17 וְנָתַתִּי פָנַי בָּכֶם—See 17:10; 20:3, 5, 6; Jer 44:11; Ezek 14:8; 15:7. This is the converse of God's promise in 26:9.

וְנִגַּפְתֶּם לִפְנֵי אֹיְבֵיכֶם—See Num 14:42. This reverses the promise in Lev 26:7. Literally this clause is "you will be struck before your enemies." However, the Niphal of נָגַף, meaning "to be struck," often takes לִפְנֵי introducing the agent of the passive verb, hence the clause means to be struck "by" the enemies (*HALOT,* s.v. נגף, Niphal).

וְרָדוּ בָכֶם שֹׂנְאֵיכֶם—See 25:43, 46, 53, where this idiom of ruling over someone is used for the mistreatment of slaves by masters.

וְנַסְתֶּם וְאֵין־רֹדֵף אֶתְכֶם׃—See 26:36, 37. This reverses the promise in 26:8.

26:18 עַד־אֵלֶּה—Here עַד means "notwithstanding" (*HALOT,* A 4) or "despite," hence the phrase means "despite these things."

לְיַסְּרָה—The Piel of יָסַר (here the so-called feminine form of the infinitive construct) in Lev 26:18, 28 means "to discipline" or "to instruct, correct," and it refers to God disciplining Israel. The Niphal of יָסַר in 26:23 has the corresponding passive sense: Israel may refuse to be "disciplined" or "corrected" by God. This verb is an educational term that was common in the Wisdom tradition. There it was used for various kinds of discipline, ranging from verbal criticism to corporal punishment.

שֶׁבַע—"Seven (times)" (also in 26:21, 24, 28) is a proverbial expression for the full, complete measure of discipline.

26:19 וְשָׁבַרְתִּי ...—This is a reversal of God's breaking of the yoke in 26:13.

גְּאוֹן עֻזְּכֶם—See Ezek 7:24; 30:6; 33:28.

וְנָתַתִּי אֶת־שְׁמֵיכֶם כַּבַּרְזֶל וְאֶת־אַרְצְכֶם כַּנְּחֻשָׁה׃—The same image is used in a slightly different way in Deut 28:23. This threat reverses the promise of rain in Lev 26:4a.

26:20 וְתַם לָרִיק כֹּחֲכֶם—See 26:16.

וְלֹא־תִתֵּן אַרְצְכֶם אֶת־יְבוּלָהּ וְעֵץ הָאָרֶץ לֹא יִתֵּן פִּרְיוֹ׃—This threat reverses the promise of good harvests in 26:4b.

26:21 וְאִם־תֵּלְכוּ עִמִּי קֶרִי—The term קְרִי (in pause קֶרִי) occurs in the OT only in this chapter and is used seven times in it (26:21, 23, 24, 27, 28, 40, 41). Its origin and sense are a matter of some dispute. On the one hand, it could be derived from קָרַר, "to be cold." In that case it would mean "coldness." But that does not fit the phrase בַּחֲמַת־קֶרִי in 26:28, which would then be "in the heat of coldness." It is most likely derived from קָרָה, "to encounter, confront." *HALOT* defines קְרִי as "hostile **encounter.**" It could also be translated "contrariness, opposition, contradiction" (see BDB). Its combination with the verb הָלַךְ, "walk," paints a rather vivid picture of a child who deliberately goes in the opposite direction of his or her parent. It is the opposite of "walking in/according to" God's statutes (26:3).

וְיָסַפְתִּי עֲלֵיכֶם מַכָּה—The noun מַכָּה has a wide semantic range in the OT. It covers any kind of a "blow" (*HALOT,* 1) or "wound" (*HALOT,* 2), including an "attack" or "slaughter" by an army that inflicts many fatalities (e.g., Josh 10:20). It can also refer to a "plague" (*HALOT,* 3, citing Lev 26:21) or "disease" sent as punishment. It is derived from the verb נָכָה, whose Hiphil occurs in Lev 26:24 (וְהִכֵּיתִי).

26:22 וְהִשְׁלַחְתִּי בָכֶם אֶת־חַיַּת הַשָּׂדֶה—This same threat, which reverses the promise in 26:6, reappears in Ezek 5:17; 14:15, 21. 2 Ki 17:25–26 reports an instance of this danger.

וְשִׁכְּלָה אֶתְכֶם—Ezekiel repeats this threat in Ezek 5:17.

וְנָשַׁמּוּ דַּרְכֵיכֶם׃—See the allusion to this in Ezek 14:15. The root שׁמם is a key word in the second part of this chapter. It is used seven times as a verb and once in a noun. God threatens to make the sanctuaries and land of Israel "desolate" and devoid of human inhabitants (26:31, 32). Thus the desolation of the land follows the devastation of the sanctuaries. The land will be a "desolation" (26:33). Its roads will be "deserted/desolate" (26:22). The land will therefore have a time when it remains "desolate" (26:34, 35, 43). Israel's enemies who take up residence in the land will be "appalled" (26:32).

26:23 לֹא תִוָּסְרוּ—This could also be translated "you will not be instructed, corrected."

26:24 וְהִכֵּיתִי—The Hiphil of נָכָה refers to God's disciplinary activity with Israel also in Jer 2:30 and 5:3, where the people refuse to accept God's discipline and be corrected. This verb is closely related in its sense to the Piel of יָסַר in Lev 26:18, 28, which likewise refers to God disciplining Israel.

26:25 וְהֵבֵאתִי עֲלֵיכֶם חֶרֶב נֹקֶמֶת נְקַם־בְּרִית—This could also be translated "I will bring a sword against you, avenging the vengeance of the covenant." This reverses the promise in 26:6. See Ezek 5:17; 6:3; 14:17; 29:8. In Lev 19:18 the root נקם is used for extrajudicial forms of payback exacted by the clan of the offended party upon the clan of the offender. Here, however, God speaks of himself as the avenger.

This reference to the sword is one of the three proverbial forms of punishment for breaking God's covenant with Israel that are mentioned here in 26:25–26: sword, epidemic, and famine (see Jer 14:12; 16:4; 18:21; 21:7, 9; 24:10; 27:8, 13; 29:17, 18; 32:24, 36; 34:17; 38:2; 42:17, 22; 44:13; Ezek 5:17; 6:11; 7:15; 12:16). The "covenant" here must be the covenant at Mount Sinai with its threat in Ex 20:5.

וְנֶאֱסַפְתֶּם אֶל־עָרֵיכֶם—Since the MT attaches this clause to the previous one, it could also be translated "so that you withdraw into your cities."

וְשִׁלַּחְתִּי דֶבֶר בְּתוֹכְכֶם—The epidemic is personified and envisaged as the Lord's agent.[7]

דֶבֶר—This could also be translated "pestilence, plague." Besieged cities were particularly prone to devastation by epidemics.

וְנִתַּתֶּם—This is the Niphal second masculine plural perfect of נָתַן with *waw* consecutive.

26:26 מַטֵּה־לֶחֶם—This is literally "the staff of bread." This idiom is most likely derived from the practice of keeping loaves of bread on a pole to keep them from getting moldy and being eaten by mice. The same metaphor reappears in Ezek 4:16; 5:16; 14:13; cf. Is 3:1; Ps 105:16.

וְאָפוּ עֶשֶׂר נָשִׁים לַחְמְכֶם בְּתַנּוּר אֶחָד—The women use one oven because they have so little flour to bake.

וְהֵשִׁיבוּ לַחְמְכֶם בַּמִּשְׁקָל—The same image for the rationing of bread reappears in Ezek 4:16.

וַאֲכַלְתֶּם וְלֹא תִשְׂבָּעוּ׃—See Hos 4:10a; Micah 6:14a.

26:27 וְאִם־בְּזֹאת—This recalls the use of זֹאת in Lev 26:16.

26:28 בַּחֲמַת־קֶרִי—This is literally "in the heat of opposition/hostility." We translated it "in anger."

26:29 This terrible threat of cannibalism is repeated in modified form in Jer 19:9 and Ezek 5:10. Cannibalism actually occurred during the siege of Samaria (2 Ki 6:26–28) and the siege of Jerusalem (Lam 4:10; cf. Lam 2:20).

26:30 These three threats are reworked in Ezek 6:3–6 (cf. Ezek 6:13–14).

בָּמֹתֵיכֶם—The term בָּמָה has traditionally been derived from the word for "back, ridge" (Deut 33:29) and, from the LXX onward, been translated as "high place." Yet that does not quite fit the evidence. Since it could be located in a valley (e.g., Jer 32:35; Ezek 6:3) and could have a chamber attached to it, it did not just designate an open air sanctuary with an altar.[8] It must be a general term for any cult place.[9] It was originally used for any place where the Lord (1 Sam 9:13, 14, 19; 1 Ki 3:4–5), or any god (Num 33:52), was worshiped. Under the influence of Num 33:52 and Deut 12:2, all these places were closed down in the reform of Josiah (2 Ki 23:8–9, 15, 19–20), and the term was used for all sanctuaries apart from the one divinely authorized central place of sacrifice in Jerusalem.

---

[7] Milgrom, *Leviticus 23–27*, 2312.

[8] Contra Haran, *Temples and Temple-Service in Ancient Israel*, 23–25.

[9] Milgrom, *Leviticus 23–27*, 2316–18.

חַמָּנֵיכֶם—This could also be translated "incense stand, incense altar." It is used also in 2 Chr 14:4 (ET 14:5); 34:4, 7; Is 17:8; 27:9; Ezek 6:4, 6. These incense altars were not used in the divine service, but were common in pagan cults.

פִּגְרֵי גִּלּוּלֵיכֶם—Ironically, the idols do not provide bodies for the gods, but are as lifeless and unclean as slain corpses.

גִּלּוּלֵיכֶם—The Hebrew word גִּלּוּלִים is a derisive dysphemism for idols. The term is derived from גָּלָל, "dung, pellets of manure" (1 Ki 14:10; Zeph 1:17; cf. Ezek 4:12, 15).

וְגָעֲלָה נַפְשִׁי אֶתְכֶם׃—This reverses God's promise in Lev 26:11.

26:31 וְנָתַתִּי—See the textual notes on 26:4.

חָרְבָּה—This could also be translated "ruin." See 26:33.

מִקְדְּשֵׁיכֶם—This, "your holy places," stands in contrast with "my sanctuary" in 26:2. See Ezek 7:24 and the textual notes on Lev 12:4.

וְלֹא אָרִיחַ בְּרֵיחַ נִיחֹחֲכֶם׃—See Gen 8:21; 1 Sam 26:19; Amos 5:21. This anthropomorphic idiom meant that God no longer accepted the sacrifices of his people.

בְּרֵיחַ נִיחֹחֲכֶם׃—See Ezek 6:13; 16:19; 20:28 and the textual notes on Lev 1:9.

26:32 וְשָׁמְמוּ עָלֶיהָ אֹיְבֵיכֶם הַיֹּשְׁבִים בָּהּ׃—See 2 Ki 17:24.

26:33 וְאֶתְכֶם אֱזָרֶה בַגּוֹיִם—See Jer 31:10; 49:32, 36; Ezek 5:2, 10, 12; 6:8; 12:14–15; 20:23; 22:15; 29:12; 30:23, 26. The same threat of scattering and pursuit with the sword is repeated in Ezek 5:2, 12 (cf. Ezek 12:14).

וַהֲרִיקֹתִי אַחֲרֵיכֶם חָרֶב—This reverses God's promise in Lev 26:6.

וְהָיְתָה אַרְצְכֶם שְׁמָמָה וְעָרֵיכֶם יִהְיוּ חָרְבָּה׃—This summarizes 26:30–33a and forms a bridge to 26:34.

26:34 אָז—This adverb, "then, at that time," is used twice in this verse and twice in 26:41 to mark the goal of the five acts of judgment by God.

תִּרְצֶה—The verb רָצָה appears twice in this verse, once in 26:41, and twice in 26:43. Its strange use with עָוֹן, "iniquity," as its object in 26:41 and 26:43 has led some scholars to postulate that in this chapter it does not mean to "accept, delight in, enjoy," as elsewhere in Leviticus, but comes from a different root (רצה II), which means to "pay for" or to "make good" and which is used here as well as in 2 Chr 36:21 and Is 40:2. *HALOT* defines the Qal of רָצָה II in Lev 26:34 and 26:43a as "to **restore** uncelebrated Sabbaths" (Qal, 2). *HALOT* explains the Qal in 26:41 and 26:43b with עָוֹן as its object as meaning "to pay, redeem" (Qal, 1). The form הִרְצָת in 26:34 is the Hiphil third feminine singular perfect with an archaic ending (GKC, § 75 m) and means "to bring for payment, have restored" according to *HALOT.* But if עָוֹן is understood as the punishment for iniquity rather than the act of sinning, then "accept" or "enjoy" makes good sense in all these passages.

שַׁבְּתֹתֶיהָ—This could also be translated "its Sabbath years." See Lev 25:2, 4.

כֹּל יְמֵי הָשַּׁמָּה—הָשַּׁמָּה is the Hophal infinitive construct of שָׁמֵם with the third feminine singular suffix (GKC, §§ 67 y; 91 e), which normally has *mappiq* (הּ◌ָ). This phrase is repeated in 26:35, and the Hophal infinitive construct also recurs in 26:43.

אָז תִּשְׁבַּת הָאָרֶץ—See 25:2; 26:35.

26:35 בְּשַׁבְּתֹתֵיכֶם—"Your Sabbaths" is contrasted with "its [the land's] Sabbaths" in the previous verse.

26:36 וְהַנִּשְׁאָרִים בָּכֶם—See 26:39. This does not, as is normally the case, refer to those who remained in the land after a devastating war (2 Ki 19:30; Neh 1:3; Jer 39:9; 40:6), but to those who survived their dispersal to foreign lands (Deut 4:27; 28:62; Is 11:11, 16).

עָלֶה נִדָּף—See Job 13:25.

וְנָסוּ מְנֻסַת־חֶרֶב וְנָפְלוּ וְאֵין רֹדֵף׃—This reverses God's promises in Lev 26:7.

26:37 וְלֹא־תִהְיֶה לָכֶם תְּקוּמָה לִפְנֵי אֹיְבֵיכֶם׃—This reverses the Israelites' status as free people in 26:13.

26:38 וַאֲבַדְתֶּם—While this means "and you will perish," the reference to survivors in 26:36, 39 implies that some will be left.

וְאָכְלָה אֶתְכֶם אֶרֶץ אֹיְבֵיכֶם׃—This reverses 26:5. Instead of the Israelites eating their fill of food in their own land, the land of their enemies will eat them.

26:39 וְהַנִּשְׁאָרִים בָּכֶם—This does not just refer to the survivors from the sword in 26:36, but to those of their number who survive the subsequent time of demoralization as refugees in a foreign land.

יִמַּקּוּ—See Ps 38:6 (ET 38:5); Ezek 4:17; 24:23; 33:10; Zech 14:12. This is the Niphal third masculine plural imperfect of מָקַק, "to rot" (*HALOT,* 1). This threat of rotting away from iniquity is repeated in Ezek 4:17 and 24:23.

בַּעֲוֹנָם—See Lev 26:40, 41, 43 and the textual notes on 5:l.

בַּעֲוֹנֹת אֲבֹתָם אִתָּם—This may be an allusion to Ex 20:5 (cf. Ex 34:7; Num 14:18; Neh 9:2; Jer 14:20; 32:18; Dan 9:16).

26:40 וְהִתְוַדּוּ אֶת־עֲוֹנָם וְאֶת־עֲוֹן אֲבֹתָם—See the textual notes on Lev 5:5. See also Neh 9:2 and the cases of this in Ezra 9:3–10:1; Neh 9:1–37; and Dan 9:1–27.

Even though this is a consecutive clause, most translators construe it as the beginning of a conditional clause. This has been rightly challenged by Steymans.[10] He argues that it describes the results of dispersal, rather than the condition for God's action.

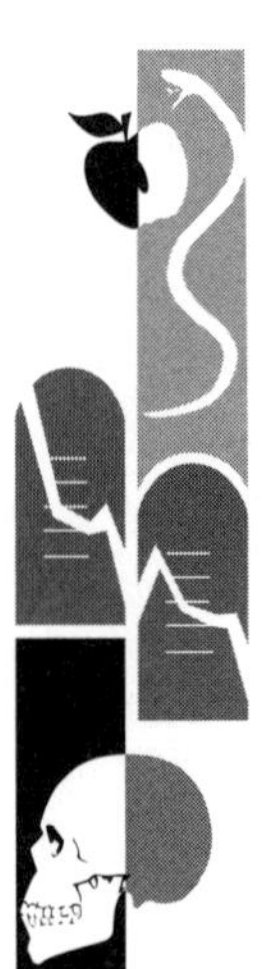

בְּמַעֲלָם—See the textual notes on 5:15. The acts of sacrilege are the violation of the commandments in 26:1–2. In Ezekiel the sin of sacrilege, caused by idolatry, the desecration of the Sabbaths, and the presentation of offerings on the "high places" (Ezek 20:27 in the context of 20:1–29), is regarded as the reason for God's punishment of Israel with the sword, famine, wild beasts, and epidemics, as well as for the desolation of the land (14:13–21) and the exile in Babylon (39:23, 26). Likewise in Chronicles, the sacrilege of the Israelites and their kings is given as the reason for Judah's humiliation by the Assyrians (2 Chr 28:19–20), for the temple's destruction (2 Chr 36:14), and for the exile (1 Chr 9:1).

26:41 אַף־אֲנִי—The phrase אַף־אֲנִי recalls Lev 26:16 and so completes the list of threats for disobedience.

אֵלֵךְ—The imperfect tense of this verb is best understood modally.

וְהֵבֵאתִי אֹתָם בְּאֶרֶץ אֹיְבֵיהֶם—This threat is an ironic reversal of God's promise to bring the Israelites into the land of Canaan (Ex 6:8).

---

[10] Steymans, "Verheißung und Drohung: Lev 26," 279–80.

אוֹ־אָז—This is literally "or then." The function of the conjunction אוֹ is uncertain. Since it does not provide an alternative to the confession of sins, it could be taken as an explicative résumé of Lev 26:40 and be translated "or rather,"[11] as in 1 Sam 29:3. Some take it as an introduction to a conditional sentence (NIV), while others hold that, as in 1 Sam 20:10, it introduces an indirect question.[12] Since the LXX reads "then" and the Syriac "and then," it seems that this is either a case of dittography, or, more likely, a corrective marginal gloss that was subsequently inserted in the text.

יִכָּנַע—This could also be translated "it [their heart] will be subdued." See the actual cases of this in 1 Ki 21:27–29; 2 Ki 22:19 ‖ 2 Chr 34:27; 2 Chr 12:6–8, 12; 30:11; 32:24–26; 33:12–13, 18–19. In each of these instances, people humbled themselves, but they did not have their hearts humbled by God.

לְבָבָם הֶעָרֵל—See Deut 10:16; 30:6; Jer 4:4; 9:25; Ezek 44:7.

26:42 וְזָכַרְתִּי—Here the verb זָכַר is used for a physical act, rather than mere mental activity.[13]

בְּרִיתִי יַעֲקוֹב—The form בְּרִיתִי (three times in this verse) could have the first common singular pronominal suffix, hence "my covenant with Jacob/Isaac/Abraham." In 26:44 בְּרִיתִי has the suffix. Or the form here could be the archaic construct form, the "covenant of" Jacob, Isaac, and Abraham (see GKC, § 90 n), referring to the covenant promises that God made to each of them. On God's covenant, see Gen 9:15, 16; Ex 2:24; 6:4, 5; Pss 105:8; 106:45; Jer 14:21; Ezek 16:60. For his covenant with Jacob, see Gen 28:13–15; 35:9–15.

בְּרִיתִי יִצְחָק—See Gen 26:2–5.

בְּרִיתִי אַבְרָהָם—See Gen 15:18–20 (cf. 17:1–8).

וְהָאָרֶץ—The Seed through whom all peoples would be blessed and the land were the main gifts that God had promised to the patriarchs in his covenant with them (e.g., Gen 12:1–3, 7; 13:15; 15:18; 26:3–4; 28:13; 35:12).

26:43 יַעַן וּבְיַעַן—This is literally "because and by the cause that." The doubling in יַעַן וּבְיַעַן makes this an emphatic conjunction (Ezek 13:10).

בְּמִשְׁפָּטַי מָאָסוּ וְאֶת־חֻקֹּתַי גָּעֲלָה נַפְשָׁם׃—This forms an inclusion with Lev 26:15a. Because it recalls that verse, the order of the direct objects is reversed.

On "ordinances" and "statutes," see Ezek 5:6; 20:13, 16.

26:44 בְּאֶרֶץ אֹיְבֵיהֶם—See Lev 26:34, 36, 38, 39, 41.

לֹא־מְאַסְתִּים וְלֹא־גְעַלְתִּים—The perfect tenses are most likely instances of the prophetic perfect that envisages what will happen as if it has already happened (GKC, § 106 n).

וְלֹא־גְעַלְתִּים—This recalls 26:11 and reverses the threat in 26:30.

לְכַלֹּתָם—See Ex 32:10, 12; 33:3, 5; Num 16:21; 17:10 (ET 16:45); 25:11.

בְּרִיתִי אִתָּם—This refers to God's covenant with the Israelites at Sinai to make them his holy people with a priestly mission to the world.[14]

---

[11] Keil, *Pentateuch*, 2:478.

[12] Elliger, *Leviticus*, 365.

[13] Schottroff, *Gedenken im Alten Orient und im Alten Testament*, 201.

[14] Hartley, *Leviticus*, 470–71.

26:45 וְזָכַרְתִּי לָהֶם—See Ps 106:45 and Jer 2:2 for this use of זָכַר לְ, meaning "to remember in favor of" someone.

רִאשֹׁנִים—This ("founders") could also be translated "previous generations." See Deut 19:14; Is 61:4; Ps 79:8.

אֲשֶׁר הוֹצֵאתִי־אֹתָם מֵאֶרֶץ מִצְרַיִם—This could also be translated "whom I brought out from the land of Egypt." See the textual notes on 19:36.

לְעֵינֵי הַגּוֹיִם—This promise is applied by Ezek 39:21–29 to the Israelites in Ezek 39:27.

לִהְיֹת לָהֶם לֵאלֹהִים—See the textual notes on Lev 11:45. This recalls the promise in 26:12 and forms an inclusion with it.

26:46 הַחֻקִּים—See the textual notes on 10:11.

וְהַמִּשְׁפָּטִים—See the textual notes on 5:10.

וְהַתּוֹרֹת—See the textual notes on 6:2 (ET 6:9).

אֲשֶׁר נָתַן יְהוָה בֵּינוֹ וּבֵין בְּנֵי יִשְׂרָאֵל—The unusual idiom נָתַן ... בֵּן ... וּבֵין is used elsewhere only in three other places: in Gen 9:12 for God's institution of the rainbow; in Gen 17:12 for his confirmation of his covenant with Abraham with the sign of circumcision; and in Ezek 20:12 for the institution of the sign of the Sabbaths.[15]

בְּהַר סִינַי—This forms an inclusion with Lev 25:1. It also recalls 7:38 and anticipates 27:34.

בְּיַד־מֹשֶׁה׃—This is literally "through the hand of Moses." See 8:36; 10:11.

Commentary

Structure

This final admonition in the book (Leviticus 26) is the second part of the speech (Leviticus 25–26) that begins with the commission of Moses in 25:1–2a and ends with the summary in 26:46. Excluding that summary, it falls into four parts: the statement of the commandments in 26:1–2; the promise of blessings in 26:3–13; the threats for disobedience in 26:14–33; and the purpose of dispersal from the land in 26:34–45.

The admonition begins with five commandments. The three prohibitive commandments and two performative commandments, both sets of which are linked together disjunctively, culminate in a formula of divine self-introduction. They are followed by a long conditional sentence with its protasis in 26:3 and its apodosis in 26:4–12. The apodosis is divided into four parts for the four blessings of obedience to God's Word, each of which is introduced by a *waw* consecutive perfect in the first person with God as the actor (26:4, 6, 9, 11). Three of these have the same verb: וְנָתַתִּי, "I will give/make" (26:4, 6, 11). While God is the actor with only one gift in the first two blessings, this increases in the third blessing with four related gifts and in the fourth blessing with three or four related gifts. These verbs are followed by other *waw* clauses that spell out the results of these gifts. These promises of blessing culminate in an expanded

[15] Steymans, "Verheißung und Drohung: Lev 26," 265–67.

formula of divine self-introduction in 26:13. This whole unit is closed off by an inclusion formed by תֵּלֵכוּ, "you will walk," in 26:3, and וָאוֹלֵךְ, "and I make you walk along erectly," in 26:13. This serves to signal that the promises of blessing are arranged in the form of a chiasm:[16]

A and A' "Walk" (26:3 and 26:12–13)
B and B' "Give/make" (26:4 and 26:11)
C and C' "Eat" (26:5 and 26:10)
D and D' "Peace" (26:6) and "covenant" (26:9)
E and E' "Your enemies," "fall before you," "by the sword" (26:7 and 26:8c)
F and F' "Pursue," "of you," "a hundred," "a hundred," "of you," "pursue" (26:8a and 26:8b)[17]

The promise of blessing is followed by a carefully crafted set of graded threats for disobedience in 26:14–33. What could be a single sentence is broken only by 26:26. This section contains five threats. Each of these is constructed as a conditional clause that is introduced by וְאִם, "but if": 26:14–15, 18, 21, 23, 27. The first protasis also functions as the introduction to all the threats as well as the first threat. The threats are arranged in an increasing order of severity to match and counter the increased resistance of the Israelites to God's Word. The compositional techniques used to communicate this escalation of punishment are shown in figure 25.

Figure 25

Degrees of Resistance and Punishment

Intensity of Israel's Resistance	*Intensity of Punishment from God*
1. If you will not **listen** to me (26:14–15),	I will do this to you (26:16).
2. If you still will not **listen** to me (26:18a),	I will *discipline* you seven times for your sins (26:18b).
3. If you still ***walk contrary*** to me, and you are unwilling to **listen** (26:21a),	I will go on to **strike** you seven times according to your sins (26:21b).
4. If you will not be *disciplined* by me, but ***walk contrary*** to me (26:23a),	I will ***walk contrary*** to you and **strike** you seven times for your sins (26:23b–24).
5. If you still will not **listen** to me, but ***walk contrary*** to me (26:27),	I will ***walk contrary*** to you in anger and *discipline* you seven times for your sins (26:28).

The repetition of certain key words and phrases creates an intricate pattern of interaction between the Israelites and their God. The Israelites are characterized by the inability to listen. That leads to their refusal to listen and accept correction, and culminates in their determined opposition to God. But God is

[16] Milgrom, *Leviticus 23–27*, 2290–91.

[17] This follows the Hebrew word order.

characterized by two things: his gradual escalation of punishment that matches their resistance, from simple discipline to "corporal punishment" and then to opposition and angry confrontation; his determination to deal justly with their sins, as is shown by the repetition of the phrase "seven times for/according to your sins."

The final section (26:34–45) is divided into parts by the use of inclusion to bracket off two sections. Thus 26:34 is linked with 26:41b by the use of אָז, "then," in both verses. It therefore brackets off a unit that contrasts God's purpose for the land with his purpose for the survivors. The part of this unit that deals with the plight of the Israelites in foreign lands is divided into two sections by the use of וְהַנִּשְׁאָרִים בָּכֶם, "and those who survive among you" in 26:36 and 26:39. On the other hand, the final part of the speech is also identified by the use of וְזָכַרְתִּי בְּרִית in 26:42 and 26:45. And this, in turn, concludes with the formula for divine self-introduction (26:45).

The three parts of the chapter are linked together by the occurrence of the rare verb גָּעַל, "loathe." This draws a stark contrast between the Lord's refusal to loathe the Israelites and their loathing of his statutes and ordinances.[18] It creates the following pattern:

A *"My soul will not loathe you"* (26:11).
- B "If you reject my statutes and your soul loathes my ordinances …" (26:15).
  - C *"My soul will loathe you"* (26:30).
- B' "They rejected my ordinances and their soul loathed my statutes" (26:43).

A' *"I will not loathe them"* (26:44).

Thus, the Lord's refusal to loathe his people overrides their loathing of his statutes and ordinances. It relativizes his own threat to loathe them if they persist in their refusal to listen to him. Besides that, the chapter is interwoven with an elaborate network of recurrent keywords and phrases: "land" (twenty-three times); "give" (fourteen times); "enemies" (thirteen times); "walk" (ten times); "the land" (nine times); a noun or verb from the root שׁבת, "sabbath" (nine times); "covenant" (eight times); "eat," "sword," "contrariness," and "be desolate/appalled" (each seven times); "your land" and "the land(s) of your enemies" (each six times).

The structure of this pericope can be outlined as follows:

I. God's final admonition with his promises and threats to the Israelites (26:1–45)
   A. Five summary commandments (26:1–2)
      1. Prohibition of idolatry with God's self-introduction (26:1)
      2. Observance of Sabbaths and reverence for sanctuary with God's self-introduction (26:2)
   B. Promises for obedience to God's Word (26:3–13)
      1. Enactment of God's Word as the condition for the reception of blessings in the land (26:3)

---

[18] Warning, *Literary Artistry in Leviticus*, 100–1.

2. The four blessings that follow its enactment (26:4–12)
    a. Regular rainfall with good harvests (26:4–5)
    b. Peace with security and victory over enemies (26:6–8)
    c. Growth of families with abundance of food (26:9–10)
    d. God's residence with his people (26:11–12)
3. Formula of divine self-introduction for God as Israel's emancipator (26:13)

C. God's treatment of the Israelites for their contempt of his Word (26:14–45)
1. God's threat of graded acts of discipline for Israel's refusal to obey his Word (26:14–33)
    a. First threat: panic (26:14–17)
        i. Refusal to listen as the reason for the punishment (26:14–15)
        ii. God's appointment of panic with sickness and military vulnerability (26:16–17)
    b. Second threat: drought (26:18–20)
        i. Ongoing refusal to listen to God as the reason for the punishment (26:18a)
        ii. God's discipline of them with a drought (26:18b–20)
    c. Third threat: wild beasts (26:21–22)
        i. Opposition to God as the reason for the punishment (26:21a)
        ii. God's attack on the family and its livestock with wild animals (26:21b–22)
    d. Fourth threat: warfare (26:23–26)
        i. Refusal to accept God's discipline as the reason for the punishment (26:23)
        ii. Military invasion with epidemic and famine in besieged cities (26:24–26)
    e. Fifth threat: devastation and dispersal after a military defeat (26:27–33)
        i. Opposition and refusal to listen to God as the reason for the punishment (26:27)
        ii. God's discipline of his people in anger with the desolation of the land (26:28–33)
2. The purpose of God's punishment by their dispersal in the lands of their enemies (26:34–45)
    a. Rest for the land (26:34–35)
        i. Enjoyment of its Sabbaths (26:34)
        ii. Compensation for the loss of Sabbaths (26:35)
    b. Submission of the survivors (26:36–41)
        i. God's demoralization of the survivors (26:36–38)
            - God's affliction of them with despondency and paranoia (26:36–37)
            - Summary of their plight (26:38)

ii. Their eventual acceptance of their plight as punishment for their iniquity (26:39–41)
   - Confession of sins as the cause of their plight (26:39–41a)
   - Acceptance of the plight as punishment for their sins (26:41b)

c. God's promise of restoration for the remnant of Israel (26:42–45)
   i. God's covenant with Abraham as the reason for restoration (26:42–44)
      - God's remembrance of his covenant with the patriarchs (26:42a)
      - God's remembrance of the land and its need for rest (26:42b–43)
      - God's refusal to annul the covenant by exterminating Israel (26:44)
   ii. God's remembrance of his covenant at Sinai as the goal of restoration (26:45)

II. Subscript about God's institution of the terms for his interaction with the Israelites (26:46)

Analysis

Without any announcement, a change of genre and tone occurs in this chapter. Most of Leviticus has thus far consisted of the communication of divine legislation to Israel and the priests. This has been interspersed with passages of admonition with warnings and promises from God in some speeches (17:10–12; 20:3–5; 25:18–22) and at the end of some of them (18:24–30; 20:22–26). But this chapter is an extended admonition about the future existence of the Israelites with him in the promised land. *It is the climax of the book.* In it God speaks personally to the Israelites. He addresses them with his promises of blessing and his threats of judgment. This chapter does not, as is commonly claimed, provide the blessings and curses that were commonly suffixed to treaties and codes of law in the ancient world.[19] Rather it proclaims how God deals with his people in grace and wrath.

The admonition begins with five commandments. They all touch on ritual matters. They are a summary of God's basic requirements for his people, the bottom line in his association with them. In them God recalled the First and Third Commandments of the Decalogue (Ex 20:3, 8) to remind the Israelites of the foundation for his interaction with them and the bestowal of his blessings on them. These commandments protected the integrity and sanctity of the divine service, the divinely instituted lifeline of Israel.

On the negative side, the flow of blessing was sabotaged most severely by idolatry. In the three prohibitions of Lev 26:1, God recalled the First Com-

---

[19] Contra Hartley, *Leviticus*, 459; cf. Milgrom, *Leviticus 23–27*, 2286–87; Wenham, *Leviticus*, 327.

mandment. The Israelites were forbidden to make puny deities for themselves by setting up idols or steles and prostrating themselves on the carved pavement in front of them. The terms that are used for these objects of homage are ambiguous. It is not clear whether they refer to an idol of the Lord or the idol of another god. The practice may be different, but the reality is the same. In either case, the Israelites served a humanly devised "god." Thus, all idolatrous cults were forbidden.

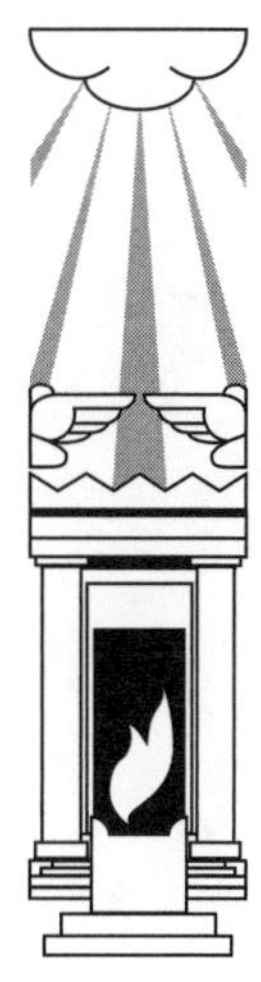

On the positive side, God established the Sabbaths and the sanctuary, so that through them he could dwell with his people and lavish his blessings on them in the promised land (26:2). There were three kinds of Sabbaths: the regular weekly Sabbaths, the seven high holy festive days of rest, and the years of rest for the land. The sanctuary was the sacred area around the altar for burnt offering and the tent of meeting (see figure 6, "Ground Plan of the Tabernacle"). It was the place for the performance of the divine service, the place where God met twice each day to receive his people and to bless them. The Israelites observed the Sabbaths by resting from work on them; they revered the sanctuary by participating in the divine service at the pilgrim festivals in a state of ritual purity, presenting the offerings to God that he himself had instituted in his law, and eating the sacred food from the offerings.

The observance of these three ritual prohibitions and the performance of these two ritual commandments were the condition for the people's enjoyment of God's four great blessings for them as an agricultural community in the land (26:3). The provision of these gifts depended on the Israelites' faithfulness in following the way of worship and life that God had instituted for them in his Word. The first of these blessings had to do with their livelihood as God's people in the land (26:4–5). God promised to give them the rain that was needed for their fields to produce plenty of wheat and barley, and for orchards to produce plenty of grapes, olives, and other kinds of fruit to eat. God's provision of bumper harvests ensured that they would have abundant food and the security that came with an assured livelihood. The second blessing was the gift of peace in the land, with the result that they would even be able to sleep out in the open because they would have nothing to fear (26:6–8). This had two sides to it. On the one hand, God would remove all animals that threatened human life, such as lions, bears, and snakes. On the other hand, the "sword" of invading armies would not weak havoc in the land. Instead, even when the Israelites were vastly outnumbered by their enemies, they would rout them with their "sword."

These two blessings are the presupposition for the third blessing, the growth of each Israelite family and clan (26:9–10). Israelite families would grow and thrive because God turned his face to care for each of them. God's promise to make his people fruitful and to multiply them confirmed his covenant with the patriarchs by fulfilling its promises. The growth of the family was matched by the promise of abundant food in 26:10, enough to eat and some left over for sale, for a large family was a mixed blessing if it lacked food and the other necessities for life. These three blessings were overshadowed by an even greater blessing, the gift of God's "dwelling" with his people (26:11–12). This fulfilled the promises that God had made in Ex 25:8 and 29:45–46 (cf. 1 Ki 6:13). Since he resided with his people in the sanctuary, he walked about with them, as he had done with Adam and Eve in the garden (Gen 3:8), and served them as their God by his proximity with them as his people and the gift of access to himself in the divine service. As long as they remained faithful to him and enacted his mandate for the divine service, "his soul," his holy being, would not "loathe" them as unfit for life with him.

This chain of promises culminates in God's presentation of himself as their liberator from slavery in Egypt. In this presentation, he solemnly declared that he had broken their yoke so that he could make them stand up straight, walk with him as free men and women, and hold their heads up high as his royal people (26:13). In contrast to pagan gods that demanded prostration from their devotees (26:1), God set his people on their feet to stand before him. He, in fact, desired to "walk" them along with him (26:13) on the way of freedom in the land, just as he had walked them through the desert to the land. That was the purpose of their deliverance. That too is his purpose in providing all these gifts for them, for if they had all these blessings, they would have no reason to fall into servitude for the lack of a secure livelihood. By his statutes he mapped out the way for them to walk as free people together with him (26:3).

The promises of blessing in 26:3–13 are followed by threats of punishment for the Israelites if they did not listen to him and if they refused to enact the service that he had instituted because they loathed his Word (26:14–33). That was no trivial matter, for they thereby annulled the operation of the covenant that he had made with them (26:15). They did not terminate it by their disobedience, for no human being could ever undo what God had done. Instead, they frustrated its operation, so that God could not accomplish what he intended through it. By their disobedience they forfeited the blessings of God's covenant; they experienced the threatened consequences of their faithlessness to God. Their increasingly adamant refusal to listen to him led to an escalation of punishment. God issued five threats, with the fifth threat as the culmination of his disciplinary activity.

First, in response to the disobedience of his people, God threatened to punish them mentally with irrational panic, a sense of fearfulness that resulted in sickness and powerlessness (26:14–17). Then, as they lost their grip and their strength ebbed away, their enemies would enjoy the fruits of their work. Worse than that, God himself turned against them. Since they had lost his protection, they would be defeated and ruled by their enemies. And that, in turn, would fuel and confirm their paranoia.

Second, if they still refused to listen to God, he would discipline them physically for their sins (26:18–20). He would break their pride by sending a drought so severe that no rain would fall from the sky and the springs would dry up on the land. As a result, all their labor would be futile; it would achieve nothing, for no grain would grow in their fields, and no fruit would be produced by their trees.

Third, if they compounded their refusal to listen to his voice by walking contrary to him, he would strike them, like a teacher caning a recalcitrant student, by unleashing wild beasts against their households (26:21–22). Since these animals robbed them of their children and their livestock, these animals would depopulate the land.

Fourth, if the people still refused to accept God's discipline, but persisted in turning away from his way, God would repay them in like kind. He would walk contrary to them and strike them even harder with the trio of punishments for violation of his covenant with them: sword, epidemic, and famine (26:23–26). This terrible trio would strike them in the wake of a large-scale invasion of the land by a well-equipped enemy that forced them to take refuge in their walled cities. There, under siege from the invading army, they would be sitting ducks for ravages of epidemics and famine for lack of bread.

Fifth, and finally, if they still persisted in their opposition to God, God would confront them directly in his anger and discipline them in the harshest possible way (26:27–33). Their enemies would defeat them and devastate their land. All that was dear to them would be taken from them. Before the siege was over, they would be forced to eat their own children to keep themselves alive. All their sacred places with their idols and incense stands would be desecrated and destroyed. Their cities would be laid to waste and the land left empty of people. In the wake of such a national catastrophe, God would scatter them among the nations as he pursued them with the sword. The end of their obstinate refusal to listen to God is summed up in a terrible sentence (26:33): "Your land will be a desolation, and your cities will be a wasteland."

The list of threats for Israel's sins is followed by a bridging section in 26:34–41, which deals with God's purpose in scattering his people among the nations. No matter how rebellious they were, their sins would not frustrate his gracious will for them and their land, for what looked like the end of God's story with them was, in fact, an interlude that prepared the ground for the restoration of his relationship with them in 26:42–45 and the fulfillment of his foundational promise in 26:11–13.

The dispersal of the people among the nations served two purposes. First, it gave the land its Sabbaths, the rest from cultivation that it had not received for as long as the Israelites had been settled on it (26:34–35). Since it had not rested every seven years, it would rest for consecutive years when it was depopulated and uncultivated. This would compensate for the years that it had not received the rest that God had ordained for it in 25:2–5. Second, the dispersal of the Israelites would humble them so completely that they would finally accept that God had punished them justly for their sins (26:36–41).

The humbling of the Israelites occurred in two stages. First, God would demoralize those who had survived the sword of battle (26:36–38). They would become so paranoid that they would flee at the sound of a leaf in the wind, even though no one was pursuing them. Since they would be too disheartened to withstand their enemies, they would be lost among the nations and eaten up by the lands of their enemies. Second, those who survived their demoralization in alien lands would learn their lesson from God (26:39–41). When they realized that they were rotting away from their iniquity and the iniquity of their ancestors, they would finally confess that they and their ancestors had been punished for two iniquities: the sin of sacrilege from involvement in idolatry and the sin of opposition to God by walking contrary to him so persistently that he had to walk contrary to them and bring them into the lands of their enemies. When they confessed their iniquities, God's punishment of them would accomplish its intended purpose. Their hearts would be humbled, and they would accept their plight as God's punishment of them for their iniquity.

Their confession of sins with its concomitant acceptance of God's punishment, however, was not the ultimate goal of God's disciplinary activity. He carried out these threats so that he could fulfill the promises that he had made in his two covenants with them: the covenant with the patriarchs and the covenant with Israel at Mount Sinai (26:42–45). He therefore promised that he would "remember" these covenants and fulfill his promises in them. That would be the reason for his intervention in the hopeless plight of his people.

On the one hand, he would remember his covenant with Abraham, Isaac, and Jacob. He therefore promised to remember his land, the land that he had promised to give to the patriarchs. Even though the Israelites forfeited their right to enjoy the blessings of the land by their disdain for its owner and their treatment of it, the land would not remain bereft of them forever; it would do without them only for as long as it needed to rest, and for as long as it took for them to accept their punishment (26:43). Moreover, because God had committed himself irrevocably to them in his covenant with the patriarchs, he promised that he would not exterminate them. He would not pay them back by rejecting them. Even though they loathed his statutes and rejected his ordinances (26:43), he would not reject and loathe them (26:44). He would not annul his covenant, but would remain committed to them.

On the other hand, even if his people failed to fulfill their side of the covenant at Sinai, he would still "remember" the covenant that he had made with them there (26:45). He would restore them that he could "be their God," even if they failed to be his people. And that's where he left the matter. He did not say what he would do or how he would accomplish all this for them. But he returned to his declaration in 26:13 and its foundational promise to be their God.

Theological Significance

In this passionate address to the Israelites, God outlined his policy for them as his holy people. He went beyond all the ritual and moral laws that he had given to them in Leviticus 1–25 so that they could share in his holiness. He looked forward to their residence in the land and, in a series of promises and threats, outlined how he intended to interact with them there as their God. In this address he made a foundational declaration of his will for them in the land of Israel. It set out the basis for his dealings with them in the land. He did not leave them in the dark about what to expect from him there, but gave them his Word to disclose the terms of their association and interaction (26:46). He set out how he would treat them and why. In his promises he listed benefits that they would receive from him if they worshiped him as he had ordained; in his threats he listed the troubles that they would experience if they failed to worship him as ordained.

The basis for their coexistence with him is summarized by five foundational commandments in 26:1–2. God committed himself to them as their God and gave them access to himself in the divine service. Their life, the land, and the blessings in the land all came from him. If the people cut themselves off from him, they forfeited all this. That was the greatest danger for them in the land. Hence he warned them about apostasy and idolatry. The two went together. If they set up idols and pillars to represent the Lord in the divine service, these objects would, in fact, involve the Israelites in the service of other gods. That was why God had forbidden them to make idols for him and perform prostration before them (Ex 20:5). As he himself declared in the formula for divine self-introduction, they had his name as their means of access to him (e.g., Lev 26:13). The use of idols desecrated God's name and the people's places of worship. On the other hand, if the Israelites remained faithful to him by observing his Sabbaths and revering his sanctuary, they enjoyed his approval and blessing. Thus orthodoxy in worship led to God's blessing, while heterodoxy in worship led to the loss of blessing from God.

The Israelites served God rightly by walking with God according to his statutes and by enacting his mandates (26:3). This included their involvement in the divine service at the sanctuary and their way of life as holy people on the land. Faithfulness to God and his Word resulted in blessing for them. They not only received all that was physically necessary for them to survive and thrive in the land, but, best of all, they enjoyed God's association with them and his personal attention to them. They benefited from his residence with him in the tabernacle and his benevolent attitude to them. He walked with them in their journey throughout history and served them as their God in the divine service.

And because he served them as their God, they, in turn, were able to live with him as his people (26:12). God had not freed them from slavery in Egypt to make them his slaves; no, he had freed them from slavery so that he could be their God and serve them as their God (26:12–13). He wanted them to be free people who held their heads up high; he wanted to keep them free and to honor them by identifying them with himself and involving them in his journey through human history. He freed them so that they could live with him as his royal sons and daughters, with all the privileges and responsibilities that came with their high status as his kinsfolk. He freed them from servitude to other gods (26:13) so that he could be their God (26:45). That was the goal of all his dealings with them, his good and gracious will for them.

Since he had such great plans for them, he would not let them frustrate his purpose for them by their disobedience of him, no matter how extreme it became. He outlined the process of rebellion in detail with some theological precision. It all stemmed from their "proud strength" (26:19) and their "uncircumcised heart[s]" (26:41). It had to do with their nature as ungodly people and their attitude of self-sufficiency. This generated their loathing and contempt for God's Word as something unfit for them and alien to them (26:15, 43). And so they refused to listen to God (26:14, 18, 21, 27). No matter what he said and what he did to discipline and correct them, they still refused to listen. Instead, they quite deliberately opposed him and lived contrary to him and his Word (26:21, 23, 27, 40). Thus their "sins" (26:18, 21, 24, 28) resulted in "sacrilege" against him (26:40). The people became involved in idolatry (26:30) and desecrated his Sabbaths and his sanctuary (26:2, 35). Yet, despite their blatant violation of his covenant with them (26:15), he would not give up on them. Their rebellion would never change his purpose for them as their God.

Since God was committed to them as their God, he would not break his covenant with them, nor would he overlook their sin that threatened their survival as his people. So right from the beginning at Mount Sinai, he told them how he would deal with them. He punished them for their sins (26:18, 24, 28) according to the severity of their sins (26:21). By these punishments he disciplined and corrected them (26:18, 23, 28). Like a loving father who resorted to physical punishment when his child failed to heed his warnings, God threatened to bring disasters on them in the land. He disciplined them to bring them back to the right worship of him. But if they did not heed his acts of discipline, he turned against them in his wrath (26:24, 28) and drove them from his land (26:33). His aim in all this was to humble their proud hearts, so that they would confess their sins (26:40) and accept their punishment (26:41).

Even though God reacted personally to the obedience and disobedience of his people, their behavior did not determine his relationship with them and his treatment of them. Instead, his own fidelity to his own Word was the determining factor. His attitude to them was determined by the two covenants that he had made with them.

On the one hand, his covenant with Abraham was irrevocable. When his people sinned and abused the land, they forfeited the blessings of that covenant; they were no longer able to be fruitful and live in the land. But God never annulled his covenant with them; he would never exterminate his people (26:44). That was the one unshakable foundation for his people, the basis of their faith and hope in him. And so God would always "remember" his covenant (26:42) and act to maintain it (26:9). Thus the sin of Israel could not annul God's covenant with Abraham.

On the other hand, God also remained committed to Israel by virtue of his covenant with them at Mount Sinai. He had rescued them from slavery in Egypt

(Ex 6:7) so that he could be their God by residing with them (Ex 29:45; Lev 26:45). That was the goal of his covenant at Sinai. It was also the goal of all his dealings with them. It is the purpose of this admonition in Leviticus 26: the commandments in 26:1–2; the blessings in 26:3–13 (as it is made clear in 26:12–13); all the threats in 26:14–33; and the promise of restoration for his penitent people in 26:34–45. His policy for them was based on his commitment to them as their God (26:1, 2, 13, 45).

Fulfillment by Christ

Jesus established the Divine Service in the church by instituting the proclamation of God's Word, Christian Baptism, and the celebration of his Holy Supper. By these most holy things, he sanctifies people and times and places. Through them the triune God gives access to his gracious presence. Through them he communicates his holiness and all his life-giving blessings.

God's people are therefore required to avoid idolatry (1 Cor 10:14–22; 2 Cor 6:16; 1 Jn 5:21), for, by worshiping God in ways that contradict his Word, they desecrate his holiness and come under his judgment (Rev 21:8; 22:15). But if they respect his holiness by listening to his sanctifying Word and receiving Baptism and the sanctifying body and blood of Jesus, they enjoy his blessings. Most do not live with God in the land of Israel. Nevertheless, they share in the divine fellowship and eternal life of the Son with the Father (John 17).

Thus, since the triune God gives access to himself and conveys his heavenly blessings to his people through the Divine Service, the reception of these blessings depends on their observance of the first three liturgical commandments of the Decalogue (Ex 20:3, 7, 8). God's people have access to him in the Divine Service, where his holy triune name is invoked and his Word is enacted. If they listen in faith to his Word in the Divine Service, they receive his bountiful blessings (Heb 4:1–16).

Yet God's people are not justified before God by keeping these liturgical commandments. God made his covenant with them as he did with Abraham. They are justified by his grace for ongoing access to his grace (Rom 5:1–2). Through Baptism he did all of these: he committed himself to them as their heavenly Father and adopted them as his royal sons; he bound himself to them and promised to walk with them in their journey from earth to heaven; he promised that through their faith in his Son they would inherit all that belongs to Christ as God's royal Son (Gal 3:23–4:7).

Nevertheless, if they refuse to worship him as he has commanded, they cut themselves off completely from him and so commit spiritual suicide (1 Jn 5:16–17). He therefore gave the first three commandments of the Decalogue to them to protect their lifeline with him, for by their right worship of him, their orthodoxy and orthopraxy in worship, they share in his holiness and enjoy his heavenly blessings on their earthly pilgrimage (Eph 1:3–14).

Those who keep his Word by their faithful involvement in the Divine Service receive four kinds of blessings from him through their interaction with him there. First, like the Israelites who had their livelihood from God in the land (Lev 26:4–5), they receive their daily bread from God, their heavenly Father (Mt 6:24–34). They therefore join with Jesus in praying for daily bread for themselves and others (Mt 6:11; Lk 11:3).

Second, like the Israelites who were promised peace in the land (Lev 26:6–8), they enjoy peace with God (Lk 2:14; Jn 14:27; Rom 5:1) and victory over all their spiritual enemies (Rom 8:31–39). They therefore join with Jesus in praying for the deliverance of the whole world from the evil one (Mt 6:13; cf. Jn 17:15).

Third, like the Israelites who were promised rich growth and God's abundant provision for them and their families in the land (Lev 26:9–10), they receive God's bountiful grace and provision for them in the church (Mk 10:29–30; Jn 1:16). They enjoy his abundant grace (2 Cor 9:14; Eph 2:7), power (2 Cor 4:7; Eph 1:19), love (Eph 3:19), and glory (2 Cor 4:17). By his Word God gives growth to the church[a] and its members.[b]

Fourth, and best of all, like the Israelites who had the promise of ongoing access to God's presence with them (Lev 26:11–13), they enjoy the indwelling of the triune God with them and in them.[c] The living God has made them[d] and their bodies (1 Cor 6:19) his holy temple here on earth, so that he dwells in them and walks about with them and is their God (2 Cor 6:16). He does not treat them as his slaves, but gives them freedom as his royal sons (Gal 5:1). They can therefore walk about with boldness and confidence, for through their union with his only Son they have open access to him and his grace.[e] His invisible dwelling in them through Word and Sacrament is a foretaste of his manifest dwelling with them forever in the new creation, where he will be with them fully as their God and they shall be his people—transparently and radiantly and completely (Rev 21:3).

Yet this privilege and these blessings must not be taken for granted by the church. Those who spurn God's Word and reject what he has so graciously instituted for them come under his judgment. They suffer the consequences of their refusal to cherish him and his Word. In his wrath God hands them over to their idols and their iniquities (Rom 1:18–32). He may cause them to experience the byproducts of their rebellion against him in failure and sickness, defeat and oppression, scarcity and drought, bereavement and oppression, dispossession and homelessness, loss of dignity and freedom, fearfulness and an uneasy conscience. He seeks to teach them the gravity of their rebellion against him and the emptiness of their idols by letting them experience the effect of life apart from him.

But God's temporal judgment upon the rebellious is never an end in itself; it is always a means to bring about their restoration. He judges them to humble them and bring them to repentance (2 Pet 3:9). If they then confess their

(a) Acts 6:7; 12:24; 19:20; Col 1:6; 3:16

(b) Col 1:10; 1 Thess 3:12; 2 Thess 1:3; 1 Pet 2:2; 2 Pet 1:8

(c) Jn 14:17, 23; 1 Jn 3:24; 4:12, 15, 16

(d) 1 Cor 3:16–17; Eph 2:19–22; Heb 3:6; 1 Pet 2:4–8

(e) 2 Cor 3:12; Eph 3:12; Heb 3:6; 4:16; 10:19, 35; 1 Jn 3:21; 5:14

sins, they can be sure that he will remember his covenant in Christ and forgive them, no matter what they have done (1 Jn 1:9). He will restore them so that they shall be his people and he will be their God. He will sanctify them so that they can enjoy the Sabbath rest of his whole creation and the fullness of eternal life with him (Heb 4:1–11).

God has blessed the church even more richly than the people of Israel. He has redeemed her from slavery to sin and the devil and has adopted her members as his royal sons. They therefore share in the eternal inheritance of his Son. He has made the church his holy temple here on earth and has given her access to his heavenly presence in the Divine Service. He therefore still encourages his people in the church to worship him faithfully and warns them against the dangers of idolatry and apostasy. He tells how he deals with them, in grace through the Gospel and in wrath through his Law. He promises the fullness of blessing to those who respect his holiness and enact his Word in the Divine Service. He also warns about the consequences of idolatry and the desecration of his holiness.

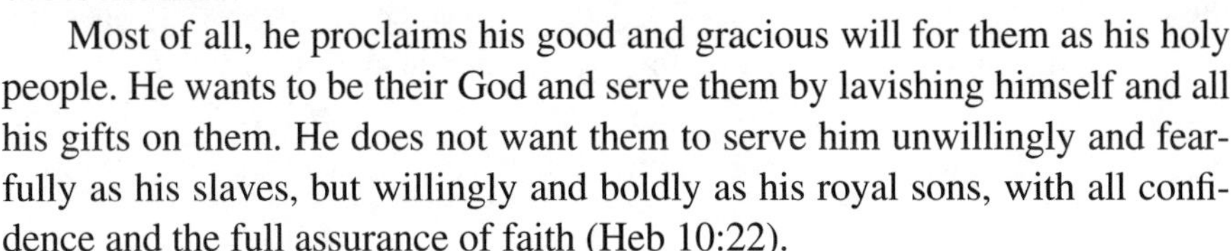

Most of all, he proclaims his good and gracious will for them as his holy people. He wants to be their God and serve them by lavishing himself and all his gifts on them. He does not want them to serve him unwillingly and fearfully as his slaves, but willingly and boldly as his royal sons, with all confidence and the full assurance of faith (Heb 10:22).

O faithful God, you never fail me;
Your cov'nant surely will abide.
Let not eternal death assail me
Should I transgress it on my side!
Have mercy when I come defiled;
Forgive, lift up, restore your child.[20]

---

[20] From "Baptized into Your Name Most Holy" by Johann J. Rambach (*LW* 224:3).

Leviticus 27:1–34

Votive Offerings and Consecrated Things

Translation

27 [1]The Lord spoke to Moses: [2]"Speak to the Israelites and say to them: When a person makes an extraordinary vow to the Lord according to the valuation of persons, [3]the valuation of a male from twenty years to sixty years [of age] is the valuation of fifty shekels of silver by the sacred shekel; [4]if it is a female, the valuation is thirty shekels. [5]If the age is from five years to twenty years, the valuation is twenty shekels for a male and ten shekels for a female. [6]If the age is from one month to five years, the valuation for the male is five shekels of silver, while the valuation for the female is three shekels of silver. [7]If the age is sixty years or over, the valuation is fifteen shekels for a male and ten shekels for a female. [8]But if anyone is too poor for the valuation, he shall station him before the priest, and the priest shall assess him. According to what the person who has made the vow can afford the priest shall assess him.

[9]"If [what is vowed is] livestock from which they may present an offering to the Lord, any one that he may give to the Lord is holy. [10]He may not exchange it or substitute another for it, either good for bad, or bad for good; if he substitutes one animal for another, both it and its substitute are holy. [11]If it [what is vowed] is any kind of unclean livestock from which they may not present an offering to the Lord, he shall station the animal before the priest [12]so that the priest may assess it. Whether good or bad [high or low], whatever the valuation of the priest, so it shall be. [13]But if he does indeed redeem it, he shall add one-fifth to its valuation.

[14]"When a person consecrates his house as holy to the Lord, the priest shall assess it; whether good or bad [high or low], as the priest assesses it, so it shall stand. [15]But if the person who has consecrated his house redeems it, he shall add one-fifth to its silver valuation, so that it may belong to him.

[16]"If a person consecrates to the Lord any field from his landholding, its valuation shall be according to its seed: a homer of barley seed is worth fifty shekels of silver. [17]If he consecrates his field on the Year of Jubilee, its valuation stands, [18]but if he consecrates his field after the Jubilee, the priest shall calculate the silver for it according to the years that are left until the Year of Jubilee, and it will be deducted from the valuation. [19]If the person who consecrated the field should redeem it, he shall add one-fifth to its silver valuation, so that it may pass to him. [20]Yet, if he does not redeem the field, but has sold the field to another person, it may no longer be redeemed. [21]When the field comes free on the Jubilee, it will be holy [belong] to the Lord as a proscribed field; it belongs to the priest as his holding.

**22“If he consecrates to the Lord a purchased field that is not part of his land-
holding, 23the priest shall calculate the amount of valuation until the Year of Jubilee, so that he may pay the valuation on that day as something holy to the Lord.
24On the Year of Jubilee, the field shall return to the person from whom he bought
it, the one to whom the landholding belongs. 25Every valuation shall be according to the sacred shekel at twenty gerahs to the shekel.**

**26“However, no one may consecrate a firstborn of the livestock which has
been designated as firstborn for the Lord, whether it is a head of cattle or a
sheep/goat, it belongs to the Lord. 27But if it is one of the unclean livestock, he
may ransom [it] at its valuation and add to it one-fifth; if it is not redeemed, it
may be sold at its valuation.**

**28“However, anything proscribed that anybody proscribes for the Lord from
all that belongs to him, whether it be a human being or livestock or any part of
his landholding, may not be sold and may not be redeemed. Every proscribed
thing is most holy to the Lord. 29Any person who has been proscribed from humanity may not be ransomed; he must be put to death.**

**30“But every tithe from the land, whether from the seed of the land or from
the fruit of the tree, belongs to the Lord; it is holy to the Lord. 31If anyone should
redeem any of his tithe, he shall add one-fifth to it. 32Every tithe of the herd or
the flock, every one that passes under the staff [of the shepherd], the tenth one
shall be holy to the Lord. 33He must not seek out the good from the bad, and he
must not substitute it. If he should make a substitute for it, then both it and its
substitute shall be holy; it cannot be redeemed.”**

**34These are the commandments that the Lord commanded Moses for the Is-
raelites at Mount Sinai.**

Textual Notes

27:2 אִ֕ישׁ כִּ֥י יַפְלִ֖א נֶ֑דֶר—See the textual notes on 7:16. The Piel of the verb פָּלָא is used with נֶדֶר for making a vow to offer an animal to God (22:21; Num 15:3). The form here (יַפְלִא) is the Hiphil, which is used with נֶדֶר as its direct object for making an extraordinary vow that went beyond the vow of a Nazirite (Num 6:1–21). In it people offered themselves (2 Sam 15:7–8; Ps 116:14–19) or a member of their family (e.g., 1 Sam 1:11) unconditionally to God as his servants.[1] The most extreme form of this practice in the ancient world was the vow of child sacrifice, which God prohibits (Lev 18:21; 20:2–5; cf. Judg 11:30–39).

בְּעֶרְכְּךָ֖ נְפָשֹׁ֥ת—See the use of the same technical term for the valuation of people vowed to God in 2 Ki 12:5 (ET 12:4). On the noun עֵרֶךְ (בְּעֶרְכְּךָ), see the textual notes on 5:15. It recurs in 27:3, 4, 5, 6, 7, 8, 12, 13, 15, 16, 17, 18, 19, 23, 25, 27. With the second masculine singular pronominal suffix, בְּעֶרְכְּךָ literally means “according to your valuation,” but the suffix is idiomatic and does not refer to any particular person, so we omit “your” from our translation. All the occurrences of עֵרֶךְ in Leviticus have that suffix.

---

1 Milgrom, *Leviticus 23–27*, 2368–69.

27:3 מִבֶּ֤ן עֶשְׂרִים֙ שָׁנָ֔ה וְעַ֖ד בֶּן־שִׁשִּׁ֣ים שָׁנָ֑ה—This is literally "from a son of twenty years to a son of sixty years." See the textual notes on 9:3. Similar phrases recur in 27:5, 6, 7.

בְּשֶׁ֥קֶל הַקֹּֽדֶשׁ׃—This could also be translated as "by the shekel of holiness" or "by the shekel of the sanctuary/the sanctuary weight." See the textual notes on 5:15. The phrase recurs in 27:25.

Regarding קֹדֶשׁ, see the textual notes on 4:6. It recurs in 27:9, 10, 14, 21, 23, 25, 28, 30, 32, 33.

27:6 Further legislation on vows made by wives and daughters is given in Num 30:2–17 (ET 30:1–16). Five shekels is the amount paid to redeem a month-old, firstborn male child (Num 18:15–16).

27:8 מָךְ—See the textual note on this verb (מוּךְ) in Lev 25:25.

מֵעֶרְכֶּ֔ךָ—The preposition מִן is used to express the comparative degree (GKC, § 133 b).

וְהֶעֱמִידוֹ֙—See 27:11 and the textual notes on 14:11. While it is possible to construe the verb impersonally, this indicates that adults would normally vow their children or their slaves to the Lord.[2]

וְהֶעֱרִ֣יךְ—This verb is used in 2 Ki 23:35 as a technical administrative term for the assessment of taxation. It recurs in Lev 27:12, 14.

תַּשִּׂיג֙ יַ֣ד—See the textual notes on 5:11.

27:9 See the cases of people making vows in Pss 50:14; 56:13 (ET 56:12); 66:13–15.

אֲשֶׁ֨ר יַקְרִ֧יבוּ מִמֶּ֛נָּה קָרְבָּ֖ן לַיהוָ֑ה—This is literally "from which they may present an offering to the Lord."

יַקְרִ֧יבוּ—See the textual note on this verb in 1:2 and the explanation in "Leviticus 1–3." It recurs in 27:11.

כֹּל֩ אֲשֶׁ֨ר יִתֵּ֥ן מִמֶּ֛נּוּ לַיהוָ֖ה—The verb נָתַן is used here as a technical term for the dedication of an animal to the Lord (cf. Ex 22:28 [ET 22:29]; 30:16; Num 3:9; 8:16).

27:10 See Lev 27:33.

לֹ֣א יַחֲלִיפֶ֗נּוּ—The Hiphil of חָלַף refers to replacement with a different species.[3]

וְלֹֽא־יָמִ֥יר—The Hiphil of מוּר refers to replacement with the same species of animal (27:33).

27:11 בְּהֵמָ֣ה טְמֵאָ֔ה—See 27:27 and the textual notes on 5:2.

וְהֶעֱמִ֥יד—The subject is the owner of the animal.

27:12 בֵּ֥ין ט֖וֹב וּבֵ֣ין רָ֑ע—This is literally "between good and between bad," that is, "whether good or bad." This phrase recurs in 27:14.[4] If the priest deems the animal to be "good," the valuation would be high, while if it is "bad," the valuation would be low.

27:13 וְאִם־גָּאֹ֖ל יִגְאָלֶ֑נָּה—The infinitive absolute is added for emphasis before the finite form of the same verb. On גָּאַל, see the textual notes on 25:25. It recurs in 27:15, 19, 20, 27, 28, 31, 33. Although the pronominal suffix "it" (יִגְאָלֶ֑נָּה) could refer back

---

2 Milgrom, *Leviticus 23–27*, 2374.

3 Milgrom, *Leviticus 23–27*, 2376.

4 See also Speiser, "Leviticus and the Critics," 135–36.

to the offerable animals in 27:9–10,[5] the context argues for its reference to unclean animals.[6]

חֲמִישִׁתוֹ עַל־עֶרְכֶּךָ׃—This is literally "one-fifth over the valuation." See 5:16; 5:24 (ET 6:5); 27:15, 19, 27, 31. Similar phrases recur in 27:15, 19, 27, 31.

27:14 יַקְדִּשׁ—See the textual note on this verb in 22:2. It recurs in 27:15, 16, 17, 18, 19, 22, 26. It is not certain how this consecration was done. The consecration could have occurred by a formal declaration, as by Micah's mother in Judg 17:3. Mention is made of consecrated gold, silver, and bronze in 2 Sam 8:11; 2 Ki 12:18; 1 Chr 18:10–11 (cf. 1 Chr 26:26, 27, 28).

כֵּן יָקוּם׃—This verb is a technical term for a legally binding transaction (Num 30:5–15 [ET 30:4–14]). It recurs in Lev 27:17.

27:16 מִשְּׂדֵה אֲחֻזָּתוֹ—This is literally "some of the field of his holding." See the textual notes on 14:34. The two words occur together also in 27:21, 22, 24, 28.

לְפִי—See 25:51; 27:18.

זַרְעוֹ—There is some debate as to whether this refers to the amount of barley produced on average by an area of ground or to the amount of seed that was used to sow it. Wenham refers to the use of זֶרַע, "seed," for harvested grain in 27:30 and so opts for the former interpretation.[7] Milgrom points out the practical difficulties in this approach.[8] He favors the latter interpretation and notes that it is supported by the rabbis. Thus a "homer" of land was the area that could be sown with a homer of barley. This method of measuring land was common in the ancient world. The assessment would then have been based on a fixed rate for a fixed area of land. The sum of fifty shekels seems to be derived from the number of years from Jubilee to Jubilee.

זֶרַע חֹמֶר שְׂעֹרִים—This is literally "seed of a homer of barley." A homer is a measure of grain (Is 5:10; Ezek 45:13; Hos 3:2). Since חֹמֶר may be related to חֲמוֹר, "donkey," it may have received its name from the amount of grain that could be carried by a donkey.[9] Estimates of its bulk vary from about three to seven bushels. It therefore amounted to one or two large bags of grain.

27:17 הַיֹּבֵל—See the textual notes on 25:10.

27:18 הַכֶּסֶף—Translated "the price" above, this is literally "the silver."

עַל־פִּי—The Masoretes read this as an adverb, "proportionately."

27:19 גָּאֹל יִגְאַל—The infinitive absolute is added for emphasis.

וְקָם לוֹ׃—See the textual notes on 25:30.

27:20 וְאִם־לֹא יִגְאַל אֶת־הַשָּׂדֶה—While this could be taken to refer to the priest as the owner of the consecrated land,[10] it most naturally refers to the owner of the land.[11]

---

5 Elliger, *Leviticus*, 387–88.

6 Milgrom, *Leviticus 23–27*, 2378–80.

7 Wenham, *Leviticus*, 340, n. 8.

8 Milgrom, *Leviticus 23–27*, 2382.

9 Levine, *Leviticus*, 196.

10 Levine, *Leviticus*, 196.

11 Milgrom, *Leviticus 23–27*, 2384.

וְאִם־מָכַר אֶת־הַשָּׂדֶה—While the *waw* could indicate an alternative case and be translated "or,"[12] the rule that all sold land reverted to the owner automatically at the Jubilee means that it refers to the failure of the owner to redeem the land that had been sold.[13] It is best translated by "and" or "but."

מָכַר—See the textual note on this verb in 25:14. It recurs in 27:27, 28. This means that the owner who had "leased" the land to another person until the Jubilee thereafter consecrated the leased land. He thereby forfeited his right to the land.[14]

27:21 וְהָיָה הַשָּׂדֶה בְּצֵאתוֹ—This could also be translated "when the field is released." See the textual notes on 25:28.

הַחֵרֶם—The noun חֵרֶם, "proscription, cultic ban, destruction," and the related verb חָרַם (used mainly in the Hiphil), are ritual terms for the consecration of a person or thing irrevocably and completely to God for destruction.[15] By it God maintained the sacral order and protected it from the ravages of chaos.[16] It was most commonly exercised in warfare against the nations for crimes against humanity and violations of the cosmic order. It was done at God's command (1 Sam 15:3) or, occasionally, as the result of a vow (Num 21:2–3). All the booty from such warfare belonged exclusively to God (Josh 7:1, 11, 12, 13, 15; 1 Sam 15:21). This consecration for destruction was also exercised at God's command against apostates in Israel (Ex 22:19 [ET 22:20]; Deut 13:13–19). This seems to be the situation in Lev 27:29. But the ruling in 27:28 seems to envisage a voluntary form of proscription in which a person devotes a slave, some livestock, or some land irrevocably to God (cf. Num 18:14; Ezek 44:29).[17] Like the Gibeonites in Josh 9:22–27, a proscribed person, most likely, belonged to the sanctuary as a slave.[18] The noun recurs in Lev 27:28, 29 (cf. Num 18:14).

לַכֹּהֵן תִּהְיֶה אֲחֻזָּתוֹ׃—Since the priests were not allowed to own any land, it belonged to the sanctuary.

27:22 שְׂדֵה מִקְנָתוֹ—"A purchased field," unlike a שְׂדֵה אֲחֻזָּה, "a tenured field," did not belong to the buyer. He therefore could only consecrate its yield to the Lord.

27:23 מִכְסַת—The noun מִכְסָה, "amount" (*HALOT*), occurs only here and in Ex 12:4. It is related to an Akkadian noun that means the share from a rented field that belongs to the owner.[19]

---

12 Brin, *Studies in Biblical Law*, 45–46; Hartley, *Leviticus*, 476; NIV; NRSV.

13 Milgrom, *Leviticus 23–27*, 2384.

14 Milgrom, *Leviticus 23–27*, 2385.

15 N. Lohfink, "חָרַם *ḥāram;* חֵרֶם *ḥērem,*" *TDOT* 5:180–99; Milgrom, *Leviticus 23–27*, 2391–96, 2417–21.

16 Milgrom, *Leviticus 23–27*, 2417.

17 Milgrom, *Leviticus 23–27*, 2396.

18 Lohfink, *TDOT* 5:199.

19 Milgrom, *Leviticus 23–27*, 2387.

בַּיּוֹם הַהוּא—The day is not the day of payment, but the Day of Atonement, since the Jubilee was proclaimed on that day (25:9), and the calculation of payment was fixed by the period of time that ended on that day.

27:24 יָשׁוּב—See the textual notes on 25:10.

27:25 גֵּרָה—See Ex 30:13; Num 3:47; 18:16; Ezek 45:12. This was the smallest unit of currency.

27:26 בְּכוֹר—Only male animals were classified as firstborn (Ex 13:12, 15). See the laws for the firstborn in Ex 13:2, 11–16; 22:28b–29 (ET 22:29b–30); 34:19–20; Num 3:11–13; 8:14–19; 18:15–19; Deut 15:19–23.

שֶׂה—See the textual notes on 5:7. This could be either a sheep or a goat.

27:27 בַּבְּהֵמָה הַטְּמֵאָה—A donkey (Ex 13:13) and a camel (Lev 11:4) would qualify as unclean livestock.

וּפָדָה—The verb פָּדָה, "to ransom," was used instead of גָּאַל, "to redeem," because it was not the person's property, but belonged to God. See 19:20. The verb פָּדָה recurs in 27:29.

וְיָסַף חֲמִשִׁתוֹ עָלָיו—This is literally "and add its fifth to it."

וְאִם־לֹא יִגָּאֵל וְנִמְכַּר בְּעֶרְכֶּךָ׃—This ruling modifies the command in Ex 13:13 and 34:20 to kill an unredeemed donkey.

בְּעֶרְכֶּךָ׃—This could also be translated "at its valuation." The money from the sale would then belong to the sanctuary.

27:28 כָּל־חֵרֶם—This is literally "any proscribed thing." See the textual notes on 27:21.

אֲשֶׁר יַחֲרִם—See 27:29.

מֵאָדָם וּבְהֵמָה וּמִשְּׂדֵה אֲחֻזָּתוֹ—This is literally "from a human being and livestock and from the field of his holding." On אָדָם, see 27:29 and the textual notes on 1:2.

The first use of the preposition מִן applies to both the following nouns. The second use of מִן could indicate that both some of the land and its produce could be proscribed.

קֹדֶשׁ־קָדָשִׁים—See the textual notes on 2:3.

לַיהוָה׃—See Num 18:14; Ezek 44:29.

27:29 כָּל־חֵרֶם אֲשֶׁר יָחֳרַם מִן־הָאָדָם—This is literally "any proscribed [person] who has been proscribed from the humankind." This goes beyond ordinary proscription that involved the handing over of a person to God. In this case, the person is handed over to destruction from the human race.

מוֹת יוּמָת׃—See the textual notes on Lev 20:2.

27:30 See also the legislation in Num 18:21–24 and Deut 12:17a; 14:22–29 (cf. Gen 14:20; 28:22; 2 Chr 31:5–6, 12; Neh 10:38b–39 [ET 10:37b–38]; 13:12; Amos 4:4; Mal 3:6–12).

מִפְּרִי הָעֵץ—This was offered in the form of olive oil and wine (Deut 12:17; 14:23; Neh 13:12).

לַיהוָה הוּא—Kings had the right to exact tithes from their subjects as taxation in the ancient world (cf. 1 Sam 8:15–17). So, since God was the King of Israel, the tithe from his land belonged to him.

27:31 וְאִם־גָּאֹל יִגְאַל—The infinitive absolute is added for emphasis.

27:32 Since the tithe was taken from the produce of the land and reckoned as a kind of annual rent for the use of God's land, this tithe was most likely taken annually from the animals born in that year, rather than from all the animals each year.[20]

כֹּל אֲשֶׁר־יַעֲבֹר תַּחַת הַשָּׁבֶט—This refers to the counting of sheep by the shepherd as they come out of the sheepfold (Jer 33:13; Ezek 20:37).

27:33 יְבַקֵּר—See Lev 13:36 (cf. Ezek 34:11, 12).

וְאִם־הָמֵר יְמִירֶנּוּ—The infinitive absolute is added for emphasis.

27:34 This final sentence stands in contrast with the concluding colophon in Num 36:13.

אֵלֶּה הַמִּצְוֹת—See the textual notes on Lev 4:2.

אֲשֶׁר צִוָּה יְהוָה—See the textual notes on 7:36.

בְּהַר סִינָי׃—This reference to Mount Sinai recalls 25:1 and so brackets off the last three chapters, Leviticus 25–27. Other references to Sinai are in 7:38 and 26:46.

Commentary

Context and Structure

Many critical scholars regard this chapter as a secondary appendix.[21] They regard this speech as out of place at the end of Leviticus and something of an anticlimax after God's passionate admonition in the previous chapter. Yet that view ignores this chapter's close association with chapters 25–26 by virtue of its discussion of redemption and the implications of the Jubilee. It is also linked quite formally with those chapters by a common emphasis on the role of Moses as the mediator of God's Word to Israel at Mount Sinai in 25:1; 26:46; and 27:34.

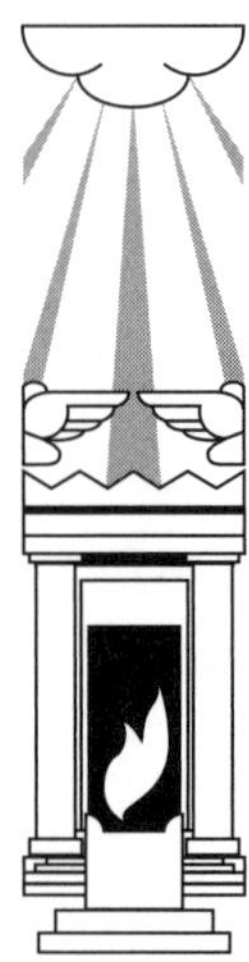

Four reasons have been given for the location of this chapter at the end of the book.[22] First, the promises made by the Israelites to God in the form of vows and acts of consecration in this chapter may be linked with God's promises to Israel in the previous chapter.[23]

Second, these laws provide the funding necessary for the maintenance of the sanctuary.[24] Through these voluntary contributions, the Israelites could therefore keep the command in 26:2 to revere the sanctuary. This association may have influenced Nehemiah to connect the obligation to present the first-born animals (Neh 10:36) and the tithes (Neh 10:39) with maintenance of the Lord's house (Neh 10:39).

Third, Leviticus 27 ensures that the book does not end on a negative note with threats of disaster, but positively with an emphasis on Israel's voluntary response to God's goodness.[25]

---

[20] Levine, *Leviticus*, 200.

[21] Elliger, *Leviticus*, 385; Noth, *Leviticus*, 14.

[22] Milgrom, *Leviticus 23–27*, 2407–9.

[23] Wenham, *Leviticus*, 336.

[24] Levine, *Leviticus*, 192.

[25] See Hartley, *Leviticus*, 479.

Fourth, these regulations for voluntary contributions to the sanctuary are the counterpart to the regulations for the divinely ordained offerings in the divine service in Leviticus 1–7. Moreover, with its legislation on the redemption of people and property, this chapter not only complements the discussion on their redemption in Leviticus 25, but also associates these acts of consecration and redemption with the emphasis in chapter 26 on God's liberation of Israel from Egypt and his promise of liberation from exile in the future.[26]

The contents of this speech are carefully arranged in three parts. The first two parts are introduced by אִישׁ כִּי, "when a person" (27:2b, 14). They are followed by a series of cases, each of which is introduced by וְאִם, "and if" or אִם, "if." The last section is introduced by the restrictive particle אַךְ, "however," in 27:26, which is repeated in 27:28 to include two further exceptions. The speech ends with a summary subscript that also serves as the conclusion for the whole book.

The various pieces of legislation are joined together by a network of key words that highlight the legislation's theological significance. Thus we have the root ערך, which appears twenty-six times, twenty-one times in the noun "valuation" and five times in the verb "assess." The phrase "to the Lord" occurs sixteen times. The noun "holiness," the noun "shekel," and the verb "redeem" each occur twelve times. And the verb "consecrate" is used eight times. The term בֵּן, "son," occurs nine times, twice in the phrase "the sons of Israel" (27:2, 34) and seven times denoting age (e.g., "a son of twenty years," that is, "twenty years of age" in 27:3). The use of בֵּן, "son," with the prepositions אֶל, "to," מִן, "from," and עַד, "until," creates a chiasm that links 27:2–7 with 27:34:[27]

A¹ "To the sons of Israel" (27:2)
    B¹ "From a son of …" (27:3a)
        C¹ "Until a son of …" (27:3b)
    B² "From a son of …" (27:5a)
        C² "Until a son of …" (27:5b)
    B³ "From a son of …" (27:6a)
        C³ "Until a son of …" (27:6b)
    B⁴ "From a son of …" (27:7)
A² "To the sons of Israel" (27:34)

Thus the phrase "the sons of Israel" forms an inclusion that frames the contents of this speech.

The structure of this pericope can be outlined as follows:

I. Introduction (27:1–2a)
   A. God's address to Moses (27:1)
   B. God's commission of Moses (27:2a)

[26] Milgrom, *Leviticus 23–27*, 2409.

[27] Warning, *Literary Artistry in Leviticus*, 97–98.

- II. Speech about the payment for vows and redemption of holy things (27:2b–33)
    - A. Payment for votive offerings (27:2b–13)
        - 1. Payment for vowed persons (27:2b–8)
            - a. Males between twenty and sixty years (27:2b–3)
            - b. Females between twenty and sixty years (27:4)
            - c. Males and females between five and twenty years (27:5)
            - d. Males and females between one month and five years (27:6)
            - e. Males and females over sixty years (27:7)
            - f. Concessional rate for poor people (27:8)
        - 2. Payment for vowed livestock (27:9–13)
            - a. Presentation of eligible livestock as offerings (27:9–10)
            - b. Procedure for the redemption of an unclean animal (27:11–13)
    - B. Redemption of consecrated property (27:14–25)
        - 1. Redemption of a consecrated house (27:14–15)
            - a. Valuation by a priest (27:14)
            - b. Redemption through payment by the owner (27:15)
        - 2. Redemption of a consecrated field (27:16–25)
            - a. Consecration of tenured land (27:16–21)
                - i. Valuation of its arable acreage (27:16)
                - ii. Valuation according to the years until the Jubilee (27:17–18)
                - iii. Option for possible redemption of the land before the Jubilee (27:19)
                - iv. Ownership of a sold field by the sanctuary at the Jubilee (27:20–21)
            - b. Consecration of a purchased field (27:22–24)
                - i. Valuation according to the years until the Jubilee (27:22–23)
                - ii. Return to its owner at the Jubilee (27:24)
            - c. The value of the shekel (27:25)
    - C. Restrictions on consecrated objects (27:26–33)
        - 1. Firstborn male livestock (27:26–27)
            - a. Sacred status of firstborn livestock (27:26)
            - b. Redemption or sale of unclean firstborn livestock (27:27)
        - 2. Proscriptions (27:28–29)
            - a. Prohibition of sale or redemption of what has been proscribed (27:28)
            - b. Execution of a person proscribed from the human race (27:29)
        - 3. Tithes (27:30–33)
            - a. Agricultural produce (27:30–31)
                - i. Sacred status of the agricultural tithe (27:30)
                - ii. Option of redemption (27:31)
            - b. Livestock (27:32–33)
                - i. Method for identifying the tithed animals (27:32)
                - ii. Prohibition of exchange or redemption (27:33)
- III. Summary conclusion (27:34)

Analysis

Moses is once again the mediator of these laws to the Israelites. They regulate the voluntary contributions that the Israelites made to God for the maintenance of the sanctuary. These contributions helped to finance its operation.

The subject matter of the first section is the payment of two kinds of vows, people and animals that have been vowed to God (27:2). People usually made such vows when they were in some kind of trouble (Ps 66:13–14), such as childlessness (1 Sam 1:11), danger of death (Ps 56:13–14 [ET 56:12–13]; Jonah 2:10 [ET 2:9]), or danger of defeat in battle (Num 21:2). If people or unclean livestock had been vowed as a gift to God, the vow was normally discharged by the payment of money.

The first unit (27:1–8) gives the fixed scale by which the Israelites could assess the value of a vowed person. People are considered apart from social status according to four categories—mature people (Lev 27:2–4), young people (27:5), children (27:6), and old people (27:7). The scale seems to be determined roughly by the productive capacity of the person. Two factors were involved in calculating the financial worth of the person: age and gender. The system is shown in figure 26.

Figure 26

Age and Valuation of Israelites

Age in Years	*Male Value in Shekels*	*Female Value in Shekels*
1/12–5	5	3
5–20	20	10
20–60	50	30
60+	15	10

The amount set for an old women shows that the lower valuation for women had nothing to do with their inherent worth, but was based on their economic status as potential employees. The standard payment for the release from vows was made according to the sanctuary shekel (27:3). An exception to this system of valuation was made for a poor person who lacked the money to pay the standard price for the discharge of a vowed person (27:8). In that case the person who had vowed to offer a member of his family to God would bring that person to the priest. The priest as God's representative would set the amount for redemption according to the economic capacity of the person.

The second part of the legislation for the discharge of vows deals with livestock (27:9–13). Here a distinction is made between ritually clean livestock, such as sheep or goats or cattle, and ritually unclean livestock, such as donkeys and camels. All animals that could be presented as offerings at the sanctuary were holy. These votive offerings (23:38) must therefore be sacrificed either as peace offerings (7:16; 22:21) or as burnt offerings (Num 15:3). Since they belonged to God, the Israelites were not allowed to substitute one species for another, such as a kid for a bull, nor could they offer an inferior animal instead of a prime specimen or vice versa. In fact, if one animal was exchanged with another animal of the same species, both would be holy (Lev 27:10). They would therefore need to be presented as offerings at the sanctuary. On the other hand, since unclean livestock, such as donkeys, could not be offered as sacrifices to the Lord, they could be redeemed (27:11–13). In that case, the animal that had been vowed to God was brought before the priest for valuation. If the owner wished to redeem it, he paid that price with an added twenty percent to compensate God for the loss of his property. If the person did not redeem it, the sanctuary presumably sold the animal.

While the first section of this speech deals with vows, the second part deals with houses and land that had been consecrated to God (27:14–25). These acts of consecration differed from the vows in two ways. They were unconditional speech acts. They did not come into effect only if the request made of God was granted by him. They also took effect immediately. The thing that was consecrated became holy as soon as its owner promised to give it to God. Most things that were consecrated to God in this way could not be redeemed. They therefore had to be presented to God. There were two exceptions to this, a house and land. Since both of these were immovable property, they could not be brought to the sanctuary.

If a house was consecrated to God, the priest assessed its value, like a modern real estate agent, and fixed its price for sale by the sanctuary or for redemption by the owner (27:15). If a piece of land was consecrated to God, the procedure was much more complicated. Once again the priest was the assessor. Four criteria determined the valuation of the land: its size as determined by the area sown with one homer of barley (27:16); the fixed rate of one shekel per year for that amount of land (27:16); the number of years that were left to the Jubilee (27:17–18, 23); and the sanctuary currency with its rate of twenty gerahs to the shekel (27:25). Thus the standard for valuation was fifty shekels per "homer" of land for the complete cycle from one Jubilee to another (27:16).

Three cases are considered. First, if a person consecrated his own field, he presumably still worked it, but paid the sanctuary the amount that had been set by the priest. He could also redeem it at any time before the Jubilee provided that he paid the assessed amount with an additional twenty percent to compensate God for his loss of property (27:16–19). Second, if a person who had already sold his land subsequently consecrated it to the Lord, he thereby forfeited his right to the land. When it was released at the Jubilee from the person who had bought it, it did not return to him as the owner, but became the property of the sanctuary as "a proscribed field" (27:20–21). In that case, the priest acted as God's attorney. Third, if a person consecrated some land that had been bought from another person, he paid the assessed amount for the land, as something "holy" to God for his use of it, up to the proclamation of the Jubilee on the Day of Atonement. As was normally the case, the land reverted to its former owner at the Jubilee (27:22–24).

The last part of the speech (27:26–33) considers three exceptions to this legislation on the valuation and redemption of people and property. First, only some firstborn male livestock could be ransomed (27:26–27). Unlike other consecrated things, a firstborn lamb or kid or calf had not been transferred by the Israelites from their property to God's property. It already was God's property because it was a firstborn male animal. But if the firstborn was an unclean animal, such as a donkey, the priest fixed its price for sale, with an additional twenty percent, to their former owner or any other buyer.

Second, anything that had been "proscribed" could not be sold or redeemed (27:28–29). If an Israelite "proscribed" any of his property, whether it was a person or livestock or land, whatever was thus proscribed was most holy; it could never be retrieved from the sacred domain and used for common purposes. Unlike the consecration of a Nazirite (Num 6:13–21), the consecration of a person by proscription was permanent. The consecration of a person by proscription to the Lord, however, is distinguished from the proscription of an Israelite "from humanity" for apostasy. Such a person had to be put to death.

Third, some tithes could be redeemed (Lev 27:30–33). Even though all agricultural tithes were holy because they belonged to God by right as the owner of the land, their owners could redeem them at cost, with the addition of twenty percent to compensate God for his loss of some holy property. But the tithe from the flock and the herd could not be redeemed. The choice of the animals was not left to the judgment of the owner, but was done by marking every tenth animal as it came out of its enclosure. The owner was not allowed to replace a superior animal with an inferior specimen. If he did, both became God's property. Nothing is said here, or elsewhere in Leviticus, about how these tithes were to be used. According to Deuteronomy, the agricultural tithes were normally eaten in sacred meals at the sanctuary (Deut 14:22–23) and given to the Levites and other poor people every three years (Deut 26:12–15). Numbers declares that all were to be given to the Levites as their livelihood (Num 28:21–24; cf. Neh 10:37–38; 13:12–13). Whatever the case, it is clear that what was tithed belonged to the sacred domain. It could only be used there.

This speech ends with a subscript in 27:34 that functions as the conclusion for the whole of Leviticus and completes the law-giving by God that began in Ex 25:1. It emphasizes two things. On the one hand, it recalls Lev 22:31 and stresses that all these commandments were part of a public tradition that God gave to all the Israelites for them to receive, enact, and hand on. On the other hand, it also stresses the role of Moses as the divinely ordained mediator of God's Word. Both these emphases stand in stark contrast with the focus in the ancient Near East on the king as the divinely appointed lawgiver and the main recipient of divine favors. In Israel Moses is the law-mediator, and Israel is the object of the Lord's benevolence as the administrator of his earthly rule.

It is significant that, unlike earlier sections in Leviticus, chapters 25–27 do not have a concluding formula of compliance. This means that the task that God gave to his people remained unfinished. What God had commanded at

Mount Sinai had still to be taught to his people and enacted by them. They could, in fact, only put this Word of God into practice once they had entered the land of Canaan. The book of Leviticus may even imply that this task would remain unfulfilled even when they took possession of the land.

Theological Significance

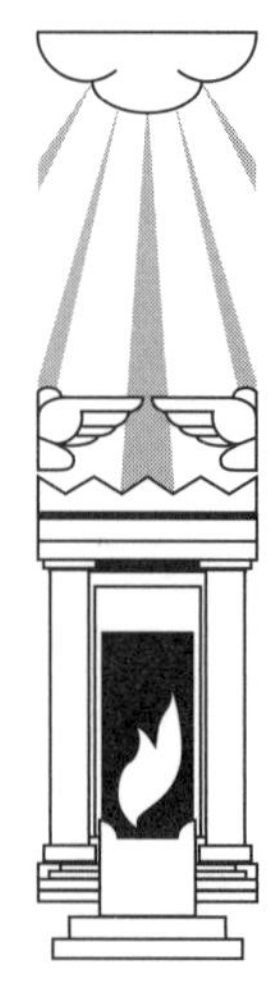

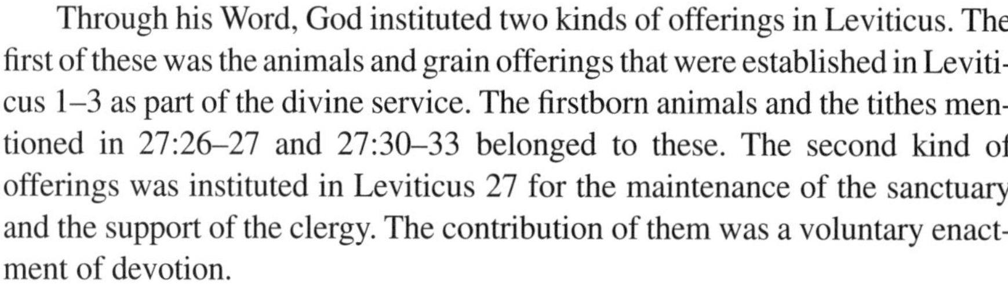

Through his Word, God instituted two kinds of offerings in Leviticus. The first of these was the animals and grain offerings that were established in Leviticus 1–3 as part of the divine service. The firstborn animals and the tithes mentioned in 27:26–27 and 27:30–33 belonged to these. The second kind of offerings was instituted in Leviticus 27 for the maintenance of the sanctuary and the support of the clergy. The contribution of them was a voluntary enactment of devotion.

We do not have an exhaustive list of such voluntary contributions in this chapter. It only mentions those that needed to be turned into money or could be exchanged for presentation in monetary form. Any person or unclean livestock that had been vowed to God was offered to him in monetary form. Thus the vow was discharged by the payment of the assessed amount. Likewise, any house or field that had been consecrated to God could be redeemed by the payment of an assessed amount. However, if a field that had been sold was consecrated to God, it could not be redeemed, but belonged to the sanctuary. But, apart from this case, neither of these contributions was exacted at the expense of anyone's divinely given livelihood. Any consecrated land that had not been redeemed reverted to its owner at the Jubilee. Thus God ensured that his sanctuary and his priesthood did not become wealthy at the expense of his people.

Apart from the votive payments and the payments from consecrated houses and fields, two other classes of offerings could be exchanged for money. Both the unclean firstborn livestock and the agricultural tithes could be redeemed by their owners. In all these cases, a surcharge of twenty percent was added to the assessed value. This compensated God for his loss of property. It also ensured that the people did not profit from the transaction. Since the money from all these transactions was holy (27:23), it belonged to God and could only ever be used for ritual purposes.

Besides these contributions of money by the Israelites to the sanctuary, mention is made of two other sources of income for the sanctuary, consecrated land that had been sold after its consecration and anything that had been consecrated to God by proscription. These constituted a special class of holy things, with those that been proscribed being designated as "most holy" (27:28). These holy things could only ever be used by the priests.

In all this, the theological implications of God's holiness are consistently applied. Some people and things become holy by the performance of certain ritual acts. These ritual acts were sanctioned by God in his Word. Through them people and things were transferred from the common domain to the sacred domain. Four such acts are mentioned: the payment of money in fulfillment of a vow; a verbal act of consecration; the presentation of clean livestock as sacrifices; and consecration by an act of proscription.

Other things were holy by right since they already belonged to God. Two such things are mentioned in this chapter: the firstborn male livestock and the tithes. Like the firstborn sons in an Israelite family, all firstborn male livestock belonged to God by historical right since he had redeemed his people from slavery in Egypt (Ex 13:14–15). The tithes belonged to God by geographical right since the land of Israel was his royal estate. All these holy things that derived their holiness from their association with God at the sanctuary were to be used for ritual purposes. They were available to support the priesthood, so that the priests could perform the divine service.

Fulfillment by Christ

At first sight, this chapter with its laws about votive offering and tithes might seem rather alien to the Gospel and somewhat irrelevant to the life of the church. It is true that Roman Catholics promote the presentation of votive offerings, and charismatic churches advocate tithing. Yet Lutherans and other evangelical Christians traditionally have been wary of promoting votive offerings and tithing because they are concerned that such practices—especially if they are required—may foster legalism and works-righteousness and contravene the freedom of Christians under the Gospel.

Yet Jesus himself had little to say about these matters. He seemed to be critical of the Pharisees for their zeal in tithing every possible product from the land (Mt 23:23–24 || Lk 11:42) and, in some cases, all their income and what they purchased with it (Lk 18:12). He did not, however, criticize tithing in itself, but only its abuse in self-promotion. He, in fact, assumed that his disciples would continue to tithe (Mt 23:23). But their tithes were to be motivated by their faith in God's justice and mercy and used to promote faith in his merciful justice by showing mercy to those in need. Likewise Jesus was critical of devoting property to God only when such vows were used to avoid the obligation to keep the Fourth Commandment (Mt 15:3–6; Mk 7:9–13).

Thus, Jesus did not abolish votive offerings or tithes. In fact, he assumed that they would continue in the church as acts of mercy rather than as legal obligations.

This final chapter of Leviticus deals with something much more important than the regulation of votive offerings and tithes. It shows how all God's people were to be involved in the stewardship of God's house. All—as they were able and as God had blessed them in the land—were to provide the material and financial resources for the maintenance of the sanctuary and the ongoing operation of the divine service.

That is just as necessary for the church as for ancient Israel. Right from the beginning of the NT church, offerings were taken in the Divine Service to provide for the work of the church and the needs of the poor. The collection of offerings was one of the four main parts of the liturgy (Acts 2:42, 44–45). Some

of the faithful even dedicated their fields and houses to God and presented the money from their sale to the apostles as holy offerings for God's work (Acts 4:34–5:11). Their gifts financed the work of the mother church in Jerusalem.

The regular presentation of offerings and the consecration of them has continued in the church to the present day. As people are moved by God's grace, they dedicate themselves, their possessions, and their money to God. In this way these offerings become holy and are used to do the holy work of God. Their presentation to God in the divine service is an act of faith that mirrors and proclaims God's justice and mercy in the incarnate Christ. Since God has dealt so generously with humanity, Christians are encouraged to be generous in giving offerings to God in the Divine Service.[a] They may even give a fixed proportion of their God-given income as their weekly tithe to their Lord each Sunday and a portion of their God-provided assets as a legacy to the church when they die. In this way they work with the triune God in the consecration of his creation. Their offerings do not just promote the liturgy of the church, but they are part of the liturgy, the holy work that God's people do in the Divine Service for the benefit of the world (Rom 15:27; 2 Cor 9:12).

(a) Rom 12:13; 15:25–27; 1 Cor 16:1–4; 2 Cor 8–9; Gal 6:6; Heb 13:16

In conclusion, this chapter seems to provide a rather anticlimactic ending to the book of Leviticus after the impassioned divine rhetoric of the previous chapter. Yet it is most appropriate that this book ends in this rather mundane and material fashion, for it teaches how God's holiness is communicated physically through physical means to God's physical people on earth.

That is what makes the offerings of God's people so significant. He sanctifies them and uses them to sanctify his people. They bear witness to a God who loves his creation and interacts physically with his people. We might prefer something more spiritual than that, but God has chosen to embody his holiness in Israel and in Christ, so that eventually the whole of his creation may be pervaded with his glory and share in his holiness.

> We give you but your own
> In any gifts we bring;
> All that we have is yours alone,
> A trust from you, our King.
>
> May we your bounties thus
> As stewards true receive
> And gladly, Lord, as you bless us,
> To you our firstfruits give.[28]

[28] From "We Give You But Your Own" by William W. How (*LW* 405:1–2).

Index